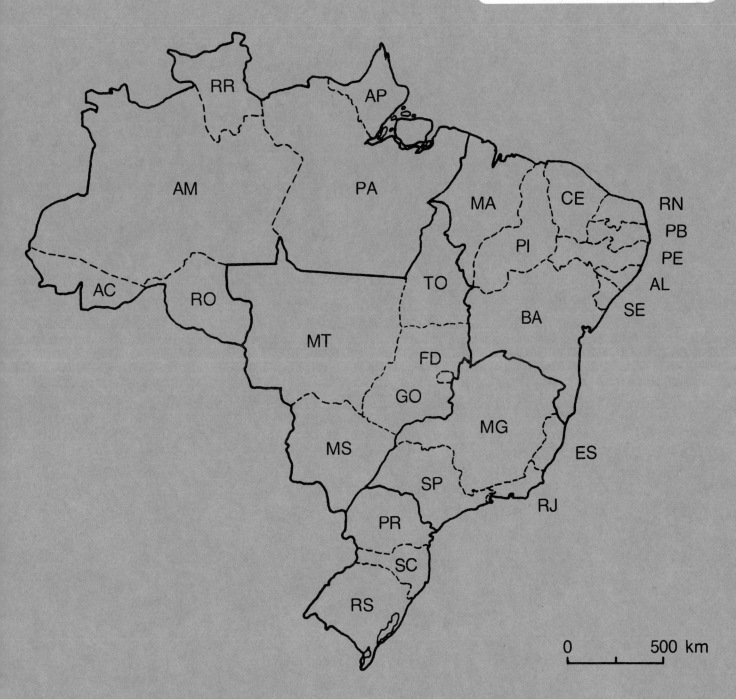

BIRDS IN BRAZIL

BIRDS IN BRAZIL

◆ *A Natural History*

◆ By Helmut Sick

Illustrated by Paul Barruel
With Color Plates by Paul Barruel and John P. O'Neill

TRANSLATED FROM THE PORTUGUESE BY

WILLIAM BELTON

Sponsored by the International Council for Bird Preservation,
Pan American Continental Section with support from the
Companhia Vale do Rio Doce

PRINCETON UNIVERSITY PRESS

PRINCETON, NEW JERSEY

Copyright © 1993 by Princeton University Press
Published by Princeton University Press, 41 William Street,
Princeton, New Jersey 08540
In the United Kingdom: Princeton University Press,
Chichester, West Sussex

Originally published as *Ornitologia Brasileira—Uma Introdução* by
Editora Universidade de Brasília, copyright © 1984 by Helmut Sick

LIBRARY OF CONGRESS CATALOGING-IN-PUBLICATION DATA

Sick, Helmut, 1910–
    [Ornitologia brasileira. English]
    Birds in Brazil : a natural history / by Helmut Sick ;
    illustrated by Paul Barruel with color plates by Paul Barruel and
    John P. O'Neill ; translated from the Portuguese by William Belton.
        p.   cm.
    Translation of: Ornitologia brasileira.
    "Sponsored by the International Council for Bird Preservation,
    Pan American Continental Section."
    Includes bibliographical references and index.
    ISBN 0-691-08569-2 (alk. paper)
    1. Birds—Brazil.   2. Ornithology—Brazil.   3. Birds,
    Protection of—Brazil.   I. International Council for Bird Preservation.
    Pan American Continental Section.   II. Title.
    QL689.B8S5313   1993
    598.2981—dc20   92-19971

The author and translator are donating their royalties to ICBP-PACS for
use in bird conservation projects in Brazil

This book has been composed in Times Roman

Printed in the United States of America

10   9   8   7   6   5   4   3   2   1

DEDICATED TO

Dr. Emilie Snethlage
(1868–1929)

PIONEER OF

FIELD RESEARCH ON

BIRDS IN BRAZIL

Contents

LIST OF TABLES

Foreword (to the Brazilian edition)

Helmut Sick, an accomplished ornithologist with an abundant, top quality scientific output that has brought him world renown, needs no further praise at the opening of this, his new book.

The book obviously has cost him many days of persevering labor, days he would certainly rather have employed in making new scientific discoveries, preferably in some distant corner where he could commune with Nature. His decision to write it must have been due to his conviction that it was the most important service he could render to the development of Brazilian ornithology and the furtherance of ornithological research among us.

The book aims at more than educating ornithologists, for it is accessible to all those who, not being students of ornithology, are merely interested in expanding their general knowledge about Brazilian birds, or only want to look up some fact or other. However, one item of interest to professional ornithologists should be emphasized. Because of Helmut Sick's vast experience (he never lets anything go by without marking it down in his notebook), the book is replete with original observations published here for the first time.

As an "introduction," the broad view the book offers could not be more detailed or complete, and it has the merit, consonant with the intention of promoting research, of making very clear how little we yet know about many aspects of ornithology.

The book also very properly treats the problem of bird conservation. This is a critical issue. The impact of civilization is having a literally devastating effect on our avifauna, and the number of species menaced by extinction is already high.

Because of its excellent quality, I do not hesitate to predict that the book will fully achieve its objective and that its contribution to the development of ornithology will be without parallel in the history of this discipline in Brazil. We owe our warmest recognition to Helmut Sick for having devoted himself with unsurpassable dedication to its preparation.

ARISTIDES AZEVEDO PACHECO LEÃO,
*Former president of the Brazilian Academy of Sciences
and member of the Comité d'Honneur of the Société
d'Etudes Ornithologiques of Paris*

A Discrete Wise Man

Among the silent Brazilians who work effectively for national progress in the field of understanding Nature, it is only just to include Professor Helmut Sick of the Federal University of Rio de Janeiro.

Born in Leipzig, he arrived in Rio de Janeiro in 1939 as a young ornithologist. I later wrote the following about what happened to him: "Recently married, he had the bad luck to leave for Brazil on the eve of the Second World War. He left his wife in Germany and disappeared into the forests of the Rio Doce to carry out a scientific mission based on an international agreement. When Brazil entered the war every German was viewed as a dangerous spy, or a potential one. As a result, he was interned on Ilha Grande. There, unable to study birds in his cell, he studied the miserable companions of his solitude: fleas, lice, termites—of the latter alone he identified eleven previously unknown species. When better times came, he was commissioned by the Central Brazil Foundation and caught malaria, which he still suffers from today."

None of this kept Dr. Sick from continuing to devote all his zeal to studying the country's avifauna, or from becoming a naturalized Brazilian citizen. By now he has written more than 160 publications on our birds and those of other countries. He refused an offer to become director of the Ornithology Section of the Zoological Museum of Berlin in favor of a place on the staff of the National Museum of Rio de Janeiro, where, in 1975, his salary was 450 cruzeiros.

This man of great scientific probity today has international renown. I, a chronicler of passing events, am not the one who says so; authoritative voices proclaim it. Despite his prestige as a scientist, he lives with extreme modesty and simplicity, far from the clarions of publicity. His book *Ornitologia Brasileira,* the work of a lifetime and of a scholar, adds relevant material to Brazil's scientific bibliography. Thank you, Professor Sick, in the name of the men, the women, and the birds of our country.

CARLOS DRUMMOND DE ANDRADE

Expressions of Appreciation

First I must applaud the insight used by Paul Barruel, of St. Jean d'Arvey, Savoie, France, in painting the plates. Sending the specimens to be painted or drawn to the artist's residence was made possible through the collaboration of the museums of Paris (Musée National d'Histoire Naturelle, Prof. D. Jean Dorst), Munich (Zoologische Staatssammlung, Dr. G. Diesselhorst), Frankfurt (Museum Senckenberg, Dr. Joachim Steinbacher), Bonn (Museum Alexander Koenig, Prof. Dr. Günther Niethammer†), London (British Museum, Natural History, Dr. James D. MacDonald), and New York (American Museum of Natural History [AMNH], Dr. Dean Amadon). I also used the collection made in the 1800s by Prince Maximilian, on deposit in the AMNH (see chapter 2). To assist the artist's work by providing him with characteristic stances of live birds, I sent Mr. Barruel sketches of birds that I had made in the field in Brazil. Mr. Barruel also drew many of the black-and-white illustrations in this book.

Among the colleagues and friends most interested in the work were the following: Dr. Eugene Eisenmann† (AMNH, New York), Dr. Philip S. Humphrey (Museum of Natural History, University of Kansas), Rodolphe Meyer de Schauensee† (Academy of Natural Sciences, Philadelphia), Dr. Alexander Wetmore† (Smithsonian Institution, Washington, D.C.), Prof. Dr. Ernst Mayr (Museum of Comparative Zoology, Harvard University, Cambridge), Dr. T. E. Lovejoy (Smithsonian Institution, Washington), Prof. Dr. Ernst Schüz (Museum für Naturkunde, Stuttgart), Paul Schwartz† (Rancho Grande, Venezuela), Dr. Maria Koepcke† (Lima, Peru), Dr. Luc Hoffmann (Tour du Valat, France), Dr. Fritz Neubaur† (Wiesbaden, Germany), Frei Tomas Borgmeier O.F.M.† (Rio de Janeiro), Dr. Étienne Béraut (Rio de Janeiro), Walter Klemm (German Embassy), and William Belton (International Council for Bird Preservation, Pan American Section).

Dr. P. L. Ames, Chicago, made the drawings of Passeriform syrinxes. Dr. Pierce Brodkorb, University of Florida, Gainesville, furnished most of the paleontological data. For this English-language edition, Dr. Herculano M. F. Alvarenga of Taubaté, São Paulo, contributed the section on fossil birds. Dr. Jürgen Haffer, Essen, Germany, authorized the reproduction of several of his maps and contributed much of chapter 4, "Biogeography and Speciation." Francisco Pontual furnished several drawings.

I appreciate the valuable cooperation of the following colleagues and friends in Brazil: Dr. Olivério M. de O. Pinto† and his successor, Hélio F. A. Camargo (Museu de Zoologia da Universidade de São Paulo), Dr. Fernando C. Novaes (Museu Paraense Emílio Goeldi, Belém, Pará), Augusto Ruschi† (Museu de Biologia Prof. Melo Leitão, Santa Teresa, Espírito Santo), H. F. Berla† (Museu Nacional, Rio de Janeiro), and Alvaro Aguirre† (former Divisão de Caça e Pesca, Museu da Fauna, Rio de Janeiro). In the body of the book I mention others.

Dr. Otto Schubart† (Pirassununga, São Paulo) devoted himself to identifying invertebrates taken from the stomachs of birds, and Dr. Graziela Maciel Barroso (Jardim Botânico, Rio de Janeiro) identified seeds found in crops and stomachs of collected birds.

Mr. Rogério Marinho tirelessly inspired me during preparation of the book.

I always enjoyed the full support of the National Council for Scientific and Technological Development (CNPq), especially in the person of Dr. Manoel da Frota Moreira,† who maintained great interest in my project. The Museu Nacional and the Brazilian Academy of Sciences, both in Rio de Janeiro, provided me full facilities for my work, and the German Consulate in Rio de Janeiro also assisted me.

I cannot fail to mention my old mentor, Prof. Dr. Erwin Stresemann† of the Museum of Zoology of the University of Berlin (see chapter 2, under E. Snethlage).

Adolf Schneider,† director of a school in Berlin-Oranienburg, came to Brazil with me in 1939, and became known through his study of the iconography of Georg Marcgrave (see chapter 2). We made field trips together in Espírito Santo until the end of 1939 (the war in Europe had begun); later, Schneider worked in the Museu Nacional, Rio de Janeiro, identifying material in the bird collections (see Schneider and Sick 1962) and made two trips to collect birds: one to the Sertão das Cobras, Rio de Janeiro, and the other to Porto Quebracho, Mato Grosso. He returned to Germany in 1942, where he died in Berlin at the end of the war.

I owe very special remembrance to my deceased wife, Marga Sick, for typing the manuscripts and for the selfless devotion with which she assumed responsibility for many other tasks related to my project.

I am deeply grateful to Dr. Aristides Pacheco Leão, former president of the Brazilian Academy of Sciences, who closely followed the progress of the project, providing me the stimulus and intellectual pleasure of his collaboration.

H. SICK

†Deceased.

Translator's Comments

The Author

Helmut Sick died on 5 March 1991 in Rio de Janeiro. Although eighty-one years old, he remained vigorous and active until his final days. During the last years of his life he devoted himself almost singlemindedly to this book. As soon as the original Brazilian version appeared in 1985, he began revising and updating it for a new edition. When events revealed that publication of a new Brazilian edition would be delayed, he concentrated on our collaboration for this English edition. When time no longer permitted significant alterations for it, he reverted to further effort on the new Brazilian edition. That work was soon cut short by his death, so this edition is likely to be his final monument.

Dr. Sick's career was one of devotion and abnegation, for he persisted in the face of economic and professional difficulties that the average scientist in other parts of the world rarely faces. Despite these problems, he remained loyal to his Brazilian birds and rejected opportunities to practice his profession elsewhere. His passing leaves a large gap in the Brazilian ornithological community, but a part of his heritage is the large number of younger Brazilian ornithologists whom he helped and influenced. He was an integral part of the movement that during the past twenty years transformed Brazilian ornithology from the province of a few elderly men to a vibrant profession studied or practiced by several hundred young men and women.

The Book

Birds in Brazil is a translation from the Portuguese of a substantially revised version of *Ornitologia Brasileira, Uma Introdução*, published in Brazil in 1985 by the University of Brasília Press. The original has gone through three printings, but almost all copies have been sold within Brazil, so the book is little known elsewhere. It was originally envisioned that the revised version would be published simultaneously in Portuguese and English, but as a new Portuguese edition is now unlikely, this volume stands as a distinct entity. Because the author continued to revise and update the text during the course of the translation, information received as recently as January 1991 has been incorporated. Dr. Sick's death occurred before he was able to answer the last set of questions I posed to him before this translation went to press. Knowing his interest in keeping up with the latest discoveries, I have, on my own responsibility, included two newly discovered antbirds, the Rondonia Bushbird, *Clytoctantes atrogularis,* and the Belem Antbird, *Cercomacra laeta,* in the species accounts and numerical summations.

Dr. Sick had a special interest in bird vocalization. Starting well before portable recording devices were available, he developed a system of notation based on his native German but with Portuguese overtones, which enabled him to recall and imitate quite accurately the thousands of bird songs and calls he had heard during his long career. Transliterating his notations into a form that would be meaningful to English speakers' ears appeared to be the most daunting of the many problems posed by this project. We tackled it over a long weekend in his Rio de Janeiro apartment, during which he read aloud each of his notations, and I transliterated them into syllables or phrases I hoped would be meaningful to ears accustomed to English. The results have built-in limitations, for every listener usually has his or her own distinctive interpretation of a bird vocalization. However, my own familiarity with many of the bird voices leads me to believe the descriptions can be helpful. In reading them, capitalized syllables should be accented.

Use of the Book

Due to the plethora of Brazilian bird and place names used here, a few hints on how to approximate Brazilian pronunciation may be helpful:

ã at the end of a word is nasalized, as in "aracuã" = aracuahng
ch is pronounced like sh in English
j is pronounced like the s in "vision"
lh is the same as ll in Spanish, pronounced as in "million" in English
nh is the same as ñ in Spanish, pronounced as in "onion" in English
ns and m at the end of a word are nasalized as in the following examples: Belém = beleng; tuim = tooeeng; mutum = mootoong; mutums = mootoongs
São combines the "soun" of "sound" with a "g" to nasalize it = soung

A number of Brazilian geographic terms, such as "cerrado" and "caatinga," cannot be satisfactorily translated and so have been unchanged. These are well explained in chapter 1, section 1.3, "Principal Habitats of Brazilian Birds."

Dr. Sick used the Brazilian phrase "consta que" (literally, "it is said that") to introduce information he accepted as probably true but about which he had neither personal knowledge nor scientific evidence at hand. I have translated this variously as "they say," "it is reported," and so on.

The figure in parentheses after the name at the beginning of each family account represents the number of species of that family found in Brazil.

One or more symbols appear after the heading in many species accounts. Their meaning is as follows:

BR = Endemic to Brazil
EN = Endangered
R = Rare
NV = Visitor from north of Brazil, not known to breed in Brazil
SV = Visitor from south or west of Brazil, not known to breed in Brazil.

Much of Sick's research was performed at a time when the city of Rio de Janeiro was situated in the state of Guanabara, a jurisdiction only slightly larger than Rio de Janeiro itself. Many of his location records were listed as "Guanabara." Guanabara was abolished as a political entity in the 1970s and absorbed by the surrounding state of Rio de Janeiro, of which the city of Rio de Janeiro became the capital. Sick's Guanabara records are designated here as "ex-Guanabara," which can be taken for practical purposes as meaning the city of Rio de Janeiro and some of its southern and western suburbs, now forming the municipality of Rio de Janeiro, roughly equivalent to a county in the United States. Another political change of the same era divided what had been, during most of Sick's research, the state of Mato Grosso, into two states, Mato Grosso and Mato Grosso do Sul. Unless otherwise specified, records herein for Mato Grosso refer to the area now comprised by these two jurisdictions.

English names for this translation have been taken primarily from Meyer de Schauensee (1970). However, during the years since that publication appeared, some species have been moved from one family to another, and new facts on habitat, behavior, and such have come to light on others, rendering their Meyer de Schauensee names misleading. When such cases involve Passerines, I have used the names selected by Robert Ridgely and Guy Tudor for the first two volumes of their projected four-volume *The Birds of South America* (vol. 1, 1989), because this work seems likely to set the standard for such matters for the foreseeable future. I have departed from this practice only where, as in the case of the Itatiaia Thistletail, *Schizoeaca moreirae,* Sick held a view different from theirs as to a bird's relationships, making it inappropriate to use their name. I am indebted to Ridgely for advancing me the list of names to be used in their forthcoming volume 2, and for bringing to my attention a few recent modifications in the spelling of scientific names.

Many non-Passerines found in Brazil also occur in Middle or North America and are therefore included in the 6th edition of the AOU *Check-list of North American Birds* (1983) and its 35th through 38th supplements. Where an English or

scientific name in these documents differs from those used by Meyer de Schauensee, I have used the AOU designation.

Readers will note that, contrary to customary practice in most English-language bird books, I have used scientific names throughout, providing the English name usually only when a species is first mentioned in a chapter and in the pertinent species accounts. This is because the English names, while generally standardized by Meyer de Schauensee, are still widely unfamiliar to the great majority of people expected to use this book, including a considerable readership for whom they would have no meaning unless accompanied by the scientific names. Although this may inconvenience some readers until they have familiarized themselves with the scientific terminology, it eliminates the equally irritating alternative of having to read both names each time a species designation is encountered. To facilitate access to these names, in the index of scientific names each name of a Brazilian bird is followed by its English equivalent, and in the index of English names the corresponding practice is followed.

Acknowledgments

To ensure that my translation meets current standards of ornithological expression, I asked a number of experts to read portions of the manuscript covering families or fields with which they were particularly familiar. All of these persons made valuable suggestions that enabled me to improve the translation. Most also had substantive comments which I sent to Dr. Sick for consideration. These usually motivated further modifications of the text. Both of us owe appreciation to Alan Brush, Mercedes S. Foster, J. William Hardy, Morton and Phyllis Isler, Helen F. James, J. Peter Jenny, James Kushlan, Joe T. Marshall, Eugene S. Morton, Charles Munn, Storrs Olson, Robert S. Ridgely, Lester S. Short, Douglas F. Stotz, Betsy T. Thomas, Melvin A. Traylor, Jr., and Richard Zusi for their help.

John P. O'Neill generously painted plates 44 and 45 especially for this edition in response to Dr. Sick's appeal. Most of the birds he portrayed are quite rare, so reference material had to come from many sources. For specimens he thanks J. V. Remsen and S. W. Cardiff of the Louisiana State University Museum of Natural Science, W. E. Lanyon, G. F. Barrowclough, and M. K. LeCroy of the American Museum of Natural History in New York, and S. M. Lanyon and D. E. Willard of the Field Museum of Natural History in Chicago. Typically, fellow artist Guy Tudor happily provided what he knew from his own experiences, as well as what he had available in his impressive personal reference collection. And, of course, Helmut Sick gathered photographs, drawings, and copies of rare publications that could be useful and added data from his often unique personal notes. To all of these people O'Neill gives a much-deserved "thanks."

Richard Georgi, Christoph Hrdina, B. Loiselle, Thomas Lovejoy, Narca Moore-Craig, Ted Parker, Carlos Quintela,

Magda Lara Resende, and David Youngman helped by safely transporting, often at personal inconvenience and expense, illustrations and revised text from Dr. Sick to me.

Great thanks is due to the Companhia Vale do Rio Doce, and especially to Agripino Abranches Viana, Maria de Lourdes Davies de Freitas, and Francisco F. de Assis Fonseca, officers of the company, for their interest and assistance in financing new color separations, prepared in Rio de Janeiro, for all the color plates except those by John P. O'Neill. This support enormously facilitated the entire project.

I am grateful to the late author, my friend of many years, for his hospitality during my visits to Rio de Janeiro to consult with him on problems relating to preparation of this English edition.

Judith May, formerly science editor at Princeton University Press, now with Oxford University Press, was instrumental in encouraging me to work with the present publishers, while Emily Wilkinson, editor in chief, has made it a pleasure to continue with Princeton. Alice Calaprice, senior editor edited the first five chapters of the manuscript and guided it through all phases of production. Elizabeth Pierson, to whom I am particularly grateful for expert advice, skillfully edited the family and species accounts.

WILLIAM BELTON
31 March 1992

Introduction

[Translator's note: Dr. Sick did not have an opportunity to revise this section before his death. I have updated the species numbers, eliminated some outdated material, and included a few explanatory remarks in brackets.]

South America, the bird continent, has over 2,650 resident species. When migrants that nest elsewhere are considered, the total comes close to 3,000. This figure is unequaled by any other region on the planet and amounts to almost a third of all the living avian species in the world. The world total is now reported to be 9,680 species (Clements 1991).

According to the latest calculations, Brazil has 1,635 species, representing 91 families or subfamilies and 23 orders. This amounts to about 55 percent of the birds recorded for the continent. I include all the species found in Brazilian territory, including territorial waters and Atlantic islands belonging to Brazil from where reliable information is available. If geographic races are considered, the total exceeds 2,500. Races and subspecies are dealt with in this book only when they are significantly distinct.

The relatively small countries of Peru and Colombia rival Brazil in number of species, not only because they share generously in the richness of Amazonian fauna, but also because they include the extraordinarily varied Andean fauna that Brazil lacks entirely except for a few relicts of Pleistocene colonization. On the other hand, Brazil has elements of the great Patagonian fauna (related to fauna of the Andes) that penetrated into the south. Bolivia, Venezuela, and Central America are also very rich in bird species, with more than 1,000 each. Brazilian bird abundance is also impressive when compared with that of mammals. Calculated on the basis of collections of J. Natterer (see chapter 2), the proportion of mammal species to that of birds is approximately 1:6. In other words, on the average one could find six bird species before finding one mammal species. In Africa mammals predominate, but the Congo region is also very rich in birds, containing more than 1,000 species.

In addition to quantity, Brazilian birds rate innumerable qualitative superlatives. For example, one of the world's largest birds, the Greater Rhea, *Rhea americana,* lives here alongside the smallest, the hummingbirds. The latter are the best aerial dancers and the most challenging birds of the hemisphere to the naturalist who tries to understand these organisms and their functioning. The largest flying birds on earth, the albatross and the condor, are found in Brazil, although each occurs only occasionally. The Harpy Eagle,

Harpia harpyja, a Brazilian resident, is the world's most powerful raptor. The fastest-flying birds, falcons and swifts, are found here. The rhea is one of the few birds in the world that has abandoned the ability to fly in favor of surface mobility. This is also a peculiarity of penguins, those regular visitors to our southern coasts who have become champions of underwater swimming, using their wings as paddles.

Among the strangest birds of the world are our potoos, *Nyctibius,* which, to avoid spoiling a camouflage indispensable to the safety of nocturnal birds during daytime roosting, have developed a system of seeing without opening their eyes ("magic eye").

Although it is unwise to discuss beauty, I can state that Brazil has various birds whose decorative virtues rate the highest international ranking. Among these are the macaws; the cock-of-the-rock, *Rupicola;* and hummingbirds such as the *Lophornis* and *Topaza.* Suitable choice of a "national bird" has not yet received proper attention. A good choice would be the Golden Parakeet, *Guaruba guaroba,* a Brazilian endemic of rare beauty that has the yellow and green colors of the Brazilian flag.

In addition to works on systematics, Brazil is well provided with catalogs of its avifauna, especially those authored by Olivério M. de Oliveira Pinto (1938, 1944, 1964, 1978, etc.), who was a veteran master of national ornithology. However, information on living birds and their multiple relations with the environment is scarce. It is precisely this feature that is my principal interest. I start, whenever possible, with observation of living birds and only later move to the study of books or materials preserved in museums. Mayr, Linsley, and Unsinger (1953) have written: "There is an unmistakable trend among taxonomists to approach their material more and more as biologists and less and less as museum catalogers." In other words, the time has passed for purely static office research. I envisage a dynamic systematics, making all possible use of the concept of geographic species or superspecies (Mayr 1942) that leads to true understanding of fauna. I aim for an ecological and biogeographic analysis of Brazilian avifauna, placed in its historic and world settings. I have brought together material on its origin, its evolution, and its phylogenetic relationships, relating it to the rest of the world.

Obedient to the concept of an "introduction to ornithology," I cannot enter into much detail. I call attention to phenomena I judge to be important, without the least pretension of being exhaustive. I usually base my comments on my own observations. My fifty years of experience as a professional ornithologist in the Neotropics has included visits to other countries of South America, and in ten years (1946–1957) as naturalist with the Central Brazil Foundation I accompanied the Roncador-Xingu-Tapajós Expedition of the Vilas Boas brothers in Mato Grosso and Pará (traveling by muleback, canoe, and single engine as well as Brazilian Air Force planes). During all this time I recorded many things, accumulating more than 8,500 pages of scientific diaries. When I use "I found" or similar phrases, I am emphasizing that I personally verified the facts. I have been unable to take advantage of many of my discoveries due to lack of support or scarcity of bibliography or equipment. A number of people have taken advantage of my information without citing my name. English-speaking authors have often not given attention to my publications in Portuguese and German, and in many cases I have lost my priority.

I worked for more than twenty years preparing a book, *Aves do Brasil* [*Birds of Brazil*]. In 1960 I started a field guide, choosing as illustrator Paul Barruel, one of the most famous in this specialty, who had just finished illustrating F. Haverschmidt's book on the birds of Suriname (1968). In the course of preparing it, the field guide (which was to include only a selection of Brazilian birds) took on the character of a treatise, like the mythological "soup of stones," and was to have been published in the early 1970s by the Brazilian Academy of Sciences, whose then president, Dr. Aristides Pacheco Leão, took particular interest in it.

The considerable lapse of time that occurred between my first presentation of the manuscript to the Brazilian Academy of Sciences and the final delivery in January 1982 required an almost complete revision to bring it up to date. There arose, among other problems, that of considering new research results on the relationship of certain groups, such as the recent elimination of the Coerebidae family and the reorganization of the Tyrannidae, published when my manuscript was practically finished. During the last twenty years, interest in ornithology, which formerly in Latin America was a discipline confined to a few specialists, grew greatly, producing a host of activities in this field, plus an immense bibliography. Such novelties included capturing birds in nylon nets for identification and banding, voice recording, and photography of birds in the field. Within a few years it became common to engage field ornithologists to lead groups of tourists interested in birds. Organizations of birdwatchers have sprung up, such as the Bird Observers' Club in Rio Grande do Sul [which has now developed into a nationwide organization].

I devote relatively little space to plumage descriptions but give more emphasis to special problems of comparative morphology and of behavior, biology, evolution, and distribution. The general structure of the book is in two parts: five introductory chapters, followed by family and species accounts of all Brazilian birds.

Introductory Chapters. [Most of these chapters have been considerably altered for the English-language edition. The sections on elemental ornithology have been omitted in the belief that English-speaking readers either would not need them or would have access to other sources. On the other hand, new sections on biogeography and speciation by Jürgen Haffer (in chapter 4) and Brazilian fossil birds by Herculano Alvarenga (in chapter 5) have been added through the generous courtesy of these experts. Chapter 2, a discussion of the history of Brazilian ornithology, remains almost unchanged. Chapter 3, on conservation in Brazil, has been entirely rewritten to emphasize the serious situation now facing the country. Brazilian terrain and vegetation and the relation of these to birds are dealt with in the first chapter, while the broad picture of Brazilian avifauna is covered in chapter 5, the last introductory chapter. These two, in particular, set the stage for the detailed information contained in the family and species accounts found in the main body of the book.]

Body of the Book. In the body of the book I provide a section on each family, to give a general idea of its characteristics, cover matters of special interest, and make comparisons with other families. The topics considered vary from family to family, according to the most important features of each group. I have avoided following a rigid pattern that is identical for all families and species. Standardization, such as is usually adopted for books of this type (for example: "identification, habitat, behavior, nesting, distribution"), would not be suitable here. I have devoted the most space to species that are particularly interesting, either ornithologically or to the general public. The fullest discussions have been given to families typical of Brazil, such as the Tinamidae, Cracidae, Psittacidae, Trochilidae, Furnariidae, and Pipridae, and to the best-known species such as the Eared Dove, *Zenaida auriculata;* Rufous Hornero, *Furnarius rufus;* Shiny Cowbird, *Molothrus bonariensis;* Rufous-collared Sparrow, *Zonotrichia capensis;* and House Sparrow, *Passer domesticus.*

Among the topics covered are morphology, including special situations such as heterogynism, cryptic species, mutations, polymorphism, albinism and variations, hybridization, gynandromorphism, molt and postembryonic development (ontogeny), and special adaptations; classification, phylogenetic relationships (also revealed by biochemical methods and ectoparasites); sounds; feeding, hunting, and fishing methods; behavior, including, for example, play and left-handedness; thermoregulation; reproduction, mating prenuptial ceremonies, sexual selection, nests, eggs, incubation, nest protection, young; parasitic species; physiological and ethological races; age; habitat and distribution; geographic races; syntopic species; migration, other movements, and invasions; enemies and other adverse factors, including the impact of weather; parasites and nest fauna; pollution, insecticides, and mortality; human utilization, hunting, and guano; supposed nuisances, sanitation problems, and abundance; synanthropic species; decline, conservation, reserves, populations; interspecific relations; hybridization in nature; artificial breeding for repopulation; domestication; popularity, legends, folklore, superstitions; common or popular names and artificial vernacular names.

When matters observed in Brazil require comparison, I have not hesitated to refer to facts observed abroad and even in other continents, in view of the educational aspect of my work. I have aspired to make this an introduction to general ornithology, based on the material in my projected *Birds of Brazil*.

My motive in approaching the subject from the greatest possible number of angles has been to stimulate new observations not only by the specialist but by the layman, especially the Brazilian hobbyist whose access to specialized literature is limited. The ornithology of every country has received very considerable contributions to the amplification of knowledge from amateurs. To recognize and know more about the extremely interesting life of birds is a first step toward stimulating sentiment in favor of conserving our presently much endangered Nature.

PART ONE

1 ◆ The Country and Its Birds

Brazil, with an area of 8,512,000 square kilometers centered in the Neotropical region, occupies 47.3 percent of South America and is fifth in the world in the size of its territory. Only the Soviet Union, Canada, China, and the United States have larger areas, and Brazil is larger than the forty-eight contiguous United States. Because birds are dependent on the environment, I outline here the great climato-geomorphologic domains of Brazil and their respective biotas or ecosystems. One should understand not only the present morphoclimatic environmental situation, but also certain aspects of the paleogeographic history of South America across the centuries that are responsible for the formation of the continent and its flora and fauna. Profound alterations of the climate and vegetation have occurred over the eons.

1.1 *Morphoclimatic Domains*

Ab'Saber (1973) recognizes six great geographic and macroecologic domains in Brazil, defined by very extensive morphoclimatic features and their principal vegetational aspects:

1. *Domain of forested lowlands of Amazonia*, covering more than 2.5 million square kilometers, a zone of labyrinthic (Amazon River) and meandering (most of the Amazon tributaries) flood plains. This domain is situated in a constantly hot and humid climate; Manaus and Santarém have an annual rainfall of about 2,000 mm, the Serra do Navio (Amapá) 2,300 mm, and Uaupés (Amazonas) 2,950 mm.
2. *Domain of the central "chapadões,"* covered by cerrado and penetrated by gallery forests and forest enclaves, with an area of about 2 million square kilometers. It is a region of upland massifs, with rainfall between 1,300 and 1,800 mm, concentrated in winter and relatively low in summer.
3. *Tropical Atlantic domain*, or domain of the "oceans of hills," an area with approximately 1 million square kilometers. Rainfall varies between 1,100 and 4,500 mm. Tropical forests originally covered more than 95 percent of the area.
4. *Caatinga domain*, over semi-arid interplateau depressions of the northeast. The areas vary between 700,000 and 850,000 square kilometers and have unequal and scanty rainfall, 350 to 600 mm annually, with great fluctuations from year to year.
5. *Domain of the araucaria plateaus*, an area of approximately 400,000 square kilometers, between 850 and 1,300 meters in altitude, covered by araucaria forests of varying density. It has a humid, subtropical climate with relatively well-distributed precipitation throughout the year, the highest elevations subject to occasional snowfall (Planalto of S. Joaquim, Lajes, and Curitibanos in Santa Catarina).
6. *Domain of mixed subtropical gaúcho grasslands*, an area of approximately 80,000 square kilometers, functioning as if it were the edge of the pampa grassland domain. It is in a temperate, humid, or subhumid zone, subject to some drought. Only limited areas are outside the annual extremes of 1,500 to 2,000 mm.

Ab'Saber (1973) emphasizes that the transition and contact zones between these great domains are so extensive that it is impossible to define the limits of the domains with precision.

With respect to the evolution of Cretaceous and Quaternary floras in Brazil, Ab'Saber concludes that all the basic patterns of vegetation must have developed between the Middle Tertiary and the Quaternary and are closely related to the present picture of Brazilian inter- and subtropical vegetation: forest, cerrado, caatinga, araucaria, and "pradaria" = "grasslands." Pradaria involves a vegetative cover of grasses with herbaceous or low-bush plants and, though rarely, trees. These floras underwent alterations due to successive climatic changes forced by the unstable paleoclimatology of Quaternary times (fig. 1).

1.2 *Terrain Types and Their Avifauna*

There are two major categories of vegetation—two standard, fundamental terrain types or phytophysiognomic formations that the public simply calls forest and field. Terrestrial avifauna can basically be classified in the same way: belonging to forest or to open country. Aquatic birds are a category apart.

1.2.1 PHYTOGEOGRAPHY

Among the various systems for classifying the phytogeographic situation of Brazil, the first and the one of greatest influence was that of Martius (1967), amply employed in *Flora Brasiliensis* (1840 to 1906, in 40 vols.), which divided Brazil into five ecological-vegetational provinces: (1) the montane forest or montane rain forest, Atlantic region; (2) the hot-dry, or caatinga, northeastern region; (3) the hot, or equatorial, rain forest, Amazonian region; (4) the extratropical, or araucaria, forest region; and (5) the montane grassland, or campo and cerrado, central plateau region.

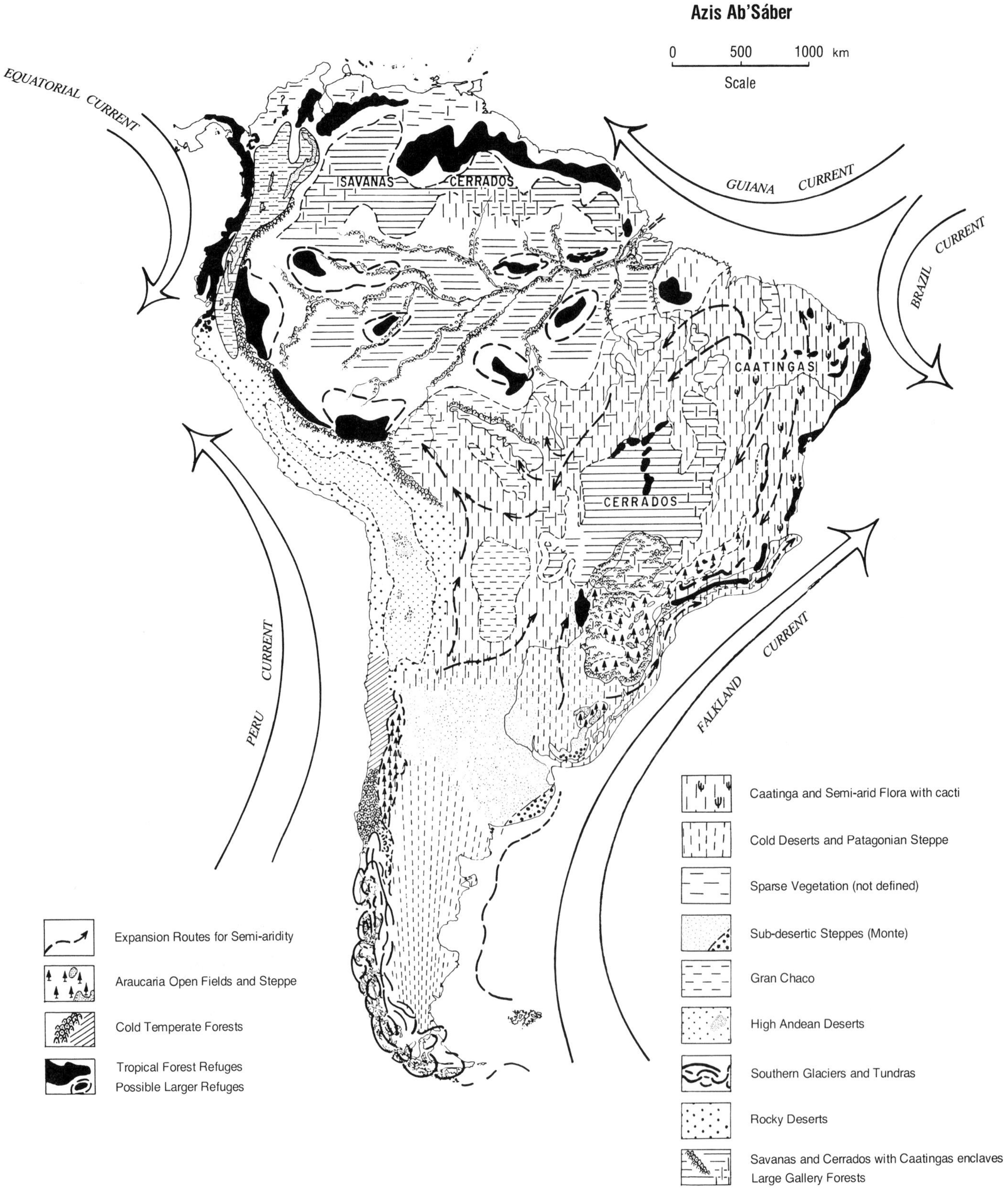

Azis Ab'Sáber

0   500   1000 km

Scale

EQUATORIAL CURRENT

GUIANA CURRENT

BRAZIL CURRENT

PERU CURRENT

FALKLAND CURRENT

SAVANAS
CERRADOS
CAATINGAS
CERRADOS

Expansion Routes for Semi-aridity

Araucaria Open Fields and Steppe

Cold Temperate Forests

Tropical Forest Refuges
Possible Larger Refuges

Caatinga and Semi-arid Flora with cacti

Cold Deserts and Patagonian Steppe

Sparse Vegetation (not defined)

Sub-desertic Steppes (Monte)

Gran Chaco

High Andean Deserts

Southern Glaciers and Tundras

Rocky Deserts

Savanas and Cerrados with Caatingas enclaves
Large Gallery Forests

Fig. 1. Natural regions of South America 13,000 to 18,000 years B.P.; first estimate. After Ab'Saber 1977.

Rodrigues (1903) recognized three great ecological zones: the Amazonian, the Mountain-Grassland, and the Maritime. Engler (1879–82) and Sampaio (1938) modified the Martius system. I have adopted the phytogeographic division of Brazil devised by Rizzini (1963, 1976–79), accepting three provinces: Atlantic, Central, and Amazonia, subdivided further into various subprovinces.

Presently the best basis for achieving better representation of the great natural spaces of our continent is Kurt Hueck's (1966) vegetation map of South America (see also Hueck and Siebert 1972) (fig. 2), on which Ab'Saber (1973) also based his work.

Brazil's primitive vegetation is today much reduced or already gone—over the centuries the victim of agriculture, mining, industry, and urbanization. Secondary formations, grasslands, and man-made semi-deserts have arisen. To replace virgin forest, at best capoeira develops. In the mid-north (Maranhão, Piauí, etc., and also in northern Espírito Santo), felling of virgin forest results in development of babaçu palm groves (Palm Zone; Sampaio 1938). Cerrado is

extremely resistant vegetation; after it is cut for pasture and later cultivated, it returns.

1.2.2 ZOOGEOGRAPHY

For zoologists, biogeographic classifications made by other zoologists are of special interest. Burmeister (1854–56) recognized three great zones for Brazil: Amazonia, Central Brazil, and the Atlantic Forest. Pelzeln (1867–71), basing his conclusions on the enormous number of birds, mammals, and other animals collected by Natterer, noted only two regions, a classification similar to that of the botanist Engler (see section 1.2.1). Wallace (1876, from Udvardy 1969) considered Brazil to have three regions: Amazonia, southern Brazil, and a piece of the pampa region. The four Brazilian "scorpiological" provinces of Mello Leitão (1937 and later) correspond to the mammalian provinces of Cabrera and Yepes (1940): the Amazonian province, the Cariri-Bororó province (northeast, central Brazil, and the northern Chaco), the Guarani province (extending to the Bolivian Chaco), and the Tupi province (coastal forests).

1.2.3 INVASIONS

Destruction of primary vegetation involves dissolution of ecosystem limits as defined here. Invasion of cerrado and caatinga bird species into neighboring forest systems can be noted where forests are disappearing. Thus, for example, open-country tinamids, such as the Red-winged and Small-billed Tinamous, *Rhynchotus rufescens* and *Crypturellus parvirostris*, have appeared in western Espírito Santo and Rio de Janeiro. The Curl-crested Jay, *Cyanocorax cristatellus*, is beginning to invade Rio de Janeiro and São Paulo. The most typical dendrocolaptid of the central Brazilian cerrado, the Narrow-billed Woodcreeper, *Lepidocolaptes angustirostris*, has been seen on Paquetá Island in Guanabara Bay, Rio de Janeiro: an isolated individual that occupied a nest and tried in vain to find a mate. Later in the book I draw attention to such cases.

1.3 *Principal Habitats of Brazilian Birds*

I propose the definition of eleven great ecological divisions where the birds of this country live, basing the vegetational aspect of Hueck and Siebert (1972) and Rizzini (1976–79). These macrohabitats, or principal ecological regions, can be divided into numerous ecological niches, to which I refer throughout the body of the book.

From the viewpoint of bird distribution, flora identification, though fundamental for the botanist, is not of major importance. The physiognomy of the habitat is what counts for birds. A dry, mesophilic forest in central Brazil, for instance, may have an avifauna very similar to that of a xerophilous forest of the caatinga. There is also the phenomenon of wide transitional bands between well-defined regions, as occurs with the vegetation (see section 1.1).

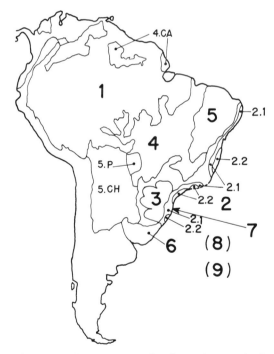

Fig. 2. Brazil's great vegetational complexes and principal bird habitats. Vegetation map adapted from Hueck and Siebert 1972. (1) Amazon rain forest. (2) Atlantic rain forest; (2.1) littoral or coastal forest; (2.2) montane forest. (3) Araucaria forest. (4) Cerrado and savannas of central Brazil, savannas north of the Amazon, restinga, and high-altitude savannas; (4.CA) Rio Branco and Amapá savannas. (5) Caatinga and Pantanal of Mato Grosso; (5.P) Pantanal; (5.CH) Chaco. (6) Gaucho region. (7) Mangrove; the arrow indicates the southern limit of mangroves on the Atlantic coast of Santa Catarina at 28°20'S. (8) Oceanic islands. (9) Aquatic environment.

1.3.1 AMAZONIAN RAIN FOREST

This rain forest is the largest forest on the planet, to which Humboldt and Bompland applied the name "Hylaea." It is the equatorial forest that extends from the Atlantic ocean to the Andean foothills, bounded to the north and south by drier formations, but including the Orinoco and Guiana lowlands. This area coincides almost exactly with that of the rubber tree (*Hevea*), which, incidentally, serves to characterize the Hylaea botanically. Brazilians speak of "legal Amazonia": an area of 5 million square kilometers that includes the states of Amazonas, Roraima, Rondônia, Amapá, Acre, Mato Grosso, and Tocantins.

The expression "Amazonian forest" is a collective designation for various types of humid forest, of which terra firme forest and várzea forest are the two basic types. There are many other formations within the Amazonian domain, such as buriti várzeas, caatingas of the Rio Negro and Rio Solimões, campinas, savannas, and small mountains with dry forest (the Serra dos Carajás, Pará, for example).

Although Amazonia is calculated to be more recent than the cerrado (see section 1.3.3), the Neotropical forest has existed for millions of years and has evolved the world's most complex group of ecosystems. Oscillations in the climate of the entire continent have produced drastic modifications in Amazonia, which once reached southeastern Brazil (see section 1.3.2 and chapter 4).

A special feature of Amazonia is the existence of different-colored rivers that also influence the flora and fauna: "white," muddy water (Rios Amazon, Madeira, and Branco); light green, transparent water (Rio Tapajós); and "black," olive-brown water (Rios Negro and Cururu) (Sioli 1962).

TERRA FIRME FOREST

This kind of forest lies beyond the influence of the rivers. It is the great, imposing, Hylaean rain forest. The terra firme forest is situated on slightly elevated (60 to 200 meters) plateaus that are undulating or cut by small streams and not subject to river flooding. The substrate is often clayey sand.

Usually the forest is stratified, with up to four identifiable strata. The highest strata (forest dome) reaches 30 to 40 meters, but not infrequently comes down to 20 meters. Emergent trees reaching 50 to 60 meters are typical. One of the most notable of these emergents is the Brazil-nut tree (*Bertholletia excelsa*), which makes up the Brazil-nut groves.

Under the top strata there is a second arboreal story, and subordinated to it another tree-bush level between 2 and 5 meters, which forms the understory, rich in palms. The wealth of trees in the Hylaea is unique; however, the dominance of certain species is only relative, and, on the other hand, numerous species are represented in a given area by only one individual. The number of trees and species per unit gives an idea of the richness of these forests: in the Belém,

Pará, region, 150 kilometers from the equator and the Atlantic, with annual rainfall of 2,800 mm or more and temperature averaging from 25°C to 26°C, 133 trees (with a trunk diameter of 10 cm at 120 cm above the ground) of 42 species can be found per hectare. On the Rio Madeira, 111 trees of 60 species are found, and in the upper Amazon even higher figures occur: 120 to 290 species of tree per hectare (Gentry 1988). In central Europe, at most 10 species per hectare are found (Kubitzki pers. com.). These censuses deepen our understanding of phytophysiognomy. The same evolution can be observed in fauna: rich in species, but few individuals per species.

Tabular roots (sapopemas) and respiratory bracing roots, similar to those of mangroves (see section 1.3.8), are conspicuous. Other typical forms are vines with thick or ladder-like stems (escada-de-macaco = "monkeyladder" [*Bauhinia*], for example). Plants living in symbiosis with ants are abundant. Normally such forests are clear and easy to pass through. The greatest obstacles are large fallen trunks. These fallen giants, together with the surrounding trees they have brought down with them, form an impenetrable thicket above which a sort of natural forest clearing appears.

VÁRZEA FOREST

This is a domain located on lowlands subject to periodic flooding by muddy, "white water" rivers during the rainy season. The forests extend onto innumerable river islands. Várzea trees are usually from 20 to 30 meters tall, but the maparajuba (*Apuleia molaris*) is a várzea forest giant that reaches 40 meters. Várzeas are cut up by small rivers and streams, called "igarapés." The understory is poor in plant life. The sumaúma (*Ceiba pentandra*), so distinctive in size and shape, grows in places of high sedimentation.

IGAPÓ FOREST

This forest is flooded by stationary water along the edges of clear, "black water" rivers. This type of forest also occurs in terra firme along stream edges. The igapó blends into the buriti groves, a beautiful formation of *Mauritia* sp. palms (see section 1.3.3).

RIVERINE FORMATIONS

This area includes sandy beaches with bushy willows (*Salix humboldtiana*) entirely covered by water during the frequently five-month-long flood season. A strip of low forest with *Cecropia*, thickets of *Heliconia*, and, locally, the jauarí palm (*Astrocaryum*) marks the actual edge of the river. The brush-covered islands disappear completely during the floods.

BIRDS OF AMAZONIA

Nowhere else in the world do so many birds live: both in total number of species and in the numbers sharing the same habitat (syntopic). The composition of these habitats changes within the same forest in ways almost imperceptible to us. Thus the fauna also changes, in an adaptation that has evolved over thousands of years; we perceive only a portion of these intimate linkages. Biodiversity is easier to understand when we study the lower animals that live in the vegetation and the soil.

The avifauna never lacks fruits, seeds, flowers, and arthropods for easy feeding throughout the year. I can give here only a vague idea of this extremely complex situation.

Amazonia is the home of the large Cracidae (curassows), many Tinamidae (tinamous; one must know the voices of the species; see below), Psittacidae (macaws, parrots, and parakeets, including the beautiful Golden Parakeet, *Guaruba guarouba*, proposed as the Brazilian national bird, endemic to the area south of the Amazon), picturesque Ramphastidae (toucans and araçaris), Picidae (woodpeckers), and many Passeriformes such as the antbirds, the most interesting of which, like the *Grallaria*, run or hop on the ground. The Pipridae, manakins, fascinate us with their dances and are famous in Amazonia, where they are called "uirapurus." It is particularly interesting to study Amazonian folklore, which often involves birds and lets one imagine the fantastic spiritual world of the Indians, traditional masters of these lands for thousands of years (see under cerrado). Typical Amazonian birds, including in the Orinoco region, are the Hoatzin, *Opisthocomus hoazin*, the trumpeters, *Psophia* spp., and the Sunbittern, *Eurypyga helias*, the latter having a range that extends to tropical Mexico and whose melodious voice, sounded at dawn and dusk, is ear-catching. There are still a reasonable number of the most powerful birds of prey, such as the Harpy and Crested Eagles, *Harpia harpyja* and *Morphnus guianensis*. Among hummingbirds of the sunny canopy, the most distinguished is the beautiful Crimson Topaz, *Topaza pella*, while brown *Phaethornis* abound in the darkest forest interior. Barbets (Capitonidae) are pantropical but in Brazil occur only in Amazonia. The Black-girdled Barbet, *Capito dayi*, is an endemic of the region. The Cotingidae stand out among the most typical Passerines, with species such as the Crimson Fruitcrow, *Haematoderus militaris*; Purple-throated Fruitcrow, *Querula purpurata*; Amazonian Umbrellabird, *Cephalopterus ornatus*; Capuchinbird, *Perissocephalus tricolor*; and Bare-necked Fruitcrow, *Gymnoderus foetidus*. The strident cry of the Screaming Piha, *Lipaugus vociferans*, is the "voice of Amazonia."

The legion of flycatchers, Tyrannidae, occurring in every strata of the forest and dominant at upper ones, challenges even the most highly trained ornithologist, who must collect specimens for proper identification.

It is difficult to observe birds of the forest roof, where flocks of tanagers and others pass through, and species such as the Slaty-capped Shrike-Vireo, *Smaragdolanius leucotis*, have their permanent habitat. The observer can well break his neck trying to see up there and identify a bird whose voice he isn't familiar with. For proper censusing of birds, day or night, it is essential to know all their voices, a process that requires hard work over months and years.

Falling fruits reveal the presence of parrots or monkeys eating in the canopy, but it is difficult to find a gap in the foliage through which to see them. Fruit scattered on the ground attracts tinamous, which are difficult to find elsewhere. Fallen trees, with their radiating disk of exposed roots, provide opportunities for nesting birds by becoming substitute embankments. Natural clearings attract forest-edge birds, including North American migrants such as warblers (Parulinae) during the northern winter. Vibrant columns of army ants are announced from a distance by the excited cries of bird flocks who foresee abundant and easy eating in the infinity of small animals fleeing from the ants. Even the most cautious birds are attracted, such as the large, terrestrial *Neomorphus* cuckoos, a notable feature of Amazonia.

Parrots, macaws, and cotingas, such as the Pompadour Cotinga, *Xipholena punicea*, fly from one emergent tree to another. One of Amazonia's best spectacles is the flights of macaw, parrot, and large icterine (oropendulas, *Psarocolius* spp.) flocks in the late afternoon as they move to their traditional roosts. Observation towers, such as the one first built in the Guama Ecological Research Area (APEG) at Belém, Pará, are very useful for seeing these movements.

It has been surprising to find species thought to belong exclusively to the upper Amazon, such as *Cephalopterus* and *Gymnoderus* (Cotingidae), on the upper Xingu and upper Tapajós.

It is most fascinating to go out at night and try to decipher the chorus of nocturnal animals—owls, nightjars, and three species of potoo, the last being among the most unusual birds of the Neotropics and the world. Among nocturnal mammals are arboreal rodents of the genus *Echimys*, and the night monkey, *Aotus*. There are batrachians with voices similar to those of birds. The song of the Rufescent Tiger-Heron, *Tigrisoma lineatum*, can be very similar to the distant roar of a jaguar, as I learned in central Brazil. On moonlit nights one can hear the rustle of the wings of the Blue-throated Piping-Guan, *Pipile pipile*, an arboreal cracid, flying from one treetop to another at the river's edge. The ventriloquial voice of a trumpeter, *Psophia* sp., roosting together with its companions, reminds us that we are in the middle of Amazonia.

Terrestrial birds are somewhat scarce in the periodically flooded forests, but during low water there is a noticeable influx of bird species, such as *Crypturellus* tinamous, that come from areas not subject to flooding, even flying across arms of rivers.

Near the Atlantic coast, as in the Belém, Pará region, the várzea forest is subject to tides and floods twice a day, when it is invaded by certain birds, such as the Green-and-rufous

Kingfisher, *Chloroceryle inda*, and the Yellow-billed Jacamar, *Galbula albirostris*.

On beaches one finds the big Large-billed Tern, *Phaetusa simplex*, and the small Yellow-billed Tern, *Sterna superciliaris*, which can be confused with the beach-inhabiting Sand-colored Nighthawk, *Chordeiles rupestris*. Flocks of Black Skimmer, *Rynchops niger*, with its fierce red beak, rest there, and the strange Orinoco Goose, *Neochen jubata*, a Neotropical endemic, appears while kingfishers, cormorants, and egrets fly by. The paucity of aquatic avifauna in Amazonia, especially along the Rio Negro, is surprising (see Anatidae). While the black water of the Rio Negro measures 0.14 grams of biomass per cubic meter, the same figure for the mixed water of the várzea of the Amazon itself is 6.2 grams, forty times more (Fittkau 1975). Even mosquitoes are missing on the Rio Negro, referred to by the local populace as a "dead" or "silent" river.

Finally I think of the birds that overfly the Amazon and its tributaries, such as the parakeets, parrots, macaws, toucans, and hawks seen by tourists traveling by ship. There are always swallows, especially during the southern winter, when thousands and thousands come from the southern part of the continent along with the Fork-tailed Flycatcher, *Tyrannus savana*, to "vacation" in the Hylaea. The local White-winged and White-banded Swallows, *Tachycineta albiventer* and *Atticora fasciata*, draw less attention, but flocks of Yellow-rumped Cacique, *Cacicus cela*, are prominent.

Habitats created in Amazonia by rivers ("river-created habitats," fig. 3) have in recent years attracted special attention from American ornithologists who have worked in the upper Amazon regions of Colombia and Peru. Remsen et al. (1983) have concluded that 15 percent of the nonaquatic birds of Amazonia are restricted to riverine habitats.

AMAZONIA–RIVER PLATE TRANSITION

Transitional regions, such as that between the Amazon and the River Plate drainage basins, in the area of the upper Rio Paraguay north of Cáceres, Mato Grosso, are of special interest. Two faunas are found there: (1) Amazonian species such as the Broad-billed Motmot, *Electron platyrhynchum*; Red-necked Araçari, *Pteroglossus bitorquatus*; Blackish Antbird, *Cercomacra nigrescens*; and Black-faced Dacnis, *Dacnis lineata*; and (2) elements typical of the cerrado and the Pantanal/Paraguayan Chaco: Red-legged Seriema, *Cariama cristata*; Collared Crescentchest, *Melanopareia torquata*; Purplish and Curl-crested Jays, *Cyanocorax cyanomelas* and *C. cristatellus*; and emberizids of the Thraupinae subfamily such as the White-banded and White-rumped Tanagers,

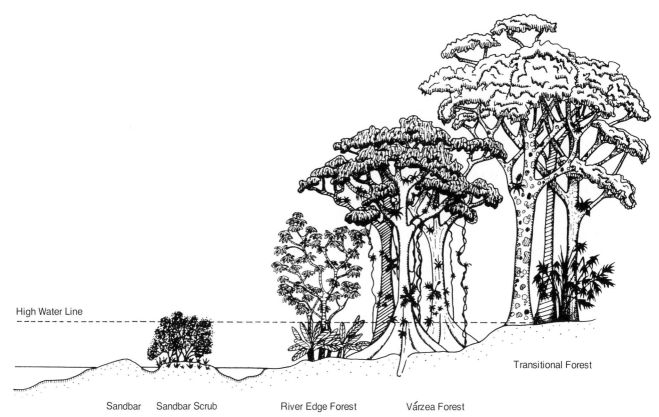

High Water Line

Sandbar   Sandbar Scrub   River Edge Forest   Várzea Forest

Transitional Forest

Fig. 3. Habitats created by a river in western Amazonia. Adapted from Remsen, O'Neill, and Parker 1983.

Cypsnagra hirundinacea and *Neothraupis fasciata* (Silva 1988). In the Rio Jauru, Mato Grosso, region I have even recorded the Andean Condor, *Vultur gryphus*, as a visitor.

COLD WAVES

In the dry season between June and September, regular cold waves occur in the upper Amazon, such as in the upper reaches of the Rio Juruá (Acre), Rio Purús (Roraima), Rio Madeira (Mato Grosso), and Rio Tapajós (Pará, personal observation). These are caused by masses of cold air invading from Antarctic regions (not from the Andes, as formerly believed). A very strong southwest wind brings instantaneous clouds (not rain), and the temperature drops from 25°C to 10°C or even lower. It is said that the waters of small rivers and lakes may cool so much as to cause fish mortality. All faunal activity is reduced. There is scarcely any bird vocalization. Insects do not fly then, and I presume feeding by insectivorous birds is quite impaired. Army ants, so important for so many Suboscine insectivorous birds of the Amazonian forest, stay in their bivouacs. Frugivorous birds are also adversely affected, for the strong wind shakes the branches of the canopy, driving away even such large species as toucans, parrots, and cotingids such as the Bare-necked Fruitcrow, *Gymnoderus foetidus*, and Spangled Cotinga, *Cotinga cayana*.

Hummingbirds and swifts disappear; they are well equipped to fall into a light torpor and thus slow down their metabolism (see Trochilidae). These cold waves (known in southern Brazil as "Friagem de São João" = "St. John's cold wave," do not last more than three to five days.

1.3.2 ATLANTIC RAIN FOREST

This body of forest in eastern Brazil runs along the littoral strip, inside the restinga (see section 1.3.4), from Rio Grande do Norte to Rio Grande do Sul. It has two sectors: littoral forest and mountain forest, each with a large number of endemics. The largest number of endemics is right in southeastern Brazil, which has about 140 forest species (Haffer 1985).

LITTORAL FOREST

This forest occurs from the northeast (where it is known as "tabuleiro" forest) to Rio de Janeiro on flat or slightly undulating terrain, from 20 to 200 meters above sea level. Climatic conditions are quite similar to those of Amazonia. Carvelas, Bahia, has 1,840 mm of rainfall annually and Ilhéus, Bahia, up to 2,124 mm. The flora and fauna are closely related to that of the Hylaea. The Atlantic forest is even more humid than that of Amazonia and thus has more Bromeliaceae, as can easily be seen. The now much-reduced forest north of the Rio Doce, in Espírito Santo and southern Bahia, closely resembles the Amazonian forest. One of the remaining pieces is in the Sooretama Refuge and the Vale do Rio Doce Company Reserve near Linhares, Espírito Santo. These forests lack the great emergent trees of Amazonia.

Amazonian elements exist among the birds of the littoral forest, such as the Red-billed Curassow, *Crax blumenbachii*; Rufous-vented Ground-Cuckoo, *Neomorphus geoffroyi*; and various Suboscine Passerines, such as cotingids of the genera *Cotinga* and *Xipholena*. Thirty non-Passerine species and sixty-seven Passerine species occur both in Amazonia and on the littoral, although they are often different subspecies (P. Müler 1973). The Red-ruffed Fruitcrow, *Pyroderus scutatus*, found also in the Andes, is a southern species in Brazil, where it also gets into high altitudes. Various other species listed here occur both in the littoral forest as well as in the coastal mountains and their interior extensions. There are various tinamous, formerly as many as six sympatric species: Solitary Tinamou, *Tinamus solitarius*, and five species of *Crypturellus*, including the endemic Yellow-legged Tinamou, *C. n. noctivagus*. Following are examples of endemic or quasi-endemic non-Passerines and Suboscines that occur in littoral forests:

ACCIPITRIDAE: White-necked Hawk, *Leucopternis lacernulata*, endemic.
PSITTACIDAE: Ochre-marked Parakeet, *Pyrrhura cruentata*; Plain Parakeet, *Brotogeris tirica*; Black-eared Parrotlet, *Touit melanonota*; Red-tailed Parrot, *Amazona brasiliensis*; Red-browed Parrot, *Amazona rhodocorytha*, all endemic. The Red-and-green Macaw, *Ara chloroptera*, formerly occurred here.
STRIGIDAE: Tawny-browed Owl, *Pulsatrix koeniswaldiana*.
TROCHILIDAE: Saw-billed Hermit, *Ramphodon naevius*; Hook-billed Hermit, *Glaucis dohrnii*; Dusky-throated Hermit, *Phaethornis squalidus*; Brazilian Ruby, *Clytolaema rubricauda*, all endemic.
BUCCONIDAE: Crescent-chested Puffbird, *Malacoptila striata*, endemic.
PICIDAE: Yellow-eared Woodpecker, *Veniliornis maculifrons*, endemic.
FORMICARIIDAE: Spot-backed Antshrike, *Hypoedaleus guttatus*; Star-throated Antwren, *Myrmotherula gularis*; Unicolored Antwren, *M. unicolor*; Rio de Janeiro Antwren, *M. fluminensis*; Black-hooded Antwren, *Formicivora erythronotos*; Alagoas Antwren, *Terenura sicki*; White-bibbed Antbird, *Myrmeciza loricata*; Black-cheeked Gnateater, *Conopophaga melanops*, all endemic.
COTINGIDAE: Banded Cotinga, *Cotinga maculata*; Black-headed Berryeater, *Carpornis melanocephalus*; White-winged Cotinga, *Xipholena atropurpurea*; Kinglet Calyptura, *Calyptura cristata*, all endemic.
PIPRIDAE: Pin-tailed Manakin, *Ilicura militaris*; Wied's Tyrant-Manakin, *Neopelma aurifrons*, both endemic.

The Tijuca Forest (Tijuca National Park), at the door of or within Rio de Janeiro, also forms part of the Atlantic littoral forest and is often the first stop for foreign visitors. It is much degraded, but the Channel-billed Toucan, *Ramphastos vitel-*

linus, and Bare-throated Bellbird, *Procnias nudicollis*, compensate for this. The Rusty-margined Guan, *Penelope superciliaris*, may appear. The Spot-winged Wood-Quail, *Odontophorus capueira*; Rufous-capped Motmot, *Baryphthengus ruficapillus*; and the secretive Barred Forest-Falcon, *Micrastur ruficollis*, reveal their presence by calling. Tinamids and large psittacids are no longer there, nor are there trogons or jacamars. The Tijuca Forest was created in the 1800s (1861) to help improve Rio de Janeiro's water-supply problem. The area had been a mosaic of coffee plantations and grew other crops and served as a woodlot. It still has centenarian trees from the primary forests alongside the great eucalyptus that were brought in from Australia.

MONTANE FOREST

This is the high-country forest existing along the coastal mountain chain from the northeast to Rio Grande do Sul. Its principal center is in the Serra do Mar and Serra da Mantiqueira, penetrating well into the interior of the states of São Paulo, Minas Gerais, Rio de Janeiro, and Espírito Santo. In its typical form it occurs between 800 and 1,700 meters. The rains in the Atlantic montane forest do not differ much from those of Amazonia, with two to four dry months. About 2,200 mm of rainfall are recorded annually in Petrópolis, Rio de Janeiro, and 3,100 mm in the Serra dos Órgãos National Park, Rio de Janeiro. The climate in the mountains is mild, with average temperatures between 14°C and 21°C; on the peaks and in the south they may fall below 0°C.

Trees may reach 30 to 40 meters in height. In the understory, palmito (*Euterpe edulis*) and high-reaching bamboos occur in great quantity, in addition to tree ferns. Multitudinous arboreal plants are a peculiarity of these forests, particularly all sizes of bromeliads, South America's most decorative plants. Rizzini (1979) lists 792 species of epiphytic plant for the mountain rain forest, headed by ferns, orchids, and mosses.

The Atlantic montane forest has a good number of endemic parrots and cotingas. A very isolated population of the Rufous-brown Solitaire, *Myadestes l. leucogenys*, lives there. There are four or five species of tinamid, with the Brown Tinamou, *Crypturellus obsoletus*, the most frequently encountered. It is, or was, the domain of the Black-fronted Piping-Guan, *Pipile jacutinga*, and Dusky-legged Guan, *Penelope obscura*. Among endemic or quasi-endemic species, the following is a selection:

ACCIPITRIDAE: Mantled Hawk, *Leucopternis polionota*
PSITTACIDAE: Blue-bellied Parrot, *Triclaria malachitacea*; Red-capped Parrot, *Pionopsitta pileata*; Vinaceous-breasted Parrot, *Amazona vinacea*
TROCHILIDAE: Scale-throated Hermit, *Phaethornis eurynome*; White-throated Hummingbird, *Leucochloris albicollis*; Black Jacobin, *Melanotrochilus fuscus*
GALBULIDAE: Three-toed Jacamar, *Jacamaralcyon tridactyla*
RAMPHASTIDAE: Red-breasted Toucan, *Ramphastos dicolorus*; Saffron Toucanet, *Baillonius bailloni*

PICIDAE: Helmeted Woodpecker, *Dryocopus galeatus*
FURNARIIDAE: White-collared Foliage-gleaner, *Anabazenops fuscus*; Pale-browed Treehunter, *Cichlocolaptes leucophrus*; Sharp-billed Xenops, *Heliobletus contaminatus*
FORMICARIIDAE: Giant Antshrike, *Batara cinerea*; Large-tailed and Tufted Antshrikes, *Mackenziaena leachii* and *M. severa*; White-bibbed Antbird, *Myrmeciza loricata*; Rufous Gnateater, *Conopophaga lineata*
RHINOCRYPTIDAE: Slaty and Stresemann's Bristlefronts, *Merulaxis ater* and *M. stresemanni*; White-breasted and Mouse-colored Tapaculos, *Scytalopus indigoticus* and *S. speluncae*; Spotted Bamboowren, *Psilorhamphus guttatus*
COTINGIDAE: Black-and-gold and Gray-winged Cotingas, *Tijuca atra* and *T. condita*; Hooded Berryeater, *Carpornis cucullatus*; Cinnamon-vented Piha, *Lipaugus lanioides*; Bare-throated Bellbird, *Procnias nudicollis* (The latter is one of the best-known components of the Atlantic forest, occurring at various altitudes. Its "anvil chorus" is the true "voice of the Atlantic forest.")
TYRANNIDAE: Bay-ringed Tyrannulet, *Phylloscartes sylviolus*; Fork-tailed Pygmy-Tyrant, *Hemitriccus furcatus*; Shear-tailed Gray-Tyrant, *Muscipipra vetula*
THRAUPINAE: Olive-green Tanager, *Orthogonys chloricterus*; Chestnut-headed Tanager, *Pyrrhocoma ruficeps*; Brown Tanager, *Orchesticus abeillei*

High-altitude species, such as the *Mackenziaena* antshrikes, sometimes descend to lower altitudes (around 200 meters) when there is continuous forest, as in the Itaguaí region and the Municipality of Rio de Janeiro. Over the centuries, certain species have scattered throughout the interior so much that it is no longer evident that they are Atlantic forest representatives. The Three-toed Jacamar, *Jacamaralcyon tridactyla*, which appears in the Paraíba valley, is such a case. The *Scytalopus* genus has begun to colonize central Brazil.

ATLANTIC FOREST OF THE NORTHEAST

In northeastern Brazil, in the states of Pernambuco and Alagoas, Atlantic forest is found both in lowlands and at higher altitudes. The one in the lowlands (which scarcely exists today; Teixeira et al. 1986) shelters a notably Amazonian fauna, providing a good idea of the former linkage with Amazonia. One of the last living witnesses of this Amazonian invasion is the Razor-billed Curassow, *Mitu mitu*. The Red-browed Parrot, *Amazona rhodocorytha*, and Bearded Bellbird, *Procnias averano*, are also found there.

The highland forest of Alagoas and Pernambuco is more like the Atlantic forest south of the Rio São Francisco. The Bare-throated Bellbird, *Procnias nudicollis*, and Black-headed Berryeater, *Carpornis melanocephalus*, are there. Two species only discovered there in 1979, Novaes' Foliage-gleaner, *Philydor novaesi*, and Alagoas Antwren, *Terenura sicki*, represent geographic replacements of the Black-capped Foliage-gleaner, *P. atricapillus*, and Streak-capped Antwren, *T. maculata*, respectively, of the Atlantic forest of southeastern Brazil, and show the earlier intimate relationship of the two bodies of forest. On the other hand, the two species document the long geoclimatic separation of the two regions, sufficient to permit a quite different evolution of such closely related taxa.

Exploration of the natural history of Brazil began in the northeast in the seventeenth century under Dutch administration (see chapter 2) and is well documented.

ARAUCARIA FOREST

Paraná Pine (*Araucaria angustifolia*), also called araucaria, exists in the high parts of the mountainous region of southern Brazil, usually above 1,200 meters in the Serra da Mantiqueira and Serra do Mar, in the latter in localities fronting on the sea. It is associated with components of the montane forest (Rizzini 1979). This is the least tropical landscape in Brazil. Araucarias immigrated into the southern Andean regions of Chile and Argentina (and from there to Brazil) from the sub-Antarctic, where there are fossils linking them to the present principal araucaria area: eastern Australia, Oceania, and New Guinea. This flora reached South America from the southern Pacific side, and not from the Atlantic. In Brazil, araucarias cannot compete with humid, subtropical forest and are eliminated when they meet. They occur semi-spontaneously from Rio de Janeiro and Minas Gerais to Rio Grande do Sul in a permanently humid climate. Curitiba, Paraná, has an annual rainfall of 1,373 mm.

The understory of the pines contains an abundance of bamboo of the genera *Merostachys* and *Chusquea*, as well as tree ferns. "Pinheirinho" (*Podocarpus lambertii*, which immigrated together with the araucaria) is especially prominent. Araucaria is sun-loving and advances over grasslands, forming groves and gallery forests.

The only bird species known to be restricted to the araucarias is the Araucaria Tit-Spinetail, *Leptasthenura setaria*. The Azure Jay, *Cyanocorax cyaneus*, always cited as a bird typical of the araucaria, occurs frequently in other types of forest. The tinamous are the same as those in the Atlantic montane forest (see section 1.3.2). In the extreme south, the Red-spectacled Parrot, *Amazona pretrei*, is periodically a bird of the araucarias, utilizing their nuts. Also cited for the araucarias are the Black-fronted Piping-Guan, *Pipile jacutinga*; Red-ruffed Fruitcrow, *Pyroderus scutatus*; Chopi Blackbird, *Gnorimopsar chopi*; Black-capped Piprites, *Piprites pileatus*; and Hooded Siskin, *Carduelis magellanica*.

1.3.3 CERRADO, GALLERY FOREST, AND BURITI GROVES, AND THEIR BIRDS

CERRADO

The cerrado, or "campo cerrado," with a very characteristic phytophysiognomy, corresponds to the "arborized savanna" of other tropical continents. The cerrado occupies an area of more than 2 million square kilometers, corresponding to 23.5 percent of the land surface of Brazil. Goiás is 69 percent cerrado and the Federal District is up to 88 percent. Cerrado is the dominant landscape of the west-central region, extending to Paraguay, Pará, Amapá, and Amazonas. The open-country phytophysiognomy of the cerrado is somewhat misleading, for in origin it was an arboreal formation. It is erroneous to consider the cerrado a secondary formation caused by fire. The large-scale development of open grassland within cerrado is secondary, and was produced by fire. Fire only modifies the cerrado. The occurrence of spontaneous fires is possible, caused by lightning or by bits of glass lying about that act as a burning lens (this only in post-Columbian times). Campo has existed alongside cerrado in central Brazil for centuries.

The cerrado is a subxerophilic formation dominated by sparsely scattered, low trees and bushes with twisted branches, thick, grooved bark, and leathery leaves. Reddish-colored termite nests are prominent on the trunks. These are a great attraction to birds, which dig holes in them for nesting. From the cerrado one gradually moves into "cerradão," whose phytophysiognomy resembles that of forest. Frequently the cerrado is very low, a successor of the open ecosystems that, until the Pleistocene, harbored a large mammalian fauna, such as horses (Equidae).[1] It is said that precursors of the cerrado receded before formations that, in the Guianas and central Brazil, existed anterior to the Cretaceous, implying, therefore, a flora much older than that of the present Amazon basin.

"Campo sujo" (dirty campo) and "campo limpo" (clean campo) and termite savannas spread over the region and, in turn, with higher humidity, give place to the buriti palm (*Mauritia vinifera*) groves of central Brazil. Rivers are accompanied by gallery forests which, in Goiás, may have a floristic and faunistic stamp of the Atlantic forest due to immigration of these flora and fauna.

BIRDS OF THE CERRADO

The Greater Rhea, *Rhea americana*, is here. The Rheiformes were already represented in the region in the upper Paleocene, about 55 million years ago (see chapter 5). Another very typical bird of the cerrado is the Red-legged Seriema, *Cariama cristata*, which has fossil ancestors in the lower Tertiary, more than 50 million years ago. Tinamids include the Small-billed Tinamou, *Crypturellus parvirostris*; Red-winged Tinamou, *Rhynchotus rufescens*; Lesser Nothura, *Nothura minor*; and Dwarf Tinamou, *Taoniscus nanus*. The last-named could be confused with the syntopic Ocellated Crake, *Micropygia schomburgkii*.

The following species are a small selection of endemics or quasi-endemics that live in the cerrado or in similar ecosystems:

---

[1] There are reasons to argue seriously that people participated in this era in Brazil (shelter in Esperança, Bahia): quartzite artifacts associated with fossilized bones of Quaternary fauna—a bear, *Arctodus*, is cited but birds have not been found, see Chapter 5.2—dating from about 300,000 years B.P. (thus before the 200,000-year Calico site in California) dated by the uranium and thorium method (Lumley et al. 1987).

FALCONIDAE: Red-throated Caracara, *Daptrius americanus*

COLUMBIDAE: Long-tailed Ground-Dove, *Uropelia campestris*; Blue-eyed Ground-Dove, *Columbina cyanopis*

PSITTACIDAE: Yellow-faced Parrot, *Amazona xanthops*, endemic, and numerous parakeets, such as the Brown-throated Parakeet, *Aratinga pertinax*, that occupy the above-mentioned termite nests.

TROCHILIDAE: Horned Sungem, *Heliactin cornuta*

BUCCONIDAE: White-eared Puffbird, *Nystalus chacuru*, widely distributed

RAMPHASTIDAE: Toco Toucan, *Ramphastos toco*

PICIDAE: Campo Flicker, *Colaptes campestris*, widely distributed

FURNARIIDAE: Campo Miner, *Geobates poecilopterus*, endemic; Pale-breasted Spinetail, *Synallaxis albescens*

DENDROCOLAPTIDAE: Narrow-billed Woodcreeper, *Lepidocolaptes angustirostris*

FORMICARIIDAE: Rufous-winged Antshrike, *Thamnophilus torquatus*

RHINOCRYPTIDAE: Collared Crescentchest, *Melanopareia torquata*

TYRANNIDAE: Campos Suiriri, *Suiriri suiriri affinis*, endemic; Ash-throated Casiornis, *Casiornis fusca*, endemic; Gray Monjita, *Xolmis cinerea*, whose melodious song is never lacking in the cerrado; Sharp-tailed Tyrant, *Culicivora caudacuta*; and Rufous-sided Pygmy-Tyrant, *Euscarthmus rufomarginatus*

CORVIDAE: Curl-crested Jay, *Cyanocorax cristatellus*, in campo cerrado; White-naped Jay, *C. cyanopogon*, in dense cerrado, endemic

THRAUPINAE: White-rumped Tanager, *Cypsnagra hirundinacea*; White-banded Tanager, *Neothraupis fasciata*

EMBERIZINAE: Cinereous Warbling-Finch, *Poospiza cinerea*, and Coal-crested Finch, *Charitospiza eucosma*

CARDINALINAE: Black-throated Saltator, *Saltator atricollis*; Blue Finch, *Porphyrospiza caerulescens*

The whooping of *Cariama cristata* is the "voice of the cerrado," but the loudest vocalization is that of *Daptrius americanus* calling in chorus. Hunters consider this bird to be gallinaceous.

GALLERY FORESTS

The Brasilia Tapaculo, *Scytalopus novacapitalis*, is an endemic of the very humid, densest gallery and river-edge forests scattered throughout the cerrado of Goiás. Of Atlantic/Andean ancestry, it was discovered in 1957 in Brasília but later found in similar forests of the high plateaus of western Minas Gerais. The very distinctive Helmeted Manakin, *Antilophia galeata*, is a conspicuous bird that is also typical of these riverine forests of central Brazil. There are also furnariids—the quasi-endemic Planalto Foliage-gleaner, *Philydor dimidiatus*, and Sharp-tailed Streamcreeper, *Lochmias nematura*, as well as the endemic paruline, the White-striped Warbler, *Basileuterus leucophrys*. The endemic Bare-faced Curassow, *Crax fasciolata*, is found in the broadest gallery forests.

BURITI GROVES

The beautiful buriti palm groves of central Brazil (in Amazonia they are miriti groves) are embedded in the heart of the cerrado in places with abundant water. A unique furnariid, the Point-tailed Palmcreeper, *Berlepschia rikeri*, is an endemic of these buritis. The Fork-tailed Palm-Swift, *Reinarda squamata*, has adapted its nest, made of pasted feathers, to their hanging fronds.

Buriti groves are rich in psittacids, including five macaws: Hyacinth Macaw, *Anodorhynchus hyacinthinus*; Blue-and-yellow Macaw, *Ara ararauna*; Scarlet Macaw, *A. macao*; Red-and-green Macaw, *A. chloroptera*; and Chestnut-fronted Macaw, *A. severa*; and two maracanãs: Blue-winged Macaw, *Propyrrhura maracana*; and Red-bellied Macaw, *Orthopsittaca manilata*. The palm fruits serve as food, and the hollow trunks offer the best shelter for nesting by psittacids, swifts (*Chaetura*), and others.

1.3.4 RIO BRANCO AND AMAPÁ CAMPOS, MINAS GERAIS AND BAHIA PLATEAUS, HIGH MONTANE CAMPOS, AND RESTINGA, AND THEIR BIRDS

RIO BRANCO AND AMAPÁ CAMPOS

These domains are similar to the open campo cerrado of central Brazil. The climate is classified as semi-humid, with a prolonged dry season. Annual average precipitation in Boa Vista, Roraima, is around 1,500 millimeters.

The avifauna of the campos of Rio Branco and Amapá is different from that of the central Brazilian cerrado, due to the existence of species that have immigrated from the northern part of the continent: Crested Bobwhite, *Colinus cristatus*; Double-striped Thick-knee, *Burhinus bistriatus*; and Eastern Meadowlark, *Sturnella magna*.

MINAS GERAIS AND BAHIA PLATEAUS

The high plateaus of Minas Gerais and Bahia, such as the Serra do Espinhaço, are another type of high montane campo. At altitudes above 700 meters there is bushy vegetation, rich in small palms (*Alagoptera-Diplothemium*) on stony ground. Various endemic birds occur: hummingbirds such as the Hyacinth and Hooded Visorbearers, *Augastes scutatus* and *A. lumachellus*; the Pale-throated Serra-Finch, *Embernagra longicauda*; and a small tyrannid, the Gray-backed Tachuri, *Polystictus superciliaris*. Recently the Cipó Canastero, *Asthenes luizae*, a member of a furnariid genus common in the extreme south of the continent and in the Andes, was discovered on the Serra do Cipó (Minas Gerais).

HIGH MONTANE CAMPOS

In the highest mountains of the southeast, the Serra Mantiqueira and the Serra do Mar (including Caparaó, Itatiaia, and

Serra dos Órgãos), mountain forests are replaced, above 1,900 meters (Itatiaia reaches 2,400 meters), by high mountain, high altitude, or "alpine" campos. This humid zone above the tropical forest may be thought of, biogeographically, as a replacement of the "páramos" of the Andes. One of the dominant plants is crisciúma-bengala (*Chusquea pinnifolia*). In part these plants reflect close affiliation with Andean vegetation at the same altitude, such as in Bolivia.

Andean/Patagonian flora and fauna immigrated during the Pleistocene. Among the birds of the high mountain campos is the endemic Itatiaia Thistletail, *Schizoeaca moreirae*, whose relatives are all in the Andes. It lives alongside another Andean form, the Mouse-colored Tapaculo, *Scytalopus speluncae*. The Band-winged Nightjar, *Caprimulgus longirostris*, is also of Andean origin. The Black-breasted Plovercrest, *Stephanoxis lalandi*, a hummingbird typical of the high mountain campos of the southeast, occurs at sea level in the mild climate of the south (Rio Grande do Sul) (Humboldt's Biogeographic Law 1805, "Voyage aux régions equinoctiales du Nouveau Continent"). There are two similar Emberizinae, the Red-rumped and Bay-chested Warbling-Finches, *Poospiza lateralis* and *P. thoracica*, the latter endemic; the genus has evolved various species in the Andes and in temperate climates of the south. The large Diademed Tanager, *Stephanophorus diadematus*, a notable singer, occupies the high mountains of the Brazilian southeast as well as eastern Argentina. The Hooded Siskin, *Carduelis magellanica*, brightens the mountain regions of Brazil the same as siskins do in the Andes and in mountainous areas of North America and the Old World. The Red-winged Tinamou, *Rhynchotus rufescens*, and Red-legged Seriema, *Cariama cristata*, have been documented in upper Itatiaia, both having immigrated from the Minas Gerais plateau.

RESTINGA

This is the coastal strip of eastern Brazil, on Holocene sands, from the ocean to the first foothills of the Serra do Mar. At the mouths of rivers and lagoons the restinga passes into mangroves. Due to its vegetation, the restinga reminds one of the cerrado ("cerrado of the littoral").

Restinga avifauna presents few special problems. It is characterized by elements also found in other open and semi-open landscapes, such as: Plain-breasted Ground-Dove, *Columbina minuta*; Glittering-throated Emerald, *Amazilia fimbriata*, a hummingbird; Tropical Mockingbird, *Mimus gilvus*; Lemon-chested Greenlet, *Hylophilus thoracicus*; Masked Yellowthroat, *Geothlypis aequinoctialis*; Black-backed Tanager, *Tangara peruviana*; Brazilian Tanager, *Ramphocelus bresilius*; Pileated Finch, *Coryphospingus pileatus*; and Hangnest Tody-Tyrant, *Hemitriccus nidipendulus*, a quite common southeastern endemic. The recently described subspecies of the Serra Antwren, *Formicivora serrana littoralis*, occurs along with an endemic restinga hummingbird, the Minute Hermit, *Phaethornis idaliae*.

1.3.5 CAATINGA AND THE MATO GROSSO PANTANAL

CAATINGA

The "Drought Polygon" is the subarid region of the northeast, having stony, sandy, or clay soils and an irregular, intense, dry season (7 to 8 months or more without rain). In the Raso da Catarina, Bahia, the caatinga spreads over a plateau cut by canyons. Its existing trees and bushes, frequently armed with spines, are leafless for months, with the bare branches having a light gray color ("caa-tinga" = "mata branca" = "white forest"). There are many succulent plants, cacti, and terrestrial bromeliads. Herbaceous plants grow only during the short rainy season. There are few grasses. The origin of the caatinga owes as little to man as does the cerrado. There is a certain resemblance to the vegetation of the calcareous outcroppings of Minas Gerais. With the coming of rain, the aspect of the caatinga alters radically, appearing like a leafy capoeira, green and flowery, with water holes. Batraquians appear, as do "seasonal" small fish that were "sleeping" in the dry bottom.

A great band of open formations connects the Brazilian caatinga to the Paraguayan Chaco, crossing the cerrado of central Brazil. It was more of a "corridor" in the upper Pleistocene than in recent millennia (Ab'Saber 1981), serving the spread of campo flora and fauna. (On Chaco birds, see Short 1975.)

A good number of avian endemics inhabit the caatinga, such as the Yellow-legged Tinamou, *Crypturellus noctivagus zabele*, and White-browed Guan, *Penelope jacucaca*. Psittacids are represented by various parakeets, such as the quasi-endemic Cactus Parakeet, *Aratinga cactorum*. The most important endemics of the northeast are the Little Blue Macaw, *Cyanopsitta spixii*, and Indigo Macaw, *Anodorhynchus leari*, found only in 1978 in the extreme northeast of Bahia. Here is a selection of other birds typical of the caatinga:

RHEIDAE: The northeast (Pernambuco) is the homeland of a subspecies of the Greater Rhea, *Rhea a. americana = macrorhyncha*, originally abundant but today scarcer than the rhea of central and southern Brazil.

COLUMBIDAE: The abundance of doves is impressive, especially the Eared Dove, *Zenaida auriculata*, which periodically expands its numbers so much that it recalls the extinct Passenger Pigeon, *Ectopistes migratorius*, of North America.

CAPRIMULGIDAE: Pygmy Nightjar, *Caprimulgus hirundinaceus*.

TROCHILIDAE: Broad-tipped Hermit, *Phaethornis gounellei*, endemic.

APODIDAE: We have found a winter roost of many thousands of Biscutate Swifts, *Streptoprocne biscutata seridoensis*, in Rio Grande do Norte; it is not yet known where they breed.

PICIDAE: There are various endemic species of piculet—Spotted, Ochraceous, and Tawny Piculets, *Picumnus pygmaeus*, *P. limae*, and *P. fulvescens*.

FURNARIIDAE: Great Xenops, *Megaxenops parnaguae*, and Red-shouldered Spinetail, *Synallaxis hellmayri*, are notable endemics. The Rufous Cacholote, *Pseudoseisura cristata*, is common.

FORMICARIIDAE: Silvery-cheeked Antshrike, *Sakesphorus cristatus*; Pectoral Antwren, *Herpsilochmus pectoralis*; and Slender Antbird, *Rhopornis ardesiaca*, are endemics. The Stripe-backed Antbird, *Myrmorchilus strigilatus*, is frequently seen. Its distribution follows the arid "corridor" that links the caatinga with the Paraguayan chaco.

PARULINAE: Flavescent Warbler, *Basileuterus flaveolus*, very typical of the caatinga.

THRAUPINAE: Scarlet-throated Tanager, *Sericossypha loricata*, is a noted northeastern endemic well known for its monotonous calling.

EMBERIZINAE: Red-cowled Cardinal, *Paroaria dominicana*, endemic.

ICTERINAE: Troupial, *Icterus i. jamacaii*, endemic, and, like *Paroaria dominicana*, one of the best-known birds of the northeast.

A very special paleontological surprise has come from the northeast. A bird feather was recently discovered alongside pterosaurs in a more than 100 million-year-old deposit on the Chapada do Araripe, Ceará. One hundred years ago the famous American naturalist, Louis Agassiz, excavated fossil fish there, but bird fossils had never been found (see chapter 5).

PANTANAL

In the above-mentioned strip linking the caatinga of northeastern Brazil to the Paraguayan Chaco lies the Pantanal of Mato Grosso, an area of 75,000 square kilometers that is the largest, richest marsh-bird region on the continent, with almost solid water cover during the high-water season (December to April). During the dry season there is water only in the lakes ("bays") and in the meandering rivers where the celebrated *Victoria amazonica* [lilypad] occurs. Pantanal vegetation is, in part, related to that of the northeastern caatinga; note, for example, the carandá (*Copernicia alba*), a palm very similar to the carnaúba (*C. cerifera*) of the northeast.

A very special attraction in the Pantanal is the groves where concentrations of large marsh birds occur, such as egrets; the Roseate Spoonbill, *Platalea ajaja*; Wood Stork, *Mycteria americana*; Jabiru, *Jabiru mycteria*; Neotropic Cormorant, *Phalacrocorax brasilianus*; and Anhinga, *Anhinga anhinga*. So-called white and black nesting colonies, together with many alligators and tame capybaras, turn the Pantanal into a great tourist attraction.

Southern Screamers, *Chauna torquata*, abound. The Limpkin, *Aramus guarauna*, is on hand. This is the home of the Pantanal Chachalaca, *Ortalis canicollis pantanalensis*, a subspecies of the Chaco Chachalaca. There are three species of macaw: the large, blue Hyacinth Macaw, *Anodorhynchus hyacinthinus*; Blue-and-yellow Macaw, *Ara ararauna*; and Red-and-green Macaw, *A. chloroptera*. There are also the

Toco Toucan, *Ramphastos toco*, and Chestnut-eared Aracari, *Pteroglossus castanotis*. The Snail Kite, *Rostrhamus sociabilis*, is common. The Black-collared Hawk, *Busarellus nigricollis*, is on hand; it is a fish specialist like the Osprey, *Pandion haliaetus*, a North American migrant that appears every year. Among Passerines, solid flocks of the Yellow-billed Cardinal, *Paroaria capitata*, referred to locally as "cavalry," are typical of the western Mato Grosso and adjacent countries.

1.3.6 GAUCHO REGION

In Rio Grande do Sul, hills and plains alternate in the "campanha." Extensive marshes spread around lakes and lagoons. Southern várzeas, with quiet waters, covered by a dense layer of marsh vegetation, floating carpets, reed beds, and thickets of aquatic bushes, represent rich biotic communities. In the pastures, high caraguatás (*Eryngium* sp.) are conspicuous, and spiny maricás (*Mimosa* sp.) are common. At the edges of streams a few groves and gallery forests remain.

Among the various subregions, the following merit attention: (1) the northern plateau of Rio Grande do Sul, extending to southern Santa Catarina, a region of campos and araucaria forests; (2) the lakes and marshes of the south, with the Taim Ecological Station; and (3) the extreme southwest, the "espinilho parkland" with its spiny algarrobos (*Prosopis* sp.), a continuation of the widespread formation of northeastern Argentina.

Rio Grande do Sul is the Brazilian state with the most waterfowl, including the largest and most impressive species: the Coscoroba Swan, *Coscoroba coscoroba*, and Black-necked Swan, *Cygnus melancoryphus*. The Chilean Flamingo, *Phoenicopterus chilensis*, appears as a visitor. The most important psittacid of the area is the Red-spectacled Parrot, *Amazona pretrei*, which gathers in great numbers in certain araucaria groves. The Monk Parakeet, *Myiopsitta monachus*, is considered a pest.

In the northern plateau and regions adjacent to Santa Catarina, one finds the Long-tailed Cinclodes, *Cinclodes pabsti*, a furnariid that is a descendant of Andean-Patagonian fauna and occupies the coldest part of Brazil. In the espinilho parkland of the southwest, one of the most notable examples of the very distinctive fauna is the large, semi-terrestrial Scimitar-billed Woodcreeper, *Drymornis bridgesii*.

The shores of Rio Grande do Sul enjoy the country's greatest influx of marine visitors, among them not a few sub-Antarctic species that appear during the southern winter (see section 1.3.9).

1.3.7 CAVE ENVIRONMENTS

The Oilbird, *Steatornis caripensis*, a nocturnal species, is a very special bird that spends half its life deep in caves, where it may be a kilometer from the entrance. It occurs in the high mountains of Roraima, on the Brazilian-Venezuelan border. To guide itself in total darkness, the oilbird has developed echolocation. Swifts, such as the *Streptoprocne* and *Chaetura*, prefer caves that are not so deep and still have a bit of light, and therefore have not developed echolocation.

1.3.8 MANGROVES

Mangroves are a pantropic, coastal vegetation that reach their southern Brazilian limit in Santa Catarina. The largest Brazilian mangrove stands, of red mangrove (*Rhizophora mangle*), stretch from the Piauí coast to Amapá, reaching widths of 50 to 60 kilometers. Their respiratory root-supports (see also the Igapó Forest, section 1.3) contribute to the unmistakable mangrove physiognomy. Mangroves, which fill estuaries, penetrate into the Amazon.

Mangroves are very rich in birds, including passerines. The Bicolored Conebill, *Conirostrum bicolor*, is found exclusively in mangroves. Other species typical of this formation are the Scarlet Ibis, *Eudocimus ruber*, and Rufous Crab-Hawk, *Buteogallus aequinoctialis*, which prey on the multitude of crustaceans living in the mud and on the trees. The Yellow-crowned Night-Heron, *Nyctanassa violacea*, is also a mangrove bird. When mangroves are quite high (*Avicennia* sp. can measure up to 6 meters) the Orange-winged Parrot, *Amazona amazonica*, may appear. The Mangrove Cuckoo, *Coccyzus minor*, is present, as are "riverine" birds such as the Masked Water-Tyrant, *Fluvicola nengeta*, and Tail-banded Hornero, *Furnarius figulus* (Rio de Janeiro). The little-known Little Wood-Rail, *Aramides mangle*, occurs. Kingfishers of all sizes fish there. From September to April the mud flats are filled with migrant Charadriiformes: plovers and sandpipers fleeing the severe northern winter.

1.3.9 AQUATIC ENVIRONMENTS

When referring to the aquatic environment utilized by birds, one must distinguish between marine and freshwater fauna.

BIRDS OF FRESH OR BRACKISH WATER

Most aquatic birds live at the edge of stagnant water, on the muddy edges of lakes: cormorants, egrets, jabirus, ducks, rails, sandpipers, and snipe. The "most aquatic" are the grebes (Podicipedidae) and the Sungrebe, *Heliornis fulica*.

Marshes are a frequent ecosystem in lowlands. The Black-capped Donacobius, *Donacobius atricapillus* (Troglodytidae), endemic to the Neotropics, is prominent. In the south one finds distinctive, endemic or quasi-endemic, wetland furnariids and emberizines such as the Black-bellied Seedeater, *Sporophila melanogaster*, and Lesser Grass-Finch, *Emberizoides ypiranganus*. The Muscovy Duck, *Cairina moschata*, well known as a domestic bird, is found wild throughout Brazil. The scarcity of aquatic birds in Amazonia is surprising (see Anatidae). As Slud (1976) wrote: "Whereas the number of species of herons (Ardeidae) increases toward

the tropics, following the general pattern, the number of ducks (Anatidae) decreases from the high latitudes toward the tropics. The ratio of water bird species to land bird species decreases drastically with decreasing latitude, being lowest in the humid tropics."

Rapids. The Brazilian Merganser, *Mergus octosetaceus*, lives in rapids, such as in the upper Rio São Francisco of Minas Gerais, and at the edge of such streams the Fasciated Tiger-Heron, *Tigrisoma fasciatum*, can be found. Both these birds are rare.

Waterfalls and miscellaneous water environments, including the famous Iguaçu Falls of Paraná, are scattered throughout the interior of the country. Some are known as "swallow falls," as in the upper Madeira (Aripuanã, Mato Grosso) and the Serra do Cachimbo (Pará). The birds here are not swallows, but swifts: the White-collared, Great Dusky, and Sooty Swifts, *Streptoprocne zonaris*, *Cypseloides senex*, and *C. fumigatus*, respectively.

The Ringed Kingfisher, *Ceryle torquata*, and certain terns fish both in fresh water and in the sea. The same applies occasionally to the Great Kiskadee, *Pitangus sulphuratus* and, in the far south, to a migrant furnariid, the Bar-winged Cinclodes, *Cinclodes fuscus*, which takes small animal life from rocks washed by the sea. During migration, herons and ducks appear on the coast, and, in the south, the Great Grebe, *Podiceps major*, is found swimming. Flamingos are highly adapted to extremely salty environments.

MARINE BIRDS

Coastal and beach environments. Gulls, terns, boobies, and frigatebirds that nest on oceanic islands are found on beaches, as are the migrant Charadriiformes mentioned in section 1.3.8, Mangroves.

Birds of the pelagic or oceanic environment. Oceanic, or pelagic, birds are ecologically distinct. They live on the open sea, far from land, and only occasionally appear on the coast, often as carcasses carried to shore by the sea. They include penguins and the procellariiform petrels, storm-petrels, and albatrosses, entering Brazilian waters after extensive migration, most coming from sub-Antarctic regions. One species, the Trindade Petrel, *Pterodroma arminjoniana*, breeds on Ilha Trindade (see section 1.3.10). The White-tailed Tropic-bird, *Phaethon lepturus*, breeds on various Brazilian Atlantic islands.

The long, 7,408 kilometers Atlantic coast of Brazil is poor in marine birds due to the meager nutrition in tropical seas. In the extreme south, with more moderate climate, the situation becomes more favorable. In contrast, the cold Humboldt Current of the Pacific is extremely rich in biomass and favors a highly varied fauna along the Chilean and Peruvian coasts.

Brazilian territorial waters were unilaterally extended by Brazil in the 1970s from 12 to 200 miles by the declaration of an "exclusive economic zone." Each island also has a 200-mile zone around it. For the purposes of this book, I treat as

"Brazilian" all oceanic birds recorded within a strip of 200 miles from the coast (see also Procellariiformes).

1.3.10 OCEANIC ISLANDS (FIG. 4)

When seen from a distance, the two principal Brazilian oceanic islands, Trindade and Fernando de Noronha, give the impression of abrupt mountains spiked with peaks rising above the sea. Fernando de Noronha is part of an undersea mountain chain of volcanic origin whose peaks emerge here to form islands. They have beaches, as well as bush and arboreal vegetation and, on Trindade, giant ferns (*Cyathea copelandi*) reaching 5 to 6 meters in height. Vegetation on all the islands has suffered the terrible effects of cutting and fire, and of introduced domestic animals on those that are inhabited.

TRINDADE

Resident birds (partly migratory) on Ilha Trindade and Martim Vaz, 1,207 kilometers from the continent, are exclusively maritime: Trindade Petrel, *Pterodroma arminjoniana*; Great Frigatebird, *Fregata minor*; Lesser Frigatebird, *F. ariel trinitatis*; Masked Booby, *Sula dactylatra*; Redfooted Booby, *S. sula*; Sooty Tern, *Sterna fuscata*; and White Tern, *Gygis alba*. The Cape Petrel, *Daption capense*; Blackcapped Petrel, *Pterodroma hasitata*; some Charadriiformes; and two swallows, the Gray-breasted Martin, *Progne chalybea*, and Barn Swallow, *Hirundo rustica*, are cited as nonbreeding migrants. The Helmeted Guineafowl, *Numida meleagris*: Domestic Pigeon, *Columba livia*; Saffron Finch, *Sicalis flaveola*; and Common Waxbill, *Estrilda astrild*, have been introduced. The Cattle Egret, *Bubulcus ibis*, has already appeared.

Disappearance of forests on Trindade, commented upon

since the beginning of the nineteenth century, was brought about by burning and lack of regeneration. Later, goats finished the rest. The forests of giant fern on Trindade have also been greatly reduced.

FERNANDO DE NORONHA

The archipelago of Fernando de Noronha, a Brazilian federal territory, is 365 kilometers from the northeastern coast. Its avifauna is interesting due to the existence of three species of landbirds: the Eared Dove, *Zenaida auriculata*, and two Passerines, the Noronha Elaenia, *Elaenia spectabilis ridleyana*, and the Noronha Vireo, *Vireo gracilirostris*. A subfossil rail has also been found (Olson 1981). Residents include: the Magnificent Frigatebird, *Fregata magnificens*; two *Phaethon* tropicbirds; three *Sula* boobies; the Sooty Tern, *Sterna fuscata*; two *Anous* noddies; and the White Tern, *Gygis alba*. Unfortunately, the island has been used by Pernambuco personnel of the former Brazilian Institute of Forestry Development (IBDF) to release cage birds confiscated on the continent. The tegu lizard (*Tupinambis* sp.) has been introduced and seriously preys upon groundnesting birds. Strict controls are needed to guarantee the natural balance of the archipelago's ecosystems.

OTHER ISLANDS

The St. Paul's Rocks are 896 kilometers from the coast (see Brown Noddy, *Anous stolidus*). The Atol das Rocas, 250 kilometers from the city of Natal and the only true coral atoll in the Atlantic, has been declared a Biological Reserve where the following marine birds breed: Masked Booby, *Sula dactylatra*; Brown Booby, *S. leucogaster*; Magnificent Frigatebird, *Fregata magnificens*; Sooty Tern, *Sterna fuscata*; Brown Noddy, *Anous stolidus*; and White-capped Noddy, *A. tenuirostris*. There are said to be 60,000 birds including some visitors. There are also marine turtles (*Chelonia mydas*) (Antas 1979).

Closer to the continent and forming part of the continental platform are the Abrolhos Islands, Bahia, 60 kilometers from the coast, where the following breed: Red-billed Tropicbird, *Phaethon aethereus*; and *Sula dactylatra*, *S. leucogaster*, *Fregata magnificens*, and *Anous stolidus* (Coelho 1981). The Moleques do Sul, Santa Catarina, only 12 kilometers from the coast, has four species of breeding marine birds: *Sula leucogaster*; *Fregata magnificens*; Kelp Gull, *Larus dominicanus*; and South American Tern, *Sterna hirundinacea*, as well as at least four terrestrial species: Black Vulture, *Coragyps atratus*; Guira Cuckoo, *Guira guira*; House Wren, *Troglodytes aedon*; and Rufous-collared Sparrow, *Zonotrichia capensis*.

1.3.11 ENVIRONMENTS ALTERED BY MAN, URBAN ENVIRONMENTS

Alteration by man of natural environments has become commonplace in Brazil, even in the most distant corners. Although a secondary forest ecosystem, untouched for many

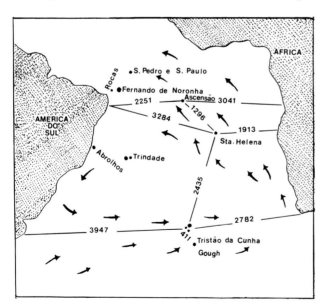

Fig. 4. South Atlantic Islands, with some distances in kilometers. The arrows indicate the principal winds on the ocean surface. After S. L. Olson 1973.

Fig. 5. Rio Branco savannas, Roraima. Habitat of Double-striped Thick-knee, *Burhinus bistriatus,* and Eastern Meadowlark, *Sturnella magna.* Photo by Harald Sioli.

Fig. 6. Amazonia/Central Brazil, upper Xingu, Mato Grosso. Meanders of the Rio Kuluene in the tall-forest habitat of the Amazonian Razor-billed Curassow, *Mitu tuberosa,* and Dark-winged Trumpeter, *Psophia viridis.* Photo by H. Sick.

Fig. 7. Amazonia/Central Brazil, upper Xingu, Mato Grosso. Habitat of Amazonian Umbrellabird, *Cephalopterus ornatus,* and Bare-necked Fruitcrow, *Gymnoderus foetidus.* Photo by H. Sick.

Fig. 8. Amazonia/Central Brazil, upper Xingu, Mato Grosso. Habitat of Sunbittern, *Eurypyga helias;* Pheasant Cuckoo, *Dromococcyx phasianellus;* Rusty-backed Spinetail, *Cranioleuca vulpina;* and Crimson-fronted Cardinal, *Paroaria baeri.* Photo by H. Sick.

Fig. 9. Buriti grove, Rio das Mortes, Mato Grosso. Habitat of Blue-and-yellow Macaw, *Ara ararauna;* Fork-tailed Palm-Swift, *Reinarda squamata;* and Point-tailed Palmcreeper, *Berlepschia rikeri.* Photo by H. Sick.

Fig. 10. Campo cerrado, Rio das Mortes, Mato Grosso. Roncador-Xingu-Tapajós expedition in 1946. Gallery forest in background. Habitat of Red-legged Seriema, *Cariama cristata,* and Red-winged Tinamou, *Rhynchotus rufescens.* Jaguars (*Panthera onca*) seized various expedition mules here. Photo by H. Sick.

Fig. 11. Caatinga, Bahia. The trees have lost their leaves. A Xique-xique (*Pilocereus gounellei*) cactus in the foreground. Habitat of Rufous Cacholote, *Pseudoseisura cristata;* Troupial, *Icterus icterus jamacaii;* and White-naped Jay, *Cyanocorax cyanopogon.* Photo by H. Sick.

Fig. 12. Caatinga, canyon in the Raso da Catarina, Bahia. Habitat of Lear's Macaw, *Anodorhynchus leari;* Blue-crowned Parakeet, *Aratinga acuticauda;* and Cliff Flycatcher, *Hirundinea ferruginea.* Photo by D. M. Teixeira.

Fig. 13. Araucaria grove, Camanducaia,
Minas Gerais, at 1400 m altitude. Habitat of
Campo Flicker, *Colaptes campestris;*
Araucaria Tit-Spinetail, *Leptasthenura
setaria;* and Chopi Blackbird, *Gnorimopsar
chopi.* Photo by H. Sick.

Fig. 14. Serra do Mar, interior of the Atlantic
forest in the Serra dos Órgãos, Rio de Janeiro,
at 1500 m altitude. Habitat of Dusky-legged
Guan, *Penelope obscura;* Giant Antshrike,
Batara cinerea; and Black-and-gold Cotinga,
Tijuca atra. Photo by H. Sick.

Fig. 15. High-montane campos of the Serra dos Órgãos, Rio de Janeiro, at 2000 m altitude. Habitat of Black-breasted Plovercrest, *Stephanoxis lalandi,* and Itatiaia Thistletail, *Schizoeaca moreirae.* Photo by H. Sick.

Fig. 16. Aparados da Serra, Rio Grande do Sul. Habitat of Sooty Swift, *Cypseloides fumigatus,* and in the grassland areas, Long-tailed Cinclodes, *Cinclodes pabsti.* Photo by M. Sander.

Fig. 17. Espinilho parkland, Rio Grande do Sul. Habitat of Checkered Woodpecker, *Picoides mixtus;* Brown Cacholote, *Pseudoseisura lophotes* (several nests of this species are in the tree in the foreground); and Tufted Tit-Spinetail, *Leptasthenura platensis*. Photo by H. Sick.

Fig. 18. Atol das Rocas, Rio Grande no Norte. Site of large nesting colonies of marine birds, such as the Sooty Tern, *Sterna fuscata,* and Masked Booby, *Sula dactylatra*. Photo by Paulo de Tarso Zuquim Antas.

Fig. 19. Marsh, Pantanal, Mato Grosso. Mixed flock of Great Egrets, *Casmerodius albus,* and Snowy Egrets, *Egretta thula,* on the ground, with a Whistling Heron, *Syrigma sibilatrix,* in the foreground, Jabirus, *Jabiru mycteria,* in background, and Wood Storks, *Mycteria americana,* in the trees.

years, may appear similar to a virgin forest, both floristically and with respect to its avifauna, serious gaps can be noted among both terrestrial and game birds, which either do not return or are killed.

Monocultures of eucalyptus and *Pinus* spp. are extremely short of birds, although eucalyptus-flower nectar attracts hummingbirds. Some avifaunal surveys in these man-made ecosystems have been made, as, for instance, in monocultures of acacia in Rio Grande do Sul (Voss and Sander 1981) in parks, university campuses, airports, and cities.

We know little about the avifauna of cane fields. In Queensland, Australia, the Swamp Pheasant, *Centropus phasianinus,* a cuckoo that was formerly rare, has found good living conditions in cane fields. Mandioca plantings have no birds.

Rice fields provide great advantages to ducks, rails, and other aquatic or wetland birds, among them the pioneer Red-breasted Meadowlark, *Sturnella militaris,* and Chestnut-capped Blackbird, *Agelaius ruficapillus,* the latter placing its nest on the rice itself. Rice culture has had an important role in the spread of the Picazuro Pigeon, *Columba picazuro,* in São Paulo (Alvarenga, pers. com.). Rice plantations offer the same inconveniences as coffee plantations and cane fields, in that they are periodically changed or even eliminated by humans.

Palm groves in the north, formerly considered a primary floristic category, have turned out to be secondary vegetation that always appears after the Amazonian forest has been chopped down. This also occurs in Espírito Santo, where similar, outlying, Amazonian-type forests exist or existed. Ordinary palm groves, as opposed to buriti groves, are very poor in birds (see section 1.3.3).

Hydroelectric installations eliminate all local fauna and attract some usually prosaic aquatic birds, such as herons, as well as the Osprey, *Pandion haliaetus,* from North America, and the Common Tern, *Sterna hirundo,* on migration (Balbina, Amazonia).

Urban environments have three categories of birds: (1) survivors of the former habitat, such as a Scissor-tailed Nightjar, *Hydropsalis brasiliana,* which I found in a protected forest patch in the Laranjeiras district of Rio de Janeiro many years ago; (2) invaders, such as another caprimulgid, the Band-winged Nightjar, *Caprimulgus longirostris* in Rio de Janeiro, the Ruddy Ground-Dove, *Columbina talpacoti* (in Belém, Pará, it is the Common Ground-Dove, *C. passerina*), and swallows; hummingbirds may have an important place in an urban environment; and (3) introduced birds, such as the exotic House Sparrow, *Passer domesticus,* and Common Waxbill, *Estrilda astrild.* Various tyrannids, such as the Tropical Kingbird, *Tyrannus melancholicus;* Great Kiskadee, *Pitangus sulphuratus*; Vermilion-crowned Flycatcher, *Myiozetetes similis*; and Yellow-bellied Elaenia, *Elaenia flavogaster*, adjust well to cities. Sometimes the Cliff Flycatcher, *Hirundinea ferruginea*, finds a substitute for cliffs on man-made structures. In certain areas, such as the southeast, the Ashy-tailed Swift, *Chaetura andrei*, often nests in residential chimneys. Happily, even some forest residents, such as antbirds, get along in cities, for example, the Lined Antshrike, *Thamnophilus palliatus*, in Rio de Janeiro, and the Barred Antshrike, *T. doliatus*, in Rio Claro, São Paulo (Y. Oniki pers. comm.) These species are foraging generalists, which facilitates their adaptation. See also synanthropic species (see chapter 5, section 5.3.5).

2 ◆ A Short History of Ornithology in Brazil, from the Sixteenth Century to the Early Twentieth Century

This is a succinct survey of the history of Brazilian ornithology. It also covers some of the individuals involved and discusses their principal fieldwork in Brazil and their publications, as well as touching on the work of others who studied material of Brazilian origin. Behind the authors stood the museums where Brazilian collections were deposited: the National Museum of Rio de Janeiro, the Museum of Zoology in São Paulo, and the Emílio Goeldi Pará Museum in Belém, Pará. The survey ends with accounts of Alípio Miranda Ribeiro and Olivério Pinto, both of whom were born in the nineteenth century but carried on their activities into our times. I make historical references throughout the rest of the book as well.

2.1 Sixteenth Century

In the era of discovery, it was a matter of pride for travelers to bring home unknown animals. These creatures served primarily to prove that new continents had been found. Showing live animals was much more informative than bringing skins, since techniques for the preparation of birds and other animal skins were very primitive, and the accounts of chroniclers were often inadequate. Pero Vaz de Caminha, who accompanied Cabral, accomplished very little when, in his letter of 1 May 1500 to Dom Manuel, the king, he wrote of "green parrots." It was even worse when scribes invented awful absurdities, as did Antonio Pigafetta, chronicler for Fernão de Magalhães (Magellan), who disembarked in the region of present-day Rio de Janeiro in 1519. Pigafetta was a "great liar" (Taunay 1934) when, for example, he described a bird without legs that laid her eggs on the back of the male who floated on the ocean, where he brooded them for weeks. This grotesque story clearly referred to legends about birds of paradise of New Guinea (not Brazil), of which Magellan's crew brought the first skins, prepared without bones or feet, claiming birds did not need feet in paradise. Birds were prepared in this way for commercial purposes.

Unknown animals obtained by seafarers often reached scientists without precise information on their origin. Thus Linnaeus named our Lesser Seed-Finch, *Oryzoborus ango-lensis*, thinking it was from Angola, Africa. The Ruby-Topaz Hummingbird, *Chrysolampis mosquitus*, was thought to have come from India. In many cases "Brazil" was given as the origin of a bird, sometimes challenging the astuteness of scientists, even into our times, to discover where in Brazil it had been found (see Indigo Macaw, *Anodorhynchus leari*).

The birds captured for sale as souvenirs or for decoration, including thousands of hummingbirds (often prepared with their wings open), came with no indication of their origin. In such cases an understanding of the technique used in preparing a skin, its typical "make-up," may offer clues as to its origin. Thus, for instance, three types of preparation can be distinguished in classic-style trade skins of hummingbirds from Colombia (Bogotá), Trinidad, and Bahia (see Trochilidae). The Bordallo and Bourgain collections in the National Museum of Rio de Janeiro are not marked with a source of origin.

In general, the first Portuguese arrivals in the New World were not much interested in the animal kingdom. For navigators, birds served only to indicate the proximity of land, and once on land they hunted them to vary their menu.

Europeans were most impressed by parrots, which were the first birds cited for the continent. Macaws figure in a variety of the first maps of Brazil drawn by the Portuguese in the period of discovery, with the most colorful birds being those on the 1502 map of Contino (see frontispiece). Sometimes, long before a scientific record was available, paintings (fig. 20) were the best source for obtaining good documentation on flora and fauna, especially when, in the beginning of the sixteenth century, techniques for preserving birds and other animals were still unknown. Birds as small as hummingbirds were thus documented. We get little from the accounts of travelers such as Ulrich Schmeidel de Straubing, who ventured into South American terrain, including Brazil, from 1534 to 1544: he reported ostriches (rheas), chickens (probably cracids such as guans), and ducks (*Cairina moschata*) being raised by aborigines.

It is to the French Calvinist missionary, Jean de Léry (1534–1611), who came to this region in the era of the illusion of a "French Antarctic," that we are indebted for valu-

Fig. 20. Painting by Hans Burgkmair, done in 1518 in Germany, showing a Red-shouldered Macaw, *Diopsittaca nobilis* (L.), on the trunk at right. Bayerische Staatsgemäldesammlungen. From Sick 1981.

able information on the birds of Rio de Janeiro (Léry 1961). The first edition of his book appeared in 1578. Persecuted by Catholics (among them the French priest, André Thévet, who knew much less about the aborigines than Léry), he lived almost as a refugee among the Tupinambá Indians, who were terrible cannibals. Thus his circumstances were ideal for understanding the Indian environment. A good linguist, he gave an excellent account of the indigenous names of birds he observed in villages, much better than other inadequate descriptions and illustrations, making it possible for his notes to be interpreted almost immediately, even when dealing with species as similar as the Rusty-margined Guan, *Penelope superciliaris*, and Dusky-legged Guan, *P. obscura*. He also referred to the Red-billed Curassow, *Crax blumenbachii*, and to the Solitary Tinamou, *Tinamus solitarius*. Certainly, however, the Indians had received the birds in trade with other Indian tribes, so *P. obscura* and *C. blumenbachii* probably did not come from the former Guanabara region, but from some place more distant from Rio de Janeiro. This would have also been the case with the Greater Rhea, *Rhea americana*, whose feathers the Indians used to make "ararojé," a type of hip pack which Léry good-humoredly likened to a basket full of chickens hanging from one's spine (fig. 21). Léry reported that the Indians did not eat their domestic chickens, but used their feathers, which they dyed red (see Phasianidae, Appendix); they used yellow toucan breasts for decoration, which later inspired Brazilian emperors to order gala mantles. Léry took down in musical notation a song of the Tupinambás about the Blue-and-yellow Macaw, *Ara ararauna*. He thus became the first to provide accurate data on the birds of Brazil, before Cristovão de Lisboa and Marcgrave (see section 2.2).

Fig. 21. Tupinambá Indians in dance costumes, in the region of present-day Rio de Janeiro, sixteenth century. The man in front has a large bunch of rhea feathers on his rump. Above him is a macaw. From Léry 1961.

In contrast, Thévet sought sensationalism, showing in his illustrated *Singularidades da França antártica* (Peculiarities of Antarctic France) a toucan with an apparently extremely heavy bill, much larger than the rest of its body, and a quadruped with a human face. His 1575 map had horrendous monsters menacing shipping on the Brazilian coast. Through Thévet's work (republished in 1878), Conrad Gesner, the great Swiss naturalist, obtained information on Brazilian birds. His very famous and well-illustrated *Historia animalium*, published in 1555, even has a description of a hummingbird.

While sixteenth-century chroniclers such as Staden, Anchieta, and Gandavo supplied valuable information almost exclusively about Indian tribes, Fernão Cardim and Gabriel Soares de Souza were much interested in fauna. Cardim, who arrived in Brazil in 1583, described the dance of the Swallow-tailed Manakin, *Chiroxiphia caudata*, and reported on the various plumage phases of the Scarlet Ibis, *Eudocimus ruber*, a subject already discussed by H. Staden in 1557. This ibis became known in Europe through Duke Karl von Croy (1560–1612). Cardim was also the first to mention the Golden Parakeet, *Guaruba guarouba*, presently the leading candidate for the "National Bird" (see Psittacidae). Soares de

Souza, in a work of 1587 (Souza 1938), wrote about morphological details of birds (for instance the scales on the tarsus of the Solitary Tinamou, *Tinamus solitarius*, and the problem of "counterfeit" parrots), as well as biological details such as the Jabiru, *Jabiru mycteria*, method of feeding its young and the pugnacity of the Tropical Kingbird, *Tyrannus melancholicus*.

2.2 Seventeenth Century

Brazilian psittacids figure among a collection of portraits, "Theatrum Naturae," painted *in vita* in aquarelle and oil between 1600 and 1614 in Germany. *Da História da Missão dos padres Capuchinhos na Ilha do Maranhão* (On the history of the Capuchin Fathers' mission on Maranhão Island), by Father Claude d'Abbeville, was published in 1614. The author also visited Fernando de Noronha, where he observed the Eared Dove, *Zenaida auriculata*, famous in the northeast. Later the report of Frei Cristóvão de Lisboa, *História dos animais e árvores do Maranhão* (History of the animals and trees of Maranhão), written between 1625 and 1631, became prominent. It contains thirty primitive plates of birds (fig. 22) and includes bats among them, as did Pliny (A.D. 23–79), who taught that bats were the only "birds" that nursed their young.

Arte de Caça de Altaneria (Art of falconry) by Diogo Fernandes Ferreira (1899), chamberlain to the king of Portugal, contains a chapter, "On the Raptors of Brazil." Ferreira mentions two raptors taken to Portugal to be used in falconry in the court of the Infante, Dom Luis (Sick 1960). Brazilian Indians do not appear to have known of this type of hunting, which could only be developed on appropriate terrain such as savannas, deserts, and unforested mountains.

Invited by Count Maurício de Nassau-Siegen, the German naturalist George Marcgrave (1610–1643) arrived in 1636 to undertake the first zoological, botanical, and astronomical scientific expedition on Brazilian soil. Marcgrave's *Historia Naturalis Brasiliae* was published in 1648 (fig. 23), and another work, by Piso and Marcgrave, appeared in 1658. According to Cuvier, Marcgrave was "the most able and most precise of all those who described the natural history of remote countries during the sixteenth and seventeenth centuries." The interest in fauna of the count of Nassau, one of the most cultured men of the era and a compatriot of Marcgrave's, contributed to Marcgrave's success. At the same time, beautiful oils were painted by Albert Eckhout, a very well known artist, and aquarelles were made, probably by Zacharias Wagener (or Wagner) and by Marcgrave himself, and annotated independently by the count of Nassau. Many of these originals, which were assembled in the *Libri picturati* but never published, were deposited in the National Library of Berlin, where they were carefully studied by A. Schneider (1938), a part of whose work I was able to observe. The pictures are of the greatest importance, for

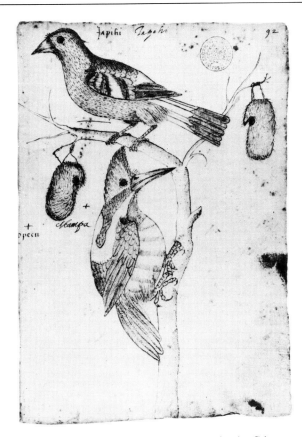

Fig. 22. Early seventeenth-century illustration by Cristovão of Lisbon showing a Yellow-rumped Cacique, *Cacicus cela,* with nest, and a Lineated Woodpecker, *Dryocopus lineatus.* From Frei Cristóvão de Lisboa, 1625–31.

Marcgrave's printed work was illustrated only with very poor woodcuts that were minimal simplifications of the originals. Among them I found the Razor-billed Curassow, *Mitu mitu mitu,* recently rediscovered, which was described by Linnaeus, based on Marcgrave's work, in 1766. No specimens collected by Marcgrave exist. During the Second World War, the *Libri picturati* were transported to Silesia and appeared to have been lost, but then were found again. They are presently deposited in the Jagiellon Library in Krakow. The so-called Thierbuch (bestiary) of Zacharias Wagener still exists (see Wagener 1964, Zoobiblion), as does the documentation of Hoflösnitz, a small hunting castle near Dresden in Saxony. Hoflösnitz contains eighty pictures of Brazilian birds painted by Eckhout in 1644, after his return to Europe (Schaeffer 1970). These pictures, more decorative than faithful to nature, adorn the ceiling of the grand salon of the castle. The birds are accompanied by the common names used in Dutch Brazil. One is a parrot used by Gmelin (1788) to describe his *Psittacus paraguanus,* which, however, existed only in Eckhout's imagination.

One of Eckhout's paintings from Pernambuco shows an African lovebird, *Agapornis* (probably *A. roseicollis,* also

portrayed in the *Libri picturati*), on the hand of a boy at the side of a pretty black girl dressed in a hat adorned with peacock feathers. Yet the only African bird that has acclimatized in Brazil (except for the Helmeted Guineafowl) is the Common Waxbill, *Estrilda astrild.*

The prince of Nassau ordered the captaincy of Rio Grande do Norte to include the rhea in its coat of arms (fig. 24) because "it is found in great abundance along the shores of the Rio Grande." Today the rhea is extinct in that state. It frequently is depicted in prehistoric rock paintings in the northeast (see Greater Rhea, *Rhea americana*).

In 1968 the Museum of Modern Art in Rio de Janeiro received some pictures from the collection of the Leningrad

Fig. 23. Baroque frontispiece from Marcgrave's *Historia Naturalis Brasiliae,* Amsterdam 1648. The Indian couple resembles the paintings of Adam and Eve of the period. Neptune, Roman god of the waters, is in the center. The animals represented only remotely resemble Neotropical animals: macaw, sloth, howler monkey with a human face, snake, hammerhead shark, land turtle, capuchin monkey, and giant anteater.

Fig. 24. Arms of Rio Grande do Norte (showing a rhea) in the seventeenth century, under the administration of the prince of Nassau. From Anon. 1986.

Academy of Sciences for an exposition. I examined these in 1982 in Leningrad. They are mostly contemporaneous copies of the original series.

2.3 *Eighteenth Century*

During his voyage to Chile in 1712, the military engineer Amédée François Frézier made port at the island of Santa Catarina, as had Dom Pernetty, companion of M. de Bougainville, in 1763. Here he found the Scarlet Ibis, *Eudocimus ruber*, the most southerly record for this species and of great interest because the bird has long been extinct in the region.

In 1783 Alexandre Rodrigues Ferreira (born in Bahia in 1756, died in Lisbon in 1815) arrived as head of the Philosophic Voyage through the Captaincies of Grão-Pará, Rio Negro, Mato Grosso, and Cuiabá, organized in Portugal to perform research for almost ten years (Ferreira 1971). It is understandable that the plan to visit Amazonia, an area closed to the curiosity of foreigners, was highly praised by the great Linnaeus in a letter to Domingos Vandelli, a former teacher of Alexandre at the University of Coimbra.

For almost ten years, from October 1783 to January 1792, Alexandre studied all aspects of the ecology of that region: flora, fauna, people—especially the indigenous populations, climate, and the exploitation of its animal, vegetable, and mineral resources, producing an enormous amount of documented information. His collections constituted the first scientific material that went from Brazil to Europe. Among the drawings can be found pictures of birds as important as the Amazonian Umbrellabird, *Cephalopterus ornatus* (Geoffroy de Saint-Hilaire, 1809), and the Nocturnal Curassow, *Nothocrax urumutum* (Spix, 1824), species that had not yet been scientifically described at that time.

A picture volume published by the Federal Cultural Council of Rio de Janeiro in 1971 provides information on the results of Rodrigues Ferreira's work, which was poorly re-

ported at the time. Among its fifty-one colored plates of birds is one that shows an artifact: a Guira Cuckoo, *Guira guira*, with the tail of another bird (a caracará?), which calls to mind the imaginary parrot painted by Eckhout in Pernambuco in the seventeenth century. As for the collections, it appears that the Lisbon Museum gave the Rodrigues Ferreira material to the Paris Museum, where Geoffroy de Saint-Hilaire prepared it. It was not stolen by Napoleonic troops during the French occupation, as is frequently suggested, but had been donated, as has been affirmed in the above-mentioned portrait volume by Arthur Cezar Ferreira Reis, the greatest authority on Amazonian history. Such gifts were already being made long before the French invasion. With permission of the local authorities, Geoffroy de Saint-Hilaire inventoried the material, which was still almost entirely stored in boxes. It was in a precarious state, and there were serious problems with the labels on the collected items. Geoffroy even saved the material from rotting, and, finally, took a minimum number of items to France. This was highly advantageous to Brazil, for in that way the most important birds, unknown to science, were promptly described. Other new species in Alexandre's collection remained forgotten in Lisbon but were later collected in portions of Amazonia outside of Brazil, with Brazil thus losing its primary claim to their discovery.

H. F. Link, a renowned scientist of that period, reported in 1798 that in company with Hoffmannsegg (see "Nineteenth Century") he met Alexandre R. Ferreira in Lisbon when he was ill and no longer involved in any scientific activity, mentioning merely that he had spent much time in Brazil. D. Vandelli (see above), aged and totally inactive, was also present.

Also deserving of mention are José Mariano da Conceição Velloso (1742–1811), a renowned botanist, who published *Aviário Brasílico* (*Brazilian Aviary*) (1800), and Diogo de Toledo Lara e Ordonhes (1752–1826), who left fragments of a *Tratado de Aves do Brasil* (Treatise of the birds of Brazil) (Taunay 1918).

2.4 *Nineteenth Century*

At the beginning of the nineteenth century the strong interest in Latin American countries solidified with the arrival of Alexander von Humboldt. Arriving in 1800 with the botanist Bompland, via the Casiquiare, in the Rio Negro, he was prohibited from entering Brazil by decision of the crown in Lisbon. Humboldt, who also included birds in his investigations (he discovered the Oilbird, *Steatornis caripensis* Humboldt, 1817, a spectacular nightbird, in Venezuela), had contact with Brazil only in 1854 when, at eighty-five years of age, he rendered the decisive opinion on demarcation of the frontier between Venezuela and Brazil (Stresemann 1950).

The first scientific bird collections to arrive in Europe after the Rodrigues Ferreira material were those of Luis Beltrão of Rio de Janeiro, F. A. Gomes of Bahia and Rio de Janeiro, and

F. W. Sieber of Pará. All these collections had been inspired by Count J. C. von Hoffmannsegg, a nobleman passionately dedicated to the natural sciences, who received Brazilian material from 1800 on. The Hoffmannsegg legacy constitutes one of the basic parts of the Berlin Museum's ornithological collection. The Gomes material includes the unusual nest of the Lesser Swallow-tailed Swift, *Panyptila cayennensis*. Sieber, who had worked for Count Hoffmannsegg in Europe as a taxidermist, came to Belém in 1800, where he remained for eleven years, in the lower Amazon region. He sent four hundred birds to Berlin, among them almost seventy species that were still unknown at the time, described by Carl Illiger and H. Lichtenstein (Berlin), C. J. Temminck (Leiden), J. Wagler (Dresden), H. Kuhl, and others. Sieber became discoverer of the Gray Tinamou, *Tinamus tao*; Brazilian Tinamou, *Crypturellus strigulosus*; Slender-billed Kite, *Helicolestes hamatus*; Vulturine Parrot, *Pionopsitta vulturina*; and various other interesting species.

Hoffmannsegg and Illiger did their best to learn more about the fauna and this fascinating, unknown country—Brazil—by encouraging collectors and promptly preparing the material they received. Thus, around 1803 Illiger wrote to Gomes: "Isn't there a cuckoo there that lays its eggs in the nests of other birds?" Gomes noted on the label of the Golden-tailed Parrotlet, *Touit surda*, Kuhl, 1820, "Periquito surdo" (Deaf Parakeet), which was used by Kuhl in choosing the scientific name of the species; surely Gomes learned what my own experience has taught: this little parrot is so tame it does not even react to the noise made by clapping—as if it were deaf. When Gomes sent a penguin from Bahia, the scientists did not want to believe it came from there (see Spheniscidae). Count Hoffmannsegg taught his collectors to use arsenic (not much used even today in Brazil, due to its poisonous character) in preparing vertebrates, which made his material highly durable. In exchange for the collection, Hoffmannsegg sent valuable books on zoology and botany to Gomes, whom he had known in Portugal. Gomes later presented them to the new public library of what is today Salvador.

With the opening of its ports in 1808, Brazil became more accessible. In 1813 Georg H. von Langsdorff came to Brazil from St. Petersburg as Russian Consul (even though he was a German). Baron Langsdorff, graduated in medicine, an enthusiastic naturalist, much traveled, and a member of the St. Petersburg Academy of Sciences, became an important figure in the progress of Brazilian ornithology. His name has been perpetuated in a hummingbird—the tiny, rare Black-bellied Thorntail, *Popelairia langsdorffi* (Temminck, 1821). Langsdorff brought G. W. Freyreiss and Friedrich Sellow, and later the Frenchman, E. Ménétriès. Langsdorff's home in Rio de Janeiro, beautifully situated overlooking the city, and his "Mandioca Ranch" (acquired in 1817), situated at the foot of Estrela Mountain, Inhomirim, Rio de Janeiro, became centers for scientists and artists. Among those received there were Wilhelm von Eschwege, founder of Brazilian mineralogy; J. Natterer, Spix, and Martius; the painter Moritz Rugendas; Hercules Florence (to whom naturalists are indebted for the original "Zoophony"); L. Riedel, a botanist; and many others. Rugendas's landscape paintings are of insuperable beauty; however, it is obvious that, strangely, he was not much interest in fauna. The few birds (parrots and macaws, for instance) and mammals that appear in his pictures are badly done. Rugendas placed two flamingos in the shade of a beautiful high, leafy forest near Mangaratiba, Rio de Janeiro—an unpardonable, misleading stupidity, for a layman might conclude that flamingos in Brazil live in dark forests and not on sunny beaches.

Freyreiss devoted himself to intensive fieldwork in eastern Brazil, making large bird collections. His material was prepared by C. P. Thunberg (Stockholm), who in 1823 described the Shrike-like Cotinga, *Laniisoma elegans*, caught near Rio de Janeiro.

Friederich Sellow, who was under the patronage of Humboldt, came to Rio de Janeiro in 1814 and worked in Brazil until 1831, when he drowned in the Rio Doce. He had traveled throughout eastern Brazil, from Bahia and Minas Gerais to Uruguay. For some time he was associated with the naturalist F. von Olfers. In Rio Grande do Sul in 1823, Sellow recorded a blue macaw that could only have been the Glaucous Macaw, *Anodorhynchus glaucus*, now probably extinct. He sent 5,457 bird skins to the Berlin Museum, including three specimens from Brazil of the now rare Brazilian Merganser, *Mergus octosetaceus*. He also collected nests, eggs, and skeletons (Stresemann 1948, 1954). In many cases, Sellow—and with him Brazil—lost priority in his discoveries because Lichtenstein, then in charge of the Berlin Museum, did not devote sufficient attention to these collections, which thereby fell behind the collections of Natterer and Spix that were immediately worked up by Temminck, who had received material from the museums of Vienna and Munich. Sellow is better known as a botanical collector, and there is now a botanical review, *Sellowia*, edited by Raulino Reitz and published by the Barbosa Rodrigues Herbarium in Itajaí, Santa Catarina. In 1981 the "Zoology" series of *Sellowia* was initiated with the article, "Aves do Estado de Santa Catarina."

Eugene Ménétriès, a young entomologist who was in Brazil from 1822 to 1825, became known in ornithology for having described such interesting birds as the Mouse-colored Tapaculo, *Scytalopus speluncae*, and the Spotted Bamboowren, *Psilorhamphus guttatus*, also a Rhinocryptidae, both originating in Minas Gerais in 1835, as well as the antbird *Formicivora deluzae* (= *grisea*). They are now in the St. Petersburg Museum. We know through Burmeister (1856) that Ménétriès was attentive to bird vocalizations and in this way found the most furtive species. His name appears in the Gray Antwren, *Myrmotherula menetriesii* (d'Orbigny, 1837), an antbird common in Amazonia.

In 1815 Prince Maximilian von Wied Neuwied arrived in Rio de Janeiro. He tramped for three years along the littoral and adjacent regions from Rio de Janeiro to the backlands of Bahia. Accompanied at first by Freyreiss and Sellow, he met F. A. Gomes in Salvador. Maximilian's travel diary, published in 1820–21, is a document of great biogeographic interest, covering everything that came along, especially fauna, flora, and aborigines. His observations compare with those of Marcgrave and Azara, the latter a contemporary authority on natural science in Paraguay (de Azara 1802–5). *Viagem* (Voyage), by Wied, published in a good Portuguese translation, has been amply reviewed by Olivério Pinto.

Maximilian filled four volumes (the *Beiträge*, Contributions to the Natural History of Brazil; there is no Portuguese translation) with 2,221 pages of studies based on his work in Brazil just on birds. The work, published 1825–33, is notable for its careful description of morphological features (partly illustrated) and for the biological details provided; he made, for example, the first observations on the unique development of the young of the Sungrebe, *Heliornis fulica*. He also reported on common names and popular legends, made very competent sketches of the countryside, Indians, and so on, which later helped artists illustrating his works to give a perfect picture of the Brazilian Neotropical environment. The scientific name of the Scaly-headed Parrot, *Pionus maximiliani* (Kuhl, 1820); Great-billed Seed-Finch, *Oryzoborus maximiliani* (Cabanis, 1851); and Black-eared Parrotlet, *Touit melanonota* (Wied, 1818), earlier known as *Urochroma wiedi* (Allen, 1889), will always remind us of the prince. Maximilian's bird collection, including many type specimens, is today under the special protection of the American Museum of Natural History in New York (see Cock-tailed Tyrant, *Alectrurus tricolor*).

This is an appropriate place for some museological observations. Old collections, such as those of Wied, were mounted, that is, the birds, mammals, and so on were stuffed to appear alive, with glass eyes, painted bills and feet—the birds frequently with open wings, perched on branches or on a board for public exhibit. At the beginning of the nineteenth century, some scientists began to prepare series of skins that were fixed to be simply lying down, as if recently dead, with the eyes and the rest of the body filled with cotton. Those responsible were accused of a selfishness that was contrary to public interest. Valuable collections, such as those of Wied, were later dismounted.

Skin series have the advantage of requiring relatively little space when shipped, and in museums they can be kept in drawers, thereby resulting in great economies of space and easier protection against harmful insects. And it is only in that way that collections can be carefully protected against daylight. This, and especially direct sunlight, discolors feathers and hairs, so eventually everything looks pale, reddish brown ("foxy," the color of the European fox), so natural coloration is almost completely lost. All that remains intact

are the measurements. Certain pigments are especially fleeting, such as the red and the intense yellow of trogons, which fade right after death and finally turn white. The magnificent orange-yellow of the cock-of-the-rock, *Rupicola* sp., also fades rapidly, to give one more example. Fading of colors is accelerated in humid climates. It is therefore necessary, in a tropical country such as Brazil, to maintain bird collections in air-conditioned areas, as is done at the Museu Goeldi in Belém, Pará.

In 1816 the botanist Auguste de Saint-Hilaire came to Rio de Janeiro, accompanied by the zoologist, Antoine Delalande. Saint-Hilaire traveled in Brazil until 1822, partly together with Langsdorff, and also collected birds. From 1818 on, his ornithological collections were prepared by Louis J. P. Vieillot. Delalande, more interested in hummingbirds (see the Black-breasted Plovercrest, *Stephanoxis lalandi* Vieillot, 1818), stayed only one year, collecting in the vicinity of Rio de Janeiro. Later he was employed by Geoffroy de Saint-Hilaire as a taxidermist.

William Swainson, an Englishman, also arrived in 1816, landing in Pernambuco and traveling to Bahia while collecting birds, fish, insects, and plants. He met Sellow and Freyreiss and returned to his country in 1818. Swainson was the second naturalist to visit Pernambuco (Marcgrave was the first). Swainson, a very well known scientist in his time, established some good genera, such as *Tigrisoma, Dendrocygna*, and *Chordeiles*, and left a pictorial record, *Birds of Brazil*, a rare work with more than eighty plates representing the most typical species. Swainson's Flycatcher, *Myiarchus swainsoni* (Cabanis and Heine, 1859), is a common tyrannid; the Royal Flycatcher, *Onychorhynchus swainsoni* (Pelzeln, 1858) (now usually merged with *Onychorhynchus coronatus*), is the famous crested bird of southeastern Brazil, and the Pearl Kite, *Gampsonyx swainsonii* (Vigors, 1825), is a small savanna hawk widely distributed in the interior.

Another Englishman, Charles Waterton, worked in Pernambuco and Maranhão at almost the same time (he arrived in 1816). The name of the Long-tailed Woodnymph, *Thalurania watertonii* (Bourcier, 1847), commemorates this naturalist, who became better known through his book, *Peregrinations in South America*, which was published in various editions.

The year 1817 became significant for natural history explorations in Brazil with the arrival of the zoologists Johannes Natterer and Johann Baptist von Spix and the botanist Carl Friedrich Philip von Martius, all part of the scientific expedition that accompanied Princess Leopoldina, later the wife of Emperor Pedro I.

Natterer (1787–1843) was the one who remained in Brazil the longest, establishing a family here and working tirelessly for eighteen years. He tramped through most of Brazil in ten great expeditions from Rio de Janeiro to Rio Grande do Sul, Goiás, Mato Grosso (where he was attacked by a strong fever that killed his Austrian companion, Sochor), Rondônia, Amazonas as far as the Colombian frontier, Roraima, and Pará. He spent the last eight years in the region of the Amazon and its tributaries, principally the Mamoré, Madeira, Rio Negro, Rio Içana, Rio Branco, and Belém areas. He did not explore the northeast (Maranhão to Bahia) due to the outbreak of civil war in Pará, a gap filled to some extent by his countryman, Otmar Reiser, who visited Bahia and Piauí in 1903. The Natterer collections contain some Pernambuco material collected by Swainson, whom he knew. Natterer married a Brazilian woman in Barcelos, upper Rio Negro, in 1831 and returned to Europe in 1835.

The Natterer collections, ordered personally by the empress of Brazil, who was much interested in the work of the naturalists, included 12,293 stuffed birds (representing 1,200 species!), more than 1,000 mammals, fish, 35,000 dry plant specimens, thousands of Indian artifacts, and so on. Saint-Hilaire, who met Natterer in Ipanema, São Paulo, wrote: "It was impossible not to admire the beauty of his birds; I did not see one dirty feather or a drop of blood."

When a modern-day layman sees the size of these old collections, he is shocked. In those times, however, large collections were necessary to build the foundations of systematics, and there was yet no risk of endangering the flora and fauna of the regions from where they came.

Natterer made many notes about characteristics that can be observed only in live or recently killed specimens, such as the iris, bill, leg, and other bare part colors, the shape of the tongue, the state of molt, contents of the crop and stomach, and anatomical details. He made observations on habitat, geographic distribution, and voice, and took parasites from the birds he prepared, all very similar to what Prince Maximilian von Wied did. Natterer's premature death did not permit him to take advantage of the results he obtained. His material was magnificently worked up by August von Pelzeln of the Vienna Museum. In many cases Natterer himself gave a name to his birds, such as *Columba cyanopis* for the Blue-eyed Ground-Dove of central Brazil, one of the rarest birds of this continent. This name, found only in Natterer's manuscripts, was used by Pelzeln to describe the new species, known today as *Columbina cyanopis* (Pelzeln, 1870). Another name published by Natterer is *Selenidera gouldii* (Natterer, 1837), considered today to be a subspecies of the Spot-billed Toucanet, *Selenidera maculirostris*.

Most of Natterer's notes were lost in a fire in the Vienna Museum in 1848, five years after his death. Philip L. Sclater (1829–1913), the great ornithologist of the British Museum, called Natterer the "prince of collectors."

John Gould (1804–81), a great English artist and scientist, produced beautiful portraits of birds of various continents, leaving more than three thousand hand-painted plates. He enjoyed the collaboration of his wife, who, however, died

early. Edward Lear, an artist and poet, joined Gould and became famous for his beautiful plate of the Indigo Macaw, *Anodorhynchus leari*, which Bonaparte used in 1856 to describe this species, which had been confused until then with the more common Hyacinth Macaw, *A. hyacinthinus*. Gould also worked in the Neotropical region, publishing monographs on hummingbirds (1849–61) and toucans (1854). He described some of our species, such as the Many-banded Aracari, *Pteroglossus pluricinctus*; Chestnut-eared Aracari, *Pteroglossus castanotis*; and Tawny-tufted Toucanet, *Selenidera nattereri*. In 1840 Gould brought the first wild budgerigar to England from Australia, thus initiating the breeding of that species in captivity (see Psittacidae, Appendix).

Prince Charles de Bonaparte, a cousin of Napoleon and a good vertebrate systematist, was a great friend and contemporary of Gould. He described the Band-winged Nightjar, *Caprimulgus longirostris*, in 1825, which I rediscovered in 1941, and the Indigo Macaw, *Anodorhynchus leari*, in 1856, which was found in the wild for the first time only in 1978.

Spix and Martius are the best-known names in the field of natural science in Brazil. Their book, *Viagem pelo Brasil nos anos de 1817 a 1820* (Voyage through Brazil in the years 1817 to 1820), has been published several times, in 1938 in a competent, scientific revision in Portuguese. Spix (1781–1826), educated in medicine, was the older and more eminent of the two; in 1815 he was charged with preparing the expedition to Brazil. The two scientists traveled together through a large portion of the country.

Various species found by Spix are among the best-known game species, showing clearly that in those days almost everything was unknown. There were ten species of Cracidae: six curassows, *Crax blumenbachii*, *C. fasciolata*, and *C. globulosa*, *Mitu tuberosa*, *M. tomentosa*, and *Nothocrax urumutum*; two guans, *Penelope jacquacu* and *P. jacucaca*; the Speckled Chachalaca, *Ortalis guttata*; and the Black-fronted Piping-Guan, *Pipile jacutinga*. The Spot-winged Wood-Quail, *Odontophorus capueira*; two tinamous, *Nothura boraquira* and *N. minor*; two trumpeters, *Psophia leucoptera* and *P. viridis*; and the Orinoco Goose, *Neochen jubata*, are also from Spix. I think it is excellent that Spix used popular Brazilian names in his nomenclature (Sick 1983). His book, *Avium species novae* (1824–25, in two volumes), was reviewed (1906) by C. E. Hellmayr,[1] one of the greatest authorities on systematics of Neotropical birds, who confirmed sixty-seven valid species, to which can be added a good number of forms that had been reclassified as subspecies, such as the beautiful Red-lored Parrot, *Amazona autumnalis diadema* (Spix, 1824).

About 1819, Spix was the first to collect the Little Blue Macaw, *Cyanopsitta spixii* (Wagler, 1832), without recognizing the importance of this discovery; he thought it was the

---

[1]Charles Hellmayr described more than 300 species and subspecies of birds. Forty-two species have his name, such as our Red-shouldered Spinetail, *Synallaxis hellmayri*, and Hellmayr's Pipit, *Anthus hellmayri*.

Hyacinth Macaw, *Anodorhynchus hyacinthinus* (Latham, 1790), a bird already known at the time. On the other hand, Spix also brought a pair of real *A. hyacinthinus*, which, thinking they were a species still unknown, he described as *A. maximiliani* (Spix, 1824), a name now relegated to the synonymy of *A. hyacinthinus*. It is interesting that Spix wrote *Arara hyacinthinus* (and not *Ara*, a genus created by Lacépède, 1799, which had priority), recognizing the correct Brazilian name "arara." Spix also wrote *Penelope jacuaçu* correctly, though later it was mutilated in Europe through lack of knowledge of Tupi, into *jacquacu* (Sick 1965). Spix noted the difference in vocalization between *C. spixii* and his *maximiliani* and distinguished the biotopes of the two: "in campis ripariis fluminis St. Francisci" for *C. spixii*, and "sylvis campestribus Provincia Goitacazes" for *A. hyacinthinus*.

The *C. spixii* specimen caught by Spix later served Wagler as the type from which to describe the species, thereby perpetuating the name of Spix. This story shows the dedicated effort that was required to remove doubts and establish the present firm nomenclature admired by all, although recently several alterations in nomenclature have occurred due to the application of new techniques to systematics.

Spix died at forty-five years of age, six years after his return, while Martius had forty-eight years available to work on his Brazilian material. He became one of the world's best-known scientists, so much so that for many the name of Spix only has meaning when associated with that of Martius. Martius himself contributed actively to the study of Brazilian fauna, as, for example, with the publication of *Nomina animalium in lingua Tupi* (1863).

In 1818 the naturalists Quoy and Gaimard were in Rio de Janeiro and visited the Serra dos Órgãos and the Nova Friburgo region. They left a well-illustrated work of 1824 that described the White-rumped Hawk, *Buteo leucorrhous*.

At the beginning of the nineteenth century, an interesting incident occurred that linked ornithology and the imperial family. The court decided to order a gala royal mantle, made of toucan breasts, for Dom Pedro I. In a decree of 25 November 1822, José Bonifácio de Andrada e Silva ordered the National Museum to deliver all but two of the Channel-billed Toucans, *Ramphastos vitellinus ariel*, in its collections (saddening the personnel of that institution, who only shortly before had collected them for the museum). A beautiful imperial mantle, which appears in various portraits of Dom Pedro I and Dom Pedro II, was made. Today it is in the Imperial Museum in Petrópolis. There is also a second mantle, made of Guianan Cock-of-the-Rock, *Rupicola rupicola*, feathers, which belonged to Dom Pedro II and appears in the oil painting by Le Chevrel in the Imperial Museum (J. C. M. Carvalho 1953).

In 1825 Peter Wilhelm Lund, a Danish paleontologist who was introduced to the natural sciences by Georges Cuvier and Alexander von Humboldt, came to Brazil, where he spent a large part of his life. Included among his multiple works on the caves of Lagoa Santa, Minas Gerais, were "Memorias" on fossil, subfossil, and recent birds. He gathered approximately forty species in his collection, all of them already known at the time, showing how advanced the knowledge of local birds already was. Lund, in his doctoral thesis, was the first to describe the lack of a muscular stomach in the *Euphonia* (Thraupinae). The ornithologists Oluf Winge and J. T. Reinhardt of the Copenhagen Museum collaborated with Lund. Reinhardt visited Brazil three times and finally published *Contribuição ao conhecimento da fauna ornitológica dos campos do Brasil* (A contribution to the knowledge of ornithological fauna of the Brazilian savannas) (1870, in Danish, now translated into Portuguese). Another publication on birds of the bone caves in Brazil is by Winge (1888), translated into Portuguese by G. Hanssen. Eugene Warming, a botanist, became better known in Brazil through publication in Portuguese of research on the origin of the cerrado and of a list of the vertebrate animals of Lagoa Santa. (See Pinto 1950 on Lund and his contribution to Brazilian ornithology.)

The celebrated French naturalist Alcide d'Orbigny, who traveled through South America from 1826 to 1833 under contract with the Argentine government, penetrated Brazil only in the far west of Mato Grosso and in the Rio Guaporé region. D'Orbigny is cited here with reference to the Glaucous Macaw, *Anodorhynchus glaucus*. He worked on his bird collections in the Paris Museum, in part together with the Baron de Lafresnaye.

The brothers Robert and Richard Schomburgk, like d'Orbigny, only skirted the frontiers of Brazilian Amazonia, touching the headwaters of the Rio Branco and the Rio Negro from the Guianas, where they worked from 1835 to 1844. Their material was worked up by Jean Cabanis of the Berlin Museum. The Schomburgks provided information on the breeding seasons and the lives of some birds.

The pharmacist Franz Kaehne, of Prenzlau, established himself in Bahia (Salvador) in 1831 and collected some birds that were among the first material taken from Brazil to Europe (to the Berlin Museum), enabling me, in 1960, to describe Stresemann's Bristlefront, *Merulaxis stresemanni*, a Rhinocryptidae.

Emílio Joaquim da Silva Maia (1808–1859; see Feio 1960), born in Salvador, Bahia, and graduated from the University of Paris, was named director of zoology of the National Museum in 1842 and studied hummingbirds, among other birds. He also commented on nature conservation. Under the title *Espécie nova e curiosa de pássaro brasileiro* (A new and curious species of Brazilian passerine), Silva Maia (1851, Trabalhos da Soc. Vellosiana: 76) wrote of a bird in the province of Rio de Janeiro that had the peculiar habit "of going under water and walking on the bottom in search of the small animals on which it feeds"—the same as the Eurasian Dipper, *Cinclus cinclus* (= *aquaticus*), of Europe, referring, he said, to observations of J. T. Descourtilz. Silva Maia concluded that the bird in question should be called *Tamnophilus aquaticus* and never returned to the matter again. I know of no Brazilian bird able to walk under water like the *Cinclus* species, Passerines found also in the Andes. In Brazil the furnariids *Lochmias* and *Cinclodes* are somewhat reminiscent of *Cinclus*, but they do not submerge.

Two French zoologists, Francis Count Castelnau and Emille Deville, in the course of a voyage to South America (1843–1847), also touched Brazil (Castelnau 1855). They collected birds and made notes on the biology of some Amazonian birds such as the Guianan Cock-of-the-Rock, *Rupicola rupicola*, and the Hoatzin, *Opisthocomus hoazin*. They took their material to the Paris Museum, where it was studied by O. des Murs, Menegaux, and C. E. Hellmayr. The latter two described the Striated Antbird, *Drymophila devillei*, in 1906.

Standing out among the best-known travelers in Amazonia are the English naturalists Alfred Russel Wallace and Henry Walter Bates, who arrived together in 1848. Wallace stayed four years, Bates eleven. Each also dedicated himself to bird study. Bates tells how he shot at the *Macrossa titan* moth, thinking it was a hummingbird that he wanted for his collection. He wrote a good description of the prenuptial ceremony of the Amazonian Umbrellabird, *Cephalopterus ornatus*, previously unknown information. (I found the first nest and egg of this species in the upper Xingu, Mato Grosso, in 1949.) The Bates and Wallace collections were identified by P. L. Sclater and Osbert Salvin. Bates's *A Naturalist on the River Amazons* (original in English, 1863), an entertaining but very correct and magnificently illustrated book, continues to be one of the most quoted publications on Amazonia. Wallace became more famous through formulating the theory of natural selection in 1859, together with Charles Darwin, basing his work on records obtained in Amazonia and the Orient.

Dr. Hermann Burmeister was in Brazil from 1850 to 1852. He went to Nova Friburgo, Rio de Janeiro, to meet C. H. Bescke, Jr., of Hamburg, a well-known dealer in natural science specimens, especially entomological material, primarily butterflies. Bescke, whose father was a famous collector, had various suppliers, so the origin of some of the material he sold was sometimes in doubt. Thus, Bescke sold to the Berlin Museum a rare nightjar, *Eleothreptus anomalus*; its origin which was probably not the Nova Friburgo region, was not indicated. Afterwards, being interested in fossils, he visited Lund and Reinhardt in Lagoa Santa, Minas Gerais.

Considering the limited time Burmeister was in the country, it is remarkable that he left us his *Compéndio dos animais do Brasil* (Compendium of the animals of Brazil) (1854–56), a very well written didactic work, in German, that gives the impression of being modern. He further published an attractive, very well illustrated volume, *Viagem ao Brasil* (Voyage to Brazil), in Portuguese, and a large-format atlas. The data on birds are frequently compilations and unreliable. Burmeister was primarily an entomologist; for example, he described *Syntermes dirus*, the large termite so appreciated by birds (see Peregrine Falcon, *Falco peregrinus*). Invited in 1856 by the Argentine government to direct the Natural Sciences Museum of Buenos Aires, he devoted himself more to paleontology. He was honored with an official funeral (1892) and a monument in Parque Centenário in the Argentine capital (Ulrich 1972).

The Frenchman Jean T. Descourtilz, who lived in the Brazilian southeast after 1851, occupies a very special place in Brazilian ornithology. He was a traveling naturalist for the National Museum from 1854 to 1855, when he died on the Espírito Santo coast. He left a valuable collection of colored plates of birds, accompanied by detailed notes on habits and customs of the illustrated species. His dedication is reflected in the choice of birds he studied, including such difficult species to observe as the Kinglet Calyptura, *Calyptura cristata*; Shrike-like Cotinga, *Laniisoma elegans*; and Sharpbill, *Oxyruncus cristatus*.

Descourtilz painted frugivorous birds perched on their favorite fruit trees. With hummingbirds he painted the flowers they prefer. Before coming to Brazil, Descourtilz served as a doctor in the French Antilles and published a Medicinal Flora of the Antilles. As a dietitian he was much interested in bird feeding and became ill after having tried the fruits of the marianeira, *Acnistus arborescens* (Solanaceae), a berry eaten by some birds but noxious to humans, being rich in saponins. Descourtilz's tongue was so swollen he was unable to talk for several days.

I cannot fail to mention Fritz Müller, a naturalist by vocation, trained in medicine, who immigrated from Germany in 1852. For some time he was a traveling naturalist of the National Museum, Rio de Janeiro, but he resided in Santa Catarina. He was particularly interested in insects and plants. While studying pollination, he also took up the study of hummingbirds. He described how a Brazilian Ruby, *Clytolaema rubricauda*, almost spoiled his research on artificial pollination of *Abutilon*, for the bird stuck its bill through the gauze with which he had wrapped the flowers. The pollen grains that had adhered to the bird's bill were wiped off by the gauze. The "Müller corpuscles" of the *Cecropia* are among the innumerable discoveries of this great scientist (see Thraupinae).

Fritz Müller's observations were much appreciated by Charles Darwin, who called Müller "the prince of observers." Darwin himself reached the Brazilian coast in 1832. He described the massacre of seabirds on the St. Paul's archipelago and on the Abrolhos, and after four months in Bahia and Rio de Janeiro, he concluded that Brazilian botany and ornithology were "too well known" (see *Diary*, ed. Nora Barlow, 1934:74). Darwin (1868) became interested in the problem of "counterfeit" parrots, the "tapiragem" of Brazilian Indians, described by Wallace (1853) (see Psittacidae).

In 1853 Karl Hieronymus Euler (Carlos Euler Senior, 1832–1901), a Swiss, immigrated to Brazil and settled as a rancher in Cantagalo, Rio de Janeiro. After having published three works on nests and eggs of the birds of southeastern Brazil, with encouragement from J. Cabanis of Berlin, editor of the *Journal für Ornithologie* from 1867 to 1868, he published more data with H. von Ihering in the Revista do Museu Paulista in 1900.

One of Euler's dedicated collaborators was Jean Roure, a bird collector resident in Muriaé, Minas Gerais, who received the first and up until today the only specimen of the Cherry-throated Tanager, *Nemosia rourei*, existing in museums and sent it to his friend Euler. Euler, sending it to J. Cabanis in Berlin, asked that the name of Roure be used for the species' scientific name. I have seen *N. rourei* in Espírito Santo (see Thraupinae). The little-known Pearly-breasted Cuckoo, *Coccyzus (euleri) juliani*, and Euler's Flycatcher, *Lathrotriccus euleri*, described by Cabanis, perpetuate the name of this great and much-quoted bird lover.

Euler was in contact with Karl Schreiner, an employee of the National Museum, who was also interested in bird reproduction. A son, Carlos Euler Junior, became an illustrious Brazilian railroad engineer (see Mabel Euler Minvielle, *Carlos Euler, Origin, Life and Work*, 1981).

La Expedición Científica Espanhola a América, 1862–1866 (The Spanish Scientific Expedition to America, 1862–1866), under the leadership of Jiménez de la Espada, began its trip through the continent of Bahia and followed the coast to Rio de Janeiro, Santa Catarina, and Rio Grande do Sul (Miller 1986; Regueiro 1983). They made contact with resident collectors such as the German, Otto Wucherer, in Bahia and the Frenchman, Auguste Bourguet, in Rio de Janeiro. The latter sold them a good collection of hummingbirds. The expedition then went to Montevideo, passed through the Strait of Magellan, and followed up along the Pacific Coast. Four members returned to Brazil, descending the Amazon to its mouth. The amphibian, *Dendrophryniscus brevipollicatus* Espada, 1870, documents this voyage.

During the 1880s the painter and traveling bird lover Paul Mangelsdorff lived in Rio de Janeiro province and left various good publications on birds of that region (*Gef. Welt* 20/21 [1891/93], for instance).

Among collecting ornithologists who worked in Amazonia during the second half of the nineteenth century, the following should be mentioned: (1) Hauxwell, an Englishman living in various parts of the upper Amazon from 1850 to 1870. His collections were worked up by Gould, Sclater, and Salvin. See, for example, the Plain-throated Antwren, *Myrmotherula hauxwelli* (Sclater, 1857). (2) G. Garlepp, a German, who also worked in the upper Amazon in 1883–84 and was advised by Count Berlepsch. (3) E. Layard, British Consul in Belém, Pará. (4) C. Riker, an American who spent some months during 1884 and 1887 in the vicinity of Santarém, Pará. His name has become better known to us due to the unusual furnariid, the Point-tailed Palmcreeper, *Berlepschia rikeri* (Ridgway, 1886), a typical representation of buriti grove avifauna. Riker was in contact with Frank M. Chapman of the American Museum of Natural History in New York. (5) W. Schulz, a German, who collected in the lower Amazon from 1892 to 1894, finding the Opal-crowned Manakin, *Pipra iris* (= *opalizans* Pelzeln), a beautiful species that had become almost legendary, for the only specimen known at that time, collected by Natterer, had been lost, so that Pelzeln had to use Natterer's field notes to describe the species. (6) Domingos S. Ferreira Pena, founder of the Belém Museum, sent a collection of birds to the National Museum of Rio de Janeiro.

The activities of other collecting ornithologists of the period are documented principally in the northeast. The Scientific Commission of Ceará, the first scientific expedition organized by Brazilians after the expedition of Alexandre R. Ferreira in the previous century, accompanied by Gonçalves Dias (Report of 1862), obtained much material that was deposited in the National Museum of Rio de Janeiro. These are the oldest items I have been able to find in the museum. The respective specimens, for example more than ninety skins of *Icterus xanthornus* (Alípio M. Ribeiro, 1928, Bol. Mus. Nac. 4[3]:19–37, apparently the Troupial, *Icterus i. jamacaii*), are recognizable only because of the splendid technique of the hunter and taxidermist, Bordallo, for they have no labels. The way this material is prepared resembles that of Bourgain, another very good taxidermist (National Museum material, characterized by the method of tying the inner toes). Bourgain's specimens, among them interesting birds such as the Little Wood-Rail, *Aramides mangle*, the South American Painted-Snipe, *Nycticryphes semicollaris*, and the Giant Snipe, *Gallinago undulata*, have a small label written in French with the day, month, year (around 1891), sex, and rarely, the place of origin.

In the mid-1880s the British anatomist, W. H. Forbes, worked in Pernambuco, a region that had not been explored since the time of Swainson. One of his finds was Forbes' Blackbird, *Curaeus forbesi* (Sclater, 1886), a species that was poorly known until very recently. Forbes (1881) himself published some results in *Ibis*.

The French entomologist, Pierre Emile Gounelle, after having worked in Minas Gerais, also moved into the northeast—Bahia, Pernambuco (1892–93), and Ceará—getting as far as Pará. Gounelle was principally interested in hummingbirds. He collected the Hyacinth Visorbearer, *Augastes scutatus*, in the Serra do Caraça in 1899 and near Diamantina, Minas Gerais, in 1903. His name has been perpetuated in the Broad-tipped Hermit, *Phaethornis gounellei* (Buccard, 1891).

Herbert H. Smith traveled in Mato Grosso and Rio Grande do Sul. His collections were worked up by J. A. Allen and F. Chapman (1891 to 1893). The National Museum of Rio de Janeiro received some duplicates.

In the meantime, Hermann von Ihering (1850–1930) had arrived in Brazil in 1880, settling in Rio Grande do Sul, where he resided for a long time as both medical doctor and naturalist, having been graduated in the two disciplines. In 1894 he was invited to direct the Museu Paulista, an office he held for twenty-two years, until 1916. His principal interest was the geographic distribution of animals in South America, and these studies contributed appreciably to his work, "História do Océano Atlântico" = "History of the Atlantic Ocean," published in 1927 in Germany shortly before his death. He was a universal scientist. He worked on all types of vertebrates and on botany and paleontology, and was a world authority on malacology.

Von Ihering did everything possible to expand the bird collections of the Museu Paulista, giving emphasis, in addition to the display collections, to assembling skin series destined exclusively to scientific study. He obtained the collaboration of various persons, such as the pharmacist Ricardo Krone, of Iguape, São Paulo, who also sent material to the National Museum of Rio de Janeiro and museums in Europe and the United States. Although birds were Krone's special interest—he was the first to describe the nest of the Bare-throated Bellbird, *Procnias nudicollis*, in 1903—he became better known for his prehistoric excavations (sambaquis). Other well-known names of the era were those of J. Zech, A. Hempel, A. Hummel, Valêncio Bueno (see *Icterus cayanensis valenciobuenoi* Ihering, 1902), and principally two traveling naturalists of the Museum, Ernst Garbe and João Leonardo Lima. Fernando Schwanda furnished important items from Maranhão, the Bare-faced Curassow, *Crax fasciolata pinima*, for instance, in the decade of the 1900s.

H. von Ihering gave as much time to systematics (classification) as to biology, using his knowledge in this field to draw morphological conclusions. He studied bird eggs and nests. At the turn of the century he had already begun to argue in favor of nature conservation, demanding a federal law on hunting and bird protection. He left more than three hundred articles, mostly on zoology, including long studies on social insects. Sometimes he published on birds together with his friend, Berlepsch. His son, Rodolfo von Ihering, who worked in fish rearing, became better known as an educator, writing such outstanding books as *Da vida dos nossos animais* = *On the Life of Our Animals* and *Dicionário dos animais do Brasil* = *Dictionary of Brazilian Animals*" (republished by the University of Brasília), excellent references based exclusively on indigenous fauna, in contrast to other Brazilian books on zoology.

Shortly after the arrival of Ihering, a Swiss, Emil A. Goeldi (1859–1917), came to Brazil, having been graduated from Jena under the well-known phylogenist, Ernst Haeckel. For a short time he was an employee of the National Museum of Rio de Janeiro and studied avifauna of the Cantagalo region of the state. In 1894 he took on the job of reorganizing the Pará Museum of Natural History and Ethnography, founded in 1866, the institution that today bears his name: Museu Paraense Emílio Goeldi. Goeldi began a systematic

study of Amazonia, bringing together good collections, especially of mammals and birds. He built a high reputation with his two popular books: *Mamíferos do Brasil* (1893) and *Aves do Brasil* (1894), the latter with an illustrated supplement, *Álbum de Aves Amazônicas* (1900 to 1906), a collection of forty-eight colored plates beautifully executed by Ernst Lohse, a sketcher, painter, and lithographer at the museum who was well acquainted with the Amazonian environment and its beauties, but was killed by revolutionaries at the door of the museum in 1930. Gottfried Hagmann, a Swiss, and H. Meerwarth, a German, both employees of the museum, also contributed at that time to the study of the birds of the region. The *Boletim do Museu Paraense* was one of the first Brazilian scientific journals with an international reputation. Goeldi returned to his homeland in 1905, where he continued to be very active as a university professor.

2.5 *Twentieth Century*

Dr. Emilie Snethlage (1868–1929) arrived at the museum in Belém in 1905 at the invitation of Goeldi, after having worked in the Berlin Museum with A. Reichenow. She was one of the first women to earn her Ph.D. in Germany, in 1904. She later took over as head of zoology and director (1914) of the Pará Museum. Oswaldo Rodrigues da Cunha, researcher and historian of that museum, has written: "Emilie Snethlage was the only woman scientist in all of South America to occupy a high administrative position in a well-known scientific institution."

Snethlage was very active in fieldwork. She sought out the most inhospitable areas of Amazonia because they were precisely the most promising in poorly known species. In 1909 she crossed between the Xingu and the Tapajós, Pará, an expedition that gave her, in addition to abundant opportunity for research on fauna and flora, the basis on which to correct maps of the region (Rios Iriri, Curuá, and Jamanxim) and to record extensive vocabularies of the Chipaya and Curuahé languages.

In those times it was an extremely arduous task for a woman to penetrate the farthest reaches of Amazonia. Emilie Snethlage almost always traveled without any other assistants than horse wranglers and paddlers. She inspired the respect of the natives by her kindly but energetic personality and by her long, thick hair, which gave her a dignity equal to that of a cacique. "Within a few hours she conquered our friendship" (Raimundo Moraes, "Os Igaraunas," 1938). An eloquent demonstration of her courage was when she, herself, amputated her own right middle finger after it had been seriously mangled by piranhas.

Francisco Queirós Lima, whom she treated as a son, and Oscar Martins worked under her direction as taxidermists. She stayed with the Museu Goeldi until 1921, when funds of the State of Pará ran out due to collapse of the rubber boom. In a short time Snethlage had become the principal authority on Amazonian avifauna, particularly that of the lower Amazon, which in ornithological literature is referred to as "Snethlage's area."

From 1922 to 1929 Snethlage was a traveling naturalist for the National Museum of Rio de Janeiro under the direction of Arthur Neiva, and later of Edgard Roquete Pinto. In 1923–24 she was in Maranhão, together with her cousin Dr. Heinrich Snethlage (1897–1939) of the Berlin Ethnology Museum, who was greatly interested in birds and who worked for three years (until 1926) in the northeast, leaving a great report with biological notes on the region's avifauna (1928), while C. E. Hellmayr (1929) undertook the systematic classification. Heinrich Snethlage also left a botanical work: the description of new species of *Cecropia*.

Emilie Snethlage visited Espírito Santo, Minas Gerais, and Bahia in 1925/26, Goiás in 1927, all the southern states as far as Rio Grande do Sul and Mato Grosso in 1928, and in 1929 went to the Serra do Caparaó, Minas Gerais, and to the Rio Madeira. In the Serra do Caparaó she met Emil Kaempfer, a German collector, who between 1926 and 1931 made large collections of eastern Brazilian birds for the American Museum of Natural History (see Hooded Visorbearer, *Augastes lumachellus*). The National Museum has a report typed by Snethlage herself on the material she collected for the museum, giving specific and subspecific identifications that are lacking only for the specimens taken on her last trip. In 1926 Snethlage became a corresponding member of the Brazilian Academy of Sciences.

Emilie Snethlage was particularly interested in zoogeography and ecology. She wanted to learn more about the evolution of vicarious forms: geographic races and "geographic species" or allospecies, the most intriguing phenomenon in the study of Amazonian fauna. Snethlage was one of the first researchers to understand this type of evolutionary action, collecting evidence with her shotgun during her well-planned surveys. She had a predilection for woodpeckers, antbirds, and vireos. In studying bird breeding she collected nests and eggs. Dedication to "field ornithology" was deprecated by the old systematists and considered a vulgar occupation fit for the collectors who furnished stuffed birds to the museums. In this way Snethlage became a pioneer (see my dedication of this book to her), although she did have predecessors in Brazil, such as Prince Wied. I have been unable to learn how much attention Snethlage gave to bird vocalization (my principal interest), which can provide valuable clues to relationships. Snethlage's collections (she also collected mammals) are the cornerstones of the ornithological collections of the museums in Belém and Rio de Janeiro.

Snethlage described approximately sixty new bird species and subspecies. Other scientists also received her material. She had contact with Count Hans von Berlepsch (1850–1915, Berlepsch Castle), Professor A. Reichenow (Berlin), Dr. R. B. Sharpe (London), A. Menegaux (Paris), Dr. Ernst Hartert (Tring, 1859–1933), C. E. Hellmayr (Munich, 1878–1944), and finally with Professor Dr. E. Stresemann (Berlin, 1889–1972, who was my mentor after 1933). Snethlage identified her material during visits to European museums. Berlepsch, whose collection, with abundant Brazilian material, was later included in the collection of the Senckenberg Museum, Frankfurt, dedicated a tyrannid genus, *Snethlagea*, to this great ornithologist. Her principal work is the *Catálogo das Aves Amazônicas = Catalog of Amazonian Birds* (1914). Other works, published in Germany, dealt with bird nesting; the most important was published post mortem in 1935. Apparently she lost a manuscript on oology of Pará avifauna during preparations for the Sixth International Ornithological Congress in Copenhagen (1926). Having struggled against malaria since 1909, Snethlage died 25 November 1929 in Porto Velho, Mato Grosso, from a heart attack during an excursion to the Rio Madeira. The cross on her grave gives only the date of her death, not that of her birth. I learned in 1941 from Fritz von Lützow, of Baixo Guandu, Espírito Santo, who had been host to Snethlage in that city, that she, believing her ornithological work in Brazil to be well advanced, was thinking of returning to Germany to write an extensive work on the birds of Brazil.

In 1894, the year Goeldi assumed direction of the Belém museum, Alípio de Miranda Ribeiro (1874–1939) became interim secretary of the National Museum of Rio de Janeiro and later chief of zoology. Carlos Schreiner, and later Pedro P. Peixoto Velho and Bruno Lobo, were his colleagues and friends. Ribeiro, an indefatigable worker with an enterprising spirit, became interested in various groups of animals, especially fish (he founded and directed the Fish Inspectorate), but also batrachians, mammals, and birds. He covered almost the entire country on scientific expeditions. He was a member of the Rondon Commission and accompanied its notable 1908 and 1909 expeditions (Commission for Strategic Telegraph Lines from Mato Grosso to the Amazon) and classified material resulting from the Roosevelt-Rondon expedition to the end. Later collections were made by botanists Frederico Carlos Hoenhne and João Geraldo Kuhlmann. The expedition continued until 1915 under the leadership of Rondon himself and Theodore Roosevelt. Others participating were Henrique Reinisch (who later worked in the Serra dos Órgãos, Rio de Janeiro; see Schneider and Sick 1962), Leo E. Miller, George K. Cherrie (the latter two in the service of the American Museum of Natural History), and, finally, Emil Stolle (see T. Roosevelt, *Through the Brazilian Wilderness*, later published in Portuguese as *Nas selvas do Brasil*). Alípio M. Ribeiro became a member of the Brazilian Academy of Sciences in 1917.

At this time Carlos Moreira, a specialist in crustaceans, worked in the National Museum. He became known in ornithology for his discovery of the Itatiaia Thistletail, *Schizoeaca moreirae* Ribeiro, 1906, one of the most common birds in the Itatiaia high country, which shows how easy it was in those days to find novelties. Eduardo Siqueira served as taxidermist. One of Ribeiro's collectors was the German rancher Rudolf Pfrimer, who lived in Goiás, and José Blaser, who obtained a pair of the rare Brazilian Merganser, *Mergus octosetaceus*, for the National Museum. Ribeiro named a subspecies from Goiás of the Maroon-faced Parakeet, *Pyrrhura leucotis pfrimeri*. Pedro Peixoto Velho brought material from Ilha Trindade in 1916. About 1911, R. Franke of Joinville made substantial bird collections in Santa Catarina that were acquired by the Vienna Museum.

Miranda visited Europe and the United States in 1911. In 1920 he published his revision of Brazilian psittacids. A good part of his work, such as his monographs on the Red-legged Seriema, *Cariama cristata* (1937), and the tinamous (1938) was included in his *Notas Ornitológicas* (Ornithological notes). Emilie Snethlage dedicated the furnariid *Syndactyla mirandae* (now a synonym of the Planalto Foliage-gleaner, *Philydor dimidiatus*) and the Buff-breasted Tody-Tyrant, *Hemitriccus mirandae*, to him.

Alípio Miranda Ribeiro was a pioneer in Brazilian zoology in the sense that, until the end of the nineteenth century, the fauna of this country was studied almost exclusively by foreign naturalists. He intended to publish a "Fauna Brasiliense," hoping to provide access to national zoology to those lacking the collection and library resources of larger scientific institutions.

Returning to the story of the museum in São Paulo, after the term of Hermann von Ihering, the activities of the zoology section were limited for a number of years to the good will of the collectors Ernst Garbe and his son; João L. Lima and his son; Hermann Lüderwaldt; and José Pinto da Fonseca. In 1929 Olivério M. de O. Pinto, a medical graduate, was taken on as an assistant in the museum, which was then under the direction of Afonso d'Escragnole Taunay. One cannot imagine a person more competent to assure, under four successive administrations, the renewed, greatly expanded, and modern development of the Museu Paulista ornithological collection and its subsequent progress within the Department of Zoology of the Department of Agriculture (terminated in 1939, today the Zoology Museum of the University of São Paulo).

Olivério Pinto carefully followed a program of methodical exploration of the country. The success of the collecting taxidermists, J. L. Lima, W. Garbe, and Emílio Dente, was demonstrated by the finding in central Brazil of the rare Blue-eyed Ground-Dove, *Columbina cyanopis*, by W. Garbe in 1940, last previously found by his father, E. Garbe in 1904,

eighty years after discovery of the species by Natterer in 1823. During expeditions to the northeast, Marcgrave's Razor-billed Curassow, *Mitu mitu mitu*, was rediscovered, and information was obtained on the possible existence of the Indigo Macaw, *Anodorhynchus leari*. Collections were obtained from Alfonso Olalla, a Colombian professional collector, later a resident of São Paulo, who was very well known for the immense quantity of Amazonian material he and other members of his family had sold to museums, such as the one in Stockholm (Count Nils Gyldenstolpe). Interchange was intensified with the Museum of Comparative Zoology of Harvard, the American Museum of Natural History in New York, and Argentine museums. A modern display of animals grouped in their natural environment was installed.

Olivério Pinto took meticulous care with everything, especially systematics, based on his deep knowledge of literature and history. His publication of the Carlos Estevão collection of skins, nests, and eggs of Belém, Pará (1953), is an important contribution to bird biology. His work, performed with extreme and exhaustive care, is also stylistically excellent. The fame of O. Pinto did not remain restricted to his field, but spread widely. For some time he had the valuable collaboration of his brother-in-law, Eurico A. de Camargo. In 1945 J. L. Peters dedicated to him the Channel-billed Toucan, *Ramphastos vitellinus pintoi*, from Goiás.

The *Catálogo das Aves do Brasil* (Catalogue of the birds of Brazil) (1938–44), by Olivério Pinto, the first volume (Rheidae to Rhinocryptidae) of which was republished by the author himself in 1978, is the starting point for any systematic ornithological work in this country. His great work, *Ornitologia Brasiliense* (Brazilian ornithology) (1964, vol. 1), remained unfinished. As the grand old man of Brazilian ornithology, he celebrated his eightieth birthday in 1976 and died in 1981. Pinto was one of the great names in international ornithology.

On the occasion of the celebration in 1986 of the 120th anniversary of the founding of the Museu Goeldi, a well-illustrated volume with text by Oswaldo Cunha, historian of the museum, was published. The bird section of the museum, after having been abandoned for many years, progressed beautifully after the institution was transferred to the National Council for Scientific and Technological Development and Fernando C. Novaes dedicated himself to the reorganization of its collections.

3 ◆ Conservation in Brazil

3.1 *History of Conservation in Brazil*

The Brazilian conservation movement has its roots in colonial times. José Bonifácio de Andrada e Silva (1763–1838), [known as the "architect of Brazilian independence"], said: "Nature has done everything for us, but we, however, have done little or nothing for Nature." The lectures of Hercules Florence (1876) were also a milestone: "Look, on all sides in this immense Brazil, with blows from the destructive machete and with fire, they are devastating broad, centuries-old forests, the refuge of unnumerable quadrupeds and birds. Once the shady retreats they need are lost, they will become increasingly rare and shy. Finally, they will totally disappear, innocent victims of the conquest by man of the wilderness. How will the exact way these animals express their sentiments or modulate their songs be preserved without zoophony." Using a modified system of musical notation, Florence, from 1831 on, developed his very original "zoophony" to symbolize the vocalizations of Brazilian animals, especially birds (Nomura 1959).

The first proposal to create national parks was made in 1876. Stimulated by the 1872 establishment of Yellowstone National Park, the world's first national park, in the United States, two parks, Ilha do Bananal and Sete Quedas, were proposed. However, it was not until 1937 that Brazil's first park, Itatiaia, was created. In 1939 Iguaçu and Serra dos Órgãos were established. In 1961 the national parks of Brasília, Caparaó, Chapada dos Veadeiros, Emas, Monte Pascoal, São Joaquim, Sete Cidades, and Sete Quedas were created, some of them in just a day. For several years the National Park Service benefited from the initiatives of Maria Tereza Jorge Pádua (Padua and Coimbra 1979).

In 1958 the Brazilian Foundation for Nature Conservation (FBCN), a nongovernmental entity, was organized through the initiative of Haroldo E. Strang, Wanderbilt Duarte de Barros, José Cândido de Melo Carvalho, Admiral Ibsen de Gusmão Câmara, and others. Its purpose has been to recommend and carry out a national conservation program for renewable and nonrenewable natural resources, especially flora and fauna, water, soil, habitats, and natural monuments, including advocating the protection of areas having scientific, historic, or esthetic value, or that have vital economic importance for the future well-being of the populace. The FBCN chose as its symbol the *curupira* of indigenous folklore (fig. 25), a good spirit who protects and defends animals and plants, unlike the "saci-pererê" (see Striped Cuckoo, *Tapera naevia*). The curupira has feet that face backward, a feature it utilizes to deceive predators and destroyers of wildlife, causing them to lose the trail or the scent of game. It also helps wounded animals recuperate.

The governmental entity responsible for nature conservation and, in particular, for national parks and other conservation units is now the Instituto Brasileiro do Meio Ambiente e dos Recursos Naturais Renováveis (IBAMA) (Brazilian Institute for the Environment and Renewable Natural Resources). It includes a wildlife department and brings together the former Special Department of the Environment (SEMA), Brazilian Forestry Development Institute (IBDF), and Superintendency of Fisheries (SUDEPE).

The great concern of Brazilian conservationists over the progressive destruction of nature was reflected in the organization of two important nongovernmental conservation organizations in 1986 that are already deeply involved. In July 1986 the Fundação Pro-Natureza (FUNATURA) was founded in Brasília to work for conservation of renewable natural resources all over the country. In September 1986 the Fundação S.O.S. Mata Atlântica was founded in São Paulo with the primary objective of preserving the remaining 5 percent of Atlantic forest and associated biomes, such as mangroves and restingas. Each has received financial assistance from abroad, especially from the United States: the International Union for the Conservation of Nature and Natural Resources (IUCN), The Nature Conservancy, The Conservation Foundation, Conservation International, and others.

3.2 *Conservation Units*[1]

As of 1989 Brazil had thirty-four national parks, nineteen federal biological reserves, and twenty national ecological stations. With a few additional "environmental protection areas" and "ecological reserves," the total area protected makes up 2.056 percent of the national territory (fig. 26).

According to world statistics, protected natural areas con-

---

[1]This section has benefited from information provided by Maria Tereza Jorge Pádua, president of Fundação Pró-Natureza (FUNATURA), and by Admiral Ibsen de Gusmão Câmara, president of the Fundação Brasileira para a Conservação da Natureza (FBCN) (= "Brazilian Nature Conservation Foundation").

Fig. 25. Curupira, logo of the Brazilian Nature Conservation Foundation (FBCN).

stitute an average of 3.2 percent of continental areas. Other such as Indonesia with 16 percent and Venezuela and Costa Rica with 8 percent each. However, using percentages as the criterion is not scientifically accurate, for the objective is to guarantee preservation of the distinctive ecosystems that each country possesses.

Various biological parks and reserves are owned by state governments, such as Carlos Botelho State Park in São Paulo, where the rare Black-fronted Piping-Guan, *Pipile jacutinga*, and the continent's largest monkey, the Spider Monkey (*Brachyteles arachnoides*), can be seen. In addition, some areas are owned by municipalities. The law provides for recognition throughout the country of "private refuges," or privately-owned properties where hunting native animals is prohibited by the owner, who is legally supported by special governmental authority. A good number of such refuges have been registered, as in the municipality of Corumbá, Mato Grosso, and in southern Brazil in Paraná. Rio Grande do Sul was a pioneer in conservation legislation, and in 1971 the Gaúcho Association for Protection of Nature (AGAPAN) was founded under the initiative of José Lutzenberger. [Lutzenberger was named Brazil's first Minister of the Environment in March 1990.]

We should be taking advantage of areas under the jurisdiction of the armed forces for faunal preservation and restocking, since trespass is prohibited in these areas. It is, however, a widely held error that nature needs to be preserved only in official parks and reserves. One must also remember that Brazil holds 33 percent of the remaining tropical forests of the planet, as well as the largest number of psittacid species, the largest number of primate species, the largest number of higher plant-life species, and the largest number of freshwater fishes.

Brazil is among the countries with the greatest biological diversity. This enormous genetic inheritance must be preserved for the benefit of present and future generations.

Information on habitats and typical avifauna of the various regions of Brazil can be found in chapter 1. See also section

Third World countries show significantly larger percentages, 3.4 on conservation problems. Immediately following are lists and discussions of the various "conservation units." The numbers in parentheses correspond to those in figure 26.

3.2.1 CONSERVATION UNITS IN BRAZILIAN AMAZONIA

State of Amazonas	Pico da Neblina National Park (23)
	Jaú National Park (22)
	Abufari Biological Reserve
	Anavilhanas Ecological Station
State of Pará	Amazônia National Park (21)
	Rio Trombetas Biological Reserve
	Jari Ecological Station
State of Rondônia	Pacaás Novos National Park (24)
	Jaru Biological Reserve
	Guaporé Biological Reserve
	Cuniã Ecological Station
State of Maranhão	Gurupi Biological Reserve
	Lençóes Maranhenses National Park (19)
Territory of Amapá	Cabo Orange National Park (20)
	Lago Piratuba Biological Reserve
	Maracá-Jipioca Ecological Station
Territory of Roraima	Monte Roraima National Park (33)
	Maracá Ecological Station
State of Acre	Serra do Divisor National Park (34)
State of Mato Grosso	Chapada dos Guimarães National Park (26)

The menace to the flora and fauna of Amazonia as a result of disorderly occupation of the region has assumed extraordinary proportions. See also the discussion in the section, "Conservation Problems," below.

3.2.2 CONSERVATION UNITS IN THE CERRADO

State of Goiás	Araguaia National Park (25)
	Chapada dos Veadeiros National Park (30)
	Emas National Park (28)
State of Minas Gerais	Serra da Canastra National Park (10)
	Serra do Cipó National Park (11)
	Grande Sertão Veredas National Park (31)
State of Piauí	Sete Cidades National Park (18)
	Uruçui-Una Ecological Station
State of Bahia	Chapada da Diamantina National Park (15)
State of Ceará	Ubajara National Park (17)
Federal District	Brasília National Park (29)

The rapid destruction of ecosystems in the cerrado region, in order to accommodate immense monocultural plantings of soybeans, rice, and sugar cane, usually involves complete destruction of gallery forests and violation of the Forestry Code's legal requirement that 20 percent of the forest be preserved. Fauna is being profoundly decimated by this insane destruction of habitats. Pests are increasing as rheas and

Fig. 26. Brazilian National Parks (map by Francisco Pontual). Circles = national parks; triangles = state capitals.

1. Lagoa do Peixe (RS)	13. Marinho de Abrolhos (BA)	25. Araguaia (TO)
2. Aparados da Serra (RS)	14. Monte Pascoal (BA)	26. Chapada dos Guimarães (MT)
3. São Joaquim (SC)	15. Chapada da Diamantina (BA)	27. Pantanal Matogrossense (MT)
4. Iguaçu (PR)	16. Serra da Capivara (PI)	28. Emas (GO)
5. Superagi (PR)	17. Ubajara (CE)	29. Brasília (DF)
6. Serra da Bocaina (SP/RJ)	18. Sete Cidades (PI)	30. Chapada dos Veadeiros (GO)
7. Itatiaia (RJ/MG)	19. Lençóes Maranhenses (MA)	31. Grande Sertão Veredas (MG)
8. Tijuca (RJ)	20. Cabo Orange (AP)	32. Fernando de Noronha, 356 km from
9. Serra dos Órgãos (RJ)	21. Amazônia (= Tapajós) (PA/AM)	the RN coast at 3°50′S 32°25′W
10. Serra da Canastra (MG)	22. Jaú (AM)	33. Monte Roraima (RR)
11. Serra do Cipó (MG)	23. Pico da Neblina (AM)	34. Serra do Divisor (AC)
12. Caparaó (MG/ES)	24. Pacaás Novos (RO)	

other natural enemies are eliminated. Gallery forests require special attention in the effort to preserve cerrados in central and south-central Brazil.

3.2.3 CAATINGA CONSERVATION UNITS

State of Piauí	Serra da Capivara National Park (16)
State of Ceará	Cuniaba Ecological Station
State of Bahia	Raso da Catarina Ecological Station
State of Pernambuco	Serra Negra Biological Reserve

3.2.4 ATLANTIC SLOPE FOREST AND ATLANTIC FOREST CONSERVATION UNITS

The Atlantic slope forest once covered an entire strip that began in the northeast and ended in the southern states of the country. This strip, which sustained Brazilians for four centuries, went unappreciated—it was violently destroyed under the impetus of development. Occupying 350,000 square kilometers, in 1985 only 3 percent of its original cover remained. The State of São Paulo, for instance, had a forest cover of about 81.8 percent, but today less than 5 percent remains, almost all of this in protected categories such as national parks, biological reserves, and ecological stations. This picture is repeated in other states such as Rio de Janeiro, Espírito Santo, Bahia, and Paraná.

State of Rio de Janeiro	Itatiaia National Park[2] (7)
	Serra dos Órgãos National Park (9)
	Tijuca National Park (8)
	Serra da Bocaina National Park[3] (6)
	Poço das Antas Biological Reserve
	Tamoios Ecological Station
	Piraí Ecological Station
State of Espírito Santo	Córrego do Veado Biological Reserve
	Sooretama Biological Reserve
	Augusto Ruschi Biological Reserve
	Comboios Biological Reserve
State of São Paulo	Juréia Ecological Station
	Tupiniquis Ecological Station
State of Minas Gerais	Caparaó National Park (12)
	Pirapitinga Ecological Station
State of Bahia	Monte Pascoal National Park (14)
	Una Biological Reserve
State of Paraná	Guaraqueçaba Ecological Station
State of Sergipe	Itabaiana Ecological Station
State of Pernambuco	Mamanguapu Ecological Station

It must be emphasized that notwithstanding the relatively large number of parks, reserves, ecological stations, and national forests in the Atlantic Slope Forest, the total amounts to only about 300,000 protected hectares under these categories. Happily there are many state parks and reserves and environmental protection areas in this badly deteriorated biome. Everything that is left of the Atlantic Slope Forest should be saved for the benefit and pleasure of future generations.

3.2.5 MATO GROSSO PANTANAL CONSERVATION UNITS

An immense wetland of about 200,000 square kilometers is situated in western Brazil between the states of Mato Grosso and Mato Grosso do Sul that includes about two-thirds of their territory. An ecosystem unique on the face of the earth, having acquired its own characteristics over the centuries, it is a mixture of Amazonia and cerrado.

State of Mato Grosso	Pantanal National Park (27)
	Taimã Ecological Station

3.2.6 SOUTHERN BRAZILIAN PLATEAU CONSERVATION UNITS

Basalt volcanic rock predominates in this region. It includes fertile soils whose traditional use for agriculture and animal husbandry has contributed to harsh deforestation. This region has been devastated in only a few decades, the violence now being aided by enormous erosion, silting, filling of valleys and rivers, and consequent flooding.

State of Rio Grande do Sul	Aparados da Serra National Park (2)
	Lagoa do Peixe National Park (1)
	Taim Ecological Station
	Aracuri-Esmeralda Ecological Station
State of Santa Catarina	São Joaquim National Park (3)
	Carijós Ecological Station
	Babitonga Ecological Station
State of Paraná	Iguaçu National Park (4)
	Superagi National Park (5)

3.2.7 MARITIME CONSERVATION UNITS

Abrolhos National Marine Park (13), in Bahia
Fernando de Noronha Marine National Park (32), in Federal Territory of F. do N.
Atol das Rocas Biological Reserve, in Rio Grande do Norte

3.2.8 CONCLUSION

Laws for protecting Brazilian fauna and flora are excellent, but they lack enforcement. (See "Conservation Problems," section 3.4, on new policies.) However, in 1982 the efforts in that direction of the then national parks director, Maria Tereza Jorge Pádua, and the then special secretary for the environment, Paulo Nogueira-Neto, earned them the Getty Prize, also called the "Nobel for World Conservation."

In view of the number of federal conservation units established in Brazil, it might appear on the surface that the situa-

---

[2]Itatiaia National Park lies in the states of Rio de Janeiro and Minas Gerais.

[3]Serra da Bocaina National Park includes parts of the states of Rio de Janeiro and São Paulo.

tion is good. However, although the number is impressive, the sum total of the areas, in relation to the size of Brazil, is insignificant at only 2 percent. Furthermore, it must be pointed out that most of the units that have been decreed have not yet been established. A large portion of their lands are still in private hands, there is inadequate control, and the administrative and scientific infrastructure is inadequate.

Two national parks have been destroyed to install dams for hydroelectric power: Paulo Afonso, created in 1948, was wiped out in 1968, and Sete Quedas, created in 1961, disappeared, also after twenty years, in 1981. Araguaia National Park was bisected by a road to service a cattle ranch established after creation of the park. Economic power is the controlling factor.

Many units have undergone drastic reduction in size, the most egregious case being that of Chapada dos Veadeiros National Park, created in 1961 with about 600,000 hectares, and through successive decrees reduced now to 60,000 hectares.

A new menace to Iguaçu Park is the helicopters that overfly the area to give tourists a better view of the falls (Andersen et al. 1989), disturbing the breeding of hawks in the area.

In conclusion, Brazilian conservation units apparently have no owner, being no man's lands where anything can happen, from fire to hunting, lumbering, mining, commercial fishing, highway construction, hydroelectric dams, transmission lines, and so forth. Of the thirty-two ecological stations, eleven still have not been legally decreed.

3.3 *The Minimal Critical Size of Ecosystems Projects*

A project underway in Amazonia is now researching the biological dynamics of forest fragments, aiming at the maintenance of ecosystems in order to establish biological base lines for planning and management of parks and reserves (Lovejoy and Oren 1981). This study is particularly important in view of the cattle-ranching projects being developed in Amazonia and the consequent deforestation of large areas. In an extensive region of primary forest north of Manaus (where even large mammals such as tapirs and jaguars are found) that has been condemned to transformation into pastureland, twelve areas between one and 10,000 hectares have been set aside to be handled by permanent reserves. In these areas, which are 500 to 2,000 meters from one another, censuses are conducted constantly of flora and fauna (particularly of birds, which are banded, and some are fitted with colored bands or radio transmitters) to study the effects of their progressive isolation, which involves a continuous impoverishment of both animal and plant species. The project was started and financed by the World Wildlife Fund-US and the Amazonian Research Institute (INPA) and expected to last for twenty years. [The World Wildlife Fund was recently replaced by the Smithsonian Institution as U.S. sponsor.]

The first data on population dynamics of all types of animals in reserves will be obtained this way, providing a basis for decisions on the size of conservation units.

Forest reserves (as well as reserves of virgin prairies, marshes, mangroves, etc.) located in the middle of a hostile, man-made environment, are similar to oceanic islands, separated from the continents to which they were linked in earlier times. Among the first to call attention to this type of dynamic biogeography were MacArthur and Wilson (1967). Reserves are subject to a similar (but not identical) rationale to that used for islands: larger islands support more species, both of animals and plants, than smaller islands.

The classic study of faunal decline due to isolation was on Barro Colorado Island, an area of 15.6 square kilometers of tropical forest that became an island when a large lake was created at the beginning of the century as part of the Panama Canal. Barro Colorado became a spectacular natural laboratory, but it failed as a good reserve, proving that the area is too small to save the most sensitive elements of its ecosystem.

Surveys undertaken in São Paulo in three residual forests of 1400, 250, and 21 hectares revealed that, in comparison with an extensive local forest that should contain about 230 species, in fact 202, 146, and 93 species of birds remained, respectively, corresponding to 87.8 percent, 63.5 percent, and 40.4 percent of their probable original status (Willis 1979).

Drastic alterations of landscapes caused by humans imply that the remaining natural environment may become too small to harbor animal species that require ample space to survive. It is impossible to preserve avifauna by providing them only the remains of a habitat, such as a patch of a few acres, and ignoring their minimum requirements. Population density of many species is low, especially in Amazonia, so the area that must be protected for their preservation is correspondingly greater.

Keeping volatile birds in small areas or patches of forest or virgin savanna, spaced between cultivated areas, impedes maintenance of their annual biological cycle. After breeding, many species undertake local migrations, usually linked to a search for different foods, such as certain fruits and seeds whose occurrence may be local and variable during the year. This is the case with toucans, parrots, and cotingids, for instance. Large birds, such as many hawks, do not immediately settle in a territory; during the first years of their life, when they are not yet breeding, they wander over a vast region. During breeding, many raptors are also accustomed to long flights in order to find adequate prey. In French Guiana it has been calculated that a Harpy Eagle, *Harpia harpyja*, needs a territory of between 100 and 200 square kilometers.

In calculating the size of a reserve, many details that may be surprising to the layman must be considered. For example, in a small area of forest, the Red-ruffed Fruitcrow,

Pyroderus scutatus, one of the largest and most colorful of endangered cotingids, cannot find, in a small area of forest, the necessary number of males and females required to complete his social group; the bird will be lost during its futile search for more companions.

Among birds in danger of extinction are the larger species, such as hawks, game birds (see below), and large fruit eaters (parrots, toucans, cotingids, etc.) that live in the canopy; species of lower strata that are "poor colonists" (Terborgh and Weske 1969), such as the Rufous-vented Ground-Cuckoo, *Neomorphus geoffroyi*; and certain terrestrial insectivores, among them the larger antbirds such as *Grallaria*. Reproduction by these birds diminishes year by year in small reserves and fails to compensate for mortality within the population, bringing the species closer and closer to extinction without the occurrence of dramatic events such as habitat destruction or hunting (Terborgh 1974). The frugivores are to some extent replaced by omnivores such as the Great Kiskadee, *Pitangus sulphuratus*, "sanhaço" tanagers, and ground doves, species typical of the forest edge.

I have found that army ants do not appear in smaller forest remnants, so the important and indispensable source of food provided by their role of flushing up insects and other small creatures for many forest birds is lacking.

There are natural fluctuations in numbers of all species of animals, including birds, that are independent of food supply; increase, decline, and extinction are frequently due to causes we do not understand. Such a process may be the result of genetic exhaustion or intraspecific imbalance and, over the course of centuries, the result of climatic change, as has so often been documented in paleontology (see Psittacidae). Epizootic diseases are capable of eradicating a species as well.

Among the limiting factors arising out of altered ecological conditions are scarcity of adequate nesting sites, such as the holes in large trees that are necessary for toucans and parrots. Large woodpeckers, such as the Robust Woodpecker, *Campephilus robustus*, are also affected due to a lack of decomposing wood where they can extract their food and construct their nests. Mid-sized woodpeckers, such as the *Piculus* and *Veniliornis*, are less affected. The Helmeted Woodpecker, *Dryocopus galeatus*, of southern Brazil is a vanishing species, but *Picumnus* piculets are even becoming common, as is the small Wedge-billed Woodcreeper, *Glyphorynchus spirurus*. In the case of *Campephilus robustus*, the considerable size of the species is significant, for it implies a normal population of a small number of individuals in a relatively extensive area. Large species, such as the larger psittacids and hawks, easily give the false impression of having a stable population even though only one or two (a pair) are present. Due to their longevity, they may be found regularly over a long period of time but not have any offspring, their reproduction being slow and limited. When such individuals die or emigrate, the species suddenly disappears. Among Neotropical avifauna there are many mid-sized and even small species that are naturally rare. Their perpetuation in limited-size areas appears to be impossible.

3.4 *Conservation Problems, Especially in Amazonia*

Since its discovery, Brazil, as is customary with new nations, has suffered a process of exploitative conquest by fire and machete. For centuries the concept of progress and development has meant a war against wildlife and nature. The only thing that has counted has been full domination by humans over the natural environment.

This mentality is still found in Brazil today. Ab'Saber (1977b) stated that "the Brazilian has had difficulty, for one reason or another, in coexisting with a forest-covered landscape." If, for example, someone buys a small rural property, the place must first be "cleaned" ("there is danger of snakes"; in early periods people were also afraid of wildcats and Indians hiding in the woods), so the trees are cut down. The forest is an impediment. Flora and fauna are not understood. "An entire cultural and social context must be altered for the Brazilian people, as a whole, to adjust their behavioral ethics to a respect for nature" (Ibsen de G. Cámara 1989). Conflict between development and nature conservation occurs in all countries.

The Amazon region is unique in having ecological conditions that have been well studied and understood only during the last forty years. The basic notions of local ecology are still little known today. Ignorance continues, which is bound to condemn new projects to failure. The victim is the Neotropical equatorial forest, whose conservation is today one of the first priorities in world nature conservation.

For those who are not up-to-date on the specific conditions of Brazil, and especially of Amazonia, here are further data, including some on Indians and local economies that clash with nature conservation. It is worthwhile for naturalists who travel in this country to know something about specific regional problems that are little known and badly interpreted outside the area.

3.4.1 SELF-SUSTAINING FOREST

Most important has been the discovery that there is a surprising scarcity of soil in 90 percent of the terra firme forests of Amazonia. The humid tropical forest of Amazonia overcomes the poverty of its substrate—the soil where it grows is usually extremely poor, often most pure sand—by becoming independent of the soil as a source of nutrients, using it only as a means of mechanical attachment and support.

The Amazonian forest is a system in equilibrium. During the day, due to photosynthesis, leaves synthesize organic material, absorbing carbonic gas and releasing oxygen. During day *and* night the leaves breathe, just like animals and microorganisms, and the reverse of photosynthesis occurs.

Thus an equilibrium between the two processes, diurnal and nocturnal, results.

In other words: the exuberance of tropical forests is due to the forest itself, which produces and recycles the nutrients for self-feeding. "Autophagous" tropical forests concentrate about 90 percent of the nutrients in their own structure (biosphere), while forests in regions with a temperate climate hold only about 3 percent of the nutrients in their biosphere and take more than 90 percent from the humus of the soil. Tropical-forest nutrients are almost exclusively accumulated within the living biomass of the forest and are being continuously recycled in a closed and constantly repeated circulation. The biomass has reached a climax and is constant.

The dense foliage of the trees protects the ground against erosion and against rapid surface runoff of rains, impeding soil compaction and maintaining permeability. Leaves catch the rain drops and let the water reach the soil in dribbles or by running down the trunks, in either case with very little kinetic energy. Half the rain that falls on Amazonian forests comes from regional recycling. Due to the high rate of evapotranspiration of this forest, the other half of the rain promptly returns to the atmosphere in the form of water vapor that recondenses and falls again as rain. Evaporation uses a great deal of thermal energy and, in this way, lowers the temperature of the forest environment. The roots of this forest are superficial, scarcely reaching groundwater. The forest thus depends on the frequency of rains.

If the tropical forest is eliminated (either by being chopped down or burned), rains and erosion will quickly carry away the few centimeters of humus, causing desertlike conditions. There are places in Amazonia that were formerly agricultural and have been abandoned for ten years, such as those along the Transamazon Highway, where there is still almost no kind of vegetation. In other parts of Brazil, such as in the temperate-climate south, good recovery of deforested areas can occur in thirty years. The Amazonian forest, once cut and burned, never returns.

3.4.2 Biodiversity

A diversity of niches and organisms adapted to them, greater than we can even imagine, can be found in the voluminous biomass produced by Neotropical forests. Until only a few years ago surveys of the total number of species existing in Amazonia indicated between 1.5 and 2 million. New estimates, based on extrapolations of the number of new species, especially insects, now go as high as 30 million. These species live in a gigantic network in which all depend, directly or indirectly, on one another, as shown in the case of pollination of the Brazil-nut tree (*Bertholletia excelsa*), one of the most characteristic trees of Amazonia and a formidable giant. Its pollination depends on only one species of bee. During months when the Brazil-nut tree is not in flower, the bee depends on the flowering of other trees in the neighboring forest. In monocultural Brazil-nut plantations, the bee cannot

survive during the long months when the trees are not in flower, so it permanently abandons the artificial plantings. The trees grow well but produce no nuts.

3.4.3 Deforestation

Cutting and fires bring an end to the marvel of the self-sustaining forest. During the past fifty years, three great waves of conquest of Amazonia menaced large parts of the region that formerly seemed untouchable. Construction of the Transamazon Highway clearly reflected the great problem of population explosion: Amazonia was occupied by immigrant colonists, "landless people." Then came the first great disillusion. Fertile soils did not exist except in a very few places already occupied by Indians. The Transamazon Highway became the "Trans-ambush," in the phrase of colonists I talked to in August 1979 in the Tapajós, Pará, region. Ultimately, lands along the Transamazon were abandoned. No vegetation, other than some invasive grasses, grows along the side of the road. The forest is not returning, and often it is not visible even on the horizon.

Then came the phase of large cattle ranches. It was officially proclaimed that Amazonia would be the largest cattle-raising region in the world. A mentality returned that had dominated Amazonia at the end of the last century, in the golden era of rubber. It brought a true second wave of conquest over the Amazonia part of the continent that had not already suffered from civilization. The lack of understanding of ecological problems, agricultural practices that were aggressive toward the environment, and the total disrespect for nature proved fatal. Facilities offered through politically motivated fiscal incentives from the Amazonia Development Bureau (SUDAM), which were purely monetary maneuvers in the incessant search for easy profits, brought ranchers and entrepreneurs from all over the planet to the forest. Amazonia was being depredated by a neocolonial concept that pushed only economic development (or simply enrichment of certain groups) without heeding the ecological, social, and sociological aspects—a predatory economics impelled by short-range interests.

Volkswagen cut down 2,000 square kilometers to plant pastures and stock them with steers. Excellent. But a few years later the plantings, including the pastures, began to degenerate. Only then did the decision makers remember the abandoned rubber monocultures (*Hevea* sp.) of Belterra and Fordlândia in Tapajós, Pará, in the 1920s. Previously unknown pests appeared and the soils became exhausted. While previously it was officially believed that pastures improved soils in Amazonia and so were subsidized, later in Rondônia it was discovered that a three-year-old pasture produced double the amount of grass of a twelve-year-old one: phosphorus declined appreciably and heavy erosion and compaction of the soil occurred (Fearnside 1985).

No one wanted to confess the failure. Damages were officially classified as improvements. Nobody spoke of the flora and fauna that had been sacrificed. Volkswagen sold out after ten years. Agriculture can last from two to three years in the region, cattle raising from five to eight years. Conversion of Amazonia to cattle raising is impossible. No benefit has accrued to Amazonia. All the profit was exported. What remained in place was sad, permanent destruction.

At the same time that the avalanche of big promoters occurred, thousands of landless people from the south, northeast, and Minas Gerais immigrated and invaded the promised forest land. These included many people who were "left over" after mechanization of large agricultural tracts in the south, as well as small miners in search of Eldorado. Just in Rondônia, the government registered more than 50,000 people per year (1988) who had abandoned their former work as producers of coffee, rice, corn, beans, rubber, and other products. The population explosion[4] in Brazil is a growing menace to nature, flora, and fauna.

The unceasing, uncontrolled migration of population to Amazonia has constantly increased the rate of deforestation. It is well known in Amazonia that ranchers cut and burn trees and plant pasture to assure that others do not enter their land, fearing squatters, land grabbers, or agricultural reform laws.

Unfortunately, farmers and ranchers in Brazil know only fire as a means of management. Fire is also popular entertainment, with illuminated hot-air balloons at the annual St. John's Day festival carrying fire as their fuel and threatening the environment wherever they fall. This spectacle is repeated every year despite being prohibited, and starts fires in the Atlantic forest (see below). Because official forest management is also accomplished with fire, the government itself has contributed decidedly to the incredible destruction in Amazonia when, for instance, through the National Institute for Colonization and Agrarian Reform (INCRA), it prepared the highway infrastructure in Rondônia by felling the forest by the most rudimentary processes and burning everything. Rondônia has, or had, one of Brazil's richest faunas, including birds.

It is precisely in Rondônia that deforestation and burning have exploded in exponential form, expanding at an estimated rate of increase of 35,000 square kilometers per year—cited in international protests as an area much larger than Belgium's 25,000 square kilometers. These calculations, made by the National Institute for Space Research (INPE) are disputed, for burning of cerrado, capoeira, and pastures is also involved, and it is said that the concentration of gases in the São Paulo atmosphere originating from the burning of sugarcane may be greater than that over Amazonia.

To accelerate drying of the forest before burning it, in Jarí, Pará, even the so-called Agent Orange defoliant, a poison of incredible destructive power, has been used. Nobody can imagine the horror that animals, which go blind before dying, suffer because of defoliants. After application, all the fauna, dead or alive, is burned, from the geckos on the ground to the birds and monkeys in the trees. Frequently not even valuable woods are saved. Fires in Jarí were so intense that they even caused violent electrical storms 10 kilometers from the scene. In 1986 a satellite detected a compact smoke screen of 65,000 square kilometers over Amazonia, produced by the innumerable fires. Newspapers wrote of "Brazil, the volcano" and "the war of fire." A hole in the ozone layer has been discovered above the Amazonia forest, similar to the one over Antarctica. The contribution of Amazonian deforestation to the "greenhouse" effect is being studied. A group from NASA has shown that the *natural* Amazonian várzea, periodically inundated each year, is a large source of methane, CH_4, in the atmosphere. This very potent gas is always cited in relation to the greenhouse effect. Larger, man-made flooding of the várzea could double the production of methane and have a global impact.

The multitude of fires in central Brazil produces "dry fog" in the dry season from June to September, causing periodic closing of all the airports. This haze in central Brazil harms fauna and flora in that it impedes production of dew, which occurs only on clear nights. Dew is the only form of precipitation at this time of year and is vital for plants and animals and a respite for humans.

3.4.4 HYDROELECTRIC INSTALLATIONS

Another wave of modernization that is destroying Amazonia is in the form of hydroelectric power dams. In the race to increase electric potential, one large plant after another is being installed, involving the flooding of immense areas. The first burst, although outside of Amazonia, was the Itaipu binational reservoir on the border with Paraguay. Six times the size of the Aswan dam, it was planned to flood approximately 1,360 square kilometers.

Areas to be flooded for hydroelectric installations in Amazonia often are not even deforested. Those responsible, acting under political pressure, have not even awaited completion of necessary topographic and rainfall studies and have flooded areas with high forest still standing. In the case of the Tucuruí, Pará, hydroelectric installation on the Rio Tocantins, it was calculated that 5.5 million cubic meters of wood were lost. This plant cost $6 billion, with much of the money coming from taxpayers of developed countries. A total of 2,430 square kilometers was flooded, creating a true ecological disaster. The decomposition of the mass of submerged material produced sulfidic gas that severely affected fauna and the Indian and European populations along the shores, and also promoted corrosion of the steel in turbines.

The dam for the Balbina plant, which generates a small

---

[4]Brazil is among the most populous countries of the world with the largest rates of population increase, similar to those of China and India. In the last forty years the population of Brazil has tripled: in 1950 there were 51,944,397 inhabitants; in 1989 an estimated 150,051,784.

amount of electrical energy for the city of Manaus, Amazonas, submerged 2,346 square kilometers over a river length of 150 kilometers. This included 1,500 islands and part of an Indian reserve. ELETRONORTE, the organization that installed Balbina, had claimed the islands would diminish the flood's impact on fauna; instead of drowning, the animals would go to the islands—foolish speculation of laymen. In reality these islands are duplicating the impact on fauna of the reservoir, since the animals that go to them are going to die because of competition for limited space. The project was presented as being generally beneficial to the plant and animal species of the region, when in reality the environmental impact has been highly deleterious. The extent of predation is incalculable (see section 3.4.7).

The plan to construct seven dams in the Xingu area of Mato Grosso has been presented to the federal government by ELETROBRAS as "the greatest national project for the end of this century and beginning of the next." In 1985 seventy-six dams were announced for Amazonia, to be built by the year 2010. While speaking proudly of progress and development, ELETROBRAS has become the undertaker of Amazonia.

To present the argument that Amazonia is too big to be destroyed is greatly to underestimate modern technology. To make perfectly clear the speed with which nature is being destroyed, I recall the example of the chain saw. It takes three and a half minutes to cut down a tree that took one hundred or more years to grow. And the chain saw is very much outclassed in deforestation by tractors and fire. The greatest danger comes from the big interests involved in the continuation of their predatory practices, protected by the permissiveness of governmental authorities. By continuing the current progressive depredation, Amazonia will be destroyed within fifty years.

3.4.5 IRON FURNACES AND WORLD HUNGER

One of the most serious problems menacing the lower Amazon region, capable of engulfing all of Amazonia in a short time, is the unlimited use of charcoal in the ovens that convert Carajás ore into pig iron for export. Carajás has 18 billion tons of iron ore. To make only 2.8 million tons of pig iron it is necessary to burn 1,000 square kilometers of forest each year.

Numerous other projects in the lower Amazon, such as cement factories, are based on charcoal use. Thousands and thousands of sawmills are established each year in the area. The price of wood on international markets keeps rising constantly, especially since the forests of southeast Asia are almost gone. A new danger for western Amazonia forests is the prolongation of the Transamazon Highway through Acre to Pucallpa, Peru, to establish a direct link with the Pacific and facilitate the export of fine woods to Japan. Thus, Amazonia's forests continue under pressure from all sides.

A great plantation of *Pinus* species, the best source of charcoal, is now under consideration for the lower Amazon. It would be available for use after sixteen years of growth (see also section 3.6).

3.4.6 INDIAN PRESENCE

The fact that Indians[5] still exist in Brazil creates problems. The most notorious situation is that during the disorderly occupation of Amazonia, the Indians have been respected no more than those people of Portuguese origin on the river edges who have been there since the time of discovery. Recent intruders, who feel important as "tamers" [of the forest], want to "cleanse" the areas of rubber tappers, Brazil-nut gatherers, Indians, and other small landholders. Their encroachments often lead to local wars, with bullets, fire, and even poison as weapons. On the Xingu in Pará, to get rid of rubber tappers and small farmers, these illegal immigrants have selectively poisoned Brazil-nut and rubber trees, the mainstays of those residents, with Tordon, a strong herbicide similar to Agent Orange. Compare this attitude with the ethics of the Kaimurá, the "uncivilized" Indians of the upper Xingu of Mato Grosso: while we believe honey exists for human consumption, they believe honey is the private property of bees and that people must ask for permission to use it, or else they commit theft. The newcomers refuse to admit that Amazonia has indigenous owners and is not a no-man's-land.

The Indians, with thousand-year-old "primitive" cultures based on Amazonia but of disputed origin (Oceanic, Japanese, or Asiatic from across the Pacific, according to linguistic evidence) are seen as obstacles when roads, hydroelectric plants, and other such installations are being planned. Fertile lands owned by Indians and mineral deposits in the subsoil of indigenous areas always attract intruders. In the middle of Ianomami territory, in Roraima, for example, between ten and twenty thousand small miners were working in 1989. The presence of Indians need not be an impediment to the national parks, unless they have been acculturated and transformed into pawns for lumber dealers, as is the case of the Pataxó in Monte Pascual National Park, Bahia.

When we penetrated the upper Xingu area of Mato Grosso in 1947 we found a dozen Indian tribes in their original villages, firmly adhering to millenial, autochthonous cultures of this continent. Not even missionaries, who were superfluous in this environment, had access to the region. The flora and fauna were untouched. Perfect equilibrium still reigned between the indigenous peoples and their natural surroundings: a true picture of the Brazil of the European discoverers of five hundred years ago.

It was impossible to maintain such an almost paradisiacal situation in a time of modern development. In 1961 the Xingu Indigenous Park was created, but the upper Xingu area

---

[5]It is estimated that in 1989 136,400 Indians lived in Amazonia. In the sixteenth century approximately two million pure-blooded indigenous persons lived there according to estimates of anthropologists.

is threatened by the same problems as other regions of Amazonia, with various dams being planned within Indian territory.

For a naturalist, the Indian, whose complex relations with his habitat make him an excellent observer of nature, is a rich source of information on flora and fauna. The names of animals and plants in the Tupi language used by present-day Indians are the same as those recorded in many publications at the time of the discovery of Brazil by the Portuguese. The ornithologist, in his or her search for certain hard-to-find birds, can utilize the knowledge of the Indians. Their feather adornments are evidence of the occurrence of distinctive species while documenting the high appreciation of beauty of the aboriginal peoples (see plate 46).

A group has been formed to work on ethnobiology. In a thesis prepared at the University of Campinas in São Paulo, A. A. Jensen in 1985 wrote on "Indigenous Systems of Bird Classification." The zoological system is seen by the Indians as groups formed by a master ("chief") species and a kingdom of other species situated at different distances, according to their degree of similarity to it. The groupings compare well with the natural discontinuities of birds recognized in the Linnean system, but there are interesting differences in the concepts of each Indian group.

The Kaiaipó, for instance, are impressive in the perfection of their understanding of fauna useful to themselves. For example, they recognize practically all the species of social stingless bees (Meliponinae), which they classified by ecological detail (Camargo and Posey 1984). Among the characters the Indians have determined to be diagnostic in separating certain types of bees is their smell. I have called attention to the typical smell of certain families of Brazilian birds, such as trogons, nightjars, and parrots. Any live or recently dead specimen belonging to one of these families can be identified by the unique smell of its plumage or flesh.

Surprisingly, just when Indians were generally being treated as a cultural embarrassment with little chance of survival, along came an initiative which, although at first it appeared to be sensationalism, has drawn the attention of the world to the problems of Amazonia. The English rock group, Sting, took the Kaiaipó Raoni Indians to seventeen Northern Hemisphere countries to arouse world opinion about Amazonia and obtain help. As a result, the Fundação Mata Virgem (Virgin Forest Foundation) was organized, linked to an educational program. As of December 1989 the campaign had produced $2 million destined for the demarcation of Indian reserves.

This is not the place to enter into further detail about indigenous peoples. It is important for two reasons to portray the Indians as an integral part of the Amazon region and obtain full support from all those interested in natural history: we can learn a great deal from them, and our collaboration is essential in saving these native peoples who are so menaced by civilization.

3.4.7 THREATS TO AMAZONIAN FAUNA, ESPECIALLY BIRDS

The data for a full discussion on the destruction of Amazonian avifauna are not yet sufficient, but I can cite the false propaganda of ELETRONORTE, builder of Amazonian electric plants, about the "benefits" of the islands behind the Balbina dam. It has been calculated that avifauna in the Balbina region includes about four hundred species (Willis and Oniki 1988) that will be dislocated or exterminated in the dam area, including the very rare Band-tailed Antshrike, *Sakesphorus melanothorax*.

More threats are constantly appearing. For instance, an area where an American group recently conducted an exhaustive survey and found an extremely rich avifauna, at Cachoeira Nazaré on the Rio Jiparaná in Rondônia, is going to be inundated.

Newspaper and magazine reports on efforts to save the animal population at the crucial time of a dam closing are pure sensationalism. When this occurred at the Brazilian/Paraguayan Itaipu dam, headlines screamed: "10,000 Animals Rescued, Now the Celebration." Not mentioned was that rescued animals released into nearby forests must now compete with those already resident there, thereby adding to the predatory impact of the operation.

The well-known limited distribution of certain Amazonian birds, such as some Formicariidae, enables us to predict the extinction of species or subspecies restricted to certain river basins. In addition, aquatic fauna are also heavily affected by the damming of rivers, which disrupts the coherence of the Amazon river system. Upstream runs of fish to their breeding grounds are interrupted. Yet surprisingly, three years after the filling of the Tucuruí, Pará dam, catches of twelve species of commercially important fish were similar to those in the prefilling period (Ataliba 1990).

3.5 *Atlantic Forest and Calcareous Forest*

The Atlantic forest is, along with Amazonia, the other principal focus of conservation efforts in Brazil. It penetrates the continent to varying distances, and even goes beyond Brazilian boundaries in the Misiones region of Argentina and in southern Paraguay.

This forest, forming a wall of vegetation along the coast, has made penetration into the interior difficult. It covered good-quality soils suitable for extensive plantings of coffee and sugarcane, and more recently wheat, cotton, soybeans, and bananas. Livestock raising prospered, and there were tree species of high commercial value. Thus the Atlantic forest was destined to disappear at the hands of humans, with almost total destruction the result.

As early as the seventeenth century, Count Mauricio of Nassau (see chapter 2) was already concerned about the destiny of the then abundant coastal forests of the northeast, precisely the area where we have now recorded the extinction of a curassow. Today most of the residual forests are small, disjunct, floristically impoverished fragments where it is difficult to discern without careful botanic studies which are primary and which are secondary forests. The total remaining Atlantic forest is estimated to be between 1 and 5 percent of its original extent. In 1911 the state of São Paulo, which lay almost entirely within the Atlantic forest, still had 64.7 percent of its area covered by forest that had originally amounted to more than 81 percent. In 1919 this had fallen to 15.6 percent, and today it is 3 percent. The Atlantic forest originally covered an area of 1.1 million square kilometers. Surprisingly, however, various birds are still not extinct, for the following reasons.

Until almost the end of the first half of the present century, large areas of primitive forest still covered part of the northeast, southern Bahia, and vast parcels of Espírito Santo, Rio de Janeiro, Minas Gerais, São Paulo, Paraná, and Santa Catarina, providing relatively good protection for the avifauna. Deforestation has accelerated since then, with ease of penetration facilitated by new roads built during the period. At the same time, the tremendous increase in population, the advance of farming and cattle raising, and the accelerated process of industrialization have opened new frontiers. Worst of all have been the fiscal inducements to reforest with exotic species, for energy and industrial purposes (see section 3.6). These were true incentives for destruction.

In the end all that was saved were forests in areas where abrupt terrain made agriculture or the raising of livestock difficult or uneconomical. Even in these areas, hunting and illegal taking of forest products such as wood, palmito, tree ferns, and ornamental plants continue, as do squatter invasions and real estate speculations near urban centers and other more accessible areas.

Meanwhile, fauna, except for the more colorful species such as large psittacids, toucans, trogons, jacamars, and game birds, has survived relatively well in islands of primary or regenerated vegetation that are the remains of fragmented ecosystems separated by large expanses of urban, cultivated, or pasture areas. However, in the near future it is going to become obvious that in many cases species thus isolated are close to the minimum size at which the population can sustain itself against the dangers of inbreeding, or they already lack enough individuals to prevent it. Various species or subspecies of lion marmoset (*Leontopithecus* sp.) have been tested in situ, and in extreme cases, ex situ, that is to say, both under natural conditions and in captivity. The Golden Lion Marmoset (*L. rosalia*), whose natural habitat was reduced to a minuscule parcel of Rio de Janeiro coastal lowland, is today in a satisfactory situation, with a captive population much larger than the wild one.

As for birds, the Razor-billed Curassow, *Mitu mitu*, in Alagoas, is the most endangered species: its survival in the wild seems unlikely. Unfortunately, human intervention through captive breeding is not producing good results in this case. Extinction of the species appears inevitable. In contrast, another cracid, the Red-billed Curassow, *Crax blumenbachii*, is maintaining a good, wild population in Espírito Santo and breeds easily in captivity, giving rise to hopes of repopulation projects. In most cases such projects are no longer feasible because there are simply no areas that are sufficiently preserved and protected to maintain wild populations.

Aside from the probable fate of *Mitu mitu*, the only Brazilian bird that I am aware has become extinct is the Glaucous Macaw, *Anodorhynchus glaucus*, once in the extreme southwest. However, by the end of this century, these will be joined by species from the Atlantic forest and even sooner from Amazonia, as a consequence of the brutal destruction of equatorial forests.

Happily, areas formerly covered by Atlantic forest have a large number of federal and state conservation units, but these cover relatively small areas and suffer from the chronic problems of such units in this country: lack of regularization of the land holdings, human residents in the interior of the reserves, and deficient inspection and control. One of the best existing reserves is the combination of Sooretama and the adjoining reserve belonging to the Companhia Vale do Rio Doce in Espírito Santo. Even there serious losses have occurred: the Red-and-Green Macaw, *Ara chloroptera*, and Black-fronted Piping-Guan, *Pipile jacutinga*, were still there as late as 1939 but have now disappeared.

The Carlos Botelho state reserve of 37,640 hectares in São Paulo is excellent, a natural location for *P. jacutinga* and for the Wooly Spider Monkey (*Brachyteles arachnoides*), the largest Neotropical primate, a Brazilian endemic.

Iguaçu National Park (170,080 hectares) in Paraná is one of the largest continuous expanses of preserved forest. For the time being, it can maintain a genetically viable population of the jaguar (*Panthera onca palustris*).

Araucaria forests are poorly represented among existing conservation units. There are good stands of this tree in the Aparados da Serra National Park (10,250 hectares) of Rio Grande do Sul and Santa Catarina, and in São Joaquim National Park (33,500 hectares) in Santa Catarina, but the latter is greatly deteriorated due both to failure to regularize its holdings and to the presence of various sawmills working within the park.

The so-called dry forest, a calcareous woodland of semideciduous trees on limestone-based soils in central Brazil (Bahia, Goiás), is greatly endangered by the charcoal industry. An interesting hummingbird species from there is the Gray-breasted Sabrewing, *Campylopterus largipennis diamantinensis* (Silva 1989).

3.6 Reforestation, Faunal Dependence, and Environmental Preservation

Reforestation in Brazil is a complex and difficult problem. There are two kinds of plantings: commercial and "ecological"; the latter means planting with indigenous species.

When reforestation is mentioned in Brazil, it is almost always understood to be commercial planting. This is easily done with exotic plants, usually species of *Pinus* or *Eucalyptus*, as well as *Gmelina* and others, all of rapid growth. This produces "energy forests," which are really just wood factories. *Pinus* plantings are the most valued. It is highly important to increase these homogeneous, artificial forests in order to save the natural ones, which become more devastated every day. In September 1989 it was reported that only 20 percent of the 36 million cubic meters of charcoal consumed annually in Brazil is from eucalyptus and pine, the remainder coming from the destruction of native forests.

It is impressive how an exotic monoculture, such as a *Pinus* plantation in Brazil, is practically equivalent to a desert so far as fauna is concerned: it lacks all the rich Neotropical fauna that depend on a great abundance of ecological niches, beginning with the rich undergrowth that is almost completely missing in these forests. In environmental circles they even speak of the desertification of Brazil with eucalyptus and pine—"the silent forests." Interestingly, *Pinus elliottii*, which has been introduced into Australia, also proves to be completely useless to local avifauna there (J. Forshaw, pers. comm.). Conditions are unsuitable, and there would be no value in bringing fauna characteristic of *Pinus* forests from the northern hemisphere, or of eucalyptus from Australia, as has been suggested.

However, exotic plants are capable of becoming favorites of Brazilian birds. The palm *Livistonia australis*, when bearing fruit, is very popular with such Brazilian birds as the *Milvago* and *Polyborus* caracaras; the Black Vulture, *Coragyps atratus*; the Reddish-bellied Parakeet, *Pyrrhura frontalis*; the Surucua Trogon, *Trogon surrucura*; and the Channel-billed Toucan, *Ramphastos vitellinus* (Espírito Santo). Eucalyptus nectar attracts hummingbirds. I have recorded fourteen Brazilian bird species of seven families eating the small fruits of yellow magnolia (*Michelia champaca*).

In part 2 of the book I give the names of many plants whose flowers, fruits, or seeds attract and nourish wild birds. Seeds inside bird feces can be collected and planted; many trees and other plants originate from this source. A simple means of obtaining feces is to collect them while banding birds, especially when working with mist nets. This is also an opportunity to induce regurgitation, or even to conduct a stomach washing to examine recently eaten foods. Works on plants attractive to birds are mentioned in the bibliography, such as those of Kuhlmann and Jimbo (1957) and Tomback (1975).

Native forests are designated as "unproductive" by Brazilian economists. The tremendous variety of tree species per hectare in Neotropical forests (see chapter 1, section 1.3.1) makes economic utilization, such as a regular supply for local sawmills, impossible. For this reason, Ludwig, in Jarí, wanting to produce paper, planted thousands of hectares of Asiatic *Gmelina arborea* (Verbenaceae) and exotic pine (*Pinus caribaea*). Today the same scheme is being used in the lower Amazon: *Pinus* is being planted, but in places that have already been deforested (see section 3.4.5).

Until a few years ago the Brazilian Forest Code officially permitted the substitution of native forests with homogeneous plantings of exotic trees "for the purpose of obtaining an economic return." Fiscal incentives were given to encourage reforestation with exotic species "for energy and industrial purposes." This meant the end of the Atlantic forest, one of the world's unique bioma, of which only 1 to 5 percent remains, although to some degree it is recoverable, unlike the humid tropical forest of Amazonia.

Some good national initiatives are seeking alternatives to exotic plants: many native tree species (most belonging to the Leguminosae family) can be as productive as eucalyptus and *Pinus*. In many cases they produce better-quality wood in addition to growing fast and leaving the soil enriched (through symbiosis with bacteria that fix nitrogen from the air) rather than depleted. At the same time, they make up an appropriate habitat for native fauna.

Some Leguminosae improve the soil and promote development of an abundant understory, generally lacking in exotic monocultures but indispensable for local fauna, especially birds. These are jacarandá, *Dalbergia nigra*; pau-brasil, *Caesalpina echinata*; pau-ferro, *C. ferrea*; angico, *Piptadenia* spp.; molungu, *Erythrina* spp.; and bracaatinga, *Mimosa scabrella* (see Hummingbirds), the last being fast-growing.

The constant deforestation and burning suffered by the Environmental Preservation Area of the Serra da Mantiqueira in São Paulo has induced airplane pilots to become winged inspectors. They have scattered Paraná Pine (*Araucaria angustifolia*) seeds from airplanes, thereby collaborating in reforestation of the area which, up to the beginning of 1990, had been "preserved" only on paper.

3.7 *Pollution: Birds as Bioindicators*

I have mentioned atmospheric pollution caused by burning (see section 3.4.3). The first indication of severe air pollution in Brazil was found in Congonhas, in the interior of Minas Gerais, where the twelve prophets, sculpted in soapstone by the great master Aleijadinho, were found to be in a process of accelerated deterioration.

New research on deposits of heavy metals in birds, in the form of residues suspended in the air and found on feathers, are impressive (see fig. 27). Specifically, this involves lead and cadmium deposits on flight feathers (remiges and rectrices), which are the feathers having the most intensive contact with the atmosphere (Ellenberg 1981; Hahn 1989). Thus, birds have become important bioindicators in the attempt to control air pollution.

Birds constitute final links in the food chain and tend, therefore, to concentrate heavy metals in feeding. Studies have been made of mercury and zinc levels in the muscular fiber of fish-eating terns (*Sterna hirundinacea* and *S. euryg-*

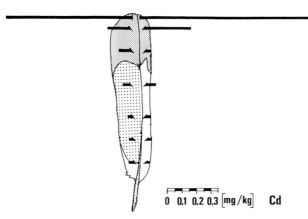

Fig. 27. Cadmium deposit on rectrix (sixth) of a domestic pigeon, *Columba livia domestica*. After Hahn et al. In Press.

natha) nesting on pillars of the Rio Niteroi bridge across Guanabara Bay (Trancoso et al. 1985). Samples of fat and blood to be analyzed can be taken from captured live birds without the need to kill them.

In Europe and the United States, and probably also in Brazil, there is a large decline in the number of raptors that, at the end of the food chain, feed principally on birds and fish (but not on rodents), in which accumulated insecticide residues are present. A statistic from Germany found the following pesticide content along the food chain: plankton, 0.04 ppm; small fish eaten by aquatic birds, 0.17–1.23 ppm (freshwater fish may reach more than 10 ppm); terns, 3.15–5.17 ppm; Common Merganser (*Mergus merganser*), 22.8 ppm. Pesticides such as DDT ingested with food are deposited mainly in fat (not in the musculature) and eggs.

The increasing pollution of rivers, which is transforming them into sewers, leads to the expulsion of birds such as kingfishers, grebes, terns, and swallows such as the White-winged Swallow, *Tachycineta albiventer*. Water behind dams becomes toxic due to lack of oxygenization (section 3.4.4). Agricultural chemical pollutants—fungicides, herbicides, pesticides, insecticides, and tick remedies—join the pollution created by leftover petroleum derivatives and industry.

Water pollution, a problem of national dimensions, can stem from the manufacture of ethyl alcohol, of which large quantities of "vinhoto," also known as "vinhaça," "restilo," or distillery broth, is a by-product. This process is highly toxic to fauna and flora and is endangering the Pantanal of Mato Grosso. The first fish kill in the Pantanal caused by one of these mills occurred in September 1981 and reached tributaries of the Rio Aquidauana and Rio Miranda, two of the rivers with the most fish in the area.

With the problem of vinhoto still unresolved (new technology to develop biodigesters of vinhoto is being reviewed, attention has moved to another serious pollution problem, again in the Pantanal but also on the Tapajós, Pará, and in Roraima, where, due to a new gold rush and intense prospec-

ting, high levels of mercury contamination were recorded in rivers. In the Poconé area of the Pantanal, more than seven hundred dredges are at work daily taking sand from river beds, silting rivers, and transforming what were formerly broad rivers into muddy creeks. Use of mercury guarantees better gold production, but with prudence it could be used in much smaller quantities. Analyses of sediments in Poconé revealed 21.9 micrograms of mercury, 44 times what is considered safe; and the water showed 8.5 micrograms, 425 times above allowable levels. The mercury index in fish from the Rio Paraguai (into which Pantanal rivers flow) became extremely high at points where the poisoned water had left the Pantanal.

The heaviest water pollution occurs in the mangroves, the site of many industrial and home development projects. The greatest concentration of heavy metals and agricultural poisons has been recorded in the Cubatão region (called "the most polluted city in the world"), where there still are, however, Scarlet Ibis, *Eudocimus ruber*, according to recent surprising reports.

Biocides, products containing Aldrin that are used on a large scale, kill both useful and harmful insects and their natural enemies. They affect birds and mammals as well as humans. Indiscriminate application of insecticides is standard practice in regions with large monocultures of soybeans and rice, such as Rio Grande do Sul. Among the first birds eliminated are open country tinamids, such as the Spotted Nothura, *Nothura maculosa*, and Red-winged Tinamou, *Rhynchotus rufescens*, for they swallow the seeds whole, like pigeons do, without crushing them.

Many years ago A. Ruschi (1950) published long lists of birds killed by spraying BHC in Espírito Santo. He also showed that insects necessary for pollination of a group of more than a hundred mango trees were practically exterminated, with the result that not a single fruit was produced.

Spraying biocides from airplanes has been shown to kill vultures and rails in Colombia, nightjars (which are outstanding insectivores) in Chile, and *Otus* owls in the United States. Fish kills occurred after application of NaPCP in Suriname rice fields to reduce the number of snails (*Pomacea*). Subsequently fifty dead Snail Kites, *Rostrhamus sociabilis*, were found, their musculature showing a high concentration of pentachlorophenol. Herons and jacanas were victims as well (Vermeer et al. 1974).

The number of cases in which birds, including cage birds, have died in Brazil due to eating food poisoned by biocides has increased, but the degree of destruction is unknown. In the *Catalog of Agricultural Remedies* published by the Ministry of Agriculture (1981), 112 products to kill insects, mites, and ticks were listed as registered, as well as 76 fungicides and 125 herbicides, many of them containing highly persistent, toxic substances such as DDT, BHC, Parathion, Aldrin, Chlordane, and Methoxychlor. The destruction of birds, particularly those in the upper links of the food chain, is probably intense. Toxic agricultural products that are prohibited for use in their country of origin, such as the United States, can no longer be imported into Brazil.

In Rio Grande do Sul studies have been undertaken on the noxious effects of insecticides, using the Spotted Nothura, *Nothura maculosa*, to test the degree of contamination with organochlorine biocides. The birds eat poisoned ticks that have dropped off cattle near their corrals.

It has been shown that the levels of DDT compounds in southern Brazil "were relatively low, lower than in many localities of North America (Risebrough et al. in litt.). But levels of Mirex (considered a potential human carcinogen) were high. Mirex is widely used against the leaf-cutting ants that pose a particular threat to fields of soybeans, which are now a major crop in southern Brazil. Blood samples taken from birds in Peru and Ecuador have shown high levels of a number of organochlorine compounds. However, the residues accumulated on the wintering grounds of North American birds do not appear to have been as important in limiting reproduction as previously thought, as in the case of the Peregrine Falcon," *Falco peregrinus* (Springer et al., in prep.)

Evidence that DDT residues in an organism affect calcification of bird eggs is apparently still lacking in Brazil. Thinning of the egg shell is the most evident symptom pointing to a high accumulation of DDT in birds (see Osprey, *Pandion haliaetus*; the phenomenon is also evident in the Peregrine Falcon, *Falco peregrinus*, and other North American birds). Possibly related to this phenomenon are the weakened eggs of the riverine tyrannid, the Black Phoebe, *Sayornis nigricans*, found by Gunnar Hoy in Salta, Argentina, in 1974.

In Rio Grande do Sul the illegal use of poisoned baits and carcasses to control vultures and wild dogs often results in the death of birds who were not targets, especially birds of prey.

Pollution of the sea with petroleum, caused by spills at PETROBRAS maritime terminals or by tanker wrecks, is responsible for deaths of many marine birds. There are relatively few birds in the Atlantic off Brazil, but autopsies of dead Procellariiformes and migrant penguins show lesions in the lungs and kidneys. Feathers of oiled birds become sticky and no longer protect the body against cold; on the high seas such birds sink. A small number reach the coast, soaked in petroleum. Apparently the problem of the "oil plague" may be resolved by bacteria: the bacteria *Pseudomonas* dissolves oil in the laboratory.

Large kills of gulls and other marine birds occur repeatedly in Bahia and São Paulo (between Itanhaém and Peruibe, for example). Their bodies are scattered over 10 to 30 kilometers of beach. But the cause of this disaster has not been clarified. (See Procellariidae.)

A large, new threat to maritime birds is the ingestion of indigestible materials that obstruct their intestines or damage the stomach walls. These are plastic materials—synthetic polymers—such as the polyethylene nodules used for packing machinery, porcelain, etc., transported by ship. The bite-sized nodules are often dumped into the sea, where they attract curious birds. Oceanic and pelagic species such as the Procellariiformes—albatrosses and petrels—are the most affected. A small ball of polyethylene has also been found in the stomach of a Lesser Golden-Plover, *Pluvialis dominica*.

3.8 *Illegal Trade in Birds: New Perspectives*

The desire to have a bird in a cage where it can be cared for and pampered is a deeply established tradition among Brazilians and cannot be totally condemned. The wish to have a cage bird is found both in the simple peasant of the interior and the ordinary laborer in the city, who immediately hangs a cage near the entrance to his new shanty. People at all levels of society do the same. One cannot imagine a shoe repair shop, open to the street, without a bird in a cage hanging in the entrance. An interesting feature of Brazil is the multitude of elaborate but empty cages: birdless cages hung in conspicuous places on balconies and terraces, as an indication that the owners like birds. A special industry makes finely finished luxury cages that serve only as decorations. In most cases a simple cage, without a bird, is considered an adequate decoration. I know of cases where an empty cage has been there for some twenty years, and will no doubt remain indefinitely.

It is very difficult for people who want a bird to understand that the most sought-after ones (interest is concentrated in certain Emberizidae, such as the Lesser Seed-Finch, *Oryzoborus angolensis*, and Red-cowled Cardinal, *Paroaria dominicana*) have today become rare and can no longer be supplied on demand. The fact that legislation exists prohibiting all commerce in native birds that are not captively bred is little known. This ignorance is explained in part by the fact that most cage bird owners know nothing, and have no interest in knowing anything, about birds in their natural surroundings. For these people, Brazilian fauna has not yet become a valued patrimony that must be protected in its natural habitat. Captive breeding of birds has been rarely undertaken, except for canaries and Australian budgerigars. Brazil has more than 170 associations of amateur bird fanciers. The other popular activity associated with birds is that of hunting "game birds" such as tinamous, guans, and ducks.

Illegal trade in birds thus continues to be an extremely serious problem, with a still heavy demand for cage birds. The long, deeply embedded tradition of every Brazilian having his own bird has permitted the trade to prosper. This trade is attractive for two reasons: (1) for many, especially certain adolescents, catching birds is more attractive than any other activity; and (2) a good profit is guaranteed—the trade in wild birds is called a "million dollar business" for good reason. Almost no one knows the law, and no one fears it.

The quantity and types of cage birds in Brazilian homes is incredible. I live in Laranjeiras, a district near the center of Rio de Janeiro, and from my thirteenth floor apartment I can hear about twenty species of caged Brazilian passerines. A similar number of different species live wild in the same district, in addition to four psittacids. Recently, a bird dealer moved into the district and brought with him a Pale-breasted Thrush, *Turdus leucomelas*, an excellent singer that cheers up all who hear it—much more than the local Rufous-Bellied Thrush, *Turdus rufiventris*, which is free but sings much less and whose song is distorted by the city. Some day the caged thrush will stop singing—it will die or escape; it will be much missed and another will be sought, in that vicious circle. I say: conserving nature does not mean prohibiting its use. However, my caveats still apply and must be continuously repeated: (1) to have one bird adapted to life in a cage, tens and often hundreds are sacrificed during capture and transportation; (2) a solitary captive bird cannot breed and is thus unable to leave descendants.

It has always been a great mystery why captive birds in Brazil sing more than wild ones, in spite of their being imprisoned in a small cage, without a mate, and unable to fly; but they sing until the lights go on at night. They exist this way for many years, apparently in perfect health.

In Duque de Caxias, Rio de Janeiro, one of the centers of illegal commerce in animals (including mammals, especially monkeys, and reptiles) between 1980 and 1983, 191 different species of birds were offered for sale, including various Red Data Book species (Carvalho 1985). Eighty species were offered on just one day. Highly valued species are "manufactured"—for example, by trimming the tail of an *Aratinga* to make an *Amazona*. The common White-eyed Parakeet, *Aratinga leucophthalmus*, is painted yellow, leaving only the remiges green, to make a Golden Parakeet, *Guaruba guarouba*. Painted individuals of this sort are exported, often deceiving foreign scientists and amateurs who do not understand Latin tricks.

In this way, Brazil's fascinating fauna is reduced to simple merchandise, and will inevitably die out. No fauna in the world could survive the waste involved in an illegal bird trade such as that in Brazil. We must remember the case of the Little Blue Macaw, *Cyanopsitta spixii*, whose last two known wild individuals were captured and sold for a fortune in 1988. The authority (formerly IBDF, now IBAMA) responsible for their protection is now in an embarrassing situation.

Beginning in the 1970s, a notable change has occurred in the Brazilian attitude. There no longer is any Brazilian newspaper that does not report something on "ecology" (confusing it with preservation), pollution, and environmental conservation. Fortunately, the Brazilian environmental movement is no longer just a fad. One result of this new outlook was the foundation of the Bird Observers' Club (COA) in 1974, which today has about nine hundred members in six of the twenty-three states of the Union. It was a complete novelty for Brazil: young people, usually students, wanting to get out to know birds in the wild. COA can be very useful in encouraging larger numbers of people to interest themselves in the conservation of nature, especially in birds. We must try to change the Brazilians' deep fondness for cage birds, persuade them to protect free, wild birds, and encourage the use of decorative cages without imprisoned birds. A practical application of the strategy of CITES (Convention on International Trade in Endangered Species of Wild Fauna and Flora, or "Washington 1973 Convention") would be a boycott of the national wild bird trade. CITES distinguishes three categories of birds: (1) the most endangered species, in which trade is not permitted except under very special license; (2) species that can be traded under a special export license; and (3) species that can be traded in accordance with restrictions established in the Convention.

Brazil has good legislation that defends its natural resources. It is in tune with the concept that problems of conservation of nature and natural resources in the modern world are intimately linked to the welfare of people and affect their health. However, this legislation needs to be more enforced and respected, which can be solved by taking immediate steps to educate the public.

The destruction of nature due to technological developments and the increase in human population throughout the world has become a grave modern risk and a foreseeable future drama. Once typical local fauna is extinct, an imminent danger everywhere in Brazilian territory, it will disappear forever from the face of the earth. The conservation of nature is a primary responsibility of any civilized people.

The current (1989) president of the Brazilian Institute for the Environment and Renewable Natural Resources (IBAMA), Fernando César Mesquita, said it very well when he referred specifically to the population of Amazonia: "It is very difficult to talk of ecology ['ecology' is customarily used in place of 'conservation'] in a country where part of the population is hungry and has to depend on fauna and other natural resources for survival." When I questioned a hunter in Amazonia National Park, he responded, "We country folk also have to eat."

Hunting of Tinamidae, Anatidae, Cracidae, Columbidae, Psittacidae, and other birds has assumed an important role in the interior of the country in the sense of supplying the rural population with meat. But it is different when, even today, "hummingbirds in rice" and "corn meal with little birds" are popular dishes in certain areas of southern Brazil colonized by Italians, and when "sportsmen" triumphantly shoot down macaws. "Scientific" collectors, who fill boxes and boxes with eggs of rare hawks, hummingbird skins, and so forth, are also a real danger.

3.9 *New Orientation*

With the change of government in 1989–90, new attitudes have emerged. IBAMA, successor to the Brazilian Forest Development Institute (IBDF), promises new policies in the vast area of Brazil's natural environment: development without destruction. The government is trying to compensate for its former neglect of nature by launching the Our Nature program.

It has now been recognized that, in the past, the preservation of nature was totally ignored. Never in the history of humanity has there been such destruction of habitats, flora, and fauna as has occurred in Amazonia, the world's richest natural resource area. Special attention will now be given to the three largest and most famous ecosystems: Amazonia, the Atlantic forest, and the Pantanal. Various proposals for self-sustaining use of Amazonian forests have already been made—for example, the creation of reserves to ensure only gradual removal of valuable forest products while the forest itself is maintained. Additional ideas are needed for the full development of Amazonia's unique environmental functions and the preservation of its biological diversity.

In order not to repeat the drama of the Transamazon Highway, any new roads must go into areas of fertile soils. The incentives that have accelerated the destruction of Amazonia, such as encouragement of cattle raising, building of sawmills, and production of pig iron, must be eliminated. The use of pastures as an "improvement" for the purpose of establishing land ownership has been one of the great motivators of the progressive deforestation of the Amazonian region.

A new type of silviculture is envisioned. Silvicultural management of terra firme virgin forests, with all its species, using the self-sustaining forest as a renewable resource, is going to be a most interesting innovation.

Technicians from IBAMA and INPE are preparing an atlas of Brazil to be presented in Tokyo, Japan, on the occasion of the International Space Year. New satellite technology is facilitating control over changes in Amazonia as well as other parts of Brazil. Good international collaboration, assisted by the international "Tropical Forests" program, is developing as well.

A "Priority Conservation Areas for Amazonia" workshop convened in January 1990, in Manaus, Amazonia. It brought together ninety-five scientists, among them Gillean Prance of the Royal Botanic Gardens, Kew (botanist), Russell Mittermeier of Conservation International (monkeys), and Ted Parker of the Louisiana State University Museum of Natural Science (birds). They discussed management of reserves in Amazonia on a scientific, botanical/zoological basis. There was general agreement that areas to be preserved must be large in order to guarantee survival of the largest possible number of species—ideally 20 percent of Amazonia, compared with 2 percent that is legally protected today. Until now, parks in the nine Amazonian countries have been established only to protect frontiers, because they are areas unsuitable for human habitation, or to protect isolated species. The protection of both flora and fauna, as now proposed, is a new concept.

4 ◆ Biogeography and Speciation

As indicated, portions of this chapter were contributed by Jürgen Haffer, in English, especially for this edition. Haffer's bibliography has been consolidated into the general bibliography.

[Haffer]: The Neotropical avifauna, comprising approximately 3,300 species, is the richest in the world. Many bird species range over huge areas of South and Middle America, whereas other species inhabit ranges of intermediate size. A surprisingly large number of species and well-differentiated subspecies are clustered in fairly restricted regions of the Neotropical lowlands, characterizing a number of areas of endemism (fig. 28): five in forested Central America, six to seven in Amazonia, and three in forested eastern Brazil, each with ten to fifty (or more) species and subspecies (Cracraft 1985; Haffer 1978, 1985, 1987a). Seven areas of endemism are known in the South American nonforest lowland regions. Most contact zones between hybridizing subspecies and closely related parapatric species cluster in intervening regions between the central portions of endemism. Another conspicuous biogeographic phenomenon in the Neotropical region is the wide disjunction of numerous closely related representative taxa (species and subspecies) of montane and lowland birds.

[Sick]: Such is the case of the extremely long-tailed nightjars, with two species in the Andes and one, the Long-trained Nightjar, *Macropsalis creagra*, in mountainous regions of southeastern Brazil. The large Red-ruffed Fruitcrow, *Pyroderus scutatus*, a cotingid, is widely distributed in the Andes of Guyana, Venezuela, and Colombia, and is a typical feature of primary forests of southeastern Brazil, Paraguay, and northern Argentina. The Whistling Heron, *Syrigma sibilatrix*, and the Fasciated Tiger-Heron, *Tigrisoma fasciatum*, and various other birds have a similar distribution. Such highly disjunct distribution shows dramatically that there was an enormous extinction of populations during the centuries before humans began to interfere.

[Haffer]: Large Amazonian rivers delimit the ranges of many bird species along their wide lower portions. However, the cumulative total of range boundaries located away from broad rivers is much larger (Haffer 1978). About one hundred species (15 percent) of the nonaquatic avifauna of the Amazon basin are restricted to habitats created by rivers, such as beaches and sandbars, sandbar scrub, river edge forest, várzea forest, transitional forest, and the water edge (Remsen et al. 1983; see also Terborgh 1985).

Depending on the genetic differentiation reached by geographically representative forms, these are ranked as species if they are (or presumably are) reproductively isolated from each other, and as subspecies of one biological species if they hybridize extensively (or presumably hybridize) along the contact zone. Geographically representative species are designated as allospecies if they are not in contact, and as paraspecies if they are in contact without (or nearly without) hybridization (semispecies *sensu strictus* are species that hybridize to some extent; Short 1969). A superspecies is composed of two or more paraspecies or allospecies which are derived directly from a common ancestor (Amadon 1966a, 1968; Selander 1971). By contrast, a zoogeographical species is a superspecies or an independent biological species (which is not a member of a superspecies; see Mayr and Short 1970).

[Sick]: A concept of these categories is the key to understanding complicated speciation and hybridization, such as that of the toucans (Ramphastidae) as explained by Haffer (1974b). The percentage of Neotropical forest birds that can be assembled in superspecies is very high in some cases: 75 percent of the chachalacas, guans, and curassows (Cracidae), jacamars (Galbulidae), and manakins (Pipridae); the aracaris and toucans (Ramphastidae) amount to as much as 85 percent. The parrots (Psittacidae), cotingas (Cotingidae), and tanagers (Thraupinae) are groups on which much work still needs to be done in this regard.

The allospecies situation becomes interesting when allospecies of the same superspecies come together again after having been isolated. They may require very similar ecological conditions and so compete as rivals. This appears to be the case with the allospecies *Pipra aureola* (Crimson-hooded Manakin) and *Pipra fasciicauda* (Band-tailed Manakin) of the superspecies *Pipra aureola* of the lower Amazon. If related species occupy contiguous areas, this special kind of allopatry is referred to as parapatric distribution and the species are parapatric.

In unusual circumstances one allospecies may penetrate, to a greater or lesser extent, into the area of another, its neighbor, and be able to hold its place there, resulting in sympatry (living in the same place, sympatric species). This happens with the Chestnut-eared Aracari, *Pteroglossus castanotis*, and Many-banded Aracari, *Pteroglossus pluricinctus*, in the upper Amazon; apparently no cross-breeding occurs (Haffer 1974b).

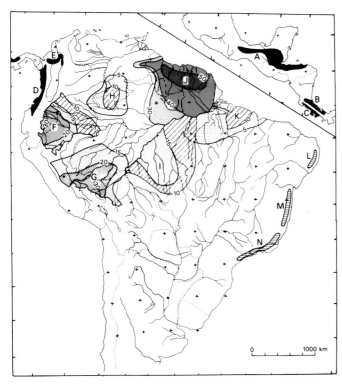

Fig. 28. Centers of species endemism in lowland forest avifauna. Trans-Andean centers (solid): (A) Guatemala (7 spp.); (B) Caribbean Costa Rica (14 spp.); (C) Pacific Costa Rica (12 spp.); (D) Chocó (32 spp.); (E) Nechí (14 spp.). East Brazilian centers (hatched): (L) Recife; (M and N) Serra do Mar. Amazonian centers (with numbers of endemic species shown by shading and simplified by omitting some displaced extensions across major rivers): (F) Napo; (G) Inambari; (H) Imerí; (I) Rondônia; (J) the Guianas; (K) Belém. Adapted from Haffer 1967, 1974b, 1975, 1978, and 1987a.

[Haffer]: In an attempt to interpret the origin of the high species diversity in the Neotropics, especially in the forested regions, and the origin of the biogeographic patterns, three theories have been proposed that may be relevant to a different degree for different faunal groups or different levels of faunal differentiation (Haffer 1974b, 1982; Simpson and Haffer 1978; Prance 1982):

4.1.1 PALEOGEOGRAPHY THEORY

Paleogeographical changes in the distribution of land and sea due to orogenic and epeirogenic movements during the Cenozoic (Tertiary-Quaternary) led to the separation and differentiation of animal populations of previously continuous biota on isolated land areas and peninsulas (Chapman 1917; Emsley 1965; Räsänen et al. 1987; Cracraft and Prum 1988). Details about the paleogeographic history of the Andean region and of central South America during the Tertiary, in particular the varying barrier effect of the Amazon River and its large tributaries, necessary to reconstruct the faunal his-

tory, remain unknown (Haffer 1974b; Cracraft and Prum 1988). World sea level was about eighty to one hundred meters lower than today during the glacial periods of the Quaternary. By contrast, during interglacial periods of raised sea level, many coastal lowlands of South America were converted into huge inland brackish and freshwater lakes extending west into the Marañón basin of eastern Peru. Under this theory, extant species and subspecies as well as their distributional patterns are thought to have originated due to large-scale changes in the distribution of land and sea during the Tertiary and early Quaternary.

4.1.2 RIVER THEORY

The development of river systems, in particular the frequently changing position of individual river channels and their floodplains in level lowlands such as Amazonia, is assumed to have caused effective separation and subsequent speciation of bird and other vertebrate populations on opposite banks (Hellmayr 1910, 1912; Snethlage 1913; Mayr 1942: 228; Sick 1967b; Willis 1969: 393; Hershkovitz 1977: 413; Caparella 1988; Cracraft and Prum 1988). The broad portions of many rivers in Amazonia, often in conjunction with their much wider floodplains, are indeed formidable obstacles for the dispersal of birds inhabiting the forest interior. They effectively separate populations of many terra firme forest bird species and subspecies [Sick]: such as, for example, separation by the lower Tapajós of two races of the Dark-winged Trumpeter, *Psophia viridis*, and by the Madeira of two allospecies (see below): *P. viridis* and the Pale-winged Trumpeter, *P. leucoptera*. [Haffer]: However, a large portion of these taxa are in direct contact in the headwater regions where the rivers cease to be effective barriers (Haffer 1982). [Sick]: Such contact of trumpeters does not occur in central Brazil on the southern affluents of the Amazon due to absence at the headwaters of those rivers of ecological and climatic conditions suitable for the existence of trumpeters. [Haffer]: Any discussion of the importance of rivers for the diversification of vertebrate faunas is incomplete without a consideration of the present and past ecological conditions in the headwater regions of rivers whose wide lower portions represent effective barriers to dispersal of many rain-forest animals.

[Sick]: How the width of a river may or may not be a barrier for fauna is objectively demonstrated by the Cactus Parakeet, *Aratinga cactorum*. This bird, an excellent flyer, colonized both sides of the Rio São Francisco in northeastern Brazil, but does not cross it unnecessarily, with the result that two subspecies have developed, one on each side of the river.

The presence of small, photophobic birds such as Formicariidae on forested islands one or two kilometers from shore in large Amazonian rivers draws attention to the fact that these birds, by flying across river channels, do more colonizing than might be expected.

4.1.3 Refuge Theory

[Haffer]: Climatic-vegetational fluctuations probably led to the isolation of forest animal populations in forest refugia (fig. 29) during arid climatic phases and of nonforest animals in nonforest refugia during humid phases of the Cenozoic (Haffer 1969; Prance 1982, 1985; critical review by Lynch 1988). Within the refugia, species populations (a) became extinct, (b) survived unchanged, or (c) differentiated to the level of subspecies or species. In Amazonia, deep forest refugia may have been separated by less humid and open forest types dominated by lianas or palms rather than by nonforest vegetation like savanna or caatinga. The original suggestion for the possible location of forest refugia in tropical America was based on consideration of current regional rainfall distribution and the surface relief, together with other geoscientific evidence. Independently, biotic distribution patterns suggested a set of core areas (areas of endemism; fig. 30) for forest organisms (Simpson and Haffer 1978; Brown 1987a,b). A comparison of these two independently derived sets of areas showed that they are, in large part, coincident, which suggested that the climatic changes and the formation of forest enclaves probably were the cause of the speciation pattern. Although probably most pronounced during the Quaternary, climatic-vegetational shifts also occurred repeatedly during the preceding Tertiary period. Geoscientific evidence from many regions in tropical America confirms the occurrence of climatic-vegetational changes during the Cenozoic (Haffer 1987b; Schubert 1988). Direct evidence for

particular areas to have supported a forest refuge or a nonforest refuge during a particular climatic period, however, is not yet available. Generally speaking, it may be too simplistic to assume alternating, prolonged periods of habitat continuity and habitat discontinuity during the Cenozoic. Rather, constantly changing climatic patterns may have caused continuous complex changes in the distribution of forest and nonforest elements during cold-arid, cold-humid, warm-arid, and warm-humid phases. Refuges may represent areas of relative habitat continuity and average survival of certain groups. During the height of at least some arid glacial phases of the Quaternary, destruction of many fragmented but still identifiable community units (e.g., rain forest) may have continued in some regions, for example, in northern South America, to such an extent that only very restricted populations of the endemic elements and many nonendemic plant and animal taxa persisted in dispersed and localized "mini-refugia" too small to register in the pollen record (Livingstone 1980).

[Sick]: A peculiar phenomenon, common in Amazonia and arising out of earlier isolation, is the insular distribution of certain very sedentary birds, such as antbirds (e.g., *Rhegmatorhina* species) in the midst of the extensive Amazonian forest. In a superwet period the jungle returned and filled the gaps in the forest, but this forest fauna was incapable of further expansion. There was no explanation for this situation before the historic interpretation that postulated "refuges," a notion that revolutionized zoogeography. The present coexistence of many similar species, such as more than

Fig. 29. Forest refuges. Distribution of presumed forest refuges in the Neotropics during dry epochs in the Pleistocene. Left: birds (after Haffer 1967 and later); middle: anoles of the *Anolis* genus (after Vanzolini et al. 1970). Right: butterflies of the *Heliconius* genus (after Brown et al. 1974).

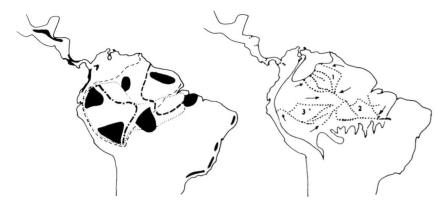

Fig. 30. Aspects of forest bird distribution in Amazonia (after Haffer 1981). Left: 6 nuclei of endemic species (black areas). Four kinds of distribution can be recognized: (1) birds of the upper Amazon (heavy dots-and-dashes); (2) birds of the lower Amazon (heavy dashes); (3) birds widely distributed in Amazonia but missing from southeastern Amazonia (light dashes); and (4) Amazonian birds missing from northeastern Amazonia (light dots). Right: contact zones of Amazonian bird species. Arrows indicate expanding faunas: (1) in the north-central region; (2) in the south-central region; and (3) in the upper Amazon.

ten *Myrmotherula* species in the same area, also became comprehensible. In certain places, twenty to forty-five sympatric species of Furnariidae and Formicariidae have been recorded.

It is impossible that these close relatives could have evolved in this same environment, no matter how varied ecological conditions may be in the present-day Amazonian forest. They must have evolved when segregated in a forest mosaic of "refuges". It should be mentioned that H. W. Bates called attention in the middle of the last century to the exis-

tence of many endemic biotas in the Amazonian forest.

[Haffer]: In contrast to lower Amazonia, no paleoecological information is yet available from the central and upper Amazonian forest region, as again pointed out by Connor (1986), Colinvaux (1987), and Salo (1987) in their critical discussions of the geoscientific basis of the refuge theory. Even if future surveys should suggest that the central and upper Amazon forest zone merely shrank in extent peripherally during arid climatic periods without fragmenting, the refuge theory would still remain a valid model for en-

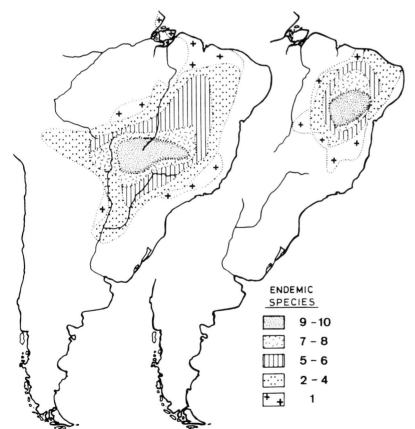

ENDEMIC SPECIES

	9 - 10
	7 - 8
	5 - 6
	2 - 4
+ +	1

Fig. 31. Superimposed ranges of ten bird species typical of the cerrado (left) and ten of the caatinga (right). Adapted from Haffer 1985. Haffer's list of species, not given here, is slightly different than mine.

vironmental forcing of evolution and the diversification of terrestrial faunas over vast regions of South America and other continents during the entire history of the earth.

[Sick]: Two other considerations are pertinent here: (1) Evolution in a Savanna Environment and Northern Immigration. The evolution of savanna (fig. 31) fauna is as interesting as that of forest fauna. (See chapter 1, section 1.3.3, on the cerrado.) A preponderant factor that limited spread of the Hylaea was the relatively dry zone that extended from southern Venezuela to northeastern Brazil, crossing the Amazon. It presumably originated with the last long, dry period, between 4,000 and 2,500 years ago. Later, with renewed expansion of the forests, the zone disappeared (Haffer 1974b). This ecological barrier, a "transamazon highway" of natural savanna, separated Upper Amazonia from Lower Amazonia and, in turn, provided savanna species new opportunities to spread, as shown in the cases of two hummingbirds, the Black-bellied Thorntail, *Popelairia langsdorffi*, and Brown Violetear, *Colibri delphinae*. Immigration from North America occurred that took advantage of savanna areas in the middle of Amazonia, such as that of the Eastern Meadowlark, *Sturnella magna*, a beautiful icterine. Its most southerly "beach head" reached the open country of the lower Tocantins, Pará. The Crested Bobwhite, *Colinus cristatus*, and Double-striped Thick-knee, *Burhinus bistriatus*, also of North American origin, were not so successful, not having managed to cross the Amazon. *Colinus cristatus* serves, north of the Amazon, as an ecological replacement for the *Nothura* spp. and the Red-winged Tinamou, *Rhynchotus rufescens*—southern tinamous that, in turn, failed to cross the Ocean River northward. I am not referring here to the great immigration of North American fauna, both mammals and birds, to South America at the time of the meeting of the two continents in much more distant times (Pliocene, 5 million years ago) when many birds of North American descent reached extreme southern South America (see Oscines).

(2) Patagonian/Andean Immigration. An immigration of Patagonian/Andean ecosystems into Brazil could have occurred during the last 2 million years (Quaternary, divided into Pleistocene, and Holocene, i.e., the last 10,000 years), during various climatic changes. Thus Brazil received various members of the Rhinocryptidae family, a group of non-Oscine Passeriformes that are generally forest-loving and widespread in the south of the continent and the Andes. The *Scytalopus* stand out among them.

Two Furnariidae have the same immigrant history: the Itatiaia Thistletail, *Schizoeaca moreirae*, and Wing-banded Cinclodes, *Cinclodes pabsti*. While the former is limited to the highest peaks of southeastern Brazil, with a moderate climate where isolated populations of bamboo (*Chusquea*) prosper, *C. pabsti* lives in open country in the extreme south of the country (see chapter 1, sections 1.3.5 and 1.3.6, and chapter 5, "Quasi-endemic Species"). It is difficult to decide whether the Brazilian representatives of these groups should be considered pioneers or relicts. A reverse dispersal of fauna, from the mountainous regions of southeastern Brazil to the slopes of the Andes, might perhaps have occurred with the Giant Antshrike, *Batara cinerea*; Rufous Gnateater, *Conopophaga lineata*; and Swallow-tailed Cotinga, *Phibalura flavirostris*.

[Haffer]: Present knowledge of the Tertiary and Quaternary history of tropical South America indicates repeated complex formations and disappearances of barrier zones over the continent through paleogeographic changes and climatic-vegetational fluctuations. Available geoscientific data, however, are insufficient to allow for the mapping of changes in distributions of land and sea or of forest and nonforest vegetation during the Cenozoic and, in particular, for the tracing of the history of areas of endemism. Therefore, no area cladograms for the Tertiary-Quaternary history of land areas and vegetational units in the Neotropics can yet be constructed for a comparison with area cladograms derived from taxonomic studies of particular groups (Haffer 1985; Cracraft and Prum 1988).

5 ◆ The Birds

5.1 *Birds of the Neotropics*

Brazil occupies a considerable portion of the Neotropical region (fig. 32), which extends from the northern edge of the Mexican rain forests at 20°N to Cape Horn at 57°S, including all of South America, Central America, and the Antilles. South of 30°S, the latitude of Porto Alegre, the moderate climate of the Pampas begins. The cold Patagonian region stretches south of 40°S.

The Neotropics are characterized by the great expanse of South American continental flatlands, including the greatest continuous rain forest in the world (Amazonia), and by the impressive Andean chain, which does not touch Brazil.

Neotropical avifauna includes many endemic species that have evolved in the region. In Amazonia (taken as an ecological unit without respect to political frontiers), out of a total of approximately 930 species, close to 44 percent are endemic and involve sixty endemic genera. Six species reach Trinidad, off the Venezuelan coast (Haffer 1974a).

The Suboscines (or non-Oscines, Clamatores or Mesomyodi), the autochthonous Passerines of the Neotropics, occupy an outstanding position: in Brazil their 582 species make up 35.6 percent of all the avifauna. Proportions are similar for all of South America. Suboscines occupy a certain number of ecological niches here that in other continents are filled by a very wide variety of other types of birds.

A small number of families hold numerical supremacy. For Brazil those richest in species are Tyrannidae, 200; Formicariidae, 167; and Furnariidae, 99; all belong to the Suboscines. The Trochilidae, with 84 species, is the largest non-Passerine group.

Omitting certain aquatic and marine birds, we can classify birds living in the Neotropics into five groups:

1. Neotropical families: Tinamidae, Rheidae, Anhimidae, Psophiidae, Eurypygidae, Cariamidae, Opisthocomidae, Steatornithidae, Nyctibiidae, Galbulidae, Bucconidae, Ramphastidae, Dendrocolaptidae, Furnariidae, Formicariidae, Rhinocryptidae, Cotingidae, Pipridae, and Phytotomidae. In certain cases, such as the Cathartidae and Momotidae that are presently exclusively Neotropical, fossils have been found in the Old World.
2. More or less extensive distribution in South and North America: Trochilidae, Tyrannidae, Troglodytidae, Mimidae, Vireonidae, and Emberizidae including Parulinae, Coerebinae, Thraupinae, Emberizinae, Cardinalinae, and Icterinae.

3. Families with pantropical distribution: Anhingidae, Heliornithidae, Jacanidae, Psittacidae, Trogonidae, and Capitonidae.
4. Families or subfamilies originating in the Old World: Phasianidae, Columbidae, Cuculidae, Corvidae, Muscicapidae with Turdinae and Sylviinae, and Motacillidae.
5. Widely distributed throughout the entire world: Anatidae, Accipitridae, Falconidae, Rallidae, Charadriidae, Scolopacidae, Laridae, Tytonidae, Strigidae, Caprimulgidae, Apodidae, Alcedinidae, Picidae (except Australia, New Guinea, and Madagascar), and Hirundinidae.

African influence in Neotropical fauna, for example the existence of the Trogonidae family in both areas, shows an ancient connection between the two continents, whose sepa-

Fig. 32. The Neotropical region (adapted from Haffer 1974b). Delineation of zoogeographic subdivisions: Cis-Andean region (dotted); Trans-Andean region (lined); Andean region (solid black). The Neotropical region extends from southern Mexico (20°N) to Cape Horn (57°S) and includes the nontropical, southern part of South America.

ration began in the Cretaceous more than 50 million years ago. In the Tertiary (Eocene) 40 million years ago, the distance between the two continents was not yet great (Short 1971).

The four African freshwater Anatidae—the Fulvous and White-faced Whistling-Ducks, *Dendrocygna bicolor* and *D. viduata*; Southern Pochard, *Netta erythrophthalma*; and Comb Duck, *Sarkidiornis melanotos*—could have crossed the Atlantic later.

5.2 *Fossil Birds, by Herculano Alvarenga*

Birds descended from arcosaurian reptiles, probably a primitive line of small, nimble dinosaurs. *Archaeopteryx lithographica*, of the Upper Jurassic of Europe, well known through about six skeletons, represents a true transition from reptiles to birds: on the one hand, it is an authentic reptile with toothed mandibles, a long tail, abdominal ribs, and no sternum; on the other, it is a true bird due to the presence of developed and fused clavicles that form the furcula, and other skeletal details, but principally due to the presence of feathers, with typical asymmetric flight feathers on the wings. Various birds of the Upper Cretaceous still had teeth, such as the Hesperornithes (*Hesperornis, Enaliornis, Neogaeornis,* etc.) and Ichthyornithes, although they already had a skeletal structure that was more avian and less reptilian.

5.2.1 FOSSIL BIRDS OF BRAZIL

The first work on Brazilian fossil birds was written by O. Winge (1888), based on material collected by Peter Lund in caves in the Lagoa Santa region of Minas Gerais. This material, from the Pleistocene epoch (partly Holocene) mostly relates to still-living species, with only one extinct form among them: *Neochen pugil*, a goose known through various bone segments to be much larger than the Orinoco Goose, *N. jubata*, that lives in Amazonia today. In 1891 Lydekker described a stork from Lagoa Santa with the name of *Paleociconia australis*, now changed to *Jabiru lydekkeri*.

After the above works came the publications of Shufeldt (1916) and Silva Santos (1950) on the finding of fossil feathers in the Taubaté basin of the state of São Paulo (Oligocene), and of Ackermann (1964), who also described a feather from the Miocene of Capanema, Pará.

Later came the works of Alvarenga (1982, 1983, 1985a,b, and 1988) describing new bird fossils from two sedimentary basins of southeastern Brazil: Taubaté, São Paulo—Oligocene; and Itaboraí, Rio de Janeiro—Paleocene. The resulting fossil (and extinct) birds of Brazil, after *Neochen pugil* and *Jabiru lydekkeri*, are as follows:

Diogenornis fragilis (fig. 33): Order Rheiformes, Family Opisthodactilidae. An extinct family very close to the Rheidae, much smaller in size than present-day rheas, about 90 cm high, with a slender bill similar to that of Galliformes

Fig. 33. *Diogenornis* reconstruction, with a modern Greater Rhea, *Rhea americana,* silhouette in the background for comparison. The much smaller size and high bill are the most notable differences. Original, H. Alvarengo.

and different from the flattened bills of modern rheas and ostriches. It is certainly the oldest representative of ratite birds within the Cenozoic Era. Its remains come from the Itaboraí basin, Rio de Janeiro, where it lived during the Upper Paleocene 55 million years ago.

Brasilogyps faustoi: Order Cathartiformes, Family Cathartidae. A fossil vulture from the Oligocene of the Taubaté basin, known only through leg bones. It was larger than the Black Vulture, *Coragyps atratus*, and smaller than the King Vulture, *Sarcoramphus papa*. It is the oldest representative of the family in South America.

Physornis brasiliensis (fig. 34): Order Gruiformes, Family Phorusrhacidae. Measured about 2 meters high and its head was the size of a horse's head. Its remains (an almost complete skeleton) were found in the Taubaté basin, where it lived in the Oligocene about 25 million years ago. *Physornis* had short tarsi and a heavy build; it was probably necrophagous. Other Phorusrhacidae, such as *Phorusrhacus* of Argentina, had long tarsi, were more agile, and certainly hunted by chase.

Paleopsilopterus itaboraiensis: Order Gruiformes, Family Psilopteridae. An extinct family very close to the Phorusrhacidae and intermediary between these and the Cariamidae (Seriemas). It lived in the Paleocene of Itaboraí, and was a little taller and certainly much heavier than present-day seriemas, but much more robust, with thicker and proportionately shorter legs. It is the oldest known representative of the Suborder Cariamae.

Taubacrex granivora: Order Gruiformes, Family Rallidae. A gallinule the size of *Gallinula*, which, judging from its anatomical characteristics, apparently was more adapted to walking than to aquatic life. Its fossilized impression in the schists of the Taubaté basin showed the stomach area full of small stones and marks left by seeds, revealing its feeding habits. From the Oligocene Epoch, it is the oldest Rallidae of South America.

Another important feature of Brazilian paleornithology is the recent discovery of a fossil feather in the Chapada do Araripe, in northeastern Brazil, proving the presence of Aves in Brazilian territory as early as the lower Cretaceous, more than 100 million years ago (Martins Neto and Kellner 1988). Although preparation of the item has not been concluded, its definite asymmetry and curvature clearly show that it is a flight feather, a remige, whether we look at the upper or lower side of the feather. It is impossible to decide whether the bird was itself a flier, or if only its ancestors were capable of flight. It can be determined that it was smaller than a pigeon because the size of remiges corresponds to wing and body size. As early as 1848 the Chapada do Araripe, Ceará, was cited by Louis Agassiz of the Museum of Comparative Zoology in Cambridge, Massachusetts, as a source of fossil fishes. Many Pterosaurians have been found there, but never before bird remains.

Brazil has various fossil birds still to be studied. Among these can be cited flamingos (*Palaelodus*), Phalacrocoracidae, and others in the Taubaté basin, and undetermined remains in the Itaboraí basin, as well as many bones from the Pleistocene epoch in central Brazilian caves. And on the Fernando de Noronha archipelago, a different species of rail

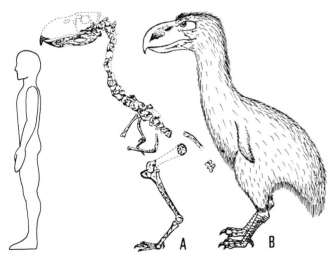

Fig. 34. The gigantic *Physornis brasiliensis* that lived in the Oligocene of southeastern Brazil, with part of the skeleton used in reconstructing the bird. At left, silhouette of a 1.75 m (5′9″) tall man, for comparison. Original, H. Alvarengo.

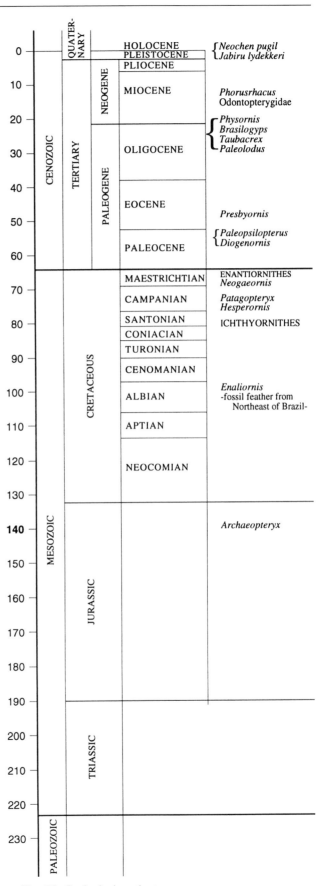

Fig. 35. Geologic time chart.

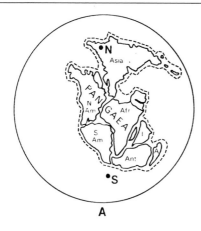

A

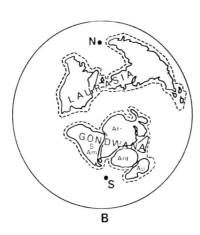

B

C

Fig. 36. Origin of the continents: (A) Pangaea; 250 million years ago all the continents were united. (B) Separation of Laurasia from Gondwana 150 million years ago. (C) The present continents 50 million years ago. Dashed lines indicate continental shelves. The drift of the continents explains the distribution of large zoological groups through geographic isolation (Holdgate 1987). Reference is made to continental drift under Tinamidae, Rheidae, and Passeriformes.

(Rallidae) that became extinct in recent times, certainly due to human action, is known today only through various pieces of the skeleton that have not yet been fully studied (Olson 1977). (See figs. 35, 36.)

5.3 *Categories of Brazilian Birds*

The composition of Brazilian avifauna is characterized by the same factors I have outlined for the Neotropical region. It seems reasonable to divide the birds of Brazil into two large groups: residents (1,492 species) and migrants (143 species). It is important to know the distribution and status of the birds as residents or migrants in the various ecosystems.

In countries such as Brazil, bird distribution is not always sufficiently understood, and gaps possibly indicate only a lack of surveys. I cover distribution here in its broadest aspects; often, however, I go into detail, especially to report previously unrecorded findings. When the text says "Southern Bahia and Minas Gerais to Santa Catarina," this means that a species such as the Rufous-headed Tanager, *Hemithraupis ruficapilla*, occurs in appropriate places within this range. When large gaps are known (see also chapter 4, Allospecies), I mention the states where occurrence of the species has been proven–for example, with the Band-winged Nightjar, *Caprimulgus longirostris*: Bahia, Minas Gerais, Espírito Santo, Rio de Janeiro, Santa Catarina, Rio Grande do Sul; so far there is only one record for either Bahia or Santa Catarina.

Among the literature on distribution, I have depended most on the publications of O. Pinto (1938, 1944, 1964) and on the first work of Meyer de Schauensee (1966). I use the designation "ex-Guanabara" (the area of the city or municipality of Rio de Janeiro, the former Federal District which was abolished in 1975) because of its great practical value for expressing the distribution of local fauna and flora. I have added many of my own previously unpublished distributional data. In the case of migratory birds and species such as hummingbirds that are found near seasonal flowers, I often give the year and the month of the respective record. When appropriate, I also give historic data (naming the year), which, in view of the constant changes in the landscape brought about by humans, is important for rare species and those expanding their ranges.

A species' distribution is normally stable. However, faunas have a certain natural dynamism: some species spontaneously expand and others contract their ranges. Human intervention can accelerate the process: see Monk Parakeet, *Myiopsitta monachus*, and House Sparrow, *Passer domesticus*. For spontaneous expansion see, for example, Cattle Egret, *Bubulcus ibis*; White-tailed Kite, *Elanus leucurus*; Red-legged Seriema, *Cariama cristata*; Guira Cuckoo, *Guira guira*; Rufous Hornero, *Furnarius rufus*; Tail-banded Hornero, *Furnarius figulus*; Masked Water-Tyrant, *Fluvicola nengeta*; Cliff Flycatcher, *Hirundinea ferruginea*; Red-breasted Blackbird, *Sturnella militaris*; and others.

Certain ecological conditions, often produced by fundamental climatic and historic changes, are necessary for the existence of each species. These are referred to in the family and species accounts in Part Two. Unfortunately, it is not possible to give more details on habitat within the framework of this book. With stenecious species, such as various members of the *Synallaxis* genus (Furnariidae), the type of habitat immediately indicates to the expert which one can be expected. Adaptation to a different ecosystem by a single species, as has happened, for instance, with the Yellow-legged Tinamou, *Crypturellus noctivagus*, is normally accompanied by alteration of the species' phenotype and evolution of a geographic race.

I frequently call attention to occurrence of various species of the same genus or family in the same place (sympatry) to provide a clearer view of the respective habitats and the pattern of their avifauna. For example, I show that two antbirds as closely related as the Spot-breasted and Plain Antvireos, *Dysithamnus stictothorax* and *D. mentalis*, may perch on the same branch in forests of the Serra do Mar, and that three antbirds—the Silvery-cheeked Antshrike, *Sakesphorus cristatus*; Stripe-backed Antbird, *Myrmorchilus strigilatus*; and Speckle-breasted Antpitta, *Hylopezus ochroleucus*—inhabit the same thickets of the caatinga, although in different niches.

To facilitate finding species that are considered difficult to encounter, such as the Slaty-Bristlefront, *Merulaxis ater*, a tapaculo, I mentioned some more common syntopic species that may serve as "guides" to locate the appropriate biotope.

There is a tendency for populations of Brazilian birds that live in hotter climates, closer to the equator, to have smaller measurements, such as in some Caprimulgidae, Psittacidae, Cotingidae, and Emberizidae. Clines are formed.

5.3.1 RESIDENT SPECIES

Every avifauna distributed over a certain expense of territory has resident species as its base—those that breed in the area and don't come only periodically or accidentally as migrants or visitors from other places (see section 5.3.3). Brazil's 1,492 resident species include representatives of all the five bird groups listed in section 5.1. I present here a brief biogeographical/ecological analysis of resident species, focusing on endemic and "nearly endemic" species and resident migratory species. Introduced species and those recently immigrated have also become residents (see section 5.3.4).

In the strictest sense, residents are sedentary species, like many forest birds (see, for example, wrens) that spend their whole lives within a restricted area, disputing their territory with other individuals of the same species, as any bird does during breeding. Whether residents are present may depend on the season of the year, especially because a species may

stay in the area in question only during the breeding season, afterward dispersing into a broader area about which little may yet be known.

Because it is almost impossible, without banding (see section 5.3.3), to distinguish individuals of the same species in a certain area, we can easily convince ourselves that the same individuals are present all year long in a given region. Indeed, some species, such as swallows, are found in the same area in all months, but the individuals are periodically replaced by others that come from elsewhere as migrants and disappear when the originals return to breed.

5.3.2 ENDEMIC SPECIES (BR)

Endemic or autochthonous species form the nucleus of the resident species group. These are species that, for historic reasons, have a limited range. They live in a certain habitat in which they may be common. South America has about 440 species of land birds with ranges smaller than 50,000 square kilometers. The United States, not counting its islands, has only 8 species in the same situation (Terborgh 1974).

According to my own counts, there are 177 endemic species in Brazil, that is, species occurring only in this country. They belong to twenty-nine families or subfamilies. In the species accounts they are noted by the letters "BR" immediately after the name, and generally receive special attention, as in comparing Suboscines and Oscines. (See also "quasi endemics," later in this section.)

COMPOSITION OF THE ENDEMIC AVIFAUNA

Considering the magnitude of Brazil's avifauna and the generally high degree of endemism in the Neotropics, 177 avian endemics, fewer than 12 percent of the 1,492 species resident in Brazil, appears disproportionately low. This is because Brazil's political frontiers do not at all coincide with the various physiographic regions. All the countries in the northern and western part of South American except Chile share the Amazonian Hylaea. Characteristic formations of southern, eastern, and central Brazil and their respective avifauna extend to Uruguay, Argentina, Paraguay, and eastern Bolivia. In this way Brazil "loses" many potential Neotropical endemic species that are "almost" Brazilian (see "quasi-endemic" species, below). Our present list of Brazilian endemics will be further reduced when the ranges of certain species, now recorded only for Brazil, are better known and have been found elsewhere, as, for instance, in Misiones, Argentina.

Some endemics, such as the two *Augastes* (Trochilidae), are allospecies, or geographic species, composing a superspecies.

Of the great number of endemic geographic races of Brazilian continental birds, I mention only special cases, such as the Yellow-legged Tinamou, *Crypturellus n. noctivagus*; Bare-faced Curassow, *Crax fasciolata pinima*; and Troupial, *Icterus icterus jamacaii*. An endemic race of the marine bird,

TABLE 5.1 Endemic Species (BR) (177 species).

Tinamidae (2)

Crypturellus noctivagus	*Nothura minor*

Accipitridae (1)

Leucopternis lacernulata

Cracidae (5)

Ortalis superciliaris	*Penelope pileata*
Penelope jacucaca	*Crax blumenbachii*
Penelope ochrogaster	

Psophiidae (1)

Psophia viridis

Rallidae (1)

Aramides mangle

Columbidae (1)

Columbina cyanopis

Psittacidae (14)

Anodorhynchus leari	*Touit melanonota*
Cyanopsitta spixii	*Touit surda*
Guaruba guarouba	*Pionopsitta vulturina*
Aratinga cactorum	*Amazona brasiliensis*
Pyrrhura cruentata	*Amazona rhodocorytha*
Pyrrhura perlata	*Amazona xanthops*
Brotogeris tirica	*Triclaria malachitacea*

Cuculidae (1)

Neomorphus squamiger

Nyctibiidae (1)

Nyctibius leucopterus

Caprimulgidae (1)

Caprimulgus hirundinaceus

Trochilidae (12)

Ramphodon naevius	*Thalurania watertonii*
Glaucis dohrnii	*Aphantochroa cirrhochloris*
Phaethornis gounellei	*Clytolaema rubricauda*
Phaethornis idaliae	*Augastes lumachellus*
Melanotrochilus fuscus	*Augastes scutatus*
Lophornis magnifica	*Heliomaster squamosus*

Galbulidae (2)

Jacamaralcyon tridactyla	*Galbula cyanicollis*

Bucconidae (2)

Malacoptila striata	*Nonnula amaurocephala*

Ramphastidae (1)

Pteroglossus bitorquatus

Picidae (5)

Picumnus varzeae	*Picumnus limae*
Picumnus pygmaeus	*Veniliornis maculifrons*
Picumnus fulvescens	

TABLE 5.1 (*Continued*)

Rhinocryptidae (3)

Merulaxis ater	*Scytalopus novacapitalis*
Merulaxis stresemanni	

Formicariidae (34)

Sakesphorus luctuosus	*Drymophila squamata*
Sakesphorus cristatus	*Terenura sicki*
Clytoctantes atrogularis	*Cercomacra brasiliana*
Dysithamnus xanthopterus	*Cercomacra laeta*
Dysithamnus plumbeus	*Cercomacra ferdinandi*
Myrmotherula gularis	*Cercomacra carbonaria*
Myrmotherula fluminensis	*Pyriglena atra*
Myrmotherula unicolor	*Rhopornis ardesiaca*
Myrmotherula urosticta	*Myrmeciza loricata*
Myrmotherula klagesi	*Myrmeciza ruficauda*
Herpsilochmus pectoralis	*Myrmeciza stictothorax*
Herpsilochmus longirostris	*Rhegmatorhina gymnops*
Formicivora serrana	*Rhegmatorhina berlepschi*
Formicivora erythronotos	*Rhegmatorhina hoffmannsi*
Drymophila ferruginea	*Skutchia borbae*
Drymophila genei	*Conopophaga melanops*
Drymophila ochropyga	*Conopophaga roberti*

Furnariidae (19)

Geobates poecilopterus	*Cranioleuca pallida*
Cinclodes pabsti	*Cranioleuca muelleri*
Furnarius figulus	*Thripophaga macroura*
Leptasthenura striolata	*Phacellodomus erythrophthalmus*
Schizoeaca moreirae	*Anabezenops fuscus*
Asthenes luizae	*Philydor novaesi*
Synallaxis infuscata	*Hylocryptus rectirostris*
Synallaxis kollari	*Cichlocolaptes leucophrys*
Synallaxis hellmayri	*Megaxenops parnaguae*
Cranioleuca semicinerea	

Dendrocolaptidae (4)

Xiphocolaptes falcirostris	*Xiphorhynchus necopinus*
Dendrocolaptes hoffmannsi	*Xiphorhynchus eytoni*

Tyrannidae (20)

Phyllomyias griseocapilla	*Hemitriccus orbitatus*
Polystictus superciliaris	*Hemitriccus nidipendulus*
Mionectes rufiventris	*Hemitriccus mirandae*
Phylloscartes roquettei	*Hemitriccus kaempferi*
Phylloscartes ceciliae	*Hemitriccus furcatus*
Phylloscartes oustaleti	*Todirostrum senex*
Phylloscartes difficilis	*Todirostrum poliocephalum*
Hemitriccus minor	*Knipolegus nigerrimus*
Hemitriccus obsoletus	*Attila rufus*
Hemitriccus aenigma	*Casiornis fusca*

Pipridae (6)

Neopelma pallescens	*Pipra nattereri*
Neopelma aurifrons	*Pipra vilasboasi*
Ilicura militaris	*Pipra iris*

TABLE 5.1 (*Continued*)

Cotingidae (9)

Tijuca atra	*Lipaugus lanioides*
Tijuca condita	*Cotinga maculata*
Carpornis cucullatus	*Xipholena lamellipennis*
Carpornis melanocephalus	*Xipholena atropurpurea*
Calyptura cristata	

Corvidae (2)

Cyanocorax cristatellus	*Cyanococorax cyanopogon*

Troglodytidae (3)

Odontorchilus cinereus	*Thryothorus griseus*
Thryothorus longirostris	

Vireonidae (2)

Vireo gracilirostris	*Hylophilus amaurocephalus*

Parulinae (1)

Basileuterus leucophrys

Thraupinae (14)

Orchesticus abeillei	*Tachyphonus nattereri*
Schistochlamys ruficapillus	*Ramphocelus bresilius*
Conothraupis mesoleuca	*Thraupis ornata*
Sericossypha loricata	*Tangara fastuosa*
Hemithraupis ruficapilla	*Tangara cyanoventris*
Nemosia rourei	*Tangara desmaresti*
Orthogonys chloricterus	*Dacnis nigripes*

Emberizinae (9)

Poospiza thoracica	*Sporophila albogularis*
Poospiza cinerea	*Sporophila melanogaster*
Embernagra longicauda	*Paroaria dominicana*
Sporophila falcirostris	*Paroaria baeri*
Sporophila melanops	

Icterinae (1)

Curaeus forbesi

---

the Lesser Frigatebird, *Fregata ariel trinitatis*, occurs on Ilha Trindade. Fernando de Noronha has endemic landbirds, an *Elaenia* and a *Vireo* (both closely related to continental species), and an extinct rail.

Out of 728 Brazilian non-Passerine species, 50 are endemics. Within this group, parrots occupy first place with 14, while the hummingbirds have 12 endemics. At 20.3 percent, endemism is high among the 69 Brazilian parrots.

The Tinamidae with 2 endemic species, the Galbulidae with 2, the Bucconidae with 2, and the Ramphastidae with one all demonstrate that for the reasons given above, Brazil has very little exclusive participation in the typical endemic families of the Neotropics.

In the Cracidae, with 5 endemics in Brazil, and the Psophiidae, with one, the matter of allospecies belonging to superspecies with ranges that extend beyond Brazil comes into focus. In the Picidae, with 5 endemic species in Brazil, we are evidently dealing in part (e.g., *Picumnus*) with geographic replacements that perhaps might more properly be considered subspecies.

There are 127 endemics among the 907 Passerine species in Brazil. As might be expected, the Suboscines, so typical for South America and with 582 species in Brazil, rank first with 95 Brazilian endemics. Of this number the 167 Brazilian species of Formicariidae contain 34 (a number greater than all the Oscine endemics), or 20.4 percent, almost as many as the two other large Suboscine families together: the Tyrannidae, with 200 Brazilian species, have 20 endemics, and the Furnariidae, with 99 Brazilian species, have 19 endemics. To these add the Dendrocolaptidae, with 37 species in Brazil and 4 endemics. The remaining four families of Suboscines are represented in Brazil as follows: Cotingidae, 9 endemics out of 36 Brazilian species; Pipridae, 6 endemics out of 34 species; Rhinocryptidae, 3 endemics out of 8 species, for a very high endemism rate of 37.5 percent; and finally, the Phytotomatidae, with just one winter migrant reaching Brazil.

Passerines that immigrated to South America after its junction with North America—the Oscines, with 325 species in Brazil—are numerically fewer than the Suboscines and include only 32 endemics. They developed mostly among the Thraupinae, which have 14 endemics among 96 Brazilian species, and the Emberizinae with 9 endemics among 64 Brazilian species. Other endemics among Oscines in Brazil are: Troglodytidae, 3 endemics among 18 species in Brazil; Corvidae, 2 endemics among 8 species; Vireonidae, 2 endemics among 16 species; and one endemic each in the Parulinae with 19 species in Brazil and the Icterinae with 35 Brazilian species.

ENDEMIC FOREST SPECIES

Brazilian forest endemics had their centers of origin in the refuges indicated on Haffer's map (fig. 28, in chapter 4), though there may have been other evolutionary centers as well.

About three-quarters of Brazilian endemics are forest species, such as the Southern Yellow-legged Tinamou, *Crypturellus n. noctivagus*; Red-billed Curassow, *Crax blumenbachii*; and Blue-bellied Parrot, *Triclaria malachitacea*. A number of hummingbirds such as the *Ramphodon* and *Phaethornis*, as well as the Crescent-chested Puffbird, *Malacoptila striata*; Red-necked Aracari, *Pteroglossus bitorquatus*; and Saffron Toucanet, *Baillonius baillonii*, are also forest birds.

Among Suboscine Passerines, forest endemics constitute a particularly large share of the antbirds. They show adaptations to various forest formations, for instance, the Glossy Antshrike, *Sakesphorus luctuosus*, to the interior of dense, dark riverine forests; and the Pectoral Antwren, *Herpsilochmus pectoralis*, and Slender Antbird, *Rhopornis ardesiaca*, to various types of dry woodland. Distribution of endemic formicariids at various levels is also noticeable: *Formicivora*, *Myrmeciza*, and *Conopophaga* near the ground; some *Myrmotherula* at middle heights; and the Rufous-backed Antvireo, *Dysithamnus xanthopterus*, in the canopy. The Rufous-tailed Antbird, *Drymophila genei*, is an endemic in high-altitude, open-country thickets.

All our tapaculo endemics are forest birds. Especially worthy of note is the Brasilia Tapaculo, *Scytalopus novacapitalis*, of central Brazil, an immigrant from Atlantic forests that moved inland along with its flora.

Endemic cotingas, especially the Black-and-gold and Gray-winged Cotingas, *Tijuca atra* and *T. condita*, are also forest inhabitants with a preference for mountainous regions. In a survey of the avifauna of southeastern Brazil, D. A. Scott and M. de L. Brooke (1985) summarized:

> The concentration of endemic species in the montane forests was evident. While the total number of species of forest birds present at any given altitude decreased steadily with altitude from over 200 species below 100 m to only 14 species in the highest patches of elfin forest between 2100 and 2200 m, the proportion of endemics (and indeed the number of species of endemics) increased steadily from sea-level to 1200 m. Above this altitude, about 50 percent of the species occurring were birds endemic to southeastern Brazil. Seventy-four endemic forest species occurred in forests at or above 1000 m above sea-level, i.e. almost half of the east Brazilian forest endemics and substantially more than half of the endemics occurring in Rio de Janeiro. Fifty-seven species occurred above 1200 m.

The majority of forest endemics among the Oscines are birds inhabiting the forest edge and the canopy, such as the "saíras" [Thraupinae]. The Bay-chested Warbling-Finch, *Poospiza thoracica*, a southern species, is typical of the Serra do Mar. The White-striped Warbler, *Basileuterus leucophrys*, is a humid, gallery-forest endemic of the tableland that lives alongside the Brasilia Tapaculo, *Scytalopus novacapitalis*. The Crimson-fronted Cardinal, *Paroaria baeri*, lives in dense, Amazonian-type gallery forests of central Brazil. The Scarlet-throated Tanager, *Sericossypha loricata*, an endemic

characteristic of the northeast, flies high from gallery forests to nearby palm groves, where it also nests. It is a transitional species with the group discussed just below.

ENDEMIC SPECIES OF CERRADO, CAATINGA, PLATEAUS, AND MILD CLIMATES

A considerable group of endemics lives in cerrado, caatinga, transitional woodlands, high plateaus, and other open or partially open habitats. The cerrado is, in reality, by origin a kind of forest and not a savanna, so the typical birds inhabiting it are arboreal (Sick 1966). This is not always clear, however, because the cerrado is often heavily interlaced with grasses, which must be a secondary phenomenon. The typically grassless cerrado became "campo cerrado," and savanna-type animal species spread across it. (See chapter 1.)

Cerrado endemics include the Lesser Nothura, *Nothura minor*; Blue-eyed Ground-Dove, *Columbina cyanopis*; Cactus Parakeet, *Aratinga cactorum*; and Yellow-faced Parrot, *Amazona xanthops*.

The caatinga of the lower Rio São Francisco had the Little Blue Macaw, *Cyanopsitta spixii*, and in a separate area with an abundance of licurí palms (*Syagrus coronata*) the most important northeastern endemic, the Indigo Macaw, *Anodorhynchus leari*, is found. (On the Hyacinth Macaw, *Anodorhynchus hyacinthinus*, see the next section, "quasi-endemic" species.) The Pygmy Nightjar, *Caprimulgus hirundinaceus*, is also a caatinga bird.

Among Suboscine Passerines, the Campo Miner, *Geobates poecilopterus* (terrestrial), as well as the Red-shouldered Spinetail, *Synallaxis hellmayri*, and Great Xenops, *Megaxenops parnaguae* (both arboreal), are inhabitants of the cerrado or caatinga. The Long-tailed Cinclodes, *Cinclodes pabsti*, a terrestrial species of open country, and the arboreal Itatiaia Thistletail, *Schizoeaca moreirae*, can be called glacial relicts or remnants (Sick 1985).

Among Oscines, the Curl-crested Jay, *Cyanocorax cristatellus*, must be highlighted as an inhabitant of cerrado and campo cerrado; the White-naped Jay, *C. cyanopogon*, also an endemic, keeps to denser formations. The Red-cowled Cardinal, *Paroaria dominicana*, and White-throated Seedeater, *Sporophila albogularis*, are typical endemics of the caatinga, while the Black-bellied Seedeater, *Sporophila melanogaster*, is an endemic of marshy areas in the south.

The Hyacinth and Hooded Visorbearers, *Augastes scutatus* and *A. lumachellus*, two hummingbirds, occupy the tops (950 to 1,600 meters) of tablelands in the interior of Minas Gerais and Bahia, rocky areas with low, xerophytic vegetation. They share these semi-arid, bushy regions with the Silvery-cheeked and Rufous-winged Antshrikes, *Sakesphorus cristatus* and *Thamnophilus torquatus*; tiny Gray-backed Tachuri, *Polystictus superciliaris*; and Pale-throated Serra-Finch, *Embernagra longicauda*. The latter represents a case of competitive exclusion with a related species, the Great Pampa-Finch, *Embernagra platensis*.

"QUASI-ENDEMIC" SPECIES

A significant portion of the resident species of southern and central Brazil have ranges extending into adjacent regions of Argentina (Misiones), and/or Paraguay, Uruguay, and eastern Bolivia, and sometimes as far as Chile (in the case of various rails). Many of these species that I call "quasi-endemic" for Brazil must have had their evolutionary center in southern or central-southern Brazil, thereby contributing decidedly to the distinctive character of these parts of Brazil and rounding out the endemic character of local avifauna. Most are forest birds, apparently originating in the Atlantic forest region, in the Serra do Mar Refuge.

Forest non-Passerines found here include Solitary Tinamou, *Tinamus solitarius*; Mantled Hawk, *Leucopternis polionota*; Black-fronted Piping-Guan, *Pipile jacutinga*; Spot-winged Wood-Quail, *Odontophorus capueira*; Slaty-breasted Wood-Rail, *Aramides saracura*; Purple-winged Ground-Dove, *Claravis godefrida*; and various parrots: Hyacinth Macaw, *Anodorhynchus hyacinthinus*; Reddish-bellied Parakeet, *Pyrrhura frontalis*; Red-capped Parrot, *Pionopsitta pileata*; Vinaceous-breasted Parrot, *Amazona vinacea*; and Red-spectacled Parrot, *Amazona pretrei*, this last a bird of the araucaria. There are three owls: the Variable Screech Owl, *Otus atricapillus*; Tawny-browed Owl, *Pulsatrix koeniswaldiana*; and Rusty-barred Owl, *Strix hylophila*. Also, the Surucua Trogon, *Trogon surrucura*; Black-girdled Barbet, *Capito dayi*; Red-breasted Toucan, *Ramphastos dicolorus*. And various woodpeckers: Mottled Piculet, *Picumnus nebulosus*; White-browed Woodpecker, *Piculus aurulentus*; Helmeted Woodpecker, *Dryocopus galeatus*; Yellow-fronted Woodpecker, *Melanerpes flavifrons*; White-spotted Woodpecker, *Veniliornis spilogaster*; and Robust Woodpecker, *Campephilus robustus*.

Among quasi-endemic forest Passerines are many Suboscines, including five woodcreepers: White-throated Woodcreeper, *Xiphocolaptes albicollis*; Planalto Woodcreeper, *Dendrocolaptes platyrostris*; Scaled and Lesser Woodcreepers, *Lepidocolaptes squamatus* and *L. fuscus*; and Black-billed Scythebill, *Campylorhamphus falcularius*; ten furnariids: Araucaria Tit-Spinetail, *Leptasthenura setaria*, a species linked to araucaria; Rufous-capped and Gray-bellied Spinetails, *Synallaxis ruficapilla* and *S. cinerascens*; Olive Spinetail, *Cranioleuca obsoleta*; Canebrake Groundcreeper, *Phacellodomus dendrocolaptoides*; White-browed Foliage-Gleaner, *Anabacerthia amaurotis*; Black-capped and Ochre-breasted Foliage-Gleaners, *Philydor atricapillus* and *P. lichtensteini*; White-eyed Foliage Gleaner, *Automolus leucophthalmus*; and Sharp-billed Xenops, *Heliobletus contaminatus*; and various antbirds, among them such notable species as the two *Mackenziaena* antshrikes and the Rufous Gnateater, *Conopophaga lineata*. Also on the list is the Giant Antshrike, *Batara cinerea*, one of the most impressive antbirds, as well as the Spot-backed Antshrike, *Hypoedaleus guttatus*, and Dusky-tailed Antbird, *Drymophila malura*.

The Mouse-colored Tapaculo, *Scytalopus speluncae*, and Long-trained Nightjar, *Macropsalis creagra*, are included, being species discovered in Misiones, Argentina; both are represented in the Andes. Three cotingas come to mind: Swallow-tailed Cotinga, *Phibalura flavirostris*; Bare-throated Bellbird, *Procnias nudicollis*; and Black-capped Piprites, *Piprites pileatus*. Finally come the Blue Manakin, *Chiroxiphia caudata*, and Greenish Mourner, *Schiffornis virescens*, and various flycatchers, such as the Shear-tailed Gray-Tyrant, *Muscipipra vetula*; Russet-winged Spadebill, *Platyrinchus leucoryphus*; Drab-breasted Bamboo-Tyrant, *Hemitriccus diops*; Southern Bristle-Tyrant, *Phylloscartes eximius*; Bay-ringed Tyrannulet, *P. sylviolus*; and São Paulo Tyrannulet, *P. paulistus*.

Among forest Oscines, which are less numerous, are found the Azure Jay, *Cyanocorax caeruleus*, and various tanagers, such as the Chestnut-bellied and Green-chinned Euphonias, *Euphonia pectoralis* and *E. chalybea*; two "saíras," Green-headed and Red-necked Tanagers, *Tangara seledon* and *T. cyanocephala*; Azure-shouldered Tanager, *Thraupis cyanoptera*; Ruby-crowned Tanager, *Tachyphonus coronatus*; and Chestnut-headed Tanager, *Pyrrhocoma ruficeps*. The Emberizinae and Cardinalinae are also on the list with several species, such as the Green-winged and Thick-billed Saltators, *Saltator similis* and *S. maxillosus*; Black-throated Grosbeak, *Pitylus fuliginosus*; Buffy-fronted Seedeater, *Sporophila frontalis*; and Uniform Finch, *Haplospiza unicolor*.

Among the most characteristic birds of the cerrado, as an arboreal formation (see chapter 1, section 1.3.3), and of the Paraguayan Chaco, as a parallel ecosystem, are the two seriemas, Cariamidae. The Dwarf Tinamou, *Taoniscus nanus*, is typical for campo cerrado and chaco open country.

Some open-country species are the Crested Black-Tyrant, *Knipolegus lophotes*; Ochre-breasted Pipit, *Anthus nattereri*; and Black-masked Finch, *Coryphaspiza melanotis*. Marshy open-country species include the Cock-tailed Tyrant, *Alectrurus tricolor*; Chestnut Seedeater, *Sporophila cinnamomea*; and Lesser Grass-Finch, *Emberizoides ypiranganus*. The Black-breasted Plovercrest, *Stephanoxis l. lalandi* is characteristic of the high campo of eastern Brazil and occurs as far as Paraguay and northern Argentina.

The most notable quasi-endemic of central and southern Brazil is the Brazilian Merganser, *Mergus octosetaceus*, of Brazil, Argentina (Misiones), and Paraguay.

5.3.3 VISITING SPECIES AND MIGRATIONS

MARKING, BANDING, AND DIRECT OBSERVATION

Sometimes the origin of visitors to Brazil is proven with precision by numbered aluminum bands placed on their legs in North America (aquatic birds, raptors, swallows, etc.);

Argentina (penguins, ducks, herons, etc.); England (Manx Shearwater, skua); Finland (skua); West Germany (terns); France (heron); Ilha Selvagem, Portugal (Cory's Shearwater), or elsewhere. Individuals banded in the Antarctic (Antarctic Giant-Petrel, Cape Petrel, skuas) and even in Australia (Antarctic Giant-Petrel) have appeared in Brazilian waters. The species most commonly found in Brazil with foreign bands are the Common Tern, *Sterna hirundo*; Blue-winged Teal, *Anas discors*; and Manx Shearwater, *Puffinus puffinus*.

To cite an example: the band of a *Sterna hirundo* that I caught alive at Atafona, São João da Barra, Rio de Janeiro, on 16 August 1975, read: "Avise Bird Band. 772-10350 Write Wash DC USA." I learned through the Office of Migratory Bird Management, in Laurel, Maryland, that this bird, when still a flightless juvenile, had been banded on 5 July 1974 near Wareham, Massachusetts.

The bands used in Argentina, provided by the Miguel Lillo Foundation of Tucuman since 1961 through the initiative of the late C. C. Olrog, request that the finder "Devuelva Instituto Lillo Tucumán Argentina" (Return to Lillo Institute, Tucuman, Argentina).

In 1978 a Brazilian bird-banding center was established, the Centro de Estudos de Migração de Aves (CEMAVE), now operating under the auspices of the Brazilian Institute for the Environment (IBAMA) in Brasília, Federal District. CEMAVE, coordinated by Paulo de Tarso Zuquim Antas, began its banding program in May 1980. Sixteen sizes of bands are used, from 1.75 mm (for siskins) to 17.5 mm (for flamingos). The size of the band is indicated by a letter; J, for example, is the size for a Chopi Blackbird, *Gnorimopsar chopi*. The complete inscription on a band appropriate for a Great Egret, *Casmerodius albus*, is: "Avise Cemave C.P. 04/034, 70312 Brasília DF." On small bands, part of the inscription is on the inside of the band. Banding a hummingbird is a problem because of its extremely short tarsus.

RESIDENT MIGRATORY SPECIES AND VARIOUS TYPES OF MOVEMENT

Genuine migration is undertaken by many resident species, especially many southern swallows and flycatchers that seek areas closer to the equator during the southern winter. Among the latter, the Fork-tailed Flycatcher, *Tyrannus savana*, an insectivorous species, stands out. One of the best-known birds in the south, its migration attracts a great deal of attention both in the south, where it breeds and its presence symbolizes spring and summer, and in Amazonia, where migrant flocks of hundreds and thousands are seen during winter. Even those in central Brazil abandon their homeland in winter and move to Amazonia. Thus some "resident" species turned up as migrant visitors in certain areas.

Thrushes, especially the Creamy-bellied Thrush, *Turdus amaurochalinus*, are among the species that emigrate in great numbers from southern Brazil and adjacent southern countries to the north in winter. Caprimulgids are also numerous among migrants from the south, the Nacunda Nighthawk, *Podager nacunda*, being conspicuous because of its diurnal habits. The American Swallow-tailed Kite, *Elanoides forficatus*, is another large-scale migrant.

Many fruit-eating birds in Brazil, such as parrots and cotingas, move about locally in search of their particular food. The Swallow Tanager, *Tersina viridis*, becomes locally abundant. Nectarivorous hummingbirds do the same to find favorite flowers with the most prized nectar.

Altitudinal migrations occur with hummingbirds, flycatchers, and emberizids in the relatively high mountains of eastern and southern Brazil, as on the Serra da Mantiqueira (Itatiaia) and the Serra do Mar, as well as the Black-fronted Piping-Guan, *Pipile jacutinga*, in Santa Catarina and Rio Grande do Sul. These movements seem minor when compared with those engaged in by birds in the spacious domain of the Andes.

Autumnal migrations often start before low temperatures arrive and before food shortages develop in the home territory, as has been shown with the Argentine population of the Vermilion Flycatcher, *Pyrocephalus rubinus* (Hudson 1920). Adults and young also move separately, so the adults are unable to guide their offspring.

So far, very little is known with respect to migrations of southern birds beyond the equator. *Podager n. nacunda* reaches Colombia. The Ashy-tailed Swift, *Chaetura andrei*, has been found in Panama. Various southern swallows (Brown-chested Martin, *Phaeoprogne tapera*; Gray-breasted Martin, *Progne chalybea*; and Blue-and-white Swallow, *Notiochelidon cyanoleuca*) also migrate to Central America, some as far as Nicaragua and Mexico.

A periodic overlapping of northern sedentary races by southern migratory races may occur, for example with swallows. In the Surucua Trogon, in winter, the southern, red-bellied race, *Trogon s. surrucura*, appears in the range of the northern, yellow-bellied race, *T. s. aurantius*.

Resident migrants also include birds such as the Purple Gallinule, *Porphyrula martinica*, which comes to Maranhão to nest only sporadically, and the Eared Dove, *Zenaida auriculata*, which appears in the northeast in enormous bands at intervals of several years.

Some landbirds are occasionally found on the high seas during migration, as, for instance, the flycatchers *Pyrocephalus rubinus* and the Many-colored Rush-Tyrant, *Tachuris rubrigastra*. The record for transoceanic migration by residents belongs to the Purple Gallinule, *Porphyrula martinica*. It occasionally reaches the farthest Atlantic islands, and even the African coast. Probably all these birds are carried by strong winds, and almost certainly they do not return to their home territories. Such movements demonstrate how colonization of oceanic islands occurs, as in the case of Fernando de Noronha, which has been populated by *Zenaida auriculata*.

Regular migration of resident species can be forced by floods, especially in Amazonia, as, for example, the Sand-colored Nighthawk, *Chordeiles rupestris*, and other river-edge birds. Amazon water levels fluctuate from 10 to 15 meters annually, a nondisastrous event except when dealing with the tidal bore (see chapter 1, section 1.3.1) at the mouth of the Amazon. In a way, floods in Amazonia resemble the tidal movements on the Atlantic coast that influence the comings and goings of egrets and of shorebirds such as sandpipers.

In central Brazil there are dawn and dusk movements of nighthawks, *Chordeiles rupestris* and the Lesser Nighthawk, *C. acutipennis* (Sick 1950a).

Another type of resident bird migration is the gathering of ducks in certain swamps during total wing molt. Duck movements (of *Dendrocygna* and others) are commonplace at various times in many places.

It is impressive how migratory birds observe a strict schedule, modified only slightly in some years by the weather. *Chaetura andrei*, for example, which disappears from Rio de Janeiro in March–April, customarily reappears in spring between 20 August and 8 September. At the Quinta da Boa Vista, in Rio de Janeiro, I recorded the first transient autumn *Turdus amaurochalinus* coming from the south several times on the same day, 20 April, in various years.

Certain birds move to communal nocturnal roosts. This happens more among non-Passerines, such as the Magnificent Frigatebird, *Fregata magnificens*; White-faced Ibis, *Plegadis chihi*; parrots; and birds of prey, such as the two *Milvago* and the Snail Kite, *Rostrhamus sociabilis*. Among Passerines such movements are observed in tyrannids and icterines. Sometimes the birds—the Yellow-headed Caracara, *Milvago chimango*, and Scarlet-throated Tanager, *Sericossypha loricata*, for instance—first assemble somewhere near the nocturnal roost but occupy it only when night falls. Movements for group roosting may continue into the breeding season, with the male participating while the female tends the nest (*Amazona* spp.). Toucan invasions occur.

VISITOR SPECIES, MIGRATORY BIRDS, AND LARGE-SCALE MIGRATIONS

By "visitors," *sensu strictus*, I mean those species that come here periodically or accidentally from other countries and do not breed in Brazil. They are not, therefore, "Brazilian" birds in the strictest sense. (On migration of resident species, see the immediately preceding section.)

Reference to migratory birds introduces the many-faceted phenomenon of bird migration, including the universally discussed problem of orientation, which receives much attention in the Northern Hemisphere but up to the present has had very little discussion in Brazil. The matter is of major interest to Brazil, because here we have migration from two directions, north and south. Because migratory birds (as well as carrier pigeons; see Columbidae) partially depend on terrestrial magnetism for orientation, it is noteworthy that the earth's magnetic equator passes through Brazil (Ceará).

This book does not deal with general subjects that are not related to specific Brazilian problems, such as migratory bird orientation and the origin of migration, which must be linked to profound climatic changes over the centuries and even to the movement of continents. Some Northern Hemisphere studies have concluded that the direction of migration may indicate the direction from which the species first came to reach its present breeding area. This does not hold up in the Americas, where the Oscine Passerines started migrating to South America, which was terra incognita for them before the junction of the two continents.

Visiting migrants either cross through Brazil or stay there for some weeks or months. In most cases birds come to Brazil during their native countries' cold winters. In general, the principal attraction is not the warmer temperature of the tropics and subtropics, but the greater food supply available in warm regions, where the succession of rainy and dry seasons has a decided influence. It still remains to be demonstrated in individual situations if more migratory birds come to Brazil when their countries of origin have especially rigorous winters than when they experience mild winters. The arrival of marine birds on Brazil's coasts also depends on strong Atlantic winds.

Long stayovers in Brazil sometimes lead to the erroneous conclusion that such migrants breed here. Usually in these cases, immature individuals that have not yet reached breeding age are involved. Among them are marine birds, Charadriiformes, and the Osprey, *Pandion haliaetus*. Rather large species reach adulthood only after a number of years. A relatively small marine bird such as the Manx Shearwater, *Puffinus puffinus*, does not start nesting until five years of age. It has been determined that the Common Tern, *Sterna hirundo*, sometimes stays in the tropics for thirty-one months before returning to its native north.

Some birds, such as the North American warblers and the Yellow-billed Cuckoo, *Coccyzus americanus*, migrate at night. Such nocturnal migrants reveal their presence to knowledgeable observers by the calls they make during flight, as in the case of rails and the Bobolink, *Dolichonyx oryzivorus*.

Migratory birds from temperate zones molt their plumage during their stay in Brazil (see swallows and *D. oryzivorus*, for example).

As already mentioned, Brazil has two main groups of visitors: those whose latitudinal migrations bring them from the north, even from as far away as the Arctic, and those from the south, from as far as the Antarctic. More come from north than south. The flocks of northern sandpipers and plovers that periodically gather on Brazilian beaches commonly number into the hundreds and thousands, ranking them among the largest gatherings of birds to be seen in Brazil;

also noteworthy are the great concentrations of northern swallows.

Among the North American birds appearing in eastern Brazil, inhabitants of eastern North America predominate, such as the Willow Flycatcher, *Empidonax traillii*, as a migrant, and the Eastern Meadowlark, *Sturnella magna praticola*, as a resident. The more northern migrant populations of North American birds normally winter farther south on this continent (see Peregrine Falcon, *Falco peregrinus*).

It is a peculiar fact that migrant birds from the Chilean coast come to eastern tropical South America instead of following the Pacific coast northward to Peru. Thus the small White-crested Elaenia, *Elaenia albiceps chilensis*, a flycatcher of southern Chile, crosses the Andes near Santiago and then migrates together with others of its species from Argentina to the Amazon, touching Brazilian territory en route, with some going beyond the equator.

Many Arctic birds that come to Brazil to "vacation" fly thousands of kilometers (see Sanderling, *Calidris alba*, and Arctic Tern, *Sterna paradisaea*).

In accordance with the different times of the year in which winter occurs north and south of the equator, migrants from those regions appear in Brazil in different seasons of the year, so they do not often meet each other. Those from the north are here between September and April, those from the south between March and September. Some individuals, however, are occasionally found in Brazil during almost the entire year.

Some species occur in both the Northern and Southern Hemispheres in similar climates (temperate or cold, sub-Arctic or sub-Antarctic) and during winter migrate toward the equator, each on its own side. This is the case, for example, with the Great Skua, *Catharacta skua*, and the Peregrine Falcon, *Falco peregrinus*. Northern *C. skua* from Scotland have been found in northeastern Brazil, while southern *C. skua*, which nest in Patagonia and the Antarctic zone, have been found as far away as southeastern and northeastern Brazil.

Falco peregrinus cassini, whose homeland is the southern extreme of South America, follows the Andes on migration and has so far only been found north as far as Uruguay on the Atlantic side, where theoretically it could meet *F. peregrinus tundrius*, which migrates as far as Argentina from the extreme north.

Some visitors do not come to Brazil regularly, but only from time to time. Thus, for example, penguins do not reach Rio de Janeiro and Bahia every year. Sometimes migrants appear only while either coming or going, evidently using a different route in each direction.

Among the longest migrations known in our region are the trans-Atlantic flights of the Purple Gallinule, *Porphyrula martinica*, to which I have already alluded. Recent immigrants have also been involved (see Cattle Egret, *Bubulcus ibis*).

Number of Visitor Species Involved

I have recorded 143 visitors, or 8.7 percent of Brazil's 1,635 species. Because this list depends on the constantly increasing number of trained field observers, the number of visiting birds—often easily recognizable species—is always growing.

Of the visitors, 105, or more than 73 percent, are non-Passerines. All but nine of these are aquatic birds (I count *Pandion* as "aquatic") and about half of these aquatic birds are maritime, such as albatrosses, petrels, jaegers, and terns. In most cases, maritime birds reach Brazilian waters from the high seas and not by flying along the coast. When observing only from land, one scarcely suspects the presence of some of these birds, which appear periodically some miles distant from the coast. An occasional albatross brought in by fishermen or a mass die-off of penguins or prions (*Pachyptila*), which are later tossed up on the beach by the waves, can demonstrate the wealth of oceanic avifauna, at least in the southern seas.

Only ten visiting species are nonaquatic non-Passerines. Six are Falconiformes, of which five are from the north, as are a cuckoo and a nighthawk. The condor and the seedsnipe come from the Andes.

There are only 38 Passerines, or 26.4 percent of the total, among the visitors. The majority of them, such as swallows, thrushes, and wood-warblers, come from the north. Among the flycatchers, five species come from the north and seven from the south.

Migrant birds that are merely geographic races of Brazilian species, for instance some native swallows and flycatchers such as the Fork-tailed Flycatcher, *Tyrannus savana*, which are very prominent during their respective periods of migration, are not included here but dealt with in the section on resident migrants, above.

Northern Visitors (NV)

These species are noted with the letters "NV" following the scientific name. Eighty-eight species come from the north, or 61.5 percent of the 143 visitors. Of these, 56 species, or 63.6 percent, are aquatic birds.

As already pointed out, waders may become very numerous along the coast. Some species, such as the Lesser Golden-Plover, *Pluvialis dominica*, do not follow the South American coast in migrating but fly from Venezuela to the Rio Negro and central Brazil. They may reach the Atlantic coast in Rio Grande do Sul. This also applies to the Buff-breasted Sandpiper, *Tryngites subruficollis*; Hudsonian Godwit, *Limosa haemastica*; and Wilson's Phalarope, *Steganopus tricolor*. It is especially noteworthy that two northern races of the Whimbrel, *Numenius phaeopus*, reach the Brazilian region, one from America and one from Europe, and that the two have been found together on Fernando de Noronha, the European race probably an accidental.

TABLE 5.2 Northern Visitors (NV) (88 species).

Procellariidae (3)

Pterodroma hasitata	Puffinus puffinus
Puffinus diomedea	

Hydrobatidae (1)

Oceanodroma leucorhoa

Pelecanidae (2)

Pelecanus occidentalis	Pelecanus erythrorhynchos

Ardeidae (3)

Ardea purpurea	Ardeola ralloides
Ardea cinerea	

Anatidae (2)

Anas acuta	Anas discors

Accipitridae (3)

Ictinia mississippiensis	Buteo platypterus
Buteo swainsoni	

Pandionidae (1)

Pandion haliaetus

Falconidae (2)

Falco peregrinus	Falco columbarius

Charadriidae (4)

Pluvialis squatarola	Charadrius semipalmatus
Pluvialis dominica	Charadrius wilsonia

Scolopacidae (22)

Arenaria interpres	Calidris pusilla
Tringa solitaria	Calidris alba
Tringa flavipes	Calidris himantopus
Tringa melanoleuca	Philomachus pugnax
Actitis macularia	Tryngites subruficollis
Catoptrophorus semipalmatus	Bartramia longicauda
Calidris canutus	Numenius phaeopus
Calidris minutilla	Numenius borealis
Calidris bairdii	Limosa haemastica
Calidris fuscicollis	Limosa lapponica
Calidris melanotos	Limnodromus griseus

Phalaropodidae (2)

Steganopus tricolor	Phalaropus fulicarius

Glareolidae (1)

Glareola pratincola

Stercorariidae (4)

Catharacta skua skua	Stercorarius parasiticus
Stercorarius pomarinus	Stercorarius longicaudus

Laridae (11)

Larus delawarensis	Sterna forsteri
Larus atricilla	Sterna dougallii

TABLE 5.2 (Continued)

Larus pipixcan	Sterna albifrons
Chlidonias niger	Sterna maxima
Sterna hirundo	Sterna sandvicensis
Sterna paradisaea	

Cuculidae (1)

Coccyzus americanus

Caprimulgidae (1)

Chordeiles minor

Tyrannidae (5)

Contopus borealis	Tyrannus tyrannus
Contopus virens	Tyrannus dominicensis
Empidonax traillii	

Hirundinidae (4)

Progne subis	Hirundo rustica
Riparia riparia	Hirundo pyrrhonota

Turdinae (3)

Catharus fuscescens	Catharus ustulatus
Catharus minimus	

Vireonidae (1)

Vireo olivaceus

Parulinae (8)

Dendroica petechia	Seiurus noveboracensis
Dendroica cerulea	Oporornis agilis
Dendroica fusca	Wilsonia canadensis
Dendroica striata	Setophaga ruticilla

Thraupinae (2)

Piranga rubra	Piranga olivacea

Cardinalinae (1)

Spiza americana

Icterinae (1)

Dolichonyx oryzivorus

The remaining thirty-two northern visitors are landbirds. Of these seven are non-Passerines, five being raptors. The Peregrine Falcon, *Falco peregrinus*, and Swainson's Hawk, *Buteo swainsoni*, have aroused the interest of the press in Rio and São Paulo, respectively. While not yet recorded in Brazil, perhaps the Chimney Swift, *Chaetura pelagica*, well known to Americans, will appear on the list soon.

Most of these birds reach only Amazonia, especially the northern and western parts. In regions close to the equator, few migrants enter the forest, almost all staying on the forest edge or in capoeira and open areas. Few migrant birds are frugivorous, many are insectivorous (Willis 1976). The Blackpoll Warbler, *Dendroica striata*, a small forest bird of extreme northern North America (Alaska, etc.), comes in small numbers to Rio de Janeiro and even beyond. Northern swallows, especially the Barn Swallow, *Hirundo rustica*, move in quantities through southern Brazil and Argentina. The Bobolink, *Dolichonyx oryzivorus*, spends the northern winter in the central plains of South America, in Mato Grosso and on the Argentine pampa.

North American field guides (Peterson's, etc.; see Bibliography), with illustrations of all the species, provide very good information on northern migrants that reach Brazil.

Southern Visitors (SV)

South America is unique in having bird migrants not only from the north but also from the south. These species are noted by the letters "SV" immediately after the scientific name. Some no doubt move eastward into Brazil, instead of coming strictly from the south. These migrants originate mostly from the many land birds in the large portion of this enormous continental mass that spreads toward the Antarctic, and from a wealth of pelagic birds in the surrounding southern seas, some coming from as far away as Australia.

Only 56, or 39.2 percent, of the total of 143 visitor species recorded for Brazil arrive from the south [north and south numbers and percentages do not jibe because *Catharacta skua* is on both lists]. Most of these, 40 species or 71.4 percent, are aquatic birds, of which 32 species are pelagic. Among the 16 landbird species in this group are 3 non-Passerines and 13 Passerines.

The field guides of C. C. Olrog and of Narosky and Yzurieta (see Bibliography) are useful for the identification of southern migrants in Brazil.

5.3.4 INTRODUCED SPECIES AND RECENT IMMIGRANTS

The Helmeted Guineafowl, *Numida meleagris*, like the pigeon, the domestic chicken, and the turkey, was brought to Brazil by the Portuguese. These domestic species, as well as the Australian budgerigar and the canary, are mentioned in the appendix to their respective families.

So far only two species of wild birds have been introduced into Brazil from abroad. These have become common and live freely in the vicinity of human habitations: the House Sparrow, *Passer domesticus*, from Europe, and the Common Waxbill, *Estrilda astrild*, from Africa.

Various European birds introduced into Uruguay, such as the Greenfinch, *Carduelis chloris*, have not yet been recorded in Brazil, perhaps only due to lack of sufficient observation. (See also gallinaceous birds [Phasianidae], where I discuss the possible practical utility of introducing exotic birds for hunting and human consumption.)

From the scientific point of view, the irresponsible introduction of exotic birds without any advance study of its consequences, practiced by amateurs everywhere in the world, should be viewed with great suspicion. It was very wisely prohibited by Brazilian Law No. 5197 of 1967 (Fauna Protection). It is never possible to foresee whether an alien species may become a pest or a menace to native fauna. Everyone in Brazil is familiar with the notorious cases of the House Sparrow and the African bee.

Native species can be introduced, as well, by taking them from one place in the country where they are native to another region where they are not. Such transplants, which science frowns upon, can lead to false identification of the local fauna. This happened with the Spotted Nothura, *Nothura maculosa*; Troupial, *Icterus icterus*; and Yellow-bellied Seedeater, *Sporophila nigricollis*.

Equally irresponsible is the indiscriminate liberation of cage birds, which is even carried out by public authorities in the name of fauna preservation. In this way the Monk Parakeet, *Myiopsitta monachus*, a pest in Rio Grande do Sul, was introduced into Rio de Janeiro.

The Cattle Ibis, *Bubulcus ibis*, originally from Africa, whose presence as a breeding bird in Brazil was proven in 1965, spontaneously immigrated to Brazilian Amazonia, presumably not from Africa but from northern South America, where it had already existed in abundance for some time.

Immigration into the city to Rio de Janeiro of the Band-winged Nightjar, *Caprimulgus longirostris*, which I have been observing for the last forty years, was also spontaneous.

5.3.5 SYNANTHROPIC SPECIES

The best-known birds in any country are the synanthropic ones: those that associate with man. The "classic" in this category is the House Sparrow, *Passer domesticus*, which is still unknown in almost all of Amazonia.

In Brazil, synanthropic birds include various ground-doves, *Columbina* spp., and some Passerines such as the House Wren, *Troglodytes aedon*; Bananaquit, *Coereba flaveola*; and some swallows. The Black Vulture, *Coragyps atratus*, is also synanthropic, unlike other vulture species. Species of the urban environment (see chapter 1) are also synanthropic. Synanthropic species also follow people into the interior, away from the urban environment onto ranches and farms.

TABLE 5.3 Southern Visitors (SV) (56 species).

Diomedeidae (6)

Diomedea exulans	Diomedea chlororhynchos
Diomedea epomophora	Diomedea chrysostoma
Diomedea melanophris	Phoebetria palpebrata

Procellariidae (15)

Macronectes giganteus	Halobaena caerulea
Fulmarus glacialoides	Pachyptila desolata
Daption capense	Pachyptila belcheri
Pterodroma incerta	Procellaria aequinoctialis
Pterodroma brevirostris	Procellaria cinerea
Pterodroma lessonii	Puffinus gravis
Pterodroma mollis	Puffinus griseus
Pterodroma macroptera	

Hydrobatidae (3)

Oceanites oceanicus	Fregetta tropica
Fregetta grallaria	

Pelecanoididae (1)

Pelecanoides magellani

Spheniscidae (3)

Spheniscus magellanicus	Eudyptes crestatus
Eudyptes chrysolophus	

Sulidae (1)

Morus serrator

Cathartidae (1)

Vultur gryphus

Phoenicopteridae (2)

Phoenicopterus chilensis	Phoenicoparrus andinus

Anatidae (4)

Anas sibilatrix	Anas platalea
Anas cyanoptera	Oxyura vittata

Accipitridae (1)

Circus cinereus

TABLE 5.3 (Continued)

Charadriidae (2)

Zonibyx modestus	Oreopholus ruficollis

Thinocoridae (1)

Thinocorus rumicivorus

Chionididae (1)

Chionis alba

Stercorariidae (1)

Catharacta skua chilensis

Laridae (1)

Sterna vittata

Furnariidae (1)

Cinclodes fuscus

Tyrannidae (7)

Elaenia albiceps	Lessonia rufa
Xolmis coronata	Knipolegus hudsoni
Neoxolmis rufiventris	Knipolegus striaticeps
Muscisaxicola fluviatilis	

Phytotomidae (1)

Phytotoma rutila

Hirundinidae (1)

Progne modesta

Emberizinae (1)

Diuca diuca

Cardinalinae (1)

Pheucticus aureoventris

Icterinae (1)

Sturnella defilippi

NOTE: At least the condor, Vultur gryphus, and the emberizid, Pheucticus aureoventris, must probably come from the west or southwest, performing more of a longitudinal than a latitudinal migration.

5.4 Population Analyses and Biodiversity

Brazil has about 1,635 bird species. The count can fluctuate for two reasons: (1) "New" species are constantly being added, having previously been listed only for neighboring regions, especially within Amazonia, or for parts of the Atlantic Ocean, from where they are usually visitors. Only very rarely these days does the number of Brazilian bird species increase because of the discovery of a species as yet unknown to science, such as recently happened with the Gray-winged Cotinga, Tijuca condita, a Serra do Mar species of very limited distribution in a previously little explored area. These circumstances are more common in the Andes (Peru, etc.), where new species are still found with some frequency. (2) The number of species is sometimes reduced in modern counts because birds considered as species are "demoted" to the level of subspecies, with the result that they no longer rank as separate species. Goeldi (1894) cited 1,680 species of birds for Brazil.

In the extreme south, Brazilian territory penetrates slightly into the Pampa region, which has a different fauna. This is reflected in the large list of birds for Rio Grande do Sul. This very positive fact compensates somewhat for Brazil's not sharing in the very rich Andean and upper Amazonian fauna that helps a relatively small country such as Colombia, with only a little more than a million square kilometers, to be richer in bird species than Brazil, with more than 8.5 million square kilometers of land surface. With respect to Andean fauna, it is interesting to note that during the Pleistocene, a small immigration of Andean flora and fauna into southern Brazil took place (see Furnariidae and Rhinocryptidae).

WE ARE indebted to T. E. Lovejoy (1974) and F. C. Novaes (1970) for the first population analyses made by net captures in bird communities of the lower Amazon. These have permitted the determination of patterns of distribution and abundance as bases for indices of density and frequency of the birds in question (see Trochilidae, Formicariidae, Tyrannidae, and Emberizidae). Lovejoy's survey, performed in part together with Novaes in the Mocambo forest (Guamá Ecological Research Area, APEG), Belém, Pará, over a number of years and at all levels (for the first time including the canopy, using high nets), is based on more than two hundred species handled; more than three hundred species occur there. Fifteen thousand individual birds were captured, processed, and released. Many species were quite rare, producing a very low index of density. This confirms the already recognized phenomenon that in the tropics the number of species of animals and plants is high but the number of individuals low.

In working up these data, it was difficult to evaluate the ease of capture of the various species (some species are never captured, while others are caught very easily) and other factors, such as local migration. Today it is universally agreed that a meticulous record of vocalizations and direct observation of the birds of the area is an essential supplement to work that has been done with nets (Remsen et al. 1983).

In the metropolitan area of Belém, an area of 1,221 square kilometers, including the municipalities of Belém and Anannindeua, 472 birds were recorded (F. Novaes, pers. com., 1987). For the Ducke Reserve (10 square kilometers), near Manaus, Amazonia, Willis (1977) made a list of 289 species, 218 of them being forest birds. Around Balta on the Rio Curanja in the upper Purus in Peruvian territory, near Brazil (the Purus crosses the center of Acre before flowing into the Amazon 1,000 kilometers downstream), O'Neill (ex-Amadon 1973) recorded 408 species of birds within a one-mile area and remarked that even more would appear with additional observation. This is because there are very few conspecific individuals and a maximum of sympatric species in that area. Bird censuses take months. Even without migrants, the Balta region still had at least 300 forest species. Amadon concluded that Amazonia by far exceeds the African Congo in wealth of bird species.

Areas that are richest in species but have very limited numbers of individuals per species are found close to the Andes in untouched, superhumid forests on flat regions of the upper Amazon. These censuses are the highest of any in the world, a classic example of biodiversity, a concept that is cited these days in the most diverse situations, even by politicians. An INPA/WWF project on Biological Diversity in Latin America (BIOLAT) is presently (1989) being conducted in Bolivia and Peru. The best conditions of natural diversity in Brazil are in Rondônia and Acre, areas still little explored, at least with regard to faunal population dynamics. For example, eleven species of *Myrmotherula* (Formicariidae) have been recorded for Rondônia (Stotz 1990). In Rio de Janeiro normally three, and a maximum of six, species are found (Gonzaga 1988). There are predictions that Rondônia, an area of 243,044 square kilometers, may be transformed into a gigantic desert by the beginning of the next century due to the current pace of uncontrolled occupation.

The list of birds for the Municipality of Rio de Janeiro, formerly the state of Guanabara, an area of 1,171 square kilometers, today stands at close to 490 species. For the state of São Paulo (247,223 square kilometers), the Iherings (1907) gave 697 species, a number confirmed by O. Pinto (1944). For the state of Paraná (199,554 square kilometers), P. Scherer Neto (1980) listed 558 species. For Santa Catarina (95,985 square kilometers), we have 544 species (Sick et al. 1981). For Brasília, Federal District (5,814 square kilometers), a cerrado area, 429 species have been recorded (Negret et al. 1984).

In an intensive study lasting more than ten years in Rio Grande do Sul, (282,184 square kilometers), Belton (1984, 1985) counted a total of 586 species [607 as of 1991], of which at least 419 breed in the state. As a result of the careful preparation of this material, Rio Grande do Sul became, ornithologically speaking, by far the best-studied state in Brazil.

It would be very difficult to compare the above-mentioned censuses, because they cover areas that are so different in size and physical characteristics and because the methodologies were so different.

In southern Brazil (São Paulo, 22°, 45/50′ S, 47/48° W), E. Willis (1979) examined three forested areas, one of 1,400 hectares with 202 bird species (175 breeding ones), another of 250 hectares with 146 species (119 breeding), and another of 21 hectares with 93 species (76 breeding). It is calculated that the number of bird species in each of the three areas must have been originally about 230. Two types of census were used: one-hour and general.

J. Vielliard has been conducting quantitative surveys (censuses) of birds since 1973. He tested three basic methods: (1) determination of the territories of the species present in a certain "block"; (2) counting all the individuals found in a certain "transect"; and (3) sampling at determined points, depending primarily on song identification. The last method, used in forest areas on the São Paulo plateau, proved to be the best in heterogeneous terrain and easiest for mathematical interpretation, giving a diversity, by the Shannon-Wiener index, of 3.89. This value is the highest so far obtained for an avian community. The qualitative ("exhaustive") survey that was carried out together with the point sampling gave a total of 272 species in 350 hours of observation in various habitats. This number of species, corrected for the time of observation and the variety of habitat, is equivalent to the values for Ecuador (Pearson 1971; Vuilleumier 1978), Peru, and Bolivia (Pearson 1977).

The MCS project (Minimal Critical Size of Ecosystems) is conducting censuses in Amazonia (see chapter 3).

5.5 Sources

5.5.1 NOMENCLATURE, BIBLIOGRAPHY, AND LISTS

In the Brazilian edition of this book I followed the system proposed by R. Meyer de Schauensee (1966, 1970) with respect to the sequence of orders, families, genera, and species. In a few exceptions I recognized other phylogenetic relationships or made an adaptation that is more suited to Brazilian conditions. I raised the flamingos to the level of an order, Phoenicopteriformes, and placed the hoatzin in a separate order, Opisthocomiformes. I included the two *Piprites*; the cocks-of-the-rock, *Rupicola*; and the Sharpbill, *Oxyruncus*, in the Cotingidae and placed the White-naped Xenopsaris, *Xenopsaris albinucha*, at the end of the Tyrannidae.

Meyer de Schauensee based his work on the system of Alexander Wetmore (1960), dean of American ornithology, and of James L. Peters's *Check-list of the Birds of the World* (see below). Unfortunately, this creates some confusion in Brazil, for here we are all accustomed to the system of Olivério Pinto, in use for fifty years. I want to take the opportunity now to point out the great importance of the books of Meyer de Schauensee, which have made it easy to find one's way among the multitude of birds on the continent. His book became my Bible.

For the English-language edition of my book, I continue to use Meyer de Schauensee's work as a base but have accepted modifications proposed in more recent volumes of Peters's *Check-list of the Birds of the World*, as well as the conclusions of the American Ornithologists' Union *Check-list of North American Birds* (1983 and supplements) as follows.

TURDINAE, SYLVIINAE. These are included as subfamilies of the large Muscicapidae family of the Old World, birds that are practically unknown in a Neotropical country such as Brazil. But from a scientific viewpoint it is of interest to know that the Turdinae and Sylviinae are closely related to the Muscicapidae, which over the millennia spread to North America and from there colonized South America. This shows the great alterations that have taken place in the movement of the continents and climates of this earth, and the changes in the ability of these birds to occupy new territory.

THRAUPINAE, PARULINAE, AND ICTERINAE. Including these three groups with very characteristic phenotypes (just like the Turdinae and Sylviinae) within the great Emberizidae family is the result of new research on this largest group of Oscine passerines, which is widely distributed throughout the world and difficult to classify.

To facilitate an understanding of recently changed scientific names, in the species accounts I cite the latest names that have been relegated to synonymy.

Before Meyer de Schauensee's publications, the only works available for Brazil were those of O. Pinto; the *Catálogo das Aves Amazônicas* of E. Snethlage (1914); *As Aves do Brasil* of E. Goeldi (1894), with his *Álbum de Aves Amazônicas* (1900–1906, re-edited by the University of Brasília); and the publications of the Iherings (1907, etc.; see also chapter 2). Thus I constantly referred to the monumental fifteen-volume catalogue of Cory, Hellmayr, and Conover (1918–1949), which covers the birds of North, Central, and South America.

The work that provides the necessary detail on species and subspecies nomenclature is the *Check-list of Birds of the World*, begun by James L. Peters in 1931, and continued by E. Mayr, J. C. Greenway, Jr., M. A. Traylor, Jr., R. A. Paynter, Jr., and others, for a total of fifteen volumes (vols. 1–6 on non-Passerines, vols. 7–15 on Passerines); several of the volumes have been revised. Also valuable is the great library of the National Museum in Rio, which is notable for its wealth of nineteenth-century works, though there is a lack of modern publications, including scientific journals.

The only nontechnical books available on Brazilian birds during recent decades have been those of Eurico Santos: *Da Ema ao Beija-flor* (From Rheas to Hummingbirds) and *Pássaros do Brasil* (Passerines of Brazil) (1938–1940). I had no records or tapes of Brazilian bird songs. In the 1960s the first recording by J. Dalgas Frisch, "Cantos de aves do Brasil," (Songs of Brazilian birds), won great popular acceptance, both inside and outside of Brazil. It was followed by "Vozes da Amazônia com o lendário canto do Uirapurú" (Voices of Amazonia with the legendary song of the Uirapurú), "Ecos do Inferno Verde" (Echos of the Green Hell), and others, as well as his book, *Aves brasileiras*, the first attempt to produce a field guide to the birds of Brazil. Then came the five monumental volumes (three on hummingbirds) of Augusto Ruschi (1979, 1981, 1982).

Also in the 1960s, Paul Schwartz of Rancho Grande, Venezuela, an authority on vocalizations of Neotropical birds, began to publish a series of records entitled "Naturaleza Venezolana" (Venezuelan nature). Schwartz collected the largest archive of Neotropical bird voices, which is now on deposit in the Laboratory of Ornithology, Cornell University, in Ithaca, New York.

The field guide to the birds of Venezuela by R. Meyer de Schauensee and W. H. Phelps (1978), with fifty-three plates, and S. L. Hilty and W. L. Brown's book (1986), with sixty-nine plates, on Colombia, are both very useful for the identification of birds of Brazilian Amazonia. These works can be consulted in those cases where, in this book, I give only the name and distribution range of Amazonian species whose ranges also extend to neighboring countries, especially Venezuela, Colombia, and Peru, where they are better known. For extreme southern Brazil, the field guides for Argentina by C. C. Olrog (1984) and by T. Narosky and D. Yzurieta (1987) for Argentina and Uruguay can be useful. These works are now being supplemented by the valuable, multivolume *The Birds of South America* by R. Ridgely and G. Tudor; the first volume, *The Oscine Passerines*, appeared in 1989.

Bibliographies at the end of each family group in this book provide additional information, though the works cited represent only a selection. In the General Bibliography I have cited other sources, including some general works on ornithology.

During my work in Central Brazil from 1946 to 1957, we had only the planes of the Brazilian Air Force to transport us; there were no roads. Today's ease of travel and the corresponding development of tourism have helped promote publications on local birds throughout the world. A Brazilian tourist agency has even compiled lists of birds, with their common names, for some regions.

Species lists for given regions are of value when they are compiled with proper standards, as the Americans have been doing for a long time. The lists, whose quality depends on their authors, become even more informative and reliable when they include the sources that were used, such as bibliographic research (B), museum collections (M), and fieldwork (C), as we did for Santa Catarina (Sick et al. 1981).

5.5.2 VERNACULAR NAMES OF BRAZILIAN BIRDS

Scientific nomenclature for birds has been established for more than two hundred years, but popular-vernacular denomination, being a product of people's imagination, is not systematized.

By "vernacular denomination" I mean two very different things: (1) popular, vernacular, or common names used by people living in the areas where the respective animals are found, which are indeed the best names for fauna (see below); or (2) vernacular names invented by technicians when no common names exist.

POPULAR NAMES

To designate a bird, people try to relate it to some characteristic, such as *coloration*: "sangue-de-boi" = "ox-blood," "polícia-inglesa" = "English policeman"; *shape of bill*: "colhereiro" = "spoonbill," "maçarico" = "tubebill"; *food*: "caramujeiro" = "snail-eater," "carrapateiro" = "tickeater"; *way of hunting*: "bico-rasteiro" = "bill-dragger"; *voice*: "vivi" (onomatopoeic); *instrumental music*: "cascavel" = "rattlesnake"; *various habits*: "pica-pau" = "wood-pecker", "dançador" = "dancer"; *nesting*; "joão-de-barro" = "John-Mud," "fura-barreira" = "wall-breaker"; *seasonality*: "primavera" = "springtime," "verão" = "sum-

mer"; *hour of song*: "maria-já-é-dia" = "it's daytime, Maria"; *habitat*: "fura-mato" = "forest-penetrator"; *human occupations*: "lavadeira" = "washer-woman," "rendeira" = "lace-maker"; and *legends*: "mãe-da-lua" = "mother of the moon." Onomatopoeic names seems strange to most people, who do not know the sounds they imitate. Such names frequently consist of phrases such as "tem-cachaça-aí" = "do you have any rum there" or "gente-de-fora-vem" = "outsiders are coming," both for the Rufous-browed Pepper-Shrike, *Cyclarhis gujanensis*; "joão-corta-pau" = "John wood-chopper" for the Rufous Nightjar, *Caprimulgus rufus*; "agua-só" = "only water" for the Giant Snipe, *Gallinago undulata gigantea*; and "chupa-dente" = "tooth-sucker" for the Rufous Gnateater, *Conopophaga lineata*. Indigenous onomatopoeic names are better. These names come from the souls of the people and form part of their culture. An old popular name, well established, passes down from father to son and never changes.

Vernacular or popular names of Brazilian birds are of Portuguese or Tupi origin, sometimes being corruptions of both. The confusion started when the Portuguese, immediately after discovering the country, applied names of European birds to those they found in Brazil. These are almost never the same species and not even related to their European namesakes. For instance, in the case of the Black Vulture, *Coragyps atratus*, because, like the Common Raven, *Corvus corax*, it is black and likes carrion, it was improperly called "corvo" = "crow." The proper solution was to use the indigenous name, "urubu."

As we know, many names are regional or local. Often, the same name may be applied to two or more species, or, on the other hand, there are some popular species (such as certain pigeons and doves) that have a profusion of regional names. For example, the male Blue Ground-Dove, *Claravis pretiosa*, is called "rola-azul" = "blue dove" and the female "rola-vermelha" = "red dove" in the same area. The Plumbeous Pigeon, *Columba plumbea*, has eight common names in Brazil; the Greater Ani, *Crotophaga major*, nine; the Shiny Cowbird, *Molothrus bonariensis*, ten; the Squirrel Cuckoo, *Piaya cayana*, fourteen; and the Blue-crowned Motmot, *Momotus momota*, sixteen. A popular bird in Germany, such as the White Wagtail, *Motacilla alba*, has more than one hundred popular names there. Still, a great many birds in this country have no individual popular name whatsoever, for in general we just say they are birds and nothing more.

The result is that Brazilian bird nomenclature has so many deficiencies that most scientists don't even dare to discuss the matter. Nevertheless, in every country that has an increasing consciousness about environmental conservation and where, in recent years, improved books about fauna have been written, common names for birds have become a matter of priority, as never before. Brazil is no exception. This is noticeable in comparison with other groups, such as lizards, which are far from being as popular as birds.

Hermann von Ihering said it well almost a century ago

(1898): "I believe it is the duty of naturalists to contribute to the examination and codification of common names of the best-known birds."

ARTIFICIAL VERNACULAR NAMES

In Argentina in 1916, a "commission to standardize the common names of Argentine birds" (Hornero 1917, 1:40) was formed. Other Spanish-speaking South American countries joined it later, but they could not reach agreement on standardizations. Much later, Olrog (1963) made another attempt to standardize the names for Argentina. But Argentine popular names also have synonyms, different authors use different names, and Argentine names are not the same as Brazilian ones: for example, for *Crypturellus* spp. Argentina uses "perdiz" = "partridge" while Brazil uses "inambu." [A new list of vernacular names for Argentine birds has just appeared. See Navas et al. 1991.]

A committee, formed in 1956 to standardize Brazil's vernacular zoological nomenclature, suffered from the death of its proponent, José Oiticica Filho of the National Museum, Rio de Janeiro, so the project was not pursued. In the 1970s a committee was organized in Rio Grande do Sul to codify the vernacular names of the birds of that state. [A list of vernacular names for Brazilian birds appeared soon after Dr. Sick's death. See Willis and Oniki 1991.]

It is a fact that even professional ornithologists in any part of the world prefer the vernacular names of their own language. Use of scientific names requires extra effort, which is applied only when there is no vernacular name. Daily experience has shown clearly that the goodwill of those who want to collaborate is quickly frustrated when they are forced to use scientific names. Lack of vernacular names also paralyzes conservation efforts: how can one work toward saving a bird that doesn't even have a name?

Scientific as well as amateur-oriented ornithological publications in English have long used the scientific name of a species only when it is first mentioned, together with the corresponding vernacular name; subsequently only the popular name, which everyone understands, is used.

Any foreigner who speaks English can find an English name for each Brazilian species in Meyer de Schauensee's book (1970), although these names are artificial and sound nothing like the popular names. The English names are still useful, for they are descriptive and aid the memory, having been created for this purpose. They have immediately been adopted by English-speaking professional ornithologists.

It is relatively easy for Americans to establish an English nomenclature for all the Latin American countries, for there are few conflicts. Working out vernacular nomenclature for the Latin American countries in their own languages is very different, for they are replete with local linguistic traditions that must be considered.

It will be a long time before mixed commissions, composed of ornithologists and philologists, have worked out a reasonable codification or even an official list (such as exists in several countries) of vernacular names for the birds of Brazil. Certainly it will never be possible to please everyone, for each region will want its local name to be used. For clarity, it will often be necessary for me to cite two or more names in this book.

THE PRACTICE ADOPTED FOR THIS BOOK

To meet the demands of this book, for which it has been essential to have at least one Brazilian name available for the principal species and headings, I have used three resources:

1. I have consulted the bibliography on the subject, especially the catalog of Brazilian birds of Olivério Pinto (1938–1944) and the great list of common names of Brazilian birds of Carlos O. C. Vieira (1936). There are numerous other sources, such as H. von Ihering (1898), *As Aves do Estado de São Paulo* (The birds of the state of São Paulo); R. von Ihering (1968), *Dicionário dos animais do Brasil* (Dictionary of the animals of Brazil); and Paulo Nogueira Neto (1973), *A criação de animais indígenas vertebrados* (Rearing of indigenous vertebrate animals). *Nomes populares das aves do Brasil* (Popular Names for the Birds of Brazil) by Gabriel A. de Andrade (1982) was published by Sociedade Ornitológica Mineira (SOM) and IBDF.

Brazil has a large stock of good popular or common vernacular names. The study of Rodolpho Garcia (1913), *Nomes de Aves em Língua Tupi* (Tupi-language bird names) is a valuable contribution to interpretation of indigenous names.

2. I collected common names during my travels throughout Brazil, asking hunters and other reliable observers, including Indians, especially those of the Tupi group of central Brazil.

3. When I did not find a common name, either in the literature or through personal informants, I adapted existing words or based my decision on important characters of the species involved, whether morphological, biological, or geographical. I coordinated my results with those of the Rio Grande do Sul committee mentioned above. In certain cases I obtained linguistic advice from Dr. Antônio Houaiss, of the Brazilian Academy of Letters. Useful suggestions for the formation of vernacular names in any language were found in Eisenmann and Poor (1946).

The criterion I adopted for choosing a particular Brazilian name was to use, whenever possible, the popular name when it could not be confused with that of another species. The difficulties, beyond those already mentioned, are many. As an example: the same name appears for birds that belong to different families, unlike in systematic zoology, as with "jacu-estalo" (Popping Guan) for the Rufous-vented Ground-Cuckoo, *Neomorphus geoffroyi*, a cuckoo that looks like a guan. It would increase the confusion to try to eliminate a reasonable popular name that has had long use like this one and substitute an unknown, artificial name that might be scientifically correct. There is no solution without some compromise.

Names referring to size (giant, large, medium, small) relate either to the comparison within the genus or among related genera. I usually eliminate the word "common" because there may be regions where the respective species is not common. To differentiate species within a genus, there is no solution (in the absence of popular names) other than to add to the name a simple, distinctive adjective (as is done with vernacular names in other languages), as, for instance, "anambé-de-asa-branca" (White-winged Anambé) for *Xipholena atropurpurea*.

I provide two names in the heading of individual species accounts when both are well known, or when one of them has a different meaning in a large part of Brazil. This is the case, for example, with the Red-winged Tinamou, *Rhynchotus rufescens*, known as "perdiz" = "partridge" in central Brazil. This name is used in extreme southern Brazil for the Spotted Nothura, *Nothura maculosa*, while *R. rufescens* is called "perdigão" there. At the end of each species account I cite,

where appropriate, the more popular names, often adding the name of the states where they are used.

Composite names are written with a hyphen, which facilitates recognition of a proper name, for instance "maria-cavaleira" (a *Myiarchus* species, Tyrannidae). I do not accept the 1943 orthographic rule on spelling geographic and personal names in hyphenated words with a small initial letter, for this can become ridiculous, as, for example, with "Pomba-do-Cabo" = "Cape Pigeon." "Cabo" = "Cape" referring to the Cape of Good Hope, whereas "cabo" would mean "handle," as, for instance, a broom handle.

[Translator's Note: Although Brazilian names are now available for all Brazilian species (Willis and Oniki 1991), Sick had particular interest in names and might not have accepted some of them. I have therefore not included Brazilian names that Sick himself did not provide. With regard to English names, see Translator's Comments at the beginning of the book.]

PART TWO

Illustrated Guide to the Orders and Families of Brazilian Birds

Order TINAMIFORMES

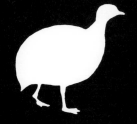

Family Tinamidae
Tinamous

p. 93

Order RHEIFORMES

Family Rheidae
Rheas

p. 106

Order PODICIPEDIFORMES

Family Podicipedidae
Grebes

p. 110

Order PROCELLARIIFORMES

Family Diomedeidae
Albatrosses

p. 112

Family Procellariidae
Shearwaters, Fulmars,
and Petrels

p. 114

Family Hydrobatidae
Storm-Petrels

p. 118

Family Pelecanoididae
Diving-Petrels

p. 119

Order SPHENISCIFORMES

Family Spheniscidae
Penguins

p. 119

Order PELECANIFORMES

Family Phaethontidae
Tropicbirds

p. 121

Family Sulidae
Boobies

p. 122

Family Pelecanidae
Pelicans

p. 125

Family Phalacrocoracidae
Cormorants

p. 126

Family Anhingidae
Darters

p. 127

Family Fregatidae
Frigatebirds

p. 128

Order CICONIIFORMES

Family Ardeidae
Herons

p. 130

Family Cochleariidae
Boat-billed Heron

p. 138

Family Threskiornithidae
Ibises

p. 140

Family Ciconiidae
Storks

p. 144

Family Cathartidae
American Vultures

p. 148

Order PHOENICOPTERIFORMES

Family Phoenicopteridae
Flamingos

p. 152

Order ANSERIFORMES

Family Anatidae
Ducks and Swans

p. 154

Family Anhimidae
Screamers

p. 164

Order FALCONIFORMES

Family Accipitridae
Hawks, Eagles, and Allies

p.166

Family Pandionidae
Osprey

p. 179

Family Falconidae
Falcons and Caracaras

p. 180

Order GALLIFORMES

Family Cracidae
Chachalacas, Guans,
and Curassows

p. 189

Family Phasianidae
Wood-Quail and Allies

p. 201

Order OPISTHOCOMIFORMES

Family Opisthocomidae
Hoatzin

p. 204

Order GRUIFORMES

Family Aramidae
Limpkin

p. 206

Family Psophiidae
Trumpeters

p. 207

Family Rallidae
Rails, Gallinules,
and Coots

p. 208

Family Heliornithidae
Sungrebes
p. 215

Family Eurypygidae
Sunbittern
p. 216

Family Cariamidae
Seriemas
p. 217

Family CHARADRIIFORMES

Family Jacanidae
Jacanas
p. 219

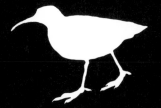

Family Rostratulidae
Painted-Snipes
p. 220

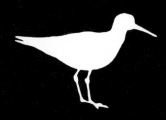

Family Haematopodidae
Oystercatchers
p. 221

Family Charadriidae
Lapwings and Plovers
p. 221

Family Scolopacidae
Sandpipers and Snipes
p. 226

Family Recurvirostridae
Stilts
p. 232

Family Phalaropodidae
Phalaropes
p. 232

Family Burhinidae
Thick-knees
p. 233

Family Glareolidae
Pratincoles

p. 233

Family Thinocoridae
Seedsnipes

p. 233

Family Chionididae
Sheathbills

p. 234

Family Stercorariidae
Skuas and Jaegers

p. 234

Family Laridae
Gulls and Terns

p. 235

Family Rynchopidae
Skimmers

p. 241

Order COLUMBIFORMES

Family Columbidae
Pigeons and Doves

p.°243

Order PSITTACIFORMES

Family Psittacidae
Parrots

p. 251

Order CUCULIFORMES

Family Cuculidae
Cuckoos

p. 278

Order STRIGIFORMES

Family Tytonidae
Barn Owls

p. 287

Family Strigidae
Owls

p. 288

Family Trochilidae
Hummingbirds

p. 321

Order CAPRIMULGIFORMES

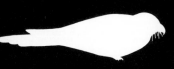

Family Steatornithidae
Oilbird

p. 299

Order TROGONIFORMES

Family Trogonidae
Trogons

p. 352

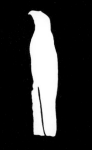

Family Nyctibiidae
Potoos

p. 300

Order CORACIIFORMES

Family Alcedinidae
Kingfishers

p. 356

Family Caprimulgidae
Nightjars and Nighthawks

p. 303

Family Momotidae
Motmots

p. 359

Order APODIFORMES

Family Apodidae
Swifts

p. 312

Order PICIFORMES

Family Galbulidae
Jacamars

p. 362

Family Ramphastidae
Aracaris and Toucans

p. 372

Family Bucconidae
Puffbirds

p. 366

Family Picidae
Woodpeckers

p. 382

Family Capitonidae
Barbets

p. 370

Order PASSERIFORMES

Suborder SUBOSCINES

Family Rhinocryptidae
Tapaculos

p. 397

Family Tyrannidae
Tyrant-Flycatchers

p. 449

Family Formicariidae
Antbirds

p. 401

Family Pipridae
Manakins

p. 487

Family Furnariidae
Horneros, Spinetails,
and Allies

p. 423

Family Cotingidae
Cotingas

p. 503

Family Dendrocolaptidae
Woodcreepers

p. 443

Family Phytotomidae
Plantcutters

p. 519

Suborder OSCINES

Family Hirundinidae
Swallows

p. 522

Subfamily Turdinae
Thrushes and Solitaires

p. 542

Family Corvidae
Jays

p. 529

Family Mimidae
Mockingbirds

p. 549

Family Troglodytidae
Wrens

p. 533

Family Motacillidae
Pipits

p. 552

Family Muscicapidae
Subfamily Sylviinae
Gnatcatchers and
Gnatwrens

p. 539

Family Vireonidae
Vireos and Allies

p. 553

Family Emberizidae
Subfamily Parulinae
Wood-Warblers

p. 557

Subfamily Icterinae
American Orioles
and Blackbirds

p. 614

Subfamily Coerebinae
Bananaquit

p. 562

Family Fringillidae
Siskins

p. 634

Subfamily Thraupinae
Tanagers

p. 563

Family Passseridae
Old World Sparrows

p. 636

Subfamily Emberizinae
Sparrows, Finches, and
Seedeaters

p. 587

Family Estrildidae
Waxbills

p. 641

Subfamily Cardinalinae
Grosbeaks and Saltators

p. 611

6 ◆ Family and Species Accounts

ORDER TINAMIFORMES

FAMILY TINAMIDAE: TINAMOUS

Tinamous have a chickenlike appearance and are well known because of their value as game birds. They comprise an important family, endemic to the Neotropics, that ranges from Mexico to Patagonia and reaches considerable altitudes in the Andes; the Puna Tinamou, *Tinamotis pentlandii,* lives at 4800 m. Tinamous form part of South America's oldest avifauna. Fossils have been found in Argentina from the Pliocene (4 million years B.P.) and in Brazil from caves in Minas Gerais from the Pleistocene (15–20,000 years B.P.).

Skeletal and karyotype (chromosomal) similarities with the ratites are great and have been confirmed by biochemical data (DNA-DNA hybridization, Sibley and Ahlquist 1982). A *Tinamus* skull is very much like that of a ratite; both are Paleognathae, having an integrated, bony palate. The fact that tinamous "still" fly leaves them apparently more primitive than the flightless ratites, which have achieved maximum adaptation to terrestrial life. Tinamous are not ancestors of the rheas but appear to be a sister group of the ratites, with which they must have had a common forebear in the extinct southern continent of Gondwanaland. A Spotted Nothura, *Nothura maculosa,* in its natural habitat may look like a miniature rhea, *Rhea* sp. The two live in the same savannas. The voice of the Brazilian Tinamou, *Crypturellus strigulosus,* is similar to that of the rhea chick. Similarities between tinamous and Galliformes are due to convergence or parallel evolution.

Morphology, Special Adaptations, and Identification

Many details of osteology, such as the skull (see above) and sternum, were well studied in the last century (see Stresemann 1927–34). Currently, comparative morphology of the tongue is also studied.

The various species are similar in general aspect but differ considerably in size. The Dwarf Tinamou, *Taoniscus nanus,*

is a bit larger than a domestic chick, whereas a female Gray Tinamou, *Tinamus tao,* weighs almost 2 kg. Tinamous have small heads, and the bill is slender and soft except in the Red-winged Tinamou, *Rhynchotus rufescens,* and *Nothura maculosa* (fig. 37). The neck appears long and slender because of its short feathers. The body is plump, with the posterior higher because of the full plumage, which is rich in powder down, which Brazilians call "ashes." The microscopic structure of tinamid feathers is unique: the terminal parts of the barbicels, or radii, are united by a solid bar, especially noticeable on the remiges (fig. 38). The wings are well developed and rounded. The tail is loose, sometimes rudimentary, and may lack the pygostyle, making the birds look bobtailed.

The legs are thick and soft, with the back of the tarsus in the *Tinamus* covered with hard, imbricated scales (fig. 39). Tarsal color may be characteristic, a useful feature in species having similar plumage patterns (see Yellow-legged Tinamou, *Crypturellus noctivagus,* and Red-legged Tinamou, *C. erythropus*). The feet have three short, relatively weak toes.

Tinamous have a penis, similar to that of ratites, ducks, and cracids, which in the *Tinamus* and *Rhynchotus,* is spiral like the hemipenis of the Squamata (lizards and snakes) without, however, being bifurcated. This structure permits quick

Fig. 37. Three different types of tinamou bills: (A) Undulated Tinamou, *Crypturellus undulatus;* (B) Spotted Nothura, *Nothura maculosa;* and (C) Red-winged Tinamou, *Rhynchotus rufescens.* After Krieg and Schuhmancher 1936.

sexing of adults especially during the breeding season. Females have a small phallic organ.

Clear sexual dimorphism is evident in the plumage of *Crypturellus strigulosus.* Usually female tinamous can be distinguished only by being larger than males, but the respective measurements may overlap when opposite sexes of two species are compared (e.g., *Nothura maculosa* and Lesser Nothura, *N. minor;* Small-billed Tinamou, *Crypturellus parvirostris,* and Tataupa Tinamou, *C. tataupa*). There are also slight size differences between certain populations of *N. maculosa.*

Sexual identification of *N. maculosa* may be achieved with 100% accuracy by measuring the osseal pelvis by palpation or with a measuring stick. Another criterion is adult iris color (male yellow, female orange-brown).

Tinamous tire rapidly when chased if they have no chance to rest. Flight is a mixture of active flying with rapid wing beats, followed by periods of gliding. Tinamids generally go only a few dozen meters and return to the ground. This weakness is not caused by poorly developed musculature but by arterial blood flow inadequate for prolonged effort. Surprising as it may seem, these birds have flight musculature (fig. 40) as highly developed (28.6–40% of total weight) as that of hummingbirds (28.3–34.4% of total weight). The quantity of this muscle is the principal reason for the tinamous' high reputation as game birds. Arterial diameter is greatly re-

stricted and the amount of blood minimal. The lungs are very small. The tinamou heart is, relative to size, the smallest of all birds (Hartman 1961), reaching only 0.16% to 0.30% of total weight, whereas this ratio reaches 1.25% in the domestic pigeon (see also Trochilidae). This deficiency in blood circulation gives a greenish white color to tinamou flesh, which, like the plumage, is so flaccid it disintegrates with the slightest impact. The skeleton is well pneumaticized (an inheritance from better fliers!), but the total weight of the bird is relatively great. Re forced, long flights, see "Behavior."

Fig. 39. (1) and (2) Solitary Tinamou, *Tinamus solitarius,* feet, showing the conformation and disposition of the scales; (3) *Crypturellus* foot, on which the different conformation of the plates can be seen.

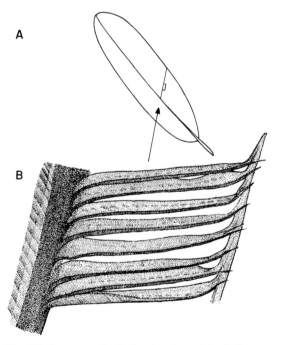

Fig. 38. Structure of a feather (remige) of the Solitary Tinamou, *Tinamus solitarius:* (A) full feather, showing location of the amplified section; (B) part of a ramus with some distal barbicels whose tips have fused into a solid bar (the barbicels of other birds are loose at the tip). Amplified ×135. After A. C. Chandler 1916.

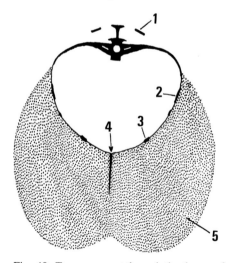

Fig. 40. Transverse cut through the thorax of a *Crypturellus:* (1) scapular; (2) rib; (3) furcula; (4) sternum with the crista sterni; (5) pectoral muscles. After H. O. Wagner 1949.

Vocalization

The principal vocalizations of tinamous correspond to the territorial songs of other birds, such as Passeriformes, and are usually the only ones perceptible. The whistles of *Tinamus* and *Crypturellus* species are loud and melodious; their low, full voices are an adaptation to their dense forest habitat, replete with obstacles that impede free circulation of sound waves. Voices of *Nothura*, which are savanna birds, are high and may have a cricketlike timbre. Interestingly, among the *Tinamus* (all forest birds), the smallest, the White-throated Tinamou, *T. guttatus*, appears to have the lowest voice, contrary to what one might expect.

Vocalization is the most useful feature in identifying tinamous and even for them must certainly be the most important means of intraspecific recognition. Each species has various slightly different whistles. In the *Crypturellus* each sex frequently has both a short and a long phrase, and the notes of the sexes are distinguishable; the voice of the female *C. strigulosus* is lower than the males.

Tinamous call more at certain times of the year, and at the peak of the breeding season they whistle tirelessly. The Undulated Tinamou, *Crypturellus undulatus*, can call uninterruptedly for 30 minutes, with notes coming one after the other at intervals of 5 to 18 seconds, with an average of 12.5 seconds. It is in this season that the Solitary Tinamou, *Tinamus solitarius*, and *T. tao* perform the "chororocado," a peculiar call sometimes given insistently for minutes on end. The male's chororocado is lower, shorter, and has a more rapid tremolo than the female's. They call from the roost.

Calling is more frequent in the late afternoon and morning. *Nothura maculosa* sings with greatest vigor for a few minutes at a certain stage of dusk. *Crypturellus strigulosus*, an Amazonian forest species, reaches its song peak in the hottest hours of the day. Tinamous, like curassows and wood-quail, periodically call even at night from the roost, especially during the full moon.

Dialects have been distinguished within some species, such as the Brown Tinamou, *Crypturellus obsoletus*, of São Paulo and Mato Grosso, and the Variegated Tinamou, *C. variegatus*, of Espírito Santo and Maranhão.

Tinamous call with the neck stretched vertically, the head tilted obliquely, and the bill open wide. When not singing they can be completely imperceptible, as if they did not exist.

Vocalizations are useful for confirming the relationship of certain species. In this way, some of the *Crypturellus* can be grouped:

1. *C. undulatus, C. erythropus,* and *C. noctivagus*
2. *C. obsoletus, C. parvirostris,* and *C. tataupa* (see also *Tinamus solitarius* and *T. tao*)

Only a few tinamous have alarm notes (e.g., *C. tataupa* and *Nothura maculosa*), or call notes. The White-bellied Nothura, *N. boraquira*, lives in the caatinga in small flocks whose members maintain contact through a constant, low cheeping that also links neighboring flocks to each other. A similar situation occurs with the woodland *Crypturellus erythropus*, but in this case associated individuals move about together less. This type of communication within a flock resembles that of gallinaceous birds such as the *Odontophorus* and *Colinus* quails. *Nothura maculosa*, which flees on the wing, sometimes gives a *tew, tew, tew . . .* that may be mistaken for wing noise but is a vocalization. There are still other vocalizations, such as the weak notes the male uses to call his young, and the young's own cries. Half a dozen different vocalizations of *Tinamus solitarius* can be distinguished. A four-month-old female *Crypturellus obsoletus* can already sing with the same rhythm as its mother, though more weakly and giving only short phrases.

Feeding

Tinamous consume berries and fallen fruits (e.g., merindibas, tangerines, and palmito fruits; the Cinereous Tinamou, *Crypturellus cinereus*, specializes in the fruits of the açai, *Euterpe oleracea*) as well as leaves and hard seeds. *Tinamus solitarius* and *Crypturellus obsoletus* were observed in São Paulo filling their crops with bamboo (*Gadua superba*) seeds. Tinamous also look for small arthropods and mollusks hiding in the carpet of rotted leaves, and they use their bills to turn over leaves and rotten sticks in search of food. They never scratch the ground with their feet like gallinaceous birds do (for an exception see "Populational Analysis . . . "). The *Crypturellus* sometimes jump to catch an insect. A captive *Tinamus solitarius* killed, dismembered, and ate a large tarantula. *T. solitarius* can be attracted by imitating a cricket.

Rhynchotus rufescens, armed with a strong, long, curved bill, digs into the earth, throws aside the dirt, and pulls out tubers and roots; it is immensely fond of grasshoppers and peanuts and swallows the latter in the shell. A single individual of this species was found to have swallowed 707 termites. The job of digging into termite nests—practiced in the same way by *Taoniscus nanus*—is facilitated if the nest has already been broken into and repaired with fresh material by the termites. *R. rufescens*, however, is capable of perforating the hard exterior of intact termite houses, opening holes several centimeters in diameter. It occasionally hunts small vertebrates such as geckos, mice, and even small snakes. Roots are taken more frequently in winter when insects become scarce.

The *Nothura* hunt ticks in pastures and take advantage of cattle moving through vegetation to catch insects (e.g., grasshoppers) that are frightened up. Of 177 *N. maculosa* examined, 109, or about 91%, had eaten both animal and vegetable materials. In a second lot of 100 individuals, 93%

had eaten vegetable materials, 7% animal matter. The immense "usefulness" of *N. maculosa* is evident from the following survey conducted in Rio Grande do Sul: of 44 plant species eaten by *N. maculosa,* 14 were harmful to plantings, pastures, or cattle. Of 28 animal species eaten, 26 were considered harmful to agriculture or livestock (Menegheti et al. 1982). These birds also dig into the earth for tender roots and tubers but on a small scale. Thus, the fact that both *N. maculosa* and *Rhynchotus rufescens* have their nostrils located at the base of the bill may have a fundamental ecological basis. It is worth noting that *Crypturellus parvirostris* appears to be the only member of its genus to have this feature; it is also the most inclined to a savanna habitat.

Tinamous drink regularly whenever there is water. They do so by sucking, not raising the head to swallow the water. Tinamous swallow small stones. The young depend on animal food.

Behavior

When suspicious, tinamous freeze instantly with the neck erect and the posterior raised, or they lie down, in which case they stand again after the first alarm and, hiding behind leaves or grass, seek a better angle from which to examine the danger. Individuals frightened by a shot sometimes feign death. The *Nothura* occasionally hide in holes. I have seen one cross a road skulking so as not to attract my attention. At each step it set its tarsus on the ground while it brought forward the other leg, always keeping the body lowered and executing all its movements in slow motion. Tinamous do not scratch the ground with their feet when searching for food (see "Feeding"), but the female makes such movements when inviting the male to copulate (see "Mating").

Tinamous fly only as a last resort, heavily and in a straight line. They are almost incapable of avoiding obstacles but maneuver relatively well when gliding to a landing. Under exceptional circumstances they make long flights; João Moojen saw a *Crypturellus tataupa* that was surrounded by fire cross the Rio Paraíba do Sul in a free flight of more than 350 m. Flights of 50 to 270 m have been recorded for *Nothura maculosa* and of 700 to 1300 m for *Rhynchotus rufescens.*

To some degree, long flights must be a regular occurrence in Amazonia because of periodic floods. These can force *Crypturellus undulatus* to fly over 500 m of open water to reach a midriver island (Remsen et al. 1983). According to observations by A. Aguirre, among others, there are considerable losses among tinamous when water invades the islands during floods. On these occasions birds such as the Great Tinamou, *Tinamus major,* try to reach terra firme but may fall into the water because the distance is too great, because they are already exhausted, or even because they hit the green wall of the river edge. Local residents make the most of these occurrences.

Tinamous make a loud noise with the wings when they

take off (*inambu* in Tupi is "y-nam-bu," "that which takes off with a roar"). Savanna species, primarily *Nothura boraquira,* produce a sonorous rustling in flight. In general, savanna species fly much better than forest species, which are adapted to tall vegetation, excepting *Taoniscus nanus,* which although a savanna species is in the process of losing its ability to fly.

Tinamous bathe in water (*Tinamus solitarius* leaves the powder down of its feathers on the surface of pools or streams) and take dust baths (*T. major, Crypturellus tataupa, Nothura*) and sun baths. *Nothura* plumage frequently takes on the color of the local earth by becoming impregnated with it. In a heavy rain birds assume an erect stance (their silhouette becoming similar to that of a bottle) and let the water run over their plumage.

The *Tinamus* roost above ground to sleep, choosing a horizontal branch no less than 2 m above ground and frequently 4 m or more. The bird goes up noisily (it can be heard from a distance), taking off almost vertically in a previously chosen trajectory that must be completely free of obstacles. Reaching the perch, it usually turns toward the side from which it came to get settled. It chooses a branch that permits it to lie on its scaly, rough tarsi, which on perches used for some time rubs off the lichens. Even on thin perches the birds do not use their toes to hold on (a detail observed by Fernão Cardim in the sixteenth century), balancing with the weight of their bodies (fig. 41). Feces do not occur beneath perches, the ground appearing to have been swept by the wind from the wings. *T. tao,* which has a smooth tarsus, sometimes perches, but on a bed of branches (Schäfer 1954).

When threatening, tinamous assume an aggressive posture

Fig. 41. Solitary Tinamou, *Tinamus solitarius,* roosting. The bird rests on the tarsus, the same as it does on the ground, not using the toes. After a photo by Werner Bokermann.

and ruffle the feathers, extending the head forward (usually without pecking) and opening the wings in readiness to flap. See also "Populational Analysis . . . ").

Populational Analysis, Annual Cycle, and Mating

To overcome the obstacles shy tinamous create for direct observation of their lives, calls are used (see "Hunting . . . "). Birds thus attracted and shot, principally during the breeding season, provide information of only moderate value in analyzing the numerical relationship between the sexes—which is the basis for the populational status of a species—because males and females may not respond to the same degree. This does provide definitive data, however, for studying development of the birds' sexual organs. In this type of hunting it makes a decided difference whether the hunter imitates a male or a female and which sex is more territorial at the time. Sometimes various individuals respond to the same call, as I have observed with *Crypturellus undulatus*.

Many tinamous are attracted by the call of their own sex. On this basis it was decided there was a predominance of *Tinamus solitarius* females. This result, however, was a consequence of the fact that the female is more aggressive than the male, responding more promptly to the call. In *Crypturellus noctivagus* the call of the male is always answered by other males. The same happens with *C. strigulosus*.

Meticulous surveys of *T. solitarius* by J. C. Magalhães have revealed that when a call is typically female, more males respond to it at the beginning of the breeding season (June–July). In August the percentage of males and females responding is balanced. And from September on the percentage of females increases. It appears, therefore, that there is numerical equilibrium of the sexes in *T. solitarius*.

Surprisingly, in *T. tao,* the Amazonian replacement for *T. solitarius,* there apparently exists a clear predominance of males, in the proportion of 2.2 to 1 (based on examination of 224 specimens from the upper Xingu collected May–September). I continue to have some doubts, for these data, like the others cited, result from birds collected by calls, not from a realistic examination of the population. One must also consider whether the population of the collecting area is intact or if previous hunting has eliminated birds that might have responded to the call. If we extrapolate for the total population, as was done by Magalhães, we get 1.5–2.0 males per female for *T. tao*. Such an excess of males would suggest a biological stockpile, with males subject to greater predation risks during brooding, a condition more aggravated in the Hylaea. There is a great difference between the respective breeding behaviors of *T. tao* and *T. solitarius*. *T. solitarius* females lay one clutch of six eggs per season, to be incubated by one male. *T. tao* females mate consecutively with two males, providing each with three eggs.

For *Crypturellus variegatus* in Guyana, an even greater proportion of males, four to one, has been reported. This species, however, presents a peculiar situation, for its breeding period is more prolonged and the female lays only one egg per nest.

Various tinamous (e.g., *T. solitarius, Crypturellus obsoletus, C. parvirostris, C. tataupa,* and *Nothura maculosa*) move about in pairs. In one place *T. solitarius* has been found paired throughout the year. Because of a lack of individual marking, we do not know how many times pair composition changes, or when. The situation is even more complicated if we consider that an individual changes behavior with age: a male may be monogamous when young and polygamous when older, as has been demonstrated in the Brushland Tinamou, *Nothoprocta cinerascens,* of the Andes. The reproductive system of the family is very efficient, as is evident from the abundance of these birds in untouched areas or when they are not hunted. Polyandry is the most certain route for the speediest multiplication.

Working with eight forest tinamou species in Amazonia, between latitudes 10°S and 15°S, Magalhães (1988 pers. comm.) identified a precise reproductive cycle that begins in May, peaks in July, and declines from September on. This breeding cycle is brought on by a period of intense light, the result of less rain and a consequent increase in the number of hours of effective sunshine. Thus, there is a light stimulus that is independent of day length, which varies very little in these low latitudes.

During courtship and to intimidate rivals, the *Crypturellus* and *Tinamus solitarius* lower their breast to the ground and raise their posterior vertically, looking much larger than they really are. In assuming this position they show the entire upper side to a frontal observer, and if seen from behind or from the side, they display the under tail coverts and lateral feathers, both highly developed and well marked. These displays may recall the respective behavior of certain pheasants (Davidson 1976). See also "Behavior."

I have recorded surprising precopulatory displays of the female *Crypturellus parvirostris*. Lowering her breast to the ground, she stretches her legs to the maximum (more to the side than backward) and scratches the ground vigorously with open toes. This may symbolize nest preparation: clearing the ground of leaves and digging a depression for the eggs. Independent of this, the female assumes a strange stance by lifting her wings to the vertical and curving her neck downward. Although the much more active female is the dominant sex, this situation may be reversed during prenuptial relations.

Territorial individuals compete by vocalizing, calling for hours on end without leaving their respective areas, mutually responding to and arousing one another. Disputes between *C. strigulosus* and *C. undulatus* are extraordinarily impressive. In fighting they use their wings rather than their feet as their primary weapon. On territorial size of forest species, see "Expansion. . . ."

Menegheti (1985) has calculated the populational density of *Nothura maculosa* in Rio Grande do Sul using the number of individuals raised by a pointer dog per unit of time.

Eggs, Paternal Care, and Young

Forest species lay in a natural depression covered with leaves alongside a tree trunk; savanna *Crypturellus*, such as *C. parvirostris*, lay in a cavity in the earth near a grass clump. The male *Rhynchotus rufescens* digs his nest in the earth, lining it with dry straw.

Eggs are generally large compared with the female's body size and vary considerably in shape. But the eggs of a large species, such as *Tinamus tao*, are no larger than those of a much smaller species, such as the Highland Tinamou, *Nothocercus bonapartei* (Schäffer 1954). The shell is so thin one can see the embryo without opening the egg. Eggs are oval or elliptical in small *Crypturellus*, becoming much more spherical in the *Tinamus* and even more so in *C. undulatus* and *C. strigulosus*.

Freshly laid tinamou eggs are among the most beautiful known: brightly uniform in color, they are as shiny as if polished or enameled and appear to be made of porcelain. This color, however, fades in a few days; for instance, *Rhynchotus rufescens* eggs change from purple or wine-colored to light plumbeous. This is one reason there is such divergence in descriptions of tinamou eggs.

Among Brazilian species eggs are colored:

1. Turquoise green or blue: *Tinamus* spp. and *Crypturellus noctivagus*
2. Chocolate or red wine: *Crypturellus* spp. (except those cited in 1 and 3), *Rhynchotus rufescens*, and *Nothura* spp.
3. Pink to gray or violaceous (*C. undulatus*, *C. soui*) or yellowish (*C. erythropus*)

The characteristic color of the eggs sometimes confirms separation of the species, as for example, with *C. noctivagus* and *C. erythropus*. Pure white eggs are said to occur occasionally, in *Rhynchotus rufescens*, for instance.

Tinamous are among the few birds in which the male incubates the eggs and rears the young, a breeding system involving polygamy (polyandry and polygyny).

The female *Tinamus solitarius* lays at intervals of three or four days; *Crypturellus strigulosus* sometimes on consecutive days. Six eggs would be a complete clutch for *T. solitarius* (Rio de Janeiro, São Paulo); however, a captive fed with a commercial mixture managed a clutch of 12. Larger clutches (*Crypturellus* occasionally have 9–16 eggs per nest) must be the product of two or more females, a conclusion reinforced by differences in size and color among eggs in the same nest. *C. variegatus* lays only one egg per clutch (Mato Grosso).

When leaving the nest the male carefully covers it with leaves (*Tinamus solitarius, T. tao, Crypturellus undulatus*) or with feathers (*Rhynchotus rufescens*), camouflaging it and thus hiding the shiny eggs.

When disturbed the brooding bird opens its wings and, leaving the nest, gives a trill, feigning injury (*Crypturellus parvirostris, C. tataupa*), thereby attracting the predator and leading it away from the nest.

I have not found a brood patch in *Nothura maculosa*. However, Magalhães advises me that at the end of October (a time when there is a high probability of brooding) he killed a male *Tinamus solitarius* that caught his attention because its belly was entirely unfeathered and the skin reddish, indicating intense vascularization.

Incubation lasts 17 days in *Crypturellus undulatus* (according to Werner Bokermann, to whom we are indebted for much valuable data on our tinamous), 19 to 20 days in *Tinamus solitarius*, and 19 to 21 days in *C. tataupa* and *Rhynchotus rufescens*.

After the last egg hatches, the chicks abandon the nest under the care of their father, who shelters them under his wings and who, to defend them, will even confront a human. In the event of danger when far from the father, the young freeze, lifting their posteriors and becoming completely one with the ground. Small *Crypturellus*, when crossing a space lacking vegetation, run like rail chicks and can be confused with rats. The plumage of the *Tinamus solitarius* chick imitates the dark, spotted pattern of dry leaves on the forest floor, whereas a prominent white spot behind the ear provides disruptive coloration. The *Rhynchotus rufescens* chick, which is similar to that of the Greater Rhea, *Rhea americana*, is entirely streaked over a very light background, producing a highly cryptic effect in the field. The *Crypturellus parvirostris* chick is uniformly brownish.

For the first few days *Tinamus solitarius* protects its young on the ground, even at night. The father only roosts high when all the chicks can accompany him. At approximately five days they can fly to a perch 1 m or more high, following their father and either clinging to his back or squatting alongside him or between his legs. The young may be of various sizes if brooding began before the clutch was complete.

During the early days while the chicks are still using their fatty embryonic matter, the father catches small arthropods to place before them. Later they become very agile at catching small insects.

The exceptional circumstance of finding a female together with chicks may be a sign that they have lost their father. I have found chicks clustered under the perch of a female *Tinamus solitarius* and have seen an adult female *Crypturellus obsoletus* with two grown young. The fact that neither the female *Nothura maculosa* nor *Crypturellus* females are adapted to care for young is easily appreciated by watching captive birds and seeing how aggressive the mother is to them.

Reproductive Potential

The reproductive period of *Tinamus solitarius* is limited, beginning in midwinter and peaking in midspring. There are two clutches (São Paulo). As verified in Mato Grosso, *T. tao* breeds earlier, peaking in midwinter. In Rio Grande do Sul, *Nothura maculosa* raises two or three clutches per year, the last in April. In captivity a male *Rhynchotus rufescens,* inseparable from two females but very aggressive toward other males, cared for three clutches from November to January. The two females continued to call and to lay eggs regularly for a total of more than 30, which under natural conditions they would surely have entrusted to other males whose nests were not yet full. I speculate that the same must occur with *T. tao* and *Crypturellus variegatus.* Two other female *Rhynchotus rufescens* laid 85 eggs between 20 May and 24 September, and a female *Crypturellus soui* isolated in captivity laid more than 20 in one season (J. C. Magalhães). A captive *Tinamus solitarius* whose eggs were constantly removed did not stop laying from August to February, producing almost 60 (Rio de Janeiro). A female *Crypturellus tataupa* in captivity with two males laid five clutches from June to September, three of them (with six eggs each) for the nest of one of the males, and the other two, with two and five eggs, for the nest of the other. In Rio de Janeiro *C. tataupa* eggs have been found in almost every month (Euler 1900).

A male *Crypturellus variegatus* may begin to incubate again while still caring for young.

Habitat, Distribution, Evolution, and Folklore

Although considered relicts of "primitive" birds, tinamous have achieved great success in South America, having adapted perfectly to the most varied ecological conditions.

In Brazil, forests hold the greater variety of species. In Rio de Janeiro, even recently, four species could be found in certain places: *Crypturellus soui, C. obsoletus, C. variegatus,* and *C. tataupa.* Earlier, *C. noctivagus* and *Tinamus solitarius* were also there. *C. soui* and *C. obsoletus* live in the dense understory of either high or low forests, whereas *T. solitarius* occupies high open forests with little undergrowth. In Amazonia there are sometimes three *Tinamus* and even more *Crypturellus* in the same forest, although each has its own ecological requirements.

These specific needs may vary according to region, as for example with *C. noctivagus. C. undulatus,* so typical of riverine forests, also lives in dry forests far from any water. *Tinamus solitarius, C. noctivagus,* and *T. tao* are not dependent on water either. During droughts they must go for months without drinking anything, for there is little dew in the forests.

As Paul Schwartz noted in Venezuela, adaptation to certain forest microhabitats creates a mosaic of parapatric distribution of similar species such as, for example, *Crypturellus undulatus* and *C. strigulosus.* When tinamous occur syntopically there is a size difference in the species (a situation similar to the guans, Cracidae); for example, *Tinamus guttatus* occurs together with larger species such as *T. major* and *T. tao.* For savanna species such as *Rhynchotus rufescens* and the *Nothura,* vegetation height is decisive. The former lives in higher vegetation, the latter in lower.

Amazonian tinamous reached the northeast (e.g., *Crypturellus strigulosus*) and, accompanying the Atlantic forest, arrived in Rio de Janeiro (*C. variegatus*). Via central Brazil, *C. undulatus* penetrated the south (interior of Paraná). *Tinamus tao,* a forest bird and our largest species, can be thought of as an allospecies of *T. solitarius,* the two forming a superspecies. Thus, they are descendants of the same ancestor, evolving because of the formation of Amazonia as a separate forest region. They may even be treated as geographic races of a single species. In the northeast there is a relict area where intergradation between *T. tao* and *T. solitarius* can be seen, demonstrating the ancient connection of the Atlantic forest with the Hylaea.

Two races of *Crypturellus noctivagus* have evolved, one dark, adapted to the wet, shady forests of eastern Brazil (*C. n. noctivagus*), and a second pale, adapted to the dry, light forests of the caatinga (*C. n. zabele*); these can be called ecological races.

Also in this genus, with its numerous forest species, I have observed that *C. tataupa* represents a transitional ecological type between forest and savanna (it is found in the caatinga together with *Nothura maculosa*). *C. parvirostris* is even more adapted to the savanna, advancing from central and northeastern Brazil to savanna areas along the Amazon. It is beginning to populate Marajó Island, Pará (see *Rhynchotus rufescens*).

Note that the southern savanna species, *Rhynchotus rufescens* and the *Nothura,* have not crossed the Amazon, being replaced there by the Crested Bobwhite, *Colinus cristatus,* a northern gallinaceous bird which in turn has not crossed from the north bank of the Amazon southward. *Nothura* distribution in the vast region of cerrados and caatingas may be quite local. I have verified that the *Nothura* may be entirely absent in vast areas, such as in Mato Grosso.[1] *N. minor* and *Taoniscus nanus* are endemic to central Brazil.

Disjunct distribution has been observed with *Crypturellus obsoletus* (which shows remarkable adaptation to such diverse climates as those of mountains and lowlands) and with *Nothura boraquira.* The latter has two populations, one in

---

[1]A very isolated population of *Nothura maculosa* has been discovered in the Roncador region of the Araguaia basin by J. C. Magalhães. Individuals are quite small and dark.

caatinga and the other in the Chaco, a case parallel to that of the Stripe-backed Antbird, *Myrmorchilus strigilatus*.

I find it interesting that Brazilian folklore became interested in the deep ecological antagonism between *Crypturellus undulatus* and *Rhynchotus rufescens*. It is said that the two were once inseparable, sometimes living in the forest, sometimes in the savanna. One day they fought and separated. *C. undulatus* went into the depths of the forest while *R. rufescens* remained in the savanna. Much later, *C. undulatus,* sad, solitary, and longing for *R. rufescens,* came to the forest edge and gave its pained cry, *Vamos fazer as pazes?* "Shall we make peace?" But *R. rufescens,* still enraged, answered *Eu, nunca mais,* "I, never again." [These Portuguese phrases resemble the calls of the two species.]

Parasites

According to L. R. Guimarães, more than 240 Mallophaga (feather lice) species are known for 45 tinamid species. Nine species were found on just one individual *Crypturellus*. The majority of ectoparasites found on tinamous are exclusive to them, some being restricted to certain genera or species. As a result, studies on Mallophaga systematics have confirmed the previous work of the ornithologists who classified these birds. From this angle, the relationship of *Tinamus solitarius* to *T. tao* and of *T. guttatus* to *T. major* is emphasized. Furthermore, each of these species has its own Mallophaga fauna.

Based on these criteria, Guimarães divided the *Crypturellus* into three principal groups:

1. *C. cinereus*
2. *C. soui, C. obsoletus, C. brevirostris, C. variegatus, C. parvirostris,* and *C. tataupa,* with emphasis on the similarity of the Mallophaga of the last two.
3. *C. undulatus, C. noctivagus, C. strigulosus,* and some other upper Amazon species

The Tinamidae are also parasitized by blood-sucking louse flies. I have found, for example, *Stilbometopa podopostyla* on *C. undulatus* (Mato Grosso) and *Olfersia holoptera* on *Rhynchotus rufescens*.

In the Parati region (Rio de Janeiro), H. F. Berla found an as yet unidentified leech on *Tinamus solitarius,* under the skin of the forehead, creating a swelling from where the parasite stretched to reach the eyeball, apparently to feed, moving over it with a motion analogous to that of a windshield wiper. This case is reminiscent of those in which nematode worms lodge themselves under the nictitating membrane of curassows, toucans, and other birds (see also Corvidae, genus *Cyanocorax*).

There are many records of nematodes, cestodes, and trematodes parasitizing tinamous (Travassos et al. 1969 and later). A malarial plasmodium (*Plasmodium pediocetti*) known in gallinaceous birds resident in Colorado, U.S., has been found in *Nothura darwinii* held captive in that state (Stabler et al.

1973). In certain fields *N. maculosa* are heavily infested with an armadillo tick they do not eat.

Mite fauna found on Tinamidae is abundant and unique; it apparently is more closely related to mites of Galliformes than to those of ratites (Gaud et al. 1972).

Enemies

Among tinamous' natural predators are wildcats, foxes, crab-eating raccoons, weasels, tayras, and opossums; it is not unusual in forests to find feathers of a *Crypturellus* taken by one of these carnivores. I learned from woodsmen in Pará that various wildcats hunt forest tinamous by preference, especially when the cats have young. A much-cited legend says that felines, especially the jaguar, can imitate the call of *Tinamus solitarius* to lure and eat it. What may happen is that in imitating the bird, the hunter attracts a wildcat (perhaps even a jaguar) which approaches assuming it will find prey.

Nests may be robbed by snakes, monkeys, opossums, and even by the Giant Anteater (*Myrmecophaga tridactyla*), which was seen on Marajó Island, Pará, breaking *Rhynchotus rufescens* eggs with its claws to suck the contents. In Cururu-açu on the upper Rio Tapajós, Pará, I found a *Tinamus major* nest being raided by a boa constrictor that was coiled around it. One egg was in the snake's esophagus, another in its stomach. Four of the beautiful, shiny, bluish green eggs were still in the nest.

The *Micrastur* are among the hawks that hunt tinamous. An Orange-breasted Falcon, *Falco deiroleucus,* caught a *Nothura maculosa* that had just taken flight in a field.

When perched, *Tinamus tao* and the other *Tinamus* that perch must be favorite victims of vampire bats (see also Cracidae) because of their very thin skin.

Hunting and Presumed Harmfulness

Tinamous are among the most important Brazilian game birds, furnishing indispensable protein to the rural populace. In Ceará it has been estimated that a family of seven consumes about 60 *Nothura* per year, in addition to more than 200 pigeons and doves and various mammals (J. Moojen 1971 pers. comm. in litt.).

A tinamou is the most esteemed trophy for any hunter, whether it be a *Tinamus solitarius,* the top prize for patiently calling in the forest, or a *Rhynchotus rufescens* or *Nothura maculosa* flushed in the field by a pointer and shot down in flight. The former method is inherited from hunting methods of indigenous peoples and has given rise to a hunting-whistle handicraft industry in southeastern Brazil, run by names such as Antônio Procópio (São Paulo) and Maurílio Coelho (Espírito Santo). The techniques of forest Indians can also be noted in hunting *T. solitarius* and other forest species with the *embaiá* (a foliage lean-to that camouflages the hunter from the eye of shy prey), a method first copied by peasants and from them by sport hunters. Traps (snares, etc.) are a traditional means of capturing tinamous, and now a new danger for *T. solitarius* is night hunting with powerful modern lanterns that easily reveal the bird on its roost.

Formerly tinamous were so numerous they were sold in urban markets, including in Rio de Janeiro. In Rio Grande do Sul, *Rhynchotus rufescens* was commercially canned until 1935.

Rhynchotus rufescens sometimes causes damage by eating mandioca and aipim roots and peanuts ready for harvest. *Nothura maculosa* frequently abandons grasslands for fields of wheat, rice, and other cultivated cereals.

Expansion, Decline, and Conservation

Crypturellus parvirostris, C. tataupa, the *Nothura,* and even *Rhynchotus rufescens* take advantage of deforestation by infiltrating cultivated areas. Introduction of very seedy grasses such as murubu (*Panicum* sp.) provides abundant food for *C. parvirostris* (Federal District). *C. tataupa* is said to show extraordinary endurance in the face of environmental change and *C. soui* to adapt well to certain secondary forests (Rio de Janeiro, Pará). *C. soui* has the advantage of requiring only a very small territory (e.g., 20 m × 50 m). J. C. Magalhães (1972) indicates that the territory of a pair of *Tinamus tao,* our largest tinamou, is approximately 10 ha.

Nothura maculosa leaves uncultivated fields for corn or cotton plantings. It also favors wheat fields of the middle planalto and Missões (Rio Grande do Sul). It is still extending its area toward the northeast (Pernambuco). Nevertheless, it is clear that savanna tinamous are endangered everywhere by the indiscriminate spread of insecticides such as Aldrin. The *Nothura* eat leaf-cutting ants poisoned by granulated baits and dead ticks that fall from cattle after dipping (it would be a useful practice to keep the cattle corralled until the ticks fall). Burning and agricultural activity between August and November harm clutches of open-country species. It is reported that tractor drivers in Rio Grande do Sul wheat fields have filled sacks with "little nothuras" while working at night, a criminal extermination (A. Closs 1971). On the modern roads of the northeast and south, nothuras are killed in large numbers all year, without the slightest use being made of them.

Forest species such as *Tinamus solitarius, Crypturellus variegatus,* and *C. n. noctivagus* are menaced by environmental destruction. The most endangered is probably the northeastern *T. solitarius pernambucensis.* Urgent measures must be taken to save our tinamous, which are among our most interesting birds.

Introductions

Tinamous have been taken by people from one place to another, including abroad, because of their great value as game birds (see *Rhynchotus rufescens*). Reference is often made to the introduction of *Nothura maculosa* in the vicinity of Campos (Rio de Janeiro) at the beginning of this century. However, Prince Maximilian of Wied, at the beginning of the last century, attributed that species to this region, which he called "campo dos Goitacazes." Perhaps *N. maculosa* really was introduced into the area despite its already being there in limited numbers. Possibly *Rhynchotus rufescens* was introduced on Marajó Island (Pará); however, its occurrence at the mouth of the Amazon has a certain parallel with that of *Crypturellus parvirostris.* See also the following paragraph and Phasianidae. "Other Exotic Phasianidae."

Captive Breeding and Hybridization

Captive breeding of tinamous is relatively easy, although until recently is was considered unpromising and practiced only rarely. It was not tried by the Indians, so there has been no true domestication, as is likewise the case with guans, curassows, and wood-quail. Rearing *Crypturellus parvirostris* in Minas Gerais and *Rhynchotus rufescens* in Rio Grande do Sul has recently given good results which could be advantageously applied to reintroductions (see also "Reproductive Potential"). In Minas Gerais *C. parvirostris* has been reared in batteries as Japanese quail have been (see below). There were three to four broods per year. It is said that tinamous are resistant to diseases that attack the domestic chicken (Nogueira Neto 1973).

Hybridization occurs in captivity between congeneric species such as *C. parvirostris* and *C. tataupa* (Zoological Garden of São Paulo) and *Nothoprocta cinerascens* and *N. pentlandii* (by Argentine breeders). *Tinamus tao* and *T. solitarius* cross easily, with the offspring fertile, as might be expected with parents so closely related.

Hybridization with domestic chickens, although frequently claimed, has not been proven. Tailless chickens are pure domestic races and not hybrids; likewise, greenish or blue eggs show the presence of the araucanian chicken of Chile (see Phasianidae, *Gallus gallus domesticus,* p. 202) in the ancestry and not hybridization with *T. solitarius.*

The confusion about *codornas,* or "quail," reared in batteries for eggs and meat should also be clarified. They are Galliformes (Phasianidae) of Japanese origin and not Tinamiformes (see Phasianidae, Appendix).

Synopsis of Brazilian Tinamidae
(number of species in parentheses)

Two natural groupings can be raised to the level of subfamilies, for they differ in features of morphology and ecology (forest or savanna, respectively):

1. Subfamily Tinaminae: genera *Tinamus* (4) and *Crypturellus* (13)
2. Subfamily Nothurinae: genera *Rhynchotus* (1), *Nothura* (3), and *Taoniscus* (1)

SOLITARY TINAMOU, *Tinamus solitarius,* Macuco
PL 1.1

52 cm; 1200–1500 g (male), 1300–1800 g (female). Largest southern species. Unmistakable. Back olive-brown, belly light gray. VOICE: a low, monosyllabic *fohn;* both male and female can call, using lower or higher notes or holding a note for variable length of time. Male usually calls less and appears not to repeat. On roosting in evening they call *foh oh oh* 3 or more times in a row. At height of breeding season both sexes give their "shororo," a full, melodious call that is prolonged and tremulous.

Eggs turquoise green. Although species likes open forest, it is common in very rough terrain with remote streams and grottoes, e.g., Serra do Mar. Forested regions of eastern Brazil from Pernambuco to Rio Grande do Sul (Aparados da Serra), Minas Gerais (upper Rio Doce), southern Goiás (forested caverns on tributaries along right side of Rio Paranaíba: Rios Meia Ponte and dos Bois), southeastern Mato Grosso (Rio Paraná, Rio Amapaí, brooding in October); also Paraguay, Argentina. Approaches *T. tao* in Mato Grosso and Goiás.

Presence of *T. solitarius* today in any forest in country is a good sign that area in question is little hunted. In many places it has become scarce or extinct. Still occurs primarily near littoral, where it can survive if last redoubts are respected and hunting is prudently managed, being suspended as soon as there is any sign of a population decline. Formerly found even in forests of Corcovado, in city of Rio de Janeiro. Represented in northeast by *macuca, T. s. pernambucensis* (BR,EN), a transitional form between typical one and *T. t. tao* of lower Amazon (see "Habitat . . ."). Northeastern form seriously endangered by deforestation but still holds out in residual forests of Alagoas (1976, 1979).

GRAY TINAMOU, *Tinamus tao,* Azulona

1300–1800 g (male), 1400–1900 g (female). Replaces slightly smaller *T. solitarius* in Amazonia. Back bluish slate gray, belly light lead gray. Voice and egg color very similar to *T. solitarius.* In Brazilian Amazonia confined to region south of lower Amazon as far as right bank of Rio Madeira and penetrates through gallery forests along streams in cerrado of central Brazil to Tangará da Serra, Mato Grosso (Bacia do Prata, W. Bokermann), and to Rio Pindaíba (Sick 1946 pers. obs.) and upper Rio das Garças, eastern Mato Grosso. Locally along eastern tributaries of Rio Araguaia in western Goiás (Jussara 1960–61); northern Goiás (Jurupi), eastern Pará (Rio Capim). Also Bolivia, Peru, Ecuador, Colombia, Venezuela, Guyana. Also called *Inhambu-açu, Inhambu-tona, Inhambu-peba* (Amazonas), *Inamu* (Kamaiurá, Mato Grosso), *Ubu* (Menaco, Mato Grosso).

GREAT TINAMOU, *Tinamus major,*
Inhambu-de-cabeça-vermelha

41 cm; 950–1150 g. Abundant and widely distributed Amazonian species. Medium sized with a rusty crown, and olive green back. VOICE: 2–10 monotonous, full, low notes, some tremulous, which frequently make up a prolonged phrase. Bluish green or greenish blue eggs rounded, like a smaller variation of *T. tao* eggs. Terra-firme forest, and várzea (Amazonas). Mexico to Bolivia, northern Mato Grosso (Teles Pires), Pará (Cachimbo and Belém). Also called *Inhambu-grande, Inhambu-serra, Inhambu-toró, Inhambu-galinha* (Amazonas), *Macuco-do-pantanal.* Includes *T. serratus.*

WHITE-THROATED TINAMOU, *Tinamus guttatus,*
Inhambu-galinha   PL 1.2

34 cm. Smallest *Tinamus.* Distinguishable by light yellow speckles on upper wing and tail coverts, chestnut under tail coverts. VOICE: a call even lower than that of *T. major:* bisyllabic, 1st note long and rising at end, 2d, given after a distinct interval, with same pitch as 1st but shorter. Eggs blue to turquoise green. Terra-firme forest, where may encounter *T. major.* Amazonia from Venezuela to upper Amazon; Bolivia, Mato Grosso (upper Rio Tapajós, upper Rio Xingu), eastern Pará (Belém). Also called *Inhambu-serra, Nambu, Macuquinho.*

CINEREOUS TINAMOU, *Crypturellus cinereus,*
Inhambu-preto

29 cm. Amazonian, almost uniformly blackish gray. Feather shafts on sides of head white. VOICE: a simple, sharp whistle, speeding up at end to 1 every 1–2 seconds. Eggs dark chocolate. Flood-prone lands with dense forest, capoeira, adjacent plantations. Abundant in várzea forest of upper Amazon. Very secretive. The Guianas and Colombia south to Bolivia and Mato Grosso, east to Amapá and eastern Pará (Belém, Marajó). Also called *Inambu-pixuna* (Amazonas) *Nambu-sujo* (Pará).

LITTLE TINAMOU, *Crypturellus soui,*
Tururim, Sururina

23 cm. Small, widely distributed forest tinamou. Immaculate brownish cinnamon with white throat, greenish legs. VOICE: a variable call, timbre always bland and tremulous, sounding like *too-ri-ring;* also longer, ascending sequences and descending whistles. Eggs chocolate colored. Edge of thick forest, dense capoeira, dry restinga forest. Sometimes roosts in vine tangles, in groups of 3–5, like Spot-winged Wood-Quail, *Odontophorus capueira.* Mexico to Bolivia and Brazil south to Espírito Santo, Rio de Janeiro, Minas Gerais, Mato Grosso. Lowlands of Rio de Janeiro to about 400 m (Serra dos Órgãos). Also called *Sovi* (Amazonas, Pará).

BROWN TINAMOU, *Crypturellus obsoletus,*
Inhambuguaçu   PL 1.3

29 cm. Typical of dense mountain forests of southeastern Brazil (Itatiaia, Petrópolis, etc.); also in certain places at sea level, e.g., forests of Baixada Fluminense (Rio de Janeiro

lowlands), where, however, it is very scarce (Rio de Janeiro; Magé, swampy area, 1969 A. Aguirre; Guapí, alongside *C. variegatus,* 1958 H. Berla; Rio de Janeiro–Petrópolis highway, Rio Iguaçu, 1948 H. Berla). Peculiar coloration: dark chocolate-chestnut with chin and throat gray; crown dark gray; legs greenish. VOICE: a very loud whistle with timbre of traffic policeman's whistle: a vibrant, simple call or a surprisingly long, complex phrase beginning hesitantly, accelerating as it rises, ending in lower tremolo. Female gives louder notes and longer series. Schematically, male gives (1) single, very loud note (combat) and (2) relatively short rising sequence, with notes emitted swiftly, without long pauses (song). Female gives (1) extremely prolonged rising sequence, with accentuated pauses at beginning but accelerated at end, and then becoming very loud (song); (2) short, rising sequence of loud, identical notes (reply to male); and (3) irregular sequence of soft, weak notes (chororo call, to attract male). There are dialects: a "trilled" timbre (São Paulo) and a "scratchy" timbre (Mato Grosso).

Eggs chocolate colored. Forests. Espírito Santo and Minas Gerais to Rio Grande do Sul, Paraguay, Argentina. There are isolated populations south of Amazon, e.g., northern Mato Grosso (Rio Peixoto de Azevedo), southern Pará (Rio Cristalino, between Serra do Cachimbo and Rio Cururu), lower Tapajós. Also Venezuela to Ecuador, Bolivia. In Andes may be confined to certain zones, e.g., 1700–2400 m. Also called *Inhambu-açu, Inhambu-bico-preto* (Iguaçu, Paraná).

Examination of bird lice suggests perhaps *C. obsoletus* of central Brazil (including *C. o. griseiventris* from south of Amazon) should be separated taxonomically from populations of upper Amazon and northern South America.

UNDULATED TINAMOU, *Crypturellus undulatus,* Jaó-verdadeiro   PL 1.4

31 cm. Common in central Brazil and much of Amazonia. Distinguished by vermiculation of upperparts and foreneck, which varies according to region (4 geographic races are recognized in Brazil); legs greenish. VOICE: a melancholy call of 3–4 syllables rising at end, *doh doh doOH? (Eu sou jaó? "Am I jaó?").* Short, trisyllabic phrase, *sou jaó,* appears restricted to female. Eggs almost spherical, light pink or light gray. Várzea and gallery forests, heavy capoeira, dry, sparse forests, cerrado. Venezuela, Guyana, Colombia, and Peru to Paraguay, Argentina, Brazil: from north and adjacent portions of northeast to centralwest as far as São Paulo, Minas Gerais, Paraná. Also called *Macucauá, Sururina* (Amazonas, Pará).

RUSTY TINAMOU, *Crypturellus brevirostris,* Chororozinho

24 cm. Amazonian. Slightly larger than *C. soui.* Like a miniature *C. variegatus* but with shorter bill (2 cm instead of 3 cm) and less spotted flanks. Legs greenish. Várzea forest, sometimes (e.g., Acre) with *C. variegatus.* Rios Negro and Madeira to Amapá, French Guiana. Includes *C. bartletti* from south of Solimões.

VARIEGATED TINAMOU, *Crypturellus variegatus,* Chororão

28 cm. Medium sized with wide range. Upperparts heavily barred with black and rusty, throat white, breast and neck intense cinnamon. Legs greenish. VOICE: a melancholy phrase of 4–6 syllables, all usually tremulous, the 1st descending and isolated from following ones, which rise: Recalls *C. soui* (sometimes its neighbor) but much louder. Eggs light chocolate. Various types of forest. The Guianas and Venezuela to Peru, northern Mato Grosso, eastern Pará (Belém); also eastern Brazil from southeastern Bahia to Espírito Santo (north of Rio Doce, alongside *C. noctivagus*), Rio de Janeiro (Guapí, alongside *C. obsoletus* and *C. soui,* 1958, 1969 H. Berla; Cachoeira de Macacu, 1963 A. Aguirre), Minas Gerais. Numbers much reduced in eastern Brazil, as with *C. noctivagus.* Also called *Inambu-onça, Inambu-relógio, Chorão.*

RED-LEGGED TINAMOU, *Crypturellus erythropus,* Inhambu-de-perna-vermelha

27 cm. Northern Amazonia species with light red legs. Upperparts dark reddish (female may be barred yellow here, like *C. strigulosus*), throat white, upper breast gray. VOICE: a clear call, *soi-so-la;* a low *woop-woop* call when birds, associated in small, scattered flocks, walk through forest. Eggs reddish gray or yellowish pink. Deciduous dry forest, islands of forest. The Guianas and Venezuela to northern shore of lower Amazon: Amazonas (Manaus), Pará (Faro, Monte Alegre), Amapá. Color of legs and eggs does not support unification with *C. atricapillus* of Amazonia and *C. noctivagus* from south, as has been proposed by some authors.

YELLOW-LEGGED TINAMOU, *Crypturellus noctivagus noctivagus,* Jaó-do-sul   BR   EN
Crypturellus noctivagus zabele, Zabelê   BR   PL 1.5

35 cm. Largest *Crypturellus.* Eastern Brazilian form, *C. n. noctivagus,* characterized by olive tarsi and brightly colored plumage: upper breast lead colored, contrasting with yellowish throat and dark red breast. Northeastern form, *C. n. zabele,* adapted to sunny environment of caatinga, paler with prominent whitish superciliary and yellow tarsi. VOICE: low and deep, 3–4 syllables, 1st accentuated, strongly descending and prolonged, others short, lacking inflection, following horizontally at even lower level; lower and fuller than voice of *C. undulatus* and distinguished by descending character of phrase. No tremolo, unlike *C. variegatus.* Voice of *C. n. zabele,* which I have heard in various parts of Bahia, is very similar, at least in macrostructure, to that of southern *C. n. noctivagus.*

Eggs light blue, fading in a few days to light gray. Southern Bahia, Espírito Santo, Minas Gerais (upper Rio Doce), and Rio de Janeiro to Rio Grande do Sul (*C. n. noctivagus:* *daó,* Rio de Janeiro; *Juó,* São Paulo; *Jaó-do-litoral,* upper Rio São Francisco). Minas Gerais to Piauí and Pernambuco (*C. n. zabele: Zabelê,* Bahia; *Jaó,* Piauí). In northwestern Bahia penetrates humid forest of river edges, but I did not hear it in same places in which less common *C. undulatus* occurs. Typical race, formerly common southeast, has become scarce or disappeared completely from some regions (ex-Guanabara). Disappearance of *C. n. noctivagus* from Atlantic forest is at least as marked as that of *Tinamus solitarius.* Locally (e.g., northern Espírito Santo, southern Bahia) syntopic with *C. variegatus.*

GRAY-LEGGED TINAMOU, *Crypturellus duidae*
Amazonia (Rio Uaupés).

BRAZILIAN TINAMOU, *Crypturellus strigulosus,* Inhambu-relógio   PL 1.6

28 cm. Medium-sized Amazonian species. Shows clear sexual dimorphism, with upperparts uniformly reddish in male (see plate), lower back and wings streaked with light yellow in female. Throat and sides of head bright ferruginous, breast gray, center of abdomen white. Tarsi gray, claws whitish. VOICE: an easily identified, melodious, prolonged, uninterrupted song, beginning with crescendo, ending descrescendo; female's somewhat lower. Birds sing when sun heats forest, competing then with stridency of cicadas. Voice recalls that of Greater Rhea, *Rhea americana,* chick. Eggs almost spherical with light lilac tone, washed with pink, resembling those of *C. undulatus* but smaller and rounder. Terra-firme forest, frequently alongside *Tinamus tao.* South of Amazon from mouth (Belém, Pará) west to Peru and Bolivia, south to Mato Grosso (upper Xingu). Also northeastern Brazil (Pernambuco, Alagoas). Also called *Macucauá-da-mata* (Amazonas). See *C. erythropus.*

BARRED TINAMOU, *Crypturellus casiquiare*

Similar to *C. strigulosus* but with black and ferruginous crossbars on back. Only in Rios Casiquiare and Uaupés region on Brazilian frontier with Venezuela and Colombia.

SMALL-BILLED TINAMOU, *Crypturellus parvirostris,* Inhambu-chororó   PL 1.9

21 cm. Smallest *Crypturellus.* Savanna species widely distributed in interior. Extremely similar to *C. tataupa* but with smaller bill (less than 2 cm) and shorter tarsus (less than 3 cm), both of which are pale red. VOICE: a prolonged sequence of sharp, harsh notes, 1st ones hesitant, then accelerating and rising but quickly descending, ending in 2–3 low trills. Female has muffled, bisyllabic call: *prrr prrr.* Calls more during hot hours of day. Eggs light violaceous-chocolate. Primary and secondary brushy open country, cerrado, cultivated fields (e.g., corn and cotton). South of Amazon from Pará (Santarém, Belém, Marajó) to northeast, east

(Minas Gerais, Espírito Santo), south (São Paulo, Paraná, Rio Grande do Sul), and centralwest Brazil. Also Peru, Bolivia, Paraguay, Argentina. Also called *Chororó* (onomatopoeic), *Inambuzinho.*

TATAUPA TINAMOU, *Crypturellus tataupa,* Inhambu-xintã

24 cm. Similar to *C. parvirostris* but larger and with bright red bill (tipped black in male). Also differs by having purplish tarsi, darker (slate) crown, dark chestnut mantle, and more contrasting design on flanks. Usually male is clearly smaller than female. VOICE: much louder than *C. parvirostris,* achieving a surprising volume for a bird this size; comprises longer or shorter series of harsh notes on a descending scale: *prrr PRRR prrr prrrr* or *prrr prrr prrr prrr prrr prrrrr.* Voices of sexes can be quite different: Male may give a long descending sequence, slightly accelerated at end (song), or just 3 well-separated, descending notes (combat). Female gives long or short descending sequence, strongly accelerated at end. When frightened a tremolo is given. Eggs pinkish light chocolate. Any secondary forest, heavy dry capoeira, caatinga, canefields (places with taller vegetation, where *parvirostris* does not enter). In northeast, east (including ex-Guanabara), south (as far as Rio Grande do Sul), and centralwest Brazil. Also Peru, Bolivia, Paraguay, Argentina. Also called *Inambumirim, Bico-de-lacre,* sometimes *Chororó,* which creates confusion with *parvirostris.*

RED-WINGED TINAMOU, *Rhynchotus rufescens,* Perdiz, Perdigão   PL 1.10

37.5 cm. Largest open-country Brazilian tinamou. Unmistakable. Strong bill used to dig up roots (see "Feeding"). VOICE: a high, plangent call of 5 syllables, 1st 2 separated from more united other 3, of which last is lower: *chiLEE-DEE—diDEE,* repeated at intervals of 16–20 seconds when singer is animated.

Eggs vinaceous or violaceous-chocolate. Birds more active in hot hours of day. Formerly abundant in savanna regions, cerrados, buriti groves (likes humid habitats); also in uninhabited highlands (Itatiaia, Rio de Janeiro, laying in November). Argentina and Bolivia to scattered campos in Hylaea south of Amazon (e.g., between Serra do Cachimbo and Rio Cururu in Pará). Recorded on Marajó Island (Pará) in 1897 and 1918 and apparently still there in certain places (Sick 1965 pers. obs.). The species being little known in that area, I believe it possibly was introduced there. It suffers from burning of fields (from August forward) in breeding season. Wherever it occurs flesh is highly appreciated, so it is suffering slow extermination from hunters. Also poisoned by insecticides and suffers from other evils of civilization. May be profiting from increase in open country in nation. Has immigrated into Minas Gerais/Espírito Santo border region since 1968, after deforestation (A. Aguirre).

Name *perdiz,* partridge, is the most common for this species in Brazil, except in Rio Grande do Sul where that term is reserved for *Nothura maculosa,* with *R. rufescens* assuming name *perdigão,* "great partridge." In last century, when certain introductions were the mode, *R. rufescens* was taken to various European countries and to U.S., but no lasting results came from those efforts.

WHITE-BELLIED NOTHURA, *Nothura boraquira,* Codorna-do-nordeste

25 cm. Relatively large, typical of our northeast. Distinguished by neat, black vertical topknot, white underparts, bright yellow tarsi, and uniformly black inner vane of primaries (in which it differs from *N. maculosa*). VOICE: a high, prolonged note, falling at end, given at intervals of 4–5 seconds (song); in timbre similar to voice of Stripe-backed Antbird, *Myrmorchilus strigilatus,* which can also be heard in same localities. A low *bit, bit, bit* . . . given by associated individuals that are mutually responsive (see "Vocalization"). When taking flight produces a loud, resonant, very typical noise: *psuit—psuit—psuit. . .*". Eggs light chocolate, less shiny than those of *N. maculosa.* Runs in small flocks. Caatinga, brushy fields, sometimes near *n. maculosa* and *Crypturellus parvirostris,* and if caatinga is dense (Piauí), even near *C. tataupa;* penetrates riverine forests (northwestern Bahia); the northeast to Minas Gerais (Pirapora), reappearing in Paraguay and Bolivia in habitat corresponding to caatinga. Also called *Codornil* (Minas Gerais), *Codorna-baiana.*

LESSER NOTHURA, *Nothura minor,* Codorna-mineira BR

19.5 cm. Restricted to central Brazil. In size resembles male *N. maculosa* but differs by more slender tarsi and feet, smaller bill, chestnut crown and back, and usual lack of barring on inner vane of outer primaries. Cerrado, sometimes in same region as *n. maculosa,* but frequents less open fields. Minas Gerais (Paracatu, Diamantina) to São Paulo (Botucatu, Itararé), Mato Grosso (Campo Grande, Chapada). Also called *Codorna-buraqueira.* See also *Taoniscus nanus,* which is even smaller.

SPOTTED NOTHURA, *Nothura maculosa,* Codorna-comum, Perdizinho   PL 1.8

23 cm. Usually best-known *Nothura.* Color changes frequently according to color of earth that impregnates plumage. Characterized by having all primaries barred with yellow (both on inner and outer vane), unlike *N. minor.* Size of sexes may vary considerably. Small individuals are no larger than those of the *minor.* VOICE: song a horizontal sequence of short, high notes that accelerate, last for approximately 8 seconds, and finish with some short notes that fall abruptly: *ti, ti, ti* . . . *tirr;* warning, given while fleeing on foot or in flight, a more distinctive, monotone sequence. Timbre of voice similar to that of a cricket abundant in same

fields (Rio Grande do Sul). Eggs dark purplish chocolate. Sparse, low savanna, cultivated fields (soybeans, corn, wheat, dry-land rice). Argentina, Uruguay, and Paraguay to Brazil (south; east; in northeast the small, light race, *cearensis;* and centralwest) but only locally, being absent in many places where *Rhynchotus rufescens* is found (e.g., Paraná, Mato Grosso). Rio Grande do Sul name *Perdiz,* "partridge," causes confusion (see *R. rufescens*). Also called *Perdizinho* (Rio Grande do Sul).

DWARF TINAMOU, *Taoniscus nanus,* Inhambu-carapé, R   PL 1.7

13 cm. Smallest tinamou, smaller than any adult *Nothura* (including *N. minor*) and little known. Yellow legs short, general aspect almost that of a small dove. Blackish back finely vermiculated with white, underparts whitish cream, breast and sides of body heavily barred with black. Flight feathers uniformly blackish without any transverse streaks. In the field a *Nothura* may be taken for *T. nanus.* Voice has same timbre as *N. maculosa* and as a cricket: *tzirrrrrr-ti-ti-ti. . .*". Trill at beginning lasts 2–3 seconds and is followed by 6–10 isolated notes, as A. Negret noted in Brasília from 1980 on; doubt existed because of confusion with Ocellated Crake, *Micropygia schomburgkii,* which occurs in same area. Cerrado, bushy savanna. Rarely flies, hides in burrows. Sometimes syntopic with *N. maculosa.* Central and southern Brazil: Goiás, Federal District (1965–67), interior São Paulo, Paraná. Also Misiones, Argentina. Comparing it with *M. schomburgkii,* I find *T. nanus* does not flick its tail the way *M. schomburgkii* does and that it has a bulkier body. Name *carapé* comes from Tupi, meaning "dwarf." See *M. schomburgkii.*

Tinamidae Bibliography
See also General Bibliography

Aguirre, A. 1957. Rio de Janeiro: Min. Agric. [*Tinamus solitarius,* biology].
Amadon, D. 1959. The subspecies of *Tinamus tao* and *Tinamus solitarius. Am. Mus. Nov.* 1955.
Beebe, W. 1925. *Zoologica* (N.Y.) 6:195–227. [*Crypturellus variegatus,* behavior]
Boetticher, H. V. 1934. *Jena Z. Naturw.* 69:169–92. [Systematics]
Bohórques, G., and N. Carnevalli. 1985. Dimorfismo sexual em *Nothura maculosa* utilizando a morfometria da pelve. *Iheringia,* Ser. Misc. 1:79–85.
Brodkorb, P. 1961. Notes on fossil tinamous. *Auk* 78:257.
Bump, G., and J. W. Bump. 1969. Spec. scient. rep. U.S. Wildlife Serv., *Wildlife* 120. [*Nothura,* behavior]
Closs, A. 1971 and other years. Publications in Rio Grande do Sul newspapers.
Conover, B. 1950. A study of the spotted tinamous. *Field Mus. Zool.* 31(37). [*Nothura,* systematics]
Davison, G.W.H. 1976. The function of tail and undertail-coverts pattern in pheasants. *Ibis* 118:123–26.
Gaud, J., W. T. Atyeo, and H. F. Berla. 1972. Acariens sarcop-

tiformes plumicoles parasitos de tinamous. *Acaralogia* 14(3): 393–453.

Guimarães, L. R. 1942. *Pap. Avuls. Zool. S. Paulo* 2:15–37 [Mallophaga]; numerous other publications on Mallophaga.

Hanke, B. 1957. Zur Histologie des Ösophagus der Tinamiden. *Bonn. Zool. Beitr.* 8(1):1–4.

Krieg, H., and E. Schuhmancher. 1936. *Verh. Ornith. Ges. Bay.* 21:1–18. [Comparison of behavior of Tinamidae, Cracidae, and Phasianidae in the field]

Lancaster, D. A. 1964. Biology of the Brushland Tinamou. *Bull. Am. Mus. Nat. Hist.* 127:273–314.

Liebermann, J. 1936. *Monografía de las Tinamiformes Argentinas, Problema de su domesticación.* Buenos Aires.

Lucca, E. J. 1985. As relações de parentesco, a nivel de cariótipo, entre Tinamiformes e Ratitae. *XII Congr. Bras. Zool.* :523.

Magalhães, J.C.R. 1972. *Troféu* 2:4–9. [*Tinamus*, behavior]

Menegheti, J. O. 1983. Aspectos da relação de coexistência entre *Nothura maculosa* e *Rhynchotus rufescens. Iheringia,* Ser. Zool. 63:27–38.

Menegheti, J. O. 1985. Observações preliminares sobre a variação anual no desenvolvimento de testículos de *Nothura maculosa* no Rio Grande do Sul. *Iheringia,* Ser. Misc. 1:71–8.

Menegheti, J. O. 1985. Densidade de *Nothura maculosa,* variacão anual. *Iheringia,* Ser. Misc. 1:55–69.

Menegheti, J. O. 1985. The growth curve of the Red-winged Tinamou, *Rhynchotus rufescens. Iheringia,* Ser. Misc. 1:47–54.

Menegheti, J. O., and T.H.A. Arigony. 1982. Insetos, aranhas e carrapatos na alimentação da *Nothura maculosa. Natureza em Revista* 9:40–45.

Olalla, A. M., and A. C. Magalhães. 1956. *Bibl. Zool.* 3. [Behavior]

Pinto, O. 1949. Sobre as raças geográficas de *Crypturellus undulatus. Hornero* 9:80–83.

Schäfer, E. 1954. Zur Biologie des Steisshuhns *Nothocercus bonapartei. J. Orn.* 95:219–32.

Sick, H. 1964. Tinamou. In A. L. Thomson, ed., *A New Dictionary of Birds.* New York: McGraw-Hill.

Sick, H. 1974. Tinamiformes. In *Encyclopaedia Britannica.* Chicago.

Silva, F., and M. Sander. 1981. Estudo sobre a alimentação da perdiz (*Nothura maculosa*) no Rio Grande do Sul. *Iheringia,* Ser. Zool. 58:65-77.

Skutch, A. F. 1963. *Condor* 65:224–31. [*Crypturellus soui*, behavior]

Stabler, R. M., et al. 1973. *J. Parasit.* 59:395. [*Plasmodium*]

Teixeira, D. M., and A. Negret. 1984. The Dwarf Tinamou (*Taoniscus nanus*) of central Brazil. *Auk* 101:188–89.

Travassos, L., J. F. Teixeira de Freitas, and A. Kohn. 1969. Trematódeos do Brasil. *Memor. Inst. Oswaldo Cruz.*

Wagner, H. O. 1949. *Festschr. Erwin Stresemann.* Heidelberg. [Anatomy]

Ward, R. A. 1957. *Ann. Ent. Soc. Am.* 50:335–53. [Mallophaga]

ORDER RHEIFORMES

FAMILY RHEIDAE: RHEAS (1)

These large, long-legged, nonflying[1] birds belong to the ratite group, represented in Africa by the Ostrich, *Struthio camelus,* the largest living bird, weighing more that 100 kg; in Australia by the Emu, *Dromaius novaehollandiae,* and the Cassowary, *Casuarius casuarius;* and in New Zealand by the kiwis, *Apteryx* spp.

Rheas, which are restricted to South America, have had ancestors on this continent since the upper Paleocene of Brazil (55 million years B.P.). There are other fossils from the Tertiary and Pleistocene. Rheas are thus among the continent's oldest birds. *Patagopteryx,* from the upper Cretaceous of Patagonia (80 million year B.P.), also appears to be linked to ancestors of the rheas (see Chapter 5.2).

The hypothesis of monophyletic origin for the ratites, now being questioned again, was suggested not only by morphological and biochemical data but by behavior and parasitological findings. The ratites' current extremely disjunct distribution indicates ancient linkages between the southern continents. It is presumed that ancestors of the Spheniscidae, as well as those of the Galliformes, Suboscines, and ratites, originated on the continent of Gondwana before the separation of Africa and South America, which is supposed to have begun during the Cretaceous, 90 million years B.P.

Osteological studies, the ultrastructure of feathers and eggshells, chromosomes, and biochemical analyses all reveal that rheas are closely related to tinamous, another an-

[1]The loss of flight occurs faster than one might think during geologic eras. Certain now-flightless birds of Hawaii that could only have reached those islands by flying across 2000 miles of open ocean, such as an ibis, stopped flying completely after becoming resident there. These organisms responded by eliminating the flight musculature and keel. Once it is known when the islands emerged from the sea, there is a basis for calculating the time necessary for these birds to lose their flying ability: much less than six million years (Olson 1983).

cient group of South American birds. Based on their skull structure, Rheidae and Tinamidae are grouped in the subclass Paleognathae, unlike all other South American birds, which are Neognathae (split palate). Ratites are highly specialized for terrestrial life. On reducing the number of toes on the foot, see *Adaptation to Habitat* in the species account.

There are two living rhea species: our Greater Rhea, *Rhea americana,* and the Lesser Rhea, *Pterocnemia pennata,* a more southerly, Andean form that does not reach Brazil.

Morphology

Ratites are distinguished from carinates by lack of the crista sterni (keel) to which the flight muscles are attached in the carinates. This feature, already visible in ratite embryos, shows the impossibility of flight for these birds. Yet existence of feathers, and their microstructure, prove that ratite ancestors were fliers. Birds that were originally nonfliers are unknown.

GREATER RHEA, *Rhea americana,* Ema   Fig. 42

Height 134–70 cm, depending on posture. Largest and heaviest Brazilian bird. Male attains 34.4 kg, female 32 kg. Soft, gray wing feathers (including "plumes" that correspond to flight feathers of other birds) are angled obliquely downward, forming a mantle that rises to a hump on back and that covers whole body except posterior, which is white and covered by short, hairlike feathers. Tail and pygostyle en-

Fig. 42. Greater Rhea, *Rhea americana,* adult male.

tirely lacking, unlike the African ostrich (in which both flight and tail feathers are transformed to plumes). Rhea is among the few birds lacking a uropygial gland. Cloaca marked by dark spot visible from a distance. Feces and urine separated, unlike other birds. Adult male has a large penis, frequently extruded from cloaca. Head and neck brownish gray, male distinguishable by black at base of neck and on upper breast and middle of upper back (*papo-preto,* "black gullet," Rio Grande do Sul). Base of neck covered by a tuft of lateral gray feathers, so black on back is only visible when bird bends forward. Adult male stockier than female, holds head higher, and has thicker neck and legs. Northeastern population (Maranhão, Pernambuco) has larger bill (*R. a. macrorhyncha*).

VOICE: In breeding season (July–September, Mato Grosso), male utters a loud, bisyllabic, ventriloquial roar, *boo-OOP* (*nan-dú*), that resembles the bellow of a large mammal, such as a steer. It prepares for this by filling the chest with air, then roaring with the bill closed. It even roars at night (November, Rio Grande do Sul). Roar can be heard for 1 km and probably much farther when wind is right. Yet there are occasions in caatinga or heavy cerrado when one cannot hear a rhea bellowing nearby. Alarm is a hoarse grunt. Lost young utter melodious whistles resembling song of Brazilian Tinamou, *Crypturellus strigulosus,* which the father answers with a light bill snapping.

Feeding: Eats leaves, including spiny and caustic ones, small fruits, seeds, insects, and especially grasshoppers. Patiently hunts flies, looking for them close to rotting flesh, and catches any small animals within reach, such as geckos, frogs, and snakes, but is not basically a snake eater. So far I have found nothing to prove the current belief that the rhea eats poisonous snakes. Neiva and Penna (1916) had the opportunity to examine the digestive tract of "many" of these birds and never found snakes.

Rhea seeks burned-over areas where it finds fallen palm fruits and dying animals. It swallows small stones or anything that might help it grind its food. The popular saying "He has the stomach of an ostrich" is applicable to the rhea. It grazes slowly and walks continuously, distancing itself almost imperceptibly and disappearing into savanna where it is hard to see in spite of its size and the low grass.

It is an excellent plant-dispersal agent. Of a group of marked seeds later recovered from feces, 66% produced new plants up to 100 m away from the point of origin. Only 25% of the seeds set out directly to germinate at the same time gave rise to new plants (Magnani et al. 199).

Adaptation to Habitat, Behavior: A terrestrial bird par excellence, the rhea "still" has 3 toes, whereas the African ostrich is reduced to 2, this being the maximum adaptation for the foot of a bird living permanently on the ground. When pursued by people, the rhea flees at high velocity, with steps of 1 1/2 m. It runs in zigzags controlled by alternately raising and lowering wings, demonstrating great utility of long wings for a flightless bird. One rhea ran at more than

60 km/hr in front of a car. When walking quietly it moves wings rhythmically. Hides by lying on ground unexpectedly and totally disappearing (perhaps behind a clump), which perhaps started legend that rhea (and ostrich) stick their heads in sand to get away from danger (from that the phrase "ostrich policy"). Tinamous behave similarly. Rhea rests sitting on tarsi and sometimes lies on stomach with feet stretched backward. During peak hot periods it pants with bill half open. It likes to bathe, enters into marshy areas, swims across rivers. Has sharp eyesight and, thanks to protruding eyes, can see in all directions. Lives in flocks and seeks company of sheep, cattle, savanna deer.

Breeding: Adult male drives away rivals and assembles a group of 3–6 females who remain together while he customarily moves about alone. Females apparently mate with more than 1 male, and there seem to be more females than males (Mato Grosso). Full polygamy governs, both polygyny and polyandry (see Tinamidae "Mating.").

Males fight by pecking, with necks entwined while whirling around in a tangle. A male courts females by stretching his wings horizontally (typical male position) and running in a circle, opening and shaking wings, then performing an ecstatic display that confounds the spectator by the exuberance of the soft, ruffled plumes which tremble with the slightest breeze. At the peak of this dance the wings seem to take on a life of their own, 1 rhea suddenly seems to be 2 or 3, and an observer cannot tell which end is which.

Rhea may lift its posterior, a display that also intimidates rivals and that resembles a similar attitude of tinamous.

For a nest male prepares a depression in ground, perhaps using a scrape excavated by a bull. Cuts nearby grass and other foliage with bill, stepping on vegetation and dragging material toward depression, resulting in a perfectly clean area of 2–3 m around nest. This produces a soft nest but may have the even more vital value of impeding enemies from sneaking up and of keeping fire from reaching eggs.

Only the male incubates. Number of eggs in each nest depends on number of females present and number of males to whom females entrust eggs. A clutch of 20–30 eggs may be considered complete. In captivity clutches of 12–18 eggs give the highest ratio of hatchings (Paschoal et al. 1990). It is said that formerly, when rhea population was much denser, 60 or more eggs would accumulate in just 1 nest, making incubation impossible. One female can lay 10–18 eggs in 1 season, at intervals of 2 days. Last eggs each female lays are infertile (approximately 30% of total). Many eggs (so-called orphans, Rio Grande do Sul) are scattered and rot on ground around nest, although the male has a strong instinct for pulling into the nest not only eggs at some meters distance but also any other object similar to an egg. During incubation the males eats not only eggs that break but flies attracted by them.

Eggs vary greatly in weight; average may be 605 g (Mato Grosso), equivalent to about 12 chicken eggs. Eggs of various sizes occur in same nest, especially because whole clutch is product of several females. Eggs are elliptical (usually not spherical like those of African ostrich), shiny, and golden, becoming white after 5–6 days in sun. It is interesting to note that the other rhea species and cassowary and emu of Australia lay green eggs (emu eggs quickly become almost black) whose color resembles that of eggs of Solitary Tinamou, *Tinamus solitarius*.

Incubating male frequently shifts position, making a complete 360° turn every 24 hours. Each time he arranges himself on clutch he pulls 2–3 eggs from edge into depression, thus guaranteeing that each of perhaps 20 eggs is regularly brooded. Incubation begins 5–8 days after females have started laying (meaning incubation periods differing by up to 12 days). Young all hatch on same day with only a few hours difference. Perhaps the loud calls uttered by embryos ready to hatch have a mutually stimulating effect that produces this synchronization. After 24 hours young can stand firmly on their own feet.

Brooding male defends nest by stretching neck horizontally and wriggling it on ground while hissing like a snake in an extremely threatening attitude. He averts small assailants with pecks and defends himself against larger ones with kicks. Animal most dangerous to clutch is large teiú lizard (*Tupinambis* sp.) which awaits male's departure to push eggs out of nest. This can result in abandonment of nest. Armadillos are also egg predators.

Strong smell given off by hatching eggs attracts many flies which chicks start to catch within 5–6 hours of hatching. They also avidly eat their father's feces, which are black at this time. The father cares for young, which forage for themselves in a well-united flock. He also cares for orphaned and stray young, so members of same "nursery" are sometimes of various ages. In event of danger young squat with neck stretched close to ground or seek safety under paternal wings. To frighten a distant enemy, male raises himself to full height and displays black around base of neck. At 6 months young are strong and almost same size as adult females. They reach maturity at 2–3 years. Outside breeding season rheas form progressively larger mixed flocks of adults and young.

Distribution, Use, and Preservation: Found in savanna and cerrado where water is available: southern Pará (savannas of Mundurucu), northeast, including Maranhão and grasslands of São Francisco valley, east, south, and central-west; also Paraguay, Bolivia, Argentina, Uruguay. Also called *Avestruz* (Rio Grande do Sul, used more for male, female being *Ema*), *Nhandu* (Tupi, Mato Grosso), *Congo* (only male, Bahia). In Ceará and Rio Grande do Norte, where rhea is extinct today, it roamed in flocks of 20–30 in early 1900s. Designated state bird of Rio Grande do Norte (see Chapter 2.2). Rhea appears in undated prehistoric rock paintings in Rio Grande do Norte in microregion of Seridó (see also Phoenicopteridae, "Habitat . . ."). Still occurs in Piauí, from where it is taken to Ceará to "clear the ranches of poisonous snakes" (R. Otoch 1987 pers. comm.) See *Feeding*.

Fences, beside preventing rheas from roaming freely, often snare them. Recreational hunts or those destined to supply feather-duster market have eliminated or drastically reduced flocks in most regions where they were once abundant. (It is said that 10 pounds of rhea plumes are not worth 1 pound of ostrich plumes). Plumes have been exported for centuries, with Cuiabá, Mato Grosso, being one of centers of this trade. This clandestine commerce continues today, the plumes being sent overseas via Paraguay. So-called feather-duster factories were nothing more than handicraft centers. It is said there was no demand for rhea plumes in Ceará at beginning of century (Malveira 1986).

In Rio Grande do Sul, cowboys used to herd rheas into corrals by surrounding them with nets or would entangle their legs by throwing bolas from horseback. Birds were set free after their plumes were pulled out, but the process was so brutal it seriously wounded most of them. For native Indians the rhea was not only a source of plumes for ornamentation but a game animal, as in the case of the Canela Indians of Maranhão and the Parecis of Mato Grosso. The latter hunted them, as well as the Red-legged Seriema, *Cariama cristata*, and Red-winged Tinamou, *Rhynchotus rufescens*, while hiding behind a *zaiacuti*, a shield consisting of a framework of sticks covered with indaiá [*Attalea* sp. palms] leaves.

In the vastness of the interior, the rhea has always been much used by rural people. Its eggs are in recipes for various delicacies; its fat is used for snake bite; its claws are used for knife handles, etc. The thighs are eaten, but the rest of the meat is very tough. The rhea keeps pastures clear of an infinite variety of insects and harmful plants, which has earned it the protection of more enlightened ranchers.

The rhea has an outstanding place in Brazilian folklore. Its plumes are used in the popular boi suribim or bumba-meu-boi dances of the northeast, and it is the theme for a series of popular verses. Indians of the Bororo nation (Mato Grosso) see the symbol of the rhea in the Southern Cross.

For some time, however, the rhea has also been considered a nuisance. In regions where soybeans, alfalfa, potatoes, and beans are grown (e.g., Rio Grande do Sul), it is accused of walking on crops and of pulling up small plants (which it in fact does), and for this it is ruthlessly slaughtered. An important natural resource is destroyed, for it is easy to raise rheas on ranches devoted to the purpose, as has been done for more than 100 years with the African ostrich, with excellent results from orderly exploitation of their plumes. Cattle and horse ranches in Rio Grande do Sul could be used for this. The Zoological Garden at Sapaucaia do Sul in that state rears and sells substantial numbers of rheas.

It is said that an initial plume crop can be obtained from 10-month-old birds, the harvest being repeated once a year. The feathers must be cut, not pulled out, for they are firmly implanted. Rheas are raised in the U.S. without problems (Wright 1977).

In spite of such great potential in a world where everything is turned to immediate profit, the rhea, if not systematically managed, is marching with long steps toward extinction.

The rhea was often the subject of prehistoric stone paintings in the northeast. In Piauí, rhea paintings (Serra-da-Capivara style) have been found from various periods from 12,000 to 9,000 or 8,000 B.C. (N. Guidon pers. comm.). The oldest figures are small, those of the final epochs enormous. There are also drawings of rhea tracks. In Argentina, where there are many and older paintings, an "impressionism" that later becomes "expressionism" is recognizable, quite comparable to classical European painting.

Rheidae Bibliography

See also General Bibliography

Blotzheim, U. G. von. 1958. Zur Morphologie und Ontogenese von Schultergürtel, Sternum und Becken von *Struthio, Rhea,* und *Dromiceius*, ein Beitrag zur Phylogenese der Ratiten. *Revue Suisse Zool.* 65(35):609–772.

Bock, W. J. 1963. The cranial evidence for ratite affinities. *Proc. Int. Orn. Cong., Ithaca*:39–54.

Britto, P. M. 1949. *Bol. Mus. Nac. Rio de Janeiro, Zool.* 89. [Rearing, behavior]

Bruning, D. F. 1975. *The Living Bird* 13:251–94. [Behavior]

Cracraft, J. 1974. *Ibis* 116:494–521. [Phylogeny]

Faust, R. 1960. *Verh. dt. Zool. Ges.*:398–401. [Rearing]

Faust, R. 1962. *Zool. Gart.* 26:163–75. [Rearing]

Hudson, W. H. 1927. *Hornero* 4:52–59. [Behavior]

Jehl, J. R. 1971. *San Diego Soc. Nat. Hist. Trans.* 16(13):291–302. [Rheidae and Tinamidae young]

Magnani, F. S., and F. R. Paschoal. 1990. Dispersão de sementes pela ema (*Rhea americana*) en condições de cativeiro. *Resumos XVII Congr. Bras. Zool., Londrina*:172.

Malveira, A. N. 1986. *O velho sertão da Bica*. Rio de Janeiro.

Olalla, A. M., and A. C. Magalhães. 1956. *Bibl. Zool.* 1. [Rheidae, behavior]

Olson, S. L. 1983. In H. F. James and S. L. Olson, Flightless Birds. *Natural History* 92(9):30–40.

Parkes, K. C., and G. A. Clark, Jr. 1966. *Condor* 68:459–71. [Relationships]

Paschoal, F. R., and F. S. Magnani. 1990. Obtenção de maior indice de nascimentos com um controle do número de ovos por incubação em ema. *Resumos XVII Congr. Bras. Zool., Londrina:* 173.

Sibley, C. G., and J. E. Ahlquist. 1981. The phylogeny and relationships of the ratite birds as indicated by DNA-DNA hybridization. *Proc. Int. Cong. Systematic and Evolutionary Biol.*:301–34.

Sick, H. 1964. Rhea. In A. L. Thomson, ed., *A New Dictionary of Birds*. New York: McGraw-Hill.

Steinbacher, G. 1951. *Zool Gart.* 18:127–31. [Behavior]

Wright, M. B. 1977. Rhea—an endangered species? *Gazette* 26(6):8–10.

ORDER PODICIPEDIFORMES

FAMILY PODICIPEDIDAE: GREBES (4)

Grebes are a widely distributed group with fossils from the lower Miocene of Europe and North America (20 million years B.P.). Their affinities with other families have not yet been clarified. The family is only modestly represented in Brazil, where members are found in rivers and lakes. See also Phalacrocoracidae, Anatidae, Rallidae (*Fulica*, coots), and Heliornithidae. There are no loons in South America.

Morphology and Special Adaptations

The legs are placed well back on the body, facilitating underwater swimming which is powered exclusively by the feet, which function like a fish tail. Grebes never use their wings while diving, holding them hidden under the dense flank plumage. The toes are unwebbed but edged with lobes that serve as paddles. Grebes leave the water only exceptionally, and when they do so they stand very erect at water's edge. They practically do not walk.

Grebes are easily differentiated from ducks by their sharp, laterally compressed bills. They fly well but take off from the water with some difficulty. During molt they completely lose the ability to fly, with all flight feathers lost simultaneously (see Anatidae). The principal features for identifying grebes are on the head. Sexes are similar. In winter grebes assume modest colors (eclipse or basic plumage). See fig. 43 for a view of the belly plumage, which provides a thick, insulating

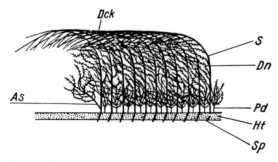

Fig. 43. Ventral plumage of Great Crested Grebe, *Podiceps cristatus,* forming a high pneumatic cushion that insulates the body against cold and humidity. Ht, skin; S, rachis of contour feather forming part of Dck, the solid, impermeable surface of the plumage; As, Dn, Pd, down. After H. Sick 1937.

air cushion, typical of and similar to that of other aquatic birds except the Anhinga, *Anhinga anhinga.* Aquatic birds have the most feathers. Fifteen thousand sixteen (15,016) contour feathers were counted on a Pied-billed Grebe, *Podilymbus podiceps.* A Chalk-browed Mockingbird, *Mimus saturninus,* had 3297, and an eagle had 7,182 (Brodkorb 1951). Male grebes may be slightly larger, as in *P. podiceps.* On skin pigmentation, see ". . . Behavior."

Vocalization, Feeding, and Behavior

Vocalizations range from the high trills of the Least Grebe, *Tachybaptus dominicus,* resembling certain rails, to the low cries of *Podilymbus podiceps,* which have the timbre of the Limpkin, *Aramus guarauna.*

Brazilian species feed on small fish, the larvae or imagoes of aquatic insects, giant water bugs (*Belostoma*), dragonflies (Aeschnidae), crustaceans, and vegetable matter. I have seen a *Podilymbus podiceps* devour a water snake (*Liophis*) 40 cm long. The very different bill shapes of the various genera indicate that their food must be different. The impressive bill of the Great Grebe, *Podiceps major,* is dagger shaped, like that of *Anhinga anhinga,* but unlike the Anhinga's it apparently is not used as a spear.

Grebes usually find their food underwater, diving expertly. The duration of their dives depends on various ecological factors such as water depth. Dives of *Tachybaptus dominicus* have been timed from 8.7 to 14.7 seconds; in Colombia *Podilymbus podiceps* has been recorded diving for 34, 37, and 43 seconds. *T. dominicus* may swim 3, 5, or even 8 m underwater, either fishing or fleeing.

Grebes have several special fishing techniques. I have seen a *P. podiceps* swim rapidly on the surface of a river so shallow the bird could not dive; it held only its head, neck, and feet underwater, touching the bill to the muddy bottom at short intervals. When a fish came out of hiding, the bird pursued it at top speed, always keeping its body at the water's surface. *P. podiceps* occasionally lets herons scare up fish for it (in the same way that anis, *Crotophaga* spp., accompany cattle); its thick bill appears to be an adaptation for crushing crustaceans. Grebes swallow quantities of feathers that accumulate in the pylorus and stomach. They ingest both their own feathers, shed while preening, and those of other birds, such as herons, they happen to find. The value, or perhaps even the need, of this practice is still under discussion. Possibly protecting the intestines against fish bones or filtering chitin from the feather mass is involved. Feather swallowing appears to be essential, for parents feed them to young. Grebes regurgitate pellets.

P. podiceps sometimes demonstrates an unusual diving technique. From a normal swimming position it sinks vertically like a stone, without the customary diving motions that involve moving the legs and projecting the head forward. I suppose the grebe "squeezes out" the considerable volume of air in its thick mattress of body feathers and thus sinks. This type of dive is used for escape, not for fishing.

Certain species, such as *P. podiceps*, frequently take sun baths. Floating quietly in the water and ruffling the plumage on the upper part of the body, they expose the skin, which is black in that area, to the sun (Storer et al. 1975).

Breeding

Grebes have specific prenuptial displays. They build a voluminous floating nest, of which only a part is above water and all is wet. *Podilymbus podiceps* lays four to six (Minas Gerais) small, elongated, white eggs with a calcareous crust. They become spotted (or entirely brown) by contact with humid vegetable detritus, especially since they are covered with this by the parent when it leaves the nest. Incubation takes 22 to 24 days for *P. podiceps*, 21 days for *Tachybaptus dominicus*. Grebes are bellicose when breeding.

The young, which at first are black with black-and-white striped heads and necks, crawl onto the mother's back. She swims with them or protects them under her wings. *P. podiceps* reportedly breaks up fish by batting them against the water surface to facilitate feeding the small young, although these are capable of swallowing quite large mouthfuls.

Migration, Enemies, and Dangers

Grebes are migratory outside the breeding season. In the southern part of the country their numbers increase in winter. This also occurs in the northeast, probably as a result of varying water levels. Among their enemies are the large carnivorous fish (e.g., the pirarucu) of Amazonia. They are parasitized by leeches on their feet. Lake and river pollution eliminates grebes.

LEAST GREBE, *Tachybaptus (= Podiceps) dominicus,* Mergulhão-pequeno   Fig. 44

23 cm. Smallest South American grebe. Grayish brown with black throat in breeding season. Wings have large white speculum, as with other *Tachybaptus,* conspicuous when bird preens or flies close to water surface. Eyes light yellow.

Fig. 44. Least Grebe, *Tachybaptus dominicus,* in nonbreeding plumage

VOICE: a sharp *tirrEE, kirr-kirr,* guttural cries that may recall voice of a capuchin monkey (*Cebus* sp.); song a raucous, monotonous sequence that sounds like whipping, recalling at a distance song of Rufous-sided Crake, *Laterallus melanophaius,* but louder. Pairs duet. Young are noisy: *bibibi* . . . . Can be found in any body of water, even a small artificial pond if this is covered with aquatic plants (e.g., roadside excavations). Southern U.S. to northern Argentina, all of Brazil.

In extreme southern Brazil there are two species:

WHITE-TUFTED GREBE, *Rollandia (= Podiceps) rolland,* Mergulhão-de-cara-branca

30.5 cm. Black, underparts chestnut. Unmistakable with bright white design on sides of head. Peru to Uruguay, Argentina, Chile, extreme southern Brazil (Rio Grande do Sul, Mato Grosso Pantanal). Common in Argentina. See *Tachybaptus dominicus.*

GREAT GREBE, *Podiceps major,* Mergulhão-grande

61 cm. Small but distinct occipital crest, long neck, and long red-and-white bill. VOICE: loud and sonorous, similar to a descending meow: "AYo, ohh-o, ohhk . . . ". Nests in Rio Grande do Sul (October, November). On migration appears on coast, fishing near surf line, at times alongside penguins (Rio Grande do Sul, August). A southern species, reaching Tierra del Fuego, Uruguay, Paraguay, Brazil (Rio Grande do Sul, São Paulo). Also called *Huala* (Chile).

PIED-BILLED GREBE, *Podilymbus podiceps,* Mergulhão

33 cm. No white in wing. Bill thick, white, and in breeding season has black band around it. Throat black. VOICE: a full *koh, kow-kow-kow;* sometimes pair duets. North America to Chile, Argentina, eastern Brazil. Frequently in reservoirs in northeast. Apparently absent west of Rio Araguaia. In same places (or slightly smaller ponds) as *Tachybaptus dominicus* but immediately distinguishable by larger size (see also Anatidae, *Oxyura*).

Podicipedidae Bibliography

See also General Bibliography

Borrero, H.J.I. 1972. *Bol. Soc. Venez. Cienc. Nat.* 29:477–86. [*Podilymbus podiceps,* feeding and breeding]

Brodkorb, P. 1951. The number of feathers in some birds. *Florida Acad. Sci.* 12,4.

Heintzelmann, D. S. 1964. *Wilson Bull.* 76:291. [Diving]

Miranda Ribeiro, A. 1927. *Bol. Muc. Nac. Rio de Janeiro* 3,3. [Mounting of a grebe carrying a chick]

Pinto, O.M.O. 1941. *Pap. Avuls. Zool. S. Paulo* 1:237–39. [Nesting]

Sick, H. 1964. *Publ. Avul. Mus. Nac. Rio de Janeiro* 49. [Protection against humidity]

Storer, R. W. 1963. Observations on the Great Grebe. *Condor* 65:279–88.

Storer, R. W. 1963. Courtship and mating behavior and the phylogeny of the Grebes. *Proc. 13th Internat. Orn. Cong., Ithaca*:562–69.

Storer, R. W. 1967. Observations on Rolland's Grebe. *Hornero* 10(4):339–50.

Storer, R. W. 1967. The patterns of downy grebes. *Condor* 69(5):469–78.

Storer, R. W. 1976. The behavior and relationships of the Least Grebe. *San Diego Soc. Nat. Hist. Trans.* 18(6):113–26.

Storer, R. W. 1976. The Pleistocene Pied-billed Grebe. In S. L. Olson, ed., *Collect. Pap. Avian Paleont., Hon. A. Wetmore,* 147–53.

Storer, R. W. 1985. Geographic variation in *Tachybaptus dominicus. Neotrop. Orn.*:31–39.

Storer, R. W., W. R. Siegfried, and J. Kinhan. 1975. *The Living Bird* 14:45–57. [Sunbathing]

Zusi, R. L., and R. W. Storer. 1969. Osteology and myology of *Podilymbus. Misc. Publ. Mus. Zool. Univ. Michigan:*139.

ORDER PROCELLARIIFORMES

The Procellariiformes bring together a large number of maritime birds, although the Charadriiformes (plovers, sandpipers, gulls, and terns) comprise the greatest share. Whereas the Charadriiformes are coastal, the Procellariiformes are pelagic. They are found especially in the Southern Hemisphere.

FAMILY DIOMEDEIDAE: ALBATROSSES (6)

Albatrosses are large oceanic birds, the majority occurring in the Southern Hemisphere. They are related to penguins but not to gulls. There are numerous fossils dating since the upper Oligocene of North America (25 million years B.P.).

Morphology, Special Adaptations, and Behavior

The family includes the largest flying birds in the world (see also Andean Condor, *Vultur gryphus*). The Wandering Albatross, *Diomedea exulans,* may have a wingspan in excess of 3.5 m and weighs about 7 kg, the body being very heavy. Fossil albatrosses were even larger. The long wings are rigid and very narrow. The tips never open to reveal individual primaries, unlike vultures, for instance. The arm is outstandingly long when seen in a skeleton.

The very robust bill is hooked and comprises several pieces. The tail is so short that a layperson seeing a captured specimen might think the rectrices had been cut off by scissors.

Albatrosses, like petrels (Procellariidae), take flight with difficulty, running several meters against the wind on the water surface or ground. They fly by gliding. Their mastery of this type of flight is based on the long arm, which has a large number of short secondaries (38–40; a duck has 12). I measured the wings of a recently dead Black-browed Albatross, *Diomedea melanophris,* at Barra da Tijuca, Rio de Janeiro, and found a wingspan of 1.94 m and a maximum width of only 18 cm in the middle of the secondaries. Unlike gulls, which fly higher, albatrosses do not beat their wings. Taking advantage of horizontal air currents over the sea, they maintain altitude without the slightest visible physical effort, even gaining height if they fly against the wind. Thus, they move low over the waves in an undulating, serpentlike trajectory, rising and descending across the wind. Without this technique albatrosses would be incapable of gliding, for their weight per unit of surface area is too great. The same dynamic gliding is used by petrels and shearwaters (*Puffinus,* etc.).

Albatrosses have large, webbed feet, similar to those of gulls, and appear to be as light as gulls when resting on the water.

Albatrosses do not vocalize in Brazilian waters. They feed on small animals, especially Cephalopoda and Crustacea that come close to the surface, and follow ships to pick up garbage. As with other Procellariiformes, half of an albatross's stomach contents consists of an oily liquid derived from its food (Prince 1980). Storms at sea do not bother them. They usually come to land only to nest (which they do not do in Brazil). Rarely they appear on our beaches, attracted by dead fish.

Migration

In this book I treat as Brazilian every oceanic bird recorded within 200 miles of the coast (the "exclusive economic" zone). Each island, such as Trindade (fig. 4, Chapter 1.3.10), has its own 200-mile-wide zone. The country's territorial waters are 12 miles wide.

Procellariiformes occur in Brazilian waters all year, most being immatures that are wandering the oceans until they reach sexual maturity (albatrosses breed at six years of age or older). Albatrosses make spectacular migrations. One *Diomedea exulans* banded in Australasia reportedly covered 4720 km in 22 days, an average of 214.5 km per day.

The number of Procellariiformes on the seas increases in the southern autumn and winter, from March to September. During this period they usually appear on our coast, especially in the southern sections, because storms have forced them toward the continent. On these occasions albatrosses appear together with petrels and boobies (these last are much less pelagic). This is a great help in judging the size of the various species, which is quite difficult on the high seas.

During their long nonbreeding phase (the juvenal phase of *D. exulans* reportedly lasts nine years), Procellariiformes in the Southern Hemisphere are carried eastward by strong westerly winds that result in latitudinal circumpolar migration covering the most productive areas of the seas.

The Neotropical region is rich in Procellariiformes because South America projects so far toward the Antarctic, home territory for many of these birds. With more high-seas observations, more pelagic birds species will be recorded for Brazil. The name *albatroz* is a corruption of *alcatraz* [widely used for a variety of other seabirds] and is not derived from *alvo*, "white."

Danger of Oceanic Pollution

I have found petroleum-soiled *Diomedea melanophris* on the beaches of Rio Grande do Sul, and on the Paraná coast a

Yellow-nosed Albatross, *D. chlororhynchos,* succumbed to the same cause. The seas are becoming full of floating plastic and abandoned nets that often kill oceanic birds. See also Procellariidae, "Mortality."

WANDERING ALBATROSS, *Diomedea exulans,* Albatroz-gigante   SV

120 cm. Largest albatross. Enormous yellow or pink bill. Nostrils open upward. Entirely snow white except for black wing tips. Immatures predominantly brown, similar to other immature albatrosses. Pelagic. Accidental on our coast, e.g., Rio Grande do Sul, Rio de Janeiro (Cabo Frio, July). Nests on subantarctic islands.

ROYAL ALBATROSS, *Diomedea epomophora,* Albatroz-real   SV

110 cm. Very similar to *D. exulans* but with smaller bill on which cutting edge of maxilla is blackish. Nostrils open forward. Occasional on coasts of São Paulo, Rio de Janeiro, Rio Grande do Sul. An individual banded as a nestling in New Zealand in October 1976 was found dead near Tramandaí, Rio Grande do Sul, August 1977.

BLACK-BROWED ALBATROSS, *Diomedea melanophris,* Albatroz-de-sobrancelha   SV   PL 2.4

83–93 cm; wingspan 2 m, wing width only 16 cm. Relatively abundant on our southern coast. Bill yellow. Short gray stripe runs across eye. Upper surfaces of wings and tail black, unlike *D. exulans* and *D. epomophora.* Rump white. Immature darker with bill, top of head, and upper side of neck blackish. Nests in Argentina (Tierra del Fuego), migrates as far as São Paulo (March), Rio de Janeiro (March, May, June, July, and other months), ex-Guanabara (June, November, December), and even farther north. Of a group of nestlings banded in Falkland Islands (Malvinas), 47 were found on our coast in February 1976: 41 between Rio Grande do Sul and Rio de Janeiro, 4 in Bahia, 1 in Sergipe, 1 in Alagoas. A nestling banded in Falklands in February was captured 32 km off coast of Rio Grande do Sul (between Solidão and Mostardas) in May 1976. Also called *Gaivotão, Antenal, Pardelão* (Rio Grande do Sul).

YELLOW-NOSED ALBATROSS, *Diomedea chlororhynchos,* Albatroz-de-nariz-amarelo   SV

79 cm; wingspan 190 cm. Smallest *Diomedea* (size of a large gull), but tail longer relative to body than in other species. Plumage similar to *D. melanophris,* but bird immediately distinguishable by black bill with bright yellow culmen. Rio Grande do Sul, Santa Catarina, São Paulo, and Rio de Janeiro in April, May, August. Not usually seen along coast but common on high seas; e.g., in May 1971 about 12 appeared 2 km off Búzios peninsula (Rio de

Janeiro). In May 1964, between Rio de Janeiro and Cabo Frio, isolated individuals as well as flocks of up to 6 were seen, the flocks always in company with equal number of *melanophris*.

GRAY-HEADED ALBATROSS, *Diomedea chrysostoma* SV

Resembles *D. chlororhynchos*, also being small with yellow culmen and mandible. São Paulo, Santa Catarina (May, Sick 1979), Rio de Janeiro (September).

LIGHT-MANTLED ALBATROSS, *Phoebetria palpebrata* SV

72 cm. Accidental in our waters. Entirely sooty with blackish head, wings, tail. Broken white eye-ring. Bill black. Rio Grande do Sul, São Paulo (August).

Diomedeidae Bibliography
See also General Bibliography

Harper, P. C., and F. C. Kinsky. 1974. *Southern Albatrosses and Petrels: An Identification Guide.* Victoria University Press.

Miranda Ribeiro, A. 1928. *Bol. Mus. Nac. Rio de Janeiro 4.* [General]

Prince, P. A. 1980. *Ibis* 122:476–88.[*Diomedea*, feeding]

Schloemp, I. M. 1990. Casos de ingestão de polímeros sintéticos em Procellariidae e Charadriidae. *Resumos XVII Cong. Bras. Zool., Londrina:* 186.

Sick, H. 1979. *Bull. B.O.C.* 99(4):116. [*Diomedea chrysostoma,* first finding in Brazil]

Teixeira, D. M., J. B. Nacinovic, I. M. Schloemp, et al. 1988. Notes on some Brazilian seabirds (3). *Bull. B.O.C.* 108(3):136–37.

Tickel, W.L.N., et al. 1968. *Emu* 68:7–20. [Migration]

Vooren, C. M., and A. C. Fernandes. 1989. *Guia de Albatrozes e Petréis do Sul do Brasil.* Porto Alegre: Sagra.

FAMILY PROCELLARIIDAE: SHEARWATERS, FULMARS, AND PETRELS (20)

These oceanic birds are similar to albatrosses in aspect and habits but generally are not as large. There is a Miocene fossil from Florida (25 million years B.P.). Procellariid remains are found in pre-Columbian archaeological sites in southeastern Brazil (see also Spheniscidae).

The numerous species visiting our shores are not easy to identify and often require specialized literature. There are considerable erroneous data in sight records, museum collections, and literature citations. A sure place to obtain specimens is along beaches where waves throw up dead or dying individuals (see "Mortality") whose heads, especially bills, permit identification. These carcasses disintegrate rapidly, however. Only one species, the Trindade Petrel, *Pterodroma arminjoniana,* breeds in Brazil, on Ilha Trindade.

Some procellariids are among the most numerous birds in the world. The total number of Sooty Shearwaters, *Puffinus griseus,* has been calculated at a billion. Certain species of Ploceidae, such as the Red-billed Quelea, *Quelea quelea,* of southern Africa, are even more abundant, being calculated at various billions.

Morphology, Behavior, and Feeding

The tubular nostrils of procellariids are attached to one another at the base of the culmen (hence the family name Tubinares, or tubenoses). The salt secretion made by the salt gland (see Laridae, "Feeding . . . ") runs to the tip of the bill through a furrow between the culminicorn and latericorn. Procellariids fly swiftly and close to the water surface, gliding and beating their wings, sometimes rapidly. They make abrupt curves, tilting the body from one side to the other.

Like albatrosses they follow a winding path, snaking over the sea to take advantage of horizontal air currents (fig. 45). They concentrate in the region of the continental shelf, where food is more abundant, to take advantage of schools of young fish and are attracted to fishing boats. The Greater Shearwater, *Puffinus gravis,* even dives to take bait, using its wings as paddles (see also *Pelecanoides*).

Prions (whale-birds), *Pachyptila,* live on plankton they filter in the bill through a system of lamellae that resemble the baleen of whales (see also Spheniscidae). Flying just above the water surface with the open bill submerged, *Pachyptila* catch zooplankton (especially crustaceans such as *Euphausia*) that come to the surface at night; many of these miniscule

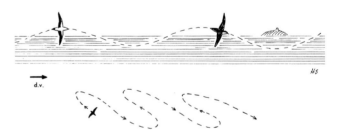

Fig. 45. Manx Shearwater, *Puffinus puffinus,* in dynamic gliding flight, seen from Copacabana Beach, Rio de Janeiro. d.v.: wind direction. Below, a vertical projection of the same flight in reduced scale. The bird advances in an ascending and descending zigzag as it accompanies the crests and valleys of the swells, becoming visible only as it rises, when it is silhouetted against the horizon. It uses the wind blowing over the ocean surface as its only propellant force, abstaining completely from wing beats. Albatrosses fly the same way on the high seas.

organisms are luminous, providing orientation for the birds. The *Pterodroma*, with their strong, hawklike bills, bite off bits from large octopuses and other cephalopods (*fura-bucho*, "belly-piercer"). Various petrel species gather where there are fish concentrations (commensalism). It has been proven that Procellariidae use smell to find food and to locate their nesting colonies on small midocean islands. The olfactory lobe/cerebral hemispheres index is, at 29% in various Procellariiformes, much greater than that of most Passerines. The index of the domestic pigeon is 20%. All Procellariiformes have a penetrating musky odor that remains indefinitely in prepared specimens and even in egg collections.

The *Pachyptila, Daption*, certain *Pterodroma*, and the Hydrobatidae (storm-petrels) are so adapted to pelagic life they are unable to walk on land or to stand. They dig subterranean galleries (*Pterodroma arminjoniana* does not) to which they can fly directly. The Antarctic Giant-Petrel, *Macronectes giganteus*, can perch on the ground like a gull, where it looks for dead animals and steals the eggs and young of shore birds, which it kills.

Migration

The Manx Shearwater, *Puffinus puffinus*, is apparently the only bird that makes annual transequatorial migrations between Europe and South America (the South Atlantic). Its newly hatched chicks accumulate such large fat deposits that they must be able to travel directly from the Irish Sea to Brazilian waters. Cory's Shearwater, *P. diomedea*, of the Madeira Islands, occasionally comes to the South American coast.

Inversely, *Puffinus gravis* breeds in the South Atlantic and migrates to the North Atlantic where it stays during the summer, returning in the southern spring. It covers 9000 km in 35 days (257 km per day). *P. gravis* is estimated to migrate 24,000 km per year and the Short-tailed Shearwater, *P. tenuirostris*, up to 35,000 km.

Numerous procellariids are scattered over the seas throughout the year, for they become adults only at five years or older and prior to that have leisure to wander the oceans (see Diomedeidae, "Migration"). Various family members, especially *P. puffinus*, have been found in Brazilian waters with bands from England. The appearance of Procellariiformes along the large rivers in the middle of the continent seems quite strange; there are various records of this for the Black-browed Albatross, *Diomedea melanophris;* Hooded Petrel, *Pterodroma incerta;* White-chinned Petrel, *Procellaria aequinoctialis;* and *Puffinus puffinus* for as far inland as Mato Grosso.

Mortality

The presence of some species, especially the *Pachyptila*, along the Brazilian coast is noticed only when kills occur.

Large numbers of dead birds are then thrown up on certain beaches without any evidence as to what caused mortality (see Spheniscidae, ". . . Mortality"). Deaths of *Puffinus gravis* on the coast of Suriname are also unexplained. It has been conjectured that lack of food in the barren tropical seas the birds cross when migrating from eutrophic Antarctic waters to correspondingly rich Arctic waters is responsible (Mees 1976). My own observations confirm this interpretation. In July 1983, 2000 Slender-billed Prions, *Pachyptila belcheri*, were found, some still alive, on 11 km of beach (L. A. Rosário and B. T. Pauli, Santa Catarina). Because those autopsied had empty stomachs, one might conclude that they died of starvation. One problem is that *Pachyptila* live on plankton or similar microscopic food whose detection in the stomach is difficult, even in fresh specimens; more samples can be obtained by brief pumping from the digestive tube. It is more significant when no fat is found and weight is below normal. After a four-day storm (winter 1987) with an east wind varying from 20 to 40 knots, a 21-km strip of beach at Cassino, Rio Grande do Sul, was examined and had 2 *Diomedea melanophris;* 50 Southern Fulmars, *Fulmarus glacialoides;* 10 *Pachyptila;* 1 *Procellaria aequinoctialis;* 1 White-headed Petrel, *Pterodroma lessonii;* and 6 *Puffinus gravis*. Many of these had food in their stomachs; cephalopods, fish, plastic (completely filling the stomach of one bird), and the feet of small procellariids (Costalunga et al. 1988). Procellariids usually flee bad weather fronts and may appear far from their normal range. They are endangered by swallowing plastics, especially polyethylene, and by petroleum pollution, which I have especially noticed with *Puffinus puffinus* in Rio Grande do Sul and Rio de Janeiro.

ANTARCTIC GIANT-PETREL, *Macronectes giganteus*, Pardelão-gigante   SV

88 cm. Size of an albatross but with much shorter, wider wings. Uniformly sooty with conspicuous light yellow bill, exceptionally large and high at base and with very long nasal tubes, extending over whole culmicorn. Flies with rapid wing beats interspersed with short glides. Fishes; attacks and devours other marine birds. Customarily vomits odoriferous stomach contents when caught, making it possible to examine its food and even internal parasites. A southern migrant; nests in Falklands and elsewhere and reaches São Paulo and Rio de Janeiro (August), being common in Rio Grande do Sul. An individual captured on 14 June 1961 had been banded as a nestling on an island south of Australia on 3 January 1961. Three individuals banded in Antarctica (South Orkneys) were found in Brazil, 2 in Rio Grande do Sul (March and June), 1 in Rio de Janeiro (June). Two cryptic (sibling) species are involved, *M. giganteus* and *M. halli*, and even hybrids of the 2 are not rare in Antarctica (Johnstone 1974). *M. giganteus* has green bill tip, *M. halli* red. Banded *halli* have been found in Uruguay but not on Brazilian coast. See Great Skua, *Catharacta skua*.

SOUTHERN FULMAR, *Fulmarus glacialoides*, Pardelão-prateado   SV

50 cm. Large with heavy body and high, pink, hooked bill. Mantle very light gray, head and underparts white. Wings have large white area at base of inner primaries, as in Cape Petrel, *Daption capense*. A southern migrant that occasionally appears in considerable numbers. Rio Grande do Sul (November), Rio de Janeiro (September), Rio Grande do Norte (São Roque). Considered a geographic replacement of Northern Fulmar, *F. glacialis*. See also "Mortality".

CAPE PETREL, *Daption capense*, Pomba-do-Cabo, SV   Fig. 46

36 cm. Most frequently seen and most abundant ship-following bird. Unmistakable with checkerboard pattern on back and 2 larger white areas on each wing. Approaches coast, having appeared in Cabo Frio (Rio de Janeiro), ex-Guanabara (November). Two individuals banded on South Orkneys were caught in Brazil in September, 1 in Santa Catarina, 1 in São Paulo, 112 km off Santos. Also called *Pintado* (a Spanish word).

TRINDADE PETREL, *Pterodroma arminjoniana*, Pardela-da-Trindade   Fig. 47

40 cm. Only procellariid that breeds in Brazilian territory. Completely sooty or with variable white on underparts, there being much variation. Seen from above in flight, small white area at base of primaries (which have yellow shafts) is promi-

Fig. 47. Trindade Petrel, *Pterodroma arminjoniana*.

nent, resembling a skua. VOICE: ternlike. Abundant on Ilha Trindade, where nests in natural cavities in phonolitic peaks or protected by low vegetation. Lays 1 white egg. Apparently breeds all year. Diurnal (unlike other petrels), consequently easy to observe. No sure data as to its approaching continent. There have been sightings, but identification by binoculars is risky. Not migratory but sometimes carried by storms as far as North America. Also called *Fura-buxo*. *P. a. arminjoniana* is a geographic replacement of Kermadec Petrel, *P. neglecta*, of Pacific and Indian Oceans (Mauritius).

Six other *Pterodroma* occasionally visit Brazilian waters. Their bodies are sometimes thrown up on beaches:

HOODED PETREL, *Pterodroma incerta*, Fura-buxo-de-capuz   SV

44 cm; wingspan 110 cm. Large chocolate-colored species, dark also under wings and tail, but with white-speckled throat, white belly. Common in south Atlantic. Breeds on Tristão da Cunha, appears in Rio Grande do Sul waters, about 100 km off coast, in reasonable numbers September–November, and dead on beaches (Cassino, November) Santa Catarina (Florianópolis, November), Rio de Janeiro (November).

The five remaining species, with even more accidental occurrences in our territory, are:

KERGUELEN PETREL, *Pterodroma brevirostris*   SV
Bahia, September 1985; Rio Grande do Sul, October 1986.

WHITE-HEADED PETREL, *Pterodroma lessonii*   SV
Rio Grande do Sul (Costalunga et al. 1988), Santa Catarina (T. R. Azevedo 1989 pers. comm.).

BLACK-CAPPED PETREL, *Pterodroma hasitata*   NV
High seas, Ilha Trindade.

SOFT-PLUMAGED PETREL, *Pterodroma mollis*   SV
Rio Grande do Sul, March.

GREAT-WINGED PETREL, *Pterodroma macroptera* SV
High seas, Santa Catarina, Rio Grande do Sul.

Fig. 46. Cape Petrel, *Daption capense,* showing the typical mottled pattern.

BLUE PETREL, *Halobaena caerulea* SV

29 cm. Similar to *Pachyptila,* forehead whitish. Búzios, Cabo Frio (Rio de Janeiro), July 1984 (Teixeira et al. 1985).

DOVE PRION, *Pachyptila desolata,*
Pardela-de-bico-de-pato SV

29 cm. Similar to *P. belcheri* but with wide, swollen bill (13.6–16 mm wide vs. 11.5 mm or less for *belcheri*) having very distinct lamellae (see "Morphology . . ."). São Paulo (July, August), Rio de Janeiro (July), Pernambuco (July). Sometimes considered conspecific with *belcheri.*

SLENDER-BILLED PRION, *Pachyptila belcheri,*
Faigão SV

28 cm. Smallest procellariid. Bill unique (see *P. desolata*). Upperparts bluish gray, underparts white. Black band on wings links scapulars to bend of wing, and this to primaries, so in flight bird shows distinctive black M (characteristic of entire genus). Gregarious, like congeners. Pelagic; recorded on coast only when kills occur. On 30 August 1972 in Búzios (Rio de Janeiro), remains of 200 individuals were counted on 1 km of beach. There were also bodies of *desolata*. On 25 August 1972, more dead *belcheri* were found on beach of Jacarepaguá (ex-Guanabara), 150 km away via beach. Surely both findings were evidence of same kill, which gives an idea of dimensions of the disaster. I do not know how many kilometers beyond these beaches bodies may have been spread. Other kills have been recorded in São Paulo (June–August) and Rio Grande do Sul (June). Also called *Gaivota* (Rio Grande do Sul), *Pardela* (ex-Guanabara).

WHITE-CHINNED PETREL, *Procellaria aequinoctialis,*
Pardela-preta SV

55 cm; wingspan 138 cm. Large with narrow wings. All sooty with chin either white (not always visible in flight) or dark like body. Bill relatively short but heavy, whitish with black design. Abundant southern migrant on high seas (Rio Grande do Sul, April), with isolated individuals appearing on beaches. São Paulo, Rio de Janeiro (April, August), Marajó Island, mouth of Tocantins (Pará). Also called *Pardelão-de-queixo-branco, Corva-de-bico-branco.* Mentioned by Marcgrave (1648).

GRAY PETREL, *Procellaria cinerea,* Pardela-cinza
SV

One found dead on beach in November 1982 at Rio Grande (32°S), Rio Grande do Sul (Vooren and Fernandes 1989).

CORY'S SHEARWATER, *Puffinus diomedea,*
Bobo-grande NV

49 cm. Same size and aspect as *P. gravis,* differing from it in lighter, brownish cap, dark-tipped yellowish bill. Migrant from north; appears on high seas off Pernambuco, Bahia, and Espírito Santo in May. Two individuals banded on Ilha Selvagem (between Madeira and Canaries) were found dead on Ceará coast (December) and in Rio Grande do Sul (Tramandaí, February). A 3d, unbanded, carcass appeared on Santa Catarina coast in December, another in Rio de Janeiro in June.

GREATER SHEARWATER, *Puffinus gravis,*
Bobo-grande-de-sobre-branco SV

50 cm; wingspan 111 cm. One of largest procellariids. Distinguishable by dark sooty cap and mantle and black wings and tail, which contrast with white collar, band at base of tail, and underparts. Bill black, webs rosy. Southern migrant that appears in considerable numbers during regular migration (see "Migration"). Comes close to coast in large flocks along Rio Grande do Sul littoral September–November; between April–May is again in Brazilian waters (Ceará, Paraíba, Bahia) on its way to North Atlantic. Sometimes flocks of 50–100 fly around ships near littoral (Búzios, Rio de Janeiro, May). A carcass was found on beach (ex-Guanabara, July). Nests in large colonies on Tristão da Cunha archipelago September–April and probably also on Falklands. Also called *Pardela.*

SOOTY SHEARWATER, *Puffinus griseus,*
Bobo-escuro SV

44 cm. Medium sized, all sooty except for white undersides of wings. Bill and webs black. Infrequent southern migrant. Rio Grande do Sul (May, August); Barra da Tijuca, Rio de Janeiro (July); Bahia. One of world's most numerous birds.

MANX SHEARWATER, *Puffinus puffinus,*
Bobo-pequeno NV

35 cm. Small, slender billed. Upperparts uniformly black, including sides of head and neck; underparts white. Breeds only at 5 years of age (see "Migration"). *P. p. puffinus* breeds in Europe (also Iceland, Bermudas; other races in Hawaii, New Zealand, etc.) and during northern winter migrates to South Atlantic where it remains some months on high seas. During this period not uncommon in our waters. In 1962, 9 individuals banded in England were found between Rio Grande do Sul and ex-Guanabara. Among these, an individual captured 16 October in Caraguatatuba (São Paulo) had been banded 45 days earlier in Skokholm, Wales, as a nestling. Another individual, found dead on northern tip of Santa Catarina island (Praia Brava) on 25 September 1980, was banded 30 August 1970 in Skokholm. Through November 1975, 80 individuals banded in England had been recorded in Brazilian waters. Banded specimens have also been found in Uruguay and Argentina. Also called *Pardela, Corva, Furabuxo.*

LITTLE SHEARWATER, *Puffinus assimilis*
One specimen captured on Fernando de Noronha 21 March 1989 (Antas 1990). There have been subsequent press

reports of a small colony there (*Jornal do Brasil*, 23 August 1990).

Procellariidae Bibliography

See also General Bibliography

Brenning, U., and W. Manke. 1971. *Beitr. Vogelk.* 17:89–103. [Migration]

Cooke, F., and L. Mills. 1972. Summer distribution of pelagic birds off the coast of Argentina. *Ibis* 114:245–51.

Costalunga, A. L., and A. Chiaradia. 1988. Sobre a mortalidade de Procellariiformes na praia do Cassino, Rio Grande do Sul. *XV Congr. Bras. Zool., Curitiba:*466.

Gill, F. B., C. Jouanin, and R. W. Storer. 1970. *Auk* 87:514–21. [*Pterodroma arminjoniana,* biology]

Harris, M. P., and L. Hansen. 1974. *Dansk orn. Foren Tidsskr.* 68:117–37. [Migration]

Haverschmidt, F. 1971. *J. Orn.* 112:459–60. [*Puffinus,* migration]

Johnstone, G. W. 1974. *Emu* 74(4):209–18. [*Macronectes,* twin species]

Mees, G. F. 1976. *Zool. Meded. Rijksmus. Leiden* 49(20):269–71. [Kills]

Metcalf, W. G. 1966. Observations of migrating *Puffinus gravis* off the Brazilian coast. *Ibis* 108:138–40.

Novaes, F. C. 1952. *Rev. Bras. Biol.* 12:219–28. [*Pterodroma,* Trindade]

Perrins, C. M., et al. 1973. *Ibis* 115:535–48. [*Puffinus,* populations]

Rumboll, M.A.E., and J. R. Jehl. 1977. Observations on pelagic birds in the south Atlantic Ocean in the austral spring. *San Diego Soc. Nat. Hist. Tras.* 1(1):1–16.

Stresemann, E., and V. Stresemann. 1970. *J. Orn.* 111:378–92. [Molt and migration]

Teixeira, D. M. 1985. Notas sobre os faigões do gênero *Pachyptila* no Brasil. *XII Cong. Bras. Zool., Campinas:*545.

Teixeira, D. M., J. B. Nacinovic, and R. Novelli. 1985. Notes on some Brazilian seabirds. *Bull. B.O.C.* 105(2):49–51.

Thomson, A. L. 1969. *L'Oiseau* 35:130–40. [*Puffinus,* migration]

Vooren, C. M., and A. C. Fernandes. 1989. See Diomedeidae Bibliography.

FAMILY HYDROBATIDAE: STORM-PETRELS (4)

These are among the smallest seabirds. A Wilson's Storm-Petrel, *Oceanites oceanicus,* weighs only 20 g, whereas an albatross, also a Procellariiform, may weigh more than 9 kg. There are fossils from the upper Miocene of California (10 million years B.P.).

Behavior

Storm-petrels are only swallow sized and fly so close to the sea that they quickly disappear behind the waves. Their erratic flight can resemble that of a bat, and they maneuver with dangling feet as if walking on the water's surface; thus the names *Calçamar, Ave de São Pedro, Petrel, Danzarin.* Their legs are so weak that on the ground they must drag themselves along on their bellies with their wings (see also Procellariidae, "Morphology . . . "). Crepuscular and nocturnal like many Procellariiformes, they are also active during the day. Re their sense of smell, see Procellariidae, "Morphology. . . ." Sea salt (sodium chloride) is excreted from salt glands through tubular-shaped nostrils in a jet similar to that of a water pistol (see Laridae, "Feeding . . . "). During storms, storm-petrels take refuge in bays and even ports. They breed on oceanic islands, outside Brazil. They are not related to swallows, swifts, or terns.

WILSON'S STORM-PETREL, *Oceanites oceanicus,* Alma-de-mestre   SV   Fig. 48

18 cm. Slender with short, almost rectangular tail. All sooty with white rump. Legs longer than tail and have yellow webs, prominent in flight. Southern visitor that nests in Falk-lands, among other places, but reaches North Atlantic. Common in Brazilian waters on high seas, tap-dancing on surface and even making small jumps while fishing; sometimes in flocks, e.g., between Rio de Janeiro and Cabo Frio (May, in association with Black-browed Albatross, *Diomedea melanophris*), or alone among islands (Santos, São Paulo, May, July); ex-Guanabara (November); Rio de Janeiro (May,

Fig. 48. Wilson's Storm-Petrel, *Oceanites oceanicus.*

August, November); Pernambuco (March). Also called *Andorinha-das-tormentas*.

LEACH'S STORM-PETREL, *Oceanodroma leucorhoa*, Tapereira   NV

21 cm. Relatively long, somewhat forked tail with edges not very clean-cut. Short legs, black webs. White rump, divided longitudinally by black area. Amapá (May, December), Bahia (February). Migrant from North Atlantic.

WHITE-BELLIED STORM-PETREL, *Fregetta grallaria*   SV

20 cm. Upperside blackish with white rump. Underside white, including under wing coverts. Very similar to *F. tropica*. On high seas between Rio de Janeiro and Bahia. (October, Coelho et al. 1985).

BLACK-BELLIED STORM-PETREL, *Fregetta tropica*   SV

Off St. Paul's Rocks and Fernando de Noronha (Teixeira et al. 1986).

Hydrobatidae Bibliography

Coelho, E. P., A. S. Alves, and M.L.L. Soneghet. 1985. Levantamento da avifauna pelágica no percurso Rio de Janeiro-Salvador a bordo do navio oceanográfico Almirante Saldanha. *XII Cong. Zool. Bras. Campinas:* 266.

Escalante, R. 1988. El Petrel de Las Tormentas de Leach, *Oceanodroma leucorhoa,* en Uruguay. *Comun. Zool. Mus. Histor. Nat. Montevideo* 12:167.

Teixeira, D. M., D. Oren, and R. Best. 1986. Notes on Brazilian seabirds, 2. *Bull. B.O.C.* 106:74–77.

FAMILY PELECANOIDIDAE: DIVING-PETRELS (1)

These small marine birds are quite reminiscent of the Alcidae (e.g., puffins, *Fratercula*) of the Northern Hemisphere—a remarkable example of convergent evolution. They swim and dive more than fly and even have block molt (see Anatidae). In diving they use the wings as paddles (see Spheniscidae). Flight is vibrant, very low above the surface of the sea.

MAGELLANIC DIVING-PETREL, *Pelecanoides magellani*   SV

20 cm. Upperparts black, underparts white. Vestigial white collar visible on side; secondaries have white tips; scapulars may (adult) or may not (immature) have white pattern. Southern coast of Rio Grande do Sul. Breeds in southern Patagonia and Chile.

Pelecanoididae Bibliography

Vooren, C. M. 1985. Migrações e ocorrência de aves marinhas na costa sul do Brasil. *XII Cong. Bras. Zool, Campinas:* 266.

ORDER SPHENISCIFORMES

FAMILY SPHENISCIDAE: PENGUINS (3)

Penguins are oceanic birds par excellence that are confined to the Southern Hemisphere. They are the most typical and most numerous birds of the subantarctic (south of 35°S) and antarctic (Antarctic Circle at approximately 66°S) zones, comprising more than 90% of the biomass of those regions' avifauna. Of the 18 species, 7 are found in South America. One breeds on the Peruvian and Chilean coast, another on the Galapagos Islands, and five on the Falkland Islands. Penguins reach Brazil only as migrants. There are numerous Tertiary fossils from the upper Eocene (40 million years B.P.). *Palaeoeudyptes,* from Seymour Island, Antarctica, reached gigantic proportions. There is a certain relationship with albatross ancestors, from which penguins became separated in the Mesozoic. Spheniscidae and Pelicanoididae take the place in the Southern Hemisphere of the Alcidae family (Suborder Alcae, Order Charadriiformes) of northern regions. Penguin bones have been found in archaeological sites (kitchen middens) about 4000 years B.P., showing that the prehistoric occupants used penguins for subsistence. These sites have also produced sculptured animal figures in polished stone with modern-type abstract design, such as a 30-cm swimming penguin.

Morphology, Special Adaptations, and Behavior

Although unable to fly, penguins descended from flying species. They lack feather tracts, the feathers being distributed equally over the entire surface like the hairs of mammals. Of all birds, penguins are best adapted to live in water and are thus highly specialized. They are heavy, and their bones are not pneumatic. They come to the surface only to breathe or rest. They can float freely and turn on their sides. They have thicker necks and bills than cormorants (*Phalacrocorax*). Penguins paddle with their wings, which have been transformed into flippers, effectively "flying" underwater. The webbed feet are used as a rudder. The first toe (hind toe of other birds) is pointed more or less forward and forms part of the web. The legs are short and situated far to the rear. The tail is very short and in some species almost rudimentary. It must be emphasized that penguins have feathers (even highly specialized ones) like other birds, so it is unfortunate that the name Impennes ("featherless") is used for the penguin superorder. The nostrils are almost imperceptible slits. Penguins have well-developed nasal glands that excrete the high concentration of sodium chloride found in sea water (see Lâridae, "Feeding . . . "). The lateral position of the eyes does not permit binocular vision. These birds see very well underwater, where they catch all their food; outside the water their vision is reduced. Apparently they are capable of underwater echolocation (see Steatornithidae).

As an adaptation to cold, penguins have a thick layer of fat and a dense cushion of feathers that holds a large amount of air. Constantly swimming to the water's surface, they produce heat through incessant movement. They swim with remarkable speed, fleeing from their enemy, the Southern Sea Lion (*Otaria byronia*), which catches only the weakest penguins. Penguins reportedly can swim 10 m per second and 36 to 40 km per hour. They can stay submerged for some minutes, the large species 30 minutes or more. They dive to depths of more than 10 m. They live on small fish, squid, and planktonic crustaceans, especially krill (*Euphausia superba*), the principal food of whales. The *Spheniscus*, with strong bills, catch schooling fish near the surface.

Penguins go ashore only where they breed or when exhausted. They walk erect, "sit" on the tail, and slide on the belly.

Breeding

Penguins breed around the end of the year in large colonies in the far south, either on oceanic islands or on the mainland coast in regions of abundant marine life, under either antarctic or subantarctic climatic conditions. The Magellanic Penguin, *Spheniscus magellanicus*, digs a burrow where it incubates. During this period it brays a lot, day and night (*burro*). The *Eudyptes* are adapted to rocky places, nesting on gravel areas without digging into the earth. Penguins' fearlessness of people is impressive.

Migration and Mortality

After breeding penguins abandon their colonies in March and are pelagic until September, usually remaining in the continental-shelf area. Travelers at sea begin to see penguins and other oceanic birds, such as procellariids and skuas, about 65 km offshore.

Penguins are brought to Brazilian waters by cold currents (Falkland Current) and storms, but they also deliberately migrate by swimming. Ninety-five percent of these birds are young of the year, surplus to the population, that do not return to their region of origin. They often arrive weakened and "shipwrecked," perhaps because of lack of nutrition in the barren tropical sea (see Procellariidae, "Mortality").

Penguins frequently suffer from aspergillosis of the respiratory tract and from worm infestations (Acanthocephala). A sodium chloride deficiency favors the development of mycosis, as shown by individuals held in captivity. Penguins are very sensitive to water or air pollution. DDT was discovered in antarctic waters in 1981. Organochlorate pesticides have been discovered in the fat of antarctic penguins.

A new and grave peril, without any selective value, now menaces penguins: petroleum pollution. Oiled plumage loses its ability to protect the body against cold. Soybean oil has been used to clean oiled penguins. The Brazilian navy has carried penguins captured on the coast out to the Falkland Current in the high seas.

Occasionally the sea throws hundreds of dead penguins onto the beaches of Santa Catarina and Rio Grande do Sul (see Procellariidae, "Mortality"). A small necrophagous crustacean (*Excirolana braziliensis*) has been found in the nasal cavity of dead penguins.

MAGELLANIC PENGUIN, *Spheniscus magellanicus*, Pingüim-de-magalhães   SV   Fig. 49

65 cm; 4.5 kg. Adult has 2 black bands across upper breast, not very visible when bird is floating. Sexes similar. Immatures lack distinctive breast marking. Immatures predominate in Brazil (see "Migration") and vary greatly in color. Chile and Argentina; colonies closest to Brazil are on coast of Patagonia.

Does not get far from land, even on migration, remaining in continental-shelf area (60–100 km offshore), where in shallower waters there are more fish (sardines) and other aquatic organisms. (This also determines occurrence of other

Fig. 49. Magellanic Penguin, *Spheniscus magellanicus*, immature, swimming.

marine birds, e.g., petrels.) Fishes in flocks, sometimes just beyond or within breaker line (Rio Grande do Sul). In winter (May–August) gets as far as Rio de Janeiro, Bahia, rarely Alagoas, even invading bays, e.g., Sepetiba, Rio de Janeiro, and Todos os Santos, Bahia. Most arrive in July and August, but birds occasionally appear as late as October. In some years beaches, e.g., Laguna, Santa Catarina, are covered with penguin cadavers after southerly and southeast winds. On 14 July 1971 an individual banded as a chick in Punta Tombo (Chubut, Argentina) on 15 January of same year was found at Barra da Tijuca, Rio de Janeiro, 2500 km away in a straight line. Three other banded *magellanicus* were recovered same year at Florianópolis, Itapema, and at Pântano do Sul, Santa Catarina, in July and August. Clips on flippers are used to mark penguins. South of São Paulo *magellanicus* sometimes appears alongside Great Grebe, *Podiceps major,* or more commonly with Neotropic Cormorant, *Phalacrocorax brasilianus* (see "Morphology"). Also called *Pato-marinho, Pato-do-mar* (Santa Catarina).

MACARONI PENGUIN, *Eudyptes chrysolophus,*
Pingüim-testa-amarela   SV

Sides of head have tufts of orange-colored feathers, linked across forehead by orange band. Antarctic and subantarctic, nests in Falklands and other subantarctic zones of world. Occasionally wanders to Rio Grande do Sul: mouth of Arroio Chui, 5 July 1964, a flock of more than 10 completely exhausted individuals. Also called *Pingüino-macaroni, Pingüino-de-penacho-anaranjado* (Argentina).

ROCKHOPPER PENGUIN, *Eudyptes crestatus,*
Pingüim-penacho-amarelo   SV

Very similar to *E. chrysolophus* but smaller and with pale yellow tufts not connected by band. There is a specimen in museum at Pelotas, Rio Grande do Sul, and a female was found dead on beach at Mostardas, Rio Grande do Sul (August 1980, F. Silva and C. Taffarel). Comes more regularly to Uruguay. Subantarctic zone, breeds in Falklands and southern South America.

Spheniscidae Bibliography

Barbieri, E., and R. M. Sperb. 1988. Tratamento de pingüins "petrolizados," *Spheniscus magellanicus. V Cong. Bras. Zool, Curitiba:*464.

Belton, W. 1978. Supplementary list of new birds for Rio Grande do Sul, Brazil. *Auk* 95(2):413.

Brenning, U., and W. Mahnke. 1971. *Beitr. Vogelk.* 17:89–103. [Migration]

Jacobus, A. L., M. Gazzaneo, and S. Momberger. 1988. Presença de *Spheniscus magellanicus* em sítios arqueológicos. *XV Cong. Bras. Zool. Curitiba:*465.

Novelli, R. 1986. Gaivotas e Trinta-réis. *Ciência Hoje* 4(24):34–37.

Pettingill, O. S., Jr. 1964. *The Living Bird* 3:45-64. [Behavior]

Sander, M., M. N. Strieder, M. V. Petry, et al. 1986. Adequação e confeção de material para a captura e anilhamento de aves marinhas: rede, anilhas e canhão. *II En. Nac. An. Aves, Rio de Janeiro:* 223.

Zusi, R. L. 1974. An interpretation of skull structure in penguins. In Stonehouse, *The Biology of Penguins.* New York: Macmillan.

ORDER PELECANIFORMES

FAMILY PHAETHONTIDAE: TROPICBIRDS (2)

These marine birds have a pantropical distribution. They resemble terns but are not related. There are fossils from the lower Tertiary (Eocene, 50 millions years B.P.) of England and the Quaternary of Bermuda (8,000 years B.P.).

Morphology, Behavior, and Breeding

Tropicbirds are pigeon sized and resemble those birds in form and in their swift, direct manner of flight, which carries them undisturbed through storms.

Their central rectrices are extremely elongated and narrowed from the middle to the end, giving a graceful appearance unequaled among marine birds. The tips of these lengthy feathers break during nesting. The bill is strong and sharp, with external nostrils (unlike boobies). The edges of the mandibles are serrated. Sexes are identical.

Tropicbirds dive into the sea from a considerable height (like boobies), submerging 3–4 m to capture fish and squid. The feet are well webbed (see Pelecanidae "Morphology"). On the Abrolhos islands their principal food is flying fish (Coelho 1981). They rest on the water with the tail raised and float with greater ease than gulls, but they cannot walk properly and cannot stand. They take flight with some difficulty and land on the belly. Their voices are ternlike.

Tropicbirds breed on oceanic islands on escarpments with holes, where they lay densely spotted eggs on sand or among stones. The eggs are unlike those of other Pelecaniformes, which are uniformly white or bluish. Two nestlings have been recorded for the Red-billed Tropicbird, *Phaethon aethereus* (Abrolhos). Tropicbirds compete with other marine birds and will oust petrels from their burrows. The long, 28-day incubation period and the youngs' 63-day stay in the nest of the White-tailed Tropicbird, *Phaethon lepturus,* are typical for birds that are little menaced during breeding.

RED-BILLED TROPICBIRD, *Phaethon aethereus,* Rabo-de-palha   Fig. 50

Length about 1 m, of which almost 40 cm is tail. White, back streaked and wings tipped with black. Inner vane of primaries dark. Bill coral red. Immature has short tail, yellow bill. Nests in Abrolhos (south of Bahia) and Fernando

Fig. 50. Red-billed Tropicbird, *Phaethon aethereus.*

de Noronha (March 1984, Teixeira et al. 1985). Apparently no record of it on Ilha Trindade. Occurs regularly in Pacific, Caribbean, other warm seas. Also called *Rabo-de-junco, Grazina* (Abrolhos).

WHITE-TAILED TROPICBIRD, *Phaethon lepturus*

Somewhat smaller than *P. aethereus,* noticeable when seen together. Differs also in all-white back and orange bill. Immature similar to that of *aethereus,* but smaller. Fernando de Noronha, Caribbean, other warm seas.

Phaethontidae Bibliography

Coelho, A. G. 1981. *Univers. Fed. Pernambuco, Publ. Avuls.* 1. [Biology]

Teixeira, D. M., et al. 1985. See Procellariidae Bibliography.

FAMILY SULIDAE: BOOBIES (4)

This is a widely distributed family of marine birds. A large number of fossils have been found, dating since the lower Oligocene of France (35 million years B.P.).

Morphology, Special Adaptations, Behavior, and Migration

Boobies are gull sized but have longer, narrower wings. The unique tail is wedge shaped. The feet have large webs (See Pelecanidae). The pointed, saw-edged bill does not have external nostrils, which may be an adaptation to avoid sea water entering the respiratory ducts as the birds hit the water

when they perform their headlong dives for fish. However, tropicbirds also make high dives but have nostrils that open externally. The most obvious consequence of having internal nostrils is that boobies must breath with their mouths open, as do cormorants. The nostrils of *Sula* embryos open externally.

An albino Brown Booby, *Sula leucogaster,* has been seen on the coast of Rio de Janeiro (Coelho et al. 1987).

Nasal glands, as in other marine birds, excrete salt. A system of subcutaneous pneumatic cushions, widely scattered on the underparts of boobies and tropicbirds, and of large air sacs in the musculature are believed to have the role of protecting the birds against the violent impact of hitting the water when they dive, but this pneumaticism is characteristic of most Pelecaniformes. The Blue-footed Booby, *S. nebouxii,* of the Ecuadorian coast reportedly dives into the sea at a speed of 100 km/hr, or 30.56 m/sec (Rüppell 1975). The Northern Gannet, *Morus bassanus* can dive more than 20 m deep. Tropical seas offer the best conditions for this type of fishing, for their waters are very transparent (because of the scarcity of plankton) and permit visibility for several meters below the surface.

The fishing method of our *S. leucogaster* is frequently unspectacular. It surreptitiously steals the bait of fishermen, and it does some group fishing. A strong head wind helps it pause in the air to observe fish schools. It catches small fish such as sardines and weakfish.

When not fishing, boobies fly in long lines close to the water, alternating a series of wing beats with a glide. To take off from the water, they need to run a few meters to get up speed, but when perched on rocks they jump into the air.

I have noted *S. leucogaster* movements along the Rio de Janeiro littoral that apparently are in the nature of regular migration. One of the first boobies banded as a nestling in Santa Catarina was recovered on Ilha do Governador, Rio de Janeiro.

Breeding

Boobies breed in island colonies. Here they become noisy, their voices like the barking of dogs. At other seasons they remain silent. The Masked Booby, *S. dactylatra,* and *S. leucogaster* nest on the ground. The latter's nest of small stones or vegetable material may be neatly arranged, depending on the locale. The Red-footed Booby, *S. sula,* reportedly builds its nest on trees or atop heaps of sticks when the woodland has been destroyed, as on Ilha Trindade, where, however, Olson (1981) found it nesting on the ground. Each species forms its own colony, separate from neighboring species. On Atol das Rocas, *S. dactylatra* nests within the great colonies of Sooty Terns, *Sterna fuscata.* Breeding activity of *S. leucogaster* has been recorded during most of the year. Colonies may have many thousands of pairs, as does *Morus bassanus* in Europe.

Boobies lay two small eggs covered with a bluish white calcareous crust which, if scratched, reveals a bluish brown background (*S. leucogaster*). They place their feet on top of the eggs, like other Pelecaniformes, apparently more to hold them and clasp them against the abdomen than to warm them, for the temperature of the feet is not high enough for incubation. They do not have brood patches. The incubation period of *S. leucogaster* varies from 40 to 42 days. Normally only one chick develops. Hatched featherless, it is susceptible to the sun and can die if not shaded. Adults and young cool themselves on hot days by panting and by fluttering the gular sac, or, when flying, the feet. The second egg is called "the insurance egg." When the first chick hatches, the second egg is thrown out of the nest.

S. leucogaster parents may reveal nervousness by picking up a stick with the bill, reminiscent of nest construction, and do the same in prenuptial displays (displacement activity). Sexes are distinguishable by the color of the bare face, which changes during the breeding cycle. Vocalizations also differ.

Guano

On the islands most used by these birds, excrement accumulates to form a substance known as guano. An analysis of this material from Ilha dos Alcatrazes (São Paulo) showed the following composition: water 6.32%; organic material 22.25%; and mineral material 71.42%, which included 0.97% nitrogen, 2.94% phosphorus, and 0.56% potash. Compared with accumulations on the coastal rocks of Peru, the quantity of guano on the Brazilian coast is small; there are a small number of producing birds, and frequent rains remove the feces at short intervals. This is also the case on St. Paul's Rocks, situated in the mid-Atlantic, where there are large colonies of *S. leucogaster;* Brown Noddies, *Anous stolidus;* and Lesser Noddies, *A. tenuirostris.* In the 1800s a small guano deposit produced by *S. sula* nesting in trees was mined on Fernando de Noronha. Both in Peru and on the South African coast, each of which has a very dry climate, the trio of boobies, cormorants, and pelicans has contributed to guano deposition. Compare the guano of insectivorous birds such as swifts (see Apodidae, "Swift Grottoes . . . ").

Nest Fauna

S. leucogaster and *S. dactylatra* nests may harbor characteristic fauna: large ticks (146 individuals of 1 species were taken from a single *S. leucogaster* nest), pseudoscorpions, and beetles of the Tenebrionidae and Trogidae families (Abrolhos archipelago, Bahia, J. Becker, in Coelho 1981).

Parasites

Boobies are parasitized by blood-sucking flies. *Olfersia aenescens* (Hippoboscidae) is a multihost species that torments other Pelecaniformes, Procellariiformes, and Charadriiformes. Nests of various tropical marine birds are said to be severely infested by argasid ticks that may transmit a fatal arbovirus causing nests and even entire colonies of *Sterna fuscata* to be abandoned.

Enemies

Like various other marine birds, boobies are pestered by Frigatebirds, *Fregata.* To escape these attacks, they jettison ballast by vomiting fish they have eaten, thus providing the

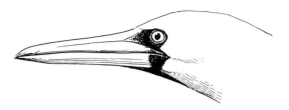

Fig. 51. Masked Booby, *Sula dactylatra.*

precise booty the frigatebird is after. Sometimes boobies try to evade a frigatebird attack by diving. On islands close to the continent, chicks are victims of vultures.

Legends and Names

Boobies are said to be the birds that drew Columbus's attention to the proximity of land. Most species of this family do not get far from shore (see also Fregatidae).

The name *alcatraz,* apparently of Arabic origin, is the more correct Portuguese designation for *Sula* species but not for the *Fregata.*

Pollution

In recent years boobies killed by eating fish poisoned by oceanic pollution have been found on the beaches of Rio de Janeiro.

MASKED BOOBY, *Sula dactylatra*, Atobá-grande
Fig. 51

86 cm. Largest booby. White, like *S. sula,* but with blackish remiges and rectrices, dark blue tone on face and throat, orange or red at base of bill, and olivaceous or plumbeous feet. Dives vertically from 10 or more m into deep water, submerging several meters in pursuit of fish. Nests on Abrolhos (September), Atol das Rocas, Fernando de Noronha. Appears periodically on Ilha Trindade. Has been observed on high seas off Recife (Pernambuco, May). Regular but infrequent visitor to certain coastal points: Cabo Frio, São Tomé bank, Macaé (Rio de Janeiro) (apparently nests at latter two, and Salvador, Bahia. Also Santa Catarina (Moleques do Sul, January 1983, 1 individual, Lenir Rosário pers. comm.). Widely distributed in Southern Hemisphere. Also called *Piloto-branco* (Albrolhos).

RED-FOOTED BOOBY, *Sula sula*,
Atobá-de-pés-vermelhos

70 cm. Small, appearing only accidentally on our coast. White, like *dactylatra,* but with smaller build and only wingtips black. Bill bluish with red base. Nests on Fernando de Noronha, Trindade. Recorded flying over high seas north of Salvador, Bahia, with *S. dactylatra* (May 1964, Vogelsang pers. comm.). Two individuals observed on Ilha Redonda, off Rio de Janeiro, being pursued by *S. leucogaster* (summer 1978, Victor Wellisch). Wide-ranging, also occurs in Pacific. Most pelagic *Sula.*

BROWN BOOBY, *Sula leucogaster*, Atobá, Alcatraz
PL 2.5

74 cm. Most common booby on our coast. Dark brown, lower breast and belly white, bill whitish. Sexes are distinguishable by bare-part colors, especially region around eye (including eyelids), which is dark bluish in male, light yellow in female. Female also has blackish spot in front of eye ("false eye"); male has dark, ill-defined loral spot. Face and feet colors match but vary according to population, age, season, and breeding phase. In general male smaller, has more color variation, and has much weaker voice (vocalization within colony). Female stands out because of heavier bill. Immature uniformly dark brown, lighter on abdomen, with light gray bill; at a distance may resemble a skua, *Stercorarius.* Nestling all white. First definitive feathers to sprout are black remiges and rectrices.

Unlike *S. dactylatra,* this species fishes by diving obliquely from medium heights, generally into shallow water near beaches and rocks, submerging completely. To take flight it runs some steps on water surface. At nightfall flies single file close to water toward islands where it roosts. Nests on islands such as those of Albrolhos archipelago (Bahia, September), Macaé (Rio de Janeiro, July), Ilhas das Cagarras (ex-Guanabara, September forward). Nest is a small concavity in ground, lightly lined (see "Breeding"). On nesting islands roosts peacefully alongside frigatebirds (see "Enemies") and does not even attack vultures perched on ground (though it attacks if they overfly). When perching on clumps of cactus (*Cereus*) sometimes punctures webs between toes (Ilha do Francês, Macaé, Rio de Janeiro). In breeding season active day and night.

Tropical and subtropical, ranging south to Paraná and Santa Catarina and may even reach Argentina. A colony on Ilha Moleques do Sul, 9.6 km off south coast of Ilha de Santa Catarina, appears to be most southerly nesting place in South America. Also Pacific Ocean and other warm-climate seas around globe. Also called *Mergulhão, Mumbebo* (Pernambuco), *Freira, Piloto, Piloto-pardo* (Abrolhos).

AUSTRALASIAN GANNET, *Morus serrator*,
Atobá-da-Austrália   SV

Superspecies *M. bassanus* of Europe (large, white, with extensive yellow on nape, black primaries, white tail or with central rectrices black) has 2 tropical replacements, very similar to each other and not separable at a distance: Cape Gannet, *M. capensis,* and Australasian Gannet, *M. serrator.* One of these was recorded on high seas off Rio Grande do Sul in July 1982 and in April 1983 by Vooren (1985). I have concluded that an individual caught off Santa Catarina coast on Ilha Moleques do Sul by Lenir Bege et al. (1987) in June 1987 is *serrator.* Length 100 cm, gular stripe only 45 mm (gular stripe of *capensis* and *bassanus* is much longer). Prepared specimen has been deposited in National Museum, Rio de Janeiro.

Sulidae Bibliography
See also General Bibliography

Bege, L. R., and B. T. Pauli, 1987. Primeiro registro de *Sula serrator* no Brasil. *III En. Nac. An. Aves*:25.

Coelho, A. G. 1981. *Univers. Fed. Pernambuco, Publ. Avuls: 1.* [Biology]

Coelho, E. P., and V. S. Alves. 1987. Um caso de albinismo no atobá-marrom, *Sula leucogaster XIV. Cong. Bras. Zool., Juiz de Fora*:402.

Howell, T. R., and G. R. Bartholomew. 1962. *Condor* 64, 1. [Temperature regulation]

Nelson, J. B. 1972. *Proc. 15th Int. Orn. Cong., The Hague*:371–88. [Behavior]

Nelson, J. B. 1978. *The Sulidae, Gannets and Boobies*. Oxford. [Monograph]

Nicoll, M. J. 1904. *Ibis* 4(8): 32–66. [*Sula leucogaster*, breeding]

Olson, S. L. 1981. See General Bibliography.

Rüppell, G. 1975. *J. Orn.* 116:168–80. [Diving]

Simmons, K.E.L. 1967. *The Living Bird* 6:187–212. [Ecology]

Vooren, C. M. 1985. Migração e ocorrências de aves marinhas na costa sul do Brasil. XII Cong. Bras. Zool., Campinas:266–67.

White, S. J., R.E.C. White, and W. H. Thorpe. 1970. Acoustic basis for individual recognition by voice in the Gannet, *Sula bassana. Nature* 225 (5238):1156-58.

FAMILY PELECANIDAE: PELICANS (2)

Pelicans are large aquatic birds found in certain areas of North and South America and the Old World. There is a Miocene fossil from Argentina (20 million years B.P.).

Morphology

The bill is disproportionately long and the tongue almost rudimentary. An elastic gular pouch (scarcely noticeable when empty) expands broadly to the sides and serves as a fishing net, not as a storage place.

Among the few distinctive external morphological characteristics of pelicans and other Pelecaniformes are the extensive webs joining the four toes, including, in contrast to the Anseriformes, the hallux.

There are many legends about pelicans. They were domesticated in ancient Egypt and venerated by the Mohammedans. The symbol of the pelican that fed its young with its own blood achieved special popularity and later became emblematic of the sacrifice of Christ. This peculiar legend was based on the fact that the pelican regurgitates food that its young feed on deep in the parental crop.

BROWN PELICAN, *Pelecanus occidentalis*,
Pelicano-pardo   NV   Fig. 52

126 cm; wingspan 2 m. Occasional visitor to northern Brazil. Flies slowly in single file flocks close to water with neck folded back. After a few wing beats, frequency of which is like that of Frigatebirds, *Fregata,* glides. Frequently glides at great altitudes for long periods. At rest on water floats like a cork, holding wings partly up and tip of bill against breast, watching fish that may pass nearby. Also fishes in shallow waters, and while flying over sea dives into water with great force. Roosts at night in mangroves. Nests

in Antilles, etc., migrating south in small numbers along continental coast as far as Amazon, sometimes going up its course (Rio Tapajós, Rio Branco). On Peruvian coast, where it is called *alcatraz,* it is among principal guano producers. Accidental on Rio de Janeiro coast (Mitchell 1957). Also called *Pelicano-do-mar.*

Fig. 52. Brown Pelican, *Pelecanus occidentalis.*

WHITE PELICAN, *Pelecanus erythrorhynchos*,
Pelicano-branco   NV

A white pelican that fished for 2 days at mouth of Guanabara Bay and flew as far as Urca was recorded by Victor Wellisch, Rio de Janeiro, in December 1960. If not an albino, it could only be this species, which normally migrates from North America only to Guatemala and accidentally to Cuba. Apparently this is the 1st record for the species in South America.

Pelecanidae Bibliography

Mitchell, M. H. 1957. See General Bibliography.

FAMILY PHALACROCORACIDAE: CORMORANTS (1)

These duck-sized aquatic birds are widely distributed throughout the world, including in cold-climate regions. They are best represented on the Pacific coast of South America, where the Humboldt Current environment favors them and where they produce important quantities of guano. Brazil has no maritime or pelagic cormorants. There are numerous fossils, the oldest being from the Eo-Oligocene of France (37 million years B.P.).

Morphology and Behavior

Cormorants have heavy bodies, narrow, hooked bills, and dark plumage (*corvos marinhos,* "maritime crows"). They swim half submerged, with the bill slightly elevated. They are expert divers, propelling themselves only with their strong, amply webbed feet and using the long, rigid tail as a rudder. The slight survival value of wings for these birds is emphasized by the fact that the Galapagos Cormorant, *Phalacrocorax harrisi,* has such small wings it has lost the ability to fly. Our cormorant does not fly badly; its wing beats are rapid and continuous, it does not glide, and it holds the neck extended obliquely. It flies high to reach distant points. Flocks may resemble those of ducks but are distinguished by very open—perhaps 160°—wedge-shaped formations that are generally interpreted as being aerodynamically advantageous, although there may be simpler explanations, such as the need to keep each individual's visual field free.

Cormorants perch at the water's edge on rocks, trees, stakes, or even cables. They stretch their wings, like vultures, to dry the plumage or for thermoregulation. Cormorants, like the Anhinga, *Anhinga anhinga,* become completely soaked during their dives, unlike other aquatic birds such as grebes and ducks.

Feeding and Food Use

As fish eaters, cormorants frequently catch prey of no commercial value, such as fish with sharp spines; a cormorant's gastric juices can dissolve these. Comorants eliminate diseased fish. In Argentina, Szidat and Nani (1951) discovered that great numbers of trematode larvae (300–500 per victim) infest the brains of certain freshwater fishes, such as *Basilichthys* species. These larvae also penetrate the eye lenses of the fish. The weakened fish become easy prey for cormorants, in whose intestines the larvae mature and reproduce.

Cormorant pellets are covered with a gelatinous membrane and contain fish otoliths and lenses which are protected by the pellet from rapid digestion and which make possible identification and quantification of the fish eaten. The pellets also contain stones which, due to their weight, must facilitate pellet ejection. Cormorants in Brazil also eat such crustaceans as freshwater shrimp (Palaemonidae) and *Pimelodus* species. They make long dives, to a depth of 20 m or more. Pairs and flocks, sometimes comprising as many as 200 individuals, as I saw in Rio Grande do Sul, gather for strategic group fishing: all swim side by side in the same direction, blocking a canal or a river inlet and diving when a fish appears and tries to escape.

Cormorants in Asia are trained to catch fish for people, much as pelicans were taught in ancient Egypt.

NEOTROPIC CORMORANT, *Phalacrocorax brasilianus*,
Biguá   PL 2.2

75 cm; 1.3 kg (male). Black with a yellow gular sac. During breeding, white feathers edge bare throat and white tuft appears behind auricular region. Immature sooty. VOICE: a cry, *bigooAH, o-AHK.* A chorus of distant individuals sounds like a motor. Nests in trees in flooded forests, in thickets of sarandi (*Phyllanthus sellowianus*), etc., sometimes among heron colonies. Light blue eggs small and covered with calcareous crust; occasional spots originate from soiling. Incubation takes about 24 days. Acid feces destroy trees but fertilize water (see Ardeidae, "Alleged Harmfulness . . . ").

Lakes, large rivers, estuaries. Does not venture out to sea but flies to islands close to littoral, e.g., Ilha Alfavaca off Rio de Janeiro, where a few nest. Sometimes fishes inside surf line and perches on beach (Rio Grande do Sul). After nesting migrates. Enormous concentrations of many thousands congregate in Amazonian region, e.g., Rios Solimões and Japurá in October. Among large flocks appearing at end of August on Lagoa dos Patos (Rio Grande do Sul), individuals were found that had been banded in May and June in Santiago del Estero, Argentina, 1400 km away (see also Anatidae, "Migration . . . ").

Mexico throughout South America. Closely related to Double-crested Cormorant. *P. carbo,* of the Northern Hemisphere.

Phalacrocoracidae Bibliography

Bó, N. A. 1956. *Hornero* 10:147–57. [Morphology, ethology]

Gales, R. P. 1988. The use of otoliths as indicators of Little Penguin, *Eudyptes minor,* diet. *Ibis* 130:418–26.

Gould, L. L., and F. Heppner. 1974. *Auk* 91:494–506. [Flock flight formation]

Schlatter, R. P., and C. A. Moreno. 1976. *Ser. Cient. Inst. Antarct. Chileno* 4:69–88. [Pellets]

Szidat, L., and A. Nani. 1951. Diplostomiasis cerebrales del Pejerrey. *Inst. Nac. Invest. Cienc. Nat., Ciênc. Zool.* 1(8):323–84.

FAMILY ANHINGIDAE: DARTERS (1)

Darters are unique aquatic birds of the world's tropical regions. The oldest fossil dates from the Eocene (40 million years B.P.) of Sumatra. Darters are clearly distinct from cormorants in morphology, oology, and ethology. *Anhinga* [pronounced "an-yeen-ga"] is an old Tupí name meaning "small head." The name was reported by Marcgrave (1648) and officialized in scientific nomenclature by Linnaeus in 1766.

Morphology and Special Adaptations

Darters have long, slender necks (20 vertebrae) which typically are angled midway, like heron and unlike cormorant necks. The long, sharply pointed, serrated bill (without a hook) is appropriate for spearing fish. The tail is even longer than a cormorant's, with a spatular form and a peculiar structure, the rectrices being rigid and transversely undulating like a sheet of corrugated metal, a design suitable for reinforcing feathers that serve as a rudder in underwater swimming. Darters, even more than cormorants, tend to sink when swimming quietly (fig. 53); the skeleton is even less pneumatic, and its air sacs do not connect with the bones. The body feathers absorb water and lose the ability to form an air cushion. This causes the bird to become heavier and facilitates diving. In grebes (Podicipedidae), the capsule of air in which the bird is enclosed provides a lifting impulse by counteracting the body weight.

Unlike other Pelecaniformes, Anhingidae undergo simultaneous molt of the flight feathers, which periodically incapacitates them for flight (see Anatidae, "Morphology . . . "). There is accentuated sexual dimorphism.

ANHINGA, *Anhinga anhinga,* Biguatinga, Carará
PL 2.1, Fig. 54

88 cm; 1.2 kg (male). Male black with large white design on wing; tail tip light (grayish). Female has light brownish neck and breast. Immature has brown back, scarcely any white in wing, yellow bill. VOICE: a croak.

Feeding and Fishing: Crawls through branches overhanging still waters to await aquatic insects, crustaceans, etc., which it catches with a quick dart of bill without leaving perch. Dives from these perches after fish, propelling itself

with feet. Sometimes opens wings during such chases but never paddles with them. Unique neck anatomy permits sudden, vigorous strikes, like a snake, spearing fish laterally with a sure thrust. I have seen an Anhinga spear a fish with the bill slightly open, the maxilla and mandible acting like 2 independent daggers that embedded themselves simultaneously in the flesh of the victim, which was about 20 cm long. To swallow its prey, the Anhinga surfaces and loosens its prey with vertical shakes of the head, then swallows it at once. It is said that several *meuás* will form a circle to try to concentrate fish in a restricted space (Maranhão). This observation may refer to the Neotropic Cormorant, *Phalacrocorax brasilianus.*

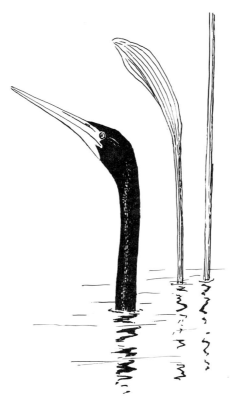

Fig. 53. Anhinga, *Anhinga anhinga,* submerged except for the head.

Fig. 54. Anhinga, *Anhinga anhinga,* adult male, resting with wings open.

Behavior and Migration: When not fishing it swims slowly, letting only a bit of its neck and head, or head only, emerge. The head is so narrow it appears to be a continuation of the neck, creating the impression that one is facing a water snake. When swimming in this position it holds the bill elevated almost vertically. Like cormorants, it flees danger by

diving. It perches on tall, dead trees and frequently holds open its wings, which are impressive in their size and concave shape. There must be 3 reasons for stretching the wings: to dry them, to gather warmth when the temperature is low, and to obtain relief from too much heat. In flight it alternates wing beats with gliding. Soars at great heights, its silhouette appearing like a slender black cross with the long tail conspicuous. Migrates locally within Amazonia.

Breeding: Lives in pairs, sometimes inside heron colonies. Nest is built on trees. Interestingly, the elongated, bluish or white eggs are not similar to cormorant eggs but resemble those of grebes (Schönwetter 1967). The Anhinga incubates like Sulidae, placing its feet on top of eggs.

Outside breeding season found in flocks or scattered among cormorants. Lives at edge of forest-bordered rivers and lakes, appears at reservoirs that have fish. Tropical South America, including all of Brazil. North to Mexico and southern U.S. Also called *Calmaria* (Rio Grande do Sul), *Peru-d'agua, Meuá.* Tupi name *biguatinga* means "a cormorant with white markings."

Anhingidae Bibliography

See also General Bibliography

Becker, J. J. 1986. Reidentification of *"Phalacrocorax" subvolans* Brodkorb as the earliest record of Anhingidae. *Auk* 103:804–8.
Marcgrave, G. 1648. See General Bibliography.
Schönwetter, M. 1967. See General Bibliography.

FAMILY FREGATIDAE: FRIGATEBIRDS (3)

Frigatebirds are typical of tropical oceanic islands. There are fossils from the Tertiary (Eocene) and also from Antillean Quaternary deposits (8,000 years B.P.).

Morphology and Behavior

The male is smaller than the female. Having extremely long, narrow, angular wings, *Fregata* are among the most elegant fliers. They are said to be among the lightest birds per unit of wing surface. The total weight of the feathers of a *Fregata* is greater than the weight of its dried skeleton. The bones are highly pneumatic, light, and elastic. A pelican with the same wingspan weighs four times as much. The tail is deeply forked, like the two blades of a scissors, and like these can be opened and closed. The tips of these "blades" may be of different lengths because of molt.

The bill is long and recurved. The legs and feet are very small with reduced webbing between the toes. Frigatebirds never alight on the surface of the sea (they would quickly become soaked) or on the beach. They rest while soaring and

roost above ground at night, their claws being appropriate for clutching firmly to branches or a nest, a fact of particular importance for the young.

Feeding

The Magnificent Frigatebird, *Fregata magnificens,* fishes on the ocean surface without wetting itself, using an elegant movement of the head. It catches fingerlings that surface in schools and flying fish. Near Ilha Grande (Rio de Janeiro) I have seen it catch a small swordfish. It also catches catfish that fishermen throw out of their nets. It breaks their three hard spines by letting them fall and catches them again in full flight, maneuvering them in the bill so as to deal with the spines. When the booty falls into the sea, there is competition with other frigatebirds or gulls. Because of their characteristic high flight, frigatebirds are more efficient in locating fishing boats than boobies or other low-flying seabirds.

Frigatebirds rob boobies and terns of already swallowed prey, pursuing them acrobatically until they vomit their meal, which the frigatebirds then catch in midair. One frigatebird may steal the booty of another, the loser usually being an immature. They even touch their victims, catching them by the tip of the tail or by the wing, and may even wound them, but I have not seen this on the Brazilian coast. The frequency of this not-always-successful predatory deportment (kleptoparasitism) depends on the local situation and size of the frigatebird population (see Stercorariidae, "Morphology . . . ").

Flying close to the sand, the Greater Frigatebird, *F. minor,* snatches newly hatched tortoises that are heading for the sea (Ilha Trindade).

The various names given to these birds throughout the world reflect their aggressive habits. Frigates were swift sailing vessels used both as warships and by pirates. In Portuguese frigatebirds are called *Aguia-do-mar,* "Sea-Eagle," and in English, "Man-o'-war-bird."

Parasites

Frigatebirds are severely attacked by the blood-sucking hippoboscid louse flies *Olfersia spinifera* (Bahia, Paraná). Restricted to this genus of birds, these parasites slip through the feathers to reach the skin and flutter about in swarms when the birds are perched.

MAGNIFICENT FRIGATEBIRD, *Fregata magnificens,* Tesourão, Rabo-forcado, João-grande   PL 2.3

98 cm; wingspread may exceed 2 m; weight scarcely 1.5 kg. Male all black with strong violaceous sheen on back. Only exceptionally does one see its red "necktie" (part of gular sac, see *Breeding*). Female has white breast. Immature has white head and underparts, brown bar on upper side of wing. Nestling has white down, with brown scapulars among 1st definitive feathers to appear.

Behavior: Using ascending air currents on mountainous littoral, this species soars together with vultures, sometimes going so high it is out of sight. Remotely resembles American Swallow-tailed Kite, *Elanoides forficatus,* but often flies with tail closed. When the 2 meet over land, the kite chases away the frigatebird. The frigatebird fishes in sea close to coast, in ports, and around fishing boats.

To bathe, it flies over fresh water, coastal lakes, and lagoons, descending to wet the tail and rise again. It then hovers clumsily and lets itself fall a few meters while shaking entire plumage, thus spreading water all over its body (Rio de Janeiro). Scratches and arranges plumage in flight. Like boobies and some other birds, has a comblike claw. In late afternoon glides in circles in flocks of about 6 toward certain tree-covered islands, e.g., Ilha Redonda, Rio de Janeiro, where it sleeps in flocks of hundreds. Goes to perch even after nightfall. May spend night soaring at great heights, letting itself be carried by breezes while napping, I suppose. Because of its light weight it can perch on slender branches, so one can speak of "arboreal seabirds."

Breeding: In breeding season, but only in nesting area, male inflates gular sac (a prolongation of cervical air sacs) which in other seasons remains covered by plumage. Sac fills until it forms a great red ball (color fades after breeding). Facing the female he moves his head and sac laterally from side to side, with head held back, while making a strange rustling. This ritual is carried out while perched on a tree, all the males displaying simultaneously when a female flies over, though males overflying colony also display. Females coo loudly. There is also bill clattering.

Nest is built in dense upper portions of trees and bushes (*Rapanea,* capororoca), sometimes on high tufts or clumps of grass (Abrolhos), or in the case of Lesser Frigatebird, *F. ariel,* even on open rocks (Trindade, Olson 1981). Destruction of vegetation may cause birds to abandon islands, as happened on Ilhas Cagarras off Rio de Janeiro. With abundant rain, vegetation may grow so as to interfere with nesting sites. Birds then seek higher trees, if there are any (Moleques do Sul, Santa Catarina, L. Rosário).

Nest is a small platform or shallow basin of branches. Material is collected by breaking off branch tips from dead trees or by taking it from neighbors. A nest left unguarded for a few minutes may be dismantled by neighbors stealing branches. This may be aggravated by a scarcity of material caused by human activity. Straw is also required. With time the loose sticks become stuck together by feces. Males are more active in nest construction.

Usually only 1 pure white egg is laid (from August forward, Santa Catarina), sometimes 2–3 (September, October, São Paulo). Sexes take turns incubating. Males may be very active at this, even invading other nests (Abrolhos, Coelho 1981). Incubation is extremely prolonged, an estimated 6.5–8 weeks (Diamond 1973). Hatching may take 24 hours in *F. minor.* Adults must constantly guard eggs and small nestlings to avoid raids by neighboring frigatebirds and vultures. Young reportedly fledge at 5 or more months. At a colony in Antilles, males abandon the areas when young are 3–4 months old and probably undergo a complete postnuptial molt. After learning to fly, young are still fed by mother for 4 months. This leads to conclusion that females only manage to nest every other year, like large raptors, and that females outnumber males.

Distribution: I know of only a few *F. magnificens* colonies on our coast, namely on Cabo Frio and Macaé archipelagoes (Rio de Janeiro), off city of Rio de Janeiro (Ilha Redonda), on Abrolhos archipelago (Bahia), Ilha dos Alcatrazes (São Paulo), along Paraná coast (Ilhas Currais, a large colony), and on Ilhas Moleques do Sul (Santa Catarina).

Wandering along coast, the species occurs from Amapá to Rio Grande do Sul and Argentina, being more frequent in the area under greater influence of the warm Brazil Current, south to São Paulo and Paraná. It is the only *Fregata* I have recorded on our coast. Migratory concentrations occur, e.g., near Santos, São Paulo, in April. An *F. magnificens* banded as a nestling on Ilha dos Currais, Paraná, in March 1984 was recovered on Dominica, Lesser Antilles, in May 1986 (Scherer Neto 1986).

Also resident on Fernando de Noronha (nesting), Cape Verde Islands, Caribbean Sea, Pacific coast of South America, Galapagos Islands, Mexico. Also called *Tesoura, Grapira* (from *grá*, an old form of *guirá*, "bird," and *pirá*, "fish"), and *Catraia* (Pernambuco). Name *Alcatraz* is said to have originally referred to *Sula* species, not *Fregata*.

Two other species occur on Trindade and Martim Vaz islands but in reduced numbers or only periodically: *F. minor* and *F. ariel*. Possibly, destruction of trees and bushes they require for nesting makes it difficult for them to remain there. On Trindade a pair of *F. minor* built their nest on a fallen log of *Colubrina* (Rhamnaceae), a tree with red wood similar to that of brazilwood.

Apparently there is no concrete information on *Fregata* reaching the mainland from those distant islands. Experience taught mariners at the time of the discovery of America that frigatebirds do not go far from their islands and consequently that their presence indicates land nearby. *F. magnificens* that nest on Ilha dos Alcatrazes (São Paulo) leave at dawn to seek food primarily near the continent, not on high seas. However, at certain periods they migrate, and sometimes, when soaring at great heights, they are carried far off by wind. This accounts for the fact that they occupy the most remote oceanic islands.

GREATER FRIGATEBIRD, *Fregata minor*

Very similar to *F. magnificens*. Male distinguishable by green sheen on back with slight violaceous tone; female has brownish rather than black throat. Immature has prominent rusty color on head and foreneck. Ilha Trindade: May, July, December (nesting). Not found there by Olson in 1975. Also Pacific Ocean.

LESSER FRIGATEBIRD, *Fregata ariel*

78 cm. Smallest *Fregata*. Male has white patch on each side of black body. Female has light brownish collar on upper neck. Trindade: August, December (nesting). Not found there by Olson in 1975. Formerly also bred on Santa Helena. *F. a. trinitatis,* described by A. Miranda Ribeiro in 1919, restricted to Martin Vaz and Trindade. More widespread in Pacific and Indian oceans.

Fregatidae Bibliography

Bege, L.A.R., and B. T. Pauli. 1989. *As aves nas Ilhas Moleques do Sul, Santa Catarina.* Florianópolis: FATMA.

Coelho, A. G. 1981. *Univers. Fed. Pernambuco, Publ. Avuls.* 1. [Behavior]

Diamond, A. W. 1973. *Condor* 75:200–209 [nesting]; also other publications.

Eyde, R. H., and S. L. Olson. 1983. The dead trees of Ilha da Trindade. *Bartonia* 49:32–51.

Guimarães, L. R. 1945. *Arq. Mus. Paran.* 4:179–90. [Ectoparasites]

Lobo, B. 1919. *Arq. Mus. Nac. Rio de Janeiro.* 22:107–58. [Nesting]

Lüderwaldt, H., and J. Pinto da Fonseca. 1923. *Rev. Mus. Paul.* 13:441–512. [Behavior]

Mahoney, S. A. 1984. Plumage wettability of aquatic birds. *Auk* 101:181–85.

Olson, S. L. 1981. See General Bibliography.

Rezende, M. A. 1987. Exploração mútua entre *Fregata magnificens* e *Sula leucogaster* estudado por rastreamento utilizando micro-transmissores. *An. III Enc. Nac. An. Aves, S. Leopoldo.*

Scherer Neto, P. 1986. Nota sobre aspectos migratórios de *Fregata magnificens. An. II Enc. Nac. An. Aves., Rio de Janeiro*:202.

ORDER CICONIIFORMES[1]

FAMILY ARDEIDAE: HERONS (21)

Most members of this widely distributed family are wetland birds. There are North American Tertiary fossils from the Eocene (40 million years B.P.) and the Pliocene (10 million years B.P.). There does not appear to be a close relationship with the Ciconiidae (Sibley and Ahlquist 1982). See also the Boat-billed Heron, *Cochlearius cochlearius.* The order is sometimes called Gressores.

I have used the nomenclature of Hancock et al. (1984)

---

[1] I have separated the flamingos, Phoenicopteridae, which traditionally have been included in the Ciconiiformes, into a distinct order.

which maintains the genera *Bubulcus* and *Butorides*. *Florida* and *Hydranassa* have been included in *Egretta*. I maintain *Casmerodius*, based on the 1983 AOU checklist.

Morphology

Herons are extremely elegant. They have long legs and toes, a slender neck, and a long, sharp bill, although the bill of the Zigzag Heron, *Zebrilus undulatus*, is relatively short. Inside the tip of the bill of the Green-backed Heron, *Butorides striatus*, and some others are very fine serrations that enable them to hold on to anything.

Size varies greatly, ranging from the Least Bittern, *Ixobrychus exilis*, scarcely the size of a jacana, to the White-necked Heron, *Ardea cocoi*, more than 1 m high. Because of the very extensible neck, short tail, and long legs, total length figures for these birds give only a vague approximation of their actual size.

The neck is notable for being two sectioned and abruptly angled, owing to the arrangement of the spinal column and to a springlike, elastic tendon that automatically positions it that way. The neck of the Anhinga, *Anhinga anhinga*, is similar. Like various other birds, herons have a comblike process on the middle toe.

Heron plumage abounds in powder, produced by three or four powder-down patches concentrated on the breast and sides of the body. This powder replaces the oil of the uropygial gland (which is little developed in herons) in maintaining feather elasticity and plumage impermeability. Changes in plumage color without molt, as I have seen in the Whistling Heron, *Syrigma sibilatrix*, are also due to feather powder.

Both the plumage and color of bare areas become more prominent in the breeding season, a phenomenon well known because of the plumes—adornment feathers on the back that develop in certain species during the nesting period (see "Alleged Harmfulness . . . ").

Sexes are similar except in the *Ixobrychus*. There are two color phases in *Zebrilus undulatus* independent of sex. Various species have juvenal plumage different from that of the adult. Some, such as the Cattle Egret, *Bubulcus ibis*, can breed at this stage. A melanistic mutation has been observed in *Ixobrychus exilis*.

Vocalization

The voice is a low, harsh, croaking, except in *Syrigma sibilatrix*. The Rufescent Tiger-Heron, *Tigrisoma lineatum*, has an elaborate "song" that consists of a prolonged phrase reminiscent of a jaguar (*Felis onca*). Bittern voices might be mistaken for those of frogs.

Feeding

Herons are unjustly defamed as destroyers of fish, for fish are only part of their diet. They also catch aquatic insects (larvae and adults, crabs, mollusks, amphibians (even *Bufo* frogs), and reptiles. The Great Egret, *Casmerodius albus*, and Pinnated Bittern, *Botaurus pinnatus*, sometimes swallow snakes and guinea pigs (*Cavea* sp.). *Ardea cocoi* occasionally takes small caiman (Mato Grosso).

Bubulcus ibis, *Syrigma sibilatrix*, the Capped Heron, *Pilherodius pileatus*, and Little Blue Heron, *Egretta caerulea*, are the most insectivorous species. The first two hunt grasshoppers far from water; the first and last make strange, lateral neck movements before releasing the sure strike that will capture a fly, for instance. Considering the force with which they move against such small prey, it is remarkable that the bill does not touch the substrate. It would be interesting to investigate whether facts here in Brazil justify the English name "tick-heron" for *Bubulcus ibis*.

B. ibis and the Snowy Egret, *Egretta thula*, take advantage of insects stirred up by cattle. *Syrigma sibilatrix* sometimes associates with the Buff-necked Ibis, *Theristicus caudatus*, while hunting insects in dry areas. In water, herons may use capybaras (*Hydrochoerus hydrochoerus*) as beaters. The Black-crowned Night-Heron, *Nycticorax nycticorax*, eats food remains that fall from the nests of other birds in the colony, not even turning down its neighbors' dead chicks. *Egretta thula* regularly catches small animals tossed onto the beach by the tide, whether they be live, moribund, or dead. *Casmerodius albus* and *Ardea cocoi* also do this.

Herons employ a variety of methods to frighten up animals hidden in the mud underwater. *Egretta thula*, for example, shakes or vibrates its toes; *E. caerulea* and *Butorides striatus* move the foot slowly like a rake. Such foot movements, which greatly facilitate fishing, are useful habits used by other aquatic birds such as the Wood Stork, *Mycteria americana*, and Southern Lapwing, *Vanellus chilensis*. I have seen an *E. thula* jumping around from here to there in a small pool as if dancing. Herons generally do not drink.

In 1966 at the Rio de Janeiro estate of E. Béraut I noticed an *E. thula* that did not eat pieces of raw meat thrown into the water near it, but left them to attract small fish. Certain *Butorides striatus* fish with bait; when the heron sees a fish, it crouches so as not to be seen and throws a lure, such as a piece of bread or an insect, to attract minnows within its reach. Young birds use inappropriate, inedible items for lures, such as feathers, but soon learn better techniques (Higuchi 1986). Herons occasionally fish by hovering over deep water, as I saw with *Nycticorax nycticorax* at the lakes in Brasília and with egrets in Amazonia during high water.

Behavior

Herons walk with long deliberate steps, as if stealing up on a danger or an opportunity. *Ardea cocoi* and *Tigrisoma lineatum* may draw attention by standing with the wings held horizontally and bottomside up, cupped like a shell, as does the Maguari Stork, *Ciconia maguari.* This posture is probably related to thermoregulation.

Herons fly slowly, with the neck drawn in (unlike storks and ibis) and the legs stretched out behind, like all long-legged birds (and descendants of long-legged types). *Nycticorax nycticorax* has a more deliberate flight, reminiscent of a hawk.

Nervousness is manifested by wagging the tail, which is held downward. *Tigrisoma lineatum* makes vertical tail movements, lowering and then rapidly lifting its tail as if impelled by a spring; the Stripe-backed Bittern, *Ixobrychus involucris,* and *Botaurus pinnatus* move their tails laterally. *Butorides striatus* rapidly spreads and closes its tail feathers.

Both *B. pinnatus* and the *Ixobrychus* bitterns freeze with the bill held perfectly vertical the instant they become suspicious of something. At such times they can pass for a stick stuck in the marsh. The *Tigrisoma* also freeze but with the neck outstretched obliquely.

Herons do not turn the head backward to sleep but hold the bill toward the front. *Nycticorax nycticorax* holds its bill vertically downward against the breast and within the plumage, hiding it completely, like *Cochlearius cochlearius.*

Some species are active during both the day and at dawn and dusk. All like rainy, dark days, when both diurnal and nocturnal species become active. In the late afternoon, when flocks of the two white egrets and of *Egretta caerulea* head for certain forested islands on the north Atlantic coast, they make a beautiful and impressive spectacle. These group roosts are not identical to the nesting colonies used day and night during the breeding period.

Breeding

Heron pairs have many displays. They build nests on trees (sometimes 10 or 20 m high) or bushes in marshes, on forested islands, and in flooded fields and mangroves. They usually nest in colonies (known as ninhais, garçais, or viveiros) which are frequently mixed, comprising various heron species as well as the Roseate Spoonbill, *Platalea ajaja; Mycteria americana;* Neotropic Cormorant, *Phalacrocorax brasilianus;* and *Anhinga anhinga.* In the Mato Grosso Pantanal, colonies of *Mycteria americana, Platalea ajaja,* and *Casmerodius albus* are known as "white nesting colonies," whereas those of *Nycticorax nycticorax, Ardea cocoi, Phalacrocorax brasilianus,* and *Anhinga anhinga* are called "black nesting colonies." Each species occupies a given area in the colony, the strongest birds generally occupying the best places. Along the coast colonies are formed on oceanic islands not far offshore, as in Rio de Janeiro (Ilha Alfavaca, *Casmerodius albus*) and Paraná (Ilha Currais, *Nycticorax nycticorax,* P. Scherer Neto). The *Botaurus* of Europe are said to be polygynous.

Eggs are uniformly greenish or bluish green (sometimes white or whitish) except those of *Syrigma sibilatrix* and the *Tigrisoma,* whose eggs are slightly spotted, something like those of rails. The incubation period is 25 to 26 days for *Egretta thula* and *Casmerodius albus* and 22 to 23 days for *Nycticorax nycticorax,* whose nestlings remain in the nest for 30 days (Rio de Janeiro).

Adults normally gather food for their chicks at great distances from the nesting site. An impressive amount of noise is produced by a nesting colony, (e.g., of *Casmerodius albus*), where all phases of the reproductive process, from pairs engaged in prenuptial displays to others with grown young, may be underway at the same time. Breeding usually occurs at the beginning or end of the dry season when food for aquatic birds is normally more abundant. *Ardea cocoi* reportedly nests in the Amazon estuary (Ilha Mexiana) in the midst of the rainy season, as do *Anhinga anhinga* and the Muscovy Duck, *Cairina moschata,* in the same area. In Amapá, *A. cocoi* has been found nesting in July with *Casmerodius albus* and *Phalacrocorax brasilianus.*

Distribution and Habitat

Half the heron genera found in Brazil also occur in the Old World. Sometimes they are the same species (e.g., *Nycticorax nycticorax* and *Butorides striatus*). *N. nycticorax* is cosmopolitan. *B. striatus,* widely distributed in warm areas of the Old World (Africa, Australia, etc.) and with a subspecies in North America, must have immigrated to the Americas from Africa, anticipating the later invasion of *Bubulcus ibis.*

Syrigma sibilatrix, a species unique in several respects, has a notably disjunct distribution. So does the Fasciated Tiger-Heron, *Tigrisoma fasciatum,* which is widely distributed along white-water rivers of the Andes and has a relict population in southeastern Brazil. The Yellow-crowned Night-Heron, *Nyctanassa violacea,* is restricted to the littoral. Certain species, such as *Botaurus pinnatus,* occur only locally. The beautiful Chestnut-bellied Heron, *Agamia agami,* is the species most adapted to woodland. *Syrigma sibilatrix* and *Bubulcus ibis* live in dry or only slightly wet areas. *Zebrilus undulatus; Botaurus pinnatus,* and the *Ixobrychus* bitterns are easily overlooked.

Migration

Populations of almost all herons fluctuate. Various species are migratory, sometimes on a large scale, as was shown by banding in northern Argentina: young *Casmerodius albus* disperse widely, up to 1200 km to the north and 700 km to the south. One *Egretta thula* was recovered 1400 km away in Paraná, another 3500 km away in Amazonia. *Bubulcus ibis* is the champion migrant, having immigrated to Brazil in the 1960s, probably via the Guianas. Recently another exotic species appeared at the mouth of the Amazon: the Gray Heron, *Ardea cinerea,* of Europe, apparently an individual that strayed. *Tigrisoma lineatum* has been recorded in England several times. Migration between the Old and New Worlds is well documented, such as the finding of an *A. cinerea* banded in France, and then two species together, the Purple Heron, *A. purpurea,* and Squacco Heron, *Ardeola ralloides,* in June 1986 on Fernando de Noronha, alongside a *Bubulcus ibis.*

Parasites and Mosquitoes

Various herons, such as *Ardea cocoi, Casmerodius albus,* and *Tigrisome lineatum,* as well as *Cochlearius cochlearius* and the Plumbeous Ibis, *Theristicus caerulescens,* are hosts to the louse fly *Olfersia palustris.*

Heron species vary in their sensitivity to mosquitoes. While fishers accustomed to spearing their prey, such as *Nycticorax nycticorax,* tolerate without difficulty mosquitoes that land on the face or legs, insectivorous birds such as *Bubulcus ibis* defend themselves vigorously against these pests (Edman et al. 1986).

Alleged Harmfulness, Use, Dangers, and Conservation

Many South American studies on the possible harm caused by herons because of their fish-eating habits have proven (1) that fish are less important in the diet of South American herons than they are in the diets of herons in colder climates, and (2) that the fish eaten are generally very small ones a few centimeters long. When larger fish are taken they are generally sick or dead. Herons catch only fish that appear close to the surface. It can even be said that the presence of herons and kingfishers in lakes and rivers is necessary to maintain biological equilibrium. The more fish predators, the more fish; the more fish, the more food for fish.

It should also be remembered that heron nesting colonies and roosts supply an accumulation of organic matter (food remains, pellets, egg shells, dead chicks, feces) that, when it falls into the water, benefits the microfauna and is reflected in an increased fish population around the nesting sites, thereby compensating for the fish eaten. It can even be said that the more fish-eating birds, the more fish. Nesting colonies also contribute to maintaining terrestrial vertebrates, such as the crab-eating raccoon (*Procyon cancrivorus*) and wildcats (*Felis* spp.) that form part of this ecosystem. The high acidity of heron feces can burn the foliage; branches also break under the weight of the birds. There are places, especially in Amazonia, where heron eggs are collected, either for local consumption or for sale, as also occurs with gull and tern eggs in other localities.

Bubulcus ibis has become very "useful": it is reported that a lone individual catches an average of 17 insects per minute when wandering through fields in search of prey.

Herons used to be greatly persecuted, particularly in Amazonia, by hunters seeking egret plumes. The birds were slaughtered at their nesting sites when they came to feed their young, the period when the plumes are most beautiful. Around 1914 in the Rio Negro region (Pará), a merchant employed 80 men to hunt egrets. A single kilogram of plumes required 300 *Casmerodius albus,* 250 *Ardea cocoi,* or 100 *Egretta thula.*

During wind and hail storms, such as occurred in ex-Guanabara in 1974, *Casmerodius albus* nestlings and eggs are knocked down to the ground. Hail storms frighten the nestlings, causing them to jump from the nest to their death, which often results not from the fall itself but from being snagged in tree branches. Strong winds can blow even an adult, such as a *Pilherodius pileatus,* from its perch, which can be fatal if it becomes entangled in branches. I have seen individual *C. albus* so soiled by petroleum that they were probably destined to die (Rio de Janeiro). A heron was found in the stomach of a pirarucu fish (*Arapaima gigas*) in Ceará, and I have seen a traíra fish (*Hoplias* sp.) catch a *Butorides striatus* fishing at the edge of a river after heavy rains. Vultures can damage nesting colonies by perching near a nest and taking eggs and nestlings when the parents leave (Mato Grosso, Pantanal), as occurs when tourists, trying to take photographs, come too close. Landowners should provide special protection to nesting colonies and group roosts, which should be made inviolate if on government property.

In the southern United States, insecticide residues (mostly DDT but also Aldrin, Dieldrin, and Heptachlor) have been found in *Egretta caerulea* eggs and chicks; *Bubulcus ibis* eggshells were 17% to 18% thinner than normal. Extensive use of insecticides and herbicides in rice plantations is menacing all the aquatic fauna on which herons depend.

Synopsis of Brazilian Herons

The diverse coloring of most species impedes a simple system. For other birds that resemble herons, see the three following families: Cochleariidae (Boat-billed Herons), Ciconiidae (storks), and Threskiornithidae (ibis). See also the Limpkin, *Aramus guarauna,* and Sunbittern, *Eurypyga helias.*

1. Essentially white
   1.1. *Casmerodius, Egretta* except *E. tricolor* and adult *E. caerulea*
   1.2. *Bubulcus, Ardeola ralloides*
   1.3. *Pilherodius*
2. Predominantly gray or bluish
   2.1. *Ardea cocoi*
   2.2. *A. cinerea, A. purpurea*
   2.3. *E. tricolor* and adult *E. caerulea*
   2.4. *Butorides*
   2.5. *Agamia*
   2.6. *Syrigma*
   2.7. Adults *Nycticorax* and *Nyctanassa*
   2.8. *Zebrilus* (see also 3.2)

3. Brown, spotted
  3.1. *Tigrisoma* (both species)
  3.2. *Zebrilus* (the respective phase)
  3.3. *Ixobrychus* (both species)
  3.4. *Botaurus*
  3.5. Immature *Agamia, Nycticorax,* and *Nyctanassa*

PURPLE HERON, *Ardea purpurea*   NV

One individual observed on Fernando de Noronha June 1986 with *Bubulcus ibis* and 1 *Ardeola ralloides.* Widely distributed in southern Europe and southern Asia. First record for New World (Teixeira et al. 1987).

GRAY HERON, *Ardea cinerea,* Garça-real-européia   NV

An individual captured December 1975 in Capitão Poço, Ourém, Pará, had been banded same year in France. Also recorded from Trinidad. See *A. cocoi.*

WHITE-NECKED HERON, *Ardea cocoi,* Socó-grande

125 cm; wingspan 180 cm; 3.2 kg. Largest Brazilian heron. Uniformly light gray with neck white, top of head, flight feathers, and some pattern on underparts black. Bill yellowish; legs blackish. VOICE: a loud *rraahb (rraahb rraahb),* a deep bass. Generally solitary. See "Behavior" on thermoregulation. Panama to Chile, Argentina, throughout Brazil. Also called *João-grande, Maguari* (see also *Ciconia*), *Baguari. Socó* means "the bird that stands on only one leg." Similar to *A. cinerea* of Old World.

GREAT EGRET, *Casmerodius albus,* Garça-branca-grande

88 cm. White. Filigree of plumes may extend behind like a short veil; these feathers reach a length of 50 cm or more, appearing at beginning of breeding season in July–August (Rio de Janeiro) (re plume hunting, see "Alleged Harmfulness . . . "). Bill and iris yellow; legs black. VOICE: a bisyllabic *ha-TA;* when flying low a *rat, rat, rat. . . .* Common on lake, river, and marsh edges. Migratory, in flocks of hundreds among a total of more than 1000 individuals resting at Lagoa de Itaipu (Rio de Janeiro) and on mudflats of Guanabara Bay (July–August), with a few *Egretta thula* intermingled (see "Migration"). North America to Straits of Magellan, throughout Brazil; also Old World. Population that nests in southern U.S. migrates as far as northern Colombia. *Casmerodius* could be included in genus *Ardea.* Also called *Garça-grande, Garça-real, Guira-tinga* (Pará). *Guará* used in Pedra de Guaratiba, Rio de Janeiro, for all white herons. See *Egretta thula* and *Bubulcus ibis.*

SNOWY EGRET, *Egretta thula,* Garça-branca-pequena   PL 4.2

54 cm. With *Casmerodius albus,* this is best-known species. All white; bill and tarsus black; lores, iris, toes yellow.

In nuptial plumage, March forward, plumes more developed, with tips turned upward. Sole of tarsus greenish in immature. Less common than *C. albus,* with which it frequently associates; distinguishable by smaller size and in flight by more rapid wing strokes. Lives in both fresh and brackish water, even on beaches, where it captures prey tossed upon sand by tide. Most of South America, throughout Brazil, north to Southern Canada. Shier than *E. caerulea,* whose immature it resembles. At a distance can be confused with *Bubulcus ibis* and looks like *E. garzetta* of Old World. See *Bubulcus ibis.* Also called *Garcinha-branca, Garça-pequena.*

LITTLE BLUE HERON, *Egretta* (= *Florida*) *caerulea,* Garça-azul

52 cm. Completely slate colored, tinged with violet on neck and head. Bill, tarsus, toes blackish. Immature white, resembling *E. thula.* Molts successively into adult plumage, which it acquires at 1 year of age. Movements slower than those of many other herons (see "Feeding"). As heron best adapted to exploiting tidal mudflats, found in intertidal zone of littoral. Southern Canada through Central America to Peru, Colombia, Brazil, along littoral as far as Rio Grande do Sul; also Mato Grosso (Pantanal), Uruguay. Hybrids occur rarely with *E. caerulea* and *E. thula;* they are conspicuous for their mixed pattern which does not change with molt (Sprunt 1954). Also called *Garça morena.*

TRICOLORED HERON, *Egretta* (= *Hydranassa*) *tricolor*

Only in north. Similar to *E. caerulea* but with white belly and rump, throat and adjacent upper breast whitish spotted with rusty. Mangroves. Northeastern U.S. to Brazil (as far as Piauí), Colombia, Peru. "Espírito Santo" (Ruschi, without basis).

CATTLE EGRET, *Bubulcus ibis,* Garça-vaqueira
Fig. 55

49 cm. First recorded in Brazil in early 1960s. Similar in appearance to *Egretta thula* but less slender and with thicker neck, giving appearance of having a crop. All white with bill, iris, and legs yellow, toes brownish. During breeding crown, breast, and back rusty, bill and legs quite reddish. Immatures have blackish bill, tarsus, and toes; sometimes breed in this plumage (Colombia). Subadults have yellow bill, black tarsus and toes, yellowish soles of feet, like a miniature *Casmerodius albus.* Said to acquire full breeding plumage and bright colors of bare parts in 1st year (Africa).

Feeding: Insectivorous. Uses a unique tactic to obtain flies, holding the head absolutely steady and close to prey while moving neck laterally to and fro in a special way (see "Feeding"). On Marajó Island I have found it associating with water buffalo (*Bubalus bubalis*), on which it perches (as it does in Africa with hippopotamuses and elephants) to widen its horizon in high grass areas. *Egretta thula* also does

Fig. 55. Cattle Egret, *Bubulcus ibis.*

this occasionally. In the Mato Grosso Pantanal it sometimes perches on deer.

Must hunt pasture spittlebugs (Cercopidae), a great curse of cattle raisers. In an examination of stomach contents by H. Alvarenga in Taubaté (São Paulo, October 1974), 23 spiders, 17 grasshoppers, 5 crickets, 8 flies, 1 caterpillar, and 2 small toads were counted.

Occurrence in Brazil: Found in low, dry fields such as those with pangola (*Digitaria decumbens,* São Paulo), facilitating the finding and capture of insects. Almost always with cattle. When cattle lie down to ruminate, it flies off to look for another grazing herd. Not a species of intertidal zone or mangroves and appears in open water alongside other herons only on migration.

First recorded in Brazil in September 1964 on Marajó Island, associating with buffalo and nesting in ample numbers with other heron species. Had been in area at least since 1962 (Sick 1965). It was subsequently found in area of Bragantina, Santa Maria, and Tracuateuá (Pará) in 1968 and 1970; upper Rio Curuá (Pará) 1984; Brasília (Federal District, 24 October 1971, a flock of 30); Rio Grande do Sul (Camaquã, from 1973 on); Mato Grosso (Pantanal, Municipality of Cáceres, 1974 and probably earlier; Rio das Mortes, Municipality of Barra do Garça, 1977); São Paulo (Taubaté, 5 October 1974, 2 specimens collected); Rio de Janeiro (ex-Guanabara) in 1976, 1 subadult with a group of wild herons in one of the ponds of the Zoological Garden in Rio de Janeiro (D. M. Teixeira); 1981 in flocks with cattle in Santa Cruz area, Rio de Janeiro; Amazonas (Manaus, 1976); Santa

Catarina (Serra da Boa Vista, 1979); Fernando de Noronha, 1986; Trindade, 1987; Atol das Rocas, Feb. 1990, a few individuals (J. Goerck). Was also reported from St. Paul's Rocks (Brazilian islands in mid-Atlantic, more than 2000 km from mouth of Amazon) in 1968, based on a photograph, but this identification was later questioned in favor of an *Egretta garzetta* (a geographic replacement of *E. thula* and very similar to it) coming from Africa or Europe, which, if correct, would be a new species for Brazil (Benson et al. 1969). See also *Colonization of America.*

It is to be expected that *Bubulcus ibis* will be found in many other parts of the country in the near future. Silva reported nesting in Rio Grande do Sul between mid-October and late December in 1980–83 (Belton 1985), but there is little other information on breeding in Brazil. Appearance of individuals with yellow tones in plumage suggests breeding in various places.

Colonization of America: B. ibis originated in Old World (Africa, southern Spain) and is believed to have begun its invasion of the Americas by the end of the 1800s. Its appearance on various oceanic islands and the fact of individuals having, more than once, sought refuge onboard ships on the high seas prove that it crosses the Atlantic on the wing (distance Dakar–Georgetown is 2800 km). Its arrival in northern South America would have been facilitated by trade winds.

Reported for Guyana between 1877 and 1882 (Wetmore 1963) and had occupied all the northern countries of South America by 1973. Reached Chile, Bolivia, and Paraguay, appearing and breeding in various parts of Argentina from 1970 on. Seen on Tierra del Fuego in 1974 and in Antarctica (South Shetlands, Schlatter and Duarte 1979). From Antilles it moved on to Florida in 1942 and has now been recorded in Canada. Its numbers have increased in Africa, and it has also colonized Australia.

It has become so abundant in northern South America (in Suriname more than 5500 individuals were counted in 1 roost in 1965; in Colombia 15,000 were estimated at another in 1966) that from there it could easily colonize other areas, e.g., Brazil, so it is unnecessary to suppose that new contingents crossed the ocean.

The decisive impulse for this population explosion and spectacular acceleration in the rhythm of *B. ibis* spread was the immense increase in cattle raising in South America during the period in question, for *B. ibis* is widely synanthropic. In Colombia and neighboring countries there is scarcely a cow that is not accompanied by 1 or more of these egrets. They walk behind cattle just as anis, *Crotophaga* spp., do, taking advantage of insects, e.g., grasshoppers, that are frightened up. Agricultural machinery is also attractive because it performs the same function for the hundreds of *B. ibis* that follow it (Colombia).

The biological potential of *B. ibis* is greater than that of many other herons for it begins to breed at the end of its 1st year and frequently has 2 broods per season. The population is customarily subject to oscillations; while in certain places it is increasing, in others it is diminishing or even disappearing, abandoning its nesting colonies. Nothing seems to indicate competition with indigenous herons, for they exploit ecologically different niches. Also called *Garça-do-gado, Garça-boieira, Garça-boiadeira* (São Paulo).

GREEN-BACKED HERON, *Butorides striatus*, Socozinho   PL 3.8

36 cm. Found wherever there is water. Unmistakable. Short, yellow legs; walks crouched like a large rail. Solitary, sometimes nests in colonies. VOICE: *kiAK* (diagnostic), *ta-tata*. Found both in continental interior and mangroves. Migratory (Rio de Janeiro). Almost all of South America (including all Brazil) to North America. Also Africa, Asia, Australia, islands of western Pacific. Considered conspecific with what was formerly called *B. virescens* of North America and Galapagos Islands; they interbreed in Central America. Thirty geographic races have been described. Also called *Socó-estudante*.

SQUACCO HERON, *Ardeola ralloides*   NV

One individual observed on Fernando de Noronha June 1986 alongside *Bubulcus ibis* and 1 *Ardea purpurea*. Widely distributed in southern Europe and southern Asia. First record for New World. (Teixeira et al. 1987).

CHESTNUT-BELLIED HERON, *Agamia agami*, Garça-da-mata   PL 3.2

73 cm. Unique proportions: bill extremely long (14–15 cm) and thin, comparable to a fencing foil; neck long, slender and angled at head end like that of *Anhinga anhinga*. Tarsus and toes surprisingly short, an adaptation to arboreal life. Our most colorful heron. Immature blackish brown with streaked breast. Lurks at edge of forest streams and lakes. Solitary but nests in small colonies. I have found fish in its stomach. Mexico to Amazonia as far as Mato Grosso. Also called *Socó-azul, Socó-beija-flor, Garça-da-Guiana*.

WHISTLING HERON, *Syrigma sibilatrix*, Maria-faceira   PL 3.4

53 cm. Multicolored, well known in southern Brazil. Appearance and behavior distinctive. Face light blue, bill pink. Yellow color appears and disappears in plumage because of abundant powder down (or a secretion of uropygial gland?). VOICE: very different from other herons: a melodious, unhurriedly repeated whistle, *i, i, i,* given with bill wide open, neck outstretched. Wings appear to be attached below axis of body; flies with neck less doubled than other herons, with short, rapid wing beats which accelerate when bird calls. Male has display flight it exhibits in front of female. Activity quite diurnal. Dry fields, rice plantations. Nests in Santa Catarina on old araucarias, where it also roosts. Rio de Ja-

neiro and Minas Gerais to Argentina, Paraguay, Bolivia; also Venezuela, Colombia (see *Pilherodias pileatus*).

CAPPED HERON, *Pilherodius pileatus*, Garça-real

Somewhat similar to *Syrigma sibilatrix*. Yellowish white, neck sometimes an intense cream color; black cap; nape with some long white feathers; region around eye and base of bill bright blue; bill reddish in center. VOICE: a ventriloquial *woop—woop—woop* given as bird lowers head in front of mate and opens nuchal crest. Solitary; rivers and lakes surrounded by forest but not common anywhere. Appears at pools alongside Transamazon Highway, which represents a new colonization. Panama to Paraguay, Bolivia, almost all of Brazil except Rio Grande do Sul. Differs from *S. sibilatrix* by white (not gray) mantle and longer bill. Also called *Garcinha, Garça-de-cabeça-preta*.

BLACK-CROWNED NIGHT-HERON, *Nycticorax nycticorax*, Savacu

60 cm. Crepuscular and nocturnal habits. Much less slender than several foregoing species, bill and legs stouter, eyes large and red. Back and top of head black; wings gray; forehead, underparts, and elongated nuchal feathers white. Immature brown and spotted, upper wing coverts and flight feathers brown, each with distinct whitish or cream spot at tip. VOICE: a croak, *o-AK* heard at night, even over cities such as Rio de Janeiro. Common. Canada to Tierra del Fuego, including almost all Brazil; also Old World. Also called *Socó, Dorminhoco, Taquiri*. See *Cochlearius cochlearius* and *Nyctanassa violacea*.

YELLOW-CROWNED NIGHT-HERON, *Nyctanassa violacea*, Savacu-de-coroa   Fig. 56

60 cm. Resembles *Nycticorax nycticorax*, with which it shares mangroves. White on head becomes more prominent in dusky light. Immature similar to that of *N. nycticorax*. Likes to warm itself in morning sun perched in mangrove canopy. Littoral of U.S. to northern Peru, southern Brazil as far as Rio Grande do Sul.

RUFESCENT TIGER-HERON, *Tigrisoma lineatum*, Socó-boi   PL 3.1   Fig. 57

93 cm. Large with extremely long bill. Adult plumage, acquired only after 2 years, distinguished by chestnut neck and grayish brown mantle, vermiculated with cinnamon. Immature, subject to some changes during molt, basically light yellow with black bars, white throat and belly, relatively short bill. VOICE: a loud "song," given during breeding season, that resembles roar of jaguar—a prolonged *ROko* . . . , initially crescendo and then decrescendo, terminating in a deep moan; also a low, deep *oh-ah* with timbre of howler monkey and a deep, monosyllabic *moo* (both sexes). When suspicious stretches neck obliquely, ruffles long nuchal

Fig. 56. Yellow-crowned Night-Heron, *Nyctanassa violacea*.

Fig. 58. Fasciated Tiger-Heron, *Tigrisoma fasciatum*, perched on a rock in river rapids. By Francisco Pontual, based on Hancock and Kushlan 1984.

plumes (which stand out like great teeth), and flips tail (see "Behavior"). Forested regions, nesting high in trees. Solitary, crepuscular; lives hidden in riverine vegetation. Central America to Bolivia, Argentina, throughout Brazil. Also called *Socó-pintado, Iocó-pinim* (Pará), *Juruku* (Jurunas, Mato Grosso). See *T. fasciatum*.

FASCIATED TIGER-HERON, *Tigrisoma fasciatum*
R   Fig. 58

Little known. Bill and legs relatively short, even in adult (culmen generally less than 95 mm). Top of head black (not chestnut as in *T. lineatum*); neck and mantle dark gray vermiculated with yellow, pattern diffuse (not dense as in *lineatum*); flanks uniformly dark gray. Unlike *lineatum*, has interscapular area of powder down. Solitary; mountain rivers with rapids, similar to its habitat in Andes where it may occur

alongside Torrent Duck, *Merganetta armata*. Perches on rocks in middle of current, in same habitat as Brazilian Merganser, *Mergus octosetaceus*. Bolivia to Argentina (Tucumán, Misiones), Colombia, Venezuela, Costa Rica. In Brazil *T. f. fasciatum* has been found in Rio Grande do Sul at Taquara by Ihering, 1882; in Mato Grosso, at Chapada, headwaters of Rio Guaporé, by G. K. Cherrie (Naumburg 1930); in Santa Catarina at Brusque by G. Hoffman, 1950; and in Goiás, at Chapada dos Veadeiros at tip of Goiás, alongside *M. octosetaceus,* by C. Yamashita, 1988.

LEAST BITTERN, *Ixobrychus exilis*, Socoí-vermelho
PL 4.3

28 cm; 64.5 g. Dwarf of group, reminiscent of a rail. Upperparts black and chestnut, underparts cinnamon. Female lacks black on back, has cinnamon upper wing coverts. *I. "neoxenus"* is a rare mutation, first described in U.S.; it has blackish upperparts, chestnut underparts (Taubaté, São Paulo, H. Alvarenga, see Teixeira and Alvarenga 1985). VOICE: song, given continuously in morning and late afternoon, a deep *rro-rro-rro . . .* ; also a croaking *raaahb,* similar to *Nycticorax nycticorax; gheh-eh.* Crawls and jumps with great agility through dense vegetation of wet marshes. Generally seen only in flight. North America to Argentina, most of Brazil (from Amazonia to southeast, northeast, Goiás, Mato Grosso, Santa Catarina). See *I. involucris.*

Fig. 57. Rufescent Tiger-Heron, *Tigrisoma lineatum*, stance when wary; the long neck plumage is fluffed out, resulting in a projection on the hind neck. Original, H. Sick.

STRIPE-BACKED BITTERN, *Ixobrychus involucris*,
Socoí-amarelo

Rusty yellow, top of head and back streaked with black. In open reed beds. The Guianas, Venezuela, Colombia, southeastern Brazil (Rio de Janeiro to Rio Grande do Sul), Uruguay, Paraguay, Argentina, Bolivia, Chile.

ZIGZAG HERON, *Zebrilus undulatus*,
Socoí-ziguezague

31 cm. Short, heavy bill; upperparts black and chestnut, transversely vermiculated with yellow. Mandible, iris, and toes may be yellow. Small marshes, moving about in dense, low vegetation near or above water. Also enters water. Moves by hopping on ground, resembling a Variegated Antpitta, *Grallaria varia* (Derek Scott). The Guianas and Venezuela to north bank of Amazon, Rondônia, Bolivia, Peru.

PINNATED BITTERN, *Botaurus pinnatus*,
Socó-boi-baio

74 cm. Large. Plumage resembles that of immature *Tigrisoma lineatum*, but with black longitudinal pattern and toes twice as long as *T. lineatum* (middle toe 12 cm). VOICE: *ro-ro-ro* when taking flight; "song" a deep, monosyllabic roar. When alarmed stretches neck vertically, assuming appearance of a fence post. Shows nervousness by lateral movements of erect tail, imitating oscillation of reeds in wind. Open marshes and reedbeds; of local occurrence. Throughout Brazil; also Mexico to Argentina. A close relative of *B. lentiginosus* of North America.

Ardeidae Bibliography

See also General Bibliography

Benson, C. W., and R. J. Dowsett. 1969. Correspondence (*Egretta garzetta*). *Auk* 86:806.

Bock, W. J. 1956. *Am. Mus. Nov.* 1779. [Ardeidae generic revision]

Borrero, H., and J. I. Borrero. 1972. *Cespedesia* 1,4. [*Bubulcus*, behavior]

Coimbra Filho, A. F. 1967. *Atas Simpos. Biota Amaz.* 7:97–103. [Nesting colonies]

Deckeyser, P., and A. J. Negret. 1978. Sur la distribution géographique du héron garde boefs, *Bubulcus ibis*, dans le région néotropicale. *Rev. Nordest. Biol.* 1. João Pessoa.

Edman, J. D., J. F. Day, and E. D. Walker. 1986. Field confirmation of laboratory observations on differential antimosquito behavior of herons. *Condor* 86:91-92.

Eisenmann, E. 1965. *Hornero:* 225–34. [*Tigrisoma*, taxonomy]

Gaviño, G., and R. Dickerman. 1972. Nestling development of Green Herons at San Blas, Nayarit, Mexico. *Condor* 74:72–79.

Goeldi, E. 1898. *Bol. Mus. Pará* 2:27–40. [Conservation]

Greenberg, R. E. 1971. *Wilson Bull.* 83:95–97. [Insecticides]

Hancock, J., and J. Kushlan. 1984. *The Herons Handbook*. London.

Higuchi, H. 1986. Bait-fishing by the Green-backed Heron, *Ardeola striata*, in Japan. *Ibis* 128:285–90.

Humphrey, P. S., and K. C. Parkes. 1963. Plumages and systematics of the Whistling Heron, *Syrigma sibilatrix*. *Proc. 13th Int. Orn. Cong.*, *Ithaca*:84–90.

Kahl, M. P. 1971. *Wilson Bull.* 83:302–03. [*Syrigma*, behavior]

Kushlan, J. A., and M. S. Kushlan. 1975. *Florida Field Nat.* 3:31–38. [*Mycteria*, breeding season]

Lancaster, D. A. 1970. *The Living Bird* 9:167–94. [*Bubulcus*, behavior]

Marin A., Manuel. 1989. Notes on the breeding of Chestnut-bellied Herons (*Agamia agami*) in Costa Rica. *Condor* 91: 215–17.

Meyerriecks, A. J. 1971. *Wilson Bull.* 83:435–38. [Behavior]

Olmos, F., and M. F. B. Souza. 1988. A new race of *Ixobrychus involucris* from northeastern Brazil. *Wilson Bull.* 100:510–11.

Olrog, C. C. 1969. *Neotropica* 15:82–88. [Banding]

Olrog, C. C. 1975. Vagrancy of neotropical cormorants, egrets, and White-faced Ibis. *Bird Banding* 46(3):207–12.

Payne, R. B., and C. J. Risley. 1976. *Misc. Publ. Mus. Zool. Univ. Michigan* 150. [Systematics and evolution in Ardeidae]

Pinto, O.M.O. 1946. *Pap. Avuls. Zool. S. Paulo* 7:45–50. [*Tigrisoma*, plumage succession]

Preston, C. R. 1986. Green-backed Heron baits fish with insects. *Wilson Bull.* 98(4):613–14.

Schlatter, R. P., and N. E. Duarte. 1979. Nuevos registros ornitológicos en la Antártica Chilena. *Ser. Cient. Inst. Antart. Chileno* 25/26:45–48.

Short, L. L. 1969. An apparently agonistic display of the Whistling Heron, *Syrigma sibilatrix*. *Wilson Bull.* 81:330–31.

Sick, H. 1965. *An. Acad. Bras. Ciênc.* 37:567–70. [*Bubulcus*, first record for Brazil]

Sprunt, A., Jr. 1954. A hybrid between the Little Blue Heron and the Snowy Egret. *Auk* 71(3):314. [Plate]

Teixeira, D. M., and H.M.F. Alvarenga. 1985. The first recorded Cory's Bittern (*Ixobrychus "neoxenus"*) from South America. *Auk* 102:413.

Teixeira, D. M., and J. B. Nacinovic. 1982. O Socó-boi, *Botaurus pinnatus*, no Rio de Janeiro. *An. Soc. Sul-Riogr. Orn.* 3:9–12.

Teixeira, D. M., and J. B. Nacinovic. 1982a. Notas sobre a garça-real, *Pilherodius pileatus*. *An. Soc. Sul-Riogr. Orn.* 3:13–15.

Teixeira, D. M., J. B. Nacinovic, and F. B. Pontual. 1987. Notes on some birds of northeastern Brazil. *Bull. B.O.C.* 107:151–57.

Wetmore, A. 1963. *Auk* 80:547. [*Bubulcus*, distribution]

FAMILY COCHLEARIIDAE: BOAT-BILLED HERON (1)

The single species in this family is restricted to tropical America. So far no fossils are known. The Boat-billed Heron, *Cochlearius cochlearius*, differs from regular herons in various morphological and behavioral particulars. Its inclusion as a tribe within the Ardeidae has been proposed. As the Cochlearini, it would go alongside the Nycticoracini (night-herons), to which it may be more closely related. Bock (1956) considered *Cochlearius* to be an aberrant type of *Nycticorax*. However, DNA hybridization reveals *Tigrisoma* to be the closest relative (Sheldon 1987). Both *Cochlearius* and *Tigrisoma* eggs are spotted on the rounded end, unlike eggs of other herons. Young *Cochlearius* lack the crest typical of young Ardeidae.

BOAT-BILLED HERON, *Cochlearius cochlearius*, Arapapá   PL 3.3

54 cm; 620 g (male). A wetland bird that looks like a heron, especially a *Nycticorax* night-heron, but differs in its peculiar, extremely wide, flat bill, whose maxilla is like an upside-down keeled boat. Large, bulging eyes immediately suggest crepuscular activity. When illuminated at night they give off an orange reflection. Both sexes may have a long, black nuchal crest (usually longer and more spectacular in male) which contrasts with light gray mantle. Pure white forehead and foreneck are impressive when seen from the front. Breast and abdomen vary from rusty to light chestnut, flanks are black, upper back is crossed by an inconspicuous black band. Juvenile is brown (lighter on forehead), with cap and nuchal crest black and belly whitish cream, lightly streaked brown. It can breed when still in transition plumage (ex-Guanabara). VOICE: *HAgagagagogo, pst-pst-pst, pit-pit-pit;* may also snap bill.

Behavior and Feeding: During the day it rests on well-shaded branches where it stays absolutely quiet, easily remaining unnoticed, its bill always lowered onto the breast as if deep in meditation. When sleeping it leans its head to one side, placing the bill so it is entirely hidden under the wing (see Ardeidae, "Behavior").

Fishes at night, at dawn and dusk, on rainy days, and rarely on clear days by walking slowly through shallow water catching amphibians, small fish, crustaceans, insects, leaves, and small mammals. Sways its body sideways, somewhat like Sunbittern, *Eurypyga helias*. Lives alone or in pairs and temporarily in small flocks. Occurs frequently in same area as night-herons, sometimes perching at their side in a dark thicket just above the water, as in an igarapé.

Breeding: When disturbed *C. cochlearius* lowers its head and opens its crest to form a marvelous fan or cockade, a most impressive display. Pairs touch bills together. I have seen a male court his companion by positioning himself behind her, daintily touching her neck plumage with his bill and trying to take her bill in his. When he succeeded, her bill was fully inside his and he closed on it. The two then began a series of strong, rhythmic movements as if wanting to intermingle even more. The ceremony lasted several minutes and gave the false impression of fighting. When the birds finally separated they made convulsive movements, as if swallowing something, and immediately started to drink. I have seen a young try to obtain food from one of its parents by the same process.

Boat-bill builds a stick nest like a heron's, placing it in branches of flooded forests, sometimes in mixed colonies with herons and Scarlet Ibis, *Eudocimus ruber*. Lays 2–3 thin-shelled eggs which vary in color from faded green to bluish-white and are covered by a light calcareous wash (Rio de Janeiro). In Central America eggs speckled with tiny dark spots have been reported. Oologists say that *C. cochlearius* eggs are more like those of ibis than of herons. Incubation lasts 23 days (Rio de Janeiro); the nestling is covered with down but differs in appearance from the young of other herons by having a level, soot-colored cap instead of a high, erect crest.

Parents, especially mother, are very aggressive in defending nest, chasing away other birds that approach and protesting vehemently against human intrusion. This aggressiveness is in notable contrast to behavior of other herons. On nest the female reveals any nervousness by lateral movements of the body. If further pressed she resorts to attacking the intruder with her crest raised, her neck fully stretched forward, and her wings half open, croaking and snapping her bill. When young are disturbed they climb branches above nest with great agility, to return when all is calm.

Habitat and Distribution: Lake and river edges with dense arboreal vegetation, aninga clumps, mangroves. Mexico to Bolivia, Argentina, almost all of Brazil; Amazonia to Mato Grosso, Goiás, Maranhão, Piauí, Bahia, Espírito Santo, Minas Gerais, Rio de Janeiro, São Paulo. Also called *Savacu, Colhereiro, Soco-de-bico-largo* (Piauí), *Arataiaçu* (Amazonia).

Cochleariidae Bibliography

Biderman, J. O., and R. W. Dickerman. 1978. Feeding behavior and food habits of the Boat-billed Heron. *Biotropica* 10:33–37.

Bock, W. 1956. See Ardeidae Bibliography.

Cracraft, J. 1967. *Auk* 84:529–33. [Systematic position]

Dickerman, R. W., and C. Juarez. 1971. *Ardea* 59:1–16. [Nesting, systematics]

Dickerman, R. W., K. C. Parkes, and J. Bell. 1982. Notes on the plumages of the Boat-billed Heron. *The Living Bird* 19:115–20.

Haverschmidt, F. 1969. *Auk* 86:130–31. [Nesting]

Mock, D. W. 1975. *Auk* 92:590–92. [Behavior]

Sheldon, F. J. 1987. Phylogeny of herons estimated from DNA-DNA hybridization data. *Auk* 104:97–108.

FAMILY THRESKIORNITHIDAE: IBISES (8)

The ibis family, which has also been called Plataleidae, is more closely related to the storks than the herons. With the family's broad, global distribution, numerous fossils since the middle Eocene (45 million years B.P.) have been found. The Sacred Ibis, *Threskiornis aethiopicus,* mummified by the Egyptians in ancient times, typifies this universally known family. The Scarlet Ibis, *Eudocimus ruber,* is one of the world's most beautiful birds.

Morphology and Identification

The bill is long and down curved or spoon shaped. The legs are not as long as in the Ciconiidae, Ardeidae, and Cochleariidae. Males and females are similar, with a certain amount of sexual dimorphism developing during the breeding period (*Eudocimus ruber;* Roseate Spoonbill, *Platalea ajaja*). Males tend to be larger. Immatures may have quite different coloring and have a shorter bill.

Feeding

Small crustaceans play an important role in the diet of *Eudocimus ruber* and *Platalea ajaja,* being responsible for the intense red pigmentation these birds show in the wild but that fades in captive specimens unless cantaxanthin or carrots are added to their diet (see also Phoenicopteridae and Vermilion Flycatcher, *Pyrocephalus rubinus*). The stomachs of various spoonbills in the Rio de Janeiro area were found to be full of barnacle larvae (*Balanus* spp.). See Anatidae, "Feeding," White-cheeked Pintail, *Anas bahamensis.*) Spoonbills engage in group fishing.

The Buff-necked Ibis, *Theristicus caudatus,* sometimes eats toads (*Bufo granulosus*), interesting in view of the fact that when eaten the poison of these batrachians is fatal to most animals except the colubrid snake boipeva (*Xenodon merremii*) (Carvalho 1940).

Behavior and Migration

Ibis fly with the neck inclined slightly downward and the wings held in a concave shape, like large shells. Their wing beats are more rapid than those of herons; sometimes they intersperse a short glide, but the White-faced Ibis, *Plegadis chihi,* does not do this on distant flights.

Ibis are gregarious, but flocks of different species keep apart. They are conspicuous when gathering to sleep or when moving to a distant site to feed. In Rio Grande do Sul the dusk flights of *P. chihi* are spectacular. At the Taim Ecological Station in January, the birds were coming and going in numerous north-south currents. Later I found them sleeping in a compact mass perched on the ground in open marshes. A

smaller number of Bare-faced Ibis, *Phimosus infuscatus,* were overflying the Taim area in an east-west direction on the way to their own separate sleeping quarters. In the Mato Grosso Pantanal, enormous flocks of *P. infuscatus* gather to fly high to their roost but return in the morning scattered and flying low in search of food. *Eudocimus ruber* appears in certain places and promptly disappears again. Banded *Plegadis chihi* from Santa Fé, Argentina, regularly spend the winter in Rio Grande do Sul. A *Platalea ajaja* banded in Rio Grande do Sul was found in Rio de Janeiro.

Breeding

Most ibis nest together in colonies. The Green Ibis, *Mesembrinibis cayennensis,* the two *Theristicus,* and *Phimosus infuscatus* breed in isolated pairs. *Eudocimus ruber* and *Platalea ajaja* nest in trees; *Phimosus infuscatus* and *Plegadis chihi* in reedbeds; and *Theristicus caudatus* on trees or rocks scattered on the savanna. Eggs vary, being solid bluish (*Phimosus infuscatus, Plegadis chihi*), green with small dark spots (*Mesembrinibis cayennensis*), white or brownish with speckles (*Theristicus* spp., *Platalea ajaja*), or light green heavily blotched with brown (*Eudocimus ruber*). Incubation varies from 23 to 24 days with *P. ajaja. E. ruber* chicks are fed by regurgitation.

Use, Decline, and Epidemiological Interest

In Amazonia *Eudocimus ruber* is valued as a pet: it rids gardens of insects and has a reputation for great cleanliness (thus the phrase *limpo como um guará,* "clean as a Scarlet Ibis"). It has become extinct in a great portion of its Brazilian range because of egg hunting, destruction of nesting colonies, and intense hunting for its feathers, used for adornment. In the Mato Grosso Pantanal a decline in *Platalea ajaja* is due to nest depredation by the Crested Caracara, *Polyborus plancus.* The spoonbill is less proficient in defense than the sharp-billed herons. Problems have been noted with *Phimosus infuscatus* because of insecticide contamination of its food. Small farmers in Santa Catarina suspect, with a certain amount of reason, that *Theristicus caudatus* contributes to dissemination of foot-and-mouth disease as its flies from one pasture to another. Normally it is protected by ranchers as a biological control that holds down the population of small noxious creatures.

PLUMBEOUS IBIS, *Theristicus (= Harpiprion) caerulescens,* Maçarico-real

73 cm. Large southern species, distinguished by much elongated nuchal feathers and full, furrowed neck plumage. Dark gray or brownish with black flight and tail feathers.

VOICE: similar to *T. caudatus* but a resonant, descending series of single syllables, *ki-ki-ki* . . . , *ghew-ghew-ghew.* . . . Marshes where it catches aquatic mollusks, e.g., *Pomacea,* as does *Plegadis chihi,* frequently its neighbor in Rio Grande do Sul. May also occur alongside *T. caudatus.* Argentina to Rio Grande do Sul, Mato Grosso (Pantanal). Uncommon, little known.

BUFF-NECKED IBIS, *Theristicus caudatus,* Curicaca   PL 3.5

69 cm; height 43 cm. Large, light-colored, with broad wings. In flight shows large white patch on upper wing surface which contrasts with all-black under surface. VOICE: loud, short cries with timbre of Helmeted Guineafowl, *Numida meleagris, kee-kee-kee* staccato, *go-GHI, tau-TA-ko.* Pairs and flocks that gather to roost vocalize together; at peak of calling they throw head back. Walks openly in dry fields, including airports, seeks burned areas; catches grasshoppers, spiders, centipedes, gheckos, snakes, rats, etc. Will sink bill into loose earth up to base to extract beetle larvae. Soars at great heights. In southern Brazil (e.g., Santa Catarina) roosts and nests in Paraná pines (*Araucaria angustifolia*) and in Amazon estuary in kapoks (*Bombax munguba*) and carobas (Bignoniaceae). Colombia to Tierra del Fuego, embracing Andes and much of Brazil, including northeast and south. Also called *Despertador* (Mato Grosso Pantanal).

SHARP-TAILED IBIS, *Cercibis oxycerca,* Trombeteiro

70 cm. Black with green sheen, purple sheen on back; skin around eye, bill, and legs red. VOICE: reminiscent of *Theristicus caudatus* but nasal and less raucous, *eg-eg.* Savannas. Venezuela and the Guianas to Colombia, Brazil, but only in northwest (Rio Negro) and west (Rio Guaporé). Also called *Tará.*

GREEN IBIS, *Mesembrinibis cayennensis,* Corocoró   PL 4.4

58 cm. Only forest ibis. Dark green, bill and legs greenish black. VOICE: a melodious *korro . . . gogogo, koRO-koRO . . . ,* with timbre of Greater Ani, *Crotophaga major.* Heard more frequently at dawn and dusk. River edges, forest lakes, aningais (Amazonia). Eats insects, worms, plants. I found a large amount of fibrous vegetable material, along with small worms and various insects, especially beetles, in intestines of 2 individuals collected at Linhares, Espírito Santo, in November 1940. Panama to Paraguay, Argentina (Misiones), Brazil (almost everywhere), e.g., Espírito Santo, São Paulo, Paraná, Rio Grande do Sul (January), sometimes isolated individuals in migration. Abundant in Amazonia. Also called *Tapicuru, Caraúna.* See Limpkin, *Aramus guarauna.*

BARE-FACED IBIS, *Phimosus infuscatus,* Tapicuru-de-cara-pelada

54 cm. Black with green sheen, forepart of head bare and light red, bill whitish (color varies), legs blackish. VOICE: a weak *ghew-ghew-ghew;* often mute. Marshes, newly plowed fields, etc. Seeks food in shallow water by walking slowly with a quarter of bill submerged, like *Eudocimus ruber.* Also eats vegetable matter (seeds, leaves). Periodically one of most numerous birds of Mato Grosso Pantanal, but uncommon or absent elsewhere. The Guianas and Venezuela to Bolivia, Paraguay, Argentina, Uruguay, Brazil (Roraima, northeast, east, south, also Mato Grosso). Also called *Maçarico-de-bico-branco, Maçarico-preto, Tapicuru, Frango d'agua* (Pantanal), *Chapeu-velho.* See *Plegadis chihi.*

SCARLET IBIS, *Eudocimus ruber,* Guará   PL 3.6

58 cm. One of world's most spectacular birds, typical of mangroves of north Atlantic coast of South America. Magnificent carmine red plumage is due to carotenoid cantaxanthin (see "Feeding"). In breeding season male bill becomes shiny black, but legs maintain light red color. Female's slimmer bill remains brownish with blackish tip, her legs stay whitish red. I have at times noted the vestige of a compact little sac of bare pink skin on each side of throat. This feature, which appears during breeding, occurs regularly in female White Ibis, *E. albus,* a more northern form. Immature dark brown with lower back and upper tail coverts white, abdomen yellowish white. Nestling covered with black down; at this age bill is straight. Now generally accepted that *E. ruber* and *E. albus* are conspecific. They breed together in Venezuelan llanos, and hybrids are fertile.

Feeding, Behavior, and Breeding: Wanders about in shallow water with tip of bill submerged, opening and closing mandibles rapidly in search of crabs, snails, and insects. Basic item in diet is small crabs, e.g., chama-maré or sarará (*Uca* sp.), and maraquani, which are abundant in intertidal zone. Species of crab varies with locality, depending on water salinity, which is different, for example, north and south of mouth of Amazon, depending on fresh-water currents that reach north coast. *Uca* is also abundant in brackish lakes and rivers. Before eating one, *E. ruber* removes the large claw. Along the coast of Amapá it appears together with the Whimbrel, *Numenius phaeopus,* a northern migrant searching for the same sararás in mud.

Always in flocks. For roosting and nesting it seeks dense vegetation, e.g., extensive mangroves (*Rhizophora, Avicennia*) and aturiás (*Macherium lunatum*). Flights to these sites are impressive, extending as far as 60–70 km from the mudflats where the birds feed during the day (mouth of Amazon). Immatures may form separate flocks.

Shares nesting colonies with *Platalea ajaja* and Wood Stork, *Mycteria americana.* Ordinarily uses already existing nests at midlevel in mangroves. I have been informed that it nests at beginning of dry season, July–September (Pará), although it is reported to breed in the Guianas in rainy season.

Distribution and Decline: There are 2 disjunct populations in Brazil, 1 in the north, the other in the south. The species formerly occurred on our coast as far south as the Island of Santa Catarina (Frézier 1712); in other words, to the southern end of Atlantic coast mangroves (28°20′S) under the influence of the Brazil Current. It was found in Paraná (Murreta, near Paranaguá, nesting colonies) by A. Saint Hilaire in 1820. As late as 1977 3 individuals were sighted on Antonina Bay, Paranaguá (Pedro Scherer Neto). Names such as Guaratuba (*guara tuba* = "many Scarlet Ibis"), a city in Paraná, perpetuate its memory in the area. There are records from the sixteenth century from the São Paulo coast, with nesting colonies being disputed between the Tupinambá and Tupiniquin tribes, who used ibis feathers to make adornments (H. Staden 1557, on the island of Santo Amaro). Surprisingly, *E. ruber* have been appearing in mangroves on the São Paulo coast at Cubatão, in the vicinity of Santos, since 1982. A good photograph was taken of a band of 42 adults in September 1984, and in the winter of 1986 as many as 82, all adults, were seen feeding in mud and shallow waters or perched on tall trees in mangroves (Bokermann 1986 pers. comm.). In January 1989 a flock of about 100 was seen there, and a pair attending a nest was even reported (Marcondes-Machado et al. 1989). The place of these current observations is close to where Staden made his while a prisoner of the Tupinambá in 1554.

E. ruber occurred in Guanabara Bay (in mangroves of Ilha do Governador) around 1929. Trustworthy observers have stated that a flock of 15–20 individuals, predominantly immatures (suggesting existence of a nesting colony not too distant), was seen between May and August 1952 at mouth of the Rio Magé in the inner end of Guanabara Bay. Other information of this type suggests that southern populations still exist (1977). In November 1979 an adult was seen at Lagoa da Tijuca (Luiz P. Gonzaga), and in February 1985 2 more (bills were not black, see above), appeared in the Guaratiba lowlands of Rio de Janeiro state (J. Nacinovic, 1 collected).

Range of *E. ruber* extends north from Brazil along coasts of all countries of northern South America to Colombia and Ecuador. It is also found in Central America, Trinidad (where it is the national bird), and sometimes the Antilles. It has been introduced into Florida, the area of *E. albus*. The latter also occurs in reduced numbers in Venezuela, where the 2 species hybridize.

E. ruber, "the most common among the aquatic bird species of the Amazon region" (Goeldi 1894), became scarce there and was totally eliminated from the southeastern part of the country. According to information gathered by H. F. Alvarenga, J. L. Freire, and F. C. Novaes (1970–72 pers. comm.), it was still relatively abundant on the Amapá coast, in such places as the mouth of the Rio Araguari, on

Ilha Vitória (nesting colonies), and in the vicinity of the city of Amapá (nesting colonies). It also visits rivers and lakes in the interior of the region. During a systematic survey made by A. L. Spaans (who overflew the Guianas and Amapá coasts from 1970 to 1972), *E. ruber* were found in the largest numbers in Brazilian territory north of 3°N, with 1 nesting colony found in the estuary of the Rio Oiapoque (Cape Orange) in August 1971. For more recent findings, see Teixeira and Best (1981). During an aerial census in 1981–82, a group of approximately 7500 adults were found near Ilha Caviana in the Amazon mouth. The birds hide in the mangroves and are easily missed, especially immatures.

E. ruber continues to exist on Marajó Island (Soure, Salvaterra, Muaná; nesting colonies, 1972), at Belém (Pirabas, Pilões, and Quatipuru bays), Vigia, and São Caetano de Odivales, Pará, and west of the mouth of the Rio Gurupi, Viseu, and Limondeoa, Pará (1972, nesting colonies). Nesting colonies found near the end of the 1800s near Arari (Marajó) and on Ilha Caviana, as well as those along the arm of the Amazon north of Marajó Island, have disappeared. I have noticed that local people use the expression *ninhal* ("nesting colony") indiscriminately both for nesting places and for roosts where ibis, egrets, etc., only sleep.

Sometimes *E. ruber* moves up the Amazon and its tributaries. Isolated individuals have appeared, for instance, on the Rio Trombetas, Oriximiná (Pará).

It inhabits the Maranhão coast (fig. 59) between Cumã (Guimarães) and Turiaçu (nesting colonies, 1972). It appears as a visitor on the Ceará littoral near Fortaleza (1973). It has been cited, erroneously, for the Mato Grosso Pantanal because of confusion with *Platalea ajaja*. The confusion is compounded by the fact that the most popular postcard sold in the Pantanal area shows a flock of *E. ruber* in flight—a photo probably taken on Marajó Island, Pará. Its occurrence in the Pantanal, where there are brackish waters, would not be so strange considering it breeds in large numbers in freshwater areas of the Venezuelan llanos. In 1984 the Venezuelan *E. ruber* colonies were reported to be moving from the littoral, where they were more disturbed, into the interior. Fifty percent of all *E. ruber* occur in Venezuela. The best habitat for them is mangroves, whose destruction is widespread because of oceanic coastal pollution and the depredations of people, who also enter the mangroves with guns and fireworks, so disturbing the birds on their nests that they abandon them.

WHITE-FACED IBIS, *Plegadis chihi,*
Caraúna, Tapicuru

53 cm. Even more slender than *Phimosus infuscatus,* which sometimes appears alongside it (Rio Grande do Sul). In aspect may resemble a curlew or Whimbrel, *Numenius* sp. Chocolate-chestnut with violet-purplish green wings and tail. Bill and legs dark, lores bare. At end of year molts to nonbreeding plumage, face taking on white that is retained

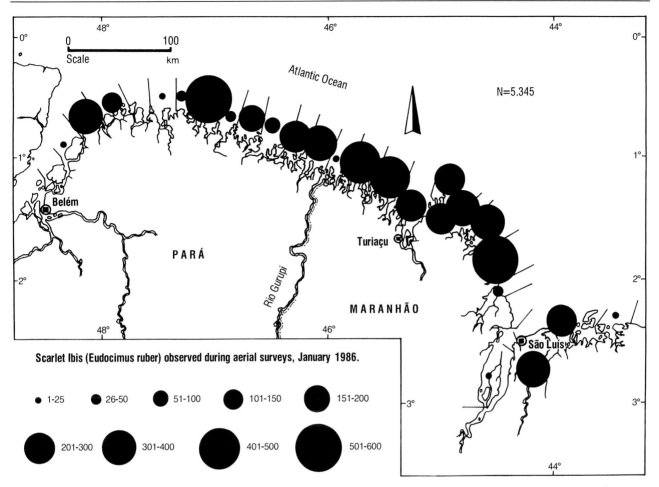

Fig. 59. Aerial census of the Scarlet Ibis, *Eudocimus ruber,* on the coasts of Pará and Maranhão in 1986. After Morrison et al. 1986.

until June/August (Weller 1962). VOICE: a low *go-go-go, quack* . . . , similar to a duck. Rice fields, open marshes. When flying a flock may be mistaken for White-faced Whistling-Ducks, *Dendrocygna viduata;* they move in wedge-shaped formations and long lines. Migratory. Individuals banded in Santa Fé, Argentina, as nestlings have been found in September and November of same year in Rio Grande do Sul, 1400 km to northeast. Chile and Argentina (Patagonia) to Bolivia, Colombia, Brazil in Rio Grande do Sul (where common), São Paulo, southern Mato Grosso. Also called *Maçarico-preto* (Rio Grande do Sul). Replaced in north by *P. falcinellus,* a very similar and cosmopolitan species that nests in Venezuela, North America, and Old World. See Limpkin, *Aramus guarauna.*

ROSEATE SPOONBILL, *Platalea ajaja,*
Colhereiro, Ajajá   PL 3.7

87 cm. Unique bill shape. Pink plumage due to presence of carotenoids cantaxanthin and astaxanthin (see *Eudocimus ruber*). Color intense only in breeding season. Matures at 3 years. Immature whitish (including head, which is feathered,

unlike adult's) with bare lores, bill and legs brownish, flight feathers black. VOICE: grunts and quacks.

In flocks feeds in shallow water by submerging "spoon" of bill and moving it from side to side, straining water. Thus catches small aquatic animals, e.g., little fish, insects, mollusks, and crustaceans, including barnacles (*Balanus*), especially larvae but also adults (as shown by pieces of shell found in stomach contents in ex-Guanabara). I have seen spoonbills perform group fishing, 10–20 individuals walking side by side fishing in shallow water (Rio Grande do Sul).

Flies with neck outstretched, somewhat resembling *Ciconia* storks, but obviously differing from these in much smaller size and in alternating a series of wing beats with a glide, like *Theristicus caudatus.* After breeding season white immatures form flocks that at a distance can be confused with egrets. Muddy beaches of interior or littoral, mangroves; nesting colonies intermingled with those of egrets, *E. ruber* (on coast), etc. Southern U.S. to Argentina, much of Brazil, including all southern regions. Nests on Ilha do Governador, at gates of city of Rio de Janeiro. A close relative of Old

World spoonbill, which is larger and all white. See also flamingos, *Phoenicopteridae.*

Threskiornithidae Bibliography

See also General Bibliography

Bokermann, C. A., and J.C.C. Guix. 1986. Reaparecimento do guará, *Eudocimus ruber,* no litoral de São Paulo. *An. II En. Nac. An. Aves, Rio de Janeiro.*

Carvalho, A. L. 1940. *Memor. Inst. Oswaldo Cruz* 35(3):375–576. [Frog eating]

Cintra, R. 1986. Nidificação e crescimento do filhote de curicaca, *Harpiprion caerulescens,* no Pantanal de Mato Grosso, *XIII Cong. Bras. Zool. Cuiabá:* 545.

Dubs, B. 1988. Beobachtungen zur Fortpflanzungsbiologie des Stirnbandibis, *Harpiprion caerulescens. J. Orn.* 129:363–65.

ffrench, R. P., and F. Haverschmidt. 1970. *The Living Bird* 9:147–65. [*Eudocimus,* general]

Frézier, A. F. 1712. In P. Berger, 1979, *Ilha de Santa Catarina, relatos de viajantes estrangeiros.* Florianópolis: Assessoria Cultural.

Marcondes-Machado, L. O., M. M. Argel de Oliveira, and E.L.A. Monteiro-Filho. 1989. Ocorrência do guará, *Eudocimus ru-* ber, no litoral de São Paulo. *Resumos V ENAV, Brasília:*12–13.

Morrison, R.J.G., R. K. Ross, P.T.Z. Antas, et al. 1985. Aerial survey of shorebirds and other wildlife in South America. *Canad. Wildlife* 148:1–22.

Morrison, R.I.G., R. K. Ross, and P.T.Z. Antas. 1986. Distribuição de maçaricos, batuiras e outras aves costeiras na região do salgado paraense e reentrâncias maranhenses. *Espaço, Ambiente e Planejamento* 4. Rio de Janeiro: CVRD/MAM.

Olrog, C. C. 1969. *Neotropica* 15:82–88. [Banding]

San Martin, P. R. 1962. *Bol. Soc. Taguató* 1:79–84. [Feeding]

Scherer Neto, P. 1982. Aspectos bionômicos e desenvolvimento de *Theristicus caudatus. Ducenia* 13(4):145–49.

Spaan, A. L. 1975. *Biol. Conserv.* 7:245–53. [*Eudocimus,* distribution]

Teixeira, D. M., and R. C. Best. 1981. *Bol. Mus. Paraen., Zool.* 104. [*Eudocimus,* distribution]

Toseli, C. 1985. Notas sobre a ocorrência de *Ajaia ajaja* nos manguezais da bahia da Guanabara. *XII Cong. Bras. Zool., Campinas:*555.

Villela, G. G. 1968. *An. Acad. Bras. Cienc.* 40:391–99. [Pigments]

Weller, M. W. 1962. *Ibis* 109:409. [*Plegadis chihi,* breeding plumage]

FAMILY CICONIIDAE: STORKS (3)

Storks, large heronlike birds, are widely distributed throughout the world. Africa is the "stork continent," with such outstanding examples as the grotesque Marabou (*Leptoptilos crumeniferus*). The White Stork, *Ciconia ciconia,* is one of the most popular birds of Europe, being considered a good luck omen and by legend responsible for bringing babies into the world. Storks are adapted to fresh water. The oldest fossil is from the lower Oligocene of Egypt (35 million years B.P.); in Brazil, 20,000-year-old fossils have been found in Minas Gerais caves.

As early as 1870 A. B. Garrod drew attention to the anatomic similarities of the Ciconiidae and New World vultures, as Ligon (1967) and König (1982) have done more recently (see Cathartidae). Biochemical research has provided confirmation: Ciconiidae and Cathartidae are close relatives that evolved from common ancestors and separated into two family groups 35 to 40 million years ago (Sibley and Ahlquist 1986). The similarity of Old World and New World vultures is pure convergence as an adaptation to carrion eating.

Morphology

The Jabiru, *Jabiru mycteria;* Maguari Stork, *Ciconia maguari;* and White-necked Heron, *Ardea cocoi,* are the largest native Brazilian birds after the Greater Rhea, *Rhea americana.* Ciconiidae have very large bills with diverse shapes and white or black-and-white plumage. Although sexes are similar, the male is more robust and generally has a different bill shape. The tail of *C. maguari* is unique. In Brazil an awkward person is popularly referred to as a *jabiru.*

Sounds and Bill Clapping

Storks are almost mute (the syrinx is rudimentary) but are able to clatter their bills, making a *peb-peb-peb* sound (*Jabiru mycteria, Ciconia maguari*). It is reported that the Wood Stork, *Mycteria americana,* clatters during copulation. *C. maguari* snorts when irritated. Young Jabirus whistle while begging food and can become noisy.

Food and Fishing Methods

Storks are omnivorous. They catch a wide variety of animals, from insects, crabs, and snails to frogs and fish. The three species that occur in Brazil have entirely different techniques for capturing prey. *Mycteria americana* remains stationary or walks slowly in shallow water (which may be covered on the surface with floating vegetation), the bill held low and slightly open with the tips underwater, and stirs one of its feet back and forth. It alternates feet in this activity, designed to frighten out animals hidden in the mud, which are seized when they touch the point of the bill, thus being caught without use of the eyes. As a result, this species seems very "calm" as it searches for food.

In contrast, *Jabiru mycteria* walks energetically to and fro with long steps and at each step submerges its bill in the water, shaking it violently to frighten up hidden fish. It leaves the water when it encounters difficulty overcoming a fish which, should it escape, is much more easily recaptured if it falls on dry ground. It catches catfish (Siluridae), whose large spines are broken by being turned over in the bill (Mato Grosso Pantanal). I have seen one of these birds jump in shallow water, also apparently to frighten animals buried in the bottom. It also catches young caiman (which it kills by beating them against a branch), turtles (*Podocnemis*), and snakes, even carrying small anacondas to its nest (Mato Grosso, Arne Sucksdorff). Sometimes *J. mycteria* carry out a regimented group operation: they march side by side toward the shore, frightening fish so they flee toward shallow water where they are easily captured.

Ciconia maguari hunts by lurking in tall aquatic vegetation. Both it and *Mycteria americana* also eat plant material. *C. maguari* hunts by sight, whereas the method of *J. mycteria* is primarily tactile and of *M. americana* almost entirely so.

For all three species the best period for feeding (and breeding) is the beginning of the dry season, when the greatest concentrations of aquatic prey occur. When the water begins to recede, storks appear in flocks with herons and other long-legged birds to search for fish or other dead or dying prey that succumb in pools that are slowly drying up in the sun. In the flatlands of Mato Grosso and Amazonia *J. mycteria* plays a significant sanitation role by devouring an incredible number of dead fish; it does not even reject large pieces of carrion torn off by vultures.

Behavior and Migration

Unlike herons, storks fly with outstretched necks. They are masters at soaring and take advantage of warm updrafts. All three species can rise so high they are lost from sight. In this way they reach the best fishing places, sometimes 30 km or more from their roosts, to which they return by the same low-energy method. They gather in wedge-shaped flocks when they fly to distant destinations (e.g., *Ciconia*). *Mycteria americana* moves regularly between the Orinoco and Amazon river systems so as always to have edge strips of shallow water available. In the Amazon basin it moves up or down river according to seasonal flooding.

Migration occurs in the south also. At the beginning of February near Capivari, Municipality of Osório, Rio Grande do Sul, a gathering was recorded of 500 to 1000 *M. americana* standing on the ground and feeding in rain-flooded pastures (F. Wildholzer). Two young *M. americana* banded in the Mato Grosso Pantanal at the end of the year were recovered in Rio Grande do Sul in February and in Santa Fé, Argentina, the following January.

Thermoregulation

Storks' long legs have an arteriovenous network (rete tibiotarsale) that facilitates thermoregulation; when the legs are wetted with urine, its evaporation results in immediate cooling (urohydrosis). Thus, the legs are frequently soiled with white (see also Cathartidae). Urination frequency to support urohydrosis increases with heat intensity and can reach once per minute, whereas normal urination occurs once in ten minutes (*Ciconia ciconia*, observed in Africa). For the jet to hit the tarsus-metatarsus precisely, this is lifted and held close to the cloaca.

Apparently the frequent wing stretching observed in storks also has a thermoregulatory function. *M. americana* opens its wings, expanding them to the maximum like cormorants and vultures. *C. maguari* has a novel habit I observed in three individuals, one of them a young bird, in Rio Grande do Sul in January 1966: the birds took a sunbath shortly before sunset, exposing their entire underparts, including under the wings, by opening them and letting the hands dangle with the drooping tips behind the tarsi. All this was in a position so erect that even the under tail coverts were exposed to the sun. The birds held themselves absolutely immobile, bills open, and remained thus for a considerable time. This way of stretching the wings (delta-wing posture), described and illustrated by Kahl (1971) for the Painted Stork, *Mycteria leucocephala,* of India, also occurs in *M. americana,* and I have even seen it in *Ardea cocoi* and the Rufescent Tiger-Heron, *Tigrisoma lineatum.*

Breeding

Both *Mycteria americana* and *Jabiru mycteria* nest in trees, the former in flooded forests in colonies that are sometimes large and include the Roseate Spoonbill, *Platalea ajaja,* and Great Egret, *Casmerodius albus.*

J. mycteria is solitary, building its nest in more prominent and usually isolated trees. These spots, which are quite strategic, are used for many years, probably by the same pair, which is eventually replaced by another. It also nests on top of palms (e.g., buritis), which may eventually kill the tree. It brings large branches, 1 m or more in length and 5 cm thick, and mountains of soft material. The nest is lined with grass. Bitter fights occur between territorial birds (September, Pantanal).

A new *J. mycteria* nest is relatively small but is enlarged at each breeding season, becoming a voluminous heap of sticks, mud, and grass that may reach a diameter of 1.5–2 m and a height of 1–1.5 m. Breeding in the Mato Grosso Pantanal occupies the entire dry season, from June to October–

November. That of *C. maguari* in Rio Grande do Sul is similarly prolonged.

C. maguari nests on the ground in rushes and reeds without trees, choosing shallow-water areas where it gathers a pile of grass and dry stems (e.g., of large Cyperaceae—papyrus) that may reach a diameter of 2 m and a height of 50 cm, similar to the nest of the Southern Screamer, *Chauna torquata*. It cleans up the vicinity of the nest, using the plants it pulls out as building material. Sometimes various pairs nest a few meters from one another. It is the only ciconiid in the world that nests on the ground, although in Venezuela it also nests in trees (Thomas 1986).

Stork eggs are pure white, nothing like those of herons. *Jabiru mycteria* lays two, three, or even four eggs. I have seen three nestlings, and four of *C. maguari*.

Mycteria americana incubation varies from 28 to 32 days, and the young fly approximately 55 days after hatching. *C. maguari* reportedly gives drink to its young by regurgitating water. If food is lacking in very dry years, storks do not breed. Kushlan (1975) demonstrated a mathematical relationship between the dry season and the breeding period of *M. americana* in Florida.

Distribution and Classification

A revision of the Ciconiidae of the world (Kahl 1972) that includes behavior of these birds among its bases provides an interesting zoogeographic perspective, revealing that the three South American species can be attributed to three different groups, each with representatives in the Old World. Thus, we have Mycteriini including *Mycteria,* Ciconiini encompassing *Ciconia,* and Leptoptilini with *Jabiru,* leading to the conclusion that our three species are less closely related to each other than to certain others of Africa and India. Inclusion of *Euxenura* in *Ciconia* is also supported by its behavior, for instance, the "up-down" display (throwing the head back and bill clapping), typical for all species of the genus; this is performed even by *C. maguari* nestlings (fig. 60).

Tenants of Arboreal Nests

The enormous heap of branches forming the nest of *Jabiru mycteria* is a point of attraction for various birds of the region, such as the Chopi Blackbird, *Gnorimopsar chopi;* Great Kiskadee, *Pitangus sulphuratus;* and Monk Parakeet, *Myiopsitta monachus,* which install their nests in its base. *M. monachus* even provides useful services to the Jabiru by reinforcing the base of the nest with material it brings to construct its own and by serving as a sentinel. The Thrush-like Wren, *Campylorhynchus turdinus,* takes soft material from the base of the nest for its own use (Mato Grosso Pantanal).

It is of epidemiological interest that assassin bugs (*Rhodnius prolixus,* Triatominae) have been observed in Venezuela

Fig. 60. Maguari Stork, *Ciconia maguari*. Young in the nest performing the "up-down" display. The bird is black with a yellow throat. Original, H. Sick.

to live in *Jabiru mycteria* and *Mycteria americana* nests. These bugs are the principal vectors of Chagas disease (the protozoan is *Trypanosoma cruzi*). The birds transport the larvae and eggs in their plumage, disseminating the vector. In Venezuela there are no *Myiopsitta monachus* which in the south could introduce assassin bugs into stork nests.

WOOD STORK, *Mycteria americana*, Cabeça-seca, Passarão   PL 4.1

95 cm; 2.8 kg. Head and neck bare and black like legs; toes pink. Plumage all white except for black flight and tail feathers. Male larger than female. Immature, whose head and neck are feathered, frequently holds light yellow, curved bill downward, somewhat like *Eudocimus ruber* does. Frequently perches off ground. Most gregarious of 3 South American species. Immatures associate together but apart from adult pairs. Nesting colonies are in flooded groves. Lives in marshes interspersed with forest. Formerly one of most common aquatic birds of Amazonia, where it is sought by hunters. Southern U.S. to Argentina, almost all of Brazil (including eastern and southern regions). Because of use of same names, both scientific and common, there is sometimes confusion with other storks, particularly *Jabiru mycteria*. Also called *Padre* (Rio Grande do Sul) and in English, Wood Ibis.

MAGUARI STORK, *Ciconia* (= *Euxenura*) *maguari*, Maguari, João-grande

140 cm; height 108 cm. White with elongated feathers on foreneck; flight feathers, greater upper wing coverts, scapular regions, and tail black. Tail bifurcate and shorter than stiff under tail coverts, which extend beyond tail feathers in a white triangle or rectangle conspicuous in flight. Thus, under tail coverts practically replace rectrices as a rudder. When

bird is standing, tips of wings look like a "black prolongation" of rear portion of body. This does not occur with *Mycteria americana,* which appears "short" and all white (its black flight feathers are covered by mantle). Bill straight, bluish gray with reddish tip. Region around eye, bare skin at base of bill, and legs red. Eyes yellow.

Nests on ground (see "Breeding"); has 2–4 young that hatch white, then quickly become blackish with prominent orange throat. Young resemble adults after 3 months (Thomas 1979). Outside breeding season gathers on open lake shores to pass night, resting lying on belly. Lives in marshes and wet tangles with little tall vegetation. In Amazonia considered a game bird like the other 2 storks. In much of South America, all of Brazil (more common in Amazonia and Rio Grande do Sul). Also called *Cauauã* (Paraná), *Cegonha, Tabuiaiá* (Mato Grosso Pantanal), *Jaburu-moleque.* See also *Ardea cocoi.*

JABIRU, *Jabiru mycteria,* Jabiru, Tuiuiú   FIG. 61

140 cm; height 107 cm; wingspan 260 cm; 8 kg. Has colossal bill (smaller in female) with slight upward curve. Bare areas coal black, occiput with some white feathers. Neck can be dilated (and is almost always grossly deformed) with red base and small reddish spot on forepart that is frequently hidden by lowered bill; this color changes in intensity, becoming scarlet, presumably through accumulation of blood, when bird is excited. In Mato Grosso Pantanal there is local variation in bare parts, with an entirely red head and neck contrasting with black bill, which may also have vestiges of red. Tarsus also red. Plumage entirely snow white, unlike *Ciconia maguari.*

Flies with neck fully extended like other storks, but because of a wad of pendant, loose flesh near base, neck looks somewhat retracted. Alternates a few wing strokes with swift

Fig. 61. Jabiru, *Jabiru mycteria.*

gliding. Nests in isolation on tall trees or palms (see "Breeding"). Young dark brown with feathers on head and body. Gathers in flocks to feed. Considered a game bird in Amazonia, its meat resembling goose in taste. Larger nestlings are more appreciated, as they are very fat. Edges of large rivers and lakes with sparse trees, humid savanna with scattered groves. When standing in open along edge of a river can be mistaken for a human. Central America to northern Argentina, Brazil (as far as São Paulo, Santa Catarina). In older literature listed as *Mycteria americana.* Also called *Tuiuiú-coral* (Mato Grosso), *Jaburu-moleque, Jaburu.*

Ciconiidae Bibliography

See also General Bibliography

Kahl, M. P. 1963. *Physiol. Zool.* 36:141–51. [Thermoregulation]

Kahl, M. P. 1964. Food ecology of the Woodstork (*Mycteria americana*) in Florida. *Ecol. Monog.* 34:97–117.

Kahl, M. P. 1971. *The Living Bird* 10:151–70. [Behavior, taxonomy]

Kahl, M. P. 1971. *Condor* 73:220–29. [*Jabiru, Ciconia,* behavior]

Kahl, M. P. 1971. *Auk* 88:715–22. [Behavior]

Kahl, M. P. 1972. *J. Zool.* (London) 167:451–61. [Taxonomy]

König, C. 1982. See Cathartidae Bibliography.

Krebs, I. R. 1978. Colonial nesting birds with special reference to the Ciconiiformes. *Wading Birds* 7:299–314.

Kushlan, J. A. 1975. *Relation of Water Level and Fish Availability to Wood Stork Reproduction in the Southern Everglades, Florida.* Tallahasse, Fla.: U.S. Dept. Int. Geol. Surv.

Kushlan, J. A. 1976. Wading bird predation in a seasonally fluctuating pond. *Auk* 93:464–74.

Kushlan, J. A. 1978. Nonrigorous foraging by robbing egrets. *Ecology* 59:649–53.

Kushlan, J. A. 1979. Effects of helicopter censuses on wading bird colonies. *J. Wildl. Manag.* 43(3):756–60.

Kushlan, J. A. 1986. Responses of wading birds to seasonally fluctuating water levels: strategies and their limits. *Col. Waterbirds* 9 (2):155–62.

Lent, H., and J. Jurberg. 1969. *Rev. Bras. Biol.* 29:487–560. [Nest fauna]

Ligon, J. D. 1967. See Cathartidae Bibliography.

Oliveira, D.M.M. 1987. Comportamento alimentar de filhotes de *Jabiru mycteria* no Pantanal de Mato Grosso. *XIV Cong. Bras. Zool., Juiz de Fora:*405.

Schulz, H. 1987. Thermoregulatorisches Beinkoten bei *Ciconia ciconia. Vogelwarte* 34:107–17.

Thomas, B. T. 1979. *Bol. Soc. Venez. Cienc. Nat.* 34, 136. [*Ciconia,* nestling plumage]

Thomas, B. T. 1981. *Condor* 83:84–85. [*Jabiru mycteria,* nesting]

Thomas, B. T. 1985. Coexistence and behavior among the three western hemisphere storks. *Neotrop. Ornith., Ornith. Monogr.* no. 36:921–31.

Thomas, B. T. 1986. The behavior and breeding of adult Maguari Storks. *Condor* 88:26–34.

Yamashita, C., and Mauro de Paula Valle. 1986. Sobre anilhamento e migração de *Mycteria americana* no Pantanal. *An. II Enc. Nac. An. Aves, Rio de Janeiro.*

FAMILY CATHARTIDAE: AMERICAN VULTURES (6)

The world's vultures are divided into two anatomically diverse groups. The Cathartidae family was created for American vultures, whereas Old World vultures are included in the Accipitridae family in the order Falconiformes.

Data on the comparative anatomy and behavior of New World vultures and storks (Ciconiidae) indicate a close relationship: these vultures do not grasp food (generally a dead animal) with their toes, but only step on it, for the first (rear) toe, being too high, cannot reach the prey, and the second toe (the inside one) does not curve downward because of prolongation of the basal phalanx (see fig. 62). The cathartid bill has perforate nostrils (nares perviae), and there is no syrinx. The birds occasionally hammer with the bill and practice urohydrosis (König 1982). Biochemical analysis has confirmed the relationship. Cathartids are storks by homology (see Ciconiidae) and carrion eaters by analogy.

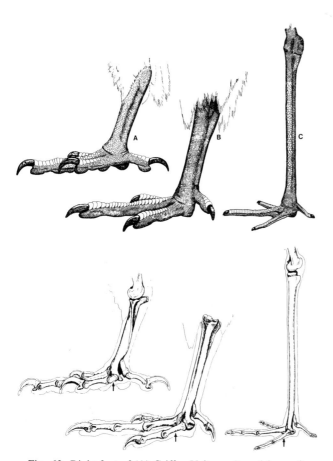

Fig. 62. Right foot of (A) Griffon Vulture, *Gyps fulvus,* of the Old World; (B) Andean Condor, *Vultur gryphus;* and (C) White Stork, *Ciconia ciconia.* Below, the respective bone structure. The arrow indicates the first (basal) phalanx of the inner toe: short in *Gyps* (Falconiformes), long in *Vultur* (Cathartidae) and *Ciconia* (Ciconiiformes). König 1982.

Some ancestors of present-day cathartids were enormous fliers; they certainly accompanied the great invasion of South America by northern mammals in the Pliocene. However, the Teratornithidae family, very akin to the cathartids, had the largest giants, such as *Argentavis magnificens* from the Patagonian Tertiary, with a wingspan of over 7 m and a weight of nearly 80 kg, the largest flying bird known. The oldest known Cathartidae fossils date from the eo-Oligocene of France and from the lower Oligocene of North America and Brazil. See Chapter 5.2.

Morphology and Special Adaptations

Cathartids have a bare head and neck, facilitating hygiene after their repugnant banquets. The thick collar of feathers at the base of the neck is usually considered to serve as an obstacle to the semiliquid repast running down into the plumage. The bill and claws are less powerful than those of birds of prey; unlike that of most Falconiformes, the hallux is elevated and short. The male may be larger than the female.

The legs being relatively long, cathartids move on the ground with long, bouncy leaps. Lacking a syrinx, they grunt or hiss loudly and thus adequately substitute the lack of a voice. The Black Vulture, *Coragyps atratus,* emits a *koaa.* While still in the egg, the young utter a sort of hoarse cry or snort. I have watched *Coragyps atratus* and the King Vulture, *Sarcoramphus papa,* open the wings and defecate on their legs ("urohydrosis," see also Ciconiidae) for thermoregulation. *S. papa* "shoots" the white, liquid feces first at one leg and then at the other, completely covering the yellow tarsi. Laboratory research has revealed that the bare parts of the head and neck also play an important role in thermoregulation (Larochelle et al. 1982). *S. papa* feathers have a strong, typical odor.

Feeding, Sanitary Service, Presumed Harmfulness, and Disappearance

As consumers of putrefying flesh, cathartids perform an important hygienic role by eliminating decomposing matter. They are apparently immune to botulism, a disease that attacks people and other birds through decayed food contaminated by the bacterium *Clostridium botulinum.* Botulinus toxins are proteins and are among the most potent poisons known. The gastric juice of vultures is so biochemically active that it neutralizes the toxins and bacteria in cadavers, thus eliminating later danger of infection. When fed fresh meat in captivity, vultures are clean and do not have a bad odor.

Coragyps atratus and *Sarcoramphus papa* are gifted with very sharp vision and when soaring high at dawn or dusk see everything and can find carcasses of large animals at a great distance. This is not so difficult considering the distinctive appearance of a dead animal and that, from an altitude of 700 m, other vultures can be seen descending to a find from as far away as 90 km. Vultures flying 3000 m high can detect an object 30 cm long. They take advantage of ascending hot-air currents around hills and mountains for upward lift, soaring for hours on end with minimum energy expenditure when the temperature is high. J. Guimarães Rosa wrote, "It is the vulture who builds castles in the air." These flights may be as much for recreation as for investigation. The fact that a jaguar covers up an animal it has killed when it cannot eat it all at once may be an adaptation to counter the visual acuity of vultures, although the jaguar usually drags its victims into dense vegetation.

The Turkey Vulture, *Cathartes aura,* and Lesser Yellow-headed Vulture, *C. burrovianus,* have a well-developed sense of smell[1] and by flying low manage to find hidden carcasses, such as a shot monkey that as it fell became stuck in a tree fork in a dense canopy, or an aracari dead on the ground under a tall Amazonian forest, as I saw in the upper Cururu, Pará. *C. aura* gets caught in traps set for small mammals in dense forest. It eats small dead animals (toads, snakes, rats) and patrols roads in search of animals hit by vehicles. It also eats feces and fruits, including those of palms such as the macaúba (*Acrocomia sclerocarpa*) and dendê (*Elaeis guineensis,* introduced from Africa), even becoming a nuisance in dendê plantations in Amazonia. *C. burrovianus* has a predilection for rotten fish. This "white meat" (as well as snakes and other reptiles) especially attracts *Cathartes* species, whereas "red meat" is the obligatory food of *Coragyps atratus.* Vultures are the great natural sanitation agents, seeking out dying animals and fallen fruit in burned-over areas. The eyes and tongues of dead animals are usually eaten first, followed by the anal area and viscera. In Africa local vultures, living on immense savannas with ample game, learn to associate the sound of a shot with the expectation of a dead animal and food for themselves.

Coragyps atratus occasionally attacks live animals unable to flee (e.g., young tortoises, newborn lambs). On islands such as the Moleques do Sul, Santa Catarina, it nests in the midst of seabird colonies, stealing everything it can get in the vicinity (Lenir Rosário pers. comm.). Captive *Sarcoramphus papa* in Rio de Janeiro proved inoffensive even to newborn kittens placed openly by their mother in the flight cage. A captive *S. papa* was unable to find hidden meat. Vultures are very fond of eating salt.

Claims that vultures spread animals epidemics such as anthrax (*Bacillus anthracis*), hoof-and-mouth disease, cholera, and salmonelloses are generally no more than speculative. Vulture concentrations at garbage dumps near airports, however, constitute an aviation danger.

There are reports of diminishing numbers of vultures in Brazil (Paraná, Rio Grande do Sul, Goiás, Rio Grande do Norte) Colombia, and Mexico. Being a carrion eater is no protection against the lethal action of insecticides, as has been amply documented in Israel. Vultures are said to die from eating poisoned cadavers, but farmers inform me the vultures detect certain poisons, such as strychnine and potassium cyanide, and save themselves by immediately vomiting the meat, which must have a repellent flavor. When vultures eat an animal killed by shooting, they run the risk of swallowing lead, which can be fatal, as has happened with California Condors, *Gymnogyps californianus.* Sometimes mummified vultures are found, which may be the result of some specific poison.

The fact that many fewer dead cattle are scattered around pastures today (because of better treatment, e.g., vaccination, etc.), thus making food for vultures scarcer, may contribute to reducing vulture numbers. Dead cattle are even removed from pastures in Rio Grande do Sul. Lack of food due to extinction of large mammals in the Pleistocene probably caused the decline of *Gymnogyps californianus.* Meanwhile, vultures continue to concentrate around slaughter houses and urban garbage dumps.

There are many literary reference to *Coragyps atratus* in the form both of severe accusation and popular acclaim. *Sarcoramphus papa* especially was used in popular medicine in Rio Grande do Sul where, after cutting off its head, people burned the rest of the bird's body to ashes to use in a tea to treat asthma. The vulture "is truly a subject of popular curiosity, due to its peaceful coexistence with death, from which it obtains its own life." (Gonzaga 1981).

Behavior

Vultures have the habit of extending their wings while they rest, like storks. At rest *Sarcoramphus papa* entertains itself by playing with its crop, which is normally hidden under feathers. On these occasions the crop looks like a great bare, red ball (gray in the immature). This must be a form of breeding-season display. Vultures are mimicked by the Zone-tailed Hawk, *Buteo albonotatus,* a unique example of aggressive mimicry. See *B. albonotatus.*

Breeding

As with so many large birds, vultures mature only after a few years. The Andean Condor, *Vultur gryphus,* which does not nest in Brazil, reaches the adult stage at eight years. *Coragyps atratus* courts the female on the ground by jumping with the wings open and in the air by demonstrating its agility with marvelous nuptial flights and zooming dives. *Sarcoramphus papa* displays while perched above or on the

---

[1]Use of smell for orientation is the exception in birds; see also "Feeding."

ground, opening and closing its wings and showing its brightly colored crown by lowering its head. It leans forward in the same way when suspicious or when observing something attentively—a position also adopted by many hawks.

Both *Coragyps atratus* and *Cathartes aura* nest well hidden among remote rocks or under roots. I was informed in northwestern Bahia that both species nest there high in dead buriti palms. *Cathartes burrovianus* is said to seek hollow trees, as does *Sarcoramphus papa,* which also builds its nest on cliffs or on top of tall trees, in the latter case probably using an old nest. In extensive, flat, forest-covered areas such as Amazonia, *Coragyps atratus* lays its eggs in holes among the roots of large fallen trees. In São Paulo, among other cities, it regularly breeds on top of high buildings.

Sarcoramphus papa lays two or three uniformly white eggs, whereas those of *Coragyps atratus* and *Cathartes aura* are heavily speckled and spotted. The incubation period and time before fledging are long, the former extending 32 to 39 days for *Coragyps* and 50 to 56 days for *Sarcoramphus.* The bodies of *Coragyps* chicks are still covered with down after 8 weeks. At 10 or more weeks they leave the nest flying. When disturbed they vomit and hiss or blow loudly.

Parents take turns at the nest, offering their little ones liquefied food and feeding them for months.

Hierarchy and Identification

In the upper Amazon sometimes four species—*Sarcoramphus papa, Coragyps atratus, Cathartes aura,* and *Cathartes burrovianus*—come together around a single carcass on the bank of a river, with the presence of even a fifth species, the Greater Yellow-headed Vulture, *Cathartes melambrotos,* possible, and perhaps even *Vultur gryphus,* whose presence in Brazil was verified only recently.

Usually it is only after *Sarcoramphus papa* is satiated that the other vultures attack the carrion. Occasionally *S. papa* permits the presence of other cathartids, such as *Coragyps atratus* and *Cathartes aura.* For this reason *C. aura* (in its role as subordinate to the "King,") has been called the "Minister Vulture" (Ceará). The presence of the strong *S. papa* is useful for other vultures, for it tears the cadaver apart more easily. In the Neotropics many insects, fly larvae, and beetles rapidly destroy carrion.

Coragyps atratus drives away *Cathartes aura* and does the same to *C. burrovianus.* The existing hierarchy, be it inter- or intraspecific, is organized according to size, strength, and hunger of the competitors. In their attacks, which are quick, they display the white marks on their wings by raising them, a tactic also used by the Crested Caracara, *Polyborus plancus.* They also kick.

It is usually difficult to distinguish *Cathartes* species in the field because there are so many variations in head color, which is ill defined in immatures. The best indicator is the color of the flight feathers.

Migration

Many vulture movements involve true migration. W. Voss and F. Silva recorded many hundred *Cathartes burrovianus* near Tapes, Rio Grande do Sul, flying from northeast to southwest in April. *C. aura* migrations also occur but are better known in Colombia and the United States. The *Vultur gryphus* appearing in Mato Grosso obviously come from a distance.

Parasites

Vultures are frequently parasitized by louse flies (Hippoboscidae). *S. papa, Coragyps atratus,* and *Cathartes aura* are hosts to *Pseudolfersia vulturina.*

Andean Condor, *Vultur gryphus,* Condor-dos-andes   SV

110 cm; wingspan may exceed 3 m; a recently hatched nestling weighs 230 g and at 6 months reaches 11–12 kg, normal adult weight. Black with thick collar of white feathers and large white area on wing. Bare head yellowish red. Male larger than female, which also has high, fleshy crest on forehead. Immature all brown but already has distinct neck band. Entire Andean cordillera, even above 5000 m. Enters Brazilian territory in Rio Jauru (Mato Grosso) region west of Cáceres (May 1973) in search of carrion accumulated during dry season and carried by river current to a certain bay on "Vulture Island," where it meets *Coragyps atratus* and *Sarcoramphus papa.* Condor remains approximately 13,000 years old recently were found in caves of the Lapa Vermelha complex at Lagoa Santa, Minas Gerais (Alvarenga pers. comm.). Flies with wings spread horizontally, somewhat like *Cathartes melambrotos.* Wings are relatively narrow, like wings of *Cathartes,* unlike those of *Coragyps atratus* and *S. papa.* Wingspan usually does not match that of Wandering Albatross, *Diomedea exulans,* but condor weighs more. *Gymnogyps californianus* of U.S. west coast now survives only in captivity.

King Vulture, *Sarcoramphus papa,* Urubu-rei   PL 6.3

79 cm; wingspan 180 cm; 3 kg. In flight reminiscent of Maguari Stork, *Ciconia maguari,* because of large amount of white and wide wings with black-and-white pattern almost the same above and below. Bare head and neck violaceous red. Fleshy, orange-yellow caruncle on cere is larger and pendant in male. Immature sooty but recognizable by size. Nestling covered with white down. Regions of mixed forest and campo, distant from urban centers. Soars very high. Mexico to Bolivia, northern Argentina, Uruguay. Becoming scarce in Brazil, being persecuted, along with large raptors, as a trophy, but still found regularly in northern, northeastern, and central Brazil. Also called *Corvo-branco, Urubu-branco.*

BLACK VULTURE, *Coragyps atratus*,
Urubu-de-cabeça-preta, Urubu-comum.   PL 6.1

62 cm; wingspan 143 cm; 1.6 kg. One of most conspicuous birds in Brazil. Commonly associates with people. Bare head and neck dark gray. Flies heavily, alternating a few rapid wing strokes with masterful soaring. Wings wide and ends are kept open in flight, with tips of 5 outer primaries distinctly visible, their bases forming a whitish area lacking in *Cathartes aura*. Rears 2 chicks, yellowish brown when newly hatched but rapidly becoming whitish, then pure white. Most gregarious cathartid, with pairs staying together in a flock. Widely distributed, has benefited from colonization of New World and is still extending range as it accompanies human occupation. It was missing, for instance, from backlands of Parecis (Mato Grosso), campos of Serra do Caparaó (Minas Gerais 1941 pers. obs.), and certain parts of Rio Grande do Sul. It is also absent from extensively forested regions (certain parts of Amazonia). Has been exterminated in certain rural areas through poisoning of cattle carcasses (Uruguay, Rio Grande do Sul). Appears to succumb to extensive spraying of insecticides (see "Feeding . . . "). Possibly lack of rising air currents in flat regions contributes to local absences in Rio Grande do Sul. North America to Argentina, Chile. Also called *Corvo*.

TURKEY VULTURE, *Cathartes aura*,
Urubu-de-cabeça-vermelha   PL 6.2

73 cm; wingspan 137–80 cm; 1.2–2 kg. Head and neck pink or red; occiput white or yellow, often streaked with blue; crown whitish or bluish; prominent feathered collar. Nestlings white. Wings and tail much longer and narrower than in *Coragyps atratus*. Light gray undersurface of all flight feathers contrasts with black under wing coverts. No white in hand area. Primary shafts blackish. Flies with wings raised at a slight angle, V-like. Beats wings slowly, accelerating flight by inclining body slightly from right to left with majestic mastery. Flies close to ground in search of small carrion. Outside cities, both in open country and forests. Canada to Argentina, Chile, throughout Brazil. Also called *Urubu-caçador*, *Jereba* (Pará), *Urubu-campeiro* (Rio de Janeiro), *Xem-xem* (Pará). See *Buteo albonotatus*, which appears to imitate the 3 *Cathartes*.

LESSER YELLOW-HEADED VULTURE, *Cathartes burrovianus*, Urubu-de-cabeça-amarela

Very similar to *C. aura* but a bit smaller. Has area of intense orange or pale yellow below eye, black spot in front of eye. Crown violet or bluish. Back plumage reaches to nape, with only yellow sides of neck remaining bare. Flies like *C. aura;* difficult to differentiate the 2 if light does not permit one to distinguish color of head or primary shafts, in *C. burrovianus* whitish, white, or straw colored (*urubu-tinga*), noticeable in flight. Usually lives away from cultivated areas, frequenting river edges bordered with trees and marshes. Mexico to northern Argentina, locally in various regions of Brazil, more common in northeast and Amazonia. Also called *Urubu-peba* (Pará).

GREATER YELLOW-HEADED VULTURE, *Cathartes melambrotos*

2d yellow-headed vulture species, from Amazonia, size of *Sarcoramphus papa*. Head less vividly colored than *C. burrovianus*, being light yellow without orange or red tinges. Crown and spot on lores blue. Flies with wings stretched horizontally, unlike *burrovianus*, and usually at greater heights. Distinguished from congeners by gray undersurface of secondaries, with rest of plumage black, including primary shafts. Forests. Along upper and lower Amazon, Pará, (e.g., Belém, Marajó, Rio Xingu, Rio Tapajós), perhaps Goiás; also the Guianas, Venezuela, Colombia, Peru, Bolivia. Described only in 1964 by A. Wetmore. This species may be the *Urubu-fidalgo* or *Urubu-pedrez* of country folk.

Cathartidae Bibliography

Alvarenga, H.M.F. 1985. Notas sobre os Cathartidae (Aves) e descrição de um novo gênero do Cenozóico brasileiro. *An. Acad. Bras. Ciênc.* 57:349-57.

Amadon, D. 1977. Notes on the taxonomy of vultures. *Condor* 79:413–16.

Antas, Paulo T. Z., and C. L. Silveira. 1980. *Int. Zoo. Yearbook* 20:202–4. [*Sarcoramphus*, rearing of]

Coleman, J. S., J. D. Fraser, and C. A. Pringle. 1985. Salt-eating by Black and Turkey Vultures. *Condor* 87:291–92.

Cracraft, J., and P. V. Rich. 1972. *Condor* 74:272–83. [Evolution]

Feduccia, A. 1977. *Nature* 266:719–20. [Relationships]

Fonseca, J. P. de. 1922. *Rev. Mus. Paul.* 13:781. [Behavior]

Gonzaga, L. P. 1981. *SOM* 24:10–11. [*Coragyps* in popular culture]

Hatch, D. E. 1970. *Auk* 87:111–24. [Temperature regulation]

Houston, D. C. 1984. Does the King Vulture, *Sarcoramphus papa*, use a sense of smell to locate food? *Ibis* 126:67–69.

Johst, E., and G. Johst. 1964. *Der Zool. Garten NF* 29:173–82. [*Coragyps*, rearing of]

König, C. 1974. *J. Orn.* 115:289–320. [Old World vulture behavior]

König, C. 1982. *J. Orn.* 123:259–67. [Systematics]

Lamartine de Faria, O. 1965. Notas para o necrólogo do urubu. *Seleções Agrícolas*, Rio de Janeiro:52–53.

Larochelle, J., J. Delson, and K. Schmidt-Nielsen. 1982. Temperature regulation in the Black Vulture. *Can. I. Zool.* 60:491–94.

Ligon, J. D. 1967. Relationships of the Cathartid vultures. *Occas. Pap. Univ. Michigan* 651.

Mendelssohn, H. 1972. *Bull. ICBP* 11:75–104. [Biocides]

Parmalee, P. W. 1954. The vultures: Their movements, economic status, and control in Texas. *Auk* 71:443–53.

Ramo, C., and B. Busto. 1988. Observations at a King Vulture (*Sarcoramphus papa*) nest in Venezuela. *Auk* 105:195–96.

Schlatter, R., G. Reinhardt, and L. Burchard. 1978. *Arch. Med. Vet.* 10(2):111–27. [*Coragyps*, spread of disease]

Sick, H. 1979. *Bull. B.O.C.* 99(4):115–20. [*Vultur gryphus*, first Brazil record]

Stager, K. E. 1964. *Contr. Sci.* 81. [Sense of smell]

Wetmore, A. 1964. *Smithsonian Misc. Collecs.* 146:6. [Taxonomy]

Yamashita, C., and M. P. Valle. 1985. Sobre as aves de hábito saprófago. *XII Cong. Bras. Zool., Campinas*:578.

ORDER PHOENICOPTERIFORMES

FAMILY PHOENICOPTERIDAE: FLAMINGOS (3)

Large and long-legged, flamingos are among the world's most picturesque birds. There are fossils from the Tertiary of North America and Europe, so it is a very old group; also from the Pleistocene of Argentina. Their systematic position is much disputed. While the flamingos historically have been attributed to the Ciconiiformes or Anseriformes, Olson and Feduccia (1980) presented a wide variety of data (osteology, myology, oology, internal parasites, ecology) that showed remote descent from the Charadriiformes (Recurvirostridae). The key fossil is *Presbyornis* (fig. 63) (see Anatidae).

Palaelodus is a genus of extinct flamingos with relatively short legs but adapted for swimming. Numerous fossil remains have been found in France and recently also in Brazil in the Taubaté basin, as yet unreported (Alvarenga pers. comm.). I prefer to place the flamingos in a separate order, near the Charadriiformes. The most interesting factor is evolution of the filtering apparatus, linked to an unusual development of the tongue, a combination vestigially perceptible in certain Charadriiformes.

Morphology

The flamingo build is exceptionally slender. The bill curved downward at an abrupt angle and provided with transverse plates resembles, by convergence, the very similar baleen of whales: one of the most notable analogies in the animal kingdom and an adaptation evolved for ingesting plankton. (See also Procellariiformes, *Pachyptila*. The structure of the flamingo filtering apparatus is basically different from that of anatids. Sexes are similar, with the female a bit smaller. The immature is variously "dirty" colored but unmistakable in general aspect. Adult plumage is acquired only at three years of age. Approximately every two years a simultaneous molt of the flight feathers occurs, similar to the en bloc molt of anatids. Two very similar flamingos appear in Brazil: the Greater Flamingo, *Phoenicopterus ruber*, in the extreme north and the Chilean Flamingo, *P. chilensis*, in the extreme south. A third species, the Andean Flamingo, *Phoenicoparrus andinus*, from Chile, appeared in 1989. The species are most easily distinguished by the color of the soft parts.

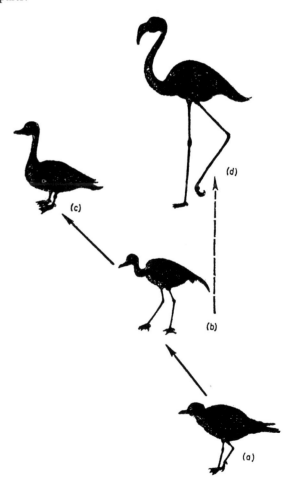

Fig. 63. Probable phylogeny of the ducks and flamingos: (a) an ancestral Charadriiform; (b) *Presbyornis*, which might have given rise to: (c) ducks and (d) flamingos. After Olson and Feduccia 1980.

Feeding and Behavior

Flamingos fish in shallow salt water with the neck curved downward and the head held so the maxilla, which is thinner than the mandible, is turned toward the muddy bottom. With this peculiar bill they filter their food, composed of miniscule aquatic animals such as fly larvae (*Ephydra* sp.), mollusks, small crustaceans (e.g., *Artemia salina*), and algae, among them some that are rich in carotenoids that give the plumage its intense red color, the same as occurs with the Scarlet Ibis, *Eudocimus ruber,* and Roseate Spoonbill, *Platalea ajaja.* Canthaxanthin, astaxanthin, and phoenicoptaxanthin have been isolated from flamingo feathers. If a flamingo does not ingest carotenoids for six months, it may suffer an 86% reduction in the level of this red pigment in its blood (Villela 1976).

The silhouette in flight is crosslike. Flamingos fly in an oblique line or in wedge formation, with the leader changing at short intervals, similar to the Maguari Stork, *Ciconia maguari;* Neotropic Cormorant, *Phalacrocorax brasilianus;* and other birds. Flamingos sometimes fly at great altitudes. They are highly gregarious but shy, using isolated beaches far from inhabited regions.

Habitat, Breeding, and Decline

These birds are found in shallow saline lakes without vegetation and at the edge of the sea. In the former they build a mud nest shaped like a small cone with the top forming a shallow dish, which reduces the danger of flooding. The nest material rapidly softens if the water rises, however, endangering eggs and young. Birds occasionally lay directly on the ground. The clutch comprises only one very large, uniformly white egg with a thick shell. The yolk is blood red because of the presence of astaxanthin (the same occurs with the beautiful turacos of Africa). Young are similar to goslings and are fed with a red secretion produced in the parent's esophagus (analogous to the "pigeon milk" of pigeons), which has given rise to stories about bloody fights among flamingos. Because their bills are still soft, two-month-old young are still fed by the parents.

Flamingos nest very irregularly. Formerly there were nesting colonies of *Phoenicopterus ruber* in southern Amapá (Lago Piratuba, inland from Cabo Norte) and on Marajó Island (Cabo Maguarinho), places that might be appropriate for establishing reserves for repopulation trials using individuals from the West Indies, where the same species occurs. The species once extended as far as Ceará, as is eloquently shown by names such as Lago dos Gansos, "Goose Lake," and by prehistoric cave paintings (fig. 64) found in Rio Grande do Norte (Souza et al. 1982). Presently it is very scarce, but apparently it still nests on the coast of Amapá north of the Rio Cassiporé (1971). It was recorded in 1978 by Teixeira and Best (1981) on Ilha de Maracá (at the SEMA

Fig. 64. Prehistoric rock painting of a flamingo, São Rafael Municipality, Rio Grande do Norte. *Pedra Ferrada,* "Branded Rock," done in red (alongside shapes of human hands) on a large, smooth block of granite (Souza and Medeiros 1982). It has not been precisely dated but is estimated to be 5000 years old, like the kitchen middens in southern Brazil (see Spheniscidae).

Ecological Station) and on the adjacent coast. It has been erroneously cited for the Mato Grosso Pantanal and other interior regions because of confusion with *Platalea ajaja* and *Eudocimus ruber.*

GREATER FLAMINGO, *Phoenicopterus ruber,* Flamingo EN Fig. 65

106 cm; height 90 cm. Light pink, wings carmine, flight feathers black, bill orange-red with white base, black tip. Legs and webbing grayish red, tarsal articulation and toes dark red. VOICE: a harsh quacking *kraaa,* almost ducklike, sounding like a shriek. Northern part of continent, Antilles and Mexico, wanders to Florida. Breeds in Amapá. Formerly as far as Rio Grande do Norte, as proven by a prehistoric painting. Menaced in its last redoubts in Amapá by spread of rice culture in lake regions, by salt works along coast, and even by increased hunting (meat and eggs are sought), a result of new roads that make access easier. Also called

Fig. 65. Greater Flamingo, *Phoenicopterus ruber.*

Ganso-cor-de-rosa (Amapá), *Maranhão.* Widely distributed in Old World.

CHILEAN FLAMINGO, *Phoenicopterus chilensis,*
Flamingo-chileno   SV

Yellowish bill with black tip. Legs pinkish gray, tarsal articulation and webbing blood red. Restricted to South America, as far as Tierra del Fuego. Winter migrant to Rio Grande do Sul, May–September, in Lagoa do Peixe and adjacent beaches, sometimes in flocks of hundreds, with brownish and different-sized immatures also appearing. Next closest colony is in Santa Fé, Argentina. Also called *Guanaco* (Rio Grande do Sul).

ANDEAN FLAMINGO, *Phoenicoparrus andinus,*
Flamingo-dos-Andes   SV

Birds of this genus have only 3 toes. Legs yellow (black in immatures), "knees" not red. An immature captured at Erval-Velho, Santa Catarina, on 19 May 1989 had been banded at Salar de Punta Negra, Antofogasta, Chile, the same year.

Phoenicopteridae Bibliography
See also General Bibliography

Bege, L.A.R. 1990. Primer Reporte de *Phoenicoparrus andinus* em Brasil. *El Volante Migratorio* 14:6.

Feduccia, A. 1976. *Auk* 93:587–601. [Relationships]

Kear, J., and N. Duplaix-Hall, eds. 1975. *Proc. Int. Flamingo Sympos. 1973, Berkhamsted.* [Pictures of all the species and subspecies]

Olson, S. L., and A. Feduccia. 1980. *Smithsonian Contr. Zool.* 316 and 323. [Evolution]

Sick, H. 1972. Espécies de Fauna brasileira ameaçadas de extinção. *An. Acad. Bras. Ciênc.* [Occurrence]

Souza, M. S. de, and O. Medeiros. 1982. *Textos Acadêmicos 2, 214, Museu Câmara Cascudo.* [Rock paintings in Rio Grande do Norte]

Teixeira, D. M., and R. C. Best. 1981. *Bol. Mus. Paraen. Zool.* 1, 104. [Distribution]

Völker, O. 1958. Die Rotfärbung des Flamingo (*Phoenicopterus*) in Freileben und in der Gefangenschaft. *J. Orn.* 99:209–17.

ORDER ANSERIFORMES

FAMILY ANATIDAE: SWANS AND DUCKS (25)

This is one of the best-known families, having benefited people through certain domesticated species, one of them the South American Muscovy Duck, *Cairina moschata.* The largest and most colorful Brazilian member is the Black-necked Swan, *Cygnus melancoryphus.* Swans are among the largest flying birds in the world.

Compared with more temperate regions to the north and south, Brazil is not particularly rich in Anatidae. Rio Grande do Sul is the area with the greatest diversity, having 20 species.

Anatidae ancestry was enigmatic until discovery of the fossil *Presbyornis* from the lower Eocene (Tertiary, 50 million years B.P.) of the United States. *Presbyornis* looks like a Charadriiform with the head of a duck. The same ancestry is attributed to the flamingos (see fig. 63). The anatids' short legs are thought to be a later acquisition, an adaptation to life in shallow saline lakes, which also led to evolution of the filtering apparatus in the bill (Feduccia 1977, Olson and Feduccia 1980).

Morphology, Special Adaptations, and Behavior

The bill is equipped with transverse lamellae (fig. 66) which, together with the very sensitive, thick tongue, form an apparatus suitable for straining miniscule animals from water or mud. This technique is comparable to that of whales that filter plankton (see flamingos, *Phoenicopterus,* and shearwaters, *Puffinus*). As in the Anhimidae (screamers), the

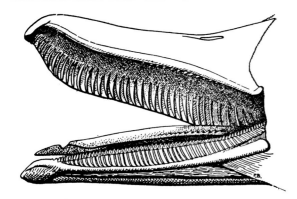

Fig. 66. Bill of Muscovy Duck, *Cairina moschata,* showing the horny lamellae of the mandibles and the horny edges of the tongue. After P. P. Grassé 1950.

lamellae are little developed in species, such as *Cairina moschata,* that live on larger food items.

Legs are short and feet are webbed, the toes having swimming membranes. At the base of the hand of *C. moschata* and of the Orinoco Goose, *Neochen jubata,* is a callous that enhances the effect of blows given with the wings during fights, recalling the spurs of Anhimidae.

Males have a copulatory organ, referred to as a "corkscrew" by country people (see also Tinamidae and Cracidae, among others). The uropygial gland is large. Its secretion is used to wax the feathers and to maintain the elasticity of their microscopic structure in perfect condition, ensuring waterproof plumage.

Most species have a conspicuous series of wing feathers (secondaries and their upper coverts) with splendid coloration (and frequently some very bright white) that form an area called the speculum. In many Brazilian species, such as the *Dendrocygna, Neochen,* and some *Anas,* there is little of the sexual dimorphism in color so evident in northern Anatidae. The male *Cairina moschata,* a polygamous species, is much larger than the female. The opposite is true with the parasitic Black-headed Duck, *Heteronetta atricapilla.*

An eclipse plumage occurs in Northern Hemisphere species, during which males acquire a modest dress similar to that of their respective females and immatures, this being part of a complete molt that includes loss of the flight feathers. They keep this plumage for about three months (the local summer), reacquiring the subsequent nuptial plumage through a further partial molt. We have more contact with this phenomenon through northern species, such as the Blue-winged Teal, *Anas discors,* that arrive here as migrant fugitives from winter (see Brazilian Duck, *Amazonetta brasiliensis*). Eclipse plumage, which to some extent correlates with the nonbreeding season, is not usually experienced by tropical and subtropical Anatidae, leading to the belief that these species are less rigid in their reproductive cycle and better able to adapt themselves to the irregularity of rainy seasons, which govern the breeding period of these birds. Some eclipse plumages are of very short duration, as in the Cinnamon Teal, *Anas cyanoptera.*

Flight of the small species is quite fast. A 300-g duck flies 33 m per second, equivalent to 118 km/hr. According to some accounts the Rosy-billed Pochard, *Netta peposaca,* may reach 88 km/hr. Anatidae fly with rapid wing beats, without gliding except when landing, and keep the neck outstretched horizontally. Some, such as the *Dendrocygna,* have sound-producing flight feathers that increase the whistling produced by the wing beats, already loud in a large, heavy species such as *Cairina moschata.*

Anatidae molt their flight feathers simultaneously (block molt, or *desasagem,* "dewinging") and are unable to fly then. At this time they are highly vulnerable to any kind of persecution and need absolute protection. They defend themselves by hiding in the most inaccessible swamps; when caught unawares in open water, they dive and may thus escape, especially if the water is ruffled by wind and hides them when they surface to breathe.[1] Block molt is more rapid than successive molt, providing a biological advantage. Small ducks can fly three weeks after they start to molt, large ducks after four.

Cairina moschata, Neochen jubata, the Black-bellied Whistling-Duck, *Dendrocygna autumnalis,* and Speckled Teal, *Anas flavirostris,* regularly perch off the ground to rest. A popular saying is "His morals are as high as a duck perch." The *Dendrocygna* sometimes rest on the ocean. The White-faced Whistling-Duck, *D. viduata,* flying at night in heavy rain, has been known to mistake the wet asphalt of a road or plaza for a river or lake and land there.

Anatids are gregarious and may associate in great concentrations.

Vocalization

Voices of most anatids are not very impressive, but the whistle of *Dendrocygna viduata* is one of the best-known voices of Brazil. The distinctive voice of the male of some species is heard only during a very short period in the breeding season, leading some people to think they are mute. The ventriloquial laugh of the Masked Duck, *Oxyura dominica,* is quite a strange sound. The duet of *Neochen jubata* is notable. Vocalization is different in anatid males and females because of a different phonic apparatus in the two sexes.

Feeding

Anatids feed on small seeds and leaves and catch worms, insect larvae, and small crustaceans. Among the floating plants eaten by *Dendrocygna viduata* are *Lemna, Azolla,* and

[1]Northern Hemisphere ducks (Oldsquaw, *Clangula hyemalis*) that had lost all their remiges managed to flee by flying low over the water with rapid wing beats, their large wing coverts substituting for the flight feathers (N. N. Kartchev 1962).

Salvinia (Magnanini and Coimbra 1964). Along the littoral of Ceará this species gorges on a small fresh-water crab appropriately called *fartura* "abundance." The White-cheeked Pintail, *Anas bahamensis,* thought of as a vegetarian, sometimes literally drugs itself with barnacle (*Balanus* spp.) larvae, to such a point that the taste of its meat is spoiled (Guanabara Bay, J. Moojen). *Cairina moschata* catches mollusks such as *Marisa planosgyra* and snails, crustaceans, small fish, and seeds (Mato Grosso, Pará). *Amazonetta brasiliensis* ducklings are expert at catching insects, even mosquitoes and flies (Coimbra Filho 1964). Ducks may contribute to the dispersal of aquatic plants, for certain seeds found in their feces are capable of germinating. An investigation of the esophagus contents of 41 *Netta peposaca* in Rio Grande do Sul showed that 75.6% by volume of the food was rice (*Oryza sativa*) and capim-arroz (*Echinochloa crusgalli*).

All Brazilian species need shallow (eutrophic) water for effective feeding. All *Anas* species and occasionally others eat by dabbling, stirring up the water and lifting their posteriors vertically. The length of the neck usually corresponds to the depth at which the ducks, as well as geese and swans, are able to pick up food without diving.

The *Oxyura* and *Heteronetta atricapilla* regularly dive for food, whereas others, such as *Dendrocygna viduata,* including ducklings, and the Fulvous Whistling-Duck, *D. bicolor,* dive only occasionally. *Oxyura dominica* can stay underwater twice as long (11–26.6 seconds) as the Least Grebe, *Tachybaptus dominicus* (Jenni 1969). The length of these dives may be more a function of ecological conditions than a characteristic of the species, with longer dives occurring where less vegetation is present in the water. It is worth mentioning that *Mergus octosetaceus,* a fish-eating species, catches all its food by diving, unlike the *Oxyura,* which feed more on the surface. Only the feet are used for underwater propulsion.

Whereas many anatids are basically primary consumers (feeding on seeds, roots, and aquatic vegetation), they change their diets during breeding to a higher trophic level, taking more aquatic invertebrates to obtain the proteins necessary for egg laying and duckling nutrition. Ducks like to wet their food in water.

Species such as the Coscoroba Swan, *Coscoroba coscoroba; Anas flavirostris;* and Silver Teal, *A. versicolor,* pasture in dry fields. Ducks are often crepuscular, using their sensitive bills to feed without visual assistance.

Breeding

Prenuptial displays are quite varied, and their analysis reveals the relationships of certain groups of species and genera within the family (e.g., see, *Oxyura* and *Heteronetta atricapilla*). Anatids are usually monogamous. Males become very jealous of their females during breeding. In its little-known display, the male *Neochen jubata* walks around stretching his wings and standing so erect he sometimes falls backward. The female accompanies the male's parade, and the two converse, using different vocalizations. *Cairina moschata* is polygamous. Males of species lacking sexual dimorphism participate in rearing the young.

The nest may be well constructed or be more rustic, but it is almost always lined with down that the female plucks from her breast (as in *Cairina moschata*).

Coscoroba coscoroba nests on dry islands in marshes, sometimes building on a platform erected by nutria (*Myocastor coypus*) (Rio Grande do Sul). *Cygnus melancoryphus* makes a mattress of leaves in the water, hiding it in flooded sarandi thickets. *Cairina moschata* and the Comb Duck, *Sarkidiornis melanotos,* nest in trees, the latter, for example, in dead buriti palms and the former among palm fronds, on large branches covered with epiphytic plants, or in abandoned nests of hawks, Jabirus, etc., situated high in the trees and sometimes as much as 5 km from water. A *C. moschata* installed herself in a hole in a buriti whose entrance was 4 m high, with the bottom only 50 cm above ground level. Ducklings leap from nests at any height while the mother awaits them on the ground to lead them to water. Sometimes *C. moschata* nests on the ground among dense vegetation (influence of domestication?).

Dendrocygna autumnalis nests in tree holes, among palm fronds, or on the ground. *D. viduata* and *D. bicolor* also tend to nest on the ground. They may build on the protected side of a tree, that is, on the side toward which the trunk is leaning, or among herbaceous vegetation or bushes near water. *Neochen jubata* and *Mergus octosetaceus* nest in tree holes, sometimes at a considerable height above ground, although the former may also hide its nest among grass or bushes at a river edge (Xingu, Mato Grosso).

Anas flavirostris uses cavities, usually on the ground, but occasionally takes advantage of the large, enclosed nests of the Monk Parakeet, *Myiopsitta monachus,* when it does not find another suitable spot (Rio Grande do Sul).

Eggs are uniformly white, greenish, or bluish. Clutches are large, reaching 14 eggs (*Amazonetta brasiliensis*). The incubation period is 25 to 26 days for *A. brasiliensis,* 27 to 29 days for *Dendrocygna viduata,* and 30 to 35 days for *Cairina moschata.* The larger *Anas* species (e.g., domestic duck) incubate for 28 days. The adult covers the eggs with down when it leaves the nest.

Duckling plumage varies with the species. *C. moschata* ducklings may be uniformly black.

Cygnus melancoryphus and *Coscoroba coscoroba* carry their young on their backs—but not while flying, as popularly believed. If humans approach, adult *Amazonetta brasiliensis* that are near the nest or leading ducklings feign injury to draw attention to themselves rather than to their nest or young.

Certain reproductive irregularities may occur, as with the *Dendrocygna,* for instance. More than one female *D. autum-*

nalis may lay in the same nest. There is a tendency to lay eggs in the nests of others, with cases known of *D. viduata* laying in nests of *D. bicolor*. A female *D. viduata* might be found herding a mixed group of ducklings of her own and of *D. autumnalis*. In the Mato Grosso Pantanal, *D. autumnalis* frequently lays in nests of *C. moschata*, which rears the adoptive young together with its own. Also, female *C. moschata* occasionally adopt young from another nest of their own species. The ducklings can be recognized by their different size. Irregularities recorded with *Dendrocygna* during laying resemble, to a degree, those of the anis (*Crotophaga* spp.). Incipient parasitism occurs in the Ruddy Duck, *Oxyura jamaicensis,* a North American counterpart of the Lake Duck, *O. vittata.*

Heteronetta atricapilla has become a parasite, always laying in the nests of others. Reportedly it occasionally even uses hawk nests (Chimango Caracara, *Milvago chimango;* Snail Kite, *Rostrhamus sociabilis.*) The ducklings run no danger, for they stay only a few hours in the nest of such a strange stepparent. The incubation period for this species is short (24–25 days, giving the intruder young a greater chance to hatch before the stepsiblings), shorter, for example, than the 24.5 to 29 days required by the Red-fronted Coot, *Fulica rufifrons,* the principal host of *H. atricapilla* in Argentina. Compared with the parasitism of other birds (e.g., Shiny Cowbird, *Molothrus bonariensis*), *Heteronetta* parasitism is perfect in the sense that it does not damage the eggs or young of the swindled species, and the duckling does not even demand feeding.

Distribution and Habitat

It is rare in other families for the same species to occur both in Brazil and the Old World, but this happens with four Anatidae. *Dendrocygna viduata* and the Southern Pochard, *Netta erythrophthalma,* are found not only in South America but also in Africa; *Dendrocygna bicolor* and *Sarkidiornis melanotos* also inhabit Africa and India, among other places. Apparently there have been trans-Atlantic crossings (see Cattle Egret, *Bubulcus ibis*).

It is interesting that Brazil has a representative of the Merginae (mergansers), a group with broad Holarctic distribution, frequently with maritime habits. Our species occurs well in the center of South America and therefore is extremely isolated from its congeners. It is not related to the Torrent Duck, *Merganetta armata,* of the Andes.

It is a peculiar fact that Amazonia, so rich in rivers and lakes, is poor in anatid species. One hypothesis is that the fish have trophic requirements somewhat similar to those of certain ducks and, being abundant, have impeded proper development of the anatids. There is a close relationship between the Amazonian forest and fish, especially in the high-water season when fish are most abundant.

Of the 20 anatid species recorded for Rio Grande do Sul

with its vast coastal marshes at Brazil's southern extremity, 80% breed there, the others appearing merely as migrants. The breeding range of a given species may be quite extensive: that of *Anas flavirostris,* for example, extends from Rio Grande do Sul to South Georgia, a subantarctic Atlantic island at the same latitude as the southernmost extremity of South America.

In contrast to the Northern Hemisphere and southernmost portions of South America, Brazil has neither truly maritime anatids nor true geese (see also *Dendrocygna*).

Migration and Broadening of Distribution

Almost all Brazilian anatids are migratory. The reasons include feeding, alterations in water levels (both excess and lack of water), and the need for safe places to sleep and molt. Thus, anatids are seminomadic.

Large concentrations of migrant anatids occur in Rio Grande do Sul, the Mato Grosso Pantanal, the northeast, and Amapá. In Amazonia there is movement because of floods, which drive away aquatic birds dependent on clear or shallow water to feed. Because of upstream flooding, ducks retreat beyond the rapids, and in the most northerly areas they move periodically from the Amazon system to that of the Orinoco. At the mouth of the Amazon the tidal bore motivates duck movements.

Flocks of *Dendrocygna viduata* and *D. autumnalis* fly to islands on the north coast of Maranhão to spend the rainy season. In the northeast, among other regions, *D. viduata* and other ducks migrate at the beginning of the year, appearing by the thousands in western Paraíba without breeding there. In Ceará flocks of this species (there called *viuvinha,* "little widow") move back and forth between the littoral and interior, which with rain becomes suitable habitat for feeding and nesting. During late afternoons in May and August on the Rio de Janeiro littoral, flocks of 50 to 150 *D. viduata,* flying low over the sea across the archipelago in front of the city of Rio de Janeiro, move west along the coast from the Maricá region toward Ilha Alfavaca.

Individual *Netta peposaca, Heteronetta atricapilla, Anas versicolor,* and Yellow-billed Pintail, *A. georgica,* banded in Argentina have been found in Rio Grande do Sul. In this way it was discovered that Argentine *N. peposaca* move in a circle that touches southern Brazil in winter. Many banded *Anas discors* from North America have been recorded, mostly in northern Brazil but also as far away as Rio Grande do Sul. The banding of 1149 *A. georgica* on the coastal region (Lagoa do Peixe) of Rio Grande do Sul from January to March has revealed a large concentration of this species, all molting wing feathers. One individual was recaptured on the Pacific coast of Chile. *Netta erythrophthalma* is greatly increasing its range. See also *N. peposaca.*

Local movements of *Dendrocygna viduata* flocks are stimulated by regular offerings of food for aquatic birds in gardens and zoological parks. At times the strident whistling of these flocks can be heard at night over cities such as Rio de Janeiro and São Paulo.

Large-scale banding is required to learn more about the routes followed by our Anatidae and about their migrations beyond our borders.

Enemies

In Amazonia caiman and large carnivorous fish are among anatids' enemies. I have found *Neochen jubata* with their feet mutliated by piranhas, one bird having lost its entire tarsus, which healed (upper Xingu, Mato Grosso 1947). Various cases of *Anas bahamensis* being devoured by pirarucus (*Arapaima gigas*) have been recorded in Ceará reservoirs, although it is possible that at least some of these victims were wounded or dead. In the Rio de la Plata watershed, including in the Rio Paraná, the dourado (*Salminus maxillosus*) is a threat to ducklings. Tegu lizards (*Tupinambis teguixin*) swim out to duck nests to suck the eggs.

Hunting, Use, and Domestication

Anatidae are an important economic resource for the country, for they provide a choice food and a source of income for businesses associated with hunting.

Duck hunting is traditionally undertaken by putting out tied or tame individuals as decoys. A curious hunting method is used by country people of Minas Gerais and the Araguaia region of Goiás: the hunter, submerged except for his head, which is masked by a gourd slowly swims or walks underwater toward his prey until he reaches birds attracted by a decoy and grabs them by the feet to pull them under the water.

Traps are also used. Those in the São Francisco region of Bahia consist of wire-fenced areas more than 1 km in extent. One single capture undertaken in January caught 5000 birds which were dried, smoked, and trucked to cities.

On Marajó Island (Pará) more modern hunting methods (shooting birds from ambush or in flight, with dogs to flush or retrieve them) have been carried to an intolerable extent by using a cannon loaded with special lead shot that kills ducks by the ton.

It is an inadmissible abuse to hunt ducks during their flightless period of wing molt, which locally coincides with the burning of fields. I learned that in 1964, 60,000 ducks, primarily *Dendrocygna autumnalis*, were killed on just one ranch in Amapá.

In Rio Grande do Sul, one of the pioneer states in natural-resource management, approximately 8000 ha of marshes for ducks and other aquatic species were reported to be under the control of hunters in 1973. Many marshes are purchased or rented for sport hunting. In 1974 there were approximately 10,000 licensed waterfowl hunters in Rio Grande do Sul. Of the 20 anatid species occurring in that state, only 5 are considered game birds: *Dendrocygna viduata*, *D. bicolor*, *Anas georgica*, *Netta peposaca*, and *Amazonetta brasiliensis*. The birds most sought after by Brazilian hunters are *Netta peposaca* and *Cairina moschata*.

All over Brazil, as well as in other countries, Anseriformes are used to beautify ponds and reservoirs. *Dendrocygna viduata* is the most valued species. In Amazonia *D. autumnalis* is often kept loose as pet in the garden. *Cygnus melancoryphus* thrives in captivity.

A wide variety of anatid species usually hybridize in captivity, proving that they are closely related. Such mixtures, which rarely or never occur in the wild, are quite undesirable from the viewpoint of preserving indigenous fauna, for hybrids produced in aviaries or in semiliberty may associate with wild flocks and become the focus of more hybridization. Most of such hybrids, even intergeneric and intertribal, are fertile, with the exception of *Cairina moschata*.

The fact that *Dendrocygna* cross among themselves but not with other anatids demonstrates the uniqueness of the genus. *D. autumnalis* has been found in archaeological sites from pre-Columbian times.

C. moschata is the only bird that South American aborigines domesticated, using the term in its restricted sense, as with the chicken. The domestic duck of the Old World, a product of human intervention over centuries, is the Peking Duck, a large, uniformly white duck with yellow bill and feet and weighing 3 kg (see *C. moschata*).

Damage, Alleged Harmfulness, and Diseases

Dendrocygna species and *Netta peposaca* may seriously harm irrigated rice, but it is imprudent to eliminate them by poisoning, as has sometimes been done, for in certain years this resulted in almost complete disappearance of *N. peposaca* from Rio Grande do Sul. In São Paulo and Goiás *D. viduata*, *D. autumnalis*, and *Amazonetta brasiliensis* damage rice fields. Rice growers in Paraná emphasize that *N. peposaca* damage comes from trampling the plants as flocks stand in sprouting rice fields.

From the public-health viewpoint, it has been a subject of speculation as to whether *N. peposaca*, sometimes a carrier of equine encephalomyelitis, might be able to bring this disease from the Santiago del Estero, Argentina, region to the Porto Alegre, Rio Grande do Sul, area.

An outbreak of botulism in *D. viduata* and *N. peposaca* has been reported from an aquatic park in Curitiba, Paraná (Schonhofen et al. 1981).

Conservation

The destruction menacing almost all wetlands is unceasing. A useful method to contain this advance, beyond the creation of national parks and reserves, would be the establishment of financial incentives for private persons and organizations to maintain their marshes as natural breeding places.

Certainly installing reserves in regular rice-growing areas would be of great value, for plantings made expressly for birds would attract ducks and other aquatic birds away from commercial production areas. This measure could be particularly important, given the fact, observed in Rio Grande do Sul, that ducks such as *D. viduata* and *D. bicolor* like to nest in rice fields.

Similar benefits would arise from proper management of ponds, by keeping aquatic plants growing around the edges of shallow reservoirs. In this way it would be possible to make up in part for other wetlands lost by filling or draining for agriculture and other purposes. Reservoirs are useful as resting places for migratory anatids. Lands useful for aquatic avifauna, such as marshes, swamps, mudflats, bogs, and flood plains, are low and covered with shallow water, either permanent or temporary, and used to be considered "useless" and unhealthful. In reality they have an important function in maintaining the natural equilibrium, being as indispensable for people as are forests. We must reconsider our economic, recreational, educational, scientific, and aesthetic values with reference to wetlands, but starry-eyed conservationism detached from the basic interests of the community gets us nowhere.

We need an international agreement to protect anatids that may cross three or four international boundaries (Brazil, Argentina, Uruguay, and Chile) twice a year.

Synopsis of Brazilian Anatidae
(number of species in parentheses)

Subfamily Anserinae

Tribe Dendrocygnini (3)
Genus *Dendrocygna*
Tribe Anserini (2)
Genera *Coscoroba* and *Cygnus*

Subfamily Anatinae

Tribe Tadornini (1)
Genus *Neochen*
Tribe Anatini (9)
Genus *Anas*
Tribe Aythyini (2)
Genus *Netta*
Tribe Cairinini (3)
Genera *Amazonetta, Sarkidiornis,* and *Cairina*
Tribe Mergini (1)
Genus *Mergus*
Tribe Oxyurini (3)
Genera *Oxyura* and *Heteronetta*

FULVOUS WHISTLING-DUCK, *Dendrocygna bicolor,*
Marreca-caneleira

48 cm. Size of a small goose, with short body, long neck, relatively long bill, long legs, and quite broad wings, all the reverse of ducks in other genera. Cinnamon brown with plumage at sides of neck furrowed in blackish, similar to geese. Flanks streaked yellow, upper tail coverts white, wings without any white, bill and very large feet lead color. VOICE: very different from congeners, with a special nasal tone, *kse-ksaya, tsi-bieh.* Crepuscular. Feeds on aquatic vegetation it takes by diving like a coot (*Fulica*). Marshes. Southern U.S. to Argentina but rare or appearing only periodically in many places. Also Africa, India. Has no geographic races. Also called *Xenxêm.*

WHITE-FACED WHISTLING-DUCK, *Dendrocygna viduata,* Irerê   Fig. 67

44 cm. Erect stance, white facial mask (lacking in immatures), finely streaked flanks, broad black wings with no white. Bill and feet plumbeous. VOICE: even sharper than *D. autumnalis, wis-wis-wieh,* female whistling more weakly. In flight resembles White-faced Ibis, *Plegadis chihi,* but does not intersperse intervals of gliding among wing strokes. Before landing circles, whistling. To take off or land flies almost vertically, unlike many other ducks, e.g., *Amazonetta brasiliensis.* Most active at dawn and dusk; overflies cities at night, whistling, especially in rainy weather. During day rests in compact flocks, remaining on foot at edge of marshes and flooded fields where it also feeds. Also perches on ocean beaches, resting during day, and even rests on ocean surface when crossing a large inlet. Tropical regions of South America to Bolivia, Argentina, Uruguay. Throughout Brazil (abundant in southeast). Also Africa, from where it colonized South America. Also called *Marreca-piadeira* (Rio Grande do Sul), *Paturi, Viuvinha* (Ceará), *Marreca-viuva* (Paraíba).

Fig. 67. White-faced Whistling-Duck, *Dendrocygna viduata,* mates caressing. After P. Scott 1957.

BLACK-BELLIED WHISTLING-DUCK, *Dendrocygna autumnalis*, Asa-branca PL 5.1

48 cm. Similar in aspect to *D. bicolor* and *D. viduata*, distinguishable by gray face, black belly, and large white patch on wing, visible only in flight. Red bill and feet. Immature grayish brown, including bill and feet. VOICE: a 4- or 5-part whistle, *jewi-jewi-ji-ji-ji,* repeated by other flock members. Grazes in low, flooded grasslands, like a goose; sometimes in mangroves. May roost high at night or for daytime sleeping, lying on tarsi. Flocks do not mix with *viduata* or other ducks. At least as crepuscular as *bicolor* and *viduata*. Unlike them, restricted to Americas. Texas to Bolivia, Argentina, a large part of Brazil (subspecies *discolor*); common in Amazonia but becomes rare, disappears, or reappears only periodically in southeastern Brazil. Also called *Marreca-cabocla, Marreca-grande-de-Marajó, Paruriaçu* (Maranhão), *Marajoara* (Goiás).

COSCOROBA SWAN, *Coscoroba coscoroba*, Capororoca

100 cm; 3.5 kg. Very large, southern, white, swanlike with black wingtips, red bill and feet. Female smaller than male. Immature marbled with brown. Young grayish white with reddish bill and feet. VOICE: a loud *GO-go goAH, coscoroba*. Marshes close to sea, lake and ocean beaches. Swims away from shore like a goose or swan, with neck stretched vertically up. Feeds in shallow water but at times gets well away from water. Patagonia and Chile to Paraguay, Brazil on Rio Grande do Sul littoral. Breeds in that state regularly, in same region as *Cygnus melancoryphus*. Also called *Pato-arminho*.

BLACK-NECKED SWAN, *Cygnus melancoryphus*, Cisne-de-pescoço-preto Fig. 68

120 cm; 4.0–5.3 kg. Wings entirely white, short compared to those of *Coscoroba coscoroba*, and the black neck appears thicker. Base of bill and feet red. Female smaller, has only a small, flaccid caruncle, and has yellowish postocular streak that extends to occiput. Immature sooty, lacks caruncles. Young has gray bill and feet. VOICE: a melodious,

Fig. 68. Black-necked Swan, *Cygnus melancoryphus,* male.

monosyllabic *ur* given in flight. Flight heavy and noisy; takes off with difficulty, completely unlike *C. coscoroba*. Floats on water to rest with neck stretched vertically. Walks very little, unlike *C. coscoroba*. Feeds while floating in water shallow enough that it can reach bottom by submerging head and neck. In extensive marshes, including brackish ones. Enjoys resting on ocean, floating in long, close, single files which quickly move away if someone appears on beach. Chile and Argentina (abundant in latter) to littoral of southeastern Brazil (Rio Grande do Sul, occasionally up to southern São Paulo). Also called *Pato-arminho, Ganso-de-pescoço-preto, Cabeça-preta, Pato-argentino* (all Rio Grande do Sul).

ORINOCO GOOSE, *Neochen jubata*, Pato-corredor PL 5.2

53 cm. Distinctive interior species of local occurrence. Stature of a goose, with exaggeratedly erect stance; neck long, surprisingly thick and ruffled, held vertically stretched. Bill and feet red. Yellowish from head to breast, chestnut on back and belly, black wings with white area. Male larger. VOICE: differs in sexes: male of a flying pair goes *shewit shewit*, female *a-ohk*. . . . Perched on beach, pair will duet, each sex using its own vocalization. Runs in a distinct manner, flies little, perches on trunks and branches. On open, rocky river beaches in hot regions. Disappearing from navigable rivers. Venezuela to Bolivia, Paraguay, Argentina, Brazil (Amazonia, central Brazil). Also called *Ganso, Marrecão-do-banhado, Marrecão, Roncador, Wa-na-ná* (Kamaiurá, Mato Grosso). Related to *Chloephaga* geese of Andes and southern South America.

SPECKLED TEAL, *Anas flavirostris*, Marreca-pardinha

41.5 cm. Southern species with short tail, speckled breast, blackish cap, yellow bill. Tierra del Fuego to Rio Grande do Sul, where it nests, through Andes to Venezuela. Also called *Danadinha, Churiazinha, Parda-pequena*. See *A. georgica*.

SOUTHERN WIGEON, *Anas sibilatrix*, Marreca-oveira SV

51 cm. Large southern migrant with prominent white area directly behind bluish bill, remotely resembling *A. discors*. Rusty flanks. Chile and Argentina to Paraguay, Brazil (Rio Grande do Sul, infrequently). Nests in extreme south of continent.

WHITE-CHEEKED PINTAIL, *Anas bahamensis*, Marreca-toicinho

37 cm. Widely distributed, easily recognized by white sides of head, white throat, cinnamon on sharp tail and posterior edge of wing in both male and female, blue bill with red base. Female similar to male but slighter, with red spot on bill and white cheeks less bright. Dives. See "Feeding." West Indies to Chile, Argentina, northern and eastern Brazil (in-

cluding Rio de Janeiro), exceptionally Rio Grande do Sul. Also called *Paturi-do-mato*.

YELLOW-BILLED PINTAIL, *Anas georgica,* Marreca-parda

60 cm. Southern species, very similar in plumage and bill color to *A. flavirostris* but differing in long, sharp-pointed tail and reddish, longer head. Tierra del Fuego to São Paulo, through Andes to Colombia. Nests in Rio Grande do Sul, including in small ponds in planalto, frequently associated with *A. flavirostris*. Also called *Marreca-danada*.

NORTHERN PINTAIL, *Anas acuta*   NV

Eight individuals in eclipse plumage observed on Fernando de Noronha in December 1988 (Antas et al. 1990). A species of Holarctic distribution. In view of frequency with which birds from Palearctic are discovered on Fernando de Noronha, it is quite possible these strong-flying ducks crossed the Atlantic from African coast.

SILVER TEAL, *Anas versicolor,* Marreca-cricri

40 cm. Small, attractive, with whitish cheeks and throat resembling *A. bahamensis*. Black cap, black-and-white streaked flanks, bill blue with yellow base. Chile and Argentina to Paraguay, Bolivia, Brazil in Rio Grande do Sul, where it nests and in certain seasons is relatively common. Also called *Quiri-quiri, Pato-argentino*.

BLUE-WINGED TEAL, *Anas discors,* Marreca-de-asa-azul   NV

38 cm. Northern migrant, size of *Amazonetta brasiliensis*. Distinguished by light blue or grayish upper wing coverts that resemble those of *A. cyanoptera* and *A. platalea*. Underparts light brown, richly spotted with dark brown. Adult male has broad white crescent directly behind black bill; this marking is poorly outlined in eclipse plumage (July–November) and is absent in female. A North American migrant that becomes periodically abundant in more northerly regions of South America, coming to northern Brazil (Pará, Maranhão) in appreciable numbers February–April; penetrates farther south, reaching Rio de Janeiro (April–August), Rio Grande do Sul (November), going as far as Uruguay, Argentina, Chile. Its presence in South America is not, therefore, restricted to period of rigorous northern winter. Between 1951 and 1978, 99 individuals banded in U.S. were found in Brazil, this being about 3% of all birds of this species recovered. Also called *Sará* (Maranhão).

CINNAMON TEAL, *Anas cyanoptera,* Marreca-colorada   SV

40 cm. Small southern migrant, bright reddish brown with black crissum and large bluish gray area on wing similar to that of *A. platalea* and *A. discors*. Southern and western South America, accidentally in Rio Grande do Sul. A sub-

species resident in North America (*A. c. septentrionalis*) migrates to northern South America in typical eclipse plumage (see "Morphology . . . ").

RED SHOVELER, *Anas platalea,* Marreca-colhereira   SV

50 cm. Southern migrant characterized by long, spatulate bill that makes bird appear larger than it is. Southern South America to Peru, Bolivia, Paraguay, Brazil, occasionally to Rio Grande do Sul, exceptionally as far as Rio de Janeiro (July).

RINGED TEAL, *Anas leucophrys,* Marreca-de-coleira

30 cm. Small, southern species with blue bill. Both males and females immediately identifiable in flight by small, round, white spot on wing. Sides of head and neck white, bordered and emphasized behind with black in male. Flooded forests alongside *Cairina moschata* (Formosa, Argentina). Northern Argentina to Bolivia, Paraguay, Brazil (Mato Grosso, Rio Grande do Sul, São Paulo: Pindamonhangaba, June 1987, H. Alvarenga).

ROSY-BILLED POCHARD, *Netta peposaca,* Marrecão

55 cm; 1 kg or more. Large, southern species. Unmistakable with large head and high bill, swollen at base and red in male, gray in female. Male head and neck black; female dark brownish. In flight a large white area is visible on black upper surface of narrow wings, which are white underneath. Breeds in certain areas of Rio Grande do Sul (Belton 1984) and appears there in flocks from western Argentina (individuals banded in Santiago del Estero, 1400 km away) which then head south to nest on Argentine littoral. Also in flocks in summer locally in Rio Grande do Sul. Appearance in Taubaté, São Paulo, in January 1988 of a male with well-developed testicles must indicate breeding in that region (H. Alvarenga pers. comm.) Favorite game bird of Rio Grande do Sul hunters. Flocks damage rice fields, sometimes more by walking on rice than by eating it. Control accomplished locally by a head bounty, as occurs with Monk Parakeet, *Myiopsitta monachus* (see "Damage . . . "). Also called *Marrecão-da-Patagônia, Pato-picazo*.

SOUTHERN POCHARD, *Netta erythrophthalma,* Paturi-preta

43 cm. Widely distributed but very local; numbers have increased considerably in recent years. Very dark brown (male brilliant) with bluish bill, wings with wide white streak crossing base of remiges, visible only in flight. Eyes red or yellow. Eastern Brazil, in Ceará (1958, 1987), Piauí, Pernambuco, Alagoas, Bahia, Rio de Janeiro (Lagoa Feia, 1965; breeding, not uncommon), São Paulo (Taubaté, 1987; breeding), Brasília, Federal District (February, August, Paulo

Antas); locally from Suriname, Venezuela, and Colombia to Argentina, Chile; also western and southern Africa.

BRAZILIAN DUCK, *Amazonetta brasiliensis,*
Pé-vermelho, Ananaí   PL 5.3

40 cm; 500 g. Small, common, with red feet. Wing speculum may appear black, green, or bluish according to light; also has prominent triangular patch that is white like axillaries. Male bill red. Between breeding periods acquires eclipse plumage (see "Morphology . . . ") which lacks contrasts, and feet become pink. Female bill bluish, hind neck black, 2 light spots on face, throat white. VOICE: *prit-prit . . . , dlewit-dlewit, et-et-et;* a surprisingly low *quaahk.* Marshes and stock ponds, even small ones with abundant low, dense vegetation. The Guianas and Venezuela to Argentina, throughout Brazil, where it is one of anatids most shot by hunters. Also called *Marreca-ananaí, Marreca-assobiadeira, Marreca-espelho.*

COMB DUCK, *Sarkidiornis melanotos,*
Putrião, Pato-de-crista   Fig. 69

82 cm; 2 kg or more (male). Unmistakable black and white color. Male neck becomes yellowish during breeding (near end of year), when tuberous growth on bill reaches maximum development, remaining flaccid and not so prominent during rest of year. Female similar but much smaller. VOICE: generally silent but capable of a loud, low roar. Flocks fly in single file, conspicuous because of birds' large black wings. Likes to perch off ground at river and lake beaches. Swampy regions. Central America to Argentina; in Brazil locally in Amazonia, northeast, centralwest, southeast, south (e.g., Espírito Santo, Rio de Janeiro, São Paulo, Rio Grande do Sul); also Africa (from where it came to South America), India, China. Also called *Pato-cachamorro* (Goiás), *Pato-argentino* (Rio Grande do Sul), *Parui* (Minas Gerais, Mato Grosso), *Pato-ganso* (Mato Grosso).

Fig. 69. Comb Duck, *Sarkidiornis melanotos,* in breeding season (crest swollen).

Fig. 70. Muscovy Duck, *Cairina moschata,* male.

MUSCOVY DUCK, *Cairina moschata,*
Pato-do-mato   Fig. 70

85 cm; wingspan 120 cm; wild adult male 2.2 kg, domesticated male up to 4.5 kg, female only a bit more than half that. A very important species, having given rise to South American domestic duck. Only bird domesticated by aborigines. Both sexes distinguished from other anatids by large, high head, as if swollen on top, owing to presence of an erect topknot, which is larger in male than female. Black with some white in wing, this being reduced or absent in female, which also has almost no caruncles at base of bill and totally lacks nuchal and frontal crests. In both sexes bill crossed in middle by whitish band. VOICE: a muffled snort.

Behavior: Perches on bare branches (e.g., of *Cecropia*) to observe surroundings, rest, and roost. Nighttime roosts, where various individuals may assemble, are evidenced by feces accumulated on ground below. Has long, sharp claws with which it clutches branches. Also uses them during fights, along with tuberosity at bend of wing, with which it can give violent blows.

Breeding: Adult male requires several females. A pair salutes each other with heads held high and clapping bills. Nests in trees (see "Breeding"). Ducklings of wild parents are all black, those of domestic birds spotted with yellow. However, spotted young in wild have been reported (Ilha Mexiana, Pará). Ducklings with black down are a more intense and shiny black when adults. Wild-phenotype parents may produce both types of young in same clutch.

Habitat and Decline: Inhabits lakes and rivers surrounded by or not very far from forest. Numbers in southern and eastern Brazil are much reduced as a result of habitat destruction and hunting. This is the aquatic bird most sought by hunters. It has become very shy because of constant persecution.

Distribution: Mexico to northern Argentina, throughout Brazil. Also called *Pato-bravo, Pato-selvagem, Asa-branca, Pato-picaço* (Rio Grande do Sul), *Zewät* (Kamaiurá, Mato Grosso), *Pato-bravo-verdadeiro.* Names *moschata, Pato-*

almiscarado, ["musky"] etc., may be derived from Muisca, name of a Colombian tribe, for this duck has no musk aroma whatsoever. Genus also occurs in Old World.

Domestication: Reared in pre-Inca Peru, being the only domestic bird (in the strict sense of the word) in South America. There is some doubt about its domestication by Brazilian natives. Father Anchieta (republished 1900) reported in 1585 that "oxen, chickens, turkeys, sheep and ducks came from Reino [the mother country]," but Souza (republished 1938) mentioned in 1587 that Indians took young Muscovy Ducks and reared them at home. The Tupinambás did not eat their domestic ducks, for they believed this would make them slow runners (Léry, republished 1961).

Under domestication there is a strong tendency for white areas of plumage to expand. This also applies to red caruncles, those birds having the most exuberant ones being called *corais,* "corals"; in wild individuals the face is black and not swollen. This "creole duck" becomes heavier than its wild ancestor. At about 1 year of age it stops growing but continues to gain weight.

Hybridization and Introduction into Old World: It is highly probable that when Brazil was first colonized by Europeans, the Portuguese introduced from the Old World, along with chickens, the large domestic duck called Peking or Pekinese, which crosses readily with *C. moschata.* The hybrid, called *paturi,* is infertile because of the remote relationship of its parents, for the Peking is a descendant of the Mallard, *Anas platyrhynchos,* a widely distributed Northern Hemisphere species from which have descended all of the world's domestic duck forms except, obviously, *C. moschata.*

In the sixteenth century Spaniards and Portuguese took *C. moschata* to Europe, where it was called Turkish Duck or Muscovite Duck, which merely meant "foreign duck."

Brazilian Merganser, *Mergus octosetaceus,*
Pato-mergulhão   EN   R   Pl 5.4

55 cm. One of the few Brazilian ducks adapted to rivers in mountainous regions, like the rare Fasciated Heron, *Tigrisoma fasciatum.* Resembles a cormorant (which may appear in same localities) but is slimmer and has thinner, narrower, serrated bill. Has nuchal crest, developed primarily in male, white wing speculum, red feet. High-country whitewater rivers that run through faults, forming rapids where it dives for fish. Flies low, calling, along river without leaving it. Perches on rocks and trees that have fallen into the water. VOICE: *krack-krack* (alarm). Nests in tree holes at river edge (July, Misiones).

Western Minas Gerais in mountains dividing Paranaíba and São Francisco basins: Serra da Canastra, 1200 m, 1979 and subsequent years when population was studied by J. M. Dietz (pers. comm.); a pair with 6 small young was photographed in August 1984 (Bartmann 1988). Also recorded on slopes of Serra Negra, Ribeirão Salitre, headwaters of Rio Dourados (G. Mattos 1973 pers. comm. and F. Sellow, prior

to 1823. See Chapter 2.4). Goiás: Chapada dos Veadeiros, 1986–87, C. Yamashita. Records from upper Tocantins 1953, Nova Roma, Pfrimer and Blaser (Miranda Ribeiro 1937, material in Mus. Nac. Rio de Janeiro). São Paulo: Itararé, Natterer and Sellow. Paraná: Salto da Ariranha, Chrostowski 1922. Santa Catarina: Blumenau, prior to 1871. An individual was seen in September 1956 by Jean Delacour above Iguaçu Falls on Argentine side. Historically better known from Misiones, Argentina, on tributaries of Rio Paraná and in Paraguay. Until recently considered one of South America's rarest birds. See "Feeding" and "Breeding."

Lake Duck, *Oxyura vittata,* Marreca-pé-na-bunda
SV

Only in extreme southern Brazil, as a migrant. Very similar to *O. dominica* but a bit larger. Male has all-black head; female has just 1 light horizontal line on side of head, lacking white superciliary of *dominica.* Tierra del Fuego to Paraguay. Common in northern Argentina (Salta), occasional in Rio Grande do Sul. Considered a representative of Ruddy Duck, *O. jamaicensis,* of North America, developing, as that species does, eclipse plumage in winter (see "Morphology . . . "). Also called *Marrecãozinho.*

Masked Duck, *Oxyura dominica,* Bico-roxo
Fig. 71

37 cm. Small, widely distributed, little noticed because it lives hidden in thick aquatic vegetation. Stiff tail, typical of genus, is lifted vertically and spread like a fan when bird displays. Male has chestnut head and neck with only mask black (see *O. vittata*). Bill high and bright blue. Wing has distinctive white spot reminiscent of *Anas leucophrys.* Female and some males (June, Minas Gerais) light brown with black on top of head and 2 black horizontal stripes on each side of head, 1 of them crossing through eye. Bill blackish. VOICE: an unusual ventriloquial cackle: a sharply descending sequence of 5 sonorous cries, similar to a human voice—*GLOO-GLOO, gloo, glo, gla.* Docile. Walks with difficulty but dives well to obtain subaquatic plants. Flies low. As a prenuptial display male swells up throat and neck, with bill a bit raised, and floats motionless on water. Lakes, flooded pastures. Texas to Argentina, much of Brazil: north, northeast, centralwest southeast (including Rio de Janeiro).

Fig. 71. Masked Duck, *Oxyura dominica,* male.

Also called *Marrequinha, Marreca-rã* (Rio Grande do Sul).
See *O. dominica*. Unusual process of swelling throat resembles *Heteronetta atricapilla*.

BLACK-HEADED DUCK, *Heteronetta atricapilla*, Marreca-de-cabeça-preta

36 cm. Small, southern species. Male characterized by combination of black head and blue bill with vertical red line on base of maxilla. Narrow white streak can be seen on open wing. Female somewhat larger, brown with light superciliary. When danger is present prefers to hide, although flies very well. Male, when ready for courtship, swells neck so it resembles bare, broadened neck of a vulture or frog (*pato-sapo*), indicating possible relationship with genus *Oxyura*. Brood parasite; eggs laid in any accessible nest situated up to 1 m above water and belonging to a bird approximately this species' size, especially such abundant aquatic birds as, in Argentina, *Netta peposaca* and coots, *Fulica* (see "Breeding"). Marshes lacking tall vegetation. Chile and Argentina to Rio Grande do Sul (November, May, in flocks), Paraguay, Bolivia. Also see "Migration."

Anatidae Bibliography
See also General Bibliography

Barratini, L. P., and R. Escalante. 1971. *Anseriformes*. Montevideo: Mus. Damasio Antonio Larrañaga.

Bartmann, W. 1988. New observations on the Brazilian Merganser. *Wildfowl* 39:7–14.

Bertoni, A. de W. 1901. *Aves nuevas del Paraguay*. Asunción.

Brettschneider, D. S. 1981. Notas sobre a alimentação do marrecão, *Netta peposaca*, em Vitória do Palmar, Rio Grande do Sul. *Iheringia* (58)31–39.

Carvalho, Cory T. 1975. *Sec. Agric., Recursos Nat.*, Bol. 16. [Duck migration]

Coimbra Filho, A. F. 1964. *Rev. Bras. Biol.* 24:383–91. [*Amazonetta*, behavior]

Coimbra Filho, A. F. 1965. *Rev. Bras. Biol.* 25:387–94. [*Cairina*, hybridization]

Coimbra Filho, A. F. 1969. *Rev. Bras. Biol.* 29:87–95. [*Anas, Netta*, distribution]

Coimbra Filho, A. F. 1969. Acêrca da proteção das espécies brasileiras da família Anatidae. *F. Bras. Cons. Nat.*, Bol. 4.

Cooke, R. G., and S. L. Olson. 1984. An archaeological record for the White-faced Whistling-Duck, *Dendrocygna viduata*, in Central Panama. *Condor* 86:493–94.

Delacour, J. 1954–64. *Waterfowl of the World*. 4 vols. London: Country Life, Ltd.

Feduccia, A. 1977. *J. Theor. Biol.* 67:715–21. [Relationships]

Jenni, D. A. 1969. *Auk* 86:355–56. [Diving]

Johnsgard, P. A. 1961. The taxonomy of Anatidae, a behavioral analysis. *Ibis* 103(1):71–85.

Johnsgard, P. A. 1965. *Handbook of Waterfowl Behavior*. Ithaca, N.Y.: Cornell University Press.

Johnson, A., and J. C. Chebez. 1985. Sobre a situación de *Merganser octosetaceus* en la Argentina. *Hist. Nat. Supl.* 1.

Madge, S., and H. Burn. 1987. *Waterfowl, An Identification Guide to the Ducks, Geese, and Swans*. Boston: Houghton Mifflin.

Magnanini, A., and A. F. Coimbra Filho. 1964. *Vellozia* 1:142–66. [*Amazonetta*, feeding]

Menezes, R. S. 1960. *Bol. Soc. Cearen. Agron.* 1:177. [Enemies]

Nacinovic, J. G. 1982. Carácteres externos em *Cairina moschata*: o Pato-do-mato. *An. Soc. Sul-Riogr. Orn.* 3:27–29.

Olrog, C. C. 1968. *Neotropica* 14:17–22. [Banding]

Olrog, C. C. 1975. El anillado de aves en la Argentina 1961–74. *Neotropica* 21(64):17–19.

Olson, S. L., and A. Feduccia. 1980. *Presbyornis* and the origin of the Anseriformes (Aves: Charadriomorphae). *Smithsonian Contr. Zool.* 323.

Ortega, V. R., F.S.C. Almeida, and A. Audi. 1987. Análise de recapturas e recuperações de aves aquáticas anilhadas pela Comp. Energética de São Paulo (CESP) 1983 a 1986. *An. III ENAV*:29.

Partridge, W. H. 1956. *Auk* 73:473–88. [*Mergus*, behavior]

Rees, E. C., and N. Hillgarth. 1984. The breeding biology of *Heteronetta atricapilla* and the behavior of their young. *Condor* 86:242–50.

Reichholf, J. 1975. *Anz. Orn. Ges. Bay.* 14:1–69. [Ecology]

Reichholf, J. 1983. Extreme Wasservogel-Armut am Rio Negro, Amazonien. *Verh. Orn. Ges. Bay.* 23:525–28.

Rossi, J.A.H. 1953. *Hornero* 10:1–17. [*Cygnus*, general]

Schlatter, R. P., et al. 1983. Ecological studies of Chilean ducks. In H. Boyd, ed., *First Western Hemisphere Waterfowl and Waterbird Symposium*. Spec. Publ. Canadian Wildlife Service.

Schonhofen, C. A., and R.G.F. Garcia. 1981. *Arq. Biol. Tecno. Curitiba* 24(4):433–35. [Botulism in ducks]

Scott, P. 1957. *A Coloured Key to the Wildfowl of the World*. Slimbridge: The Wildfowl Trust.

Silva, F. 1986. Movimentos de dispersão da marreca-parda, *Anas georgica*, recuperações e recapturas. *An. II ENAV*, Viçosa.

Teixeira, D. M., and J. B. Nacinovic. 1981. Notas sobre a marreca preta *Netta erythrophthalma*. *An. Soc. Sul-Riogr. Orn.* 2:19–22.

Weller, M. W. 1968. *The Living Bird* 7:169–207. [*Heteronetta*, behavior]

Weller, M. W. 1968. *Wilson Bull.* 80:189–212. [Behavior]

Weller, M. W. 1969. *Iowa Agr. Stat.*, J-7677:89–130. [Migration]

Weller, M. W. 1969. *Wildfowl* 20:55–58. [Danger of exotic species introduction]

Wildholzer, F. L., and W. A. Voss. 1978. Procriação de Cisne-de-pescoço-preto em cativero. *Natureza em Revista* 5:24–29.

FAMILY ANHIMIDAE: SCREAMERS (2)

This endemic South American group is so distinctive that in the past it was placed in a separate order. However, its members are Anseriformes, the existence of rudimentary lamellae in the bills of *Anhima* and *Chauna* proving their true relationship with the Anatidae and suggesting that the Anhimidae are not "primitive" members of the group but more evolved types that have abandoned the filtering technique of feeding (Olson and Feduccia 1980). The fact that the Anhimidae are not web-footed gives them a certain gallinaceous appearance.

Chauna remains have been found from the Pleistocene of Argentina (20,000 years B.P.).

Brazil has two widely distributed species, one southern, the other Amazonian. A third, which does not occur here, is restricted to northwestern South America.

Morphology, Special Adaptations, and Behavior

Screamers are bulky birds with a deceptively gallinaceous bill. It is hard to realize that the plates outlined on the inside of the maxilla (less visible in the mandible) are vestiges of the complicated filtering apparatus of ducks (see fig. 66 in Anatidae). Screamers have sturdy, short legs and enormous toes (an adaptation to their wetland environment) which, unlike those of other Brazilian Anseriformes, lack webbing. They swim only occasionally and slowly; the young, however, do so with ease.

Screamers are the only birds whose ribs lack processi uncinati, which contribute decisively to thorax rigidity. They have two spurs at the bend of the wing that are powerful weapons when the wings are used to defend the nest (see also Wattled Jacana, *Jacana jacana,* and Southern Lapwing, *Vanellus chilensis*). There is little documentation on fights between Southern Screamers, *Chauna torquata,* but sometimes the horny spur coverings (which are not very tightly fixed and are shed periodically like the plumage) are found buried in the breast flesh of these birds. The feather arrangement is not divided into pterylae and apteria.

The skin is spongy and provided with a system of interlacing spaces connected to the air sacs and lungs, as in pelicans. This sponginess extends to the toes. The plumage, when pressed in the hands, makes strange popping noises. The short neck is held outstretched during flight. The wings are very wide and the flight heavy and noisy. During hot hours of the day *C. torquata* may soar so high that it disappears from sight and can be mistaken for a vulture or large hawk, unusual behavior for Anseriformes and more like the Ciconiidae. Anyone overflying marshes by plane will see screamers flying easily from one place to another. Screamers molt their flight feathers successively, not en bloc like Anatidae.

Screamers roost in treetops where they can pass for vultures. They enjoy bathing, getting so wet they can scarcely take off in flight. They dry their wings outstretched. Periodically they gather in flocks, sometimes of hundreds, for local migration (Argentina, Uruguay). Sexes are similar, with the female smaller.

Sounds

Screamers frighten enemies with a snakelike hiss and by clapping the bill lightly. A ventriloquial *boo* can be heard, probably coming from the spongy skin. Their calls are deep and loud with a melodious background. Pairs duet, the male having the lower voice. The calls are also dimorphic, in a way resembling the Orinoco Goose, *Neochen jubata.*

Feeding

Screamers eat leaves of aquatic plants and grass and take arthropods and any small, dead animals they find while grazing.

Breeding

Nesting is by pairs. They show affection, caressing each other mutually on the head with the bill. Their large nest of leaves and stems in the marsh may be similar to that of the Maguari Stork, *Ciconia maguari.* The nest of the Horned Screamer, *Anhima cornuta,* is low and partially floating.

C. torquata lays two or three white eggs (which turn yellow as they become dirty), similar to those of large Anatidae; *A. cornuta* lays two brownish olive eggs. Pairs take turns at incubation, which for *C. torquata* varies from 44 to 45 days. They cover the eggs when leaving the nest.

Use, Collisions

Screamers are not valued as game, for the spongy skin is often repugnant. Local people in the south dislike *C. torquata,* and those in the north hate *A. cornuta,* for each warns untamed cattle or game (e.g., deer) of the approach of cowboys or hunters. They are good sentinels, responding to any disturbance with their very loud calling, which can also be provoked by shots or firecrackers.

Various curative powers are attributed to the forehead "horn" of *A. cornuta.* It is regarded as a preventative and is famous as a powerful snakebite remedy, as the Pernambuco Indians taught Count Mauricio de Nassau in the seventeenth century.

When the first electric lines were installed near *C. torquata* habitat in Rio Grande do Sul, these birds caused innumerable accidents which later were almost entirely eliminated by greater separation of the lines (Tessmer 1989).

HORNED SCREAMER, *Anhima cornuta,* Anhuma
Fig. 72

80 cm; height 61 cm; wingspan 170 cm; 3150 g. Amazonian species with a peculiar frontal appendage, or "horn," implanted in skull; resembling an antenna, it may be either straight or curved back or forward, sometimes almost reaching tip of bill and touching ground when bird eats. This appendage, which sprouts hidden in crown plumage of young bird, is elastic but breakable in adult, but grows back. Plumage black and white. In flight a light brown streak is noticeable on front edge of large black wings. Legs black. Immature dark brown with short horn.

Fig. 72. Horned Screamer, *Anhima cornuta*.

VOICE: pair sings a somewhat ventriloquial *WEEboo WEEboo* "song" together, female starting and male responding with a slightly deeper voice. This is interpreted by local people as *João Gomes, que comes tu? Minhoca, minhoca,* "John Gomes, what do you eat? Worm, worm." Also a series of melodious *uo, uo, uos* . . . ; *hoo-OOM-hoo* like a large pigeon or curassow. Marshes and even small swamps and ponds in forest. Lives in pairs and family groups and in small to slightly larger flocks. Emigrates when river branches or lakes inhabited in rainy season dry up (upper Rio Xingu, Mato Grosso). Almost throughout Amazonia and extending into interior Ceará, Bahia, Minas Gerais (Parque do Rio Doce), Mato Grosso (where in northern Pantanal both this

species and *C. torquata* can be heard in same place), São Paulo, Paraná (Rio Paracaí). Also Bolivia, Colombia, Venezuela, the Guianas. Common where aquatic avifauna is generally abundant and thus in places distant from civilization. Also called *Inhuma, Inhauma, Unicorne, Licorne.* State bird of Goiás.

SOUTHERN SCREAMER, *Chauna torquata,* Tachã
PL 5.5

80 cm. Large-headed, crested, southern species. Dark grayish brown, neck banded by a black choker emphasized by another of white down. Upper surface of black wing has large white area visible in flight; under wing surface all white. Area around eye, legs, and not-always-visible bare ring around neck red. VOICE: very loud, recalling a goose, audible at a distance of more than 3 km; song consists of pair duetting *GRYa-graGRA,* female's voice considerably weaker; also a *shlarew* when suspicious. When calling, head is raised and shaken. Pairs converse while flying, male crying a low *ta-HAH,* female responding with a high *tew-hew.* In flight resembles a seaplane maneuvering clumsily, with feet half dangling. Perches for hours on trees. Forms large flocks for overnighting in marshes, standing in shallow water. At any time of year there may be large or small gatherings of individuals that apparently do not breed but graze together peacefully. In some areas (Rio Grande do Sul) believed to compete with sheep for forage. Argentina and Bolivia to Mato Grosso, Rio Grande do Sul, São Paulo. Also called *Inhuma-poca, Chajá, Anhuma-do-pantanal* (Mato Grosso).

Anhimidae Bibliography
See also General Bibliography

Haffer, J. 1968. Notes on the wing and tail molt of the Screamers, the Sunbittern, and immature Guans. *Auk* 85(4):633–38.

ORDER FALCONIFORMES[1,2]

FAMILY ACCIPITRIDAE: HAWKS, EAGLES, AND ALLIES (44)

These hawks form a great, cosmopolitan family. Latin America is the richest but least investigated region for raptors. More than ten genera, including *Harpagus, Rostrhamus,* *Leucopternis, Buteogallus,* and *Harpia,* are restricted to the Neotropics. Family members are easily recognizable by the hooked bill and sharp claws, characteristics they share with

[1] The Cathartidae, the New World Vultures, which were the first Falconiformes family, have been transferred to the Ciconiiformes, after the Ciconiidae.

[2] In the introductory material for the families of this order, I cite members of the entire order, for in this case their separation into families is of secondary interest.

the Osprey, *Pandion haliaetus,* and falcons. The owls are a somewhat similar group. The oldest accipitrid fossils are from the eo-Oligocene of France (37 million years B.P.); they have also been found in the Brazilian Pleistocene (15–20 million years B.P.).

Morphology

Accipitrids vary in form, some being the size of a thrush, others having a wingspan of almost 2 m. The Harpy Eagle, *Harpia harpyja,* is unquestionably the world's most impressive raptor. One of the decisive anatomical characteristics of the Falconiformes is the shape of the sternum and pectoral girdle; when a hawk is prepared as a museum skin, this part of the skeleton should be kept with it.

Bill shape varies greatly, with the presence of two strong teeth on either side of the maxilla of the *Harpagus* being a distinctive feature reminiscent of the *Falco* (Falconidae). In various genera the basal phalanges of the second toe are fused. The Snail Kite, *Rostrhamus sociabilis,* has a comblike structure on the middle toe that must be useful in removing snail mucous from its plumage. The vision of eagles is two (not ten) times sharper than that of humans.

The primaries molt from the center to the tip of the wing, that is, the molt starts with the first (farthest inside) and ends with the tenth, (farthest out)—unlike the Falconidae, whose molt begins with the fourth primary, from there descending toward the tenth and ascending to the first. In large species a wing feather may last two years or more, resulting in various generations of remiges being used simultaneously. In general, Accipitridae have wider and more rounded wings than Falconidae. They soar a great deal, sometimes interspersing a few rapid wing beats.

In Brazil sexes are almost always similar in color, except in the Long-winged Harrier, *Circus buffoni,* which exhibits accentuated sexual dimorphism in this respect. Male and female are generally told apart by size. The female is frequently larger that her mate, even by as much as a third, and may appear to be a different species (e.g., *Accipiter, Harpia harpyja*). This reverse sexual dimorphism, which is clearer when weights rather than sizes of the sexes are compared, is more pronounced in species such as the *Spizastur, Accipiter,* and *Falco,* which catch relatively large and active birds; less pronounced in rodent and insect predators such as the *Buteo;* and almost absent in carrion eaters such as *Polyborus.* The fact of the female being larger may be based on the modus vivendi of the pair, to keep the much more aggressive male from becoming a danger to his mate (Amadon 1975). The large female is the best defender of their offspring. She takes advantage of this time of inactivity to molt her flight feathers. Molt of the remiges takes various months. The male molts after the young have been reared. Birds of prey frequently have both ovaries developed instead of just the left one, as in other birds.

Immatures often lack the most distinctive characteristics of adults. For a long time the juvenile Gray-bellied Hawk, *Accipiter poliogaster,* was believed to be a separate species, called *A. pectoralis.* The error was only discovered after the two plumage phases had been considered independent species for more than 100 years. Large hawks keep their immature plumage for more than a year, for which reason more individuals are seen in this dress or in mixed subadult plumage. To complicate the matter even further, some species have melanistic phases (e.g., Hook-billed Kite, *Chondrohierax uncinatus;* White-tailed Hawk, *Buteo albicaudatus;* Crested Eagle, *Morphnus guianensis*). It is said that the black phase may appear regularly in young individuals, as in the Red-backed Hawk, *Buteo polyosoma,* of the Andes. Perplexing similarities exist between nonrelated species, as in the Rufous-thighed Kite, *Harpagus diodon,* and Bicolored Hawk, *Accipiter bicolor,* or *A. poliogaster* and the Slaty-backed Forest-Falcon, *Micrastur mirandollei* (Falconidae).

Conspicuously colored "pants" (tibias) are frequently an outstanding feature. The pattern and color of the tail are of major importance for species identification. Some, such as the American Swallow-tailed Kite, *Elanoides forficatus,* and *Harpia harpyja,* have plumage full of powder. When the latter shakes itself it raises a cloud of powder. The base of the bill, the cere, and the legs are often brightly colored.

Vocalization

During the breeding season hawks and eagles utter cries that are similar in various species. These are usually composed of high whistles, which sound strange coming from large birds such as eagles. The Harris' Hawk, *Parabuteo unicinctus,* with a low, hoarse cry, is an exception. Certain species (e.g., Roadside Hawk, *Rupornis magnirostris*) vocalize all year.

Feeding and Hunting Methods

Brazilian accipitrids show a clear preference for arthropods such as grasshoppers, assassin bugs, ants, wasps, termites, and spiders. They also hunt reptiles, amphibians, and rodents. The Crane Hawk, *Geranospiza caerulescens,* the *Spizaetus,* and others catch bats. The Great Black-Hawk, *Buteogallus urubitinga,* catches snakes, even poisonous ones. Some species specialize. *Rostrhamus sociabilis* and the Slender-billed Kite, *Helicolestes hamatus,* for instance, eat only aquatic snails, and the Rufous Crab-Hawk, *Buteogallus aequinoctialis,* only crabs. To a lesser extent *Chondrohierax uncinatus* and the Black-collared Hawk, *Busarellus nigricollis,* are the same with relation to land snails and fish, respectively. *Geranospiza caerulescens* has an especially mobile intertarsal articulation which facilitates its exploration of certain cavities. Individual specializations also develop. Certain individual Savanna Hawks, *Buteogallus meridionalis,* know how to find subterranean, blind, burrowing snakes (*Leptotyphlops*) that come out in the rain.

Various species, such as *Buteogallus meridionalis, B. urubitinga, Buteo albicaudatus,* and the Plumbeous Kite, *Ictinia plumbea,* seek burning areas to capture, either on the ground or in flight, animals frightened or overcome by smoke. The *Harpagus, Ictinia plumbea, Accipiter, Rupornis magnirostris, Leucopternis, Chondrohierax uncinatus,* the Ornate Hawk-Eagle, *Spizaetus ornatus,* and others use army ants and bands of monkeys or coatis as beaters. Some species occasionally eat carrion: *Buteogallus urubitinga, Geranospiza caerulescens,* and the Crowned Eagle, *Harpyhaliaetus coronatus;* or fruit: *Elanoides forficatus* and *Buteogallus urubitinga.*

Large females often hunt animals larger than those caught by males, thus avoiding competition. The Zone-tailed Hawk, *Buteo albonotatus,* is interesting in its perfect imitation of a *Cathartes* vulture, thereby giving the impression of being incapable of attacking live prey. E. Willis (1966) observed how one, after circling with wings spread horizontally like a Black Vulture, *Coragyps atratus,* and later lifting them in the way the Turkey Vulture, *Cathartes aura,* does, descended and caught a bird in flight close to an isolated tree. No bird in the vicinity gave any alarm, for the perfectly disguised hawk was not recognized as dangerous. Such aggressive mimicry (see Ramphastidae, "Aggressive Mimicry") has also been suspected in *Accipiter bicolor pileatus,* an able bird hunter that mimics the insectivorous *Harpagus diodon* (Amadon 1961).

As for feeding frequency, everything leads to the belief that in nature *Harpia harpyja* hunts only twice a week, therefore requiring larger prey, such as a simian. It can fast for one or two weeks. It brings food once a day for its nestling, however, but even then may intersperse intervals of up to five days during which it suspends feeding (Fowler et al. 1964). Usually hawks hunt only a few hours per day, perhaps three, and their success is more limited than is generally believed—11% for the Eurasian Sparrowhawk, *Accipiter nisus,* the great European bird hunter. In California it was found that only 39% of White-tailed Kite, *Elanus leucurus,* attacks against rodents were successful (Warner and Rudd 1975). See also Falconidae.

Birds of prey (including Pandionidae and Falconidae) employ two principal hunting methods.

1. The raptor keeps watch from a branch or other perch, from where it launches out against any prey that happens along on land or water. These species customarily have short toes, as for example, those of the *Buteo* and *Harpyhaliaetus coronatus.* When the victim, such as a rat, is on the ground, it is literally "pinned down" by the predator.

In a variation of this method the bird hovers before falling on its prey, as with *Elanus leucurus,* the *Circus, Pandion haliaetus,* and certain falcons. This is a special adaptation for habitats where high perches are lacking. *Buteo albicaudatus* stops in midair instead of hovering, remaining still for up to several minutes as if suspended by an invisible wire, thanks to its stratagem of flying into a strong wind (especially in mountainous terrain) with the wings outstretched and immobile. In this way it scrutinizes the ground in search of prey. Other species patrol by flying close to the ground to catch insects perched on leaves or snails that rise to the surface of the water. *Buteo* are attracted to giant worms (*Glossoscolex* sp.) that may reach 1 m or more in length with a diameter of up to 5 cm and that remain close to the surface, coming out of the ground on rainy days. This kind of experience probably helped a *Rupornis magnirostris* in São Paulo catch a false coral snake (*Erythrolamprus aesculapii*) and a jararaca (*Bothrops jararaca*) (Sazima pers. comm.). The evolution of a facial disk, like those of *Harpia harpyja* and *Circus buffoni,* must facilitate localization of victims through the orientation furnished by even the softest sounds, a reminder of the owls. A further technique to be included under this heading is that employed by *Chondrohierax uncinatus* and *Geranospiza caerulescens* and described in the species accounts.

2. The raptor pursues insects or birds flying by. Sometimes the hunter seeks its victims by actively flying; sometimes it awaits the passerby while sitting on a perch from which it launches out in pursuit. Hunters of this kind, such as the *Accipiter* and *Falco,* usually have long toes and rough soles in order to better hold the prey, which does all it can to escape. These birds are capable of knocking down victims almost their own size, but usually they are only a third or half their own weight. *Elanoides forficatus,* the *Ictinia* and *Daptrius,* and various *Falco* catch large termites when swarming.[3] The Gray-headed Kite, *Leptodon cayanensis,* and *Daptrius* (Falconidae) consume hornet larvae and the hornets themselves in large quantities.

Prey is captured with the feet and at once carried to the mouth to be devoured. Some species, such as *Elanoides forficatus* and *Elanus leucurus,* occasionally do so without even perching when catching swarming ants. Small prey is swallowed whole; only when a larger bird is caught in the talons does the raptor tear out at least the flight and tail feathers before eating it. It is interesting to study remains scattered on the ground, for these can provide us with interesting data both on the hunter and hunted (see also Falconidae).

The various species and individuals develop their own techniques to deal with prey; for instance, a *Buteogallus urubitinga* ate only the large hind legs of amphibians it caught (Espírito Santo). Regurgitated pellets contain only feathers, hairs, and scales that have been eaten, for unlike owls, Falconiformes usually can digest bones. They usually produce one pellet per day, depending on circumstances.

Hawks have three principal types of aerodynamic specialization for hunting:

---

[3]When *Elanoides forficatus* finds a caterpillar on a leaf while flying, it takes both the leaf and caterpillar and later lets the leaf fall.

1. Short, rounded wings and a long tail, a combination appropriate for maneuvering in thick forest. Examples: *Accipiter, Spizaetus, Harpia,* and *Micrastur.*
2. Long, wide wings with "open tips" (the outer primaries visible during flight, as in the vultures) and a short tail, a combination appropriate for soaring in open spaces. Examples: *Buteo, Busarellus, Geranoaetus,* and *Leucopternis,* as well as the vultures.
3. Narrow, closed wings and a medium tail, for skilled hunters on the wing above the forest or in open country. Examples: *Ictinia* and *Falco.*

Birds of prey, like owls, usually do not drink.

Breeding

Male *Harpagus, Rostrhamus, Spizaetus,* and *Circus* make aerial displays. Little is known about the nesting of Brazilian species. *Buteo albicaudatus,* an open-country species, builds on trees or on rocks among umbellifers (*Eryngium* spp.); *Circus buffoni* nests on the ground in marshes. *Rostrhamus sociabilis* often nests in colonies, sometimes in reedbeds. *Harpia harpyja* builds a large nest like that of the Jabiru, *Jabiru mycteria,* and there are cases where one nest has been used consecutively by both species. The Black-chested Buzzard-Eagle, *Geranoaetus melanoleucus,* breeds on rocky escarpments.

Eggs are usually spotted and highly variable in color, even in the same clutch. Uniformly white or dirty white eggs are the rule with the *Ictinia* and *Spizaetus, Buteo albicaudatus, Buteogallus meridionalis, Harpyhaliaetus coronatus, Geranospiza caerulescens,* and Gray Hawk, *Buteo nitidus;* but *Buteogallus meridionalis* and the *Ictinia* also have spotted ones. A *Harpia harpyja* egg, not yet soiled, was gray with a heavy white wash filling the pores over the entire surface. Variation is so great that the presence or absence of a design on hawk eggs has little taxonomic importance.

A *Harpyhaliaetus coronatus* egg weighs 100 g, with 10 g of that shell; that of *Harpia harpyja* weighs 113 g; of *Coragyps atratus* (Cathartidae) 105 g. Some species lay only one egg (e.g., *Buteogallus meridionalis, Busarellus nigricollis*).

The incubation period for a small species such as *Elanus leucurus* is 30 to 32 days; for large species it is 50 days or more (*Harpia harpyja,* 52 days). Although there frequently are two eggs, it is common for only one nestling to survive, as for example, in *H. harpyja.* It is said that the interval between hatching of the two chicks and the aggressive tendencies of the larger one have a decided influence on the elimination of the younger ("cainism"). If the first chick is lively when its younger sibling hatches, the latter has little chance of surviving.

The female *Morphnus guianensis,* which guards the nest while, as in so many cases, the male brings food, brings back a branch with green leaves whenever she does leave and places it around the nest. She also cleans the nest of food remains (Bierregaard 1984).

The young of large species depend on paternal care for half a year or more, reaching adulthood only at two to three years of age. They may breed while still in immature plumage, as *Rostrhamus sociabilis* does, for instance. Large species such as *Harpia harpyja* do not nest every year.

The tayra (*Eira barbara*) [a mustelid mammal resembling the fisher] has been cited as a predator on the nest of *Morphnus guianensis.*

Migration

Elanoides forficatus and *Ictinia plumbea* disappear from southern regions (from Espírito Santo south) during our winter. *Harpia harpyja* was said to be migratory in Rio Grande do Sul. One October, W. Voss saw about a thousand *Rostrhamus sociabilis* in Sapucaia do Sul, Rio Grande do Sul, flying from north to south against a strong wind. They reportedly abandon the Taim area in April and May.

Some North American hawks reach Brazil as migrants: the Mississippi Kite, *Ictinia mississippiensis;* Swainson's Hawk, *Buteo swainsoni;* and Broad-winged Hawk, *B. platypterus.* The finding of *B. swainsoni* predominantly in western and southern Brazil (including four individuals banded in the U.S.) suggests that this hawk has a route similar to that of certain North American shorebirds, such as the Lesser Golden Plover, *Pluvialis dominica,* that travel from Venezuela directly to the upper Amazon and Central Brazil, reaching the Atlantic coast in Rio Grande do Sul.

Rostrhamus sociabilis travels at dusk, gathering to roost in certain flooded groves. The Chimango Caracara, *Milvago chimango,* also makes similar local migrations.

Parasites

Louse flies (Hippoboscidae) are common. *Leucopternis polionota,* for example, harbors *Olfersia raptatorum.* I have found two other species, *Lynchia nigra* and *Ornithoica vicina,* on *Rupornis magnirostris,* and *L. nigra* has also been found on the Peal Kite, *Gampsonyx swainsonii,* and *Ictinia.*

A microfilarial parasite, *Microfilaria rojasi,* has been described from the blood of *Ictinia plumbea* (Mazza et al. 1927).

Reaction of Other Birds to Raptors

Certain birds give a special alarm cry when a raptor appears (see also Strigiformes), but they do not always discern whether a raptor is or is not dangerous to them (see Hirundinidae). Thus, for example, the Grassland Sparrow, *Ammodramus humeralis,* is frightened by a *Buteogallus aequinoctialis,* which eats only crustaceans, and the Gray-breasted Martin, *Progne chalybea,* attacks *Rostrhamus sociabilis,* which is exclusively a snail eater. Just the generalized pattern of a bird of prey terrorizes some birds.

It is amusing to see how a Yellow-headed Caracara, *Milvago chimachima,* a falcon that is sluggish by nature, accelerates its flight, makes abrupt turns, and even lets itself fall a long way when fleeing from a Tropical Kingbird, *Tyrannus melancholicus,* chasing right on its tail.

Larger hawks harass smaller ones. I have seen the Chimango Caracara, *Milvago chimango,* chase *Buteogallus meridionalis, Geranoaetus melanoleucus,* the Crested Caracara, *Polyborus plancus,* and even vultures.

Association of the Manatee with the Snail Kite

It has been determined in Amazonia through telemetry, that the manatee (*Trichechus inunguis*) likes to linger under collective roosts of *Rostrhamus sociabilis* (R. Best pers. comm.). Apparently this is a phenomenon similar to that which I recorded in egret colonies: the feces that accumulate under these bird colonies provide a wealth of nutrients that promote more aquatic plant and animal growth.

Alleged Harmfulness, Usefulness, Use as a Symbol, Decline, and Preservation

Hawks and eagles are frequently accused of catching domestic animals. They occasionally do catch a chick or dove or even a chicken or pigeon, but there is no doubt that such "damage" is amply compensated by the large number of animals they consume that are considered "worthless" or even "noxious," antiquated and inadequate classifications unworthy of a cultured people. The fact is that birds of prey play an indispensable role in faunal equilibrium as regulators of selection. They help avoid excessive populations of rodents and small birds and eliminate defective individuals (before these can pass on their defects to descendants) or sick ones, thus avoiding epidemics. It has been shown in North America that in regions where raptors have declined, rodent populations have increased rapidly. In rare cases, birds of prey such as *Polyborus plancus* (Falconidae) may become a true nuisance. The names of hawks tend to emphasize their dangerous aspects: *gavião-pega-pinto,* "chick-catching-hawk"; *pega-macaco,* "monkey-catcher"; etc.

Most hawks are menaced by habitat destruction and indiscriminate hunting. *Rostrhamus sociabilis* is indirectly driven out by the introduction of *Tilapia* (Cichlidae), herbivorous fish that eradicate the aquatic plants in which the hawk's only food, a snail, lives. It is also hurt by the incessant drainage of marshes for agriculture and road building. On the elimination of *R. sociabilis* by biocides, see Chapter 3.7.

Information is lacking on the deadly effects of insecticides on Brazilian raptors, but everything leads me to believe that such effects exist. The raptors most in danger are those that live on birds and fish (see Pandionidae). Predators on mammals are usually not so harmed. The concentration of pesticides in *R. sociabilis* eggs and nestlings in Florida is frightening (Sykes 1985). Until recently, scientific institutions and private egg collectors did considerable harm to birds of prey. It has been suggested that eggs of popular species be marked, thereby making them valueless for collectors without hurting the birds (Olsen et al. 1982).

I want to emphasize that forest-dwelling native peoples, although they use flight and tail feathers of the larger species for headdresses and arrows, are not a problem. Indians of the Xingu (Mato Grosso) keep a *Harpia harpyja* in captivity as a periodic source of flight and tail feathers (a primary can be 50 cm long), thereby guaranteeing their feather source while at the same time saving the lives of other individual birds. These Indians know nothing of the custom of hunting with birds of prey that is practiced, preferably with trained falcons (falconry), in the Old World and by South American aborigines in Chile and Peru. It is reported that *açores,* "birds of prey," used to be taken from Brazil to Portugal to be employed in this way (Diogo F. Ferreira 1616).

Builders of the Catete Palace [in Rio de Janeiro] were well advised to decorate it with the sculpture of a bird of prey with a crest—a somewhat exaggerated principal feature—doubtless having in mind *Harpia harpyja.* The Municipal Theater of Rio de Janeiro, in contrast, was decorated with a foreign eagle, which might be justified by the international attractions shown there.

One of the species least affected by human activity is *Rupornis magnirostris.* Small *Accipiter* species live so hidden in the densest thickets that often their presence in the vicinity of cities is not even noticed. *Buteo albicaudatus* is extending its range, taking advantage of deforestation. Another open-country species, *Elanus leucurus,* is increasing its numbers in various parts of the extensive area where it occurs.

Synopsis of Brazilian Accipiters
(number of species in parentheses)

1. The kite group: *Elanus* (1), *Gampsonyx* (1), *Elanoides* (1), *Leptodon* (1), *Chondrohierax* (1), *Harpagus* (2), *Ictinia* (2), *Rostrhamus* (1), *Helicolestes* (1). These are relatively docile hawks usually insectivorous or living on mollusks. They are partly gregarious; sexes are similar. With the exception of *Elanus,* all are restricted to the Americas.
2. *Accipiter* (4), a genus with numerous species in both the New and Old Worlds; rounded wings and long tails; excellent hunters. The female is much larger than the male.
3. *Buteo* (7) and allies: *Rupornis* (1), *Geranoaetus* (1), *Parabuteo* (1), *Leucopternis* (6), *Busarellus* (1), *Buteogallus* (3), and *Harpyhaliaetus* (1). Long, broad wings and short tail, appropriate for soaring. Sexes similar. Of the seven genera, only *Buteo* occurs in the Old World.
4. Crested hawks, American "eagles": *Morphnus* (1), *Harpia* (1), *Spizastur* (1), and *Spizaetus* (2). Powerful hunters; the female larger than the male. *Geranoaetus* and *Harpyhaliaetus* (see above) can also be considered "eagles."

5. Harriers, *Circus* (2), cosmopolitan marsh birds, and *Geranospiza* (1), Neotropical. Slender hawks; the female larger than the male.

WHITE-TAILED KITE, *Elanus leucurus*, Peneira

35 cm. Long wings and tail. Upperparts light gray like a gull, upper wing coverts forming a wide black spot. Sides of tail white. Underparts white with black spot on wing in hand area. Immature streaked, back brown. Hunts by hovering slowly against wind, examining ground from an altitude of about 30 m; holds wings quite elevated, feet dangling with toes closed. Eats small mammals (e.g., Marsupialia, jupatis, Rodentia; see "Feeding . . ."), geckos, insects. In savannas with sparse trees perches on wires, flicking tail. Argentina and Chile to North America. All of Brazil, becoming locally common. Increased numbers have also been noted in North and Central America, where it has benefited from agricultural development. Appears even in planted areas in cities such as Rio de Janeiro (on Ilha do Governador), Brasília (Federal District), Porto Alegre (Rio Grande do Sul). Also called *Gavião-peneirador*.

PEARL KITE, *Gampsonyx swainsonii*, Gaviãozinho
PL 8.4

22 cm; 113 g (female). Smallest hawk in Brazil, size of a thrush, related to *Elanus* and *Elanoides*. VOICE: *kit-kit-kit, tsi ew, ew, ew, ew*. Eats insects and geckos which it spies from perch. Shakes tail while perched. Customarily soars at great heights. River edges, cerrado. Central America to northern Argentina. Northern, northeastern, and centralwestern Brazil, also reaching western Minas Gerais (São Francisco), western São Paulo. In general aspect similar to a falcon, which is confirmed by order of its molt (for which reason I would rather include it among Falconidae). However, anatomic details and mallophagan lice indicate it is a kite. Also called *Cri-cri* (Pantanal, Mato Grosso).

AMERICAN SWALLOW-TAILED KITE, *Elanoides forficatus*, Gavião-tesoura   PL 7.1

60 cm; wingspan 120 cm. Deeply forked tail, like that of Magnificent Frigatebird, *Fregata magnificens*, very distinct. Slender body, short legs and toes. VOICE: *bit-dlewit-dlewit*. Flies quietly over forest, often in flocks, in search of termite or ant swarms. Also perches on termite nests to capture insects as they exit en masse for nuptial flight. Normal flight resembles that of a gull. Skims over trees in search of caterpillars, geckos, even fruits of murici [*Byrsonima* sp.] and red camboatá (*Cupania vernalis*). Also hunts vine snakes and frogs, catches wasps with large stingers. Sleeps in tall, defoliated trees. Birds from southern regions emigrate in winter, as do mountain populations from Espírito Santo. As a result of such movements, periodically appears in larger flocks. North America to Argentina, throughout Brazil.

North American form *E. f. forficatus*, differs from our *E. f. yetapa* by longer wings and tail, back with greenish or bluish, rather than purple, sheen. Winters in South America. A young bird banded in Florida on 17 June 1965 was shot in Curiúva, Paraná, on 22 December 1965. Other marked individuals have been found in Mato Grosso (October, November).

GRAY-HEADED KITE, *Leptodon cayanensis*, Gavião-de-cabeça-cinza

54 cm. Forest species uncommon outside Amazonia. Head gray, back blackish, underparts white with under surface of tail and wings barred black. Immature has white head with black cap, white under wing coverts. VOICE: a guttural *keyo, keyo keyo . . . ,* resembling *Chondrohierax* and *Herpetotheres*. Eats insects, including hornets, frogs, arboreal geckos, small birds. In forest openly observes scene from a tree branch. Mexico to Argentina, forested regions of Brazil, including Rio de Janeiro (Teresópolis), São Paulo (e.g., Boracéia and coastal zone), Rio Grande do Sul. Includes *L. forbesi* of northeast, presently being studied by D. M. Teixeira (1987) in Alagoas.

HOOK-BILLED KITE, *Chondrohierax uncinatus*, Caracoleiro   PL 9.3

42 cm. Long, wide wings; long tail; bill notably hooked and strong. Lores have bright orange spot; eyes white. Plumage highly variable, frequently with brown upperparts and gray barred underparts (adult). There are black individuals with 2 gray bands on tail, others with all-white abdomen. Immature has rusty collar. VOICE: *HAY-tetetete*. From medium heights in forest, marsh edge, etc., slyly watches for snails which, unlike *Rostrhamus sociabilis*, it swallows in shell. Catches arboreal snails and large, terrestrial *Strophocheilus;* also spiders, insects. Also hunts by jumping from branch to branch. Circles in reconnaissance flights. Mexico to Argentina; northern Brazil south to São Paulo, Minas Gerais, Goiás, Mato Grosso. Also called *Gavião-de-bico-de-gancho*. See *Geranospiza*.

RUFOUS-THIGHED KITE, *Harpagus diodon*, Gavião-bombachinha

33 cm. Appears to be mimicked by *Accipiter bicolor pileatus* (see "Feeding . . ."). Gray with uniformly chestnut pants and under wing coverts (visible in flight) and, like *H. bidentatus*, with black streak down center line of throat. Immature has streaked underparts, chestnut pants. VOICE: a rhythmic whistle, *WEEoo-WEEoo-wit*, while flying above forest. Eats large insects (e.g., cicadas). Occasionally joins cohorts of *Eciton* army ants. Rather open forest. The Guianas to Paraguay, Argentina, Brazil: the north, northeast, west, south. See *Accipiter bicolor, A. striatus,* and *Ictinia plumbea*.

DOUBLE-TOOTHED KITE, *Harpagus bidentatus,* Ripina   PL 8.2

33 cm. Small, stocky, with thick, 2-toothed bill. Upperparts and side of head gray, underparts rusty with abdomen and pants barred white. Throat "divided" (see *H. diodon*). Female more distinctly barred on underside. Immature brown above streaked white below with uniformly white pants. Frequents various tree levels, spying out insects and geckos both in forest and at edge. Disposition somewhat lazy, like *H. diodon*. Mexico to Bolivia; Brazil in Amazonia, northeast, east, including Rio de Janeiro. Compare immature with *Rupornis magnirostris* and *H. diodon*.

PLUMBEOUS KITE, *Ictinia plumbea,* Sovi   PL 7.4

34 cm. Small, common, with long, narrow wings, resembling a *Falco*. Entirely slate gray with under surface of primaries deep chestnut. Eyes red, as in *Harpagus bidentatus;* legs orange. Immature has streaked, white underparts with white spots on top of head. VOICE: *hee-hi hee-hi, jip-jip.* Hunts and eats ants, termites, and other insects in full flight, catching them with its small feet, which it often dangles. Seeks out burned-over areas where it catches small reptiles on ground (Minas Gerais). Likes to associate in flocks. Mexico to Argentina, throughout Brazil, though it disappears from south in winter. Also called *Gavião-sauveiro, Gavião-pomba.*

MISSISSIPPI KITE, *Ictinia mississippiensis*   NV

Northern representative of genus; periodically appears from North America. Differs from *I. plumbea* in absence of chestnut on flight feathers and in dark, brownish (not yellow) tarsi and all-black tail. Gets as far south as Paraguay (October–February), Argentina. One banded in Texas was recovered in Bolivia, thus having passed through Brazil.

SNAIL KITE, *Rostrhamus sociabilis,* Caramujeiro   PL 7.7

41 cm. Unmistakable wetland species with extremely hooked bill. Male slate gray with white at base of tail, visible from above and below. Cere and feet orange. Female and immature have whitish superciliaries and throat and cream-streaked underside, resembling immature *Milvago chimachima* or *Buteogallus meridionalis*. VOICE: a bleating *hehh-gheh-gheh-gheh-gheh* or a cry, *koreea*. A mollusk eater; lives on aquatic apple snail (*Pomacea*, Ampullariidae), being absolutely dependent on these gastropods. Finds them by overflying marshes and descending with legs dangling to grasp a snail with 1 foot, sometimes transferring it to bill at once. If it picks up an empty shell, it simply lets it fall. Once it has its prey, it perches to eat. Holding snail between toes of 1 or both feet and introducing sharp, recurved maxilla between internal face of operculum and columella, it cuts columellar mus-

cle which immediately weakens mollusk's resistance. It then pulls whole snail from shell and swallows it while empty, unharmed shell falls to ground. By observing this process, Hugo de Souza Lopes of the Oswaldo Cruz Institute, Rio de Janeiro, in 1956 developed a perfect technique for obtaining soft parts of the snail without destroying the shell, using a blade shaped like the kite's bill. Around a favorite perch, which may be a mere heap of earth, shells and operculi of prey accumulate, the latter in smaller numbers because they are occasionally eaten by the bird. Locally, e.g., Mato Grosso Pantanal and Venezuela, captures crabs of genus *Dilocarinus*. In Florida one was observed with a small turtle. See Limpkin, *Aramus guarauna.*

Roosts in flocks, sometimes large ones, which are conspicuous as they fly at dusk to roosting places in large marshes. Often nests in colonies. Makes elegant display flights, with loops and dives, in breeding season. Endangered by biocides (see "Alleged Harmfulness . . ." and "Migration"). Florida and Mexico to Argentina, Uruguay, Brazil wherever there are marshes. Also called *Gavião-de-aruá* (Amapá).

SLENDER-BILLED KITE, *Helicolestes hamatus*

Amazonian species similar to *Rostrhamus sociabilis* (and sometimes included in *Rostrhamus*), having same bill type and living exclusively on aquatic mollusks. All gray without any white. Areas around eye and base of bill yellow-orange; iris white (not dark, like *R. sociabilis*). Tarsi yellow or red. Immature has 2–4 white bars on tail; black tarsi. Always makes forays directly from a perch, a technique little used by *R. sociabilis*. Amapá (Macapá) and Pará (Belém, Santarém) to Peru, Venezuela, Suriname.

BICOLORED HAWK, *Accipiter bicolor,* Gavião-bombachinha-grande

35 cm. Forest species with grayish upperparts, light gray underparts. Pants and under wing coverts chestnut, latter sometimes white, especially in Amazonian population. I saw an individual in Espírito Santo join a band of *Cebus* monkey to catch insects scared up by simians, and another in Rio Grande do Sul catch a Rufous-bellied Thrush, *Turdus rufiventris*. Mexico to Argentina, Chile, throughout Brazil. In south, *A. b. pileatus* is similar to *Harpagus diodon* (see "Feeding . . .").

TINY HAWK, *Accipiter superciliosus,* Gavião-miudinho

26 cm. One of smallest raptors, with relatively short tail. Upperparts slate gray; underparts and white pants densely barred with narrow brownish bands, recalling Barred Forest-Falcon, *Micrastur ruficollis*. Low, tangled forest, also canopy of tall forest. An able bird hunter, can catch hummingbirds. Central America to Argentina, much of Brazil:

Fig. 73. Sharp-shinned Hawk, *Accipiter striatus erythronemius*, immature female.

Amazonia (Serra do Cachimbo, Pará) to southeast and south (Santa Catarina).

GRAY-BELLIED HAWK, *Accipiter poliogaster*, Tauató-pintado

49 cm. Most robust *Accipiter*. Upperparts brownish black, underparts white, tail barred black. Immature, believed until recently to be a separate species, *A. pectoralis*, resembles *Spizaetus ornatus* in coloration (see this species and "Morphology"). Of local occurrence and little known. Northern South America to Bolivia, Argentina, northwestern and centralsouthern Brazil, including Rio de Janeiro, São Paulo, Rio Grande do Sul.

SHARP-SHINNED HAWK, *Accipiter striatus*, Gavião-miúdo   Fig. 73

30 cm. Small—male only thrush size—and exceptionally slender, with very long tail and toes, dainty body. Flanks and pants uniformly rusty. Hunts small birds. Food of an *A. striatus* in U.S. 97.7% birds, 2.3% mammals (Storer 1966). Usually stays hidden in thick forest but occasionally flies openly from one woodland to another, displaying barred underparts. Also frequents vicinity of buildings. North America to Argentina, central and southeastern Brazil (including ex-Guanabara) to Rio Grande do Sul. Includes *A. erythronemius*.

BLACK-CHESTED BUZZARD-EAGLE, *Geranoaetus melanoleucus*, Aguia-chilena

66 cm; wingspan almost 2 m. Large, southern species with tail so short that in flight it scarcely projects beyond rear line of very wide wings. Head quite protruding. Upperparts slaty,

upper wing coverts forming wide, whitish gray area. Underparts white, upper breast brownish. Immature streaked, has longer tail. Eats carrion. Has been seen breaking up a Rufous Hornero, *Furnarius rufus,* nest to get at nestlings. A great soarer. Open and mountainous regions. Tierra del Fuego through Andes to Colombia, Venezuela. Also Brazil in Rio Grande do Sul, where it nests, occasionally São Paulo, Minas Gerais (Caraça, July 1974), northwestern Bahia (Serra do Cipó, August 1976), Piauí, Rio Grande do Norte (nesting, October), Maranhão.

WHITE-TAILED HAWK, *Buteo albicaudatus*, Gavião-de-rabo-branco   PL 9.6

55 cm. Large savanna species, relatively common in open area. Wings long and wide; white tail with black subterminal band is short. Scapulars have large, rust-colored spot. White of underparts sometimes extends to chin. Some individuals all black except for white tail. Immature has gray tail finely barred with black, spotted belly. VOICE: *gliehh klia-klia-klia, ghewli . . . ,* latter given during impressive nuptial flights. Eats large insects, toads (e.g., *Bufo marinus,* of which it eats only legs), rats, opossums, snakes. After rains catches large earthworms (*Glossoscolex giganteus,* Oligochaeta) that may be more than 1 m long (Itatiaia, Rio de Janeiro). Soars often. Campo, cerrado, buriti groves, high campo (e.g., Itatiaia). Southwestern U.S. to Argentina. Does not reach Amazonia. Is extending its presence in eastern Brazil because of deforestation. May appear near large urban centers (city of Rio de Janeiro). Also called *Gavião-fumaça.* See *Polyborus plancus,* which has similar tail, and *Buteogallus meridionalis.* May be considered a geographic replacement for *B. polyosoma,* an Andean species.

ZONE-TAILED HAWK, *Buteo albonotatus*, Gavião-de-rabo-barrado

50 cm. In flight almost perfectly imitates *Cathartes aura,* differing in black feathered head, which is not glabrous and "barren" like *Cathartes,* and in more rectangular tail crossed by 3 distinct gray bands. Immature's tail finely barred. Pounces on small terrestrial animals (see "Feeding . . ."). Open landscapes, e.g., caatinga, alongside *Cathartes.* California to Paraguay, sparsely in Brazil in Marajó (Pará), northeast (Ceará, Pernambuco, where relatively common), Paraná.

SWAINSON'S HAWK, *Buteo swainsoni*, Gavião-papa-gafanhoto   NV

50 cm. Relatively large, broad-winged, northern migrant. Immatures predominate in Brazil, distinguishable by blackish design on upper breast, white throat outlined in black. Gregarious and insectivorous. Famous for mass appearances in Central America during southward migrations in northern autumn. Winters primarily in Argentine pampas where it

hunts grasshoppers (*langostero*, "grasshopper," Argentina). In November 1974 some individuals surprisingly appeared right in São Paulo (Campos Elíseos). There are also reports from Acre (February, an individual banded in Oklahoma, U.S.), Pará (Serra do Cachimbo, August), Maranhão, Mato Grosso (Rio das Mortes, stomach contents: grasshoppers), Paraná (January), Rio Grande do Sul (November 1977, banded as a nestling in Alberta, Canada, in July of same year). See "Migration."

BROAD-WINGED HAWK, *Buteo platypterus*, Gavião-de-asa-larga   NV

Northern migrant. There are reports from northwestern Amazonia (December), southwestern Mato Grosso.

WHITE-RUMPED HAWK, *Buteo leucorrhous*, Gavião-de-sobre-branco

35 cm. Small, sooty black, woodland species with white upper and under tail coverts, rust-colored pants. Spies out prey (e.g., small rats) in forest. Shakes tail when perched. Flies in circles above forest. Rio de Janeiro (in mountains) to Rio Grande do Sul, Paraguay. Also in Andes.

GRAY HAWK, *Buteo nitidus*, Cavião-pedrez

43 cm. Upperparts light gray, underparts finely barred gray and white. Tail crossed by 2-cm-wide white subterminal band. Bases of immature's primaries yellowish. VOICE: similar to *Rupornis magnirostris* but more prolonged. Savanna edges. U.S. to Argentina, northern and southeastern Brazil, including Rio de Janeiro (Nova Friburgo). Also called *Asturina nitida,* a name I prefer.

SHORT-TAILED HAWK, *Buteo brachyurus*

43 cm. Another typical small species with short tail, upperparts and sides of head black in adult, brown in immature. Underparts pure white. There is a blackish phase. Mexico to Argentina, throughout Brazil, including Rio de Janeiro.

ROADSIDE HAWK, *Rupornis magnirostris*, Gavião-carijó   PLS 7.2, 8.1

36 cm. Most abundant hawk in Brazil, extending into big cities wherever there are enough trees. Rusty area at base of primaries (less accentuated than in *Ictinia plumbea*) unmistakable. Immature has streaked belly. VOICE: *WEEEEeh* (corresponding to song), *et-et-ghee ghee, ghi, ghi, ghi.* Hunts large insects, geckos, small snakes, birds such as doves and House Sparrows, *Passer domesticus*. Seizes bats in their daytime roosts. One individual, trying to take a nestling out of a *Furnarius rufus* nest, paid with its life, for while attempting to withdraw, its head became stuck and it died. Pairs fly in open with rapid wing beats, describing circles and drawing attention by their characteristic cries. Appears even

in entirely treeless areas (Rio Grande do Sul). Mexico to Argentina, throughout Brazil. Also called *Indaié, Gavião-pega-pinto*. Differs notably from any *Buteo* I know. Rusty area on wing recalls Grasshopper Buzzard, *Butastur rufipennis,* of Africa. See *Milvago. R. magnirostris* and *Buteo nitidus* (see above) differ from true *Buteo* in molt of primaries (Stresemann 1960).

HARRIS' HAWK, *Parabuteo unicinctus*, Gavião-asa-de-telha

48 cm. Blackish brown with chestnut scapulars and pants; base and tip of tail white; cere and feet yellow. Said to capture birds and rodents. Open country with sparse trees. Southern U.S. to Bolivia, Argentina, Uruguay. Locally not uncommon in central and southeastern Brazil, including Rio de Janeiro, Espírito Santo.

WHITE HAWK, *Leucopternis albicollis*, Gavião-pomba-da-amazônia

49 cm. Medium sized. White with black-spotted back. Wide wings with coverts and tertiaries tipped white. Short, black tail with base and wide terminal band white. Cere plumbeous; legs light yellow. VOICE: a prolonged, high whistle, *zhewEEee-eh.* Hunts small mammals, reptiles, amphibians, large insects. Has been seen devouring a yellow-breasted toucan (Amapá). Perches openly at forest edge and often patrols with circular flights, drawing attention because it is so white. Mexico to Bolivia, Amazonian Brazil as far as Mato Grosso (Rio das Mortes), northern Maranhão. "Espírito Santo" (Ruschi, without foundation).

MANTLED HAWK, *Leucopternis polionota*, Gavião-pombo-grande   EN

52 cm. Large, similar in plumage to *L. lacernulata*. White tail with black base. Immature has streaked head and upper neck. VOICE: a sequence of high whistles, *bibibi . . . , beee-eh.* Hunts not only birds and geckos but guinea pigs (*Kerodon rupestris*) in area of Jequitinhonha, Minas Gerais. Soars low over high forests. Alagoas to Rio Grande do Sul, Argentina (Misiones), Paraguay. Sometimes in same region as *lacernulata.* In Rio de Janeiro only in mountainous areas (Serra dos Órgãos, Itatiaia). See *Leptodon cayanensis.*

WHITE-NECKED HAWK, *Leucopternis lacernulata*, Gavião-pomba   BR   PL 7.3

43 cm; wingspan 96 cm. Broad wings, short tail, underparts white with some black markings on under surface of wings. Tail white with black base and narrow black subterminal band. With pure white color (see also other *Leucopternis*), it is conspicuous from a distance, perched at forest edge or describing circles as it flies low over forests of Serra do Mar, where it frequents primarily valleys. Catches beetles, spiders, small snakes, etc., on ground. Restricted to

eastern Brazil (fig. 74), from Alagoas to Santa Catarina (including ex-Guanabara). See *L. polionota*.

BLACK-FACED HAWK, *Leucopternis melanops*

One of 2 smaller, black-and-white Amazonian species, relatively rare in Brazil. North of Amazon (see fig. 74).

WHITE-BROWED HAWK, *Leucopternis kuhli*, Gavião-vaqueiro

The other of 2 smaller, black-and-white Amazonian species, relatively rare in Brazil, this one with orange cere and legs. South of Amazon (see fig. 74).

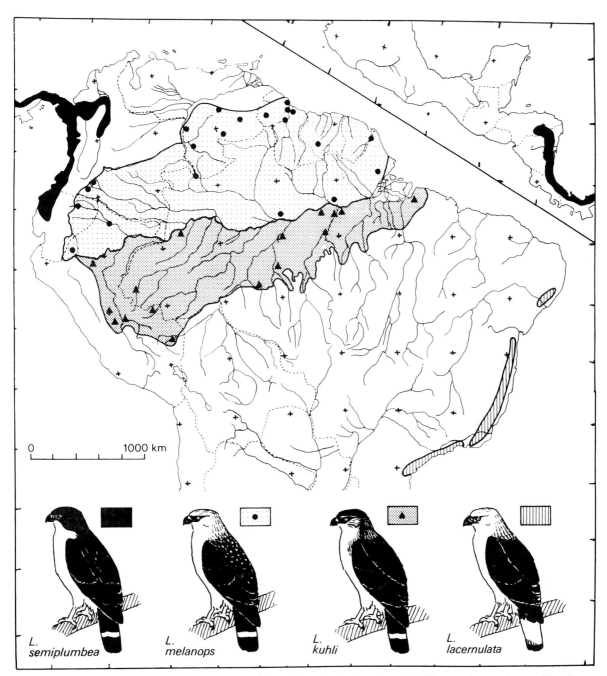

Fig. 74. Distribution of four *Leucopternis* species. After Haffer 1987a. The three Brazilian species may be considered geographic races or allospecies. *L. lacernulata* is isolated in the Atlantic forest; *L. melanops* and *L. kuhli* are separated by the Amazon.

SLATE-COLORED HAWK, *Leucopternis schistacea,*
Gavião-azul

46 cm. Uniformly slate gray, tail with white band. Cere
and legs orange. Spies out frogs, crabs, fish, water snakes,
etc. Shady banks of rivers and lakes. Venezuela to Bolivia,
Amazonas, Pará (Rio Guamá), Amapá. See *Geranospiza
caerulescens.*

BLACK-COLLARED HAWK, *Busarellus nigricollis,*
Gavião-belo

51 cm. Unusual, with long, wide wings contrasting with
extremely short tail. Head white, rest of body ferruginous.
Has black spots on upper breast, primaries, and tail. Head
and underparts of immature yellowish and streaked. VOICE: a
bisyllabic cough, *he-ehh,* resembling Greater Ani, *Crotophaga major,* or Dusky-legged Guan, *Penelope obscura.*
Also nasal whistles. Fishes; toes spiked on underside and
talons long and recurved, like Osprey, *Pandion haliaetus,*
appropriate for grabbing fish. Also eats aquatic insects and
mollusks. Soars for hours on end. Mexico to Argentina; almost all of Brazil wherever there are extensive swamps,
marshes, flooded fields, or mangroves, e.g., Mato Grosso,
eastern part of Marajó Island (Pará). Also Rio de Janeiro.
Also called *Gavião-lavadeira* (Mato Grosso). See *Buteogallus meridionalis* and *B. aequinoctialis.*

SAVANNA HAWK, *Buteogallus (= Heterospizias)
meridionalis,* Gavião-caboclo   PL 9.4

55 cm. Large, relatively common savanna species. Almost all ferruginous with long, broad, bright reddish wings,
resembling an eagle except for black tips on all flight feathers
and brown on part of upper wing coverts. Black rectrices are
crossed in middle by white band and have whitish tips. Reddish underparts so finely barred with black that this is imperceptible at a distance. Immature dark brown but has rusty
wings and pants; superciliary and striated underparts yellowish white; tail gray and black. VOICE: a prolonged whistle,
eeeeee-eh. Spies out amphibians, large insects, crabs, lizards
(*Ameiva* and *Iguana*), snakes, occasionally birds such as
Guira Cuckoo, *Guira guira,* (see "Feeding . . ."). Seeks out
burning areas where it hunts only a few meters from flames,
walking slowly over ground. Perches erectly on fences or
mounds of earth. Savannas, marsh edges, mangroves, cerrado. Panama to Argentina, throughout Brazil. Also called
Casaca-de-couro, Gavião-telha (São Paulo), *Gavião-
fumaça* (Mato Grosso), *Gavião-tinga* (Pará). Immature may
resemble a young *Rostrhamus sociabilis.* See *Busarellus
nigricollis* and *Buteogallus aequinoctialis.*

RUFOUS CRAB-HAWK, *Buteogallus aequinoctialis,*
Caranguejeiro

44 cm. Most common mangrove hawk. Resembles
B. meridionalis but has shorter wings, tail, and legs. Head,
neck, and upperparts blackish brown, upperside of wings
with black tips and edges and large rusty area. Underparts

rusty, barred black; tail blackish with whitish tip and narrow
bar. Area around eye yellow. Feeds exclusively on crabs.
Circles at great heights. Mangroves. Venezuela and the
Guianas to Brazil, from mouth of Oiapoque to São Paulo,
Paraná (Paranaguá). Not recorded for Santa Catarina, although mangroves extend to there. Also called *Gavião-do-
mangue.* See *Circus buffoni.*

GREAT BLACK-HAWK, *Buteogallus urubitinga,*
Gavião-preto

63 cm. Eaglelike silhouette but short toes and rather long
legs. Black with secondaries barred gray and with white on
base of tail. Cere and legs yellow in *B. u. urubitinga,* the
South American race. Immature dark brown and striated.
VOICE: quite loquacious, giving a prolonged series of rapid
*bi, bi, bi*s. . . . Hunts at forest edge and in marshy places for
frogs (including large *Ceratophrys,* of which it eats only
large hind legs), geckos, snakes (including poisonous ones),
rats, insects. Takes young egrets and spoonbills that have
fallen from nest, does not spurn carrion (Mato Grosso).
Fishes well. Likes fruits (e.g., of cajá-mirim, *Spondias
lutea*). Mexico to Argentina throughout Brazil. Not uncommon. Also called *Gavião-caipira, Gavião-caripira* (Pará;
cari = "grasper," *pora* = "fish"), *Urubitinga, Tauató-preto,
Gavião-fumaça, Cauã* (Minas Gerais). See immature *Spizaetus tyrannus.*

CROWNED EAGLE, *Harpyhaliaetus coronatus,*
Águia-cinzenta

66 cm; 2950 g. Large southern species with characteristic
nuchal topknot, broad wings, short tail, relatively long legs,
short toes. Almost uniformly dark gray, a bit lighter on underparts. Tail tipped white with white band crossing it. Cere and
legs yellow. Immature has cream-colored superciliary,
whitish streaking on underparts. VOICE: a long sequence of
*glee, glee, glee*s. . . . Indolent in disposition, perches on
posts, stakes, or on ground. Hunts armadillos, among other
animals. Semicrepuscular. Open country, e.g., Pantanal. Argentina to Bolivia, Brazil: southern Mato Grosso and Rio
Grande do Sul, Rio de Janeiro (Tinguá, Nova Friburgo),
Maranhão. See *Buteogallus urubitinga* and *Geranoaetus
melanoleucus.*

CRESTED EAGLE, *Morphnus guianensis,*
Uiraçu-falso   EN R

85 cm. Similar to immature *Harpia harpyja* but clearly
less stocky, even appearing svelte, with longer and more
slender tarsi, toes slimmer, crest not divided into 2 "horns,"
tail longer and fuller. In one plumage stage shows black bars
on belly (*M. "taeniatus"* of upper Amazon) but never has
black on upper breast like *H. harpyja.* Watches for guans
(Cracidae) and trumpeters (Psophiidae) under fruit trees. Virgin forest. Guatemala to Bolivia, Argentina (Misiones). Formerly in many parts of Brazil south to Mato Grosso (Chapada

dos Parecis, Juruena) and Rio Grande do Sul but now very rare. Also called *Gavião-de-penacho.*

HARPY EAGLE, *Harpia harpyja,* Gavião-real
EN PL 9.7

105 cm; height 57 cm (male)–90 cm (female); wingspan to 2 m; 4.8 kg (male), 7.6–9 kg (female). Majestic in size and unequaled in strength. The world's most powerful raptor but not the largest. Wings broad, round, relatively short. Legs short and stout, tarsi and toes extremely strong. Talons enormous (hallux claw measures 7 cm), bill incomparably powerful. Head and eyes relatively small, latter facing forward. There is a suggestion of a facial disk, resembling that of an owl, which must improve hearing. Gray head has long, soft topknot divided into 2 black spikes whose feathers frequently dangle and become visible from front. Mantle and upper breast black. Breast, belly, and under surface of wings white, the latter and thighs streaked with black. Tail has 3 gray bands. Iris light gray. Immature when it leaves nest has immaculate white underparts; requires more than 4 years to attain full adult plumage. VOICE: a strident, prolonged *weeee-eww.*

Feeding and Behavior: Keeps watch from heights of primary forest at edge of rivers with rapids (Amapá) and near salt banks where many animals come to lick the salty earth (Mato Grosso, Pará). Among its prey are sloths (*Bradypus didactylus,* Amapá, Rio Tocantins, Rio Cururu, Pará); curassows (*Crax alector,* Amapá, and *C. fasciolata,* Cururu, Pará; Goiás); monkeys (*Ateles* sp. and *Cebus cai,* Cururu, Pará, and Xingu, Minas Gerais, respectively); fawns, including those of caatinga deer (*Mazama simplicicornis,* Goiás, Minas Gerais); Hyacinth Macaws, *Anodorhynchus hyacinthinus;* Red-legged Seriemas, *Cariama cristata;* armadillos (Goiás); and cachorro-do-mato (*Dusicyon thous,* Itatiaia, Rio de Janeiro). It is fast and powerful in attack, capable of carrying an agouti or young peccary to the top of a tree; very heavy prey, e.g., a large sloth, are dragged to a fallen tree. It tears apart its prey, including those with tough skin and musculature, e.g., sloths. In Amapá I saw one ripping the skin of a sloth into strips 2 cm wide, but in spite of its strong bill and talons it only managed to scratch the skin on the animal's head. It is not bothered by porcupine (*Coendou* spp.) spines. It cuts snakes of average diameter (5 cm) in 2 and eats them immediately.

In inhabited areas attacks dogs, chickens, lambs, and kids (Goiás, Espírito Santo, Rio Grande do Sul). Is chased away from ranches, for occupants fear it may attack children, though this is unlikely. Reportedly pursues humans approaching its nest, as do certain macaws. Flies with rapid wing beats, then immediately soars. In hot hours of day circles over forest and adjacent savannas.

Breeding: Nest is a pile of branches the bird rebuilds and retouches with each use. In Amazonia it is placed on very tall trees, e.g., giant ceiba (*Ceiba pentandra*), Brazil-nut (*Bertholletia excelsa*), or tucoari, that dominate surrounding forest, permitting occupants to survey full horizon. It may also be hidden among dense shoots of a split top, or in crown of a *Mauritia* palm in areas with extensive buriti groves. The birds approach by sneaking through the forest and going up only when they reach the right tree. Two eggs are laid between September and November (Goiás), but only 1 nestling survives (Mato Grosso) (see "Breeding").

Hunting, Mythology, and Usefulness: H. harpyja has always been a prized trophy, either for Indians or hunters. In the Xingu (Mato Grosso) between 1947 and 1957, I found cages (*apuin*) in which the chiefs kept these birds in order to periodically cut (not pull out) the extraordinarily long flight and tail feathers. These prisoners, taken as nestlings, are considered the personification of the chief, and when the owner dies they are killed or succumb to hunger (Carvalho 1949). *H. harpyja* has often been a feature of Indian mythology (Zerries 1962). Other hunters keep the talons as amulets and eat the meat.

Distribution and Decline: Mexico to Bolivia, Argentina, and a large part of Brazil. Presently rare in less remote areas and quite scarce in southeastern Brazil, but reasonably common in Amazonia. Around 1960 it still occurred regularly north of Rio Doce, and in 1937 it nested near Pontal (Espírito Santo). A pair was observed for some months in upper Itatiaia (Rio de Janeiro 1973). It occurred in Guaramirim and Mafra between 1948 and 1950 and on Rio do Peixe in 1968 (Santa Catarina). Also on Rio Gravataí, Rio Grande do Sul, and until at least 1958 migrant individuals appeared in summer in this state. Also called *Gavião-de-penacho, Guiraçu* (*uirá, guirá* = "bird," *açu* = "large"), *Harpia.* See *Morphnus guianensis* and *Spizaetus.*

BLACK-AND-WHITE HAWK-EAGLE, *Spizastur melanoleucus,* Gavião-pato

56 cm. Small hawk-eagle with topknot; long, fully feathered tarsi; formidable talons. Snow white, including the pants, with topknot, small mask, and mantle black. Base of bill, iris, and tarsi yellow. Hunts toads and birds such as caciques, *Psarocolius* spp.. Perches on tall trees, likes to soar. Forest and savanna adjacent to river banks. Mexico to Argentina. Sparsely scattered around Brazil, including in southeast. Also called *Apacanim-branco.*

ORNATE HAWK-EAGLE, *Spizaetus ornatus,* Gavião-de-penacho EN PL 9.1

67 cm; wingspan 140 cm. Svelte, impressive bird with tarsi densely feathered to base of toes. Wings short and rounded; tail, legs, and talons exceptionally long. Has long, full topknot (not divided, as in *Harpia harpyja*) which it frequently raises vertically like the tip of a spear rising above head. Immature has all-white head and underparts, with only pants barred black; topknot brownish. VOICE: high whistles, accompanied by a quiver of wings, while circling over for-

est in breeding season. Hunts birds, small mammals, reptiles in tall forest, catching them on the ground or in trees. Mexico to Argentina, throughout Brazil. On slopes of Serra do Mar (Rio de Janeiro) is sometimes alongside *S. tyrannus*. Has become scarce. Also called *Apacanim*. See immature *Accipiter poliogaster* and *Morphnus guianensis;* also *S. melanoleucus*. The genus *Spizaetus* is not restricted to the Americas.

BLACK HAWK-EAGLE, *Spizaetus tyrannus,* Gavião-pega-macaco   PL 9.2

72 cm. Black with abdomen and pants finely speckled white. Topknot shorter and broader than *S. ornatus*. Immature has whitish head, streaked underparts. In flight wings have an almost elliptical silhouette, not as broad as *S. ornatus,* from which it also differs by holding long tail less open when fanned. VOICE: melodious, high whistles, *eeeeee-eh-i, i, i, i, i, ew-ur,* the bird conspicuous when it does this while circling above forest. Hunts mammals more than birds. Said to habitually eat primates, among them probably marmosets. Bats (*Artibeus jamaicensis*), probably caught in their daytime roosts, perhaps in rolled-up leaves (H. F. Berla), have several times been found in stomach contents of this species. Mexico to Argentina, throughout Brazil, less scarce than *S. ornatus*. Also called *Papa-mico, Papa-macaco* (Rio de Janeiro), *Apacanim*. See *Buteogallus urubitinga*.

LONG-WINGED HARRIER, *Circus buffoni,* Gavião-do-mangue   PL 7.5

50 cm. Attractive wetland species, unmistakable with extraordinarily long, narrow wings and tail. Well-marked facial disk of light lines on a dark background resembles that of an owl. Color highly variable, except for wing and tail pattern. Male has slaty upperparts; forehead and superciliary white; flight feathers, wing coverts, and tail light gray, barred black; rump and belly white, latter speckled black. Female and immature dark chestnut, streaked on underparts, pants rusty. There is a black or dark chestnut mutant (polymorphism, in both sexes), but wing and tail patterns remain unaltered. Female larger than male. Hunts frogs, cavies, other small animals. Perches on ground. Flies low and elegantly over marsh vegetation, soaring with smooth veerings from right to left, reminiscent of *Cathartes*. Also hovers. Venezuela and the Guianas to Argentina, Chile. Locally in eastern Brazil (Amapá; Marajó, Pará; Espírito Santo; Rio de Janeiro), where rare, and in central Brazil (Mato Grosso, western São Paulo). More frequent in south (Paraná, Rio Grande do Sul). See *Buteogallus aequinoctialis,* which is also called *Gavião-do-mangue*.

CINEREOUS HARRIER, *Circus cinereus*   SV

Second species of this genus, rarer and smaller than *C. buffoni,* with underparts finely barred with ferruginous. A southern Andean species that reaches Rio Grande do Sul, Santa Catarina. May be considered a representative of Northern Harrier, *C. cyaneus,* a North American and Old World species.

CRANE HAWK, *Geranospiza caerulescens,* Gavião-pernilongo   PL 9.5

46 cm. Hawk of unusual proportions, with slight body, broad wings, long tail, extremely long legs extending beyond tail in flight. Outer toe very short, intertarsal articulation highly mobile—special adaptations for inspecting cavities and especially for pulling tree frogs out of bromeliads by feeling among leaves with feet (Bokermann 1978). In Amazonia almost uniformly bluish gray, resembling *Leucopternis schistacea,* but more slender and behaves differently. Two white bands on tail, 3rd wide one on underside of base of primaries. Feet red. No yellow at base of bill. VOICE: utters a strange *waah-o* at dusk. Catches cockroaches, frogs, geckos, bats, etc., pulling them out of holes in trees, bromeliads, and other epiphytic vegetation, which it examines partly while flying and partly climbing and walking, balancing itself with wings and tail open. Also robs bird nests, taking chicks. May have a strong odor on neck plumage, perhaps connected with its habit of eating certain similar-smelling tree frogs. Circles over forest. Woodland interspersed with savanna, sometimes in tree tops, marsh edges, mangroves. Mexico to Argentina, locally throughout Brazil.

Accipitridae Bibliography
See also General Bibliography

Albuquerque, J.L.B. 1985. Notes on distribution of some Brazilian raptors. *Bull. B.O.C.* 105:82–84.

Amadon, D. 1961. *Condor* 63:178–79. [*Harpagus,* relationships]

Amadon, D. 1975. *Raptor Research* 9:1–11. [Sexual dimorphism]

Amadon, D. 1982. A revision of the sub-Buteonine hawks (Accipitridae). *Am. Mus. Nov.* 2741.

Belton, W. 1972. *Am. Birds* 26:565. [*Elanus,* range expansion]

Bierregaard, R. O., Jr. 1984. *Wilson Bull.* 96:2–5. [*Morphnus,* nesting]

Bokermann, W. 1978. *Rev. Bras. Biol.* 38(3):715–20. [*Geranospiza,* behavior]

Brown, L., and D. Amadon. 1968. *Eagles, Hawks and Falcons of the World.* New York: McGraw-Hill.

Carvalho, J.C.M. 1949. Observações zoológicas e antropológicas na região do alto Xingu. *Publ. Avul. Mus. Nac. Rio de Janeiro* 5.

Contino, F. 1972. Elementos sobre alguns rapaces del noroeste argentino. *Inst. Invest. Recursos Nat. Renov.,* Serie Fauna 1.

Eisenmann, E. 1963. *Auk* 80:74–77. [*Ictinia,* migration]

Eisenmann, E. 1971. *Am. Birds* 25:529–36. [*Elanus,* range expansion]

Ferrelra, D. F. 1899. *Arte da caça de altanaria.* Lisbon (original of 1616).

Foster, M. S. 1971. Plumage and behavior of a juvenile Gray-headed Kite. *Auk* 88:161–63.

Fowler, J. M., and S. B. Cope. 1964. *Auk* 81:257–73. [*Harpia,* behavior]

Haverschmidt, F. 1970. *Auk* 87:580. [*Rostrhamus,* behavior]

Klein, B. C., L. H. Harper, R. C. Bierregaard, et al. 1988. The nesting and feeding behavior of *Spizaetus ornatus*. *Condor* 90(1):239–41.

Lehmann, F. C. 1959. *Noved. Colomb.* 1:169–95. [*Spizastur, Spizaetus, Morphnus*, etc., behavior]

Lopes, H. S. 1956. *Rev. Bras. Biol.* 16:535–42. [*Rostrhamus*, bill]

Matthäi, H. 1977. *Die Rolle der Greifvögel, insbesondere der Harpye und des Königsgeiers, bei ausserandinen Indianern Südamerikas*. Renner, Honenschäftlarn.

Oliveira, R. G. 1982. *An. Soc. Sul-Riogr. Orn.* 3:20. [*Buteogallus meridionalis*, feeding]

Olsen, J., T. Billet, and P. Olsen. 1982. A method for reducing illegal removal of eggs from raptor nests. *Emu* 82:225.

Olson, S. L. 1982. The distribution of fused phalanges of the inner toe in the Accipitridae. *Bull. B.O.C.* 102:8–12.

Plótnik, R. 1956. Afinidad entre los generos *Elanoides y Gampsonyx*. *Rev. Invest. Agric.* 103:313–15.

Sick, H. 1979. *Bull. B.O.C.* 99(4):115–20. [*Geranoaetus melanoleucus, Buteo swainsoni*, distribution]

Simmons, R. 1988. Offspring quality and the evolution of cainism. *Ibis* 130:339–57.

Storer, R. W. 1966. Sexual dimorphism and food habits in the North American Accipiters. *Auk* 83:423–36.

Stresemann, E., and V. Stresemann. 1960. Die Handschwingensmauser der Tagraubvögel. *J. Orn.* 101:373–403.

Sykes, P. W., Jr. 1985. *Condor* 87:438. [*Rostrhamus*, pesticides in eggs and nestlings]

Teixeira, D. M. 1987. *Bull. B.O.C.* 107(4):152. [*Leptodon forbesi*]

Voous, K. H. 1968. Distribution and geographic variation of *Buteo albicaudatus*. *Beaufortia* 208.

Voous, K. H. 1969. Predation potential in birds of prey from Suriname. *Ardea* 57:117–48.

Warner, J. S., and R. L. Rudd. 1975. *Condor* 77:226–30. [*Elanus* behavior]

Weick, F. 1980. *Birds of Prey of the World*. With L. Brown. Hamburg: P. Parey.

Willis, E. O. 1966. A prey capture by the Zone-tailed Hawk. *Condor* 68:104–05.

Willis, E. O. 1988. A hunting technique of the Black-and-white Hawk-Eagle, *Spizastur melanoleucus*. *Wilson Bull.* 100 (4):672–75.

Zerries, O. 1962. Die Vorstellung vom zweiten Ich und die Rolle der Harpye in der Kultur der Naturvölker Südamerikas. *Anthropos* 57:889–913.

FAMILY PANDIONIDAE: OSPREY (1)

This family has only one living species which is almost cosmopolitan. There are fossils from the Pliocene of Florida (10 million years B.P.), and other fossil species are known from the Oligocene of Egypt. The Osprey (*Pandion haliaetus*) is closely related to the Accipitridae but is distinguished by several anatomical features. It appears in South America only as a migrant. Sexes are alike, and the immature is similar to the adult.

OSPREY, *Pandion haliaetus*, Águia-pescadora
NV PL 6.6

57 cm. Large, strong-billed species that almost never gets far from large expanses of water. Unmistakable with long, angular wings and ruffled nape feathers. Head and underparts white. A wide black stripe behind eye continues to blackish brown back. Breast has dark pattern. In flight a black spot is evident on under surface of wing near bend. VOICE: shrill, repeated whistles.

Feeding and Behavior: P. haliaetus is a fish eater, but observations in Brazil indicate it occasionally captures a bird or mammal. It often catches a fish after lengthy hovering, which is quite conspicuous because of bird's broad wingspan. It dives at 80 km/hr at a fish near waters surface, hitting violently with wings beating vertically and feet stretched forward. It may submerge for an instant, going as deep as 1.5 m. With sharply recurved talons and spikelike modifications on soles of feet, it manages to grasp its smooth, slippery prey. It is also aided by its reversible outer toe which, like that of an owl, turns backward to support hallux in the capture. After fish is captured with both feet, it is shifted to be carried head forward. This is different from the way other hawks hold their prey and is well portrayed in logo of the International Council for Bird Preservation of an Osprey carrying a fish. The success of Osprey attacks is usually considerable, estimated at 20% to 80% or more. Lives on lakes, large rivers, estuaries, and close to coast. Fishing is facilitated by calm, transparent water.

Occurrence: Migrates from North America as far as Argentina and Chile. Sporadic throughout Brazil except in northeast, where records are lacking. It has been observed in Amazonas (28 individuals banded in U.S.), Pará (17 banded), Amapá, Bahia, Minas Gerais, Goiás, Espírito Santo, Rio de Janeiro (including ex-Guanabara), São Paulo, Paraná, Mato Grosso, and Rio Grande do Sul, with most of the records in Amazonia, central Brazil, and Rio Grande do Sul. More numerous at end and beginning of year but may be seen at any time. Has been recorded in Brazil in all months, giving rise to assumption that it breeds here, but up to present this is unproven. Most of these sightings are of young birds still unable to breed or of adults in nonbreeding season. *P. haliaetus* matures only at 2 to 3 years, when it goes to its homeland to nest, but it returns here regularly to avoid northern winter.

Records of U.S. Bird Banding Laboratory in Laurel, Maryland, show 58 Osprey recovered in Brazil between 1937 and 1987, in some years 3, 4, or even 5 individuals. Forty-seven of them were shot. One, collected in Ilhéus (Bahia) in August, was banded as a nestling near New York City in June of the previous year. A 2d, captured on the Rio Pacas (Mato Grosso) in September, and a 3d, from the Rio Madeira (Amazonas) in October, had been banded as nestlings in Maryland in July, 1 of them the same year, only 85 days before its capture in Brazil. An individual banded 28 June 1959 was killed 28 December 1975 and thus was 16 years old.

While here an Osprey occupies a territory where it stays for weeks or even months; for roosting it perches on rocky hills (ex-Guanabara). Four individuals appeared on the same lake in December in Rio de Janeiro (Magnanini and Coimbra Filho 1964). Perched it may resemble a Yellow-headed Caracara, *Milvago chimachima*, because of white head, but it always has a ruffled nape and larger ocular stripe. It also has an impressive, eaglelike aspect. Also called *Gavião-caipira, Guincho, Gavião-do-mar*.

Decline: In U.S. it was severely endangered by biocide water pollution, especially by DDT, the concentration of which increases by more than 100 times along the food chain in which the Osprey is the last link. Thus, while phytoplankton may show a DDT index of 0.04 ppm, in fish it increases to 0.10–0.17 ppm. Feeding on DDT-contaminated prey, Osprey may lay eggs with 13.8 ppm DDT. Inadequately calcified in the oviduct, the eggs are highly susceptible to breaking during incubation. In Maine Osprey egg shells were 31% thinner than normal, and in Connecticut 81% of 185 eggs did not hatch (Peterson, in Hickey 1969). Prohibiting DDT use in U.S. has been highly beneficial for fish-eating birds such as *P. haliaetus* and Bald Eagle, *Haliaeetus leucocephalus* (U.S. national bird)—so much so that Osprey, which was close to extinction there, is again common to abundant in suitable habitats. In Brazil the use of these chemicals continues on a large scale.

Pandionidae Bibliography

Ames, P. L. 1966. *J. Appl. Ecol.* 3, suppl.:87–97. [Insecticides]
Hickey, J. J. 1969. *Peregrine Falcon Populations*. Madison, Wisc.: Univ. Wisconsin Press.
Magnanini, A., and A. F. Coimbra Filho. 1964. *Vellozia* 1,4. [Avifauna of Guanabara]

FAMILY FALCONIDAE: FALCONS AND CARACARAS (16)

These birds of prey are distinct from the Accipitridae, not only anatomically, but also biochemically (electrophoretic analysis), behaviorally, and in the way they molt. It is estimated that the Falconidae and Accipitridae split approximately 68 million years ago. Falcons have certain similarities to the owls, which could be due to convergence. There are fossils from the eo-Oligocene in France (37 million years B.P.) and from the lower Miocene in Argentina (20 million years B.P.).

Morphology

This family has as little homogeneity as the Accipitridae. Whereas the Red-throated Caracara, *Daptrius americanus*, has a gallinaceous aspect, falcons are the most elegant fliers imaginable. The bill and feet are weak in the four caracaras; *Falco* bills, with a large tooth on the maxilla, are as sharp as wire snippers. The perfected vision of Falconiformes is attributed especially to the existence of two foveas centralis, similar to those in Alcedinidae and Apodidae. An interesting osteological feature is a spinal fusion that stiffens the body (and can absorb the shock of the strike when catching a bird in flight); some vertebrae are fused to form the notarium. For lack of this, the Pearl Kite, *Gampsonyx swainsonii*, was transferred to the Accipitridae. However, the Laughing Falcon, *Herpetotheres cachinnans*; *Micrastur* forest-falcons; and American Kestrel, *Falco sparverius*, also lack that fusion (Storer 1982).

The Crested Caracara, *Polyborus plancus*, and the *Daptrius* caracaras have brightly colored, bare faces. There is sexual dimorphism in size, which can be highly accentuated in *Falco* (the female being considerably larger than the male). In *Falco sparverius* there is sexual dimorphism in coloration.

Regarding molt, see the Accipitridae. The Falconidae have the most aerodynamic form among the hawks. Their narrow pointed wings are less adequate for soaring than those of accipiters.

Vocalization

This is more varied than in the Accipitridae. *Herpetotheres cachinnans* and certain *Micrastur* are notable for having elaborate songs and for their loquacity, being able to vocalize continuously for ten minutes or more, more notes being added at each repetition. Mated pairs usually duet. They usually call only at dawn and dusk. In twin species such as the Barred Forest-Falcon, *Micrastur ruficollis*, and Lined Forest-Falcon, *M. gilvicollis*, the voices serve perfectly for species identification, which is a great help, for the two may occur in the same forest (Amazonia).

Daptrius americanus, one of the noisiest hawks, has orgies of vehement vocalization that may remind one of the collective cacophony of chachalacas [Cracidae]. The Chimango Caracara, *Milvago chimango*, also sometimes sings in chorus. *Polyborus plancus* throws its head back at the peak of its hoarse song, an expressive gesture also occasionally made by the *Milvago*.

Hunting Methods and Feeding

In the Accipitridae I have already mentioned the hunting tactics of birds of prey in general. The most powerful fliers of all birds are the larger Falconidae. The Peregrine Falcon, *Falco peregrinus,* has an unhurried cruising speed of 40 to 50 km/hr, and it is said that when it launches after prey in an almost vertical dive, with its wings half closed, it reaches 75 m/sec (270 km/hr). When chasing a pigeon (which flies at 90 km/hr or a bit more), however, it is not always successful. In Europe the success of *F. peregrinus* in hunting birds of various sizes is calculated at a maximum of 22%; on average it is much lower, from 10% to 12%. The species is credited with the ability to see and attack a pigeon feeding on the ground 1 to 1½ km away, although normally it does not make such distant chases. Usually it knocks down birds in flight (it often flushes nervous, perched flocks in order to catch them flying), letting them fall to the ground but returning immediately to retrieve them. It can also catch terrestrial prey grabbing it from above and carrying it away but never pinning it against the ground as the *Buteo* do. It is more attracted by birds that have some white in the plumage.

Only the talons are used to capture victims (see below for an exception), which are rapidly killed by a blow from the terrible, sharp tooth, which severs the spine. The falcon first eats the head and then the breast muscle, holding it with one foot. When *F. peregrinus* finishes its meal, the victim's wings are usually still united by the pectoral girdle. Unlike other hawks, *F. peregrinus* does not tear out the flight feathers of its prey.

There is a great deal of exaggerated talk about the daily intake of birds of prey. The fact is that a male falcon weighing 600 g needs about 100 g of meat, equivalent to about two doves. The female, weighing 1000 g, requires 150 to 180 g per day. If she eats a pigeon weighing about 300 g, she can fast on the following day or be content with some small prey item.

The *Micrastur* forest-falcons are true acrobats, hunting in dense forest somewhat like the *Accipiter* do. Their presence frequently surprises the most experienced human hunter, for they can pick up a tinamou that has been shot even before the hunter reaches it. In Minas Gerais an Orange-breasted Falcon, *Falco deiroleucus,* caught a Spotted Tinamou, *Nothura maculosa,* flushed by a dog. The *Micrastur* follow army ants, which frighten up animals of all sizes and attract many birds; they also take birds caught in mist nets. It is interesting that *Micrastur* hunting in dense forest and captive *Falco peregrinus* walk on the ground without difficulty in spite of not being adapted to a terrestrial life. The *Falco* have a short

tarsus, the *Micrastur* a long one. *Polyborus plancus* moves about very well on the ground as it seeks animal life exposed by plowing.

The Slaty-backed Forest-Falcon, *Micrastur mirandollei,* a rare species, has evolved a curious but efficient hunting method: perched low in dense forest, it gives a series of ventriloquial notes that attract birds, similar to what happens when an owl is discovered by a flock of Passerines (see pygmy-owls, *Glaucidium* spp.). The hawk then finds it easy to catch one of the more daring but innocent birds, among them probably some North American migrants unaware of the dangers of the tropical forest.

On the beaches of Amazonia, the *Daptrius* seek eggs of tortoises and hidden-necked turtles (*Podocnemis* spp.).

Herpetotheres cachinnans is famous for eating bats and snakes; it hunts bright red coral snakes, both the false corals (*Apostolepis assimilis* and *Oxyrhopus trigeminus*) and the true poisonous one (*Micrurus lemniscatus*). All three were found in the stomach of one *H. cachinnans* from Goiás (I. Sazima). Another false coral (*Simophis rhinostoma*) and a *Micrurus* were victims of an Aplomado Falcon, *Falco femoralis,* and still another false coral was taken by a Yellow-headed Caracara, *Milvago chimachima*. Possibly the snakes were caught during rains or plowing, or even already dead. The *Milvago* clean pests from cattle. The Black Caracara, *Daptrius ater,* (and probably *Milvago* also) sometimes takes botfly larvae and ticks from wild animals, a matter of great interest for it demonstrates a situation that existed before domestic animals were introduced on the continent.

An interesting symbiotic relationship is said to exist between the tapir (*Tapirus terrestris*) and *Daptrius ater*. The tapir begins to squeal on hearing the call of the caracara, which then goes to the tapir, for it likes eating its ticks. The tapir lies down, belly up, so the bird can get at the parasites.

Caracaras are omnivorous, eating fruits, garbage, and carrion. They seek burned-over areas. In the Mato Grosso Pantanal, the *Polyborus plancus* population is increasing because of an abundance of caiman carcasses. The caracaras then become a danger to nestlings such as those of spoonbills (A. Sucksdorff pers. comm.). *Daptrius americanus* tears apart the nests of even the most aggressive hornets in order to eat their succulent larvae. *Falco sparverius* and *F. femoralis* are among the insectivorous falcons. I have seen an *F. femoralis* use its feet to catch flying termites, occasionally trying to catch them directly with its wide open mouth. This latter technique, unusual for a hawk, was nevertheless the only one I saw an *F. peregrinus* use in a swarm of large red termites (*Syntermes dirus*) (see Sick 1989). *Milvago chimango* has a special aptitude for taking advantage of new food sources, thus being able to play the trophic role of various other species and easily become synanthropic. Occasionally it raids nests of other birds, as do the *Micrastur* and *Daptrius*. Some species, such as *Herpetotheres cachinnans,* the

Micrastur, the Bat Falcon, *Falco rufigularis*, and sometimes *F. peregrinus*, tend to hunt at dawn and dusk in order to catch bats.

Behavior

Curiously, Falconidae perched on the nest let their feces fall perpendicularly, whereas most Accipitridae squirt them far off. They like to bathe in rain, as I have observed with *F. rufigularis*. *F. sparverius* shakes its tail, as do other small raptors such as *Gampsonyx swainsonii* and the White-rumped Hawk, *Buteo leucorrhous*. *Milvago chimango* and *Daptrius americanus* are gregarious, the former gathering by the hundreds to roost in marshy places after first assembling on the ground in the savanna (Rio Grande do Sul). *D. americanus* lives constantly in small flocks. The *Milvago* and *Polyborus plancus* are proving to be quite synanthropic, having benefited from the expansion of livestock ranching.

In Bahia I once saw a *Falco femoralis* "amuse itself" by chasing, without trying to capture, a group of Passerines that included a flock of Grassland Yellow-Finches, *Sicalis luteola;* various Red-cowled Cardinals, *Paroaria dominicana;* Chestnut-capped Blackbirds, *Agelaius ruficapillus;* Shiny Cowbirds, *Molothrus bonariensis;* and a Red-breasted Blackbird, *Sturnella militaris*—a rare documentation of bird "amusement" (see also Hirundiniidae, "Behavior"). I have also seen the same thing with *F. peregrinus* chasing sandpipers.

Breeding

Most falcons do not build nests, instead occupying ones already made by other birds. Thus, *Milvago chimango* uses piles of sticks assembled by the Firewood-Gatherer, *Anumbius annumbi*, or Monk Parakeet, *Myiopsitta monachus*, as a platform. Falcons tend to nest in high places, and even forest hawks—*Micrastur ruficollis* and *M. gilvicollis*—that hunt in the lower and middle levels install themselves at a good height. An *M. ruficollis* occupied a spacious hole in an old araucaria, access to which was through a small entry about 6 m high (Itatiaia, Rio de Janeiro, 1973, E. Gouvêa). An *M. gilvicollis* in Peru reportedly made a nest in the open on the edge of the canopy of a high tree, but it seems probable to me that the nest was built by another species.

Falco sparverius and *F. rufigularis* regularly nest in tree holes, including those made by woodpeckers. The former even uses cavities in posts, buildings (e.g., concrete bridges), cliffs, embankments, terrestrial termite nests, or a *Colaptes* nest, and when nothing better offers itself, will take advantage of an abandoned *Myiopsitta monachus* nest (Rio Grande do Sul). Also, according to reports from outside Brazil, *Falco deiroleucus* selects tree holes, whereas *F. femoralis* uses any existing tree platform (e.g., the nest of another bird), as does *F. sparverius* on rare occasions. *Her-*

petotheres cachinnans breeds in large tree holes or in holes in rocky escarpments (Raso da Catarina, Bahia) without lining them. *Polyborus plancus* makes a crude nest of branches in a tree or, lacking one, builds directly on the ground. I found a *Milvago chimango* in a deep nest, lined with wool, that it apparently built itself. It also may use nests of other birds as a base (see above) or install itself on the ground.

Incubation is 28 days in *Polyborus plancus* and 20 to 30 days in *Falco sparverius*. As with many Falconiformes, the male *F. rufigularis* obtains food for the two or three nestlings while the female guards the nest. Three nestlings (two males and a female, Rio de Janeiro) have been recorded for *Micrastur ruficollis*. According to information gathered in other countries, young *Micrastur* abandon the nest after 35 to 40 days.

Migration and Movement

Falco peregrinus from North America is a regular migrant to Brazil during the Northern Hemisphere winter; one other northern species, the Merlin, *F. columbarius*, was recorded once at sea off our coast. During the Southern Hemisphere winter there are migratory movements of *F. femoralis* in southernmost Brazil. At the same time, isolated *Milvago chimango* migrate well to the north of their usual nesting areas. *M. chimango* also moves about at dusk and dawn (see "Hunting Methods . . .").

Parasites

Falcons, like the Accipitridae, are often parasitized by hippoboscid flies. I have found *Lynchia nigra* on *Herpetotheres cachinnans, Micrastur gilvicollis, Milvago chimachima,* and *Falco sparverius*. The *Milvago* and *Polyborus plancus* are hosts to *Olfersia raptatorum*.

Alleged Harmfulness and Conservation

Few birds are as aesthetically valuable as raptors, especially falcons. Let them knock down a few pigeons, whose numbers are a thousand times greater than theirs, and be it always remembered that raptors hunt to eat, not to "rob." The usefulness of *Milvago chimachima* is obvious to all. Its existence is supported by livestock raising. It is absurd to list a species such as *Polyborus plancus* as noxious when, because hunters have limited knowledge of bird identification, other raptors will be sacrificed in error. In the northeast raptors are considered game birds.

Synopsis of Brazilian Falcons
(number of species in parentheses)

1. Purely Neotropical species, thought to be the ancestral group of birds of prey:

1.1. Savanna or forest-edge species: *Herpetotheres* (1), *Daptrius* (2), *Milvago* (2), *Polyborus* (1)

1.2. Forest species: *Micrastur* (4)

2. A cosmopolitan genus: *Falco* (7), all open-country hunters, with *F. rufigularis* above the high forest. Only three— *F. rufigularis, F. femoralis,* and *F. sparverius*—are found with frequency in Brazil.

LAUGHING FALCON, *Herpetotheres cachinnans,* Acauã   PL 8.3

47 cm. Easily recognizable and well known. Large-headed, reminiscent of an owl. Creamy yellow or whitish on head contrasts with black area around eyes which continues back to form nuchal collar. Black tail densely barred with white. In flight a conspicuous light area is visible near wingtip.

VOICE: well known for duet of mated pair, an uninterrupted sequence that may last 9 minutes or more, unfolding with an almost dramatic tone: a low laugh, *gogogo . . . ,* introduces a sequence of loud *kwa*s which continue for perhaps 4 minutes until they finally start an equally long series of trisyllabic cries, *a-cua-ahng,* this being most impressive part. I have also observed an individual giving a long, horizontal series of bisyllabic cries while its mate simultaneously produced an ascending phrase of single cries, finally changing to *a-cua-ahng.* There are superstitious translations of call, e.g., *Deus quer um,* "God wants one." Sings by preference at dawn and dusk, sometimes during night. There is a curious legend reflecting fascination this bird's song inspires, saying that whoever hears this voice will become so enraptured that, overcome by a strange spell, he or she will feel impelled to imitate it.

Feeding and Behavior: Famous (originally among Indians and then through witch doctors [of other cultures]) for exterminating snakes, this falcon does in fact eat them, but in most cases they are inoffensive species, e.g., vine snakes, *Philodryas* and *Liophis.* If a bird carries away a still-live snake, it trails horizontally in an undulating line ½ m long behind flying bird. Also catches poisonous species, e.g., coral snake. In certain areas (Minas Gerais, Bahia) prefers to catch bats, standing watch before cliffs. Apparently has not yet been proven that it catches vampire bats (*Desmodus* spp.) (see Strigiformes). Forest borders, cerrado, river edges, isolated trees where it may remain immobile for hours. Mexico to Brazil. Local and temporary throughout Brazil, including Rio de Janeiro, ex-Guanabara. Also called *Macauá, Acanã.*

COLLARED FOREST-FALCON, *Micrastur semitorquatus,* Gavião-relógio   PL 8.6

53 cm. Large, uncommon, long tailed. Long tail and legs more conspicuous than in congeners. Color variable, but bird always recognizable by rusty or white collar and dark, crescent-shaped spot in auricular region, reminiscent of facial disk of a *Circus* harrier. There are as many individuals with pure white underparts as with solid ferruginous ones. Tail usually has 3 narrow white bars visible; tip also white. VOICE: recalls *Herpetotheres cachinnans* but sequences normally lack intense gradation. Songs may go on 10–20 minutes or more, well beyond dusk. Male frequently duets with female, which sings higher. Also a loud, isolated cry, *oh-a,* is repeated at intervals of 3–4 seconds. Like its congeners, is more active at dusk; has large eyes. Flies, runs, and jumps through branches and on ground with enormous agility as it pursues birds, small mammals, geckos, large insects. Forest borders; low, sparse, dry woodland. Mexico to Argentina, with occurrences scattered all over Brazil. Also called *Gavião-mateiro, Tem-tem.*

BARRED FOREST-FALCON, *Micrastur ruficollis,* Gavião-caburé   PL 8.5

36 cm. Slender, little-known, but not rare in dense, secondary forests and at times found near and even in cities. Silhouette resembles an *Accipiter* but wings even more rounded, tail longer (157–87 mm). Two geographic races occur in Brazil: southern one (*M. r. ruficollis,* see plate) brown, Amazonian one (*M. r. concentricus*) dark gray on upperparts and white barred with black below but with no reddish areas, in which it is similar to *M. gilvicollis.* Both races have reddish brown iris, bare face, orange-yellow feet. However, I have seen greenish yellow on area around eye on typical form (*M. r. ruficollis*), in which males usually are more barred than females, a feature already visible in fledglings.

VOICE: a monotonous, sharp *keyak,* repeated tirelessly at dusk, dawn, or on rainy days at intervals of approximately 2 seconds. Sometimes utters 4–6 consecutive *keyak*s. Loudest vocalization is a group of more varied syllables that might be classified as a song: *keyo-keyuh-keyOH ko ko ko,* at times accompanied by an ascending phrase from mate. Lives well hidden in dense forest, revealing itself only by voice. Hunts insects (e.g., large beetles), small birds, geckos, small snakes in lower, shadiest portion of forest. Takes advantage of army ants as beaters (see also "Hunting Methods . . ."). Mexico to Argentina, Bolivia, southcentral and eastern Brazil, including Mato Grosso (upper Rio Xingu, *M. r. concentricus*), Rio de Janeiro (ex-Guanabara), Rio Grande do Sul (*M. r. ruficollis*). Also called *Gavião-mateiro, Gavião-rasteiro.* See *M. gilvicollis.*

LINED FOREST-FALCON, *Micrastur gilvicollis,* Gavião-mateiro

34 cm. Twin to *M. ruficollis,* with relatively long wings (165–98 mm) but short tail (135–61 mm), no reddish. Under tail coverts often white and unstreaked. Iris white, face bare, feet orange. VOICE: less sharp, a sobbed *oh-ah,* an isolated cry repeated at intervals, or 2 consecutive cries, *oah oah,* also repeated at intervals (diagnostic; *ruficollis* has nothing like it). Also a standard song similar to *ruficollis.* Amazonia

south to Mato Grosso (Teles Pires), Bahia, northern Espírito Santo (Rio Doce). Also called *Tauató-i* (Kamaiurá, Mato Grosso), *To-to-i* (Kaiabi, Mato Grosso). May occur in same area as *ruficollis* (Bahia, Espírito Santo).

SLATY-BACKED FOREST-FALCON, *Micrastur mirandollei*

Rare Amazonian species reminiscent of adult *Accipiter poliogaster* but with obvious *Micrastur* silhouette. Voice similar to *M. semitorquatus*. South to Espírito Santo. See "Hunting Methods . . . ."

BLACK CARACARA, *Daptrius ater*, Gavião-de-anta

41 cm. Black, base of tail white, throat bare and yellow, legs orange. Immature has some white bars on tail and bare, orange face. VOICE: like *Milvago chimachima,* to which it is similar in almost all behavioral aspects. Omnivorous; eats larvae of large beetles (Cerambycidae), ants, amphibians, reptiles, Passerine nestlings, small mammals, fish. Picks ticks off tapirs and deer; likes buriti (*Mauritia*) and dendê (*Elaeis*) nuts as well as other fruits. Seeks burned-over areas. River banks, forest openings, and near ranches. Northern South America south to Maranhão, Mato Grosso, Bolivia. Also called *Caracará-i, Ka-ka-zi* (Kamaiurá, Mato Grosso), *kai-a-nó-na* (Waurá, Mato Grosso), *Cã-cã* (Amazonas). See "Hunting Methods . . ." re "symbiosis" with tapir.

RED-THROATED CARACARA, *Daptrius americanus,* Gralhão   Fig. 75

50 cm. Peculiar, showy species. Black and white with broad wings, long tail. Bare face and throat red, as are legs. Yellow bill; weak talons. VOICE: a noisy bird, song consisting of an accelerating sequence of *gheh*s . . . turning into a *ka-ka-ka* . . . that resembles cackling of a hen and culminating in full loud cries, *ka-o*, with timbre of a parrot or even a macaw, which are repeated by flock, even in flight. Sings more in morning and late afternoon when flying to collective roost. Eats hornet larvae taken from nests it tears apart in trees and later descends to finish up on ground, being indifferent to stings of most formidable wasps. Also takes hornets, bees, termites, seeds, fruits. On beaches searches out eggs of turtles and tracajás [hidden-necked turtles, *Podocnemis unifilis*]. Flies heavily as it goes through forest canopy and cerrado. Amazonia north to Mexico, south to Piauí, Mato Grosso, interior São Paulo. Also called *Alma-de-tapuio* (Maranhão), *Cã-cã, Caracará-preto, Cacão.* Considered by public to be a relative of jays; could also be thought of as an extraordinary cracid. The Wayampi (Amapá) include the *Ka-kã* among toucans.

YELLOW-HEADED CARACARA, *Milvago chimachima,* Carrapateiro   PLS 6.5, 7.8

40 cm; wingspan 74 cm. Probably best-known hawk in country, associated with cattle raising. In south replaced by

Fig. 75. Red-throated Caracara, *Daptrius americanus.*

M. chimango. Head, neck, and underparts yellowish white. Short, black postocular stripe; bare face orange. Wings long with clearly defined white patch. Immature brown, head and underparts streaked white, nuchal collar yellow; wing pattern is typical one of adult. VOICE: a whistled *kilieh* rendered constantly in flight; *TSAYre-TSAYre* when fighting. Its voice is one of most typical sounds of cattle ranches. Frequents pastures and corrals, both of cattle and horses, picking ticks and botflies off animals. Can become addicted to eating flesh from steers with back wounds, perching on unhappy animals as if taking off ticks. When cattle are unavailable eats caterpillars (including hairiest ones) and fish, hunts swarming termites, patrols roads and beaches (of either fresh or salt water) in search of dead animals, eats garbage, feces, fruits, raids birds nests. Has been seen capturing a false coral snake (*Erythrolamprus aesculapii*) (Mato Grosso) and eating caterpillar of *Dirphia araucariae* moth, a pest of Paraná pines (São Paulo, Vila and Carvalho 1972).

Central America to northern Uruguay, northern Argentina. All of Brazil, including Rio Grande do Sul (except along its southern border), where it meets *M. chimango* and where one *chimachima* may be found among 20 *chimango*. Its "soft," characteristic flight resembles *Polyborus plancus*. See also *Herpetotheres cachinnans* and Osprey, *Pandion haliaetus.* Also called *Pinhé* (São Paulo), *Cara-pinhé, Caracará-i* (Amazonas), *Caracará-branco* (Rio Grande do Sul), *Chimango-branco* (Rio Grande do Sul), *Papa-bicheira* (Marajó Island, Pará). Immature may resemble that of Snail Kite, *Rostrhamus sociabilis;* also similar to that of *M. chimango.*

CHIMANGO CARACARA, *Milvago chimango,*
Chimango

Southern species similar to *M. chimachima.* All brown, head and underparts slightly lighter. Upper tail coverts and area in wing white. Immature similar but darker than that of *M. chimachima.* VOICE: a prolonged, typical whistle, frequently followed by hoarse calls, *eeeeee-a, eeeeee a-CHA CHA CHA, CHEEeh-KEEeh, KEEeh, KEEeh,* that distinguish it perfectly from *chimachima.* In general less loquacious than that species. Some occasionally sing together, recalling chorus of *Daptrius americanus.*

Feeding and Behavior: Particularly energetic, able to adapt to the most varied foods. Plays role of *M. chimachima,* picking parasites off cattle, and of vultures, eating carrion and competing with *Polyborus plancus* along roadsides. Learns to steal turtle eggs (*Pseudemys dorbigni,* Rio Grande do Sul), surprising reptile in act of laying. Looks for burned areas where it meets Savanna Hawk, *Buteogallus meridionalis,* and gathers by hundreds to follow a plow. Also approaches coast where it occurs with Brown-hooded Gull, *Larus maculipennis,* and Southern Lapwing, *Vanellus chilensis.* Steals nestlings, even attacks adult birds.

Unlike *M. chimachima,* has a steady flight, somewhat reminiscent of a *Falco.* Aggressive against other raptors; I have seen it attack *Buteogallus meridionalis;* Black-chested Buzzard-Eagle, *Geranoaetus melanoleucus;* Lesser Yellow-headed Vulture, *Cathartes burrovianus;* and *Polyborus plancus.* Assembles on ground in large flocks at dusk, perhaps on a plowed field. Savanna, cultivated fields, ocean beaches, any kind of open landscape. Tierra del Fuego to Paraguay, Rio Grande do Sul, Santa Catarina. I have also found it in Minas Gerais (Juiz de Fora, June; Serra da Canastra, February). Very well known in Rio Grande do Sul, where *chimango* is a nickname [for a political group] used in such phrases as "Don't waste your ammunition on a chimango," and where it is common, to some extent replacing *chimachima.*

CRESTED CARACARA, *Polyborus plancus,*
Caracará   PL 6.4

56 cm; wingspan 123 cm. Very well known, large, black and white with yellow or red cere, bare face. Nuchal crest gives head a distinctive look. Long legs have yellow tarsi. Wing pattern similar to *Milvago chimachima,* a much less imposing species. Immature brown with streaked breast, violet or light yellow face, yellowish or whitish legs; quickly distinguished as this species by head shape. Face color changes from red to yellow when bird becomes excited, difference having nothing to do with sexual dimorphism. VOICE: a deep, low *rrak.* Song a composite phrase, a snorting *rak, rak, rak-RAah,* with head thrown back violently during last part.

Feeding and Behavior: Omnivorous; eats live and dead animals of all kinds. Often found on roads and in burns, also at ocean's edge, sometimes in flocks. Does not reject even most caustic centipedes; likes geckos, snakes, amphibians, snails; raids egret and spoonbill nests (Mato Grosso Pantanal) and even those of its *Milvago* "cousins." Walks on ground like a chicken, jumps, becomes soiled in sticky grass [*Mellinis minutiflora*] and ashes. Scratches earth with feet in search of peanuts and beans, gathers fruits of dendê palm. Attacks newborn lambs and on this account considered noxious in some parts. Follows tractors plowing fields to catch earthworms, including giant worm (see Accipitridae, "Feeding . . .").

Folklore: Considered by some Indians to be a bad-luck bird, it is nevertheless an appreciated source of feathers for forest tribes of upper Xingu (Mato Grosso). In Brazilian folklore *P. plancus* is symbol of a sad, intrusive person but also of a daring, rapacious one, well personified in famous ballad, among many that mention it, that goes, *Caracará, lá no sertão . . .,* "Caracara, there in the outback. . . ." Ceará peasants say caracara carries burning sticks that it drops to burn dry fields, a legend existing in other continents with very dry regions, e.g., Australia, with other raptors as principal actors.

Inhabits any open region, where it is often only hawk around. Southern U.S. to Tierra del Fuego, throughout Brazil. Also called *Carancho, Caracarai* (Marajó, Pará), *Gavião-de-queimada.* Population north of Amazon grades into northern form of species. *P. p. cheriway,* having lower back all black.

PEREGRINE FALCON, *Falco peregrinus,*
Falcão-peregrino   NV R   PL 7.6 Fig. 76

37–47 cm. Largest *Falco* in Brazil and an almost cosmopolitan species. Appears in Brazil only as a migrant from North America. Upperparts light bluish gray, well-defined malar stripe ("tear") black. Underparts white, barred black (sometimes only slightly) in adult, streaked in immature. Feet sulfur yellow. Female clearly larger than male. Of 3 birds caught in Brazil, 2 males measured: wing 30–33 cm; tail 13–15 cm; total length 38.0 cm; weight 600 g. One female measured: wing 36 cm; tail 16 cm; total length 46.3 cm; weight 950 g. Wings long and pointed, tail medium long. In flight resembles a pigeon but wing beats more solid, less accentuated, occasionally interrupted by gliding. Never descends with wings held up in a V like a columbid, tail more wedge-shaped, head less blocky, more rounded. VOICE: *tsewke-tsewke-tsewke,* heard when 2 individuals meet, more commonly with approach of northern spring and when breeding in far north. Open landscapes, also in cities because of habit of nesting in its homeland on skyscrapers and rocky cliffs.

Habitat, Records: A northern migrant recorded throughout Brazil; e.g., Amazonas (December), Pará, Pernambuco (February), Bahia (March), Minas Gerais (January, March, April), Paraná (April), Santa Catarina (November), São

Fig. 76. Peregrine Falcon, *Falco peregrinus,* logo of The Peregrine Fund, Inc.

Paulo, Mato Grosso, Rio Grande do Sul (October, November, March, April), and Rio de Janeiro (ex-Guanabara, see below). For more data on distribution, including recovery of individuals banded in North America, see below.

Feeding: Feeds on birds it catches in flight (see "Hunting Methods . . ."). Smaller male contents itself with doves and average-sized birds; female especially catches pigeons and birds the size of a Purple Gallinule, *Porphyrula martinica* (ex-Guanabara), or of a Lesser Golden Plover, *Pluvialis dominica* (Mato Grosso). Has been seen hunting parakeets (*Brotogeris* sp.) in Amazonia. In Rio de Janeiro I have seen it at dusk chasing bats and large red termite (*Syntermes*) swarms, catching insects directly with its wide-open mouth (see "Hunting Methods . . ."). In a Rio Grande do Sul environment of beaches and lakes, its menu can be abundantly rich in aquatic birds, as has been recorded by A. J. Witeck of Rio Grande. In 3 years (1985–87) the following victims of *F. peregrinus* were noted: 11 Charadriiform species; 7 rails; 2 grebes; 1 Stripe-backed Bittern, *Ixobrychus involucris;* 1 Whistling Heron, *Syrigma sibilatrix;* and 2 ducks (fig. 77). This diet is much like that of falcons living in similar environments in other parts of globe. Apparently does not hunt mammals on ground (European data) and flushes birds perched there.

The Peregrine Falcon in the City of Rio de Janeiro: *F. peregrinus* is present in Rio from beginning of October (earliest I have recorded it is 4 October) to end of April. It has usually been observed more frequently in center of city and in Santa Teresa, Laranjeiras, São Cristovão, Méier, etc., in February. Favorite spot for these falcons in Rio was for some years the Mesbla tower, where I observed it regularly from 1950 on, usually solitary individuals that made it their headquarters. In certain years *F. peregrinus* was famous for weeks on end as the "Mesbla Hawk," and in 1959 it reached the front page of the newspapers.

From 1977 on a peregrine was observed in the Cidade Universitária, Ilha do Fundão. Always perching in the same place on the University Hospital, it was captured and banded in April 1983, being recaptured 5½ months later (E. Pacheco pers. comm.). During the interval it must have bred in Canada or Alaska. It was recaptured twice more and continued to appear until April 1989—one more beautiful example of the faithfulness of birds to certain places during migration, corresponding to their better-known territoriality at the nesting site. This bird was under observation for 12 years before it failed to appear in late 1989 or in 1990. The life span of the North American form (*F. p. anatum*) has been estimated at 10–20 years. *F. peregrinus* is also observed regularly in São Paulo and some other cities. Records in rural districts (see below) increased after bird became known, beginning with my observations in Rio de Janeiro.

Although before 1950 *F. peregrinus* was almost unknown in Brazil (Pinto 1938), shortly thereafter it became so popular that any hawk appearing in an urban environment (e.g., *Milvago; Polyborus;* Roadside Hawk, *Rupornis magnirostris,* etc.) was called a "falcon," including some Swainson's Hawks, *Buteo swainsoni,* that surprisingly appeared in the center of São Paulo (see *B. swainsoni*).

Fig. 77. Peregrine Falcon, *Falco peregrinus,* pursuing a duck. After Sick 1960.

Systematics, Selection, and Migration: As clarified in late 1960s (White 1968), a northern population, *F. p. tundrius,* coming from arctic and subarctic tundra of Canada, Alaska, and Greenland, can be distinguished from *F. p. anatum,* a more southerly North American population of which the portion in the eastern U.S. became extinct in 1970s. Its decline was due primarily to eating birds poisoned by organochlorine pesticides, which caused poor calcification of eggs which broke in the nest. In 1970 shells were 15–20% thinner than in 1947 (Hickey 1969). The situation subsequently improved in U.S., but heavy use of pesticides in countries through which falcons migrate remains a problem.

As is customary, more northerly, even arctic, populations go farther south in migration, to regions near Antarctica. Round trip involves at least 22,000 km if falcon flies in a straight line, as it probably does, guided by instinct. Various other migratory birds have a very similar itinerary (see sandpipers, terns, and Bobolink, *Dolichonyx oryzivorus*).

Rigorous selection results in scarcely 30% of nestlings surviving for 1 year, a conclusion reached during a survey of *F. p. anatum* in U.S. I have also recorded yearlings between October and April. Evidently they do not prolong their vacation all year, unlike immature Ospreys (see *Pandion haliaetus,* Occurrence). *F. p. tundrius* ranges as far as Chile. An individual banded in Canada was captured 4 months later in Argentina. Possibly it might meet its southern replacement, *F. p. cassini,* resident in extreme south of continent, which migrates north during our winter as far as Colombia, following Andes. Individuals found breeding in Colombia and Ecuador in southern summer (December–February) must belong to an Andean population linked to *cassini.* Study of recoveries of falcons banded in North America revealed that individuals from both *tundrius* and *anatum* areas penetrate far into south. Thus, both races may appear in Brazil on migration. Of 37 falcons banded in North America between 1973 and 1985 and subsequently recovered, 19 were recovered in Brazil. One, banded 18 August in the Yukon, Canada, not far from Arctic Circle, was recovered on 25 December of same year at Iguaçu, Paraná. Another, banded in Alaska, was found in Rio Madeira region (Amazonas, 7°10'S). Another, banded in Texas, was found in Minas Gerais (20°S), and a 4th, banded in California, was found in Santa Catarina (28°S). All had been banded as nestlings.

Repopulation of eastern U.S. with individuals reared in captivity and of very diverse ancestry (some even from Old World; artificial insemination was used) has undoubtedly affected natural migratory instinct adversely.

More northerly falcons, *tundrius,* are smaller and lighter in color than *anatum.* Smaller size of *tundrius* has evolved in response to fact that this population spends much more time in regions with a hot or temperate climate than in cold climate of its native land. In this way it "escapes," as it were, the rule (formerly Bergmann's Rule, now modified) that postulates a larger size for boreal or antarctic forms.

ORANGE-BREASTED FALCON, *Falco deiroleucus,* Falcão-de-peito-vermelho   R

35 cm average; male about 30 cm, female about 40 cm, the difference between sexes being the same as in *F. peregrinus.* Stocky, with stature of a small *peregrinus* and color similar to *F. rufigularis* but, when adult, with upper breast reddish instead of black, barred white. Lower breast, flanks, and under surface of wings black with yellowish edges and round spots. Immature with forebreast rusty cream, streaked black. VOICE: *actseeck-actseek,* corresponding to *peregrinus* in Suriname (Haverschmidt 1963) or similar to *rufigularis* in Ecuador and Guatemala (Jenny and Cade 1986).

Hunts *Columbina* doves. In Ecuador and Guatemala catches *Aratinga* parakeets and *Streptoprocne* swifts in large numbers in flight (Jenny and Cade 1986), usually above canopy of high forest. Cerrado semiopen country, forest edges. Mexico to Argentina, Bolivia, throughout Brazil, but rare. Apparently nothing known about breeding in Brazil. Recorded in vicinity of city of Amapá (Amapá); Santarém, Marajó Island, Serra do Cachimbo (Pará); Piauí; Bahia; Serra do Cipó (Minas Gerais); Cantagalo (Rio de Janeiro); Paraná; Santa Catarina; Rio Grande do Sul; Cuiabá, Rio São Lourenço (Mato Grosso); Rio Claro (Goiás). May be confused with a large *rufigularis,* but with a specimen in hand one quickly notes powerful feet (middle toe 4–5 cm, only 3–3.5 cm in *rufigularis*) which are much larger and heavier than those of *peregrinus,* which it replaces in Neotropics, a surprising fact suggested by E. Stresemann as early as 1924.

BAT FALCON, *Falco rufigularis,* Cauré   PL 8.9

26 cm; 120 g (male), 200 g (female). Quite small, black with breast and belly barred with white. Throat, upper breast, and sides of neck rusty yellow or white, abdomen and thighs chestnut. Immature has yellowish under tail coverts, barred black. VOICE: *ghi, ghi, ghi . . . , tsreeee-i, kit,* possibly recalling a tern. Famous as an able hunter. At dusk catches bats and moths just above canopy of tall forests; during day catches dragonflies, grasshoppers, birds, occasionally even swifts (Apodidae) and larger birds such as aracaris (Ramphastidae). Also hunts small rats and geckos, which it gets on ground. Pairs roost high on dead branches in cultivated patches at river edges and in forest. In Amazonia considered a symbol of happiness and credited with building large felt nests of Lesser Swallow-tailed Swift, *Panyptila cayennensis.* Mexico to Bolivia, northern Argentina; throughout Brazil wherever there are forests, except Santa Catarina and Rio Grande do Sul but including Rio de Janeiro, ex-Guanabara, São Paulo, without being common anywhere. Also called *Coleirinha, Tem-tenzinho.* Often called *F. albigularis.* See *F. deiroleucus,* which at first glance appears to be a larger replica. In Neotropics *F. rufigularis* replaces *F. subbuteo* of Old World.

APLOMADO FALCON, *Falco femoralis*,
Falcão-de-coleira   PL 8.7

36 cm. Easily identified, peculiar savanna species. Slender with quite long wings and tail. Abdomen less red than *F. rufigularis*. Wide white superciliaries meet on nape; distinct malar stripe. Open wing shows clear, whitish trailing edge. Secondaries have wide white tip, well pronounced in flight, unlike *rufigularis* and *F. deiroleucus*. Immature has streaked white underparts. VOICE: *ee-ee-ee*. Hunts close to ground in campos, restingas. Sometimes hovers. Eats insects, swarming termites, geckos, bats (*Molossus ater*), occasionally birds and even poisonous snakes, e.g., jararaca (*Bothrops* sp.). Seeks burned areas. Not usually rare. Periodically in small migrant flocks (restinga, Rio de Janeiro, August). U.S. to Tierra del Fuego, throughout Brazil. See *F. deiroleucus* and *F. peregrinus* immature. Also called *Gavião-pombo* (São Paulo).

MERLIN, *Falco columbarius*, Esmerilhão   NV

Stray visitor, a single individual having been caught on Dutch ship a short distance from Bahia coast (November 1963), apparently having come from Palearctic (Iceland?).

As a curiosity, I draw attention to the fact that Diogo Fernandes Ferreira (1899) in his *Arte de Caça de Altaneria* mentions a "white gyrfalcon, as white as a pigeon . . . taken on a ship near Brazil while crossing the sea" (from Sick 1960). This could refer to Gyrfalcon, *F. rusticolus*, a circumpolar species, or to an albino of some other species.

AMERICAN KESTREL, *Falco sparverius*,
Quiriquiri   PL 8.8

25 cm. Vies with *F. rufigularis* as smallest falcon. Unmistakable head design: 2 lateral streaks and 2 black spots on nape, resembling eyes (an "occipital face," much less convincing than that of Ferruginous Pygmy-Owl, *Glaucidium brasilianum*). Accentuated sexual dimorphism already evident in nestlings ready to fledge. Male's tail and back uniformly ferruginous, tail feathers with wide black subterminal band and white tips; wings gray. Female's wings rusty like back and spotted with black; tail has numerous black bars. VOICE: *gli-gli-gli, ee-i, i, i, i*. Eats geckos (e.g., *Ameiva*), large insects, e.g., grasshoppers. Also catches mice, small snakes. At dusk tries to catch bats, not always successfully, though individuals may specialize in this. Perches on telegraph posts and wires. Shakes tail. Occasionally hovers, and when flying may resemble a large swallow. Does not adapt as well to city life as *F. tinnunculus* of Old World (to which it is similar in aspect and which is sometimes considered its geographic replacement). However, does occur in Rio de Janeiro, Porto Alegre (Rio Grande do Sul). I saw one enter under a roof tile to sleep (Iguaçu, Paraná). Savanna and quasi-desert, where it may be common. Requires a minimal vegetation. Northern Alaska to Tierra del Fuego, throughout Brazil except in forests.

Treating *F. sparverius* as a close relative of *F. tinnunculus* is unsupported by osteological data: latter has a notarium lacking in *F. sparverius* (see "Morphology").

Falconidae Bibliography
See also General Bibliography

Albuquerque, J.L.B. 1982. Observations on the use of rangle by the Peregrine Falcon, *Falco p. tundrius*. *Raptor Research* 16(3):91–92.

Beebe, W. 1950. *Zoologica* (N.Y.) 35:69–86. [*Falco rufigularis*, behavior]

Burnham, W. A., J. P. Jenny, and C. W. Turley. 1989. *Maya Project, Progress Report 2*. Boise, Idaho: The Peregrine Fund.

Cade, T. J. 1974. *Proc. Conf. Raptor Cons.*, Colorado: 89–104. [*Falco peregrinus*, conservation]

Coelho, E. P., M. Soneghet, and V. Alves. 1987. *An. II ENAV*: 190–191. [*Falco peregrinus*, capture and recovery in Rio de Janeiro]

Fischer, W. 1962. *Der Wanderfalke*. Wittenberg: Neue Brehm Büch.

Goeldi, E. A. 1898. *Bol. Mus. Paraen.* 2:430–42. [*Falco rufigularis*, legends]

Haverschmidt, F. 1963. *J. Orn.* 104:443–45. [*Falco deiroleucus*, Surinam]

Hickey, J. J. 1969. *Peregrine Falcon Populations*. Madison, Wisc.: University of Wisconsin Press.

Jenny, J. P., F. Ortiz, and M. D. Arnold. 1981. First nesting record of the Peregrine Falcon in Ecuador. *Condor* 83:387.

Jenny, J. P., W. A. Burnham, T. Vries, et al. 1983. Analysis of Peregrine Falcon eggs in Ecuador. *Condor* 85:502.

Jenny, J. P., and T. J. Cade. 1986. Observations on the biology of the Orange-breasted Falcon, *Falco deiroleucus*. *ICBP Birds of Prey Bull.* 3:119–24.

Risebrough, R. W., A. M. Springer, S. A. Temple, et al. Observaciones del Falcon Peregrino, *Falco peregrinus*, en América del Sur. *Rev. Bras. Biol.* In preparation.

Schwartz, P. 1972. *Condor* 74:399–415. [*Micrastur*, voice and taxonomy]

Sick, H. 1961. *Auk* 78:646–48. [*Falco peregrinus*, behavior]

Sick, H. 1989. Der kanadische Wanderfalke, *Falco peregrinus tundrius*, in Brasilien. *Mitt. Zool. Mus. Berlin. 65 Suppl. Ann. Orn.* 13:27–36.

Springer, A. M., W. Walker II, R. W. Risebrough, et al. Acumulação de organoclorados no Falcão Peregrino, *Falco peregrinus*, na América do Sul. *Rev. Bras. Biol.* In preparation.

Stresemann, E. 1924. *J. Orn.* 72:429–46. [Taxonomy]

Stresemann, E. 1943. *Orn. Mber.* 51:100–101. [*Falco deiroleucus*, size]

Stresemann, V. 1958. *J. Orn.* 99:81–88. [Primary molt confirming homogeneity of the Falconidae]

Vila, W. M., and C. T. Carvalho. 1972. *Brasil Florestal* 3(10):25–28. [*Milvago*, feeding]

Vuilleumier, F. 1970. *Breviora* 335. [Taxonomy]

Wattel, J. 1964. *Ardea* 52:225–26. [*Falco columbarius*, occurrence]

White, C. M. 1968. *Auk* 85:179–91. [*Falco peregrinus tundrius*, taxonomy]

ORDER GALLIFORMES

FAMILY CRACIDAE: CHACHALACAS, GUANS, AND CURASSOWS (24)

The cracid family contains the most important gallinaceous birds of South America, for the Neotropics have few representatives of the other families in this order, which is ecologically "complemented" or supplemented by other taxons such as the tinamous (Tinamidae), trumpeters (Psophiidae), and even the Hoatzin, *Opisthocomus hoazin* (Opisthocomidae)[1] in Amazonia (see also Anhimidae). The cracids are a sister group of the Phasianidae and of the Megapodiidae (of Australasia). Sibley et al. (1988) propose an Order Craciformes comprising two Suborders: Craci (Cracidae) and Megapodii (Megapodiidae).

Cracids are among the most ancient avifauna of the New World; there are various fossils from the Tertiary (Eocene, 50 million years B.P.) of North America and from the Pleistocene of Brazil (Minas Gerais, 20,000 years B.P.). They are presently distributed from the southern United States (Texas) to Uruguay and northern Argentina.

Morphology, Special Adaptations, and Identification

Cracids are the only arboreal Galliformes. Sizes vary from that of a Greater Ani, *Crotophaga major,* to that of a turkey (fig. 78). Although the Brazilian species[2] comprise four distinct biotypes (chachalacas, guans, piping-guans, and curassows), they have a basically homogeneous aspect. They frequently show a plume or crest (more prominent in piping-guans and curassows) and a bare throat, and guans and piping-guans have a brightly colored dewlap that is conspicuous in the forest darkness. Curassows have red or yellow at the base of the bill and on the cere (even blue and green occur), with the base of the bill frequently swollen, which makes the brilliantly colored area even larger. The swellings on the bills of the *Crax* are fleshy and enlarge during breeding, unlike the Razor-billed Curassow, *Mitu mitu,* whose swollen bill is solid.

Cere and appendage (caruncle and wattles) color descriptions have very confusing, for authors are frequently familiar only with subadult individuals or museum skins where the cere and appendages are deformed and discolored. No one was aware of the great variation produced by age and

Fig. 78. Comparison of tinamid and cracid sizes: (1) Red-winged Tinamou, *Rhynchotus r. rufescens;* (2) Undulated Tinamou, *Crypturellus u. undulatus;* (3) Chaco Chachalaca, *Ortalis c. canicollis;* (4) Dusky-legged Guan, *Penelope o. obscura;* (5) Blue-throated Piping-Guan, *Pipile pipile cumanensis;* and (6) Bare-faced Curassow, *Crax fasciolata sclateri.* After Krieg and Schuhmancher 1936.

time of year. European scientists, dependent on live imported birds, sometimes received individuals from different localities without knowing it. They then put together pairs composed of two species from different places, with consequent errors in identification. The bare parts of the head are very important in classifying the *Crax* and *Pipile.* Scars I have examined on male Wattled Curassows, *Crax globulosa,* and Black Curassows, *C. alector,* are the same color as the cere of the individual involved: red or yellow, respectively. The bright bills of curassows, which identify the birds at a distance, are incredibly conspicuous in the forest shadows

---

[1]The Hoatzin, *Opisthocomus hoazin,* is often included in the Galliformes; I have put it in a separate order.

[2]The non-Brazilian genera—*Oreophasis, Penelopina,* and *Chamaepetes*—are distinctive.

where their black plumage blends completely with the surroundings.

Plumage also gives problems, especially in the *Penelope* and *Ortalis*. *Crax* females sometimes have various phases, as in the non-Brazilian Great Curassow, *C. rubra*. Females tend to vary more than males (heterogynism, see Formicariidae, "Morphology"), as in the geographic races of the Bare-faced Curassow, *C. fasciolata*. I (Teixeira and Sick 1981, 1986) have pointed out color variation in *Crax* adults: (1) a yellowish instead of white abdomen; (2) white tip of the tail absent without being worn (*C. fasciolata*) or present (Red-billed Curassow, *C. blumenbachii*); and (3) marbling of the wings in female *C. globulosa*.

Publication of the well-illustrated book *Curassows and Related Birds* by Jean Delacour and Dean Amadon (1973) now greatly facilitates identification. Dr. Jesús Estudillo López of Mexico is also a world authority on cracids.

Cracids have long necks and tails and large wings. They take flight immediately upon being surprised. Their pectoral musculature is well developed, but flying capacity in most is reduced, although it serves very well to help a bird escape through foliage to reach the canopy. Piping-guans fly relatively well.

The legs are long and strong, being longest in the curassows, which also have a longer and narrower pelvis, being the most terrestrial cracids. Cracids walk majestically through open forest with long steps. Under normal conditions, when the clumsy-flying Dusky-legged Guan, *Penelope obscura*, wants to get to a distant grove, it crosses the intervening campo on foot, thereby arousing much less attention from possible enemies than if it flew. Guans, the most arboreal of the group, have shorter legs. When they run through the branches they may resemble monkeys, but they do not make the least noise. Cracids have long toes and a well-developed hallux situated on the same level as the foretoes; even the heavy curassows can grasp thin branches with the greatest ease, frequently holding various branches or vines at once. When they reach the canopy they hide in the leaves or glide off silently, thus escaping the most assiduous observer.

Sexes are similar, except in *Crax* curassows other than *C. alector*. Males have an intromissive organ, as I have observed in *Mitu mitu* and the Blue-throated Piping-Guan, *Pipile pipile nattereri*. There is sexual dimorphism in iris color. The iris of the male *Penelope obscura* is red and that of the female chestnut, a difference already well marked in the first year. Such is also the case for certain other *Penelope*, such as the White-browed Guan, *P. jacucaca*, and White-crested Guan, *P. pileata*, but not for the Rusty-margined Guan, *P. superciliaris*. The male *Crax blumenbachii* has a chestnut iris, the adult female red, and the young female yellowish brown. The *Crax* also show sexual dimorphism in tarsus color, and leg color can be a specific character in the *Penelope* and *Crax*. The dewlap of *Penelope* and *Pipile* is larger and more vividly colored in the adult male, especially during the breeding season. Later it turns dull.

Immature plumage is similar if not the same as that of the adult. For example, a young male *Crax blumenbachii* still accompanying its mother appears to be a smaller replica of its father, a fact that sometimes led earlier researchers to consider a young bird in perfect adult plumage to be a different species. In less than six months young cracids reach adult size but not weight. I have noted that the crests of immature *C. blumenbachii* (both sexes) are higher than those of adults, for the feathers are less curved. There is erroneous information in the literature on a brown plumage of immature cracids, arising from the occasional appearance of some brown feathers in the black plumage of certain *Crax* and *Mitu* individuals (schizochroism). When *Penelope obscura* is reared in captivity, some molt occurs before six months of age; a 40-day-old bird, still much smaller than an adult, has rapidly changing, different juvenal plumage. The head and neck pattern resembles that of the domestic chick (the throat is white), and body plumage is pale without the white markings of the adult. At 90 days it is almost the same as an adult. It is notable that the male Highland Guan, *Penelopina nigra,* of Central America acquires its definitive black plumage only in its second year, being brown like the female before.

Studying the color of down-covered chicks is interesting and now much easier because of frequent captive breeding of several species. I have recorded sexual dimorphism in Black-fronted Piping-Guan, *Pipile jacutinga*, chicks: the male's superciliary is white or whitish, the female's light brownish, as I learned in 1974 with U. Schadrack in Blumenau, Santa Catarina. G. Scheres (pers. comm.) observed the same thing in *P. pipile gravi* and states that there is a similar situation in the chicks of various *Crax* species bred in Belgium (e.g., *C. blumenbachii, C. fasciolata, C. alector*). The sex of older *fasciolata* chicks is indicated by the growing flight feathers: all black in males, barred in females. There is already evidence of a penis in chicks. On possible hybrids with species of other families, see "Hunting . . . ."

Vocalization

Vocalizations are generally quite similar in related species but vary greatly among the four biotypes. Chachalaca vocalizations consist of a highly rhythmic, ventriloquial cackling with a very hard timbre. The fact that a pair is duetting can be perceived only with great difficulty, and it is even more difficult when various individuals of a flock, or neighboring pairs, sing simultaneously (see also Spot-winged Wood-Quail, *Odontophorus capueira*). The song of the large Chaco Chachalaca, *Ortalis canicollis,* can be heard for more than 2 km. The male trachea is elongated, forming a large loop in the chest (fig. 79). Apparently this distinctive feature serves more to lower the voice than to amplify it; male voices are an

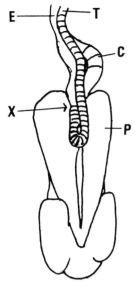

Fig. 79. Trachea of the Dusky-legged Guan, *Penelope obscura bronzina*, female, showing the tracheal loop and its entrance (X) into the thorax. (C) spinal column; (E) esophagus; (P) Musculus pectoralis. Varjão de Guaratuba, São Paulo, October 1969.

octave below female voices. As early as 1829 Hercules Florence noted that chachalaca pairs sing alternately, the female higher. It is possible to start these birds singing by ringing a bell.

When guans are alarmed the force and hoarseness of their voices are impressive. They have a looped trachea like the chachalacas, which can be felt in a live bird. Conclusions on the significance of the tracheal loop are hampered by the fact that it is present in certain *Penelope* species and absent in others. Within species there is little variation in the form of the trachea, so it is very useful in classification and determination of species relationships. The voice of *Penelope obscura* resembles the braying of a burro and differs completely from that of *Pipile pipile* and *P. jacutinga*, whose high, thin calls resemble those of an Amazonian antbird. The *Pipile* have normal tracheas with no looping.

The curassows (*Crax, Mitu,* and *Nothocrax*) have low, deep, ventriloquial songs similar to the sound obtained by blowing into a bottle; hunters say the bird is "booming." This is one of the lowest voices heard among our avifauna; the phrases are bi- or tripartite and well accentuated: for example, *hm-hm-HM hm-hm-HM* (*Crax fasciolata*) or *hm-hm-HM hm-HM-hm-HOOO* (Nocturnal Curassow, *Nothocrax urumutum*).

With wings held close to the body and tail lowered, *Crax blumenbachii* booms by first throwing its neck forward and panting through its open bill. Then it retracts its neck and lowers its head. Closing the bill and pointing it toward its breast, the bird begins to sing with bill and eyes closed. The trachea, full of air and with its upper portion closed, serves as

a resonating chamber. The trachea of male curassows is shaped differently than in chachalacas and guans, being distinguished by its strong lateral compression (and consequent change in width). During the breeding period curassows prefer to sing at dawn or at night while on their perches. It is very difficult to locate the boom of a curassow, especially in the forest where the sound may come from two males in different places (curassows are extremely territorial). The boom of a curassow at one's side (in captivity) may be almost inaudible to us, but the female attends it from a distance. A male in the presence of a female will often stretch and beat its wings heavily after booming. Certain species, such as *Crax globulosa* and the Yellow-knobbed Curassow, *C. daubentoni* (not Brazilian), apparently never boom. The warning or alarm signal is a cough followed by a whistle. The alarm of *C. globulosa* is surprisingly soft.

Instrumental Music

Guans and piping-guans are noted for the extremely loud, strange noises they make with their wings when flying from one treetop to another, perhaps 50 m away. This activity is more intense at the beginning of the breeding season. The bird takes off from a branch, glides for a moment, makes the noise and glides again, then flies normally to perch on another branch, generally a bit lower than that from which it took off.

Hunters use the terms *rasgar,* "ripping," or *riscar asas,* "scratching wings," for the noise made by piping-guans and *rufar as asas,* "ruffling the wings," for guans, which very well characterize these sounds. The ripping of piping-guans closely resembles the noise made by ripping a thick cloth or the noise of a large tree falling; that of the guans is similar to the ruffling of a drum. In either case there is always a double sound, but with *Pipile pipile* a weak, diatonic *dak* is also noted. It is difficult to observe details, for this music is almost always performed in the dark, at dusk, dawn, and on moonlit nights, as I verified on the upper Xingu where I observed *P. pipile.*

It is certain that the outermost primaries, which have an abrupt thinning at their outer end, act as sound-producing remiges (fig. 80). This adaptation is much less evident in guans than in piping-guans. Apparently certain *Penelope* species (e.g., *P. superciliaris*) only ruffle their wings under exceptional circumstances, whereas the large Spix's Guan, *P. jacquacu,* of Amazonia and its southern replacement, *P. obscura,* do it as intensely as the *Pipile.* The ripping of *Pipile* can be heard for 1 km or more, depending on local terrain. Female *Pipile* have the same modification of the primaries but appear not to make any sound.

The impossibility of precise observation during these displays has led hunters to declare that such noises are produced by friction of the wings against the tarsi while perched and that narrowing of the primaries is just the result of the vane

Fig. 80. Wing of a Blue-throated Piping-Guan, *Pipile pipile nattereri*, male. The three or four outer primaries are sound-producing remiges. After Sick 1965.

wearing against the claws. In captivity, *Pipile* reportedly make a ripping while flying from a perch to the ground.

Feeding

Guans eat fruits, leaves, and shoots, such as those of the murici [*Byrsonima* sp.] and caneleira [Lauraceae]. Chachalacas like mandiocão (*Didymopanax*), and I have seen *Penelope obscura* eating *Podocarpus* fruits (Campos de Jordão, São Paulo). They attend the fruiting of certain palms, such as the palmito (*Euterpe edulis*) and licuri (*Syagrus*). Clutching a clump of palmito fruits, *Pipile jacutinga* swallows several, taking the pulp into its crop and regurgitating the hard seeds which rain down on the foliage of the understory and attract the attention of hunters. Cracids must play a role in disseminating various plant species; country people of the south say *Penelope obscura* "plants" erva-mate. On occasion they descend to the forest floor to pick up fallen fruits. They enjoy eating tree flowers.

Cracids hunt mollusks, grasshoppers, tree frogs, and other small animals. *Crax blumenbachii* takes even large centipedes and dangerous spiders such as *Lycosa*. It is said that *Ortalis canicollis* periodically overstuffs itself with caterpillars. Cracids seek out salt banks to eat salty earth (Mato Grosso, see Psittacidae, "Feeding"). Small stones are always found in their stomachs.

Cracids drink at river edges, sucking like pigeons with the bill held underwater, so their swallowing of the liquid can be seen from the rhythmic motion of the throat.

Behavior

Impetuous opening and closing of the tail is a special signal of excitement among guans and curassows. It is even more notable when the tail feathers have white tips (see *Mitu*). All cracids have a head-shaking tic. Even chicks do it, and it intensifies when the birds become excited or are in the

presence of people. I first thought this nervous habit was perhaps linked to the occurrence of nematodes in their eyelids (see "Parasites . . ."). This common motion is performed in two ways: the *Crax* shake their heads laterally, the *Mitu* back and forth. Any excitement is also reflected in movement of the crown feathers. This is more noticeable in genera having crests (the curassows, for instance) and even more so in females of certain species having a white-barred pattern. Chachalacas, piping-guans, curassows, and *Penelope jacucaca* wallow in dust and enjoy sunbaths. Unlike other gallinaceous birds, cracids do not scratch the ground in search of food. *P. jacucaca,* when surprised feeding on the ground, squats on the caatinga sand, hoping thus to escape detection (Reiser 1924). In the late afternoon before roosting, cracids become very restless, in a way reminiscent of thrushes (see Turdinae, "Behavior"). I have noted this nervousness—apparently anxiety about finding a good place to sleep—in both guans and piping-guans. They always sleep at the same roost, a place that can be identified by the pile of feces accumulated over months if there is another branch below the roost (*Crax fasciolata*). On moonlit nights *C. fasciolata* becomes very restless on the roost and even abandons it to perch in another nearby spot. For other behavior, see "Morphology . . ." and "Instrumental Music."

Breeding

Cracids, unlike tinamous, are monogamous. The male feeds the female, turning and graciously lowering his head, the way parents feed their young (see below). Pairs caress each other on the head (e.g., *Ortalis*). The male *Crax blumenbachii* chases the female on the ground, displaying his white crissum and "sweeping" the ground with his tail. However, display of the crissum and abdomen, which become visible from behind when a bird lifts its tail, can be seen regularly in *C. blumenbachii,* including in females when they preen. Little is known about nuptial displays of Brazilian cracids (see "Vocalization" and "Instrumental Music"). A curassow pair reportedly requires a territory 2 to 3 km in diameter and fights vigorously against intruders of the same species. Birds move about constantly in their territories, preferring certain portions, and move from branches to ground and vice versa. Territories of species of different genera, such as those of *Mitu tuberosa* and *Crax fasciolata,* may overlap. It would be interesting to use radio tracking to determine the daily movements of a pair.

Pairs build a small nest in vine tangles, sometimes high in trees or on branches over water, or even on fallen trunks. They also use abandoned nests of other birds. *Pipile jacutinga* may lay on heavy limbs, branching trunks, or rocks, almost doing without construction material. Occasionally *Penelope superciliaris* also nests on rocks in the forest (Espírito Santo). *P. obscura* may install itself on a branch among bromeliads whose leaves it tramples to form a nest. Chachalacas, which live permanently in small flocks that defend their territory against neighboring flocks, tend to nest in groups.

Eggs are large and uniformly white but may become covered with dirt and turn yellowish. Curassow eggs are like those of the Horned Screamer, *Anhima cornuta*, except they have a very rough instead of smooth surface (especially those of *Mitu*). They may vary greatly in size and shape, even those laid by a single female (e.g., *Penelope, Mitu*). *Penelope* eggs are smooth. The incubation period for the Speckled Chachalaca, *Ortalis guttata*, is reportedly 21 days; for *Pipile pipile* 24 days; for *Penelope superciliaris, P. obscura bronzina,* and *Pipile jacutinga* 28 days; for *Crax fasciolata* 30 days; and for *Mitu tuberosa* 30 to 32 days. *Penelope obscura* lays two clutches annually (Rio de Janeiro).

There are two or three nestlings. When only two, they are of opposite sexes, as I recorded among wild *Crax blumenbachii* in Espírito Santo. They hatch with the eyes open and can move about freely immediately, balancing on branches and even flying, reaching considerable heights among the foliage. During the first days they walk around under the mother's large tail, being called back when they wander away (*C. blumenbachii*). During this period they scarcely eat, living on fat reserves. Later they actively take food (e.g., insect larvae, termites, fruit) offered by the mother, who lowers her bill. The prize may be a regurgitated pellet, which is presented in the same way (*Ortalis, Penelope obscura*). Young *C. blumenbachii* are inseparable from their mother even after four months.

In the early days of life the flight feathers of *Ortalis canicollis* grow to 2 cm in length, and the still down-covered chick uses its wings when it moves around through the branches. In general the young are quite competent at making high, long jumps, moving up through the branches with great ease. They sleep perched under the wings of the mother (curassows) or of both parents (chachalacas). Even when grown they sleep alongside the adults. They accompany their parents for some months (*Crax fasciolata, Mitu mitu*) and for this reason many of the "pairs" shot down consist of an adult female and a young (male or female). Immatures, when independent, unite in flocks separate from the adults (*Penelope*).

Distribution, Evolution, and Nomenclature

Taxonomic revisions (Vuilleumier 1965; Vaurie 1968; Delacour and Amadon 1973) have provided a better understanding of the relationship and distribution of the Cracidae. Apparently all members of a genus, such as *Crax* or *Mitu*, have allopatric distribution (fig. 81), excluding or replacing each other geographically, which suggests superspecies status. But various species, one from each genus, may live in the same forest, as for example, *Crax fasciolata, Mitu tuberosa,* and *Penelope jacquacu* in the upper Xingu, Mato Grosso. In Vaupés, Colombia, *Crax alector, Nothocrax urumutum, Penelope jacquacu,* and the Lesser Razor-billed Curassow, *Mitu tomentosa,* are syntopic. With this kind of

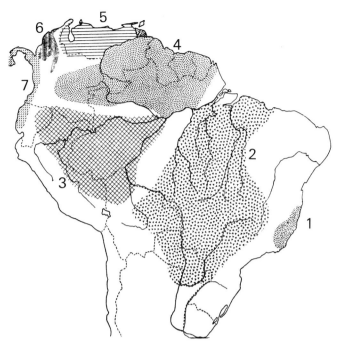

Fig. 81. Distribution of curassows of the genus *Crax,* strictu mensu, including four Brazilian species (1–4): (1) Red-billed Curassow, *C. blumenbachii;* (2) Bare-faced Curassow, *C. fasciolata;* (3) Wattled Curassow, *C. globulosa;* (4) Black Curassow, *C. alector;* (5) Yellow-knobbed Curassow, *C. daubentoni;* (6) Blue-billed Curassow, *C. alberti;* (7) Great Curassow, *C. rubra.* These seven forms can be considered members of a superspecies, *C. rubra.* The map gives only an idea of the distribution. After Vaurie 1968. In addition to these, there are also curassows of the genera *Mitu* and *Nothocrax.*

coexistence, the sympatry of *Crax* and *Mitu* species is eloquent proof that *Mitu* cannot be included in *Crax,* as Delacour and Amadon (1973) did.

The *Pipile* also replace each other geographically, although there appears to be a possibility of hybridization when two of them meet. All the *Pipile* could be considered geographic races of one species. There is no need to suppress the generic name *Pipile* in favor of *Aburria* (Delacour and Amadon 1873). *Pipile* species, widely distributed on this continent, constitute a very different unit from the Wattled Guan, *Aburria aburri,* a monotypic genus restricted to the Andes from Venezuela to Peru. *Pipile* and *Aburria* do have similar wing shapes. My conclusions on nomenclature are the same as those suggested by the Second International Cracid Symposium in Caracas, Venezuela, in February–March 1988.

The chachalacas, *Ortalis,* also replace each other, no two species occurring in the same place (fig. 82). All Brazilian species (except *Ortalis canicollis*) may be considered allospecies constituting a superspecies; they can even be thought of as geographic races of a single species.

Sympatry is sometimes simulated when ecological or altitudinal exclusion occurs, as happens in the *Penelope* (fig.

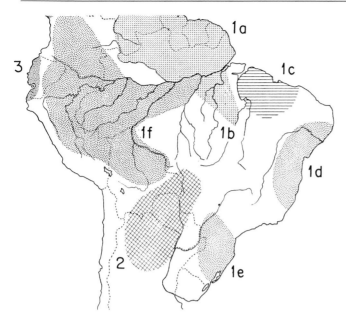

Fig. 82. Distribution of *Ortalis* chachalacas: (1a) Little Chachalaca, the superspecies *O. motmot,* and its five allospecies: (1b) Rufous-headed Chachalaca, *O. ruficeps;* (1c) Buff-browed Chachalaca, *O. superciliaris;* (1d) White-bellied Chachalaca, *O. araucuan;* (1e) Scaled Chachalaca, *O. squamata;* and (1f) Speckled Chachalaca, *O. guttata.* (2) Chaco Chachalaca, *O. canicollis.* (3) Rufous-headed Chachalaca, *O. erythroptera* (non-Brazilian). After Delacour and Amadon 1973.

83). *P. superciliaris,* a small species, appears to be locally sympatric with five large species of the same genus: *P. jacucaca, P. pileata, P. jacquacu, P. obscura,* and the Chestnut-bellied Guan, *P. ochrogaster. P. obscura* lives in the Serra dos Órgãos where *P. superciliaris* does not penetrate, but both meet while frequenting certain fruit trees in the foothills of the Serra do Mar (Rio de Janeiro). Both reportedly occur together on the São Paulo littoral. In Espírito Santo *P. superciliaris* lives both in the hot lowlands (Rio Doce) and mountains (Limoeiro, Jatiboca), where *P. obscura* apparently does not exist. In Central Brazil and Amazonia *P. jacquacu* and *P. ochrogaster* live in tall forest, whereas *P. superciliaris* lives in the same region at the forest edge and in cerrado. *P. superciliaris* meets *P. jacucaca* in the caatinga of Piauí.

One can conclude that about 75% of the cracids may be considered members of superspecies. Such a high percentage is also observed in Galbulidae and is even higher in Ramphastidae (Haffer 1974b).

Movement and Migration

Outside the breeding season curassows may form small flocks made up solely of male or females. *Pipile pipile* in Mato Grosso make local migrations up or down river. In Rio Grande do Sul at the end of the last century, *P. jacutinga* was reported as migratory. It arrived in May–June (winter) in flocks of 4 to 16 individuals, nested, and disappeared in December (summer). In Santa Catarina real invasions of this species were recorded in cold winters; normally their movements occurred there during the fruiting of the pindaúba [*Xylopia frutescens*] in March–April, with flocks of 10 to 15 individuals appearing (see Ramphastidae, "Migration"). Cracid flocks I have seen in various regions have always been composed of only one species.

Parasites and Vampire Bats

Nematodes (Spiruroidea) are common under the nictitating membrane of cracids. *Thelazia lutzi* lives in the eye of *Penelope; T. anolobatia* in the eye of *Crax fasciolata.* See also "Behavior." As nothing appears to be known about the origin of these worms, which usually have an interesting life cycle, I cite what is known of *Oxyspirura mansoni* which occurs in the conjunctival sac of the domestic chicken (Phasianidae) and which has veterinary importance as the cause of oxyspirurosis. The fertile egg of the parasite cannot develop in the eye of the host without first passing through an intermediate host, in this case a cockroach (*Pycnoscelus surinamensis*) which being occasionally eaten by chickens, infects them. The larvae abandon the insect in the crop of the bird and reach its eye through the mouth and tear ducts.

Roosting cracids are threatened by blood-sucking vampire bats, such as *Diaemus youngii* (Phyllostomidae), which also attack chickens that do not sleep in hen houses. The bat, accommodating itself under the luxurious ruffled plumage, cuts the skin of the toe, heel, or tarsus or around the cloaca (Sazima and Uieda 1980; Sazima pers. comm. 1987).

I have found clusters of ticks on the face of *Mitu mitu* (Xingu, Mato Grosso).

Hunting, Decline, and Conservation

Cracids constitute one of the most endangered groups of birds in Latin America. More than a third of the species are in danger of extinction because of forest destruction and illegal hunting. Many more species will be endangered if prompt measures are not taken.

In the Caracas symposium of 1988 (see "Distribution . . ."), the following seven Brazilian species were indicated as candidates for the *Red Data Book: Penelope jacucaca, P. ochrogaster, P. pileata* (all three insufficiently known), *Pipile jacutinga* (CITES, Ap. I), *Mitu mitu* (extinct in wild), *Crax globulosa,* and *C. blumenbachii.* Various extraordinary family members occur in the Andes and in Central America and Mexico, such as the Horned Guan, *Oreophasis derbianus,* and Helmeted Curassow, *Crax pauxi.*

Cracids are among the most important game birds, still relevant in the diet of rural Amazonians in spite of having rather dark meat. The principal attraction in hunting *Pipile*

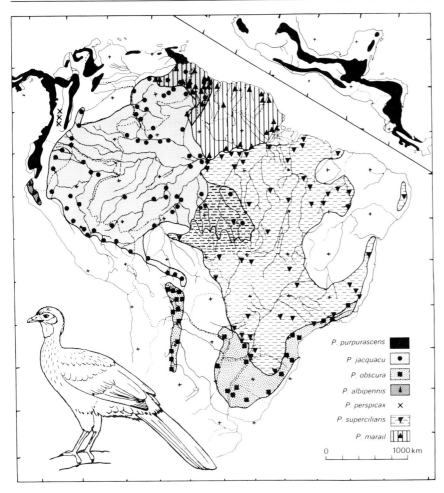

P. purpurascens

P. jacquacu

P. obscura

P. albipennis

P. perspicax

P. superciliaris

P. marail

0   1000 km

Fig. 83. Distribution of some *Penelope* guans, after Haffer 1987a. The two small, eastern species, Marail Guan and Rusty-margined Guan, *P. marail/superciliaris*, form a superspecies and are partially sympatric with one of the five large species that form another superspecies. The White-browed Guan, *P. jacucaca*, occurs in the white space in northeastern Brazil, living to some extent alongside *P. superciliaris*.

jacutinga in the southeast is to render the abundant fat it accumulates during the principal forest fruiting season (May–August).

Curassow feathers are widely used by Indians in making arrows, aprons, etc. Curassows are sought primarily for the wild-bird trade. Even non-Brazilian species appear in the cages of fanciers.

In southeastern Brazil deforestation and indiscriminate hunting have drastically reduced cracid populations, such as those of *Penelope obscura bronzina* in São Paulo. However, *P. o. obscura* is reportedly common in secondary forests in northern Argentina (Scott and Brooke 1985). *Pipile jacutinga* has become scarce throughout its range. It was the victim of colonization in northern Paraná, which became an important coffee-producing area. Photographs taken between 1930 and 1940 show hunters alongside a pyramid of these birds in the Londrina region, where the species no longer occurs. At that time *P. jacutinga* were sold in street markets in Porto Alegre, Rio Grande do Sul (Sick 1969).

The incredible abundance and tameness of *P. jacutinga* in the past can be understood from a report from Fritz Müller (see Chapter 2.4) to Charles Darwin, written in Itajaí, Santa

Catarina, on 9 September 1868: "I myself saw how half a dozen jacutingas were killed, one after the other, in the same tree. A neighbor told me that, two years ago, he had killed about 100 jacutingas in just one guarajuva tree. During the cold winter of 1866 so many jacutingas appeared in the lowlands of the Rio Itajaí that in a few weeks approximately 50,000 were killed."

Mitu mitu was one of the first birds of Brazil to be described and to become extinct in the wild. Chachalacas, not being forest birds, are the least bothered by environmental alterations.

The good reproductive potential of captive cracids should be taken advantage of to obtain individuals for repopulation programs. The migratory habits of *Pipile jacutinga* make its conservation in small areas difficult; it requires palmito groves.

Although cracids domesticate rapidly, captive breeding has rarely been attempted until recently. Although there is not now and never was an Indian village without some cracid as a mascot, there was no true domestication, even among the most developed pre-Columbian cultures. Today it is common practice to place eggs of *Penelope obscura*, or any other species, under hens (which were not available in pre-

Columbian times) for brooding. Breeding of *Ortalis* and *P. obscura* is called "very easy" (Nogueira Neto 1973), it being a question only of appropriate feed and cages. Four layings per year of *P. obscura* have been obtained with the use of brooders. Estudillo López of Mexico says cracids are disease resistant but do not tolerate cold weather. In Brazil leading cracid breeders are the Zoobotânica Mario Nardelli in Rio de Janeiro and the CRAX-Society for Wildlife Management and Breeding Research of Roberto M. A. Azeredo of Belo Horizonte.

Ortalis canicollis pantanalensis of Mato Grosso is esteemed as a sentinel and reacts to any unusual happening on the ranch, like the Southern Lapwing, *Vanellus chilensis,* of the south and the trumpeters, *Psophia,* of Amazonia. Hybridizations occur in captivity between various curassows and even between genera, such as *Crax fasciolata* x *Penelope* sp., and *Pipile pipile cumanensis* x *Ortalis canicollis.* Such mixing, which is restricted to captive environments, demonstrates the close relationships within the Cracidae. Hybridization, loved by fanciers, is profoundly undesirable from the conservationist's viewpoint, the more so because the hybrids are at least partially fertile. I know of no concrete evidence of hybridization of *Ortalis* species with domestic chickens "to obtain better fighting cocks." There is talk of hybrids with guinea fowl (Numididae), but such mixing would seem difficult. The hybrid brought forth by Ruschi and Amadon (1959) must have been a cross between a guinea fowl and a domestic chicken (Amadon 1973 pers. comm.).

SPECKLED CHACHALACA, *Ortalis guttata,* Aracuã PL 10.6

48 cm. As in other *Ortalis,* bare red throat feathered along median line so appears fully feathered on live bird. Lacks pronounced dewlap. Outer tail feathers rusty. Color similar to *O. araucuan.* VOICE: a rhythmic, penetrating song that may resemble guinea fowl, with 5 syllables, *ha-ga-GAA-gogok,* hurriedly repeated (*aracuã* is onomatopoetic). Runs in small flocks in low woodland, groves, palm groves. Upper Amazon to left bank of lower Tapajós and to upper Xingu, Mato Grosso (not shown on fig. 82). Replaced elsewhere in Brazil by 5 very similar forms that occupy separate areas:

LITTLE CHACHALACA, *Ortalis motmot*

50 cm; 500 g (male). Head chestnut. VOICE: *sha-sha-LA* (3 syllables). Lower Rio Negro (Manaus) to Venezuela, the Guianas, Amapá.

RUFOUS-HEADED CHACHALACA, *Ortalis ruficeps*

Similar to *O. motmot* but smaller. Lower Tapajós (right side) and lower Xingu as far as Araguaia.

BUFF-BROWED CHACHALACA, *Ortalis superciliaris*

42 cm. Resembles *O. guttata* but with light superciliary. Breast lacks whitish half-moon transverse spots. Belém to Piauí, northern Goiás.

WHITE-BELLIED CHACHALACA, *Ortalis araucuan*

Similar to *O. guttata* but with white instead of brown belly. VOICE: *retoko.* Pernambuco, Bahia, Minas Gerais, Espírito Santo.

SCALED CHACHALACA, *Ortalis squamata*

50 cm. Relatively large, similar to *O. araucuan* but with gray belly. Southeastern Mato Grosso, São Paulo, Paraná, Santa Catarina, Rio Grande do Sul.

CHACO CHACHALACA, *Ortalis canicollis pantanalensis*

54 cm; 600 g. Almost size of *Penelope superciliaris.* Head and neck gray. Only in southwestern Mato Grosso. VOICE: *HAra-kaka, tororo-terere,* a very loud call interpreted by local people as *Quero casar pelo natal,* "I want to marry at Christmas," or *Quero matar . . . ,* "I want to kill. . . ." Lower cries, *HAYghe, ghe, ghe, ghe,* uttered with open bill. Ventriloquial cries, given with closed bill, *wooik* (warning), *sha-ka, ka, ka* (fright, belligerence). Seldom goes to ground. Gallery and secondary forests, palm groves. Bolivia to Argentina. Also called *Arancuã, Jacu-anão.*

RUSTY-MARGINED GUAN, *Penelope superciliaris,* Jacupemba PL 10.5

55 cm; 850 g. Smallest *Penelope* and most widely distributed south of Amazon. Bare, red dewlap more prominent (triangular) in male. Shows rudimentary crest. Wings have distinctive, wide, rusty borders. Breast has whitish design. Iris red in both sexes. VOICE: a harsh *hayohh, gogo, hahaha.* Also ruffles wings (see "Instrumental Music"). Forest border, capoeira, forest groves in cerrado, caatinga, river and lake edges. Sometimes sympatric with one of large *Penelope.* South of Amazon and Madeira through central, northeastern, and southeastern Brazil to Paraguay. Also called *Jacucaca* (Rio de Janeiro). Considered a geographic replacement of Marail Guan, *P. marail.*

DUSKY-LEGGED GUAN, *Penelope obscura,* Jacuguaçu, Jacuaçu PL 10.4

73 cm; 1200 g. Sizable southern species. Dark greenish bronze with faint whitish superciliary. No rusty pattern on wing. Mantle, neck, and breast finely streaked with white. Legs blackish, unlike other guans. VOICE: a loud, harsh cry, *oaaaao;* a melodious ascending sequence, *o, o, o, o, o . . . ;* a loud cough or bark, *wow; gaaaak* (alarm). Ruffles wings *pat, pat, pat . . . ,* a loud, rough drumming interrupted in middle of sequence by a pause (see "Instrumental Music"). Tall forest. Southeastern and southern Brazil from Minas Gerais and Rio de Janeiro to Rio Grande do Sul; also Uruguay, Paraguay, Argentina, Bolivia. In mountains in Rio de Janeiro (e.g., Itatiaia, Serra dos Órgãos), where normally it is only *Penelope,* and on littoral and in Serra do Mar in São Paulo, where it has become scarce and sometimes occurs alongside *Pipile jacutinga.* It is a geographic replacement of *Penelope jacquacu* (see fig. 83).

SPIX'S GUAN, *Penelope jacquacu,* Jacu-de-Spix

Also large and dark but with light superciliary, intensely chestnut underparts. Legs reddish. VOICE: a whistle, *PEEoo,* which if imitated by a hunter attracts the bird; also a long descending note with bill closed (alarm). Ruffles wings like *P. obscura.* Upper Amazon to Rio Tapajós (Mato Grosso), Bolivia, Colombia, left bank of Rio Negro, Guyana. Zoologist J. B. von Spix, traveling companion of C.F.P. von Martius, named it *jacúaçu,* correctly taking name given the species by indigenes, with *jacquacu* later being adopted by scientists based on a spelling error in Spix's text, which happened because of European ignorance of indigenous languages then. Considered a geographic replacement of *P. obscura* but has different tracheal morphology.

MARAIL GUAN, *Penelope marail*

Medium sized, plumage with clearly visible green reflections. Short tarsus is an adaptation to arboreal life. North of lower Amazon from Amapá to Itacoatiara (Amazonas), the Orinoco. See *P. superciliaris.*

WHITE-BROWED GUAN, *Penelope jacucaca,* Jacucaca   BR

73 cm. Large, dark, cinnamon colored, with white streaks, black crest. Wide white superciliaries meet on forehead. Caatinga. Quite terrestrial. Only in northeast: Piauí, Ceará, Paraíba, Bahia. Together with *P. ochrogaster* and *P. pileata* forms a superspecies.

CHESTNUT-BELLIED GUAN, *Penelope ochrogaster,* Jacu-de-barriga-castanha   BR

77 cm. Very large with reddish brown crest. Whitish superciliary contrasts with black eyebrow which extends in a streak around auricular region and throat. *P. jacutinga* and *P. pileata* also have this feature. Abdomen bright chestnut. Forest interspersed with savanna. Only in middle of central Brazil, from western Minas Gerais and Goiás to eastern Mato Grosso (Rio das Mortes, Poconé).

WHITE-CRESTED GUAN, *Penelope pileata,* Jacu-de-cocoruto-branco   BR

Large; unmistakable with white, loose crest and heavy chestnut neck and underparts. Green mantle. Restricted to southern margin of Amazon, from lower Madeira to Xingu (Gorotire and Altamira) as far as eastern Pará (Ourém), Ma-

ranhão (Rio Grajaú), Tocantins (Rio Caiapó, Alvarenga pers. comm. 1989).

BLACK-FRONTED PIPING-GUAN, *Pipile jacutinga,* Jacutinga   EN   PL 10.7   Fig. 84

74 cm; 1.1–1.4 kg. Typical of southeast, white and shiny black. Crown feathers quite elongated, face feathered black. Base of bill shiny whitish blue, area around eye bare and plaster white. Wide, sparsely feathered dewlap red posteriorly but forepart lilac above, bright blue below. Male more robust with brighter bill and dewlap, latter larger and more rounded. "Typical" dewlap found only in breeding season; later shrinks and fades. VOICE: a long, high, descending *i-eww,* reminiscent of Sharpbill, *Oxyruncus cristatus* (Cotingidae). See "Instrumental Music." Tall forest abundant in palmito (*Euterpe edulis*), whose fruits are favorite food of *P. jacutinga.* Makes altitudinal migrations in Serra do Mar (São Paulo), following fruiting of this palm, in which ripening occurs earlier at lower levels. Periodicity of its appearances has been observed in Paraná and Rio Grande do Sul (see "Movement . . .").

Distribution and Decline: Formerly nested at all altitudes in Serra do Mar region, in rough, thickly forested country with scattered rocks, and still occurs there, but in greatly reduced numbers. Was common in area of present Serra do Órgãos National Park (Rio de Janeiro) in early 1900s (1915–17, R. Vieira). North of Rio Doce (Espírito Santo) was regular in magnificent forests of hot lowlands, alongside local *Crax blumenbachii* (pers. obs. 1939). Existed in Sooretama Reserve (Espírito Santo) until 1953 and is probably still there but rare. I also found it in southern Bahia (Monte Pascoal National Park 1977). In 1940s it occurred in mountainous regions of Espírito Santo (at about 1000 m). It has disappeared from most of places where it was common, including valleys of great rivers of São Paulo and Paraná, where it could be found in any woodland (see Hunting . . ."). Occurs sporadically near Foz do Iguaçu (Paraná 1977, 1979), São Paulo (Ilha de São Sebastião and Carlos Botelho State Park 1987), Itatiaia (Rio de Janeiro 1978), Santa Catarina (1979). Originally occurred from southern Bahia to Rio Grande do Sul, Paraguay, northern Argentina. Along Rio Paraná its range borders that of *P. pipile grayi.*

In rest of South America this side of Andes it is replaced by a group of closely related forms that replace each other geographically, all being grouped in *P. pipile,* whose typical form, *P. p. pipile,* is found only in Trinidad, off Venezuelan

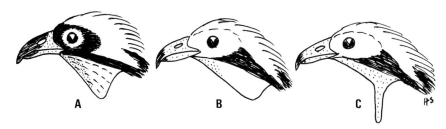

Fig. 84. Three Brazilian forms of *Pipile:* (A) Black-fronted Piping-Guan, *Pipile jacutinga* (Espírito Santo); (B) Blue-throated, or Natterer's, Piping-Guan, *P. pipile nattereri* (upper Xingu, Mato Grosso); and (3) Blue-throated, or Gray's Piping-Guan, *P. pipile grayi* (Pantanal, Mato Grosso). Original, H. Sick.

coast. These forms differ in color of bare face and shape of dewlap, as well as in extent of white in wings, form of crest feathers, and sheen on black portions of plumage.

BLUE-THROATED PIPING-GUAN, *Pipile pipile nattereri*, Cujubi Fig. 84

74 cm; 1.1–1.3 kg. Common over a vast area extending from upper Araguaia and Rio das Almas (Goiás) to upper Xingu (Mato Grosso), upper Guaporé and upper Paraguay (Rondônia), Madeira, Purus (Amazonas), Tapajós (Pará). Unlike *P. jacutinga* has completely bare, white face. Dewlap triangular and larger in male, similar to that of *jacutinga* in color but without any feathering. Forepart blue (no lilac), the rest red. VOICE: various whistles, *wit* (call), *kooeeeoo, bak-bak* (warning), an ascending sequence of various *ooeees* similar to song of Scale-backed Antbird, *Hylophylax poecilinota* of Amazonia. Rips wings (see "Instrumental Music"). Gregarious, in flocks of up to 30 or more. Riverine forests.

Replaced on southern bank of Amazon by *P. p. cujubi*, identified by smaller area of white in wing and crest. The Madeira, lower Tapajós, and lower Xingu to eastern Pará. Also called *Jacubim, Jacutinga.*

In Mato Grosso Pantanal replaced by *P. p. grayi* (fig. 84), well characterized by pure white, thread-shaped wattle hanging from a dewlap without any red whatsoever. Reaches Rio Piquiri (Mato Grosso) region, area of *P. p. nattereri;* apparently sometimes gets into valley of Rio Ivaí (Paraná), within range of *P. jacutinga.* Also Paraguay, Bolivia, southern Peru.

P. p. cumanensis found in northwest and extreme north. It has wide, triangular, all-black dewlap (not blue, as shown in Delacour and Amadon 1973). Upper Rio Negro and Solimões to Peru, Colombia, the Guianas.

BARE-FACED CURASSOW, *Crax fasciolata*, Mutum-de-penacho PL 10.3

83 cm; 2.7 kg (female)–2.8 kg (male). Widely distributed inland species, generally best-known curassow, found in most zoological gardens. Male black with white abdomen (typical of all *Crax*) and broadly white-tipped tail, by which it differs from all other Brazilian *Crax* (see variations, "Morphology"). Bill and cere sulfur yellow. This is only curassow with bare skin (black) around eye. Legs blackish. Female richly barred with white, base of mandible yellowish, legs reddish. Young male has yellow on bare skin below eye.

Some color differences can be seen in Amazonian form, *C. f. pinima* (BR, R). Base of male's maxilla more swollen and reddish, crest denser, white tip of tail feathers more extensive, tarsi purplish. Female has less apparent, finer white barring than typical form described above; topknot black with white spots (not the opposite, as in *C. f. fasciolata.*)

VOICE: a high whistle, *PSEEEEew,* with timbre of Long-tailed Tyrant, *Colonia colonus* (irritation); barks a *koa,*

Fig. 85. Wattled Curassow, *Crax globulosa.*

wayoo, oo-OO (fright, warning); a loud whisper, given after *waayoo* (frightened on perch at night). See "Vocalization" re song. Riverine forests, woodland edges; in mornings and evenings wanders along local beaches. South of Amazon from Tapajós to Maranhão, across central Brazil to western São Paulo, Paraná, Minas Gerais; also Paraguay, Argentina, Bolivia. In Maranhão and eastern Pará *pinima* race still occurs in reasonable numbers in forests of Rio Pindaré (Maranhão 1977, pers. obs.) alongside *Mitu tuberosa.* Also in Ourém (eastern Pará 1978). Found in fanciers' collections in Pará and Rio de Janeiro (1977, 1978). In southeastern Pará name *mutum-pinima* is applied to females of *C. fasciolata. Pinima* = "full of speckles."

WATTLED CURASSOW, *Crax globulosa*, Mutum-fava Fig. 85

82 cm. Western Amazonia. Male characterized by highly developed globular red caruncle on base of maxillar culmen and 2 lobes of same color on base of mandible. Legs gray. Female, with "normal" red bill, has rusty under tail coverts and abdomen (not white like male). Some females have barred wings, very similar to *C. blumenbachii.* Sometimes a little white appears in female's crest. VOICE: a loud cough ending with a descending whistle similar to that of other curassows; a long, descending, soft trill, *oo, oo, oo . . . ,* that could pass for a Passerine voice (warning voice), a vocalization very different from *blumenbachii* and other curassows I know. I have never heard this curassow boom (see "Vocalization"). Upper Amazon from Rio Solimões to Manaus (Amazonas), Rios Madeira and Guapore. Also Bolivia, Colombia. Also called *Mutum-açu.* See *C. blumenbachii,* which can be quite similar. They appear to be geographical replacements.

RED-BILLED CURASSOW, *Crax blumenbachii*, Mutum-do-sudeste BR EN

84 cm; 3.5 kg. Restricted to southeastern Brazil. Male similar to male *C. globulosa,* also without white at tip of tail. Base of bill red. Vestiges of a maxillar caruncle may appear

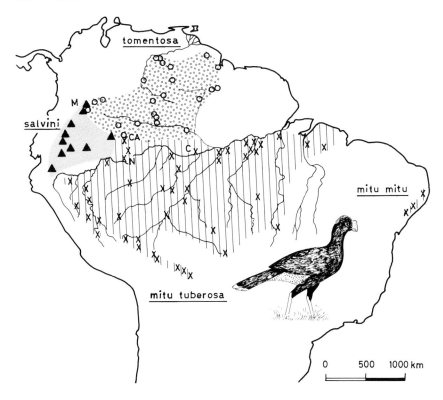

Fig. 86. Distribution of the Razor-billed Curassow and allies, *Mitu mitu* superspecies (after Haffer 1985). Explanation: Crosses and vertical hatching—*M. mitu* (male illustrated); closed triangles and shading—*M. salvini;* open circles and dots—*M. tomentosa.* Symbols denote locality records. C = Codajás, Brazil; N = Puerto Narino; CA = Caquetá region; M = Macarena region, Colombia.

during breeding but it never reaches great size of *globulosa.* In breeding season males show trace of a pair of lobes at base of mandible and sometimes small red caruncles below eyes. Abdomen white, legs black. Sometimes difficult to distinguish well-developed *blumenbachii* males from slightly developed *globulosa* males; females can also be quite similar, since that of *globulosa* sometimes also has barred wings. Female *blumenbachii* has thighs and wings densely vermiculated with rusty, large topknot richly barred with white. Abdomen rusty; bill gray with black base, legs red. Immature's crest larger (see "Morphology"); at 4 months it is still smaller than its mother's but is same color. Adult male iris chestnut, female's orange-red. VOICE: re song, see "Vocalization"; a low *woop* while quietly foraging on ground, changing to *eeee-oooo* when disturbed by something; cackles in fighting or when frightened; takes off in flight from ground with an *irk-irk-irk;* also other vocalizations. Tall primary forest in hot, humid regions. Originally from Bahia to Minas Gerais and Rio de Janeiro (e.g., Paraíba do Sul valley), its former presence attested by names of various villages or geographic features (Rio Mutum, Mutum Creek, Vargem do Mutum) in northeastern Rio de Janeiro. Presently restricted to an extremely small number of areas in southern Bahia (including Monte Pascoal National Park, 1977) and northern Espírito Santo (Sooretama Reserve) and to reserve of Cia. Vale do Rio Doce, where there is a good wild population. At CRAX-Society breeding facility (see "Hunting . . .") there is (1989) a healthy population of *blumenbachii,* a valuable source for reintroducing the species into forested areas of southeastern Brazil.

BLACK CURASSOW, *Crax alector,* Mutumporanga

3.2–3.6 kg. Replaces *C. globulosa* in most of area north of Amazon (east of Rio Negro). Male's plumage similar to that of *globulosa,* lacking white tail tip. Bill without caruncles, base slightly swollen and yellow, tending toward orange or red in most western form, *C. a. erythrogenis.* Plumage black with violaceous, not greenish, sheen. Most notable feature of species, topknot feathers, curlier than those of *C. fasciolata.* Tarsi greenish horn, toes gray. Female almost identical to male, showing vestiges of white in black feathers of crest. Amapá to Rio Negro, Colombia, Venezuela, the Guianas.

AMAZONIAN RAZOR-BILLED CURASSOW, *Mitu tuberosa,* Mutum-cavalo   PL 10.1

89 cm; up to 3.8 kg. Common in forests of southern Amazonia. Largest Brazilian curassow. Topknot feathers smooth and flat, lacking curliness of *Crax.* Culmen elevated, forming a high hump, with base of red bill much swollen. Abdomen chestnut in both sexes, there being no sexual dimorphism in color. Male somewhat larger. Lateral tail feathers have distinct white tip, fully visible in 2-month-old individuals. VOICE: *ooAH* coughed, *kuwik* (warning); song low, ventriloquial, with timbre identical to *Crax* and *Nothocrax* and a 3-part *HM-hm-hm HM-hm-hm HOO* characterized primarily by strongly accented final note. South of Amazon from western Maranhão to Mato Grosso (Guaporé, Tapajós, Xingu), eastern Peru; also Bolivia (fig. 86). Also called *Mutum-de-várzea, Mutum-piri, Mutum-etê.*

Fig. 87. Razor-billed Curassow, *Mitu mitu,* the head showing the bare auricular area and unswollen culmen. The base of the bill is pink, the front half whitish. This is the first female in the collection of P. Nardelli, obtained and studied in 1976. After Sick 1980, illustration altered.

RAZOR-BILLED CURASSOW, *Mitu mitu,*
Mutum-do-nordeste   BR   EN   Fig. 87

Extinct in wild. Smaller than *M. tuberosa.* Replaced it in residual forests of northeast. Bill moderate sized, not swollen, anterior half whitish; area around ear bare; tail all black or with outer tail feathers showing slender, whitish brown tip. Mentioned in 1st significant scientific work on Brazilian fauna (Marcgrave 1648) as originating in Pernambuco. Its existence was well documented through a good, unpublished, contemporaneous watercolor (see Chapter 2.2). True existence of this form was questioned for a long time until its 1951 rediscovery by Olivério Pinto in Alagoas. Survived in that state until recently. The only individuals in captivity were obtained by Pedro Nardelli in Alagoas since 1976 and are in the Mario Nardelli Zoobotanical Collection in Nilópolis, Rio de Janeiro. The species' survival can only be assured by captive breeding. Also called *Mitu, Mutu* (Marcgrave, Pernambuco). *M. mitu* can be considered a superspecies that includes *M. tuberosa* as an allospecies.

LESSER RAZOR-BILLED CURRASOW, *Mitu tomentosa,*
Mutum-do-norte

84 cm. Replaces *M. tuberosa* north of Amazon. Lacks crest and any swelling on red bill. Tail has wide chestnut terminal band, abdomen chestnut. Gallery forests. Upper Rio Negro and Rio Branco to Guyana, Venezuela, Colombia.

NOCTURNAL CURASSOW, *Nothocrax urumutum,*
Urumutum   PL 10.2

58 cm. Small, size of a large domestic hen. Crown feathers lie flat but can be raised into a high crest. Resembles a guan in color but in manner and voice is a typical curassow. Only distinctive mark is bare area around eye: a brilliant, almost phosphorescent, yellow curved strip. Sexes similar but female lacks any modification of trachea. VOICE: song (see "Vocalization") more melodious than *Crax* or *Mitu,* ending

in a descending moan with timbre of a large pigeon, given when bird is already roosting in total darkness. I have noted longest sequence of phrases early at night (8:00–10:00 P.M.), with fewest before dawn (2:00–3:00 A.M.). Behavior similar to other curassows. Right bank of Madeira to Purus and Peru, upper Rio Negro to Venezuela, Colombia. Also called *Mutum-bastardo, Falso-mutum.*

Cracidae Bibliography
See also General Bibliography

Caziani, S. M., and J. J. Protomastro. 1988. The fruit availability and consumption by *Ortalis canicollis* in the Argentine Chaco. II Symp. Int. Cracidae, Caracas.

Coimbra Filho, A. F. 1970. Sobre *Mitu mitu* (L., 1766) e a validez das suas duas raças geográficas. *Rev. Bras. Biol.* 30(1):101–09.

Davis, L. J. 1965. Acoustic evidence of relationships in *Ortalis. Southwest Nat.* 10:288–301.

Delacour, J., and D. Amadon. 1973. *Curassows and Related Birds.* New York: Am. Mus. Nat. Hist.

Eley, J. W. 1982. *Wilson Bull.* 94:241–58. [*Penelope,* systematics]

Estudillo López, J. 1977. *World Pheasant Assoc. Journ.* 2. [*Nothocrax*]

Ihering, H. v., 1885. *Ges. Orn.* 97–184. *Pipile jacutinga,* migration]

Krieg, H., and E. Schuhmacher. 1936. See Tinamidae Bibliography.

Lapham, H. 1970. A study of the nesting behavior of *Ortalis ruficauda* in Venezuela. *Bol. Soc. Venez.* 28:291–329.

Oliveira, R. G. 1982. O Jacutinga, *Pipile jacutinga,* no Rio Grande do Sul. *An. Soc. Sul-Riogr. Orn.* 3:16–19.

Pinto, O.M.O. 1938. Sobre as jacutingas de Mato Grosso, con referência especial à validez de *Pipile cumanensis grayi. Bol. Biol. Nov. Sér.* 3, 2.

Pinto, O.M.O. 1952. *Pap. Avuls. Zool. S. Paulo* 10:325–34. [*Mitu,* rediscovery]

Rodrigues, H. O., et al. 1970. *Atas Soc. Biol. Rio de Janeiro.* 13:5–6. [Nematodes]

Ruschi, A., and D. Amadon. 1959. A supposed hybrid between the families Numidae and Cracidae. Proc. First Pan-African Orn. Congr. *Ostrich, Suppl.* 3:440–42.

Sazima, J., and W. Uieda. 1980. Feeding behavior of the White-winged Vampire Bat, *Diaemus youngii,* on poultry. *J. Mamm.* 61:102–4.

Scheres, G. 1985. Hokkozucht in Volieren auch in Westeuropa. *Geflügel-Börse* 17:11–12.

Sick, H. 1964. Curassow. In A. L. Thomson, ed., *A New Dictionary of Birds.* New York: McGraw-Hill.

Sick, H. 1965. *Pap. Avuls. Zool. S. Paulo* 17:9–16. [*Penelope,* distribution]

Sick, H. 1970. *Condor* 72(1):106–8. [Feeding]

Sick, H. 1979. *Bull. B.O.C.* 99(4):115–20. [*Crax fasciolata pinima,* occurrence]

Sick, H. 1980. *Condor* 82:227–28. [*Mitu m. mitu,* morphological characteristics]

Teixeira, D. M., and H. Sick. 1981. *Bol. Mus. Nac. Rio de Janeiro, Zool.* 299. [*Crax blumenbachii, C. globulosa,* morphology, chicks]

Teixeira, D. M., and H. Sick. 1986. Plumage variation and plumage aberration in Cracidae. *Rev. Bras. Biol.* 46:777–79.

Vaurie, C. 1968. *Bull. Am. Mus. Nat. Hist.* 138, 4. [Taxonomy]

Vuilleumier, F. 1965. *Bull. Mus. Comp. Zool. Harvard* 134(1). [Evolution]

Wagner, H. O. 1953. Die Hokkohühner der Sierra Madre de Chiapas/Mexico. *Veröff. Museum Bremen* A,2,2:105–28.

Wagner, H. O. 1960. *Z. Tierpsychol.* 17(3):364–75. [Domestication]

FAMILY PHASIANIDAE: WOOD-QUAIL AND ALLIES (4)

This group of Galliformes, the most important in the Old World, is sparsely represented on this continent. However, there are fossils of the Tertiary Oligocene (30 million years B.P.) from Canada and of the Pleistocene (22,000 years B.P.) from Brazil. Members include the Domestic Fowl, *Gallus gallus domesticus* (see appendix), the Peafowl, *Pavo cristatus,* and the pheasants, which gave their name to the family. These were brought to Brazil by early colonists, the Portuguese bringing the domestic chicken and guineafowl from Europe and Africa, respectively. For practical purposes, these birds are replaced in South America by the Cracidae and Tinamidae.

Brazilian Species

Native Brazilian species all belong to the genera *Odontophorus* and *Colinus* of the subfamily Odontophorinae. They are small, terrestrial birds having high, hard bills with serrated edges on the mandible, short, sturdy legs, and strong toes. The tail is well developed but much shorter than in the Cracidae. The head has a crest that does not flatten, unlike the tinamous, the only local birds that resemble them.

Pairs duet (*Odontophorus*). They readily scratch the earth (something tinamids do not do), eating small arthropods, mollusks, berries, and seeds. They are valued game birds and are easily caught in traps.

The Crested Bobwhite, *Colinus cristatus,* is a northern savanna bird that recently immigrated from North America. Its dispersal was delayed by the Hylaea, and it apparently only reached the Amazon (Amapá) in our times.

The *Odontophorus* wood-quails (various similar species) are well known throughout Brazil and resemble the Hazel Grouse, *Bonasa bonasia,* of Europe. They are broadly distributed through forested regions of the subtropical and tropical zones of the New World, from Central America to Paraguay.

CRESTED BOBWHITE, *Colinus cristatus,*
Uru-do-campo   Fig. 88

21 cm. Small, open-country gallinacean of northernmost South America. Brown with neck and underparts spotted white, black, and ferruginous. Crest straw-colored in male, dark brown in female. VOICE: song, given in breeding season (September forward), consists of a strident bi- or trisyllabic phrase, *ew-ew-kooWYT;* sometimes pair duets, with male frequently perched on higher spot (mound of earth, etc.). Voice similar to its close relative, Bobwhite, *C. virginianus,* of U.S. Terrestrial, lives in flocks of 3–6. When "grazing," feeds on small seeds (e.g., "stick-tights") and insects (e.g., ants). If pursued, flock disperses, preferably by running, to reunite again soon, members cheeping like domestic chicks.

In flight male distinguished by more erect posture. Sleeps on ground under bent-over grass. Replaces southern tinamous (e.g., Spotted Nothura, *Nothura maculosa,* and Redwinged Tinamou, *Rhynchotus rufescens*) in savanna regions north of Amazon, a faunal barrier that impedes advance of quail southward and of tinamous northward. Crosses roads, invades cleared land and plantings, approaches homes where it finds food remnants, becoming truly synanthropic. Central America to the Guianas, Venezuela, Brazil along Braço

Fig. 88. Crested Bobwhite, *Colinus cristatus sonnini,* male singing.

Norte (Amapá) to north bank of Amazon and Roraima. Syntopic with terrestrial icterine Eastern Meadowlark, *Sturnella magna,* another immigrant from north. At edge of capoeira meets Little Chachalaca, *Ortalis motmot.* Also called *Perdiz, Uru.*

SPOT-WINGED WOOD-QUAIL, *Odontophorus capueira,* Uru, Capoeira   PL 10.8

24 cm. Common, small, crested, forest gallinacean. Sexes similar, male somewhat stockier. Immature has reddish bill, underparts spotted whitish, not all gray as in adult. VOICE: song a vigorous, sonorous sequence of bisyllabic notes, *ooROO-ooROO-ooROO,* that may be prolonged for some minutes, slightly undulating and sometimes so slow it almost seems to stop. Given on roost before sleep in breeding season and especially at dawn and dusk and on moonlit nights. Pairs duet. I observed that male starts singing and female soon joins him, singing a similar counterpoint of monosyllabic notes, *kloh-kloh-kloh,* clearly perceived when female occasionally sings alone. Rest of flock does not interfere with singing pair, but as soon as it stops, another pair starts. Also other vocalizations, especially some weak, tremulous notes, *bew, bew, bew . . . ,* given before roosting for sleep, that resemble peeping of chicks and serve to maintain contact with members wandering over ground. Also louder whistles, for alarm *wit, wit, wit . . . .*

Behavior, Feeding, and Tameness: Walks in flocks on floor of shady forests and capoeira, a flock perhaps comprising some pairs or families (parents and grown young from last nesting). Such groups, which defend their territories from other neighbors, remain united even when a female is brooding. Avoids flight, preferring to flee by running. Depending on circumstances, may lie on ground to hide. When perched very close to one another, individuals warm each other and do mutual preening. Has a special predilection for succulent berries of pokeweed (*Phytolacca decandra*). In 1800s it was possible to catch wood-quail with a snare (F. Müller 1863). In Itatiaia, while picking at fallen araucaria nuts on forest floor, flocks always returned after being frightened (Luis P. Gonzaga).

Breeding: Apparently breeds monogamously, according to field and captive observations, from August to November. Nests on ground, sometimes in a hole (e.g., of an armadillo), but always by building a shelter of dry leaves with a side entrance and solid roof. Eggs white but rapidly become yellowish or even reddish from dirt. Apparently more than 1 female occasionally lays eggs in same nest, for clutches of more than 12 have been found. Reported incubation for *O. gujanensis* in Costa Rica is 26 days, only 18–19 days for *capueira.* Only female broods and takes charge of young, whose color is generally blackish but difficult to describe. Young nidifugous, hide in cavities or even holes in ground.

Ceará to Rio Grande do Sul, southeastern Mato Grosso, Paraguay, Argentina (Misiones). *Uru,* onomatopoeic name, means "bird" in Guarani and more specifically "small gallinacean." Replaced in Amazonia by various closely related species, 2 of which occur in Brazil.

MARBLED WOOD-QUAIL, *Odontophorus gujanensis*

Underparts reddish brown, eye region bare and orange (not red, as in *O. capueira*). VOICE: similar to *capueira* but less hurried and lower. I noted song of male in northern Mato Grosso as a trisyllabic *GOO-guru, GOO-guru, . . . ,* onomatopoeically symbolized in name given it by local residents *Corcovado,* "hunchback." Counterpoint of female is *ko, ko, ko. . . . Pará, Mato Grosso, Anapá.* Also called *Uru-i* (Kaiabi, Mato Grosso).

STARRED WOOD-QUAIL, *Odontophorus stellatus*

Underparts chestnut. Amazonas.

Phasianidae Appendix

DOMESTIC FOWL, *Gallus gallus domesticus,* Galinha-doméstica

The "chickens" cited by chroniclers from first half of sixteenth century forward as being found in indigenous villages could only have been Cracidae, since domestic fowl reached these people later. The domestic fowl was not well dispersed in central Brazil even in 1947, for Indians who knew it from expeditions of the Central Brazil Foundation appreciated it more for the rooster's crow than for the eggs or meat—an interesting parallel with the enthusiasm of the Japanese for the cry of the domestic quail (see *Coturnix japonica*). Léry (republished 1961) reported that the Tupinambás of the Rio de Janeiro region raised chickens they had obtained from the Portuguese more for the white feathers than for the meat. There was no need for domestic animals, for game was abundant and easy to get.

The domestic fowl, brought by Cabral's men on the first authentic disembarkation of Europeans on 22 April 1500 in Bahia, is a descendent of the Red Junglefowl, *G. gallus,* from Sumatra.

A domestic fowl variety called Araucana Fowl, Chilean Hen, Creole Chicken, or Pre-Hispanic Chicken (*G. inaurus* or *G. castelloi*) is erroneously assumed to be a hybrid of *G. gallus domesticus* and *Tinamus solitarius.* The araucana lacks a tail ("anurous," having the occygeal vertebrae or pygostyle absent) but has some feather tufts on the head and green legs; it lays light blue, turquoise blue, or greenish blue eggs and is noted for its combative disposition. It is generally considered a creation of the Araucana Indians of Chile, but everything leads to the conclusion that it was introduced there from islands in the Pacific.

JAPANESE QUAIL, *Coturnix japonica,*
Codorna doméstica

18.5 cm. Also called *codorna caseira,* "house quail," or *codorniz.* Size of a small Spotted Nothura, *Nothura maculosa,* with short (0.8 cm), sturdy bill. In recent years has been used as a regular egg factory, as it was long ago in Orient, from where it was imported. It was reared 600 years ago in Japan for voice of male. Starts laying at 38 days of age and lays intensely for 18 months, often producing more than 300 eggs per year. Eggs are speckled, unlike those of our "quail" of the *Nothura* genus. It is used experimentally in tests for insecticide toxicity.

This quail does not occur in the wild in Brazil. Attempts to introduce it as a new game bird in Minas Gerais were destined to failure because, due to domestication, its wings have atrophied and its incubation instinct has weakened. Probably predation by hawks and small carnivores also contributed to its extinction. Introduction of crosses between *C. japonica* and European Quail, *C. coturnix coturnix,* which is larger, takes off faster when flying, and has unaltered maternal instincts, has been considered. In my view, however, this would not be advisable, for prejudicial competition with our native "quail" could arise.

OTHER EXOTIC PHASIANIDAE

Considering the decline of native game birds in regions with intensive agriculture and livestock raising, it would be reasonable to consider introducing the Ring-necked Pheasant, *Phasianus colchicus torquatus,* an Asian native that has long been well established in Europe and North America as a game bird. It could be reared on farms and then liberated, as has been done in various South American countries. I have the impression its introduction would not be prejudicial to native birds. Attempts to do this in Santa Catarina failed because of predation by carnivores such as opossums and rats, as has occurred in other South American countries. However there has been success on islands, such as off the coast of Chile. A recent undertaking to rear pheasants for game was started in São Paulo (Maia 1986).

To me it appears inadvisable to introduce *Colinus virginianus,* which could easily compete with *C. cristatus* and with tinamids. Apparently the California Quail, *Callipepla californica,* now established in Chile and Argentina, has not yet been introduced into Brazil.

Phasianidae Bibliography

See also General Bibliography

Maia, J.L.S. 1986. Faisões (*Phasianus* spp.) criados com finalidades cinegéticas. *XIII Cong. Bras. Zool., Cuiabá:* Comun. 567.
Skutch, A. F. 1947. *Condor* 49:217–32. [*Odontophorus,* behavior]
Wilhelm, O. 1963. *Rev. Chil. Hist. Nat.* 55:93–107. [Araucana chicken]

FAMILY NUMIDIDAE: GUINEAFOWL

HELMETED GUINEAFOWL, *Numida meleagris,*
Galinha-d'angola

This African savanna gallinacean has been introduced and domesticated in many countries with hot or mild climates. *N. m. galeata* was brought to Brazil from Cape Verde Islands off west coast of Africa by Portuguese at start of colonization, as shown by *Bestiary* of Zacharias Wagener of Dutch period, 1637–1644. Marcgrave (1648) also mentioned Crested Guineafowl, *Guttera pucherani,* of West Africa. *N. meleagris* is characterized by vividly colored bare head topped by a casque, wattles at base of mandible, and gray plumage speckled white. Sexes similar, but adult male has larger casque and wattles, although these are dependent on age. VOICE: a loud *TOH-fraca, TOH-fraca,* uttered only by female. Male has another loud vocalization, different and little known to anyone, given while perched on a high point.

Lives in flocks. Eggs small and pointed, brownish with a very hard shell. Clutches may be large, 20 or more, and even up to 100 eggs have been reported when many females lay together.

Although it prefers to move away from buildings to nest in forest, it usually is unable to hide from backwoods people who seek its eggs, thereby preventing its return to wild state. If it escapes it falls victim to carnivores.

Introduced in 1960 on Ilha Trindade, its existence there is facilitated by an absence of predators such as fox and by presence of domestic pigs (Becker 1965 pers. comm.) which apparently eliminated rats that had been introduced earlier. I have removed *N. meleagris* from the list of Brazilian birds. Also called *Galinhola, Conquém, Galinha-d'Africa, Galinha-da-India, Galinha-da-Numídia, Galinha-da-Guiné, Angolinha, Capote, Cocar, Picota, Pintade;* in Bahia name *Sacuê* is derived from an African dialect. Breeders obtain varieties such as "harlequins," "whites," etc. Other species of family, e.g., Vulturine Guineafowl, *Acryllium vulturinum,* are kept in amateur breeders' aviaries.

Numididae Bibliography

See General Bibliography

ORDER OPISTHOCOMIFORMES

FAMILY OPISTHOCOMIDAE: HOATZIN (1)

This family consists of one species that is restricted to arboreal vegetation in flooded Amazonian terrain. It is the most notable product of bird evolution in the world's greatest river systems, the Amazon and Orinoco, which are poor in endemic aquatic and marsh birds. A Tertiary fossil, *Hoazinoides magdalenae,* has been found in Colombia (from the Miocene, 18 million years B.P.), which suggests affinities with the Cracidae (Miller 1953).

The claws on the wings of the young, very probably a secondary adaptation, recall the classic existence of such claws on Jurassic birds (*Archaeopteryx,* see Chapter 5.2). It is quite probable that *Archaeopteryx,* provided with three powerful hooks, had a similar technique of wing support for crawling over forest branches and to avoid having the head and body hang down in front. We know almost nothing, however, about the habitat of *Archaeopteryx.* Certainly it had highly developed feathers, very similar to those of modern birds, proving that it was capable of flying well.

The Hoatzin has usually been included among the Galliformes, near the Cracidae, which seems reasonable to me, taking into account the impression created by the live bird.

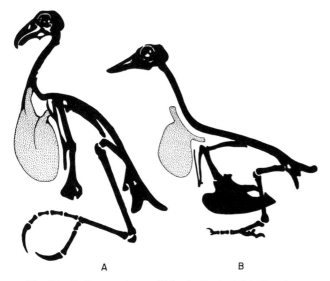

Fig. 89. Skeleton and crop (light shading) of (A) Hoatzin, *Opisthocomus hoazin,* compared with (B) Domestic Pigeon, *Columba livia domestica.* The Hoatzin's voluminous crop extends into the thorax, profoundly altering the latter's organization. After Böker 1937.

More research is needed. Immunological analyses suggest affinity with the Galliformes. The microscopic structure of the feathers (similar to the Cracidae) supports this. Characters reminiscent of the Cariamidae have been suggested. Electrophoretic analyses, showing that egg-white proteins of the Hoatzin are essentially different from those of the Galliformes but fit well within the ani (Crotophaginae, Cuculidae) pattern, have not been confirmed. Being very familiar with the Hoatzin in the field, I never thought of a similarity between *Opisthocomus hoazin* and the Guira Cuckoo, *Guira guira,* a theory advocated by discoverers of the supposed biochemical affinity between the two families.

The Opisthocomidae must have gone through a long, independent evolution. On the one hand they kept part of their primitive ancestral organization, but on the other they evolved new specialized characters. Thus, it has been difficult to understand their phylogenetics, and the Hoatzin's descent remains an enigma. It being such a peculiarly organized bird, it appears prudent to place it in its own order, as Stresemann (1934) and Stegmann (1978) did, without pushing one tendency or the other.

Morphology

Among the Hoatzin's most notable anatomical characters is the extrathoracic double crop (fig. 89) (there are also two intrathoracic crops) which restricts the furcula and anterior portion of the keel of the sternum, displacing the flight musculature. This system of crops, 50 times larger than the stomach, permits digestion of the hard, caustic foliage of aroids, etc., of the Hoatzin's amphibious world and makes up 13% of the bird's total weight, a unique fact in the Class Aves. Another peculiar feature is the structure of the fossa nasalis, which diverges as much from that of the Galliformes as it does from the Cuculiformes (Bang 1971). The wing claws give the young an archaic appearance.

HOATZIN, *Opisthocomus hoazin,* Cigana   PL 10.9

62 cm; 816 g (male). Unmistakable, resembling a strange guan decorated with a high, rigid, permanently erect crest. Region around eye shiny blue, contrasting with bright colors of plumage (*cigana* = "gypsy" = dressed in extravagant clothing). Eyelashes prominent. Bill high and short. Small

body, when seen from the side, is hidden by broad wings which bird holds loosely and drooping, giving impression of a bulky bird. Black tail long and wide, has a broad, cream-colored terminal band that contrasts sharply when seen on underside as tail hangs vertically. Sexes similar but female has shorter crest. VOICE: a low, hoarse series of *gaah-gaah-gaah*s . . . uttered periodically in chorus for several minutes and sometimes 1 or more prolonged *shehh*s, resulting in a great racket. When neighboring flocks sing at same time, these phrases, which constitute song, resemble mutter of Greater Ani, *Crotophaga major,* which occurs in same places and whose loud croak (warning) is similar to other cries of Hoatzin. In defending its nest, hisses like a snake. Also other vocalizations.

Habitat, Behavior, Feeding, and Aninga Patches: Inhabits *aningais,* patches of aninga (*Montrichardia* spp., Araceae), aquatic plant formations, mangroves, and other flooded forests of Amazonia, living in pairs that make up small flocks. Perches on any sort of branch, slender, thick, or sloping, and tries to grasp various small twigs at same time with toes, as cracids do but without their sure grasp. Sits with breast against branch, lying on a callous formed at free end of sternum (sternal perching) which functions as a "skid." When frightened or trying to intimidate enemies, raises its wings high and opens them, producing a whirring with the hard, rough feathers and displaying bright chestnut flight feathers which contrast with large black spot surrounded by white which simulates an over-sized eye on underside of secondaries. This is repeated at short intervals and is somewhat reminiscent of uneasiness of trumpeters (Psophiidae). Moves clumsily through branches, breaking feathers in its efforts to grasp them with open wings. Feet, although large, frequently falter, and it sometimes falls into water. Flight heavy and noisy.

In spite of its phlegmatic disposition, active around the clock. Rests during day, especially in hottest hours. Cries more likely to draw attention at night and become spectacular on moonlit nights. Also feeds at night.

Eats new leaves, flowers, and fruits of aninga and of black mangrove, a Verbenaceae (*Avicennia*) abundant among true mangroves; also *Cecropia, Cassia,* etc., water hyacinth (*Eichornia*), and new grass growing high enough to reach lowest levels of swamp forest. This great deglutinized vegetable mass fermenting in crop produces the characteristic Hoatzin odor ("stinking bird").

Breeding: Reproduction occurs during the rainy season, beginning at its start. Pairs are evident in flock because the 2 members always perch together. They nest by preference in turiazais (aquatic plant formations) (May–June, Marajó, Pará) making a small, flat nest of twigs atop a big branch that could be the work of a Green-backed Heron, *Butorides striatus.* Two, rarely 3 very peculiar eggs: oblong, cream to pink, richly spotted with lilac, etc., reminiscent of certain rail eggs. Incubation lasts approximately 28 days. Nestling

has uniformly brown down. Its 1st and 2d toes are provided with sharp claws, moved by appropriate musculature, which let it grasp effectively with toes and creep through dense branches like an arboreal lizard. Also supports itself by placing chin and bill on branches, like young anis and parrots do. Claws are lost with molt to definitive plumage. I have found these claws hidden under feathers of museum specimens with adult plumage. When frightened, young jump into water and even dive, swimming with wings and feet. On such occasions they may be in danger from aquatic predators, depending on water depth. Apparently they do not return to the nest. When not driven from nest, young leave it only after 2–3 weeks, thus qualifying more as nidicolous than nidifugous. Small anis behave similarly but lack hooks on wings and live on dry land. Parents feed young with odoriferous mess that fills their crops, a habit recalling pigeons. Nest is tended by a flock of young from previous broods. Simulated copulations are engaged in by a pair and even by other flock members in front of rivals, an impressive demonstration of who is the real boss. Sometimes 2 nests are only a few meters from each other.

Distribution, Use, and Decline: Formerly the most abundant bird in the aningas that are common along edges of rivers, lakes, and igarapés of great Amazon and Orinoco river systems south to lower Rio das Mortes (S. Domingos, Mato Grosso), upper Rio Paraguay, and Bolivia. Also in the Guianas and Venezuela. Although not considered a game bird, its eggs are savored and its meat is not disdained, being much sought after for bait. Its feathers are used in making fans. Today it is no longer found close to cities.

Opisthocomidae Bibliography
See also General Bibliography

Bang, B. 1971. *Acta Anatómica Suppl.* 58 (ad 79):1–76. [Nasal fossa]

Barnikol, A. 1953. *Zool Jb. Syst., Okol.* 81:487–526. [Comparative anatomy of the crop and separation of *Opisthocomus* as an order]

Beebe, W. 1909. *Zoologica* (N.Y.) 1:45–66. [Behavior]

Brush, A. 1979. *Biochem. Syst. and Ecol.* 7:160. [Immunological data]

Bühler, P. 1986. *J. Orn.* 127:487–507. [*Archaeopteryx,* current conclusions]

Goeldi, E. 1886. *Bol. Mus. Paraen.* 1:1–4. [Behavior]

Grimmer, J. L. 1962. *Nat. Geog. Mag.:* 391–400. [Behavior]

Guimarães, L. R. 1940. Malófagos da Cigana, *Opisthocomus hoazin. Arqu. Zool. S. Paulo* 1:283–318.

Magalhães Pinto, and D. C. Gomes. 1985. *Memor. Inst. Oswaldo Cruz* 80(2):213–18. [Nematodes, *Hoazinstrongylus*]

Miller, A. H. 1953. A fossil Hoatzin from the Miocene of Colombia. *Auk* 70:484–89.

Queiroz, K. de, and D. A. Good. 1988. *Auk* 105:29–35. [Scleral ossicles of *Opisthocomus*]

Rutschke, E. 1970. *Zeitschr. Wiss. Zool.* 181(3/4):331–52. [Feather structure]

Sibley, C. G., and J. E. Ahlquist. 1973. *Auk* 90:1–3. [Electrophoretic analyses]

Sick, H. 1964. Hoatzin. In A. L. Thomson, ed. *A New Dictionary of Birds*. New York: McGraw-Hill.

Sick, H. 1985. Hoatzin. In B. Campbell and E. Lack, eds., *A Dictionary of Birds*. Vermillion, S.D.: Buteo Books.

Stegmann, B. C. 1978. *Publ. Nutall Orn. Club*, no. 17. [Relationships]

Strahl, S. D. 1988. The social organization and behaviour of the Hoatzin, *Opisthocomus hoazin*, in central Venezuela. *Ibis* 130:483–502.

ORDER GRUIFORMES

FAMILY ARAMIDAE: LIMPKIN (1)

The Limpkin is a long-legged, snail-eating bird. There is only one living species, but there are fossils from the middle Tertiary (lower Oligocene, 30 million years B.P.) of Argentina. South America lacks true cranes (Gruidae), although they exist in North America, where very old fossils have also been found (Tertiary, Eocene), including flightless forms, showing that the order is well established in our hemisphere.

Morphology and Parasites

Limpkin proportions are similar to those of ibis. The adult male trachea (fig. 90), twisted in various curves to amplify the volume of the voice, is similar to that of cranes. Electrophoretic analyses show more affinity to the Gruidae than to the Rallidae. The long hallux and black plumage of the chick suggest relationship with the rails. The bird lice of *Aramus* demonstrate no affinity with rails but point to a relationship with the Threskiornithidae.

Fig. 90. Trachea of limpkin, *Aramus guarauna*, male. The enlarged part is the syrinx. After Maynard, from Rüppell 1933.

LIMPKIN, *Aramus guarauna*, Carão   PL 3.9

70 cm. Looks a bit like Bare-faced Ibis, *Phimosus infuscatus*, and Green Ibis, *Mesembrinibis cayennensis*, but stockier and bill straighter. Dark brown with white throat, white streaks on head and neck. At a distance appears all black. Legs black, base of mandible yellow. Sexes similar but female smaller. VOICE: loud and full, a long cry frequently followed by 3–4 short cries, e.g., *krayo-ke, karOW* (from this comes name *Carão*); repeats these frequently at dawn and dusk and throughout night. When Limpkins begin to call, inhabitants of Amazonia believe water level of rivers will not rise any further.

Feeding: Basic food consists of aquatic snails *Pomacea* (= *Ampularia*) *guyanensis* and *Marisa planosgyra*, which also constitute typical food of Snail Kite, *Rostrhamus sociabilis*, whose technique for extracting meat of this prey is totally unlike that of *A. guarauna*. Latter places snail firmly in mud, apparently without securing it with toes, then hammers it with its sharp, slightly curved bill. It then lifts mollusk and shakes it, finally throwing pieces of or all of extracted meat into air, catching and swallowing them and letting fall the shell, which is usually slightly split at edges, sometimes completely perforated. Unlike *R. sociabilis*, *A. guarauna* can capture this prey in dense vegetation or even from shallow-bottomed lakes. It even manages to swim short stretches. In other regions it reportedly takes terrestrial mollusks and geckos. Incidentally, *Marisa planosgyra* is also sought by Muscovy Duck, *Cairina moschata*.

Behavior: Takes flight easily, flying with outstretched neck and legs held slightly downward. Wing beat has singular rhythm. Lives in marshes and flooded fields where it walks openly, often entering water up to its belly. Thanks to long toes, can walk on floating plants. One of birds most frequently seen flying low over extensive marshes. Sometimes roosts on tall trees. When frightened makes abrupt movements with neck and dips tail downward, opening rectrices slightly in a gesture unlike that observed in rails. After breeding gathers in flocks. Emigrates in dry season, returning with start of rains.

Breeding: Lives in pairs, making large, deep, basket-shaped nest atop tall marsh vegetation. Eggs cream colored and richly spotted, reminiscent of crane eggs. Young nidifugous with black down like rail chicks.

Florida and Mexico to Bolivia, Argentina, throughout Brazil.

Aramidae Bibliography

Eichler, W. 1949. Mallophagen von *Aramus scolopaceus. Festschrift von Erwin Stresemann*:249–52. Heidelberg: Carl Winter.

Rüppell, W. 1933. Physiologie und Akustik der Vogelstimme. *J. Orn.* 81:3.

Snyder, N.F.R., and H. A. Snyder. 1969. *The Living Bird* 8:177–224. [Behavior]

FAMILY PSOPHIIDAE: TRUMPETERS (3)

These gallinaceouslike birds are typical of Amazonia. Their phylogenetic relationships are still under discussion, there being similarities both to the Galliformes and Gruiformes. Electrophoretic analyses of egg-white protein have confirmed relationship with the rails. DNA–DNA hybridization apparently indicates closer ties with the cranes. So far no fossils are known. The eggs are so peculiar that oology does not help clarify their relationships.

Morphology

Small-headed (*Jacamim* in Tupi means "he who has a small head") and with a curved neck, their feathers are so short they look velvety. The bill is strong and curved. The wide, drooping wings, together with the long, fringed plumage of the mantle, give the body a heavy look which contributes to a hunchbacked appearance. The tail is short and soft. The legs are long and the toes short, but both are strong. Sexes are similar, though the male is slightly smaller.

Vocalization

Their voices are ventriloquial, an effect produced by vibrating compressed air in two thoracic air sacs connected to the trachea. These can be seen filling during a low growling that introduces the song itself, a muffled "pectoral" sequence given with closed bill: *ooo-ooo-ooo . . . ,* gradually diminishing in intensity and ending in a prolonged, descending syllable. This noise can be imitated by blowing into a bottle. The birds sometimes sing while roosting at night.

Their alarm vocalization resembles the high crying of guineafowl mixed with the grunting of pigs. They communicate with each other through a monosyllabic, muttered *woop* as they walk along the ground.

Feeding and Behavior

Trumpeters eat insects (termites, ants, etc.), centipedes, seeds, berries, etc. Evidence of feeding activity can be seen in places where ground litter has been disturbed to expose the soil. They eat carrion (*urubu-do-chão, urubu-da-terra,* "ground vulture," upper Rio Curuá, Pará) and are said to chase snakes.

They walk peacefully in flocks through shady forests (preferably on terra firme), rhythmically shaking their wings and zigzagging along established trails under leadership of one individual, probably the most experienced. When frightened they fly up to nearby branches and then, jumping, flying, and calling, continue to considerable heights.

To intimidate rivals during courtship, or simply because they are excited, they run and jump in circles on the ground. In a show of nervousness they lower the neck and raise the wings, vertically tossing up the "mantle" (wings and dorsal plumage) in a display that is impressive because of the long, colorful plumes in this area. These plumes serve as the principal specific character. Such movements may recall the famous dances of cranes. Couples caress each other on the head. At dusk they become restless until they have gone to roost, as do other birds, such as guans.

A Gray-winged Trumpeter, *Psophia crepitans,* was seen rubbing its plumage with a millipede, thus using the animal's caustic secretion the same way as in anting.

Breeding

Trumpeters reportedly use spacious holes well up in hollow trees in the forest. The eggs are rounded and white with a rough shell. The incubation period is 27 days (R.M.A. Azeredo). Chicks are light chestnut spotted with gray, similar to those of cracids such as *Crax* species, but with longer legs.

Parasites and Use

I have frequently found nematodes on the nictitating membrane under the eyelids.

Trumpeters can be completely tamed. When living semidomesticated, they are used by native Indians as sentinels and by others as pets.

Fig. 91. Distribution of three allopatric species of trumpeter, *Psophia*, that can be considered members of a superspecies, *P. crepitans*. Included is the range of *P. c. napensis*. After Haffer 1974b.

Distribution and Evolution

Trumpeters are presently found in three distinct, geographically separated forms (fig. 91). Having descended from the same ancestor (monophyletic), they evolved in forest refuges of a semidestroyed and reduced Hylaea during dry epochs. The present three species may therefore be considered as allospecies composing a superspecies, remaining separated by the widest parts of the great rivers after the resurgence of Amazonia in its present form. In this way the Madeira and Amazon constitute impressive barriers between populations of the Dark-winged Trumpeter, *Psophia viridis*, and those of the other two forms. In the headwaters of the southern tributaries of the Amazon, where the narrower rivers do not form insuperable obstacles and would permit possible contact, I have not found trumpeters because of ecological conditions incompatible with these exclusively humid equatorial forest birds. This is why populations inhabiting both sides of the middle and lower Tapajós and its headwaters have not entered into contact.

GRAY-WINGED TRUMPETER, *Psophia crepitans*, Jacamim-de-costas-cinzas

Closely related to *P. leucoptera*. Rear sections of mantle gray mixed with ochre. North of Amazon and Rio Negro to Venezuela, the Guianas, Amapá. Also north of Rio Solimões to Colombia, Peru.

PALE-WINGED TRUMPETER, *Psophia leucoptera*, Jacamim-de-costas-brancas

Rear portions of mantle white (*P. l. leucoptera*, on west bank of Madeira to Peru, Bolivia) or ochraceous (*P. l. ochroptera*, between lower Solimões and lower Rio Negro). Latter form might be considered a race of *P. crepitans*, into whose area of northern Amazonia it fits better (see fig. 91).

DARK-WINGED TRUMPETER, *Psophia viridis*, Jacamim-de-costas-verdes   PL 11.1

49 cm; height 46 cm; 1071 g (female). Best-known Brazilian trumpeter. Back olivaceous brown or very green. The Madeira to Belém (Pará), northern Mato Grosso. Forms 2 distinct geographic races, separated by lower Tapajós. *P. v. viridis*, with bright green mantle, shiny blue tips on upper wing coverts, and light yellowish bill and feet, is on left bank. On right bank, *P. v. dextralis* has much darker mantle, lacks green and blue almost entirely, has black legs and bill.

Psophiidae Bibliography

Haverschmidt, F. 1963. *J. Orn.* 104:443. [*Psophia crepitans*, eggs]

Haverschmidt, F. 1964. Trumpeter chapter. In L. A. Thomson, ed., *A New Dictionary of Birds*. New York: McGraw-Hill.

Sick, H. 1969. Psophiidae. In Grzimek, B. 1972. *Tierleben*. Zurich: Kindler.

FAMILY RALLIDAE: RAILS, GALLINULES, COOTS (28)

This peculiar, cosmopolitan family has many known fossils from the New and Old Worlds, including Brazil. Rails probably originated in the Old World tropics.

Morphology and Special Adaptations

Sizes vary from that of a domestic fowl chick to that of a small goose. The legs and toes are long. All lack swimming membranes except the coots, *Fulica*, which have lateral swimming lobes, resembling the Sungrebe, *Heliornis*, in this adaptation. The tail is short. The considerable length of the bill, neck, and legs often causes the "total length" designation to be vague or illusory, as with the Ciconiiformes and Charadriiformes.

The family can be divided by external appearance into two informal groups: the rails, which move primarily by walking, although they can swim well; and the gallinules and coots, which are generally seen swimming although they walk very well. Apparently forest life can be considered their original disposition (as with the Slaty-breasted Wood-Rail, *Aramides saracura,* and Uniform Crake, *Amaurolimnas concolor*), whereas aquatic adaptation (as in the Spot-flanked Gallinule, *Porphyriops melanops;* Common Moorhen, *Gallinula chloropus;* and the *Porphyrula* and *Fulica*) is a secondary specialization (Olson 1973).

Rails are well camouflaged by their plumage. The white design on the flanks and under the tail of *Gallinula chloropus* creates an admirably disruptive effect.

The bill and feet are vividly colored, the former often greenish and sometimes showing other bright colors. The feet are frequently reddish.[1] In the nonbreeding season the bright colors are lost.

Gallinules, moorhens, and coots have a frontal shield which is more developed in males. In the White-winged Coot, *Fulica leucoptera,* this shrinks after the breeding season. *Gallinula chloropus* and the Red-gartered Coot, *Fulica armillata,* have a brightly colored garter on the tibiotarsus just below the "pants," visible only when the bird is in certain positions.

Sexes are generally similar, though the male is usually larger with a longer and slightly different-shaped bill. Sketchy sexual dimorphism is visible in the head pattern of the Ocellated Crake, *Micropygia schomburgkii.* Immatures have smaller and indistinctly colored bills, and their plumage may differ from that of adults, as with the Plumbeous Rail, *Rallus sanguinolentus;* Spotted Rail, *R. maculatus; Porphyriops melanops; Gallinula chloropus;* and the *Porphyrula* and *Laterallus.*

As is evident from the hallux, the toes are quite long in the aquatic species, facilitating walking on floating plants. The laterally compressed body and silky plumage combine to offer an extraordinary capacity for slithering through the most tangled marsh vegetation, but this is not accentuated in the gallinules and coots. The *Aramides, Laterallus,* and *Neocrex* roost above ground.

Rails fly well, although they have a tendency not to fly during the day. On oceanic islands, flightless rails have evolved whose wings have been reduced to vestigial remnants under a mantle of piliform feathers (Inaccessible Rail, *Atlantisia rogersi*). There is even a flightless *Gallinula* on Gough Island in the mid-Atlantic.

The flight feathers of aquatic species—*Rallus, Aramides, Porzana, Laterallus* [except Russet-crowned Crake, *L. viridis*], *Gallinula, Porphyrula,* and *Fulica*—molt simultaneously, whereas successive molt occurs in *Amaurolimnas concolor, Laterallus viridis, Micropygia schomburgkii,* the Paint-billed Crake, *Neocrex erythrops,* and all campo or forest species. Only birds able to hide in marshes can endure simultaneous molt of all the flight feathers, for this implies

full loss of flight—for three to four weeks in *Fulica.* However, it has the advantage of terminating more rapidly than successive molt.

When frightened, the rallids' dangling-legged flight is short and awkward. Coots typically fly close to the water, as if running over the surface, displaying the white wing speculum (if they have one) and garter. The *Fulica* dive, though with some effort.

Various species, such as the Clapper Rail, *Rallus longirostris,* live in littoral regions with brackish water, in mangroves and corresponding ecosystems. Their interorbital (nasal) glands are highly developed and excrete excess salt (see Laridae, "Feeding . . ."). In Brazil two outstanding cases of adaptation to life on dry land are *Micropygia schomburgkii* and *Laterallus viridis,* the latter also being a diurnal, not a crepuscular bird, that sings in the hottest hours of the day.

Vocalization

Because of the withdrawn, crepuscular habits of these birds, it is almost essential to know their voices, which year-round are sometimes uttered in impressive choruses (e.g., Gray-necked Wood-Rail, *Aramides cajanea,* and *Rallus sanguinolentus*), mostly in the late afternoon, at dawn, and when it rains (according to popular belief, they announce the coming of rain). They also duet (e.g., Blackish Rail, *Rallus nigricans; Aramides cajanea;* Ash-throated Crake, *Porzana albicollis*); male and female phrases may be different. They frequently call when frightened by a loud noise, such as a shot. Warning vocalizations differ between the sexes (*Fulica armillata*) and serve to distinguish males from females. Until recently, ignorance of the voice of *Amaurolimnas concolor* was an obstacle to learning the distribution and abundance of the species.

In central Brazil the Tupi Indians tried to convince me that the noisy calling of *Aramides cajanea* was not only a chaos of voices but was accompanied by the noise resulting from gas expelled from the cloaca! I have found references to this picturesque legend in *Tratado da terra e gente do Brasil* by Fernão Cardim (republished 1939), who arrived here in 1583 and who, when referring to the Tupis of the littoral, said the following about this bird: "It has a strange song, for whoever hears it assumes it to be a very large bird although it is small, for it sings with its mouth while at the same time it makes another sonorous, intense, loud, but not very smelly tone with its rear end, which can be frightening." This "other tone" may correspond to a ventriloquial *bo, bo, bo . . . ,* a modest counterpoint accompanying the loud *três-potes* ["three-pots"] that I have sometimes heard when nearby; possibly it is the female's voice. As for *A. saracura,* I have noted, together with the very loud *bAHik,* an independent, weak, hoarse sound undoubtedly produced in the trachea. The duet of *A. saracura* is so perfectly synchronized that full

---

[1]In the species accounts I often do not mention the color of the tarsus if it is red.

attention is required to discover that two individuals are singing. Cardim, not knowing about duets, wrote of their "curious ability to sing two notes at the same time." Rails can produce whisper song.

The croaks and peeps of amphibians sometimes are thought to come from rails. It is also possible to mistake capybara and tapir whistles as well as caiman snorts and, in the extreme south, the nasal voice of the nutria (*Myocastor*) for rail calls.

Feeding

Rails are omnivorous and enjoy grass and corn shoots as well as small water snakes such as *Helicops* (found in stomachs of *Rallus nigricans* and *R. sanguinolentus*). They pick insects and larvae from cattle droppings near marshes and are caught in traps baited with corn or oats.

The large species (*Aramides*) steal eggs of other aquatic birds. Coots gather plants from the bottom of shallow lakes, probably aided by their claws, which can be enormous (e.g., *Fulica leucoptera*) and are also used as weapons in fights between rivals. Plants taken from lake bottoms by coots may attract ducks that try to steal this sought-after food (kleptoparasitism). In North America the opposite frequently occurs: coots rob rails (Olson pers. comm.). Rails regurgitate pellets.

Behavior

All rails have restless dispositions and reveal their nervousness by almost constant movement of the short tail, which is lifted vertically (unlike the tinamous), an especially conspicuous movement in those with a white "tail light" (under tail coverts), such as the gallinules and *Rallus longirostris* and *R. maculatus*. Important specific characteristics are exhibited in this way (see *Laterallus* spp.). Chicks whose tail feathers are just sprouting already do this tail tilting.

Although certain species, such as the Rufous-sided Crake, *Laterallus melanophaius*, are abundant and live near human habitations, they usually go unnoticed because they remain hidden, revealing their presence only by their voices.

The Red-and-white Crake, *L. leucopyrrhus*, *Gallinula chloropus*, and others customarily moisten their food before swallowing it. Various species probe the mud with their bills, like snipe, leaving a series of small holes in their trail.

Breeding

Little is known about the prenuptial displays of rallids, but some observations have been made of captive birds. The male and female caress each other on the head and sleep together on the nest, where the male feeds the female (*L. leucopyrrhus*). Nests are large, durable, made of leaves, partially covered, have a small lateral entrance, and are placed on bushes and vines or sometimes in holes (*Laterallus*), occasionally far from water. *Aramides cajanea* and probably others build a nursery nest near the incubation nest that is used for about a month by parents and young (Teixeira 1981). *Micropygia schomburgkii* builds a spherical nest 200 × 140 × 170 mm made entirely of grass, with a very small entrance on the upper side. It is hidden among field grasses and holds two shiny, white eggs 25 × 19.3 mm (A. Negret 1984, Brasília).

Eggs (up to 7 for *Gallinula chloropus* in Minas Gerais) are variously colored with speckles on a yellowish, pinkish, or white background, except for *Laterallus viridis* and *L. leucopyrrhus* which have pure white eggs. Incubation lasts 16 to 17 days for *Gallinula chloropus* in ex-Guanabara; 15 to 16 days for the Purple Gallinule, *Porphyrula martinica*, in Maranhão; and 21 to 25 days for *L. leucopyrrhus*. Chicks are usually covered with black down, and various species have a red mark at the base of the bill. *Aramides cajanea* chicks are black with reddish heads; those of *Gallinula chloropus* have a diminutive frontal shield (larger in the male) and blue skin above the eye and remain in the nest four days although they can walk well when two days old. The parents, which are extremely aggressive at this stage, feed the very shy chicks for 20 days. The chicks take food from the tip of their parents' bills. Sometimes young from the last clutch help their parents rear their younger siblings.

A mother occasionally carries a chick by holding it by the neck (*Rallus*). The first toe of the chicks of some species has a claw that is useful in getting through the most tangled vegetation. The young give location calls to help their parents find them (*Aramides*).

Distribution, Migration, and Isolated Populations

Genera such as *Rallus, Porzana, Gallinula,* and *Fulica* are widely distributed throughout the world. *Fulica* penetrates into the Andes and Northern Hemisphere but in Brazil is a southern genus. *Gallinula chloropus* is cosmopolitan.

The strong tendency of Rallidae to scatter is evident from their nocturnal flights. On rainy nights they overfly cities such as Rio de Janeiro, where their voices can be heard (*Rallus nigricans, Laterallus melanophaius, Aramides cajanea*). They may smash against illuminated windows: a Little Wood-Rail, *Aramides mangle,* flew against the Hotel Simon in Itatiaia, Rio de Janeiro, and a *Neocrex erythrops* was found in the gardens of the Museum of Natural History in Belo Horizonte.

What seems to be disjunct distribution may arise from lack of appropriate habitat or simple lack of records for birds that are so difficult to see. The sedentary condition of small isolated populations may produce partial albinism, presumably a consequence of inbreeding, as I observed in Espírito Santo in 1940 with *L. melanophaius*.

Some species are long-distance migrants, especially *Porphyrula martinica, Gallinula chloropus,* and the *Fulica.* The first two even venture to overfly the Atlantic, with *P. martinica* being the only Neotropical bird to make "regular" transatlantic flights. Everything indicates that such exploits are involuntary, the birds being carried by wind over the South Atlantic. *P. martinica* must be able to rest on the surface of a calm sea. Of 12 individuals captured on the African coast, 10 were immatures (Winterbottom 1965). A *Rallus maculatus* was found 500 km off the coast of Espírito Santo (September, J. T. Nichols).

In 1973 a Quaternary sub-fossil rail of medium size with atrophied wings was discovered on Fernando de Noronha, apparently distinct from rails of the South American continent (Olson 1977).

Parasites

Aramides saracura is host to the louse fly *Olfersia holoptera,* which is also found on the Red-winged Tinamou, *Rhynchotus rufescens.* I have found leeches feeding while attached to the toes of the Giant Wood-Rail, *Aramides ypecaha,* in Rio Grande do Sul marshes.

Usefulness and Supposed Harmfulness

Gallinules are valued as game birds, especially in the northeast where *Porphyrula martinica* is important to hunters and supplies necessary protein to the populace and where destruction of eggs and birds is almost total. *P. martinica* and *Aramides cajanea* are sometimes accused of destroying rice when the plants sprout.

Synopsis of Brazilian Rallidae
(number of species in parentheses)[2]

1. Small, multicolored rails: *Porzana flaviventer, Laterallus* (6) (see PL 11), *Micropygia* (1), and *Coturnicops* (1). The first and last two have white speckles on the upperparts.
2. Medium-sized rails: *Rallus* (4), with *R. maculatus* streaked with white; *Porzana albicollis* (see PL 11), *Amaurolimnas* (1), and *Neocrex* (1)
3. Large rails: *Aramides* (5) (see PL 11)
4. Gallinules, moorhens, and coots: *Porphyriops* (1), *Gallinula* (1) (see PL 11), *Porphyrula* (2) (see PL 11), and *Fulica* (3)

PLUMBEOUS RAIL, *Rallus sanguinolentus,* Sanã

30 cm. Very similar to *R. nigricans* but with brilliant blue at base of maxilla, scarlet at base of mandible and on legs. Immature brown, lighter on underparts, with some black spots on wings, black bill and legs; bill shorter than adult's. VOICE: song *tsewWIT, tsewWIT . . . tsewrrr,* almost always

in chorus at dusk; warning a loud, coarse note similar to that of Helmeted Guineafowl, *Numida meleagris.* Broad marshes and oxbow lakes covered with aquatic plants. A southern Andean species: Tierra del Fuego to Rio de Janeiro. "Espírito Santo" (Ruschi, without foundation). Also called *Saracura-do-banhado.*

BLACKISH RAIL, *Rallus nigricans,* Saracura-sanã

31 cm. One of most abundant rails in areas it inhabits. Color identical to *Aramides saracura* (which is distinctly larger) but all-green bill longer and curved. VOICE: warning a high whistle, *tirit, kirk, PEEoo,* very similar to cry of Roadside Hawk, *Rupornis magnirostris;* song a composite phrase, beginning with an ascending series of piglike grunts, with bellows in background, and ending with a clear, descending tremolo. Lives in any sort of marsh, frequently close to houses and alongside *Laterallus melanophaius.* Colombia to Brazil (Pernambuco to Rio Grande do Sul, Goiás, Federal District), Paraguay, Argentina (Misiones). Similarity to *R. sanguinolentus* would suggest a close relationship which is denied by disparity between their voices.

SPOTTED RAIL, *Rallus maculatus,* Saracura-carijó

27 cm. Blackish brown entirely mottled with white; white tail-light. Bill green with red base. VOICE: *PEEoo,* also low snorts. Humid marshes and buriti groves. Mexico to Argentina; also northern and southeastern Brazil (to Rio Grande do Sul). See *Coturnicops notata.*

CLAPPER RAIL, *Rallus longirostris,* Saracura-sanã-dos-mangues

31 cm. Relatively large with long, orange, slightly decurved bill. Grayish brown with rusty breast and sides of abdomen barred brown and white; white tail light. VOICE: a loud clacking, *kek-kek-kek.* Restricted to littoral in mangroves. U.S. to South America, including Brazil from Pará (Marajó) to Santa Catarina.

UNIFORM CRAKE, *Amaurolimnas concolor,* Saracurinha-da-mata

23 cm. Unique in almost all-dark rusty chestnut color. Iris and legs red, bill green. VOICE: a sequence of about 6 notes, *tooee,* 1st ones louder. Shallow, clear creeks bordered with palms in shady tall forest (north of Rio Doce, Espírito Santo) and low, wet swampy forest (Rio de Janeiro, L. P. Gonzaga). Mexico to Amazonia and to eastern Brazil, sparsely to Espírito Santo, São Paulo.

LITTLE WOOD-RAIL, *Aramides mangle,* Saracura-da-praia   PR   PL 44.9

32 cm. Similar to *A. cajanea* but smaller with shorter bill and foreneck lacking any gray. Rusty underparts, pale in

[2]See also the Sunbittern, *Eurypyga helias;* Wattled Jacana, *Jacana jacana;* and the *Butorides, Ixobrychus,* and *Zebrilus* herons.

immature, begin just below white throat. Bill green with red base. Muddy beaches with mangroves, adjacent forest. Common in mangroves in Alagoas (Teixeira et al. 1989). Eastern and southern Brazil from Belém (Pará, F. Novaes pers. comm.) and Maranhão to Rio de Janeiro, Itatiaia, September 1959 (see "Distribution . . ."). Also called *Saracura-do-mangue.*

GRAY-NECKED WOOD-RAIL, *Aramides cajanea,* Três-potes PL 11.3

39 cm. Because of large size and loud song, generally our best-known rail. Head and neck gray; rest of underparts (except black belly) and inner vane of remiges (visible in flight) ferruginous; under wing coverts rusty yellow, barred black. Bill green. VOICE: a well-syncopated phrase, *TERres-pot TERres-pot TERres-pot pot pot* (hence onomotopoeic vernacular name *três-potes,* "three-pots"), frequently sung in duet or in chorus with more distant individuals; duet is an extremely loud, impressive performance that may go on for several minutes; warning is a sharp *wett.* See also "Vocalization." Marshes with tall vegetation; mangroves; edges of rivers, lakes, and igarapés; tall, humid forest, sometimes distant from water; sugarcane plantations; etc. Also close to cities. Mexico to Bolivia, Argentina, throughout Brazil. Also called *Sericóia* (Espírito Santo), *Chiricote.*

GIANT WOOD-RAIL, *Aramides ypecaha,* Saracuraçu

46 cm. Largest Brazilian rallid, similar to *A. cajanea* but larger and with only foreneck gray. Breast and flanks an unusual pinkish hue, belly light gray. Rump and tail black, noticeable when bird raises tail or flies. VOICE: extremely loud and harsh, a trisyllabic *keyo-BYke* . . . repeated about 6 times; other multisyllabic motifs are sometimes followed by a low moan, *BY-kare, BY-kare, BY-kare KOa,* a sequence initiated with a series of simple *keyuh, keyuh, keyuh*s . . . reminiscent of cries of an *Amazona* parrot. Edge of marshes. Local in northeastern and central Brazil: Piauí, Bahia, Minas Gerais, Mato Grosso; more abundant in south: Rio Grande do Sul, Paraguay, Uruguay, Argentina.

SLATY-BREASTED WOOD-RAIL, *Aramides saracura,* Saracura-do-mato

34 cm. Same mantle color and shape as *A. ypecaha* but has all dark gray underparts except for white throat and black crissum. VOICE: song a series of loud, harsh, monotonous cries, *byk-byk-byk* . . . , beginning with *kew* . . . , *ko* . . . ; (see "Vocalization"); alarm a loud *kee, kee, kee* . . . ; also *wet, wet, wet.* . . . Marshy areas bounded by forest, forest in rugged country; crosses long stretches of forest lacking water. Espírito Santo (mountainous regions) and Rio de Janeiro (including ex-Guanabara) to Rio Grande do Sul, Argentina (Misiones), Paraguay. May look like a large *Rallus nigricans,* sometimes its neighbor in marshes.

RED-WINGED WOOD-RAIL, *Aramides calopterus,* Saracura-de-asa-vermelha

Upper Juruá region (Amazonas). Extends as far as Ecuador.

ASH-THROATED CRAKE, *Porzana albicollis,* Sanã-carijó PL 11.2

27 cm. Relatively small, common in eastern Brazil. Upperparts speckled with black, legs brownish or greenish, bill without any red. VOICE: call *bewrewt;* warning *keAH;* male song consists of a melodious hum ending in a typical full, prolonged syllable, *grrrrrrehhhyo,* while female constantly "barks" a *kehrre.* . . . Open reed beds and marshes. The Guianas and Venezuela to Bolivia, Argentina, Brazil from north (Óbidos, Pará) to center (southern Goiás) and south (Rio Grande do Sul).

YELLOW-BREASTED CRAKE, *Porzana flaviventer*

14 cm. Upperparts speckled white, superciliary and underparts yellowish, flanks streaked black. Similar to *Laterallus* spp. It has been suggested that this species be placed in the genus *Poliolimnas* of Asia and Australasia (Olson 1970). Locally from the Guianas to Argentina, northern and eastern Brazil (Rio de Janeiro, São Paulo).

GRAY-BREASTED CRAKE, *Laterallus exilis,* Pinto-d'água

17 cm. Similar to *L. melanophaius* but with hindneck chestnut, underparts lacking rusty tints. Breast gray, black under tail coverts barred white. Legs light chestnut. Tall grass near water. Central America to Amazonia, Pernambuco (Igaraçu), Mato Grosso (Porto Quebracho), Paraguay. Found from Pleistocene of Florida. Includes a 1980 specimen from Paraíba which was identified as *L. levraudi,* a Venezuelan endemic.

RUFOUS-FACED CRAKE, *Laterallus xenopterus*

18.5 cm. Known in Brazil only from Brasília National Park, Federal District. Similar to *L. melanophaius* but with upper wing coverts heavily barred white, breast cream colored, under tail coverts black. Bill gray, legs greenish gray. Partially flooded, dense, tall grass (A. Negret). Also in Paraguay.

RUFOUS-SIDED CRAKE, *Laterallus melanophaius,* Pinto-d'água-comum PL 11.4

17.5 cm. Smallish, abundant. Plumage has contrasting ferruginous and pure white. Under tail coverts also ferruginous (unlike *L. exilis, L. xenopterus,* and *L. leucopyrrhus*). Legs greenish. VOICE: call a high peep, *tsewp-tsip* (similar to a chick [*pinto*], thus the name); warning *psieh;* song a prolonged, loud trill (e.g., 6 seconds), *tsewrrr* . . . , fuller than Yellow-chinned Spinetail, *Certhiaxis cinna-*

momea, which frequently lives in same places; a short, smooth, repeated *tsewrrr* uttered even at night in flight on migration. Well-flooded marshes. In some small marshes there is a tendency for albinism to develop (Espírito Santo). Central America to Bolivia, Argentina, northern and eastern Brazil south to Rio Grande do Sul. Also called *Açanã, Frango-d'água.* See *L. leucopyrrhus.*

RED-AND-WHITE CRAKE, *Laterallus leucopyrrhus,* Pinto-d'água-avermelhado

17.5 cm. Southern species, similar to *L. melanophaius* but with crown and hindneck chestnut (not olivaceous), under wing coverts white (not streaked black), under tail coverts black and white in female, white in male—never rusty as in *L. melanophaius.* Legs red, unlike those of 3 preceding species. VOICE: a resonant trill, descending at end. Argentina north to Rio de Janeiro, where it may occur alongside *melanophaius.*

BLACK-BANDED CRAKE, *Laterallus fasciatus*

18 cm. Chestnut head, neck, and breast; dark green mantle; light rusty belly streaked with black. Only in upper Amazon region, along Rios Solimões and Purus as far as Ecuador, Peru, Colombia. See *L. viridis.*

RUSSET-CROWNED CRAKE, *Laterallus viridis,* Siricora-mirim

18 cm. Unusual among rallids in its adaptation to dry environments. Upperparts olivaceous brown, top of head and underparts rusty, sides of head gray. Legs red. VOICE: an even more prolonged trill than *L. melanophaius,* with timbre of a domestic canary, beginning as if "choking," then flowing freely without pause and descending to continue without undulations, ending with spaced notes; alarm *kewrr.* In completely dry fields of thatching grass or brush, frequently far from any water (e.g., on hills below Sugar Loaf in Rio de Janeiro). The Guianas and Venezuela to Rio de Janeiro, Mato Grosso. It has been proposed to place it in a separate genus, *Rufirallus,* in consideration of its special form of molt and color of its eggs (see "Breeding"). Together with *L. fasciatus,* it could be included in genus *Amaurolimnas.* See *Micropygia schomburgkii,* which also lives far from water.

OCELLATED CRAKE, *Micropygia schomburgkii,* Maxalalagá

13 cm. Minuscule; size of a Rufous-collared Sparrow, *Zonotrichia capensis.* Bill short; upperparts brown, speckled with white and outlined in black. Underparts light rusty yellow, abdomen white, bill greenish blue. VOICE: *prrrssss,* like rasping of a grasshopper. Dry fields with tall grass. Squats when pursued but does not fly badly. Appearing at edges of burned fields as a refugee from its habitat and doped by smoke, it becomes easy prey for Aplomado Falcon, *Falco*

femoralis, as I have observed in Brasília. Central America to Venezuela, locally in central (Goiás, Mato Grosso) and eastern (Bahia, São Paulo) Brazil. Unlike Dwarf Tinamou, *Taoniscus nanus,* its occasional neighbor in central Brazil, carries tail raised and has much longer, reddish legs. Also called *Perdigão.* Could be included in genus *Coturnicops.*

SPECKLED CRAKE, *Coturnicops notata,* Pinto-d'água-carijó

12.7 cm. Tiny, with short legs and toes. Blackish brown, upperparts speckled with black and white, foreneck streaked white, rest of underparts barred white. VOICE: a trisyllabic *koowee-cack* uttered at night (Teixeira and Puga 1984). Rice plantations, locally from Argentina and Uruguay to Venezuela, the Guianas. In Brazil in São Paulo, recently in Taubaté (H. Alvarenga), and Rio Grande do Sul. See also *Rallus maculatus.*

PAINT-BILLED CRAKE, *Neocrex erythrops,* Turuturu

18 cm. Robust physique in spite of small size. Bill short with bright red base. Upperparts uniformly olivaceous brown, underparts slate gray, throat white, flanks streaked black and white. Immature has even shorter bill, without red. Legs red. VOICE: a descending trill, ending with some harsh notes. Forest edges. Venezuela and Colombia to Argentina, Paraguay, Brazil: Pará, Pernambuco, Bahia, Minas Gerais (Belo Horizonte), Espírito Santo, São Paulo, Mato Grosso (upper Xingu, September). See *Porzana albicollis.*

SPOT-FLANKED GALLINULE, *Porphyriops melanops,* Frango-d'água-carijó

25 cm. Like a small *Gallinula,* bobs its head while swimming and is quickly recognized by this tic. Bill and narrow shield light green, contrasting with blackish face. Back tinged with bright chestnut, flanks spotted with large, round, white marks. Immature has chestnut instead of gray head, lighter cheeks. VOICE: song an accelerated sequence; usually silent. Lakes and ponds with abundant floating vegetation. Argentina and Chile to Brazil (Rio Grande do Sul to Ceará); locally in Andes.

COMMON MOORHEN, *Gallinula chloropus,* Frango-d'água-comum PL 11.6

37 cm. Widely distributed, also found in North America and Old World. Unlike *Porphyrula martinica,* has scarlet shield; white streaks on flanks; large, 2-part tail light; green legs with red garter. Immature blackish brown with abdomen whitish; bill, shield, and legs lack bright colors. VOICE: a sharp *kewrrrk,* a strident *ki-ki.* Bobs head as it swims, with bill held downward. When walking shows red garter. Frequents lakes, including brackish ones. In winter numbers in southern Brazil increase because of immigration of birds

from farther south. Occurs in most of continent and throughout Brazil. Reaches Tristão da Cunha archipelago, aided by west winds (see also *P. martinica*). Also called *Jaçanã-galo* (northeast), *Peituda* (Rio de Janeiro). Fossils of this genus are known from upper Pliocene of North America. See also *Fulica rufifrons*.

PURPLE GALLINULE, *Porphyrula martinica*, Frango-d'água-azul   PL 11.5

35 cm. Generally our best-known gallinule. Unlike *Gallinula chloropus*, has flat, whitish blue shield, yellow legs, undivided white tail light. Immature similar to that of *G. chloropus* but yellowish brown; may resemble a young sandpiper or jacana. VOICE: a high *te-te-te, tik-tik-tik*, a low *dog;* also notes or phrases sounding like mutters or screeches. Perches on posts, clutches bunches of reeds (*Typha*) like a bittern. Flies well, with legs stretched out behind and held together with feet crossed.

Breeding in Maranhão: Large numbers appear in Maranhão at beginning of rainy season (January–February) and nest there April–June during normal years (when there is no drought), remaining until November. From March forward they are heavily hunted and eggs (4–8 per clutch) are also taken. From July on adults are particularly vulnerable, being fat and unable to fly because of simultaneous molt of flight feathers. "Jacana rice" is most esteemed regional dish and is available March–November. A closed season from April to June has been recommended (Aguirre 1962).

Distribution and Migration: Widely distributed wherever there are marshes, occurring from southeastern U.S. to Argentina, throughout Brazil. Being migratory, disappears completely in winter from southern Brazil. Shows up to rest on ships at sea 100 or more km from coast (March). Frequently crosses Atlantic, being found annually on Tristão da Cunha archipelago 3200 km away from American shores and on southern coast of West Africa. Also appears on Santa Helena and Ascension, perhaps coming from Tristão da Cunha (Winterbottom 1965) or carried by west winds that blow above easterly trade winds. Has also been recorded in Azores and South Georgia (see "Distribution . . ."). Also called *Jaçanã* (Maranhão), *Tauá-tauá-azul* (Amapá). See *P. flavirostris*.

AZURE GALLINULE, *Porphyrula flavirostris*, Frango-d'água-pequeno

27 cm. Similar to immature *P. martinica* but much more slender and with longer tail; neck, breast, and sides of head bluish gray; bill and shield yellowish green; legs ochre yellow. Very wet bogs with tall vegetation and buriti groves, sometimes alongside *P. martinica*. There is little information on this species, which is frequently confused with *martinica*. The Guianas to Argentina; Amazonian, central, southern, and eastern Brazil (Rio de Janeiro, Minas Gerais). Also called *Tauá-tauá-branco* (Amapá).

Fig. 92. Red-gartered Coot, *Fulica armillata*.

RED-GARTERED COOT, *Fulica armillata*, Carqueja-de-bico-manchado   Fig. 92

47 cm. Largest Brazilian coot weighing 1 km. In Brazil appears only in south. Slaty soot with head and neck shiny black. Wings without any white. Tail light less prominent than in *Gallinula chloropus*. Red garter. Bill and shield both yellow but shield lighter. Red marks on bill vary with age and season; migrant individuals appearing here usually have only a scarlet line separating bill and shield. May also have a red spot at base of mandible. Red garter visible when bird kicks vigorously or stretches its leg backward to scratch, rest, or perch at water's edge. VOICE: a high *pit:* male, *kwit, kwit, kwit;* female, *terr-terr-terr;* this sexual difference is noticeable mostly during breeding (Navas 1956). Dives with some effort. Lakes edged with aquatic vegetation. Tierra del Fuego and Chile to southern Brazil as far as São Paulo (June), Rio de Janeiro (ex-Guanabara, August; Cabo Frio, February, March, June). Name *carqueja* comes from a plant, *Baccharis,* of same name that has winged stems resembling toes of *Fulica*. Also called *Galinha-d'água* (Rio Grande do Sul), *Gallareta de ligas rojas* (Argentina). At a distance may be difficult to separate from *F. leucoptera*.

WHITE-WINGED COOT, *Fulica leucoptera*, Carqueja-de-bico-amarelo

42 cm. Similar to *F. armillata* but with tips of inner secondaries white, conspicuous in flight. Black underside of tail has an inverted white V. Bill whitish or light yellow, shield sulphur yellow, lemon, or pink. No garter. VOICE: *keyuh, keyuh, keyuh. . . .* Shallow, open marshes. Tierra del Fuego and northern Chile to Bolivia, Paraguay, Uruguay, Brazil: Rio Grande do Sul, nesting in October; Campinas, São Paulo, on migration, January (Dean Greenberg). Apparently a geographic replacement of Coot, *F. atra*, of Europe.

RED-FRONTED COOT, *Fulica rufifrons*,
Carqueja-de-escudo-roxo

46 cm. Distinguished by purple shield and yellow bill with purple base. No white in wing, no garter. Shows large, white, 2-part tail light when it takes off and fans tail, which is longer than in *F. armillata* and *F. leucoptera*. Marshes with dense vegetation, where it swims vigorously, bobbing head. Could be mistaken for *Gallinula chloropus*. Tierra del Fuego and Chile to Uruguay, southeastern Brazil in Rio Grande do Sul, Santa Catarina (probably nesting), São Paulo (June).

Rallidae Bibliography

See also General Bibliography

Aguirre, A. C. 1962. *Arq. Mus. Nac. Rio de Janeiro* 52:9–20. [*Porphyrula*, northeast]

Anders, K. 1981. *Zool. Beitr.* 27:175–84. [Caudal area anatomy of *Gallinula* and *Fulica*]

Dickerman, R. W., and F. Haverschmidt. 1971. *Wilson Bull.* 83(4):445–46. [*Rallus*, plumage]

Gonzaga, L. P. 1984. Censo de uma população de *Amaurolimnas concolor* no sudeste do Brasil. *XI Cong. Bras. Zool., Belém:* 353–54.

Jacob, J., J. Plawer, and P. Rosenfeld. 1979. Gefiederwachskompositionen von Kranichen und Ralle. *J. Orn.* 120(1):54–63.

Navas, J. R. 1956. *Hornero* 10(2):119–35. [*Fulica*, vocalization]

Navas, J. R. 1970. *Rev. Mus. Argent. Cienc. Nat.* 10(4):65–85. [*Fulica*, plumage]

Negret, A., and D. M. Teixeira. 1984. *Micropygia schomburgkii* of Central Brazil. *Condor* 86:220.

Olson, S. L. 1970. *Auk* 87:805–08. [*Porzana flaviventer*, systematics]

Olson, S. L. 1973. *Smithson, Cont. Zool.* 152. [Evolution in the South Atlantic]

Olson, S. L. 1973. *Wilson Bull.* 85:381–416. [Classification]

Olson, S. L. 1977. In S. D. Ripley, *Rails of the World.* Boston: David R. Godine. [Fossil rails]

Ripley, S. D. 1980. *Rails of the World.* Boston: David R. Godine.

Ripley, S. D., and B. M. Beehler. 1985. Rails of the World, a compilation of new information, 1975–1983. *Smithsonian Contr. Zool.* 417.

Sick, H. 1979. *Bull. B.O.C.* 99(4):115–20. [*Laterallus xenopterus*, first record for Brazil]

Stiles, F. G. 1981. *Wilson Bull.* 93(1):107–08. [*Amaurolimnas*, behavior]

Storer, R. W. 1981. *Wilson Bull.* 93:137–44. [*Laterallus*, morphology and distribution]

Teixeira, D. M. 1981. *Bol. Mus. Paraen., Zool.* 110. [*Aramides cajanea*, behavior and nesting colony]

Teixeira, D. M., and M.E.N. Puga. 1984. Notes on *Coturnicops notata. Condor* 86:342–43.

Ventura, P. E. C., and J. Ferreira. 1982. Observações sobre a minúscula saracura *Porzana flaviventer. An. Soc. Sul-Riogr. Orn.* 3:23–26.

Winterbottom, J. M. 1965. American Purple Gallinule in South Africa. *Ostrich* 36:90.

FAMILY HELIORNITHIDAE: SUNGREBES (1)

Sungrebes are delicate aquatic birds, remotely similar in aspect to a *Podiceps* grebe. In addition to the Neotropical species described here, a second family member is found in Africa and a third in Asia. Fossils are not known. Although apparently related to the Rallidae, sungrebes have a very characteristic aspect of their own. Their mallophagous fauna is similar to that of rallids, but their shared biotope could facilitate exchange of such parasites.

Morphology

Sungrebes have slender necks, sharp bills, long wings, wide, long tails, and short, strong legs. The toes are lobed like those of coots. The thorax is much compressed in a dorsal/ventral sense (not laterally as in rallids), which gives a peculiar, flattened shape to the body. The primaries molt simultaneously, leaving the bird flightless.

SUNGREBE, *Heliornis fulica*, Picaparra   Fig. 93

28 cm. Well-defined black-and-white pattern on head and neck. Mantle brown, underparts yellowish gray, bill red (from which it gets name *marrequinha-de-bico-roxo*, "little purple-billed duck"). During breeding period female's cheeks become tinged with cinnamon (barely visible in male) and eyelids with red. Feet yellow; toes have black rings. VOICE: a full, loud cry, *ohk*, repeated 3–10 times, resembling voice of Pied-billed Grebe, *Podilymbus podiceps*.

Feeding and Behavior: Catches beetles, ants that have fallen into water, dragonflies, spiders, and small crabs. Swims swiftly near water's edge, where it is easily overlooked. Perching on trunks or branches not far above water, it reaches them by crawling over obstacles, at which time

Fig. 93. Sungrebe, *Heliornis fulica*.

bright color of feet is noticeable. Roosts at night hidden among vines but always over water into which it slips noiselessly when disturbed or frightened. Dives very well but infrequently unless being chased. Takes off with ease, flying close to water's surface, and has been known to fly into a wall at night (Lagoa Juturnaiba, Rio de Janeiro), showing that it can undertake long flights, like the rallids.

Breeding: In breeding season swims in circles, holding its neck outstretched horizontally close to water with half-raised wings. Nest is a poorly arranged platform of sticks in branches above water. Two oblong, yellowish white eggs are finely speckled with cinnamon. Incubation period of 11 days is extremely short, and chick at hatching is poorly developed, almost in an embryonic state. Father is more active in caring for young, sheltering them in a cavity under his wing and protected by feathers (fig. 94). Young reportedly are carried this way even during swimming and in flight. This practice, unique among birds, was discovered 150 years ago in Brazil by Prince Maximilian of Wied but was documented with more detail in the 1970s in Mexico (Alvarez del Toro 1971). More advanced young ride on their father's back, even during dives, like grebes. Young are not nidifugous (Ruschi 1979).

Habitat and Distribution: Inhabits small, deep, shady rivers with still waters and no aquatic vegetation but bordered with root and vine-covered banks. Occurs in lowland forests where it replaces grebes. In Amazonia found in igarapés, larger rivers, and lakes bordered with floating vegetation (where it encounters Least Grebe, *Tachybaptus dominicus*). Can survive in sunny, dammed waterholes alongside high-

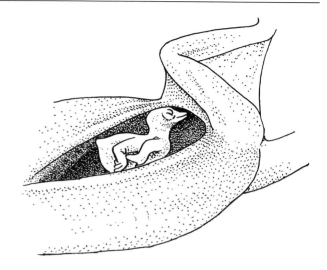

Fig. 94. Recently hatched sungrebe chick, *Heliornis fulica,* sheltered in a cavity under the father's wing. After M. A. del Toro 1971, adapted.

ways (Maranhão, Pará). Individuals, probably driven from roosts, are sometimes caught in nets on nocturnal fishing expeditions. Mexico to Bolivia, Argentina, throughout Brazil, except in extreme south. Also called *Ipequi, Ananaí, Dom-dom* (onomotopoeic, Amapá).

Heliornithidae Bibliography
See also General Bibliography

Alvarez del Toro, M. 1971. *The Living Bird* 10:79–88. [Breeding]

FAMILY EURYPYGIDAE: SUNBITTERN (1)

This monotypic family contains one of Amazonia's most characteristic birds, although it is not an endemic. It is more closely related to the Gruidae than to the Rallidae. No fossils are known.

Morphology

With its slender, delicate, elegant silhouette, the Sunbittern, *Eurypyga helias,* somewhat resembles a small egret. The neck is exceptionally thin and has a graceful S-shaped curve. The bill is long, straight, and sharply pointed. The wings are disproportionately large and wide. Sexes are similar.

SUNBITTERN, *Eurypyga helias,*
Pavãozinho-do-Pará   PL 11.7

45 cm. Admirable wing design, complemented by tail, is frequently displayed when bird is irritated (see plate). Even 2-week-old chicks display this way, pirouetting in nest. Large, brightly colored, eye-shaped spots, suddenly dis-

played, an effective means of frightening possible predators, including people. (Such terrifying marks are found on many insects, especially butterflies.) VOICE: a melancholy trill, *rrrrrrew* or *ioo-rrrrrew,* with timbre similar to whistle of Cinereous Tinamou, *Crypturellus cinereus,* which inhabits same regions. Also other vocalizations, e.g., a loud *ia,* a *tshrrrrra,* a strange whistle, a croak, and a snap, *klak.*

Feeding and Behavior: Perches on branches or logs that have fallen into water, on stones, or directly on ground at edge of rivers and igarapés, where it lurks for insects, frogs, small fish, crabs, etc., that it catches by slowly sneaking up on them. Often makes a smooth, lateral, swaying motion, sometimes with entire body, other times only with posterior, while head and legs remain stationary. Young start early to practice these peculiar movements, which are somewhat reminiscent of Cattle Egret, *Bubulcus ibis,* and Boat-billed Heron, *Cochlearius cochlearius.* Low flight is quiet like that of a nocturnal bird. Occurs alone or in pairs.

Breeding: Nest is a shallow cup, often located high on branches above or close to water and made of fibers, roots, and leaves that have been previously dipped in mud. One or 2 large, buffy eggs with chestnut and gray spots are incubated by parents for 26–27 days, each brooding for 2 days without interruption, as do certain marine birds. Parents try to keep intruders away from nest by pretending to be wounded or by turning against enemy, raising and stretching wings and tail to assume an imposing appearance, simultaneously hissing like a snake. Nestlings actively take food from parents' bills. They remain in nest 21–25 days, despite having hatched alert and typically feathered like nidifugous birds such as plovers.

Domestication and Distribution: Easy to tame and will live in semidomestication. Mexico to Bolivia, Brazil: throughout Amazonia to southern Mato Grosso (northern Pantanal), Goiás, Piauí. Also called *Pavão-papa-moscas.*

Eurypygidae Bibliography

Coimbra Filho, A. F. 1965. *Rev. Bras. Biol.* 25:149–56. [Breeding]
Frith, C. B. 1978. The function of the display and coloration in the Sunbittern. *Avicult. Mag.* 84:150–57.
Lyon, B. E., and M.P.L. Fogden. 1989. Breeding biology of the Sunbittern (*Eurypyga helias*) in Costa Rica. *Auk* 106:503–7.
Riggs, C. D. 1948. The family Eurypygidae: a review. *Wilson Bull.* 60:75–80.
Skutch, A. F. 1947. A nest of the Sun-bittern in Costa Rica. *Wilson Bull.* 59:38.
Wennrich, G. 1981. Zuchterfolge und Verhalten von Sonnerallen (*Eurypyga helias*) im Vogelpark Walsrode. *Gefiederte Welt* 105:145–50, 167–72.

FAMILY CARIAMIDAE: SERIEMAS (1)

Seriemas are large, long-legged birds of archaic appearance that are restricted to the Western Hemisphere. Ancestral fossils have been found from the Tertiary (lower Oligocene and Miocene, 30 million years B.P.) of Argentina as well as in North America (attributed to Suborder Cariamae). The oldest ancestor, however, comes from the Brazilian Paleocene (55 million years B.P.). The gigantic South American Phorusrhacidae were related to the seriemas but are not direct ancestors. Surprisingly, Phorusrhacidae have been found in the Tertiary of France (Mourer-Chaviré 1981).

As a group whose ancestry is controversial, the Cariamidae's inclusion in the Gruiformes is provisional. There is some relationship to the *Psophia.* The two present cariamids are part of the evidence pointing to the existence of very early semiopen landscapes (going back to the beginning of the Tertiary) as precursors of the present cerrado in South America. The non-Brazilian species is the Black-legged Seriema, *Chunga burmeisteri,*[1] which lacks the tuft of feathers on the head, is smaller, has black legs, and is a forest bird from Paraguay and northern Argentina. The forest origins of the Red-legged Seriema, *Cariama cristata,* a ground bird, can be seen in the fact that it nests in trees, a convergence with raptors. See *Breeding.*

RED-LEGGED SERIEMA, *Cariama cristata,*
Seriema   Fig. 95

90 cm; 1400 g. Has broad, "hard" wings, long tail. Gray with slight brown or yellowish tints. Clump of erect, forward-facing feathers, creating a martial appearance, grows at base of bill, which is sturdy and red like legs. Bird has a menacing look that recalls a *Neomorphus* ground-cuckoo. One of few birds with eyelashes. Sexes similar.

Fig. 95. Red-legged Seriema, *Cariama cristata.*

[1]In 1980 an individual Black-legged Seriema, *Chunga burmeisteri,* was found in the hands of workers on the Itaipu Dam construction camp in Paraná: possibly the bird was caught on the Paraguayan side of the river (Clodoaldo Abreu Filho, pers. comm.).

Vocalization: Song is a long phrase composed of strident cries that sound melodious at a distance and can be heard for more than 1 km. They sound like *glo* and come slowly at the beginning, accelerating as song progresses to a climax. Then they successively diminish, though they may be quickly restarted. Bird seeks a high piece of ground and sings with mouth well open, throwing head back at peak of song. At beginning of breeding season it calls before daybreak. When starting in morning it utters the notes so far apart it is difficult to realize it is a seriema preparing its concert. Song is widely known and most prominent one heard in rural regions, especially in cerrado. Also has other vocalizations: when irritated, as when wanting to devour a large prey, gives a growl. When courting and sometimes when resting, utters a squeak.

Feeding and Behavior: Eats grasshoppers and other arthropods, rodents, lizards, and other small animals, including an occasional snake. Reputed to devour a "great number" of snakes, but this is apparently exaggerated; thus, the saying "where there are seriemas there are no snakes" is not precisely so. It is not immune to snake poison. Kills larger prey, e.g., a small rat, by holding it in bill and beating it violently against ground. With a live mouse it secures its footing, lifts its head as far as possible, then lowers its head and throws prey to ground with full force, killing it after successive throws. Will step on an animal it has caught, but toes, adapted to fast running, are too short to grab anything (a captive bird did use claw of its inner toe while tearing apart a mouse with bill). Smaller prey, e.g., a gecko, is swallowed whole. Tears wings off ground-doves, tears snakes into pieces. Does not like dead animals. Always begins to eat victims at head. Most of its time is spent pertinaciously hunting small insects on ground or in low vegetation, walking slowly with head held low. Enjoys drinking.

When defecating ruffles all its plumage, especially on neck, becoming a great bundle of feathers completely different from its normal shape. Also assumes grotesque positions when defending itself.

When creeping through sparse branches of cerrado trees, jumps as high as 1 m, aided by a wing stroke. Clutches thick bark firmly with very sharp claws, large claw of 2d toe giving special service. Roosts high in trees at night, squatting on branch and sleeping with neck drawn in and head forward, not hidden under scapulars.

Moves about in pairs or small flocks. Flies only when tenaciously followed or to reach a roost. If chased by a car reaches 40 or even 70 km/hr before taking flight. During day rests by lying on its legs on ground; sometimes moves about a bit in this position, corresponding to our "walking" on our knees.

Takes dust- and sunbaths; for latter it first lies on tarsi, then on belly, and finally rolls over on side and raises its free wing, appearing to be dead. Hides by lying on ground behind a fallen log, and if appropriate carefully stays there to escape observation by a presumed enemy. To confront an immediate danger it leans forward, opening wings and tail to display impressive pattern, especially that of tail, and ruffles head and neck plumage. Perches on posts to extend visual horizon.

Breeding: In breeding season, male, to appear more intimidating or to impress female, stretches wings laterally and turns them to face forward, displaying contrasting design of remiges, whose pattern resembles that of certain raptors with which there are even other distant external similarities, especially with Secretary-bird, *Sagittarius serpentarius,* of African savanna, a species of *incertae sedis* in systematics.

During courtship walks with solemn steps, extending neck up to maximum while holding bill vertically downward; entire plumage is held close to body, but neck crest is raised slightly to one side.

In cerrado nests in trees, constructing a fair-sized nest of fragile twigs and branches, lining bottom with cattle manure, mud, or dry leaves. Tree must be such that bird can move up in jumps, supplemented by short flutters, to nest, which may be 4–5 m above ground. Usually lays 2 white, slightly pinkish eggs spotted with chestnut. Spots may be covered by external coating of shell but are visible when pieces of shell are held up to light. Oological characters are somewhat similar to those of Rallidae. Mates take turns at incubation, which lasts 26–29 days. Chick (only one is reared) covered with long, pale brown, hairlike down with brown spots; has dark brown bill, dark gray legs, is reminiscent of a young vulture or raptor. Leaves nest at 12 days. At this stage utters a series of cries to attract attention of parents; though only a few weak whistles, they have timbre of adult song.

Parasites: Nematode worms (Spiruroidea), e.g., *Oxyspirura brevipenis,* collected by Natterer in 1824, and *O. altensis* live in eyes.

Habitat and Distribution: Lives in cerrado, campo sujo, and bleak highlands of southeastern Brazil (Itatiaia). Progressive deforestation is contributing to its expansion by providing new areas of favorable habitat. Absent, for example, from Paraíba valley (Rio de Janeiro) at beginning of 1900s, but a few years ago began to penetrate Rio de Janeiro lowlands and Amazonia, taking advantage of unlimited devastation produced by Belem-Brasília highway.

Argentina, Uruguay, Paraguay, and Bolivia to central and eastern Brazil as far as western Mato Grosso (Chapada dos Parecis), southern Pará (locally in Serra do Cachimbo); not in savannas of Rio Cururu (upper Tapajós, Pará) in 1957 or in Serra Norte (Municipality of Marabá, Pará) in 1969; it had not reached Amazon as of 1973. Occurs in Maranhão (Barra da Corda, Imperatriz). Also called *Sariema* (Ceará).

Cariamidae Bibliography

Almeida, A.C.C. 1988. Comportamento reproductivo de *Cariama cristata. XV Cong. Bras. Zool., Curitiba*:497.

Alvarenga, H.M.F. 1982. Uma gigantesca ave fóssil do Cenozóico Brasileiro: *Physornis brasiliensis* sp.n. *An. Acad. Bras. Ciênc.* 54(4):697–712.

Burmeister, H. 1937. *Rev. Mus. Paul.* 23:91–152. [Natural history, original of 1853–54]
Frieling, H. 1936. *Z. Morph. Ökol. Tiere* 30,5 [Ecological adaptations]
Heinroth, O. 1924. *J. Orn.* 77:119–24. [Ontogeny]
Mourer-Chauviré, C. 1981. Première indication de la présence de

Phorusrhacidés, famille d'oiseaux géantes d'Amerique do Sud, dans le Tertiaire européan: *Ameghinornis* nov. gen. *Geobios* 14:637–47.
Rodrigues, H. 1962. *Rev. Bras. Biol.* 22:371–76. [Nematodes]
Schneider, K. M. 1957. *Beitr. Vogelk.* 5:168–83. [Vocalization]
Vanzolini, P. E. 1948. *Rev. Bras. Biol.* 8:377–400. [Snake eating]

ORDER CHARADRIIFORMES

The Order Charadriiformes can be divided into two suborders that include the following families occurring in Brazil:

1. Charadrii: Jacanidae, Rostratulidae, Haematopodidae, Charadriidae, Scolopacidae, Recurvirostridae, Phalaropodidae, Burhinidae, Glareolidae, Thinocoridae, and Chionididae
2. Lari: Stercorariidae, Laridae, and Rynchopidae

FAMILY JACANIDAE: JACANAS (1)

Jacanas are graceful aquatic birds with very lightweight bodies. They occur also in Africa and Asia. There are fossils from the Pliocene (5 million years B.P.) and Pleistocene of Brazil, and possibly even from the Oligocene of Egypt (30 million years B.P.).

Morphology and Special Adaptations

Jacanas resemble gallinules, although they do not swim. Apparently they are not related to the Rallidae but are close to the Rostratulidae.

The legs are very long and the toes exceedingly long and delicate. The elastic claws are needle sharp. The hallux claw, which curves upward, measures more than twice the length of those on the foretoes (4.5 cm vs 2 cm in the female). This is a most appropriate adaptation to living on carpets of floating vegetation where it is impossible to swim and where even a rail gets bogged down. When walking where it is partially dry, jacanas nearly step on their own toes.

WATTLED JACANA, *Jacana jacana,*
Jaçanã, Piaçoca   Fig. 96

23 cm. Probably most common Brazilian marsh bird. Black with chestnut mantle, bill yellow, membranous frontal and lateral lobes red. Frequently displayed remiges yellowish green. Sharp, yellowish spur on bend of wing serves as a weapon, like that of Southern Lapwing, *Vanellus chilensis*.

Sexes similar but female much larger (159 g vs 69 g for male). Immature resembles that of Purple Gallinule, *Porphyrula martinica,* or even a sandpiper, being more easily recognized by wings, which are like adult's. VOICE: alarm a loud, strident *wert-wert* while lifting wings.

Behavior: Walks with long steps over water hyacinth, sal-

Fig. 96. Wattled Jacana, *Jacana j. jacana,* in the typical raised-wing position; a juvenal at the side.

vinia, and other floating plants in search of insects (e.g., beetles), mollusks, small fish (when one jumps out of water and lands on a leaf), seeds. Wings often held open, typical behavior for young and reminiscent of various sandpipers. Acts as a sentinel, alert to any change in situation, like *V. chilensis.*

Breeding: Polyandry, known for other *Jacana,* confirmed by Ferreira (1983) in a 3-year survey of a Rio de Janeiro population marked with color bands. Female territory includes 2–3 male territories. One female laid 2 successive clutches, incubated by 2 males for 21–28 days. In both clutches, each densely spotted, yellowish chestnut egg was smaller than its predecessor, although all were laid by same female. Male expels female from vicinity of nest, which is on water lily leaves. To lure away possible enemies from nest or young, it uses same technique as Charadriidae, pretending to have a broken leg and acting as if unable to fly (feigning).

Young are nidifugous and walk on aquatic plants immediately after hatching. They are already extremely long-legged and can dive. In face of danger father sometimes flees by running with chicks under his wings, only shanks of their legs dangling in view.

Vicious battles may occur between 2 females disputing a male. If intruding female manages to expel "legitimate" one, intruder becomes aggressive against young, even though they are well defended by father and may even kill them.

Male then gives more attention to clutch laid by intruding female (Emlen et al. 1989).

Habitat, Migration, Enemies, and Distribution: Lives in marshes and small bogs, e.g., those formed by excavations along highways. In nonbreeding season migratory and forms flocks. Appears transitorily, as in mountain regions where it does not breed. Perches on rocks in rivers. In Amazonia is preyed on by pirarucu fish (*Arapaima gigas*). Most of tropical America east of Andes, including throughout Brazil. Also called *Cafezinho, Menininho-do-banhado* (Rio Grande do Sul), *Enxofre, Casaca-de-couro* (Minas Gerais), *Marrequinha* (Bahia). Replaced in Central America, Mexico, and Antilles by Northern Jacana, *Jacana spinosa,* a close relative that lacks lateral lobes at base of bill.

Jacanidae Bibliography

Emlen, S. T., N. J. Demong, and D. J. Emlen. 1989. Experimental induction of infanticide in female Wattled Jacanas. *Auk* 106:1–7.

Ferreira, Ildemar. 1983. "Comportamento reprodutivo da jaçanã, *Jacana jacana* no Est. do Rio de Janeiro." Thesis, Universidade Federal de Rio de Janeiro.

Jenni, D. A., and C. Collier. 1972. *Auk* 89:743–65. [Behavior]

Osborne, D. R., and G. R. Bourne. 1977. *Condor* 79(1):98–105. [Breeding, feeding]

Silva, F. 1971. *Estudos Leopoldenses* 18:331–43. [Behavior]

FAMILY ROSTRATULIDAE: PAINTED-SNIPES (1)

These wetland birds, superficially similar to snipes, were unknown in Brazil until the 1960s. They also occur in Africa, Asia, and Australia. Fossils have not been found.

SOUTH AMERICAN PAINTED-SNIPE, *Nycticryphes semicollaris,* Narceja-de-bico-torto   Fig. 97

20 cm; 65.5 g (male). Southern species with much shorter, heavier bill than Common Snipe, *Gallinago gallinago;* pink, tactile tip down-curved and broadened. Tail soft, so short and narrow it appears missing in live bird. Wings quite large with conspicuous white spots, lacking on *G. gàllinago.* Prominent white marks low on either side of neck extend along back to form a yellowish, V-shaped band. Sexes similar. Immature distinguishable from *G. gallinago* by bill shape.

Behavior, Distribution, and Breeding: Seeks shellfish in shallow water, describing semicircles with bill, keeping tip submerged while rapidly opening and shutting mandibles. Having a calmer disposition than *G. gallinago,* takes flight without calling (thus the name *narceja-muda,* "mute snipe"). Flies slowly in straight line, without zigzagging; does not go as high as *G. gallinago,* instead descending promptly with legs dangling.

When frightened freezes in place, leaning toward presumed danger with bill almost touching ground and displaying almost entire upper side; yellow and white streaks, which cut body outline into various longitudinal pieces, thus produce a unique, cryptic effect (disruption).

Fig. 97. South American Painted-Snipe, *Nycticryphes semicollaris.*

I have not seen courtship rituals. Soft tail does not produce sound (see *G. gallinago,* Scolopacidae).

Eggs oblong, not top-shaped like those of *G. gallinago,* and almost completely covered with dark spots. Marshes, rice fields. Rio de Janeiro (including ex-Guanabara), where it breeds in May, São Paulo, Santa Catarina, Rio Grande do Sul to Paraguay, Argentina, Chile.

Rostratulidae Bibliography

Höhn, E. O. 1975. *Auk* 92:566–75. [Notes on *Nycticryphes*]
Neithammer, G. 1966. *J. Orn.* 107:201–4. [Anatomy]
Pitman, C.R.S. 1964. Painted Snipe. In A. L. Thomson, ed., *A New Dictionary of Birds.* New York: McGraw-Hill.
Sick, H. 1962. *J. Orn.* 103:102–7. [Occurrence, behavior]

FAMILY HAEMATOPODIDAE: OYSTERCATCHERS (1)

Oystercatchers are cosmopolitan marine birds. There are fossils from the Pliocene of North America (5 million years B.P.). The bill is hard and straight, higher than it is wide, resembling an engraver's tool. Sexes are similar. They nest in sand, the eggs similar to those of sandpipers and gulls.

AMERICAN OYSTERCATCHER, *Haematopus palliatus,* Piru-piru PL 12.4

46 cm. Robust, long-legged, with scarlet bill and eyelids, yellow iris, pink legs. Rump and broad wing stripe white. Bill hard without specialized tip, like those described in 1st group of bill types in Scolopacidae. VOICE: a strident *kwip . . . , kleet, piru-piru;* song a trill that rises at beginning, falls at end.

Feeds on clams, barnacles, snails, etc., cutting musculature of clams by using bill as a plier and then opening valves by "gaping" (see *Arenaria* and Icterinae, "Feeding") or using bill like chisel to break them. Restricted to ocean edge, on beaches and rocks exposed to wave action. North America to southern South America, including entire Brazilian coast, where it nests (e.g., Rio Grande do Sul, November). Closely related to Eurasian Oystercatcher, *H. ostralegus,* of Old World. Also called *Baiacu, Batuíra-do-mar-grosso, Bejaqui* (Rio Grande do Sul), *Cã-cã-da-praia* (Rio Grande do Sul).

Haematopodidae Bibliography

Escalante, R. 1958. *Condor* 60:191–92. [Taxonomy]

FAMILY CHARADRIIDAE: LAPWINGS AND PLOVERS (10)

This is a cosmopolitan family of aquatic birds. Fossils have been found from the Tertiary of North America and Europe and from the Pleistocene of Brazil (20 million years B.P.). There are only four resident species in Brazil and six that arrive as migrants. In appearance and comportment the Charadriidae frequently resemble the Scolopacidae. For this reason I cover the two families together in the entry in this section entitled "Visiting Species: Identification, Behavior, and Large-scale Migration" and in the entry in Scolopacidae on bill and tarsus adaptations.

Brazilian Species

I urge using the term *batuira* when referring to the Charadriidae in Portuguese, reserving *maçarico*[1] for the Scolopacidae.

Native Brazilian plovers are the Southern Lapwing, *Vanellus chilensis;* Pied Lapwing, *Hoploxypterus cayanus;* Collared Plover, *Charadrius collaris;* and, in the extreme south, a recent addition, the Two-banded Plover, *C. falklandicus.*

The first-named is one of the most celebrated birds of Brazil. Sexes are similar. Food is predominantly animal (see Scolopacidae, "Bill and Tarsus Adaptations"). Searching for food in shallow water, *Charadrius* customarily scrape their feet over the sand, scaring up hidden prey such as small crustaceans.

Plovers nest in small hollows scraped in the earth. The eggs are top- or pear-shaped, a form that causes them to roll around their own axis and not laterally. Being spotted, they blend perfectly with the ground. When frightened off their nests, adults feign injury to lure away the enemy. If someone discovers a nest, a *Charadrius* may roll its eggs to a neighboring spot to save them. The young are nidifugous. The male *Vanellus chilensis* becomes aggressive, even toward humans. Ranchers know it to be a better sentinel than dogs, for it alerts the dogs.

In Amazonia plovers are periodically driven away by floods that inundate their habitat (river beaches and shallow marshes). The resulting migration is not just an irregular movement but a periodic annual occurrence. The dislocated

---

[1]There is also the *maçarico-preto* or *tapicuru,* the White-faced Ibis, *Plegadis chihi,* of the Order Ciconiiformes. When *maçaricos* are spoken of in Rio Grande do Sul, often *P. chihi* is understood.

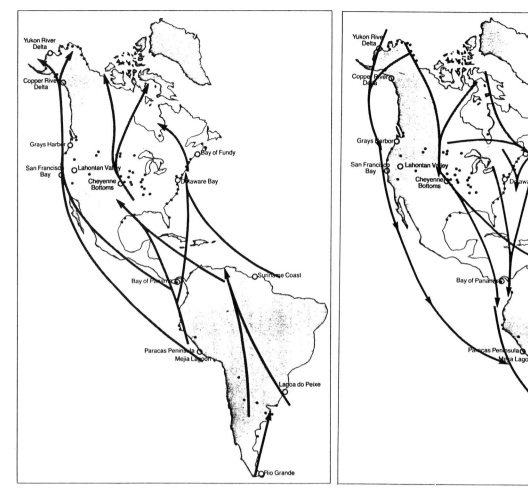

Fig. 98. The principal northbound and southbound migration corridors of migratory shorebirds in the Americas are shown schematically, superimposed on maps of the Western Hemisphere Shorebird Reserve Network. The network, established by an international consortium of public and private organizations, currently consists of more than 90 sites divided into two categories: hemispheric reserves (circles), defined by an international panel of biologists as supporting either more than 250,000 birds or at least 30% of a species' population moving along a migration corridor; and regional reserves (dots), defined as supporting more than 20,000 birds or 5% of a migrating population. From Myers et al. 1987. Left: northbound; right: southbound.

birds go through a nonbreeding period at this time. When the water recedes, they immediately initiate breeding, as do other beach birds such as terns and ducks. The four Brazilian species do not associate with visiting flocks.

Visiting Species: Identification, Behavior, and Large-scale Migration of Charadriidae and Scolopacidae

Six of the ten Charadriidae are migrants, four of them coming from North America: the Black-bellied Plover, *Pluvialis squatarola;* Lesser Golden-Plover, *P. dominica;* Semipalmated Plover, *Charadrius semipalmatus;* and Wilson's Plover, *C. wilsonia;* and two from the southern Andean region: the Rufous-chested Dotterel *Zonibyx modestus,* and Tawny-throated Dotterel, *Oreopholus ruficollis.* These latter are rare in Brazil, reaching only the extreme south during the

southern winter, especially in July–August. Of the Scolopacidae, 20 are migrants.

Identifying migrant shorebirds is not normally easy, because when the birds are in Brazil (the northern winter) they wear their modest nonbreeding plumage, which is similar in most species (eclipse plumage). This is also similar to the plumage of immatures, which are more numerous. The earliest individuals to arrive here usually still show remains of their beautiful nuptial plumage, often black (e.g., in both *Pluvialis*) or bright rusty (e.g., in Red Knot, *Calidris canutus,* and Sanderling, *C. alba*), which they regain beginning in February, before returning to the Northern Hemisphere to breed. I found a *C. canutus* in full breeding plumage on 29 March in Rio Grande do Sul. These conspicuous plumages provide perfect camouflage for these birds on the summer boreal tundra.

Among the most important diagnostic characters, after

total length, are length and color of the legs; length, form, and color of the bill (the last is not always clear because of mud); and presence of a white pattern in the wings or tail (as seen in flight). The fact that individuals of the same species differ considerably in size (e.g., Pectoral Sandpiper, *Calidris melanotos,* and Buff-breasted Sandpiper, *Tryngites subruficollis*) may cause confusion. In many cases comparing associated species facilitates identification. Much that has been said about the Charadriidae applies also to the Scolopacidae. Other details can be found in North American field guides.

It is common for migrant plovers to act tame, perhaps because they are inexperienced immatures or because they come from remote polar regions where they are not confronted by firearms.

These northern birds, fugitives from the boreal winter, are common, arriving here in large numbers beginning around the end of August (figs. 98A and 98B). Frequently they continue on to Argentina. They migrate day and night, unlike swallows. None breed in Brazil, but they may, as in their summer quarters, occupy small feeding territories (e.g., *Pluvialis dominica*). They return to North America in March–

April, the northern spring, to breed starting in May. Some individuals, usually immatures, remain in the tropics all year. At the peak of migration they gather at the water's edge ("shorebirds") in hundreds and even thousands, especially *Calidris alba.* They frequently form mixed flocks. They like to fly in close formation, with the whole flock maneuvering impressively in perfectly synchronized fashion, swirling without ever colliding (see Hirundinidae, "Migration"). Censusing shorebird flocks has to be done by estimates. First the total number is estimated; then a second count is made, calculating one or more parts of the flock and extrapolating to the whole.

Since 1974 the Canadian Wildlife Service and Manomet Bird Observatory in Massachusetts have conducted an International Shorebird Survey (iss) to gather data on the distribution and migration of these birds. The census is conducted in South America in two periods, between 21 August and 20 November (arrival of the migrants) and between 11 March and 31 May (return). In January 1986 flights over the Maranhão and Pará coast were made in a dual-turbine helicopter of the Vale do Rio Doce Co. as part of this international census (fig. 99). In addition to specific surveys, such as on

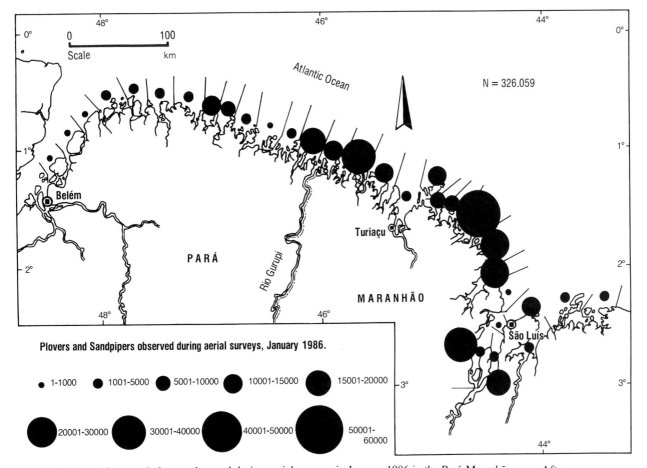

Fig. 99. All sandpipers and plovers observed during aerial surveys in January 1986 in the Pará-Maranhão area. After Morrison et al. 1986.

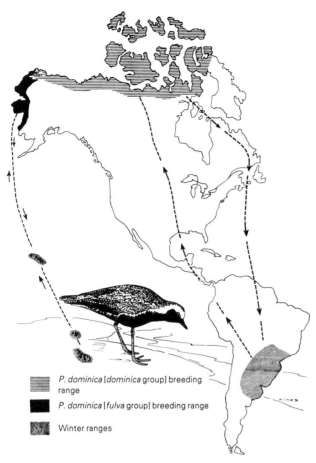

P. dominica [dominica group] breeding range

P. dominica [fulva group] breeding range

Winter ranges

Fig. 100. Migration of the Lesser Golden-Plover, *Pluvialis dominica*. The eastern [*dominica*] group migrates from northeastern Canada nonstop across the North Atlantic to the Venezuelan coast and on to central Brazil and Argentina. It returns on a westerly route. The illustrated individual is in breeding plumage, seen in Brazil only at the beginning and end of these migrants' winter sojourn. After Lincoln 1950.

C. alba, censusing was done by grouping sandpipers and plovers by size: small, medium, and large. In Maranhão the "small" birds were estimated to number 40,000, the majority probably *C. pusilla*. All sandpipers and plovers together totaled 60,000. In April 1983 calculations on the density of *C. canutus* made on the beach at Cassino, Rio Grande do Sul, gave estimates of 149 individuals per km. In May the figure diminished to 31, before the species disappeared completely.

Distances covered by shorebirds are among the greatest known for migratory birds. *C. alba,* for example, one of the most abundant shorebirds in Brazil, breeds beyond the Arctic Circle and must fly about 10,000 km to reach Rio de Janeiro, 5000 km more to reach Tierra del Fuego. Shortly afterward it covers the same distance back to the Arctic. It does not hurry, spending weeks traveling and stopping to eat and rest. Going north it usually stops less. A *C. canutus* color banded at Lagoa do Peixe, Rio Grande do Sul, was identified 13 days

later at Delaware Bay in the U.S., 7600 km away. To cover such distances the birds must accumulate large fat reserves, which is clearly indicated by the great amount of weight they gain while at Lagoa do Peixe (see also Parulinae, "Northern Migrant Species"). Species such as the Ruddy Turnstone, *Arenaria interpres,* can cover 800 km in a day doing the major part at night. This species has been seen in daylight 48 km off the coast of Recife (October) and flying south 160 km out to sea at approximately 10°S.

Certain species, such as *Pluvialis dominica,* do not usually follow the Atlantic coast, as do *P. squatarola* and *C. alba,* but fly directly via Colombia and Venezuela to the upper Amazon and from there to central Brazil, finally reaching Paraguay and the interior of Argentina (fig. 100). Some reach the Brazilian coast only in the extreme south. Others that follow this route are the Phalaropodidae and certain Scolopacidae, such as the Stilt Sandpiper, *Calidris himantopus; Tryngites subruficollis;* Upland Sandpiper, *Bartramia longicauda;* Hudsonian Godwit, *Limosa haemastica;* and Eskimo Curlew, *Numenius borealis.* Some species, such as *Pluvialis dominica,* opt for different routes coming and going. In coming, *P. dominica* flies directly from Nova Scotia to Venezuela. Returning it follows the Andes and crosses the Gulf of Mexico. Thus, a species may appear in a given area in Brazil only when coming or going. It is important to watch for banded individuals.

Colored Flags for Regions and Countries of the New World

Marking Charadriidae and Scolopacidae with colored bands was organized in 1984 by the Pan American Shorebird Program (PASP) under J. P. Myers, then of the Philadelphia Academy of Natural Sciences, and financed by the World Wildlife Fund/US. The system is designed to standardize marking of these birds throughout the hemisphere, using traditional metal and color bands with a new system: a small flag placed on the bird's tarsus-metatarsus. The flag is made of the same material as the color bands, with a trailing end that is visible to field workers at a distance. Study is still needed to determine whether color marking may disturb the birds' social life. The codes for the various countries were published in *Volante Migratorio,* no. 1:16–21, and later perfected in *Volante Migratorio,* no. 3, as follows:

Canada	White
United States	Dark green
Central America	
Mexico	Red over yellow
Honduras	Red over gray
Costa Rica	Red over black
Guatemala	Red over orange
Nicaragua	Red over dark green
Belize	Red over light green
El Salvador	Red over blue
Panama	Red over white

Antilles	
Haiti	Yellow over red
Puerto Rico	Yellow over dark green
Dominican Republic	Yellow over white
Venezuela	Black
Suriname	Light green
Northern South America	
Colombia	Light green over yellow
Ecuador	Light green over red
Guyana	Light green over dark green
French Guiana	Light green over blue
Peru	Yellow
Brazil	Blue
Central South America	
Bolivia	Orange over red
Paraguay	Orange over yellow
Uruguay	Orange over blue
Argentina	Orange
Chile	Red

Hunting and Decline

Some species, such as *Pluvialis dominica* and *Bartramia longicauda,* are or have been treated as game birds and sold in the marketplace. This resource is not inexhaustible, as the case of *Numenius borealis* clearly shows. In Ceará sandpipers and terns (*Sterna*) are caught with bait on the beach (L. C. Marigo pers. comm.).

SOUTHERN LAPWING, *Vanellus chilensis,* Quero-quero   PL 13.2

37 cm. One of most appreciated birds among ranchers. Unmistakable with nuchal crest, large white area on wing (visible in flight), and white at base of tail. Spur at bend of wing remains hidden under plumage, as in *Hoploxypterus cayanus* and Wattled Jacana, *Jacana jacana.* Red spurs are displayed to rivals or enemies by raising wing or in flight, when they are prominent. VOICE: *tero-tero,* uttered day and night. Sometimes adopts a fishing tactic similar to that of certain herons, frightening up insect larvae and small fish hidden in mud by stirring rapidly with a foot. Marshes and pastures where it nests on ground; is seen on roads far from water. Very common in certain places, e.g., Rio Grande do Sul, where in winter its ranks are swollen by immigrants. Central America to Tierra del Fuego, throughout Brazil. Also called *Téu-téu, Espanta-boiada* (Minas Gerais), *Chiqueira.* See Double-striped Thick-knee, *Burhinus bistriatus,* and *Hoploxypterus cayanus.*

PIED LAPWING, *Hoploxypterus cayanus,* Batuíra-de-esporão   PL 13.3

22 cm. Elegant and unmistakable, brilliantly colored with black, white, and brown but without crest. Wing spur, eyelids, and legs red, bill black. VOICE: call a bisyllabic *tweet-tweet;* song a high trill, *tewtewtew. . . .* Sandy beaches of large rivers, primarily in Amazonia, nesting alongside

Large-billed Tern, *Phaetusa simplex.* Also along ocean, muddy lake shores. Tropical South America south to Bolivia, Paraguay, Argentina (Misiones), Paraná and Mato Grosso in Brazil.

BLACK-BELLIED PLOVER, *Pluvialis squatarola,* Batuiruçu-de-axila-preta   NV

30 cm. Migrant with circumpolar distribution similar to *P. dominica.* Differs from it in black axillaries, prominent in flight. VOICE: a strident, trisyllabic *tli-ew-i.* Beaches along entire Brazilian Atlantic coast, including Rio de Janeiro (October, June), ex-Guanabara (August), São Paulo, Rio Grande do Sul. Occurs as far south as Argentina. Does not penetrate into interior of continent. Also in Old World.

LESSER GOLDEN-PLOVER, *Pluvialis dominica,* Batuiruçu   NV   PL 13.1

26 cm. Large plover from Arctic. Adults arrive still wearing remnants of breeding plumage (underparts black, September), in which they resemble *P. squatarola.* VOICE: a low *tlewit.* Dry places with short grass, e.g., airports, football fields. Large numbers land on deserts of earth scraped bare by Transamazonian Highway in heart of Hylaea (September–October). Abundant in central Brazil until end of February. Migrates as far as Argentina and Chile but scarcely appeared on northern and eastern littoral of Brazil (Bahia, November; Espírito Santo, October) until recent years, when it has been seen almost regularly (Rio de Janeiro). In south (Rio Grande do Sul) not unusual on ocean beaches, sometimes with Greater Yellowlegs, *Tringa melanoleuca,* and *Charadrius semipalmatus.* Also in Old World. Also called *Maçarico-do-campo, Batuira-do-campo.*

SEMIPALMATED PLOVER, *Charadrius semipalmatus,* Batuíra-de-bando   NV   PL 13.5

18 cm. Common North American migrant with distinct white nuchal collar. Bill quite short with yellow base; feet yellow; colors inconspicuous in immature. Muddy or sandy beaches of littoral along entire Brazilian coast and as far south as Argentina. Two banded individuals, captured on Rio Tocantins estuary (Pará, January and April), had been banded in Ontario and New Jersey, respectively. May be considered conspecific with Common Ringed Plover, *C. hiaticula,* of Old World, which occasionally reaches Neotropics as a migrant (Trinidad). Also called *Pinga-pinga* (Rio Grande do Sul). Clearly stockier than Collared Plover, *C. collaris.*

TWO-BANDED PLOVER, *Charadrius falklandicus,* Batuíra-de-coleira-dupla

19 cm. Two black or blackish bands across breast. Beaches, nests mostly in southern South America. Moves in small numbers to Rio Grande do Sul and in 1986 found nesting at Lagoa do Peixe. Also called *Maçarico-da-Patagonia.*

COLLARED PLOVER, *Charadrius collaris*, Batuíra-de-coleira PL 13.4

15 cm. Attractive Brazilian species with upperparts tending toward ferruginous (lacking in *C. semipalmatus*), no white on nape. Black breast band frequently narrows at center. Bill black; legs quite long and light pink. VOICE: *tilip, tewrew*. Remains paired all year. Shows nervousness by bobbing. Sandy or muddy places, sometimes far from water; lays eggs in open without making slightest effort to prepare a nest. Found more in interior than near salt water. Prefers dunes and areas of pioneer vegetation. Mexico to Bolivia, Argentina, Chile, throughout Brazil. Also called *Batuíra-da-costa*.

WILSON'S PLOVER, *Charadrius wilsonia* NV

Similar to *C. semipalmatus* but with heavier, black bill. Northern migrant to Brazilian coast: Pernambuco (September–May) to Bahia.

RUFOUS-CHESTED DOTTEREL, *Zonibyx modestus*, Batuíra-de-peito-tijolo SV

19 cm. Southern migrant in winter plumage, immature brown with white superciliary and abdomen. In nuptial plumage breast reddish, bordered below with black. Coastal and lake shores. Occurs in extreme south of continent, arriving on migration in Rio Grande do Sul (where it becomes relatively common in April, May, June) and rarely to São Paulo (May).

TAWNY-THROATED DOTTEREL, *Oreopholus ruficollis*, Batuíra-de-papo-ferrugíneo SV

27 cm. Rare southern migrant, distinguishable from all others. Has aspect of a small *Vanellus chilensis* and size of *Pluvialis dominica* but with longer and more slender bill, long legs, short toes. Back gray or brownish streaked with black and yellow, throat bright cinnamon, belly pale yellow with black area in center. With wings open, white shafts and bases of primaries are visible. VOICE: *drewde-lewdel-lewdel*; on migration usually silent. Savannas, rice plantations. Occurs in south of continent, migrating to Ecuador and extreme southern Brazil, in Rio Grande do Sul May–July, sometimes in large flocks (Belton 1984).

Charadriidae Bibliography
See also General and Scolopacidae Bibliographies

Andrade, M. A., R. Otoch, D. M. Hassett, et al. 1988. Salinas de Macau, Rio Grande do Norte: uma importante região para aves aquáticas migratórias no Brasil. *An. IV ENAV*:17.

Belton, W. 1973. *Auk* 90:95. [*Oreopholus ruficollis*, recorded in Brazil]

Duffy, D. C., D. C. Schneider, and N. Atkins. 1984. Paracas Rejoined—Do Shorebirds Compete in the Tropics? *Auk* 101:199–201.

Fernandes, A. C., and C. M. Vooren. 1987. Sobre a densidade sazonal de *Calidris canutus* and *C. fuscicollis* na praia de Cassino, Rio Grande do Sul. *XIV Cong. Bras. Zool., Juiz de Fora*:407.

Hoerschelmann, H. 1970. *Zool. Anz.* 184, 5/6. [Ecological adaptations]

Maclean, G. L. 1972a. *Auk* 89:299–324. [Clutch size]

Maclean, G. L. 1972b. *Zool. Africana* 7(1):57–74. [Behavior]

Milléo-Costa, L. C. 1985. Aspectos comportamentais de *Vanellus chilensis*. *XII Cong. Bras. Zool., Campinas*:536.

Mitchell, M. H. 1954. *Wilson Bull.* 66(2):139–40. [Migration]

Morrison, R.I.G., R. K. Ross, and P.T.Z. Antas. 1986. Distribuição de maçaricos, batuíras e outras aves costeiras na região salgada paraense e reentrâncias maranhenses. CVRD/GEAMAM, *Espaço, Ambiente e Planejamento*, 4.

Myers, J. P., R.I.G. Morrison, P. Z. Antas, et al. 1987. Conservation strategy for Migratory Species. *Amer. Scientist* Jan./Feb.:19–26.

Novaes, F. C., and T. Pimentel. 1973. *Publ. Avul. Mus. Para.*, no. 20 [Feeding]

Olson, S. L. 1981. Natural history of vertebrates on the Brazilian islands of the mid South Atlantic. *Nat. Geo. Soc. Res. Reports* 13:481–91.

Peterson, R. T. Various North American field guides. All species are illustrated; see General Bibliography.

FAMILY SCOLOPACIDAE: SANDPIPERS AND SNIPES (24)

This cosmopolitan family of aquatic birds is related to the Charadriidae. There is extensive fossil documentation from the upper Eocene of France (40 million years B.P.). Brazilian fossils also have been found, from the Pleistocene (20,000 years B.P.) in Minas Gerais.

The only two species recorded as resident in Brazil are the Common Snipe, *Gallinago gallinago*, and Giant Snipe, *G. undulata*. Both are wetland species valued as game birds and famous for the noise (instrumental music) they make during their twilight nuptial flights.

Bill and Tarsus Adaptations in Scolopacidae and Charadriidae

Bill shape varies greatly according to the specific food taken and the strategy employed to get it. Two principal types can be recognized:

1. Hard rhamphotheca, the tip of the bill without special differentiation: genera *Vanellus*, *Pluvialis*, *Charadrius*, *Arenaria*, *Tringa*, and *Actitis*. Prey is found visually or acoustically, being caught on the surface of shallow waters or

mud (as in the intertidal zone). *Arenaria* captures animals by turning over stones, using the bill as a lever and "gaping" (see Icterinae "Feeding"). It digs in the sand and is sometimes necrophagous. Birds with this type of bill are capable of catching swift prey. The Spotted Sandpiper, *Actitis macularia,* for instance, sometimes hunts swarming termites, and the Southern Lapwing, *Vanellus chilensis,* occasionally goes after hornets (northeast) and sometimes exploits recently plowed land to capture small creatures, competing then with the Crested Caracara, *Polyborus plancus.* It is common for sandpipers such as the Greater Yellowlegs, *Tringa melanoleuca,* to enter water up to the belly and to swim a little, even without webbed feet.

2. Flexible rhamphotheca, sensitive bill tip: genera *Calidris, Numenius, Limosa,* and *Gallinago.* They find prey predominantly by feel, catching slow-moving creatures, some of which are subterranean. The Least Sandpiper, *Calidris minutilla,* captures larvae of aquatic beetles and vegetable material (eastern Pará). *Gallinago gallinago* sticks its bill (which resembles that of the Kiwi, *Apteryx,* of New Zealand) in the bog up to its base, opening it only at the tip to snatch a worm. Its nostrils are right next to the forehead plumage. For this reason snipes, which are fresh-water birds, require soft, very wet soils to take full advantage of their peculiar bills. Their activities are revealed by holes that remain on the surface of the mud if it is not too soft. This adaptation does not prevent snipes from hunting insects perched on leaves or on the ground when opportunity offers. Like *Vanellus chilensis,* which sporadically eats small seeds and berries, snipes do not completely reject vegetable matter, perhaps as a result of a scarcity of animal food. They also use sand and mud banks exposed at low tide.

Sandpipers can bring plants from one continent to another through live seeds in their droppings, as many other migratory birds must do.

Gallinago undulata catches frogs, whereas the Whimbrel, *Numenius phaeopus,* digs into coastal bogs in search of small crabs, sinking its long bill halfway in.

The length of the tarsus-metatarsus may be partly an ecological adaptation in the sense that a longer tarsus may mean more time spent in high vegetation or deeper water.

While resting on the beach, sandpipers regurgitate pellets containing chitin from exoskeletons of arthropods they have eaten.

Visiting Species

The 22 Scolopacidae migrants all come from hyperboreal regions. Fourteen are restricted to the New World; two, the Pectoral Sandpiper, *Calidris melanotos,* and Semipalmated Sandpiper, *C. pusilla,* extend their ranges to include Siberia, whereas the remainder—the Ruddy Turnstone, *Arenaria interpres;* Red Knot, *Calidris canutus;* Sanderling, *C. alba;* Ruff, *Philomachus pugnax;* and *Numenius phaeopus*—have

circumpolar or Holarctic distributions. Among the North American Scolopacidae that arrive here are three geographic representatives of Old World forms, as their practically identical voices reveal: see Solitary Sandpiper, *Tringa solitaria; T. melanoleuca;* and Spotted Sandpiper, *Actitis macularia.* Adults all arrive molting into eclipse plumage, looking similar to the immatures, which outnumber them (see Charadriidae, "Visiting Species . . .").

Numenius phaeopus hudsonicus from North America occasionally meets *N. p. phaeopus* from the Old World on Brazilian soil (Fernando de Noronha).

The Eskimo Curlew, *N. borealis,* which as recently as the 1800s was a frequent migrant to the Argentine pampas and also occurred in Brazil, is presently almost extinct.

I have included some observations on migration, etc., of the following Scolopacidae: *Arenaria interpres, Calidris canutus, C. melanotos, C. alba,* and *Tryngites subruficollis* in the introductory section of the Charadriidae. All these species are covered extensively in North American bird books.

Usually there is no competition between migrants and resident birds, but such is possible, as was noted in Peru between an *Arenaria interpres* and a Seaside Cinclodes, *Cinclodes nigrofumosus* (Furnariidae) (Atkins 1980).

RUDDY TURNSTONE, *Arenaria interpres,*
Vira-pedras   NV   Fig. 101

22 cm. Stocky, arctic sandpiper with short, sturdy bill, relatively short, orange legs. White streak through wing, another crossing lower back, and a 3d across base of tail form conspicuous design in flight. Underparts white. Immature has brown breast. VOICE: *kyeh, kikiki.* Sometimes eats dead animals (remains of fish, etc.). Not uncommon along rocky ocean shores, picking at algae-covered rocks for mollusks,

Fig. 101. Ruddy Turnstone, *Arenaria interpres,* in immature plumage.

small crustaceans. On methods of hunting, see "Bill and Tarsus Adaptations. . . ." Occasionally in interior: Petrópolis, Novo Friburgo (Rio de Janeiro), Mato Grosso. Entire Brazilian coast as far as Argentina. On migration, see "Visiting Species." Also called *Agachada.*

SOLITARY SANDPIPER, *Tringa solitaria,*
Maçarico-solitário   NV

18 cm. Throughout Brazil as a lone migrant. At water's edge, including among trees, and in flooded excavations, biotopes not often used by other sandpipers. Upper wing all black, unlike *Actitis macularia,* which bobs posterior part of body; this species lifts forepart of body upward. A geographic replacement for Green Sandpiper, *T. ochropus,* of Old World, which it greatly resembles in all respects, including ecological requirements and voice, a limpid whistle, *dlooit-dlooit.*

LESSER YELLOWLEGS, *Tringa flavipes,*
Maçarico-de-perna-amarela   NV PL 12.2

26 cm. One of most abundant visiting shorebirds in wettest areas of interior as well as littoral. Rump and tail whitish; no white in wing; legs bright yellow. Muddy, open river and lake beaches. Throughout Brazil to Tierra del Fuego. An individual caught on São Paulo coast (November) had been banded 3 months earlier in Massachusetts. See *T. melanoleuca,* with which it frequently associates. Also called *Batuíra, Maçarico-da-praia.*

GREATER YELLOWLEGS, *Tringa melanoleuca,*
Maçarico-grande-de perna-amarela   NV

35 cm. Very similar to *T. flavipes* but clearly larger and with longer bill that tends to curve slightly upward, unlike straight bill of *flavipes.* VOICE: loud, with timbre of Campo Flicker, *Colaptes campestris, jew-jew-jew (jew).* Beaches, flooded savannas, probably throughout Brazil, including central Brazil and Amazonia, to Tierra del Fuego. Less numerous than *flavipes.* Also called *Chirolito* (Rio Grande do Sul). A geographic replacement of Old World's Greenshank, *T. nebularia,* which it resembles, including in voice. See Hudsonian Godwit, *Limosa haemastica.*

SPOTTED SANDPIPER, *Actitis macularia,*
Maçarico-pintado   NV PL 12.5

19 cm. Slender, almost unique in bobbing its body while walking (see *Tringa solitaria*) and for short wing strokes, somewhat like those of *Bartramia longicauda.* Upperside of wings has white line (see *T. solitaria*), underside black with white area in center. Blackish spots on breast in breeding season. VOICE: song resembles *T. solitaria: pit, dlewit-dlewit.* Stony, muddy river edges, almost always in vegetation, frequently in mangroves where it roosts overnight on roots and branches. In most of Brazil. In Amazonia periodically very active (September, singing in breeding plumage), as if it were nesting. Also called *Rapazinho* (Rio Grande do

Sul), *Maçariquinho.* A geographic replacement of Old World's Common Sandpiper, *A. hypoleucos,* and could be considered a geographic race of it. Genus *Actitis* could be included in *Tringa.*

WILLET, *Catoptrophorus semipalmatus,*
Maçarico-de-asa-branca   NV

38 cm. Large, uncommon migrant, distinctive in flight. Upperparts light gray, underparts white. Open wings show wide white streak with black trailing edge; rump white. Legs dark bluish, unlike *Tringa melanoleuca.* Littoral. Pará and Rio Grande do Sul (December). Breeds on Venezuelan coast (May).

RED KNOT, *Calidris canutus,*
Maçarico-de-papo-vermelho   NV

26 cm. Arctic migrant to our coast (fig. 102). Piauí, Rio de Janeiro (November), São Paulo, Rio Grande do Sul. Appears on our shores both as a migrant and wintering bird. Principal wintering ground is in Tierra del Fuego. On distances and speed of return to Arctic, see Charadriidae, "Visiting Species . . . ."

LEAST SANDPIPER, *Calidris minutilla,*
Maçariquinho   NV

13.5 cm. Miniscule arctic species. Compared with *C. pusilla* has more slender bill, browner mantle, streaked breast, yellowish green legs. VOICE: a prolonged *trrooit.* Abundant

Fig. 102. Red Knot, *Calidris canutus,* migration follows the continental coasts. After Rappole et al. 1983.

on our northern coast, also common at edge of fresh water and in brackish marshes. On feeding, see "Bill and Tarsus Adaptations . . . ." In Pernambuco September–March, south to Bahia. Once in Rio Grande do Sul.

BAIRD'S SANDPIPER, *Calidris bairdii,* Maçarico-de-bico-fino   NV

17.8 cm. First recorded in Brazil in Torres, Rio Grande do Sul, September 1975 (Belton 1978). Similar to *C. melanotos* but with black, not yellow, legs. Common migrant in Chile and Andean region. See *C. pusilla* and *C. minutilla.*

WHITE-RUMPED SANDPIPER, *Calidris fuscicollis,* Maçarico-de-sobre-branco   NV

18 cm. White rump. VOICE: *tsri, tsri,* high like a bat. A migrant to all regions of Brazil (fig. 103). Mud flats, pastures, flooded areas, beaches, frequently far from water.

PECTORAL SANDPIPER, *Calidris melanotos,* Maçarico-de-colete   NV

22 cm. Migrant both to interior and coast, as far as Rio Grande do Sul. Pastures, flooded areas. Varies greatly in size. See *C. bairdii.*

SEMIPALMATED SANDPIPER, *Calidris pusilla,* Maçarico-rasteirinho   NV   PL 13.7

15 cm. Quite small but plump with heavy black bill, broad at tip like that of congeners (except *C. bairdii*). Legs black. VOICE: a short, harsh *prrewt.* Regularly accompanies *C. semipalmatus.* Comes from Arctic, where it breeds June–July in Canada and Alaska. Of 458 individuals captured and banded in Pará (14), Maranhão (74), Ceará (47), Pernambuco (270), and Rio Grande do Sul (53), most were molting (flight feathers and into basic plumage) on arrival in September–October. By January adults had begun to reacquire breeding plumage. Two individuals banded in U.S. and Canada were recovered in Amazon estuary (January and April). Reaches Argentina, Chile. See *C. minutilla* and *C. alba.*

SANDERLING, *Calidris alba,* Maçarico-branco NV   PL 12.6

20 cm. Generally most commonly seen Arctic sandpiper on our beaches. Resembles *C. pusilla,* with which it often associates, but clearly larger and whiter with large white streak through wing. Mantle pale gray. VOICE: *plit.* Accompanies movement of waves on beach, moving its small legs with extraordinary speed. Occurs along entire Brazilian coast. Small flocks even frequent beaches in cities such as Rio de Janeiro (Copacabana, at night) and near Recife (Pernambuco) from end of August until mid-May. As late as last week of April, birds in breeding plumage were recorded on Rio Grande do Sul coast. Breeding starts in June north of Arctic Circle. By mid-August adults begin to appear again along our coast. Thus, these birds spend very little time in the Arctic and then come to the Southern Hemisphere, crossing

Fig. 103. White-rumped Sandpiper, *Calidris fuscicollis,* migration penetrates the continent. After Rappole et al. 1983.

subtropical and tropical regions (see Peregrine Falcon, *Falco peregrinus*). They concentrate in certain places (e.g., Rio Grande do Sul, November) by the hundreds but go as far as Tierra del Fuego.

STILT SANDPIPER, *Calidris himantopus,* Maçarico-pernilongo   NV

20 cm. Uncommon migrant. Beaches. Northern, central (Araguaia, Aragarças, Goiás, October), and southern (Rio Grande do Sul) Brazil. Similar to Curlew Sandpiper, *Calidris ferruginea,* of Old World.

RUFF, *Philomachus pugnax*   NV

23–29 cm (male). Widely distributed in Old World, common in Europe. Casual in Americas. Rio Grande do Sul (Taim, Lagoa do Peixe, October 1985, March). Famous for variable nuptial plumage of males and fights between rivals.

BUFF-BREASTED SANDPIPER, *Tryngites subruficollis,* Maçarico-acanelado   NV

21 cm. Small head, short bill, slender neck, yellow legs. Underparts cinnamon, contrasting in flight with pure white underwing. Resembles a small *Bartramia longicauda.* Associates with Lesser Golden-Plover, *Pluvialis dominica.* Dry, open, short-grass fields. Amazonas (October), Rondônia, Rio Grande do Sul (November, January).

UPLAND SANDPIPER, *Bartramia longicauda,*
Maçarico-do-campo   NV

30 cm. Unique appearing, with small, pigeonlike head, slender bill and neck, and long tail, all unlike *Pluvialis dominica,* with which it sometimes occurs. Yellowish brown with black bars on underside of wings, which are often raised; legs yellow. Dry or flooded fields, burns, cattle corrals. In south may appear alongside Greater Rhea, *Rhea americana.* Usually perches on posts, even in trees. Roraima (October), Pará (February), Bahia, São Paulo, Santa Catarina, Rio Grande do Sul (October), Mato Grosso (September), Goiás (September). An individual banded in Canada was recovered in interior of Ceará. Also called *Batuíra-do-campo.*

WHIMBREL, *Numenius phaeopus,* Maçaricão
NV   PL 13.6

42 cm. Easily singled out by size (male reaches 350 g) and long, decurved bill, vaguely similar to that of Scarlet Ibis, *Eudocimus ruber,* with which it sometimes associates. Wings and rump lack any pattern. VOICE: a melodious whistle, *ew-ew-ew.* Arctic migrant. Found in intertidal mangroves. Re feeding see "Visiting Species." Relatively abundant in northern Brazil: Amapá (January–February), Maranhão (July), Piauí (September), Pernambuco (end of September forward). Central north coast of Brazil is its most important wintering area. Becoming somewhat scarce in south (Cabo Frio, Rio de Janeiro, November); ranges to Tierra del Fuego, which it must reach via Pacific coast, where it is numerous (Peru, Chile). North American birds, *N. p. hudsonicus,* have been found on Fernando de Noronha in association with European form, *N. p. phaeopus,* which has white rump (July 1973, Olson 1981). Also called *Maçarico-real, Maria-rita* (Maranhão).

ESKIMO CURLEW, *Numenius borealis,*
Maçarico-esquimó   NV   EN

33 cm. Canadian breeder, once a common migrant to Brazil. By 1920s so scarce it can be considered practically extinct. Slightly larger than *Pluvialis dominica.* Bill more slender, less curved, smaller than *N. phaeopus.* Inner vane of remiges all dark, uncrossed by light streaks. Recorded in mid-1800s in small flocks in Argentine pampa, alongside *P. dominica* and *Bartramia longicauda,* September–February. Also documented in Brazil (Amazonas, Mato Grosso, São Paulo, September–November). Between 1819 and 1830 Natterer collected 9 specimens, most in Ypanema, São Paulo, There is 1 well-mounted specimen in National Museum (Rio de Janeiro) but it lacks any indication of origin, which may be Brazil. Among latest records of species are 1 from Louisiana, another from Massachusetts, both on migration in 1970. Also James Bay, Ontario, Canada, 1976. In 1981, 23 individuals were counted in Texas, providing new hope for survival of species (Gollop et al. 1981).

HUDSONIAN GODWIT, *Limosa haemastica,*
Maçaricão-de-bico-virado   NV

38 cm. Uncommon migrant. Somewhat resembles *Tringa melanoleuca* but larger, bill distinctly curved upward. White rump contrasts with black tail. Shallow, highly saline water of lakes and estuaries. Rio de Janeiro (November), São Paulo, Paraná (August), Santa Catarina (October), Rio Grande do Sul (October), Mato Grosso, Guaporé. Principal wintering ground is in Patagonia.

BAR-TAILED GODWIT, *Limosa lapponica*   NV

From Old and New World (Alaska) tundras. One individual found on Fernando de Noronha 16 December 1988 (Antas et al. 1990).

SHORT-BILLED DOWITCHER, *Limnodromus griseus,*
Narceja-de-costas-brancas   NV

29 cm. Uncommon migrant. Coast, south to Bahia and Rio Grande do Sul (Belton 1984).

COMMON SNIPE, *Gallinago gallinago,*
Narceja, Batuíra   Fig. 104

30 cm; 115–23g. One of 2 Brazilian snipe. Long, straight bill, relatively short tarsi, long toes. Lives hidden in bogs and marshes, nesting in grass. Flushes only when closely approached. See *G. undulata.* SOUNDS: utters an unresonant *atch.* Flies swiftly with bill angled downward, zigzagging, rising frequently to good heights. Conspicuous during breeding because of impetuous diving flights at dusk and on moonlit nights, when it makes a loud sound reminiscent of a bleating goat, *uh-uh-uh . . .* in an ascending phrase lasting 1–2 seconds. "Bleating" is not, however, a voice; it originates in stiff, curved, laterally spread outer rectrices (controlled by strong muscles). Descending with great speed, bird throws itself to one side and lets itself fall 10–15 m while air flow is

Fig. 104. Common Snipe, *Gallinago gallinago paraguaiae.*

channeled by wings to tail, which vibrates like a musical instrument. Short wing movements (11 per second) even make it possible to modulate the sound. Bird can bleat even during short descents. One bleat last 2 seconds and occurs each 6–8 seconds. At height of breeding season male, perched on ground, cries *ke-ke-ke-* . . . or a bisyllabic *pi-kYER* . . . . Migratory in nonbreeding season, appearing in open bogs alongside visiting species, including at edges of brackish waters. In south numbers are augmented by immigrants from adjacent countries. Nests throughout South America. Usually considered conspecific with North American and Old World snipes. Also called *Bico-rasteiro, Corta-vento.* See *G. undulata* and South American Painted-Snipe, *Nycticryphes semicollaris* (Rostratulidae).

GIANT SNIPE, *Gallinago undulata,* Narcejão, Galinhola

47 cm. World's largest snipe. Bill, very heavy at base, may exceed 13 cm in length. Weight 420–500 g. A giant replica of *G. gallinago* (weighing 3–4 times more), it is surpassed among Brazilian Charadriiformes in size only by *Burhinus bistriatus* (Burhinidae). Sluggish disposition, difficult to flush. Squats or flees by walking slowly with long steps. Even more nocturnal than *gallinago.* SOUNDS: at dawn (less often at dusk) and at night flies high over its territory uttering its distinctive call, 2–5 sonorous cries like *HO-go, go* or *GA-ga, ga* with a human timbre, translated by country people as *agua-só, o-rapaz,* or *rola-pau.* These sequences fall off, becoming successively softer; 1st ones are trisyllabic, last one, which is weak, is monosyllabic. Also produces a loud buzz, *sch,* lasting about 4 seconds, which can be compared to noise of a bogged-down truck or buzzing of large bee swarm; i.e., completely different from "goat bleat" of *gallinago.* I assume that this noise, which can be somewhat modulated (probably by wing movements) and usually precedes vocalization, is produced by a diving flight. It is very difficult to observe this activity at night. Sometimes I have heard voice and buzzing simultaneously. In other

Fig. 106. Giant Snipe, *Gallinago undulata gigantea,* recently hatched chick. Approximate range in Brazil. After Teixeira et al. 1983.

Gallinago, outer rectrices are responsible for such instrumental music, but in *undulata* they are neither narrow nor stiff. Tail of this species (fig. 105) is very short and hidden between coverts but has a large number (14) of rectrices.

Performs its musical flights almost all year. According to my records in Rio de Janeiro they occur in all months except July and August. Other records of its vocalization are: Bahia, Goiás, Federal District (December, January); São Paulo (November–January). Calls more on hot, rainy nights. Lives in várzeas, inaccessible bogs, small wetlands with abundant vegetation. Nests in September in grass, has 2–4 light brown eggs with dark spots. Chick (fig. 106) black, finely spotted white, completely different from *gallinago* chick, which has reddish chestnut pattern with black-and-white design. Occurs both in lowlands (ex-Guanabara and Lagoa Feia, Rio de Janeiro) and mountainous regions (Rio de Janeiro, Minas Gerais). Found in reduced numbers in many places but is only discovered by those who know voice, for it flies during day only if stepped on; a very protective custom, for if it flies it is unlikely to escape being shot by a trained snipe hunter, unlike *gallinago,* which is much more difficult to hit. Often syntopic with *gallinago* and sometimes, as in Rio de Janeiro, with *Nycticryphes semicollaris.* Also lives in drier areas where other snipe do not exist. Northern South America to Paraguay, Uruguay. In eastern and central Brazil subspecies *G. u. gigantea* occurs. E. V. Kozlova of Leningrad (pers. comm. 1965), the greatest Charadriiforme specialist, has called my attention to the fact that *gigantea* probably should be treated as a separate species. Also called *Agua-só, O-rapaz* (both onomatopoeic), *Batuirão.*

Scolopacidae Bibliography

See also General and Charadriidae Bibliographies

Antas, P.T.Z., and I.L.S. Nascimento. 1988. Análise dos dados de anilhmento de *Calidris pusilla* no Brasil de 1981 a 1988. *IV Enc. Nac. Anilh. Aves, Recife:*18.

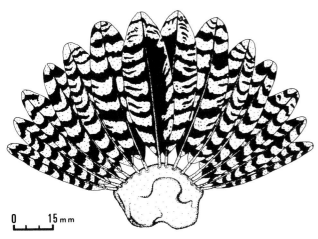

Fig. 105. Fanned tail of Giant Snipe, *Gallinago undulata;* the coverts have been removed. After H. Seebohm 1886.

Atkins, N. 1980. Possible competition between *Cinclodes nigrofumosus* and *Arenaria interpres. Condor* 82:107–8.

Belton, W. 1978. Supplementary list of new birds for Rio Grande do Sul, Brazil. *Auk* 95:413–15.

Fjeldsö, J. 1977. *Guide to the Young of European Precocial Birds.* Strandgarden: Skarv. Nat. Publ.

Gollop, J. B., T. W. Barry, and E. H. Iversen, 1981. Eskimo Curlew, a vanishing species? *Saskatchewan Nat. Hist. Soc.* 17.

Hayman, P., J. Marchant, and T. Prater. 1986. *Shorebirds: An Identification Guide.* Boston: Houghton Mifflin.

Olson, S. L. 1981. Natural history of vertebrates on the Brazilian islands of the mid South Atlantic. *Nat. Geo. Soc. Research Reports* 13:481–91.

Seebohm, H. 1886. *The Geographical Distribution of the Family Charadriidae.* London.

Teixeira, D. M., M. E. Mendez Puga, and J. B. Nacinovic. 1983. Notas sobre a biologia do narcejão, *Gallinago undulata gigantea. An. Soc. Sul-Riogr. Orn.* 4:7–9.

Vooren, C., R. Novelli, and A. Krob. 1984. Migration and trophic ecological relationships of the birds of Cassino beach. *XI Cong. Bras. Zool., Belém:*330–31.

FAMILY RECURVIROSTRIDAE: STILTS (1)

Stilts are very long-legged birds that also occur in temperate zones of other continents and at considerable altitudes in the Andes. There is a fossil from the eo-Oligocene of France. Other, disputed fossils come from the lower Tertiary of North America. *Juncitarsus* (Olson and Feduccia 1980) from the middle Eocene of North America (45 million years B.P.) shows intermediate characteristics between stilts and flamingos (see Phoenicopteridae).

BLACK-WINGED STILT, *Himantopus himantopus,* Pernilongo   PL 12.1

38 cm. Exposed tarsus and tibia together measure 16 cm. Unmistakable. Amount of white on head and back varies with age, time of year, and geographic region. Large, all-black wings conspicuous. Immature brown. VOICE: varied, loud, like a bark, *kow,* or a soft *wett,* that may be gull- or ternlike. Muddy edges of lakes, marshes, mangroves, rice plantations. Nests in bogs. Eggs like those of Southern Lapwing, *Vanellus chilensis.* U.S. to northern South America (*H. h. mexicanus*) and to westcentral and southern Brazil as far as Argentina and Chile (*H. h. melanurus,* with white area between base of neck and interscapular region). Common in certain areas, e.g., Rio Grande do Sul, Amazon estuary, Campos lowlands (Rio de Janeiro). Also called *Maçaricão, Quero-quero-da-praia* (Rio Grande do Sul), *Pernalonga, Cachorrinho* (Rio Grande do Sul).

Recurvirostridae Bibliography
See General Bibliography

FAMILY PHALAROPODIDAE: PHALAROPES (2)

Phalaropes migrate here from the north. There are Pleistocene fossils (50,000 years B.P.) from North America. Phalaropes are notable for the shape of their toes, which are edged with a lobed swimming membrane. Females are larger than males and during breeding (which does not occur in Brazil) are more brightly colored. Sex roles during courtship are reversed, with the female more active.

WILSON'S PHALAROPE, *Steganopus tricolor,* Pisa-n'agua   NV   PL 12.3

21 cm. Delicate in appearance, no others like it. Neck slender, bill needle-sharp. Prominent black stripe behind eyes. Legs greenish. VOICE: weak and low, drawing little attention. Quiet disposition; runs along muddy shores, moves into flooded fields. The only "sandpiper" that swims frequently, bobbing head nervously. Floats like a cork, wings and tail lifted obliquely like a small gull. In shallow water runs swiftly in small circles, pecking here and there to catch miniscule animals (plankton, Rio Grande do Sul). Arriving from North America, goes as far as Tierra del Fuego. Mato Grosso (August), Rio Grande do Sul (November, January).

RED PHALAROPE, *Phalaropus fulicarius*   NV

19 cm. May recall Sanderling, *Calidris alba,* but has black postocular spot and yellow at base of bill, which is not slender like that of *Steganopus tricolor.* Coming from Arctic, migrates mostly along Pacific coast of South America where it is largely pelagic, resting on sea, but 1 was found at Aripuanã, Mato Grosso, March 1979 by Paul Roth.

Phalaropodidae Bibliography

Sick, H. 1979. *Bull B.O.C.* 99(4):115–20. [*Phalaropus fulicarius,* recorded for first time in Brazil]

FAMILY BURHINIDAE: THICK-KNEES (1)

The long-legged thick-knees are widely distributed around the globe. They are quite different in appearance from other Charadriiformes, apparently being related to a primitive type of Charadriiforme from the upper Cretaceous of North America. There are fossils from the lower Miocene of North America and from the Pleistocene of Kansas and the Bahamas. These birds' particular characteristic is the thick heel, erroneously referred to as knee.

DOUBLE-STRIPED THICK-KNEE, *Burhinus bistriatus*
Téu-téu-da-savana   Fig. 107

43 cm; 700 g (male). Bulky with short bill and toes. Large yellow eyes indicate twilight habits and when illuminated at night give strong reddish reflections. Upperparts streaked earth color, top of head blackish, belly and wing stripe white. VOICE: resembles Southern Lapwing, *Vanellus chilensis;* heard only at night.

Flies well. Moves about in pairs in dry savanna with low vegetation. Appears along dirt roads and is unwary enough to let itself be run over. During day hides in grass, lying on tarsi (thermoregulation?). Its presence can be discovered by its tracks in sand. When pursued, squats, even laying head on ground. Insectivorous, frequently eats leaf-cutting ants. Lays eggs on ground, preferentially among manure pieces.

Normally only north of Amazon, where locally common. Amapá and Roraima to Venezuela, Colombia, Mexico. Rarely it occurs beyond its range, e.g., a pair at airport in Belém, Pará (November, D. Oren). Like *V. chilensis,* can be semidomesticated on ranches. Also called *Maçaricão, Pintão* (Amapá). A close relative of Old World *Burhinus.*

Burhinidae Bibliography

Natterer, J. 1871. In A. v. Pelzeln, *Zur Ornithologie Brasiliens.* Vienna. [Vocalization]

Fig. 107. Double-striped Thick-knee, *Burhinus bistriatus.*

FAMILY GLAREOLIDAE: PRATINCOLES (1)

These are small crepuscular birds that remotely resemble terns because of the deeply forked black tail that is white at the base. Widely distributed in warmer parts of the Old World, such as southern Spain.

COLLARED PRATINCOLE, *Glareola pratincola,*
Andorinha-do-deserto   NV
23 cm. An individual found on Atol das Rocas 9 March 1990 (Antas 1990). This family had not previously been recorded in the Americas.

Glareolidae Bibliography
See General Bibliography

FAMILY THINOCORIDAE: SEEDSNIPES (1)

These are predominantly Andean birds that also occur in Patagonia. They are the size of a small dove but with a more rounded aspect and short, thick necks, bills, and legs. The wings are strong, the flight is fast, and their manner of walking shows their relationship to the Charadriiformes.

LEAST SEEDSNIPE, *Thinocorus rumicivorus,*
Puco-puco-menor   SV

One individual, an unlikely visitor, found in humid fields among sand dunes at Lagoa do Peixe, Rio Grande do Sul, 26 April 1990 (Antas 1990). Dark with white throat and belly.

Thinocoridae Bibliography
See General Bibliography

FAMILY CHIONIDIDAE: SHEATHBILLS (1)

The Snowy Sheathbill is an unusual Antarctic seabird. Fossils are unknown. The bill is short and high, the base of the maxilla being covered by a supplementary dome that at a distance resembles the compound rhamphotheca of the Procellariiformes, to which it is not related. It appears to be related to the Laridae.

SNOWY SHEATHBILL, *Chionis alba,*
Pomba-antártica   SV   Fig. 108

39 cm. Rare migrant, with pigeonlike aspect. Immaculate white with bare pinkish skin and caruncles on face. Bill greenish with black tip. Feet gray. VOICE: croaking; normally silent. Flight pigeonlike. Gregarious. Water's edge, walking and hopping on beach and over rocks exposed to wave action where there is abundant flora and fauna. Eats small animals, dead or alive, and refuse. In Patagonia I have seen it regularly patrol gull and penguin colonies in search of broken eggs, etc., acting as a garbage collector. Rests on sea and swims well but does not have webbed feet. Nests in Antarctica, migrating from there as far as Rio Grande do Sul (Cassino beach, Rio Grande do Sul, May 1973, W. Belton).

Fig. 108. Snowy Sheathbill, *Chionis alba.*

Chionididae Bibliography

Belton, W. 1974. Two new southern migrants for Brazil. *Auk* 91:820.
Scherer Neto, P. 1985. Nova ocorrência do Pomba-Antártica no Sul do Brasil. *An. Soc. Sul-Riog. Orn.* 6:19–20.

FAMILY STERCORARIIDAE: SKUAS AND JAEGERS (4)

These pelagic species of the polar zones are related to gulls and have short legs and webbed feet like they do. There are Pleistocene fossils from North America.

Morphology and Behavior

Being birds of prey, they have a hooked bill, a compound maxillar rhamphotheca, and long, sharp claws. The female is usually larger. They fly swiftly close to the water surface and catch floating animals, dead fish, and trash and threaten other seabirds, such as terns, forcing them to vomit food they have eaten. They then catch it in midair like frigatebirds do (kleptoparasitism). They are even more aggressive in their breeding areas, where they will catch a bird by a wing or tail tip or force a landbird to fly over the sea where it can be victimized more easily.

I have seen a Great Skua, *Catharacta skua,* chase even a Kelp Gull, *Larus dominicanus,* though unsuccessfully (Guanabara Bay, Rio de Janeiro). Shorebirds become alarmed at its presence.

Immatures wander through the tropics for years on end and so occur with some frequency on South American shores. Some return to their homelands after 31 months away, as do some terns.

GREAT SKUA, *Catharacta skua,*
Gaivota-rapineira-grande   SV, NV

60 cm. Size of a large gull but with much wider, arched wings. Body all dark brown, often with cinnamon spots. White area at base of primaries is more sharply defined than a similar mark on Parasitic Jaeger, *Stercorarius parasiticus.* Usually flies higher than *S. parasiticus,* sometimes dives

precipitously to ocean surface. Southern forms (*C. s. antarctica, C. s. maccormicki, C. s. lonnbergi,* and especially *C. s. chilensis*) and northern ones (*C. s. skua*) may appear along our coast, as proven by banded individuals coming from (a) Antarctica (S. Orkney, Graham Land), with a specimen found in Santa Catarina (July 1963), another in Ceará (December 1974), and 2 in Pernambuco (October, December) from Tristão da Cunha and Cormorant Island; and (b) Scotland, 1 specimen in Maranhão (February 1974), another in Ceará (March 1970), a 3d in Piauí (March 1974, banded in Reykjavik, Iceland, July 1973). In Guanabara Bay I quite regularly record solitary individuals (May, June). I assume they are coming from southern regions where they breed in November (Patagonia). Identification of various forms (considered by some to be independent species), especially the more frequently seen immatures, is difficult. There are crosses between *maccormicki* and *lonnbergi.*

POMARINE JAEGER, *Stercorarius pomarinus,* Gaivota-rapineira-pomarina   NV

51 cm. Smaller than *Catharacta skua,* larger than *S. parasiticus.* Immature very similar to that of *S. parasiticus.* Rounded tail elongated. Northern migrant; gets as far south as Uruguayan and Argentine coasts. Recorded in Tapajós Pará, estuary May 1960.

PARASITIC JAEGER, *Stercorarius parasiticus,* Gaivota-rapineira-comun   NV   PL 14.1

47 cm. Dark brown, more hawk- than gull-like. Wings relatively narrow and angular. Central rectrices elongated

into a point, scarcely noticeable in immature. Underparts and neck yellowish white to varying degree, often with prominent clear pattern of bars. All-dark individuals occur. Often rests on water, likes to perch on pieces of floating wood. A regular migrant from Northern Hemisphere to our coast, as in Guanabara Bay (between Rio de Janeiro and Ilha de Paquetá) in January (the largest number), March–May, and September–December. An individual captured on Ilha do Governador 2 June 1970 had been banded in Föglö, Finland, as a chick. A 2d, banded in Scotland, was captured near Maceió (Alagoas) in May. Mingles with concentrations of *Sterna* spp. in migration. Occasionally goes up Amazon and even Rio Negro (Barra do Rio Branco, Roraima, August). Reaches Tierra del Fuego. Also called *Bandido, Rabo-de-junco, Dizimeiro.* See *Catharacta skua, S. pomarinus,* and Procellariidae, *Puffinus.*

LONG-TAILED JAEGER, *Stercorarius longicaudus,* Rabo-de-junco-preto   NV

Coming from high northern latitudes, has been recorded in Uruguay and Argentina. A January 1979 sighting on Guanabara Bay (J. M. Grugan). Very distinctive tail shape, with central rectrices 10 cm longer than the rest. Underparts pure white, cap black. Pelagic, reaching South Atlantic via high seas.

Stercorariidae Bibliography

Escalante, R. 1972. *Auk* 89:663–65. [*Stercorarius pomarinus,* occurrence]

FAMILY LARIDAE: GULLS AND TERNS (25)

Laridae are cosmopolitan aquatic birds with ancient fossil evidence from the lower Tertiary (Eo-Oligocene of France, 37 million years B.P.) and the Miocene of North America.

Morphology and Identification

Gulls and terns have long wings, short legs, and completely webbed feet (palmiped), except in the White Tern, *Gygis alba,* where the webbing is reduced. Sexes are similar, but the male is frequently more robust.

Tern plumage has two distinct phases, the very short breeding phase, acquired by prenuptial molt and characterized by black on the forehead, and the winter or nonbreeding phase, acquired by postnuptial molt. Both phases are highly variable in terns of the genus *Sterna,* our principal Laridae group, which during sexual repose become whiter, have the cap (which is black in nuptial plumage) spotted with white, and have faded bill and foot color. This nonbreeding dress is similar to that of immatures (see South American

Tern, *Sterna hirundinacea*). Thus there is great variation in color in the same species, depending on age and stage of the individual reproductive cycle. In Brazil breeding individuals often lack complete breeding plumage. The situation can become even more complex when two populations of a single species, one southern and the other northern, which breed at different times of the year, periodically intermingle, as appears to occur with the Cayenne Tern, *Sterna eurygnatha.*

The lovely silvery tint on the primaries of various tern species comes from refracted light in the microscopic structure of the feathers which lack pigmentation in this area. It is curious to note that *Gygis alba,* with immaculate white plumage, has coal black skin, whereas the Brown Noddy, *Anous stolidus,* has white skin, both probably for reasons of thermoregulation. It is said that a bird with white plumage absorbs only 16% of solar energy, whereas a black bird absorbs 33%. Black skin facilitates absorption of solar heat.

Brazilian Laridae may be divided into two groups:
  1. Gulls: tail rounded and bill curved downward. There are

only three resident species—Kelp Gull, *Larus dominicanus;* Brown-hooded Gull, *L. maculipennis;* and Gray-hooded Gull, *L. cirrocephalus*—and three migrants from the north—Ring-billed Gull, *L. delawarensis,* Laughing Gull, *L. atricilla,* and Franklin's Gull, *L. pipixcan.* They are concentrated on the coast of eastern Brazil. See also skimmers, skimmers, albatrosses, and petrels.

2. Terns: (*trinta-reis* roughly "thirty pennies," a name given these birds because of their abundance at certain seasons) forked tail (except *Anous*), narrower wings, and straighter, sharp-tipped bill, held pointed downward in flight. Ten resident species and eight migrants have been recorded. Of the former, only two are relatively numerous along the coast: *Sterna hirundinacea* and *S. eurygnatha;* in the interior the Large-billed Tern, *Phaetusa simplex,* and Yellow-billed Tern, *S. superciliaris,* are very common on the edges of large rivers such as the Amazon and its tributaries. Four species—the Sooty Tern, *S. fuscata; Anous stolidus;* Lesser Noddy, *A. tenuirostris;* and *Gygis alba*—are resident on oceanic islands (Trindade, etc.), so there is almost no opportunity to see them on the mainland coast. See also tropicbirds and boobies.

Identifying some terns, such as the Common Tern, *Sterna hirundo,* and Arctic Tern, *S. paradisaea,* requires full scientific documentation such as that in North American treatises. Only with considerable experience can one identify these birds in the field, especially since most are similar in size. In addition, one must remember that identification is made more difficult by periodic alternations in plumage and bill color, the latter being one of the most distinctive characters in the breeding period. Migrant species usually appear only in postnuptial plumage, their least characteristic phase. Immatures may present the same identification difficulties as do nonbreeders.

Feeding and Special Adaptations

Gulls are generally omnivorous, being attracted on the coast by dead fish thrown on the beach or into the water, by road-killed animals, and by garbage dumps. *Larus maculipennis* is periodically insectivorous, adapting itself to agriculture and taking advantage of plowing (Rio Grande do Sul) like its European representative, the Common Black-headed Gull, *L. ridibundus. L. dominicanus* is one of the species that drops robbed eggs in order to break them. Gulls and terns produce pellets that permit monitoring their food. Gull pellets resemble those of owls.

Most terns dive forcefully to capture fish or crustaceans swimming near the surface. They fly at lower speeds when patrolling for prey. At any given moment a bird may hover by beating its wings rapidly, keeping its body vertical and holding its head downward to observe the water. Immediately it launches itself after its chosen prey, submerging (rarely to 1 m) for an instant. Terns follow schools of young fish that surface while being pursued by larger ones, or they fish in

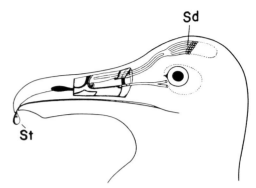

Fig. 109. Salt excretion by a gull. The salt glands (Sd) separate out a liquid containing more than 5% sodium chloride which passes through the mucous membrane of the nostrils and drips from the tip of the bill (St). After Kaben and Schwarz 1970.

surf where fish are tossed to the surface. The Large-billed Tern, *Phaetusa simplex,* catches young turtles (*Podocnemis*). *P. simplex* and *Sterna hirundinacea* sometimes catch swarming termites. The Gull-billed Tern, *Gelochelidon nilotica,* habitually hunts over dry land, catching insects perched on leaves of grass or in flight; occasionally it also fishes like other terns, but without submerging, a technique also used by *Gygis alba* and *Sterna fuscata,* the latter being a master of gliding flight. *S. fuscata* is the only tern that rapidly becomes water soaked, but manages to take flight, although with difficulty.

Seabirds' constant contact with salt water creates an interesting physiological problem, for their kidneys cannot eliminate such a high level of sodium chloride. A gull would have to excrete 2 liters of urine to eliminate the salts ingested in 1 liter of sea water, so to meet the problem a special mechanism (fig. 109) has evolved, the transformation of the supraorbital glands (which usually serve as olfactory glands) into salt-secreting glands. Thus, elimination of excessive salt is possible without compromising the organism's moisture balance. This excretion is so intense that one can see from a distance a highly concentrated solution of sodium chloride, saltier than the sea, drip from the bill of a *Larus dominicanus* approximately 15 minutes after it has drunk. This extrarenal mechanism for excreting salt is similar to that of marine reptiles. Gulls and terns protect themselves from the heat of the sun by displaying their large feet and by panting.

The white or gray color of most species facilitates association of these naturally gregarious birds in an open habitat which permits light objects to be seen at a distance. This serves for orientation both when searching for food and when gathering to rest or to form nesting colonies.

Breeding

Little is known about nesting of Brazilian species. Research is difficult because they sometimes do not breed regularly in the same place, as has been shown with

Sterna eurygnatha, which breeds in winter (July, August) in Rio de Janeiro. *Phaetusa simplex* and *S. superciliaris,* along with the Black Skimmer, *Rynchops niger,* nest in Amazonia as soon as beaches appear after the annual floods. The situation with *Gelochelidon nilotica* is similar. To a certain degree, colonial nesting may be considered an antipredatory adaptation.

Terns are aggressive near the nest, attacking intruders with low dives and bombarding them with feces. They breed on the ground, on beaches, or among low vegetation in flat places, as with *Sterna superciliaris, S. eurygnatha,* and *Phaetusa simplex. S. hirundinacea* seeks the steep edges of rocky islands. *Gygis alba* frequently lays directly on bare branches, which, mutatis mutandis, is also the case with *Anous tenuirostris,* which may also build on cliffs, making a console cemented with guano. On St. Paul's Rocks, *A. stolidus* makes a rudimentary nest on rocks. Eggs are similar to those of the Charadriidae and Scolopacidae but more oblong and less shiny. Whereas the weight of a *Sterna hirundo* egg does not exceed 14% of the mother's weight, that of *Gygis alba* is about 34% of the mother's weight. Chicks are nidifugous, but those of *S. hirundinacea* are still fed by the mother when far from the hatching place and already able to fish. Young *Gygis alba* remain for some weeks in the locale where born, firmly grasping a bare branch with long, strong claws.

Gulls are frequently the most dangerous enemies for neighboring gulls, cannibalizing their eggs and young. For this reason, and to avoid exposing the nest to too much sun, they stay on the nest a great deal.

Tern colonies on oceanic islands have hundreds or thousands of pairs, as with *Sterna fuscata,* probably the most abundant tropical seabird. Young Sandwich Terns, *S. sandvicensis,* are said to recognize their parents by their individual voices, facilitating their finding each other in the midst of a colony where one nest is alongside another. Mated tern pairs usually stay together, even on migration (see below).

Distribution and Migration

I have already called attention to the relative scarcity in tropical and subtropical seas, as compared with higher-latitude waters, of birds such as Procellariiformes and Pelecaniformes which are pelagic or share the same habits. This applies to species of the present group, so larids are not abundant along the Brazilian coast. The zone dominated by the Brazil Current (which comes from the equatorial region) lacks conditions especially favorable to the microorganisms that sustain most fish, which in turn are the primary food of seabirds. Murphy (1936) wrote in his classic work on birds of the South Atlantic: "In general the water of the Brazil current (altitude of Cabo Frio) is very warm and very blue, which is the equivalent of saying that it is relatively poor in plankton, fish-life, etc." Only around oceanic islands such as Trindade and Fernando de Noronha, where the influence of the cold Falkland Current is more accentuated, are conditions better

and fauna more abundant. The paucity of larids, especially gulls, in Amazonia is strange, a phenomenon also evident with other aquatic birds such as anatids.

The number of resident gulls and terns periodically increases, either because of immigration of southern contingents of *Sterna eurygnatha* and *S. hirundinacea* or because of floods, especially in Amazonia, that drive out riparian birds such as *Phaetusa simplex* and *S. superciliaris.* Pelagic species such as the *Anous* appear periodically on islands only to breed and then disappear. *Larus cirrocephalus* must have immigrated in a not-so-distant epoch from Africa, and *L. maculipennis* is a similar case. Gulls in Brazil are essentially coastal birds.

Among migrants is *Sterna paradisaea,* widely distributed in the Northern Hemisphere, whose migrations are among the longest and most prolonged known. It flies from the Arctic to the Antarctic, as do various shorebirds, making a round trip of 35,000 km (fig. 110). Banding has shown that parents and young of northern terns embark together toward the south after the breeding period. Almost all stop in the tropical zone where the immatures remain for up to two and a

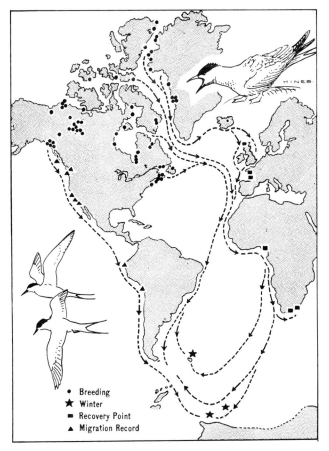

Fig. 110. Migration of the Arctic Tern, *Sterna paradisaea.* The eastern North American population migrates to the Atlantic coast of Europe and Africa and later spreads throughout the South Atlantic, reaching the coasts of South America and Antarctica, its wintering area. After Lincoln 1950.

half years, like skuas and jaegers, only then returning to their native land to breed, having successively changed their juvenal plumage for nuptial dress. The practice of banding and meticulous studies of molt on museum specimens have permitted accumulation of data on the destination and development of some of these birds. For us, banding in North America has been of the greatest use, with hundreds of terns banded in the U.S. and Canada, especially *S. hirundo*, having been caught in Brazil. Individuals with colored bands may appear.

Use and Dangers

Eggs are consumed on a large scale by fishermen. Those of *Gelochelidon nilotica* in the Amazon estuary (Ilha Mexiana, Pará), of *Sterna hirundinacea* in Santa Catarina, and of *Larus maculipennis* in Rio Grande do Sul are all taken by local people. In the Abrolhos, *Anous stolidus* eggs are eaten.

The presence of humans in a nesting area during the breeding season, especially before the chicks hatch, greatly disturbs the colonies and places them at the mercy of predators such as vultures, caracaras, and *Larus dominicanus*. The same happens in heron and frigatebird colonies.

During a storm an *S. hirundinacea* flew into the pillar of the Rio–Niteroi bridge and fractured its skull (Maciel 1987).

RING-BILLED GULL, *Larus delawarensis*, Gaivota-de-Delaware   NV

47 cm. Rare northern migrant. Distinguishable by black ring around tip of bill. One individual, amidst other, different "gulls," was caught near Tefé (Amazonas, November 1968). It had been banded 5 months earlier near Canada–U.S. boundary. Apparently 1st record of species in South America.

KELP GULL, *Larus dominicanus*, Gaviotão
PL 14.3   Fig. 111

58 cm. Only large gull in Brazil. White with back and upper wing surface black, tips of secondaries white. In adult plumage, acquired only in 4th year, subterminal white spot on outer primary is conspicuous at a distance. Yellow bill has red spot on mandible, short of tip, which fades in nonbreeding season. Eyelids red, iris whitish, legs greenish. Immature spotty brown with highly variable dark gray or blackish

Fig. 111. Kelp Gull, *Larus dominicanus*, immature.

brown bill and feet, dark brown iris. VOICE: *keh-ohh, kyo-kyo-kyo.* . . . Along Brazilian coast north only to Espírito Santo and Rio de Janeiro. Nests in winter in small numbers on offshore islands, e.g., near Cabo Frio, Rio de Janeiro. More common in more southerly regions, breeds in Rio de la Plata area August–September. Usually the only gull in Guanabara Bay, although it is not frequent. Concentrations of immigrant flocks, as in Santos, São Paulo, in April, may number more than 100. Does not get far from coast. Occurs as far as Tierra del Fuego as well as on Pacific coast of South America, Africa, New Zealand. Considered a replacement for Great Black-backed Gull, *L. marinus*, of North America and Europe, which has light flesh-colored legs. Also called *Cau-cau*.

LAUGHING GULL, *Larus atricilla*   NV

41 cm. Occasional migrant from north. Small with dark gray mantle, all-black outer primaries, secondaries with white tips. Recorded in Amazon estuary as far as Maranhão. One caught at Lagoa do Peixe, Rio Grande do Sul, July 1985.

GRAY-HOODED GULL, *Larus cirrocephalus*, Gaivota-de-cabeça-cinza

43 cm. Similar to *L. maculipennis* but larger, not so white, and with darker mantle and light gray head (during breeding, November). The 2 external primaries have limited area (2–4 cm) of white before tip. Bill brown, eyelids and feet red, iris yellow. Only vestiges of gray remain on head in nonbreeding plumage. There are few certain records of its occurrence in Brazil. Rio de Janeiro (Lagoa de Araruama, May, July, November), sporadically in other places: Maranhão, southern Mato Grosso, Santa Catarina (May), Rio Grande do Sul. Also Paraguay, Bolivia, Uruguay, Argentina, Pacific coast of South America, and Africa, from where it immigrated. Also called *Tiribique* (Rio de Janeiro).

FRANKLIN'S GULL, *Larus pipixcan*   NV

Extraordinary migrant from interior of North America that usually migrates along Pacific coast. Fernando de Noronha (P. Antas 1988 pers. comm.).

BROWN-HOODED GULL, *Larus maculipennis*
Gaivota-maria-velha

42 cm. Upperparts light gray, underparts white. Head brown in breeding season, otherwise white with black spot behind cheeks. Bill, eyelids, and feet red, iris brown. External primaries have large area with white spots, separated from white tip by black streak. Much variation in remiges pattern according to time of year and age of individual. In flight more white shows in primaries than in *L. cirrocephalus*. Immature has brown wing coverts and tertiaries. Spots before and behind eye blackish, like occiput. Tail has sooty apical bar. Common in eastern Rio Grande do Sul. Along river and lake edges, catching insects in flight and in

plowed fields where it looks for insect larvae, etc. Sometimes alongside Chimango Caracara, *Milvago chimango*. Also on coast. Nests in most southerly parts of South America, including in Rio Grande do Sul marshes (November). Occasionally recorded in states of São Paulo, Rio de Janeiro, Alagoas, western Mato Grosso. Replaces *L. ridibundus* of Old World, to which it is very similar in appearance, voice, and ecological requirements. See *L. pipixcan*.

BLACK TERN, *Chlidonias niger*　NV

Slender, widely distributed in Northern Hemisphere, recorded in 1986–87 at Lagoa do Peixe, Rio Grande do Sul, and Maricá, Rio de Janeiro. An individual banded in Berlin, Germany, in 1984 was recovered in Macau, Rio Grande do Norte, in September 1986.

LARGE-BILLED TERN, *Phaetusa simplex*, Trinta-réis-grande　PL 14.2

43 cm. Unmistakable with wing pattern and considerable size of lemon yellow bill. Bare skin on face and throat red; feet yellow. Immature has brownish crown, shorter bill. VOICE: *gheh-gheh, ga-gaa-a, ghehh*, may recall *Rynchops niger*. River and lake beaches where nests in colonies with *R. niger* and *Sterna superciliaris*. Common in Amazonia. Young prized by Indians of upper Xingu as pets (September). South to Uruguay, Argentina. Outside breeding season also in estuaries and on coast. Also called *Gaivota, Alā* (Juruna, Mato Grosso). See *Sterna eurygnatha* and *Rynchops niger*.

GULL-BILLED TERN, *Gelochelidon nilotica*, Trinta-réis-de-bico-preto

36 cm. Looks like a small *Larus* because of small bill but has forked tail. Top of head and bill black, upperparts relatively dark gray. Flies low above fields behind dunes. Insectivorous. Sometimes fishes like other terns but does not dive, catching prey by flying low above surface. Nests in remote muddy areas as soon as they have dried after rainy season floods (Amazon estuary, August). Atlantic coast of South America from the Guianas to Argentina (including Rio de Janeiro, Rio Grande do Sul). Also U.S., Old World.

SOUTH AMERICAN TERN, *Sterna hirundinacea*, Trinta-réis-de-bico-vermelho　PL 14.5

41 cm. Common southern maritime species with scarlet bill and feet. More robust build than *S. hirundo* or *S. paradisaea*. Outside breeding season forehead white, although individuals with patchy forehead are common. Immature has brown spotted upperparts, black bill. Recently fledged juveniles show brownish streak on forewing, design of same color on tertiaries, and some dark spots on back; outer vane of remiges and rectrices dark gray, not light. VOICE: *chirrik, kiaarrr*. Tierra del Fuego to Bahia. Among nesting places is Macaé archipelago, Rio de Janeiro, where it accompanies *S. eurygnatha* (July), and Ilha das Cagarras (ex-Guanabara).

In 1986 nested at 17 places in Guanabara Bay, the largest area being on the Rio–Niteroi bridge (Maciel 1987). Also on Pacific coast. Also called *Gaivota*. See also *S. maxima*.

COMMON TERN, *Sterna hirundo*, Trinta-réis-boreal　NV

36 cm. Regular migrant with red bill that is more slender than that of *S. hirundinacea*. Forepart of head white in nonbreeding season when it appears in Brazil. Penetrates interior up large rivers such as Tocantins, Araguaia (I obtained a specimen near Aragarças, between Goiás and Mato Grosso, in October), and São Francisco (2 specimens found near Pirapora, Minas Gerais, both banded in U.S.). From 1927 to 1987, 330 individuals that had been banded in U.S. were recovered in Brazil. Of these, 110 have been captured at Lagoa do Peixe since 1984. Most appear between November and February, but there are records for every month of year. One individual caught on Ilha das Flores (ex-Guanabara) on 1 April 1950 had been banded 16 years earlier on Weepecket Island, Massachusetts. An individual banded as a nestling on 17 June 1972 in Schleswig–Holstein, Germany, was recovered on beach at Cidreira, Rio Grande do Sul, 10 December 1977. In recent years large concentrations have been recorded at Lagoa do Peixe, with estimates of 12,000 sleeping there. Between 1985 and 1987, 839 were banded there; it was later learned that most came from east coast of U.S., between Virginia and Massachusetts. See *S. paradisaea*.

ARCTIC TERN, *Sterna paradisaea*, Trinta-réis-ártico　NV

38 cm. Northern migrant, apparently very uncommon. Extremely similar to *S. hirundo* but with shorter bill, tarsi (15.6 instead of 18.9 mm), and toes. Feet tiny; tail more deeply forked in adults. More pelagic than *hirundo*, apparently does not penetrate into continent. Two individuals banded in U.S. were recovered in Rio de Janeiro (March) and Santa Catarina (November). Found in Rio Grande do Sul in December and March. On migration, see "Distribution. . . . "

ANTARCTIC TERN, *Sterna vittata*, Trinta-réis-antártico　SV

38 cm. Rare subantarctic migrant, similar to *S. paradisea* but with underparts gray, not white. Recorded on our coast only in nonbreeding plumage, with white forehead, in southern winter. Found in Santa Catarina, Rio de Janeiro.

SNOWY-CROWNED TERN, *Sterna trudeaui*, Trinta-réis-de-coroa-branca

35 cm. Easily recognized southern species with wide black stripe behind eyes. Underparts gray, bill pinkish orange with black subterminal band. Subadult bill black with yellowish tip. VOICE: *gaaa-a, kit-kit, kirit*. . . . Common in Rio Grande do Sul at ocean shore and in marshes where it breeds (No-

vember), sometimes alongside *Larus maculipennis*. Rarely as far north as Rio de Janeiro.

FORSTER'S TERN, *Sterna forsteri*   NV

Accidental northern migrant, size of *S. hirundo,* with large, black eye spot. Pernambuco.

ROSEATE TERN, *Sterna dougallii*   NV

Northern migrant, accidental as far south as Bahia. Same size as *S. hirundo.* Nine banded individuals from U.S. have been caught in north (Pará) and northeast (Maranhão, Piauí, Ceará, Rio Grande do Norte, Paraíba).

SOOTY TERN, *Sterna fuscata,* Trinta-réis-das-rocas

40 cm. Oceanic island species, only tern with black upperparts, resembling *Rynchops niger.* Forehead and underparts white. Young sooty, speckled white. Forms large colonies on Atol das Rocas, Fernando de Noronha, Trindade, etc. An estimate made in March 1982 at das Rocas placed breeding population at about 120,000 birds (Antas 1986). Accidental at mouth of Amazon (Pará). On wetting plumage, see "Morphology . . . ."

YELLOW-BILLED TERN, *Sterna superciliaris,* Trinta-réis-anão   PL 14.6

25 cm. Smallest Brazilian tern. In breeding season bill all yellow. Third, 4th, and 5th outer primaries blackish, conspicuous in flight. In nonbreeding season crown gray, streaked with black. Immature has blackish bar on wing, base and tip of bill blackish. Young have brown spots on wing. VOICE: *kit kit, ooeh-tetete.* Nests on beaches of lakes and big rivers, frequently associating with *Phaetusa simplex.* In Amazonia alongside Sand-colored Nighthawk, *Chordeiles rupestris,* which it resembles. Immatures and adults in winter plumage occasionally reach coast on migration; breeding occurs there in Rio Grande do Sul (Belton 1984). The Guianas to Argentina, Bolivia, Colombia. Sometimes meets *S. antillarum* (ex-Guanabara, December). Also called *Te-ne-nígu* (Juruna, Mato Grosso).

LEAST TERN, *Sterna antillarum*   NV

Northern migrant, very similar to *S. superciliaris,* but short, thin bill (29–34 mm instead of 35–40 mm) has all-black mandible in nonbreeding season when it comes to Brazil. Only 2 outer primaries are blackish gray. Immature has contrasting black bars on wings, black bill. Restricted to littoral. Pará, Maranhão (July), Piauí, rarely to Rio de Janeiro. Replaces *superciliaris* in North America and Antilles.

ROYAL TERN, *Sterna maxima,* Trinta-réis-real
NV   PL 14.4

49 cm. Largest tern. Nuchal feathers ruffled, orange-red bill very heavy; feet black. Immature has streaked crown, spotted mantle, yellowish bill and feet. Lives in small flocks on coastal rocks (e.g., Rio de Janeiro, July). Found in nonbreeding plumage with white forehead in almost all months of year near Cabo Frio, Rio de Janeiro (A. Pacheco Leão pers. comm.). Northern Hemisphere, where it breeds, to Argentina. Individuals in breeding plumage (top of head black) and young observed in Uruguay (September–October) suggest nesting not far away.

CAYENNE TERN, *Sterna eurygnatha,* Trinta-réis-de-bico-amarelo

41 cm. Large with yellow bill, black feet with yellowish soles, black on top of head, including forehead, during breeding; nuchal plumage long and ruffled. In prolonged nonbreeding season, entire upper part of head white, with black only around eyes, on nuchal crest and in area connecting them; bill loses bright yellow color. Immature and subadult similar but have only forecrown white and black design on tertiaries; bill color quite variable, may be yellow spotted with black or black with yellow tip. Juvenals have blackish design on upper wing coverts. Nests from Lesser Antilles to Patagonia. Common along our coast from Bahia to Rio Grande do Sul, with limited information on nesting. Abundant on southern littoral; I found a colony (associated with *S. hirundinacea*) on Ilha dos Papagaios, off Macaé, Rio de Janeiro, In July 1963. There was a small colony in Guanabara Bay (Maciel 1987) and a large one on 4 islands off littoral of Espírito Santo, with *hirundinacea*, with an estimated 1000 eggs (Moure et al. 1985). Number of wandering individuals increases periodically (Rio de Janeiro, Rio Grande do Sul), probably through immigration of Uruguayan and Argentine populations (which have longer bills) which breed September–January. This is southern replacement of *S. sandvicensis,* a species widely distributed in North America and Europe, and could properly be included as a subspecies of *sandvicensis.*

SANDWICH TERN, *Sterna sandvicensis acuflavida* NV

Northern migrant with smaller bill (black with yellow tip) than *S. eurygnatha.* An individual banded in extreme south of U.S. (Mississippi coast, July 1964) was captured in Rio Grande do Norte in August 1966. Four specimens recently collected in Guanabara Bay, in April, May, July and September (Teixeira pers. comm.). Specimens cited in literature for Rio de Janeiro (Pelzeln 1871), São Paulo (Pinto 1938), and Uruguay (Escalante pers. comm.) have proven to be *eurygnatha,* not *sandvicensis.*

BROWN NODDY, *Anous stolidus,* Andorinha-do-mar-preta

38 cm. Bird of oceanic islands. Unlike other terns, lacks forked tail. Dark sooty with gray crown, white forehead.

Abrolhos, Fernando de Noronha, Atol das Rocas, Trindade, and St. Paul's Rocks where it, *A. tenuirostris,* and Brown Booby, *Sula leucogaster,* are only breeding birds. A dead specimen was found at Barra da Tijuca, Rio de Janeiro, May 1987 (Teixeira pers. comm.). Also called *Benedito* (Abrolhos). See *A. tenuirostris* and Wilson's Storm-Petrel, *Oceanites oceanicus.*

WHITE-CAPPED NODDY, *Anous tenuirostris*

This 2d species of genus is smaller with crown all whitish. Fernando de Noronha, St. Paul's Rocks, Trindade.

WHITE TERN, *Gygis alba,* Grazina

33 cm. Only pure white tern. Bill extremely sharp-pointed and black, eyes large and dark. VOICE: a nasal *rret, rret, ga, ga, ga.* Catches small fish on surface of sea, not diving like other species, and fishes more at twilight. Lays egg on rocks, sand, or often in fork of a slender branch, without using any nesting material. So tame it can be caught by hand. Fernando de Noronha, Trindade (where Grazinas Peak figures on old maps), Abrolhos (in passage). See Tropicbirds, *Phaethon.*

Laridae Bibliography

See also General Bibliography

Antas, P.T.Z. 1987. Análise dos dados de anilhamento de *Sterna hirundo* na Lagoa do Peixe, Tavares, Rio Grande do Sul. *III ENAV, S. Leopoldo:*32.

Buckley, P. A., and F. G. Buckley. 1984. Cayenne Tern new to North America, with comments on its relationship to Sandwich Tern. *Auk* 101:396–98.

Burger, J. 1974. *Auk* 91:601–13. [*Larus maculipennis,* behavior]

Escalante, R. 1968. *Condor* 70:243–47. [*Sterna maxima,* distribution]

Escalante, R. 1973. *Condor* 75:470–72. [*Sterna eurygnatha,* distribution]

Escalante, R. 1973. *V. Cong. Lat. Am. Zool.* 1:85–96. [*Larus dominicanus,* plumage]

Escalante, R. 1985. Taxonomy and conservation of austral-breeding Royal Terns. In *Neotrop. Ornith.,* Ornith. Monogr. no. 36.

Grant, P. J. 1982. *Gulls, a guide to identification.* Vermillion, S.D.: Buteo Books.

Hutchison, R. E., J. G. Stevenson, and W. H. Thorpe. 1968. *Behaviour* 32:150–57. [*Sterna,* vocalization]

Johnston, D. W. 1979. *Condor* 81:430–32. [*Sterna fuscata,* uropygial gland]

Kaben, U., and D. Schwartz. 1970. *Zool. Gart.* 39:133–46. [Salt excretion]

Maciel, N. C. 1987. Nidificacão de *Sterna hirundo* na Baia de Guanabara, Rio de Janeiro. *II ENAV, Rio de Janeiro:*207–8.

Moure, R. P., H. S. Sá, E. C. Perrone, et al. 1985. Ocorrência de colônias de reprodução de *Sterna eurygnatha* e *S. hirundinacea* no Espírito Santo. *XII Cong. Bras. Zool., Campinas:* 261.

Rutschke, E. 1965. *J. Orn.* 106:307–12. [Feather structure]

Saunders, H. 1877. *Proc. Zool. Soc.* 45:794–800. [*Anous,* nesting]

Schmidt-Nielsen, K., et al. 1958. *J. Phys.* 193:101–7. [Sodium chloride excretion]

Sick, H. 1979. *Bull. B.O.C.* 99(4):115–20. [Occurrence of *Larus delawarensis, Sterna sandvicensis acuflavida*]

Sick, H., and A. P. Leão. 1965. *Auk* 82:507–8. [*Sterna eurygnatha,* nesting]

Voous, K. H. 1968. *Ardea* 56(1/2):184–87. [*Sterna eurygnatha,* geographic variation]

Voous, K. H. 1979. *Bull. B.O.C.* 97(2):42–44. [*Sterna eurygnatha,* distribution]

FAMILY RYNCHOPIDAE: SKIMMERS (1)

Skimmers are unique water birds related to the Laridae. They also occur in Africa and India, each of which has a different species. Fossils are unknown. Some authors include the Rynchopidae in the Laridae.

Morphology and Special Adaptations

The bill has an exceptional shape, unique among birds. It is highly compressed laterally with the mandible much longer than the maxilla. The maxilla has a groove into which the mandible fits, the latter having been reduced to an elastic blade, similar to a letter opener, with oblique furrows. The furrows apparently function like surface stabilizers on airplane wings to avoid lateral movements (e.g., oscillations produced by water pressure) of the very thin, submerged lower rhamphotheca. The maxilla has similar furrows which are less distinct and differently oriented. The bill is well supplied with blood and nerves which permit tactile orientation while fishing and facilitate regeneration of the mandible tip, which sometimes breaks. In captivity the mandible grows excessively, demonstrating how intense the water pressure must be against the rhamphotheca when used in "plowing."

This natural deformity of the bill is so great that the skimmer cannot pick up food off the ground without turning its head to the side, but it can take small objects off the water surface, like terns do. The nestling initially has a "normal" bill, taking food from its parents' bills or catching it on the ground.

The *Rynchops* are the only birds with a slit-shaped pupil,

Fig. 112. Black Skimmer, *Rynchops niger,* "plowing" the water. The sketch in the upper right corner shows it approaching a submerged prey and then lowering its head to catch it. Sketch after Zusi 1962.

like that of a cat—an important systematic character but one for which it is difficult to find any "use," either in nocturnal fishing, which is guided by bill touch, or on sunlit beaches. The eyes are small, unlike those of owls. The feet are disproportionately small, with moderately developed webs that are scarcely used. The male is larger than the female.

BLACK SKIMMER, *Rynchops niger,*
Corta-água, Talha-mar   Fig. 112

50 cm. Resembles a gull but with longer, narrower wings. Tail forked. Upperparts sooty black; forehead, hind margin of wings, and underparts white. White tips on secondaries considerably more extensive on southern individuals (*R. n. intercedens,* which range as far north as Rio das Mortes, Mato Grosso). Feet and bill red, latter with black tip. Immature has sooty upperparts, white collar. VOICE: a prolonged, monosyllabic *gaa-a,* unlike Large-billed Tern, *Phaetusa simplex.* Calls primarily at night, most loquacious around dawn. Spends day on beaches, preferably those of quiet islands in large rivers, sleeping with bill lowered in a unique posture.

Feeding and Behavior: When fishing flies just above water holding bill constantly open, submerging mandible from a third to two-thirds of its length, as if "plowing" water. Flight

must be steady and absolutely horizontal to keep bill in correct position, and wing beats must be short so wingtips do not touch water. In this way bird catches small fish and shrimp just below water's surface. When mandible touches something, bird brakes by opening tail and closes bill by lowering maxilla. Usually it immediately bows head so far it may be below flanks. Then it stretches the neck forward again and swallows prey while continuing flight. Fishing efficiency may be very high: 1 bird caught a small fish every 3 seconds for 6 minutes (Zusi 1959, Texas). The head is never submerged to pursue fish.

Sometimes skimmer spirals down from a few meters above water to catch a fish seen from a distance. Does not dive like terns, approaching prey on a horizontal, not vertical, trajectory. Flight notably elegant and swifter than a gull. Prefers to fish at twilight and at night, in both clear and turbid waters, deep or shallow, sometimes so shallow mandible almost touches muddy or sandy bottom. Does not fish among floating plants but does use small, shallow ponds in flooded areas (Mato Grosso Pantanal). Reportedly hits water with bill to make fish reveal their presence, the same as "promombó" fishing [which causes fish to jump into a canoe with a fire burning in it]. There is no foundation for allegation that *R. niger* food consists of plankton. On a Rio Trombetas, Pará, beach a skimmer chased a newly hatched tortoise as if it wanted to catch it—probably an act of play.

Breeding: Lays 2–3 densely spotted eggs in a sizable excavation in sand. Pairs nest close to each other, frequently near a colony of *Phaetusa simplex* and, like these, begin to lay as soon as beach is exposed after annual flood (Amazonia). When a human approaches nesting beach in a canoe, skimmers immediately fly close to water in a straight line toward canoeist to inspect the situation but do not attack; terns fly in high circles and dive swiftly against an intruder that approaches nest or young. In this way terns provide protection for skimmers.

Habitat and Distribution: Lives on large rivers and lakes of Brazil. On migration also on coast, at least in estuaries (e.g., Espírito Santo, Rio de Janeiro, São Paulo, Amapá). Accidental as far as Tierra del Fuego. Also in North America, where it occurs on coast. Also called *Bico-rasteiro, Corta-mar, Ga-gãnha* (Waurá, Mato Gross), *Paaguaçu.*

Rynchopidae Bibliography

Schildmacher, H. 1931. *Orn. Monatsber.* 39(2):37–41. [Bill morphology]
Zusi, R. L. 1959. Fishing rates in the Black Skimmer. *Condor* 61(4):298.
Zusi, R. L. 1962. Structural adaptations of the head and neck in *Rynchops nigra. Publ. Nuttall Orn. Club,* no. 3.

ORDER COLUMBIFORMES

FAMILY COLUMBIDAE: PIGEONS AND DOVES (23)

Pigeons and doves are widely distributed over the globe and very well represented in the New World. They probably originated in the Old World tropics and immigrated early to the Americas. There are few fossil records, the oldest being from the lower Miocene of France (20 million years B.P.). Gigantic, flightless forms (dodos) from the Mascarene Islands (Indian Ocean east of Madagascar), which have been extinct for about 30 years, were long attributed to the Columbiformes but are now awaiting new classification.

The Columbidae constitute a natural grouping whose relationship with other orders has not yet been clarified. There are remote similarities with Psittaciformes and Charadriiformes.

Morphology

Pigeons are homogeneous and unique: the head is small and round, the bill weak and covered at the base by the cere, which is swollen in the Rock Dove, or Domestic Pigeon, *Columba livia domestica*. The body is heavy and the plumage full and soft, being rich in powder which keeps the microscopic structure of the feathers flexible, thereby substituting for the secretion of the frequently-absent uropygial gland. When *C. l. domestica* bathes, the water surface quickly becomes covered with powder from its feathers (see Tinamidae, "Behavior"). The feathers fall out at the least impact.

Legs and toes are soft and generally red. The hallux is well developed, an adaptation to arboreal life. Sexes are usually similar, but the male is more brightly colored. There is accentuated sexual dimorphism in the Scaled Pigeon, *Columba speciosa*, and in *Claravis* and *Geotrygon*.

Columbids have a pronounced wing design called a "speculum." The neck is sometimes conspicuous with beautiful metallic reflections, especially in *Columba livia domestica*. A cinnamon-colored mutation occurs in both sexes of the Ruddy Ground-Dove, *Columbina talpacoti*.

The popularity of pigeons and ground-doves has resulted in a profusion of regional names that create real confusion because they mutually contradict each other as to their true meaning.

Vocalization

Voices of Brazilian species are often limited almost exclusively to a territorial song, which is schematized and low, uttered with the bill closed. Voices of species in the same genus are very similar, being distinguished by timbre, rhythm, and inflection. Those of the Eared Dove, *Zenaida auriculata*, and Scaled Dove, *Scardafella squammata*, are peculiar. Sometimes there are voice differences between the sexes (e.g., *Leptotila*). A warning vocalization of the Plumbeous Pigeon, *Columba plumbea*, is distinctive.

The song is sung repeatedly during the usually-long breeding period. At the peak of the mating season the Pale-vented Pigeon, *Columba cayennensis*, sings in the middle of the night and at dawn (northwestern Bahia, August). Whereas wild pigeon males vocalize with frequency to call their absent mates, the domestic pigeon sings more at the approach of his own or any other female. Pigeons rustle their feathers and beat their wings (see "Behavior").

Feeding

Normally granivorous or frugivorous, almost all columbids feed on the ground. Moving the bill rapidly, they turn over dead leaves to uncover seeds and fallen fruits. This motion (which is generalized, not used just for certain situations) is also used to get seeds that have fallen into a crack, throwing them up to the surface where they are taken at once. Seeds are eaten whole without cracking them, filling the crop, where digestion takes place. Columbids are important dispersers of plants, because the seeds are not crushed in their small stomachs. For this reason they are also easily poisoned by insecticide-treated seeds.

Favorite fruits include those of the canela-murici (Rio de Janeiro) and aturiá (*Drepanocarpus*, Amazon estuary, Pará). *Columba cayennensis* likes marmelo-do-campo (*Croton* sp.), and the Picazuro Pigeon, *C. picazuro*, enjoys beans (northeast). The Purple-winged Ground-Dove, *Claravis godefrida*, is attracted by fruiting bamboo. It is commonly believed that the flesh of *Columba plumbea* becomes bitter when the bird eats large quantities of mistletoe. During breeding *Zenaida auriculata* takes mollusks (Gastropoda) and millipedes, apparently to meet its calcium need. Both *Geotrygon* species, in addition to fruits and seeds, eat some insects and other small creatures.

Columbids in large numbers frequent places where there are banks of salty earth: *barreiros* (central Brazil, Paraná). In the northeast these are called "licks" and are sought out by

Zenaida auriculata and *Claravis godefrida.* The walls of the crop of a *Z. auriculata* collected while foraging in one of these areas may be completely lined with a thin layer of siliceous earth.

Columbids are avid drinkers (*Z. auriculata* goes to springs 30–40 km away), collecting at the edges of rivers, lakes, and river-bottom wells. Unlike most birds, they suck water without raising their heads, a more rapid and efficient process. Sucking involves a peristaltic movement of the esophagus, pumping the water with the bill submerged. Tinamidae, Psittacidae, nectivorous birds such as Trochilidae, certain Passerines such as the *Dacnis* and *Coereba,* and the Common Waxbill, *Estrilda astrild,* and Mousebirds (Coliidae) of Africa use a similar technique. In the upper Xingu (Mato Grosso), of 12 columbid species (including 5 *Columba*), only *Columba cayennensis* came regularly to drink at the edge of the river, morning and evening.

Behavior

Columbids fly well, *Columba livia domestica* being considered excellent (see Falconidae, "Hunting Methods"). *Zenaida auriculata* flies low and swiftly. Columbids produce a whistling noise, and some, such as *Claravis* and *Leptotila,* have sound-producing flight feathers. *Geotrygon,* which live hidden in the lower levels of the forest, have silent flight. On wing beating, see "Breeding."

Columbids move on the ground by walking with rapid, tiny steps, stopping the head for an instant at each step, like chickens, to better observe their surroundings. They never hop. They "yawn" like parrots and hummingbirds, without, unlike mammals, inhaling deeply. They do not hide their heads among the back feathers to sleep. They enjoy bathing. It is interesting that after the male *Columba livia domestica* treads the female, she frequently "treads" him.

Columbina talpacoti shows nervousness by raising one or both wings. When an adversary is considered weaker, the nearer wing is raised as if to hit it; in a contrary situation the far wing is lifted as a sign of submission. At the peak of confused excitement, both wings go up. Similar behavior has been noted in the Common Ground-Dove, *C. passerina,* and *Scardafella squammata. Columba livia domestica* also fight by beating each other with their wings. The White-tipped Dove, *Leptotila verreauxi,* shows nervousness by teetering its tail.

Small, terrestrial, forest species, such as the Ruddy Quail-Dove, *Geotrygon montana,* and *Claravis godefrida,* easily escape observation. Any columbid may suffer the strange "fright molt" with remiges and other feathers falling out, when captured.

Breeding

During courtship the male bows before the female (*Columba, Zenaida, Columbina, Leptotila*). Mates mutually caress each other on the head and feed each other with material regurgitated from the crop, especially moments before copulation. When wanting to attract attention while flying, they clap the upper side of the wings above the back (*Columba livia domestica,* both sexes, but more violently in the male). The Gray-fronted Dove, *Leptotila rufaxilla,* also claps its wings, interspersing the claps between its usual moans. *Columba cayennensis, C. plumbea,* and *Zenaida auriculata* make display flights. The first of these is tireless in flying around buriti groves and gallery forests (Bahia), frequently gliding with its wings tilted upward like *C. livia domestica.*

Mates are inseparable. They make such flimsy nests that from below the eggs can be seen through the bottom. In this case lack of hygiene is useful in that nestling feces accumulate on the twig platform and give it greater stability. The *Geotrygon* keep their nests clean, swallowing eggshells and nestling feces.

Sometimes columbids use abandoned nests of other birds. *Columba picazuro, Columbina passerina,* and the Plain-breasted Ground-Dove, *C. minuta,* usually lay on the ground, as does *Zenaida auriculata* in part of its range. The latter gathers in flocks that can become enormous. Possibly ground nesting is a primitive character of the family. The male *Scardafella squammata* brings the nesting material (Lordello 1954).

Columbids usually lay two pure white eggs shaped the same at each end, but *Columba speciosa, C. cayennensis, C. plumbea* (Amazonas) and the Spot-winged Pigeon, *C. maculosa,* lay only one. *Geotrygon* eggs are light brownish or pink. Mates incubate with dedication; covering the eggs is a necessity given their lack of protective coloring. *Geotrygon* are an exception; their eggs are protectively colored, which permits frequent absence of the pair. Injury is feigned to lead a predator away from the nest (*Columbina talpacoti, Geotrygon montana, Leptotila*), a habit well represented among species that nest or had ancestors who nested on the ground.

The incubation period is 16 to 19 days for the *Columba* (17 days for *C. livia domestica*); 14 days for *Zenaida auriculata, Scardafella squammata,* and *Leptotila verreauxi;* 12 to 13 days for *Columbina talpacoti;* and only 11 days for *Geotrygon montana,* which must be close to the minimum incubation period known. The male *Scardafella squammata* incubates from morning until 4:00 or 5:00 P.M. and is then replaced by the female.

Northeasterners insist that air temperatures govern *Zenaida auriculata* incubation, irrespective of the parents' actions, a curious belief already mentioned in 1877 by the writer A. B. Menezes.

Nestlings are nidicolous, being fed by the parents with "pigeon milk," a cheesy material produced by the digestive epithelium of the crop, which is highly developed in both sexes during the breeding period. This "milk," regurgitated and taken by the nestlings from the parents' bills, is rich in fat (25–30%), proteins (10–15%), and lecithin (5%), but has no carbohydrates. The protein supply so necessary for the young is thus guaranteed even if the parents consume only vegetable material (see also "Feeding"). Crop milk is also produced by flamingos (see Phoenicopteridae, "Breeding") and by the male Emperor Penguin, *Aptenodytes forsteri.* Other birds substitute insects for "milk." As the nestlings grow, seeds are added to their diet in increasing amounts, as recorded for *Zenaida auriculata* (Bucher and Nores 1973). *Leptotila verreauxi* and *Scardafella squammata* leave the nest at 15 days of age. Certain species, such as *Columbina talpacoti,* breed all year, sometimes using the same nest for consecutive clutches. In Brasília 7 reproductive cycles were recorded in 12 months for *C. talpacoti* (Couto 1985).

Habitat and Synanthropic Tendencies

Most Brazilian species, particularly the smaller ones, live in savanna regions, benefiting from deforestation and expansion of agriculture. In this way typically cerrado and caatinga forms, such as *Zenaida auriculata, Scardafella squammata,* and the Picui Ground-Dove, *Columbina picui,* have invaded Espírito Santo as a result of the "northeastification" that has taken place there. Ground-doves are the most frequently seen birds in caatinga.

Eight columbid species may occur in the same area. Some adapt perfectly to city life, as exemplified by *C. talpacoti,* which has become the most abundant flier in big cities such as Rio de Janeiro, outnumbering even the House Sparrow, *Passer domesticus. Columba picazuro* has begun to use urban areas. See also *C. livia domestica.*

Migration

After breeding, most columbids, especially savanna or semi-open country species such as *Columba picazuro* and the Spot-winged Pigeon, *C. maculosa,* gather in flocks. Banding of *C. picazuro* in Poconé, Mato Grosso, revealed regular migration to the Paraguayan chaco.

In southern Brazil migration coincides with the southern autumn and winter. Columbids then appear in regions where they are not seen in other months. Pinto (1954) recounts that *Claravis godefrida* sometimes appeared in great abundance in the Itatiaia area. The same is reported for the Blue Ground-Dove, *C. pretiosa,* in Espírito Santo and Mato Grosso and, mutatis mutandis, in Amazonia with *Geotrygon montana,* lost migrants of which are sometimes found in the center of Manaus (A. Whittaker pers. comm.). Vertical migration occurs on mountains such as Itatiaia (*Columba plumbea*). *Zenaida auriculata* is one of the few landbirds that have colonized Fernando de Noronha Island. The periodic migrations of *Z. auriculata* in northeastern Brazil are unique (see "Enemies . . .").

Parasites and Diseases

Columbids are frequent hosts to louse flies (Hippoboscidae), the so-called *almas-de-pombo,* "pigeon souls."

Columba cayennensis and *Scardafella squammata* harbor *Stilbometopa columbarum; Columbina talpacoti, Scardafella squammata,* and the *Leptotila* host *Microlynchia pusilla.* On the occurrence of blood parasites and public health significance, see *Columba livia domestica.* The drastic decline in the Chilean Pigeon, *C. araucana,* in Argentina and Chile 30 years ago was caused by Newcastle disease and avian pox (Cubillos et al. 1979, Casas and Peña 1987).

Enemies and Other Dangers, Hunting, Alleged Harmfulness, and Decline

Columbids often fall victim to carnivorous mammals and birds of prey. Ground-doves such as *Columbina talpacoti* are caught while they sleep by the false vampire bat (*Chrotopterus auritus*), which devours the entire bird, starting with the head (Peracchi et al. 1976).

Storms may kill small doves. Eight ground-doves were found dead in a small bamboo grove after a hail storm (Nova Friburgo, Rio de Janeiro). Other birds, such as the Rufous Hornero, *Furnarius rufus;* House Wren, *Troglodytes aedon;* Double-collared Seedeater, *Sporophila caerulescens;* Rufous-collared Sparrow, *Zonotrichia capensis;* and a thrush were also affected but on a smaller scale. *Columbina, Geotrygon,* and other doves are among the birds that regularly fly into white walls of houses built in the woods.

Large pigeons are esteemed as game birds. The average consumption for a Cariri (Ceará) family with five children between ages 12 and 20 is 80 to 100 pigeons and 120 doves per year, in addition to Spotted Nothuras, *Nothura maculosa,* and numerous rodents (J. Moojen 1955 pers. comm.). En masse appearances of *Zenaida auriculata* in the northeast are a valuable economic asset. It then becomes the principal source of protein for regional inhabitants, and exploitation becomes an "industry," with clear divisions of labor among those who hunt, those who remove feathers, and those who salt the birds.

Wild species, such as *Columba picazuro,* that cause damage to new plantings and *C. livia domestica,* which causes problems in cities (São Paulo and Paraná), are combated by poisoning (see "Feeding").

Among wild species that are becoming scarce is *Claravis godefrida.* The decline of *Zenaida auriculata* has been compared to the extinction of the Passenger Pigeon, *Ectopistes migratorius. Z. auriculata* is a synanthropic species considered to be a pest in Argentina. Its increasing scarcity in the northeast is a local phenomenon.

Captive Breeding

Captive breeding of Brazilian columbids such as *Columba picazuro* holds promise; it was also practiced by Indians in eastern Mato Grosso (Tapirapé). *Zenaida auriculata,* a gregarious bird accustomed to living in large concentrations, is one of the least demanding species for rearing in a confined environment.

Synopsis of Brazilian Columbids
(number of species in parentheses)

The 23 species can be arranged in 3 categories. Some congeners are so similar ("twin species") that distinguishing between them is difficult. This is the case with *Leptotila verreauxi* and *L. rufaxilla; Columba plumbea* and *C. subvinacea; Claravis pretiosa* and *C. godefrida;* and *Geotrygon montana* and *G. violacea.* To complicate things further, sometimes both members of the same "pair" live in the same forests, in the same habitat.

1. Large species: *Columba* (8)
2. Medium species:
   2.1. *Leptotila* (2)
   2.2. *Claravis* (2)
   2.3. *Geotrygon* (3)
   2.4. *Zenaida* (1)
3. Small species:
   3.1. *Scardafella* (1)
   3.2. *Uropelia* (1)
   3.3. *Columbina* (5)

ROCK DOVE, *Columba livia domestica*
Pombo, Pombo-doméstico

38 cm. Introduced into Brazil in sixteenth century as a domestic bird; continues as such, but some individuals have become wild, shy, and independent of human care, thus justifying inclusion in list of Brazilian birds.[1] It would be interesting to determine whether there are places in Brazil where it nests on cliffs, far from human habitation. Only rarely have I seen it perch in abandoned quarries (Rio de Janeiro).

Domestic pigeon, kept for 5000 years by Asians, descended from wild *C. livia* of Mediterranean Europe, from which it inherited habit of nesting on cliffs. Now finds city buildings ideal substitute. Perching on window sills and fluttering down into plazas among skyscrapers of large cities, this pigeon is only bird to provide us pleasure (if we overlook its filth) of its presence. Pigeon excrement, called "columbina," is a rich fertilizer similar to guano.

Public Health Significance: Feral pigeons are beginning to cause problems in Brazil with the filth they create and because they may transmit diseases. They are susceptible to Newcastle disease, a virus common in chickens. Of 455 individuals examined in São Paulo, 14% were infected with the protozoan *Toxoplasma gondii.* There are few references to toxoplasmosis in Brazilian birds: in the domestic chicken; *Passer domesticus;* and Red-legged Honeycreeper, *Cyanerpes cyaneus* (Bueno et al. 1962). *C. l. domestica* is attacked, like other domestic birds (chickens, turkeys,

ducks), by ornithosis, an illness closely related to psittacosis and caused by a *Miyagawanella.*

Among their ectoparasites, the prominent hippoboscids are well known. These dorso-ventrally flattened flies, size of a common house fly, are found on many birds. They slide swiftly over the plumage to quickly disappear again among feathers or fly to another bird. They suck only bird blood.

The true alma-de-pombo in the Americas is *Pseudolynchia canariensis,* carrier of the hematozoon *Haemoproteus columbae* which is called the "perfect parasite" in that it does not damage its host. In Rio de Janeiro I have found this pigeon hosting another hippoboscid: *Microlynchia pusilla.* I have noticed that a pigeon becomes nervous when an insect, such as a fly, flies around it, as if it foresees bad luck, and have noticed the same thing with cracids.

Population control of this pigeon (and of other vertebrates considered to be pests, e.g., rats) can now be undertaken by the relatively benign method of contraception. Even the young, given "pigeon milk" by medicated parents, become sterile (Sturtevant 1970; see also *Passer domesticus, Rivalry and Longevity*).

Pigeon Fanciers: The origins of pigeon keeping are lost in time. One of its branches is the breeding of ornamental varieties, a sophisticated and expensive pastime. There are about 140 varieties originating from artificial selective processes, all with the domestic pigeon. Prominent among them are the "crowned pigeon," "pouter," and "fantail," also bred in Brazil. There is an International Columbophile Federation with headquarters in Belgium.

The carrier pigeon, one of the numerous descendants of the domestic pigeon, was used in antiquity as a messenger. Trained for competitions, it can cover 800–1000 km/day. It has been a challenge to physiologists to explain its orientational ability. Contrary to what one might expect, the conclusion has now been reached that vision plays an insignificant role in its aerial navigation, for individuals have occasionally returned at night, even when fitted with darkened contact lenses. The fact is that the orientation mechanism of the carrier pigeon remains unknown. The theory indicating the earth's magnetic field as its basis has not yet been well explained.

Carrier pigeons fly at an average speed of 50 km/hr and can reach 66 km/hr. A record was made in Brazil in 1972: the pigeon "Jacuí" and 2 others flew from Teresina (Piauí) to Belo Horizonte (Minas Gerais), a distance of 1700 km in a straight line and perhaps 3000 km as flown. Jacuí took 2 weeks, dying shortly afterward. Another record was a course flown from Corumbá (Mato Grosso) to Porto Alegre (Rio Grande do Sul), a straight-line distance of 1500 km, by the pigeon "Itati," which spent 34 hours en route. The absolute record was made by "Charlie," from Guernsey, England, who in 1986 crossed the Atlantic, 4700 miles, and landed in Fortaleza, Ceará, in good physical condition.

---

[1]The Collared Dove, *Streptopelia decaocto,* of the Old World is frequently bred in captivity. It sometimes escapes and reproduces in the wild, for instance on islands in Guanabara Bay (Rio de Janeiro). See also Eared Dove, *Zenaida auriculata.*

Pigeon shooting contests have caused disputes between shooters and environmentalists and have several times been prohibited.

In 1961 during the building of Brasília, a large dovecote was constructed on the Esplanade of the Ministries.

SCALED PIGEON, *Columba speciosa*,
Pomba-trocal   PL 15.5

30 cm. One of largest Brazilian species, unmistakable with red bill and scaly appearance of whole neck. Female has dark brown back contrasting with chocolate head. VOICE: a song divided into 5 phrases, alternating prolonged syllables with short ones: *ghelooo gloo-GLOOO gloo-GOOO gloo-GOOO goo-glooo-OO*. Forest canopies, but nests on lower branches. Mexico to Argentina, hot regions throughout Brazil. Also called *Pomba-carijó, Pomba-divina, Pomba-pedrês*. See *C. fasciata* and *C. picazuro*.

BAND-TAILED PIGEON, *Columba fasciata*

On Venezuela/Brazil border; 3 specimens collected on Cerro Uei-tepui (Phelps and Phelps 1962). In Andes region as far as Argentina.

PICAZURO PIGEON, *Columba picazuro*,
Asa-branca, Pombão

34 cm. Largest native Brazilian columbid, size of *C. livia domestica*. Upper side of wing crossed by white band, more visible in flight. Scaly semicollar restricted to hind neck, unlike *C. speciosa*. Ring around eye has some red. VOICE: a low, deep, harsh song of 3–4 syllables, *goo-goo-GOOOoo, GOOOoo-goo-goo-goo*. Groves, gallery forests, caatinga. Frequently on ground. Migratory, like many pigeons, extending range and appearing in large numbers as deforestation proceeds. The northeast to Rio Grande do Sul, Goiás, southern Mato Grosso, Bolivia, Argentina. In southern portions of Brazil frequently the only sizable species. Also called *Pomba-trocal, Pomba-trocaz, Pomba-carijó* (Rio Grande do Sul), *Pomba-verdadeira*.

SPOT-WINGED PIGEON, *Columba maculosa*,
Pomba-do-orvalho

33 cm. Large; dark gray; wing sooty, speckled white. On migration associates with *C. picazuro*. A southwestern species. Southern Peru to Argentina, Uruguay, Brazil in Rio Grande do Sul (espinilho parkland, nesting October). Also called *Pombão*.

PALE-VENTED PIGEON, *Columba cayennensis*,
Pomba-galega

32 cm. Generally most common large species in hot lowlands. Top of head, neck, mantle, and breast vinaceous; rest of plumage bluish gray, nape with metallic reflections. Tips of flight feathers light brown, prominent in flight. VOICE: similar to *C. speciosa* but higher and faster, *gooo GOOK-*

GOOK-gooo. Forest edge, perches on isolated trees, e.g., cecropias along river banks. Mexico to Argentina, Uruguay, throughout Brazil. Gathers in flocks in nonbreeding season. Also called *Pomba-legítima, Picuçaroba, Pomba-mineira, Pocaçu, Caçaroba, Pomba-do-ar*. See "Vocalization" and "Breeding."

RUDDY PIGEON, *Columba subvinacea*,
Pomba-amargosa-da-Amazônia

22.8 cm. Very similar to *C. plumbea* but smaller; deep vinaceous with brownish mantle. Internal vane of primaries chestnut. VOICE: *koo-OO, koo-OO, oo, koo-oo*, similar to *C. plumbea plumbea* of south but higher and suave, unlike sympatric *C. p. pallescens*. Tall forest. Panama to Bolivia, Brazil: Mato Grosso (upper Xingu), Maranhão. Also called *Pomba-do-vinagre*.

PLUMBEOUS PIGEON, *Columba plumbea*,
Pomba-amargosa

34 cm; 231 g. Large with long, wide tail. Almost uniformly plumbeous gray with small, faint, light spots at base of hind neck. VOICE: a loud song of 4 clear syllables, *kooo KOO-koo kooo* (*um só ficou*, "only one remained") with a diatonic note uttered every 5 seconds. Warning a monosyllabic, harsh moan, *rrooo;* see *C. subvinacea*. At height of breeding season rises above forest on display flights, mounting vertically and gliding down in spirals to perch on another branch. Lives hidden in leafy treetops of tall forest, both in cold areas (Serra do Mar, Serra da Mantiqueira, etc.) and hot ones, e.g., Rio São Francisco, Minas Gerais. See "Feeding." Rio Grande do Sul to Amazonia, where meets its twin species, *C. subvinacea*. Also called *Picaçu, Caçaroba, Pomba-verdadeira, Guaçaroba, Was kost' die Kuh* ("How much does the cow cost?," German colonists in Espírito Santo).

EARED DOVE, *Zenaida auriculata*,
Avoante, Pomba-de-bando   PL 15.3

21 cm. Slender savanna species that in flight may resemble a sandpiper. Has 2 almost horizontal black streaks on each side of head and some black spots on wings. Tail feathers, particularly outer ones, have generous white tip set off by black subterminal band, prominent when bird perches. Immature at about 3 weeks of age has head, neck, and wings triangularly streaked with white or yellowish and large white spot on lores. VOICE: a phrase of 4 low whistles, the 2 middle ones together, *ooo OOO-OOO oo*.

Open country, even that almost devoid of taller vegetation, cerrado, caatinga, cultivated fields, pastures. Antilles to Tierra del Fuego, discontinuously throughout Brazil, including Fernando de Noronha Island, where abundant. Recently reached northeastern Espírito Santo, taking advantage of deforestation. Called *Ribaça* (Rio Grande do Norte), *Pararé* (Mato Grosso), *Guaçuroba-pequena, Arribaçã, Pomba-do-meio* (Rio Grande do Sul), and many other names. A southern replacement of Mourning Dove, *Z. macroura,* of North America. *Z. auriculata noronha,* a subspecies described from Fernando de Noronha, also occurs in northeast to Maranhão, Bahia. See *Columbina picui* which is smaller and has white in wing. Ecological niche of *Z. auriculata* is similar to that occupied in Old World by *Streptopelia* (see *Columba livea domestica*).

Eared Doves in the Northeast: At intervals of 2–3 years *Z. auriculata* becomes extremely numerous in northeast (Piauí, Ceará, Rio Grande do Norte), appearing April–June by the thousands to form compact flocks whose sizes place them among the world's most spectacular bird migrations. Apparently they are attracted by the abundant fruiting of marmelo-do-campo (*Croton* sp.) which occurs after the heavy rains that usually fall between November and March, as determined by A. Aguirre, to whom we owe the first reliable information about the species.

The recovery pattern of 26,000 banded *Z. auriculata* showed a movement in the caatinga paralleling the rains (Antas 1986). This was the first Brazilian example of migration detected by banding. The caatinga, situated in the 550–750-mm average annual rainfall zone, has a seasonal precipitation pattern that moves from the centralwest to Rio Grande do Norte. The rainiest trimester gradually moves from southwest to northeast. The rains cause the caatinga to resprout, blossom, and fruit. When the seeds mature and fall is the ideal time for the ground-feeding, granivorous *Z. auriculata.*

The range of the local form, *Z. a. noronha,* the *arribaçã,* the only one to participate in this migration, covers only the northeast (Maranhão, Piauí, Ceará, Pernambuco, Bahia, Fernando de Noronha); other races occur in Amazon estuary (Marajó, Mexiana), west (Santarém savannas, etc.), and southern Brazil (Bahia southward).

Regional people believe the *arribação,* "migration," [literally "arrival"] comes overseas from Africa and that "the more are killed, the more appear." In the eyes of country people, this supposition is amply confirmed by an occasional accumulation of dead doves thrown up on beaches. A pair of *Z. auriculata* was seen about 50 km from Fernando de Noronha flying toward the continental coast (Oren 1984).

Separate dove feeding, drinking, and breeding areas are spoken of. It nests among macambiras (*Bromelia laciniosa*) and xique-xique cactus (*Pilocereus gounellei*) during the March–June period. One of these congregations may cover an area 1 km × 5 km (average size) and be active for 60–70 days. The outback people pursue the doves with every means, even at night ("spotlighting"), primarily at their drinking spots, which may be water holes dug at the time to attract them. The height of the brutality is that the "hunters" usually poison the water in the water holes, using a poison that only affects the doves, not people. Salt licks are another place doves are found.

In Ceará, a "poor" site exploited in 1959 furnished about 100,000 birds in a week and about 300,000 in the 21 days it

was used. In Paraíba in 1953, 1 man managed to get 400 birds in 1 night; another on the same occasion got 800. The doves, once salted and dried (each then weighs 60 g), are packed in 50-kg bales, 100,000 loading a 6-ton capacity truck. Eggs are sold by the liter. Consequently, during certain periods these doves are an important factor in the diet and economy of local populations, not to mention the rich booty they represent for predatory mammals, birds, and reptiles that gather at their sites.

Nesting: In the northeast *Z. auriculata* nests on sand, protected by spiny vegetation. On Fernando de Noronha it lays on rocks among marine birds (boobies; Brown Noddy, *Anous stolidus*), as noted by the first explorers (Abbeville 1614). In the Amazon estuary (Ilha Mexiana) it also nests on the ground among underbrush. In some regions (e.g., Ecuador) it builds nests in trees or on the ground. In Rio Grande do Sul in 1971 we found nests in trees. The same occurs in São Paulo, Argentina, and Venezuela. Perhaps it adapts its habits to habitat changes (deforestation). It also lays eggs on the ground in São Paulo and Paraná. In Paraíba there were 6–7 nests per sq m (R. von Ihering 1968). See also "Breeding."

Potential for Harm, Decline, and Conservation: It is interesting that in spite of its numbers in northeast, it has not yet become a nuisance, for there are no plantings such as soybeans. It eats sprouting seeds. When its natural habitat is altered by agriculture, it is almost certain to become a pest, as occurred in Colombia for soybeans and in Argentina (Córdoba) for monocultures such as sorghum. In the latter area 85% of its food is composed of cultivated grains, especially sorghum, wheat, and millet (Bucher 1970), with birds always abundant and roosts of 1–5 million. It seems unlikely there will be a major influx of monocultures in the northeast that might enable *Z. auriculata* to become a problem, as it is starting to be in soybean plantations in Paraná.

The area favorable to dove concentrations in the northeast must now be only half what it was in the early 1900s when almost all the "drought polygon" was suitable for breeding (Aguirre 1976). Certain gathering places need to be protected by creating reserves to perpetuate the typically northeastern spectacle of *Z. auriculata* population dynamics. It is a unique local phenomenon that recalls the gatherings of the famous *Ectopistes migratorius;* once one of the most numerous birds on earth, it became extinct in the early 1900s, being apparently dependent on the effect of very large assemblages. The hundreds to which its population was reduced were not enough to assure survival. The situation of *Z. auriculata* is different (see "Enemies . . . "). Creation of 3 northeastern reserves to protect the migration has been proposed to adjust for the fact that they do not lay every year in the same colonies (Aguirre 1976).

BLUE-EYED GROUND-DOVE, *Columbina cyanopis,*
Rolinha-do-planalto   BR   R   PL 44.10

15.5 cm. Rare species of central Brazil. Similar to *C. talpacoti* but with chestnut head, upper wing coverts with blue spots, under wing coverts cinnamon. Open savannas, on ground, like ordinary ground-doves. Known only from a few museum specimens. Mato Grosso (Cuiabá), southern Goiás (Rio Verde), western São Paulo (Itapura). See Chapter 2.4. Also called *Pombinha-olho-azul*.

COMMON GROUND-DOVE, *Columbina passerina,* Rolinha-cinzenta

15 cm. Head, neck, and breast scaled with black. Flight feathers cinnamon like *C. minuta,* but this species even more terrestrial. Prefers very open places, may invade cities, e.g., Belém (Pará). From southern U.S. to northern Brazil, south to southern Bahia.

PLAIN-BREASTED GROUND-DOVE, *Columbina minuta,* Rolinha-de-asa-canela

14 cm. Lighter-colored than *C. talpacoti.* Underside of wings and bases of remiges cinnamon, prominent in flight. When frightened squats on ground. Locally in fields, restingas, and caatingas, where it may be most common small dove. Likes dense, low vegetation, unlike *C. passerina.* Apparently does not invade cities (Rio de Janeiro). Mexico to Paraguay, southern and central Brazil. Also called *Rolinha-caxexa* (northeast).

RUDDY GROUND-DOVE, *Columbina talpacoti,* Rola, Rolinha   PL 15.2

17 cm. Usually best-known Brazilian ground-dove. Male has contrasting light gray head. Under wing coverts regularly displayed when bird is threatening or feels threatened (see "Behavior"). Immature has yellowish spots on wings. VOICE: a continuous, monotonous *oo, oo-oot* series of 6–16 notes, given almost all year. Any semiopen area, coffee plantations, wetlands. Although normally seeks food on ground, adapts perfectly to city life, even to increasing verticalization of buildings, where it explores balconies and porches (with or without plantings); rummages for food on parapets, service areas, inside rooms; and even sings territorial song. Flies from heights of one building to another instead of returning to ground, then lets itself fall as if by parachute, also a new adaptation. Nests in city (Rio de Janeiro) on beams under tiles, on porches of buildings, in sheds, and in space where a window air conditioner had been removed. Has become most abundant bird of metropolitan areas such as Rio de Janeiro. Meets *Columba livea domestica,* which ignores it, on tops of buildings, and less often *Passer domesticus,* which does not go to great heights. Individuals fight furiously trying to steal food from one another. Mexico to Bolivia, Paraguay, Argentina, throughout Brazil. Also called *Rola-caldo-de-feijão, Rolinha-comum, Rola-cabocla* (Paraíba).

PICUI GROUND-DOVE, *Columbina picui,* Rolinha-branca

16 cm. Unmistakable with large white area in wing and white sides of tail. Shiny, blue-black band crosses high on wing. VOICE: a very typical song, about 6 bisyllabic *gooLOO*s. Savannas with sparse trees, also cities. In certain regions, e.g., Minas Gerais, abundant, especially in caatinga. Range spreading with deforestation; has now immigrated into northwestern Espírito Santo. In southern areas (Rosário, Argentina) has become a pest but is far from being as abundant as *Zenaida auriculata.* Colombia to Bolivia, Chile, Argentina, Uruguay. Southwestern and northeastern Brazil. Also called *Rolinha-pajeú* (Paraíba), *Rolinha-pintada.*

BLUE GROUND-DOVE, *Claravis pretiosa,* Pomba-de-espelho

19 cm. Clearly larger than the *Columbina.* Male bluish gray with black spots on wing and sides of tail. Female brown with chestnut wing spots, yellowish bill. VOICE: song a series of *OO*s . . . , low and simple. Forest edge, restinga, etc., also near dwellings. Mexico to Argentina, throughout Brazil. Also called *Rola-azul, Rola-vermelha* (male and female, respectively, northeast).

PURPLE-WINGED GROUND-DOVE, *Claravis godefrida,* Pararu   R

23.5 cm. Similar to *C. pretiosa* but considerably larger. Male with 2 wide, copper-chestnut wing bars, and white sides of tail. Female brown with sepia-violet wing bars. VOICE: song a full *oo-OOT.* Lives on ground hidden in thick woods, bamboo groves, etc. Primarily in mountains (Serra dos Órgãos, Itatiaia) in Rio de Janeiro region. Fifty years ago appeared around Teresópolis (Rio de Janeiro) in flocks of 50–100 in November–December, when giant bamboo (*Gadua superba*), bamboo (*Bambusa* sp.), and criciúma (Gramineae) were loaded with seed, staying until autumn. Recently has become noticeably scarcer, although it reappeared in 1975, perhaps due to bamboo cycle. Southern Bahia to Santa Catarina (formerly including bamboo groves in ex-Guanabara), Paraguay. Also called *Pomba-espelho.*

LONG-TAILED GROUND-DOVE, *Uropelia campestris,* Rola-vaqueira   PL 15.4

17 cm. Long, graduated tail with white tips, sulfur yellow feet and eyelids. VOICE: song *WAH-oo* . . . , sounding like *tew* . . . at a distance; resembles song of Collared Crescentchest, *Melanopareia torquata* (Rhinocryptidae), with which it is syntopic. Savannas of central Brazil as far as Amapá, Marajó, northeast, western Minas Gerais Bolivia. Walks on ground with tail lifted, unlike *C. talpacoti.*

SCALED DOVE, *Scardafella squammata,* Fogo-apagou   Fig. 113

19.5 cm. Unique in scaly appearance. Remiges have rufescence, prominent in flight and reminiscent of *C. passerina.* Sides of tail white like *C. picui.* VOICE: characteristic song a trisyllabic *oo GOO-GOOO* (*fogo-apagou,* "fire went out"). Makes loud rattlelike noise with wings: *prrrr(oh)-*

Fig. 113. Scaled Dove, *Scardafella s. squammata.*

tststs (hence the name *rola-cascavel,* "rattlesnake ground-dove"). Dry savanna, cerrado, gardens. Venezuela to Paraguay, Argentina (Misiones), Brazil: northeast and central Brazil to São Paulo, southern Mato Grosso, Paraná, Rio Grande do Sul. Immigrated around 1928 to Colatina region (Espírito Santo). Also called *Rolinha-carijó, Fogo-pagô, Rola-pedrês, Felix-cafofo* (Paraíba), *Paruru.*

White-tipped Dove, *Leptotila verreauxi,* Juriti
Pl 15.1

26.5 cm. One of best-known species, twin of *L. rufaxilla.* In flight white tips of outer rectrices and cinnamon underside of wings prominent. VOICE: song melancholic and ascending, sounding like a question: *oo-OOO* (male): *oo-oo-OOO, prr-prr-prr-OOO* (female). Hot areas; capoeiras (from which it makes expeditions into savanna), forest edge, cerrado. Absent from top of Serra do Mar (Rio de Janeiro). Southern U.S. to Bolivia, Argentina, almost all of Brazil. Also called *Pu-pú* (Rio Grande do Sul). See *L. rufaxilla.*

Gray-fronted Dove, *Leptotila rufaxilla,* Gemedeira

Extremely similar to *L. verreauxi* but somewhat larger. Forehead more distinctly white, iris dark without orange ring. Hind neck bluish, tending toward violaceous (not metallic green as in *verreauxi*). Breast purplish. VOICE: song a deep, descending moan, *oooooo.* Interior of primary or secondary forest, in lowlands or highlands (e.g., ex-Guanabara), alongside *L. verreauxi.* Venezuela to Bolivia, Argentina, Uruguay, much of Brazil. Also called *Juriti.*

Ruddy Quail-Dove, *Geotrygon montana,* Pariri

24 cm. Relatively common terrestrial bird, twin of *G. violacea.* Conspicuous sexual dimorphism: male has dark purplish rufous upperparts, sides of head with whitish horizontal line above a dark line, underparts ochraceous, tail

chestnut. Female olive brown. VOICE: similar to *L. rufaxilla* —descending, lower basso profundo, more prolonged: *koooooo,* resembling a ship's fog horn. May give this note each second for a minute or longer. Forest interior or capoeirão. Walks with bill held a bit downward, takes flight silently, roosts low. On ground resembles a quail or tinamou, easily passes unnoticed. Mexico to Bolivia, Argentina, Paraguay; almost all of northern, eastern, southern Brazil. Also called *Pomba-cabocla, Juriti-vermelho, Juriti-piranga.* See *G. violacea.*

Violaceous Quail-Dove, *Geotrygon violacea,* Juriti-vermelha

Similar to *G. montana* but with whitish forehead (similar to *L. rufaxilla*) and without contrasting pattern on face. Upper back intensely purplish violet (male). White belly (eye-catching in female). Central America to Bolivia, Argentina (Misiones), eastern Brazil (Alagoas to Paraná), also Pará Belém). Sometimes in same forests with *G. montana* (e.g., north of Rio Doce, Espírito Santo) but much less well known. Also called *Juriti-da-mata, Cabocla-violeta.*

Sapphire Quail-Dove, *Geotrygon saphirina*

A sight record from Benjamin Constant, Amazonas (Willis 1987). Occurs in neighboring Peru, Ecuador, Colombia.

Colombidae Bibliography
See also General Bibliography

Abbeville, C. de. 1614. *Da História da Missão dos Padres Capuchinos na Ilha do Maranhão.*

Aguirre, A. C. 1964. *As avoantes do Nordeste.* Rio de Janeiro: Min. Agric.

Aguirre, A. C. 1976. *Distribuição, costumes e extermínio da "avoante" do nordeste,* Zenaida auriculata. Rio de Janeiro: *An. Acad. Bras. Ciênc.*

Bucher, E. H. 1970. *Consideraciones ecológicas sobre la paloma,* Zenaida auriculata, *como plaga en Córdoba.* Minist. Economia y Hacienda.

Bucher, E. H. 1982. *Biotrópica* 14(14):255–61. [*Zenaida auriculata,* colonial breeding in northeastern Brazil]

Bucher, E. H., and M. Nores. 1973. *Hornero* 11:209–16. [*Zenaida auriculata,* feeding]

Bueno, R. C., et al. 1962. *Arq. Inst. Biol. S. Paulo* 29:231–70. [Pigeon, diseases]

Carvalho, C. T. 1957. *Bol. Mus. Paraen.* 7. [*Columbina passerina, C. talpacoti,* behavior]

Casas, A. E., and M. R. de la Peña. 1987. Algunos datos sobre la situación actual de la Paloma Araucana, *Columba araucana,* en la Argentina. *Nótulas Faunísticas* 3.

Cintra, R. 1988. Reproductive ecology of *Colombina talpacoti* on the Central Plateau of Brazil. *Wilson. Bull.* 100(3):443–57.

Couto, E. A. 1985. "O efeito da sazonalidade na população da rolinha, *Columbina talpacoti,* no Distrito Federal." Thesis. Tese Inst. Ciências Bio. Univ. Brasília.

Cubillos, A., R. Schlatter, and V. Cubillos. 1979. Diftero-Viruela Aviar en Torcaza, *Columba araucana*, del sur de Chile. *Zbl. Vet. MedB.* 26:430–32.

Eston, M. R. 1989. "Aspectos do comportamento reprodutivo da rolinha fogo-apagou, *Scardafella squammata*." Thesis. Dep. Ecol. Inst. Biociências, Univ. São Paulo.

Goodwin, D. 1970. *Pigeons and Doves of the World.* London: Brit. Mus. Nat. Hist.

Goodwin, D. 1973. *Bull. B.O.C.* 93:103–08. [*Columba plumbea*, etc., behavior]

Ihering, R. v. 1937. *Hornero* 6,1. [*Zenaida auriculata*, behavior]

Ingels, J. 1989. Beobachtungen an Roten Erdtauban (*Geotrygon montana*) in Surinam. *Trochilus* 10:43–78.

Lordello, L.G.E. 1954. Contribuição à História Natural do Parú (*Scardafella squammata*). *An. Esc. Sup. Agric. "Luiz Queiroz", Piracicaba* 2:13–21.

Nogueira Neto, P. 1980. "Notas sobre aspectos ecoetológicos de alguns Columbidae e Psittacidae indígenos." Thesis. Dep. Ecol. Inst. Biociências, Univ. São Paulo.

Peracchi, A. L., et al. 1976. *Rev. Bras. Biol.* 36:179–84. [Bat predation]

Pinto, O.M.O. 1949. *Arq. Zool. S. Paulo* 7:241–324. [Monographic sketch]

Rodrigues, M., R. Pucetti, and R. Galetti. 1987. Ocorrência e aspectos comportamentais de *Columba picazuro* en áreas urbanas de Campinas. *XIV Cong. Bras. Zool., Juiz de Fora*:409.

Skutch, A. F. 1964. *Wilson Bull.* 76:211–47. [Behavior]

Storer, R. W. 1970. Independent evolution of the Dodo and Solitaire. *Auk* 87:369–70.

Sturtevant, J. 1970. *Science* 170:322–24. [Sterilization of pigeons]

Vale, M. P., and C. Yamashita. 1987. Migração de *Columba picazuro. An. II ENAV*:201.

Willis, E. O. 1987. Primeiro registro de *Geotrygon saphirina* e *Grallaria* sp. cf. *eludens* no oeste do Brasil. *XIV Cong. Bras. Zool.*:423.

Willis, E. O., and Y. Oniki. 1987. Invasion of deforested regions of São Paulo state by the Picazuro Pigeon (*Columba picazuro*). *Ciência e Cultura* 39(11):1064–65.

ORDER PSITTACIFORMES

Family Psittacidae: Macaws, Parakeets, Parrots, and Allies (69)

Psittacids are distributed throughout the world's tropics, from where they have radiated to the subtropics and even to cold areas such as Patagonia. Their fossils are poorly represented in the lower Tertiary of Europe and in the Pleistocene (20,000 years B.P.) of Brazil. The family is so old its phylogeny is speculative. Relationship with the pigeons is substantiated by electrophoretic analysis of egg whites and eggshells of the two groups.

Brazil is richer in parrots than any other country in the world, with even the largest species, the macaws, living here. This wealth was already evident in the first maps, from 1500 on, in which Brazil was shown as the "Land of Parrots" (*Brasilia sive terra papa-gallorum*).

Morphology

Few orders are as distinctive as this one, with immediate recognition possible despite extreme size variations, the weight of Brazilian species ranging from 26 g (Blue-winged Parrotlet, *Forpus xanthopterygius*) to 1.5 kg (Hyacinth Macaw, *Anodorhynchus hyacinthinus*). Nevertheless, compared to Australasian parrots, ours are quite homogeneous. This is partly because South America, which long remained isolated, is geographically somewhat uniform. In Brazil the unusual psittacids are the Red-fan Parrot, *Deroptyus accipitrinus*, and Vulturine Parrot, *Pionopsitta vulturina*. On uniformity of Neotropical species, see "Endoparasites. . . ."

Parrots have high, recurved bills with a cere at the base, like those of raptors. The weight of a macaw's head is impressive because of the colossal bill; that of a 940-g macaw reaches 180 g, 19% of the bird's total weight. The head of a domestic hen weighing 1220 g accounts for only about 3% of its total body weight. Parrots are described as "round-billed" birds (fig. 114). The maxilla is movable, being attached to the skull by a "hinge" that permits extra movement and increases the power of the bill in opening hard seeds. (The maxilla of all carinate birds is movable to a certain extent—rhynchokinesis.) In large species such as the *Anodorhynchus* and *Amazona*, a notch of varying size may form at the center of the mandibular tomia. Variations in this cut may be interpreted as an individual characteristic or as a manifestation of age, food, or even sex (the notch is deeper in the male). The maxillary ramphotheca is internally folded with transverse ridges that serve in grinding up seeds while the thick tongue, sensitive and densely covered with taste buds, presses the food against the grooves, holding and maneuvering it skill-

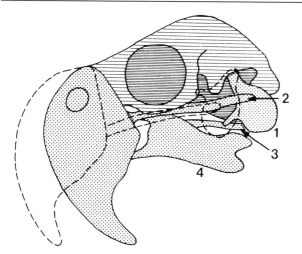

Fig. 114. Kinetics of the upper jaw of a macaw skull:
(1) quadrate bone; (2) jugal bar; (3) pterygoid bone;
(4) palatine bone. Dashed line: protraction of the jaw
(pterygoid and palatine bones omitted). After Starck,
from Peters 1987.

fully to facilitate action of the mandible or entire bill in chewing a hard item. The mandible can also move horizontally, like a sled. Analysis of the functional morphology of the bill and tongue, together with the method of drinking, is of special interest (Homberger 1980).

Parrots have large crops in which they hold food for their chicks for hours. P. Roth (1986 pers. comm.) has concluded that the crop of the Little Blue Macaw, *Cyanopsitta spixii* (practically extinct; see species account), must be relatively small because the parents bring food to the nestlings with great frequency. Psittacids have sharp vision, possessing two retinal foveae.

The tarsus is very short, with the fourth (external) toe pointing backward along with the first (hallux) on a zygodactyl foot like that of woodpeckers and toucans. Toe mobility is controlled by a peculiar musculature (Berman 1984).

The wings are long and strong. The plumage is short, stiff, and full of powder (see the *moleiro*, "miller," Mealy Parrot, *Amazona farinosa*). The uropygial gland tends to atrophy and even to disappear completely (see Columbidae, "Morphology"; also Homberger 1976). Psittacids give off a strong, typical odor which is noticeable with macaws at more than 2 m and may resemble the smell of honey, though it is different in various genera. Green coloring predominates among Brazilian species, frequently with red "markers" on the wing and tail feathers, shoulder, edge of the wings, or even coverts, especially the under wing coverts, producing a colorful effect when revealed in flight or during courtship (e.g., see White-eyed Parakeet, *Aratinga leucophthalmus*). A wing speculum is also spoken of, constituted by the secondaries in the *Amazona* and by the upper wing coverts in certain *Brotogeris*. (See ". . . Color Alterations" on the subject of yellow or blue individuals.) Unlike Australian cockatoos, none of our

species have a crest, but there is a trend toward plumes, most notably in *Deroptyus accipitrinus*.

The bare region around the eye varies in extent. It may be a narrow circle, often brightly colored, as in the *Anodorhynchus, Aratinga, Pyrrhura, Brotogeris,* and *Amazona,* and may be highlighted by a second circle of brightly colored feathers, as in the Peach-fronted Parakeet, *Aratinga aurea.* It may extend to the lores, as with *Cyanopsitta spixii,* or to the entire face (*Ara*) and even to the base of the mandible. The bare strip of swollen skin surrounding the bill (mainly the mandible) is the principal characteristic of the *Anodorhynchus.* There are frequently parallel or circular lines of small feathers on the bare face; the skin of the unfeathered areas is generally white (most of the *Ara, Aratinga,* and *Pyrrhura*) but may be yellow (*Anodorhynchus* and Red-bellied Macaw, *Orthopsittaca manilata*) or even blackish (*Cyanopsitta spixii;* Sun Parakeet, *Aratinga solstitialis;* Maroon-faced Parakeet, *Pyrrhura leucotis;* Festive Parrot, *Amazona festiva*). The eyelid may be a noticeably different color than the eye-ring, as in the Indigo Macaw, *Anodorhynchus leari.*

I recognize six species of true macaws for Brazil: three *Anodorhynchus: hyacinthinus, leari,* and *glaucus;* and three *Ara: ararauna, macao,* and *chloroptera* (see "Systematics . . .") .

Identification of Sex and Age

Sexes are usually similar, although the male is usually stockier, primarily in the bill, and has a squarer head— differences more discernible when an adult pair is seen side by side. In long-tailed species, especially the macaws, the male has a longer tail, but care must be taken not to confuse females with short-tailed young which generally fly with their parents. The male Blue-headed Parrot, *Pionus menstruus,* is a deeper blue; the same effect can be seen in the green of the Blue-bellied Parrot, *Triclaria malachitacea,* whose male has a lilac-colored spot on the breast. A pronounced plumage difference is also seen in the Red-capped Parrot, *Pionopsitta pileata,* the male having a "red hat," and in *Forpus xanthopterygius,* the male of which develops a characteristic blue rump while still a nestling. See also the *Touit.*

Surprisingly, the White-fronted Parrot, *Amazona albifrons,* of Central America and Mexico shows distinctive sexual dimorphism (only the male has red in the wings), making it ideal for field studies.

In adults, pelvic breadth, which is easily felt in the live bird, may be diagnostic: narrow in the male, broader in the female. This difference can sometimes be seen in perched individuals: the male's feet are closer together. This measurement is infallible in the Spotted Nothura, *Nothura maculosa.*

Sex identification in parrots has always aroused great interest, for males are considered to be the better "talkers." I thought I had found the key to this problem: ask the Indians.

But a Turquoise-fronted Parrot, *Amazona aestiva,* said to be a male by the Iaulapiti of the Xingu began to lay eggs two years later. Today there are three sure ways to sex a bird lacking external sexual dimorphism: fecal analysis, blood analysis, and laparatomy, or endoscopy.

Apparently there is sexual dimorphism in the iris color of *Amazona aestiva:* studies with various individuals have shown the male to have an orange-yellow iris, the female orange-red. It is not yet known whether this dimorphism extends to other *Amazona;* it can only be determined with certainty by laparatomy on individuals of the various species. It is not an impossible hypothesis, however, for in various species of Australian Cacatuinae, sexual dimorphism is found precisely in different iris coloration: males have a black iris, females reddish brown. However, before characterizing diversity of iris color as sexual dimorphism, we must bear in mind that this can also be related to age: young *Amazona* and *Pionites,* for example, have a brown iris that changes to red or orange-yellow when they are adults (see above). The Chestnut-fronted Macaw, *Ara severa,* has a dark chestnut iris until six months of age; then it turns yellow.

As soon as a Blue-and-yellow Macaw, *Ara ararauna,* loses its nestling down, it is identical to its parents in plumage except for dark edges on the wing coverts and a chestnut instead of white iris. Still, it is impossible to generalize as to the age at which psittacids obtain their definitive iris color. This process varies from genus to genus, and in some genera from individual to individual, except with the *Amazona,* where individuals at about eight months have their definitive iris color. All immature psittacids have less vividly colored plumage than the respective adults.

Head color varies in the *Amazona* from individual to individual, independent of sex, with no two birds the same. It is known that flavism (an excess of yellow feathers) can play a role in this. Color may vary until the bird reaches sexual maturity: an *A. aestiva* may have a yellow streak on its head that is more accentuated after the first molt. The presence or absence of red on the lower back of *A. festiva* is related to age: a bird's first plumage shows no red, the first red feathers beginning to appear at approximately one year.

Natural and Artificial Color Alterations

The green color of various Brazilian psittacids is sometimes replaced by a beautiful bright reddish yellow. The incidence of light on melanin reflects a structural blue color that, superimposed on yellow, makes the feather look green. The reddish yellow appears with elimination of the melanin. Such individuals are called "counterfeits," a term used as early as 1648 by Marcgrave.

This phenomenon occurs both in nature and in captivity; sometimes one sibling may be "normal" and the other yellow, as I saw in *Amazona farinosa* taken from a nest at Belém, Pará. I also saw a yellow individual with the usual red pattern in a flock of 30 *A. aestiva.* It had normal relations with others of the flock and was followed by a "normally" colored young that was begging (Serra da Mantiqueira, Municipality of Camanducaia, southern Minas Gerais, February 1953). Birds may be greenish yellow (called *canela,* "cinnamon," by breeders) and have a normal iris, or they may be golden yellow, the tint of the red feathers intensified and the iris red, recalling albinism. It is not unusual for certain psittacids, after some years in captivity, to become spotted with yellow. Also, yellow feathers appearing on captive specimens may be replaced with normal ones at the next molt.

I have seen xanthochroism in the Blue-crowned Parakeet, *Aratinga acuticauda;* Cactus Parakeet, *A. cactorum;* Reddish-bellied Parakeet, *Pyrrhura frontalis;* Monk Parakeet, *Myiopsitta monachus* (in captivity); Plain Parakeet, *Brotogeris tirica;* Tui Parakeet, *B. sanctithomae;* Scarlet-shouldered Parrotlet, *Touit huetii;* Yellow-headed parrot, *Amazona ochrocephala;* and *Pyrrhura leucotis, Forpus* sp., *Amazona festiva, A. aestiva, A. farinosa,* and *Triclaria malachitacea.* It also occurs in macaws (*Ara*). Luteinistic individuals have sometimes been considered to be new species, the Yellow-sided Parakeet, *Pyrrhura hypoxantha,* for instance. Schizochroism is well known in the canary and the Australian Budgerigar, *Melopsittacus undulatus* (see appendix), of which a yellow race was bred long ago.

Cyanism has occurred in a wild population of *Brotogeris tirica* (upper Serra do Cubatão, São Paulo). Captured individuals from this source bred in captivity. The same blue occurred in offspring of a "normal" pair of this species in the Munich Zoo at the beginning of the twentieth century. This type of mutation has been observed in the Yellow-chevroned Parakeet, *Brotogeris chiriri; Amazona aestiva; A. ochrocephala panamensis; Forpus xanthopterygius;* and *Myiopsitta monachus.* There are also blue Australian Budgerigars. Partial elimination of the pigment ("pastel blue") has been noted in *Amazona aestiva* and the Orange-winged Parrot, *A. amazonica.* Pale mutants occur in *Myiopsitta monachus* and in the Blue-winged Macaw, *Propyrrhura maracana* (the blues and the greens become very light, while the red does not change).

Early explorers such as de Souza (republished 1938), de la Condamine (1745), and Spix and Martius (republished 1938) mentioned a technique known as *tapiragem* that was used by the Indians, primarily those of Amazonia (there is also a record from Santa Catarina, Pernetty 1979), to artificially produce the yellow color so appreciated by these forest people. The travelers reported that the process involved pulling out the wing and tail feathers of the parrot at molting time and rubbing the area vigorously with material rich in carotenoids; some mentioned fat and frog (probably *Dendrobates tinctorius*) blood used by the Tupinambás, whereas others cited the "lard" of fish such as the pirarara (*Phractocephalus hemiliopterus*), a red substance used by the Araguaian tribes. Applications of fat from the river dolphin (*Inia geoffroyensis*) are also mentioned. They said yellow feathers would sprout after a period of treatment and that these also were pulled out. The next set of feathers would be yellow without need of further action. They also said a similar effect could be obtained with roots and fruits given as food. It is not always clear whether this information came from the authors' personal observations or was cited from other naturalists, travelers, or the Indians themselves. It is known, however, that the Indians usually keep certain techniques secret. A. R. Wallace (1853, 1864), who described the tapiragem of the Uaupés Indians, later reported that the same phenomenon was produced on local parrots by aborigines of the Moluccas Islands in the Orient.

The subject was investigated by G. G. Villela (1968). Attempts to reproduce color alterations by this technique under scientifically controlled conditions failed, strengthening the conclusion already reached by many that tapiragem never existed. Nevertheless I can state on the basis of my own experience with museum collections of feather work that there appears to be more luteinistic material than could be expected under natural conditions. The feathers in question are more commonly *Amazona* flight and tail feathers, although I have also seen completely yellow macaw tail feathers. Red, a natural color in these birds (e.g., tail spots on *Amazona*), is maintained and even emphasized in counterfeit individuals—on the edges of dorsal feathers of *A. aestiva*, for instance. It must be admitted that psittacid pigments, whether yellow or red, are still little understood.

I conclude that the Indians had, and still have, a technique corresponding to the classic tapiragem which is a controlled source for producing yellow feathers, which along with red ones, were always the most sought after to own or the most valuable to trade. Although altered feathers are more frequent in old collections, I have also found recent material that could well be the product of artificial chromatic modification.

It is hard to imagine how feather color can be altered without feeding a pigment before molt. Breeders mix carotenoids with the food of scarlet ibis, canaries, etc., to intensify feather color. Another process is to feed dendé [palm] oil, producing an intense yellow color but causing serious liver lesions. The pigments eaten are deposited in the growing feather by the blood.

A process widely used by illegal dealers in wild birds is to discolor fully developed feathers, probably with oxygenated water. It is common to see entirely discolored *Aratinga leucophthalmus* with only their flight feathers having the original green. These are then sold as young Golden Parakeets, *Guaruba guarouba*. However, immediately after the first molt new feathers come out in their original colors. Until the molt is complete the bird has mixed green and yellow plumage. It is also common to see individual Red-shouldered Macaws, *Diopsittaca nobilis,* with the tail cut and the forehead discolored so they can be sold as young *Amazona aestiva.*

Vocalization and "Cerebralization"

American psittacids are thought of as very noisy. Among the loudest voices, in addition to those of the macaws, is the cry of the Short-tailed Parrot, *Graydidascalus brachyurus.* To distinguish the cries of the various species requires long and constant practice. Certain vocalizations of each species are diagnostic, especially those given in flight. It is usually possible to recognize the genus, if this expresses a genuine relationship and is not artificial, as is presently the case with the *Ara,* which includes such so-called macaws as the Golden-collared, *Propyrrhura auricollis; P. maracana; Orthopsittaca manilata;* and *Diopsittaca nobilis,* all birds with vocalizations totally unlike those of the macaws and closer to the *Aratinga* (see "Systematics . . ."). Vocalizations of the true macaws are as unique as they are impressive, well stated by João Guimarães Rosa: *Avista-se o grito das araras,* "Hark the cry of the macaws." It is obvious that neither voice nor behavior justify inclusion of *Guaruba guarouba* in the *Aratinga,* as generally accepted today. Vocalizations alert us to the need for more research to clarify the systematic position of these species.

The natural repertoire of an *Amazona* is abundant; for example, more than 25 different cries of *A. albifrons,* of Mexico, have been registered (Levinson 1980).

Mated pairs of *Brotogeris* duet, as do *Triclaria malachitacea* and *Ara ararauna.* The phrasing of *T. malachitacea* recalls the song of a thrush. An *A. ararauna* at 14 months is still unable to pronounce the vigorous *arara* of an adult. Parrots indulge in great chattering and singing activity in their collective roosts, culminating in an overwhelming din. In captivity they are stimulated by any sort of sound—water dripping from a shower, for instance. *Maitaca* or *Maritaca* [Brazilian parrot names] are nicknames for a person who talks too much: "He talks like a maritaca" (Minas Gerais).

The inclination to imitate random sounds appears on rare occasions in wild individuals. I have heard a *Pionus menstruus* imitate the croak of a toucan, although more quietly than the model (Xingu, Mato Grosso, 1951), and a *Brotogeris tirica* copy a Smooth-billed Ani, *Crotophaga ani,* to perfection (north of the Rio Doce, Espírito Santo, 1954). A semidomesticated Vinaceous-breasted Parrot, *Amazona vinacea,* surprised me with its perfect imitation of a Tataupa Tinamou, *Crypturellus tataupa,* living in the vicinity. A similarly semidomesticated Red-fan Parrot, *Deroptyus accipitrinus,* imitated the various vocalizations of a Great Kiskadee, *Pitangus sulphuratus,* in the garden. Wild parrots do not learn to imitate as well as pets do, for they lack the incessant repetition of unusual sounds that captive individuals hear. Indirect proof of this comes from the case of a talking parrot that for some time was in the custody of a veterinarian who did not talk with it. It stopped talking. In Trinidad dialects peculiar to certain populations were recorded in the song of *Amazona amazonica,* implying extensive imitation in the wild (Nottebohm et al. 1969). Parrots have few fright and alarm vocalizations (e.g., *T. malachitacea*). The begging of chicks is a characteristic sound (see *Pionus*).

Various species, and especially certain individuals, learn to pronounce words, imitate music, bark, cough, laugh, etc., to perfection. (I credit this ability also to the Squirrel Cuckoo, *Piaya cayana*). It cements their position as favorite companions of humans, especially as they also become very tame. When trained as a young bird, *Amazona aestiva* is the best talker among Brazilian psittacids. It continues to learn for several years, however, and success or failure may depend on the individual bird. Good talkers are also found among other species, such as *Diopsittaca nobilis*, *Amazona ochrocephala*, and *Aratinga leucophthalmus*. Macaws, parakeets, and others (*Brotogeris chiriri*, *Myiopsitta monachus*, *Forpus* spp., and *Deroptyus accipitrinus*) learn to say words. They "understand" situations sufficiently to appear to be acting logically, but their talk generally is nothing but pure mimicry. I must emphasize that psittacids are good at "conditioned mimicry." This ability is demonstrated when a parrot calls "hello" when the telephone rings, or cries "tasty" while awaiting a food it especially likes, or even says "enter" on hearing the doorbell ring. They can also scandalize with obscene phrases and profanity. In the upper Amazon, Salesian nuns taught a parrot to sing the religious hymn "Thirteenth of May." It is particularly impressive when parrots "talk" in an unknown language: Count Mauricio of Nassau, in Pernambuco in the seventeenth century, even employed an interpreter so he could understand one that spoke in Tupi. Alexander von Humboldt told of another that used words from the language of an extinct tribe.

There is no doubt that psittacids are among the world's most "intelligent birds. The intracerebral weight index of a Blue-and-yellow Macaw is 28.07 according to Portmann (1947), reaching the highest level of the Class, even surpassing that of Corvidae (Passeriformes). The lowest index, 2.9, is that of the domestic chicken; that of a raptor reaches 8.3. Research is underway to test the mental faculties of parrots; an *Amazona aestiva*, for instance, learned experimentally to distinguish seven shapes and numbers of dots in order to reach a tidbit hidden in a covered glass; even an individual more than 40 years old demonstrated its skill in these experiments, although it did not achieve the success of a young bird of the same species. See also "Behavior."

Parrot and macaw voices are very loud. City police received a complaint that a parrot "made wild noises before six in the morning, disturbing the peace."

Feeding, Salt Banks, Smell, Drinking, and Migration

Psittacids seek food in the tops of the tallest trees, such as sapucaias [Lecythidaceae], as well as in certain fruit-bearing bushes. Crawling through branches they use their bill as a

third foot; the feet serve to grasp food and carry it to the mouth. On "southpaws," see "Behavior."

They prefer fruit seeds to pulp, even being so choosy as to reject pulp; nevertheless, the Jandaya Parakeet, *Aratinga solstitialis jandaya*, and *A. aurea* eat cashew pulp. They are attracted by fruit trees such as mangos, jaboticabas, guavas, oranges, and papayas. It is surprising how certain isolated fruit trees are frequented year after year in the bearing season by these "customers," who require a good sense of direction, for such temporary sources sometimes demand extensive travel. For this reason certain species appear only periodically and after gorging themselves disappear to unknown destinations where they breed. I have noted in the Brazilian northeast that macaws are more widely scattered during the rainy season when there are more food sources.

The fruits of many palm species, especially the buriti (*Mauritia*) but also the tucum [*Bactris setosa*], bocaiúva [*Acrocomia* spp.], carandá [*Copernicia alba*], and acuri are favorite foods, being taken even from the ground, whether fallen because of fire or because they are ripe. *Anodorhynchus hyacinthinus* runs along the ground to pick up fruits of stemless palms such as the catolé (*Syagrus*), piaçaba [*Attalea* or *Leopoldinia*], and a bushy tucum (*Astrocaryum*) in the cerrado close to buriti groves (Bahia). In the Mato Grosso Pantanal it descends to the ground to gather acuri fruits regurgitated by cattle (A. Pacheco Leão pers. comm.). In the caatinga *Anodorhynchus leari* takes licuri (*Syagrus coronata*) fruits from the ground. Various species eat palmito fruits (*Euterpe edulis*) and like seeds of the oil palm [*Elaeis guineensis*] and jaracatiá [*Jaracatia dodecaphylla*]. *Ara ararauna* likes fruits of the bacuri [*Platonia insignis*], combaru, jatobá (*Hymenaea*), mandovi and, especially of the pequi (*Caryocar brasiliensis*), a tree typical of central Brazil and of great value to indigenous people. Experienced hunters say that fruits taken by psittacids are also good eating for people. However, in Frias, Argentina, *Aratinga acuticauda* has been observed eating cinamomo (*Melia azedarach*) fruits, which are listed as poisonous in specialized reference literature (see Chapter 2.4.). The birds crush pits, destroying the seeds, thus becoming predators that do not help spread the plants. *Brotogeris tirica*, *Forpus xanthopterygius*, the Scaly-headed Parrot, *Pionus maximiliani*, and certainly others seek imbaúba (*Cecropia*) fruits.

Even species with the most powerful bills enjoy the still-soft stones of unripe fruits such as sapucaias (*Lecythes*) and Brazil nuts (*Bertholletia excelsa*). The Red-and-green Macaw, *Ara chloroptera*, is among the psittacids most regularly found in Brazil-nut trees. A captive *Anodorhynchus hyacinthinus* broke coconuts by holding them by the "eyes" and beating them full force against a cement floor. See also "Morphology" on bill use.

The *Aratinga*, *Pionus maximiliani*, *Amazona vinacea*, and others eat buds, flowers, and tender leaves, including those of eucalyptus. *Anodorhynchus hyacinthinus* likes palm shoots. Corn, banana, coffee, and cacao plantings are popular. The Black-hooded Parakeet, *Nandayus nenday,* comes to rice fields and *Forpus* to grass. *N. nenday* and *Myiopsitta monachus* often eat on the ground, running easily over newly plowed terrain seeking food like pigeons. *Aratinga aurea* also descends to the ground to eat seeds of certain low-growing cerrado plants. *Pyrrhura frontalis* eats cones of the slash pine (*Pinus elliottii*) and like so many other birds is fond of the hot pepper *Capsicum fructescens. Pionus maximiliani* has been seen gnawing the tips of tall eucalyptus until they look decrepit (Pinto 1946). In the south the nuts of Paraná pine (*Araucaria angustifolia*) and the small fruits of *Podocarpus lambertii* are a great attraction, especially for the Red-spectacled Parrot, *Amazona pretrei,* and *A. vinacea.*

Pionopsitta pileata cuts off the end of branches loaded with small *Rapanea* (Myrsinaceae) fruits and carries them to the bill with one foot. *Pyrrhura frontalis* and *Pionus maximiliani* eat flowers this way. The position of fruits on the end of branches is a plant strategy to attract seed dispersers such as birds; from the plants' viewpoint, psittacids are destroyers.

In the upper Rio Negro (Rio Uaupés, Amazonas) parrot flocks descend on midriver rapids to take advantage of the many small animals found among the Podostemonaceae growing on rocks under a thin layer of swiftly running water; they also like the miniscule fruits of these peculiar plants. I have seen *Pyrrhura frontalis* do the same at Iguaçu Falls (Paraná). In the Rio Aripuanã (upper Madeira, Mato Grosso) the Golden-winged Parakeet, *Brotogeris chrysopterus,* fishes for algae and aquatic snails (Roth 1982), and there have been additional observations of mollusk, worm, and beetle-larvae eating. Thus it is not surprising that captive parrots are much attracted to *Tenebrio molitor* larvae as well as to meat (even when rotten) and bones. In the cerrado of Minas Gerais a flock of *Aratinga aurea* was seen catching winged termites on the ground as they came out of a terrestrial termite nest; possibly the parakeets had had contact with termites when they excavated their nest in an arboreal termite nest (Sazima 1988). The Kea, *Nestor notabilis,* of New Zealand is truly carnivorous.

Parakeets, parrots, and macaws all gather in quantity at salt outcroppings, barreiros, in the forest and along river banks (in the dry season) to eat earth (Mato Grosso, Amazonas, Pará; see also Columbidae, "Feeding"). It is amusing to see them stumping along on the ground with their extremely short legs and large in-turned feet ("to parakeet" is to walk pigeon-toed). They cling to the vertical surface of the salty river banks, supporting themselves with the tail, *Ara macao* and *A. chloroptera* especially producing a marvelous spectacle in sunny places. I have had the earth of a barreiro on the Rio das Mortes, Mato Grosso, analyzed. The results have not yet been published. I am impressed with the high degree

of sodium (Na) and magnesium (Mg), but there are no chlorides. In the Mato Grosso Pantanal blue macaws look for salt (NaCl) put out for cattle. Eating small stones is vital for any psittacid.

Psittacids have the most numerous (300–400) and most varied taste buds of all birds. Pigeons have only 50 to 75 but still are almost as sensitive to taste as parrots. Most birds have 100 to 200 buds (Rensch and Neunzig 1925). Psittacids reject bitter tastes, unlike emberizids. Let it here be said that birds can distinguish the same taste characteristics we do: salty, sour, bitter, and sweet, the last almost always attractive. There is good evidence that *Amazona* can find a favorite food hidden nearby through smell. The olfactory bulbs of *Melopsittacus undulatus* are small (Bang and Cobb 1968).

Psittacids come morning and evening to lake edges to drink, sometimes from great distances, as in the case of *Cyanopsitta spixii.* They also drink rainwater from tree hollows, and *Amazona amazonica* even drinks saltwater at the ocean's edge. Psittacids drink by suck-pumping the liquid.

Seasonal movements in search of food occur with almost all species. *Pionopsitta pileata* appears in some numbers in July in the mountains of Itatiaia, Rio de Janeiro, where it is rare in summer (Pinto 1954). Regular migrations of this species have been recorded in Paraná (Scherer Neto and Müller 1984).

Behavior

Large psittacids fly somewhat heavily, resembling ducks in the rhythm of their wing beats; they are, however, capable of flying tight curves and of letting themselves fall vertically while turning to one side to reach a perch in a treetop. Parakeets move swiftly, sometimes intermingling a closed-wing interval within a series of rapid wingbeats (*Aratinga*). The *Pionus* have a peculiar way of maintaining themselves in the air with a wing stroke that goes farther below the body than that of any other psittacid. In the forest on a short flight they move without the least sound, whereas *Pyrrhura frontalis* loudly rustles its wings going from one branch to another in the same tree. *Amazona* males and females fly so close together that the pair, even when flying in a flock, may appear to be a large, fabulous, four-winged bird.

Immobility and silence are the best defenses. An individual that has just perched or is frightened freezes, staring at the supposed danger. Even a brightly colored species in the open blends so well with its surroundings that it seems to magically evaporate. The *Brotogeris,* when menaced by some danger, sometimes hang head-down from a branch. Once the danger passes, they come out screeching.[1] A *Forpus xanthopterygius* can hang by one or both feet for a long time and can even preen in this exotic position. Its slow movements in walking, crawling, or eating appear prudently

---

[1]Guimarães Rosa: *Varam o ar caturritas: explosão de verde e gritos, periquitos,* "They sweep the air, an explosion of green and shrieks—parakeets."

calculated to conceal itself even better. In the forest it betrays its presence mostly by the noise of fruits it lets fall to the ground.

Contentment and tranquility are signaled by roosting birds through a clicking produced by rasping the mandible against undulations on the surface of the "palate." This procedure is used to eliminate food residue that has accumulated between the ridges (*Ara, Amazona, Pionus*). In captivity alertness is shown by vigorously shaking the entire plumage (e.g., *Ara, Amazona, Pionus*). This is also used as a sort of greeting when a familiar person approaches. After preening, bits of dandrufflike follicle remain on the plumage and are picked off with the bill. The feathers are then shaken to rid them of remnants and to realign those mussed during preening.

Parrots show many signs of emotion. The already pinkish face of a young *Ara ararauna* becomes redder when one fondles it (as if it were blushing); the pure white face of the adult also becomes slightly red when the bird is angered, and the pupil closes to a tiny point. I have seen the same phenomenon in *Amazona* when irritated or making a great physical effort (e.g., when "talking"). The pupils alternately open and shut constantly in excited individuals.

Slowly raising the foot, very typical parrot and macaw behavior, is agonistic. Hissing like a snake is another sign of irritation (see *Deroptyus* under "Breeding"). The narrow yellow band around the bill of *Anodorhynchus hyacinthinus*, hidden under ruffled feathers during repose, becomes a colorful signal in an agonistic situation. The yellow periodically alters in intensity. *Deroptyus accipitrinus* and *Amazona vinacea* frequently elevate their ruffs. Other Neotropical psittacids, such as other *Amazona* and the *Aratinga*, that lack long feathers on the nape also do this. They also frequently ruffle the cheeks and throat. The strongest agonistic reaction involves putting the bill forward, hissing, and raising and lowering the body (*Amazona, Ara*).

Both *Amazona amazonica* and *A. aestiva* are frequently "southpaws," so the left foot is better developed. These individuals are almost incapable of perching with the left foot, it being entirely adapted to picking up things to carry to the mouth, and can only stand firmly with the right foot. I do not know whether the picture (Pl 17) of the Red-browed Parrot, *A. rhodocorytha*, using its right foot to carry food to the bill is based on actual observation by the artist. Among 56 Brown-throated Parakeets, *Aratinga pertinax*, from Venezuela, half were southpaws (McNeil et al. 1971). Among 18 individuals of 13 Neotropical species (*Amazona, Ara, Aratinga*, and *Brotogeris*) kept in captivity and tested 20 times, 75% were left-footed. The *Brotogeris* and *Ara* were generally 100% left-footed. They were never observed passing an object from one foot to the other (Friedmann et al. 1938). Australian psittacids are also predominantly left-footed. The degree of "footedness" is often the same as in humans (Rogers 1980). The anatomical basis for this is still unknown. Could it be greater development of one side of the brain and of the mus-

culature of the left side? The anatomist S. Berman (1984), who dissected the rear extremity of six *Amazona albifrons*, lost the opportunity to make a quantitative study comparing the two sides. Left-footedness is also predominant in hawks. I have also found left-footedness in Galbulidae (*Jacamaralcyon*). Certain psittacids, such as the Golden-tailed Parrotlet, *Touit surda*, scarcely use the feet for eating or don't use them at all.

Parrots like to bathe in rain, sometimes while hanging head-down among wet foliage. In captivity they also take dust baths—the White-bellied Parrot, *Pionites leucogaster*, for instance. They will make long daily flights to reach a bathing place, possibly near a salty river bank. During drought *Brotogeris* gather by the hundreds at bathing places, perching at the water's edge, splashing, and covering certain stretches of rocky rivers, such as the Curuá, in Pará, like a green carpet (Adolfo Kindel pers. comm.).

Amazona parrots yawn like other birds. Most Neotropical psittacids scratch the head by extending the leg under the wing, but *Forpus xanthopterygius* does the reverse. Stretching can have a "contagious" effect: for example, when an *Amazona farinosa* extends its left wing and leg, a *Brotogeris chrysopterus* perched to its right may extend its right wing and leg.

To sleep they gather in flocks; the circadian migrations of red macaws and certain parrots constitute a truly spectacular phenomenon in Amazonia. Each flock keeps separate, not associated with other groups, even of the same species. In Amazonia macaws and parrots prefer to pass the night in small gallery forests separated from the continuous forest where they spend the day. During high water they seek flooded islands in the middle of large rivers, roosting in the tree canopy undisturbed by the water below. *Forpus xanthopterygius* sometimes roosts in flocks in the crowns of rather open, small trees isolated in grassland; I once counted 34 in one small tree (Rio de Janeiro). There is more detail about flock roots of *Amazona pretrei*, a southern species, in the species account. Small flocks of *Pyrrhura* may sleep together in a tree hole.

With a caged *Amazona* one can see how it sleeps on its perch: it stands on only one leg, hiding the other foot (usually the one used to carry food to the bill) in the belly plumage. Like so many other birds, psittacids turn the head completely around and hide it in the back plumage. A *Deroptyus accipitrinus* wanting to sleep crawled under a cloth or a newspaper where it lay stretched out on its belly, demonstrating its instinct to spend the night protected in a hole. With captive *Pyrrhura* one can also see that they usually sleep not perched but clinging head up to a vertical cloth or similar substrate. *Amazona* give some evidence of dream activity, similar to that which I have observed in toucans. Certain species (or is it only individuals?) do not defecate during the night.

Psittacid abilities are widely exploited, as for instance, at Parrot Jungle in Florida and at Loro Parque in Tenerife. There

Fig. 115. Some typical stances of the White-fronted Parrot, *Amazona albifrons,* of Mexico. Upper left: lifting the foot as an agonistic signal against an approaching individual; upper right: pair playing, one biting the foot of the other; lower left: the male, left, passing regurgitated food to the stooping female; lower right: copulation, the male at left. After Levinson 1980.

one can see macaws riding bicycles, responding to questions, finding a red cube among several of various colors, etc. Such exercises are taught, but there are also playful activities. I have seen tame parrots and macaws lie on their backs and "play" with small stones held in their feet, almost like a child. An *Ara chloroptera* amused itself with a large bolt, tirelessly putting on and taking off the nut (Deckert and Deckert 1982). Pairs also tease each other, one pushing another, for instance. A flock of parakeets may perch atop a tree loaded with flowers, such as a yellow ipé, and immediately start to cut off the flowers without eating any, just for fun. Keller (1975) made a detailed analysis of the play activities of *Nestor notabilis* of New Zealand.

Tools are also used. A tame *Ara chloroptera* used a piece of wood or similar object as a toothpick, holding it between the tongue and the creases of its palate to clean its spacious mandible.

I have seen a captive *Deroptyus accipitrinus* with lowered head, completely ruffled feathers, and feet close together move rapidly in long, energetic hops to make a loud noise on the metal floor of its cage—an entirely unusual movement for our psittacids.

A most interesting behavioral detail is the way American psittacids copulate, entirely unlike psittacids in the rest of the world. There mounting occurs—that is, the male mounts the female during copulation, as is customary with birds—but this is not the case with Neotropical psittacids. For example, a male *Amazona* remains at the side of the female (generally on the left), firmly clutching the perch with one foot. He then places the other foot and a wing over the female and the two rub their cloacae together (fig. 115). During this process macaws sometimes raise their long tails vertically, a very curious sight.

Brereton (1963), working with Australian psittacids, proposed a "social index" with ten categories of sociability and reached some taxonomic conclusions.

Breeding and Predation

Psittacids live strictly in pairs and, so far as known, stay together for life, at least in the larger species. Consorts are assiduous in their attention to each other, mutually preening and sometimes caressing each other while hanging head-down from a branch (*Aratinga acuticauda*). Macaw pairs even lick each other's faces. Males regurgitate food for their females and court them by walking before them with the tail open, exhibiting the beautiful red spots (*Amazona amazonica*) or the large yellow areas of the tail feathers (*Pionopsitta vulturina*) which are invisible when the tail is closed. These fine effects are even more highlighted when the birds are seen perched in trees against the light. *Ara chloroptera* pairs undertake lengthy flights circling over their territory, always staying close together and sometimes interspersing almost vertical dives. *Deroptyus accipitrinus* displays with an undulating flight, alternating wing beats with gliding. *Guaruba guarouba* continues to be gregarious during breeding. Re copulation, so different from the majority of birds, see "Behavior."

Mates frequently remain together in the nest, even during the day. Near the nest they are extremely cautious and escape the most careful observation, so little is known about their breeding. They like to approach the nest by crawling up vines. On hearing a strange noise they emerge halfway from their hole to inspect the surroundings and, if frightened, come out one after the other without making the slightest sound. A *Pionus maximiliani* may stay for hours at the entrance to its nest, exposing only its head and remaining absolutely immobile while surveying its surroundings. *Anodorhynchus hyacinthinus,* which inhabits open regions, becomes openly aggressive, even toward people. The *Pyrrhura* and *Myiopsitta monachus* chase vultures and hawks crossing their territory; *Deroptyus accipitrinus* defends its nest with a snakelike hiss and by raising its magnificent neck piece while executing a strange, lateral oscillation of its body. The most secretive behavior does not stop local residents, especially Indians, from finding nests that then become the "property" of the finder with the privilege of annually taking the young, ensuring a good source of revenue (see also Ramphastidae, "Enemies . . . ").

Psittacids nest in hollow trunks of palms (e.g., buriti) and other trees, taking advantage of openings caused by rotting, as does *Triclaria malachitacea* (Camargo 1976). They compete for holes with other psittacids, woodpeckers, aracaris, and the Bat Falcon, *Falco rufigularis.* They try to excavate holes in dead trees or in live ones with dead sections and sometimes install themselves in palm crowns. Although associated with araucarias, *Amazona pretrei* does not appear to nest in them because they generally do not have holes. A lack of usable holes can be a limiting factor for psittacids. Many existing holes are occupied by bees, wasps, and ants, and there is also competition from small vertebrates such as possums and marmosets. Parakeets gnaw retort-shaped nests in arboreal termite nests whose interior provides a favorable microclimate with constant temperature and humidity. *Aratinga aurea* excavates its nesting holes especially in nests of the termite *Constrictotermes cyphergaster. Brotogeris versicolurus* prefers *Nasutitermes* nests, the texture of which is not so hard (A. Negret pers. comm.).

Nandayus nenday uses fence posts or palms. *Ara chloroptera, Anodorhynchus hyacinthinus,* and *Aratinga leucophthalmus* sometimes nest in rocky cliffs. In the karstic region of Minas Gerais *Amazona aestiva, Aratinga leucophthalmus,* and *A. aurea* regularly breed in holes in eroded rock and sometimes in banks. The Cuban Parrot, *Amazona leucocephala,* of Cuba and the Bahamas nests in holes in the ground. *Anodorhynchus leari* and *Aratinga acuticauda* nest in canyons of the Raso de Catarina, Bahia. The tail of a macaw on the nest may be seen at the entrance, as I observed with *Anodorhynchus hyacinthinus.* In both the Pantanal and the area of Rio das Mortes (Mato Grosso) it sometimes nests in tight quarters in hollow branches of large trees. A macaw's prolonged occupancy of a small nest hole results in wear on the tail which can be a sign of nesting. Generally the entrance is placed such that it is difficult to see from the ground. In captivity *Ara ararauna* even burrows holes in the ground to nest.

Forpus xanthopterygius is a regular tenant of the Rufous Hornero, *Furnarius rufus,* whose old nests it is accustomed to occupying, laying on the already existing lining made by the original landlord or by a Saffron Finch, *Sicalis flaveola,* which may have been a previous tenant. Reportedly it may also add a few twigs or leaves of its own to the nest. Occasionally a pair of these parrotlets take over by force a nest still occupied by the hornero and its feathered young. I have seen this species use a hole previously occupied by a Long-tailed Tyrant, *Colonia colonus.* It also uses hollow fence posts.

Parrots and macaws cushion the bottom of their cavities with pulverized wood obtained by scraping the walls, thus facilitating absorption of liquid feces. *Myiopsitta monachus* constructs a large twig nest in tree branches, unique among psittacids. Several pairs work together on the structure, but each has its own nest within. Sometimes they establish themselves in the base of a stork or hawk nest.

Eggs are rounded, white, relatively small, and are incubated primarily by the female, who is visited and fed by the male in the incubation chamber. *Amazona pretrei* lays three to four eggs. Small flocks attracted by *Podocarpus* fruits have had a ratio of three to five young for two adults (W. Voss and F. Silva pers. comm.). *A. aestiva* and *A. vinacea* lay four eggs; *Pyrrhura frontalis* five to eight; and *Forpus xanthopterygius* three to five. Whereas the eggs of the last named are smaller than those of a Shiny Cowbird, *Molothrus bonariensis,* the eggs of *Ara chloroptera* reach 50×35.5 mm.

The incubation period is 30 days for *Ara chloroptera;* 29 for *Triclaria malachitacea;* 28 for *Deroptyus accipitrinus;* 26 for *Aratinga solstitialis* and *Brotogeris tirica;* 25 to 26 for *Pyrrhura frontalis* and *Nandayus nenday;* 24 for *Ara severa;* 22 to 23 for *Pionites melanocephala;* and only 18 for *Forpus xanthopterygius.* Parents feed chicks by regurgitating food, which may be almost liquid, the male being more active in this duty. This food contains nothing produced by the birds themselves, unlike the "pigeon milk" of columbids. The nestling's mandible is very wide at the base, like a shell, which facilitates receiving the "gruel." The offspring of two species as similar as *Amazona amazonica* and *A. aestiva* have different voices. Begging of young *Myiopsitta monachus* resembles the bleating of a goat kid. In a group of three male and three female *Guaruba guarouba* (private zoo of E. Bérault, Rio de Janeiro), all attended the 14 young hatched within a few days of one another. The mother tries to clean the nesting cavity by pushing aside filth absorbed by the wood dust on the bottom so it will not stick to the chicks' plumage. Young are frequently attacked by bird botflies and can die from this.

Young *Pyrrhura frontalis* leave the nest after a month and a half, those of *Forpus xanthopterygius* at five weeks, of *Amazona* species after two months, and of *Ara ararauna* at 13 weeks. Young of an *A. chloroptera* left at 103 days.

I have seen *Amazona vinacea* with four young, *A. pretrei* and *A. xanthops* with four eggs, and up to eight eggs (from two females?) with *Forpus xanthopterygius.* A captive female *Forpus* laid seven eggs. The number of young may be estimated by seeing a pair flying followed by its offspring. Young birds leave their parents only when they start to breed again. The young of a large clutch (*Myiopsitta monachus,* up to nine eggs) differ greatly in size because several days may intervene between hatching of the first and last egg, for the parents begin to incubate as soon as the first egg is laid. The smaller young catch up with the larger ones in ten days.

Large species, *Amazona* for instance, start to reproduce late in their third or fourth year. It has been reported that the Glaucous Macaw, *Anodorhynchus glaucus* (apparently extinct now; see species account), in the wild laid two clutches of two eggs per year. A captive *Forpus xanthopterygius* may produce five clutches in the same period. In Bahia *Amazona* nest from September on.

Breeding does not totally inhibit social contact with the flock. Mates certainly keep to themselves more during incubation, but apparently even during this period the male parrot [*Amazona*] continues to participate in a collective roost, returning to the nest at dawn to care for his family. Flocks seen during the breeding season must generally be made up of immature individuals. It would be interesting to use radio tracking on macaws and parrots to learn more about individual movements.

Snakes (e.g., caninana, *Spilotes* sp.), toucans, monkeys, and tayra (*Eira barbara*) [a mustelid mammal] are considered to be nest predators. A whole clutch can be killed by African bees occupying the nesting hole. In the early 1900s in Goiás *Anodorhynchus hyacinthinus* was "heavily persecuted" by the Harpy Eagle, *Harpia harpyja* (Neiva and Penna 1916). An Orange-cheeked Parrot, *Pionopsitta barrabandi,* has been captured by a Barred Forest Falcon, *Micrastur ruficollis* (Roth 1983).

Nest Fauna of Myiopsitta, *Importance of Sanitation, and Psittacosis*

Interiors of the stick nests of *Myiopsitta monachus* usually harbor various arthropods that find a favorable microclimate there, similar to that existing in furnariid edifices. The situation is ideal given that the stability, continuous use, and colonial grouping of the structures guarantee continuity for several generations of arthropods, some of which suck the blood of the unfeathered young. After the young abandon the nest the parents do not clean the incubation chamber but simply place a new lining over the old. An assassin bug (*Psammolestes coreodes,* Reduviidae, Triatominae, in Argentina, Paraguay, and Brazil) and a louse (*Psitticimex urituri,* in Argentina) live there. Other assassin bugs sometimes present in *M. monachus* nests are *Triatoma delpontei* and *T. platensis,* both carriers of *Trypanosoma cruzi* which produces Chagas' disease. See also Ciconiidae, "Tenants of Arboreal Nests," and Furnariidae, "Use of Furnariid Nests . . . ." *M. monachus* nests occasionally are occupied by various climbing mammals and by some other birds, even the Chimango Caracara, *Milvago chimango;* Plumbeous Ibis, *Theristicus caerulescens;* and a duck.

Psittacosis, a type of ornithosis disease acquired through contact with psittacids and some other birds (e.g., pigeons) contaminated with *Chlamydia psittaci* (an etiological agent intermediate between a bacterium and a virus), does not have as severe effects in Brazil as it does in the Northern Hemisphere. The illness manifests itself as an atypical pneumonia or grippe. Human psittacosis is practically unknown in Brazil but can be cured with tetracycline derivatives. Seemingly healthy psittacids may be carriers of this infection, which appears to be widespread among macaws, parakeets, parrots, and even other birds. Other ornithoses have been found in more than 130 bird species but not in Brazil.

Myiopsitta *Nests as a Cause of Electric Short Circuits*

In areas where *M. monachus* occurs, originally only in the extreme south, their bulky, often shared nests of sticks (they may even use wire) may cause short circuits and fires when placed on rural electric posts. See also Furnariidae, "Furnariid Nests as Obstacles . . . ."

Evolution and Distribution

With more than 100 species, South America takes first place by a wide margin as the continent with the most psittacids. Brazil stands out with 69 species, followed by Colombia with 51 and Venezuela with 49. In comparison, Australia has 52 species, New Guinea 46, and Africa, including Madagascar, only 35. The total for the world is about 345 species. Australasia shines because of its variety of types and its splendidly colored species, among them the cockatoos. We are indebted to the Australian Joseph M. Forshaw and his illustrator, William T. Cooper, for a magnificent monograph on psittacids of the world, published in 1973.

In Brazil, Amazonia is the richest psittacid region, both in individuals and species. *Brotogeris versicolurus* is among the most abundant species of the Hylaea; a singular concentration of macaws, parrots, and other psittacids lives in the "Gerais" [open country with palms, often dwarf types] and adjacent regions of the northeast, which have abundant buriti groves.

The diversity of psittacids (both of species and subspecies) in Amazonia was promoted by periodic subdivision of the tropical forest during the Pleistocene. Wildlife then withdrew to forest "refugia," resulting in the evolution of quite diverse forms that I consider to be allospecies composing superspecies. This occurs, for example, in the *Pionites;* the *Pionopsitta* (in which I include *Eucinetus* and *Gypopsitta,* fig. 116); and *Brotogeris versicolurus* and *B. chiriri.* In the *Pionopsitta,* evolution of marked differences on the head has masked the relationship between various species whose close affinity is documented by their similar wing and tail color patterns. As of now, transitional forms between the respective species are almost unknown.

Dispersal of the open-country *Aratinga pertinax,* a north-

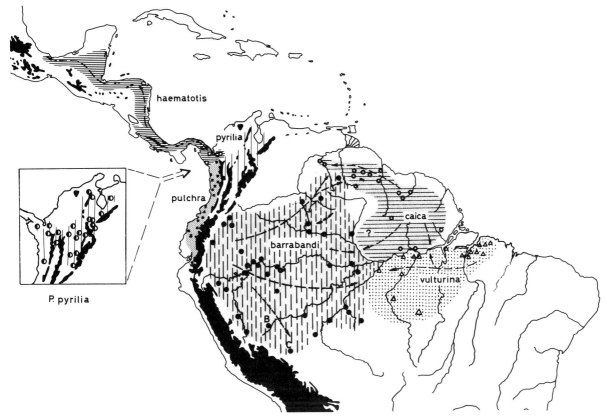

Fig. 116. Distribution of the Caica Parrot and allies, *Pionopsitta caica* (after Haffer 1970). Open circles and horizontal hatching: *P. caica;* closed circles and vertical dashes: *P. barrabandi;* open triangles and stippling: *P. vulturina;* half-solid circles and vertical hatching: *P. pyrilia;* solid squares and shading: *P. pulchra;* open squares and dense horizontal hatching in Middle America: *P. haematotis* (only the easternmost records are plotted). Symbols denote locality records.

ern replacement for *A. cactorum,* suggests existence of an ancient connection of open landscapes between northern and southern Amazonia during the arid Pleistocene periods.

Geographic races have evolved, as in the *Pyrrhura* and *Forpus.* Sometimes such populations, as in *Pionus maximiliani* and *Amazona vinacea,* show a progressive increase (cline) in size from north to south, accompanying a decrease in temperature (former Bergmann's Law, now modified). A geographic substitution of very different forms occurs in the Blue-cheeked Parrot, *Amazona dufresniana;* Red-tailed Parrot, *A. brasiliensis;* and *A. rhodocorytha.*

Psittacids are among the few birds that have been identified at archaeological sites. At a Rio de Janeiro kitchen midden 3,000 to 4,000 years old, a macaw (probably *A. chloroptera,* H. Alvarenga pers. comm.) has been found. A parrot with open wings sometimes figures in prehistoric pictographs.

Systematics and Nomenclature

Psittacid systematics are still unclear. It is certain that New World psittacids are distinctly separate from those of the Old World both in morphology and ethology. Biochemical research has confirmed this.

American psittacids have been united in the subfamily Arinae. There is considerable convergence in the similarities of many species, as for example in skull structure (Smith 1975). Similarity does not always prove relationship, and clear differences do not always mean greater phylogenetic distance. Morphological variations among American psittacids are greater than they appear at first glance.

The true, and sometimes unexpected, proximity of certain species is proven by intergeneric hybridization in captivity (there is no hybridization in nature). For example, all macaws hybridize, including the *Anodorhynchus. Propyrrhura maracana* has hybridized with *Pionites melanocephala,* and *Nandayus nenday* with the *Aratinga.* This is not the place to debate systematics and nomenclature at length. I only want to call attention to the case of the macaws, the world's most notable psittacids. The problem is that the pretty, generic name *Ara* Lacépède, 1799, under which we now classify the true, nonblue macaws, was later applied (in the 1800s but also in current day literature) to other barefaced species, the *maracanãs,* which are definitely not macaws. I recognize six true macaws for Brazil: *Ara ararauna;* the two red ones, *A. macao* and *A. chloroptera;* and the three blues, *Anodorhynchus hyacinthinus, A. leari,* and *A. glaucus. Ara severa* is not far away. *Cyanopsitta spixii* is not a macaw.

Four macaw species with bare faces—an attractive character for museum taxonomists but useless for classification—have erroneously been included in *Ara: maracana, auricollis, manilata,* and *nobilis* (Sick 1990). They are not macaws, being more closely related to the *Aratinga* group, both in behavior and voice. At the moment in the International Committee for Nomenclature we can only revalidate the previous names of the four species, those used by O. Pinto (1938) for our maracanãs: *Propyrrhura maracana, P. auricollis, Orthopsittaca manilata,* and *Diopsittaca nobilis.* The Blue-headed Macaw, *Ara couloni,* also belongs to the maracanã group.

Interestingly, anyone in the interior of Brazil who knows local fauna speaks of the four above-mentioned species as maracanã and finds it absurd to call them *arara,* "macaw." Happily, in the 1986 *Novo Dicionário Aurélio da Lingua Portuguesa* (= "*New Aurelio Dictionary of the Portuguese Language*") under "Maracanã" the names *Propyrrhura, Diopsittaca,* and *Orthopsittaca* appear, based on Olivério Pinto's catalogue.

We know the scientific name is just a formula. This becomes a problem with the generic name *Ara,* which is based on the onomatopoeic indigenous name *arara*[2,3], extremely well known in Brazil and with a very limited meaning applied exclusively to the six species mentioned above. As a result, anyone in Brazil discovering the name *Ara* in the literature feels safe concluding that the bird in question is a macaw—a mistake in the case of the maracanãs. Thus scientific necessity and practical advantage in Brazil counsel abandonment of the name *Ara* for the four maracanãs to avoid confusion between the two types of bird.

What identifies maracanãs immediately are their voices: cries similar to those of genuine members of the *Aratinga* (*Aratinga* is another artificial genus in which *Guaruba guarouba* has been erroneously placed). Maracanãs do not have the cries *ara* or *arara* in their repertoires, these being copyrighted by the true macaws. The importance of ethology in psittacid classification is emphasized by the surprising fact that the way New World psittacids and those of the rest of the world copulate is essentially different (see "Behavior").

Endoparasites, Ectoparasites, and Conclusions about Psittacid Relationships

Bird-lice studies suggest the existence of subfamilies in the Psittacidae, among them the Arinae, which includes all American psittacids. Such studies may confirm separation of the Arinae from other Psittacidae of the world.

The Arinae have only one genus of mallophaga (*Paragoniocotes*) with four evolutionary lines that match evolution of the Psittacidae themselves. As for their occurrence on various genera, a first line appears on the *Pionopsitta, Pionus,* and *Amazona;* a second only on *Amazona,* along with

the first line; a third on the *Ara, Aratinga, Pyrrhura, Forpus,* and *Brotogeris;* and a fourth on *Aratinga, Forpus,* and *Brotogeris,* along with the third (L. R. Guimarães pers. comm.). An *Amazona pretrei* medicated in Rio de Janeiro with a laxative evacuated a large quantity of worms (*Ascaridia hermaphrodita*).

Popularity, Longevity, and Use

A much-cited legend says discovery of this continent was due to a flock of parrots that Columbus's flotilla followed. This would scarcely have been possible unless the ships were very close to land, for parrots do not venture out over the sea except between the coast and nearby islands. There are similar legends about other birds.

Parrots and parakeets have always been the favorite pet birds in Brazil, liked by everyone because of their ability to imitate the human voice. A parrot considers its owner to be its companion and is antagonistic to other people. It demonstrates this affection by regurgitating its craw contents, which in the wild would feed its mate or young. They give no preference to persons of one or the other sex, being more acoustically than visually oriented. They feel "offended" if not given appropriate attention and are extremely jealous of other pets. They may attain great age in captivity. A *Pyrrhura* and a *Triclaria malachitacea* lived 27 years, an *Amazona aestiva* 42 years, an *A. ochrocephala* 50 years, and an *Ara macao* more than 64 years. Ages of up to 80 years are spoken of for parrots, something like cranes, reputed to be the longest-lived birds. One parrot lived throughout four generations of a human family.

The great esteem enjoyed by American psittacids since the discovery of the New World is shown by their use in art. Only 50 years after the discovery of America, *Amazona* parrots and macaws were portrayed in Flemish tapestries for Wawel Castle of King Sigismundo Augusto of Krakow, now part of Poland. England imported macaws very early (Gesner 1555). Among paintings by Lazarus Roting between 1600 and 1614 in Nuremburg, Germany (Stresemann 1923), are two Brazilian species, one *Ara severa* and one *Aratinga aurea,* which also appear in the work of Marcgrave (1648). *Ara severa* was scientifically recorded by Linnaeus in 1758, whereas *Aratinga aurea* was only recorded in 1788 by Gmelin. On the famous altar of H. Burgkmair in Munich, painted in 1518, there is a *Diopsittaca nobilis.* Possibly, however, this was added to the picture around 1600 (Sick 1981). A picture painted by Lucas Cranach in 1502–03 in Vienna, Austria, contains an *Ara macao,* a species that had already appeared on maps in 1500.

Psittacids, beginning with macaws, are used for food, with even small species such as the *Touit* being hunted. The Golden-tailed Parrotlet, *T. surda,* and *Pionopsitta pileata* are

---

[2]The name *maracanã* comes from *maracá,* a very noisy Indian percussion instrument. The name *Maracanã* of the famous Rio de Janeiro football stadium is derived from a small river of this name that crosses the city.

[3]*Ara* may be a version of *guirá,* "bird," and *arara* may mean "large bird." In Aymará *arara* means "talker" (Garcia 1913).

reportedly so unwary as to be easily caught with snares (F. Müller 1868 in Möller 1915–20). One of the first species cited in the literature as a game bird is *Anodorhynchus glaucus*, apparently now extinct. *A. hyacinthinus* continues to be shot for food today along the Transamazon Highway. *Amazona amazonica* was formerly sold in quantity in markets.

I have already spoken of how much aborigines value psittacid feathers for decoration. In colonial Brazil *Ara macao* flight feathers were used in place of domestic goose feathers for writing. On the large illegal trade in psittacids, see "Trade . . . ."

Abundance and Noxiousness

In the early 1800s Hercules Florence reported that there were about 80 macaws in an Apiacá Indian village of 80 inhabitants on the Rio Arinos in central Brazil. In colonial Brazil psittacids were so abundant that an ancient chronicle recommended "taking special care to eliminate some birds that eat a fourth of the bread of a whole district." *Aratinga aurea*, even in 1948–49, was unquestionably a pest in the cornfields of Barra de São Francisco, Espírito Santo (G. Mattos pers. comm.).

Some species, such as *Myiopsitta monachus, Nandayus nenday, Aratinga aurea, A. solstitialis,* and *Pyrrhura frontalis,* even today feed in corn fields, orchards, etc. Macaws chew shoots of the bocaiúva (*Acrocomia* spp.), killing it. Because this palm provides good wood for fence posts, *Anodorhynchus hyacinthinus* is shot in Mato Grosso. I have heard that the same species is killed by cowboys because it frightens cattle, making them hard to round up. This recalls a relatively recent story from the interior of Ceará where cowboys complained that the noise of roosting parrots interfered with their work. In Goiás *Amazona xanthops,* unpopular as a pet, does some damage to crops. On the Transamazon Highway, flocks of *Pionus menstruus* feed in rice fields whenever they can find a perch that will sustain their weight. *Myiopsitta monachus* is considered a nuisance, flocking in corn and sorghum fields. Having benefited from the planting of field crops and eucalyptus (which it uses for nesting), it has begun to multiply explosively as a result of food abundance and a sharp decline in predators.

Captive Breeding and Synanthropic Tendencies

It is said that when Brazil was discovered, a psittacid called *anapuru* (a name also used for the Lesser Swallow-tailed Swift, *Panyptila cayennensis*) was bred in the houses of coastal natives. Captive breeding of Brazilian species is undertaken only rarely, and by amateurs, but with good re-

sults. Under appropriate conditions *Forpus xanthopterygius* reproduces easily; even macaws will lay one clutch after another when the nestlings are taken away and raised artificially. A pair of *Ara ararauna* in Rio de Janeiro produced two clutches (one of three, the other of four eggs) in five months, from which four young resulted.

Captive breeding of psittacids clearly can be much more efficient and rapid than in the wild; however, it works for only a few generations because of the effects of endogamy, or consanguinity—a standard problem in captive breeding.

Of the 69 Brazilian species. N. Kawall of São Paulo (1976) indicates that 39 have been reared in captivity, based on his own experience and that of other known breeders (usually abroad) and from the literature. Kawall observes that long-tailed species (macaws, *Aratinga,* etc.) are easier to breed that short-tailed ones (e.g., *Amazona, Pionus, Pionites*). We need to organize official breeding centers for rare species in the hope of reestablishing them in the wild—but how? When a reasonable number of birds are available for repopulation, a safe area cannot be found: the freed birds are almost certain to be recaught. This is probably what has happened in the case of *Cyanopsitta spixii,* now practically extinct, although it was reared in captivity for some years in the 1960s by A. R. Carvalhães of Santos.

Myiopsitta monachus frequently becomes synanthropic. In Santa Catarina wild pairs of *Pyrrhura frontalis* installed themselves under a tile roof, gnawing through a slat to facilitate entry (R. Reitz pers. comm.).

Trade, Decline, Extinction, and Conservation

At present psittacids have become rare near large population centers and roads. Hundreds of parrots from Bahia are shipped clandestinely by truck between April and June to southern markets (Geraldo T. Mattos 1974 pers. comm.). One thousand *Anodorhynchus hyacinthinus* reportedly left Brazil illegally in 1982. In 1979 just one dealer in Western Germany had a stock of 200 of this species, certainly all from Brazil. West Germany imported 7438 *Amazona aestiva* in 1980. In 1986 in just one shipment from Argentina to London–Singapore, 600 *A. a. xanthopteryx* were found. As long as 60 years ago, between 3000 and 6000 *Amazona* parrots (primarily *A. aestiva*) and 20,000 to 30,000 long-tailed South American psittacids (Neunzig 1930) were sold. The high esteem for parrots goes far back. I have already mentioned that the first maps of Brazil were decorated with three Red Macaws. The situation today, almost 500 years later, is just the same: psittacids continue to be the most attractive birds in the entire world, avidly sought after for pets. Now we hear of a real "parrot mania" in the United States.[4]

---

[4]Between October 1979 and June 1980 more than 200,000 psittacids (in a total of 442,000 birds) were imported into the United States, with 94,000 coming from South America, 70,000 from the Pacific region, and 37,000 from the Afro-Asian region (Roet et al., 1980). At Delhi in 1981, all the psittacids of the world were included in the species protected by CITES, Appendix II, except the Australian Budgerigar and two other domesticated

Australian species. The 1988 annual report of the International Council for Bird Preservation states: "Tens of thousands of parrots were reported leaving Argentina, Venezuela and Mexico on an annual basis; as many as 500 Hyacinth Macaws, *Anodorhynchus hyacinthinus,* (possibly down to just 2,500 birds in the wild) are still being smuggled out of Brazil each year."

The great majority of amateur cage-bird fanciers consider their parrots to be like puppies, if not toys and showpieces, without taking any interest in the conditions under which these birds live in the wild. How many tens of thousands of birds had to be captured and perish for that number to reach market! Even worse, many eggs and young are lost as they are taken from the nest, for frequently the tree is cut down to get at them, thus eliminating favored nesting places. Dead palm trees, the best places for nesting, are often the first to be cut because they are easily removed. Arboreal termite nests, so common in the cerrados and caatingas and used by parakeets for refuges, may in degraded forests to some extent be an adequate substitute for holes in large trees.

I want to emphasize that lack of food resulting from elimination of fruit trees may become a problem. For example, pau-rosa (*Aniba duckei* and *A. roseodora,* Lauráceae), large fruit trees of the primary forest much sought by macaws, parrots, and other fruit-eating birds such as toucans and cotingas, were never common but are now much scarcer in vast areas of the Hylaea because of unregulated exploitation (they produce an essence used for fixation of perfumes, formerly one of the most important products of Amazonia).

Among the most menaced psittacids are large woodland species of eastern Brazil such as *Amazona brasiliensis, A. pretrei, A. rhodocorytha,* and *A. vinacea.* I have already mentioned *Cyanopsitta spixii* and *Anodorhynchus glaucus* and must include *A. leari.* This family has the largest number of forms on my list of endangered species. The situation is rapidly becoming acute because of complete habitat destruction and uncontrolled persecution of the most interesting species, which are those most valued in the clandestine traffic. One of the first successful attempts to actively protect our species was the creation of an ecological station in the Esmeralda region of Rio Grande do Sul in 1975 by the Special Secretary for the Environment (SEMA) to protect the "conclaves" of *Amazona pretrei.*

Key to Identification of Brazilian Species
(number of species in parentheses)

Study of psittacids, including all Brazilian species, is facilitated by various monographs, especially those of Reichenow (1878–83) and Forshaw and Cooper (1973).

1. According to the tail: South American species may be divided superficially into three groups according to tail type:
   1.1. Long tail, sharp-pointed or wedge-shaped: *Anodorhynchus* (3), *Cyanopsitta* (1), *Ara* (5), *Aratinga* (7), *Nandayus* (1), *Pyrrhura* (10), *Myiopsitta* (1), *Brotogeris tirica, B. versicolurus,* and *B. chiriri.* The maracanãs: *Propyrrhura* (2), *Orthopsittaca* (1), *Diopsittaca* (1), and *Guaruba* (1), plus *Ara severa* and *A. couloni* numbered among the *Ara* above.
   1.2. Tail long and wide: *Triclaria* (1) and *Deroptyus* (1)
   1.3. Tail short, truncated, rounded, or wedge-shaped: *Touit* (4), *Pionites* (2), *Pionopsitta* (4, including *Gypopsitta*),

Graydidascalus (1), *Pionus* (3), *Amazona* (11), *Brotogeris chrysopterus, B. cyanoptera, B. sanctithomae,* and *Forpus* (3)

2. According to color:
   2.1. Blue: four sizable species: *Anodorhynchus hyacinthinus, A. leari, A. glaucus,* and *Cyanopsitta spixii.* Also *Ara couloni,* with maracanã plumage.
   2.2. Blue and yellow: only one large species, *Ara ararauna*
   2.3. Predominantly red: two large species, *Ara macao* and *A. chloroptera*
   2.4. Predominantly yellow or orange: *Guaruba guarouba* and *Aratinga solstitialis.* Yellow also occurs more or less extensively on so-called counterfeit (luteinistic) individuals.
   2.5. Green: separation by tail length is required in the multitude of species of this color; the *Aratinga, Forpus, Touit, Pionus,* and *Amazona* are distinguished by various characters, but it is not always easy to discern the species in the genera. Among the remaining species, the maracanãs (formerly all included in the *Ara*) merit special attention: *A. severa, A. couloni* (bluish), *Propyrrhura maracana, P. auricollis, Orthopsittaca manilata,* and *Diopsittaca nobilis.* The genus *Brotogeris,* as presently conceived, is heterogeneous.

   One should be alert for the color of the secondaries (speculum) and tail feathers, which usually remain hidden but show up at a distance when the bird, perched in the top of a tree, preens its feathers, or when the male greets the female. Red on the shoulder, edge of the wing, secondaries, and under wing coverts (in *Aratinga leucophthalmus* they are bicolored, scarlet and yellow) is prominent in flight.

   Colors of the foreparts of the head, bare region around the eye, and bill are important for identification and are frequently conspicuous in flight. The bill is especially noticeable when it is reddish, as in *Aratinga acuticauda* (pink maxilla), *Pionus menstruus,* and some *Amazona* (red base of the maxilla). The northern and southern populations of *Diopsittaca nobilis* are differentiated by bill color.

   Immatures do not always have the characteristic colors on the plumage or bare parts.

3. I would name the following as unusual Brazilian species: *Nandayus nenday, Myiopsitta monachus, Pionites leucogaster, P. melanocephalus,* and *Deroptyus accipitrinus.* See also the *Pionopsitta* (4 species) and *Pionus fuscus.*

HYACINTH MACAW, *Anodorhynchus hyacinthinus,* Arara-azul-grande   PL 16.3

93 cm; central tail feathers 55 cm; 1.5 kg. A giant among macaws and world's largest psittacid. Bill enormous, appearing larger that skull, and lacking maxillar tooth (unlike *Cyanopsitta*) but with more or less pronounced notch on mandible. Almost all cobalt blue, so dark it looks black at a distance; underside of flight and tail feathers black. Eye-ring, eyelids, and band around base of mandible yellow; latter may appear as a half moon or disappear under adjacent feathers when bird is resting with bill closed. I have sometimes seen

yellow skin on underside of wings of certain paired individuals in flight (sexual dimorphism?). Both sexes show yellow longitudinal band on sides of black tongue. VOICE: a very loud croaking, *kraaaa, ara; TRAra, TRAra* (warning): *kraaaa, kraaaa, kraaaa* . . . (1 of a pair), *rraaaaka, rraaaaka* . . . (other of pair); in Rio das Mortes (Mato Grosso) region I noted a different croak terminating in *ee,* a penetrating *trarrrEE-arrEE.*

Buriti groves, gallery forests, adjacent cerrado, nests in buriti palms and other hollow trees, in cliffs in Bahia, Piauí, Minas Gerais. Occurs in Mato Grosso (Pantanal, Rio das Mortes), Goiás (especially in north of state, in area of Rio Tocantins), Minas Gerais (midcourse of Rio São Francisco), Bahia (upper Rio Preto, Barreiras), southern Piauí (Correntes), southern Maranhão, Pará (along Transamazon Highway, east and west of Altamira) Rios Capim and Cupari (Bates 1863); also recorded by Goeldi (1897) on northern edge of lower Amazon in Marajó. Also eastern Bolivia, northernmost Paraguay. Frequently alongside *Ara ararauna.* Although not rare now, could become endangered soon by tremendous illegal trade (see "Trade . . ."). Total wild population estimated in 1988 to be only 2500 individuals. In 1987 we included species on Appendix I of CITES as "an endangered species, commerce prohibited without special license." *Arara-preta* (Mato Grosso), *Arara-una* (*una* = "black" in Tupi), *Arara-hiacinta.* See next 3 species.

INDIGO MACAW, *Anodorhynchus leari,*
Arara-azul-de-Lear.   BR EN PL 16.1

71 cm; central tail feathers 40 cm; 940 g. Very similar to *A. hyacinthinus* but clearly smaller with more slender build, despite powerful, toothless bill. Head and neck greenish blue, belly faded blue, back and upper side of wings and tail dark blue (cobalt). Eye-ring relatively light yellow, eyelid light blue, white, or slightly bluish (not black as in *hyacinthinus*); iris chestnut (like *hyacinthinus*).

Most important mark distinguishing *leari* from *hyacinthinus* is lappet forming a large, almost triangular, light sulfur yellow spot, paler than eye-ring, on each side of base of mandible. Lappet projects prominently on live bird and never disappears underneath plumage (unlike narrow mandibular band of *hyacinthinus*); when bird is observed from front, each lappet looks like 2 superimposed protuberances separated by a pleat that disappears when bill is open; on a dead bird they are flat and unimpressive. Lappet bordered below by a group of forward-facing feathers that completely hide a very narrow yellow strip bordering base of mandible. Upper edge of maxilla, half hidden by frontal feathers, may also be yellow, as in *hyacinthinus.* Mouth black inside, sides and base of tongue extensively yellow, appearing as a continuation of lappets when bird opens bill, as with *hyacinthinus.* VOICE: a hoarse, relatively high *ara-ara, trrAHra.*

Described by Bonaparte in 1856, *A. leari* was known only through specimens of unknown origin ("Brasil") maintained in live bird collections, where it was valued as a great rarity.

As late as 1937 O. Pinto wrote, "Exact information is lacking. Brazil?" Finally it was proposed to adopt region of Juazeiro, in northern Bahia, as probable source of *leari,* based on an individual purchased in that city (Pinto 1950). It having been impossible to find *leari* in the wild, Voous (1965) proposed it be considered a hybrid between *A. hyacinthinus* and *A. glaucus.* This was impossible, both for morphological and distributional reasons. Lappet of *leari* shows relationship only with *glaucus;* in plumage *leari* is in fact intermediate between *hyacinthinus* and *glaucus.*

Together with D. M. Teixeira and L. P. Gonzaga, I found home range of *leari* in Raso de Catarina in northeastern Bahia (December 1978). This was a true discovery, not a rediscovery. It is the only macaw of that region. For living quarters it uses rock caves in the most precipitous canyon walls. Its favorite food is the fruit of the licuri palm (*Syagrus coronata*) which it finds on the ground. Part of its range is the Raso de Catarina Ecological Station created in 1975 by the Special Secretary for the Environment. Preservation of the species is in doubt. Yamashita in 1985–86 estimated its population at about 60 individuals living in 2 colonies in the Raso and showing indications of difficulty: fault bars on feathers and probable inbreeding. In addition to feathers very abraded by friction with sandstone, broken feathers were found that had not yet fully emerged from follicle. Perhaps *leari* is in a process of decadence such as I suppose occurred with *glaucus.* In May 1986, J. K. Hart of Houston, Texas, counted 22 and 30 birds, respectively, in the 2 colonies. *A. leari* is a geographic replacement of *A. glaucus;* the 2 species, constituting relict populations and being widely separated by *A. hyacinthinus,* form a superspecies.

GLAUCOUS MACAW, *Anodorhynchus glaucus,*
Arara-azul-pequena   EN

68 cm; central tail feathers 39.5 cm. Smallest blue macaw (not counting *Cyanopsitta spixii*), with large, heavy bill. Similar to *A. leari,* having same type lappet. Below lappet is same arrangement of forward-facing feathers hiding narrow yellow strip that descends along lateral edge of mandible. Plumage even lighter than *leari:* head, neck, back, wings, tail, and belly faded greenish blue. Throat blackish.

Lived in lowlands with palms (tucum, mucujá), along river edges, excavating nest sites on high banks of Rio Paraguay, also nesting in hollow trees (Labrador 1767 and Azara 1802–05, in Goeldi 1894). In early 1800s common along Rio Paraná near Corrientes, Argentina. Crew of anthropologist A. d'Orbigny, navigating Paraná in 1837, used meat of this macaw ("so leathery it can't be eaten", d'Orbigny 1835–38), which is probably extinct today in that region. I have not found any record of this macaw on Brazilian part of Rio Paraná. However, a report from F. Sellow (in Stresemann 1948) says that in December/January 1823–24 a blue macaw nested in cliffs near Caçapava, Rio Grande do Sul, which could only be *glaucus.* Saint-Hilaire (1936) noted in 1820 in Santa Catarina a relatively small, very common macaw with greenish blue plumage and a yellow circle around eye, which also must have been *glaucus*. At end of 1800s species was designated "very rare" (Holmberg 1895) in northeastern Argentina and in Uruguay (Zotta 1944). The disappearance of this macaw at a time when its range was little touched by civilization leads me to suspect a natural decline, a genetic exhaustion of the species (see also *A. leari*), or maybe even a natural catastrophe caused by disease, as perhaps occurred with the Carolina Parakeet, *Conuropsis carolinensis* (Ridgely 1980).

I have been unable to find either individuals living in captivity or specimens recently seen or collected in the wild. The species is even rarer than *leari* in museum collections. I have personally examined most of the existing *glaucus* specimens. The only 2 in the American Museum of Natural History are from Paraguay, having been received from the Zoological Garden of London in 1886 and 1898. The last died in 1912. The 2 specimens in the British Museum also come from Paraguay; the only specimen in the Paris Museum is from Corrientes, Argentina.

Three specimens were recorded in the Amsterdam Zoo, which traditionally had this macaw. One died in 1862, another was acquired in 1863 and died in 1867, and a 3d that arrived in 1868 was not subsequently mentioned. There was no information about the source of these birds (K. H. Voous pers. comm.). A specimen was in the Berlin Zoo in 1892 (Neunzig 1921). Jean Delacour informed me (1974) that between 1895 and 1905 he found an individual in the Paris Acclimatization Garden where it lived for several years. This was the only live specimen this illustrious French ornithologist, who died in 1985, saw in his long life. Possibly some *glaucus* specimens have been traded in amateur circles and others were not recognized, passing as *leari* or *hyacinthinus*. This totally negative summary seems to indicate that the species is really extinct. *A. glaucus* is a geographic replacement for *A. leari*.

LITTLE BLUE MACAW, *Cyanopsitta spixii*, Ararinha-azul   BR   EN   PL 16.2

57 cm. A bit more than half the size of *Anodorhynchus hyacinthinus* but with tail proportionately longer and very long, narrow wings (features unique to this species)—unlike all other Neotropical psittacids, including other macaws. Slender black bill with large tooth on maxilla. Blue, wings and tail darker, head quite light, sides of head below eye light gray. Iris mustard yellow. Young has whitish face and culmen, dark brown iris. VOICE: *kreh, krreh-krreh, kra-ark* (Roth). In flight slow wing beats distinctive. Likes to perch on tips of high, dead branches. Occurs in extreme northern Bahia (Juazeiro, Spix, see Chapter 2.4). Typical habitat, as P. Roth discovered in 1985–86, is dry caatinga crossed by valleys of small tributaries of Rio São Francisco. Along these temporary streams an open gallery forest appreciably higher than surrounding caatinga has evolved, formed by

caraibeiras (*Tabebuia caraiba*) in which bird nests in holes made by large woodpeckers. Eats fruits and seeds, especially of Euphorbiaceas such as *Jatropha* and *Cnidoscolus*. During local migrations also appears in buriti palm groves, as I saw at Formosa do Rio Preto on 25 December 1974 when 7 individuals flew over. Numbers have been extremely reduced by illegal trade. In June–July 1990 on an expedition financed by International Council for Bird Preservation, L. C. Marigo and others found 1 male associating with a group of *Propyrrhura maracana* in the same place Roth made his observations. A video made by F. Pontual shows how 1 individual in the flock of 7 *P. maracana* (3 pairs and 1 lone, probably a female) sought out the *spixii* (probably a male), which reacted with reserve. Might it have been the last *spixii* living in the wild, as expedition members concluded? I don't want to believe that. It is important to note that extermination of *spixii* is not due to habitat destruction but to its tenacious pursuit by bird dealers in search of a fortune. See also "Captive Breeding . . . ."

BLUE-AND-YELLOW MACAW, *Ara ararauna*, Arara-de-barriga-amarela, Canindé   PL 16.6

80 cm. Upperparts blue, underparts yellow. Throat and lines of facial feathers black. VOICE: most typical call a penetrating *kewaaaaaa*. Várzeas with buriti and babaçu groves, etc., forest edge. Central America to Brazil as far as São Paulo and formerly Santa Catarina (L. Choris 1822), Bolivia, and Paraguay. Also called *Arara-amarela*. Inappropriate name *ararauna*, given in 1758 by Linnaeus, who did not know meaning of this word of Indian origin (*arara-una* = "black macaw"), must be retained for reasons of priority.

Closely related to this species is *A. glaucogularis* (ex *caninde*), with less impressive head and bill, throat and tiny feathers of face blue, not black. Bolivia; has not been recorded for Brazil.

SCARLET MACAW, *Ara macao*, Arara-canga

89 cm. Similar to *A. chloroptera* but less stocky with large yellow area on wing. White face is entirely bare, not crossed by lines of red feathers like *chloroptera*. Also, voice not as loud. Forests, river edges. Mexico to Amazonia as far as northern Mato Grosso (Marmoré), southeastern Pará (Gorotire, Rio Fresco), Bolivia. Also called *Arara-piranga, Arara-vermelha-pequena*. This macaw figured as a decoration on 1st map of Brazil, made in 1500. Discoverers of Brazil must have found *macao* in last decade of fifteenth century in northern part of continent where it reaches coast.

RED-AND-GREEN MACAW, *Ara chloroptera*, Arara-vermelha-grande   PL 16.7

90 cm; 1.5 kg. Similar to *A. macao* but without yellow on wing. VOICE: prolonged *AHH-ra, AHH-ra* in flight; *arAT arAT*. Formerly common on coastal rivers with forested edges in eastern Brazil, originally reaching as far as Espírito

Santo, state of Rio de Janeiro, interior Paraná, southern Mato Grosso; still frequently found in Amazonia, sometimes alongside *macao,* to which immature individuals showing some yellowish green on upper wing coverts have a certain resemblance. Forests, groves. Panama to Paraguay, northern Argentina. Also called *Arara-verde.*

CHESTNUT-FRONTED MACAW, *Ara severa,* Maracanã-guaçu

50 cm. Largest maracanã. Similar to other maracanãs. White face crossed by lines of tiny black feathers, like pattern of *A. chloroptera;* bill black; pants, shoulders, and underside of wings and tail red, conspicuous in flight; forehead chestnut. VOICE: *AHHaarra, AHHaarra, AHHaarra* while perched, similar to *A. ararauna.* Also other vocalizations, e.g., *ghehh* in flight. Gallery forests, buriti groves. Panamá to Bolivia; Brazil from Amazonia to Bahia, Mato Grosso. Also called *Ararinha-de-fronte-castanha.* An Amazonian species seldom seen in captivity in Brazil.

BLUE-HEADED MACAW, *Ara couloni*

41 cm. Green with blue head and flight feathers; no white on face. Upper side of tail reddish. Maracanã-type voice. Not a macaw (see "Systematics . . . "). Forest edges. Found 27 June 1986 by T. Parker in Acre. Also adjacent Peru.

BLUE-WINGED MACAW, *Propyrrhura maracana,* Maracanã-do-buriti

41 cm. Forehead, parts of back and belly red; upper base of tail rusty; bare face pale yellow, white around eyes; bill black. Young similar to those of *Ara severa.* VOICE: *gheh; kreh kreh kreh,* similar to other maracanãs and *Aratinga.* Forest edges, buriti and other palm groves. Argentina and Paraguay to Maranhão (including Rio de Janeiro). Some authors include in *Ara.* Also called *Ararinha.*

GOLDEN-COLLARED MACAW, *Propyrrhura auricollis,* Maracanã-de-colar

41 cm. Similar in general aspect to other maracanãs but easily distinguishable by yellow collar (reddish in immature) at base of hind neck. Bare face pale yellow, not chalk white. VOICE: similar to other maracanãs, not to macaws. Groves, gallery forests. Mato Grosso (Pantanal) to Paraguay, Bolivia, Argentina. Some authors include in *Ara;* obviously not a macaw (see "Systematics . . . ").

RED-BELLIED MACAW, *Orthopsittaca manilata,* Maracanã-de-cara-amarela   PL 16.4

44 cm. Bare face bright yellow, breast scaly grayish, abdomen crimson, bill black. VOICE: reminiscent of *Aratinga leucophthalmus.* Gallery forests, buriti groves. Venezuela to Brazil (Amazonia, Mato Grosso, Goiás, Piauí, western Bahia). Also called *Maracanã-do-buriti, Ararárana* (Mato Grosso). Some authors include in *Ara,* which is unsatisfactory (see "Systematics . . . ").

RED-SHOULDERED MACAW, *Diopsittaca nobilis,* Maracanã-nobre   PL 16.5

35 cm. Forehead blue; shoulders and under wing coverts scarlet; underside of flight feathers yellowish; face white. Population north of Amazon (*D. n. nobilis*) has all-black bill; those to south (*D. n. cumanensis* and more southerly *D. n. longipennis*) have whitish maxilla. Size increases noticeably and progressively from north to south (see "Evolution . . . "). VOICE: similar to *Aratinga.* Cerrado, palm (buriti) groves, forest edge. Venezuela and Suriname to Brazil: Mato Grosso, Goiás, São Paulo, Rio de Janeiro, northeast states. Some authors include in *Ara* (see "Systematics . . . "). See *Aratinga leucophthalmus* and *Orthopsittaca manilata.*

GOLDEN PARAKEET, *Guaruba guarouba,* Guaruba BR   PLS 16.8, 44.7

34 cm. Has aspect of an *Amazona* but with long tail, very unlike *Aratinga.* Unique in golden color, green flight feathers, and white tail feather shafts (adult). Young have yellow feathers with green shafts and marbling, tail feathers all green. VOICE: *greh, greh, greh,* softer than *Aratinga;* during courtship, prolonged and strident *kewo.* . . . Behavior unlike *Aratinga;* e.g., amusing themselves in a treetop, a pair will silently hook bills together with one perched, the other hanging below perch flapping its wings. Much biological data, including on voice (see "Vocalization . . . "), support omission of *G. guarouba* from *Aratinga;* its ethology is reminiscent of macaws (*ararajuba* = "yellow macaw"). Favorite food is açaí (*Euterpe* sp.) fruit. Very gregarious, even during breeding. Lives in tall forest canopy when not seeking fruit at lower levels, always in small flocks.

Maranhão to western Pará, across lower Tocantins and Xingú to Tapajós and beyond, Transamazon Highway, Pará (fig. 117). Mentioned by Fernão Cardim in Bahia (see Chapter 2.1) at end of sixteenth century as an extremely valuable bird from Maranhão, having a commercial value equivalent to that of 2 slaves. As one of most beautiful Brazilian endemics, it is best choice for national bird, even having national colors green and yellow, unique among the world's national birds. See Rufous-bellied Thrush. Compare with yellow *Amazona* and *Aratinga solstitialis* individuals. *Ararajuba* (Tucano, Maranhão), *Tanajuba.* *Guaruba* is derived from Tupi: *guará,* "bird," *yuba,* "yellow."

BLUE-CROWNED PARAKEET, *Aratinga acuticauda,* Periquitão

33 cm. Green with fore part of head blue; shows red only on inner vane of tail feathers, conspicuous when bird opens tail to perch; area around eye bare and white; maxilla pink or light brown; mandible black; feet yellow, brownish, or orange. VOICE: low and croaking. Open country with scat-

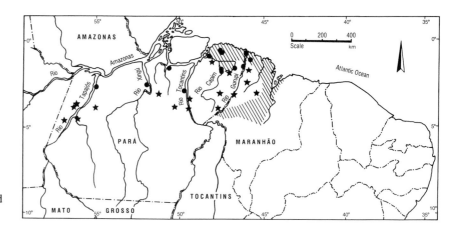

Fig. 117. Distribution of Golden Parakeet, *Guaruba guarouba*. Solid circles: museum specimens; stars: recent observations; hatched: area of former occurrence. Adapted from Oren and Novaes 1986.

tered trees, caatinga, buriti groves (Bahia). Locally from Venezuela to Bolivia, Paraguay, Argentina, but not in Amazonia; abundant in northwestern Bahia; alongside *Nandayus nenday* in Mato Grosso Pantanal. Also called *Maracanã, Periquito-de-pé-rosa, Periquito-de-bico-rosa*.

WHITE-EYED PARAKEET, *Aratinga leucophthalmus*, Periquitão-maracanã

32 cm. Head shape "oval"; green, including lores, with some red feathers on sides of head and neck; only lesser under wing coverts red, greater being yellow and conspicuous in flight. Region around eye bare and white, iris orange, bill light horn color. VOICE: a characteristic *chirrri*. Forest edge, common in many places. Sometimes nests in limestone caverns (Mato Grosso). The Guianas to Argentina; almost all of Brazil. Also called *Araguari, Maricatã* (Minas Gerais).

SUN PARAKEET, *Aratinga solstitialis*, Jandaia
PL 17.8

31 cm. Much more slender than *Guaruba guarouba*. Bill black. There are 3 distinct geographic races (semispecies):
(1) Sun Parakeet, *A. s. solstitialis* (Jandaia-amarela), intensely orange with only flight feathers and some wing and tail coverts bluish green. The Guianas to Roraima and southern side of Amazon: Santarém, Coatá, Pará. Also called *Jandaia-sol, Cacaoé*.
(2) Jandaya Parakeet, *A. s. jandaya* (Jandaia-verdadeira), only head and underparts orange, mantle green. Maranhão to Pernambuco, eastern Goiás.
(3) Flame-capped Parakeet, *A. solstitialis auricapilla* (Jandaia-de-testa-vermelha), dark green with only fore part of head and abdomen washed with red. Southern Bahia to Paraná.
VOICE: loud *kree-krew-kree*. Forest edge, secondary forests, cultivated regions, carnauba palm groves, etc. Common in Minas Gerais. Also called *Periquito-de-cabeça-vermelha, Cara-suja* (Minas Gerais), *Jandaia-sol*. See *A. aurea*.

DUSKY-HEADED PARAKEET, *Aratinga weddellii*, Periquito-de-cabeça-suja

Only in extreme west (Amazonas, western Mato Grosso).

BROWN-THROATED PARAKEET, *Aratinga pertinax*, Periquito-de-bochecha-parda

25 cm. Similar to *A. cactorum* but region around eye has yellow feathers (like *A. aurea*) and cheeks sepia, not green. Open country. Panamá and Antilles locally to Suriname, Brazil (Roraima; southern Pará, Rio Cururu); must occur in other open areas of Amazonia. Has many geographic races and is northern replacement of *cactorum*, with which it forms a superspecies.

CACTUS PARAKEET, *Aratinga cactorum*, Periquito-da-caatinga   BR

25 cm. Green with characteristic yellow breast and orange-yellow belly. VOICE: typical *cri, cri, cri.* . . . Abundant in caatingas and cerrados of northeast. See *A. pertinax*, also "Evolution . . . ."

PEACH-FRONTED PARAKEET, *Aratinga aurea*, Periquito-rei, Periquito-estrela   PL 17.9

27 cm; 84 g. One of our best-known and most abundant psittacids. Bright yellow forehead and feathered eye region. Cerrado, secondary forest, cultivated fields, mangroves. Right bank of Amazon to Bolivia, Paraguay, Argentina. In almost all of Brazil; locally north of Amazon (e.g., Faro, Pará, Suriname). Also called *Jandaia, Ararinha, Maracanã-de-testa-amarela* (Amapá). See *A. solstitialis auricapilla, A. pertinax*, and *Brotogeris sanctithomae*.

BLACK-HOODED PARAKEET, *Nandayus nenday*, Periquito-de-cabeça-preta   Fig. 118

32 cm. Green with black mask and black undersides of wings (visible in flight), red pants. VOICE: *krehh.* . . . Open country, frequently walking on ground; sometimes alongside *Myiopsitta monachus*. Argentina to Bolivia, Paraguay, Bra-

Fig. 118. Black-hooded Parakeet, *Nandayus nenday.*

zil (as far as southwestern Mato Grosso, where it is most common psittacid, appearing in flocks of more than 100). Also called *Maracanã, Príncipe-negro.*

OCHRE-MARKED PARAKEET, *Pyrrhura cruentata,* Fura-mato BR

29 cm. Relatively large, dark green with blackish crown and nape, reddish lores and cheeks. Has conspicuous rusty yellow area on sides of upper neck. Breast bluish; shoulder, belly, and underside of tail red (the last characteristic of various *Pyrrhura*). Lives inside tall forest, hidden in canopy. Coastal zone of southern Bahia to northeastern São Paulo, where locally somewhat common. Introduced into Tijuca National Park (ex-Guanabara) in 1969–70 with specimens confiscated from the market. Also called *Cara-suja, Tiriba.*

Two very similar species have been recorded in the cerrados and dry woodlands of southeastern Mato Grosso, Bolivia, and Paraguay:

BLAZE-WINGED PARAKEET, *Pyrrhura devillei*

27 cm. Red and yellow shoulder and under wing coverts. May be a race of *P. frontalis;* also called *P. borellii.*

GREEN-CHEEKED PARAKEET, *Pyrrhura molinae*

27 cm. Lacks red on forehead. Top of head brown, upperside of tail red. Secondary forest. A 3d "species" that could occur in same region is "*Pyrrhura hypoxantha*" (Corumbá),

which is merely a yellow mutation of *P. molinae* (See "Natural and Artificial Color . . . ").

REDDISH-BELLIED PARAKEET, *Pyrrhura frontalis,* Tiriba-de-testa-vermelha PL 17.10

27 cm. Frequently most common parakeet in southeastern Brazil. Flies in small, tight flocks. Green (including cheeks) with auricular zone brownish. Forehead, belly, and underside of tail red. Eye-ring white. VOICE: *tseh, tseh, tseh . . .* in flight; song *CHIrrra.* Forest edges, orchards. Bahia to Rio Grande do Sul, southern Mato Grosso, Uruguay, Paraguay, Argentina. In mountains in Rio de Janeiro. Also called *Tiriva, Cara-suja.*

PEARLY PARAKEET, *Pyrrhura perlata,* Tiriba-pérola BR PL 44.8
(includes *P. rhodogaster,* Tiriba-de-barriga-vermelha)

24 cm. Green with shoulder and under wing coverts red, cheeks green, foreneck scaly chestnut, flanks blue. Adult of nominate race develops carmine red on belly and was described as *P. rhodogaster.* This name enters the synonymy of *P. perlata perlata* because the type of the species was an immature without carmine, found in captivity by Spix. Three other races recognized for Maranhão, Pará, and Mato Grosso (fig. 119) do not develop red on belly. VOICE: *tieww, kritieww,* confirming that the 4 geographic representatives belong to same species.

MAROON-FACED PARAKEET, *Pyrrhura leucotis,* Tiriba-de-orelha-branca PL 17.11

21 cm. One of smallest long-tailed parakeets and smallest *Pyrrhura.* Face dark brown with contrasting whitish auricular spot (lacking in central Brazilian population in Goiás, *P. l. pfrimeri*). VOICE: *ki-ki-ki.* Forest edge. Northern Venezuela and Ceará to São Paulo, Goiás. An attempt was made to introduce it into ex-Guanabara (see *P. cruentata*). Also called *Querequetê* (Espírito Santo), *Fura-mato-pequeno.* See *P. picta.*

PAINTED PARAKEET, *Pyrrhura picta,* Tiriba-de-testa-azul

23.5 cm. Similar to *P. leucotis* but with yellow auricular spot. Forehead blue; center of breast feathers black. Populations of upper Amazon (Juruá, Purus, Madeira) have red mask (*Ararinha-de-cabeça-encarnada, P. p. lucianii,* and *Tiriba-do-juruá, P. p. roseifrons*). Gallery forests. The Guianas and Colombia to northern Mato Grosso, Goiás. Also called *Marrequém-do-igapó.*

In the upper Amazon basin there are three more species, all with the underside of the tail blackish brown:

FIERY-SHOULDERED PARAKEET, *Pyrrhura egregia*
Roraima and Venezuela.

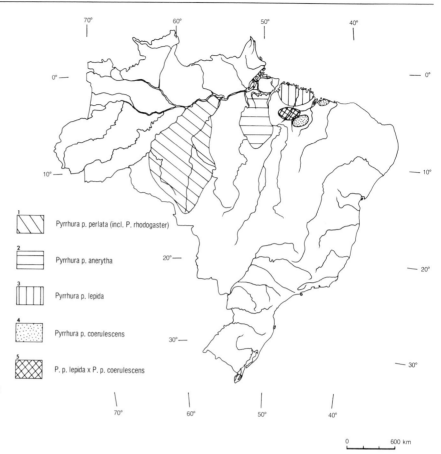

Fig. 119. Geographic races of Pearly Parakeet, *Pyrrhura perlata:* (1) *P. p. perlata* (including *P. rhodogaster*); (2) *P. p. anerytha;* (3) *P. p. lepida;* (4) *P. p. coerulescens;* (5) transition area between 3 and 4. Original map, P. Roth.

Legend:
1. Pyrrhura p. perlata (incl. P. rhodogaster)
2. Pyrrhura p. anerytha
3. Pyrrhura p. lepida
4. Pyrrhura p. coerulescens
5. P. p. lepida x P. p. coerulescens

0   600 km

MAROON-TAILED PARAKEET, *Pyrrhura melanura*

Distinguishable by orange speculum that recalls *Brotogeris chrysopterus;* Amazonas, between Rios Negro and Solimões.

ROCK PARAKEET, *Pyrrhura rupicola*

Acre (Municipality of Rio Branco, May 1968), Peru, Bolivia.

MONK PARAKEET, *Myiopsitta monachus,* Caturrita

30 cm. Stocky, long-tailed parakeet; green without any red; blue flight feathers; head and foreneck grayish; breast with white bars; bill yellow. In flight may resemble a small hawk.

Breeding: Highly resistant nest is built of dead, spiny branches with lateral twigs and of green branches of bougainvillea, etc., carried with heavier end in bill. In Rio Grande do Sul prefers to nest in eucalyptus trees at average height of 10 m, either at tip of a branch or against trunk. Also uses utility poles and high-tension electric towers. Entrance to nest is through a shaft directed obliquely or vertically downward. Male and female work independently using only bill, not feet. They arrange material of upper part obliquely, suggesting a roof, in a way reminiscent of collective nests of certain African weaver-birds that also have entrances pointing down-ward. Birds prepare a lining by pulverizing branches and dry leaves and continue to improve nest as long as they use it.

Various pairs normally associate and build close to each other in same tree, forming a colony. They may set themselves up side by side, resulting in a "composite" nest with 4–8 openings, 1 for each pair. In this way the "ball" becomes very large, reaching perhaps 1 m in height and more than 10 kg (recorded up to 200 kg), sometimes heavy enough to break the supporting branch. Any large animal approaching colony is announced with a great racket; 1 bird, lying on its belly in a nest entrance and invisible from a distance, acts as sentinel.

Photographs taken from ground have created an erroneous impression, perpetuated in various illustrations, about architecture of nest, as if it were round with a lateral entrance when in reality its form is quite variable and entrance customarily low. See also "Breeding" and "Nest Fauna. . . ."

Use of Nests by Other Animals: Abandoned nests, offering a well-protected chamber, are used by wood rats (Cricetidae) and marsupials (*Didelphis*). Occasionally other birds take advantage of them, e.g., Speckled Teal, *Anas flavirostris;* American Kestrel, *Falco sparverius;* House Sparrow, *Passer domesticus.* I have seen a Black-backed Tanager, *Tangara peruviana,* carry material to the upper part of a nest in Rio Grande do Sul. Chimango Caracara, *Milvago chimango,* and Crested Caracara, *Polyborus plancus,* may also use it as a platform for laying eggs (see also "Nest Fauna . . ."). Small nests may be confused with those of Firewood Gatherer, *Anumbius annumbi* (Furnariidae), being constructed of same material but differing in location of entrance (above in the Passerine).

Habitat and Distribution: Lives in open country but needs trees for nesting. Change in native landscape from primarily low woods to groves or isolated tall trees such as eucalyptus has provided excellent places for shelter. Abounds in southern and southwestern Rio Grande do Sul, also southern Mato Grosso, Bolivia, Paraguay, Uruguay, and certain parts of Argentina. Has been introduced in Rio de Janeiro on navy's Enxadas Island (breeding there in palms since 1969, Churchill C. Maia). In 1986 nested on Fundão and Governador islands.

Population explosion of *Myiopsitta* is related to human-induced environmental changes such as deforestation, elimination of predators, eucalyptus cultivation, and especially the provision of easy food sources. With its well-finished nest, which it uses all year, it can also live in temperate regions such as the U.S. (New York), Germany (Berlin), Austria. Also called *Papo-branco* (Mato Grosso), *Catorra*, *Periquito-do-pantanal*.

Harmfulness: In Uruguay and Argentina considered a pest to be combated, its range linked with corn, sunflower, sorgum, wheat, barley, millet, and fruit cultivation. In cattle-raising and mixed farming regions where crop-growing is less intensive, degree of "infestation" is significantly lower (see "Abundance . . ."). To combat it, mechanical means are recommended, e.g., tearing nests apart or burning them. Ideal is to fight the pest without destroying the species and not to use chemical means under any circumstances.

BLUE-WINGED PARROTLET, *Forpus xanthopterygius*, Tuim   PL 17.12

12 cm; 26 g. Our smallest psittacid. Male has large blue patches on wing and lower back. Female all green, almost uniformly so except for yellowish on head and flanks. VOICE: very distinctive: *wiss-wiss,* song *TSIlip-tsiptsip-TSIlip-tsiptsip.* Forest edge. Nests in *Furnarius rufus* houses (see "Breeding"), holes in termite nests, rarely nests of Red-rumped Cacique, *Cacicus haemorrhous.* Northeastern, eastern, and southern Brazil to Paraguay, Bolivia. Also upper Amazon to Peru, Colombia. There are various geographic races. Migratory like other parakeets. For a long time it was called *F. passerinus,* with eastern Brazilian populations designated *F. p. vividus.* Also called *Tapa-cu, Quilim.* Blue and yellow mutations occur in Bahia and other regions (see "Natural and Artificial Color . . .").

GREEN-RUMPED PARROTLET, *Forpus passerinus*, Periquito-do-espírito-santo

12 cm. The true *F. passerinus.* No blue on rump. In northern part of range seems to overlap partially into same regions as *F. xanthopterygius.* The Guianas to Brazil (Roraima, Amazonas, Pará, Amapá).

DUSKY-BILLED PARROTLET, *Forpus sclateri*, Tuim-de-bico-escuro

12 cm. Very dark green with wing and lower back dark bluish violet. Maxilla blackish. Restricted to heart of Amazonia, from Belém (Pará) to Bolivia, Colombia. See *Brotogeris sanctithomae,* which has almost same build.

PLAIN PARAKEET, *Brotogeris tirica*, Periquito-rico   BR

24.5 cm. Long-tailed, all green except for bluish flight and central tail feathers. Forest edge, parks and gardens inside cities, e.g., Rio de Janeiro, São Paulo. Eastern Brazil from Bahia to Santa Catarina. A blue mutant has appeared along coast (see "Natural and Artificial Color . . .").

CANARY-WINGED PARAKEET, *Brotogeris versicolurus*, Periquito-de-asa-branca

21.5 cm. Green Amazonian species with all secondaries and their coverts whitish yellow. Riverine forests and prairies; abundant on Amazon delta (Belém), being most numerous psittacid there, its racket heard everywhere. Amapá and Pará to Peru, Colombia. Also called *Periquito-da-campina, Periquito-de-asa-amarela* (Amapá). Also called *Tirica virescens.* It is northern version of *B. chiriri.* Introduced in California, Costa Rica. Erroneously spelled *B. versicolorus.*

YELLOW-CHEVRONED PARAKEET, *Brotogeris chiriri*, Periquito-de-encontro-amarelo   PL 17.13

23.5 cm. Central Brazilian form, perhaps a geographic race of *B. versicolurus.* Green with large sulfur yellow speculum. Differs from *versicolurus* by more densely feathered lores. VOICE: *chiri, chiri-ri.* Cerrado, gallery forests, etc., common in interior. Mato Grosso and Goiás to southern Pará (Serra do Cachimbo, August and October), Maranhão, Bahia, Minas Gerais, São Paulo; also Bolivia, Paraguay, Argentina. A visitor in Rio de Janeiro (including ex-Guanabara, January, April, October). Appearance in such northerly regions as southern Pará may also be attributed to migration. See *B. chrysopterus.*

COBALT-WINGED PARAKEET, *Brotogeris cyanoptera*, Tuipara-de-asa-azul

20 cm. Chin pumpkin-colored, underside of wings blue. Recorded only in upper Amazon, Rios Negro and Purus, to Bolivia, Venezuela.

GOLDEN-WINGED PARAKEET, *Brotogeris chrysopterus*, Tuipara-de-asa-laranja   PL 16.11

18.5 cm. Stocky Amazonian species with tail less than half as long as *B. tirica.* Pumpkin-colored speculum. Low woodland. Locally common. Venezuela to Amazonia, apparently excluding headwaters of southern affluents of Amazon, to Maranhão and Piauí. Includes *B. tuipara* and *B. chrysonema*. See *Pyrrhura melanura* (which has long tail, scaly breast).

TUI PARAKEET, *Brotogeris sanctithomae*, Tuipara-estrelinha

17 cm. Only slightly larger than a *Forpus*, with short, pointed tail. Green with forehead and curved strip behind eye yellow. Along Amazon from Amapá and Belém to Peru; locally abundant. Also called *Estrelinha-do-Pará, Periquito-testinha* (Amapá), *Tuim* (Amapá").

SAPPHIRE-RUMPED PARROTLET, *Touit purpurata*, Apuim-de-costas-azuis

17 cm. Like a miniature *Amazona*. Dark green with sepia scapulars, blue rump, intensely red tail feathers except center ones. Female's outer tail feathers have greenish black tips. Forests. Eastern Pará (Belém) to the Guianas, Venezuela, Colombia.

BLACK-EARED PARROTLET, *Touit melanonota*, Apuim-de-cauda-vermelha   BR   EN

16 cm. Unlike *T. purpurata* has sepia back and rump. VOICE: a characteristic rattling, *tewrew-tewrew* (in flight timbre may recall song of Boat-billed Flycatcher, *Megarynchus pitangua*). High forests of Serra do Mar, in southern Bahia and São Paulo, also occasionally ex-Guanabara and Itatiaia (Rio de Janeiro). In 1946–48 still relatively common near Xerem, Rio de Janeiro. Also called *Apuim-de-costas-escuras, Papagainho*. There is a good illustration on a Brazilian stamp (see *Amazona brasiliensis*).

SCARLET-SHOULDERED PARROTLET, *Touit huetii*, Apuim-de-asa-vermelha

16 cm. Differs from *T. purpurata* and *T. melanonota* in lacking sepia on upperparts; cheeks and wing areas blue; under wing coverts red. Female's outer tail feathers greenish yellow, not red. VOICE: a strident *klooit* in flight. Tall forests, generally in canopy. Pará (Rio Cururu, Serra do Cachimbo, Marabá, Belém) to Venezuela, Ecuador, Peru. Also called *Curiquinha*.

GOLDEN-TAILED PARROTLET, *Touit surda*, Apuim-de-cauda-amarela   BR   EN   PL 16.10

16 cm. Green with yellow face, sepia scapulars, golden tail feathers. Forest edge. Pernambuco to Espírito Santo, São Paulo, Goiás, both in mountains (Espírito Santo, Rio de Janeiro) and lowlands (Rio de Janeiro, Cabo Frio, 1970). Also called *Papagainho, Periquitinho, Periquito*. Rare but still common in late 1800s in lower Tietê (São Paulo). See *T. purpurata, T. melanonota*, and Chapter 2.4.

BLACK-HEADED PARROT, *Pionites melanocephala*, Marianinha-de-cabeça-preta

23 cm. Northern version of *P. leucogaster*. Black cap, green lores. Yellow collar more intense in male. Feet and bare region around eye lead-colored. The Guianas and Venezuela to Amazon; also Colombia, Peru. Also called *Periquito-de-cabeça-preta*.

WHITE-BELLIED PARROT, *Pionites leucogaster*, Marianinha   PL 16.9

23 cm. Southern Amazon species. Head yellow; underbelly white; pants green (*P. l. leucogaster*, lower Amazon) or yellow (*P. l. xanthomeria* and *P. l. xanthurus*, upper Amazon); bare skin around eye blackish, not whitish. There is an intermediate population between *P. l. leucogaster* and *P. l. leucurus* in upper Xingu and upper Tapajós (Novaes 1981). VOICE: a strident, prolonged, tremulous *tsrrrri-tsrrrri*, in timbre sometimes reminiscent of tapir call, hence the name *Periquito-d'anta*, "Tapir Parakeet." Forests along rivers. South of Amazon from Bolivia to northern Mato Grosso (upper Xingu), southern (Serra do Cachimbo) and eastern Pará (Belém). This is a southern version of *P. melanocephala*, with which there appears to be some hybridization along Peruvian border (Haffer 1977).

RED-CAPPED PARROT, *Pionopsitta pileata*, Cuiú-cuiú

21 cm. Like a very small maitaca [*Pionus* sp.]. Color of adult unmistakable: male green with top of head red; female all green with blue forehead; both with bluish shoulder and tail, dark gray bill. VOICE: *chi, chi, shiluh, shiluh, kloo-looEE, kloo-looEE . . .* (monosyllabic in flight, recalling *Brotogeris tirica*, sometimes its neighbor). Does not gather in large flocks. Likes *Podocarpus* and cambuí [*Myrcia sphaerocarpa*] (São Paulo) fruits. Tall forests of Serra da Mantiqueira (Itatiaia, Campos do Jordão), Serra do Mar (Bocaina, Serra dos Órgãos), and mountains of Espírito Santo. Breeds on Paraná plateau in summer; in winter moves to Atlantic coastal forest (Scherer Neto and Müller 1984). Southern Bahia to Rio Grande do Sul, Argentina (Misiones), Paraguay. Still in reasonable numbers in Paraná and adjacent states. Also called *Maitaca-da-cabeça-vermelha* (Bahia), *Curica-cuiú*.

ORANGE-CHEEKED PARROT, *Pionopsitta barrabandi*, Curica-de-bochecha-laranja

24 cm. Same aspect as *P. pileata*. Multicolored, head and neck black, cheeks and leading edge of wing orange; shoulder and under wing coverts scarlet. Forests along rivers. Upper Amazon from southern Venezuela and Rio Negro to Rio Madeira and northern Mato Grosso (see fig. 116.). Belongs to subgenus *Eucinetus*, in which I also include *P. caica* and *P. vulturina*.

CAICA PARROT, *Pionopsitta caica,* Papagainho, Curica

23 cm. All-black head; scaly yellow collar; wings without any red, unlike *P. barrabandi* and *P. vulturina.* VOICE: a strident *ewlit* (perched). Replaces *barrabandi* north of Amazon (Manaus, Amapá). Also called *Papagainho, Curica.*

VULTURINE PARROT, *Pionopsitta vulturina,* Curica-urubu   BR   PL 17.6

22 cm. Unique with bare, black head, emphasized by sulfur yellow collar. Under wing coverts red as in *P. barrabandi,* for which it can be considered a geographic replacement. Skin color of head of immature orange or pumpkin colored, sparsely covered by black "hairs" invisible from a distance. Immatures lack collar of yellow and black feathers; form flocks independent of adults. Head of young birds covered with feathers with yellow bases. VOICE: *iz-teret-teret, tre-TRAYeh . . .* (in flight). Restricted to south of lower Amazon, from eastern Pará to Rio Madeira and south to Serra do Cachimbo (southern Pará). Also called *Urubu-papaguá, Pirí-pirí, Periquito d'anta.*

SHORT-TAILED PARROT, *Graydidascalus brachyurus,* Curica-verde

22 cm. Unique Amazonian species with short tail, heavy bill. Green with base of wing wine-colored (invisible when perched because of back feathers), base of tail feathers reddish. VOICE: a soft *kurik,* a sequence of strident *kia, kia, kias. . . .* Canopy of forests at edges of rivers and lakes. Locally abundant. Amapá to Rios Solimões and Juruá, Peru, Colombia. Also called *Curiquinha, Curica-pequena.*

BLUE-HEADED PARROT, *Pionus menstruus,* Maitaca-de-cabeça-azul, Suia

27 cm. Very similar to *P. maximiliani* but with brighter colors. Head, neck, and breast intense cobalt blue, conspicuous even in flight; auricular region blackish; bill black with red at base of maxilla. Some red tints often show in middle of throat. Immature lacks any blue, and red is pale; sometimes forehead reddish. VOICE: *ksht-ksht, kari-karitz* (like Tupi name given it in Mato Grosso); young begging, *TEret.* Costa Rica to Bolivia, Mato Grosso, Goiás, Rio de Janeiro; in certain regions (e.g., lower Rio Doce, Espírito Santo) sympatric with *maximiliani.* Also called *Curica, Maitaca-de-barriga-azulada.*

SCALY-HEADED PARROT, *Pionus maximiliani,* Maitaca-de-Maximiliano   PL 17.7   Fig. 120

27 cm. Stocky with short tail. In appearance very similar to *P. menstruus.* Common in eastern Brazil. Head slightly blackish green, almost without blue; bill yellow with blackish base; under wing coverts red like *menstruus;* some tail feathers with red base. VOICE: *krek . . . , maiTAK-maiTAK.* Flies in a peculiar manner, holding wings well below body. Tall forests, araucaria groves, gallery woodland. The north-

Fig. 120. Scaly-headed Parrot, *Pionus maximiliani,* showing the characteristic low wing beat.

east (Maranhão, Piauí, Pernambuco, Alagoas) and east (including ex-Guanabara) to southern Brazil (including Rio Grande do Sul, Goiás, Mato Grosso); also Bolivia, Paraguay, Argentina. Also called *Baitaca.*

DUSKY PARROT, *Pionus fuscus,* Maitaca-roxa

27 cm. Notable for shades of sepia in plumage. Auricular region has conspicuous white pattern; base of bill yellow; undersurface of wing blue (not green as in *P. maximiliani*); under tail coverts carmine as in congeners. Brazil (Maranhão, Pará, Amazonas) to Columbia, Venezuela. Also called *Curica* (Amazonas, *Papagainho-roxo.*

RED-SPECTACLED PARROT, *Amazona pretrei,* Papagaio-da-serra   EN

32.5 cm. Small, southern species, splendidly colored with mask, bend of wing, alula, upper coverts of primaries, and pants scarlet; base of maxilla orange. "Green" individuals monitored in captivity with shoulders, metacarpal margin, and upper primary coverts with little or no red were females and similar to Alder Parrot, *A. tucumana,* of Andean slopes. VOICE: *SPLEEeh-kreh-klay, quero-quero,* full cries mixed with strident whistles resembling *Pionus* and parakeet voices. Restricted to principal regions where Paraná pine (*Araucaria angustifolia*) grows, feeds by preference on nuts of this coniferous tree. As slow ripening of pine nuts extends over many months, this food guarantees nourishment for birds for a good part of year. Another important source of food is fruit of *Podocarpus* sp. which ripens early in year (January, February) before pine nuts. Originally from São Paulo to northern Argentina, now recorded only in Rio Grande do Sul (possibly extending to Santa Catarina) according to observations and information gathered by William Belton 1970–83 (Belton 1984).

Breeding, Annual Reunions, and Preservation: Like other parrots becomes extremely secretive in breeding season, which occurs around end of year (see "Breeding"). In autumn begins to gather in flocks that are especially conspicuous when flying toward some distant forest. Even makes regular migrations in March–April, first described in 1800s for Taquara (Rio Grande do Sul) region, but it did not nest there (Berlepsch and Ihering 1885).

In May 1971 an araucaria grove was discovered in Esmeralda area of Rio Grande do Sul where these parrots gathered in great numbers. Based on a proposal by Belton, SEMA in 1974 established an ecological station there. In May 1972 we had the opportunity to observe the great flocking of *A. pretrei* in Esmeralda and, as usual, to note interesting details. The parrots entirely covered some branches and tree crowns and appeared very agitated, moving suddenly from one place to another, "conversing" uninterruptedly and making an extremely loud hubbub. As dusk advanced, the mass of parrots suddenly took flight and increased its screeching even more until it became a constant din. In flocks that now dispersed, now merged, the birds wheeled over the grove in large circles. From time to time they moved away a bit but quickly returned. After 15–30 minutes of these circular flights (during which they sometimes interspersed a short pause on the tops of the tallest araucarias) they were finally ready to retire. As night fell they perched on the trees where they slept. We estimated that several thousand were present. In the flocks that flew in to the roost and those that later overflew the grove, there were 2 groupings: (1) pairs that flew very calmly and (2) individuals that flew in small groups (2–4), chasing each other tenaciously. The latter appeared to be mostly young birds but also included adults.

These roosting assemblages occur from April to mid-July, coincident with ripening of the pine nuts. After these conclaves the parrots disappear, with only the odd pair remaining to nest. The young hatch in December.

May and June censuses by the Rio Grande do Sul branch of the Bird Observers Club in 1987 and 1988 showed approximately 8000 individuals; in 1989 they amounted to 10,000. It was thus a severe shock when only 31 birds appeared in 1990. This must be due to a shift in their roosting place—an unusual circumstance that leads one to suspect a drastic reduction in the number of parrots, which could affect the survival of the species. The traditional roosts having been destroyed, and this now being where what is probably an important portion of the total population meets, the species has become highly vulnerable. Also called *Serrano, Charā, Charão* (Rio Grande do Sul), *Maragato*. An illustration of *A. pretrei* has appeared on a Brazilian postage stamp (see *A. brasiliensis*).

RED-LORED PARROT, *Amazona autumnalis,* Cavacué

37 cm. Large species of northeastern Brazil. Forehead, lores, and speculum red; crown bluish lilac. Between Rios Negro and Solimões (*A. a. diadema*) to Venezuela, Ecuador, Mexico. Periodically common near Manaus (Ducke Reserve Forest). Also called *Papagaio-diadema.*

RED-TAILED (= BLUE-CHEEKED) PARROT, *Amazona brasiliensis,* Papagaio-de-cara-roxa
BR   EN   PL 44.4

36 cm. Very local southern species. Green with forehead and lores red (without orange); crown and throat purplish; sides of head blue; edge of wing red; no red speculum; greater wing coverts and tertiaries conspicuously edged with yellow; tail feathers with greenish yellow tips, outer ones with wide red subterminal band; bill horn color, without red. VOICE: in flight *kraaaa-kraaaa; kli-kli; kehlik; KRAYo* (similar to *A. aestiva*). Forest. Originally from São Paulo to Rio Grande do Sul, now restricted to southeastern São Paulo coast (Municipality of Pariquera-açu, Camargo 1962) and Paraná. Nests on forested islands in Paranaguá Bay, Paraná (Scherer Neto 1989). Can be considered a geographic replacement of *A. rhodocorytha*. A good illustration of this little-known species, taken from Forshaw and Cooper (1973), is on a postage stamp published by the Postal and Telegraphic Service in 1980. (See also *A. pretrei, A. vinacea,* and *Touit melanonota* in same series.) *A. brasiliensis* is on list of species protected by CITES, Appendix I: most endangered species. Currently being studied by Scherer Neto.

RED-BROWED PARROT, *Amazona rhodocorytha,* Chauá   BR   EN   PL 17.4

37 cm. Typical of eastern Brazilian forests. Forepart of head and base of maxilla intense red; lores (also throat in Alagoas) orange; speculum and tail spots red; edge of wing green. VOICE: typical and full *koyOK-koyOK, kow-ow* (thus vernacular name), *noAT-noAT; alo, alo, alo . . . ; kray-o* (in flight). High forest, both in Serra do Mar and high regions of interior (eastern Minas Gerais), and coastal lowlands. Alagoas to Rio de Janeiro (Marambaia 1986, Ilha Grande, Poço das Antas 1968, and Silva Jardim). Appears to be a geographic replacement of *A. brasiliensis* and of *A. dufresniana* of the Guianas. Also called *Jauá.*

FESTIVE PARROT, *Amazona festiva,* Papa-cacau

35 cm. Northern species with green forehead and dark rusty red lores; a little blue behind eye. Lower back red, unusual for this genus and conspicuous in flight; absent in immature (see "Identification . . ."). No speculum. VOICE: a full *kyay-ow, kyay-lo,* repeated. North of Amazon from Mexiana Island and Amapá to northwestern Brazil, Colombia, Guyana; also from west of Rio Madeira to Peru. Locally abundant (upper Amazon); partial to cacao plantations; sometimes found with *A. ochrocephala* in Roraima.

YELLOW-FACED PARROT, *Amazona xanthops,* Papagaio-galego   BR

26.5 cm. No larger than a *Pionus,* typical of dry portions of central and northeastern Brazil, with different characteristics than other *Amazona.* Head and belly yellow; sides of body (and sometimes cheeks) orange, with much variation; perhaps there are 2 phases, with males more brilliant; feather edges dark green, creating a scaly pattern; bill light pink. Immature and certain adults have green bellies. VOICE: *KREWe, KREWe . . . ; grayo-grayo-totototo* in flight. Cerrado, caatinga, gallery forests. Locally common. Interior of Piauí to Bahia, Minas Gerais, Goiás, Mato Grosso (Rio Araguaia), as far as western São Paulo (Rio Paraná). Also called *Papagaio-goiaba, Papagaio-de-barriga-amarela, Curau* (Brasília). Inclusion in *Amazona* is questionable. See *A. ochrocephala,* which it resembles in yellow head and ecology.

TURQUOISE-FRONTED PARROT, *Amazona aestiva,* Papagaio-verdadeiro PL 17.1

35 cm; 400 g. Parrot most sought-after for a pet, being famous as best "talker" (see "Vocalization . . . "). Forehead and lores blue; yellow of head extends above and behind and thus around eye, unlike *A. amazonica.* Speculum, shoulder, and bases of tail feathers (normally invisible) scarlet. Bill black (adult male). There are predominantly yellow individuals (see "Natural and Artificial Color . . . "). Immature may have all-green head. There are 2 geographic races: *A. a. aestiva* with red shoulders (Brazil) and *A. a. xanthopteryx* with shoulder, lesser upper wing coverts, and head yellow. Latter resembles *A. ochrocephala* but forehead blue (Bolivia, Argentina; it is heavily commercialized, see "Trade . . . "). In Mato Grosso Pantanal there is an area of transition (mixed red and yellow shoulder). Adult iris orange-yellow (male) or red-orange with thin red outer ring (female); immature has uniformly chestnut iris (see "Identification . . . "). VOICE: *krik-kiakrik-krik-krik, KRAYo* (very typical), *rak-OW* in flight; a melodious song, *drewwo drOOo-drOOo-drOOo drewoh drewwee dew;* begging of young, *ga, ga, ga, ga,* recalls Black-billed Magpie, *Pica pica,* of Northern Hemisphere.

Humid or dry forests, palm groves, river edges. Found in interior of country, frequently alongside very similar *A. amazonica.* The northeast (Piauí, Pernambuco, Bahia) through central Brazil (Minas Gerais, Goiás, Mato Grosso) to Rio Grande do Sul, Paraguay, northern Argentina, Bolivia. Absent from coastal areas, unlike *amazonica.* Also called *Papagaio-de-fronte-azul, Curau, Papagaio-grego, Papagaio-comum, Ajuru-etê, Trombeteiro* (Mato Grosso), *Louro* (the name used for all domesticated parrots [*Amazona*] in Brazil; it is even more generalized in Spanish, being used for various psittacids). See *A. ochrocephala.*

YELLOW-HEADED PARROT, *Amazona ochrocephala,* Papagaio-campeiro

38 cm. Large northern species, partly an open-country bird. Head, neck, and pants yellow; shoulder, speculum, and tail spots scarlet. Head color may vary, being intermingled green and blue. Light gray bill, maxilla sometimes with red

base. Immature almost without yellow. Dry deciduous forests at edge of open country. Mexico to northern South America (where common), from there to Pará (Marajó, Rio Tapajós), Amazonas, Acre, northern Mato Grosso. Also called *Papagaio-de-Suriname.* See *A. xanthops,* with which, to some extent, it shares a similar habitat, and *A. aestiva,* which has blue forehead.

ORANGE-WINGED PARROT, *Amazona amazonica,* Curica, Papagaio-do-mangue PL 17.3

34 cm. Much like *A. aestiva* but a bit smaller and with wing bend green or yellowish, not red. Most reliable differentiating characteristics are pumpkin-colored (not scarlet) speculum and tail spots prominent in flight even when seen from side or directly below. Blue on head more concentrated above eyes than on forehead; front part of cheeks and often forehead yellow. Does not usually have yellow feathers around eyes, unlike *aestiva.* VOICE: *kurik-kurik* (thus the name *curica*), *KEEro-KEEro-KEEro, dlo-dlo-dlo,* etc.; young begging, *gheh, gheh, gheh, gheh.* Forests. Common in Amazonia. Along Atlantic coast uses mangroves, eating fruits of certain species and nesting in trunks of larger ones. Flies to forested islands to roost and probably nests on them when they are safer from human predation than nearby mainland (e.g., Rio de Janeiro). Colombia, Venezuela, and the Guianas to Paraná, western São Paulo, Rio de Janeiro. Also called *Aiuru-curuca* and *kuritzaká* (Kamaiurá, Mato Grosso), *Curau* (Mato Grosso). Extensive range overlaps almost all of that of more restricted *aestiva.*

MEALY PARROT, *Amazona farinosa,* Papagaio-moleiro

40 cm. Largest Brazilian *Amazona,* with relatively long tail. Green, with entire plumage, especially hind neck, covered by a white powder (thus the name; reflections from this powder produce an attractive haze. One particle of this powder measures $1/1000$ mm or less). Occiput blackish violet; crown frequently with some yellow, blue, and red. Bill and area around eye white. Speculum and wing edge scarlet; tail feathers amply tipped with light green and sometimes red on basal portion. VOICE: a loud, melodious *kruhh-urk . . . , kurrIK;* a typical phrase it repeats is *chop, chop, chop.* Tall, extensive forests. Mexico to Bolivia, northern Mato Grosso, eastern Pará; also eastern Brazil from Bahia to eastern Minas Gerais, São Paulo. Also called *Juru, Juru-açu, Curica.*

VINACEOUS-BREASTED PARROT, *Amazona vinacea,* Papagaio-de-peito-roxo PL 17.2

35 cm. Beautiful southern species whose scaly, vinaceous purple breast pattern (more intense in male) recalls *Deroptyus accipitrinus,* especially because *A. vinacea* also has neckpiece of elongated feathers it frequently raises like *Deroptyus.* Lores, forehead, base of bill, chin, shoulders, speculum, and base of outer tail feathers red. More colorful,

larger birds and less colorful, smaller birds appear in bird trade from southern and northern populations, respectively. VOICE: *TAYo-TAYo, krayo-krayo* . . . . Dry forests of interior, araucaria groves, edges of groves in open country. Still relatively common in Santa Catarina and Minas Gerais. According to a survey conducted in northern Espírito Santo at end of 1970s and early 1980s, the species suffered a tremendous reduction in numbers in 1970s. In 1 area successively deforested by ranchers there, 80, 38, 12, and 5 young were produced in 4 consecutive years. Its extermination there within a year was predicted (Duce Fortaleza, 1983, *O Canarinho*, March–April; in September 1990 it stated: "the 'crau-crau' no longer exists in Espírito Santo"). Southern Bahia to Rio Grande do Sul, Paraguay, northern Argentina. Also called *Jurueba, Quero-quero, Téu-téu, Curraleiro*.

RED-FAN PARROT, *Deroptyus accipitrinus*, Anacã
PL 17.5

35 cm. Amazonian species notable for large ruff of red erectile feathers with wide blue border. In northern Amazonia forehead whitish (*D. a. accipitrinus*, see plate). Female larger. VOICE: a strident bark, *kwiAH-kwiAH-kwiAH-ghi-ghi-ghi, HEEa-HEEa-HEEa* . . . . Forests, forest edge. The Guianas to southern Pará (Serra do Cachimbo, nesting), northern Mato Grosso (upper Rio Xingu, Rio Tapajós), Amazonas (Rio Madeira), Rondônia, Maranhão, Colombia, northeastern Peru. Flies more rapidly than an *Amazona* and has long-tailed silhouette; could be mistaken for an unusual hawk. Also called *Hia, Curica-bacabal* (Maranhão).

BLUE-BELLIED PARROT, *Triclaria malachitacea*, Sabiá-cica   PL 44.5

29 cm. Unique southern species with relatively long, wide tail. Deep green, of a shade unlike that of other psittacids. Male has purplish blue abdomen, bright white bill. Female not as deep green, lacks blue underparts. Old males may show red instead of blue feathers on belly. Blue on male said to begin appearing as a nestling but may take longer. VOICE: in flight strident cries, *kri-kri-kri*, similar to a parakeet; flutelike song reminiscent of White-necked Thrush, *Turdus albicollis*, but a bit harsh and louder: *ewer-ewer jewlewt-jewlewt* (male), accompanied by female with a soft *jot, jot, jot*. . . . Dry forests of Serra do Mar at midaltitudes (300–700 m, Rio de Janeiro), adjacent forests of interior mountain regions. Outside breeding season also occurs on coast (Parati, Rio de Janeiro). Southern Bahia and Minas Gerais to Rio Grande do Sul, southern Mato Grosso (Campo Grande). Also called *Araçuaiava, Cica. Sabia-cica* in Tupi = "Mother of the Thrush."

Psittacidae Appendix

The Budgerigar, *Melopsittacus undulatus* (*Periquito australiano*), of which many varieties are bred in Brazil, does not appear capable of surviving without human assistance. There has been no lack of attempts to introduce it so it could breed in a semiwild state (ex-Guanabara, Minas Gerais, Santa Catarina). The world population of this species in captivity was estimated to be 500 million in 1983. See also Chapter 2.4.

Psittacidae Bibliography
See also General Bibliography

Arndt, T. 1983. *Südamerikanische Sittiche-Pyrrhura*. Walsrode: Horst Müller.

Arndt, T. 1983. Neue Erkenntnisse über den Artstatus des Blausteiss Sittich *Pyrrhura p. perlata* Spix. *Spixiana* 1983, suppl.:425–428.

Arndt, T., and P. Roth. 1986. Der Rotbauchsittich *Pyrrhura rhodogaster* im Vergleich mit den verschiedenen Unterarten des Blausteissittichs *Pyrrhura perlata*: Vorschlag für nomenklatorische und systematische Änderungen. *Verh. Ornith. Ges. Bay.* 24:313–17.

Arrowood, P. C. 1980. Importation and status of *Brotogeris versicolorus* in California. In *Conservation of New World Parrots, Proc. ICBP Parrot Working Group Meeting, St. Lucia.* 1980:425–429.

Berman, S. L. 1984. The hindlimb musculature of *Amazona albifrons. Auk* 101:74–92.

Braun, H. 1952. *Z. Tierpsych.* 9:40–91. [Mental faculties]

Brereton, J. Le Gay. 1963. Evolution within Psittaciformes. *Proc. 13th Int. Orn. Cong., Ithaca.* 1962:499–517.

Brockmann, J., and W. Lantermann. 1981. *Agaporniden*. Stuttgart.

Caccamise, D. F. 1980. *Wilson Bull.* 92:376–81. [*Myiopsitta*, development]

Camargo, H.F.A. 1962. *Pap. Avuls. Zool., S. Paulo* 15:67–77. [*Amazona brasiliensis*, distribution]

Camargo, H.F.A. 1976. Sobre o ninho de *Triclaria malachitacea. Pap. Avuls. Zool., S. Paulo* 29:93–94.

Condamine, C. M. de la. 1745. *Relation Abrégée d'un Voyage fait dans l'Interieur de l'Amérique Méridional.* 8 vols. Paris: Chez la Veuve Pissot.

Deckert, G., and K. Deckert. 1982. Spielverhalten und Komfortbewegungen bei *Ara chloroptera. Bonn. Zool. Beitr.* 33:269–81.

d'Orbigny, A. D. 1835–38. *Voyage dans l'America meridional.* Vol. 1:220–21.

Fallavena, M.A.B., and F. Silva. 1988. Alimentação de *Myiopsitta monachus* no Rio Grande do Sul. *Iheringia*, Ser. Misc. 2:7–11.

Forshaw, J. M., and W. T. Cooper. 1973. *Parrots of the World.* Melbourne: Lansdowne Press.

Friedmann, H., and M. Davis. 1938. "Left-handedness" in parrots. *Auk* 55:478–80.

Haffer, J. 1977. *Bonn. Zool. Beitr.* 28:269–78. [*Pionites*, distribution, hybridization]

Hardy, J. W. 1966. *Auk* 83:66–83. [Evolution]

Hohenstein, K. F. 1987. Werkzeuggebrauch bei Papageien, *Anodorhynchus hyacinthinus. Gef. Welt* 111(12):329–30.

Holmberg, E. L. 1895. *Territorio VI, La fauna de la República argentina*, 513.

Homberger, D. 1976. "Vergleichende Untersuchungen zum Fress-verhalten der Papageien." Thesis. University of Zurich.

Homberger, D. 1980. Functional morphology and evolution of the feeding apparatus in Parrots, etc. In *Conservation of New World Parrots, Proc. ICBP Parrot Working Group Meeting, St. Lucia*, 1980:471–85.

Hoppe, D. 1981. *Amazonen*. Stuttgart.

Kawall, N. 1976. Psitacídeos brasileiros. *SOM* 11:22–27.

Keller, J. 1975. Das Spielverhalten der Keas (*Nestor notabilis*) des Zürcher Zoos. *Z. Tierpsych.* 38:393–408.

Kenning, J. 1975. *Gef. Welt* 99:64–66. [*Deroptyus*, captive breeding]

Kollar, K. 1968. Die Ernährungsweise einiger Papageien. *Zool. Gart.* 35:218–23.

Lantermann, W. 1986. *Trochilus* 7:3–37. [*Pionus menstruus*, reproduction in captivity]

Lantermann, S., and W. Lantermann. 1986. *Die Papageien Mittel- und Südamerikas*. Hannover: Schaper.

Lent, H., and J. W. Abalos. 1946. *An. Inst. Med. Reg., Tucumán* 1(3):337–48. [Nest fauna]

Lent, H., and J. H. Jurberg. 1965. *Rev. Bras. Biol.* 25:349–76. [Nest fauna]

Levinson, S. T. 1980. The social behavior of the White-fronted Amazon (*Amazona albifrons*). In *Conservation of New World Parrots, Proc. ICBP Parrot Working Group Meeting, St. Lucia*, 1980:403–18.

Low, R. 1972. *The Parrots of South America*. London.

Low, R. 1980. *Parrots, Their Care and Breeding*. Dorset.

Low, R. 1988. *Gef. Welt* 112(9):246. [Breeding of *Triclaria*]

Machado, L.O.M. 1971. *Ciência e Cultura* 23:270. [Hybridization]

McNeil, R., et al. 1971. *Ibis* 113:494–99. [*Aratinga*, behavior]

Meyer, A. B. 1882. Über den Xanthochroismus der Papageien. *SB, Akad. d. Wiss., Berlin.* 24:517–24.

Miranda Ribeiro, A. 1920. *Rev. Mus. Paul.* 12:1–82. [Monograph]

Müller-Bierl, M. 1985. *Gef. Welt* 109:193. [Yawning]

Müller-Bierl, M. 1988. *Arara, eine textkritische Untersuchung.* Minden: Philler.

Neunzig, K. 1921. *Die fremdländischen Stubenvögel.*

Neunzig, K. 1930. *Sber. Ges. naturf. Freunde Berlin:*67–78. [Captivity]

Nichols, T. D. Since 1984. *The Amazona Newsletter.* Seattle: Amazon Society.

Nottebohm, F., et al. 1969. *Animal Kingdom:*19–23. [*Amazona*, vocalization]

Novaes, F. C. 1981. *Bol. Mus. Paraen., Zool.* 106. [*Pionites*, structure of the species]

Oren, D. C., and E. O. Willis. 1981. New Brazilian records for the Golden Parakeet. *Auk* 98:394–96.

Oren, D. C., and F. C. Novaes. 1986. Observations on the Golden Parakeet, *Aratinga guaruba* in Northern Brazil. *Biol. Cons.* 36:1–9.

Peters, D. S. 1987. Mechanische Unterschiede paläognather und neognather Vogelschädel. *Nat. & Museum* 117(6):173–82.

Pinto, O.M.O. 1946. *Aves brasileiras da família dos papagaios.* São Paulo: Instituto de Botânica.

Pinto, O.M.O. 1950. *Pap. Avuls. Zool., S. Paulo.* 9(24):364–65. [*Anodorhynchus leari*]

Portmann, A. 1947. Études sur la Cérébralisation chez les Oiseaux; 2, Les indices intra-cérébraux. *Alauda* 15:1–15.

Reichenow, A. 1878–83. *Papageien.* Kassel. [Iconography]

Rensch, B. 1925. *J. Orn.* 73:514–39. [Color alteration]

Ridgely, R. S. 1980. In *Conservation of New World Parrots, Proc. ICBP Parrot Working Group Meeting, St. Lucia*, 1980:233–84.

Roet, E. C., D. S. Mack, and N. Duplaix. 1980. In *Conservation of New World Parrots, Proc. ICBP Parrot Working Group Meeting, St. Lucia*, 1980:21–55.

Rogers, L. J. 1980. Lateralization in the Avian Brain. *Bird Behav.* 2:1–12.

Roth, P. 1982. "Habitat-Aufteilung bei sympatrischen Papageien des südlichen Amazonasgebiets." Thesis. University of Zurich.

Roth, P. 1983. Observations on the Orange-cheeked Parrot. *Bird World—Amer. Avicult. Gaz.* 6(3):26–28.

Roth, P. 1984a. Repartição do Habitat entre Psitacídeos simpátricos no Sul da Amazônia. *Acta Amazonica* 14:175–221.

Roth, P. 1984b. Freilandbeobachtungen an Rotbauchsittichen, *Pyrrhura rhodogaster. Verh. Ornith. Ges. Bay.* 24:137–40.

Roth, P. 1984c. Comentário sobre a tiriba-do-Pará (*Pyrrhura perlata*) e a tiriba-de-peito-vermelho (*Pyrrhura rhodogaster*). *Res. XI Cong. Bras. Zool.:*351.

Roth, P. 1987a. A last chance to save Spix's Macaw. *Oryx* 21:73.

Roth, P. 1987b. Ararinha-azul: um passo da extinção. *Ciência Hoje* 5, no. 30.

Saint-Hilaire, A. de, 1936. Viagem à Província de Santa Catarina (1820). Nacional, São Paulo, *Brasiliana* 58.

Sazima, I. 1988. Peach-fronted Parakeet, *Aratinga aurea*, feeding on winged termites in southeastern Brazil. Unpublished manuscript.

Scherer Neto, P. 1989. "Contribuição a biologia do papagaio-da-cara-roxa *Amazona brasiliensis* (L., 1758)." M. Sc. thesis. Univ. Fed. Paraná.

Scherer Neto, P., and J. A. Müller. 1984. Aspectos bionómicos de Cuiú-cuiú, *Pionopsitta pileata. Arq. Biol. Tecno. Paraná* 27:391–99.

Schittko-Kienle, S. 1985. *Gef. Welt* 109:134–36. [Yawning]

Sick, H. 1957. *Auk* 74:510–11. [*Touit huetii*, occurrence in Brazil]

Sick, H. 1959. *J. Orn.* 100(4):413–16. [*Aratinga pertinax*]

Sick, H. 1963. *J. Orn.* 104(3–4):441–43. [*Aratinga pertinax*]

Sick, H. 1979. *Bull. B.O.C.* 99(4):115–20. [*Pyrrhura rupicola*, first discovery in Brazil]

Sick, H. 1979. *Alauda* 47(1):59–60. [*Anodorhynchus leari*, discovery]

Sick, H. 1980. In *Conservation of New World Parrots, Proc. ICBP Parrot Working Group Meeting, St. Lucia*, 1980:439–44. [The blue macaws]

Sick, H. 1984. Brasilianischer Ara 1502/3 in Europa gemalt. *J. Orn.* 125(4):479–81.

Sick, H. 1990. Notes on the nomenclature of Brazilian parrots. *Ararajuba* 1:109–10.

Sick, H., D. M. Teixeira, and L. P. Gonzaga. 1979. *An. Acad. Bras. Ciênc.* 51(3): 575–76. [*Anodorhynchus leari*, home range]

Sick, H., and D. M. Teixeira. 1980. *Am. Birds* 34(2):118–19 [*Anodorhynchus leari*, first photographs taken in the field]

Sick, H., L. P. Gonzaga, and D. M. Teixeira. 1987. A arara-azul-de-Lear, *Anodorhynchus leari* Bonaparte, 1856. *Rev. Bras. Zool.* 3(7):441–63.

Silva, F. 1981. Contribuicão ao conhecimento da biologia do papagaio charão, *Amazona pretrei. Iheringia*, Ser. Zool. 58:79–85.

Smith, G. A. 1975. Systematics of Parrots. *Ibis* 117:18–68.

Souancé, M. C. de. 1857. *Iconographie des Perroquets.* Paris. [Color illustrations of *Anodorhynchus glaucus* and *A. leari* on the same plate]

Stresemann, E. 1923. *Verh. Ornith. Ges. Bay.* 15(3):308–15. [Seventeenth-century paintings of psittacids]

Stresemann, E. 1948. *Zool Jb., Syst Ökol. und Geogr. der Tiere* 77:401–25. [*Anodorhynchus glaucus*, occurrence in Brazil]

Teixeira, D. M. 1985. Plumagens aberrantes em Psittacidae neotropicais. *Rev. Bras. Biol.* 45:143–48.

Völker, O. 1942. Die gelben und roten Federfarbstoffe der Papageien. *Biol. Zentralbl.* 62:8–13.

Völker, O. 1965. *Mitt. Naturf. Ges. Bern* 22:201. [Pigments]

Voous, K. H. 1965. Specimens of Lear's Macaw in the Zoological Mus. Amsterdam. *L'Oiseau et R.F.O.* no. 35(special):152–54.

Wallace, A. R. 1864. On the Parrots of the Malayan Region. *Proc. Zool. Soc. London:*288.

Yamashita, C. 1987. Field observations and comments on the Indigo Macaw (*Anodorhynchus leari*), a highly endangered species from northeastern Brazil. *Wilson Bull.* 99:280–82.

Zotta, A. R. 1944. *Lista Sistemática de las Aves Argentinas.* Buenos Aires: Museo Argentino de Ciênc. Nat.

ORDER CUCULIFORMES

FAMILY CUCULIDAE: CUCKOOS (19)

[Translator's note: Sick treats the Guira Cuckoo, *Guira guira,* as an ani along with the Smooth-billed Ani, *Crotophaga ani,* and Greater Ani, *C. major.* Where the term *ani* is used herein without further qualification, it refers to all three species.]

This cosmopolitan family probably originated in tropical regions of the Old World and long ago immigrated to the New World where it has now become quite differentiated. Fossils are poorly represented in the lower Tertiary of Europe and North America and in the Pleistocene of Brazil (Minas Gerais). Some authors include the Hoatzin, *Opisthocomus hoazin,* in the Cuculiformes.

Morphology and Special Adaptations

The body is slender and the tail long and graduated, as can easily be seen in the Squirrel Cuckoo, *Piaya cayana,* and anis, all among the best-known birds of Brazil. In the *Dromococcyx* the tail is extraordinarily long, broad, and soft. Sometimes the upper tail coverts reach the tips of the rectrices. The bill is strong and curved; the foot is zygodactyl (two toes forward, two to the rear) and less specialized than that of woodpeckers. Body skin is black, sometimes in surprising contrast to the white plumage. The iris is frequently red, at least in adults. Sexes are similar. The body odor is strong and characteristic, especially in *Crotophaga.* I can smell it at several meters distance (particularly when they are gathered in groups at night), and it can attract blood-sucking bats and carnivores.

Cuckoos are highly adept at jumping and running through branches; *Guira guira* seems to sneak through the foliage. Most go to the ground to eat, where they run with great agility, keeping the tail lifted and even threading their way through tall grass. The forest-dwelling *Neomorphus* are truly terrestrial. Flying ability varies greatly; *Guira guira* resembles a kite tossed across the savanna to the mercy of the wind; *Piaya cayana* glides down from the treetops, and the *Coccyzus* and *Dromococcyx* have a zooming flight almost like pigeons, at least over short distances. In mountainous regions flocks of *G. guira* are very able at using strong air currents to move long distances by holding their wings in a V, ascending or descending without a single wing beat.

The inside of the mouth of an ani nestling has several bright, whitish spots that show up remarkably against their red background (fig. 121). Such markings help the adults place food in the chick's mouth, especially in dark nests. There are two groups of spots, one in the roof of the mouth (1,2) and the other around the tongue (3,4). Between 2 and 3 is the opening of the esophagus. Anything placed between these marks provokes a swallowing reflex. The marks in *Crotophaga* and *Guira* are slightly different. There is a similar arrangement in the mouths of nestlings of some other cuckoos, such as the *Coccyzus* and the Great Lizard-Cuckoo,

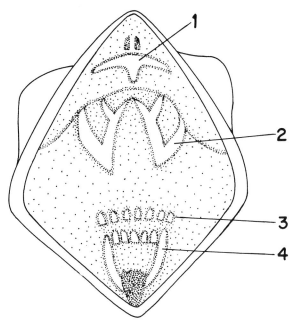

Fig. 121. Open mouth of a Smooth-billed Ani, *Crotophaga ani*, nestling showing the white marks (1 and 2) on the roof of the mouth and (3 and 4) around the tongue. The tip of the tongue is black. See the text for further explanation.

Saurothera merlini (New World), and the couas, *Coua*, of Madagascar (Appert 1970). This recalls also the Estrildidae, African Passerines (see Common Waxbill, *Estrilda astrild*, a species introduced into Brazil) whose nestlings have developed a somewhat different, sometimes even seemingly phosphorescent, arrangement of the mouth that is very efficient in the dark, enclosed nests where they are reared. There is no doubt that the grotesque appearance of the colorful, open mouth of the above-mentioned cuckoos can also serve to frighten predators, especially when the markings resemble large eyes and the nests are open, as in the case of our anis and the Madagascar *Coua*.

Vocalization

Crotophaga ani has more than 12 different vocalizations (Davis 1940). It has two alarm notes: one causes all flock members to perch in very visible places to examine the situation; another, uttered when a hawk approaches, causes the entire flock to disappear instantly into the woods. *Guira guira*, which has an impressive, very loud song, also has a full repertoire. The croaking of anis may recall jays, whereas the cooing of the Ash-colored Cuckoo, *Coccyzus cinereus*, and of *Neomorphus* ground-cuckoos is pigeonlike. The Striped Cuckoo, *Tapera naevia*, and the *Dromococcyx* have high notes they sing at intervals for hours on end, not even stopping at night. The song of *T. naevia* varies in certain regions. *Piaya cayana* is extremely loquacious at the height of the breeding season: it utters its territorial call 96 times per minute and scarcely stops for hours on end; sometimes it mimics other birds, exceptional for a non-Passerine. *Crotophaga ani* amuses itself with low chattering in a quite varied way, sometimes giving the impression it is trying to mimic another bird or even a human voice. This chatter recalls the murmured conversations of corvids such as *Pica* and *Garrulus*. The Greater Ani, *Crotophaga major*, sings in chorus. *Piaya cayana* can snarl with its bill open, resembling the growl of the Toco Toucan, *Ramphastos toco*. Some cuckoos click their bills, especially the *Neomorphus*, which intensify it into a very loud rattle. I have noted a "double" voice in *Dromococcyx*, apparently produced simultaneously but independently by the two bronchi (see Cotingidae, *Procnias*).

Feeding

Cuckoos are essentially carnivorous, eating grasshoppers, fleas, spiders, millipedes, etc; *Neomorphus* can catch centipedes 11 cm long. They also prey on large, hairy, urticant caterpillars and on geckos and mice. They reportedly can eliminate the lining of their large stomach, expelling it when it is loaded with irritating caterpillar hairs. *Guira guira* regurgitates pellets.

Crotophaga ani feeds primarily on grasshoppers it catches while accompanying cattle. It is a popular belief that anis are great tick eaters, but of 98 *C. ani* stomachs examined, only 1 had ticks (Köster 1971). *C. ani* sometimes undertakes group hunts in pastures when cattle are absent. I have seen it watch for animals fleeing from grass and brush fires, calmly perched only 2 m from high flames. Sometimes it catches insects in flight or takes small snakes and frogs. Occasionally it raids other birds' nests, taking House Sparrow, *Passer domesticus*, nestlings or breaking through the roof or sides of the spherical nest of the Bananaquit, *Coereba flaveola*, to get at its contents. Sometimes it just kills the birds without eating them. I recorded this also with a *Piaya cayana* that threw two Lined Seedeater, *Sporophila lineola*, nestlings out of a nest without eating them. *Crotophaga ani* even devastates Rufous Hornero, *Furnarius rufus*, nests, in spite of the difficulty of entering their "ovens." It also follows tractors plowing fields. Occasionally it uses army ants as beaters. These are highly important for the *Neomorphus*, which easily catch grasshoppers, cockroaches, daddy longlegs, large centipedes, and ants that may be clinging to other birds. I have also seen *Crotophaga major* attracted to army ants. Eating large daddy longlegs brings the caustic odor of these arachnids to the *Neomorphus* plumage. *Neomorphus* also follow peccary herds. Anis fish in shallow water and periodically eat fruits, berries, small palm fruits, and seeds, especially in the dry season when arthropods are scarce.

In the upper Amazon, squirrel monkeys (*Saimiri*) accompany large flocks (150 or more) of *C. major* which frighten up many insects (Ayres 1985).

Behavior

Cuckoos enjoy sunbathing and dustbathing (e.g., *Coccyzus, Tapera naevia, Guira guira*), and sometimes their plumage is strongly tinged with the color of the earth or with ashes or charcoal, especially if the anis have first made their feathers sticky by running through grass that sheds a honeylike substance. In the morning and after rains they perch with open wings to dry themselves. Anis are quite sensitive to humidity. The plumage of an individual that is incubating and unable to seek protection under large leaves becomes soaked. To keep warm at night, *G. guira* and *Crotophaga ani* roost in closely packed lines or pile up in disorderly heaps. Sometimes one will run over the backs of the others to force its way into the lineup. They seek out patches of bamboo for night roosting, sometimes in company with icterines. *G. guira* may die of cold in winter. Anis engage in mutual preening. A *C. ani* that I once caught pretended to be dead and then unexpectedly escaped. *G. guira* may become aggressive with a hawk, such as the Roadside Hawk, *Rupornis magnirostris,* if one appears in its territory.

Breeding

It is well known that the European Common Cuckoo, *Cuculus canorus,* which gave its name to this family, is a notorious brood parasite; it lays its eggs in the nests of other birds for them to incubate. In Portugal a *cuco* is a man whose wife is unfaithful to him. In Brazil there are three parasitic cuckoos: *Tapera naevia;* the Pavonine Cuckoo, *Dromococcyx pavoninus;* and Pheasant Cuckoo, *D. phasianellus.* The other Brazilian cuculidae are not parasites, but there are other irregularities in their breeding.

Ani eggs are relatively large; those of *Crotophaga ani* comprise 14% of the female's body weight; those of *C. major* 20.8%; and those of *Guira guira* 17% to 25%. *Coccyzus* and *Piaya* eggs are "normal." The parasitic species lay small eggs, comprising 3.2% to 8.3% of the weight of the respective bird (among Old World species), a notable adaptation for a relatively large parasite that lays eggs in the nests of small birds. The eggs of a 70-g *Turdus* thrush comprise about 10% of the female's weight.

Egg color for some species is as follows:

1. Uniformly green: Dark-billed Cuckoo, *Coccyzus melacoryphus*
2. White, sometimes stained by the chlorophyll of fresh leaves brought by the birds into the nest: Mangrove Cuckoo, *Coccyzus minor,* and *Piaya cayana*
3. Greenish blue, covered with a calcareous crust, scratched by turning the eggs during incubation: *Crotophaga ani* and *C. major; Guira guira* eggs are much larger, with a sea green background covered with a network of calcareous white in high relief all over the surface
4. Pure greenish or bluish white: *Tapera naevia*
5. White, finely speckled with brown: *Dromococcyx*
6. Uniformly yellowish white: Rufous-vented Ground-Cuckoo, *Neomorphus geoffroyi*

Breeding of Nonparasitic Species

Several of the world's Cuculidae, especially in the Palearctic, are not parasitic.

The male feeds the female, more often when he arrives with the intention of copulating. The male *Piaya cayana* delivers a caterpillar to the female and then copulates. *Crotophaga ani* customarily brings food when he visits the female in the nest; when copulating he continues to hold the nuptial present (a caterpillar, spider, small fruit, etc.) until after the act and may then eat it himself.

Pairs of *Coccyzus melacoryphus* and of *P. cayana* rear their young in a small nest, made by themselves, that may resemble a pigeon nest. Sometimes a female lays in the nest of another. Among the cuckoos that rear normally is *Neomorphus geoffroyi,* a solitary, terrestrial, forest species.

Because of the many irregularities, it is difficult to discern the breeding pattern of the extremely gregarious anis. *Crotophaga ani,* although it forms pairs, lives in flocks that occupy group territories all year. They may even kill an individual of another flock that comes close to their collective nest. Within the group, individuals threaten one another, indicating the existence of a hierarchy.

Although some ani pairs have individual nests, more frequently they associate with one or two other pairs of the flock to build a collective nest, lay eggs, and rear their offspring together with the cooperation of grown young of previous clutches. The nest is large and deep and may be attended by 6 to 10 birds and have 10, 20, or more eggs placed in various layers. The clutch of one female is estimated to have 4 to 7 eggs. Birds coming to the nest regularly bring a green leaf, like other cuckoos, filling the interior of the nest and making it more difficult to manage the fresh eggs. The leaves are not used to cover the eggs, as has been erroneously stated; sometimes they are placed right under the eggs. Fresh eggs may become buried in the bottom of the nest, escape normal incubation, and fail to hatch, joining other rotten eggs from earlier clutches. Counting these abandoned eggs, a nest that has been used several times may have 50 or more eggs.

One can understand such confusion only by marking all the individuals and their eggs, as Köster (1971) did with *Crotophaga ani* and Vehrencamp (1977) did with the Groove-billed Ani, *C. sulcirostris* (a non-Brazilian species). The dominant female throws many eggs out of the nest. The male plays a large role in incubation, always incubating at night.

The male *Guira guira* dances with open wings around the female on the ground. I saw a pair copulate while running on the ground. The male vigorously stepped on the female's tail, pinning her to the ground, then climbed on her back but immediately jumped off to her side and copulated while perched on the ground beating his wings and covering her with his right wing. Mounting, therefore, did not occur (because they were on the ground?), as in *Amazona* parrots. During the entire act the male pecked the female's head.

Nesting of *G. guira* is similar to that of *C. ani*. There are both individual and collective nests. A female that has constructed a nest and not yet begun to lay throws out eggs that are laid there by other females. If the laying female finds the nest where she wants to lay occupied by another bird, she lays on the ground, similar to what occurs with *C. ani*. Adults do not always take good care of nests with eggs, sometimes abandoning them. Both sexes have brood patches. In Argentina *G. guira* reportedly lays its eggs in nests of other species sometimes. This may be pure carelessness, but it also could be incipient parasitism. I saw in Espírito Santo what has been observed in Paraguay: *G. guira* laying in *C. ani* nests and participating in incubation there, contributing further to the confusion regarding these nests. It appears that change in the nesting instinct of anis is governed more by their intense gregariousness than by incipient parasitism. Lost eggs are also found under trees where *G. guira* sleep, and I have found a similar situation with *C. major*.

Incubation is short, lasting 13 to 16 days in *C. ani* and 15 days in *G. guira*. Young *C. ani* less than a week old leave the nest at the slightest disturbance but return to be warmed by their parents (behavior similar to that of *Opisthocomus hoazin*). At 10 days they already sleep outside; they abandon the nest definitively at 8 weeks (Köster 1971).

About six young at a time may be reared successfully. Young, like those of parasitic cuckoos, leave the nest before they are able to fly, while the tail is still short, and are fed for some weeks by stepparents or parents. The whole flock defends the nest and nestlings against intruders and helps feed the young. Sometimes *Crotophaga ani* nests are found in groups. The total lack of effort to hide their nests and the constant turmoil throughout the day near them frequently lead to the loss of eggs or young to predators.

Breeding of Parasitic Species

The nesting instinct has been entirely lost in *Tapera naevia* and the *Dromococcyx*. These have become true parasites, no longer making a nest and laying all their eggs in certain Passerine nests. We still know very little about the details of this parasitism. The eggs are small, being adapted to the hosts; *T. naevia* eggs are almost the same size as those of Spix's Spinetail, *Synallaxis spixi*, a furnariid not even half the cuckoo's size. This is the phenomenon of aggressive mimicry. The discrepancy between parasite and host is even greater in the case of the *Dromococcyx*. The parasite's egg has a more resistant shell and a shorter incubation period than those of its host, guaranteeing that it hatches before its pseudosiblings.

There is much speculation on the evolution of Cuculidae

parasitism (see Reichholf 1982–83). The parasitism of American cuckoos developed independently of that in the Old World and took a different direction. Conclusions reached from studies of *Cuculus canorus* cannot be applied to Neotropical cuckoos. In Brazil this parasitism also exists among icterines (e.g., Shiny Cowbird, *Molothrus bonariensis*) and ducks (see *Heteronetta*). The gregariousness of anis cannot be taken simply as a stage leading toward parasitism.

Migration

I have the impression that *Coccyzus melacoryphus* emigrates during the cold months in Rio de Janeiro. A North American species, the Yellow-billed Cuckoo, *Coccyzus americanus,* is a large-scale migrant.

Parasites

Nematode worms (Spiruroidea) are sometimes found in the eyes of cuckoos. *Oxyspirura brasiliensis* has been described from *Crotophaga major* on the Serra do Cachimbo, Pará. I have found louse flies (*Lynchia latifascies*) on *Piaya cayana* in Mato Grosso.

Reaction of Other Birds to Cuculids

Species such as *Guira guira, Piaya cayana*, and *Tapera naevia* are recognized like owls, as possible enemies and are attacked by other birds, such as the Tropical Kingbird, *Tyrannus melancholicus*. Ground-doves are frightened when *G. guira* appears. *G. guira* in turn scares away hawks (see "Behavior").

Ani Nests Used by Other Animals

Large, deeply cupped, abandoned ani nests are sometimes used by other birds, such as the Cattle Tyrant, *Machetornis rixosus*. and Saffron Finch, *Sicalis flaveola*, which are incapable of building without certain aids. Small mammals, especially marsupials, and snakes take over these nests, sometimes after preying on their contents.

Abundance and Decline

Guira guira, Crotophaga ani, and to some extent the *Coccyzus* are benefited by the disappearance of tall forest. They immigrate into regions where they were formerly unknown and become the most common bird along roadsides.

Because of their heavy, weak flight they are frequently hit on roads. Strong winds carry them out to sea. I found two *G. guira* on the Ilha Cagarra Grande, Rio de Janeiro, 5.5 km off the coast. Two *C. ani* appeared on a small island off the coast of Espírito Santo, 10 km from Guarapari (A. Aguirre).

Anis are adversely affected by insecticides, a fact all the more lamentable because crops benefit from the presence of the birds.

Neomorphus geoffroyi, a sensitive species of primary forests, is endangered by disappearance of its natural habitat, especially in eastern Brazil where *N. g. dulcis* and *N. g. maximiliani* live.

Folklore and Superstitions

Indigenous mythology includes the *Saci-Pererê,* the *Matinta-Pereira,* etc., which are associated with *Tapera naevia.* The behavior of this bird and of the *Dromococcyx,* which are heard but not seen because they live secretively, has given rise to popular fantasies that have encircled them in an aura of legend and mystery. The meat of *Crotophaga ani* is claimed to have curative powers against venereal diseases and asthma, to cite an example of superstitions current among back-country people.

Synopsis of Brazilian Cuculids[1]

Subfamily Phaenicophaeinae
   Coccyzus pumilus
   Coccyzus cinereus
   Coccyzus americanus
   Coccyzus julieni
   Coccyzus minor
   Coccyzus melacoryphus
   Piaya cayana
   Piaya melanogaster
   Piaya minuta
Subfamily Crotophaginae
   Crotophaga major
   Crotophaga ani
   Guira guira
Subfamily Neomorphinae
   Tapera naevia
   Dromococcyx phasianellus
   Dromococcyx pavoninus
   Neomorphus geoffroyi
   Neomorphus squamiger
   Neomorphus rufipennis
   Neomorphus pucheranii

DARK-BILLED CUCKOO, *Coccyzus melacoryphus,* Papa-lagarta   PL 15.8

28.3 cm. Long-tailed, a bit larger than Creamy-bellied Thrush, *Turdus amaurochalinus.* When young fledge they have white underparts. VOICE: a ventriloquial *ga-ga-ga-go-go;* song a decrescendo sequence of 8 snorted *goas;* a monosyllabic growl. Also vocalizes at night. Lives secluded in forests, dense capoeira, riverside vegetation at medium levels. Apparently migrates in winter (Rio de Janeiro). Northern South America to Bolivia, Paraguay, Argentina, throughout Brazil, where relatively common. Also called *Cucu* (Rio Grande do Sul).

Five other *Coccyzus,* all of local occurrence and very similar to *C. melacoryphus,* have been recorded for Brazil:

ASH-COLORED CUCKOO, *Coccyzus cinereus,* Papa-lagarta-cinzento

24 cm. Gray, eyes and area around them red, tail relatively short, not graduated but with white tip. Cerrado intermingled with savanna, capoeira. Argentina to Mato Grosso, Goiás, Bahia.

YELLOW-BILLED CUCKOO, *Coccyzus americanus,* Papa-lagarta-norte-americano   NV

Yellow mandible, white underparts. Remiges show large rusty area when wings are open. Regular migrant from North America, coming to Brazil during northern winter. Travels at night, sometimes flying into brightly lit walls. Piauí (December), Rio de Janeiro (January, March), Minas Gerais, São Paulo, Rio Grande do Sul (February), Rondônia (June), Mato Grosso to Argentina. It is the eastern North American race (*C. a. americanus*) that emigrates to Brazil, a situation corresponding to that of Eastern Meadowlark, *Sturnella magna,* an icterine.

PEARLY-BREASTED CUCKOO, *Coccyzus julieni,* Papa-lagarta-de-Euler

Similar to *C. americanus* in color of mandible and underparts but lacks rusty area in wing. VOICE: a ventriloquial *kyoa.* . . . Capoeira. Venezuela to Argentina, Rio de Janeiro, Paraná, Mato Grosso. Not common anywhere.

MANGROVE CUCKOO, *Coccyzus minor,* Papa-lagarta-do-mangue

Yellow mandible. Coastal mangroves from Mexico to Amazon estuary.

DWARF CUCKOO, *Coccyzus pumilus*

21 cm. Throat and upper breast rusty, contrasting with gray head and upper neck. Seen in Maracá, Roraima, December 1987 (A. Whittaker pers. comm.)

SQUIRREL CUCKOO, *Piaya cayana,* Alma-de-gato PL 15.6

47 cm. One of showiest birds, resembling a squirrel when it slips through branches. Immature has shorter tail, bill and region around eyes gray instead of green, eyes brown. VOICE: a loud *pi-kwa;* warning *ki-ki-ki;* a ventriloquial *heh-gogo;* a prolonged sequence of *wewp wewp wewps* . . . with perhaps 16 notes in 10 seconds or 96 notes per minute (proclaiming

---

[1] *Cuculus canorus,* of the Old World, mentioned in the text, belongs to the Cuculinae, which do not occur in the Americas.

territory). While chattering sometimes imitates other birds, e.g., Great Kiskadee, *Pitangus sulphuratus,* giving cuckoo a reputation among country folk as an idler. A hard rasping *rrrrr* (see "Vocalization"). Moves about in pairs. Forest, forest edge (but in canopy), cerrado, cerradão. Mexico to Argentina, throughout Brazil, where there are 6 geographic races. Also called *Rabo-de-palha, Chincão.* There are 2 similar species in Amazonia:

BLACK-BELLIED CUCKOO, *Piaya melanogaster,* Chincoã-bico-vermelho

36 cm. Scarlet bill, gray cap. VOICE: a strident *pi.* Treetops, sometimes in same forests as *P. cayana.* Pará to Mato Grosso.

LITTLE CUCKOO, *Piaya minuta,* Chincoã-pequeno

28 cm. Like a dark, miniature *P. cayana,* sometimes alongside it at river edges. VOICE: *tseh,* resembling a tree frog; a melodious *ki-OH.* Raises and lowers tail gently. In dense growth at forest edges. Locally abundant (e.g., Amapá). The Guianas and Colombia to Goiás, Mato Grosso, Bolivia.

SMOOTH-BILLED ANI, *Crotophaga ani,* Anu-preto   Fig. 122

36 cm. One of most frequently seen birds in cultivated areas; always in flocks. All black with peculiar raised hump on maxilla. VOICE: a melodious whistle, *tewlit, ani,* resembling that of Whimbrel, *Numenius phaeopus; eweh;* song a slow sequence of *glews. . . ;* also ventriloquial vocalizations (see "Vocalization").

Regularly takes advantage of cattle to frighten up insects (e.g., grasshoppers), a feature that may have become important only after colonists introduced domestic animals. If there are no steers, pigs, or other animals, a flock will sometimes spread out in a semicircle on ground, each separated from the other by 2–3 m. They stay attentive and still, but when an insect appears, closest bird jumps and catches it. From time to time flock moves forward. Common opinion that this species is a large consumer of ticks has not yet been proven. In hundreds of stomach contents examined by various scientists (especially J. Moojen in Minas Gerais and Mato Grosso), Koster (1971) found only 1 tick and the others none, even when an ani was seen pecking on the hide of an animal. When an ani jumps onto the leg of an animal it probably is catching a horse fly (Tabanidae), not a tick. When it perches on the back of a steer it generally does so only to improve its field of vision. It is possible, however, that certain individuals or even entire populations of *C. ani* do eat ticks, a hypothesis also applicable to *C. sulcirostris.* The odd tick found in an ani's gizzard could have been taken on the ground or on vegetation. The ani/cattle relationship is similar to that between cattle and Cattle Egret, *Bubulcus ibis.*

Most common inhabitant of areas where there are aban-

Fig. 122. Smooth-billed Ani, *Crotophaga ani.*

doned fields. Open country with clumps and groves, among pastures and gardens. Along highways often almost the only bird regularly seen in small flocks. Prefers humid areas, unlike *Guira guira.* A weak flier; has a hard time against a breeze, and a stronger wind can carry it far away. Florida to Argentina, throughout Brazil. Also called *Anu-pequeno, Anum* (Pará). See "Breeding"; also *C. major.*

GREATER ANI, *Crotophaga major,* Anu-coroca

46 cm. Distinctly larger than *C. ani,* with shorter crest to maxilla that is lacking in immatures. Plumage has greenish luster. Adult has greenish white iris. VOICE: a deep *oaak;* a melodious *kew-urre;* a monotonous *wow, wow, wow . . . ,* a well-synchronized, prolonged, unisonal phrase that starts out at full strength and then oscillates slightly without increasing, like an amphibian chorus that stops as if on command. Moves about in flocks of at least 3–4 pairs. Has individual or collective nests, the latter sometimes with 20 or more eggs. Near water or flooded areas, in dense forests at river edges, marshes and mangroves. In Amazonia a neighbor of *Opisthocomus hoazin.* Usually distant from human habitation. Panama to Argentina, throughout Brazil in suitable places. Also called *Anu-peixe.* See "Feeding."

Fig. 123. Guira Cuckoo, *Guira guira*.

GUIRA CUCKOO, *Guira guira*, Anu-branco   Fig. 123

38 cm. Almost as well known in south as *Crotophaga ani*. Feathers on top of head constantly erect. Yellowish white, bill orange (gray in immature), tail with black band. VOICE: call and cry in flight a high, strident *ee-eh, ee-eh, ee-eh;* warning *i-i-i-i;* a loud *kooeet* announces presence of a hawk; song a strongly descending, decrescendo sequence of melodious *glewwews;* a low cackling, resembling *Opisthocomus hoazin.* Fifteen basic calls have been recorded (Mariño 1986). When perched cocks tail and throws it onto back. Always in flocks. See "Breeding."

Formerly restricted to dry savannas and cerrado of interior (see *C. ani*); in last 100 years has penetrated fields of deforested areas. Unknown in Cantagalo, Rio de Janeiro, region as late as about 1870. In early 1800s reportedly was only recently immigrating into eastern Brazil. Disappears when an open area becomes forested. Southeastern Amapá and Amazon estuary (savanna islands, e.g., Mexiana and eastern part of Marajó) to Bolivia, Argentina, Uruguay. Missing from forested parts of Amazonia. Also called *Anu-galego, Alma-de-gato, Gralha* (Rio Grande do Sul), *Guira* (from Tupi, "bird"), *Quiriru* (Amapá), *Piririguá* (Maranhão, Piauí).

STRIPED CUCKOO, *Tapera naevia*, Saci
PL 15.7   Fig. 124

29 cm. Well known by voice but very difficult to see. Black alulas always prominent when bird moves. Feathered young has large yellow patches on upperparts; foreneck and breast vermiculated with black, even after tail is grown and bird has become independent. VOICE: a loud bisyllabic whistle, *ew ee,* most common vocalization, regularly and constantly repeated (July–January, Minas Gerais), even at night from roost. In certain regions (e.g., northeast) whistle is only monosyllabic, in other areas it is trisyllabic. Can be heard for almost ½ km. Other vocalizations include 4 whistles that move up scale, with a 5th descending, *si si si sisi,* and a simple, piercing note.

When avidly seeking bits of food on ground, opens wings and projects large, black alulas forward, giving impression of a 3-headed or 4-winged animal (*tico-tico-de-três-cabeças,* "three-headed-tico-tico," Santa Catarina, or "four-winged cuckoo." See also White-banded Mockingbird, *Mimus triurus*). At times projects alulas without opening wings. This is also done by young when frightened (see *Breeding*).

Breeding: Parasitic. In Brazil its eggs are found in large, enclosed, stick nests of furnariids such as Spix's Spinetail, *Synallaxis spixi;* Pale-breasted Spinetail, *S. albescens;* Plain-crowned Spinetail, *S. gujanensis;* Sootyfronted Spinetail, *S. frontalis;* Chotoy Spinetail, *S. phryganophila;* Yellow-chinned Spinetail, *Certhiaxis cinnamomea;* Common Thornbird, *Phacellodomus rufifrons;* Red-eyed Thornbird, *P. erythrophthalmus;* and Greater Thornbird, *P. ruber.* Only *C. cinnamomea* and the *Synallaxis* have been observed as hosts rearing the cuckoo. Its egg is only a bit larger than that of *S. spixi* and is rounder. For example: a *T. naevia* egg was 21.3 × 16.9 mm, weight 3.4 g; an *S. gujanensis* egg 20.4 × 14.4 mm, weight 2.5 g. Female *T. naevia* weighs 47 g, female *S. gujanensis* 18 g. Apparently *T. naevia* also lays in enclosed, globular nests of some tyrannids (*Myiozetetes, Todirostrum*). In certain regions a large portion of *Synallaxis* and *Certhiaxis* nests are molested by this cuckoo, 1 or 2 cuckoo eggs being found in each nest. Cuckoo egg's incubation period reportedly is shorter than host egg's, the cuckoo hatching after 15 days, the *S. gujanensis* after 18. Young cuckoo develops rapidly. Tip of its bill is a sharp pliers (fig. 125), the right tool for finishing off pseudosiblings (Sick 1981), a fact confirmed by Morton and Farabaugh (1979) and

Fig. 124. Striped Cuckoo, *Tapera naevia,* hopping on the ground while extending the alulas, giving the impression of a bird with three heads or four wings. After Sick 1953.

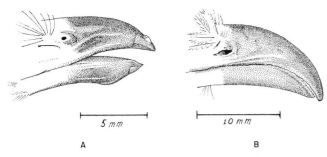

Fig. 125. Striped Cuckoo, *Tapera naevia*. Bills of (A) nestling and (B) adult. The tip of the nestling's bill is shaped like a pliers, suitable for giving fatal bites to other young in the nest. Nestling collected and studied by the author 11 November 1941, Linhares, Espírito Santo.

Salvador (1982). Situation resembles that of young Indicatoridae (Piciformes) of Africa and Asia, such as Lesser Honeyguide, *Indicator minor*, whose young are born with a sharp hook at tip of maxilla and mandible, a powerful weapon with which they kill pseudosiblings. Pseudosiblings of *T. naevia* disappear shortly after cuckoo hatches and are not usually found dead under nest, being carried away by parents. Eggs in a nest where a *T. naevia* has hatched also disappear, including other *Tapera* eggs if present. Direct observations are still lacking on placement of egg by cuckoo. Entrance and adjoining gallery of *Synallaxis*, etc., nests are very narrow. I have found *Certhiaxis* nests opened near the incubation chamber, which must have been the work of a *Tapera*. The owners of such a nest do not abandon it but immediately start to mend the damage. Young cuckoo defends itself in nest by hissing like a snake and even "striking" (snake display) by jumping forward and moving its large, black alulas. Young cuckoo abandons nest early (18 days of age), when still unable to fly, but runs swiftly and continues to be fed by stepparents.

Habitat, Distribution, and Folklore: Inhabits open country with bushes and bogs, both in lowlands and mountains such as Mantiqueira, Minas Gerais, to 1400 m. Mexico to Bolivia, Argentina, throughout Brazil. Also called *Sem-fim, Peitica, Tempo-quente, Peixe-frito* (Bahia), *Pitica* (Pará), *Peixe-frito-seu-veríssimo* (name applied to individuals that use the prolonged phrase). Name *Saci*, although it can be considered onomatopoeic, suggests even more a link with the Saci-Pererê of folklore, a notorious "deceiver," for this bird, with the very high timbre of its voice, fools us as to its whereabouts.

PAVONINE CUCKOO, *Dromococcyx pavoninus,* Peixe-frito-pavonino   PL 15.9

28.5 cm. Skulking forest bird, revealing its presence only by voice at dawn and at night. Extremely long tail and upper tail coverts. Foreneck ferruginous without dark spots (see *D. phasianellus*). VOICE: a whistle with timbre of *Tapera naevia*, with 4–5 syllables: *ew i ew ew, ew-i ew-i i;* also a

bisyllabic response, like *Tapera*. Parasitic. Lays eggs in bag-shaped nests of tiny tyrannids such as Ochre-faced Tody-Flycatcher, *Todirostrum plumbeiceps* (fig. 126), Eared Pygmy-Tyrant, *Myiornis auricularis,* and *Hemitriccus* and in open formicariid nests (Plain Antvireo, *Dysithamnus mentalis*). It would be impossible for this bird to enter a *Todirostrum* nest. It must introduce egg with bill or lay while holding onto outside of nest, "tossing" egg into incubation chamber. Adult *D. pavoninus* weighs 48 g, *T. plumbeiceps* only 5.9 g. Edge of tangled forests and dense secondary woodland. Northern South America south to Paraguay, Argentina. In Brazil in Amazonia, Mato Grosso, Goiás, Rio de Janeiro, São Paulo, Paraná. See *D. phasianellus*.

PHEASANT CUCKOO, *Dromococcyx phasianellus,* Peixe-frito-verdadeiro

36 cm. Similar to *D. pavoninus* but larger, throat and breast with blackish spots on whitish background. VOICE: similar to *pavoninus* but lower and ending in a tremolo, *eweerrew;* tremolo is replaced by simple whistles in an ascending sequence if bird is more excited, *eww eww dewrew,* which sounds much like *pavoninus*. Sings at dawn and night. Parasitic, eggs being found in enclosed tyrannid nests (*Myiozetetes* and Pied Water-Tyrant, *Fluvicola pica*) and open formicariid nests (Barred Antshrike, *Thamnophilus doliatus*). Thick forests, at low levels above ground, like *pavoninus*. Mexico to Bolivia, Argentina, and locally throughout Brazil: Amazonia to Rio Grande do Sul, including Rio de Janeiro and São Paulo. Also called *Täzin* (Kamaiurá, Mato Grosso), *Tchimina* (Juruna, Mato Grosso).

RUFOUS-VENTED GROUND-CUCKOO, *Neomorphus geoffroyi,* Jacu-estalo   PL 15.10

51 cm. Shy, terrestrial, size of a small guan, with broad crest raised vertically at least provocation. Long legs, relatively short toes. Triangular blue area behind eye is covered with feathers when bird is at ease. Juvenal has short tail and blackish plumage but already has blue mark on side of head.

Fig. 126. Young of a Pavonine Cuckoo, *Dromococcyx pavoninus* (left), fed by an Ochre-faced Tody-Flycatcher, *Todirostrum plumbeiceps* (right). After H. Neunteufel 1954.

VOICE: song a low, monosyllabic descending note, *OOOOoo*, with timbre of Gray-fronted Dove, *Leptotila rufaxilla*. Notes come at intervals of 3–4 seconds over several minutes, their low timbre similar to "moan" of curassows. When restless produces a loud snapping or even a clacking with bill, resembling gnashing of imposing teeth of White-lipped Peccary (*Tayassu pecari*).

Behavior: Although basically terrestrial, regularly perches to expand its horizon, to rest (letting wings fall onto branch), to preen, and to sleep at night, when it lies on branch like a chicken. In full motion even alights on vertical shoots and raises tail at 45° angle. When running on ground may resemble a squirrel. A permanent client of army-ant (*Eciton*) columns; also said to seek out fire-ant hordes (*Solenopsis*). Investigates heaps of dry branches, armadillo holes, empty terrestrial termite nests. See also "Feeding."

Breeding: In 1941 in Espírito Santo I observed a pair caring for a chick, eloquent proof that this species raises its own offspring and is not parasitic. A nest found in September 1977 by P. Roth (Aripuanã, Mato Grosso) was a small assemblage of heavy sticks lined with green leaves, 2.5 m above ground. It had 1 yellowish white egg without spots. Castelnau (1855) referred to the breeding of *Neomorphus pucheranii*, mentioning 2 eggs a pair was brooding (probably information from an Indian). Eggs of *N. rufipennis* are in oological collections.

Tall virgin forest from Central America to Bolivia, Mato Grosso, Goiás, Minas Gerais, and Espírito Santo north of Rio Doce, the frontier of Amazonian fauna. In southern part of range becomes very scarce as a result of deforestation and disturbance of remaining woodlands. Also called *Jacu-porco, Jacu-queixada, Aracuã-da-mata.* Name *Jacu-taquara,* used for Rufous-capped Motmot, *Baryphthengus ruficapillus,* causes some confusion with *Neomorphus.*

In Amazonia *N. geoffroyi* is replaced by various forms that are very similar both in morphology and ecology:

SCALED GROUND-CUCKOO, *Neomorphus squamiger*
BR
South of lower Amazon; may be considered a geographic race of *N. geoffroyi*.

RED-BILLED GROUND-CUCKOO, *Neomorphus pucheranii*

Upper Amazon. Reported to have reddish bill, reddish bare areas on face.

RUFOUS-WINGED GROUND-CUCKOO, *Neomorphus rufipennis*

Upper Rio Branco northward. All *Neomorphus* appear to replace each other geographically.

Cuculidae Bibliography
See also General Bibliography

Appert, J. M. 1970. *Zool. Jb. Syst.* 97:424–53. [*Cova*, biology]

Ayres, J. M. 1985. *Pap. Avuls. Zool. S. Paulo* 36(14):158. [*Crotophaga major,* association with monkeys]

Davis, D. E. 1940. *Auk* 57:179–218. [*Crotophaga ani,* behavior]

Davis, D. E. 1940. *Auk* 57:472–84. [*Guira guira,* behavior]

Davis, D. E. 1941. *Auk* 58:179–83. [*Crotophaga major,* behavior]

Davis, D. E. 1942. *Quart. Rev. Biol.* 17(2):115–34. [*Crotophaga,* social nesting, phylogeny]

Haverschmidt, F. 1961. *J. Orn.* 102:353–59. [*Tapera,* behavior]

Ihering, H. v. 1914. *Rev. Mus. Paul.* 9:371–410. [Biology, classification]

Köster, F. 1971. *Bonn Zool. Beitr.* 22:4–27. [*Crotophaga ani,* behavior]

Loflin, R. K. 1982. Ani male apparently killed by other anis while attempting to parasitize nest. *Auk* 99(4):787–88.

Loflin, R. K. 1983. Communal behavior of *Crotophaga ani. Dis. Abstracts Int.* 44:5

Makatsch, W. 1955. *Der Brutparasitismus in der Vogelwelt.* Neumann.

Mariño, J.H.F. 1986. Análise da communicação sonora no anu-branco, *Guira guira. II ENAV,* Rio de Janeiro: 221.

Moojen, J. 1942. *Bol. Mus. Nac. Rio de Janeiro, Zool.* 4. [*Crotophaga ani,* feeding]

Morton, E. J., and S. M. Farabaugh. 1979. *Ibis* 121:212–13. [*Tapera,* behavior of young]

Neunteufel, A. 1954. *Orion* 9:45–46. [*Dromococcyx,* parasitism]

Pinto da Fonseca, J. 1922. *Rev. Mus. Paul.* 13:785. [*Tapera,* behavior]

Reichholf, J. 1974. *Bonn. Zool. Beitr.* 25:118–22. [*Crotophaga, Guira,* habitat, flock size]

Reichholf, J. 1982–3. Die Evolution des Brutparasitismus beim Kuckuck, *Cuculus canorus. Verh. Ornith. Ges. Bay.* 23:479–92.

Rodrigues, H. O. 1962. *Rev. Bras. Biol.* 22:371–76 [Nematodes]

Salvador, S. A. 1981. Desarrollo de una nidada comunal de Pirincio, *Guira guira. Hist. Nat.* 2(4):29–31.

Salvador, S. A. 1982. Estudio de parasitismo del Crespin, *Tapera naevia. Hist. Nat.* 2(10):65–70.

Sariego, J.C.L., and L. O. Marcondes Machado. 1985. *Crotophaga ani,* estrategias alimentares em comparação com *Machetornis rixosus XII Cong. Bras. Zool., Campinas:* 281–82.

Sick, H. 1949. In *Festschrift Erwin Stresemann:* 229–39. [*Neomorphus,* breeding]

Sick, H. 1953. *Bonn. Zool. Beitr.* 4(3–4):305–26. [*Tapera, Dromococcyx,* ecology]

Sick, H. 1953. *Rev. Bras. Biol.* 13:145–68. [*Tapera, Dromococcyx, Neomorphus,* behavior]

Sick, H. 1981. *J. Orn.* 122:437–38. [*Tapera,* elimination of pseudosiblings]

Skutch, A. F. 1966. *Wilson Bull.* 78:139–65. [*Piaya, Crotophaga,* ecology]

Vehrencamp, S. L. 1977. Relative fecundity and parental effort in communally nesting anis, *Crotophaga sulcirostris. Science* 197:403–5.

ORDER STRIGIFORMES

FAMILY TYTONIDAE: BARN OWLS (1)

These cosmopolitan owls are more dispersed in hot regions. Numerous fossils exist from the upper Tertiary and Pleistocene (including from Brazil). The oldest known, *Ogygoptynx*, from the North American Paleocene, shows intermediate characteristics between Tytonidae and Strigidae.

Although barn owls are separated from other owls for various reasons, such as structure of the syrinx and position of the legs, they and the Strigidae appear to be monophyletic. *Tyto* could be treated as a tribe or subfamily of the Strigidae. This is corroborated by new biochemical data and by a hybrid produced in captivity between *Tyto* and *Rhinoptynx*, two very different owls although of similar size.

Morphology and Behavior

The Barn Owl, *Tyto alba*, is a slender bird with a long "face" and a heart-shaped facial disk that contrasts with the round ones of other owls. The eyes disappear in a longitudinal slit of feathers when the bird is frightened during the day. For major details on the eyes and ears of the barn owl, see Strigidae, "Morphology . . . ." The legs are long and "knock-kneed." The toes are covered with bristles, and the claw of the middle toe has a comblike structure similar to that of herons and nightjars.

If disturbed, it sways its body sideways. When frightened and unable to flee, it throws itself belly up to face the danger with its powerful claws upraised. Although truly nocturnal, it has been seen to hunt geckos under a hot sun (Haverschmidt 1970).

BARN OWL, *Tyto alba*, Suindara   Fig. 127

37 cm. Unmistakable with slender build and light coloration, underparts and face white (*coruja-branca*, "white owl"). VOICE: a loud cry, *craish*, (*rasga-mortalha*, "shroud-ripper") given frequently in flight and commonly heard at night over cities such as Rio de Janeiro. A snore, just like a human snore, is given during courtship period by a pair dueting, female responding during intervals when male is silent. Similar snoring sound is frequently given by young, which thereby reveal their presence in nest. Also a rhythmic whistling, produced from daily sleeping roost. Also a *tic-tic-tic . . .* in nocturnal flight; this sound is not known through-out entire range of species, but I have noted it in various parts of Brazil and Argentina, and it also occurs in Suriname and in Antilles (Jamaica). It resembles certain noises produced by some bats when hunting on the wing. This *tic* did not figure in Bühler and Epple's survey (1980) which recorded 18 different *Tyto* vocalizations in Germany. When frightened during the day or when it wants to scare something, it hisses loudly and may snap its bill like other owls.

Feeding: Eats small vertebrates: rodents, marsupials, bats, amphibians, reptiles and small birds but usually does not attack pigeons or swallows in nearby nooks. Surveys of bone deposits scattered in caverns of Lagoa Santa, Minas Gerais, considered to originate primarily from remains of *T. alba* pellets or food balls (see also Strigidae, "Feeding"), revealing that 87% were from rats (with *Carterodon sulcidens* in 1st place), 10% from marsupials, 2% from birds, and 1% from bats (Carnevalli 1973). Examinations of stomach contents in Espírito Santo showed more than 90% from rats. In cities such as Rio de Janeiro *T. alba* lives on black rats (*Rattus rattus*), brown rats (*R. norvegicus*), and house mice (*Mus*

Fig. 127. Barn Owl, *Tyto alba*, showing the typical position of the "bandy" legs. Original, Paul Bühler.

musculus), as I have verified in National Museum at Quinta da Boa Vista; pellets from there measured 50 × 34 × 27 mm, sometimes only 35 × 32 × 21 mm. In pellets examined in Espírito Santo the following bats were found, all of them insectivorous: *Molossus rufus* (Molossidae), *Myotis nigricans* (Vespertilionidae), *Tonatia brasiliensis, Lonchoglossa ecaudata* (Phyllostomatidae), and *Peropteryx macrotis* (Emballonuridae). Evidence of *T. alba* taking blood-eating bats is the exception, though they sometimes share caves with them (Pernambuco). J. Moojen found 2 vampires (*Desmodus*) in *T. alba* pellets in Salvador, Bahia. When *T. alba* and vampires (*Desmodus* and *Diphylla*) were put together in a flight cage, the bats attacked the owls, which did not eat the bats (A. Ruschi 1953). Insects (beetles) are not lacking in the diet, and House Sparrows, *Passer domesticus,* are among the birds taken.

At night it skillfully hunts rats near human habitations ("living rat trap"). Although only half the weight of a Great Horned Owl, *Bubo virginianus, T. alba* is said to eat as many or more rodents than this larger bird. It is therefore among the world's most useful birds as measured by economic benefit to people.

Ninety pellets from 2 individuals living in a São Paulo forest revealed seasonal variation in food: in summer (December–February) pellet contents were 90.5% grasshoppers and beetles, 7.2% rodents; in winter (June–August) 89.8% rodents, 7.2% grasshoppers (Motta 1988). This demonstrates abundance of easily caught insects in summer in a subtropical climate.

In protected places such as caves, bones from owl pellets remain preserved for a long time; feathers and hairs, however, are destroyed by insect larvae and rapidly disintegrate. Pellets that fossilized in African caverns reveal that millions of years ago owls ate animals that today are extinct. Much of our knowledge about vertebrates (some already extinct) of the Antilles, for instance, comes from examination of *T. alba* pellets. In central Brazil the rat *Carterodon sulcidens,* described by Lund in 1841, was for a long time known only through remains found in *T. alba* pellets.

Breeding: Eggs are long, oval (unlike those of other owls), pure white, and laid directly on the substrate or in a bed of decomposed pellets. Incubation takes 30–34 days, carried out primarily by female, who is fed by male. According to observations outside Brazil, parents feed young in 2 phases, as do various nocturnal mammals: (1) from dusk to midnight and (2) at dawn. Father hunts and mother feeds young, which may be of quite varied sizes. Larger ones receive whole mice, smaller only small pieces. Grown young may help feed younger siblings, but if there is a food shortage they may devour them. In complete dark hungry chick actively seeks bill of mother, who calls to it. There is no begging (Bühler 1981). Young abandon nest at approximately 2 months of age. Even in temperate climates breeding continues almost all year as long as food is abundant.

Habitat and Distribution: Prefers to nest in attics of old houses, under roof tiles, in church steeples, pigeon roosts, grottoes. Sleeps during day, sometimes in palm trees. Adapted readily to buildings of new capital Brasília, and today lives under roofs of its large apartment complexes. Particularly noticeable in cultivated terrain. In South America as far as Tierra del Fuego, throughout Brazil. Also called *Tuidara* (from Tupi, "what is traditionally not eaten"), *Coruja-católica* [= "Catholic owl"], *Mocho-das-cavernas* (Minas Gerais). Thirteen geographic races are recognized for the Americas, showing how sedentary this owl is after having spread throughout the world over the centuries.

Tytonidae Bibliography

Bühler, P. 1972. *Institut f. leichte Flächentragwerke.* Univ. Stuttgart, Mitt. 4:39–50. [Bone structure]
Bühler, P. 1981. The feeding behavior of the Barn Owl, *Tyto alba. Ökologie Vögel* 3:183–202.
Bühler, P., and W. Epple. 1980. *J. Orn.* 121:37–70. [Vocalization]
Carnevalli, N. E. D. 1973. *SOM* 5:8–9. [Feeding]
Dias, V. S. 1985. *XII Cong. Bras. Zool., Campinas:*581. [Feeding]
Flieg, G. M. 1971. *Auk* 88:178. [*Tyto* x *Rhinoptynx*]
Haverschmidt, F. 1962. *J. Orn.* 103:236–42. [General]
Haverschmidt, F. 1970. Barn owls hunting by daylight in Suriname. *Wilson Bull.* 82:101.
Mones, A., A. Ximenez, and J. Cuello. 1973. *V Cong. Lat. Am. Zool.* 1:166–67. [Pellets]
Motta, J. C., Jr. 1988. Alimentação diferencial da suindara *Tyto alba,* em duas estações do ano em S. Carlos, São Paulo. *An. Sem. Reg. Ecol. S. Paulo* 6:357–64.
Payne, R. S. 1962. *The Living Bird* 1:151–61. [Prey location]
Payne, R. S. 1971. *J. Exp. Biol.* 56:535–73. [Acoustic location of prey]
Ruschi, A. 1953. *Bol. Mus. Biol. Prof. Melo Leitão,* Biol. 13. [Feeding]
Schneider, W. 1964. *Die Schleiereule, Tyto alba.* Wittenberg: Neue Brehmbüch.

FAMILY STRIGIDAE: OWLS (20)

Owls are distributed over all the continents except Antarctica and probably originated in the Old World. There were already owls in the lower Tertiary (Eocene, Protostrigidae) of North America, with the Strigidae represented in the United States since the Tertiary. A Pleistocene specimen has been found in Minas Gerais, and there was a large, flightless owl in the Pleistocene of Cuba.

Similarities with both nightjars and hawks can be interpreted in part as analogous, linked to nocturnal life or hunting methods. See Tytonidae. No relationship with other orders has yet been discovered.

Morphology, Special Adaptations, and Identification

Size varies considerably: a Great Horned Owl, *Bubo virginianus,* weighs 20 times more than a *Glaucidium* pygmy-owl. Plumage is extremely soft. Flight is silent, an adaptation to dusk and nocturnal life made possible by a feather structure (fig. 128) that eliminates even ultrasonic components that could both reveal the owl's presence when it is hunting and interfere with its own acoustic orientation (Thorpe and Griffin 1962). Species with daytime habits, such as the *Glaucidium;* Short-eared Owl, *Asio flammeus;* and fishing owls, *Ketupa* and *Scotopelia,* of Asia and Africa respectively, have a "harder" flight. The same holds true for individuals of nocturnal species whose flight feathers are worn.

The lores have bristles whose bases are surrounded by sensitive cells, probably of taste (Herbst's corpuscles). There is a prominent facial disk of feathers (particularly studied in the Barn Owl, *Tyto alba,* see Tytonidae) which fulfills an important role as a sound reflector. Using a mobility provided by folds in the skin, it amplifies sound volume and helps locate prey by ear. The owl ear appears to act as a radar microphone placed at the focal point of a parabola. The sound is captured by the facial disk (acting as a parabola) and is then sent to the ear—the "microphone" (fig. 129)—whose external opening, due to a movable fleshy fold, is in front of the focal point of the disk, facing backward, like the microphone of a radar (Bühler 1989). As in all birds, the feathers

Fig. 129. Outer ear of the Spectacled Owl, *Pulsatrix perspicillata.* The longest feathers, behind the ear opening, help locate noises, serving as a directional microphone. After Böker 1937.

covering the ear have a peculiar, sparse structure that permits sound penetration. The asymmetry of the external ears, another special feature of owls, apparently aids in focusing. The left side focuses downward, the right side upward. Another asymmetry exists, that of the syrinx. The great width of the skull of owls also evolved as a function of their highly developed hearing. The ear tufts that are typical of certain owls and lacking in others have no connection whatsoever with their true ears.

The internal ear, or labyrinth, of owls is highly developed. Some owls, among them *Tyto alba,* can catch a live rat in absolute darkness, guided only by sound (Payne 1971). An infrared film has revealed that *T. alba* even closes its eyes at the instant it catches a mouse. A Tengmalm's Owl, *Aegolius funereus,* of Europe, is reported to have found a small rat at a distance of 48 m in open forest (Kuhk 1966). Owls locate a moving animal by using only part of the ample spectrum of frequencies making up the noise produced, and their ability to perceive extremely weak sounds is perhaps even more important than hearing high frequencies (Konishi 1973). *T. alba* is said to react especially to frequencies between 3000 and 9000 Hz. The capability of the owl ear appears to us as miraculous as the capability of the nose of macrosomatic mammals such as dogs. New research is attempting to show that owl hearing is similar to that of humans (Martin 1986).

It is remarkable how owls discern which of the multitude of sounds are the ones of vital interest to them, such as the faint rustle of a mouse walking on the ground. Certain species in addition to *T. alba,* such as the Rusty-barred Owl, *Strix hylophila;* Striped Owl, *Rhinoptynx clamator;* and Stygian Owl, *Asio stygius,* are reputed to have the best hearing. The facial disk is not well developed in the Ferruginous Pygmy-Owl, *Glaucidium brasilianum,* which hunts by day. It is interesting to note that there are hints of facial disks in crepuscular hawks, such as *Micrastur,* and in species, such

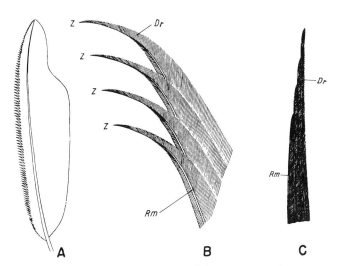

Fig. 128. Edge of the outer vane of the outermost primary of: (A and B) Tengmalm's Owl, *Aegolius funereus,* and (C) White-throated Needletail, *Hirundapus caudacutus.* The "teeth" (Z) of the owl feather, amplified in (B), reduce or eliminate flight noise. Dr = distal barbules; Rm = barb. After Sick 1937.

as *Circus,* that hunt like *T. alba* by flying low over cane, grass, and marsh.

Owls have large, farsighted, almost immobile eyes which are telescopic in shape (unlike those of hawks), resulting in a very limited visual field, a disadvantage compensated for by the extreme mobility of the head, which has a 270° action radius. Their sight is not inferior to their hearing. At night the pupil opens, permitting all available light to enter. This happens at death, when it is barely possible to record the iris color. The opposite occurs during the day or when the bird is disturbed, the iris closing and the pupil diminishing to a pinpoint. Owls see well in daylight. Iris color is often important for identifying species, although it is hard to observe in the dark, at least for humans. There is more intraspecific variation in eye color than was previously thought. Even siblings may have completely different eye color (see below under *Otus,* Oliveira 1984). Unlike nightjars' eyes, the eyes of most of our owls do not reflect when a strong light is focused on them.

When looking at something attentively, owls move the head laterally, which must assist in adjusting for parallax. Nervousness is manifested by a rapid lowering and raising of the upper eyelid; a relaxed owl closes its eye by slowly drawing the lower eyelid upward, like most birds.

The outer toe (fourth) can voluntarily be turned backward to reinforce the hallux in securing prey (fig. 130), for the axis of the prey is directed forward, not crosswise, in relation to the hunter's body (see Osprey, *Pandion haliaetus*). Owls, unlike hawks, have intestinal diverticula, each comparable to a cecum, producing a different type of black, fetid feces. They do not have a crop.

Highly cryptic plumage, similar to that of nightjars and potoos, hides owls during their daytime roosting, a vital function that causes the color and pattern of most species to

be much alike and makes identification by external characters more difficult. There is much individual variation, so it is unusual to find two similar-appearing individuals in the same area. Many owls have a ferruginous color variation, or phase, perhaps brought about by ecological conditions (adaptation to the environment or effect of humidity). Sometimes the rusty color is dominant only on the upper- or underside of the body. Museum skins become reddish with age. Very fresh specimens may have a pinkish fluorescence under the wings, produced by porphyrins (e.g., Tropical Screech-Owl, *Otus choliba,* and *Asio flammeus*). Molt of tail feathers may be almost simultaneous, as in the Burrowing Owl, *Speotyto cunicularia.* A curious color pattern or a face on the back of the head is a feature of the *Glaucidium.* The American Kestrel, *Falco sparverius,* shows a similar design.

Sexes are similar, the female sometimes larger. A special feature of owls is replacement of natal down by a second generation of plumes, similar to fleece, which is still in place when the nestling fledges. These feathers cover the body when the flight and tail feathers already resemble definitive plumage and enable the bird to fly. In *Pulsatrix* and *Lophostrix* the down is yellowish or whitish, making a showy contrast with the black facial disk.

There are Brazilian bats larger than *Otus* species that can be mistaken for owls in the forest. A bat flight-silhouette is distinguished by lack of a tail, which is substituted by the feet outstretched behind. The leaf-nosed bat (*Phyllostomus hastatus*), a carnivorous species (it even eats birds) that occurs almost throughout Brazil, has a wingspan almost equal to that of an *Otus* or even greater (65 cm). However, bats fly faster than owls or nightjars.

Vocalization

It is an error to assume, because of our own difficulty seeing in the dark, that acoustic communication, either intra- or interspecific, is more important for nightbirds such as owls and nightjars than it is for diurnal birds. The "song" of owls, given frequently or exclusively during breeding, is for us the best means of specific identification. However, it is not easy to convey how a voice sounds by describing it in words.

First we must get to know the symphony of rich Neotropical fauna that are active at dawn, dusk, and during the night, for the voices of certain owls (e.g., *Otus*) and nightjars may sound similar to those of amphibians. In Espírito Santo I heard the very loud voice (audible 500 m away from the forest) of the tree frog *Phrynohyas (Hyla) mesophaena,* living in arboreal bromeliads in the canopy of virgin forest, singing at twilight. Mammals may also contribute to the confusion of the crepuscular and nocturnal chorus, as I learned in central Brazil, where the bellow of the Ke-re-ruá (Kamaiurá, Mato Grosso), or porcupine rat (*Echimys armatus*), an arboreal animal that lives in riverine forests, may be taken for the voice of a large owl. The same can occur north of the Amazon (Rio Trombetas) with another nocturnal

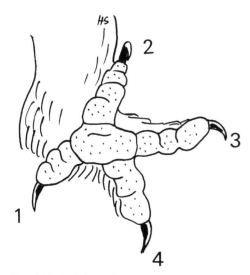

Fig. 130. Left foot of Great Horned Owl, *Bubo virginianus,* at the moment of catching prey. Note the radial placement of the toes. Original, H. Sick.

porcupine rat (*Dactylomys dactylinus canescens*), whose cry is a bisyllabic *kórro-kórro*. Another surprise in Amazonia is the deep *hoot-oot* of the nocturnal monkey, *Aotus* sp., which resembles a toy automobile horn and could be attributed to an owl. Alexander von Humboldt, who described this little monkey, noted how noisy the nighttime tropical jungle is in contrast to the quasi-silence reigning during the day. There are similar problems with identification of rail voices.

I concentrate here on owl vocalizations that correspond to song in other birds. Among the very similar *Otus*, voice becomes a deciding factor in classification.

Both sexes sing. Pairs of various species, such as *Strix hylophila*, sing a duet or dialogue, their phrases differing somewhat according to sex. That of the female may be a bit different, higher and hoarser in *Otus, Bubo, Pulsatrix,* and *Glaucidium brasilianum*, for example. Two neighboring males may carry out an intense conversation (*Otus*). The higher voice of the female (who is heavier than the male) is explained by the female's smaller syrinx (Miller 1934). They do not open their bills when they call. In southeastern Brazil, singing activity is great in August and September, but the weather must be hot and calm. The "rattle" of the young *Speotyto cunicularia* is a peculiar vocalization. *Glaucidium* young utter a *zisi, si, si* resembling the alarm of the Sharp-tailed Streamcreeper, *Lochmias nematura* (Furnariidae). All owls, including the young, snap their bills.

A better understanding of owl vocalization is going to reveal the existence of as yet undescribed species, in the *Glaucidium* genus, for example.

Feeding

Insects (grasshoppers, beetles, cockroaches, etc.) usually predominate in the diet of Brazilian species, with even a large owl such as a *Pulsatrix* being mostly insectivorous. Droppings around the entrance to the gallery leading to the nest of *Speotyto cunicularia* attract beetles (Scarabaeidae) which serve as food for the owl. Large and more powerful species catch rodents, marsupials (opossums), bats (including vampires, recorded as food of *Rhinoptynx clamator*), lizards, and frogs. *Pulsatrix* and *Asio stygius* also hunt bats.

Ecologically, successful hunting for forest rats implies sparse vegetation on the forest floor, so the ground is exposed. *Glaucidium brasilianum* sometimes carries a bird (perhaps a House Sparrow, *Passer domesticus*) into the dense foliage where it eats the head and abandons the rest, which hangs there rotting. I know the European *Glaucidium* (which lives in a moderate climate with a rigorous winter) is much given to storing food such as small rats, depositing them on a limb for later use. *G. brasilianum* has perfected a tactic of using its "occipital face" when hunting. *Speotyto cunicularia* may raid Spotted Tinamou, *Nothura maculosa*, nests and occasionally eats scorpions. When army ants are active at night, owls such as the *Otus* harvest the animals they frighten up.

As in hawks, individual specializations may obscure interspecific differences. The Spectacled Owl, *Pulsatrix perspicillata*, for example, learns to feed on crabs at the river edge (Guyana); *Bubo virginianus* occasionally catches chickens on their roosts, and *Glaucidium* do not hesitate to snatch a pet bird out of its cage in full daylight. In central Brazil the large owls frequent salt banks to hunt (see Psittaciformes, "Feeding"). The daily ration of *B. virginianus* is reported to amount to approximately 10% of its own weight.

Hunting activity of nocturnal species is greatest at dusk and during the early night hours until approximately 9 P.M. However, there must be some modification of this schedule when moonlight improves visibility and creates shadows. As explained under "Morphology," owl orientation is usually more acoustic than visual, unlike that of nightjars.

A sated, captive *Speotyto cunicularia* forced a passing mouse to take refuge in a burrow from which it later recovered the tasty morsel.

When the stomach of a diurnal owl is examined it is usually empty. This makes all the more important owl diet surveys conducted by examining regurgitated pellets or balls, which contain skulls, etc., of mammals (sometimes of great interest for recording rare species of wild rodents); bills, feet, and claws of birds; and the chitinous parts of arthropods. In Europe even bones of shrews, minuscule mammals having a total length of 71 mm (Vogel 1970; see also Trochilidae, footnote 1), have been identified. These skulls are often found broken, but the teeth (a maxillar dental series scarcely measures 6 mm) are conclusive. It is remarkable how the digestive juices of owls strip the most delicate bones of flesh and tendons. Hair, feathers, and scales remain unaltered. Vegetable material in pellets comes from the intestinal contents of the rodents eaten. Pellets vary according to the species of owl and its diet; those of *Tyto alba* are more compact than those of other owls. Eating a number of small animals produces larger and more numerous pellets than eating one large animal. It is reported that *Bubo virginianus* pellets, although formed in the stomach in 8 to 10 hours (observed by X ray), are expelled only after 16 hours. They may measure 45 × 25 mm. Pellets are found below daytime roosts and around nests.

The gastric juice of hawks, in contrast, does digest bony material. Unlike hawks, owls often devour their prey intact without cleaning it. When preparing a bird, owls customarily cut off and do not swallow the bill and feet. When pellets are examined for several consecutive years, periodic cycles of noxious rodents may be revealed (Wendland 1975).

Behavior

Nocturnal habits are rare in birds, attributable to less than 5% of the class. *Speotyto cunicularia* and *Asio flammeus* are diurnal. The *Glaucidium* are also to some extent. Most owls are crepuscular, like nightjars. In absolute dark only the Oilbird, *Steatornis caripensis,* and the *Collocalia* swifts of

Asia move about. Both have evolved echolocation. There are records of *Otus choliba* taking advantage of artificial light to hunt beetles.

Owls like to bathe in rain. *S. cunicularia* takes dust baths and runs rapidly on the ground. Re other behavior, see other subtitles, such as "Feeding" and "Breeding."

Breeding

Owls breed in the abandoned nests of other birds. *Rhinoptynx clamator* and *Bubo virginianus* sometimes lay in grass on the ground. *Otus choliba*, the *Ciccaba*, and the *Glaucidium* nest in hollow trees and the latter also in woodpecker holes. In the cerrado *Otus choliba* may occupy an arboreal termite nest opened by parakeets. When trees are lacking, *G. brasilianum* may occupy a hole in a terrestrial termite nest (Pantanal, Mato Grosso); in Argentina it was even found to lay eggs in a Rufous Hornero, *Furnarius rufus*, nest. *Speotyto cunicularia* installs itself in holes in the ground, being attracted by armadillo burrows and by holes in the base of terrestrial termite nests which the pair, taking turns, widens. They excavate a wide, more or less horizontal, gallery using both their feet and, to a lesser extent, their bills. They line the nesting cavity with manure or dry grass. *Asio flammeus* constructs its nest on the ground, taking advantage primarily of the grass growing around the chosen spot. Its nest resembles that of the Long-winged Harrier, *Circus buffoni*, which may be its neighbor.

Eggs, frequently three, are almost round, sometimes oval; the form varies a great deal, even within a clutch (*Speotyto cunicularia*). They are pure white, although those of *S. cunicularia*, when fresh, are slightly pinkish. Incubation in this species is 23 to 24 days, that of *Asio flammeus* 27 to 28 days, and that of *Bubo virginianus* 28 days. The female usually begins to brood after laying the first egg, resulting in different hatching dates and quite diverse sizes in the young—differences that are still evident when they fledge at three to five weeks. On plumage of nestlings, see "Morphology."

Distribution and Habitat

Six of the 11 genera occurring in Brazil (*Otus*, *Bubo*, *Glaucidium*, *Ciccaba*, *Strix*, and *Asio*) are also found outside the Americas; *Asio flammeus* is a cosmopolitan species. Of the remaining five American genera, four (*Lophostrix*, *Pulsatrix*, *Rhinoptynx*, and *Aegolius*) are Neotropical and one (*Speotyto*) ranges from Tierra del Fuego to Canada. *Lophostrix* appears to be related to *Pulsatrix* and to the African genus *Jubula*. *Ciccaba* might be considered Neotropical, but it includes a widely distributed African species.

Certain species such as *Otus choliba* and *Rhinoptynx clamator* also live in cities wherever there are sufficient trees (e.g., certain districts of Rio de Janeiro). *Speotyto cunicularia*, a savanna species, profits from deforestation.

Parasites

Owls, like certain other birds (e.g., Cracidae), suffer from nematodes that live under the nictitating membrane of the eye, as I found in central Brazil. For example, *Oxyspirura brevisubulata* was discovered in *Otus choliba*. Louse flies (Hippoboscidae) also occur, as for instance, *Olfersia nigra* on *Rhinoptynx clamator* and *Tyto alba*, and *Olfersia fusca* on *Glaucidium brasilianum* (Rio de Janeiro). I found *Lynchia americana* on *Speotyto cunicularia* (Mato Grosso).

Reaction of Other Birds to Owls

Discovery of an owl in its daytime hideout irritates certain birds, especially Passerines, whose warning cries attract neighbors and reveal the presence of the owl to all, including people. Only certain bird species fuss about owls, among them hummingbirds and small hawks, such as the Roadside Hawk, *Rupornis magnirostris*, which manages to catch them, as they are easy prey during the day. When birds begin to mob it, an owl endures it for a while with indifference but finally leaves to seek another hideout. Some birds are also alarmed by owl vocalizations such as that of *Glaucidium brasilianum*, a notorious bird hunter. An imitation of a *Glaucidium* voice can be used to test whether this owl lives in a certain area. If it does not, other birds ignore the imitated voice. For centuries hunters on various continents have attracted birds by exposing a tame, tied owl or by imitating owl hoots.

Conservation, Folklore, and Accidents

Owls merit our full protection. All of them benefit people by their incessant destruction of insects and rodents. This is a case where I do not hesitate to emphasize the utilitarian viewpoint. We have to fight the bias against these birds: defamatory, baseless rumors brought in part from Europe, where they also lack any foundation. Such lies generate and spread antipathy to these most interesting creatures whose nocturnal lives render them mysterious and feared, giving them fame as harbingers of ill fortune. It is a sign of a backward mentality to speak of the *agoureiros*, "foreboding calls," of owls. The great poet J. Guimarães Rosa stated, "The owl does not augur evil: he just knows the secrets of the night." Indians revere owls, and backwoodspeople attribute to the pygmy-owl the power of bringing good luck. The curious occipital face of pygmy-owls is interpreted by Indians as meaning that they have four eyes and can thus quickly detect any danger. People with night duties speak of "owling." For the ancient Greeks, owls were the symbol of wisdom because of their large eyes.

With greater traffic on highways, certain owls such as *Speotyto cunicularia*, *Asia flammeus*, *Rhinoptynx clamator*, and *Tyto alba* are in increasing danger of being run over (see also Caprimulgidae, "Behavior").

The Screech-Owls, Genus Otus

[Translator's note: Since the author's death the *Otus* genus has been further elucidated by Marshall et al. (1991). Because of Sick's particular interest in this subject and his correspondence with the authors relating to it, I draw attention to their paper. I have used the English names they use, but in downgrading *guatemalae* to subspecific status, as Sick chose not to do, they have assigned its English name, Vermiculated Screech-Owl, to another species. I have therefore resuscitated Protean Screech-Owl, a name they discarded, to provide an English designation for Sick's *O. guatemalae*.]

Five species of *Otus* screech-owls have been recorded for Brazil. Separating them on the basis of morphology is difficult, but it is usually possible through vocalization.

1. *Morphology:* When looking at these small owls in the field at night close up with a bright light, it is almost impossible to recognize the species. The same applies for daytime observation.

Size differences are minor, and the measurements of different species may overlap. Only the extremes are clear: the Tawny-bellied Screech-Owl, *O. watsonii*, of Amazonia is "small," and the Long-tufted Screech-Owl, *O. sanctaecatarinae*, of the southeast is "large." The others are intermediate. An ordinary *O. choliba* may be near the size of *O. watsonii;* the Variable Screech-Owl, *O. atricapillus;* or Protean Screech-Owl, *O. guatemalae. O. atricapillus* is not far from *sanctaecatarinae*. In museum collections a *sanctaecatarinae* may appear enormous alongside the others. The real size difference can be well recognized without measuring by comparing the feet and bills of these specimens. Sexual dimorphism (female larger is the general rule with owls) is little pronounced in *Otus*. Collected specimens need to be weighed with a Swiss Pesola scale.

Iris color is an important diagnostic character. The basic difference is between a light yellow iris and a dark brown one. This feature, however, is not entirely reliable. *O. choliba* siblings have been found, one with yellow iris, the other with brown. I have collected a *sanctaecatarinae* in Rio Grande do Sul with a brown iris, but the typical color for this species is yellow. Two hours after death the iris has shrunk and become invisible. Iris color may be linked to plumage phase (see below): a dark brown iris in the dark phase, a yellow iris in the red phase (Marshall pers. comm.)

Describing plumage to differentiate the species enters into details that cannot be provided here. Tremendous variation exists which must be shown in illustrations. No two individuals are alike. There is also polymorphism, as in most owls and nightjars, with gray and red phases, ("phases" being used in the sense of the permanent color of an individual's plumage). It is also important whether the plumage is fresh or worn, depending on the breeding period. Immatures may be slightly different.

The following difference exists in the pattern of the remiges: In *O. choliba* the inner vanes of the primaries show wide, light bars, whereas in *O. atricapillus* they are almost uniformly dark. The inner vane of the primaries of *O. sanctaecatarinae* is almost as dark as that of *atricapillus* (fig. 131).

One must also consider whether hybridization occurs, which should be expected when geographic races are under consideration. Plumages fade in museums. Every effort to clarify *Otus* systematics based on plumage only has failed, and some have even contributed to the confusion. *Otus* relationships are a very difficult taxonomic problem in which definitive answers can be expected only by using modern methodology: recording voices of individuals that are subsequently collected and genetic research. As *Otus* are locally common, limited collecting for such studies does not adversely affect the species.

2. *Vocalization:* Territorial songs of Brazilian *Otus* usually indicate the specific identification of individuals (although geographic variation does exist). Doubt may arise in cases of *atricapillus/guatemalae* and *atricapillus/sanctaecatarinae*. The size of the individual has an influence, with large ones louder and lower (see *sanctaecatarinae/atricapillus*). The voice of the female (who vocalizes less) is a little higher (see "Vocalization"), except in *sanctaecatarinae*, whose female has an extraordinary gargle. The *Otus* sing on hot nights with absolutely no wind, more in September in southeastern Brazil. Beyond territorial song, dealt with here extensively, there are other vocalizations.

3. *Distribution and Ecology:* There is a tendency for the various forms of *Otus* to replace one another geographically. This has led to the decision to "downgrade" certain species to geographic races. Thus, *guatemalae* may be considered only subspecifically different from *atricapillus*. I have no evidence of *atricapillus* existing alongside *sanctaecatarinae* in Rio Grande do Sul.

Comparative ecological studies are still lacking to define the habitats of the various species and geographic representatives. König (1989) provided some data of this type. The perfect adaptation of plumage color and design to the appearance of bark and branches of owls' daytime roosts is one of the most remarkable examples of cryptic evolution.

Marshall (1989 pers. comm.), the premier authority in the difficult field of *Otus* species throughout the world, separates the large *O. sanctaecatarinae* from the smaller *O. atricapillus* as valid species and believes *O. guatemalae* to be a geographic race of *atricapillus*, since he recognizes hybridization of the latter two in Bolivia. He states that there is no hybridization between *O. sanctaecatarinae* and *O. atricapillus* in Paraguay and Misiones, Argentina. I prefer to treat the Brazilian species of the *O. atricapillus* complex as allospecies that constitute the superspecies *atricapillus*. Allopatric distribution appears evident. There is no proof of hybridization, and to prove such crossing would be difficult.

Fig. 131. Lower side of the fifth primary of (a) Tropical Screech-Owl, *Otus choliba;* (b) Black-capped Screech-Owl, *Otus atricapillus;* and (c) Long-tufted Screech-Owl, *Otus sanctaecatarinae.* Actual size. Drawings by F. Pontual.

A   **B**   **C**

TROPICAL SCREECH-OWL, *Otus choliba,* Corujinha-do-mato   PL 18.2

22 cm; wingspan 54 cm; wing 160–73 mm; 97–134 g. Usually most common species, with short ear tufts difficult to see in twilight. Iris yellow with exceptions (see "The Screech-Owls . . ."). VOICE: song an accelerating, ascending sequence, *gur-go-go-go-go* or *gurrrrrkooKOO; ke-ke-ke, queea, guaa,* etc. Forest edge, cerrado, orchards, cities, where it occasionally hunts large insects attracted by street lights. Costa Rica to Bolivia, Paraguay, Argentina, throughout Brazil. Also called *Corujinha-orelhuda, Pirê-cuí* (Kajabi, Mato Grosso). Occurs alongside *O. atricapillus* and *O. sanctaecatarinae.*

VARIABLE SCREECH-OWL, *Otus atricapillus,* Corujinha-sapo

24 cm; wing 176–86 mm; 114–23.8 g. Top of head black (with slight, very fine, ferruginous pattern), well differentiated from lighter back with abundant ferruginous pattern. Long ear tufts with outer vein all black. Iris color varies: dark brown in dark phase (typical), dark yellow or yellowish brown in red phase. VOICE: an absolutely horizontal and homogeneous, smooth, melodious phrase (fig. 132), at a distance sounding like a tremolo, *rrrrrroo* (close up sounds like *oooo* . . .), with or without a crescendo, last note lower and end abrupt. This may resemble croaking of marine toad (*Bufo marinus ictericus*). Phrases may last 5–14 seconds. When irritated by playback, bird produces longer phrases with rougher notes, approaching timbre of female's voice, the *oo* turning to an *ah*. Under such circumstances voice approximates *sanctaecatarinae.* To be certain the population in question is really *atricapillus* and not *sanctaecatarinae,* it is useful to listen for the distinctive voice of the *sanctaecatarinae* female.

My finding of *O. atricapillus* on Fazenda Barreiro Rico, property of J. C. de Magalhães, Anhembi, São Paulo, in November 1969 in a good semideciduous forest at 560 m, reopened the study of this species, which was only known until then through a few museum specimens not connected with its voice (then unknown). Meanwhile, Magalhães made excellent recordings of the species, which is common there. They proved that *atricapillus* is not synonymous with the

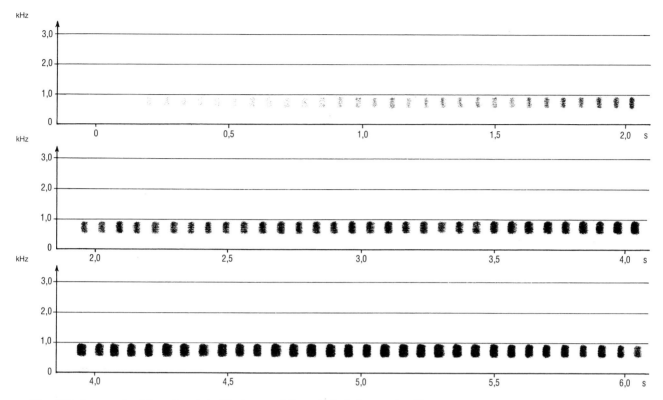

Fig. 132. Sonagraph of the voice of the Black-capped Screech-Owl, *Otus atricapillus*.

larger *sanctaecatarinae*. Indications on the ranges of the 2 species need to be reviewed. Apparently *atricapillus* also occurs in Misiones, Argentina (Straneck, in König 1989) and Paraguay (Foster, Marshall pers. comm.). I found 4 *atricapillus* specimens from São Paulo in the São Paulo Museum. Vocalization of *atricapillus* is very similar to *guatemalae* and also to *Otus hoyi* König 1989 from northern Argentina.

PROTEAN SCREECH-OWL, *Otus guatemalae*

Voice similar to *O. atricapillus*. Only in extreme north of Brazil. Reported from Roraima and Venezuela and from other countries, but proof lacking. See introduction to *Otus*. Probably a race of *atricapillus*.

LONG-TUFTED SCREECH-OWL, *Otus sanctaecatarinae*

Wing 180–202 mm; 155–211 g. Largest southern species, confused until recently with *O. guatemalae*. The situation has been clarified by W. Belton's collections and recordings in Rio Grande do Sul from 1970–79. Long, broad ear tufts; iris yellow (typical), orange-yellow, or brown. VOICE: a trill similar to *guatemalae* but louder (not always noticed because bird is larger), slower, shorter. May be slightly ascending or descending (fluctuations I have not noticed in *atricapillus*) and may move to rougher notes. Female produces a loud, low, hoarse *bababa . . . ,* completely unlike voices of other Brazilian *Otus*. Belton (1984) found it to be quite common in

forests of Rio Grande do Sul, sometimes alongside *choliba*. Apparently does not occur with *atricapillus* (my own observation). National Museum in Rio de Janeiro has specimens from Santa Catarina (Snethlage 1928), Paraná (1948), Uruguay (Arroyo La Mina, near Brazilian border, 1969). I found 1 specimen from Santa Catarina and 1 from Paraná in the São Paulo Museum.

TAWNY-BELLIED SCREECH-OWL, *Otus watsonii*

22 cm; wing 167–68 mm; 115 g. Small, long, wide ear tufts with outer vanes and tips black; iris chestnut, or exceptionally, yellow. In central Brazil (Mato Grosso) a ferruginous phase is often found. VOICE: low and full, song beginning with long, horizontal notes, then passing to faster, descending notes and ending with low trill (*O. w. ustus*); voice quite unlike other Brazilian *Otus*. Interior of Amazonian forests (upper Xingu); anajá palm groves in forest (Rio das Mortes, Mato Grosso). Venezuela to Bolivia, Mato Grosso, Pará, Amapá. Also called *Urukú-reá* (Kajabi, Mato Grosso), *Koro-koeá* (Kamaiurá, Mato Grosso), *Ko-ko-koi* (Juruna, Mato Grosso), *Bu-bu* (Waura, Mato Grosso).

CRESTED OWL, *Lophostrix cristata*, Coruja-de-carapuça

39.5 cm. Unique with long, soft ear tufts whose partly white coloring rises out of a facial V that is also white. Underparts finely vermiculated. In juvenile plumage of white down, black facial disk similar to *Pulsatrix perspicillata* but has ear tufts. VOICE: a low, descending *rrrroo*. Forest canopies. Venezuela to Bolivia, northern Mato Grosso, Pará.

GREAT HORNED OWL, *Bubo virginianus*, Corujão-orelhudo, Jacurutu

52 cm; over 1 kg. Continent's largest owl, size of a Crested Caracara, *Polyborus plancus,* but appearing larger. Ear tufts wide, erect, always visible. Underparts densely barred brown and whitish, throat pure white. VOICE: a deep song of 4–5 equal syllables, 2d or 3d accentuated, with a typical interval after 4th: *oo oo OO oooo oooo*. Phrases are sometimes only 2–3 syllables. Male and female voices similar but female's higher. Forest edge, groves and savanna, usually near water. Forms pellets (see "Feeding"). North America to Tierra del Fuego, locally in Amazonia, central western Brazil (e.g., southern Mato Grosso, where not rare), northeast, east. Also called *Mocho-orelhudo*.

SPECTACLED OWL, *Pulsatrix perspicillata*, Murucututu

48 cm. Large, without ear tufts, face with pure white design (unlike *P. koeniswaldiana*), breast with brown band, belly uniformly white or yellow. Iris orange or yellow. Nestling has white down and black facial disk. VOICE: a descending sequence of ventriloquial *ko-ko-kos* . . . , accelerated and weaker at end, well symbolized by name *murucututu*. Tall forest. Mexico to Bolivia, Paraguay, Argentina; probably throughout Brazil, not rare in Amazonia. In south apparently sometimes replaces *koeniswaldiana* in hot lowlands. Also called *Corujão, Mocho-mateiro*. See *P. koeniswaldiana* and *Lophostrix*.

TAWNY-BROWED OWL, *Pulsatrix koeniswaldiana*, Murucututu-de-barriga-amarela   PL 18.3[1]

44 cm. Similar to *P. perspicillata* but smaller, especially bill and feet. Face with wide yellowish superciliary, belly yellow with faint cinnamon bars. Iris chestnut. Young similar to that of *P. perspicillata*. VOICE: a low phrase, very similar to and with timbre of *perspicillata: brrr BRRR brrr brrr* or *oot OOT oot oot oot*. Female responds promptly in a higher pitch. Tall forest. Typical of southeast, mountains of Espírito Santo, Rio de Janeiro, ex-Guanabara, and Minas Gerais to Paraná, Paraguay, Argentina (Misiones).

LEAST PYGMY-OWL, *Glaucidium minutissimum*, Caburé-miudinho

14 cm. Scarcely the size of *Passer domesticus*. Similar to *G. brasilianum* but with crown speckled (not streaked) with white. Tail with 3–4 (not 6–8) light bands. VOICE: a bi- or trisyllabic *ooo-ooo, ooo-ooo-ooo,* sometimes more syllables, descending, with timbre and force similar to notes of an *Otus;* entirely unlike *brasilianum,* which may occur in same area. Forests, very local in occurrence. Mexico to Paraguay, Mato Grosso, Goiás, Minas Gerais, Rio de Janeiro, Espírito Santo.

AMAZONIAN PYGMY-OWL, *Glaucidium hardyi*, Caburé-da-Amazônia

Similar to *G. minutissimum* but with shorter tail (up to 52 mm) and completely different vocalization: a monotonous staccato. Canopy. Amazonia, northeastern Atlantic forests (Vielliard 1989).

FERRUGINOUS PYGMY-OWL, *Glaucidium brasilianum*, Caburé   PL 18.5

16.5 cm; wingspan 31 cm. Genus includes smallest Strigidae; the 63-g average weight of *G. brasilianum* is less than half that of one of our *Otus*. Male clearly smaller than female. Head and eyes small compared with those of other owls (except *Asio flammeus*). Nape has 2 black spots resembling eyes, sometimes outlined by a large, white "superciliary," forming occipital face (see below). There is a rusty phase in which tail usually does not have light bands. VOICE: a horizontal sequence of 10 or more monotonous notes in a slower or faster rhythm, *tuh-tuh-tuh* . . . , *wit, wit, wit,* sometimes followed by harsh syllables such as *churroop-churroop, turr, turr, turr*. Female's voice quite a bit higher. Frequently sings during day, perched in an open place, defying surrounding birdlife.

Occipital Face: False, occipital face is more showy than real one, which does not stand out from mottled plumage; this species can completely fool either a bird or person. An approaching bird probably tries to avoid the frightening occipital face by moving in toward the front, thinking to surprise its enemy from behind when in reality it is going directly into the "lion's mouth." At this instant the owl pounces in flight and captures the most daring. I have had a chance in the field to confirm the highly disturbing effect of the occipital face of this owl. The fact that the occipital face becomes visible only when the bird ruffles its feathers is the reason this pattern is not usually noted in museum specimens, in which the plumage is smoothed.

Feeding and Behavior: Catches birds such as *Passer domesticus,* sanhaçu tangers, and occasionally hummingbirds, eating head of prey first. Although bravery of this owl is exaggerated, attacks on birds twice its size have been witnessed. For example, a Northern Pygmy-Owl, *G. gnoma,* captured a California Quail, *Callipepla californica,* in U.S. Catches frogs, geckos, and even small snakes on ground during brightest and hottest hours of day under full tropical

---

[1]The individual painted by P. Barruel, which was loaned to the artist by the Paris Museum (and not seen by the author), is not very typical. Pay more attention to the text.

Fig. 133. Burrowing Owl, *Speotyto cunicularia grallaria.*

sun. Whispering flight is swift and agile, recalling a miniscule hawk. Nervousness is reflected in tail movements upward and sideways. Active day and night. Forest edges,
cerrado, tree plantings. Arizona and Mexico to Argentina,
northern Chile, throughout Brazil. Also called *Caburé-do-
sol.* See *G. minutissimum.*

BURROWING OWL, *Speotyto cunicularia,*
Buraqueira, Coruja-de-campo   Fig. 133

23 cm. Unmistakable. Small, long-legged, terrestrial owl,
diurnal in habits. Plumage frequently has earth-colored, reddish traces. VOICE: Multiple vocalizations, especially a loud,
harsh cry resembling voice of Yellow-headed Caracara,
Milvago chimachima, to which it adds strident *kit-kit*s.
Young threaten intruders with a rattle quite similar to that of a
rattlesnake, something that, coming from inside a burrow,
might truly frighten a hunter or woodsman (aggressive sound
mimicry); also snorts. Perches erect, unlike nightjars, on
termite nests, stakes, wires, including along roadsides, bowing continuously and moving head sideways. Hovers like
American Kestrel, *Falco sparverius.* Apparently also hunts
at night. An individual may occupy various burrows, running
from one to the other. Takes refuge in its burrow when a
larger predator appears. Attacked during day by Fork-tailed
Flycatcher, *Tyrannus savana,* as if it were a hawk. Savannas,
pastures, restingas. Expanding because of forest destruction.
Occupies bare hills in cities such as Rio de Janeiro and is
colonizing extensive open areas of Brasília. Individuals

killed on highways can give an idea of local abundance.
Canada to Tierra del Fuego, including almost all of Brazil,
where it is locally common.

BLACK-BANDED OWL, *Ciccaba huhula,* Coruja-preta

35 cm. Lacks ear tufts. Black, finely barred all over with
white; bill and feet yellow. VOICE: a loud phrase, *et-et-et-
kwayya.* Locally in tall forest, araucarias in south. Venezuela
to Paraguay, Argentina, Amazonia, the northeast, Minas
Gerais, Rio de Janeiro, Santa Catarina, Mato Grosso. Also
called *Mocho-negro.*

MOTTLED OWL, *Ciccaba virgata,* Coruja-do-mato

34 cm. Lacks ear tufts, underparts clearly streaked. Tall forest. Venezuela to Bolivia, Argentina, Amazonia (where more
common), Espírito Santo, Rio Grande do Sul. *C. borelliana*
occurs in south. See *Rhinoptynx clamator.* Also called *Mocho-
carijó.*

RUSTY-BARRED OWL, *Strix hylophila,*
Coruja-listrada   PL 18.1

35 cm. Unmistakable with distinct, blackish brown streaks
on underparts. VOICE: a low *rrrrroh;* a rhythmic, descending
sequence, *goo goo goo goo goo oo, oo, oo, oo,* with timbre
of Dusky-legged Guan, *Penelope obscura.* Duets occur; also
a prolonged cry, *i-ew-eh.* Forest edge. Common in mountains
of southeast. Rio de Janeiro and Minas Gerais to Rio Grande
do Sul, Paraguay, Argentina.

STRIPED OWL, *Rhinoptynx clamator,*
Coruja orelhuda   PL 18.4

37 cm. Relatively large with prominent ear tufts and contrasting, longitudinal color pattern. VOICE: varied; a prolonged
sequence of *out-out-out*s . . . unlike voice of any other Brazilian owl; loud cries, *ee-i, kyehh-ehh;* other vocalizations.
Pellets with bones of large rodents and of bats, including
skulls of vampire bat *Desmodus rotundus,* have been found
(Serra do Timóteo, Pernambuco, Galileu Coelho). Relatively
common in open areas with groves, cerrado, caatinga, even
in cities (e.g., Rio de Janeiro, in Laranjeiras). Venezuela to
Bolivia, Paraguay, Argentina, Uruguay, throughout Brazil,
except forested areas of Amazonia. Also called *Coruja-gato*
(Pernambuco), *Mocho-orelhudo.* See *Asio stygius.* Marshall
(pers. comm.) considers this species to be an *Asio.*

STYGIAN OWL, *Asio stygius,* Mocho-diabo

38 cm. Large ear tufts and streaked underparts like those of
Rhinoptynx clamator but upperparts and facial pattern blackish with light forehead. Iris yellow. Cerrado, araucarias,
even exotic plantings of *Pinus* spp., sometimes alongside
R. clamator but much rarer (Mato Grosso). Locally from
Mexico and Antilles to Paraguay, Argentina; also Amazonia,
centralwest, south; recently found in Paraná and Rio Grande
do Sul.

SHORT-EARED OWL, *Asio flammeus,*
Mocho-dos-banhados

Slender with long wings and short, almost invisible ear tufts. Underparts finely streaked. Because of diurnal habits, unmistakable. Living in extensive marshes, hunts openly in plain daylight, flying low over wetlands. Movements recall Long-winged Harrier, *Circus buffoni.* Perches on ground, hovers. Being migratory, may appear in any savanna area and gathers in flocks (Chile). Having come from North America, spread through Andean America to Tierra del Fuego. São Paulo to Rio Grande do Sul but apparently not found in rest of Brazil. Widely distributed in northern portions of Old World. Few birds in the world have such a complex distribution. Also called *Coruja-dos-campos.* See Nacunda Nighthawk, *Podager nacunda.*

BUFF-FRONTED OWL, *Aegolius (= Gisella) harrisii,*
Caburé-acanelado

20 cm. Small, little known, without ear tufts. Upperparts blackish; forehead, facial disk, and underparts uniformly intense yellow. With distinct white spots on wing and tail, somewhat resembles *Speotyto cunicularia.* Iris yellow. VOICE: an extensive, horizontal sequence (e.g., lasting 8, 10, or 15 seconds) of hurried *oos,* which can become more vigorous. Sparse forest and cerrado. In central planalto (Goiás, 1000 m), Brasília, northeast (Ceará, Pernambuco, Alagoas), São Paulo, Paraná, Rio Grande do Sul, Argentina, Uruguay. Also in Andes (Venezuela). Inclusion in *Aegolius,* which is broadly distributed in Northern Hemisphere, is tentative.

Strigidae Bibliography

See also General Bibliography.

Bock, W. J., and A. McEvey. 1969. The radius and relationship of Owls. *Wilson Bull.* 81(1):55–68.

Borrero, J. 1967. Notas sobre hábitos alimentarios de *Asio stygius. Hornero* 10:445–47.

Bühler, P. 1989. Anpassung des Kopf-Hals-Gefieders der Schleiereule (*Tyto alba*) an die akustische Ortung. *Proc. Int. 100. DO-G Meeting,* 1988:49–55.

Burton, J. A., ed. 1973. *Owls of the World.* New York: E. P. Dutton.

Dice, L. R. 1945. Minimum intensities of illumination under which owls can find dead prey by sight. *Am. Nat.* 79:385–416.

Grimm, R. J., et al. 1963. *Auk* 80:301–06. [Pellets]

Hardy, J. W., B. B. Coffey, Jr., and G. B. Reynard. 1988. *Voices of the New World Nightbirds* (revised edition). Gainesville, Fl.: Ara Records.

Hekstra, G. P. 1982a. "A Revision of the American Screech Owls (*Otus*)." Dissertation. University of Amsterdam.

Hekstra, G. P. 1982b. Description of twenty-four new subspecies of American *Otus. Bull. Zool. Mus. Univ. Amsterdam* 9(7): 49–63.

König, C. 1989. Eine neue Eule (Aves:Strigidae) aus Nordargentinien. *Stuttgarter Beitr. Naturk.* S.A, no. 428.

Konishi, M. 1973. *Am. Scient.* 61:414–24. [Prey location]

Kuhk, R. 1966. *An. Ornith. Ges. Bay.* 7:714–16. [*Aegolius,* behavior]

Marshall, J. T., Jr. 1967. Parallel variation in North and Middle American Screech-owls. *West. Found. Vertebr. Zool. Monogr.* 1.

Marshall, J. T., R. A. Behrstock, and Claus König. 1991. Special Review of *Voices of the New World Owls (Strigiformes: Tytonidae, Strigidae)* by J. W. Hardy et al. 1990. *Wilson Bull.* 103(2):311–15.

Martin, G. R. 1986. Sensory capacities and nocturnal habitat of owls. *Ibis* 128(2):266–77.

Miller, A. H. 1934. The vocal apparatus of some North American Owls. *Condor* 36:204–13.

Miller, A. H. 1947. The structural basis of the voice of the Flammulated Owl. *Auk* 64:113–35.

Norberg, R. A. 1977. Occurrence and independent evolution of bilateral ear asymmetry in owls and implications on owl taxonomy. *Phil. Trans. R. Soc. London* B280:375–408.

Oliveira, R. G. 1980. Observações sobre a coruja orelhuda *Rhinoptynx clamator* no Rio Grande do Sul. *Rev. Bras. Biol.* 40(3):599–604.

Oliveira, R. G. 1981. A ocorrência do Mocho-diabo, *Asio stygius,* no Rio Grande do Sul. *An. Soc. Sul-Riogr. Orn.* 1:9–12.

Oliveira, R. G. 1984. Diferença na cor da iris em dois caburés-de-orelhas, *Otus choliba,* irmãos de ninho. *An. Soc. Sul-Riogr. Orn.* 5:15–19.

Payne, R. S. 1971. *J. Exper. Biol.* 56:535–73. [Acoustic location of prey]

Räber, H. 1949. *Behavior* 2(1–2). [*Asio* and *Strix,* hunting behavior]

Salvador, S. A. 1981. *Hist. Nat.* 2(7):49–52. [*Asio flammeus,* nesting]

Scherer Neto, P. 1985. Notas bionômicas sobre o mocho-diabo, *Asio stygius,* no Paraná. *An. Soc. Sul-Riogr. Orn.* 6:15–18.

Schlatter, R., J. Yáñez, H. Núñez, et al. 1982. Estudio estacional de la dieta del pequén, *Athene cunicularia,* en la precordillera de Santiago. *Medio Ambiente* 6(1):9–18.

Schwarzkopf, J. 1963. Proc. *13th Int. Orn. Cong., Ithaca:*1059–68. [Auditory system]

Silva Porto, F., and R. Cerqueira. 1984. Dados preliminares sobre os hábitos alimentares da coruja-buraqueira, *Athene cunicularia,* na restiga de Maricá. *XI Cong. Bras. Zool., Belém:* 326.

Storer, R. W. 1972. *Auk* 89:452–55. [*Lophostrix*]

Thiel, H. 1968. Die Porphyrine der Vogelfedern. *Zool. Jb. Syst.* 95:147–88.

Thorpe, W. H., and D. R. Griffin. 1962. *Ibis* 104:256–57. [Ultrasonic components]

Vielliard, J. 1989. Uma nova espécie de *Glaucidium* da Amazônia. *Rev. Bras. Zool.* 6(4):685–93.

Vogel, P. 1970. *Z. Säugetierk.* 35:173–85. [Shrew, *Suncus etruscus*]

Wendland, V. 1975. Dreijähriger Rhythmus im Bestandswechsel von *Apodemus flavicollis. Oecologia-Berlin* 20:301–10.

ORDER CAPRIMULGIFORMES

FAMILY STEATORNITHIDAE: OILBIRD (1)

The Oilbird is a gregarious, cave-dwelling, nocturnal bird of the Andes and their foothills, related to the potoos, Nyctibiidae (also endemic to the Neotropics), and more remotely to the Podargidae and Aegothelidae of Australasia. There is only one *Steatornis;* the family is monotypic.

OILBIRD, *Steatornis caripensis,* Guácharo   Fig. 134

43 cm. Rusty chestnut speckled with white, especially on wings. Sexes similar. Appearance does not immediately suggest a nocturnal bird. Head small with strong, hooked bill (resembling that of an owl) encircled with bristles. Eyes small, unlike those of owls and nightjars, with red reflections when illuminated by a flashlight. Wings quite long and narrow, wing-span a bit over 1 m. Tail also quite long and graduated. Flight not swift but bird is very agile within limited space offered by caves. Flight silhouette against night sky is falconlike. Legs short and weak, feet small. Perches on belly on rocks, in a half-fallen-forward position. Unlike swifts, unable to cling to vertical walls. Plumage not soft like that of other nightbirds.

SOUNDS: While flying in a cave makes very loud cries, *grehh,* producing a deafening sound when many call together, as they always do. Flying outside of caves, gives a guttural *karr-karr.* In depths of caves where there is absolute darkness, emits a high *kli* . . . (frequencies reach 12 kHz) that serves for echolocation, corresponding to our sonar. This kind of acoustic orientation occurs in insectivorous bats (e.g., *Saccopteryx bilineata* of central Brazil) and certain swifts (*Aerodramus = Collocalia*) of the Indo-Pacific region. The auditory nuclei of *S. caripensis* are the largest known, perhaps because of echolocation, and are similar to those of *Collocalia* (Cobb 1968). The *Steatornis* syrinx is illustrated in Van Tyne and Berger (1959). Bat sonar is much more efficient than that of oilbirds, permitting the capture of insects in flight.

Feeding: This is the only frugivorous, nocturnal bird. Feeds on fruits of various forest trees (e.g., Lauraceae) and of palms, flying 50 or more Km to find a meal, orienting itself by sight and probably also by smell. Tears off fruits with bill while hovering. Swallows them whole, regurgitating pits later in caves where it spends day.

Breeding: Colonies established only in deep caves, e.g., 650 m in from entrance of famous Oilbird Cave near Caripe, Venezuela, from where Humboldt described species in 1817 (fig. 135) (and where I made my observations). Roosts and builds nest on rock outcroppings 30–40 m up near roof of cavern. Regurgitated pits serve as nesting material, being glued to substrate with birds' own excrement. Female lays 2–4 eggs which are incubated by pair for approximately 33 days. Development of young is very slow, taking 4 months. During this period nestlings accumulate an incredible amount of fat, becoming much heavier than parents, but they thin down before flying. Local residents kill young to extract a valuable oil (hence the name "oilbird").

Distribution: Guyana and Venezuela (also Trinidad) to

Fig. 135. Oilbird, *Steatornis caripensis,* adult and nestling. Sketch by Alexander von Humboldt, made 18 September 1799 in an oilbird cave in Venezuela, from which Humboldt described the species. The sketch has been retouched by an artist.

Fig. 134. Oilbird, *Steatornis caripensis.* Original, M. Werneck de Castro.

Roraima (Brazil), Ecuador, Colombia, Peru, Bolivia, and Panamá at altitudes of 7–3500 m. In Venezuela many oilbird colonies are known. Since 1978 I have been receiving information from Venezuelan speleologists on oilbird colonies on the Venezuela/Brazil border, such as in the Urutaní caves, whose entrances are in Venezuelan territory at an altitude of 1300 m but whose end is 228 m away in Brazilian territory.

Steatornithidae Bibliography
See also General Bibliography

Anonymous. 1977. Catastro Espeleológico Nacional. *Bol. Soc. Ven. Espel.* 8(16):199–231.

Bosque, C. 1986. Actualización de la distribución del Guácharo, *Steatornis caripensis* en Venezuela. *Bol. Soc. Ven. Espel.* 22:1–10.

Cobb, S. 1968. On the size of the auditory nuclei in some Apodiformes and Caprimulgiformes. *Auk* 85:132–33.

Griffin, D. R. 1953. Acoustic orientation in the Oil Bird, *Steatornis caripensis*. *Proc. Nat. Acad. Sci.* 39(8):884–93.

Humboldt, A. von. 1817. Mémoire sur le Guacharo de la caverne de Caripe. *Recueil d'Obs. de Zool. e d'Anatomie* no. 2.

Pye, J. D. 1985. Echolocation. In B. Campbell and E. Lack, eds., *A Dictionary of Birds*. Vermillion, S.D.: Harrell Books.

Snow, D. W. 1961. The natural history of the Oilbird, *Steatornis caripensis* in Trinidad. *Zoologica* (N.Y.) 46:21–48 and 47:199–221.

Stolzmann, J. 1880. Observations sur le *Steatornis* péruvien. *Bull. Soc. France* 5:198–204.

FAMILY NYCTIBIIDAE: POTOOS (5)

Potoos are nocturnal birds restricted to the hottest regions of the New World. They are related to the nightjars (Caprimulgidae), oilbirds (Steatornithidae), and frogmouths (Podargidae, of Australasia). A Common Potoo, *Nyctibius griseus,* fossil from the Pleistocene (20,000 years B.P.) is known from Lapa da Escrivaninha, Lagoa Santa, Minas Gerais.

Morphology and Special Adaptations

This is a well-defined group with only one genus and few species. Potoos are among the most bizarre creatures of this continent. The head is wide, flat, and largely occupied by the uncommonly large eyes and mouth. When the eyes are closed, two incisions (fig. 136) are noticed in the upper eyelid which in 1940 I attributed to a mechanism for covering the eyeball, which protrudes greatly (Long-tailed Potoo, *Nyctibius aethereus,* and *N. griseus*). In 1952, however, I concluded that these incisions are slits through which the bird can observe its surroundings with "its eyes closed", that is, without opening its eyelids. It thus has the effect of a "magic eye," a conclusion also reached by J. I. Borrero (1974). When the eye is open the incisions in the upper eyelid are visible as small cuts. By day the large eyes of a nightbird are very conspicuous (see also Caprimulgidae), so the birds quickly shut their eyes if they become wary. In this situation potoos then take advantage of their "magic eye," a unique adaptation among birds. When illuminated at night by a flashlight, the eye produces a reddish or orange reflection visible at a great distance (see also Caprimulgidae).

The mouth resembles that of a gigantic toad. The tip of the bill is hooked, the maxilla has a tooth, and the mandible is elastic. A man's fist will fit inside the mouth of one of the large species. The mouth skin is heavily vascularized and serves for thermoregulation when the bird is under full sun on its daytime roost, as frequently happens. On these occasions the bird pants with its mouth constantly held a bit open, exhaling excess heat through the large surface of the vascular system of the throat. This habit can be seen in the young in the "nest." The brain is quite small. Wings and tail are long and hard, the plumage being less soft than that of owls and nightjars, although abundant powder is produced by powder down concentrated in an area on either side of the rump. There is a large uropygial gland. *Nyctibius aethereus* may accumulate abdominal fat to a thickness of 5 mm.

Potoos do not have rictal bristles or vibrissae (unlike nightjars), except the small Rufous Potoo, *N. bracteatus,* of Amazonia. This must have an ecological basis: *N. bracteatus* hunts in the interior of the Amazonian forest, whereas the other potoos hunt at the edge or above the forest and even in open country. Thus, the same speculation regarding the function of bristles arises as with the nightjars.

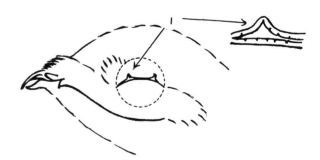

Fig. 136. "Magic eye" of the Common Potoo, *Nyctibius griseus*. The upper eyelid has two incisions (I), each corresponding to a "magic eye," permitting the bird to observe its surroundings with its eyes closed. Upper right: enlargement of one of the incisions. The projecting eyeball and the compact arrangement of the feathers above the eye enable vision upward and backward without moving the head. Original, H. Sick, Xingu, Mato Grosso, February 1952.

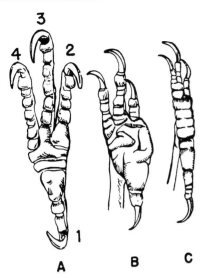

Fig. 137. Right foot, seen from below, of (A) Plumbeous Pigeon, *Columba plumbea;* (B) Common Potoo, *Nyctibius griseus;* and (C) American Pygmy Kingfisher, *Chloroceryle aenea.* Evolution of a broad, well-padded sole in the potoo (less in the kingfisher). The larger size of the pigeon foot makes its sole appear more padded than it is. Toes numbered. After H. Böker 1935.

The tarsi are quite short. The toes are long, wide, and fleshy at the base, forming a large sole surface like a hand, a special adaptation for prolonged, complete immobility during the day (fig. 137). Unlike nightjars, potoos do not have a comblike claw. Sexes are similar.

Vocalization and Folklore

The voice of *N. griseus,* one of the most impressive bird voices of Brazil, resembles a human lament and is widely but erroneously attributed to all its congeners. Flightless young can already sing a little, very quietly. On rare occasions I have heard vocalizations other than the song; an alarm cry and small cries of the young.

There are various indigenous legends about the song of *N. griseus.* For country people of Amazonia, its flight and tail feathers have the power to protect the chastity of young girls. To achieve this, a mother sweeps under her daughters' hammocks with a broom made of these feathers.

Feeding

Potoos hunt insects (large moths and beetles) like nightjars and tyrant flycatchers do (returning to the perch from which they flew) or pursue their prey in full flight like swallows. They fly with the bill closed, catching insects one by one. The maxillar tooth must serve to cut up moth wings. When such wings are found scattered through the woods, they are usually remains of bat meals. Stories of potoos awaiting their meals perched with the bill open, using the mouth as a trap

(which happens with the frogmouths, *Podargus,* of Asia), are nothing more than fable. *N. griseus* gorges itself on termite swarms, probably catching several at a time. Potoos take lice or other insects perched on leaves. They also exploit rotten stumps, for larvae of beetles that live in dead trees and pieces of decomposing wood have been found in potoo stomachs. They thus take advantage of the incredible abundance of nocturnal insects in Neotropical forests, which is also an inexhaustible food source for the numerous nightjars and owls. Both adult and young potoos are normally very fat.

Behavior

Potoos never perch on the ground like nightjars; they hold themselves erect when they perch on stumps and branches. If molested during the day they stretch themselves even more and lift the head until the bill is pointed vertically up and the tail touches the trunk, a very slow process, controlled by the bird, which observes the danger through the slits in its eyelids ("magic eye," see "Morphology . . . "). They can thus be confused with a dead branch tip, end of a broken palm leaf, stake, etc., in a camouflage so efficient that the bird permits close approach in the certainty it will not be noticed. With this "branch mimicry" potoos occupy a niche not used by any other bird in this region. At ease the potoo lowers it head, napping, and its bill is pointed forward or even a little down, while the tail hangs loosely vertical. The underside of the tail feathers is sometimes impregnated with a green film that I presume to be algae (or fungus?), rubbed on by contact with the humid bark; this is similar to the situation with sloths (Mammalia, Bradypodidae), which has long been known (see Picidae, "Parasites . . . "). Potoos use favorite daytime perches in their territories for years on end.

Another notable adaptation for staying at a fixed perch for 12 hours of tropical daylight is that a potoo does not let its excrement drop but shoots it far away, like a hawk. The perch stays clean and the white excrement does not betray the bird's presence.

At night potoos perch on exposed branches (e.g., those of cecropia) in a transverse position. They fly high and steadily, often gliding, which suggested to Prince Maximilian of Wied the picturesque name *aetherius.* They may then resemble a strange hawk, an oilbird, or a very large nightjar. Captured individuals try to frighten their enemy by opening the mouth silently, but they do not and cannot peck.

Breeding

Potoos lay one speckled egg in a natural cavity on the end of a broken tree trunk or branch a few meters above ground. The egg is so securely boxed in that on one occasion not even a shot was sufficient to knock it down; this happened when I was collecting an *N. griseus* I did not know was brooding. The shot broke the upper part of the egg, which did not even move. Potoos brood in an erect position. I have found only males incubating during daytime. I presume the female incubates at night. The vertical position is also assumed when the adult bird covers a small chick or by the chick itself when it is alone on the branch and observes any movement near its tree. The instinct to adopt a vertical stance manifests itself early, so the chick clutches the wood tenaciously.

Adults feed their offspring by regurgitation. With the young staying seven weeks (51 days are reported for *N. griseus*) in the "nest," and calculating the incubation period at 33 days, we have a total of 84 days, one of the longest development periods I know of for South American birds and one more eloquent testimonial to the extraordinary efficiency of potoo camouflage, for this proves that they manage to survive well despite an extraordinary mode of life. For some time after the bird is already able to fly, the white down of the young, pushed by the definitive feathering, remains like a mantle on the tips of the definitive tail feathers.

GREAT POTOO, *Nyctibius grandis,* Mãe-da-lua-gigante

54 cm; 1 m; 360–600 g. Size of a Great Horned Owl, *Bubo virginianus,* with coloring of *N. griseus,* though often whitish; iris brown. VOICE: song a very loud, monosyllabic cry, *groaaaa,* repeated at intervals of approximately 12 seconds in a consecutive series of perhaps 28 cries; a bark, *wow.* When disturbed by spotlighting, a male uttered isolated *grook*s. Likes to perch in tall trees with white bark that perfectly matches its light plumage. Locally from Chiapas, Mexico, to Mato Grosso, São Paulo, Rio de Janeiro. I found a male brooding 12 m up in a large souari nut tree [*Caryocar brasiliense*]; the single egg was on a thick, horizontal branch, well distant from trunk (upper Xingu, Mato Grosso, July 1949). Also called *Urutau, Choralua.* Sometimes alongside *N. griseus* (Mato Grosso).

LONG-TAILED POTOO, *Nyctibius aethereus,* Mãe-da-lua-parda EN

Wingspan 98 cm; 434–47 g. Almost as large as *N. grandis.* Very dark brown; iris greenish chestnut or bluish gray. VOICE: a mild, melodious cry, strongly accented in middle, *aoo-OO-uh* (Peru, Hardy et al. 1989). Often perches close to ground, even on stakes in open. Locally from southern Venezuela to Paraguay; in eastern and southern Brazil as far as Paraná. Includes *N. longicaudatus* of Amazonia. Sometimes alongside *N. griseus* (Espírito Santo). Probably endangered.

COMMON POTOO, *Nyctibius griseus,* Urutau
PL 18.6

37 cm; wingspan 85 cm; 159–87 g (male). Most common species. Like other potoos, has prominent tuft of feathers in front of eye, reminiscent of ear tufts of certain owls; this typical projection disappears when eye is opened. Color is variable, either browner or grayer, breast with compact black pattern. Iris amber yellow. VOICE: a melancholy song (which seems to come from a larger, distant bird, or from a human): 5–7 consecutive full cries, beginning harshly, in a descending sequence, and weakening at end, *poh-o oh oh oh oh; call *rak* (in flight). A well-feathered male still unable to fly gave some weak notes (begging?) and then began to sing, 4 very quiet notes (Renato Pineschi). Forest edge, semiopen terrain with palms and other scattered trees, cerrado. Occurrence irregular. Two potoos have been reported breeding 500 m from one another, separated by a predominantly savanna area. Easily escapes detection. Costa Rica to Bolivia, Argentina, Uruguay, all of Brazil, sometimes in cities (Rio de Janeiro). Also called *Mãe-da-lua, Kuá-kuá* (Juruna, Mato Grosso), *Urutavi* (Kamaiurá, Mato Grosso). *Urutau* comes from Tupi, "ghost-bird."

WHITE-WINGED POTOO, *Nyctibius leucopterus*
BR R PL 44.1

300 mm; (wing 209 mm). Clearly smaller than *N. griseus,* with large white area on each upper wing covert which, together, form a prominent V on back. Described by Wied in 1821 from Vitória da Conquista (not Caravelas), Bahia, but never again mentioned. A potoo recently encountered near Manaus that attracted attention because of voice, similar to that of Sunbittern, *Eurypyga helias,* has been identified as *N. leucopterus* (J. W. Hardy pers. comm.). *N. maculosus* of Andes is a different species.

RUFOUS POTOO, *Nyctibius bracteatus*

230 mm. Smaller with prominently white-spotted, bright rufous plumage. VOICE: a descending *boobooboo* . . . resembling a small owl (*Otus* or Least Pygmy-Owl, *Glaucidium minutissimum*) from Amazonia (T. Parker pers. comm.). Forest interior (see "Morphology . . ."). Found 80 km north of Manaus, Amazonas, in Forest Fragment Dynamics Project area. Also in Guyana, Colombia, Ecuador, Peru.

Nyctibiidae Bibliography
See also General Bibliography

Borrero H., J. I. 1970. *The Living Bird* 9:257–63. [Behavior]
Borrero H., J. I. 1974. *Condor* 76:210–12. [Eye]
Goeldi, E. A. 1900. *Bol. Mus. Paraen.:*210–17. [Behavior]
Hardy, J. W., B. B. Coffey, Jr., and G. C. Reynard. 1989. *Voices of the New World Nightjars.* Gainesville, FL.: ARA Records.
Schulenberg, T. S., S. Allen, D. F. Stotz, et al. 1984. *Le Gerfaut* 74:57–70. [Separation of *Nyctibius leucopterus, maculosus,* and *griseus*]
Sick, H. 1951. *Vogelwelt* 72:40–43. [Eggs]
Sick, H. 1953. *Wilson Bull.* 65(3):203. [*Nyctibius grandis,* vocalization]
Skutch, A. F. 1970. *The Living Bird* 9:265–80. [Behavior]
Wetmore, A. 1919. *Proc. U.S. Nat. Mus.* 54:577–86. [Anatomy]

FAMILY CAPRIMULGIDAE: NIGHTJARS AND NIGHTHAWKS (23)

This is a cosmopolitan group of nocturnal birds found especially in hot regions. There are tertiary fossils (Eocene/Oligocene) from France; remains of *Nyctidromus* and *Hydropsalis* exist from the Pleistocene (20,000 years B.P.) of Lagoa Santa, Minas Gerais. The Neotropics are particularly rich in species, which suggests they had their origin in this part of the world. Six species live in central Brazil. Phylogenetic relationships of the Caprimulgiformes with the Strigiformes are evidenced by egg proteins. The Aegothelidae (Owlet-Nightjar) family of Australasia, which nests in tree holes, appears to be a link between the Caprimulgidae and Strigidae.

Morphology and Special Adaptations

The nightjars, a general name for members of this family, are close to the potoos in having the bill transformed into a very wide mouth. The nightjar mouth can be expanded considerably, both laterally (from 2.5 to 4 cm) and vertically. The mandible is highly elastic, even having a median articulation called the intramandibular syndesmotic articulation. As a result these birds have a large gular sac that is highly vascularized and sensitive, functioning as a net to capture insects. The skull (fig. 138) is large because of the size of the mouth (the brain is quite small) and is spongy, similar to that of owls (involving "sandwich" structures to reduce weight, better known in airplane construction). A *Caprimulgus* skull, measuring 5 × 3 cm, weighs, with the mandible, only 0.45 g (Bühler 1972). Whereas the mouth is always large, bill length varies considerably and may be so short that it is hidden in the plumage, as in *Nyctiprogne*. In seeking diagnostic characters for African nightjars, Jackson (1985) concluded that it is more useful to measure the tomia than the culmen.

The bill is surrounded by bristles: modified contour feathers with strong shafts and no barbs (except at the base), linked to a special musculature that moves them (fig. 139). The tip of each bristle is broad and narrow, looking through a microscope like a button that is coming unbuttoned. The skin around the bristles is rich in Herbst corpuscles. The bristles may be tactile organs (this has not been proven) that correspond to the sensory hairs of cats and rodents. The bristles expand the reach of the open mouth during hunting and may be useful in capturing insects. They have also been suspected of having a chemical-receptor taste function. Caprimulgiformes have a relatively large olfactory bulb (Bang and Cobb 1968) which might serve to select the insects the birds capture. It is also possible that the bristles protect the large and entirely exposed eyes against insect strikes during hunting. The Band-winged Nightjar, *Caprimulgus longirostris,* has very long bristles. It does not hunt inside forests. Compare the Rufous Potoo, *Nyctibius bracteatus,* which also has bristles. The *Chordeiles* and *Nyctiprogne,* nightjars whose ways of life are not essentially different, lack prominent bristles.

The eyes are large, movable, and placed laterally and so high they give a visual field directed upward and somewhat to the rear, in great contrast to owls, providing defense against attacks and an enlarged view for hunting. Provided with a tapetum lucidum, the eyes reflect light strongly, like those of the Nyctibiidae, with a generally green glow that may vary (green, orange, white) according to the angle of observation and distance. Eyesight is the nightjars' sharpest sense. They differ from owls in not having a facial disk (whose function is acoustic), although they have very good hearing. The claw is serrated, as in the barn owls and some other birds. Feet are quite small.

Various species are similar in the color and design of their

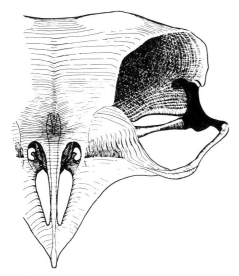

Fig. 138. The extremely broad skull of a nightjar is the foundation for the unusually large mouth opening. After Bühler 1970.

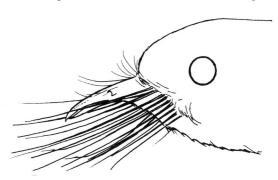

Fig. 139. Bristles around the bill of a Band-winged Nightjar, *Caprimulgus longirostris*. Original, H. Sick.

cryptic plumage, making identification difficult (see below). More distinctive are the white markings in the wing or tail, as well as a frequently V-shaped gular mark with the angle pointing forward which is revealed full-sized when the bird calls. These white markings, more developed in males, are important for a nocturnal bird, for the white shows up brightly in the crepuscular light and aids the male display by being apparent in flight or when deliberately exposed by a rapid opening and closing of the wings and tail as the bird perches (as in *Caprimulgus longirostris*). The white on both the fore and after extremities of the Blackish Nightjar, *C. nigrescens,* has an effectively confusing function, for when the bird is perched it is scarcely possible to distinguish its head from the tip of its tail. The effect of strongly reflective white parts is augmented by the microscopic structure of the feathers, as happens with the silvery remiges of terns. Plumage and skin are delicate. The body emits a strong, characteristic odor.

The degree of darkness of the plumage indicates the birds' habitat. The Pauraque, *Nyctidromus albicollis,* and Scissor-tailed Nightjar, *Hydropsalis brasiliana,* for example, blend perfectly with dead leaves on the ground. *Caprimulgus nigrescens* has adapted to the color of black stones, and the Pygmy Nightjar, *C. hirundinaceus,* to the yellow sand of the light, sun-baked caatinga. The Sand-colored Nighthawk, *Chordeiles rupestris,* inhabiting open river beaches, has become ternlike in color and even in voice and mode of life, resulting in one of the most interesting products of Amazonian avifaunal evolution. Still other nightjars with river-edge habitat, such as the White-tailed Nightjar, *Caprimulgus cayennensis,* and Ladder-tailed Nightjar, *Hydropsalis climacocerca,* have evolved quite white coloring. There are individual and/or regional differences (*Caprimulgus longirostris*) in plumage color, recalling the ferruginous and gray phases of owls. The size of species (e.g., of *Nyctidromus albicollis* and *Hydropsalis brasiliana*) diminishes as they approach the equator.

Caprimulgids may fall into a torpid sleep, like hummingbirds and swifts, to get through periods of cold and lack of food, a situation more frequent in moderate climates. A captive North American nightjar spent four days in torpidity (Marshall 1955).

Sounds

Recognizing the voices of these birds is indispensable to learning about their occurrence and population densities in a given area. The oft-cited cries that are the origins of the Brazilian onomatopoeic names *bacurau* and *curiango,* widely used for many caprimulgids, are produced exclusively by *Nyctidromus albicollis* and are the best-known nightbird voices in Brazil. Voices of most other species are entirely different. On the importance of acoustic communication

among nightbirds, see Strigidae, "Vocalization." Some species have a series of different vocalizations (see Least Nighthawk, *Chordeiles pusillus; C. rupestris;* and *Nyctidromus albicollis*). Certain types of Brazilian nightjar vocalizations can be classified:

1. Gargling and croaking, like an amphibian: Lesser Nighthawk, *Chordeiles acutipennis;* Nacunda Nighthawk, *Podager nacunda;* Ocellated Poorwill, *Nyctiphrynus ocellatus;* Little Nightjar, *Caprimulgus parvulus; C. rufus; C. nigrescens;* and *Chordeiles rupestris. Chordeiles pusillus* has a voice of this type and also of the following type.
2. Strident whistling: Short-tailed Nighthawk, *Lurocalis semitorquatus;* Spot-tailed Nightjar, *Caprimulgus maculicaudus; C. cayennensis;* and *C. longirostris.* A more resonant whistle is produced by *Caprimulgus hirundinaceus* and *Chordeiles pusillus.*
3. Chirping like a cricket: *Hydropsalis brasiliana*
4. Cries of *bacurau* and *curiango: Nyctidromus albicollis.* Band-tailed Nighthawk, *Nyctiprogne leucopyga,* and Silky-tailed Nightjar, *Caprimulgus sericocaudatus,* have calls with the same timbre as *Nyctidromus albicollis.*

Caprimulgid vocal activity, which becomes intense during the breeding season, is greatest at dawn and dusk and when there is moonlight. They then repeat their phrases at intervals of only a few seconds. Birds mark territories by flying from one perch to another while singing. When irritated by playback, *Nyctidromus albicollis* and *Caprimulgus sericocaudatus* utter some disgruntled-sounding low notes.

I do not yet know whether the autumn and winter singing activity I have noted in *Hydropsalis brasiliana* in Rio de Janeiro (ex-Guanabara) is linked to breeding activity. To sing it perches near the ground on a stump or fallen log, or on branches. Some species always sing perched high in forest trees (*Nyctiphrynus ocellatus, Caprimulgus rufus*). *Lurocalis semitorquatus* and *Chordeiles pusillus* regularly sing in flight. Nightjars call with the mouth almost closed, thereby increasing the ventriloquial character of the voice. The song of *Hydropsalis brasiliana* is so high pitched it can easily pass unnoticed.

In the Municipality of Rio de Janeiro I have noted several times that local *H. brasiliana* and *Caprimulgus longirostris,* after not having sung in months, sing very actively at the end of a heavy storm.

Although their plumage is extremely soft and their flight so silent they move like passing shadows, various species produce snaps or other noises with the wings when flying during courtship or in defense of their territory (*Caprimulgus maculicaudus;* Sickle-winged Nightjar, *Eleothreptus anomalus; Hydropsalis brasiliana*). These noises are probably produced by the primaries in the same way that a flag flaps or a napkin is snapped. Batting one wing against the other above the body, as pigeons do can also be presumed. A variety of noises are produced, possibly by various methods (see *H. brasili-*

ana). In the dark it is impossible to see what is happening. Perched birds also beat their wings against the substrate (see "Behavior").

Feeding

Nightjars are insectivorous. *Nyctidromus albicollis,* the *Hydropsalis,* and others hunt by taking off from the ground and returning. It is evident that they use the light of the night sky to see and chase insects. The unusual size of their mouths facilitates catching insects in low light and is not an adaptation for taking large insects. The principal hunting of nightjars, based on visual perception, is restricted to dawn and dusk or moonlit hours. They perch on the substrate and localize the insects against the clear sky, as they also do in flight. Caprimulgids lack the ability to find insects by echolocation like bats or by acute hearing like owls, both of which work in complete darkness, as was well analyzed by Bühler (1987). In central Brazil various nightjar species hunt around burning fields, *Podager nacunda* doing so even by day along with swifts. Insects that are caught stick in the mouth in a thick mass, as can be seen in a bird taken while hunting, which shows that the insects are not swallowed individually. The full gizzard of a nightjar may contain many hundreds of insects, such as winged ants and termites. The stomach of a *P. nacunda* in Uruguay contained 238 insects belonging to 8 orders, 9 families, and 16 species, with Hemiptera (138 bugs, mostly Pentatomidae prejudicial to rice crops) and Orthoptera (62 individuals) predominating. A *Chordeiles minor* examined in the U.S. had 2175 insects in its stomach, almost half of them queen ants caught during the swarming of these Hymenoptera. It was calculated that the weight of the food taken from the stomachs of two other individuals of this species was 24.6% and 25.4% of the weight of the birds with empty crops. The large stomach capacity of caprimulgids compensates for their lack of a crop. Nightjars are usually very fat. They are menaced by the unlimited use of insecticides.

I have verified that they sometimes pick up small stones and pieces of burned wood, perhaps for their salt content.

Behavior

Unlike potoos, nightjars perch in a squatting position, lying on their bellies, most of them on the ground. On branches they usually perch longitudinally, which provides excellent camouflage. This stance is facilitated by their reduced number of toe segments (phalanges)—the outer toe has only four instead of five. To sleep during the day, *Lurocalis semitorquatus* roosts high (e.g., 14 m) on a thick branch. The *Hydropsalis* and *Chordeiles* sometimes perch transversely. During floods *Chordeiles rupestris* perches on branches without difficulty, although at nesting time it uses only beaches.

During the day a roosting nightjar does not sleep but only takes naps. It notices any change in its surroundings, observing through a narrow slit between the eyelids; it does not have the "magic eye" of the potoos, which is a more sophisticated solution to avoid exposing the shiny eyeball, the only uncamouflaged part of its body, which is prominent in full daylight. Nightjars see as well in daytime as owls.

When disturbed they raise and lower the head, move the body laterally, stretch the wings as if preparing to flee, or beat the wings against the ground or branch like *Chaetura* swifts (e.g., *Nyctidromus albicollis, Caprimulgus rufus, C. longirostris, Hydropsalis brasiliana*). They fly very well and are true acrobats in the air, combining the swooping flight of swifts with the oscillating flight of the Southern Lapwing, *Vanellus chilensis.* They can remain stationary in the air like a hummingbird when catching insects attracted by a light, hovering perfectly. They like to hunt over open areas such as airfields. A *Podager nacunda* was sucked into the turbine of a jet, which fell. They walk rapidly with small steps, whether along the length of a branch before roosting or on the ground to pick up earth, etc.

Various caprimulgids perch on roads, flying up in front of vehicles (*mede-leguas,* "league-measurer"). They seek asphalt highways that hold the heat of the sun during the night and attract insects. They are frequently run over, and in that way a rare species such as *Eleothreptus anomalus* may be discovered. Unhappily, where traffic is intense the bodies of these delicate birds are completely destroyed in a short time and disappear rapidly. I have found that most of those hit are young birds.

The large gular sac serves well for thermoregulation, as can be seen in a species such as *Caprimulgus nigrescens* which sits on rocks exposed to the burning sun. Sometimes they drink from lakes and rivers while skimming over the surface (*Chordeiles*). They take dust baths.

When their voices are not heard and they do not appear on roads, nightjars attract little attention. Although abundant in regions such as central Brazil and Amazonia, they are almost unknown to the general public. The occurrence of several species in the same area in the Neotropics suggests certain ecological and trophic adaptations.

A few species, such as *Chordeiles acutipennis* and *Podager nacunda,* leave their hiding places in the afternoon before sunset to hunt in flocks, flying at great heights above water and fields, exploiting different strata. *Chordeiles rupestris* is diurnal. Swallows gathered at a roost before dusk may be frightened up by a nightjar swooping by, probably because they confuse its silhouette (nighthawk) with that of a raptor (Carajás 1984, L. P. Gonzaga).

The nocturnal habits of most of these birds have led the public to call a person who goes out at night a *bacurau.* Bacurau is also a name given to black people (Rio de Janeiro). To become a *curiango* is slang for a worker, such as a bus driver, to get the night shift. The name *Caprimulgus* comes from a European fable that these birds with unusually large mouths suck milk from nanny goats.

Breeding

It remains to be demonstrated how nightjar breeding activity is synchronized with the moon cycle, for increased light guarantees optimum conditions for, and thereby facilitates, feeding the young (see above).

Nightjars are closely tied to their territories, being attracted like a magnet when they hear the voice of their species in the area where they live.

Prenuptial displays are difficult to observe except with *Chordeiles rupestris,* a species with diurnal habits that can easily be seen on the beaches of Amazonia. The male courts the female by stretching his neck vertically, swaying from right to left as he walks. He keeps his throat very much inflated and his tail fully open, displaying the white on each (fig. 140). Suddenly he sits and stretches horizontally, touching the ground with his swollen throat (which almost obliterates the bill) while maintaining the position of his tail.

Nightjars do not build nests. They lay directly on the ground, sand, or stones, or in the case of *Lurocalis semitorquatus,* on a broad branch perhaps 10 m up. Usually they lay two eggs which are elliptic (equipolar), heavily speckled, and highly cryptic. *Nyctiphrynus ocellatus* eggs are slightly pinkish white, the rounded end with fine red spots (Teles Pires, Mato Grosso). *Lurocalis semitorquatus* and *Caprimulgus parvulus* lay white eggs. *C. nigrescens,* an Amazonian species, lays only one egg (Mato Grosso, Pará), as does *Nyctidromus albicollis* in certain regions and *Chordeiles acu-*

Fig. 140. Sand-colored Nighthawk, *Chordeiles rupestris,* male, in two display postures. Above, erect; below, lying down. Rio Trombetas, Pará, September 1979. Original, H. Sick.

tipennis. It has been shown that the number of eggs per clutch generally diminishes as one moves closer to the equator. However, a *Nyctiphrynus ocellatus* clutch consists of two eggs whether in the mountains of Espírito Santo or in northern Mato Grosso.

When eggs are exposed to the sun, as is common with those of *Chordeiles rupestris* and *Caprimulgus nigrescens,* incubation must serve to protect them from excessive heat rather than to keep them warm. A chicken embryo is said to be able to stand temperatures up to 42.2°C.

Occasionally a tendency to nest in colonies is noted (*Caprimulgus parvulus, Chordeiles rupestris*). Adults with eggs or young feign injury when frightened; when unable to flee (e.g., if caged), they threaten with the bill open.

A pair takes turns on the nest. Incubation lasts 18 to 19 days in the Common Nighthawk, *Chordeiles minor,* of North America. Parents are very sensitive to disturbance and move elsewhere, pulling the eggs while walking backward a few meters and even carrying newly hatched chicks in flight (once recorded with *C. acutipennis* in Rio de Janeiro. It is very difficult to see how the bird would carry the young—I suppose with the feet.) Moving young is rare in birds but occurs with aquatic birds and rails.

When surprised by people, a young bird tries to frighten them by opening its bill, displaying its wide red mouth, and hissing like a snake. It also oscillates its head slightly, reminiscent of similar movements executed by certain poisonous snakes before striking (even the strike is made by the young Striped Cuckoo, *Tapera naevia*). It may intensify its response by rapidly opening its wings to simulate a larger size.

Parents feed their young by regurgitating a ball of insects held together with sticky saliva. The nestling receives the food by entering the parent's bill up to the forehead (the parents do not insert their bills into the nestling's bill). At only a few days of age nestlings are very agile, walking around the area where they were hatched and depositing their white excrement at a distance so as not to draw attention to their presence.

Small young of *Nyctidromus albicollis* will approach a person who talks very quietly; apparently they confuse the human voice with the call by which the parents cause them to abandon the nest in case of danger. Young *Caprimulgus nigrescens* reportedly abandon the "nest" at 16 to 18 days.

Synanthropic Tendencies

Caprimulgus longirostris, a southern Andean species typical of regions with subtropical and temperate climates, has recently adapted to sea level in Rio de Janeiro, where it lives and nests on rooftops, like *Chordeiles minor* of the U.S., which long ago became habituated to urban environments. *Hydropsalis brasiliana* is also beginning to show this sort of ecological plasticity. While *C. longirostris* is an immigrant to the urban scene, *H. brasiliana* is a remnant of the original fauna.

Internal Movements and Migration

In central Brazil during the breeding season I have seen certain species, especially *Chordeiles rupestris, C. acutipennis,* and *C. pusillus,* move in flocks at sunset toward the east, as if trying to hasten the arrival of dusk by fleeing from the still-light west; they return immediately afterward in the dark (Sick 1950b). *C. rupestris* is periodically driven away by regular floods in Amazonia and gathers in flocks (*bacurau-de-bando,* "flock-nightjar") shortly after its young become independent. It can be seen in flocks of 250 hunting over the Rio Madeira, Amazonas, for example, during floods when beaches are nonexistent.

There are many instances of large-scale migration induced by the southern winter. *Podager nacunda, Chordeiles acutipennis, C. pusillus,* and *Caprimulgus parvulus* appear then in flocks and later disappear completely, as can be observed in central and southern Brazil (Mato Grosso, Goiás, Minas Gerais, Espírito Santo). *Podager n. nacunda,* the large southern race, has been found in July (southern winter) in Colombia alongside the resident *P. n. minor* (Wetmore 1968). *Chordeiles minor* comes from North America during the northern winter (fig. 141).

Fig. 141. Common Nighthawk, *Chordeiles minor,* breeding area (cross-hatched) and wintering area (stippled). After Rappole et al. 1983.

Parasites

I have frequently found louse flies (Hippoboscidae) on nightjars (Mato Grosso). *Chordeiles acutipennis, Podager nacunda,* and *Hydropsalis brasiliana* are hosts of *Pseudolynchia brunnea. H. brasiliana* also hosts *P. nigra.*

Identification

Identification of most caprimulgids, particularly the females, requires considerable practice and specialized literature. Among the numerous Brazilian species, the long-tailed *Hydropsalis* and *Macropsalis,* as well as *Podager nacunda,* are outstanding for their general appearance. The two genera of scissor-tailed nightjars are distinguished by the configuration of their central tail feathers. In the *Hydropsalis* they are prolonged, forming a projecting blade between the two outer extensions; in *Macropsalis* the central projection is lacking. *P. nacunda* can resemble a Southern Lapwing, *Vanellus chilensis.* It is surprising how the pure white belly of *P. nacunda,* a species that begins to fly early, in the late afternoon, becomes pink during sunset. Best known is *Nyctidromus albicollis,* which differs in appearance from other caprimulgids.

The large fish-eating bat (*Noctilio leporinus*), with long, narrow wings but almost no tail, may pass for a nightjar hunting insects over lakes, rivers, and ocean bays; it occurs locally almost throughout Brazil, including the east (e.g., Cabo Frio, Rio de Janeiro).

SHORT-TAILED NIGHTHAWK, *Lurocalis semitorquatus,* Tuju

27 cm. Stocky forest species, notable for length (21–22 cm) and rigidity of unbanded wings. Tail short with whitish tip. Tertiaries and scapulars marbled with white. Abdomen cinnamon, barred black. VOICE: draws attention with loud *tooit* whistle while overflying forests and even cities such as Rio de Janeiro. Approaches immediately on hearing an imitation of its call. Roosts in canopy of tall trees, lying longitudinally on thick branches, where it also lays eggs. Panama to Argentina. Probably throughout Brazil to Rio Grande do Sul. Also called *Curiango-coleiro* (Rio Grande do Sul).

LEAST NIGHTHAWK, *Chordeiles pusillus,* Bacurauzinho

16.5 cm; wingspan 38 cm. One of smaller species, with highly variable brown tones in plumage. Trailing edge of wing markedly whitish, quite visible in flight. Both sexes have white stripe across primaries. Tail feathers of male tipped white. VOICE: often used in flight; *bit-bit* (weak); *kor-rewt, kew, kew, kew-kerrewt* (resonant); a monotonous, full, froglike croaking; *ewt-ewt-EEo* (melodious); also other vocalizations. Brushy, open country (campo sujo). Begins to hunt a little before sundown, sometimes alongside *C. acu-*

Fig. 142. Sand-colored Nighthawk, *Chordeiles rupestris:* above left, flying alongside a Yellow-billed Tern, *Sterna superciliaris;* and below, perched on the beach. After Sick 1950.

tipennis. On migration abundant in pastures. Venezuela and Colombia to Mato Grosso, Minas Gerais, the northeast.

SAND-COLORED NIGHTHAWK, *Chordeiles rupestris,* Bacurau-da-praia   PL 14.7

19 cm. Extraordinarily similar to Yellow-billed Tern, *Sterna superciliaris,* in whose company it lives on Amazonian beaches, where it nests and flits about in full daylight (fig. 142). Differs from tern by round head and short bill. VOICE: *rob-rob, KWOa,* etc., *grehh* (resembling the tern voice), *rrrrrr-wo-wo-wo* (song, given perched or in flight). Also on rocky islands in rivers. Sometimes catches swarming termites alongside Fork-tailed Flycatcher, *Tyrannus savana.* During floods that cover beaches and islands, gathers in flocks of hundreds, perching alongside one another on branches overhanging rivers. See "Internal Movements . . ." on migrations at dusk and to escape floods. Venezuela to upper Amazon as far as Xingu (Mato Grosso) and Bolivia. Also called *Bacurau-branco, Bacurau-de-bando.*

LESSER NIGHTHAWK, *Chordeiles acutipennis,* Bacurau-de-asa-fina   PL 19.2

21.5 cm; wingspan 50 cm. Generally common, medium sized, easily seen when it hunts in afternoon, often at great heights. Wings long and narrow with white stripe. White V on throat, but this is barely outlined in female. Male has white subterminal tail band. VOICE: *shrop, shrop-gogogogogo* (in flight); song (perched) a melodious purring, resembling a toad. Usually perches on branches. Open country, campo cerrado, restinga. California to Bolivia, Argentina, almost all of Brazil, including east, south (Rio de Janeiro, São

Paulo), centralwest. Also called *A-ku-kú* (Juruna, Mato Grosso).

COMMON NIGHTHAWK, *Chordeiles minor,* Bacurau-norteamericano   NV

23 cm. Very similar to *C. acutipennis* but stockier. White stripe on primaries is closer to base of feathers, noticeable when one knows *acutipennis.* Frequently flies during day; roosts on horizontal branches to sleep during day, e.g., 4 m high in capoeirão. Recorded in Maranhão (February), Rio de Janeiro (January, December), São Paulo, Mato Grosso, Rio Grande do Sul (São Leopoldo, October–March; on a rainy day 20 individuals were hunting together; Tampson 1987). Nests as far south as Panama.

BAND-TAILED NIGHTHAWK, *Nyctiprogne leucopyga,* Bacurau-cauda-barrada

19 cm. Slender, northern species, quite dark, without white spots on wings but with white band across middle of tail. VOICE: *glok, glok, glok . . . ,* unhurried, sometimes bisyllabic, *gole-kwak.* Forests at river edges; periodically gregarious. Amazonia to Mato Grosso (upper Xingu), Piauí, French Guiana, Colombia.

NACUNDA NIGHTHAWK, *Podager nacunda,* Corucão

29.5 cm; wingspan 71 cm; 205 g. Stockiest species. Short tail, unmistakable in size, pure white belly, white area on lower throat, and wide white stripe on primaries. Tip of tail also white in male. VOICE: *pro-pro-pro . . . ;* song toadlike, with prolonged sequence, *t-rrohh ttt-rrohh* or *prrr-doo.* Flies in full daylight, perches on stakes, periodically in flocks (Mato Grosso, Rio Grande do Sul). Hunts over cities under urban illumination (Cuiabá, Mato Grosso) and under airport lights (Belo Horizonte, Minas Gerais, Federal District). Open country, cerrado. On migration sleeps in campo limpo, and is invisible until it takes off at one's feet. Venezuela and Colombia to Bolivia, Argentina, throughout Brazil. Flight silhouette resembles Short-eared Owl, *Asio flammeus;* prominent white can make it look like *Vanellus chilensis,* at whose side it sometimes flies during day, primarily on migration (December–January, Espírito Santo), or even like a Gray Monjita, *Xolmis cinerea.*

PAURAQUE, *Nyctidromus albicollis,* Curiango, Bacurau   PL 18.7

30 cm. Our best-known species. Has red and gray phrases. Tail long, not forked. White wing stripe and large, white streaks on tail feathers occasionally displayed on short, vertical flights, when they become prominent, even at night. VOICE: call *ba-bacoorau;* warning *dog, groh-groh-groh;* song *go-bee-oo, gril-woo, cohrianGOO;* see also "Sounds." Forest edge, open capoeira, on ground. Southern U.S. and Mexico to Bolivia, Paraguay, and Misiones, Argentina; all of Brazil

where there are forests, including Rio Grande do Sul. Also called *Ju-jau, Ibijau* (Kamaiurá, Mato Grosso), *A-ku-kú* (Juruna, Mato Grosso).

OCELLATED POORWILL, *Nyctiphrynus ocellatus,* Bacurau-ocellado

21 cm. Unique, slender, strictly forest species. Blackish chestnut with round white spots on belly, absent on all other species. VOICE: song a harsh *breh-oo*. Forest interior; perches on high branches to sing but nests on ground like most other nightjars (see "Breeding"). Colombia to Argentina, locally in most of Brazil, including Espírito Santo, Rio de Janeiro, Paraná, Mato Grosso, but not Rio Grande do Sul.

RUFOUS NIGHTJAR, *Caprimulgus rufus,* João-corta-pau

28 cm. Stocky with long, broad tail; 3 outer rectrices of male have large subterminal yellowish white spots, usually visible only when tail is fanned. No white stripe in wing; throat has scaly yellow pattern. Female has yellow at tip of tail. VOICE: *jook-bakbak-BRAo* (*João-corta-pau*, "John-cut-wood"). Forest edge, where it perches on branches to sing. Costa Rica to Bolivia, Argentina, almost all of Brazil, including Amazonia, southeast, centralwest. Formerly placed in genus *Setochalcis*. Also called *Maria-faz-angu* (Pará). See *C. sericocaudatus*.

SILKY-TAILED NIGHTJAR, *Caprimulgus sericocaudatus*

Little-known, very similar to *C. rufus*. Unlike it, has more graduated tail, and in male 3 outer rectrices have wide terminal white (not yellowish) band on both vanes which becomes narrower farther in, a decoration also visible on closed tail. Internal vanes of primaries all black (not barred with cinnamon, unlike *rufus*). VOICE: a trisyllabic *doh-diew-lewt* with timbre of *Nyctidromus albicollis,* sung in extensive sequences of 3 minutes or more, without slightest modulation and no interval, while perched on a low branch (R. Straneck, Iguaçu, August). Pará (Santarém), Espírito Santo (Vitória, September), Paraná (Curitiba), Paraguay, Argentina (Misiones), eastern Peru.

BAND-WINGED NIGHTJAR, *Caprimulgus longirostris,* Bacurau-da-telha

23 cm. Primaries have wide white (yellow in female) stripe. 3 or 4 outer rectrices on each side have large terminal white spot and 1–2 lesser basal stripes (fig. 143). White spot on edge of wing is prominent when perched bird moves wings. These adornments are poorly outlined on female. VOICE: song a high whistle, *bilooEET,* given at intervals of 1–3 seconds. Colombian Andes (where I found it in paramos at 3300 m), Chile, southern Argentina. Also tepuis of Roraima and Venezuela.

Rediscovery in Brazil and Invasion of the City of Rio de Janeiro: One hundred seventeen years after it was last seen in Brazil, I rediscovered this species in high campos of Serra do

A **B**

Fig. 143. Rectrices (from the right side, seen from above) of two nightjars: (A) Band-winged Nightjar, *Caprimulgus l. longirostris* (Rio de Janeiro); and (B) Spot-tailed Nightjar, *C. maculicaudus* (Xingu, Mato Grosso).

Caparaó in Espírito Santo (Jatiboca 1940). I later obtained records from Serra do Caparaó, eastern Minas Gerais (1941); Serra dos Órgãos and Itatiaia, Rio de Janeiro, and Serra da Mantiqueira, southern Minas Gerais, above 1300 m (1956); Rio Grande do Sul (1972); Bahia (Raso da Catarina, 1979); and Santa Catarina (1979). Everything leads me to believe it breeds in most of these places. The almost complete lack of records of the species in Brazil until recently must be due to lack of attention to it by ornithologists and to complete lack of information on its voice. Apparently it immigrated to ex-Guanabara (city of Rio de Janeiro) subsequent to 1955, where it now lives in many neighborhoods (Santa Teresa, Laranjeiras, Urca, Copacabana, Leblon, etc.), perching on roofs and walls which substitute for stones and rocky places. Reveals its presence by voice, more frequently near dawn; almost always flies only after nightfall. Perches on buildings, as in Laranjeiras, Copacabana, and Leblon, where it catches termites fallen on sills of illuminated, closed windows, perhaps on a 15th floor. Rarely can be seen hunting termites swarming around street lights. Sometimes combines life in its original environment in mountains with its recently adopted life among human buildings, as I saw in Caraça, Minas Gerais, at 1450 m, where it regularly perches over door of church to catch insects attracted by electric lights at school. In Rio de Janeiro sings almost all year but sometimes stops for a week or more. I found a clutch of 2 eggs atop an old building in Santa Teresa, Rio de Janeiro, in September 1973. I think it nested on the roof of the National Museum at the Quinta da Boa Vista in 1969. In Argentina (with a different climate) it also sometimes penetrates into cities (Buenos Aires, during migration?). See *C. maculicaudus*.

WHITE-TAILED NIGHTJAR, *Caprimulgus cayennensis*

Male has more white than *C. longirostris*, including white belly. VOICE: a penetrating note, *siBEEeh*. Edge of rivers. Only in extreme north, in Roraima, Amapá, the Guianas, Costa Rica. See *C. candicans*.

RORAIMAN NIGHTJAR, *Caprimulgus whitelyi*

Roraima (Dickerman and Phelps 1982).

WHITE-WINGED NIGHTJAR, *Caprimulgus candicans*, Bacurau-rabo-branco

23 cm. Resembles *C. cayennensis* and *C. longirostris*, with wing stripe, abdomen, and lateral rectrices white. Orissanga, São Paulo; Cuiabá, Mato Grosso; Goiás (a small flock in August, T. Parker III); Emas National Park (A. Negret 1984 pers. comm.); Paraguay.

SPOT-TAILED NIGHTJAR, *Caprimulgus maculicaudus*, Bacurau-rabo-maculado

19.5 cm. Slender savanna species with wide local distribution. Rectrices have 4 round spots and white tip (fig. 143) but no marking on wings. VOICE: *bitSEwit, tsiwit*, recalling *C. longirostris*. In flight snaps flight feathers. Humid savannas, e.g., buriti groves. Mexico to Bolivia. May be common where it occurs, but due to lack of observers known from only a few places in all of Brazil: Mato Grosso (Xingu 1948); south to Espírito Santo (Linhares 1976), Rio de Janeiro (Baixada Fluminense, area of Oswaldo Cruz Institute 1951; Itaguaí 1962; Poço das Antas 1981); São Paulo. Locally common in Marajó, Pará.

LITTLE NIGHTJAR, *Caprimulgus parvulus*, Bacurau-pequeno   Fig. 144

20 cm. Abundant in bushy open country (campos sujos). Throat, stripe on external primaries, and spots on tip of tail all white. Lower throat has black spots and some white bar-

Fig. 144. Little Nightjar, *Caprimulgus parvulus*.

ring. Female lacks white markings. VOICE: *druee-dro-dro-dro-dro-dro-dro-dro*, with timbre of a xylophone. Perches on stumps to sing. Migratory; appears in large numbers in Minas Gerais in October. Venezuela to Bolivia, Argentina, throughout Brazil to Rio Grande do Sul. See *C. hirundinaceus* and *Chordeiles acutipennis*.

BLACKISH NIGHTJAR, *Caprimulgus nigrescens*, Bacurau-de-lajeado

19.5 cm. Very dark Amazonian species. White lateral spot on throat and white-tipped tail make it difficult to distinguish one end of bird from the other when it is perched. Female lacks any white features. VOICE: *bit-bit*; song *rad, kwo-ak*. On black rocks among sparse vegetation (see "Morphology . . ."). The Guianas and Venezuela to Bolivia, northern Mato Grosso, Pará, Maranhão. See *Chordeiles pusillus*.

PYGMY NIGHTJAR, *Caprimulgus hirundinaceus*, Bacurauzinho-da-caatinga   BR

16.5 cm. As small as *Chordeiles pusillus*. Very light brown, perfectly adapted to sunny environment of caatinga. Wing stripe and tips of outer 2 rectrices white in male; female has no white marks. VOICE: a single syllable, *WEEe*, sometimes fuller; a short confused phrase with timbre of *Nyctidromus albicollis*. Perches on sand or stones. Restricted to northeast. See *C. parvulus* and *Chordeiles acutipennis*.

LADDER-TAILED NIGHTJAR, *Hydropsalis climacocerca*, Acurana

28 cm. This is Amazonian version of *H. brasiliana*. Wing stripe, underparts, and tail almost entirely white. VOICE: call *krip-krip*. River edges, river islands, frequently perching on branches. Venezuela to Bolivia, Acre, northern Mato Grosso, Pará (Tocantins).

SCISSOR-TAILED NIGHTJAR, *Hydropsalis brasiliana*, Bacurau-tesoura   PL 19.1

Adult male 40 cm, tail accounting for more than ²/₃ of total length; immature male only half that; female 27.5 cm. Neither sex has white wing stripe. In south (southern Mato Grosso, Rio Grande do Sul) nuchal collar yellowish (*H. b. furcifera*); in northern part of range nuchal collar reddish chestnut and bird smaller (*H. b. brasiliana*). SOUNDS: voice an extremely high *tsig* (in flight), sounding like voice of a cricket or bat. Song a prolonged sequence of *tsips* . . . , one note per second just like a cricket, sometimes for minutes on end—e.g., 3 minutes with an interval of a few seconds and then continuing—while perched crosswise on a small branch or other substrate, sometimes in flight. Produces various noises with wings: a muffled beat in flight or when perched, a ruffle (*bo, bo, bo, bo, bo* . . .) while flying up fast or coming down in pursuit of another individual; after perching on ground male sometimes produce a muffled *bo, bo, bo, bo, bo,* possibly by beating wings against ground.

Forest borders, cerrado, campo sujo, parks, on ground. In Rio de Janeiro shows a tendency to adapt to residence in city. In Laranjeiras I have observed it at Nossa Senhora Cenáculo convent (at foot of a capoeira-covered hill); at dusk and dawn perches on roofs to sing, from where it also hunts, launching out from and returning to roof, like *Caprimulgus longirostris,* which occurs in same place. South of Amazon to Bolivia, Paraguay, Argentina, Uruguay, including all of eastern and southern Brazil. Also called *Curiango-tesoura.* See *H. climacocerca* and *Macropsalis creagra.*

Long-trained Nightjar, *Macropsalis creagra,* Bacurau-tesoura-gigante   Pl 18.8

Male 76 cm, tail accounting for ³/₄ of total length; a side tail feather can measure 61 cm (Bocaina, Rio de Janeiro), with central ones only 5 cm; female 32 cm, conspicuous for pattern of large yellow spots on lower throat. Clearly stockier than *Hydropsalis brasiliana,* with broader wings and tail; crown dotted (not streaked) with black. Quiet. Lives in forests, hunts well in dark at edge of roads crossing through forest, the same as *Hydropsalis.* Espírito Santo to São Paulo (Guaratuba, Santos), Rio Grande do Sul (Novo Hamburgo, Torres), and Misiones, Argentina. In northern part of range (Espírito Santo, Rio de Janeiro) found only in mountains, e.g., Serra dos Órgãos, Itatiaia. Apparently has low population density and is threatened by deforestation in its very limited range. Of Andean descent but is strictly a forest bird and one of darkest-colored species. Also called *Curiango-tesoura.*

Sickle-winged Nightjar, *Eleothreptus anomalus,* Curiango-do-banhado

20 cm. Small, stocky. Male has short, uniquely shaped wings: primaries are recurved like sabers, have white tips, and must serve to produce a loud noise during display flights. Foreneck typically streaked and speckled with yellowish white. Outer tail feathers tipped whitish. Female has "normal" wing, without white. Marsh edges. Brasília, Federal District, Minas Gerais, and São Paulo to Rio Grande do Sul, Uruguay, Argentina. See *Chordeiles pusillus.*

Caprimulgidae Bibliography

See also General Bibliography

Blem, C. R. 1972. *Wilson Bull.* 84:492–93. [Stomach]

Bühler, P. 1970. Schädelmorphologie und Kiefermechanik der Caprimulgidae. *Z. Morph. Tiere* 66:337–99.

Bühler, P. 1972. Sandwichstrukturen der Schädelkapsel verschiedener Vögel—zum Leichtbauprinzip bei Organismen. *Mitt. 4 Inst. f.leichte Flächentragwerke.* Stuttgart.

Bühler, P. 1987. Zur Strategie des Beutefangs der Caprimulgidae. *J. Orn.* 128(4):488–91.

Hardy, J. W., B. H. Coffey, and G. B. Reynard. 1988. *Voices of the New World Nightbirds.* Revised edition. Gainesville, Fl.: ARA Records.

Hardy, J. W., and R. Straneck. 1989. The Silky-tailed Nightjar (*Caprimulgus sericocaudatus*) and other neotropical Caprimulgids: Unraveling some mysteries. *Condor* 91:193–97.

Hartert, E. 1897. *Das Tierreich.* Berlin. [Taxonomy]

Howell, T. R. 1959. *Wilson Bull.* 71:19–32. [Thermoregulation]

Jackson, H. D. 1985. Mouth size in *Macrodipteryx* and other African Nightjars. *Bull. B.O.C.* 105(2):51–54.

Marshall, J. T. 1955. Hibernation in captive goatsuckers. *Condor* 57:129–34.

Mills, A. M. 1986. The influence of moonlight on the behavior of goatsuckers, Caprimulgidae. *Auk* 103:370–78.

Roth, P. 1985. Breeding biology of the Blackish Nightjar, *Caprimulgus nigrescens,* in western Brazil. *Le Gerfaut* 75:253–64.

San Martin, P. P. 1959. *Bol. Soc. Taguató.* 1:51–55. [Feeding]

Sick, H. 1950a. *Rev. Bras. Biol.* 10:295–306. [*Chordeiles rupestris,* behavior]

Sick, H. 1959. *Bol. Mus. Nac. Rio de Janeiro, Zool.* 204. [*Caprimulgus longirostris,* rediscovery in Brazil]

Sick, H. 1963. *Vellozia* 1:107–16. (GB) [*Caprimulgus longirostris,* distribution]

Sick, H. 1979. *Bull. B.O.C.* 99(4):115–20. [*Caprimulgus longirostris,* adaptation to new environments]

Straneck, R., R. Ridgely, M. Rumboll, et al. 1987. El nido de *Lurocalis nattereri. Comun. Mus. Argent. Cien. Nat. Zool.* 4(17):133–36.

Tampson, E. 1987. Notas preliminares sobre a presença do bacurau norte-americano, *Chordeiles minor,* no morro do Espelho, São Leopoldo, Rio Grande do Sul. *Acta Biol. Leopold.* 9(1): 133–36.

Udvardy, M. de F. 1951. Heat Resistance in Birds. *Proc. 10th Int. Orn. Cong. Uppsala,* 1950:596–99.

Wetmore, A. 1968. Additions to the list of birds recorded from Colombia. *Wilson Bull.* 80(3):325–26.

ORDER APODIFORMES

FAMILY APODIDAE: SWIFTS (15)

Widely distributed throughout the world, swifts are well represented in the Neotropics, where the largest species, *Streptoprocne*, are also found. The name *andorinhão* [literally "big swallow"] applies to both large and small species. Fossils are known from the lower Miocene of France (20 million years B.P.) and from the Pleistocene of Brazil (20,000 years B.P.).

The grouping of swifts and hummingbirds in the same order is disputed, as is any close relationship with the "pico-Passerines." The structure of the musculus splenius capitis, similar in Apodidae and Trochilidae, which facilitates neck movements during rapid chasing of insects, can be interpreted as convergent evolution (Zusi and Bentz 1982). Swifts appear to have some relation to the Caprimulgiformes.

The general public does not know anything about *andorinhões*, "swifts"; they are all *andorinhas*, "swallows." Thus, geographic names such as *gruta de andorinhas*, "swallow grotto," and *cachoeira de andorinhas*, "swallow falls," certainly refer to swifts.

Morphology and Special Adaptations

Swifts and swallows are superficially similar, especially in the short neck and wide-based bill which serves each to capture insects in flight (see also Caprimulgidae, referred to generally as nightjars).

The wings of swifts, birds that are essentially aerial, are notably long, narrow, and stiff[1] (fig. 128). They are long because of the great length of the 9 or 10 primaries and narrow because of the 8 to 11 shortened secondaries. The longest primary of a swift is three times as long as a secondary. In a swallow this primary is only double that of a secondary. Although reinforced, the humerus and ulna are short, whereas the hand bones are extremely long. The total length (tip of bill to tip of tail) is misleading in swifts, for their closed wings extend far beyond the tip of the tail, except in species with long rectrices of the genera *Panyptila* and *Reinarda* (see Band-rumped Swift, *Chaetura spinicauda*, and Short-tailed Swift, *C. brachyura*).

Only rarely do swifts have more than 10 rectrices (unlike swallows, which have 12). In the *Chaetura* the rachis is prolonged beyond the vane, forming a kind of rigid spine. In this genus the tail, with its series of small spines, is still so short it sometimes appears to be missing. This is never the case with swallows.

The feet are very small (*apodis*, literally "without feet"), and the toes are incapable of clutching branches or wires, unlike those of the Hirundinidae and Trochilidae. The relatively short hallux may be directed toward the sole of the foot or forward. In the Lesser Swallow-tailed Swift, *Panyptila cayennensis,* all four toes are clearly oriented toward the front (pamprodactyl). The feet of newly hatched young, however, are zygodactyl (two toes forward, two back). The calluses on the metatarsus, an adaptation for support on abrasive surfaces, correspond to the heal pads of Piciform nestlings.

Swifts rest clinging to rough vertical surfaces with their strong, sharp, curved claws, firmly fixed with the body supported on the above-mentioned callosity and rigid tail (fig. 145). Although quite resistant, the rectrices and outer primaries thus suffer great wear. Those of the *Streptoprocne* lose the curved outline at their ends in only a few months. The terminal spines of the rectrices may be completely worn away, generally a certain sign that the individual is breeding, for it implies much time spent on the rough rock surrounding the nest.

There is good convergence of the visual field of the eyes (see "Flight . . . "). The feathers of the lores are lowered to avoid impeding the view.

The salivary glands are highly developed and periodically, during breeding, become much larger for use in nest building, as in the Trochilidae. The basic digestive function of saliva is minimal.

The ability to fall into a torpor is a rare adaptation of swifts; they become completely immobile on their roost (see also Trochilidae, "Reaction to Cold"). I have verified that in the Serra do Mar, above 800 m, the Ashy-tailed Swift, *Chaetura andrei,* does not leave its chimneys on cold, rainy days, remaining in a semisomnolent state. Individuals that have been properly investigated show a reduction in respiratory rate and body temperature.

The skin is resistant, similar to that of hummingbirds. Sexes are similar, but there may be clear sexual dimorphism in the Chestnut-collared Swift, *Cypseloides rutilus,* with only the male having red on the lower throat.

---

[1]The former name of the order, now abandoned, was *Machrochires,* "those with large hands."

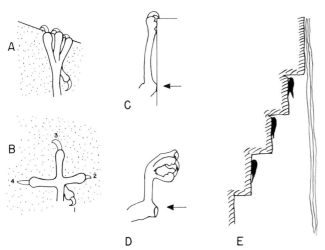

Fig. 145. How a swift clings to a wall. Gray-rumped Swift, *Chaetura cinereiventris,* left foot, disposition of the toes: (A) hanging from an edge; (B) clinging to a rough, vertical wall. White-collared Swift, *Streptoprocne zonaris,* right foot: (C) hanging from an edge, using outer toe and tarsus, seen from the side. Note the callus on the tarsus (arrow) supported against the wall, providing counterpoise to the hooked claw; (D) the same foot, loose, showing the callus. (E) Three sleeping *S. zonaris* clinging to a wall behind a waterfall. Original, H. Sick.

Vocalization

Swift vocalizations are simple, with the song a somewhat more elaborate phrase. The *Streptoprocne* cry in chorus in the late afternoon (see "Breeding . . ."). The *Chaetura,* especially *C. andrei,* if bothered at rest, either alongside the nest or in flocks, beat their wings strongly against the substrate in a menacing manner. The sound produced is unlike that made by pigeons beating one wing against the other.

Flight and Feeding

Swifts catch all their food in flight. It has been calculated that the Common Swift, *Apus apus,* of Europe, the size of our *Chaetura,* flies 1000 km a day just to feed itself. They may therefore go far afield in search of food, as is attested by research on the droppings of the Biscutate Swift, *Streptoprocne biscutata,* in the Serra do Bico da Arara (Rio Grande do Norte), which contained obvious evidence of insect remains (e.g., leaf-cutting ants) unknown in the region.

The Apodidae live in continuous movement, competing with hummingbirds as the most dynamic birds of our planet. With their constant, zooming flight, they, and especially the Chaeturinae, are equal to the fastest hawks (*Falco* spp.). The normal velocity of *Apus apus* was measured by a pilot flying alongside at 103 km/hr. In a diving flight they reach 150 km/hr, a figure I accept as reasonable for large species such as the *Streptoprocne.* Swifts far outdo the velocity of swal-

lows. They are swift by nature, having no "need" for rapid flight, unlike falcons, which must be speedier than the prey they chase. A solid screen of feathers that swifts can control by muscles protects their eyes from the pressure of air currents created by motion. The rest all hinges on aerodynamics. At such velocities the slightest shock, against a utility wire for instance, is fatal. If placed on the ground, some swifts have great difficulty taking flight.

Swifts catch very small insects. Four hundred ants were found in the stomach of one White-collared Swift, *Streptoprocne zonaris,* and 300 ants plus numerous other tiny insects in two others. In Venezuela a female of the same species had 800 winged *Azteca* ants in her stomach.

Swifts fly with the bill closed, capturing their prey individually as do other birds such as swallows. They are farsighted, being among the birds that can focus both monoptically and bioptically, and have two foveae, one central, one lateral.

They take advantage of fires, where myriad arthropods, even nonfliers such as small spiders, are carried up by the strong mass of ascending air. They gather insects off water surfaces (where they also drink) and beetles from leaves that happen to be blowing in the air. I have seen *S. zonaris* capture large leaf-cutter ant queens as they come out of the nest. In the act of catching the insect they cut off the fat abdomen and let fall the thin cephalothorax. In *Panyptila cayennensis* and the Fork-tailed Palm-Swift, *Reinarda squamata,* small ants and termites comprised about 90% of the diet. They capture both male and female ants. So-called aerial plankton also figures in the diet of the Apodidae. Carried by wind, it does not require a swift flier to capture it, so swifts get it merely by flying against the wind, as swallows do.

Swifts have the ability to reduce their velocity abruptly, switching to hovering like hummingbirds, as when they exploit a stationary swarm of small Hymenoptera or slowly flying termites. The *Chaetura* move in chimneys, descending and ascending vertically. The same technique is used by the *Streptoprocne* and *Cypseloides* when they change perches on the walls where they sleep.

I have noticed in the Serra do Mar (Rio de Janeiro) that during low fog and rain the *Chaetura* hunt close to the ground or go above the clouds. Swifts generally fly higher than swallows, often being seen above tall forests where swallows seldom appear. Certain species, such as the *Cypseloides,* have a greater propensity for hunting at high altitudes. Only under certain atmospheric conditions that keep the insects in the lower strata will all of them hunt low above ground, where they meet swallows. These are the best opportunities to observe plumage color well. They fly at twilight to hunt swarming termites, going to considerable heights when there is no wind, and can be confused with bats then, especially short-tailed species such as the Short-tailed Swift, *Chaetura brachyura.* On extensive flights ahead of storms, see "Swift Grottoes. . . ." If there is a food shortage during cold, rainy weather, they spend the whole day roosting (see "Morphology . . . "). This is the beginning of the torpor that enables them to better withstand periods of cold and food scarcity.

In the Indo-Pacific region swifts have been observed hunting under artificial light. I have seen *Cypseloides* regurgitate pellets, although swift feces contain chitin. Swifts bathe in flight, in the rain.

Breeding and Special Adaptations in Nesting

During the breeding season swifts display by adopting a different type of flight (*Streptoprocne, Cypseloides, Chaetura*). *Chaetura andrei,* among others, frequently flies in groups of three in elegant swirls, holding the wings almost immobile and arched, with occasional interspersed rapid wing beats.

The *Streptoprocne,* which along with the *Cypseloides* are the most gregarious, gather in large circling flocks that utter cries at certain intervals as if obeying a command. Independently of this, certain individuals fly silently in undulant revolutions near their companions. They ascend abruptly, then immediately come down closing their wings. They point the bill partially downward, apparently to give maximum display to the white nuchal area, which is separated from the forecollar in *S. biscutata,* a detail visible at a distance on these occasions. I have seen in-flight copulation attempted in both *Chaetura* and *Streptoprocne.*

Apodidae nesting, which I have studied in Brazilian species since 1941, is one of the most interesting evolutionary problems. Notwithstanding the enormous variation in nesting habits in this family, there are some fundamental elements, including some based on morphological adaptations. For example, the size and productivity of their salivary glands (see "Morphology . . .") increases greatly during the breeding season because saliva is used to glue the nesting material, however diverse this may be in different species. The extreme in this regard is the Edible-nest Swiftlet, *Collocalia fuciphaga,* of the Orient, which builds only with saliva, producing the famous edible nests.

The *Chaetura* build a nest of dried twigs which they break from the crowns of trees as they fly over the branches. They paste this material with saliva inside tree holes, chimneys, attics, and other building cavities, even in underground culverts and on the walls of wells (*C. brachyura*). The saliva hardens like mason's grout.

I only noticed the use of residential chimneys (fig. 146B) as a substitute for trees for roosting or nesting after 1945, but since then it has become common (*C. andrei* and Gray-rumped Swift, *C. cinereiventris*). Formerly, when the forest was still dominant, the *Chaetura* sought trees for nesting. As more and more masonry homes became available, swifts discovered chimneys to be convenient shelters, for in southern Brazil many home fireplaces are not used in the warm season, which is precisely when these birds appear to nest. The number of "house" swifts, one pair per chimney, will increase as the number of homes (and chimneys) increases and the forests diminish and as the number of swifts that were reared in these artificial shelters increases. This is one of the rare cases in which a wild bird with special requirements has managed to replace them advantageously as its natural habitat has become degraded. In Amazonia (Belém, Pará) the use of home chimneys was noted in 1960. Adoption of chimneys by *C. brachyura* was observed in the 1930s in Trinidad. Most species reveal their presence in the roost by peeping or warbling almost constantly, even at night.

The *Streptoprocne* and *Cypseloides* make nests of moss and other soft materials, firmly amalgamated with saliva and lined with fragments of vegetable material. They generally place them in humid locales having rock walls and cliffs, near waterfalls, and in dark, dripping grottoes (fig. 146A). The Great Dusky Swift, *Cypseloides senex,* builds its solid "throne" near waterfalls or on cliffs (Iguaçu, Paraná), entirely exposed to daylight, something uncommon for an Apodidae. Both genera enjoy being sprayed by drops of water. Geographic names such as Saltos dos Dardanelos e Andorinhas, ("Falls of the Dardanelles and Swallows," Rio Aripuanã, Mato Grosso) refer to these swifts. On the south coast *Streptoprocne* frequent slits in rocky islands and grottoes opening toward the sea.

The *Cypseloides* nestling develops a luxurious down that protects it against the cold and humidity of its nest site. To reach their nest or nocturnal roost, *Cypseloides* sometimes must fly through waterfalls. I have seen a *C. senex* washed away by a waterfall manage to get out of the water downstream and fly away (Serra do Cachimbo, Pará). I was told that birds sometimes are killed in such situations. Sometimes during floods the water increases so much that the *Cypseloides* can no longer reach their nests. In Asia and the Orient various swifts, such as the *Collocalia* and the Giant Swiftlet (or Waterfall Swift), *Hydrochous gigas,* live in this same situation.

Swifts have been seen nest building in the bracing of an operating water wheel (A. Ruschi). This odd place was first used by a *Cypseloides* and two years later by a *Streptoprocne.* The *Cypseloides* often nest close to one another.

Other Brazilian species are susceptible to humidity. *Panyptila cayennensis, Reinarda squamata,* and the White-tipped Swift, *Aeronautes montivagus,* build in dry places with vegetable wool and soft feathers they pick up in full flight. *A. montivagus* makes its nest in rock crevasses or vertical pipes. *R. squamata* and *P. cayennensis* eschew cavities and caves for well-finished incubation chambers of their own making, where they brood in the dark; the projection that holds the eggs forms part of the front wall, not being independently attached to the nest's substrate as is the saucer of *Chaetura.* The *Reinarda* nest is well protected by the fan of a hanging palm leaf (fig. 146C), whereas the suspended nest of *Panyptila* is totally exposed (fig. 146D), the species being entirely independent of a need for protection.

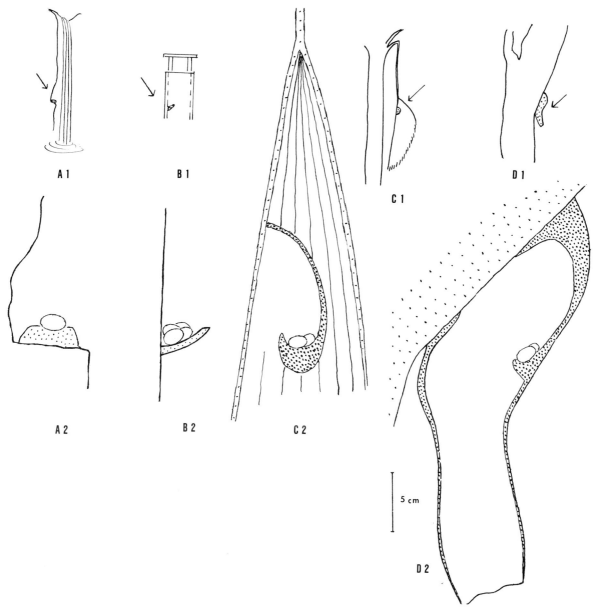

Fig. 146. Types of nests of Brazilian swifts: (1) general view, (2) close up. (A) Great Dusky Swift, *Cypseloides senex,* small ledge on a cliff alongside a waterfall. (B) Ashy-tailed Swift, *Chaetura andrei,* saucer made of twigs, glued to the wall inside a hollow tree or a chimney. (C) Fork-tailed Palm-Swift, *Reinarda squamata,* bag of feathers, glued inside the fold of a buriti leaf. (D) Lesser Swallow-tailed Swift, *Panyptila cayennensis,* large felt tube, glued to a tree trunk. After Sick 1948, 1955, and 1958.

Whereas the *Reinarda* nest is fluffy, being sufficiently protected from intemperate weather by the leaf, *Panyptila* requires one that is protected against rain and storms and has resolved the problem by perfecting a feltlike finish; the pair does not hurry over construction of the nest, which takes a little more than a month but may go on for more than two.

Reinarda squamata begins nest construction by gluing separately, feather by feather, along the vein of the palm leaf, as if marking out the boundaries of the construction area. It first builds the middle, ring-shaped part, then the upper part, and finally the lower part, with the egg-holding shell in the

final phase (Carvalho 1962). The bird fixes the feathers by holding its bill to the substrate and vibrating its head, an act that must facilitate expelling the saliva. It normally takes more than 30 days to complete its nest, although there are cases of less than a month and others of more than three months. The mates take turns at the job.

Eggs are quite elongated and white (yellowish in *Streptoprocne*). The three miniscule eggs of *R. squamata* are similar to those of hummingbirds and have a rosy tone due to the transparency of the shell. Sometimes eggs of this species are found glued to the feathers forming the substrate, which apparently occurs during the laying and not as a result of a deliberate act by the bird. In the course of incubation they become unstuck and can be turned freely, which is indispensable for their proper incubation. Sometimes eggs of this species fall from the nest as a result of unfortunate movements by the parents or because the supporting leaf is blown by the wind. *Chaetura andrei* lays three to four eggs, the *Cypseloides* only one or two.

Incubation takes 19 days on the average for the Chimney Swift, *Chaetura pelagica*, and 21 days for *R. squamata*. The young hatch naked, without even natal down. Those of *Cypseloides* develop a dense mantle of gray semiplumes in less than two weeks, an important adaptation to the extremely humid environment of the nest. Newly hatched birds are blind, opening their eyes on the fifth or sixth day (*R. squamata*) or as much as two weeks after hatching (*Chaetura pelagica*).

Nestlings cling fast to the nest, which appears to be essential in the case of *R. squamata,* whose nest is greatly exposed to shaking by the wind. Newly hatched *Chaetura* develop a strong instinct to creep a little way up the wall to which their nest is fixed. Nestlings usually stay three weeks in the nest and two more weeks hanging on the nearby walls (*C. brachyura*). They are fed by their parents with miniscule insects, some still alive, stuck together by the hundreds in balls brought in the gular sac. A single nest is frequently attended by three or four adults, probably immatures that cooperate in brooding and feeding the new young. Each pair requires a full residential chimney for itself (*C. andrei, C. cinereiventris*). One nest found with nine young probably involved more than one female. The nesting season corresponds with the rainy season when there is a greater abundance of insects.

Swift Grottoes and Silos, Guano, and Migration

The *Streptoprocne* gather in certain grottoes to spend the night, locales that probably have been traditional for centuries, with hundreds and even thousands of individuals congregating. I have studied such grottoes occupied by *S. zonaris* in Itatiaia, Rio de Janeiro, and in the Serra do Caraça, Minas Gerais. All were quite humid. At the Torres promontory in Rio Grande do Sul, the thousands of *S. zonaris* that converge there at evening to pass the night in rocky grottoes bathed by the sea are most impressive (W. Voss).

In Rio Grande do Norte at the Serra do Bico da Arara (Fazenda Ingá, belonging to Luis G. M. Bezerra) there is a great concentration of *S. biscutata*. Their droppings and pellets accumulate on the cave floor, forming an insupportably odiferous organic fertilizer which is sold on the spot. In 1975 production reached 50 tons. It is used in agriculture on the Seridó meadows and is considered more effective than cattle manure or chemical fertilizers (L. Bezerra pers. comm.). Analysis of this guano shows it to be a valuable nitrogen compound, although it is poor in phosphorus and potassium. An analysis I had made in 1973, through the Technology Center of the Ministry of Agriculture (Rio de Janeiro), showed the following percentages: water 13.16%; ash 5.48%; organic nitrogen 9.64%; ammoniacal nitrogen 2.50%; oxide of phosphorus 1.4%; and oxide of potassium 0.10% percent. Guano of insectivorous birds differs from the classic guano of seabirds (see Sulidae, "Guano") which are fish eaters. It would be interesting to compare swift guano with the "cave phosphate" (chiropterit, Eisentraut 1938) of insectivorous bats.

In Suriname in chimneys occupied by large flocks of *Chaetura brachyura* roosting together, an "impenetrable layer" of guano was formed (Haverschmidt 1958). The accumulation of feces, etc., (biodeposition) in caves where swifts breed, however, is usually small.

A good-sized flock of *Chaetura andrei* gathered over various months in the silo of the Passa Tempo ranch in Minas Gerais (Andrade and Freitas 1987). One cannot speak of a "colony," for the swifts come there only to roost together. There were 127 in October 1985, 250 in November, 420 in December, and 542 in January, but in February the numbers started to decrease until the birds were completely gone in April 1986. Samples collected revealed that "club" members had small gonads and perfect plumage, no molt, which probably means they were young and not yet breeding. In winter the whole flock emigrated like the rest of the population of that area. Large-scale banding will clarify the situation. In Suriname Haverschmidt recorded two clubs of this type, one with 1000 birds. Twenty specimens collected were in complete molt and had small gonads, suggesting they had probably finished breeding. There is insufficient information on swift cycles in Suriname. See the clubs of the Blue-and-white Swallow, *Notiochelidon cyanoleuca,* in Hirundinidae, "Migration."

The outstanding flight ability of swifts lets them flee areas of bad weather. They let themselves be pushed away by storms but quickly return, taking advantage of their unequaled flight ability. Thus, before or after passage of a cold front (*andorinhão-do-temporal* = "storm swift") they may appear in greater or lesser flocks of transitory character in regions where they are not normally found, as I frequently observed in ex-Guanabara.

"Thunder flights" of swifts and certain swallows are known throughout the world and reflect the great sensitivity of these birds to adverse air currents that dislocate the aerial plankton that is their food (Voipio 1970).

Night flights at great altitudes, like those recorded with radar in Europe for *Apus apus,* have not yet been noted for Brazilian species. However, it is worth mentioning that in Rancho Grande, Venezuela, on nights with strong wind and rain or thick fog, individual *Streptoprocne zonaris* hit illuminated windows (Beebe 1949).

After breeding swifts become truly migratory. *Chaetura*

andrei disappears from almost all of southern Brazil, although records of migrant flocks are not lacking for the winter (Rio de Janeiro, Sick 1958). Southern representatives of this species, *C. a. meridionalis,* appear during the southern winter in Colombia and even Panama. They gather during this period by the hundreds to sleep in certain chimneys, apparently arriving from a distance, sometimes from above the clouds as I saw in the Serra do Mar (Rio de Janeiro). They clutch the walls of the chimney, huddled close together warming one another, forming a dense carpet like bats in their diurnal roosts. In Rio Grande do Sul in the winter, *C. cinereiventris* uses certain spacious chimneys for flock roosting. These are occupied night after night by flocks that may contain hundreds of individuals (Novo Hamburgo, São Leopoldo, W. Voss). *C. cinereiventris* is recorded regularly throughout the winter in the southeast. The origin of migrant individuals of *Chaetura* and *Streptoprocne* can be deduced by identifying the geographic race to which they belong. In southeastern Brazil *C. andrei* returning in August (ex-Guanabara and Rio de Janeiro) are taken as precursors of spring.

Migrations of *Streptoprocne biscutata* that I discovered will be clarified by differences in morphology (only now recognized) between the northern and southern populations and by systematic banding. Banding is also going to bring understanding of the *Chaetura* clubs (see above). *Reinarda squamata* moves about within Amazonia.

Chaetura pelagica comes to western South America during the northern winter. Its entry into Brazil has not yet been proven. The long migrations of this species, which probably were already taking place in the upper Tertiary in eastern North America, must have been caused by Pleistocene climatic changes, like so many other migrations from one continent to the other. The greatest landbird migrations known are by the White-throated Needletail, *Hirundapus c. caudacutus,* which breeds as far north as northern Siberia and winters in southern Australia and Tasmania (Mees 1985).

Enemies, Other Dangers, and Longevity

Perils for swifts are evident during nesting. Predation of *Chaetura andrei* by snakes must occur in buriti groves in Mato Grosso (see Icterinae, "Enemies"). When this swift takes up residence in chimneys, it may die of asphyxiation or burns. I have found eggs, nestlings, and nests (these glued together with saliva, melted by the heat) in the bottom of chimneys.

At Iguaçu Falls, Paraná, a Peregrine Falcon, *Falco peregrinus,* was seen pursuing a *Cypseloides senex* (W. Andersen, October 1982).

I documented a rare event: after a storm at night I found some fallen trees at the forest edge. A branch had hit a trunk on which a *Panyptila cayennensis* had fixed its felt nest. The nest that sheltered the pair and one nestling was crushed (Ilha Grande, Rio de Janeiro, November 1944). There is a record in Brazil of a *C. senex* colliding with an airplane.

I have the impression that swifts are diminishing in number, like swallows and nightjars, victims of unrestricted pesticide use.

Dexter (1979) observed the life of a banded *Chaetura pelagica* in the U.S. for 14 years, without knowing where it went during the local winter; it probably migrated to South America.

Distribution and Ecology

Most South American species belong to the subfamily Chaeturinae, which includes the genera *Streptoprocne, Cypseloides, Chaetura, Collocalia,* and *Hydrochous. Chaetura* also occur in warm regions of the Old World, whereas *Collocalia* are restricted to the oriental/Australian region (see "Breeding . . ."). The Giant Swiftlet, *Hydrochous* (= *Collocalia*) *gigas* (Java, etc.) is very similar to our *Cypseloides,* which is also clear from the nest, an important character in the difficult evaluation of the relationships of this family (Becking 1971).

The dependence of certain South American Chaeturinae on tree holes is or was a limiting factor in their dispersal and continues to be the main reason swifts are more often seen in forested regions. *Chaetura andrei,* however, by adapting to hollow trunks of palm trees, such as the buriti (*Mauritia vinifera*), conquered the vast savanna region of central Brazil. The same palms have become the environment par excellence for *Reinarda squamata,* mutatis mutandis. On adaptation to life in chimneys, see "Breeding . . . ."

The two *Streptoprocne* species are quite different in their adaptation to the environment: *S. zonaris* likes humidity, *S. biscutata* dry areas.

Identification

Chaetura identification can be difficult, even in the museum, and requires complete scientific documentation. There are twin species in the other genera also (*Streptoprocne zonaris* and *S. biscutata; Cypseloides senex* and *C. fumigatus*). In 1962 a new *Cypseloides* species was described for Colombia, while another was described for Venezuela in 1972. The best means of identification is usually the voice, which requires much experience to distinguish.

Speed of flight, seeing the birds against a clear sky, and association of various species together all hamper identification of most swifts in the field. The last factor, however, can be both a problem and a help in that it facilitates comparison. Collecting these birds, often essential for specific diagnosis, is also a problem. I draw attention to the existence in Brazil of the White-thighed Swallow, *Neochelidon tibialis,* a forest bird that is similar to the *Chaetura.*

The genera *Aeronautes, Panyptila,* and *Reinarda* are restricted to the Americas and belong to the Apodinae. Recognizing them is easy, and their separation from European members of the same subfamily is obvious due to both plumage color and nesting habits.

WHITE-COLLARED SWIFT, *Streptoprocne zonaris,* Andorinhão-de-coleira, Taperuçu   PL 19.4

21.2 cm; wingspan 53 cm; 122–34 g. Largest Brazilian species, characterized by continuous white collar (not continuous or only slightly visible in immature; see *S. biscutata*). VOICE AND DISPLAYS: a strident chittering, *chee . . . , klieh . . . ,* often uttered as song, primarily at beginning of breeding season (July forward, ex-Guanabara) when flock of 50–100, sometimes even 500, conspicuously circles or spirals at great heights in late afternoon. Collective song may coincide with 1st swarming of termites, attracted by electric lights. After performing acrobatics for some time in heights, flock retreats in a straight line or follows in zooming flight some turbulent river through forest, as I have observed in Serra do Mar.

Roosts collectively on cliffs near waterfalls, by the hundreds or thousands, frequently with *Cypseloides senex,* or in dark, humid grottoes along forest streams. Clings head up, leaning right or left and observing surroundings. Mates separate somewhat from flock when breeding. Mexico to Bolivia, Argentina, throughout Brazil, except in extensive flat regions (e.g., certain sectors of Amazonia), for it requires grottoes and cliffs to sleep and nest. In savanna areas of Paraná (Municipality of Palmares, etc.), because of lack of rocky cliffs, takes advantage of openings in sandstone underneath savanna surface. During day moves far from roost, flying in flocks, but such flights have nothing to do with migration (see "Flight . . . "). Geographic races distinguishable by size and width of collar. Also called *Andorinhão-foguete, Gaivota* (Minas Gerais). See *S. biscutata* and the *Cypseloides.*

BISCUTATE SWIFT, *Streptoprocne biscutata,* Andorinhão-de-coleira-falha

20.8 cm. Less well known. White collar interrupted on sides by gaps of 1½–2½ cm. White mark on foreneck tends to form a diamond instead of a strip. Forehead and lores light brown, chin and throat have white feathers with brown edges and black rachis. Breeds in dry grottoes in Minas Gerais (Ibitipoca Park, 1600 m, Lima Duarte) October–December. In Rio Grande do Norte, Municipality of Acari, in Seridó region, Serra do Bico da Arara, there is a "swallow grotto" where this species roosts (without breeding) in large numbers February–October. In August 1986 it was estimated that 8000–10,000 birds entered cave and in August 1978 90,000–100,000. Guano deposit (see "Swift Grottoes . . . ") there has been exploited for many generations by Bezerra family. Locally these birds are believed to come from Dakar, West Africa. In fact, as of February 1989 we do not yet know

where Seridó swifts breed: it is a different population (with smaller measurements, which I describe as *S. b. seridoensis*) from that of Ibitipoca, which belongs to already known *S. b. biscutata* (Sclater 1865) whose summer residence area is still unknown. Large-scale banding will reveal the facts on the 2 forms. Although it roosts in dry caverns, it hunts around waterfalls, as in Itaimbezinho, Rio Grande do Sul, where it meets *S. zonaris* and Sooty Swift, *Cypseloides fumigatus.* Widely distributed in eastern Brazil, from northeast (Piauí, Ceará) to Argentina (Misiones), including Rio de Janeiro: Serra do Órgãos (August), Itatiaia (December, January).

GREAT DUSKY SWIFT, *Cypseloides senex,* Andorinhão-velho-da-cascata

18 cm. Large, sooty colored, with head and pattern on bend of wing lighter. Edges of various feathers whitish. Head may convey a false idea that it is white, primarily on forehead. Tail about 63 mm. Immature has light edges on most of feathers. VOICE: entirely unlike *Streptoprocne zonaris,* song being a *ti-ti-ti* followed by a buzz, *tirr-tshaarr;* terminal rasp may resemble warning of a House Wren, *Troglodytes aedon.* Lives by hundreds near waterfalls ("swallow waterfalls"), over which birds flutter, looking from a distance like a swarm of mosquitoes. During day they hunt high over forests. On nesting, see "Breeding. . . ." Upper Madeira (Aripuanã, Dardanelos, Mato Grosso) and Serra do Cachimbo (Pará) to São Paulo (Salto do Itapura), Paraná (Iguaçu), Paraguay, Argentina (Misiones), in association with *S. zonaris.* See *C. fumigatus,* which under certain light conditions may look very similar. On similarities with *Collocalia* and collision with an airplane, see "Breeding . . . " and "Enemies . . . ."

SOOTY SWIFT, *Cypseloides fumigatus,* Andorinhão-preto-da-cascata

15 cm. Southern species that almost looks like a large *Chaetura.* Entirely sooty, tail about 48 mm. Immature has white, scaly design on belly. Smaller than *C. senex;* may weigh scarcely half what that species does (44 g vs 60–98 g). Foot slender. Near waterfalls on littoral. Flies in flocks of 3–6, occasionally associates with a flock of *Streptoprocne.* Southeastern Brazil (Rio de Janeiro to Rio Grande do Sul), northern Argentina. Also called *Andorinha-das-tormentas* (Rio Grande do Sul).

TEPUI SWIFT, *Cypseloides phelpsi*

14.5 cm. Sooty with reddish collar and breast. Tail relatively long, soft, forked. Recorded in Roraima. Pantepui (southwestern Venezuela), northwestern Guyana.

CHESTNUT-COLLARED SWIFT, *Cypseloides rutilus*

Very similar to *C. phelpsi.* Observed once in Brasília (A. Negret 1984 pers. comm.). Widely distributed in Andes and the north of continent as far as Mexico.

CHAPMAN'S SWIFT, *Chaetura chapmani,*
Andorinhão-de-Chapman

12.5 cm. Stocky with bluish black plumage. Tail wide and black, unlike *C. brachyura,* sometimes its neighbor at forest edge. The Guianas to Colombia and northern Brazil in Amapá, Pará (Belém), Mato Grosso, Acre. May form an allospecies with *C. pelagica.*

CHIMNEY SWIFT, *Chaetura pelagica,*
Andorinhão-migrante

The fact that this species' appearance in Brazil has not yet been proven (although it is expected) requires its exclusion from the Brazil list.

13 cm. Similar to *C. chapmani* and *C. andrei* but differing from former by having narrower remiges, smaller feet, and more uniformly sooty coloring on upperparts, with only wings black. A migrant from North America, coming to South America during northern winter. Various individuals banded in U.S. have been recovered in Peruvian Amazonia and Colombia but none in Brazil (up to 1987). An observation made by E. T. Gilliard in Manaus, Amazonas, in March 1943, with hundreds of *Chaetura* roosting inside a chimney, could have been of Brazilian swifts, probably *andrei* in migration, and not of *pelagica* as recorded in report. *C. pelagica* adapted long ago to use of human habitations. VOICE: similar to *andrei,* a repeated *tsrrruit* that resembles call of White-crested Tyrannulet, *Serpophaga subcristata.* On migration follows Pacific coast of South America in great numbers as far as Chile, where it is only *Chaetura* (in great contrast to situation in Brazil), which facilitates its identification there.

GRAY-RUMPED SWIFT, *Chaetura cinereiventris,*
Andorinhão-de-sobre-cinzento

11.5 cm. Much shorter wings than *C. andrei,* black upperparts except for extensively light gray rump (see *C. spinicauda*). Throat whitish, tail relatively large (unlike *C. brachyura* and *C. andrei*). VOICE: a harsh, distinctive *chree-chree-chree.* Forests. Seeks chimneys for sleeping and nesting, like *andrei,* and usually frequents same areas in southern Brazil, except that *andrei* is not seen, like this one, in small numbers regularly throughout winter (Rio de Janeiro, ex-Guanabara). Central America to upper Amazon (Madeira, Acre), eastern and southern Brazil (including Rio Grande do Sul), Argentina (Misiones).

PALE-RUMPED SWIFT, *Chaetura egregia*

Known only from a few specimens. Larger than and may be a geographic replacement for *C. cinereiventris,* with bronzed back (instead of bluish), whitish rump. Acre (September), northern Mato Grosso (Serra do Roncador, August–September), Bolivia.

BAND-RUMPED SWIFT, *Chaetura spinicauda,*
Andorinhão-de-sobre-branco

11.7 cm. Amazonian species with much shorter wings (102–06 mm) than *C. brachyura,* sometimes its neighbor on forest edges. Tail relatively large, giving impression of a larger bird than *brachyura.* Upperparts black (including tail) except for rump which is crossed by distinct, narrow whitish band. VOICE: *sri-sri-sri,* resembling *C. cinereiventris* more than *C. andrei.* Forest openings. Costa Rica to northern South America as far as Rio Purus (Amazonas), Serra do Cachimbo (southern Pará), Belém (eastern Pará, where common), Amapá, Maranhão.

ASHY-TAILED SWIFT, *Chaetura andrei,*
Andorinhão-do-temporal   PL 19.3   Fig. 147

11.5 cm. Usually most common species outside Amazonia. Tail short; plumage dark sooty; throat, rump, and tail lighter. VOICE: *tip tip tip,* adding as a song a *tli-ti-tit.* Overflies forests and cities, nests in hollow trees (e.g., palms, Minas Gerais and Goiás), chimneys (eastern and southern Brazil). Nest unknown until 1946. From March forward migratory, roosting in flocks in residential chimneys (e.g., Teresópolis, Rio de Janeiro, where seen in flocks of up to 700, Sick 1958). See also "Swift Grottoes. . . ." In Parati, Rio de Janeiro, I found a roosting flock in an open space in a bamboo and mud wall covered with bricks. Swifts entered the 2.5-m wall through a high hole. Southern race, *C. a. meridionalis,* larger and lighter, occurs from Argentina and Paraguay to central Brazil (Mato Grosso, where nests October–November), southern Brazil (Rio de Janeiro, ex-Guanabara, where nests end August–January), and northwest. In migration crosses equator, reaching Roraima (May), Suriname (August), northern Venezuela (September), Colombia (August), Panama (August).

Fig. 147. Ashy-tailed Swift, *Chaetura andrei meridionalis,* alongside its nest in a chimney. Teresópolis, Rio de Janeiro.

SHORT-TAILED SWIFT, *Chaetura brachyura,*
Andorinhão-de-rabo-curto

10.5 cm. Delicate Amazonian species with sizable (115–20 mm) wings and extremely short tail which makes it shorter than *C. spinicauda.* Black, including underparts, but with light brown rump and tail. VOICE: *tsew-tsew-tsewdewlewdel,* resembling *C. andrei,* which is not usually in same region, except on migration. Nests in downspouts, wells, chimneys, etc. Common in open landscapes of north (savanna, forest edge), regularly flies over cities such as Belém and Macapá. The Guianas, Venezuela, and Colombia to Peru, Mato Grosso, Pará. May be a neighbor of *C. chapmani* and *C. spinicauda.*

WHITE-TIPPED SWIFT, *Aeronautes montivagus,*
Andorinhão-serrano

11 cm. In mountains near Venezuelan border. Throat, foreneck, and abdominal stripe white. VOICE: *tsirrrrr,* resembling Tropical Kingbird, *Tyrannus melancholicus.* Lives in forest, sleeps and nests in rocky crevasses (see "Breeding"). Venezuelan Andes, Roraima, Bolivia. See *Panyptila cayennensis.*

LESSER SWALLOW-TAILED SWIFT, *Panyptila cayennensis,* Andorinhão-estofador

13 cm. Small but stocky with forked tail normally held closed. Bluish black with throat, collar, and spots on lores and side of rump white, the latter quite visible in flight. VOICE: a bisyllabic *gsh-gsh, spit-spit, ps-psioo* and a warble. Solitary, usually hunts over tall forest. Lives in south alongside *Chaetura cinereiventris* and in north with *C. spinicauda,* from which it differs by more impetuous flight.

Has large "felt" nest (glued vegetable fiber, degree of felting varying greatly with individuals). Nest has a bottom entrance and is glued to tall trees with smooth bark or on underside of roof eaves. Similar in shape to a wool sock hung by sole, with the degree of felting or amalgamation reaching its maximum in upper portion, which acquires appearance of solidified mud. Amount of saliva used there is so great it becomes almost impermeable. Narrow internal support where 2 eggs lie is built later and resembles a shelf. Lower part of nest (below egg shelf) is a spacious hanging tube in which nonbrooding parent stays. In many cases this section resembles a fine, almost transparent cloth; it tears in a high wind but is later mended. Nests are longer or shorter (30–100 cm), yellow or whitish depending on material used (vegetable fiber and a few feathers). Bird depends on certain fibers for construction, e.g., seeds of *Forsteronia* (Apocynaceae), *Tillandsia* (Bromeliaceae), and kapok, *Ceiba pentandra* (Bombacaceae), which it gathers only in certain regions and seasons (Sick 1947). Appearance of nest varies greatly according to its age and exposure, newer and better-protected ones (e.g., inside a house) being fluffier and less dense. Older nests become darker under influence of felting action and inclement weather. Nest may be attached to its support over its full length. I have ascertained that nests are used in successive breeding seasons, probably by same pair, but birds do not always sleep in nest.

On Tapajós in Pará I learned that it is not unusual for eggs or nestlings to fall out of nest when it is shaken by arrival of an adult.

Mexico to northern Mato Grosso (Rio Xingu) and Maranhão and from Bahia to São Paulo, always in warm areas. Relatively common in Amazonia and is confused by local people with Bat Falcon, *Falco rufigularis,* which is thought to be builder of these nests. Pieces of nest are treasured by country folk as a powerful amulet that will bring good luck, for this falcon is considered to be happy beyond comparison. Also called *Anapuru* (southern Pará).

FORK-TAILED PALM-SWIFT, *Reinarda squamata,*
Tesourinha

13 cm; 11 g. Very slender with long, deeply forked tail usually held closed in flight, assuming form of a spear. Upperparts blackish with greenish sheen, feathers edged cream. Underparts grayish white. VOICE: a harsh, high *ks-ks,* very distinctive.

Depends completely on palms with fan-shaped leaves, on surface of which it roosts and nests. Particularly looks for buriti (*Mauritia vinifera*) in central Brazil and miriti (*Mauritia flexuosa*) in Amazonia. Shares entire distributional range of these palms. Also uses carnaúba (*Copernicia cerifera*) and exotic palms that have same palmate leaf (e.g., *Livistonia*). Uses both old, vertically hanging leaves and green, almost horizontal ones, placing nest next to spine. Nest consists of a wad of soft, loose feathers, more narrow above and wide and open below, where entrance is. Attached laterally by saliva to veins on surface of supporting leaf. Egg shelf is a reinforced fold of wall opposite supporting leaf and has shape of a more ample and concave shell than that of *Panyptila cayennensis,* giving greater security to continually swaying nest contents. Nest's internal walls get more saliva and lose flaky appearance of exterior (see "Breeding"). Common for 2 or more pairs to nest in same palm.

In northeastern cities such as Crato, Ceará, residents complain of filth created by this species, which nests and sleeps in hanging leaves of palms (some exotic) planted in parks—a situation reminiscent of the polemic against flocks of migrant swallows perched in street trees in interior of São Paulo. The Guianas and Venezuela to Mato Grosso, Goiás, Minas Gerais, Bahia. In part of its range migratory, disappearing after March and reappearing in November (Borba, Rio Madeira, Amazonas). Also called *Poruti* (Amazonas").

Apodidae Bibliography

Alvarez, F., and F. Hiraldo. 1972. *Ardeola* 16:137–43. [Formation of a claw on the thumb]

Andrade, M. A., G. Mattos, and M. V. Freitas. 1986. Notas sobre a nidificação e anilhamento de *Streptoprocne biscutata*. *XIII Cong. Bras. Zool. Cuiabá:*555.

Andrade, M. A., and M. V. Freitas. 1987. Notas sobre o anilhamento de *Chaetura andrei* no estado de Minas Gerais. *II ENAV, Rio de Janeiro:*192–93.

Becking, J. H. 1971. *Ibis* 113:330–34. [*Collocalia, Cypseloides,* nesting]

Beebe, W. 1949. *Zoologica* (N.Y.) 34:53–62. [Migration]

Carvalho, C. T. 1960. *Rev. Bras. Biol.* 20:305–25. [*Panyptila,* pterylosis]

Carvalho, C. T. 1962. *Pap. Avuls. Zool. S. Paulo* 14,32. [*Reinarda,* pterylosis, nesting]

Collins, C. T. 1963. *Condor* 65:324–28. [*Cypseloides,* juvenile plumage]

Collins, C. T. 1968. *Bull. B.O.C.* 88:133–34. [Distribution]

Collins, C. T. 1968. *Am. Mus. Nov.* 2320. [*Chaetura,* behavior]

Collins, C. T. 1968. *Bull. Fla. St. Mus. Biol. Sci.* 2:257–320. [*Chaetura,* behavior]

Collins, C. T. 1972. *Contr. Sci. Nat. Hist. Mus. Los Angeles* 229. [*Cypseloides,* taxonomy]

Dexter, R. W. 1979. Fourteen-year life history of a banded Chimney Swift. *Bird Banding* 50(1):30–33.

Eisentraut, M. 1938. Fledermausdung, Chiropterit und sonstiger Fossildung. *Rohstoffe des Tierreichs* 1(2):2217–27.

Fischer, R. B. 1958. *Bull N.Y. St. Mus.* 368. [*Chaetura pelagica,* monograph]

Hartert, E. 1897. In *Das Tierreich.* Berlin. [Taxonomy]

Haverschmidt, F. 1958. *Auk* 75:121–30. [*Panyptila,* nesting]

Haverschmidt, F. 1958. Schornstein als Massenschlafplatz von *Chaetura brachyura* in Surinam. *J. Orn.* 99:89–91.

Hellmayr, C. E. 1908. Südamerikanische Formen von *Chaetura. Verh. Ornith. Ges. Bay.* 8.

Howell, T. R. 1961. An early reference to torpidity in a tropical swift. *Condor* 63:505.

Johnston, D. W. 1958. Sexual and age characters and salivary glands of the Chimney Swift. *Condor* 60:73–84.

King, B. 1987. The waterfall swift, *Hydrochous gigas. Bull. B.O.C.* 107(1):36–37.

Lack, D. 1956. *Auk* 73:1–32. [Nesting]

Lincoln, F. C. 1944. *Auk* 61:604–9. [*Chaetura pelagica,* migration]

Medway, Lord. 1962. The relation between the reproductive cycle, moult, and changes in the sublingual salivary glands of the Swiftlet *Collocalia maxima. Proc. Zool. Soc. London* 138:305–15.

Medway, Lord. 1970. Untersuchungen über die Biologie der Salanganen von Südost-Asien (Studies on the biology of the edible-nest Swiftlets of south-east Asia). *J. Orn.* 111:196–205.

Mees, G. F. 1985. Comments on species of the genus *Hirundapus. Proc. Kon. Nederl. Akad.* 100(88):63–73.

Orr, R. T. 1963. Comments on the classification of swifts of the subfamily Chaeturinae. *Proc. 13th Int. Orn. Cong., Ithaca:*126–34.

Sick, H. 1947. *Rev. Bras. Biol.* 7:219–46. [*Panyptila,* nesting]

Sick, H. 1948. *Auk* 65:169–74. [*Reinarda,* nesting]

Sick, H. 1948. *Auk* 65:515–20. [*Chaetura andrei,* nesting]

Sick, H. 1950. *Rev. Bras. Biol.* 10(4):425–36. [*Chaetura andrei,* ecology]

Sick, H. 1951. *J. Orn.* 93(1):38–41. [*Chaetura,* adaptation to chimneys]

Sick, H. 1955. *Acta XI Cong. Int. Orn., Basel:* 618–22. [Nesting]

Sick, H. 1958. *Vogelwarte* 19:248–53. [*Chaetura,* migration]

Sick, H. 1958. *Auk* 75:217–20. [*Panyptila,* evolution of nesting]

Sick, H. 1959. *Auk* 76:471–77. [*Chaetura,* breeding]

Sick, H. 1969. Chaeturinae. In Grzimek's *Tierleben.* Zurich.

Sick, H. 1991. Distribution and subspeciation of the Biscutate Swift, *Streptoprocne biscutata. Bull. B.O.C.* 111(1):38–40.

Sick, H., M. A. Andrade, G. Mattos, et al. 1987. Anilhamento de *Streptoprocne biscutata,* em Rio Grande do Norte. *III ENAV S. Leopoldo:*21.

Snow, D. W. *Zoologica* (N.Y.) 47:129–39. [*Chaetura, Cypseloides,* biology]

Voipio, P. 1970. On "thunder-flights" of the House Martin, *Delichon urbica. Orn. Fennica* 47:15–19.

Wetmore, A. 1957. *Auk* 74:383–85. [*Chaetura,* classification]

Zimmer, J. T. 1945. A Chimney Swift from Colombia. *Auk* 62:145. [First record of *Chaetura pelagica* in South America, 1931]

Zimmer, J. T. 1953. Studies of Peruvian Birds, no. 64. The swifts, family Apodidae. *Am. Mus. Nov.* 1609.

Zusi, R. L., and G. D. Bentz. 1982. Variation of muscle in hummingbirds and swifts and its systematic implications. *Proc. Biol. Soc. Wash.* 95:412–20.

FAMILY TROCHILIDAE: HUMMINGBIRDS (84)

This is one of the largest and most interesting bird families, totaling more than 320 species in the three Americas, most heavily concentrated in the Andean region near the equator. Thus, Colombia has 143 species, Brazil fewer than 90. Nevertheless, in the area of the Municipality of Rio de Janeiro, 28 species have been recorded. The greater abundance of hummingbirds in the Andes has led to the deduction that these birds are sensitive to extremely high temperatures.

Hummingbirds are exclusively American. Fossils are known only from the Pleistocene of Brazil and from the Antilles (10,000 to 20,000 years B.P.). They are very distinctive, having few marked affinities with other bird families. Grouping with the swifts (Apodidae) in an order known as Macrochires was proposed by Fürbringer (1888). See Apodidae, "Morphology . . . ." Hummingbirds have some affinities with the Passerines. Their resemblance to sunbirds of Africa and Australasia and to honeyeaters of Australasia (Passeriformes) is merely analogous; the Nectariniidae have difficulty hovering before flowers when they want to sip nectar, preferring to perch on the corolla, like coerebinae, and are therefore less specialized than hummingbirds. There is also a superficial resemblance to jacamars (Galbulidae), giving rise to the latter being called *beija-flor-grande* ["large hummingbird"] by laypeople.

Morphology

Hummingbirds are among the world's smallest warmblooded vertebrates.[1] The smallest Brazilian species are the Frilled Coquette, *Lophornis magnifica* (1.5–2.8 g); Horned Sungem, *Heliactin cornuta* (1.8–2 g); Reddish Hermit, *Phaethornis ruber* (1.8–2.5 g); and Amethyst Woodstar, *Calliphlox amethystina* (2.3–2.8 g). Species such as the Black-throated Mango, *Anthracothorax nigricollis* (6.7 g), and Swallow-tailed Hummingbird, *Eupetomena macroura* (9.2 g), pass as "large," being larger than some flycatchers. The relatively great length of some species comes from elongated bills and tails, the latter frequently exceeding the length of the body. The largest Brazilian species are the Crimson Topaz, *Topaza pella* (13–18 g), and Saw-billed Hermit, *Ramphodon naevius* (9–10 g). The largest species in the family, the Giant Hummingbird, *Patagona gigas* (21 g, the size of a swallow) lives in the Andes. All hummingbirds have thick skin and resistant feathers.

They have long, thin bills and a narrow mouth that can be opened wide (see "Mating," nuptial display of *Phaethornis ruber*). Some, like the *Ramphodon, Glaucis, Colibri,* and *Avocettula,* have the end of the maxilla serrated, suggesting its use as a saw or improved ability to hold smooth objects. The serrations may extend to the mandible, which may be shaped like a draftsman's compass (e.g., certain White-vented Violetear, *Colibri serrirostris,* individuals). The bill of the Black-eared Fairy, *Heliothryx aurita,* is shaped like an awl, enabling it to pierce flower corollas. Compare the different morphology of immature bills. *Ramphodon* exhibits sexual dimorphism in the bill, the male's being straight and ending in a hook, the female's gently curving, undoubtedly indicating a difference in feeding. Female *Phaethornis* usually have a shorter, more curved bill. The tongue (fig. 148) is very long and extensible, with a split, capillary tip. A species' bill might measure 15 mm, its tongue 30 mm. Bill length is adapted to the callyx depth of flowers on which the species feeds. The hyoids supporting the base of the tongue reach the forehead under the skin, resembling, mutatis mutandis, the woodpeckers. The neck is long and flexible. Hummingbirds have a distinctive nape muscle, the musculus splenius capitis (see Apodidae, "Morphology . . . ").

The wing is long. The hand is equal to or longer than the extremely short arm. The sternum is relatively large. Flight muscles comprise a quarter to a third of the total weight. See "Flight." Hummingbirds have 10 large primaries but only

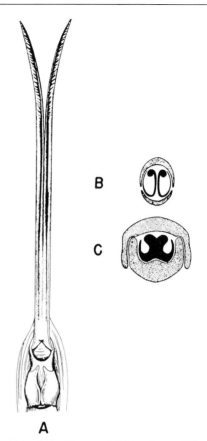

Fig. 148. Tongue of White-throated Hummingbird, *Leucochloris albicollis*. (A) General view, showing the fringed, forked tongue tip. (B) Transverse cut of bill and tongue, near the tip of the bill, showing two tubes. (C) Cut at the middle of the bill, where the maxilla broadly overlaps the mandible, forming a vacuum, like a suction pump. After H. Böker 1937.

6 to 7 secondaries; the Wandering Albatross, *Diomedea exulans,* a master of gliding flight, has 37 secondaries.

Among the most notable features that distinguish hummingbirds and provide the basis for their extreme activity is the relatively large heart (fig. 149), which comprises 1.9% to 2.5% of total body weight. In the House Sparrow, *Passer domesticus,* the heart comprises only 1.39% of total body weight; in humans it is only 0.5%. The relative size of the hummingbird heart is the greatest known in birds; that of tinamous is the smallest. The lungs are large and simply structured, facilitating a rapid breathing rate. There are no valves. Lung volume and the connected air sacs make up 14% to 22% of a hummingbird's total weight, resulting in a large permeable surface that facilitates oxygen absorption. The breathing rate of a resting hummingbird is 260 inhalations per minute (29 in a pigeon). It is estimated that the heart of a flying hummingbird moves the blood 100 times faster

---

[1]The smallest mammals in the world, the shrews, belonging to the Soricidae (Insectivora), weigh about the same: *Suncus etruscus* of the Mediterranean weighs 1.8 to 2 g; *Microsorex hoyi* of northern North America weights 2.3 g. The miniscule marsupial of Brazil, *Microdidelphys sorex,* is close to the shrews in size. A bat only 3 cm long and weighing 2 g was discovered in Thailand in 1974. Being a flier, the bat is even more appropriate for comparison with hummingbirds.

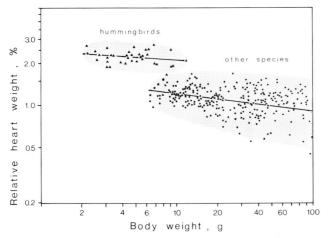

Fig. 149. Relative weight of bird hearts: hummingbirds at left, nonhummingbirds at right. An 8-g hummingbird has a heart 71% heavier than that of a nonhummingbird of the same weight (Johansen, Berger, Ruschi, et al. in press).

than a human heart moves blood. On body temperature, see "Reaction to Cold . . . ."

The feet are small with strong toes and long, hook-shaped claws; they clasp small branches well but do not serve for walking (except in one Andean species that hops). The wings are used for even the shortest moves. Some hummingbirds grasp the leaves of flowers they visit with their feet while continuing to beat their wings. There must be a functional reason for the *Phaethornis* and similar genera having the three front toes linked.

The splendid iridescent metallic colors that distinguish hummingbirds result from diffraction and reflection of light by the microstructure of the feathers and therefore vary with the direction of the sun's rays, as in diamonds and drops of oil. Study of hummingbird feathers with the electron microscope is opening new horizons.

Various chromatic effects from the feathers produced by incident light from various angles, and by transmitted light, depend on a bird's individual actions. A hummingbird moves certain areas of its plumage, the crest or the lateral tufts of the neck, for instance, or turns its body to obtain the most surprising results—all this in hovering display flights before the female. Evolution has resulted in some remarkable effects (e.g., see the *Lophornis*). The name *colibri*, more used in French and German, is derived from the Carib tongue and means "resplendent area." There are various derivations for the Tupi name *guainumbi*, among them *guirá-mimbig*, "scintillating bird."

Species living in forest shadow, such as *Phaethornis* (*hermit* refers to monk's garb), have modest plumage. Sometimes they have a bright marking, such as the white tip of the long tail, which the bird moves back and forth when perched, drawing attention from afar.

Young males normally look like females. The male Brazilian Ruby, *Clytolaema rubricauda*, acquires the first bright

green feathers on its underparts after 50 days, and in the fourth month the red throat patch is prominent. Its nuptial plumage is complete at 8 or 9 months. The Minute Hermit, *Phaethornis idaliae*, keeps its subadult plumage, quite distinct from that of the adult, for 18 months. Young *Florisuga, Melanotrochilus, Anthracothorax,* and *Polytmus* also have plumage different from the adults. Immatures may differ from adults in the rough (instead of smooth) surface of the sides of the maxilla (Ortiz-Crespo 1972).

Unlike most birds, the Stripe-breasted and Blue-tufted Starthroats, *Heliomaster squamosus* and *H. furcifer,* undergo two normal molts per year: the nuptial (basic molt for all birds) and postnuptial. With the postnuptial molt (beginning in July) they acquire a nonbreeding, or eclipse, plumage in which they lose the blue crown and red throat, becoming similar to females (see Anatidae, "Morphology . . ."). They regain nuptial plumage in October. A nonbreeding plumage also occurs in *Calliphlox amethystina:* various adult males held captive in Europe had their shiny throat feathers replaced by white and gray ones during a period of six to eight weeks in the local autumn.

Females of most species are modestly colored. Old females may progressively acquire attractive plumage similar to that of the adult male, as in the White-necked Jacobin, *Florisuga mellivora.* Female Black Jacobins, *Melanotrochilus fuscus,* and *Colibri* are similar to their brightly colored males. Females of modestly colored forest species such as the *Ramphodon, Phaethornis,* and the Sombre Hummingbird, *Aphantochroa cirrhochloris,* are similar to their males.

Most hummingbirds known only by the "type specimen" used to describe them, and others of doubtful origin, are probably hybrids. This conclusion was reached with the "species" *Augasma* and *Eucephala,* for instance, which may be hybrids between a *Thalurania* and the Blue-chinned Sapphire, *Chlorestes notatus.* American museums have at least 14 hybrids of American hummingbirds, with a total of only 15 species in the United States (Short et al. 1966). Hybridization between different species, which appears to be more common than previously recognized, may result from a lack of any close relationship between pairs (see "Mating"). This occurs with other polygamous birds that do not form fixed pairs during breeding, such as birds of paradise and manakins. A number of hybrids have been recorded among captive hummingbirds. A. Ruschi observed copulation between different species in his flight cages, for instance Violet-capped Woodnymph, *Thalurania glaucopis* × *Melanotrochilus fuscus.* Hermaphrodites are also found.

Vocalization

Most hummingbirds have shrill voices resembling those of insects or bats. At times their vocalizations are almost inaudible to human ears although they are evident from movements of the head or throat feathers, as I have noted in

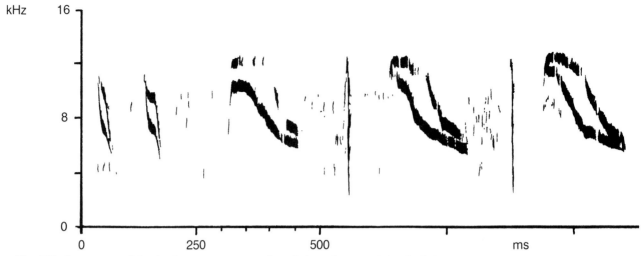

Fig. 150. Spectogram of the simultaneous utterance of two independent sounds by the Ruby-topaz Hummingbird, *Chrysolampis mosquitus,* after Vielliard 1983. A long note (140–200 ms) shows the superposition of two pure, modulated frequencies, each from 10–12 kHz to 6–7 kHz, which are harmonically unrelated.

Melanotrochilus fuscus, a relatively large species with an extremely high voice reaching above 12 kHz (Vielliard pers. comm.). Sometimes movements of the mandibles show that the bird is singing (e.g., see Gilded Hummingbird, *Hylocharis chrysura*). There are different vocalizations to express aggression, alarm, etc., and these are frequently given in flight. The White-throated Hummingbird, *Leucochloris albicollis,* and *Clytolaema rubricauda* are examples of species with loud voices. Various modestly colored hummingbirds that live hidden in the forest, such as the *Ramphodon, Glaucis, Phaethornis,* and *Aphantochroa,* also have loud voices.

Songs of the various species are quite different, but the high frequencies make their study difficult. Sonograms are indispensable, for they reveal many details. Species that sing in groups (see "Mating") hold their collective territories for years. This permits development of local differences in phraseology, noted in Trinidad, for instance, in the Little Hermit, *Phaethornis longuemareus,* implying a learning process among individuals. The intense singing activity of these hummingbirds is almost beyond imagining. One *P. longuemareus,* a very small forest species, sang on average every two seconds, with few interruptions on the day it was observed, resulting in a total of 12,000 songs per day (Snow 1968). In the songs of certain hummingbirds two independent sounds are made simultaneously, produced in the two bronchi. Thus, the Ruby-topaz Hummingbird, *Chrysolampis mosquitus,* utters an unmistakable *tlEE, tlEE, tlEE* (fig. 150). Also compare the *Procnias* (Cotingidae).

Among open-country species *Colibri serrirostris* and the *Augastes* are tireless singers. *Leucochloris albicollis* has two song types, as apparently occurs with *Hylocharis chrysura* and probably others. They sometimes sing in flight, *Ramphodon naevius,* for example. Female vocalizations are much

less complex. There is also "instrumental music" among males (see "Mating").

Feeding and Color Discrimination

Sugar is the basic food. A 3-g *Hylocharis chrysura* in perfect health, observed by W. Scheithauer in a cage in Germany during a 16-hour day, consumed 22 g of sweetened water containing 2.2 g of honey, an amount equivalent to 73% of the bird's weight. In addition, the same bird captured 677 *Drosophila* flies weighing 0.8 g (each one weighed 1.2 mg), equivalent to 27% of the bird's weight. The total daily intake of this hummingbird was 25 g—eight times its own weight. The voracity of hummingbirds is well known, leading to the most absurd exaggerations, such as "some manage to consume up to almost thirty times their own weight in food" (Ruschi 1986). A man consuming proportionately as much as a hummingbird that consumed only half its weight in sugar would have to eat 58.9 kg of bread. The energetics of a warm-blooded animal (the hummingbird is not fully "warm-blooded," see "Reaction to Cold . . . ") depend on its size: the smaller it is, the more it has to eat, relatively, and the more oxygen it uses, producing more energy—in summary, it has a higher metabolism.

The carbohydrates in nectar give hummingbirds the immediate energy needed for their hovering flight and their continuous flitting about. Unlike insects such as bees, trochilids prefer flowers with diluted nectar, up to a bit above 20%, whereas bees use concentrations of up to 70% or 80% (Baker 1975). Measurements made by Snow and Teixeira (1982) in the Brazilian southeast indicate sugar concentrations of 15% to 31% for flowers visited by hummingbirds. The low concentration of sugar in flowers pollinated by hummingbirds reduces competition from bees that are physiologically more dependent on a high concentration (Bolton et al. 1978). Hummingbirds do not accept acid nectar such as that produced by certain flamboyants. The timing of nectar secretion by *Heliconia* is adapted to the visits of *Phaethornis,* which fly at dawn (Stiles 1979), in the same way that maximum intensity in perfume production by certain flowers coincides with the time of greatest activity of their pollinating insects.

The tongue/bill combination of a hummingbird is a capillary mechanism that functions like a water pump. The hummingbird must absorb the liquid as rapidly as possible, for it drinks while hovering. It must visit thousands of flowers a day to meet its requirements and may visit more that 200 *Salvia* flowers, one after the other. The common case of a hummingbird systematically using an extensive area of flowers of the same species has been called "trap-lining." The long tongue is introduced into the nectaries. *Thalurania glaucopis,* for instance, has a 1.8-cm bill; with the tongue extended it can reach 4 cm. It is unnecessary to insert the bill into very small corollas, but it is always inserted into the tubes of feeder bottles. The head is stuck deeply into large flowers and disappears completely in the enormous funnel of *Datura* (Solanaceae). Extremely long bills like those of the Long-tailed Hermit, *Phaethornis superciliosus,* and Great-billed Hermit, *P. malaris,* are probably an adaptation for exploiting flowers with deep corollas (see "Pollination"). Small species such as *Calliphlox amethystina* and the *Lophornis,* which have short bills, seek out small flowers, for instance gervão preto (*Stachytarpheta*), *Phlox, Salvia rufa,* and esporinha (*Delphinium*). Along with nectar they accidentally take a certain amount of pollen (see "Pollination").

Whereas the "normal" position of the bill is horizontal when sipping, there are many exceptions, as in the case of a visit to Nymphaeaceae flowers that just barely appear above the water surface. This requires an almost vertical position of the hummingbird's bill as it hovers above the flower.

Thalurania glaucopis, Phaethornis ruber, and others sometimes perforate flower tubes from outside in a direct attack at the coveted liquid, as with the always half-shut flowers of *Malvaviscus arboreus,* or they take advantage of openings made by the Bananaquit, *Coereba flaveola,* bees (especially *Euglossa* species), and wasps: what I call "illegitimate acquisition" of nectar (see also "Morphology" and "Pollination"). Hummingbirds sometimes grasp flowers, such as those of *Hibiscus,* to open a hole with their claws. They peck at succulent fruits, such as persimmons, and sip sap dripping from a slashed branch or trunk. They are among the most assiduous visitors to perforations made by sapsuckers, small North American woodpeckers. In Colombia hummingbirds use perforations made by the Acorn Woodpecker, *Melanerpes formicivorus* (Kattan and Murcia 1985).

Hummingbirds are highly sensitive to colors, as is suggested by the widely varied colors of their plumage. They examine colored items lying around in gardens, head scarves, and the red-and-white stakes of land surveyors. Bees, in contrast, are color-blind, confusing red with black. Ornithophily is usually characterized by the red color of the flowers; thus bees are eliminated as competitors. See also "Pollination". The colored "nests" of bromeliads are inspected even when they have no flowers. Hummingbirds may become habituated to certain colors associated with obtaining their favorite food. Bright color and nectar abundance are principal characteristics of flowers attractive to hummingbirds. Although it is frequently said that red, the brightest of all colors, is the preferred color of hummingbirds, it must be pointed out that the individual experience of a hummingbird and its capacity to learn to exploit the best sources available at the moment are highly important factors. They apparently can recognize color change in *Malvaviscus arboreus* flowers: they look for flowers in which the bright scarlet has begun to fade, which coincides with the beginning of nectar production (Gottsberger 1971). Young, inexperienced individuals sip at any flower, whereas adults are selective.

Insignificant-appearing flowering bromeliads with miniscule, colorless flowers are not neglected. Red- or yellow-flowered epiphytic and terrestrial bromeliads are among the plants most sought by hummingbirds. Small bromeliads in the Teresópolis region of Rio de Janeiro visited by hummingbirds include, according to A. Abendroth, *Vriesia lubbersi, V. procera, V. petropolitana, V. carinata,* and *Neoregelia sarmentosa. Fuchsia* species with colorful red flowers, common in rain forests such as that of the Serra dos Órgãos, Rio de Janeiro, are also sought (see also "Pollination").

In Espírito Santo in one day at one white-flowered eucalyptus tree, approximately 100 hummingbirds of one species were counted, and at another 14 species were recorded. See also "Return to Territory . . . ." In its native Australia, eucalyptus is especially used by the Meliphagidae. Another imported Australian plant much appreciated by hummingbirds is *Grevillea* sp. (Proteaceae). Other white flowers also much sought by hummingbirds are those of orange trees and of ingazeiro [*Inga* spp.]. Elimination of an orange grove may result in disappearance of the Versicolored Emerald, *Amazilia versicolor,* from the vicinity.

The flowers of mistletoe (*Psittacanthus,* Loranthaceae), which grow on fig trees, Myrtaceae, tabebuias, etc., are attractive to many hummingbirds; the flower clusters appear like a great yellow or red flame on the crowns of the trees they parasitize. Ruschi (1950) cites nine species as visitors to the very nectariferous *Psittacanthus dichrous* that blooms along the coastal strip of Espírito Santo in January and February: the Glittering-throated Emerald, *Amazilia fimbriata;* Planalto Hermit, *Phaethornis pretrei; P. ruber; P. idaliae; Eupetomena macroura; Colibri serrirostris; Chlorestes notatus; Thalurania glaucopis;* and *Calliphlox amethystina.*

Knowledge of the flowers favored by certain species may often be the key to finding hummingbirds. Because flowering is restricted to certain periods, appearance of the respective hummingbirds is similarly restricted. Once flowering is ended, the birds disappear to unknown destinations.

Apparently rain increases the problem of exploiting nectar from flowers, which explains why hummingbirds appear at sugar-water feeders in greater abundance during rainy periods.

Another natural source of sugared liquid for hummingbirds is licking or sucking seepage from ripe fruits, such as wild figs (*Ficus* spp.), along with wasps and flies. Plant lice larvae (*Xyloccus* sp., Coccidae) excretions are a special situation. These insects suck the thin bark of bracaatinga (*Mimosa scabrella*), a legume widespread in the south (Paraná to Rio Grande do Sul). The excretion exudes from a capillary tube 2 to 5 cm or even longer, projecting from a soft, black, sooty mass of fungus, *fumagina,* held together by the excretion, which covers the bark and insects. The liquid being available only on the underside of branches and trunks, the best means of obtaining it is by hovering, an easy maneuver for hummingbirds. In Santa Catarina one October, in half an hour on one 12-m high bracaatinga, I counted seven species of birds, some in pairs, feeding on this excretion: *Leucochloris albicollis;* Tropical Parula, *Parula pitiayumi;* Black-backed Tanager, *Tangara peruviana;* Diademed Tanager, *Stephanophorus diadematus;* Ruby-crowned Tanager, *Tachyphonus coronatus;* Green-winged Saltator, *Saltator similis;* and Rufous-collared Sparrow, *Zonotrichia capensis.* When bees such as the irapuã arrive to feed, the hummingbirds retreat.

Arthropods (insects and arachnids) provide hummingbirds with the proteins indispensable for growth of their young. They catch insects in flight, hovering before a swarm of small flies, or like flycatchers simply fly out from a perch and immediately return to it. When a hummingbird catches a flying insect with its bill, as with tweezers, and is unable to suck it up with its long tongue as it does in the calyx of flowers, it lets it go and catches it again with the open mouth, which is very narrow for such a maneuver. Apparently it also catches insects while flying rapidly with the mouth open. Among insects caught by hummingbirds are quantities of blackflies, gnats, and mosquitoes, including *Culex, Anopheles, Simulium,* and *Phlebotomus,* vectors of tropical diseases such as filariasis, yellow fever, malaria, and leishmaniasis. This is an important contribution to public health. They scavenge insects from spider webs, from cracks and holes in walls (*Phaethornis pretrei* is called *limpa-casa,* "house cleaner"), or from tree bark. They catch very small Hymenoptera on leaves and water surfaces, and they of course fly from flower to flower in whose corollas live great numbers of miniscule insects gorging on nectar, together with the small spiders that prey on them—as occurs in orchid flowers and in the corolla tubes of bromeliads. It is suspected that a forest species such as the Pale-tailed Barbthroat, *Threnetes leucurus,* may be predominantly insectivorous. Sometimes they let an insect

that has been caught fall, only to catch it again. Tiny balls regurgitated by hummingbirds contain arthropod chitin.

They like to lick ashes, as I have seen in the Scale-throated Hermit, *Phaethornis eurynome.* Very tame hummingbirds, attracted by the salt content of sweat, have been known to lick a person's face. They frequently clean their bills, wiping now on this side, now on that.

Flight

Hovering flight is the hummingbirds' strong point. The smaller the species and the shorter the wing, the greater the frequency of the wing beat; the male *Calliphlox amethystina* reaches 80 strokes per second, producing a very high-pitched sound; the female reaches "only" 70, and her humming sound is lower pitched. Frequency is measured by stroboscope. *Lophornis, Popelairia, Discosura, Heliactin,* and the smaller *Phaethornis* also have very high frequencies. The male *Lophornis magnifica* reaches 58 wing beats per second, the female 52, and *Phaethornis ruber,* the smallest *Phaethornis,* 48 to 51. The wing sounds of these hummingbirds are similar or equal to those of insects of almost the same size and wing-beat frequency, such as the mamangaba-bee (*Bombus* sp.). The wing-beat frequency of a honeybee is 250 per second, that of a mosquito, producing its frightening, high whine, 500 per second. A hummingbird with more "normal" capacity, such as the Glittering-bellied Emerald, *Chlorostilbon aureoventris,* reaches 30 beats per second.

Brazilian hummingbirds with the lowest wing-beat frequency and lowest-toned hum are the *Ramphodon* and *Campylopterus* (14 beats per second). A mockingbird (*Mimus*) has the same frequency; a *Passer domesticus* reaches 20; and a *Sporophila* 32 (M. Berger pers. comm.). Small hummingbirds flying in a straight line make 47 to 74 km/per hr. The average velocity of a *Phaethornis superciliosus* was measured by Gill (1985) at 11.5 m/s (= km/hr). During chases and nuptial flights velocity is certainly even higher. The great writer João Guimarães Rosa, an incomparable observer of nature, wrote, "Just a scintillating instant without past or future: a hummingbird," and he later spoke of "a constellation of colibris."

Vibration of the flight musculature reaches very high values (100 Hz), the same as found in a rattlesnake's rattle. Hummingbirds can fly forward, backward, sideways, and up and down and can stop instantly at any point, just like a helicopter. They can even move backward and up while hovering. Sometimes they fly on their backs. Their mastery is revealed in the sudden shift from one extreme to another: while hovering or flying slowly, a bird will switch to its fastest escape flight, as can often be seen with *Calliphlox amethystina.* Hummingbirds are unable to soar; the wing is comparable to a propeller blade.

Hummingbirds have a tendency when hovering in front of

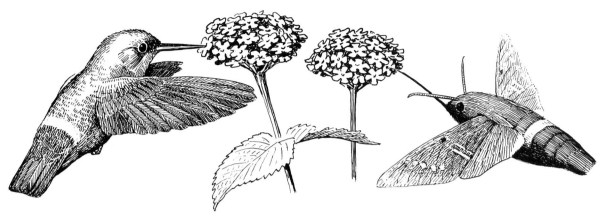

Fig. 151. Coquette (*Lophornis* sp., female) and moth (*Aellopus* sp.) at a camará flower (*Lantana* sp.).

a flower or feeder to lift the tail to the horizontal or even higher, giving a somewhat grotesque aspect to species such as male Black-bellied Thorntails, *Popelairia langsdorffi,* and *Calliphlox amethystina,* causing their slender, elongated tail feathers to look like upright, erected spines. *Melanotrochilus fuscus* stretches its tail until it almost points forward. Some move the tail backward and forward at intervals as they hover without moving from the spot; see also prenuptial displays (e.g., *Phaethornis ruber*).

The similarity between hummingbirds and insects reaches its high point in the case of some sphinx moths. *Aellopus* species such as *A. fadus* even have the white band of *Lophornis* on their spindle-shaped abdomens; the long proboscis imitates the bird's bill; *Aellopus* has also developed a small tail that moves like a hummingbird tail. The only difference is in the presence or absence of antennae. The method of hovering in front of a flower is common to both, although the moth is usually more timid. There are other sphinx moths resembling hummingbirds, such as the *Oryba.* Thus it is not surprising that legends exist describing the metamorphosis of a hummingbird into a moth, or more precisely, saying that the hummingbird develops from a caterpillar, the same as a moth. A good picture showing the insect alongside the bird, both hovering before neighboring flowers, can be found in the work of Bates (1863; see my Chapter 2.4) (fig. 151).

Behavior

Hummingbirds are generally considered to be very tame; however, I have the impression that they are not really docile but fearless by nature. Certain species and individuals are more timid.

During their most active hours they are very aggressive, not only against individuals of the same species and other hummingbirds but also against other birds, even large ones such as vultures that pass near their perches. Such attacks appear to be more in fun than by compulsion and can be confused with flights linked to mating. They may even in-

volve physical contact with an adversary hummingbird, and sometimes both fall to the ground, clasping each other. Hummingbirds are among the first birds to attack owls at their perches during the day (see "Parasites . . ."). A pygmy-owl, *Glaucidium* sp., can be used to attract hummingbirds. Females near the nest are among the most bellicose. Some, such as the *Lophornis,* are not very aggressive, at least against other species.

When an individual begins to consider a sugar-water feeder its own, its defense of such an easy food source is impressive. In the wild a hummingbird may defend a certain flowering plant from which it feeds. *Calliphlox amethystina,* by perfecting its flight to a point that permits immediate action and departure, has freed itself from the pecking order in disputing flowers and feeders.

Territoriality, which with male birds in general primarily means possession of a good food source, should also guarantee better prospects for a female. In hummingbirds, males and females defend separate territories, not only against individuals of the same species but against other species (Cody 1968).

They bathe on leaves moistened by dew and rain and may even fly against a twig with tiny leaves, ruffling their feathers under the improvised shower. They take baths in the rain (occasionally ten or more perched on a wire), fly through the spray of a waterfall or lawn sprinkler, and immerse themselves rapidly in clear running water and in pools in bromeliad funnels. They need all this washing because of their constant contact with the viscous liquid of flowers. They like to sunbathe. The feet play an important role in hygiene, although a comblike claw has not evolved. Hummingbirds scratch themselves on any part of the body, including the back. To clean the bill they pull it through the closed fist, to the best of my knowledge a unique phenomenon among birds (fig. 152). Yawning is common.

Some species, *Clytolaema rubricauda, Leucochloris albicollis,* and the *Thalurania,* keep flying until dusk. *Eupetomena macroura* continues to catch insects when it is

Fig. 152. Hummingbird cleaning its bill by pulling it through its closed foot. Drawing by F. Pontual, based on a photograph of the White-tailed Starfrontlet, *Coeligena phalerata,* of Colombia, by J. S. Dunning.

Fig. 153. Stance of a hummingbird according to ambient temperature. In cold weather (left) the tarsi are hidden in the woolly plumage of the abdomen and the body plumage is ruffled. In hot weather (right) the tarsi and feet are exposed, the plumage is smoothed, and the bird is panting. Udvardy 1983.

almost dark. Hummingbirds have been observed in full activity under fluorescent lights at 2:00 A.M. in Rio de Janeiro, when sunrise was at 6:12 A.M. (Sick and Teixeira 1981); the birds sang and chased each other; see also "Pollination."

In stretching themselves after resting, hummingbirds follow a routine similar to other birds (see Psittaciformes, "Behavior"): the bird stretches one wing downward and simultaneously spreads the tail on the same side in a half fan. Then it performs the same movements on the other side and, finally, lifts both wings and spreads the full tail.

They sleep perched openly on a slender branch with the bill forward and the head slightly elevated in a position similar to that assumed in rain and when singing. They frequently place the wings under the tail.

Reaction to Cold, Hibernation

It has been noted that hummingbirds that are active during cold periods hide their tiny feet in the woolly white feathering of thighs and abdomen, an act of thermoregulation (fig. 153).

Hummingbirds are among the few birds (certain swifts and nightjars; see also Bucconidae, "Behavior," White-eared Puffbird, *Nystalus chacuru*) with the ability to hibernate. They fall into a lethargic sleep during cold weather, an ecological adaptation to survive abrupt drops in temperature

(fig. 154). Although large-scale hibernation is not known in Brazil (as it is in Chile, where live hummingbirds have been found in rock crevices beneath snow), hibernation has been observed here on cold nights. The birds (*Eupetomena macroura, Clytolaema rubricauda,* and *Chrysolampis mosquitus*) remain immobilized for several hours during which they can be caught by hand. Everything leads to the belief that all hummingbirds can hibernate, a phenomenon more accentuated in the rigorous winter of southern regions. This has been known since ancient times by Chilean Indians who informed the missionaries, and J. Gould noted it in the beginning of the last century. Hibernation does not occur when the female is on the nest incubating or brooding the nestlings (see also "Nest Care . . . ").

During its torpid sleep a hummingbird's temperature, 40° to 42°C during the day, falls to that of the ambient air, perhaps 24°C at night. We can deduce that hibernation is the metabolic magic by which a hummingbird makes its food last from evening until morning—a space of 12 hours in the tropics. When a hummingbird is cold, it begins to shiver, thus producing heat.

Mating

The breeding season brings a series of extremely variable events. In a primary phase the male sings and displays in a certain place to draw the attention of any female of his species. He proclaims a territory that he defends against other males of his species, unless there is a grouping of various males (see below). In a second phase the male makes nuptial flights before a certain female. In most cases these consist of very rapid actions that are difficult to observe in detail as, for instance, when the tiny birds rise to considerable altitudes in the bright light of the tropical sun, or in a dense, shady forest full of obstacles. The most detailed accounts of "nuptial parades" have been made by A. Ruschi, who has used, in part, observations in large flight cages where many species bred. I can give here only a vague idea of the many events.

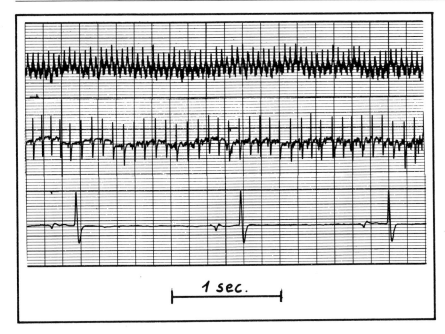

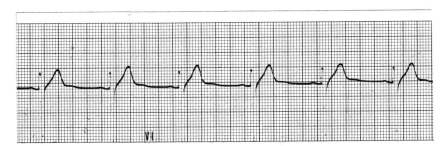

Fig. 154. Electrocardiograms of hummingbirds (Johansen, Berger, Ruschi, et al., in press). Above: EKG of Amethyst Woodstar, *Calliphlox amethystina,* in flight: heart rhythm 1240 per minute. Center: EKG of Violet-capped Woodnymph, *Thalurania glaucopis,* resting after flight: heart rhythm 635 per minute, body temperature 41.2°C. Below: EKG of Frilled Coquette, *Lophornis magnifica,* in lethargic sleep: heart rhythm 42 per minute, body temperature 12.0°C, ambient temperature 10.5°C. For comparison: EKG of a 25-year-old man in complete repose: heart rate 60 per minute. The frequencies are similar but the physiological conditions are completely different.

Male and female *Eupetomena macroura* and *Melanotrochilus fuscus* make zigzag flights together (fig. 155). Males of some species make flights that skim above the perched female, whereas *Lophornis magnifica* flies circling around the female, rising in a spiral flight and performing other acrobatics.

The effects of brilliant and bizarre plumage are instinctively "calculated" by the male to take best advantage of the courted female's vision, taking into consideration the momentary position of the sun, which influences the quality of the colors (see also "Morphology" and "Evolution . . ."). All the more reason for male *Heliomaster squamosus* and *H. furcifer,* who lose the showiest parts of their plumage after the breeding season, to stop their displays, for they lack endocrine motivation.

Male *Phaethornis* open the bill and display the mouth, tongue, and mandible, all of which have conspicuous bright colors. The male *P. ruber,* while flying around the perched female, darts his extremely long tongue in and out at short intervals, creating a most curious spectacle. Displaying the tongue must have evolved from the act of eating and of darting out the tongue after eating, a common action with all hummingbirds.

Lophornis and *Popelairia* even display their miniscule feet. The Festive Coquette, *L. chalybea,* displays the bright blue bare skin on his crown.

Display of the spread tail is frequent and reveals surprising features. Thus two very similar species, *Phaethornis eurynome* and *P. pretrei,* demonstrate the difference in the shape of their fanned tails, a feature "normally" scarcely visible.

Both voices and sounds originating from flight movements, such as buzzes and snaps, "instrumental music" (*Lophornis, Popelairia, Melanotrochilus*), are also used in nuptial displays. *Campylopterus* make a goatlike bleat. It can be very difficult to determine whether one of these acoustic phenomena is vocalization or instrumental music, especially when performed in flight. Finally, courtship ends with the union of the sexes on a branch, the male hovering above the perched female. Afterward the pair separates. One can observe a hummingbird species frequently for many years without seeing any particularly interesting display until suddenly one occurs. This happened to me with *Phaethornis ruber.*

Sometimes a male will display by flying in front of another male perched singing on "his" branch. Once the demonstration is over, the perched male pursues the visitor and expels him. Sometimes a solitary male attempts to display before a

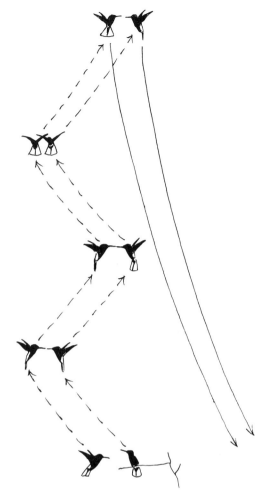

Fig. 155. Nuptial flight of the Black Jacobin, *Melano-trochilus fuscus*. The pair zigzags upward. The points at which the male and female stop in front of each other are approximately 10 m apart. Finally the pair descends in a dive. Original, H. Sick.

certain leaf, even going as far as copulating (*Threnetes*). A *Eupetomena macroura* has been seen courting a Ruddy Ground-Dove, *Columbina talpacoti,* and a Common Waxbill, *Estrilda astrild* (H. Berla).

Any male perceiving the approach of another bird, male or female, of his species is disposed to advertise his presence and accelerate his singing, tail fanning, etc. The readiness of males to copulate immediately must contribute to the production of hybrids (see "Morphology").

Males of some species, such as certain *Phaethornis,* gather in "clubs" to sing. Apparently such groups develop when local population density is very high, as is obvious, for example, in the case of *Phaethornis superciliosus* in Amazonia and the Black-breasted Plovercrest, *Stephanoxis lalandi,* in the south.

Each male has one or several branches, generally low in the forest, where he sings tirelessly during the larger part of the day for months on end. It has been estimated that a

Phaethornis longuemareus occupies its "spot" from 67% to 92% of daylight hours (see also "Vocalization"). This situation somewhat resembles that of polygamous birds such as cotingas and manakins. It is notable that the *Phaethornis* lack accentuated sexual dimorphism, unlike other "court birds" that live promiscuously. On supposed interspecific relations (hybrids) see "Morphology."

Nest Care and Types of Nests

Nesting is the exclusive responsibility of the female. Rarely a second adult (sex?) will appear at the nest, making a short visit, as I observed with *Phaethornis pretrei;* in this species two females occasionally feed the same young. An apparent male attending a nest may be a female in progressive plumage, which is similar to that of the adult male.

Brazilian hummingbirds have three types of nest structures, as A. Ruschi recognized some years ago. The first and second types are elongated; the third is semispherical and usually the best known to laypeople. Binding of the material, both in the nest and to the support, is done with spider web and webbing of insects such as embiids and psocids, firmly amalgamated with saliva: hummingbirds possess large salivary glands (compare with swifts). The female wraps the nest with the webs, working on the wing or attaching them while her feet are on the support but often with the wings in motion. She can work with her bill while clutching the nest and beating her wings. To compact the webs in the nest the feet are used alternately. The inside bottom of the nest is usually a bit more spacious than the top, thus impeding the eggs from falling out. The form of the nest varies according to the substrate. It must be in an exposed position to facilitate access by the female in flight.

1. Nests of *Ramphodon, Glaucis,* and *Threnetes* are elongate with a tail-like appendage and are suspended from a palm leaf, a *Heliconia,* or such. They are built of fine roots, fibers, and even horsehair, resulting in a woven net through which the eggs can be seen. Some lichens and vegetable detritus are fixed to the external walls. The caudal appendage gives equilibrium to the nest. The general shape of this type of nest is similar to fig. 156A, but the material and construction (transparent) are different.

2. Nests of *Phaethornis* (fig. 156A) have an elongated conical form with a more or less long, pendant tail which may serve as a counterweight. The shape is similar to type 1, but the material employed is different, being soft: vegetable fibers and detritus are accumulated in a thick mass. Using slender roots, the nests are suspended over shady ravines from the interior face of leaves of palm, fern, banana, *Heliconia,* etc. Because of the weight of the nest, the leaflet or leaf tip folds over and the rest of it protects the nest. The nest may be affixed to a simple hanging electric wire inside a house, as *pretrei* likes to do.

3. Nests of most species are shaped like a solid bowl—a

small throne—made of bromeliad kapok and other soft materials such as threads from tree-fern blades; the outer wall is covered with fragments of leaves, lichen, moss, etc., firmly glued with cobweb, a technique similar to that used by various tyrannids, such as the elaenias. The consolidated surface of these nests may resemble nests of certain swifts (e.g., Lesser Swallow-tailed Swift, *Panyptila cayennensis*) that apply abundant applications of saliva. The *Topaza* create a pink, rubberlike, elastic mass (the nest stretches as the nestlings grow) using woolly fibers of pteridophytic ferns (*Osmunda*) mixed with a liquid (probably saliva, regurgitated nectar, or sap) and spider web (Ruschi 1986); they do not cover the surface with lichens, leaving the nest with a "nude" appearance.

3.1. A nest placed openly on a more or less horizontal branch or in a fork is typical of *Eupetomena, Colibri, Anthracothorax, Chrysolampis, Lophornis, Thalurania, Leucochloris, Polytmus, Amazilia* (fig. 156B), *Aphantochroa, Clytolaema, Topaza, Augastes,* and *Calliphlox.*

3.2. A nest fixed on a grass stalk, slender root, or hanging wire is typical of *Stephanoxis, Chlorostilbon* (fig. 156C), and *Hylocharis.*

3.3. A nest placed on the dorsal side of a large horizontal leaf is typical of *Melanotrochilus, Chlorestes,* and *Heliothryx.*

The most serious danger for nest types 2 and 3 is rain. Lacy-textured nests of type 1 let the water escape. Many young die in rainy years. Covering the nest surface with lichens and other hard materials gives a certain amount of protection against rain and is also good camouflage. The best safeguard is to construct under embankments, bridges, and inside houses (see *Phaethornis pretrei*). The nesting time of *Chlorestes notatus,* which builds in the open on the base of

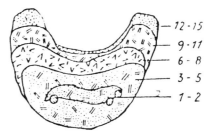

Fig. 157. Pace of nest construction of a *Lampornis* (non-Brazilian) hummingbird in Mexico, showing construction phases over a 15-day period. Wagner 1952.

palm fronds, corresponds with the period of highest rainfall (Belém, Pará), but it protects itself by choosing the margin of a leaf protected by other leaves above it. In Costa Rica hummingbirds nest at the peak of the rainy season (Skutch 1969).

The disadvantage of water-absorbent kapok in a nest is partly compensated for by the thermal effect of a thick wall. Hummingbirds living in colder climates make thicker walls than do species in tropical climates. A warm nest protects the incubating female and nestlings from going into hibernation (see "Reaction to Cold . . . "). The night temperature of a nest warmed by a female is usually 10°C higher than the ambient air temperature (Howell and Dawson 1954).

Hummingbirds are susceptible to too much sun and even abandon nests with eggs when there is insufficient shade; nestlings die in nests overexposed to sun. Nevertheless, there are nests of type 3.1 (e.g., Hyacinth Visorbearer, *Augastes scutatus,* a mountain species) that are entirely exposed to sun and rain but protected from wind.

A female *Chlorostilbon aureoventris* may take ten days to finish her nest before laying the first egg. *Glaucis hirsuta* needs five to ten days; nest construction begins with the lower part, below the egg chamber, and proceeds upward (fig. 157). Females of all species continue to bring nesting material after starting to incubate.

Sometimes two or three suspended nests of *Chlorostilbon* or *Phaethornis* are superimposed, probably having been built by the same female who has held her territory for years. A group of six superimposed *P. pretrei* nests using the full length of a hanging electric light wire in a generator shed that I saw in Paraná looked like a continuous roll 60 cm long. The nest in use at the time (with two nestlings) was on the free end under the roll. Only the length of such a support limits the number of superimposed nests. Sometimes the same nest is used repeatedly.

One hummingbird nest was found made of hair and cockroach wings, upholstered inside with kapok.

Eggs and Young

Hummingbirds lay two elongated eggs (which are shaped like caiman eggs). In their minuscule nests two equal-ended eggs take best advantage of the tight space. Rarely three eggs

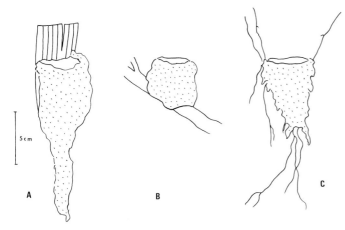

5 cm

Fig. 156. Sketches of hummingbird nest types. (A) Dusky-throated Hermit, *Phaethornis squalidus,* nest suspended on upper side of a palm leaf. (B) Glittering-throated Emerald, *Amazilia fimbriata tephrocephala,* nest placed solidly on a branch. (C) Glittering-bellied Emerald, *Chlorostilbon aureoventris,* nest hanging under a bank, suspended from a grass stem and roots. Adapted from A. Ruschi 1949.

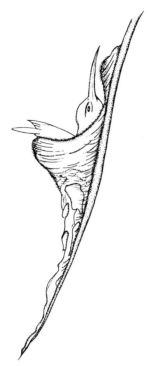

Fig. 158. Position of *Glaucis hirsuta* in nest. After Novaes and Carvalho 1957.

are found, probably laid by two females, as has been recorded especially in the case of *Glaucis hirsuta*. Only two young develop. Each egg is about the size of a white bean.

Eggs are large relative to the size of the mother. A *Chlorostilbon aureoventris* egg weighs 0.42 g, the female 3 g. Laying is normally on alternate days. The white eggs sometimes turn red from contact with lichens included in the internal nest structure. This color may also be transmitted to the incubating bird (e.g., Dusky-throated Hermit, *Phaethornis squalidus),* deceiving observers unfamiliar with this phenomenon which was recorded by Burmeister in 1850, who drew attention to the fact that the color of the lichen, *Spiloma roseum,* is activated by the heat of the brooding bird.

When the female returns to the nest to incubate she immediately sits on the eggs, as do most birds. If there are no eggs yet she may perch on the edge of the nest for hours, perhaps because laying is imminent. *Ramphodon, Glaucis, Threnetes,* and *Phaethornis* perch on the nest with the bill pointed upward, turned toward the leaf to which the nest is attached (fig. 158). Incubating females of any species distract themselves with their long tongue, opening and moving the bill and sometimes catching tiny insects that perch within reach. The male does not participate in incubating or feeding the young.

The incubation period varies according to species and weather. Fifteen days have been recorded for *Thalurania glaucopis,* 12 to 13 for *Lophornis magnifica.* Hatching may

coincide with the blooming of flowers not available during the incubation period, facilitating feeding of the young. The female removes the eggshells, letting them fall over the edge of the nest; or the shells and even an egg that failed to hatch may be left to be ground into the nest bottom. Efforts to clean the nest are minimal.

Young hatch quite undeveloped. They are bare or sparsely covered with fuzz, and their bills are short. At 10 days their eyes open. They are fed a paste the mother regurgitates and places in their throats after touching their heads to make them open their bills. Semilethargic young on cold mornings are force-fed. The mother regurgitates several rations of food on one visit, introducing her bill deeply into the esophagus of each nestling until she reaches the crop.

To feed the offspring the mother perches on the edge of the nest, with her wings still fluttering in the case of suspended nests like those of *Glaucis* or *Phaethornis;* sometimes she feeds while hovering above the nest. To receive food, nestlings of *Phaethornis,* etc., have to bend their necks backward because they are facing the side of the nest attached to the leaf (the same as the mother). This position facilitates their defecating outside the nest, as they do every 15 minutes or so.

A. Ruschi reported that in *Phaethornis pretrei* arthropods form 90% and nectar 10% of the food in the first few days; after the tenth day the proportion of nectar rises. For an initial period of about a week the young are regularly brooded by the mother. When regular food and warmth are lacking, the young become lethargic (see "Reaction to Cold . . . ").

Young leave the nest at three weeks of age but may remain up to 35 days when food is scarce (*Eupetomena macroura*). A few days ahead they test their wings while firmly clutching the bottom of the nest. Fledglings stay for some days in the vicinity of the nest and may even return to it for the night (*Glaucis hirsuta*). Although nestlings are silent, newly fledged young beg loudly (location call, *Anthracothorax*). Certain *Phaethornis pretrei* individuals may nest five times in a year, as I noted in Rolândia, Paraná (see "Nest Care . . ."); the nest remained vacant only eight to ten days. It has been reported that most hummingbird species nest once or twice a year, which also depends on the individual.

Evolution and Distribution

Brazil is not particularly rich in hummingbirds compared to Ecuador and Colombia. The center of trochilid evolution is in the Andes, precisely on the equator where at altitudes above 800 m the largest number of hummingbirds occur. They reach altitudes of 5000 m around Chimborazo, Cotopaxi, etc. From there they spread to Tierra del Fuego and Alaska, becoming scarcer the farther away they get.

The most intense evolution has occurred in the genus *Phaethornis,* sedentary forest species, of which 19 occur in Brazil. Some hummingbirds, such *P. superciliosus* and the

Fork-tailed Woodnymph, *Thalurania furcata,* have developed various subspecies.

Certain geographic forms, such as the *Augastes,* may be considered allospecies that comprise a superspecies; they are distinctive endemics of the eastern part of the central plateau. In the Serra do Caraça, Minas Gerais, an ecological race has evolved from *Augastes scutatus* (Grantsau 1967). The Wedge-billed Hummingbird, *Augastes* (= *Schistes*) *geoffroyi,* a resident of the eastern slope of the Andes, reaches the upper Rio Negro region in a bioclimatic situation similar to that of the central plateau.

In *Threnetes,* forest hummingbirds of Amazonia, evolution is most evident in the tail feather color, often revealed when the bird fans its tail, an outstanding behavioral character. *Lophornis* has also evolved impressively; the various species of this genus are distinguished by the form and color of lateral neck tufts that play an important role in nuptial display and are thus subject to strong selective pressure.

Existence of a typically open-country hummingbird like *Heliactin cornuta,* both in cerrados of central Brazil and on savannas of Amapá and Suriname, now widely separated by the present Hylaea, suggests probable connection of those plains before the great expansion of Amazonian forest in the Quaternary. It can be objected, however, that *Heliactin* moves about with great facility and should be capable of a distant penetration; there are analogous cases of this type among Andean hummingbirds occupying disjunct areas with identical bioclimatic character.

Other notable cases of disjunct distribution are those of the Brown Violetear, *Colibri delphinae,* and *Popelairia langsdorffi. C. delphinae* is a scrub-country species of the mountainous region of interior Bahia; it also exists in an equivalent situation north of the Amazon. *P. langsdorffi* occurs in the Atlantic forest and reappears in the upper Amazon. *Lophornis chalybea* lives in the southeast and certain areas of Amazonia. Apparently many populations have become extinct over a vast region.

Eastern Brazil became another center of hummingbird evolution: *Ramphodon, Stephanoxis,* and *Clytolaema* are genera restricted to this region; *Melanotrochilus, Aphantochroa,* and *Leucochloris* have similar distribution. *Phaethornis* is present in the southeast with two typical forms: *P. eurynome* and *P. idaliae.*

Stephanoxis lalandi, typical of high mountaintops in the southeast (Serra do Mar, Mantiqueira) and of the extreme south, is one of the few Brazilian mountain hummingbirds. To a certain extent the *Augastes* (see above) are also.

A. Ruschi (1963–76) recorded the number of hummingbird species in some Brazilian states (of course their areas and the extent to which they have been explored are very unequal): Amazonas 38; Pará 41 (Belém area 21); Amapá 32; Maranhão 30; Pernambuco 24; Bahia 37; Minas Gerais 38; Espírito Santo 37; Rio de Janeiro 34; Guanabara (now the Municipality of Rio de Janeiro) 27; São Paulo 32; Paraná 32; Santa Catarina 25; Rio Grande do Sul 25; Mato Grosso 33; Goiás 28; Federal District 22. The currently calculated total number of species in Brazil is 84.

Abundance

Hummingbird abundance depends on the place and season. The period when the greatest number of individuals and species are constantly present in the region of Teresópolis, Rio de Janeiro, for instance, runs from the end of February to November, corresponding to the dry season. In March at a small farm near that city, with many flowers and feeders, I counted 9 hummingbird species in half an hour. This number rose to 11 on the same day after additional observation. In April in the garden of a house in Petrópolis, Rio de Janeiro, I observed 10 species in less than half an hour. At the São João ranch, Macaé de Cima, Rio de Janeiro, 19 species have been recorded but not at the same time. A. Ruschi recorded 28 to 32 species on the terrace of his house in Santa Teresa in October; the most common was *Melanotrochilus fuscus,* of which 150 were caught in one day. In all of these cases the attraction of sugar-water bottles is a decided influence, for we are dealing with an environment artificially improved to attract hummingbirds (see "Conservation . . ."). Hummingbirds appear on well-planted terraces of buildings in Copacabana, Rio de Janeiro.

In certain cases the number of individuals in a given area under natural conditions is impressive. In forests of the Amazon estuary (lower Rio Guamá), *Phaethornis superciliosus, Threnetes leucurus,* and the Gray-breasted Sabrewing, *Campylopterus largipennis,* are the non-Passerines with the highest frequency and population density, as shown by net captures during a survey conducted by F. C. Novaes. The fact is surprising because these strictly forest hummingbirds are scarcely ever seen (they do, however, reveal their presence by their voices). In the same region forest hummingbirds are notable for the number of species: 7 in capoeira and várzea forests and 5 in terra-firme forests. In the same areas only the flycatchers, with 9 species in capoeira, and the antbirds, with 10 species in capoeira and várzea and 13 in terra firme, outdo the hummingbirds. In the Atlantic forest (Rio de Janeiro) there are often three *Phaethornis* in the same area (*P. pretrei, P. eurynome, P. squalidus*). Ruschi reported four *Phaethornis* (*P. superciliosus, P. malaris, P. ruber,* and Straight-billed Hermit, *P. bourcieri*) in the Serra do Navio (Amapá); in the same habitat there are two to three *Threnetes* species.

Return to Territory and Migration

Hummingbirds are good at orientation, which helps them find the nectar-producing flowers on which they depend. In experiments carried out by A. Ruschi between 1940 and

1944, a banded *Clytolaema rubricauda* was captured 2 km from the banding site 30 minutes after banding. A banded *Melanotrochilus fuscus* traveled 30 km with a change of 455 m in altitude in only one day, from a jenipapo tree [*Genipa americana*] to a eucalyptus, proving what was suspected, that a feeding area may be very extensive. In experiments with banded hummingbirds liberated far from the place of capture, *C. rubricauda, Phaethornis idaliae,* and *Lophornis magnifica* could not return from more than 15 km away. However, *Phaethornis pretrei, Melanotrochilus fuscus,* and *Anthracothorax nigricollis* returned from 85 km away, flying from sea level on the coast at Vitória, Espírito Santo, to Santa Teresa at 700 m, a distance covered by the *Phaethornis* in two and a half hours. These results confirm a fact observed in many birds, including carrier pigeons, and demonstrate that it is also true of hummingbirds: transported adult individuals tend to return to their native soil. Species such as *Phaethornis ruber* and *Chlorostilbon aureoventris* are apparently sedentary.

Documentation also exists on spontaneous movements of hummingbirds. In the winter in southeastern Brazil, altitudinal migration occurs in the Serra da Mantiqueira and Serra do Mar. Populations of *Clytolaema rubricauda, Colibri serrirostris,* and *Leucochloris albicollis* living at altitudes of 700 to 1400 m in spring and summer descend in the fall. At least some individual *Stephanoxis lalandi,* which occupy the highest parts of those mountains and the plateau of Rio Grande do Sul in the summer, descend in winter. In the Andes there are many mountain species of hummingbirds, not all of which migrate in winter.

Seasonal north-south migrations occur. Individual *Chrysolampis mosquitus* banded in Paraná have been captured in Santa Teresa, Espírito Santo, and southern Bahia. This helps explain observations made in the Rolândia region of Paraná that *Chrysolampis* appears there in spring (arriving in October) and disappears in April. Reversing this, *Melanotrochilus fuscus* appears in Rolândia in autumn (March–April) and disappears in September, thus meriting the name *beija-flor-de-inverno* ["winter hummingbird"]. In Sapucaia do Sul, Rio Grande do Sul, in July, midwinter, a congregation of more than 50 *Melanotrochilus* has been observed, attracted by the pinkish flowers of *Dombeya wallichii* (Sterculiaceae) (W. Voss). In Macaé de Cima, Rio de Janeiro (1000 m), *Melanotrochilus* disappears in winter and returns in October, although it reappears in certain winters (E. Garlipp). The return, after months of absence, may occur on the same or almost the same day: 14 and 15 October 1973 and 1976 respectively for *Chrysolampis mosquitus* (M. Maier, Rolândia). Hummingbird phenology in São Paulo shows heavy migration during eucalyptus flowering in March and April, followed by a general emigration in winter; see also "Feeding . . ." (Vielliard and Silva 1986).

Large-scale migrations have been recorded outside Brazil. Hummingbirds exploit the Juan Fernandez Islands of Chile by making an ocean crossing requiring a nonstop flight of 667 km.

Pollination

Hummingbirds play an important role in the pollination of many plants, especially the bromeliads, one of South America's most characteristic plants, whose evolution has perhaps proceeded parallel with that of hummingbirds. Many Brazilian plants are spoken of as trochilogamous, this constituting one of the most interesting Neotropical contributions to the ornithophily of plants. Stiles (1985), working in Costa Rica, estimates that ornithophily in the humid Neotropics is not common, involving no more than 3% to 4% of the total flora and 7% to 10% of the flora of any one habitat. Among bromeliads pollinated by hummingbirds are *Aechmea, Billbergia, Vriesia, Tillandsia,* and *Dyckia.*

It has long been suspected, and now proven, that hummingbirds are sensitive to ultraviolet waves (waves under 400 nanometers) (Bowmaker 1988)). This is one more notable adaptation of hummingbirds to certain flowers that attract their pollinators by reflecting ultraviolet sunlight invisible to humans. We do not know what color the hummingbirds see.

On the basis of Martius's *Flora Brasiliensis,* O. Porsch (1924, 1929) mentioned many plants probably pollinated by hummingbirds. Botanist J. S. Decker (1934), working in southern Brazil, named 58 plant families (more than 200 species) he saw pollinated by hummingbirds.

The salvia, *Salvia patens,* studied by A. Abendroth, appears to be an example of special adaptation to pollination by hummingbirds. It is an herbaceous plant with blue flowers, native to Mexico, that is frequently cultivated in cities of the Serra do Mar, Rio de Janeiro. Hummingbirds, especially *Eupetomena macroura,* like its flowers. The flower has a mechanism apparently constructed especially to take advantage of hummingbird visits. This is located on the filaments supporting the anthers. The two long filaments each have two sections, joined a little below the midpoint. The upper section is the longer, with the anthers on one end; the other end projects, lightly arched, into the tube of the corolla. Articulation with the lower section is a bit short of the end, permitting movement of the upper section, including the anthers, within the tube. These stick out of the mouth of the tube a bit and rest on the upper petals. The hummingbird arrives and inserts its bill into the flower tube; the bill automatically lifts the free ends of the filaments slightly, causing the anthers to lower and deposit pollen on the crown of the visitor.

Coevolution of plant and hummingbird (*Phaethornis*) is evident with various species of *Heliconia,* which have great boat-shaped bracts that perfectly imitate the bill shape of *P. pretrei.* F. G. Stiles (1979) has gathered further details on this in Costa Rica. The problem of guaranteeing cross-fertilization remains. The various species of *Heliconia* each deposit their pollen on a certain part of the hummingbird bill

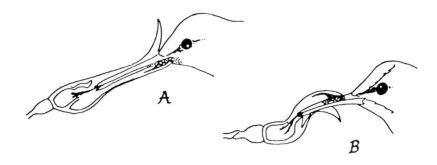

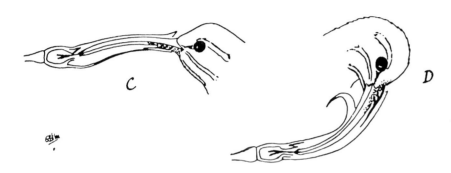

Fig. 159. Mechanisms of *Heliconia* flowers to guarantee cross-pollination. (A and B) *H. latispatha* and *H. imbricata*, pollinated by non-Phaethornithinae. (C and D) *H. umbrophila* and *H. irrasa*, pollinated by *Phaethornis*. The hummingbird introduces the bill exactly to the point at which the tongue will reach the nectar chamber. Stiles 1979.

to avoid interspecific pollination (see fig. 159). Snow and Teixeira (1982) believe it probable that in the Atlantic forest of the Brazilian southeast *Phaethornis eurynome* and *Heliconia velloziana,* both endemic there, have coevolved.

It is interesting that after meticulous research Melin (1935) concluded that existence of a flower truly adapted (in color, morphology, etc.) to visits by birds has never really been proven. Visits to flowers by birds such as hummingbirds is not a phenomenon of adaptation, only simple use of the plants by the birds.

Efficient pollination, occurring in various ways, is important for plants. For example, a hummingbird visiting a certain plant first goes to the lowest flowers, which are oldest and have well-projecting stigmas and anthers that have already separated from their filament. Only afterward does the hummingbird move to upper flowers that have recently opened and have pollen that sticks to its bill, etc., and is carried to another plant. Pollen also adheres to a hummingbird's crown, nape, breast, belly, axillaries, and tail. The hummingbird head is wide, facilitating contact with the anthers and stigmas of flowers. The bill and forehead sometimes carry a thick layer of creamy white or brown pollen. In the Teresópolis region of Rio de Janeiro, *Colibri serrirostris* is often conspicuous due to being covered with masses of pollen from the orchid *Rodriguezia* (A. Abendroth); an explosive opening of the pollinating apparatus is triggered by the hummingbird.

Among flowers pollinated by hummingbirds (*Glaucis, Phaethornis*) are those of *Stanhopea,* an orchid with a very strong, rotten stench that attracts insects. Plants pollinated by bats are generally characterized by a bad odor, whereas those pollinated by insects are typically fragrant. *Bifrenaria, Laelia, Oncidium,* and *Cattleya* are other orchids pollinated by hummingbirds.

Some plants, like the flor-de-papagaio ["parrot flower"], *Euphorbia* (*Poinsettia*) *pulcherrima,* are sought by hummingbirds only in certain places and never in others. Hummingbirds are not found at the flowers of quaresmas (*Tibouchina,* etc., Melastomataceae, plants very important to birds because of their small fruits) or *Cassia* species (Leguminosae, much sought after by bees) because these plants do not furnish nectar, only pollen.

I have already referred to occasional nocturnal hummingbird activity related to feeding (see "Behavior"). I saw a *Phaethornis ruber* sipping at a flower by the light of the illuminated home of Sra. Fávia S. Lobo on Ilha do Governador, Rio de Janeiro, at 8:00 P.M. on a dark October night when the sun had set at 5:57. J. S. Decker (1936) reported that *Datura suaveolens* (Solanaceae), whose flowers normally open at night and are adapted to pollination by large moths, also receives hummingbird visits "between 8 and 10 at night." Decker (1934) recorded the same phenomenon with cactus, for example on a species of *Epiphyllum;* he proved that certain night-blossoming *Cereus* species are pollinated by hummingbirds, apparently *Phaethornis*, in the early morning hours before the flowers close.

Fritz Müller (1878) reported that he did not know of any flowers pollinated exclusively by hummingbirds but that during the severe Santa Catarina winters when scarcely any butterflies and bees are on the wing, certain plants such as *Abutilon* and *Fuchsia* are visited almost exclusively by hummingbirds. See also Chapter 2.4. Even today there are no known flowers pollinated only by birds.

Pollination of *Fuchsia* sect. *Quelusia* has been studied by Berry (1989), who considers its flowers especially adapted to hummingbird visits: they are red, odorless, pendulous, and tubular in shape. In this connection he mentions *Colibri serrirostris*, *Stephanoxis lalandi*, and *Leucochloris albicollis*.

Although it was long believed that hummingbirds do not orient by smell, it has been revealed (Goldsmith et al. 1982) that the olfactory lobes of hummingbirds are sizable relative to the hemispheres (index of 14%; see Procellariidae, "Morphology . . . "). Ornithophilous flowers reportedly have no smell and are generally larger than entomophilous ones. Considering that ornithophilous flowers are usually red, it is interesting that Neotropical *Heliconia*, pollinated by hummingbirds, have red bracts, unlike *Heliconia* of the Pacific, whose flowers are white and entomophilous.

Hummingbirds do not pollinate when they use holes in the side of the corolla or pierce the flowers to suck nectar (illegitimate acquisition of nectar, "thievery," see "Feeding . . . ").

Association with Wasps

A relationship between *Phaethornis ruber* and a small, solitary wasp (*Pison* sp., Sphecidae) has been recorded in Belém, Pará. The voluminous base of 8 of 13 nests of this forest hummingbird contained 1 to 13 larval cells of this wasp, complete with larvae and spider prey. The *Phaethornis* sometimes captured one of the wasps to eat (Oniki 1970). *Pison* cells were also found in a nest of the Yellow-breasted Flycatcher, *Tolmomyias flaviventris*, in the same region.

Parasites, Enemies, and Other Dangers; Longevity

Young hummingbirds are severely parasitized by botflies. Sixty-four adult botflies, *Philornis insularis*, hatched from a *Thalurania glaucopis* nest placed in a closed jar. These, added to the larvae I removed from two young that had fledged from the nest, brought the total to approximately 80 botflies from this nest.

I once enclosed a recently abandoned *Chlorostilbon aureoventris* nest in a glass jar and later found 17 adult botflies whose larvae (pupated in the bottom of the nest) had developed in the two chicks, one of which died at five days of age. Small hummingbird nestlings die from harboring many botfly larvae.

It is reported that hornets not only compete with hummingbirds at flowers but can sting them mortally. Ruschi (1950) reports that a hunter-hornet (*Campsomeris* sp.) guarding a flowering cluster of mistletoe (*Psittacanthus dichrous*) attacked a *Chlorestes notatus* the moment it arrived at one of the flowers. The hummingbird fled several times but was finally stung and fell to the ground. Although rescued by the observer, it died. It is reported that 0.6 mg of bee venom are mortal for a 100-g bird; a bee sting injects 0.2 mg of venom. In Costa Rica Gill et al. (1982) noted that stingless bees of the genus *Trigona* flying constantly around the red flowers of a *Passiflora* kept *Phaethornis superciliosus* from approaching in a third of the cases. I have known of cases in which army ants invaded a hummingbird nest and killed the nestlings. The *Eciton* are incapable of tearing apart a bird.

I used to believe that the large praying mantises I saw lurking on flowers by day and clutching, head downward, the wire from which the feeder bottle was suspended at dusk would have a hard time capturing hummingbirds. However, I have found three records that occurred in the U.S. with the Ruby-throated Hummingbird, *Archilochus colubris*, the only species in the Eastern U.S. (Butler 1949, Hildebrand 1949, Murray 1958). Efforts to save the hummingbird, being tightly held by the insect, were successful in two cases. It was difficult to separate the combatants, proving that the mantis is quite capable of killing a hummingbird.

There have been cases of trochilids (e.g., *Amazilia*, *Phaethornis*) being caught accidentally in spider webs (see also Hirundinidae, "Usefulness . . . "). The possibility that the victims are consumed by the resident spider cannot be discarded. The frequent conjecture that tarantulas actively hunt hummingbirds was supported by Sybilla Merian who, in her famous work *Metamorphosis Insectorum Surinamensis* (1705), pictured a tarantula feeding on a hummingbird. This illustration, however, is unconvincing and unfortunate, for the hummingbird is an imaginary one and its nest, shown at the side, has four eggs, something that never occurs (Haverschmidt 1970). It is quite probable that tarantulas do sometimes reach hummingbird nests. Ruschi saw a tarantula capture a female *Melanotrochilus fuscus* that was searching for nesting material close to the ground. The spider carried the hummingbird close to a tree where it tore it open through the back and ate the viscera. Plate 26 in vol. 4 of Ruschi's *Aves do Brasil* (1986) is not credible: as W. Bokermann has informed me, a nocturnal tarantula and a diurnal snake are involved, both of which live on the ground; the acrobatics of the spider on a slender branch could only be forced. Bokermann states that tarantulas prefer cold-blooded animals. A captive tarantula (*Grammostola* sp., body length 5–6 cm without legs) can kill a newborn mouse with its poison. By cutting up and ingesting the victim, the aracnid makes such good use of it that finally not even a small bone remains (Bücherl 1951).

Snakes and lizards (e.g., *Anolis*) eat hummingbird eggs when they find them. Pygmy-owls, *Glaucidium;* small, swift hawks such as the Sharp-skinned Hawk, *Accipiter striatus;* Great Kiskadees, *Pitangus sulphuratus;* cats; and snakes (e.g., *Oxybelis*) occasionally catch hummingbirds. The pygmy-owls, crepuscular and even diurnal in habit, are natural enemies of hummingbirds, with sometimes six or more hummers quickly finding one. The hummingbirds then make feinted attacks, during which the occipital face (see Strigiformes, "Feeding") of the pygmy-owl must sometimes become fatal for them.

A Great Egret, *Casmerodius albus,* has been seen to catch a hummingbird that approached the egret from the back at head level. After briefly manipulating the victim in its bill, the egret let it fall. Kingfishers can also be dangerous (M. A. Andrade pers. comm.). Usually hummingbirds escape this type of danger by their very rapid flight. They are afraid of dragonflies (Odonata) but drive away butterflies.

A *Phaethornis pretrei* was taken from the stomach of an electrocuted opossum (*Caluromys philander*) (R. B. Pineschi). The hummingbird was probably caught at night while sleeping.

The large, red flowers of the African tulip tree (*Spathodea campanulata*), an African ornamental widely planted in Brazil, are a problem. In Angola up to 200 meloponid bees (and other small insects) were found dead in its flowers. The same thing happens in Brazil. Hummingbirds have not been found dead near the flowers, and it is impossible to determine if they die at a distance, but it would be easy to make tests in a flight cage. P. Nogueira Neto (1970) lists this tree under "undesirable plants."

Hummingbirds sometimes fly into white walls and glass windows but frequently escape death from these accidents, unlike other birds such as pigeons, thereby demonstrating their notable durability (thick skin, etc., see "Morphology").

Hummingbird longevity under natural conditions, as recorded by A. Ruschi, is five to eight years; in captivity some reach twice that age.

Use, Slaughter, and Research

Hummingbirds, like other multicolored birds and egrets, were intensely hunted in the nineteenth century to supply the European and North American fashion industries. In 1847 S. A. Bille, commander of the Danish corvette *Galathea* on its research cruise around the world, had his interest aroused by the shop of Mme. Finot, a French modiste who specialized in making adornments for dresses and hats from hummingbird skins. Bille made one of the first protests against destruction of Brazilian fauna: hummingbirds "die by the thousands so their brilliant feathers can adorn our elegant ladies." At the same time E. J. Silva Maia (1851) of the National Museum in Rio de Janeiro drew attention to the fact that hummingbirds in this area had diminished in numbers and that some had disappeared completely.

The Brazilian hummingbird trade was centered in the Recôncavo, Bahia, where skins were typically prepared with the tail fanned out. The most valued was the *beija-flor-cabeça-de-fogo* ("fiery-headed hummingbird"), *Chrysolampis mosquitus.* One collector supplied 40 hummingbirds per day of various kinds. In a London auction 37,603 hummingbird skins from Brazil, other parts of South America, and Trinidad were sold. Eight thousand hummingbirds were used on just one ladies' shawl in 1905. At the beginning of the 1800s one London merchant imported from the Antilles over 400,000 hummingbird skins in one year. Colombia furnished the most sought-after species.

In those days natural resources of this type seemed endless. Until the trade in wild animals in Brazil was prohibited in 1967, hummingbirds were the principal raw material for the manufacture of artificial flowers from feathers, a practice that, unhappily, from time to time returns to style. Even in the 1930s hundreds of hummingbirds, particularly *C. mosquitus,* were sold in the market of Salvador (J. Becker pers. comm.). The great loss of hummingbirds in times past to use in fashions corresponds to modern mortality from unrestricted use of pesticides. In pineapple plantations, for instance, which are much used by hummingbirds, they die by hundreds and thousands.

Incredible as it may seem, the custom still exists among residents of the Caxias do Sul region of Rio Grande do Sul of eating hummingbirds in a dish known as *passarinhos com polenta,* "little birds with corn meal." And in every part of this country there are children who, for lack of anyone to educate them about nature, go around with slingshots shooting hummingbirds that hover near flowers or sugar-water feeders.

In their eagerness to create rarities or novelties, unscrupulous merchants offer fakes, using the skins of two species to make an artifact. This falsification has also occurred with butterflies.

The rarity of certain hummingbird species in collections has sometimes arisen from the fact that they originated in little-known regions, as in the case of the Hooded Visorbearer, *Augastes lumachellus.* After their rediscovery in these areas, the collection of dozens or hundreds of birds by irresponsible persons, as has occurred in recent years, has become the greatest danger to their survival.

Immediately after Brazilian ports were opened, hummingbirds aroused intense interest among naturalists. P. A. Delalande, who came to this country in 1816 together with A. Saint-Hilaire, was one of the first great scientific collectors of trochilids. In 1843 E. J. Silva Maia of the National Museum in Rio de Janeiro described an Amazonian hummingbird species (Green-tailed Goldenthroat, *Polytmus theresiae*) and in 1851 published his observations on the "habits and customs of some hummingbirds." Between 1849 and 1861 the famous hummingbird monograph by J. Gould appeared. In 1900 E. Hartert published his work *Trochilidae,* and in 1921 E. Simon published *Histoire Naturelle des Trochilidés.* Simon was a famous spider specialist. Later J. Berlioz did outstanding research, and we are indebted to A. Ruschi, an enthusiast/fancier without a solid scientific foundation, who from 1933 until his recent death provided most of our information on hummingbirds. Hummingbirds have become one of the most popular and most studied bird families of Brazil.

Conservation, Feeders, and Repopulation

Species with limited distribution, especially those living in forests, run the risk of extinction due to destruction of their native habitat. This is especially true of the Hook-billed Hermit, *Glaucis dohrnii,* a species of northern Espírito Santo and southern Bahia where deforestation has reached alarming proportions and has already caused the disappearance of species of several families. Other forest hummingbirds are in the same situation.

Hummingbird conservation can be facilitated by replacing their original food sources through systematic cultivation of plants with nectariferous flowers. To attract hummingbirds to gardens, preference should be given to malvaceous plants with large red flowers that bloom all year, such as *Malvaviscus.* The use of sugar-water bottles with the feeding tube painted red is a very efficient method used for years on a large scale by A. Ruschi in Santa Teresa, Espírito Santo.

A mixture of 15% to 25% cane sugar (e.g., 4–6 parts water to 1 part sugar, or ⅔ water and ⅓ sugar) is recommended. Higher concentrations, lack of cleanliness of the bottles, or addition of honey provoke fermentation of the liquid in our climate and cause mycosis of the tongue, which may prove fatal to the birds. To avoid access by ants, it is advisable to hang the bottles from a wire wrapped in cotton soaked in lubricating oil. Bees and wasps can be kept away by applying a repellent that drives them off by its odor. This does not bother hummingbirds, which have a poorly developed sense of smell. If any poisonous substance is placed on the bottles, great caution should be taken to prevent it reaching the tube into which the birds insert their bills. Setting out plates of sweet poisoned liquid to kill insects is dangerous for hummingbirds and other birds, such as the Bananaquit, *Coereba flaveola.*

At night sugar water is sought by bats, who can drink it while hovering like hummingbirds; nectarivorous bats are a New World specialty. Bottles should always be hung in the same place, and it is a good idea to put out several to avoid, at least to some extent, fights between hummingbirds.

If the bottles are kept full over a period of time, gradually more individuals will establish themselves permanently in the area and also start to nest, resulting in effective settlement or resettlement of a population. At the aforementioned ranch at Macaé de Cima, it took three months for the first hummingbird to appear at the bottles. Some years later these little birds were swarming around the buildings. They have 22 bottles of 150–500 ml. One winter, from July 2 to 10, they used 3 k of sugar in 15 l of water daily. Two to five hummingbirds were at a bottle at one time, with ten species competing. Without individually marking the birds there was no sure way to count the total number, but it was estimated that 100 or more individuals were present simultaneously (Elisabeth Garlipp; see also "Abundance").

Hummingbirds can become addicted; when the bottles are taken in for cleaning, the most assiduous clients become very nervous searching for their favorite food. Certain individuals or species will not come to the bottles, some really never. As a result it is almost certain that more hummingbirds are in a given area than are recorded at the bottles. When the bottles are withdrawn, the hummingbirds disappear.

A. Ruschi made a great effort to repopulate many places in Brazil with hummingbirds. In May 1956, for example, he released 450 birds in the Botanical Garden of Rio de Janeiro. He sent shipments of hummingbirds to many other cities to encourage breeding these birds in captivity. Hummingbirds were furnished for national and international expositions. Ruschi himself spoke of 20,000 hummingbirds used in this way, a number reminiscent of the consumption of hummingbirds for Paris fashions. There was insufficient research to determine whether the transferred hummingbirds stayed in their new areas. I believe it is almost certain that these birds did not stay and were lost.

Identification Data

Subdividing the Trochilidae is impossible (Hartert 1900) except for the following groupings: Phaethorninae (*Ramphodon, Glaucis, Threnetes,* and *Phaethornis*) and Trochilinae (the remaining genera).

The chance of observing hummingbirds closely—in front of flowers and feeders—provides an opportunity to distinguish details that normally are seen only when a bird is in the hand. It is even better because certain distinctive features, such as on the sides of the head and neck, the abdomen, and under the wings, are frequently lost on stuffed specimens. Hummingbirds flit fearlessly in front of our eyes and stop to drink with an immobility created by a thousand movements. With insufficient light or when observed against the sky, their brightest colors are not always seen, for green, blue, and red may appear black. Not even spectacularly colored areas, such as the gorgets of *Clytolaema* and *Heliomaster,* stand out under such conditions. Pollen smears can sometimes simulate light-colored markings, especially on the head. Mandible color, so important for distinguishing species such as the *Phaethornis,* is completely lost after death, and the same is true for the feet. Sometimes it is useful to know one diagnostic character for the bird as seen from the front and another from the rear (see *Phaethornis pretrei* and *P. eurynome*).

Identification of the members of some genera, especially *Phaethornis, Thalurania,* and *Amazilia,* requires specialized literature or more complete illustrations. Some cryptic species, as in *Phaethornis,* occur in the same areas. Identification of certain species is not easy even when good comparative material is at hand. In some cases agreement is lacking on whether certain forms should be considered good species or simply geographic races. *Thalurania furcata* has been divided into eight Brazilian subspecies. Identification of females is frequently facilitated by appearance of the respective males in the same place.

1. Size
   1.1. Very small: *Lophornis* (Pl 20), *Popelairia* (fig. 168), and *Discosura* (fig. 169), all three with a white, whitish, or light cinnamon band on the lower back (see item 7); *Calliphlox* (Pl 20), female with sides of the body cinnamon; *Phaethornis ruber* and *P. idaliae* ("hermit" type, see item 5.4.1). All are conspicuous because of a high hum in flight. *Doryfera* and *Klais* are also small.
   1.2. Larger species: *Topaza* (Pl 20), found only in Amazonia, and *Ramphodon naevius,* only in the southeast. *Eupetomena* (Pl 20) is also long.
2. Bill
   2.1. Long and decurved: *Glaucis, Phaethornis* (Pl 20), and *Polytmus;* less curved in *Threnetes*
   2.2. Surprisingly long and straight: *Heliomaster* (Pl 21). *Doryfera* also has a long, straight bill with a slightly upturned tip.
   2.3. Short, the tip sharply curved upward: *Avocettula* (fig. 167)
   2.4. Bill color is often diagnostic, sometimes involving only the mandible, which is best seen from below when the bird opens its bill to yawn or during the nuptial display (e.g., *Phaethornis*). As with other birds, the bill becomes discolored in prepared specimens; it may then appear whitish, while in life it was plumbeous, red, or yellow.
3. Tail
   3.1. Tail bifurcated to varying degrees, for example: *Eupetomena* (Pl 20), *Thalurania* (Pl 20), *Popelairia* (fig. 168; item 10.2.2.), *Heliodoxa, Heliomaster* (Pl 21), and *Calliphlox* (Pl 20)
   3.2. Tail with elongated central feathers: *Phaethornis* (Pl 20) and *Heliactin; Topaza* (Pl 20) with subcentral feathers elongated; *Heliothryx* (Pl 20) with sharply graduated tail
   3.3. Racket-tailed: *Discosura* (fig. 169)
   3.4. Tail chestnut-colored (translucent): *Glaucis, Chrysolampis* (Pl 21), *Lophornis* (Pl 20), *Hylocharis sap-*

phirina, Clytolaema (Pl 20), *Topaza* (Pl 20), and *Augastes lumachellus. Anthracothorax* also has a tail that is chestnut in transmitted light but violet purple in incident light (Pl 21).
   3.5. Tail brilliant golden bronze: *Hylocharis chrysura*
   3.6. Sides of tail whitish or white: *Threnetes leucurus, Florisuga, Melanotrochilus, Heliothryx,* and *Heliactin*
4. Distinctive head shape
   4.1. Topknot: *Stephanoxis* (Pl 21), *Lophornis* in part (Pl 20), and *Heliactin*
   4.2. "Onion head" (forehead plumage extends beyond nostrils): *Chrysolampis* (Pl 21)
5. General coloration (principal species)
   5.1. Green or green and blue: *Eupetomena* (Pl 20), *Chlorestes, Chlorostilbon* (Pl 21), *Thalurania* (Pl 20), *Hylocharis cyanus* (Pl 21), *Chrysoronia,* and *Polytmus*
   5.2. Green with more or less extensive white on underparts: *Florisuga* (item 9), *Leucochloris* (Pl 21), *Amazilia* (Pl 21), *Heliothryx,* and *Heliactin*
   5.3. Upperparts green, underparts gray: *Campylopterus, Klais, Stephanoxis, Aphantochroa;* females of various species such as *Chrysolampis, Stephanoxis* (Pl 21), *Chlorostilbon* (Pl 21), and *Thalurania* (Pl 20)
   5.4. Green restricted to upperparts, underparts brown
      5.4.1. Tail long, often white-tipped: *Phaethornis* ("hermit,"[2] see item 3.2, Pl 20). *P. ruber* has a "normal" tail (see item 1.1).
      5.4.2. Tail not elongated: *Ramphodon* (item 1.2), *Glaucis* (item 2.1), *Threnetes* (greenish breast, item 2.1), female of *Clytolaema* (Pl 20). An eye-catching brown design occurs also in immatures of *Florisuga, Melanotrochilus, Colibri, Anthracothorax,* and *Polytmus.*
   5.5. Sooty, auricular patch blue: *Colibri delphinae*
   5.6. Extensively dark red: *Chrysolampis* (item 4.2, Pl 21) and *Topaza* (item 1.2, 3.2, Pl 20)
6. Small white spot behind eye
   Various species have a well-marked, small, white spot behind the eye, e.g.,: *Campylopterus, Klais, Stephanoxis* (Pl 21), *Polytmus, Aphantochroa* (Pl 21), *Clytolaema* (Pl 20), *Augastes, Heliomaster,* and *Calliphlox* (Pl 20). Situated at the widest point of the head and visible even from behind and in poor light, it must be an important marker in life but is little noticed or invisible in stuffed specimens. As a result it is often not even mentioned by authors who know these birds only through museum specimens.
7. White band
   Whitish or cinnamon-tinged on the lower back, including females: *Lophornis* (Pl 20), *Popelairia,* and *Discosura;* see also item 1.1.
8. White tufts on the side of the belly
   These occur in various hummingbirds, e.g.,: *Eupetomena, Colibri serrirostris, Chrysolampis, Discosura, Chlorestes, Thalurania, Aphantochroa,* and *Heliomaster. Topaza* has white thighs. See also *Melanotrochilus* (item 10).

---

[2]*Hermit* is not a suitable name, considering the biology of these hummingbirds. The males of various *Phaethornis* are found in singing "clubs," and all are very active in pursuit of females. A good name would be *Schattenkolibri,* "shade hummingbird."

9. Green with a showy white patch on the throat or nape
   9.1. White throat: *Leucochloris* (Pl 21)
   9.2. Large white spot on the nape: *Florisuga*
10. Extensive black
   10.1. Black and white without any green: *Melanotrochilus* (fig. 166)
   10.2 Underparts black or blackish
      10.2.1. All underparts black: *Doryfera* and *Melanotrochilus*
      10.2.2. Only the belly black or sooty: *Chrysolampis* (items 4.2, 5.6) and *Popelairia* (items 1.1, 3.1)
      10.2.3. Underparts white with a black median stripe: female *Anthracothorax* (Pl 21) and *Avocettula* (item 2.3)
11. Sparkling patch on the throat or sides of the head
   11.1. Throat red: *Chrysolampis* (Pl 21), *Clytolaema* (Pl 20), *Heliomaster* (Pl 21), and *Calliphlox* (Pl 20). *Polyplancta* has a red spot on the breast.
   11.2. Green throat contrasting with the rest of the underparts: *Popelairia* (fig. 168), *Topaza* (Pl 20), and *Augastes* (elongated in a "necktie")
   11.3. Violet patch on the sides of the head: *Colibri delphinae* and *C. serrirostris* (Pl 21)
12. Feet
   Generally black but sometimes light (yellow, yellowish, or light flesh color), e.g., *Threnetes,* certain *Phaethornis,* and *Topaza*

BLUE-FRONTED LANCEBILL, *Doryfera johannae,* Bico-de-lança

10 cm. Bill long (2.6–2.7 cm), straight, with tip tilted slightly upward; tail short; dark green above with violaceous forehead; black below. Roraima and adjacent countries. See *Avocettula.*

SAW-BILLED HERMIT, *Ramphodon naevius,* Beija-flor-grande-do-mato   BR

16 cm. Very "large," brown species of southeastern Brazil. Heavily black-streaked breast, wide, unelongated tail (unlike *Phaethornis*), light brown lateral tail feathers. Bill sturdy with wide base (giving it a certain snipelike, *Gallinago,* air), ending in a hook (male) or mildly curved (female). Mandible yellow. Female and immature have small black spot on throat. VOICE: *chak;* 3–6 high whistles in a sharply descending sequence, *tsee-tseww-tseww (-tseww);* a more modulated and prolonged stanza given in flight; *it-it* resembling *Galbula* and with timbre similar to Pin-tailed Manakin, *Ilicura militaris.* Bobs tail. Deep forest shade of escarpment. Seeks tiny bromeliad flowers (e.g., *Neoregelia, Billbergia*). Espírito Santo and Minas Gerais to Rio Grande do Sul.

HOOK-BILLED HERMIT, *Glaucis dohrnii,* Balança-rabo-canela   BR   EN   PL 45.7

12 cm. Similar to *Ramphodon naevius* but with almost straight bill and whitish mandible. All tail feathers uniformly metallic bronze with lateral ones (4 on each side) white-tipped. Upperparts greenish bronze; underparts cinnamon; superciliary and malar regions white; postocular area black. VOICE: a descending stanza like *R. naevia* and *G. hirsuta.* Restricted to forests. Visits same flowers, such as those of lemon tree and of epiphitic bromeliads, as *G. hirsuta,* sometimes at same time. Sometimes included in *Ramphodon.*

RUFOUS-BREASTED HERMIT, *Glaucis hirsuta,* Balança-rabo-de-bico-torto

13 cm. Stocky with long, curved bill, light yellow mandible. Underparts rusty; tail feathers chestnut with wide black subterminal band and white tip, except central ones which are green and not elongated. VOICE: a descending and decrescendo sequence, *sst-sst-sst;* song *ee-ee-eww-eww-eww-eww-eww,* softer than *Ramphodon naevius.* Panama to Bolivia, almost all of Brazil. Includes *Threnetes grzimeki* Ruschi from Espírito Santo, which is immature *G. hirsuta.*

PALE-TAILED BARBTHROAT, *Threnetes leucurus,* Balança-rabo-de-garganta-preta

11 cm. Amazonian species resembling *Glaucis hirsuta* but with slightly curved bill lacking serrations on maxilla; mandible gray. Black throat edged with horizontal rust-colored band; feet yellow. Color of tail feathers varies drastically according to region; yellowish white with black tips on lateral ones (Amapá, Pará, Maranhão; *T. l. medianus*), light cinnamon (upper Amazon, Juruá; *T. l. cervinicauda*), or white (Roraima, *T. l. leucurus*) (see also forms mentioned below and "Evolution . . . "). Female and immature have paler throat patch. VOICE AND DISPLAYS: song a high *tsit-tsit-tseri.* Constantly moves tail up and down. When another individual approaches or when flying in front of a female, flares out tail and moves it backward and forward like a pendulum, exposing large light area on lateral tail feathers while also displaying throat pattern. Numerous at lower levels of dark forest but does not attract attention except by voice. Most abundant non-Passerine in terra-firme forests around Belém, Pará, and equally common in várzea forests. See also "Feeding". The Guianas, Venezuela, and Colombia to Bolivia, Amazonas, Pará, Maranhão. Sometimes alongside *Glaucis.* See *T. niger.* Includes *T. loehkeni* Grantsau from Amapá, considered by Hinkelmann (pers. comm.) to be a subspecies of *leucurus.* Also includes *T. cristinae* Ruschi from Amapá, which appears to be identical to *loehkeni.*

SOOTY BARBTHROAT, *Threnetes niger*

11 cm. Greenish black, tail without any white. Rio Oiapoque (Amapá) region, on border with French Guiana, to Serra do Navio.

LONG-TAILED HERMIT, *Phaethornis superciliosus,* Besourão-de-rabo-branco

15.5 cm. "Large," common in forested parts of Amazonia. Mandible red or orange. Frequently alongside *Threnetes.*

Abundant in capoeiras of Amazonian estuary. Mexico to Bolivia, Amazonian Brazil (Amazonas, Pará, Amapá). Has several geographic races.

GREAT-BILLED HERMIT, *Phaethornis malaris*, Besourão-de-bico-grande

16 cm. Twin species of *P. superciliosus,* from which it is distinguished by being Brazilian trochilid with longest bill (46–47 mm). Base of mandible red or pink. The Guianas to Amapá and sympatric with *superciliosus*. Includes *P. margarettae* Ruschi 1972 from Espírito Santo as a subspecies (L. Gonzaga and C. Hinkelmann pers. comm.).

SCALE-THROATED HERMIT, *Phaethornis eurynome*, Rabo-branco-de-garganta-rajada   Fig. 160

15.5 cm. Similar to *P. pretrei* but with even longer bill, yellow mandible, clearly striped throat. Rump same color as back but feathers bordered with rufous. Subcentral tail feathers less elongated than in *pretrei,* making tips of central ones look more isolated. VOICE: peeps a *tsieww, tsuit; klip-klip-klieh,* etc. Sometimes several individuals sing in a small area. Lower levels of forest and capoeira. In northern part of range typical of mountainous regions, alongside *pretrei,* both being devoted customers of gravatás-de-ninho (*Neoregelia* and *Nidularia*). Southeastern Brazil from Espírito Santo to Rio Grande do Sul, Paraguay, and Misiones, Argentina. Black-billed Hermit, *P. nigrirostris* Ruschi 1973, is perhaps a variety of *eurynome,* to which it is similar but with a more curved, all-black bill. So far known only from Nova Lombardia Reserve, Espírito Santo, where I saw it in 1977.

WHITE-BEARDED HERMIT, *Phaethornis hispidus*, Besourão-cinza

14 cm. Very light colored, pale gray, not brownish. Sunny cerrado of central Brazil, flying from one grove to another. Peru to Bolivia, Brazil in Roraima, Acre, Amazonas, Mato Grosso (as far as Tapirapoã). See also *P. nattereri.*

STRAIGHT-BILLED HERMIT, *Phaethornis bourcieri*

North of Amazon (Pará, Amapá) and adjacent countries; also Tapajós, Pará.

NEEDLE-BILLED HERMIT, *Phaethornis philippi*

Only in western Brazil (Tapajós, Madeira) as far as Peru.

DUSKY-THROATED HERMIT, *Phaethornis squalidus*, Rabo-branco-miúdo   Fig. 161

12 cm. Relatively small with color like *P. eurynome,* including yellow mandible. VOICE AND DISPLAYS: *ew-TSEE ew-TSEE;* a much varied trill ending in *tsrrr (tsrrr, tsrrr)* and other hurried phrases, e.g., *TSEH-wat, wat, wat,* all forming part of collective song various males that gather in certain areas perching 20–30 cm above ground; hovering over another individual it emits a *chaa, chaa.* Oscillates tail while

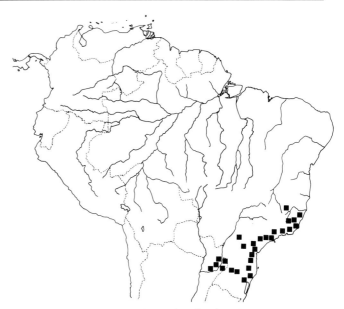

Fig. 160. Scale-throated Hermit, *Phaethornis eurynome*. Original, C. Hinkelmann, in press.

singing. When a congener approaches, opens tail, lifts it above horizontal, and intensifies singing. Deep forest, living at low levels. Southeastern Brazil. Locally abundant (ex-Guanabara).

STREAK-THROATED HERMIT, *Phaethornis rupurumii*

Replaces *P. squalidus* in Amazonia, from Orinoco to Mato Grosso.

SOOTY-CAPPED HERMIT, *Phaethornis augusti*

Only in extreme north (Roraima and adjacent regions).

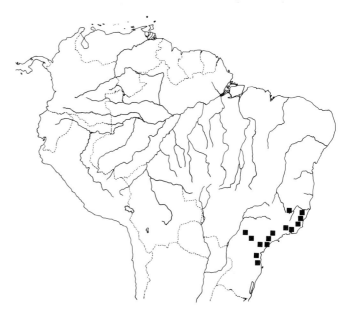

Fig. 161. Dusky-throated Hermit, *Phaethornis squalidus*. Original, C. Hinkelmann, in press.

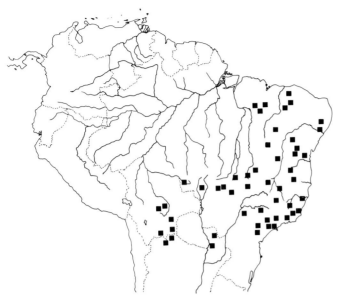

Fig. 162. Planalto Hermit, *Phaethornis pretrei*. Original C. Hinkelmann, in press.

Fig. 163. Cinnamon-throated Hermit, *Phaethornis nattereri* (circles). Broad-tipped Hermit, *Phaethornis gounellei* (squares). Original, C. Hinkelmann, in press.

PLANALTO HERMIT, *Phaethornis pretrei*, Rabo-branco-de-sobre-amarelo   PL 20.4   Fig. 162

15 cm. Abundant in eastern and central Brazil. Has regularly graduated, long tail edged white. Underparts (including throat) and upper tail coverts uniformly cinnamon, unlike *P. eurynome*, its occasional neighbor; base of mandible red. VOICE AND DISPLAYS: *swit* (in flight), song *wist-wist-wist, tseeeh-tseeeh-tseeeh*. Bobs tail. Prenuptial flight involves prolonged chasing of female low in dense forest while both vocalize. Forests, tree-filled gardens among houses, where sometimes nests; likes vicinity of running water (see "Nest Care . . . "). Maranhão to Santa Catarina, Goiás, Mato Grosso.

BUFF-BELLIED HERMIT, *Phaethornis subochraceus*

Only in extreme west (western Mato Grosso, Descalvados, to Bolivia).

CINNAMON-THROATED HERMIT, *Phaethornis nattereri*, Besourão-de-sobre-amarelo   Fig. 163

14 cm. Similar to *P. pretrei* but smaller and with lateral tail feathers bordered rufous, not white. Mandible yellow. Maranhão, Piaui, Mato Grosso (Tapirapoã, alongside *P. hispidus*, which is larger), Bolivia. Includes *P. maranhaoensis* Grantsau, which is male of *nattereri* (Hinkelmann 1988).

BROAD-TIPPED HERMIT, *Phaethornis gounellei* BR PL 45.6   Fig. 163

9.5 cm. Tail feathers have even broader white tip than *P. pretrei*. Restricted to northeastern Brazil, in Piauí, Ceará, Bahia.

REDDISH HERMIT, *Phaethornis ruber*, Besourinho-da-mata

8.6 cm; 1.8–2.2 g. One of smallest Brazilian hummingbirds. Tail relatively short with central tail feathers only slightly prolonged and lacking white tips; rump and underparts bright rufous; breast with black spot (male); mandible yellow. VOICE AND DISPLAYS: song *si-SEE-SEE-sisisisisisi*. Flies low with a sharp buzz similar to that of a large bee. I have seen a 3-phase prenuptial display showing increasing intensity of movement; I repeat here only the fundamentals: (1) Male executes a slow, silent, horizontal pendulum flight, slightly above and in front of perched female. At each extreme of pendulum, emphasizing rigid rhythm of the action, he turns his body outward. He holds the tail elevated so the white "underpants" appear to the female as the extreme rear end of the body. His body is held relatively immobile, permitting a view of every detail of plumage, etc., while the rapidly moving wings are invisible. Bill, yellow inside, is open and pointed toward female while tongue is held slack like a dangling worm. From time to time he produces a muffled, *daDA, daDA, daDA* with wings. (2) Male changes stance completely, pointing bill upward and puffing out breast while still continuing pendulum flight, though at a more accelerated rhythm. (3) Finally he performs a frenetic flight before female, appearing like a dark, horizontal streak, and sings *dlewit, dlewit, dlewit . . . .* Lower levels of forest, capoeira, yards, gardens, but easily overlooked. The Guianas and Venezuela to Bolivia, Brazil as far as São Paulo.

In the upper Amazon there are two more small species:

GRAY-CHINNED HERMIT, *Phaethornis griseogularis*

9.5 cm. Similar to *P. ruber* but with center part of tail feathers black. Venezuela to northern and western Brazil.

LITTLE HERMIT, *Phaethornis longuemareus*

10 cm. Similar to *P. ruber* and *P. griseogularis*. Mexico to Rio Negro, lower Tapajós. See "Vocalization" and *P. idaliae*.

MINUTE HERMIT, *Phaethornis idaliae*,
Besourinho   BR   Fig. 164

As small as *P. ruber*. Immature or subadult male has short tail, very dark plumage with almost black throat and breast, lemon yellow mandible. Differs appreciably from adult, which has long central tail feathers with extensive white tips, chestnut throat. Female reddish with long central tail feathers. Restingas, etc., locally common. Bahia to Rio de Janeiro Sometimes considered a geographic replacement of Amazonian *P. longuemareus*.

GRAY-BREASTED SABREWING, *Campylopterus largipennis*, Asa-de-sabre

12 cm. Stocky, distinguished by wing being angled at level of hand because of very elongated rachises of primaries (fig. 165). Underparts dark gray; lateral tail feathers white on outer half. Female similar but lacks elongation of primaries. VOICE: Alarm a loud *oEH;* song much varied. Flight heavy (see "Flight"). Capoeira, forest. In várzea forests of Belém (Pará) region it is one of most abundant non-Passerines alongside *Threnetes* and *Thalurania furcata*. Isolated pairs have been found above 1000 m in small ravine forests in

Fig. 165. Gray-breasted Sabrewing, *Campylopterus l. largipennis,* right wing, showing the extremely broadened rachises of the primaries.

Minas Gerais. The Guianas to Ecuador, Bolivia, Brazil: Amazonas, Pará, Maranhão, Mato Grosso, Minas Gerais (Diamantina, Grão Mogol, Serra do Caraça).

On the frontier with Venezuela there are two more species:

RUFOUS-BREASTED SABREWING, *Campylopterus hyperythrus*

BUFF-BREASTED SABREWING, *Campylopterus duidae*

It is worth mentioning here that a Mexican species, the Violet Sabrewing, *Campylopterus hemileucurus,* which has the same unusual wing formation, makes a noise similar to the bleating of a goat (see Common Snipe, *Gallinago gallinago*) when skydiving before the female. This probably also occurs with other *Campylopterus* species.

SWALLOW-TAILED HUMMINGBIRD, *Eupetomena macroura,* Tesourão   PL 20.1

18 cm. One of largest and most bellicose trochilids. Deeply forked tail takes up almost ⅔ of total length. Head and neck blue, rest of plumage brilliant dark green. VOICE: a loud *tsak;* a weak twitter interspersed with *cha-cha-cha.* Re nuptial flight, see "Mating." Capoeira, gardens. The Guianas to Bolivia, Paraguay, throughout Brazil except certain re-

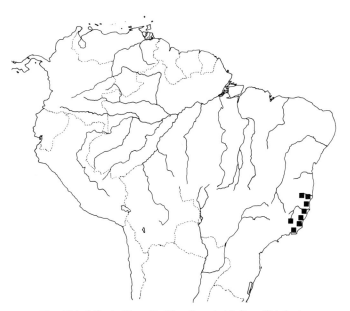

Fig. 164. Minute Hermit, *Phaethornis idaliae.* Original, C. Hinkelmann, in press.

gions of Amazonia; common in many places. See *Thalurania glaucopis.*

WHITE-NECKED JACOBIN, *Florisuga mellivora,* Beija-flor-azul-de-rabo-branco

11 cm. Adult male unmistakable with large white nuchal patch; head blue, back brilliant green, belly and tail feathers white, latter with black tips. Female green above with green-spotted white underparts, green tail. Immature male has cinnamon stripe on side of throat, slightly resembling immature *Melanotrochilus fuscus.* Forest, often in canopy of tallest trees (*beija-flor-da-copa,* "canopy hummingbird"). Mexico to Bolivia, Amazonia, Mato Grosso, Maranhão; one of most widely distributed hummingbirds. Related to *M. fuscus;* see also "Morphology."

BLACK JACOBIN, *Melanotrochilus fuscus,* Beija-flor-preto-e-branco   BR   Fig. 166

12.6 cm. Typical of eastern Brazil. Eye-catching, contrasting colors of tail are displayed when bird spreads it into a white fan divided in 2 by black center feathers, or by rapidly opening and closing it, creating a blinker effect. White of tail extends to flanks and forms band across crissum. Sexual dimorphism not accentuated. Immature has wide chestnut band on sides of throat; younger individuals are black almost completely spotted with brown, have cinnamon or black tail with only lateral feathers white.

Seems to remain immobile in air more than other hummingbirds, displaying arrestingly beautiful contrasts. Nuptial flight (see fig. 155) consists of zigzag chases of female; pair mounts to heights, stopping as they rise about every 20 m to hover in front of each other; then return at once to their perch where they arouse each other by opening and closing wings. On migration, see "Return to Territory. . . ." Forest edges, capoeira, gardens, banana plantings, frequently in tops of tall trees. Alagoas to Rio Grande do Sul; can be periodically abundant, e.g., it is most frequently observed hummingbird in Macaé de Cima, Rio de Janeiro, in summer.

Fig. 166. Black Jacobin, *Melanotrochilus fuscus,* sipping nectar.

BROWN VIOLETEAR, *Colibri delphinae,* Beija-flor-marron-de-orelha-azul

12.2 cm. Sooty with cinnamon under tail coverts, only throat and tail greenish. Auricular spot brilliant blue like *C. coruscans.* Semiarid rocky areas, open fields, mesas with xerophytic vegetation (*carrasco*). Bahia (Serra do Sincorá, Andaraí, alongside *Augastes lumachellus*) and primarily Roraima and Andes.

SPARKLING VIOLETEAR, *Colibri coruscans*

14 cm. "Large," sparkling green and blue. Only in mountains of frontier with Venezuela (Roraima) and in Andes.

WHITE-VENTED VIOLETEAR, *Colibri serrirostris,* Beija-flor-de-orelha-violeta   PL 21.5

12.1 cm. Distinguished by postauricular purplish blue spots that can be taken for a collar. White under tail coverts. Immature has brownish tones, white belly and malar stripes. Extent of serrated maxilla varies (see "Morphology"). VOICE AND DISPLAYS: *ttt . . . ; tsip-TSIP-tsap,* etc.; sings this song from sunrise to sunset (hence the name "singing hummingbird"). Male hovers stationary before perched female, raising his neck tufts forward and upward. Semiopen country, cerrado, sea-level restinga; also common in high country above timber line (e.g., Itatiaia), descending to valleys in autumn (see "Return to Territory . . ."). Bolivia and northwestern Argentina to Mato Grosso, Goiás, Bahia, Espírito Santo. See *C. coruscans* and *C. delphinae.*

BLACK-THROATED MANGO, *Anthracothorax nigricollis,* Beija-flor-preto   PL 21.6

11.4 cm. Male so dark it often appears all black. Tail color somewhat like *Clytolaema.* Female has much different color pattern (making her look like another species), similar to female *Avocettula.* Immature has white streaks mixed with rusty on underparts. Capoeira, forests. Frequents canopy. Panama to Bolivia, Argentina, all of Brazil. See *Melanotrochilus.*

GREEN-THROATED MANGO, *Anthracothorax viridigula*

Exclusively Amazonian, similar to *A. nigricollis* but with green throat. The Guianas and Venezuela to Maranhão, Pará (Santarém).

FIERY-TAILED AWLBILL, *Avocettula recurvirostris,* Beija-flor-de-bico-virado   R   Fig. 167

8.5 cm. Unique with short (8 mm), abruptly up-curved bill. Maxilla serrated. In plumage both male and female greatly resemble *Anthracothorax nigricollis.* The Guianas and Venezuela to Roraima, Amazonas, Pará (Monte Alegre, Santarém, Belém), Maranhão, Piauí. Rare in Brazil. See *Doryfera.*

Fig. 167. Fiery-tailed Awlbill, *Avocettula recurvirostris*. Original, H. Sick.

RUBY-TOPAZ HUMMINGBIRD, *Chrysolampis mosquitus*, Beija-flor-vermelho   PL 21.1

9.2 cm. One of most famous species; head appears horizontally broadened because of prominent forehead plumage and singular nuchal hood ("onion head"); splendid colors generally appear very dark if inadequately illuminated, with only translucently rusty tail outstanding. Has more iridescent feathers than any other hummingbird. Female bronze-green on upperparts, dirty white below with lateral tail feathers tipped white. During courtship male pursues female as soon as he sees her perched, flitting around her with opened tail, creating an effect as spectacular as that of contrast between glittering gold breast and hood of short, erect, constantly moving feathers. On migrations, see "Return to Territory . . . ." Sparse forest, cerrado, caatinga. Colombia and Venezuela to Bolivia. Also central Brazil as far as the northeast and in eastern Brazil (Bahia, Minas Gerais, Espírito Santo, infrequently ex-Guanabara and Paraná). This was species most sought by skin merchants (see "Use . . . ").

VIOLET-HEADED HUMMINGBIRD, *Klais guimeti*, Beija-flor-de-cabeça-roxa

8.5 cm. Resembles *Stephanoxis lalandi* but lacks crest and has more slender bill, black lores, bright white postocular spot. Amazonas (Javari), Roraima, and adjacent countries.

BLACK-BREASTED PLOVERCREST, *Stephanoxis lalandi*, Beija-flor-de-topete   PL 21.3

8.5 cm. Male unmistakable, being Brazilian species with longest crest, point of which is turned upward and often broken and short (nonadult male or molting). Populations in southern states (São Paulo to Rio Grande do Sul) have larger, blue (not green) crest, very dark violet underparts (*S. l. loddigesi*). Female has small, white postocular spot, white-tipped tail. VOICE: high like an insect: song *tsri, tsi-tsi* and a repeated *tsilli-tsilli-tsilli*. Gathers in groups to sing. A high-country or cold-climate species; in northern part of range (Espírito Santo, Minas Gerais, Rio de Janeiro) reaches highest altitudes (e.g., 2900 m in open country of Serra do Caparaó, Espírito Santo, and Itatiaia, Rio de Janeiro, etc.) where abundant. In winter descends to 1500 m (Itatiaia) and lower (900 m, Novo Friburgo, Rio de Janeiro). I found it at 1400 m in Itatiaia singing vigorously in September–October. In planalto of Rio Grande do Sul, reaching sea level (Porto Alegre) in winter (*S. l. loddigesi*). Southeastern Brazil from

Espírito Santo and Minas Gerais to Rio Grande do Sul and as far as Paraguay and northern Argentina. See female *Chlorostilbon aureoventris* and *Klais guimeti*.

FRILLED COQUETTE, *Lophornis magnifica*, Topetinho-vermelho   BR   PL 20.5

6.8 cm. Well-known southern species, by conventional measurements smallest Brazilian hummingbird. Elongated, white, lateral feathers of male neck, united in a great tuft, fan-shaped and end in green band that becomes black at feather tips. Female and immature lack crests and tufts but have white throat speckled cinnamon; rump band whitish, bill less intensely red. SOUNDS AND DISPLAYS: *gr-gr; piu-piu-piu . . . ;* a monotonous and prolonged *si-si*. During nuptial display male raises red crest and expands lateral neck tufts, moving them while he executes a slow flight or hovers in front of female who remains perched, turning her body sideways simultaneously; suddenly he rises in acrobatic flight, returning in a dive as if to collide with her, but stopping close and producing a loud, rustling *rrrep,* after which he goes up again. Capoeira, country estates, flowery gardens. Restricted to central and southeastern Brazil. Bahia to Rio Grande do Sul, Mato Grosso, Goiás. Also called *Beija-flor-magnífico,* "magnificent hummingbird." See other 4 Brazilian *Lophornis* and *Calliphlox*.

TUFTED COQUETTE, *Lophornis ornata*, Tufinho-vermelho

6.8 cm. Crest and long, lateral neck tufts cinnamon. Latter narrow and graduated with rounded green tips. Restricted to north of Amazon from Amapá and Roraima to Venezuela, the Guianas.

DOT-EARED COQUETTE, *Lophornis gouldii*, Topetinho-do-Brasil-central

7 cm. Similar to *L. ornata* but with narrow, white, lateral tufts with green tips. Forest edge, cerradão. Maranhão and southern Pará (Serra do Cachimbo) to northern Mato Grosso (upper Xingu), Goiás, Bolivia.

FESTIVE COQUETTE, *Lophornis chalybea*, Tufinho-verde

7.4 cm. Green crown but no red crest; bill black; tuft feathers narrow, elongated, green with white tips. Nuptial displays involve male hovering before female to display crown spot of bare, cobalt blue skin by holding bill against chest and raising forehead feathers while holding lateral tufts forward so they look like packets of colored toothpicks. According to A. Ruschi, blue crown patch (which is same color as eyelids) is more intense in breeding season. Forests. Venezuela to Bolivia, Amazonian Brazil (Amazonas, Roraima, Mato Grosso, southern Pará); also southeastern Brazil (e.g., Serra da Mantiqueira, Serra do Mar) from Espírito Santo and Minas Gerais to Santa Catarina.

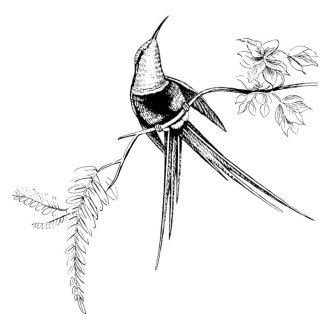

Fig. 168. Black-bellied Thorntail, *Popelairia langsdorffi,* male. Sketch by A. von Koenigsmarck, after J. Gould 1854.

PEACOCK COQUETTE, *Lophornis pavonina*

8 cm. No red crest but has long, wide green tufts on a large black anteapical spot. Roraima to Venezuela, Guyana.

BLACK-BELLIED THORNTAIL, *Popelairia langsdorffi,* Rabo-de-espinho   R   Fig. 168

12.5 cm (male); 7 cm (female). Male has long, slender, spinelike tail; green with white band on lower back and red band across breast; belly black. Female has "normal," short tail, generally dark with rump band, tip of tail, and line on side of throat white. SOUNDS AND DISPLAYS: male raises, opens, and closes tail while flying. In grazing flights over female he produces popping noises, e.g., *rrep,* apparently by beating tail feathers against each other. He flies around female slowly, displaying forward projecting feet while opening and wiggling toes. Mountainous and rocky regions with treelike vegetation (Bahia). Bahia to Rio de Janeiro (including ex-Guanabara, where rare); also upper Amazon west of Rios Madeira and Negro to Venezuela, Colombia, Peru.

RACKET-TAILED COQUETTE, *Discosura longicauda,* Bandeirinha   R   Fig. 169

10.4 cm. Distinguished from all others by "banners" at end of outer tail feathers. Brilliant green with whitish band across lower back, white on flanks. Female has short, bifurcated, tail tipped light brown and similarly colored rump band. Tree-studded open country, seeks flowers of cashew

trees, ingás, *Leonotis, Vochysia,* eucalyptus. Northern South America to Roraima, Amapá, Pará; also in northeast and east of Brazil as far as Minas Gerais, Espírito Santo, Rio de Janeiro (Tinguá). Also called *Pavãozinho.*

BLUE-CHINNED SAPPHIRE, *Chlorestes notatus,* Beija-flor-de-garganta-azul

8.9 cm. Dark green with blue chin; bill black with base of mandible orange; female has white underparts mixed with green. Shady places, secondary woodland, igapó forest. Frequently in canopy. Abundant in lower Amazon. Venezuela, the Guianas, and Pará to eastern (including ex-Guanabara), northern, and central (Goiás) Brazil. See *Chlorostilbon aureoventris* and *Hylocharis cyanus.*

GLITTERING-BELLIED EMERALD, *Chlorostilbon aureoventris,* Besourinho-de-bico-vermelho   PL 21.2

8.5 cm. One of most common species in eastern Brazil. Brilliant green with black-tipped red bill. Female distinguished by curved white line behind eyes and white-tipped tail. VOICE AND DISPLAYS: *tsr;* squeaky song tireless. In prenuptial displays male dives down in skimming flights over perched female, moving from side to side while cheeping continually. Open capoeira, gardens. Maranhão to Rio Grande do Sul, Mato Grosso, Uruguay, Paraguay, Bolivia.

Fig. 169. Racket-tailed Coquette, *Discosura longicauda,* male.

BLUE-TAILED EMERALD, *Chlorostilbon mellisugus*
7.5 cm. All-black bill. Amazonia.

FORK-TAILED WOODNYMPH, *Thalurania furcata,*
Beija-flor-tesoura-verde
9.7 cm. Similar to *T. glaucopis* but with belly violet-blue. Color of under tail coverts varies according to region; e.g., black with white border (*T. f. furcata*) on northern shore of lower Amazon; all black (*T. f. baeri*) from Maranhão to Ceará, Minas Gerais, Goiás, Mato Grosso. Forests. Abundant in várzea forests in lower Amazon estuary, alongside *Threnetes* and *Campylopterus*. Mexico to Bolivia, Paraguay, Argentina, all of Brazil except extreme south, reaching as far as Paraná.

LONG-TAILED WOODNYMPH, *Thalurania watertonii*
BR
11.5 cm. Tail longer than *T. glaucopis*. Restricted to northeastern coast in eastern Pará and from Pernambuco to Bahia.

VIOLET-CAPPED WOODNYMPH, *Thalurania glaucopis*, Tesoura-de-fronte-violeta PL 20.2
11.1 cm. One of best-known species of eastern Brazil. Brilliant green with violet-blue cap, white tufts on crissum, steel blue rectrices, black bill. Female has dirty white underparts, lateral tail feathers with white tips, forehead and underparts sometimes washed with cinnamon. VOICE AND DISPLAYS: song *tirip-trip-trip-ti-tri*. . . . In nuptial displays male makes semicircular flights around perched female while displaying iridescent crown and breast. Forest, capoeira, gardens. Abundant in Rio de Janeiro: 6 males were counted simultaneously near a feeder in July. Bahia and Minas Gerais to Rio Grande do Sul, Uruguay, Paraguay, Argentina (Misiones), southern Mato Grosso. See *T. glaucopis* and *T. watertonii*.

RUFOUS-THROATED SAPPHIRE, *Hylocharis sapphirina*, Beija-flor-safira
9 cm. Green chin; under tail coverts and tail (against light) chestnut, but under incident light tail varies from bronze to steel blue and neck and breast appear brilliant purplish blue. Red bill has black tip. Female has whitish underparts with cinnamon chin. Forests, forest edges, capoeira. Often in canopy. Locally common. Northern South America to Rio Madeira (Amazonas), Belém (Pará). Also eastern Brazil from Bahia to São Paulo, Paraguay, Argentina. See *H. cyanus*.

WHITE-CHINNED SAPPHIRE, *Hylocharis cyanus,*
Beija-flor-roxo PL 21.7
8.8 cm. Head, neck, and breast violet-blue, chin whitish, bill red with black tip. Female grayish white. VOICE: song *TSEboo-tsi-i-i-i-i-i-i-i, HITsi . . . ; gogogo*. One of most

timid species in capoeira. Northern South America to Bolivia, all of Brazil except extreme south.

GILDED HUMMINGBIRD, *Hylocharis chrysura,*
Beija-flor-dourado
10.5 cm. Relatively large. Coppery golden green with intensely sparkling golden green tail. Black-tipped red bill. Female similar. VOICE: surprisingly loud song, *tsi-TSI-tsi-tsi*, descending at end; has another phrase, so high it is almost inaudible, that can be observed by noting movement of mandibles. Forest, cerrado, capoeira, country gardens. Frequently in canopy. Minas Gerais to Mato Grosso, Goiás, Rio Grande do Sul; also Uruguay, Bolivia. See *Chlorostilbon, Chlorestes,* and *Chrysuronia oenone.*

GOLDEN-TAILED SAPPHIRE, *Chrysuronia oenone*
9 cm. Reminiscent of a *Hylocharis* with coppery gold tail. In extreme west (Benjamin Constant), also adjacent countries as far as Venezuela.

WHITE-THROATED HUMMINGBIRD, *Leucochloris albicollis*, Papo-branco PL 21.4
10.5 cm. Typical of southeastern Brazil. Stocky, unmistakable with white throat and belly separated by green breast band. White-tipped tail feathers conspicuous when bird opens and closes tail at brief intervals. Sexes similar. VOICE: *tsewt, tsrrr;* has 2 quite different song types: *TSI-tsi-tsi-tsi-tsi-tsi-tsi* and a much-varied twitter. Can switch from one type to the other under same conditions. Capoeira, gardens, orchards. Minas Gerais and Espírito Santo to Rio Grande do Sul, Paraguay, and Misiones, Argentina. In north (Espírito Santo, Rio de Janeiro) of range abundant in mountainous regions. Also called *Cuitelo* (São Paulo).

WHITE-TAILED GOLDENTHROAT, *Polytmus guainumbi*, Beija-flor-dourado-de-bico-curvo
10 cm. Relatively "large" open-country species with long, curved bill; light red base on mandible. Golden greenish bronze with distinct whitish line behind eye and white-tipped tail. Immature an eye-catching chestnut-toned rufous. Fields, marshes, restinga. Amazon estuary (Marajó, etc.) to Mato Grosso, São Paulo, Paraguay, Argentina; also northern South America. See *P. milleri* and *P. theresiae.*

TEPUI GOLDENTHROAT, *Polytmus milleri*
Only in extreme north, Roraima to Venezuela.

GREEN-TAILED GOLDENTHROAT, *Polytmus theresiae*
Amazonia (e.g., Rios Negro and Purus) to the Guianas, Peru.

OLIVE-SPOTTED HUMMINGBIRD, *Leucippus chlorocercus*
Extreme western Brazil to Peru, Ecuador.

MANY-SPOTTED HUMMINGBIRD, *Taphrospilus hypostictus,* Peito-carijó

10 cm. Underparts, except belly, covered with green spots. Peru to Bolivia, northern Argentina, Mato Grosso (Cáceres).

WHITE-BELLIED HUMMINGBIRD, *Amazilia chionogaster,* Beija-flor-verde-e-branco ˎ

Almost the same distribution as *Taphrospilus hypostictus,* from Peru to Bolivia, northern Argentina, Mato Grosso.

WHITE-CHESTED EMERALD, *Amazilia chionopectus*

Only in extreme north, Roraima to Venezuela, the Guianas.

VERSICOLORED EMERALD, *Amazilia versicolor,* Beija-flor-de-banda-branca

8.5 cm. Green with pure white, longitudinal stripe on underparts that is narrow on throat and chin, wider on belly. Base of mandible orange. Capoeira, country gardens. Venezuela to Paraguay, Argentina, all of Brazil, including southeast from Bahia to Rio Grande do Sul; includes *A. rondoniae* Ruschi 1982 from Porto Velho, Rio Madeira, Rondônia. *A. v. brevirostris* is considered a separate species by some.

GLITTERING-THROATED EMERALD, *Amazilia fimbriata,* Beija-flor-de-garganta-verde   PL 21.8

8.5–11 cm. Widely distributed. In Brazil 5 geographic races have been identified, 1 of them "large" and coastal (*A. f. tephrocephala,* Espírito Santo to Rio Grande do Sul), the white-bellied "beach hummingbird." VOICE: *TSI-tsitsi TSI-tsitsi . . . .* Capoeira, restinga. Northern South America, throughout Brazil to Paraguay, Bolivia.

SAPPHIRE-SPANGLED EMERALD, *Amazilia lactea,* Beija-flor-de-peito-azul

9.5 cm. From chin to breast brilliant blue that turns violet; belly bluish green with well-defined white center streak. Base of mandible orange. Forest, capoeira, gardens. Relatively common in mountainous regions. Amazonas to Bahia, Minas Gerais; also Venezuelan and Bolivian Andes.

PLAIN-BELLIED EMERALD, *Amazilia leucogaster,* Beija-flor-de-barriga-branca

Eastern Pará (Belém) to Piauí, Pernambuco, Bahia; also Venezuela, the Guianas.

GREEN-BELLIED HUMMINGBIRD, *Amazilia viridigaster*

Only in extreme north, Roraima to Venezuela, Guyana, Colombia.

SOMBRE HUMMINGBIRD, *Aphantochroa cirrhochloris,* Beija-flor-cinza   BR   PL 21.9

11.8 cm. "Large," well-characterized by dark gray underside, small postocular mark, rump spot, and white tufts on crissum. VOICE: a loud *tsewk-tsewk,* and a melodious *tsiu.* Sings often and loud but squeakily. Capoeira, country estates. Eastcentral Brazil from Pernambuco to Rio Grande do Sul, Goiás, Mato Grosso.

BRAZILIAN RUBY, *Clytolaema rubricauda,* Beija-flor-rubi, Papo-de-fogo   BR   PL 20.8

12 cm. Stocky forest species of southeast. In forest shadows male, when not in motion, looks almost black, with only a tiny white postocular spot (also present in female) to distinguish him. In sunlight red throat, if seen at a certain angle, becomes golden. Forehead, crown, and breast sparkling. Female and young male much different, with cinnamon on underparts. VOICE AND DISPLAYS: Loud, full voice draws attention, *ew-uh;* warning in flight *tikeh, tikeh, tikeh . . . ; tirreh, tirreh . . . ;* an incessant song, *TIK-tirrr. . . .* In nuptial play flies around female in semicircles while rapidly opening and closing tail, to great effect due to light color of tail feathers. Concomitantly displays brilliant areas of throat and crown, which sparkle surprisingly even in deep forest shadows. Forest interior, tree-filled gardens, banana plantations. Espírito Santo and Minas Gerais to Goiás, Rio Grande do Sul. Also called *Topázio.* See *Polyplancta aurescens.*

GOULD'S JEWELFRONT, *Polyplancta aurescens,* Beija-flor-estrela

21.1 cm. Amazonian species somewhat resembling *Clytolaema rubricauda.* Green with black and blue crown, brown chin, red breast band. Female similar to male but chin and crown green. Forests. Venezuela to eastern Peru, Amazonas (Solimões, Juruá), southern Pará (Cururu, Serra do Cachimbo).

BLACK-THROATED BRILLIANT, *Heliodoxa schreibersii,* Estrela-de-garganta-violeta

11.5 cm. Steel blue, forked tail, longer than *Thalurania.* Upperparts green, underparts black, lower throat with purple spot. Female has long whitish line below eye. Ecuador, Peru, upper Rio Negro (Amazonas).

Two more species of the genus occur in Brazil:

VELVET-BROWED BRILLIANT, *Heliodoxa xanthogonys* Venezuela to Roraima.

PINK-THROATED BRILLIANT, *Heliodoxa gularis* Colombia and Peru to Amazonas.

CRIMSON TOPAZ, *Topaza pella,* Beija-flor-brilho-de-fogo   PL 20.6

20 cm (male). Our largest hummingbird. Tail accounts for more than 1/2 of total length. Male unmistakable with elongated tail feathers that cross about halfway down, golden throat patch, and metallic red belly contrasting with snow-

white "underpants" and light, flesh-colored feet. Female, lacking elongated tail, measures only 12 cm and is green with red throat, resembling *Clytolaema;* underside of wings and sides of tail extensively rufous, as in male. VOICE AND DISPLAYS: a loud *tsak.* In prenuptial displays male hovers before perched female opening and closing tail, scissoring elongated tail feathers, or even spreading tail like a fan. When feathers of gorget are raised and lowered they change from green to sparkling bronze or opaque black, like a light that goes on and off. Gallery forests, frequently in canopy. The Guianas and Venezuela to eastern Ecuador, Roraima, Amapá, open country northeast of Belém (Pará), where formerly common in both city and surrounding area. Even more abundant near Brazilian border with Venezuela and the Guianas. See *T. pyra.*

FIERY TOPAZ, *Topaza pyra*

Replaces *T. pella* in upper Amazon. Similar to it but inner secondaries black, lateral tail feathers blackish violet, not cinnamon. Upper Rio Negro (Amazonas) to Venezuela, Colombia, Ecuador.

HOODED VISORBEARER, *Augastes lumachellus,* Beija-flor-de-gravatinha-vermelha BR

9 cm. Distinctive species of central Bahia with forehead and gorget sparkling green, gorget highlighted by black below, small red "necktie," white breast band, and coppery red tail. Almost no sexual dimorphism. VOICE: *shrreb, shrreb, shrreb* and a squeaky song interspersed with trills and metallic popping sounds. Semiarid stony regions at tops of mountains and mesas between 950 and 1600 m (topographically comparable to Venezuelan tepuis) that are scrubby and rich in cacti, bromeliads, Velloziaceae, orchids. Restricted to Bahia, between Morro do Chapéu, Andaraí, and Barra da Estiva (Chapada Diamantina, Serra de Sincorá, etc.) where not rare, living alongside *Colibri serrirostris* and *C. delphinae.* See also Pale-throated Serra-Finch, *Embernagra longicauda.*

Described in 1838, it was later considered possibly extinct because of lack of information on its origin (the literature merely read "Brazil, probably Bahia"), for its range was so limited and access was so difficult before the existence of good roads and automobiles. Its rediscovery in 1928 by E. Kaempfer only became public knowledge in 1959 when A. Ruschi announced it based on the Kaempfer collection in the American Museum of Natural History in New York. In 2 days more than 20 singing males can be found in a small area. Also called *Beija-flor-da-Serra-Pelada,* "Bald Mountain Hummingbird." See *A. scutatus.*

HYACINTH VISORBEARER, *Augastes scutatus,* Beija-flor-de-gravatinha-verde BR PL 45.1

8 cm. Southern replacement for *A. lumachellus,* to which it is similar but with gray "necktie," pink breast band, blue belly, green tail. Female has whitish breast band, bluish gray belly, gray-tipped outer tail feathers. There are 2 distinct ecological races in Serra do Caraça (Minas Gerais), one in rocky area with low vegetation (to 2000 m, *A. s. scutatus*), other, in area of gallery forests (1000–1200 m, *A. s. ilseae*), that is smaller and has purple instead of blue belly and bluish green instead of bronze-green upperparts. Apparently this is a genetically fixed local ecological race (Grantsau 1967). I have seen *A. s. scutatus* feed from Compositae flowers such as *Dasyphyllum velutinum* (Caraça, June and July) and *Stachytarpheta glabra,* a Verbenaceae (Cipó, February). Male pursues female and immediately courts her by hovering, projecting his gorget forward, raising nuchal plumage, fanning tail, and "screeching" ceaselessly. Habitat similar to that of *A. lumachellus,* with which it forms a superspecies. On Serra do Espinhaço, Minas Gerais, from Montes Claros, Grão Mogol, and Diamantina to Serra do Cipó, Belo Horizonte, Ouro Preto, Conselheiro Lafaiete.

BLACK-EARED FAIRY, *Heliothryx aurita,* Beija-flor-de-bochecha-azul PL 20.3

12.5 cm. "Large" with white, wedge-shaped tail with black central feathers; straight, black bill. Female and immature have longer tails and lack postauricular blue spot but have greenish brown speckles on throat and breast. Spreads and closes tail rapidly, like *Melanotrochilus,* producing a lively effect due to black and white tail feathers. On bill shape, see "Morphology," Forests, canopies. Uncommon. Bahia to Santa Catarina, Goiás, Mato Grosso, Bolivia. Also Maranhão, Pará, and north of Amazon as far as the Guianas, Colombia.

HORNED SUNGEM, *Heliactin cornuta,* Chifre-de-ouro

11 cm. Dainty savanna species, long-tailed and unmistakable with split crest divided into 2 golden red horns. Crown greenish blue, underparts white, throat black. Sharply graduated and lanceolate-shaped tail white with black-tipped green center feathers. Female lacks horns, has brown throat, slightly shorter tail. One of our smaller and speediest species. VOICE AND DISPLAYS: a very high mouselike squeak. In nuptials male flies around perched female with tail fanned, raising and lowering sparkling horns and ruffling "necktie." Typical of tree-covered savannas of interior and of cerrado, caatinga, mountain, and mesa regions with low vegetation. In northeast (Maranhão to Alagoas), east (interior of Sergipe, Bahia, Minas Gerais, São Paulo), and central Brazil as far as Rondônia, Acre, Bolivia. Also savannas of Suriname and Amapá. See "Evolution . . . ."

LONG-BILLED STARTHROAT, *Heliomaster longirostris,* Bico-reto-cinzento

10.5 cm. Characterized by long, straight bill; similar to *H. squamosus* and *H. furcifer* but with almost rectangular tail; throat red like *squamosus* and *furcifer* (but changes momentarily to dark green while top of head stays green) but breast and flanks gray, malar line, postocular spot, 2 longitudinal black streaks, and lower back feathers white. VOICE: *tling-tling-tling*. Cerrado, cultivated fields, groves, sometimes alongside *furcifer,* perhaps in same *ipê-roxo* in Mato Grosso. Mexico to northern South America, across Amazonia to Bolivia, Acre, Mato Grosso, Goiás, Federal District, São Paulo, Paraná, Maranhão, Piauí, Ceará.

STRIPE-BREASTED STARTHROAT, *Heliomaster squamosus,* Bico-reto-de-banda-branca
BR   PL 21.10

11.2 cm. Similar in aspect to *H. longirostris* but with deeply forked tail like *H. furcifer.* In addition to glittering red throat and lateral tufts on neck, distinguished by longitudinal white stripe dividing green underparts. Throat becomes gray after postnuptial molt (see "Morphology"). Female has gray underparts, throat speckled crimson and black, white-tipped lateral rectrices. Restricted to eastern Brazil. Maranhão to São Paulo, Goiás. Locally common, e.g., in Serra da Mantiqueira.

BLUE-TUFTED STARTHROAT, *Heliomaster furcifer,* Bico-reto-azul

12 cm. Red throat like *H. squamosus* and *H. longirostris* but lateral head tufts blue like underparts. Bird appears almost black under certain light conditions. After breeding plumage becomes similar to that of female (see "Morphology"), which has white underparts. Male flies before female as if going up and down an invisible staircase, maintaining body in a vertical position and projecting erected neck fans forward. Cerrado, sparse woodland. Colombia to Bolivia, Argentina, Uruguay; central and southern Brazil (Goiás and Mato Grosso to Rio Grande do Sul).

AMETHYST WOODSTAR, *Calliphlox amethystina,* Estrelinha, Tesourinha   PL 20.7

8.6 cm (male); 7.5 cm (female); 2.5 g. One of smallest species. In breeding season adult male unmistakable with deeply forked tail and large, glittering, reddish pink amethyst gorget. Female has short, unforked, white-tipped tail. Unlike similar-sized *Lophornis,* lacks white rump band but does have white spot on lower flank that is prominent in flight. Short, white postocular streak, chestnut flanks contrasting with white area farther up. Female's throat speckled. See "Morphology" re eclipse plumage; in this phase adult male distinguished from immature by longer tail.

Attracts attention because of strange humming it makes (see "Flight . . ."). Because of its dexterity, it is less nervous than other species and does less zigzagging. Expert at ascending and backward flight. Constantly opens, closes, and bobs tail when poised before a flower. In courting female,

male approaches very slowly while vibrating wings to maximum. In a progressively accelerated backward and forward movement he moves away and immediately returns while producing at every change of direction, a loud pop sounding like crack of a whip. Sometimes female reacts by taking off from her perch and fleeing backward, always watching male. Forest edges, caatinga, country gardens. Frequently found in canopy. The Guianas and Venezuela to Bolivia, Paraguay, Argentina. Throughout Brazil, not rare in northeast, southeast, or south. Also called *Beija-flor-mosca* (Rio Grande do Sul), *Besourinho-ametista, Besoura-zumbidor.*

Trochilidae Bibliography
See also General Bibliography

Baker, H. G. 1975. *Biotrópica* 7:37–41. [Feeding]

Behnke-Pedersen, M. 1972. *Kolibrier.* Skibby, Denmark.

Berger, M. 1974. Energiewechsel von Kolibris beim Schwirrflug unter Höhenbedingungen. *J. Orn.* 115:273–88.

Berger, M., and J. S. Hart. 1972. *J. Comp. Phys.* 81:363–80. [Respiration]

Berger, M., and K. Johansen. 1980. *Verh. Dtsch. Zool. Ges.* 307 [Torpor]

Berlioz, J. 1944. *La Vie des Colibris.* Paris.

Berlioz, J. 1959. *L'Oiseau* 29:261–77. [Trade]

Berry, P. E. 1989. A systematic revision of *Fuchsia* sect. *Quelusia* (Onagraceae). *An. Missouri Bot. Gard.* 76:532–84.

Bille, S. A. 1854. *Beratung an Corvetten Galatheas Reise.* [Trade]

Bokermann, W. C. A. 1978. *Rev. Bras. Biol.* 38:259–61. [*Stephanoxis lalandi,* breeding]

Bolton, A. B., and P. Feinsinger. 1978. *Biotrópica* 10(4):307–09. [Nectar concentration]

Bowmaker, J. K. 1988. Avian colour vision and the environment. *Acta 19th Cong. Int. Orn. Ottawa:* 1284–94.

Bücherl, W. 1951. Estudos sobre a biologia e a sistemática do gênero *Grammostola. Memor. Inst. Butantan* no. 1.

Burton, P.J.K. 1971. Some observations on the *splenius capitis* muscle of birds. *Ibis* 113:19–28.

Butler, C. 1949. Hummingbird killed by praying mantis. *Auk* 66:286.

Cody, M. L. 1968. *Condor* 70:270–71. [Territory]

Decker, J. S. 1934. *Ber. Deutsche Schule São Paulo.* 56:54–74. [Hummingbirds as flower visitors]

Decker, J. S. 1936. *Aspectos Biológicos da Flora Brasileira.* São Leopoldo.

Descourtilz, T. 1960. *Beija-flores do Brasil.* Translation and critique by Carlos Drummond de Andrade and O. M. O. Pinto, respectively, from the original *Oiseaux-Mouches orthorynques do Brésil,* 1831 (sic). Rio de Janeiro: Livr. S. José.

Dorst, J. 1951. *Mém. Mus. Hist. Nat., Zool.* 1:125–260. [Feather structure]

Faegri, K., and L. Van Der Pijl. 1979. *The Principles of Pollination Ecology.* Oxford: Pergamon.

Fritsch, E., and K. L. Schuchmann. 1988. The *Musculus splenius capitis* of hummingbirds, Trochilidae. *Ibis* 130:124–32.

Gill, F. B. 1985. Hummingbird flight speeds. *Auk* 102:97–101.

Gill, F. B., A. L. Mack, and R. T. Ray. 1982. Competition between Hermit Hummingbirds (Phaethoninae) and insects for nectar in Costa Rican Rain Forest. *Ibis* 124:44–49.

Goldsmith, K. M., et al. 1982. *Condor* 84:237–38. [Smell in hummingbirds]

Gonzaga, L. P., D. A. Scott, and N. S. Collar. 1988. O Beija-flor *Ramphodon dohrnii* na Reserva Florestal da C.V.R.D. em Porto Seguro, Bahia. *XV Cong. Bras. Zool. Curitiba:* 473.

Gottsberger, G. 1971. Colour changes in petal in *Malvaviscus arboreus* flowers. *Act. Bot. Neerl.* 20:381–88. [Color discrimination]

Gottsberger, G. 1972. *Osterr. Bot. Z.* 120:439–509. [Floral biology]

Gould, J. 1849–61. *Monograph of the Trochilidae*. London.

Grant, K. A., and V. Grant. 1968. *Hummingbirds and Their Flowers*. New York: Columbia University Press.

Grantsau, R. 1967. *Pap. Avuls. Zool. S. Paulo* 21:21–31. [*Augastes*, ecological race]

Grantsau, R. 1968. *Pap. Avuls. Zool. S. Paulo* 22:57–59. [*Phaethornis maranhaoensis*]

Grantsau, R. 1969. *Pap. Avuls. Zool. S. Paulo* 22:245–47. [*Threnetes loehkeni*]

Grantsau, R. 1988. *Os beija-flores do Brasil*. Rio de Janeiro: Expressão e Cultura.

Greenewalt, C. H. 1960. *Hummingbirds*. Garden City, N.Y.: Doubleday.

Hartert, E. 1900. *Das Tierreich*. Berlin. [Taxonomy]

Hartman, F. A. 1954. Cardial and pectoral muscles of Trochilidae. *Auk* 71:467–69.

Haverschmidt, F. 1970. *Alauda* 38:274–77. [Tarantulas]

Hildebrand, E. M. 1949. Hummingbird captured by praying mantis. *Auk* 66:286–87.

Hinkelmann, C. 1988. On the identity of *Phaethornis maranhaoensis* Grantsau, 1968 (Trochilidae). *Bull. B.O.C.* 108(1):14–18.

Hinkelmann, C. 1988. Comments on some recently newly-described species of hermit hummingbirds. *Bull. B.O.C.* 108(4):159–69.

Hinkelmann, C. 1988. "Taxonomie, geographische Variation und Biogeographie der Gattung *Phaethornis* (Aves Trochilidae)." Thesis. Universität Bonn.

Hinkelmann, C. 1989. Notes on the taxonomy and geographic variation of *Phaethornis bourcieri* with the description of a new subspecies. *Bonn. Zool. Beitr.* 40:99–107.

Howell, T. R., and W. R. Dawson. 1954. *Condor* 56:93–97. [Temperature]

Johansen, K., M. Berger, A. Ruschi, et al. In press. Heart rates in hummingbirds.

Kattan, G., and C. Murcia. 1985. Hummingbird association with Acorn Woodpecker sap trees in Colombia. *Condor* 87:542–43.

Köster, F., and H. Stoewesand. 1973. *Bonn. Zool. Beitr.* 24:15–23. [Structure of hummingbird fleas]

Lasiewski, R. C. 1963. *Physiol. Zool.* 36:122–40. [Oxygen consumption]

Lasiewski, R. C., and R. Lasiewski. 1967. Physiological responses of Hummingbirds. *Auk* 84:34–48.

Mebbs, A. J. 1974. *Gefied. Welt* 98:167–69. [*Calliphlox*, etc., captivity]

Melin, D. 1935. *Contribution to the Study of the Theory of Selection II. The Problem of Ornithophily*. Uppsala Univers. Arsskr. 16.

Merian, Sybilla. 1705. *Metamorphosis Insectorum Surinamensis*.

Müller, F. 1878. See General Bibliography under Möller, A. 1915–20.

Murray, J. J. 1958. Ruby-throated Hummingbird captured by praying mantis. *Wilson Bull.* 70:381.

Nogueira Neto, P. 1970. A criação de abelhas indígenas sem ferrão (Meloponinae). São Paulo: Chácaras e Quintais.

Novaes, F. C., and C. T. Carvalho. 1957. Observações sobre a nidificação de *Glaucis hirsuta*. *Bol. Mus. Para. E. Goeldi, Zool.* 1.

Oniki, Y. 1970. Nesting behavior of *Phaethornis ruber*, and occurrence of wasp-cells in nests. *Auk* 87:720–28.

Ortiz-Crespo, F. I. 1972. *Auk* 89:851–57. [Bill morphology]

Pearson, O. P. 1954. *Condor* 56:317–22. [Energy]

Pearson, O. P. 1960. *Bull. Mus. Comp. Zool. Harvard* 124:92–103. [Hibernation]

Pinto, O.M.O. 1943. *Pap. Avuls. Zool. S. Paulo* 3:265–84. [Trade]

Poley, D. 1968. Experimentelle Untersuchungen zur Nahrungssuche und Nahrungsaufnahme der Kolibris. *Bonn. Zool. Beitr.* 19:111–56.

Porsch, O. 1924. *Jahrb. Wiss. Bot.* 63:553–706. [Flowers pollinated by hummingbirds]

Porsch, O. 1929. *Jahrb. Wiss. Bot.* 70:181–277. [Flowers pollinated by hummingbirds]

Portmann, A. 1950. In P. P. Grassé, *Traité de Zoologie*, 15:245. [Circulation]

Primak, R. B. 1975. Interference competition between a hummingbird and Skipperflies (Hesperiidae). *Biotropica* 7:55–58.

Reichholf, H., and I. Reichholf. 1973. *Bonn. Zool. Beitr.* 24:7–14. [Hummingbird fleas]

Ruschi, A. 1949 and forward. *Bol. Mus. Biol. Prof. Melo Leitão.* Series Biologia, Zoologia, Proteção a Natureza e Divulgação.

Ruschi, A. 1972. *Beija-flores*. Mus. Biol. Prof. Melo Leitão.

Ruschi, A. 1982. *Beija-flores do Espírito Santo*. São Paulo: Editora Rios.

Ruschi, A. 1982. Uma nova espécie de beija-flor do Brasil: *Amazilia rondoniae*, n. sp. *Bol. Mus. Biol., Zoologia* 100.

Ruschi, A. 1986. *Aves do Brasil*, vol. 4, Beija-flores. Rio de Janeiro: Expressão e Cultura.

Ruschi, A. 1986. *Aves do Brasil*, vol. 5, Beija-flores. Rio de Janeiro: Expressão e Cultura.

Scharnke, H. 1931. *J. Orn.* 79:425–91. [Tongue morphology]

Scheithauer, W. 1966. *Kolibris*. Munich.

Schuchmann, K. L. 1979. *J. Orn.* 120:311–35. [Metabolism temperature dependency]

Schuchmann, K. L. 1983. *J. Orn.* 124:65–74. [Behavior of young]

Short, L. L., and A. R. Phillips. 1966. More hybrid hummingbirds from the United States. *Auk* 83(2):253–62.

Sick, H., and D. M. Teixeira. 1981. *Auk* 98:191–92. [Activity under artificial light]

Silva, J.M.C. 1990. Comentários sobre *Campylopterus largipennis diamantinensis*. *XVII Cong. Bras. Zool., Londrina:* 166.

Silva Maia, E. J. 1851. *Velosiana*:45–52. [Behavior]

Simon, E. 1897. *Cat. Trochilidés*. Paris.

Simon, E. 1921. *Histoire Naturelle des Trochilidés.* [Synopsis and catalogue]

Skutch, A. F. 1973. *The Life of the Hummingbirds.* New York: Crown Publishers.

Snow, B. K. 1973. *Wilson Bull.* 85:163–77. [*Phaethornis, Threnetes, Glaucis,* behavior]

Snow, B. K. 1974. *Ibis* 116:278–97. [*Phaethornis guy,* behavior]

Snow, D. W. 1968. *The Living Bird* 7:47–55. [*Phaethornis longuemareus,* behavior]

Snow, D. W., and D. L. Teixeira. 1982. Hummingbirds and their flowers in Southeastern Brazil. *J. Orn.* 123:446–50.

Stanislaus, M. 1937. *Z. f. Morphol. u. Ökol. d. Tiere Bd.* 33:261–89. [Lung morphology]

Stiles, F. G. 1977. Coadapted competitors: The flowering seasons of hummingbird-pollinated plants in a tropical forest. *Science* 198:1177–78.

Stiles, F. G. 1978. Taste preference, color preference, and flower choice in hummingbirds. *Condor* 78(1):10–26.

Stiles, F. G. 1978. Ecological and evolutionary implications of bird pollination. *Am. Zool.* 18:715–27.

Stiles, F. G. 1979. Notes on the natural history of *Heliconia* in Costa Rica. *Brenesia* 15, suppl. 151–80.

Stiles, F. G. 1980. Ecological and evolutionary aspects of bird-flower adaptations. *Acta 17th Cong. Int. Orn., Berlin:*1173–78.

Udvardy, M.D.F. 1983. *Condor* 85:281–85. [Thermoregulation]

Vielliard, J. 1983. *Bol. Mus. Biol. Prof. M. Leitão, Biol.* 58. [Vocalization, sonagrams]

Vielliard, J., and W. R. Silva. 1986. Migrações de beija-flores no interior do Estado de São Paulo. *II ENAV, Rio de Janeiro.*

Vogel, P. 1974. *Z. Säugetierk.* 39:78–88. [*Suncus etruscus*]

Wagner, H. O. 1952. *Veröff. Mus. Bremen* A(2):1–44. [*Lampornis,* biology]

Wagner, H. O. 1954. Versuch einer Analyse der Kolibribalz. *S. Tierpsych.* 11:182–212.

Wagner, H. O. 1966. *Meine Freunde die Kolibris.* Berlin.

Zimmer, J. T. 1950. *Am. Mus. Nov.* 1449 and subsequent issues. [Taxonomy]

Zusi, R. L., and G. D. Bentz. 1984. Myology of the Purple-throated Carib and other Hummingbirds (Trochilidae). *Smithsonian Contr. Zool.* 385.

ORDER TROGONIFORMES

FAMILY TROGONIDAE: TROGONS (9)

The trogons are a small group with splendid plumage, worthy of symbolizing the exuberance of the tropics. Well represented in the Neotropics (especially in Central America), they also occur in Africa and the Oriental region, although in reduced diversity. Their appearance is distinctive, and their phylogenetic relationships are obscure. They appear to be linked to the Coraciiformes. There are fossils from the lower Tertiary (Eocene/Oligocene) of France and from the Pleistocene of Brazil (Lapa da Lagoa do Sumidouro, Minas Gerais, 20,000 years B.P.).

The most famous trogon is the Resplendent Quetzal, *Pharomachrus mocinno,* one of the world's longest-tailed birds, sacred to the Mayans and Aztecs and now on the Guatemalan coat of arms. It does not occur in Brazil, where all species of this family are well known as *surucuás.*

Morphology

Medium-sized, the smaller ones (Violaceous Trogon, *Trogon violaceus,* and Collared Trogon, *T. collaris*) are only thrush sized. The bill is short and strong, broadened at the base, serrated along the tomia (except in *Pharomachrus*), and surrounded by bristles reminiscent of other birds such as nightjars. The neck is short, the eyes large and dark. The eyelids, which have eyelashes, are sometimes brightly colored (a specific character that may differ to some extent among males, females, and immatures or during the non-breeding season).

The convex wings are deeply curved because of the twisted shape of the flight feathers, an adaptation to flying in leafy tropical forest that permits sudden vertical ascents and descents as well as tight curves. When resting they often place their wingtips under the long, rectangular, strongly graduated tail, which hangs vertically or frequently inclined forward.

The most notable anatomical character, unique among birds, is the foot structure (fig. 170). The feet have two toes in front and two behind, like woodpeckers, but in this case the front ones are the third and fourth toes (instead of the second and third) and the hind ones the first and second (instead of the first and fourth), forming a "heterodactyl" ("nonstandard toe conformation") foot. The short legs, small, weak feet,

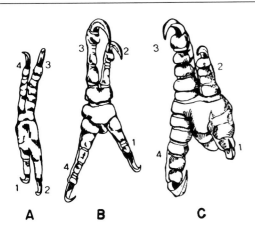

Fig. 170. Feet of three bird species that have two hind toes, seen from below: (A) Black-tailed Trogon, *Trogon melanurus*, left foot, toes 1 and 2; (B) Channel-billed Toucan, *Ramphastos vitellinus*, right foot, toes 1 and 4; and (C) Mealy Parrot, *Amazona farinosa*, right foot, toes 1 and 4. After Böker 1935.

and wide sole like that of nightjars are appropriate for quiet perching but are not useful for jumping or hopping. The skeleton is fragile, with the skull surprisingly thin.

The skin is extremely thin, like silk paper, whereas the plumage is dense but loose, falling out at the least touch, as with nightjars. The bright color of the ventral feathers (red or yellow) fades rapidly after death, even when kept in the dark, and becomes white if the specimen remains exposed to daylight. The red pigment (zooerythrine) found in the quetzal is the carotenoid cantaxanthin, a lipochrome similar to that found in the Scarlet Ibis, *Eudocimus ruber,* and in spoonbills and flamingos. In captivity the appearance of red depends on food. Thus, a yellow-bellied species such as the White-tailed Trogon, *Trogon viridis,* may acquire red tints on the underparts if it eats lots of carotenoids. Sexual dimorphism is usually marked.

Young resemble their mothers. Young *T. collaris;* Masked Trogons, *T. personatus;* and Black-throated Trogons, *T. rufus,* are brown; in species such as *T. viridis,* where the female is gray, the young are also gray. The sex of young Surucua Trogons, *T. surrucura,* can be determined by tail color. The definitive color of the eyelids and bill is fixed at six months of age.

The fresh flesh and viscera of trogons have a distinctive odor.

Vocalization

The ventriloquial voice has the timbre of a hen turkey (hence the name *perua-choca,* roughly "brood-hen turkey," given to the Blue-crowned Trogon, *T. curucui*) and is a sequence of monotonous notes repeated more insistently in the breeding season (even on moonlit nights, in spite of their being very diurnal birds). They sometimes sing whisper song. Female vocalizations resemble those of males but are less resonant. They respond to each other mutually at the beginning of breeding. There are also warning cries and a peculiar vocalization of nestlings that is different from the croaking they do when receiving food, consisting of an ascending, accelerated sequence similar to the song, persistently repeated at short intervals, as with *T. rufus* and *T. surrucura;* see also *T. curucui.* The vocalization of two syntopic species may be very similar, such as that of *T. s. surrucura* and *T. viridis* in São Paulo. Trogons tend to sing all year.

Feeding

By flying through the foliage and hovering, trogons catch large caterpillars, including hairy ones, and large arthropods such as cicadas, beetles, and spiders, as well as small insects such as ants. They hunt like flycatchers, sallying out from a branch for a few meters and then returning to it. *T. rufus* occasionally takes advantage of army-ant activity. They eat berries, palm and cecropia fruits, etc., which they take in flight while opening the tail wide to brake. They regurgitate pits that have been swallowed. I have found leaves in the stomach of *T. rufus.*

Behavior

Trogons live alone or in pairs. The body stance is erect. Their disposition is very calm, but when irritated they move the tail forward and upward. Short flights are swift and efficient. While flying longer distances (e.g., crossing a valley) the flight is undulating.

Breeding

A male fans his tail in front of a female, exposing the typical pattern of the rectrices. Nests are made in abandoned arboreal termite nests, old wasp nests, rotting dead trees, and in thick tree-fern trunks (*T. surrucura,* Rio Grande do Sul).

T. viridis and *T. surrucura* burrow an upward-sloping tunnel that leads to an incubation chamber in the center of the termite nest (fig. 171); *T. collaris* and *T. rufus* make less elaborate nests. The brightly colored eyelids shine phosphorescently in the darkness of the hole.

Trogons lay two to four white, yellowish, or bluish eggs without markings. These become dirty during incubation, for the incubation chamber is not even lined. An incubation period of 18 days or a bit more has been reported for *T. rufus.* The female broods in the afternoon and at night, the male in the morning. The parents take turns providing food for the young, which consists almost entirely of insects, including large ones mashed up in the parents' bills.

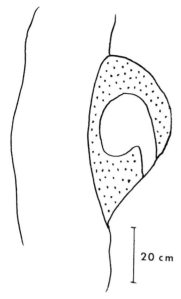

20 cm

Fig. 171. Nest of Surucua Trogon, *Trogon surrucura aurantius,* dug by the bird in an arboreal termite nest. Jatiboca, Espírito Santo. Original, H. Sick.

Nestling feces remain in the nest, wetting the bottom of the cavity in spite of the porosity of the termite nest material and exuding a repugnant odor of rotting meat that attracts flies whose larvae develop there in profusion. Members of a clutch may be quite different in size if it consists of four small nestlings. Apparently the parents begin to brood with the first egg (*T. surrucura*). *T. rufus* nestlings fledge at 14 to 15 days. There seem to be more males than females.

Habitat, Evolution, and Migration

Trogons are forest birds, with certain species living in dry, sparse woodland or in bamboo thickets. They appear at the woodland edge and even fly out to isolated trees near the forest.

In the more northerly regions of Brazil various *Trogon* species may occur in the same area. In Rio Grande do Sul, two, *rufus* and *surrucura,* are found. In the Serra dos Órgãos (Rio de Janeiro) three have been recorded, all with yellow bellies: *viridis, rufus,* and *surrucura.* On the upper Xingu (Mato Grosso) I found four: *melanurus, viridis, collaris,* and *curucui;* around the Serra do Cachimbo at least five: *melanurus, viridis, rufus, collaris,* and *violaceus;* and a bit more to the north, in the upper Rio Cururu, this total goes up to six with the inclusion of *curucui,* and the Pavonine Quetzal, *Pharomachrus pavoninus,* is also there. In the area of Belém, Pará, five species have been recorded: *melanurus, viridis, rufus, curucui,* and *violaceus.* Each species occupies its own niche, which is defined by the level, height, and density of the forest.

The existence in eastern Brazil of a geographic race of *T. surrucura* with a yellow belly and of another with a red belly is particularly interesting for it proves that the region underwent, temporarily, a total split in the habitat of these trogons, permitting development of two such different forms in their respective refuges. Subsequently the two races again entered into contact around Rio de Janeiro.

Inhabitants of southern regions are migratory during the southern winter, invading the domain of adjacent populations living to the north (*T. surrucura*).

Numbers and Decline

Trogons are relatively common in their natural surroundings and can be easily observed. Their luxuriant multicoloration reveals rather than protects them and makes them easy targets for their enemies, although it has advantages in breeding by facilitating conquest of a mate and repelling other males.

They are quite trusting, which becomes fatal when people appear on the scene, for the birds can even be hit with a switch. They are hunted for their meat and are among the first birds to disappear in areas under pressure from civilization. They have become totally extinct in the vicinity of the city of Rio de Janeiro.

Identification Data

It is a group of very homogeneous appearance. Beyond the belly color and under tail pattern, distinctive characters are the eyelid color, existence or absence of some white feathers adjacent to the eyes, whether the upper wing coverts are vermiculated or not, and crown color (identical to that of the back or not). It is especially important to observe the under tail, which requires finding a favorable angle. Presence of the female helps, for she is brown only in *T. collaris, T. personatus,* and *T. rufus.* With the latest changes in scientific nomenclature there is a certain amount of confusion, so I give, as usual, the principal synonymy.

1. Belly yellow or orange
   1.1. Underside of tail black with white barring: *T. viridis* (female and immature, Pl 22), *T. rufus* (male and female), *T. violaceus* (male and female)
   1.2. Underside of tail black with longitudinal white design: *T. viridis* (male, Pl 22), *T. surrucura aurantius* (male and female, fig. 172)
2. Belly red
   2.1. Underside of tail uniformly black: *Pharomachrus pavoninus* (Pl 22), *T. melanurus* (adult male and female)
   2.2. Underside of tail black with white barring: *T. collaris* (male and female, Pl 22), *T. personatus* (male and female), *T. curucui* (male and female), *T. melanurus* (immature), *Pharomachrus pavoninus* (immature)
   2.3. Underside of tail black with white longitudinal design: *T. s. surrucura* (male and female, fig. 172)

3. Upperside of central tail feathers:
   3.1. greenish/bluish with black tip: males of all species
   3.2. blackish with indistinct black tip: females, except
     T. collaris and *T. rufus*, which have brown upper tail
     feathers with black tips

PAVONINE QUETZAL, *Pharomachrus pavoninus*,
Surucuá-açu   PL 22.2

34 cm; 158 g (male). Amazonian quetzal whose female resembles that of *P. mocinno* (see introduction). Unlike Central American congener, prolongation of upper tail coverts only suggested, scarcely reaching or only slightly passing beyond tips of rectrices. Upper wing coverts also elongated. Bill yellow with red base. Female similar to male but less brilliant with head brownish, tips of outer tail feathers with whitish barring, bill black with red base. In immature outer vane of flight feathers yellowish brown, bill black. VOICE: song a sequence of 5 melodious notes, *ew ewwo-ewwo-ewwo-ewwo;* warning a descending tremolo. Interior of tall forest (Weske pers. comm., in litt., Peru). Upper Amazon from right bank of Tapajós and upper Rio Negro to Bolivia, Peru, Venezuela. See *Trogon melanurus*.

BLACK-TAILED TROGON, *Trogon melanurus*,
Surucuá-de-cauda-preta

31.5 cm. Both sexes have red belly and all-black tail, as in *Pharomachrus pavoninus*, but face, throat, and wings black, latter vermiculated with white. White band across breast, eyelids red, bill yellow (female has only mandible yellow). In immature upperparts dark gray (not green like adult), outer vane of 3 outer tail feathers finely barred whitish, eyelids black, white spot behind eye. VOICE: a monotonous *wow . . . ;* alarm (very typical) *KWA-kwa*. Forest edge, gallery forests. Sometimes alongside *P. pavoninus* and *T. collaris*. Panama to Bolivia, northern Mato Grosso, Maranhão. Also called *Surucuá-tatá*.

WHITE-TAILED TROGON, *Trogon viridis*,
Surucuá-grande-de-barriga-amarela   PL 22.1

30 cm; 93 g (male). Widely distributed. Male similar to smaller *T. surrucura aurantius* but has light blue eyelids. Outer tail feathers have longitudinal streaks that are wider at tips. Upper wing coverts lack white barring (unlike *T. surrucura*). Female and immature gray, wings vermiculated with whitish, outer tail feathers barred white. VOICE: a sequence of loud *kyows . . . ,* last tone lower. Humid or dry forest in both lowlands and mountains. In Serra do Mar (Rio de Janeiro) sometimes alongside *T. surrucura* and *T. rufus* (which also has yellow belly). Panama to Bolivia, Amazonian Brazil, southern Bahia, western Minas Gerais, southern São Paulo, southern Mato Grosso. Also called *Curuxuá, Capitão-do-mato, Urukuá* (Kamaiurá, Mato Grosso).

COLLARED TROGON, *Trogon collaris*,
Surucuá-de-coleira   PL 22.3

22.5 cm. Quite small with red belly and noncontrasting eyelids. Female has distinct white postocular spot, rusty central tail feathers. The form restricted to coastal forests of eastern Brazil (*T. c. eytoni*) has narrower white pectoral band, narrower barring on tail feathers. VOICE: song a sequence of "*ewuhs . . . ,* phrase beginning with a diatonic note; warning a melodious and rising *prrrr*. Forest, sometimes alongside *T. viridis* and *T. curucui*. Mexico to Bolivia and Brazil, locally to Mato Grosso, Rio de Janeiro. See also *T. curucui* (male) and *T. rufus* (female).

MASKED TROGON, *Trogon personatus*

22.5 cm. Similar to *T. collaris*. Female has black forehead and upper wing coverts. Only in extreme north from northern South America to Roraima, Bolivia.

BLACK-THROATED TROGON, *Trogon rufus*,
Surucuá-de-barriga-amarela

26 cm. Widely distributed. Male has coppery green upperparts and breast, light blue eyelids, wings and tail barred black and white. Upperside of central tail feathers green in male and brown in female with wide black tips. Belly yellow, bill greenish yellow. Female brown, similar to female *T. collaris* but with belly light yellow, eyelids light lead gray. Immature similar to female but upper wing coverts have whitish spots and there are connected white spots before and behind eyes. Feet pink, not black. VOICE: a slow sequence, *ew-uhh . . . ,* weaker than *T. viridis*, slightly crescendo, with a total of 5–6 notes and 1 diatonic note; song, higher than *T. personatus*, easily imitated. Forest, not rare in mountains of southeast, alongside *T. surrucura* and *T. viridis*, and Amazonia alongside *T. melanurus*. Honduras to Amazonia, Mato Grosso, southern Bahia to Rio Grande do Sul, Paraguay, and Misiones, Argentina.

SURUCUA TROGON, *Trogon surrucura*,
Surucuá-de-peito-azul   Fig. 172

26 cm. Southern species. Two races occur with different belly color. One, orange-bellied, *T. s. aurantius*, from Bahia to Rio de Janeiro and eastern Minas Gerais; other, red-bellied, *T. s. surrucura*, from Rio de Janeiro and Minas Gerais to Rio Grande do Sul, Goiás, southern Mato Grosso, Paraguay, northern Argentina. Both have blue head and breast, bright green back, wings speckled white, underside of outer tail feathers with extensive longitudinal white design and tip. Eyelids yellow, or orange in red-bellied race. Female and immature gray with tiny spot before and behind eye and white vermiculation on wings; longitudinal white tail pattern reduced. Male young distinguished when still small by wide, shiny, black tip to central tail feathers, lacking in female. VOICE: an ascending sequence of 14–17 full *dius . . .* or

*kwa*s . . . with last syllable lower, like *T. viridis;* warning *kiarrr; kwo-kwo-kwo.* Forest, cerradão. Both forms found in mountains regions of southeastern Brazil (Itatiaia, Rio de Janeiro) in winter; there is an area of transition between them in Rio de Janeiro (e.g., Nova Friburgo). Sometimes alongside *T. rufus* and *T. viridis.* See *T. viridis* and *T. curucui.*

BLUE-CROWNED TROGON, *Trogon curucui,* Surucuá-de-barriga-vermelha

25 cm. Male similar to that of *T. collaris,* differing in yellow eyelids and blue (not green) crown. Female has gray upperparts and foreneck, 2 small white spots before and after eye, tail with black and white barring. VOICE: reminiscent of *T. viridis.* In an immature that already flew perfectly, I noted a melodious sequence that ended with a low note, a vocalization unlike that of adult (Rio das Mortes, Mato Grosso). Colombia to Bolivia, Paraguay, Argentina; Amazonian and central Brazil, eastern Brazil from Maranhão to Rio de Janeiro. Also called *Peito-de-moça* (Pantanal de Mato Grosso), *Perna-choca, Dorminhoco* (Ceará). See *T. surrucura.*

VIOLACEOUS TROGON, *Trogon violaceus,* Surucuá-miudinho

22 cm. Amazonian, even smaller than *T. collaris.* Yellow belly. Male has blue head and breast, green back, tail with black and white barring, yellow eyelids. Female and immature similar to female *T. surrucura aurantius* but tail barred. VOICE: reminiscent of *T. melanurus* but weaker. Forest edges. Mexico to Bolivia, Amazonas, Mato Grosso (Tapirapoã), eastern Pará.

Fig. 172. Surucua Trogon, *Trogon s. surrucura,* male. The underside of the tail appears almost entirely white.

Trogonidae Bibliography

Pinto, O.M.O. 1950. *Pap. Avuls. Zool. S. Paulo* 9:89–136. [Classification]
Skutch, A. F. 1956. *Auk* 73:354–66. [Behavior]
Skutch, A. F. 1959. *Wilson Bull.* 71:5–18. [Behavior]

ORDER CORACIIFORMES[1]

FAMILY ALCEDINIDAE: KINGFISHERS (5)

This cosmopolitan group is of Oriental origin. Most species occur in tropical and subtropical zones. The family is poorly represented in the New World, though there are kingfishers from Tierra del Fuego to Alaska. Fossils from the lower Tertiary have been found in North America and Europe and from the Pleistocene in Brazil (Lapa da Escrivaninha, Minas Gerais, 20,000 years B.P.).

A proposal has been made to establish the order Alcediniformes, characterized by the peculiar structure of the inner ear (columella/stapes, Feduccia 1977). This order would comprise the Alcedinidae, Momotidae, Todidae, and Trogonidae.

In southern Brazil kingfishers are called *martim-pescador,*

[1]This order is very heterogeneous. In addition to the families mentioned here for Brazil, it includes the hornbills (Bucerotidae) and hoopoes (Upupidae) of the Eastern Hemisphere, among others.

pica-peixe, or *flecha-peixe;* in Amazonia *ariramba-da-mata-virgem* (see Galbulidae, "Morphology . . . ").

Morphology and Identification

Unlike Old World species, Neotropical kingfishers are quite homogeneous in appearance but very diverse in size. The dwarf of the group, the American Pygmy Kingfisher, *Chloroceryle aenea,* weighing scarcely 13 g, is less than one twentieth the size of the largest species, the Ringed Kingfisher, *Ceryle torquata,* which reaches 320 g. All Alcedinidae have proportionately large bills and are capable of regenerating large losses of the rhamphotheca. The tongue is short, unlike that of the Picidae, to which they have a slight resemblance due to head shape. The neck is short.

The wings appear short, but the arm is relatively long, only the hands and primaries being shortened, differing in this from other birds that dive into the water to fish, such as boobies, Sulidae. Apparently they move the wings underwater, rowing or using them as rudders. The tail is medium sized. The small feet, inappropriate for swimming, show advanced syndactylism (all three front toes are united at the base, the third and fourth up to the middle, see fig. 137).

The plumage is dense, smooth, and close to the body, adapted to an aquatic life. There is sexual dimorphism, already visible in fledglings (Amazon Kingfisher, *Chloroceryle amazona*).

Vocalization

The call and alarm are explosive and may culminate in a strident rattle. *Chloroceryle amazona* and the Green Kingfisher, *C. americana* (both sexes), utter an almost melodious phrase that corresponds to a song.

Feeding and Behavior

Kingfishers perch on isolated branches overhanging water or on stakes or wires with the nuchal feathers ruffled, the wings drooping, and the tail moving slightly up and down but sometimes lifting to the vertical. They observe aquatic life from these lookouts with the bill held vertically downward, then launch out after fish, water-beetles, and insect larvae that float or appear close to the surface. They catch their prey with the bill like boobies and terns but are not always successful. Calculations on the success of kingfisher dives in the Old World give figures of 36% to 53%. They also fish by hovering in full flight, like terns, sometimes letting themselves fall from heights of over 10 m obliquely into the water with the wings held close to the body (*Ceryle torquata* and *Chloroceryle amazona*). When the prey is reached underwater, the wings are opened to brake the motion, the prey is caught, and the bird returns to the surface by paddling with the wings.

Focusing on prey underwater, which is difficult because of refraction, must be facilitated by having two foveae, one central and one lateral, enabling both monocular and binocular vision, an adaptation also found in swifts, swallows, hawks, and terns, all birds that hunt in rapid flight. Fishing becomes difficult or impossible in turgid waters during or after rains or in waves or rough waters, so the Alcedinidae become insectivorous to a certain degree or emigrate at these times (see "Migration"). The nictitating membrane, a thin, transparent skin, protects the eyeball during dives.

Herons walking in shallow water sometimes act as beaters for fishing kingfishers. On Ilha Grande (Rio de Janeiro) I saw a kingfisher attract small fish by letting its feces fall into the water. I also saw *Chloroceryle amazona* sometimes perch on beaches where it hopped around catching crabs. When a large prey is caught, they beat it against the perch to kill it. This also breaks up the skeleton, fins, and any stingers on the fish, which is swallowed head first.

Ceryle torquata has twice been observed catching a Swallow-tailed Hummingbird, *Eupetomena macroura,* and carrying it away (M. A. Andrade). A Green-and-rufous Kingfisher, *Chloroceryle inda,* brought a batrachian for its young (L. Gonzaga). Kingfishers regurgitate small friable pellets containing bones, scales, and chitin fragments.

Numerous Old World species, accepted as the most primitive of the family, live in forests and feed on terrestrial arthropods, insects, crustaceans, etc. Fishing is considered to be a specialization that evolved independently in various Alcedinidae groups in different parts of the world.

The small species fly rapidly, close to the water's surface. *Chloroceryle amazona* frequently flies higher, and *Ceryle torquata* even overflies cities such as Rio de Janeiro. They bathe by diving shallowly into water.

Breeding

Kingfishers live in pairs, nesting in banks. A shortage of such places may cause a concentration of *Ceryle torquata* nests, as I saw near Oriximiná, Rio Trombetas, Pará. They also use railroad embankment slopes (e.g., those of ICOMI in Amapá). I found *Chloroceryle americana* nesting in a large terrestrial termite nest, 2.5 m in circumference and the same height above ground, 20 m from the Rio Sapão in northwestern Bahia. More than 20 holes of the same size, but with various finishes, were scattered over its surface (most facing the river), probably reflecting years of work. After excavating their nest kingfishers show considerable wear on the bill, which quickly grows back.

In excavating, the front toes, connected at the base, serve as a shovel. The pair takes turns making the long, twisted, gallery, 1–2 m in length, which opens into a widened area where two to four rounded, pure white eggs are laid directly on the substrate. Females of *Chloroceryle americana* and *C. amazona* reportedly brood at night; during the day the pair divides this task. In *Ceryle torquata* the sexes change over every 24 hours. The incubation period for *Chloroceryle amazona* in Costa Rica is 22 days. Hatching of a chick may be prolonged for one or two days in *C. americana*. Chicks are born bare, featherless, and especially strange looking (fig. 173), for the mandible projects well beyond the tip of the maxilla (prognathous), as occurs with nestling Piciformes. This difference in length disappears at approximately 11 days because of more rapid growth of the maxilla (*C. amazona*). Like jacamars and woodpeckers, young have a callus on the tarsus that they lie on to support themselves on the hard bottom of earth or detritus.

Fish-eating Alcedinidae feed their nestlings tiny fish. In a short time the nest interior is carpeted with food remains, for nothing is done about sanitation. In spite of this the nestlings remain clean except for their bills and feet. They fledge at 29 or 30 days (*C. amazona*), or even at 35 days or more for *Ceryle torquata*.

African kingfishers live in flocks that help the breeding pair by bringing food for the young, most of whom would die without this collaboration.

Habitat

The notable size variation among the five Brazilian species suggests more or less accentuated trophic separation as well as ecological specialization. Thus, both the large species, *Ceryle torquata* and *Chloroceryle amazona*, inhabit the edge of larger water bodies where they fish openly. *Ceryle torquata* also occurs at the ocean edge. *Chloroceryle aenea* and *C. americana* do not leave protective riverine vegetation, living more along small water courses where they are easily overlooked, and in the case of the latter, also in marshes. *C. inda* is the one that most enters forests wherever there is water, such as flooded várzea woodland, and is therefore the species of most local occurrence outside Amazonia. Mangroves offer advantages for all kingfishers as long as water salinity is not important.

Migration

Movements occur in Amazonia during the floods (e.g., on the Rio Madeira in May), apparently because of the difficulty of fishing in turgid water (see "Feeding . . ."). Small flocks of *Ceryle torquata* assemble. Similar situations occur on a larger scale with ducks and other riverine birds. The Belted Kingfisher, *Ceryle alcyon,* of North America is truly migratory, reaching northern South America.

Alleged Harmfulness and Decline

Kingfisher invasions of an uncovered tank of fingerlings obviously displease the owner, but everything should not be viewed from the standpoint of profit and money. A minimum of sacrifice is necessary to avoid destruction of these birds.

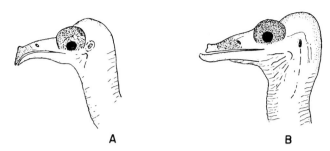

Fig. 173. Day-old Coraciiformes: (A) Turquoise-browed Motmot, *Eumomota superciliosa*, from Central America, with a hooked bill; (B) Ringed Kingfisher, *Ceryle torquata*, with projecting mandible. After A. F. Skutch 1947.

Often their natural habitat is ruined by filling streams or by pollution. The only European kingfisher, *Alcedo atthis*, up to 16.5 cm, is valued by fish breedings, for it preferentially catches slow-moving, sick, or defective individuals.

Polluted water courses are abandoned by Alcedinidae. In addition to petroleum and industrial pollution, there is danger from prey saturated with insecticides.

RINGED KINGFISHER, *Ceryle torquata,*
Martin-pescador-grande   PL 22.4

42 cm; 305–41 g. Unmistakable in large size and enormous bill (8 cm) which sometimes has reddish hues. Can be reminiscent of a night-heron (*Nycticorax*). Underparts and female under tail coverts chestnut. Female and young male have blue-gray breast band. Throat white. VOICE: a penetrating *kwat* that can be heard at a distance, repeated at regular intervals in flight, so a bird's arrival can be anticipated; also *chat-yat-yat* (hence the name *matraca,* "rattle"); *egeh.* . . . Perches on rocks and tall dead trees at water's edge. Lives along large rivers, lakes, lagoons, mangroves, ocean edge, wherever there are banks or rocks in which it can nest. Moves from island to island and appears at small pools on long flights. Overflies mountains and cities. Migrates in Amazonia (see "Migration"). Southern Texas to Tierra del Fuego, throughout South America. Also called *Ariramba-grande* (Pará), *Matraca* (Rio Grande do Sul), *Caracaxá*. Can be considered an allospecies of *C. alcyon* of North America. Genus *Ceryle* (but not *Chloroceryle*) also occurs in Asia and Africa.

AMAZON KINGFISHER, *Chloroceryle amazona,*
Martim-pescador-verde, Ariramba-verde

29.5 cm. Clearly smaller than *Ceryle torquata*. Upperparts metallic green, often appearing bluish gray. Collar, starting at base of bill, and underparts white (yellowish in female). Flanks streaked. Male with rufous breast band; female spotted green here. VOICE: *krad, kech;* song, both sexes, a sequence of whistles *it . . . ji . . . chew-chew . . . tse-tse-tse.* Habitat and numbers similar to *C. torquata* but less frequent along coast and does not fly as high. Mexico to Argentina, throughout Brazil. Also called *Martim-gravata* (Rio Grande do Sul).

Fig. 174. Green Kingfisher, *Chloroceryle americana*, male, flying low over water.

GREEN KINGFISHER, *Chloroceryle americana,*
Martim-pescador-pequeno   Fig. 174

19 cm. Usually most common kingfisher. Almost a smaller replica of *C. amazona,* but upperparts very dark green, contrasting with prominent silky white band connecting base of bill with nape, which is crossed by nuchal crest. Base of outer tail feathers white. Male has white underparts with chestnut breast; in female these are, respectively, yellowish and spotted green. VOICE: *ta-ta,* reminiscent of Sunbittern, *Eurypyga helias,* frequently its neighbor in Amazonia; warning *TI-ti; trr-trr-trr,* etc; song a twittered, descending sequence similar to *amazona* but weaker, *kli-kli-kli-kli-kli.* Lakes with abundant aquatic vegetation, edges of large and small rivers, mangroves. Texas and Mexico to Argentina, throughout Brazil.

GREEN-AND-RUFOUS KINGFISHER, *Chloroceryle inda,*
Martim-pescador-da-mata

22 cm. Retiring, found at edge of creeks in shady forest. Relatively abundant in várzea forest cut by igarapés, a region periodically inundated. Also at edge of relatively open rivers (Rio Parnaíba, Piauí). Sometimes alongside *C. aenea.* Color similar to *aenea* but lacks white collar, underparts entirely rusty, throat lighter. Female characterized by mixed black-and-white breast band. VOICE: a loud *kreh, chip-chip-chip.* Nicaragua to Bolivia, Brazil on Rio das Mortes (Mato Grosso) and Goiás. Along Atlantic littoral as far as Rio de Janeiro, Santos (São Paulo), Santa Catarina (Colônia Hansa). Also called *Ariramba-pintado* (Amazonas).

AMERICAN PYGMY KINGFISHER, *Chloroceryle aenea,*
Arirambinha   PL 22.5

12.5 cm (2.7 cm of which is bill); 11–16 g. Only ½ the size of *C. americana.* Female similar to male but has white breast band. Edges of water courses with dense vegetation, where easily overlooked. Mexico to Amazonia, Bolivia, Argentina (Misiones), Santa Catarina, São Paulo, Rio de Janeiro (Poço das Antas, Majé), Espírito Santo (Sooretama), Minas Gerais, Bahia, Pernambuco, Mato Grosso. Also called *Ariramba-miudinho.*

Alcedinidae Bibliography

See also General Bibliography

Reyer, H. V. 1981. Königsfischer in Afrika. *Deutsche Orn.-Gesellschaft,* Melk.
Skutch, A. F. 1947. *Auk* 64:201–17. [Chick development]
Skutch, A. F. 1957. *Condor* 59:217–29. [Behavior]
Skutch, A. F. 1972. Studies of Tropical American Birds. *Publ. Nuttall Orn. Club.* 10:88–101.

FAMILY MOMOTIDAE: MOTMOTS (4)

The motmots are Neotropical forest birds that have spread from Central America. A Miocene (upper Tertiary) fossil has been found in Florida (Becker 1986). Pleistocene fossils of 20,000 years B.P. have come from the Minas Gerais grottoes of Escrivaninha, Marinho, Sumidouro, and Capão Seco. The family also existed in Europe. Motmots are related to the Alcedinidae and Trogonidae through the peculiar morphology of the inner ear (see Alcedinidae).

Morphology and Formation of Caudal Spatulas

Jay-sized, motmots have a strong, curved bill with serrations on the tomia that vary in degree from species to species. The tongue is relatively long, the wings short and rounded. Miranda Ribeiro (1931) called attention to two bony projections at the angle of the wing. In Brazilian species the tail is long and the plumage profusely colored. Legs are short, and the toes are not so joined as in the Alcedinidae, with only the two outer front toes (third and fourth) together. Sexes are similar.

The most prominent characteristic of several motmots are the spatulas at the end of the elongated central tail feathers, which contribute greatly to the birds' beauty. The true importance of the spatula relates to behavior, for they serve for signaling (see "Behavior"). There have always been doubts as to how these are formed, with a variety of conjectures on the problem. Most authors agree that the bird pulls off the pertinent portions of its tail ("The tail has a small subapical stretch lacking barbs, which have been cut off by the bird itself, for its own decoration. This is perhaps unique among birds," Ihering 1967). I do not accept this interpretation. The feathers in question develop normally until they reach or almost reach normal length, at which time they have no gap near the end but show a slight strangulation in the distal region of the vane at the point where the space that creates the spatula will later open. This occurs when the feather reaches a certain age. The barbs (rami) in the portion in question become very brittle at the base, as if perforated, and within a short time break off by themselves or with the slightest rubbing against vegetation or the walls of the nest. The size of the gap is fixed and preshaped in its structure, as I verified with material in the Berlin Museum in 1933. This prior formation of the gap guarantees the integrity of the spatula, which always stays the same size. Thus, theories of its creation by active efforts of the bird or as a result of nest size are invalid. Certain species, such as the Rufous-capped Motmot, *Baryphthengus ruficapillus,* of southeastern Brazil, that share the same behavior do not acquire spatulas and retain their central rectrices intact like the rest of the tail, demonstrating a less advanced evolutionary stage.

Vocalization

Motmots fill the woods with a low, melodious bellow that is their version of song and dominates certain forests at dawn and dusk. They begin to call while it is still dark and usually stop before sunrise. Their vocalizations have the timbre of those of a pigeon or frog. Pairs "converse" with similar voices. Voice is often the only indication that *Baryphthengus ruficapillus* is present.

Feeding

In the same way as puffbirds (Bucconidae) and jacamars (Galbulidae) do, motmots pick arthropods off leaves and branches in flight. They also catch butterflies and accompany army-ant swarms, catching animals such as beetles, caterpillars, centipedes, or occasionally a small rodent, a nestling of some other bird, or a fleeing gecko. They descend to the ground (hence the name *galo-do-mato,* "forest cock") where they turn over rotten sticks and fallen leaves. They beat prey against the substrate to kill it. I have found stomachs full of blue berries in two *Baryphthengus ruficapillus* (one from Espírito Santo, one from ex-Guanabara). They eat *Heliconia* fruits and regurgitate pellets.

Behavior

Motmots live alone or in pairs. They perch low and usually remain immobile for considerable periods of time (attracting little attention as long as they do not move the tail), like the Galbulidae; the Great Jacamar, *Jacamerops aurea,* may resemble the Blue-crowned Motmot, *Momotus momota.* They do not stray from the tallest trees and bushes. *Baryphthengus ruficapillus* takes dust baths.

The tail is a precise indicator of every emotion; brusk lateral and vertical movements are alternated. *B. ruficapillus*

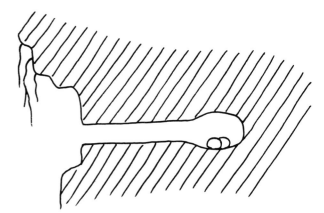

Fig. 175. Nest of Rufous-capped Motmot, *Baryphthengus ruficapillus,* in a bank in the forest. Original, H. Sick.

sometimes cocks its tail as high as the top of its head. Pendulumlike movements are a feature (*pássaro-pêndulo,* "pendulum-bird"); the strangest is when the tail is stopped at whatever angle, as if stuck. The spatula unquestionably augments the optical effect of such movements.

Breeding

Motmots dig nesting galleries 60 cm to 2 m long (fig. 175), altering direction if they meet an obstacle. Sometimes they use burrows excavated by other animals, deepening them even more to make access more difficult for intruders. The pair works together, throwing earth backward with the feet. While such work is in progress the bill is often encrusted with mud. Apparently they are unable to turn around inside the gallery, even when incubating. I have always seen them come out of their burrows backward, which is the effective way of maintaining intact the long, delicate tail, although I have found *Momotus momota* individuals with worn tails and broken spatulas.

The eggs, rounded and shiny, pure white, are laid directly on the bottom of the incubation chamber. Parents take turns incubating and feeding the young. An incubation period of 17 to 21 days has been recorded for Central American species. Newly hatched chicks resemble those of kingfishers but have a hooked bill (see fig. 173). Despite the filth of the nest, whose interior soon is boiling with flies and their larvae, the young fledge with perfect plumage after approximately one month. Lack of available banks may result in nests of two pairs being close, but they are definitely not gregarious. Apparently they have only one clutch per year (Espírito Santo, Rio de Janeiro) and use the nesting burrow as a refuge only during the breeding period.

Parasites

Motmots are among the hosts of the ocular nematodes; *Oxyspirura cephaloptera* was discovered on *Momotus momota* by J. Natterer in the early 1800s. The same worm occurs in the eyes of the Troupial, *Icterus icterus croconotus.*

They are also parasitized by louse flies (Hippoboscidae) such as *Olfersia fusca,* found on *Baryphthengus ruficapillus.*

Folklore

Legends, such as those of the Pareci Indians (Mato Grosso) referring to the acquisition of fire by people, explain the singular form of the tail: *Baryphthengus martii* caused the gap in the rectrices by carrying an ember on its tail.

BROAD-BILLED MOTMOT, *Electron platyrhynchum,* Udu-de-bico-largo

37 cm. Very similar to *Baryphthengus ruficapillus* but with wider and more depressed bill having clear indentation along length of culmen. Chin shiny greenish blue; tail, with or without spatulas, strongly graduated. VOICE: much different than other species, a strange, nasal cry: *eh-o eh-o, qua-qua,* reminiscent of a *Selenidera* (Ramphastidae) voice. Primary or secondary forest. Honduras to Bolivia, locally in Brazilian Amazonia (Rios Juruá, Purus, Madeira, and Tocantins, of northern Mato Grosso and Goiás).

RUFOUS-CAPPED MOTMOT, *Baryphthengus ruficapillus,* Juruva   PL 22.6

42 cm. Has black mask like other species, but typical black spots on breast sometimes absent (molt). Plate shows southern form (*B. r. ruficapillus*), *jacu-taquara,* with intact tail lacking spatulas; rarely, incipient spatula formation visible. VOICE: a ventriloquial *BOOoooooo, do-DOOG-doog-doog-doog-doog,* a dry *rrrrew, go-go-go.* Interior of shady forests. Central Brazil (Goiás: *B. r. berlai*) to eastern Brazil from Bahia and Minas Gerais to Rio Grande do Sul (including ex-Guanabara), Paraguay, and Misiones, Argentina (*B. r. ruficapillus*). Also called *Bururuk* (Botocudo), *Jeruva, Pururu, Formigão* (Bahia); southern name *jacu-taquara* leaves room for confusion with Rufous-vented Ground-Cuckoo, *Neomorphus geoffroyi dulcis.* In Goiás sympatric with *Momotus momota.*

RUFOUS MOTMOT, *Baryphthengus martii,* Udu

Replaces *B. ruficapillus* in Amazonia. Head, neck, and underparts deep rusty; tail spatula well defined, unlike *ruficapillus.* VOICE: *HOOtoo,* a sequence of *hoot, hoot, hoots.* . . . Nicaragua to Bolivia, Amazonia (upper Amazon and Rios Negro, Juruá, and Tapajós). Sometimes considered a geographic race of *ruficapillus.*

BLUE-CROWNED MOTMOT, *Momotus momota,* Udu-de-coroa-azul   Fig. 176

44 cm. Best-known Brazilian motmot, showing typical spatulas. Unlike others, lacks rufous on head. Black mask

Fig. 176. Blue-crowned Motmot, *Momotus momota;* note the perfectly shaped tail spatulas.

and cap bordered with blue. VOICE: a deep *HOO-doodoo; dek,* like a blow on a hollow log; song a sequence of *hoo-oo-oo-oo-oo-oo-oo-oos.* Woodlands and gallery forests, sometimes quite dry and open. Mexico to northwestern Argentina, central Brazil, western São Paulo, the northeast (Maranhão, Piauí, Paraíba, Alagoas); in Goiás meets *Baryphthengus ruficapillus.* Also called *Uritutu* (Mato Grosso), *Jeruva.*

Momotidae Bibliography

Becker, J. J. 1986. A fossil Motmot (Momotidae) from late Miocene of Florida. *Condor* 88:478–82.

Miranda Ribeiro, A. 1931. *Bol. Mus. Nac. Rio de Janeiro* 7(2). [Morphology]

Rodrigues, H. O. 1964. *Atas Soc. Biol. Rio de Janeiro* 8:33–35. [Nematoda]

Skutch, A. F. 1964. *Ibis* 106:321. [Behavior]

Skutch, A. F. 1971. *Wilson Bull.* 83:74. [Behavior]

Stager, K. E. 1959. *Cont. Sci. Nat. Hist. Mus. Los Angeles,* no. 33. [Taxonomy]

Wagner, H. O. 1950. *Auk* 67:387. [Behavior]

ORDER PICIFORMES

FAMILY GALBULIDAE: JACAMARS (14)

Jacamars are one of the typical Neotropical families. They are usually considered to be related to puffbirds (Bucconidae), but certain affinities with the Alcedinidae have recently been highlighted by biochemical data. Fossils are unknown to date.

Morphology

In aspect (sharp, awl-shaped bill; long, graduated tail; etc.) and life history (feeding, nesting, etc.) they are similar to Old World bee-eaters (Meropidae, Coraciiformes), one of the most interesting cases of convergent evolution.

The slender bill, almost always held obliquely (like hummingbirds), and brilliant, metallic, golden green plumage of unrivaled beauty have led people to confuse them with hummingbirds (thus the names *beija-flor-grande,* "large hummingbird"; *chupa-flor-da-mata-virgem,* "virgin forest flowersucker"; and *beija-flor-d'agua,* "water hummingbird"). Indians, who understand the jacamars' completely different modus vivendi, do not make this mistake. The birds are also known as *jacamares,* an indigenous name. Jacamars also resemble the Alcedinidae, which explains the origin of the Amazonian name *ariramba-da-mata,* "forest kingfisher." Unlike kingfishers, however, they have long tongues that are "normal" compared with those of woodpeckers.

The Chestnut Jacamar, *Galbalcyrhynchus leucotis,* has a heavy bill, very similar to those of the Alcedinidae. The bill of the Great Jacamar, *Jacamerops aurea,* resembles that of the motmots (Momotidae), a companion family with similar habits. The *Galbula* bill is daggerlike and can be used as such, as has occurred in fights between captive individuals.

The legs are short and weak, the feet quite small and zygodactyl, with the second and third toes in front and the first and fourth behind, a character distinguishing all Piciformes and some unrelated families (Psittacidae, Cuculidae) but which is not a decisive feature in systematics. The two front toes are linked at the base, forming a "shovel" (see Alcedinidae, "Morphology"). There is a tendency toward toe reduction: in the *Brachygalba* the inner rear toe is short, and in the Three-toed Jacamar, *Jacamaralcyon tridactyla,* the hallux has disappeared, leaving only three toes, the fourth toe being the hind one. In this genus the first metacarpal (thumb) is well developed.

Bill and eye color (see "Identification Data") are diagnostic. The *Brachygalba* attract attention by their light blue, seemingly enameled iris. That of *Jacamaralcyon tridactyla* is yellowish brown or red, according to age.

Sexes are often recognizable by throat color, a difference already accentuated in the young before fledging. Galbulidae flesh has a strong odor, similar to that of Trogonidae.

Vocalization

The voice can be heard at a distance and consists of high, melodious whistles. Jacamars are quite loquacious. When caught, individuals snap the bill.

Feeding and Behavior

Operating from favorite perches on thin branches, jacamars search out passing insects. They usually address their attention obliquely upward, not down. When prey appears they launch out to pursue it in a short, swift charge, returning with the booty to the perch they left, where they beat larger items against the branch to break the wings and more resistant chitinous parts, thereby easing the eating. I have, however, seen the Rufous-tailed Jacamar, *Galbula ruficauda,* swallow butterflies without breaking the wings. The pincerlike bill is as efficient in this type of chase as are the entirely different bills of some other insectivorous birds, such as nightjars and swallows.

Jacamars capture butterflies, including those with thick abdomens, such as Hesperidae, and large ones, such as *Morpho* and *Papilio,* and are perfectly able to separate out the unpalatable species, which they do not molest. They also catch bees (Meliponidae), wasps, winged ants, small beetles, cicadas, and dragonflies. The food of *Galbula ruficauda* may be up to 85% Hymenoptera (Mato Grosso). Wasps and bees have been found in the stomach of *Galbalcyrhynchus leucotis,* a species with a different "snout." *Jacamerops aurea* gleans insects perched on leaves. Jacamars regurgitate pellets containing chitin.

Whereas species such as *Galbula ruficauda* and the Yellow-billed Jacamar, *G. albirostris,* hunt at low levels on the edge of and in the forest, the Paradise Jacamar, *G. dea,* and Brown Jacamar, *Brachygalba lugubris,* exploit the space above the forest, perching on dead branches in the tops of tall trees In the upper Xingu (Mato Grosso) I recorded four galbulids (*Brachygalba lugubris, Galbula ruficauda, G. dea,* and Bronzy Jacamar, *G. leucogastra*) in the same region occupying different niches. The bright green species live in the lowest part of the forest. I have verified in the Belém area that both the Purple-necked Jacamar, *Galbula cyanicollis,* and Green-and-rufous Kingfisher, *Chloroceryle inda,* only appear in várzea forests when these are flooded, a twice-daily occurrence due to the tides.

Galbula ruficauda even hunts at night, revealing its presence by the noise it makes beating insects against branches. Jacamars have the custom, like puffbirds, of remaining for long periods on their perches, moving only the head; they are, however, considerably more active than the Bucconidae.

I have noted left-footedness in *Jacamaralcyon tridactyla* during the intense effort of one excavating a nesting hole (see Psittacidae, "Behavior").

Breeding

Breeding involves pairs or occasionally three to five individuals, probably family groups. *Jacamaralcyon tridactyla* is gregarious and may form small colonies. Jacamars excavate their nests in sandy or clay banks, usually in the forest alongside a trail or creek. Sometimes they use terrestrial termite nests (*Galbula ruficauda*) or rotting tree trunks (*Jacamerops aurea*). In flat forest areas where there are no banks, they may use earth lifted by the roots of a fallen tree if the layer is thick enough, for they usually dig deep galleries. The incubation chamber may have more than one access route (*Jacamaralcyon tridactyla*), which confuses enemies. While working on the nest the bill gets dirty, for they loosen the earth with the mandibles, which are much more resistant than they appear. Although very small, the feet are used to get debris out of the tunnel (thus the names *cavadeira,* "digger," and *fura-barreira,* "barrier-breaker"). I have seen a *J. tridactyla* with the foreclaws of the left foot completely worn down.

Eggs are round, shiny, and pure white. Although two to four are usually recorded (in Rio de Janeiro *Galbula ruficauda* lays two clutches per year of four eggs each), *G. r. rufoviridis* is reported to lay only one egg in Amazonia. The male brings insects for his mate, sometimes preparing them (e.g., breaking the wings of moths) before delivery, such deference being a sure sign of nesting. Both parents brood unstintingly, for 20 to 23 days in *G. ruficauda.* The same species in captivity, with abundant food, took only 18 days.

G. ruficauda chicks hatch with dense whitish down, unlike most Piciformes. The mandible of recently hatched birds projects somewhat, a strange feature that disappears after a few days (see Alcedinidae "Breeding"). Nestlings have a spiny, soft callous on the tarsus, similar to that of Picidae, Alcedinidae, etc., an appropriate substitute for the cushion-

ing that is entirely absent from their nest. Although even minimal hygiene is lacking, the chicks keep perfectly clean. They give the full song of the adults but with low volume. They fledge at 21 to 26 days and promptly acquire adult plumage but are recognizable by their shorter bills.

Jacamaralcyon tridactyla galleries that are occasionally exposed on high banks lacking vegetation may serve as swallow perches.

Distribution and Evolution

Various species are geographically isolated, being frequently separated in Amazonia by wide rivers. *Galbula ruficauda rufoviridis* and the Green-tailed Jacamar, *G. galbula,* are kept apart by the Amazon itself and by the lower Tapajós (fig. 177). Nevertheless there are cases in which two species occupy adjoining areas not separated by any distinct geographic barrier, as in the case of the White-chinned and Bluish-fronted Jacamars, *Galbula tombacea* and *G. cyanescens,* in the upper Amazon. Hybrids of these allopatric species, which have achieved reproductive isolation, are un-

Fig. 177. Distribution of the Green-tailed Jacamar and allies, *Galbula galbula* species group (after Haffer 1974). Open squares: *G. galbula*. Stars: *G. r. ruficauda* (only peripheral records are shown); includes the ranges of the clinal forms *G. r. brevirostris* and *G. r. pallens*. Solid triangles: *G. r. rufoviridis* and *G. r. heterogyna* in eastern Bolivia. Open circles with center cross: *G. cyanescens* (cy). Open circles: *G. tombacea* (to). Crosses: *G. pastazae* (pa). Plumage color is mostly metallic green (hatched) and rufous (stippled). Mountains over 2000 m are in black. Symbols denote locality records.

known. Their identical ecological requirements result in competitive exclusion.

To make it perfectly clear that these species are close relatives, it is convenient to designate them as allospecies constituting a superspecies. Thus, I recognize the superspecies *Galbula galbula* made up of the following allospecies: *G. galbula, G. ruficauda* (which includes *G. rufoviridis* and *G. melanogenia*), *G. tombacea,* and *G. cyanescens. G. albirostris* is another superspecies, having *G. cyanicollis* as an allospecies. According to Haffer (1974), 76% of Brazilian Galbulidae species may be considered superspecies components. A similar pattern of geographic exclusion occurs in Amazonia in toucans, parrots, and Passerines such as cotingas and manakins.

Although most jacamars inhabit hot, tropical regions, the distinctive *Jacamaralcyon tridactyla* occupies mountainous areas in southeastern Brazil. Apparently all Galbulidae are sedentary. See "Feeding and Behavior."

Abundance and Decline

Certain species, such as *Galbula ruficauda,* are abundant in their natural habitat but become scarce or disappear under the pressure of civilization, as occurs in the vicinity of cities.

Identification Data

There are two chromatic types:

1. Green and/or ferruginous species: *Galbula* spp. (except *G. dea; G. leucogastra* is green and white), *Jacamerops aurea,* and *Galbalcyrhynchus leucotis*
2. Black (or blackish brown) and white species: *Galbula dea, Brachygalba* spp., *Jacamaralcyon tridactyla*

There are also two tail types: the most common is long and graduated, but some species have short, triangular tails (*Brachygalba* and *J. tridactyla*).

The black, yellow, or red bill may also be diagnostic, both for species and subspecies, to some extent corresponding to the color of the feet and the bare region around the eyes.

CHESTNUT JACAMAR, *Galbalcyrhynchus leucotis,* Ariramba-vermelha

21.6 cm. Characteristic of upper Amazon, with very strong bill and rectangular tail, resembling a kingfisher. Feet relatively large. Chestnut with blackish head, wings, and rectrices; white cheeks. The Solimões (Amazonas) to Colombia.

PURUS JACAMAR, *Galbalcyrhynchus purusianus*

Bill and feet red, no white on cheeks. Replaces *G. leucotis* in upper reaches of Rios Purus and Juruá (Amazonas) to Bolivia, Peru. Apparently does not hybridize with *leucotis,* for which reason I consider it a separate species.

BROWN JACAMAR, *Brachygalba lugubris,* Ariramba-preta

16.5 cm. Widely distributed, quite small with short tail, very long bill. Blackish with throat lighter, abdomen white. Bill color varies from black (northern population, *B. l. lugubris,* south to northern Goiás) to yellow on mandible and base of maxilla, as does eye-ring color (southern population, *B. l. melanosterna,* Rios Curuá and Cururu in Pará to Mato Grosso, Goiás, western Minas Gerais, western São Paulo). Iris light blue. VOICE: a very high whistle, *hilew;* call *dihewee;* song *hi, i, i, i, i, i, i, i-hi-dewwee.* Dense forest edges, river shores. The Guianas and Colombia to Bolivia, Brazil as far as São Paulo, Maranhão, Piauí.

WHITE-THROATED JACAMAR, *Brachygalba albogularis*

Similar to *B. lugubris* but with white on throat and sides of head. A geographic replacement for *lugubris;* found on frontier with Peru and in Rio Purus region (Amazonas).

THREE-TOED JACAMAR, *Jacamaralcyon tridactyla,* Cuitelão   BR   PL 44.2

18 cm. Southern jacamar with only 3 toes (see "Morphology"). Similar to *Brachygalba lugubris* but with top of head quite ruffled, streaked with brownish yellow. Throat black, center of underparts white. Bill black, iris brown or red. VOICE: a sequence of short whistles, weaker than *Galbula ruficauda.* River edges with bushes and isolated trees in rough country; frequently perches on stalks of tall grass. Found in small flocks. Locally from Espírito Santo (in mountains) and Minas Gerais (Paraiba valley) to Paraná (Rio Paraná). Also called *Violeiro* (Minas Gerais). See "Feeding . . . " and "Breeding."

YELLOW-BILLED JACAMAR, *Galbula albirostris,* Ariramba-de-bico-amarelo

19 cm. Widely distributed in northern Amazonia. Similar to *G. ruficauda* but with bill, feet, and region around eyes bright yellow. Claws and bill tip black. Breast ferruginous (not green), like belly and sides of tail. VOICE: warning a *trratrra.* The Guianas, Venezuela, and Colombia to Rio Solimões, Peru (*G. a. chalcocephala*), north bank of Amazon (*G. a. albirostris*). In Amapá sympatric with *G. galbula* and *G. leucogastra.*

PURPLE-NECKED JACAMAR, *Galbula cyanicollis*   BR

Face blue, not green; male throat ferruginous, not white as in *G. ruficauda.* Replaces *G. albirostris* south of Amazon. Javari (Amazonas) region to eastern Pará, Maranhão, Goiás, Mato Grosso. I accept it as a species, for there is no report of intergradation with *albirostris.* In Belém (Pará) area sympatric with *G. ruficauda rufoviridis, G. dea,* and *Brachygalba lugubris.*

GREEN-TAILED JACAMAR, *Galbula galbula,*
Ariramba-de-cauda-verde

20 cm. Similar to *G. ruficauda rufoviridis,* having black bill and green breast, but tail green above, black below. Forest. The Guianas and Colombia to Rio Negro, Amapá, and between lower reaches, of Rios Tapajós and Madeira. May be considered a replacement of *G. ruficauda* (see fig. 177).

RUFOUS-TAILED JACAMAR, *Galbula ruficauda,*
Bico-de-agulha-de-rabo-vermelho   PL 23.2

22 cm; 23 g (male). Well distributed. Bill black, throat white (male) or rusty (female), breast green, sides of tail rusty. VOICE: a limpid, repeated whistle; an accelerated sequence ending with downward trill. Edge of dense vegetation, river banks, marshes. Also interior of sparse, dry woodland in savanna regions. Mexico to Bolivia, northeastern Argentina (Misiones). In Brazilian Amazonia (Roraima) typical form (*G. r. ruficauda*) has ferruginous chin and tail (only 2 central rectrices are green). South of Amazon *G. r. rufoviridis* has rusty tail with green tips, 4 central rectrices green, chin white; extends to Mato Grosso, Goiás, and in eastern Brazil as far as Rio de Janeiro, Paraná (see fig. 177). Southern form was long considered a separate species. Also called *Beija-flor-grande, Ariramba-da-mata-virgem, Beija-flor-d'agua, Jacamarici, Bico-de-sovela, Sovelão* (Minas Gerais).

WHITE-CHINNED JACAMAR, *Galbula tombacea*

This and *G. cyanescens* are replacements for *G. ruficauda* in upper Amazon (see fig. 177). Both have black bills and rusty sides of head; throat, like breast, predominantly green; chin white. In this species crown sooty. Apparently they do not cross with *ruficauda,* so I consider them valid species.

BLUISH-FRONTED JACAMAR, *Galbula cyanescens*
See *G. tombacea.*

BRONZY JACAMAR, *Galbula leucogastra,*
Ariramba-acobreada

21 cm. Upperparts and breast bronzy green; throat and abdomen white; bill black. VOICE: even higher than *G. ruficauda;* a rhythmic sequence, *eww-hihi heww-heehee heww.* Interior of tall, dry forest. Eastern Venezuela, the Guianas, Amapá, and western Pará to upper Amazon, Peru, Mato Grosso on Teles Pires (upper Tapajós) and Xingu (Suiá-missu). See *G. dea.*

PARADISE JACAMAR, *Galbula dea,*
Ariramba-do-paraíso   Fig. 178

31 cm. Tail extremely long, comprising more than ¹/₂ total length. Black and white with forehead brownish, wings and tail lustrous green. VOICE: a descending sequence of rounded whistles, sometimes accelerated, *glewweh . . . ,* resembling

Fig. 178. Paradise Jacamar, *Galbula dea amazonum.*

a woodcreeper or even a hawk heard from a distance; also a different, low call, *ghib-ghib-rrehha.* River edge forest, frequently perched high on dead branches. The Guianas and Colombia to Bolivia, northern Mato Grosso (upper Rio Xingu), Pará (Serra do Cachimbo, Belém). Also called *Upianá.*

GREAT JACAMAR, *Jacamerops aurea,*
Ariramba-grande-da-mata-virgem   PL 23.1

29.5 cm. Family giant, somewhat resembling Broad-billed Motmot, *Electron platyrhynchum,* without spatulas. Female lacks white on throat. VOICE: a high whistle, loud and monosyllabic, initially ascending, then descending, *bi ew,* as if it were a hawk, and with timbre of Rusty-margined Flycatcher, *Myiozetetes cayanensis.* Frequently silent. Streams in high forest. Costa Rica to Bolivia, southern and eastern Pará (Rio Cururu), Goiás. Also called *Uirá-piana, Jacamaraçu.*

Galbulidae Bibliography

Fry, C. H. 1970. *An. Acad. Bras. Ciênc.* 42:275–318. [Ecology, comparison with Meropidae]
Haffer, J. 1974. *Publ. Nuttall Orn. Club* 14:313–44. [Speciation]
Sclater, P. L. 1882. *A Monograph of the Jacamars and Puff-Birds or Families Galbulidae and Bucconidae.* 4 vols. London.
Skutch, A. F. 1968. *Condor* 70:66–82. [Behavior].

FAMILY BUCCONIDAE: PUFFBIRDS (23)

Puffbirds are very distinctive American arboreal birds. Fossils of the lower Tertiary (Eocene) have been found in North America and of the Pleistocene in Brazil (Lapa da Escrivaninha and Lagoa Santa, Minas Gerais: 20,000 years B.P.).

Morphology

Bucconidae have certain similarities to the Alcedinidae, possibly of phylogenetic origin. The Swallow-wing, *Chelidoptera tenebrosa,* is frequently confused in the field with a swallow, whereas the Rusty-breasted Nunlet, *Nonnula rubecula,* may recall a small tyrannid.

The head is large and noticeably broad. The eyes are recessed under projecting eyebrows, and the adult iris is bright white, light yellow, or red. The strong bill, with a rounded culmen, is frequently hooked and is surrounded by thick bristles or vibrissae (see Caprimulgidae "Morphology . . . "), hence the term *capitão-de-bigode,* "mustachioed captain." The bill may be red or white. The wings are generally short and the legs almost invisible. The feet are small and zygodactylous. The narrow tail on a resting bird is like a narrow board. The eyelids are sometimes swollen and prominently colorful (*Nonnula, Chelidoptera*).

The soft, fluffy (puffbird) plumage creates the impression of larger, heavy bodies than they really have. The head feathers are usually ruffled, and the malar stripe is prominent. Colors are modest but frequently spotted; the bill may be the most brightly colored feature. Sexes are similar, with the female perhaps somewhat larger but less colorful than the male. Immatures have shorter bills. Their flesh has a strong odor, similar to that of the Galbulidae and Trogonidae.

Vocalization

Puffbirds whistle, often so high (to the point of resembling a bat voice) that it is difficult to locate the vocalist. These high notes are surprising coming from such robust, coarse-appearing birds. The songs are similar to those of the Galbulidae.

Male and female may sing in response to one another (e.g., White-eared Puffbird, *Nystalus chacuru*). The Yellow-billed Nunbird, *Monasa flavirostris,* has a full, melodious voice, giving its lengthy phrases in chorus while gathered in small assemblages. These songs are among the most pleasant heard in their respective areas and may recall vocalizations of cotingids such as the Purple-throated Fruitcrow, *Querula purpurata.*

Chelidoptera tenebrosa often sings in flight. Whereas some periodically become loquacious, not even keeping quiet at night (e.g., *Nystalus chacuru*), others, such as the *Malacoptila* and *Nonnula,* are quiet and easily overlooked. When disturbed puffbirds snap the mandibles (e.g., *Nystalus chacuru* and the *Nonnula*).

Feeding

They hunt insects, such as beetles, which they wait for while perched. They catch the insects in flight with an audible snap and then return to the perch they left to beat the prey against a branch before devouring it. *Chelidoptera tenebrosa* resembles a bat or a large butterfly during such sallies, with elegant, gravity-defying maneuvers. Sometimes it hovers. It likes to eat termites and ants flying in swarms. *Nystalus chacuru* and others also catch perched arthropods and lizards, millipedes, centipedes, daddy longlegs, scorpions, and even velvet worms (*Peripatus*), which I have found in an *N. chacuru* stomach. *Malacoptila* and *Monasa* prove that puffbirds also find food by digging into the ground, perhaps while excavating to nest. Some (*Notharchus, Nystalus, Monasa*) also eat vegetable material. They eject small pellets containing the thick chitinous remains of consumed insects. They drink water that has accumulated in the rosettes of leaves.

Behavior

Puffbirds have sluggish dispositions and are tolerant of other birds. They remain stationary for long periods, only turning from time to time and twisting the head (the bill usually is held a bit elevated), showing they are observing everything and not sleeping as country people indicate by the names they give them (*dormião,* "sleeper," or *preguiçosos,* "lazy ones"). In spite of their detached air, they are not stupid (*joão-bobo,* "john-stupid") but depend on their mimicry. Thanks to their cryptic plumage and their relative immobility they manage to escape notice by the sharpest observers. They prefer to roost on the tip of a stake or branch, favorite spots they use for years on end. They also perch on electric wires (*Nystalus chacuru* and Pied Puffbird, *Notharchus tectus*). Sometimes they perch longitudinally on branches (see Caprimulgidae, "Behavior"). When changing perches they fly, not hop, through the branches. In certain situations they walk backward with tiny steps. They are clumsy on the ground. Sometimes *Chelidoptera tenebrosa* perches on the ground other than during the drudgery of nesting (see "Breeding"). They rest (e.g., *Nystalus chacuru*) lying with the belly on the branch while the nictitating membranes are brought over the eyes.

When vigilant they assume an erect position. *N. chacuru* reveals nervousness by tail movements like those of the motmots (Momotidae), with slow sideways oscillations as well as circular movements. Sometimes the tail is stopped while not on the axial line, creating a strange impression. Puffbirds adopt an oblique stance when frightened. When caught they feign death in order to flee unexpectedly (e.g., *N. chacuru*).

Flight is rapid and horizontal, usually over only the short distances required by their varied forest or cerrado habitats. *Chelidoptera tenebrosa*, which has relatively large wings, is an excellent soarer and actively flies long distances above the forest and dives from treetops to the ground. Its flight is sufficiently vigorous to let it attack passing swallows and hawks, it being the puffbird most adapted to life in sunny, open areas. *Nystalus chacuru* also lives in sunny places; the *Malacoptila*, *Nonnula*, and *Monasa* are shade lovers with comparatively larger eyes. Puffbirds enjoy bathing in rain. I have seen the White-fronted Nunbird, *Monasa morphoeus*, take a dust bath.

N. chacuru periodically lives in what are apparently small family flocks (parents with offspring). They sleep perched on branches, side by side. In Paraguay is was determined that the Spot-backed Puffbird, *Nystalus maculatus*, does not leave its galleries during cold hours, being immobilized by a lethargic sleep, such as we know with certain hummingbirds (J. Unger, from Steinbacher 1962).

Breeding

For nesting, puffbirds dig a gallery in rough terrain, in a bank (thus the name *fura-barreira*, "barrier-breaker"), or sometimes even on flat ground (*Chelidoptera tenebrosa*, *Nystalus maculatus*) or in arboreal termite nests (*Notharchus tectus* and White-necked Puffbird, *N. macrorhynchus*). In this regard it is interesting to note that the termites immediately restore walls opened by the puffbird but leave the chamber made by them, the same as occurs with trogons and psittacids. Puffbirds also use already existing holes. When they work on wood, their hammering can be heard at a distance (*Notharchus, Nonnula*).

As the gently descending gallery becomes deeper they rake the debris to the entrance, from where *Malacoptila, Nonnula,* and *Monasa* carry it away in the bill, thereby avoiding an accumulation of fresh earth in front of the nest that might reveal its presence. The entrance to the nest (fig. 179) of *Chelidoptera tenebrosa*, burrowed into muddy earth in a forest opening, is smooth and oval and marked by a hill of earth like that near a rat hole, which would not be noticed if the excavation were made in sandy soil (as in the cerrado or at the edge of the beach) where the pile would disintegrate.

Nystalus chacuru uses railroad embankments for nesting (Corumbá, Mato Grosso). During the excavation it soils its bill, feet, and feathers, altering its natural color somewhat, especially in red-earth regions. At the gallery entrance two furrows can be seen, made by the bird's two feet. The Black Nunbird, *Monasa atra*, may use armadillo burrows for nesting.

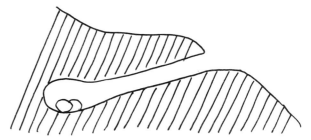

Fig. 179. Nest of a Swallow-wing, *Chelidoptera tenebrosa*, in a pasture. Limoeiro-Jatiboca, Espírito Santo. Original, H. Sick.

The incubation chamber may be bare (*Notharchus*) or lined with a bit of grass and dry leaves (*Malacoptila, Nonnula, Chelidoptera*). The entrance is sometimes camouflaged with leaves and branches piled up by the birds (*Malacoptila, Monasa, Nonnula*). They lay two to three pure white, shiny eggs. There is no nest sanitation, and the bottom is alive with fly larvae (*Chelidoptera tenebrosa*). In *C. tenebrosa* both pair members incubate for 15 days (A. Ruschi pers. comm.). The young hatch bare, blind, and with black or red skin and a short bill. I have noted small calluses on the tarsi of *C. tenebrosa* nestlings, recalling other Piciformes. The White-whiskered Puffbird, *Malacoptila panamensis*, fledges at 20 days.

The pair takes turns in its responsibilities for nest, eggs, and young. *C. tenebrosa* becomes aggressive with other birds, a vulture, for instance (see "Behavior"). Sometimes the pair receives help from another adult in feeding its young, and although neighboring pairs visit each other mutually and in a friendly way, sometimes there are fights among the females. This species has a tendency to nest in dispersed colonies.

The nest is sometimes used as a dormitory. *Nonnula rubecula* has been seen entering its nest backward, blocking the entrance with its head, good protection against enemies such as snakes which are immediately confronted with the bill of their prey. Fires, frequent in the cerrados of central Brazil, probably do not reach the incubation chambers of Bucconidae.

Distribution and Evolution

In various cases the distributional pattern and differentiation of Bucconidae in Amazonia show geographic exclusion (e.g., in *Malacoptila* and *Nonnula*). Some species spread as far as the Atlantic forest. In the heart of the Hylaea the breadth of the principal rivers act as geographic barriers that impede dispersal and preserve the integrity of the respective populations, which might compete if they were sympatric. We still lack a good understanding of the phylogenetic affinities of the various species. Species as similar as the Black-fronted Nunbird, *Monasa nigrifrons*, and *Monasa morphoeus* are extensively sympatric.

Migration and Local Movement

After breeding *Chelidoptera tenebrosa* gathers in certain regions in flocks of 20 to 30 individuals, giving the impression of migratory concentrations (May–June, Goiás). Apparently *Nystalus chacuru* is migratory in the extreme south. Forest species such as *Nonnula* sometimes accompany mixed bird flocks for a while.

Identification Data

1. Black with large white areas: *Notharchus* (see also *Chelidoptera*)
2. All black or black with some white marks; bill red, yellow, or black: *Monasa, Chelidoptera*
3. Almost uniformly brown without very distinct markings; small size: *Nonnula* (Pl 23). See also *Malacoptila rufa, M. fusca,* and *M. striata.*
4. Brown with uniformly white underparts: *Nystalus chacuru*
5. Brown with prominent varied pattern on underparts: *Bucco tamatia* (Pl 23)
6. Brown with black collar: *Bucco capensis*
7. The same as 5 but with black upper breast: *B. macrodactylus*
8. Brown with spotted underparts: *Nystalus striolatus, N. maculatus,* and *Micromonacha lanceolata*

WHITE-NECKED PUFFBIRD, *Notharchus macrorhynchus*, Capitão-do-mato   Fig. 180

26 cm. Widely distributed. Sizable, resembling at a distance Amazon Kingfisher, *Chloroceryle amazona,* because of strong bill, white collar, and black pectoral band (which varies in width). Belly white (northern form, *N. m. macrorhynchus*) or brownish (southern form, *N. m. swainsoni*).

Fig. 180. White-necked Puffbird, *Notharchus macrorhynchus.*

VOICE: very high for a bird this size, suggesting a Galbulidae or Emberizinae. Descending sequences of melodic whistles, frequently trisyllabic, sometimes ascending and accelerated or decreasing with surprising changes of rhythm, such as song, *ewi-ewi . . . dibewle-dibewle-dibewle;* calls harsh but also partly melodious. Quiet forest in top branches of tallest trees. Also at lower levels. Mexico to Bolivia, Paraguay, Argentina (Misiones); Amazonian Brazil as far as Mato Grosso (upper Rio Tapajós, upper Rio Xingu), Maranhão. Also eastern Brazil from Espírito Santo to Santa Catarina (*N. swainsoni*). Also called *João-do-mato, Bico-de-latão* (Minas Gerais), *Macuru.* See *N. ordii* and *N. tectus.*

BROWN-BANDED PUFFBIRD, *Notharchus ordii*

20 cm. Similar to *N. macrorhynchus* but smaller. Upper Amazon. Venezuela to Rios Negro and Tapajós.

PIED PUFFBIRD, *Notharchus tectus,* Capitão-do-mato-pequeno

15.5 cm. Amazonian, almost a small replica of *N. macrorhynchus.* Head, wings, and tail spotted white; eyebrows light. VOICE: high like a bat: tremulous *peet . . . rri . . . , bee-bibibi.* Riverine forests, generally perching high. Costa Rica to Amazonia as far as lower Tapajós (Pará) and Maranhão. When seen from below resembles Bronzy Jacamar, *Galbula leucogastra.* Also called *Macuru, Rapazinho-dos-velhos.*

CHESTNUT-CAPPED PUFFBIRD, *Bucco macrodactylus,* Rapazinho-de-boné-vermelho

14 cm. Smallest of 6 similar Amazonian species (*B. tamatia, B. capensis, Nystalus striolatus, N. maculatus, Micromonacha lanceolata*). Cap ferruginous, eyebrow and malar stripe white like underparts, black band across upper breast. Mask and bill black. Upper Amazon to Rios Negro and Tapajós. See *B. capensis.*

SPOTTED PUFFBIRD, *Bucco tamatia,* Rapazinho-carijó   PL 23.5

17 cm. Heavily spotted underparts, white malar stripe set off by black spot below it. On sides of upper back a white spot may appear, visible at a distance. Bill black. VOICE: short, weak, melodious tremolos. Gallery forests, palm groves. Frequently found in tops of leafy trees. Northern South America to upper Rio Tapajós, upper Rio Xingu (Mato Grosso), eastern Pará. Also called *Rapazinho-dos-velhos, Tacuru* (Kamaiurá, Mato Grosso), *Ia-kuru-aib* (Kaiabi, Mato Grosso). See especially *Nystalus maculatus.*

COLLARED PUFFBIRD, *Bucco capensis,* Rapazinho-de-colar

17.5 cm. Upperparts brown, underparts whitish with large black pectoral band extending around hind neck. Bill orange.

Northern South America to mouth of Amazon and south to Rondônia.

WHITE-EARED PUFFBIRD, *Nystalus chacuru,* João-bobo, Dormião   PL 23.4

18 cm. Best-known species outside Amazon. Pure white puffy cheeks, conspicuous white collar separated by black area. Underparts lack any black design but are often soiled with earth. Bill red. Immature belly spotted dark brown; upperparts barred yellow; bill short, blackish. VOICE: a trisyllabic phrase, tremulous and descending, male and female responding to each other *tewrew tewrew tewrew* (February) with timbre of Small-billed Tinamou, *Crypturellus parvirostris,* often its neighbor in central Brazil; song a prolonged, descending sequence that fades out at end, *tewrew . . . ,* sung at all hours of day but most eloquently between sundown and nightfall when entire local population participates in singing; warning *rr-rr-rr.* Savannas with scattered trees, cerrado, cultivated fields (coffee groves, etc.), alongside railroads, perched on electric wires. Common in many places. Upper Rio Madeira (Amazonas), Maranhão, northeastern Brazil, and eastern Peru to Rio Grande do Sul (including Rio de Janeiro and ex-Guanabara), Paraguay, Bolivia, Argentina (Misiones). Apparently migratory in south. Also called *Macuru, Pedreiro, Sucuru, Tamatiá* (São Paulo), *Capitão-de-bigode, Fevereiro* (Minas Gerais), *Colhereiro.*

STRIOLATED PUFFBIRD, *Nystalus striolatus,* Rapazinho-estriado

18 cm. Similar to *N. maculatus* but with yellowish breast streaked black. Forest fringes. Eastern Pará (Belém), locally through western Amazonia to Mato Grosso (Rio Guaporé), Bolivia.

SPOT-BACKED PUFFBIRD, *Nystalus maculatus,* Rapazinho-dos-velhos

18 cm. Similar in size to *N. chacuru* and with red bill but without white on head. Lower throat and collar yellowish brown; breast and belly white spotted with black, like *Bucco tamatia.* VOICE: song an undulating phrase, *tewre-tewtewre-tewtewre.* Low, dry forest and caatinga, where common. Frequently in same region as *N. chacuru.* Cuiabá, Rio das Mortes, and Araguaia (Mato Grosso) to Maranhão, Pernambuco, Bahia, Minas Gerais, Paraguay, Argentina, Bolivia; also north of Amazon (Oriximiná, Pará). Also *Fura-barreira* (Pernambuco), *Macuru.* See *N. striolatus.*

CRESCENT-CHESTED PUFFBIRD, *Malacoptila striata,* João-barbudo   BR   PL 23.3

20.5 cm. Unmistakable southern species. "Comma" at base of bill may be shiny white; white of lower throat not always visible. VOICE: a high whistle that could well be that of a small tyrannid: *bieh, bieh, bieh . . . ,* a horizontal sequence of 10 or more notes. Silent most of year. Interior of dark forests with an abundance of fallen leaves; forest edges with grass. Southern Bahia to Minas Gerais, Santa Catarina (including ex-Guanabara); also Maranhão. Also called *João-doido.* See *Bucco capensis.*

In Amazonian Brazil *Malacoptila striata* is replaced by three related forms that lack the black breast band:

RUFOUS-NECKED PUFFBIRD, *Malacoptila rufa*

18 cm. Back uniformly brown; crown gray, streaked white; sides of head and nuchal collar ferruginous. Bill black with greenish base. VOICE: an ascending phrase, *eww, eww, eww-ew, ew.* Forest. Upper Amazon (Rios Ucayali and Juruá to upper reaches of Tapajós and Xingu (Mato Grosso), eastern Pará. Also called *Junurá* (Kaiabim, Mato Grosso).

WHITE-CHESTED PUFFBIRD, *Malacoptila fusca*
Orange bill. North of Amazon, including Amapá.

SEMICOLLARED PUFFBIRD, *Malacoptila semicincta*
Upper Purus to Bolivia, Peru.

LANCEOLATED MONKLET, *Micromonacha lanceolata,* Macuru-papa-mosca

12.5 cm. Dwarf of family. Bill heavy; upperparts reddish brown; forehead, lores, and underparts white, latter streaked black. Forest. Costa Rica to upper Amazon as far as Rio Ucayali and upper Juruá (Amazonas).

RUSTY-BREASTED NUNLET, *Nonnula rubecula,* Macuru   PL 23.6

14 cm. Widely distributed. Small, characterized by relatively slender, short bill and distinctive white pattern on face. Forest interior. Venezuela and Suriname to Rio Negro, Rio Juruá, Rio Tapajós, Amapá, northern Pará, Piauí, Goiás, eastern Brazil (Minas Gerais and Bahia to Paraná); also Paraguay, Argentina (Misiones).

Three other *Nonnula* are found in Amazonia:

GRAY-CHEEKED NUNLET, *Nonnula ruficapilla*

13.5 cm. Crown reddish; swollen eyelids red in adult, yellowish brown in immature. Usually silent. Could pass for a small tyrannid. Tall high forest, gallery forest. Panama to Rios Juruá (Amazonas) and Guaporé, upper Rio Paraguay, upper Rio Xingu (northern Mato Grosso).

FULVOUS-CHINNED NUNLET, *Nonnula sclateri*
Upper Juruá and upper Purus to west of Madeira.

CHESTNUT-HEADED NUNLET, *Nonnula amaurocephala*   BR
North of lower Solimões.

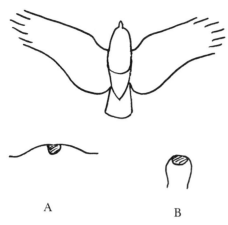

A   B

Fig. 181. Swallow-wing, *Chelidoptera tenebrosa,* typical views in flight. Wing position: (A) horizontal; (B) lowered. Original, H. Sick.

BLACK-FRONTED NUNBIRD, *Monasa nigrifrons,* Bico-de-brasa

27.5 cm. Largest Bucconidae, size of a large thrush. Uniformly dark gray with black flight and tail feathers, bill flesh-colored or brick red. Juvenal has brown forehead and chin, resembling *M. morphoeus.* VOICE: full and suave: call *kewuh;* a prolonged phrase of complex, melodious whistles, accelerated and rising at end, e.g., *hewluh . . . tewrr-tewrr,* uttered by a group of perched individuals of both sexes, sometimes on same branch, one close to the other, each moving its tail slowly in circles or with a rowing motion, or even just raising and lowering it. Various types of forest, also palm groves (e.g., babaçu); treetops. Colombia and Ecuador to Bolivia, northern Amazonas (Óbidos), eastern Pará, Piauí, central Brazil, Minas Gerais, western São Paulo. In certain areas, e.g., upper Rio Xingu, Mato Grosso, found alongside *morphoeus.* Also called *Tanguru-pará.*

WHITE-FRONTED NUNBIRD, *Monasa morphoeus,* Bico-de-brasa-de-testa-branca

27.5 cm. Similar to *M. nigrifrons* but with yellowish white mask covering forehead and chin. Ecology and distribution similar to *nigrifrons.* Honduras to Colombia, Rios Negro and Juruá, eastern Pará (Belém), Piauí, Bahia, Espírito Santo, Rio de Janeiro, Mato Grosso, Bolivia. Also called *Tanguru-pará, Biu-biwit* (Kamaiurá, Mato Grosso), *Bico-de-fogo, Bico-de-cravo* (Bahia), *Juiz-do-mato* (Amazonas), *Sauni* (Pará).

BLACK NUNBIRD, *Monasa atra,* Bico-de-lacre

27 cm. Black with red bill. Slight white design in upper wing coverts. Underside and bend of wing white. VOICE: a sequence of whistles, *trew-dewelewt, trrew-dewelewt . . . ,* sometimes 3 individuals together, giving effect of ringing a bell, a lament that lasts for minutes. Venezuela and the Guianas to north of Amazon from Rio Negro to Amapá. Also called *Tanguru-pará.*

YELLOW-BILLED NUNBIRD, *Monasa flavirostris*

20 cm. Similar to *M. atra* but smaller, bill yellow. Upper Amazon. Colombia and Peru to Rios Negro and Purus (Amazonas). Also called *Tanguru-pará.*

SWALLOW-WING, *Chelidoptera tenebrosa,* Urubuzinho, Andorinha-do-mato   Fig. 181

16 cm. Unusual in aspect and behavior. Black bill short, slender, curved. Plumage black to dark gray with white rump and under wing coverts, rusty yellow abdomen. Lower eyelids chalky white, contrasting with dark face. Wings disproportionately long and wide; in flight holds tips open like a vulture or *Buteo* hawk. Tail quite short. VOICE: varied: warning *tsi-tse-tse;* high, clear, repeated *DEE-didi* whistles resembling Spotted Sandpiper, *Actitis macularia,* represent song and are uttered either perched or in flight. Forest edge (e.g., small cultivated clearings) in tops of tall trees on bare branches from where it hunts insects while plunging in elegant curves (see "Behavior"). With ability to hold wing forward, it is capable of real acrobatics; swoops away over forest easily and conspicuously with slightly undulating flight. Often seen on boat trips through Amazonia, for it likes river-bank vegetation. On ground and on nest resembles a swallow (*Andorinha-do-chão,* "ground swallow"). During breeding perches on bushes and stakes. Northern South America to Bolivia, Mato Grosso, São Paulo. Also called *Andorinha-cavadeira* (Espírito Santo), *Miolinho, Taterá* (Amazonia), *Taperaí* (Kaiabi, Mato Grosso).

Bucconidae Bibliography
See also General Bibliography

Haverschmidt, F. 1950. *Condor* 52:74. [Behavior]
Skutch, A. F. 1948. *Wilson Bull.* 60:81–97. [Behavior]
Skutch, A. F. 1958. *Ibis* 100:209–31. [Behavior]

FAMILY CAPITONIDAE: BARBETS (4)

This is a Pantropical family of forest birds that are abundant in Africa and Asia but are represented by only a few species in the Neotropics, where they are concentrated primarily in the upper Amazon. There is a Tertiary (Miocene) fossil from Europe; a Capitonidae cited by Lund, found at Lagoa Santa (Minas Gerais), is presently believed to be a recent Bucconidae. The Capitonidae having been proven not to be monophyletic, its abandonment has been proposed, with transfer of all Capitonidae species to various Ramphastidae subfamilies. A Capitoninae subfamily, formed by the Neotropical *Capito* and *Eubucco* genera, is considered to be monophyletic with the Ramphastinae subfamily (Prum 1988).

Morphology

Barbets approach the puffbirds (Bucconidae) in aspect because of the large head and heavy bill surrounded by bristles. These bristles are relatively inconspicuous when compared with those of Old World species, which are responsible for the English name *barbets*. The [Brazilian] name *capitão-de-bigode*, "mustachioed captain," is more appropriate for the Bucconidae. The tongue is relatively long, and the legs are short with large, zygodactylous feet (see Galbulidae, "Morphology"). The plumage is brightly colored with scarlet, yellow, black, and white, sometimes reminiscent of toucans. The Lemon-throated Barbet, *Eubucco richardsoni*, is predominantly green. Sexes are different, as can already be seen in young about to fledge.

Vocalization

The loud, low, gruff voice (*roncador*, "roarer," is a popular name) causes one to expect a much larger bird, for it is audible 1 km away. The song is monotonous. In late afternoons during breeding season the male and female perch close together and utter prolonged phrases in a unisonal duet wherein the female's voice can be heard as the weaker. The singing of one pair stimulates others to sing. Vocalization is associated with certain forced positions and rhythmic movements typical for each species. The Scarlet-crowned Barbet, *Capito aurovirens*, for instance, grunts with the bill lowered almost vertically, although the body remains erect.

Feeding

Barbets feed on shoots and small fruits such as berries from various Melastomatacea and *Cecropia* fruits. They normally come down from the canopy to feed. They hold fruits with their toes to pound them, thus managing to tear even the largest ones into pieces. They come to orange and other kinds of orchards, soiling their throat plumage with juice. They catch small animals such as spiders and insects and hammer on wood and termite nests in search of arthropods.

Behavior

Capitonidae perch erectly with a stance similar to that of Bucconidae. They move around with long jumps, making a commotion in the foliage like aracaris. This similarity, as well as that of their exuberant coloring, is reflected in the name *tucanuí*, "small toucan," given them by the Kaiabi Indians.

Barbets are more active than Bucconidae, although they are equally trusting. Their flight is straight but they go only short distances. Wide rivers are insuperable obstacles (see "Distribution . . ."). When irritated they bob the tail. They like to sunbathe. They live in high, leafy, forest branches (unlike the African and Asiatic Capitonidae which occur in open country). From a distance they look like brightly colored fruits in the tops of the tallest trees. In this strata and within their area (e.g., upper Rio Juruá, Acre, and Rio Beni of Bolivia) they are among the dominant birds.

After the young fledge the family becomes gregarious, participating in flocks with tanagers, cotingas, and other fruit-eating birds. They also sleep together, sometimes using larger holes in which various individuals fit at the same time, like the aracaris.

Breeding and Parasites

Barbets burrow their nests into dead trees where the rotted wood makes the work easy, for their bills are not right for chiseling like woodpeckers, whose holes, like any other, they sometimes use. The pair takes turns preparing the hole. The uniformly white, shiny eggs are similar to those of Picidae and are laid on a mattress of "sawdust" produced by the birds in the bottom of the nest cavity. Incubation is only 13 days in a Central American species. Young hatch naked and blind with a large tarso-metatarsal callus. The parents keep the nest perfectly clean and sleep in it with the nestlings, whose growth is slow. I have found botfly larvae (*Philornis* sp.) on Black-girdled Barbets, *Capito dayi*.

Distribution and Evolution

The Pantropical distribution of the Capitonidae is as interesting as the similar distributional pattern of other families, such as the Trogonidae. Discovery of fossil representatives at 49° north latitude in Germany shows how global climatic conditions have changed and how tropical species were able to adapt as they found suitable living conditions in places far from those to which they are presently restricted (Prum 1988).

The scarcity of Capitonidae in Amazonia may be attributed to competition with toucans and woodpeckers, the former restricted to the Neotropics, the latter abundant on this continent. Whereas South America has only 12 Capitonidae, there are 41 in Africa, which has few Picidae. Note, however, that Capitonidae are more dependent on soft wood than are Picidae, so the efficiency of Picidae in excavation could even favor establishment of Capitonidae by providing them with more ready-made nesting holes. In this context, one recalls the Dendrocolaptidae and Furnariidae.

The Amazonian species occur in a series of populations of varying color that are separated by wide rivers. Some of these forms, formerly accepted as species, are now treated only as geographic races or, when there is no hybridization, as allospecies composing a superspecies (see Galbulidae, "Distribution . . . ").

Identification

Distinguishing the various forms requires specialized literature that records small details of color. There are two green-backed species: *Capito aurovirens* and *Eubucco richardsoni*, and two with black backs: *Capito dayi* and the Black-spotted Barbet, *C. niger*.

SCARLET-CROWNED BARBET, *Capito aurovirens*, Capitão-de-bigode-de-boné-vermelho

17.2 cm. Green-backed with scarlet (male) or whitish (female) crown, orange throat and breast, greenish abdomen. Base of bill may be yellow (male). VOICE: a loud *croo-croo-croo*. . . . Upper Amazon (Colombia, Peru) to Rio Negro and Tefé (Amazonas).

BLACK-GIRDLED BARBET, *Capito dayi*, Capitão-de-bigode-de-cinta   PL 44.3

17.2 cm. Back black with center white. Crown scarlet (male) or black (female), throat brownish, flanks black, under tail coverts scarlet like those of toucans, bill whitish. VOICE: a low *booboobo*. . . . South of Amazon from Rio Javari (Amazonas) to Tocantins (Pará), south to Rios Guaporé and Teles Pires (Mato Grosso); also Bolivia. Also called *Tucanuí* (Kaiabim, Mato Grosso).

BLACK-SPOTTED BARBET, *Capito niger*, Capitão-de-bigode-carijó   PL 23.7

17.5 cm. Back black, forehead and throat scarlet. On lower Rio Tapajós, *C. n. brunneipectus* has brown breast. VOICE: song harsh and slowly rhythmic, reminiscent of Blue-crowned Motmot, *Momotus momota;* call *trra-trra,* hard and low. The Guianas and Venezuela to Bolivia and from upper Amazon on left bank to Amapá and on right bank to Rio Tapajós (Pará). Relatively abundant on upper Juruá (Acre). Also called *Caboclo-velho, Roncador.* Includes *C. auratus.*

LEMON-THROATED BARBET, *Eubucco richardsoni*, Capitão-de-bigode-limão

15 cm. Smallest Brazilian species, with green back. Male crown, sides of head, and chin red; throat lemon yellow; breast reddish. Female has green crown, yellow superciliary, gray throat. Colombia and Peru to Rios Juruá and Madeira (Amazonas).

Capitonidae Bibliography

Miranda Ribeiro, A. 1929. *Bol. Mus. Nac. Rio de Janeiro* 4. [Morphology]

Prum, R. O. 1988. Phylogenetic interrelationships of the barbets (Capitonidae) based on morphology with comparison to DNA-DNA hybridization. *Zool. Jour. Linnaean Soc.* 92:313–43.

Ripley, S. D. 1945. *Auk* 62:542–63. [Morphology, relationships]

Sick, H. 1958. *Condor* 60:339. [*Capito dayi,* distribution]

Skutch, A. F. 1944. *Auk* 61:61–88. [Behavior]

FAMILY RAMPHASTIDAE: ARACARIS AND TOUCANS (21)

These arboreal birds are restricted to the Neotropics, being distributed from Mexico to Argentina. They are among the most picturesque and best-known features of American continental fauna and of the tropics in general. Old fossils have not been found up to the present, though there are remains of the Toco Toucan, *Ramphastos toco,* from the Pleistocene (20,000 years B.P.) of Lagoa Santa, Minas Gerais.

The Ramphastidae are related to ancestors of the Capitonidae and Picidae but not to the hornbills (Bucerotidae, Coraciiformes) of Africa and the Orient, which have equally unusual bills. A new phylogenetic analysis, based on morphological and paleontological characteristics and on DNA-DNA hybridization, has led Prum (1988) to include all the Capitonidae (including those of the Old World) in the Ramphastidae, distributing them in various subfamilies.

Morphology

These birds are exceptional because of their almost monstrous bills, the length of which may exceed that of the body (*R. toco* and the Red-billed Toucan, *R. tucanus*) and which, in spite of being hard and sharp enough to lacerate human skin, are light, porous, and translucent when seen against the light. Toucans are very sensitive to lesions on the bill caused, for example, by lead shot. The tomia are toothed and sharp.

Evolution of bill color has produced most surprising results, and changes in appearance of the bill have become more important than those of plumage. The existence of "teeth," in addition to colorful arabesques, makes it all the more conspicuous, with the ornamentation being characteristic in various species. Even the inside of the bill is brightly colored, contrasting with the outside. Thus, the Channel-billed Toucan, *R. vitellinus,* has a black bill whose inside is blood red, producing a shock effect when the bird opens its mandibles. The inside of the bill of *R. toco* is the same brilliant color as the outside, whereas the mouth is lead colored. In collected specimens the bright colors of the ramphotheca are lost or changed, so there is little information about this important feature, for most studies have been done in museums.

This unusual decoration of the ramphotheca apparently serves two purposes. It is a "signboard" with a brightly colored, frightening aspect to restrain attacks of other animals and frighten rivals. Its creates for its owner an appearance of strength beyond what in fact it has, being frightening to all who see it and especially to other birds, the creatures having the most contact with toucans. Thus, the anthropomorphic interpretation that it has a "terrifying set of teeth" may be valid to a certain degree. In fact, a toucan's peck can be a formidable weapon.

The second function of the bill could be that of attracting a mate, although the importance of color in interspecific recognition must not be so great since there is considerable hybridization between individuals with diversely colored bills (e.g., between *Ramphastos t. tucanus* and *R. t. cuvieri*). Identification appears to be primarily by voice. It is interesting to note that sixteenth-century naturalists, who received only the bills of toucans, concluded that they must be a peculiar adaptation of aquatic birds for fishing.

Immatures have shorter, differently proportioned bills that are less toothed, poorly colored, and soft. Nestlings of only a few days have a triangular-shaped bill due to the width of the base. In young *R. vitellinus* and Red-breasted Toucans, *R. dicolorus,* the top of the head is not differentiated from the culmen as in adults. In adults the nostrils become invisible in the base of the bill (*R. toco*). The long tongue is like a feather (*Pteroglossus* = "feather-tongue"). The region around the eye is bare and richly colored and becomes enlarged with ruffling of the head feathers, sometimes revealing a different color. In this way both sexes of the Curl-crested Aracari, *Pteroglossus beauharnaesii,* display a ruby red patch behind the bare area around the eye that normally stays hidden, unlike a second streak of bare red skin alongside the crown plumage. The Lettered Aracari, *P. inscriptus,* can enlarge the red triangle behind its eye. Eyelids and iris are also brightly colored, with iris and bare periophthalmic region colors sometimes varying according to geographic area (see *R. vitellinus*). In certain aracaris (Spot-billed Toucanet, *Selenidera maculirostris,* and Red-necked Aracari, *Pteroglossus bitorquatus*) the pupil gives the false impression of a horizontal slit instead of a "normal," round, centered pupil because of the presence of a dark streak through the iris. The iris color of nestlings is dark chestnut and then changes, 10 to 15 days after hatching, to a bright color, blue, for example, in *R. dicolorus,* even before they can fly (Oliveira 1985).

Plumage is showy, although it does not achieve the variety of the bill. The lower throat is often prominent and may vary within the same species from egg-yolk yellow to pure white, thereby distinguishing geographic races (*R. vitellinus*). The upper and/or under tail coverts are important features (see "Enemies, Utility . . . ").

The foot is zygodactyl, as in parrots and barbets. The uropygial gland is divided, as in woodpeckers. Sexes are similar, except in the Green Aracari, *Pteroglossus viridis,*

and the *Selenidera.* The adult male is usually heavier and frequently recognizable by having a longer and more colorful bill than the female. Cases may occur where the male bill is shorter (*R. toco*). Morphologically the Saffron Toucanet, *Baillonius bailloni,* and *Pteroglossus beauharnaesii* are very isolated species.

Aggressive Mimicry

A good example of aggressive or competitive mimicry is the unique phenomenon of the occurrence in the upper Amazon of two sympatric and syntopic toucan species, one the large *Ramphastos tucanus cuvieri,* the other the small *R. vitellinus culminatus,* both with white throats and yellow upper tail coverts. The smaller and weaker species, which elsewhere, as in southeastern Brazil, has a yellow throat and red upper tail coverts, in Amazonia imitates the larger species in order not to be expelled by it from the best fruit trees. The color change in the smaller bird is perfect in the sense of being effective from all viewing angles: front, above, or below. It is not important that the two species' vocalizations are completely different: the smaller one must remain quiet when it wants to eat, so as not to reveal its identity in the presence of the larger one in the same tree (see "Vocalization"). Thus, morphological mimicry demands a change in behavior for the illusion to be complete. The favorite fruit of toucans is that of the ucahuba (*Virola* sp., Myristicaceae); it has a red aril that could be considered a perfect food. Toucans are important disseminators of these plants (see "Feeding").

Character convergence in sympatric species has attracted the curiosity of scientists (e.g., Moynihan 1969, Cody 1969). Its causes can be various. The aggressive mimicry of toucans is a rare phenomenon studied in the 1970s by Paulini Filho and Vielliard (1983). The imitation of a vulture by the Zone-tailed Hawk, *Buteo albonotatus,* and the parasitism of cuckoos are other cases of aggressive mimicry.

Vocalization

A grunt, cry, or bark: the song of *Ramphastos tucanus* is one of the dominant voices of Amazonia, with long, complex phrases that appear cheery and melodious at a distance.

Toucans vocalize more in the morning, evening, and after rains. Several individuals of the same species will gather in the highest treetops, bowing, turning sideways, displaying the throat, rump, and brilliant bill, assuming the most extravagant postures, and mutually stimulating each other. Neighboring toucans synchronize their vocalizing, waiting, up to a point, for a colleague to finish before responding. When *R. tucanus* calls it throws its head up in a display that is showy even at a distance. *Selenidera* aracaris live hidden in the forest; their grunts resemble those of a toad. The rattle of *Ramphastos toco,* commonly assumed to be produced by clapping the mandibles together, is actually given with the bill open. Apparently there are differences in male and female vocalizations. Aracaris sometimes attempt to imitate the voices of other birds, as has best been analyzed for the Emerald Toucanet, *Aulacorhynchus prasinus,* in Mexico by H. O. Wagner (1944).

The voice is a sure way of recognizing that toucans as different as *Ramphastos vitellinus culminatus* and *R. v. ariel* belong to the same species, for they share the same voice. The same occurs with *R. t. tucanus* and *R. t. cuvieri,* whose bills can be very different in color (see "Distribution . . . "). Voice, so important in interspecific orientation, must be suppressed in cases where evolution of aggressive mimicry in plumage has not been accompanied by acoustic mimicry. Both developed in the parasitic Viduinae of Africa.

The late afternoon cries of toucans announcing the close of day give South American forests one of the most characteristic flavors of the Neotropical environment. Their absence is a certain indicator of rapacious human activity.

Feeding

Toucans are basically frugivorous and like the fruits of fig (*Ficus*), guava (*Psidium*), mandioqueira (*Didymopanax*), caruru-bravo (*Phytolacca*), and palms such as the palmito, açaí (*Euterpe*), bacobá (*Oenocarpus*), and many others. They come to coffee plantations and orchards to eat green fruits and may descend to the ground in orchards for fallen fruit (*Ramphastos toco* and *R. dicolorus*). Like the Black-fronted Piping-Guan, *Pipile jacutinga,* thrushes, and others, toucans enjoy the fruits of red pepper (*Capsicum fructescens*). I have found *Baillonius bailloni* and *Selenidera maculirostris* eating *Cecropia* fruits. Wild fruits dispersed by birds, such as those of the Laraceae, tall hardwoods of the primary forest, are an important resource that may be locally abundant (see also "Migration"). When dealing with small fruits, such as capororocas (*Rapanea* spp., Myrsinaceae), the *Selenidera* break the branch and work it over, tossing it up and moving it from one side of the bill to the other until they have removed all the fruits; then they let the branch fall. Breaking off a branch is reminiscent of certain psittacids, whose technique of using the foot is even more advanced. Toucans are among the great seed dispersers. They regurgitate pits and pellets with various seeds unharmed. Larger seeds with resistant coatings are said to germinate even after 200 to 300 hours in a bird's intestine.

Whereas aracaris are more vegetarian, toucans will take any small animal, beginning with spiders, crickets, and cicadas. *Ramphastos vitellinus* captures swarming termites by perching on an arboreal termite nest and catching insects from its surface or in full flight. They investigate anything that appears to be a bird's nest, including the balls of vegetable material forming kiskadee and becard nests; these heaps are torn apart and overturned without bothering to look for the entrance. Not even hanging nests of colonial icterines

such as the Yellow-rumped Cacique, *Cacicus cela,* escape; toucans (*Ramphastos tucanus cuvieri* and *R. toco*) and aracaris (Chestnut-eared Aracari, *Pteroglossus castanotis*) arrive at these colonies, sometimes in flocks, each species independently. They appear to divide the work, but there is no true group collaboration, each individual doing what it likes. While some perch openly on branches, displaying and calling as if wanting to intimidate the caciques, others fly directly to a nest, entering through the opening to take the eggs or nestlings. During these attacks a nest may fall from its branch, but the attackers do not go down to take the prey that has fallen with it. Apparently the presence of wasps, so often found in the midst of these icterine colonies, is not a deterrent. The icterines may flee and disappear silently into the understory before the predators alight near their nests. However, there is no lack of records of toucans being expelled by a frontal attack of wasps or cagafogo bees (*Trigona* sp.). See Icterinae, "Enemies." A tame toucan perched high on a terrace dived against House Sparrows, *Passer domesticus,* and doves feeding on the ground.

Toucans also investigate holes, such as those of woodpeckers, if the entrance is sufficiently wide. Hooded Siskin, *Carduelis magellanica,* nestlings installed high in the tops of araucarias (Santa Catarina) are easy prey for *Ramphastos dicolorus.* Toucans catch bats at their daytime roosts. Recently fledged young, recognizable by their short bills, are more avid for flesh and become a danger to any bird's nest. The long bill serves as a handy pincer, but there remains the problem of getting the food from the tip of the bill to the distant mouth: with a rapid to-and-fro head movement they toss small mouthfuls, even a tiny insect, directly into the esophagus. Larger prey is torn apart by holding it down with one or both feet. When swallowing food they hold the bill upward.

Behavior

Toucans and aracaris are very restless, never stopping as they hop through the trees on their strong legs and feet. They move the tail laterally or cock it vertically. In flight their appearance is made the more curious by the colossal bill stretching forward; after a few rapid beats the wings are held still against the flanks and altitude is lost. This produces an undulating trajectory that can be seen even when they beat the wings uninterruptedly. *Ramphastos toco* may follow a brief period of short wing beats with a more prolonged glide in a straight or almost straight horizontal course, during which the wings are held open. When a flock crosses an opening, it does so single file.

Both toucans and aracaris make a characteristic noise while flying that reveals their presence to an observer who, on the floor of the closed forest, cannot see them; these effects are obtained through outer remiges that have become modified for sound production. With the exception of *R. toco*

Fig. 182. Chestnut-eared Aracari, *Pteroglossus castanotis,* sleeping. The tail comes up automatically to cover the head. Original, H. Sick.

they avoid overflying extensive water bodies. Aracaris fly rapidly, even swiftly, for short distances, their tails forming a counterbalance for the enormous bill.

R. tucanus likes to bathe in foliage that has been wet by rain. A tame aracari, arriving at its "bathtub" (a jaboti, *Erisma calcaratum,* bark) sometimes would submerge only its bill and shake its head, thus taking an imaginary bath. It is a beautiful sight to see toucans drinking water from the cups of epiphytic bromeliads such as the *Vriesia,* which are abundant in the canopy of the fine forests of the southeast.

In the late afternoon toucans that live in flocks become restless and gather in groups that at sunset fly to certain spots where they sleep together. Perched on a branch and ready to sleep, they turn the head back and cover it with the raised tail (fig. 182), hiding the bill under the scapulars, a strange position apparently related to their habit of sleeping in cavities, but they assume the same position when sleeping on a branch. Lifting the tail is automatic; when they become sleepy all their muscles relax and the tail is pulled up over the back by dorsal tendons without the bird making the slightest effort. Simultaneously they double the legs, perching with the belly on the substrate, exactly like a chicken on its roost.

Apparently aracaris always spend the night in holes, sometimes several together, filling the cavity. Occasionally there are one or more individuals too many who have to seek other shelter. It is difficult to find out where toucans sleep if they are not caring for eggs or nestlings. I first learned from Indians in central Brazil that they use leafy treetops for nocturnal roosting, perching side by side in bodily contact. A sleepy, tame aracari looking for a good resting place shoved its bill into my clothing, showing its instinct for introducing its bill, the most sensitive part of its body, between its compa-

nions, and thus also avoiding mosquito bites on its bare face. I observed dream activity in this same individual: it made very slight movements similar to those induced by mosquito bites. On this occasion it sometimes sighed, so quietly that it could only be heard at very close range. Toucans "yawn" (see Columbidae, "Behavior").

Breeding

Pairs feed each other, bringing food, such as a handful of berries, in the esophagus. Standing in front of its mate, the bird doing the feeding rapidly expels its booty like a revolver shot into the half-opened bill of the receiver, who swallows the gift. It is generally accepted as true that only the male feeds the female, the usual rule with many birds. However, E. Béraut has observed in sexed individuals of *Pteroglossus beauharnaesii* that the female calls the male into the interior of the nest by offering food. Toucan pairs engage in mutual preening and meet in the incubation chamber where they strike bills in friendly fashion.

For nesting, ramphastids choose an already existing hole or slit situated high in a tree. *R. toco,* for example, uses hollow buriti palms, as do many psittacids (Rio das Mortes, Mato Grosso). In Minas Gerais it frequently nests in earth banks, and in the cerrados of Mato Grosso it uses terrestrial termite nests that have been opened by the Campo Flicker, *Colaptes campestris.* An *R. dicolorus* tore the honeycombs out of a wasp nest in a hole where it wanted to nest (Itatiaia, Rio de Janeiro, E. Gouvêa). Aracaris look for woodpecker holes and even fight with the owners.

The toucan bill is not useful for carpentry in hard wood, but sometimes the birds tear out chunks of rotten wood to enlarge a hole or its entrance. They cushion the bottom of the chamber with wood from the nest itself and do not carry in material. *Pteroglossus castanotis* occasionally uses an empty arboreal termite nest.

Ramphastids lay two to four small eggs that are elliptic and dull white but may turn chestnut with dirt that can be washed off (earth, in the case of *R. toco*). The weight of an *R. vitellinus ariel* egg reportedly is equivalent to only 5% of the female's weight. The birds are extremely cautious when they have eggs or nestlings, which hampers discovery of the nest. This explains why ramphastid eggs are so rare in oological collections. The incubation period of *R. vitellinus,* recorded by A. Ruschi for a captive, was 18 days, during which the female incubated alone but was fed by the male.

Young hatch bare and blind with a tarsal-metatarsal callus (fig. 183) composed of spiny scales on which they support themselves by placing the legs lateral to the body and lying on the belly with the head turned toward the back. These heel pads, characteristic of Piciformes, occur in a modified way in Alcedinidae, Psittacidae, and Apodidae (see the last, "Morphology").

Young are prognathous: the mandible is prominent (see

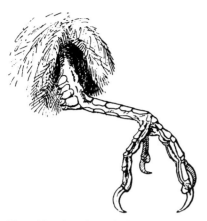

Fig. 183. Right foot of a just-fledged Toco Toucan, *Ramphastos toco*. The heel has scales that protect the tarsus when the bird lies on the uncushioned wood bottom of the nest. After Krieg 1948.

also other Piciformes and Coraciiformes). *R. toco* nestlings reveal their presence by their loud begging inside the nest hole when parents are absent. Both male and female feed the nestlings, offering many insects. Cleaning the cavity is difficult, for the excrement is semiliquid; regurgitated pits (palmito nuts, etc.) accumulate in the chamber. Finally the parents can empty the hole. Captive *R. vitellinus* young abandon the nest 25 to 30 days after hatching; they begin to feed themselves only 8 or 10 days later. A Keel-billed Toucan, *R. sulfuratus*, of Central America was still almost bare at three weeks and only left the nest at 47 days. The tarsal calluses fall off after departure from the nest.

Distribution and Evolution

Ramphastids were subject to ample speciation as a result of Pleistocene climatic changes. They evolved in a fragmented Hylaea whose parts became refuges for all forest fauna during this dry period. Later, accompanying a new expansion of the Amazonian forest in a more humid period, they again entered into contact, crossing freely, for they had not achieved reproductive isolation (e.g., *Ramphastos v. vitellinus,* and *R. v. culminatus*). Another evolutionary center became established outside the Amazon in southeastern Brazil, where *R. dicolorus* arose (fig. 184).

The process of geographic replacement of *R. t. tucanus* and *R. t. cuvieri* is similar to that of the various forms of *R. vitellinus. R. t. cuvieri,* from the upper Amazon, managed to advance farther east to the south of the Amazon, for there was no significant competition there. No more than two *Ramphastos* species live in any place, and in Amazonia there is always one large one, belonging to the superspecies *R. tucanus,* and another small one, belonging to the *R. dicolorus/ R. vitellinus* group. The local and periodic sympatry of *R. dicolorus* and *R. vitellinus ariel,* two species of similar

build, constitutes an exception; *R. dicolorus* is by preference a montane bird.

Proving the existence of broad zones of hybridization among the small forms of the *R. vitellinus* group, as well as among the large *R. t. cuvieri* and *R. t. tucanus,* studied in detail by J. Haffer (1974), has been of the utmost importance. One result of these surveys has been the elimination of species or subspecies such as *R. "theresae"* and *R. "osculans"* which were nothing more than hybrids from transition zones. *R. toco,* the only open-country ramphastid, which moves with greater facility and occurs over an immense area, has almost no phenotypic variation.

Aracari distribution conforms to a pattern similar to that of the toucans, although areas of crossing have not been found, with allopatric or parapatric distribution predominating (figs. 185 and 186). In *Selenidera,* ramphastids of limited movement, it is notable that evolution functioned primarily on bill color; all *Selenidera* can be considered allospecies composing a superspecies.

In Amazonia the lower courses of the Rios Negro, Madeira, Tapajós, and the Amazon itself, all of which are very wide, have the distinct effect of geographic barriers to the spread of members of this and other families, something that does not occur in the much more narrow upper courses of these rivers. Still, one must remember that downstream there are often numerous forested islands that could serve as support bases for crossing a wide river.

Voice is generally more constant than morphological characters such as bill color, plumage, etc., and can serve to

Fig. 184. Distribution of forms of Channel-billed Toucan, *Ramphastos vitellinus,* and Red-breasted Toucan, *Ramphastos dicolorus.* After J. Haffer 1974.

Fig. 185. Distribution of Black-necked Aracari superspecies, *Pteroglossus aracari*. After J. Haffer 1974.

test the degree of relationship, as is evident to those such as myself who orient themselves primarily by vocalization. Thus it can be noted that the voices of *Ramphastos vitellinus culminatus* and *R. v. ariel* are the same, this also being the case for *R. tucanus cuvieri* and *R. t. tucanus*. It remains to be

Fig. 186. Distribution of Spot-billed Toucanet superspecies, *Selenidera maculirostris*. After J. Haffer 1974.

pointed out that the *Dios-te-dé* vocalization characteristic of these latter birds is pronounced in the same way by their Central American replacement, the Chestnut-mandibled Toucan, *R. swainsonii*. The very similar voices of the *Selenidera* suggest a close relationship.

Haffer concluded that 85% of the ramphastids belong to superspecies or to geographic species, that is, forms descended from a common ancestor that exclude each other geographically. The superspecies concept better clarifies the degree of relationship (where a geographic race is not under consideration) and therefore is of great value in understanding zoogeography. The above-mentioned percentage is the highest so far calculated for a group of Neotropical birds. See also Galbulidae and Cracidae ("Distribution . . . ").

The aggressive mimicry of *R. v. culminatus* is a highly interesting evolutionary development.

Migration

After the breeding season ramphastids associate in monospecific flocks, wandering through the forest in search of their favorite fruits, at which time certain fruit trees may simultaneously hold a variety of species, such as *Ramphastos vitellinus*, *R. tucanus*, *Pteroglossus castanotis*, *P. inscriptus*, and *P. beauharnaesii*, in the upper Xingu, Mato Grosso. Such an encounter is caused only by the abundance of food and would not occur in other situations. Even a *Selenidera maculirostris*, a furtive species that usually lives alone, hidden in dense forest, may appear in a "good" fruit tree. Flocks of aracaris and toucans do not mix in flight.

Toucan invasions in certain years result in extraordinary concentrations that attract all the local residents for a large-scale, easy hunt (Amapá, eastern Pará). The birds are shot for food, with the bill saved as a souvenir. On one of these occasions one hunter easily killed 50 birds in one day (Porto Platon, Amapá). During one invasion observed in Amapá, *R. tucanus* came out of the forest headed north. When they reached the Rio Araguari, only those that left the southern shore flying high managed to cross; those that started out on a lower trajectory fell into the water. The same thing was observed on the Rio Oiapoque where, according to reports, such migrations are more frequent (B. S. Pascoli pers. comm.).

The same species invaded Belém, Pará, in June 1934 or 1936 together with smaller contingents of *R. toco*. The birds came from south-southeast of the city, starting slowly to increase until their numbers were considerable; they perched on street trees, roofs, fences, chicken houses, and utility poles, from where they invaded houses. This siege, in which 1000 or more toucans participated, lasted a fortnight with heavy losses for the invaders. Those that escaped with their lives headed for the north side of the city. By the end of the month there was no vestige of the migratory horde (E. K.

Silveira). On another occasion, around 1920, a large number of *R. vitellinus* appeared in the vicinity of Belém, "from the islands," in other words, from the north (R. Siqueira).

Invasions of *R. dicolorus* have also been recorded in southern Brazil during the southern winter, at the same time that flocks of thrushes head north (Santa Catarina, Paraná, June and July). The same thing happens in Misiones, Argentina, with *R. dicolorus, R. toco,* and to a lesser extent *Pteroglossus castanotis.* Anticipated cold or drought and a resulting scarcity of wild fruits sometimes leads to an invasion of these birds into plantations. At the end of winter, in August, most toucans disappear (Neunteufel pers. comm.).

In the Taió, Santa Catarina, region during the fruiting of pindaúba (*Xylopia* sp., Anonaceae), large movements of *R. dicolorus* regularly occurred in March–April in the 1930s. The birds always came from the same direction. Residents presumed the toucans made a great circle and that the same individuals appeared in the same place at certain intervals (C. Neideck pers. comm.) See also Cracidae, Black-fronted Piping-Guan, *Pipile jacutinga.*

Parasites

I have examined various ramphastids harboring nematodes under the nictitating membranes. Nestlings suffer from botflies. There are other blood-sucking flies, such as various species of louse fly, *Stilbometopa ramphastonis,* for instance, and *Ornithoica confluenta,* which lives on *Ramphastos vitellinus ariel.* A *Giardia tucani* was found in the intestine of the same species. Two malaria sporozoans, *Plasmodium pinotti* and *P. huffi,* have been described from aracaris.

Enemies, Utility, Decline, Conservation, and Folklore

Among the few enemies of ramphastids are monkeys and the Ornate Hawk-Eagle, *Spizaetus ornatus.* A Great Horned Owl, *Bubo virginianus,* captured a *Ramphastos vitellinus* that was probably sleeping on a branch and not in a hole.

They are persecuted by people because their flesh is tasty, they are valued as trophies, and their bills are used in popular medicine. *R. toco* nests, built in earth banks, are considered the property of the youngsters who discover them, who will later take and sell the nestlings. Indians used the magnificent toucan rump feathers in their adornments, as documented by Léry in 1557 (Léry 1961). The Brazilian monarchs Pedro I and Pedro II used a mantle, in the form of a poncho made of *R. vitellinus* breasts, as a gala robe. Yet another imperial mantle was made of Guianan Cock-of-the-Rock, *Rupicola rupicola,* feathers (see Chapter 2.4.).

In regions where they still exist in good numbers, ramphastids may damage orchards and gardens. Their visits to planted crops are more frequent when wild fruits become scarce.

Toucans and aracaris were formerly so abundant as to be sold in the markets of cities such as Rio de Janeiro. They have now disappeared from many places. They are frequently victims of their own curiosity, being easily attracted by their own whistles. This feature was described and illustrated by Bates (1863) when he had wounded a *Pteroglossus beauharnaesii* and quickly found himself surrounded by a dozen of these birds.

Conservation of toucans in small reserves is almost impossible because of their restless nature and their gregarious and migratory habits. When repopulation is contemplated, their need for large tree holes for nesting must be considered. Such holes are not abundant, even in virgin forests. Conservation of ramphastids is of real interest, for they are among the most distinctive features of Brazil's avifauna.

It is curious that the toucan has become ridiculous in Brazilian legend. The toucan, with his enormous bill, wanted to become king of winged creatures. He hid inside a tree trunk, letting only his large bill show. Seeing the size of his bill, the birds were disposed to accept him as king. However, when the toucan came out of the hole, the thrush cried "Hey, dumb guys, he's nothing but nose!" and the toucan was left demoralized.

Identification Data

1. Aracaris. There are three types:
    1.1. *Aulacorhynchus*
    1.2. *Pteroglossus* and *Baillonius*
    1.3. *Selenidera*

Whereas *Baillonius* is monospecific, there is a great deal of speciation in *Pteroglossus* and *Selenidera* that demands careful attention to bill and underpart coloration. *Pteroglossus* is frequently seen from below, making it easy to discern the three species that occur in the same area of Belém, Pará (*P. aracari, P. bitorquatus,* and *P. inscriptus*) and unnecessary to see the bill. All *Pteroglossus* and *Baillonius* have red upper tail coverts; the *Selenidera* have red under tail coverts. Along the Brazilian littoral, only *Pteroglossus aracari, Baillonius bailloni,* and *Selenidera maculirostris* occur. The *Aulacorhynchus* are green.

2. Toucans. I recognize four species for Brazil:
    2.1. Small: *Ramphastos vitellinus* and *R. dicolorus*
    2.2. Large: *R. tucanus* and *R. toco*

In eastern Brazil only *R. vitellinus ariel* and *R. dicolorus* occur. *R. toco* begins to appear in the interior. Brazilian Amazonia is dominated by *R. vitellinus* (with yellow or white breast) and *R. tucanus* (with black or red bill).

All the toucans have red under tail coverts. However, upper tail covert color varies and becomes important in diagnosis. The same is true for the color of the iris and of the bare region around the eye. In Amazonia two extensive areas of hybridization of both large and small forest toucans result in a mixture of characters that create confusion if one is unaware of the situation.

CHESTNUT-TIPPED TOUCANET, *Aulacorhynchus derbianus,* Tucaninho-verde

38.5 cm. One of a group of small Andean ramphastids little known in Brazil. Green with black bill, red at base and tip; throat whitish; tip of tail chestnut. Mountains along Venezuelan frontier (Serra Tapirapeco) and to Bolivia.

EMERALD TOUCANET, *Aulacorhynchus prasinus*

Found in Acre, July 1989, by B. Forrester. Venezuela, Colombia, and Ecuador to Peru.

CHESTNUT-EARED ARACARI, *Pteroglossus castanotis,* Araçari-castanho   PL 24.5

43 cm. Best-known and most common aracari of central and eastern Brazil. Cheeks, throat, and nape chestnut. Red band on belly broadened on sides. Multicolor bill with bright yellowish white "teeth" and yellow band around base of bill set off by red area. Basal part of maxilla extensively black, anterior part caramel. VOICE: a penetrating *PSEEa, psip, chuhrik.* Tall forest, often in canopy like most congeners and toucans. Colombia to Bolivia, Paraguay, south-central Brazil (Mato Grosso, Goiás, Minas Gerais, São Paulo, Paraná, Rio Grande do Sul), and Misiones, Argentina. A geographic replacement of *P. aracari,* which it meets in interior of Paraná, São Paulo, southern Goiás. See also *P. pluricinctus.* Also called *Tucani* (Kamaiurá, Mato Grosso).

BLACK-NECKED ARACARI, *Pteroglossus aracari,* Araçari-de-bico-branco   Fig. 187

43 cm. Replaces *P. castanotis* in eastern Brazil. Unmistakable with white maxilla, black culmen, black mandible, and lack of red at base of bill, which also lacks "teeth." Narrow reddish band on belly. VOICE: call a bisyllabic *biditz;* warning *spierrr.* Forest. In Espírito Santo found both in hot lowlands (Rio Doce) and mountains (Limoeiro, 1000 m). The Guianas and eastern Venezuela to northern Mato Grosso (Rios Teles Pires, Tapajós, and Suiá-missu; occasionally on Rio Xingu) and as far as eastern Pará and Maranhão. Also in

Fig. 187. Black-necked Aracari, *Pteroglossus aracari,* alert stance.

northeast, east, south (to Santa Catarina). Formerly common on coastal strip (Rio de Janeiro, etc.) where presently extinct in most areas. Found alongside *P. bitorquatus* and *P. inscriptus* in Belém, Pará, area; in Amapá sympatric with *P. viridis.* Also called *Camisa-de-meia, Culico* (Minas Gerais), *Tucano-de-cinta, Araçari-da-mata* (Rio de Janeiro), *Araçari-minhoca* (Rio de Janeiro). Can be considered a superspecies, together with *P. castanotis* and *P. pluricinctus.*

MANY-BANDED ARACARI, *Pteroglossus pluricinctus,* Araçari-de-dupla-cinta

43 cm. Similar to *P. aracari* but with 2 bands: narrow black one on breast and wide, reddish black one on belly. Upper Amazon from upper Rio Negro to Venezuela, Peru. Also southern Pará (Serra do Cachimbo, June 1956, specimen collected). Can be considered a geographic replacement of *aracari.* Locally sympatric with *P. castanotis.*

GREEN ARACARI, *Pteroglossus viridis,* Araçari-miudinho

33 cm. Smallest *Pteroglossus.* Underparts uniformly yellow, head black (male) or chestnut (female). Bill yellow, black, and red, without transverse design on mandible. Venezuela and the Guianas to Amapá. Geographic replacement of *P. inscriptus,* with which it forms a superspecies.

LETTERED ARACARI, *Pteroglossus inscriptus,* Araçari-miudinho-de-bico-riscado

33 cm. Very similar to *P. viridis,* from which it differs by having fine black design on bill. Only female has chestnut throat. VOICE: a loud *ta-RAT, ra-AHK, kehkehkeh,* recalling warning of a large kingfisher. Eastern Pará to Rios Madeira (Amazonas) and Guaporé (Mato Grosso) as far as Bolivia. Also Maranhão, Pernambuco (*P. i. inscriptus*). In upper Amazonas (west of Rio Madeira) represented by *P. i. humboldti,* which has black mandible.

RED-NECKED ARACARI, *Pteroglossus bitorquatus,* Araçari-de-pescoco-vermelho   BR

36 cm. Small with nape and breast crimson (weakly so in immature); maxilla yellowish green; mandible all black (Rio Madeira to northwestern Mato Grosso, *P. b. sturmii*) or white with black tip (Rio Tapajós to Rio Tocantins, *P. b. reichenowi,* and eastern Pará to northern Maranhão, *P. b. bitorquatus*). VOICE: *uhrit, uhrit,* very different from *P. aracari.* See *P. flavirostris,* which replaces it geographically in upper Amazon and with which it forms a superspecies.

IVORY-BILLED ARACARI, *Pteroglossus flavirostris,* Araçari-de-bico-de-marfim

36 cm. Similar to *P. bitorquatus* but with bill uniformly ivory, "teeth" outlined in black. Venezuela and upper Rio Negro to upper Rio Solimões, south of which it is replaced

(as far as Peru and Bolivia) by *P. f. mariae,* which has brown mandible.

CURL-CRESTED ARACARI, *Pteroglossus beauharnaesii,* Araçari-mulato   PL 24.6

42 cm. Unique in "lacquered," hardened, and curved head feathers ("frizzle-headed"). VOICE: loud and deep, quite unlike other aracaris, *rrep, reh-reh-reh;* a penetrating *ghe-ek ghe-ek.* . . . Upper Amazon to south of Rios Solimões and Madeira (Amazonas), upper Tapajós, and upper Xingu (Mato Grosso) to Bolivia, Peru. In upper Xingu lives alongside *P. castanotis* and *P. inscriptus* without associating with them or with toucans. A unique species that would have been better left in genus *Beauharnaisius.*

SPOT-BILLED TOUCANET, *Selenidera maculirostris,* Araçari-poca   PL 24.8

33 cm. Quite different in aspect, color, and behavior from the several foregoing species. Shows accentuated sexual dimorphism. VOICE: a sequence of low, deep, guttural croaks: territorial cry or song, of both sexes, *growwa* or *ehho,* which could pass for voice of a large toad; fighting, *gheh-eh.* Shady interior of forests, where easily overlooked, unlike aracaris. Bahia and Minas Gerais to Rio Grande do Sul and Misiones, Argentina. Also called *Araçari-tirador-de-leite* (Minas Gerais). In Amazonia replaced by closely related forms that are allospecies or even geographic races of same species. They are distinguished primarily by bill color:

GOULD'S TOUCANET, *Selenidera gouldii,*

Brown bill with white base, maxilla with large black spot, mandible with smaller one. Bare periophthalmic ring intense green, iris bluish green. VOICE: *growaak, growaak* . . . , similar to *S. maculirostris.* South of lower Amazon to northern Mato Grosso (upper Rio Xingu), Maranhão, Ceará. Also called *Tchu-ria-ha* (Juruna, Mato Grosso).

GUIANAN TOUCANET, *Selenidera culik,* Araçari-negro

Black bill with crimson base, shiny blue region around eye. Female has gray underparts. North of lower Amazon to lower Rio Negro, Venezuela. Also called *Araçari-negra.*

TAWNY-TUFTED TOUCANET, *Selenidera nattereri*

Chestnut bill, streaked black. North of lower and middle Solimões to the Guianas, Venezuela.

GREEN-BILLED TOUCANET, *Selenidera langsdorffii*

Bill almost all black with dull olive base. South of Solimões and in Rio Purus area.

GOLDEN-COLLARED TOUCANET, *Selenidera reinwardtii*

Replaces *S. langsdorffii* north of Solimões. Reddish on base of bill. The two are probably conspecific.

SAFFRON TOUCANET, *Baillonius bailloni,* Araçari-banana   PL 24.7

35 cm. Unique species of eastern Brazil, unmistakable with extensive yellowish coloring. Related to *Pteroglossus* by morphology and behavior. VOICE: *pre-tet, psett psett* . . . , sometimes accelerated; in flight *spitz-spitz; tseh-tseh-tseh;* melodious whistles, *gooee-gooee-gooee,* like those of a *Celeus* woodpecker. Vocalizations are unlike those of other aracaris. Mountainous regions, e.g., Limoeiro (Espírito Santo), Itatiaia, Serra dos Órgãos (Rio de Janeiro). Espírito Santo and Minas Gerais (Viçosa) to Rio Grande do Sul, Argentina (Misiones), eastern Paraguay; also Pernambuco (Serra Negra). Introduced into ex-Guanabara, Rio de Janeiro.

CHANNEL-BILLED TOUCAN, *Ramphastos vitellinus,* Tucano-de-bico-preto

46 cm. A group of small forms with yellow or white throats according to region. They justify inclusion in a single species on basis of voice and bill shape. Culmen clearly compressed and not arched or rounded as in other toucans such as the large *R. tucanus cuvieri,* which is very similar in plumage to *R. v. culminatus;* this character is visible at a distance in live bird if one pays attention. VOICE: *iaaar, iewwr,* very low, almost bisyllabic, unlike *R. dicolorus.* Also called *Tucano-gritador, Reu-reu.* Four geographic races have been described:

1. *R. v. ariel* (Pl 24.3). Throat orange-yellow; periophthalmic region blue (Amazonian population) or crimson (eastern Brazil population). Yellow band at base of bill; culmen black with blue base. Pará south of Amazon to mouth of Rio Madeira (Amazonas), Maranhão; also the northeast (locally in Pernambuco and Alagoas) to southeast (Santa Catarina). On Island of Santa Catarina sometimes alongside *R. dicolorus* (Lenir R. Bege pers. comm.) For more on distribution, see below.

2. *R. v. vitellinus.* Throat yellow, broadly bordered with white, giving impression, when seen from side, that throat is white. Periophthalmic region, band around base of bill, and base of culmen blue. North of lower Amazon (Amapá) to Rios Negro and Branco and eastern Venezuela. Also called *Tucano-pacova* (*pacova* = "banana").

3. *R. v. culminatus.* Throat white, sometimes washed with citrine (immature). Looks like a small replica of *R. tucanus cuvieri* except for bill shape. Periophthalmic region blue, bill black with base of maxilla and culmen greenish yellow, base of mandible bluish. Upper tail coverts yellow, not red as in *R. v. ariel* and *R. v. vitellinus.* Western Venezuela to upper Amazon, Bolivia, northwest and central Brazil. Also called *Tucano-pequeno-de-papo-branco.* See also "Aggressive Mimicry."

4. *R. v. pintoi.* Can be thought of as a hybrid population between *R. v. culminatus* and *R. v. ariel.* Small with white or slightly yellowish throat. Upper tail coverts and bases of maxilla and mandible yellow. Base of culmen blue. Central

Brazil (Goiânia, Goiás to central Mato Grosso). Also called *Canjo* (Meinaco, Mato Grosso).

In areas of contact, different forms of *R. vitellinus* produce hybrid populations that show intergradation in color of breast, rump, bill, and periophthalmic skin. There are 2 large areas of hybridization of *R. v. culminatus* with its eastern counterparts, one north and one south of Amazon. In Rios Branco and Negro regions this form passes gradually into that of *R. v. vitellinus*, and between Rio Madeira and northern Goiás *R. v. pintoi* does the same with *R. v. ariel*.

In Amazonia *R. v. culminatus* lives alongside *R. tucanus cuvieri*, even perching in same tree, from which it is expelled by larger "twin." Such competition is not very serious, however, and both species get along well in same forests. See "Aggressive Mimicry." *R. v. ariel* found in mountainous regions of Espírito Santo, on southern slopes of Serra da Mantiqueira (Itatiaia, 600 m; Rio de Janeiro), and on São Paulo and Paraná littoral, occasionally with *R. dicolorus,* this one being typical species of planalto. The two may feed in the same palmito. In Rio de Janeiro *R. v. ariel* is a resident of lowlands, being replaced in Serra dos Órgãos above 600 m by *R. dicolorus*.

RED-BREASTED TOUCAN, *Ramphastos dicolorus,* Tucano-de-bico-verde   PL 24.2

48 cm. Southern species, somewhat larger than *R. vitellinus,* with yellow throat and green bill somewhat different in shape from *vitellinus,* for although compressed, shorter, and higher, it looks more compact. Maxillar "teeth" well developed and highlighted by blood red. Unlike *R. vitellinus ariel,* throat broadly bordered with light yellow; no light band at base of bill as in *vitellinus*. VOICE: similar to *vitellinus* but more nasal and dry, *ek, rret, rrayt*. This toucan gets farthest south, along with *R. toco*. Espírito Santo, Minas Gerais (Serra do Caraça), and Goiás to Rio Grande do Sul, Paraguay, northern Argentina. In Rio de Janeiro typical of mountainous areas (e.g., Serra dos Órgãos and Itatiaia). On São Paulo littoral sympatric with *R. vitellinus ariel,* at least periodically and partially. On upper Rio Paraná meets *R. v. pintoi* but does not interbreed. In Santa Catarina rare hybrids between *dicolorus* and *vitellinus* have been mentioned. Has been proposed to combine *R. vitellinus* and this species into a superspecies. Name has been erroneously written as *R. "discolorus."*

RED-BILLED TOUCAN, *Ramphastos tucanus,* Tucano-grande-de-papo-branco   PL 24.1

55 cm; about 600 g. Only large forest species of Brazilian Amazonia. Bill enormous with smoothly arched culmen (unlike *R. vitellinus*). Has evolved into 2 races:

1. *R. t. tucanus*. Sides of maxilla crimson, upper tail coverts citrine yellow. Lower Orinoco (Venezuela) and the Guianas to lower Rio Negro, Manaus (Amazonas), Amapá, Marajó (forested part, see *R. toco*), eastern Pará, Maranhão. Also called *Pia-pouco, Quirina*. Also called *R. monilis*.

2. *R. t. cuvieri*. Sides of maxilla black; upper tail coverts orange. Upper Orinoco and upper Amazon (Rios Negro, Solimões, Madeira) to northern Mato Grosso (Rio Guaporé and upper Rio Xingu) and southern Pará. Also called *Johät"* (Kamaiurá, Mato Grosso), *Jo-kuá-kuá* (Iaulapiti, Mato Grosso).

The 2 races meet north and south of Amazon, forming in each case an extensive area of hybridization. Hybrids can be distinguished by mixed color of bill (sides of maxilla between black and red) and by citrine yellow or orange rump. In same forests as *R. vitellinus culminatus*.

VOICE: identical in the 2 races, giving rise to various onomatopoeic names, *pia-pouco* (Amazonas), *cachorro,* and *Dios-te-dé* (Colombia, Venezuela). Best way to express voice would be with a well-articulated sequence of various syllables, *iOK-pet-pet (pet) . . . , rro-het rro-het iew-het iew-het het iew-het,* sounding melodious at a distance; can also resemble barking of a dog pursuing game. It is the "singing toucan," unlike *vitellinus*. Also has a very different vocalization: *rrroEEeh gwa, gwa, gwa . . . ,* which at a distance sounds only like an *EE-ehh* that resembles *vitellinus*. One of the most loquacious Amazonian birds.

TOCO TOUCAN, *Ramphastos toco,* Tucanuçu   PL 24.4

56 cm; about 540 g. Largest toucan, unmistakable with unusual orange bill, of various shades, with large, black, oval spot at tip of maxilla; this mark shines unbelievably when seen with light on it. Periophthalmic bare skin orange or sulfur yellow, eyelids blue. Throat white, frequently tinged with citrine yellow and edged with red, but varying, even in a molting individual. Rump white, crissum red as in other toucans. Young have short yellow bill lacking black spot, skin around eyes whitish, throat yellow. VOICE: a low, deep snore, *rrrraa, rrro-rrro,* lower and less resonant than cry of *R. vitellinus* or *R. dicolorus;* a toad in Minas Gerais makes exactly the same *rrrraa* as a distant *R. toco; rrret;* a murmuring, vocal *te, te, te . . .* (see "Vocalization"). Gallery forests, cerrado, groves; the only Brazilian ramphastid that does not live exclusively in forests. Frequently overflies open country and wide rivers. Likes to perch on tall trees. Less sociable than other toucans. Widely distributed in savanna regions of interior, from Amazonia (e.g., Amazon mouth and formerly Manaus) to Paraguay, Bolivia, Argentina. Does not reach eastern Brazil littoral. Moves from one savanna area to another, taking advantage of deforested areas. Appears around airports, along recently opened roads in Hylaea. Also from Amapá littoral to the Guianas, middle Rio Branco. Also called *Tucano-boi* (Rio Grande do Sul).

Ramphastidae Bibliography
See also General Bibliography

Carini, A. 1943. *Arq. Biol. S. Paulo* 27(253):14–16. [Parasites, giardia]

Carvalho, J.C.M. 1953. *Publ. Avul. Mus. Nac. Rio de Janeiro* no. 10. [Utility]

Gould, J. 1854. *Monograph of the Ramphastidae.* London.

Haffer, J. 1974. *Publ. Nuttall Orn. Club* 14:179–312. [Speciation]

Höfling, E., and J. P. Gasc. 1982. *An. Acad. Bras. Ciênc.* 54(4):755–56. [Analysis of toucan bill movements]

Lange, R. B. 1967. *Araucária* 1:1–3. [Behavior]

Novaes, F. C. 1949. *Rev. Bras. Biol.* 9:285–96. [Systematics]

Oliveira, R. G. de. 1985. Mudança na cor da iris em *Ramphastos dicolorus. Sulornis* 6:18–21.

Paulini Filho, H. F., and J.M.E. Vielliard. 1983. Primeiro caso da biologia de aves reportando um fenómeno de mimetismo descoberto entre dois dos dispersores ultra especializados de Myristicaceae. *V Encontro Regional de Química, Araraquara.*

Pineschi, R. B. 1989, in preparation. Myrsinaceae do Itatiaia e sua utilização pela avifauna.

Sick, H. 1979. *Bull. B.O.C.* 99(4):115–20. [*Baillonius bailloni,* distribution]

Van Tyne, J. 1955. *11th Cong. Int. Orn., Basel:* 362–68. [Evolution]

Wagner, H. O. 1944. Notes on the life-history of the Emerald Toucanet. *Wilson Bull.* 56(2):65–76.

FAMILY PICIDAE: WOODPECKERS (46)

The woodpeckers are nearly cosmopolitan in distribution, being absent only from Australia, New Guinea, New Zealand, Madagascar, and Antarctica, with the Neotropics the region richest in species. There is a close relationship between American and Old World woodpeckers, especially those of South America and Africa. Fossils from the upper Tertiary (Pliocene) have been found in North America, and recent species have been found in the Pleistocene deposits (20,000 years B.P.) of Lagoa Santa (Minas Gerais).

The most closely related family is the Capitonidae, with which the Picumninae show more similarity in their molt than they do with the Picinae (Stresemann and Stresemann 1966). Piciformes are usually considered to be the non-Passerines most closely related to Passeriformes.

Morphology and Special Adaptations

Brazilian species vary in weight from 10 g to 200 g. All are immediately recognizable by their strong, straight, chisel-shaped bills which they use to hammer with such force that the brain requires protection against excessive shock. This is provided by adaptations of the skull and musculature (protractor pterygoidei). The neck musculature is very strong, and there are special adaptations of the vertebrae. Mobility of the maxilla, another important anatomic feature of the Picidae, is reduced in those species that hammer most vigorously. The sharp bill also serves as a pincer. The bill of the male is frequently larger, indicating different feeding (see "Behavior").

The wormlike tongue is extremely long, sometimes five times longer than the bill (fig. 188). The retracted hyoid muscles arise from underneath the skin of the nape, curve forward, and end in the forehead or even penetrate into the base of the maxilla (e.g., in *Colaptes*) (fig. 189). Similar conditions occur in hummingbirds. In *Picumnus* the hyoids may be coiled in the orbital cavity. Short hyoids are considered to be a primitive character, but there could have been secondary reductions. The tip of the tongue has special adaptations (see "Feeding").

Another adaptation is the development of the mandibular gland (glandula picorum), which is larger in those species, such as *Colaptes,* that feed on ants and termites. The abundant secretion acts as a sticky glue that gives the tongue the holding capacity of a limed branch.

The legs are short, the feet zygodactyl (fig. 190), unlike those of the Dendrocolaptidae (Passeriformes), which also creep (see Dendrocolaptidae, "Morphology"). The outer rear toe can be moved laterally to grasp round trunks. The slen-

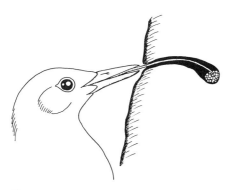

Fig. 188. Woodpecker sticking tongue into a slit to take out insect eggs. There are woodpeckers whose tongue is five times longer than the bill.

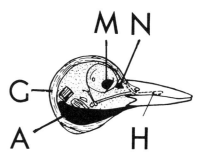

Fig. 189. Tongue glands and supports of the Green-barred Woodpecker, *Colaptes melanochloros:* (A) mandibular gland; (M) maxillary gland; (N) nasal gland; (G) geniohyoid; (H) "horn" of the hyoid. After W. R. Goodge 1972.

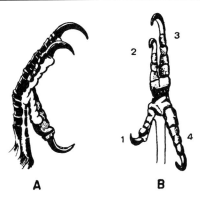

Fig. 190. Zygodactyl foot of Green-barred Woodpecker, *Colaptes melanochloros:* (A) left foot; (B) seen from below. After Böker 1937.

derest trees are even "hugged." Species that dig into the wood most vigorously need stronger feet to hold on but have correspondingly reduced climbing capacity. Stability is increased by the tendency to rest the tarsus on the bark (e.g., *Campephilus*). The piculets, *Picumnus*, are among the most energetic hammerers and have relatively gigantic feet.

Except in *Picumnus* the tail is transformed into a support for use on vertical substrates, thanks to its very rigid rachises, which are longitudinally grooved, apparently to increase their strength. The black color of these feathers is caused by melanin, which gives greater resistance to the structure (this is usual among birds). Use of the tail to support the body is different than in dendrocolaptids and is reflected in the skeleton (pygostyle). To climb a tree trunk, woodpeckers "jump" upward with feet together, "sitting" on the tail at each stop. *Veniliornis* descend a vertical trunk backward, sometimes for quite a distance, in the manner of dendrocolaptids. The piculets, with soft tails, more often frequent the tips of branches, recalling certain furnariids. However, they also perch on branches and thin vertical trunks, using the tail as little as when hanging under a branch or going down a trunk head first, possible only because of the exceptionally strong feet. I draw attention to the very different structure between the tails of woodpeckers and woodcreepers (see Dendrocolaptidae, "Morphology"). Sexes are similar, but the male is distinguished by a malar stripe (e.g., in *Celeus, Dryocopus*) or red spot on the crown or nape (as in *Veniliornis*). There are other types of dimorphism, as in the White Woodpecker, *Melanerpes candidus,* and Checkered Woodpecker, *Picoides mixtus.* Typical male coloring shows in the plumage of nestlings (e.g., head reddish yellow in Yellow-fronted Woodpecker, *Melanerpes flavifrons*). It is confusing that young females may have more red than in adult plumage, as in *Veniliornis* and *Melanerpes:* the female Yellow-tufted Woodpecker, *M. cruentatus,* has a reddish nuchal spot that is lost in adulthood. Young males may also present this "inversion" relating to the presence of red, as in the Crimson-crested Woodpecker, *Campephilus melanoleucos,* in which young males appear older and more colorful that adult males. This sort of chang-

ing immature plumage pattern is a feature of many Picinae but is lacking in the Picumninae. Young Picumninae can be told from adults by the color of the crown (all black or streaked, without red), a pattern linked to behavior.

Many mutations or morphs have originally been described as species, such as *Dryocopus erythrops* (= Lineated Woodpecker, *D. lineatus*) and *Melanerpes rubrifrons* (= *M. cruentatus*).

Woodpeckers give off a typically strong, resinous odor that is more intense in certain species (e.g., Blond-crested Woodpecker, *Celeus flavescens,* and Chestnut Woodpecker, *C. elegans jumana*). I do not believe this odor has any connection with their food, as has been suggested by others. It is a smell from the plumage, perhaps arising from greases of the uropygial gland or from the feathers themselves. The phenomenon has been studied in Asiatic woodpeckers (Bock and Short 1971). Re odor in other birds, see Caprimulgidae and Trogonidae ("Morphology").

Vocalization and Drumming

All have a territorial "song" and various calls. When an individual's territorial song is played on a loudspeaker, the respective bird is immediately attentive and comes to it. These vocalizations are complemented by "instrumental music," drumming, which must not be confused with drilling. The latter is the process of seeking food or of building a nesting cavity, whereas the former is performed on dead trees, loose bark, hollow trunks, and even sheet metal with the exclusive purpose of producing noise in defense of territory. The substrate is chosen to provide good amplification of the fullness and reach of the noise, which may exceed that of the voice. This results from the blows of the bird against the substrate, not from vibration of the latter, as is sometimes claimed. A woodpecker has been seen drumming on a glass insulator on a telephone pole. The timbre varies according to the substrate used. Thus the Mottled Piculet, *Picumnus nebulosus,* produces a very loud drumming when it hammers bamboo, the noise resembling the song of the horned frog (*Stombus*), an unusual terrestrial amphibian. In Bahia I heard some arboreal batrachians that have voices very similar to woodpecker drumming, which has a characteristic rhythm for each species and genus. Drumming involves 30 to 40 or even more blows per second and differs with individuals.

The large *Campephilus* (= *Phloeoceastes*) such as the Red-necked Woodpecker, *C. rubricollis,* and Robust Woodpecker, *C. robustus,* do a bisyllabic drumming that may sound like a voice. *Dryocopus lineatus* produces a monotonous, prolonged sound; this latter type of drumming, produced by various woodpeckers, may sound almost identical to our ears when originating with related species, but the differences are usually revealed in a sonagram. In the case of *Campephilus melanoleucos* I have noted not only a bisyllabic but a monotone drumming. *Celeus flavescens* drums weakly.

This instrumental music, like song, serves to mark territory, warn rivals, and as a means of communication between male and female. There are true duets, sometimes with one of the pair drumming from the nesting cavity. Drumming may to some extent replace song, being, like it, linked to the breeding cycle and performed only periodically.

Feeding

Woodpeckers are attracted to trees parasitized by a wide variety of insects and their larvae; frequently these are scale insects, Homoptera, that are very injurious to the plants. Woodpeckers locate insect larvae, such as those of beetles that are invisible in the wood, by the noise these small creatures make while gnawing. A White-spotted Woodpecker, *Veniliornis spilogaster,* hits lightly on the bark trying to find cavities under it that are revealed by a hollow sound. When it finds a promising spot, it starts to hammer vigorously, perforating the bark to exploit the cavity with its sticky tongue, whose sharp tip, provided with tactile corpuscles, spears the prey (fig. 191). Woodpeckers reveal their presence by the noise they make working throughout the day.

See "Breeding" on the importance of older or dead trees for woodpeckers. Food such as beetle larvae, etc., is furnished for certain woodpeckers by stumps, branches, and fallen logs, all of which are removed in cultivated forests. The *Picumnus* are fond of ant larvae and pupae.

I have taken 2094 ants from the crop of a Campo Flicker, *Colaptes campestris,* and 1489 termites from that of a *Celeus flavescens.* Ants and their eggs and larvae constitute the favorite food of many Brazilian woodpeckers. *Dryocopus lineatus* does not even fear the biting ants (*Azteca*) that live in cecropia. I found many stinging termite soldier heads in the feathers around the bill of a *Colaptes campestris,* which regularly opens large terrestrial termite mounds. Its work is

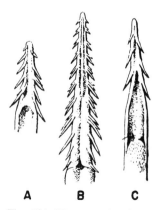

Fig. 191. Three woodpecker tongue tips covered with sharp barbs: (A) Blond-crested Woodpecker, *Celeus flavescens intercedens;* (B) Red-necked Woodpecker, *Campephilus rubricollis trachelopyrus;* and (C) Green-barred Woodpecker, *Colaptes melanochloros nattereri.* After Steinbacher 1955.

facilitated when it returns to an already raided termite nest that has been repaired with still fresh earth. *Melanerpes candidus* opens wild bee nests (see "Use of Nests . . ."), even breaking into large wasp nests to take the meaty larvae and honey. Sometimes it takes an insect in flight. Occasionally certain species, the Red-stained Woodpecker, *Veniliornis affinis,* for instance, accompany army-ant columns to catch the arthropods they scare up.

I have verified that the Field Flicker, *Colaptes campestris campestroides,* at times breaks into nests of the Rufous Hornero, *Furnarius rufus.* I have not yet been able to determine if this is to take out and eat the young. If this were to occur, we would have a parallel with a European species, the Great Spotted Woodpecker, *Dendrocopos major.* This predatory attitude would explain the fear that woodpeckers sometimes instill in other birds. I have noted, for instance, that the presence of a *Colaptes* irritates certain birds such as the Saffron Finch, *Sicalis flaveola;* Sayaca Tanager, *Thraupis sayaca;* and Yellow-bellied Elaenia, *Elaenia flavogaster.*

Not a few tropical species, such as *Celeus flavescens, Campephilus melanoleucos, Melanerpes flavifrons, M. candidus,* and *Veniliornis affinis,* like fruits such as papaya, persimmon, banana, and orange, as well as seeds and small cecropia fruits. In Espírito Santo I observed that berries of pokeweed (*Phytolacca decandra*), a 1.5-m bush, were favorites of three Picidae: *Campephilus robustus, Melanerpes flavifrons,* and the Green-barred Woodpecker, *Colaptes melanochloros.* The long, mobile tongue is quite effective in licking up juice of soft fruits. A certain periodic change in diet can be noted, with fruit consumption greater in winter when insects are scarcer. Fritz Müller (1878) hypothesized that "woodpeckers" searching for nectar and insects pollinate the flowers of certain Bombacaceae (*Carolinea*). Woodpeckers living in cold climates store seed for later use, an activity observed by C. Yamashita in the interior of São Paulo among a flock of *M. flavifrons,* probably a trait inherited from ancestors living in cold climates (see Corvidae, "Feeding . . ."). *Colaptes campestris* occasionally makes holes in isolated adobe houses in the country; possibly the whitewashed earth has a flavor it likes. In Argentina this species perforated the tile wall of a shed, leaving ten holes 5 to 7 cm in diameter; it is believed the bird was attracted by insects (Achenbach pers. comm.). In Brazil I saw where a *C. campestris* hammered the wall of an abandoned building but did not make a significant hole.

The various species occurring in the same area usually differ in size, adaptation to one strata or another, and technique of approaching food, by creeping up trees or hopping on the ground. They also have different ways of obtaining it; chiseling, excavating, probing, or catching insects on the surface of the substrate. The size of the bill and tongue contributes to this feeding specialization. Behavior merely reflects anatomy. Various species exploit ecological niches very close to one another, but there is little competition. The

Dendrocolaptidae and Capitonidae may be woodpecker competitors. The piculets, *Picumnus,* forage especially on the tip of branches, twigs, and slender vines, usually dead ones, in search of arthropods (ants), an open ecological niche when not used by *Xenops* species (Furnariidae); they hammer constantly like large woodpeckers.

To prevent woodpecker damage to utility poles in the United States, the wood is sprayed with a nonpoisonous repellent.

The rectangular cuts frequently found on bamboos of eastern Brazil, such as in the Serra do Mar near Rio de Janeiro, are not the work of woodpeckers but probably of rodents—but which? The bamboo rat (*Kannabateomys amblyonyx*) eats bamboo shoots. Beetles (Curculionidae, J. Becker pers. comm.) cannot be discarded as a possibility. See also Dendrocolaptidae, "Food . . . ," and fig. 218.

There is another interesting tree-lesion phenomenon found in various parts of Brazil that is not the work of woodpeckers, as might be supposed when recalling the sapsuckers (*Sphyrapicus* spp.) of the Northern Hemisphere. These lesions are made by marmosets (*Callithrix* spp.). With their lower front teeth these small simians perforate certain trees, such as paudoce (*Vochysia rufa*), in search of their copious latex (Coimbra Filho 1972).

Behavior

Forest woodpeckers live alone except for *Melanerpes candidus, M. cruentatus,* and *M. flavifrons.* They, along with *Colaptes campestris,* live in groups.

Most of our woodpeckers are strictly arboreal, chiseling tirelessly. They seek out different strata in the forest, at medium levels or up in the tops, and certain parasitized trees, trunks, or branches, the sexes perhaps feeding separately because of different adaptations such as bill length (see "Morphology . . . ").

The *Picumnus* are the least specialized, although they are very efficient in most aspects of arboreal life. Their ability to advance head down is similar to that of Northern Hemisphere nuthatches (*Sitta* spp.), but their temperament is totally different: they are very active and move rapidly like other woodpeckers, though their flight is direct and not undulating. They perch vertically on horizontal branches like any Passerine. The restriction of various *Picumnus* species to certain limited ranges must indicate specific ecological requirements that are still unknown.

The former *Chrysoptilus,* now included in *Colaptes,* regularly descend to the ground. *Colaptes melanochloros* hops through the branches horizontally like a jay (a strange means of locomotion for a woodpecker, except for *Colaptes campestris* and the *Picumnus*). *C. campestris* has become truly terrestrial, but when it wants to escape it still heads for trees, posts, or large stones. In this adaptation to terrestrial life there are interesting parallels to the Dendrocolaptidae; the

adaptation of *C. campestris* to hopping and walking on the ground is similar to that of the most terrestrial dendrocolaptid, the Scimitar-billed Woodcreeper, *Drymornis bridgesii,* sometimes its neighbor in Rio Grande do Sul.

Woodpeckers, especially those that have contact with earth and grass, soil their plumage. Arboreal species such as *Dryocopus lineatus* have the same problem with resin (see also ". . . Fungi"). They scratch themselves by hanging onto a vertical trunk with one foot. *C. campestris* takes dust baths.

The flight of Picidae follows an undulating course. They alternate a series of rapid wing beats with folding the wings, gaining and losing altitude respectively in the process. They always sleep in holes, where they also protect themselves from heavy rain. Most construct cavities just for sleeping. They retire early to sleep, but that doesn't stop a *Dryocopus lineatus* from feeding and only after sundown seeking a perch by flying from the cerrado to a nearby grove (Goiás). Some *Melanerpes flavifrons* and *M. cruentatus* assemble to sleep in the same shelter (each species by itself), like aracaris. Woodpeckers start their activities late, not being early risers.

Woodpeckers are aggressive. When caught by people, they defend themselves by pecking, not with mandible closed as when chiseling, but partly open, leaving two marks on the hand of the person holding them. When sleeping in holes they lie down, like parrots, or clutch the side in a vertical position, as if creeping up a tree.

Breeding

There are different displays with mates and between rivals. The elegant *Melanerpes cruentatus* (and *M. flavifrons*) display with a variety of positions and movements while perching close to one another. *Campephilus melanoleucos* produces a loud buzzing with the wings when mates meet each other in flight. In the breeding season *Melanerpes candidus* demonstrates by flying over the treetops, screaming. A *Colaptes campestris* will raise and then quickly lower its wings before its mate, repeating this gesture various times at short intervals; the pair calls together while flapping wings. I have seen two male White-barred Piculets, *Picumnus cirratus,* perform a silent, symbolic struggle: each perched exactly in front of the other on opposite sides of a slender stalk separating them, in such a way that one appeared to be the mirror image of the other, and "hammered" with the bill in the direction of his opponent without touching the stem (fig. 192). The most interesting part of this ceremony was the abstention from using any acoustic effects, although on other occasions *P. cirratus* drums loudly.

Mates work with great dedication to made a cavity in wood, in many cases one for each breeding period. They especially look for dead trees, such as those standing after fires or whose heartwood has been weakened by fungus. They like to work on palms and cecropias and use trees killed by lightning. They prefer to excavate on the side leaning

Fig. 192. Symbolic fight between two male White-barred Piculets, *Picumnus c. cirratus*. Original, H. Sick.

toward the ground, to make protection against rain and defense of the entrance easier. Location of the entrance has a decided influence on the microclimate in the nest, it being important that the nestlings not get too hot. They frequently work on more than one hole. The entrance exactly corresponds to the birds' body size, to exclude larger birds and predators. Thus, the mouth of a *Dryocopus lineatus* nest is clearly larger than that of *Campephilus melanoleucos,* a slightly smaller species.

In Goiás *Colaptes campestris* builds its nest in terrestrial nests of the termite *Cornitermes cumulans* and occasionally in the arboreal nests of another, *Constrictotermes cyphergaster,* so never has to use tree trunks.

In a tree plantation in Minas Gerais I found a dead vertical branch of a large guapuruvu [*Schizolobium parahybum*] with nests of three woodpecker species (*Picumnus* sp., *Colaptes melanochloros, Veniliornis* sp.), one above the other, almost adjoining, which demonstrates how, in a landscape impoverished by people, a suitable site attracts these birds. According to reports, all three appeared in that locale simultaneously. Destruction of primary forest deprives them of a multitude of trees, among them the oldest and largest, which are those required for nesting. They also need holes for sleeping. In exceptional circumstances they use arboreal termite nests for these purposes (e.g., *Dryocopus lineatus*), as do mediocre hole diggers such as puffbirds and trogons. The *Picumnus* like to use soft agave (*Agave americana*) stems but are capable of excavating in hard wood. When it does not find trees, *Colaptes campestris* looks for semirotted posts or stakes (as do other species) or excavates in terrestrial termite nests or in cuts or banks along rivers or roads. It scrapes the debris out with its feet. In the karstic zone of Minas Gerais, *Melanerpes candidus* apparently uses holes in the rocks for nesting.

Melanerpes flavifrons and *M. cruentatus* are gregarious. Within each species they install their nests close to one another, with the respective owners visiting each other and evidently living in peace. An isolated nest of *M. flavifrons* was attended by more than three males and at least two females, helping to bring food (C. Yamashita).

Woodpeckers lay two to four pure white, shiny eggs. The bottom of the incubation chamber is usually covered with small bits of wood produced during construction, for woodpeckers do not carry material into the nest. With *Campephilus melanoleucos* this layer is a fine sawdust, appropriate for absorbing any kind of liquid. The two mates take turns incubating. A. F. Skutch noted 12 days of incubation for a Central American *Melanerpes* and 14 days for a *Picumnus,* short incubation times. Unlike Passerines, a brood patch appears in both sexes and all genera (Short 1982). Embryonic development in the Picidae generally is rapid, but postembryonic development is slow (see below).

Chicks hatch bare and blind but are not insensitive to light, for they raise their heads (expecting to be fed) when light is obstructed by blocking the nest entrance. They are even more sensitive to noise on the trunk near the nest announcing the arrival of parents with food. They immediately stop their noise and begging, however, when the parents give an alarm signal from outside. In the embryo the mandible is much longer than the maxilla (see Alcedinidae, "Breeding") and both end in a hard tip with which the eggshell is sawed at hatching. A white, soft swelling at the base of the mandible must help the parents locate the nestlings' gullets in the dark chamber. It is said that nestlings only open their bills to receive food after the parent touches this spot. Food consists of conglomerate balls of insects regurgitated by the parents (e.g., *Dryocopus lineatus, Colaptes*) or of insects carried in the tip of the bill (e.g., *Melanerpes, Picumnus*). Picidae nestlings have tarsal calluses, like toucans. Larger nestlings like to cling to the inner walls of the chamber. Even when only a few days old and still blind they begin to hammer "in play." A bit later they become noisy and finally give the characteristic song of the parents from the nest. The nest is kept clean. Nestling feces are wrapped in a white film forming a small sack the parents carry outside. This process develops in many birds, especially Passerines. The smallest nestling frequently does not survive. One of the parents customarily sleeps with the young, as is done with the eggs.

Nestlings remain in the incubation cavity for a long time, five weeks, for instance, in a medium-sized species such as a *Melanerpes.* This can be interpreted as an adaptation relating to security of the young. Even after acquiring the ability to fly, the young, their sex now recognizable, still remain under the care of their parents and return to the nest to sleep (*M. flavifrons*).

Distribution and Evolution

Woodpeckers show great geographic variation, resulting in a large number of geographic races (e.g., in the Golden-green Woodpecker, *Piculus chrysochloros,* or Little Woodpecker, *Veniliornis passerinus*). More diversified and usually well-isolated species exclusively occupying an area (allopatric distribution) are considered to be allospecies that compose a superspecies, as occurs with *Colaptes melano-*

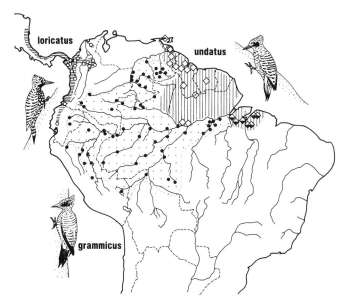

Fig. 193. Range of the Waved Woodpecker and allies, *Celeus undatus* superspecies; males illustrated (modified after Haffer 1974b). Open squares and vertical hatching: *C. u. undatus;* half-solid squares and vertical hatching: *C. u. multifasciatus;* closed circles and stippling: Scale-breasted Woodpecker, *C. grammicus;* open circles and horizontal hatching: Cinnamon Woodpecker, *C. loricatus.* Symbols denote locality records.

chloros and the Spot-breasted Woodpecker, *C. punctigula;* the Scale-breasted Woodpecker, *Celeus grammicus,* and Waved Woodpecker, *C. undatus* (fig. 193); *C. flavescens* and the Pale-crested Woodpecker, *C. lugubris;* and *Melanerpes cruentatus* and *M. flavifrons.*

Interesting parallel evolution has occurred in the genera *Dryocopus* and *Campephilus. Dryocopus lineatus* and *Campephilus melanoleucos* are extremely similar species, both sometimes living under the same ecological conditions. They differ in the bill and other small morphological details (e.g., toe length), head color (demonstrating the importance of the malar stripe in intraspecific recognition), and sound production.

The close relationship between Neotropical and Old World species is patent in the presence of the same genera in the two hemispheres (*Picumnus, Celeus, Dryocopus,* and *Picoides*). This relationship is most conspicuously documented by the *Picumnus:* there are three species of *Picumnus* and *Sasia* (a related genus) in southern Asia and one in Africa. Thirty forms are listed for Brazil (Pinto 1978), the majority of which must be geographic representatives. The piculets appear to have originated in the New World. The similarity of Neotropical woodpeckers with those of Africa is startling.

Our terrestrial *Colaptes campestris* corresponds to Africa's Bennett's Woodpecker, *Campethera bennettii,* which lives in wooded savanna south of the Congo (Short 1982, Fry 1983).

The abundance of woodpeckers in Amazonia may perhaps be connected to the scarcity of Capitonidae, since the two families have similar ecological requirements (see Capitonidae, "Distribution . . . "). Exactly the reverse occurs in Africa, where the latter predominate, but in Asia both are numerous.

Movements

The *Veniliornis* and other forest species associate temporarily with mixed flocks of woodcreepers, tanagers, and other Passerines that wander through the woods. *Picumnus* accompany these Passerine flocks even more often. *Colaptes campestris* migrates short distances over savanna areas. *Picoides mixtus* apparently makes seasonal movements, and this is probably also the case with other southern species, such as the White-fronted Woodpecker, *Melanerpes cactorum.*

Parasites, Nest Fauna, and Fungi

I have found nematodes under the skin of the head, neck, and tibio-tarsal joint and in the abdominal cavity of Brazilian species. It has been reported that ants, so often the food of woodpeckers, may transmit tapeworms (Cestoda) found in these birds (Eichler 1936).

Woodpeckers are sometimes hosts to louse flies (Hippoboscidae) such as *Olfersia fusca* (*Veniliornis affinis*). They carry arthropods, primarily pseudo-scorpions, which take residence in their nests and cling to their plumage (*V. affinis,* Mato Grosso).

L. P. Gonzaga (1980) found filamentous fungi and yeasts in the feathers of *Celeus flavescens* which may have been responsible for yellowish and greenish coloring on the throat, breast, and back that had caught our attention.

Use of Nests by Other Animals, Usefulness, and Alleged Noxiousness

No birds are more useful than woodpeckers to animals incapable of excavating their own shelter. Among these are many birds, such as Dendrocolaptidae, Furnariidae, Cotingidae, such Tyrannidae as *Colonia* and *Myiarchus,* Bucconidae, parakeets, aracaris, and many others. North of Brasília holes made by *Dryocopus lineatus* were occupied by the Yellow-faced Parrot, *Amazona xanthops* (October–November, C. Yamashita). I also know that the Turquoise-fronted Parrot, *Amazona aestiva;* Scaly-headed Parrot, *Pionus maximiliani;* and Bat Falcon, *Falco rufigularis,* opportunistically take advantage of woodpecker holes. Some tenants, such as certain Bucconidae, are themselves capable of digging such holes but use those of woodpeckers because of "laziness." Small mammals also benefit, such as the golden lion tamarin (*Leontopithecus rosalia*), reptiles, amphibians, and lesser animals.

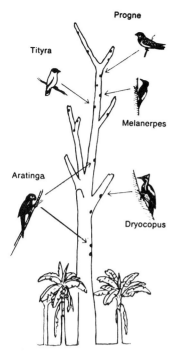

Fig. 194. Dead tree in Peru (approximately 25 m high) with holes dug by woodpeckers. Six pairs (five species) of birds nested there at the same time, among them two pairs of woodpeckers. After Koepcke 1972.

Woodpeckers are often badly compensated, for their "tenants" often take possession of these accommodations by force, expelling the builders. Tityras, *Tityra* (Tyrannidae), do this, filling the woodpecker's house with the leaves and twigs they need as a cushion for their eggs and nestlings. The woodpecker, which uses only the remains of wood left over from excavation of the hole (see "Breeding"), throws out the tityra's material but finally gives up and leaves. Aracaris eat eggs and nestlings before occupying the holes of the woodpecker, which patiently constructs another. In the upper Amazon of Peru, Maria Koepke recorded six pairs of birds (among them two different woodpeckers) simultaneously nesting in woodpecker holes in a single tree (fig. 194).

In general woodpeckers are very useful to people because they destroy large quantities of insects and larvae harmful to wood (e.g., long-horned beetles, Cerambycidae). *Melanerpes candidus* is the natural enemy of the irapuá (*Melipona ruficrus*), providing valuable service to citrus growers by opening nests of this indigenous bee in search of its larvae and pupae. The type specimen of *Trigona ceophloei* was found in the stomach of a *Dryocopus lineatus.*

It is also undeniable, however, that certain woodpeckers sometimes cause damage in orchards and sugar-cane fields. In the cacao zone *Celeus flavescens;* the Cream-colored Woodpecker, *C. flavus; Dryocopus lineatus;* and *Campephilus robustus* are accused of causing serious damage to cacao pods. Local people say these woodpeckers perforate the fruits and return after they have attracted insects. Still, it appears to me the birds probably attack primarily fruits that are already infested.

Decline and Popularity

At the end of the last century Ihering already considered the Helmeted Woodpecker, *Dryocopus galeatus,* to be a rarity. Apparently it is a species in danger of extinction. This may be for ecological reasons. In Europe the Middle Spotted Woodpecker, *Picoides medius,* is disappearing because of the elimination of oak trees (*Quercus* spp.); formerly it was more common there. We know almost nothing about the ecological adaptations of Brazilian woodpeckers. In North America and Cuba we have the famous case of the Ivory-billed Woodpecker, *Campephilus principalis,* which is almost extinct.

Reforestation with eucalyptus and pine (*Pinus*) does not favor the survival of woodpeckers, and the same is the case with native capoeira, where trees large enough for them to install their nests are lacking.

Woodpeckers are quite susceptible to insecticides. Their presence can even serve as an indicator that the respective environment is intact, with the number of species present giving a clue to forest health. The popular appeal of woodpeckers is reflected in the fact that rudimentary, muzzle-loading shotguns are called "woodpeckers."

Identification Data
(number of species in parentheses)

Field recognition of certain *Picumnus, Piculus,* and *Veniliornis* can be difficult if not impossible. The bright red on the head of certain individuals does not help much in determining the species, for it may indicate only age or sex. Red on the malar region is the male marker for *Colaptes, Celeus,* and *Dryocopus.* Separation of the large, red-crested, black-and-white species (group 7) also requires careful attention.

Picidae taxonomy was reviewed by L. L. Short (1982), giving weight to ecological factors. He proposed including *Chrysoptilus* in *Colaptes* and including *Tripsurus, Leuconerpes,* and *Trichopicus* in *Melanerpes. Dendrocopos* was replaced by *Picoides,* and *Phloeoceastes* was included in *Campephilus.* Considering that in Brazil these changes in nomenclature are not yet well known and that complete abandonment of the former names (used in the catalogues of O. Pinto, etc.) would lead to confusion, I cite the old names in parentheses.

1. Piculets, *Picumnus* (13): Identification of most is only possible using a complete list of their characters. Adult males have red on the crown (see Pl 25), except *P. aurifrons.* The female crown is black speckled with white; juveniles are speckled brown.
2. Flickers, *Colaptes* (1): *C. campestris* (Pl 25.3)

3. Relatively large green woodpeckers, semiterrestrial: *Colaptes* (= *Chrysoptilus*) (2) (Pl 25.8)

4. Medium-sized green woodpeckers, *Piculus* (5): generally with more or less extensive bright yellow on the head (Pl 25.9). See also item 5.

5. Small green woodpeckers, *Veniliornis* (6): there are several very similar species, usually distinguished by the mantle color and pattern. Presence of red on the head varies with age (Pl 25.10). See item 4.

6. Medium or large-sized chestnut-colored woodpeckers, *Celeus* (8):

   6.1. Only in Amazonia: *C. elegans* (Pl 25.5), *C. grammicus,* and *C. undatus*

   6.2. With the head and crest yellow or ferruginous: *C. flavescens* (Pl 25.6), *C. lugubris, C. flavus, C. spectabilis,* and *C. torquatus*

7. Large woodpeckers with a red crest (2 genera, 6 species):

   7.1. With a white line on the side of the neck and a barred belly: *Dryocopus* (= *Ceophloeus*) *lineatus* (Pl 25.1), *D. galeatus,* and *Campephilus* (= *Phloeoceastes*) *melanoleucos*

   7.2. Only a black and white mark on the side of the red head: *Campephilus* (= *Phloeoceastes*) *robustus* (with barred belly: Pl 25.4), *C. rubricollis* (uniformly chestnut belly), and *C. leucopogon* (uniformly black belly)

8. Medium-sized black-and-white woodpeckers with or without colors: *Melanerpes* (4) and *Picoides* (1).

   8.1. Multicolored with black, red, yellow, and white: *Melanerpes* (= *Tripsurus*) *flavifrons* (Pl 25.2) and *M. cruentatus*

   8.2. Black-and-white: *M.* (= *Leuconerpes*) *candidus* (see fig. 195) and *M. cactorum* (both with yellow markings), *Picoides* (= *Dendrocopos*) *mixtus* (small, Pl 25.7)

WHITE-BARRED PICULET, *Picumnus cirratus,* Pica-pau-anão-barrado   PL 25.11

10 cm. Woodpeckers of this dwarf genus have an average weight (about 11.5 g) that is only ⅓ that of other small species, e.g., *Veniliornis*. Nape feathers often form small crest. Black-and-white pattern of tail, crown, and nape generally the same in various *Picumnus*. In *P. cirratus* upperparts uniformly brown, underparts densely barred. Male crown and forehead red. Immature head uniformly brown. SOUNDS: voice a high, descending *tsirrrr,* sometimes prolonged and modulated, also given by immature; *tsirit, tsick.* Drums a *trrrr.* On male rituals, see "Breeding." In not too dense woodlands, at medium height, generally at tips of branches; frequently clings to underside of branches; hammers violently, clinging with exceptionally powerful feet (see "Morphology . . . "). Opens holes in fallen cecropia leaves stuck among branches to take out small ants which it also finds in stems of samambaia-das-taperas (*Pteridium aquilinum*). The Guianas to Bolivia, Paraguay, northern Argentina, Brazil.

In south (Paraná, São Paulo, Rio Grande do Sul, Misiones, Paraguay) represented by Ochre-collared Piculet, *P. c. temminckii,* which has cinnamon on sides of head and clear white spot at rear edge of eye. VOICE: *tsirrrr, si-si-si . . . .* Forest edges, capoeira. In Rio Grande do Sul found locally alongside *P. nebulosus.*

Of 13 Brazilian *Picumnus,* 4 of which are endemic, *cirratus* is best known. Crosses occur, e.g., *P. cirratus* × *P. varzeae* and *P. albosquamatus guttifer,* showing their close relationship (Short 1982).

WHITE-BELLIED PICULET, *Picumnus spilogaster*

Resembles *P. cirratus,* with spotted belly. Only on border with Venezuela (Roraima).

WHITE-WEDGED PICULET, *Picumnus albosquamatus,* Pica-pau-anão-escamado

10 cm. Typical of cerrados of central Brazil. Mantle punctuated with white, underparts whitish scaled with black. VOICE: *si-si-si . . .* in descending sequence. Maranhão to western São Paulo, Minas Gerais, Mato Grosso, Bolivia. Includes *P. guttifer* of Mato Grosso.

VARZEA PICULET, *Picumnus varzeae,* Pica-pau-anão-da-várzea   BR

10.5 cm. Dark brown with feathers of underparts outlined with whitish. On islands near Óbidos and Faro (Rio Jamundá) in Pará and Amazonas.

SPOTTED PICULET, *Picumnus pygmaeus,* Pica-pau-anão-pintalgado   BR

10 cm. Typical of northeast. Upper- and underparts speckled with white, somewhat like *P. varzeae.* VOICE: extremely high, resembling bat squeaks, *tsirrrrr, tsi, tsi, tsi.* Capoeira, forests of caatinga and mountains (in outback). Maranhão, Piauí, Bahia to Minas Gerais (Rio São Francisco). "Espírito Santo" (Ruschi, without basis). See other caatinga species: *P. fulvescens, P. limae.*

ORINOCO PICULET, *Picumnus lafresnayi*

Back uniformly green, underparts barred. Only in extreme northwestern Brazil, from lower Rio Uaupés to Colombia. Includes *P. pumilus.*

GOLDEN-SPANGLED PICULET, *Picumnus exilis,* Pica-pau-anão-de-pintas-amarelas

9 cm. Upperparts green or greenish, speckled with black or black and white. Underparts whitish or yellowish, barred black. Mantle with yellowish speckles. VOICE: *tsilit, tsirrrr.* Capoeira, capoeirão. Venezuela to Amapá; also Maranhão, Pernambuco, southern Bahia to Espírito Santo. Sometimes syntopic with *P. fulvescens.*

GOLD-FRONTED PICULET, *Picumnus aurifrons,* Pica-pau-anão-dourado

7.5 cm. Smallest *Picumnus.* Upperparts olivaceous (locally barred yellow), breast barred, belly streaked, crown yellow gold (male). VOICE: *tsirrrit-tsit-tsit,* reminiscent of a hummingbird. Upper Amazon to northern Mato Grosso (upper Xingu), southern Pará (Serra do Cachimbo), Rio Tocantins, Belém (eastern Pará). Includes *P. borbae,* with red, not yellow, crown; from Rio Tocantins to Peru.

MOTTLED PICULET, *Picumnus nebulosus,* Pica-pau-anão-carijó

10.2 cm. Southern species characterized by streaked belly. Elongated black nuchal feathers have white tips. SOUNDS: a hum, *tsewrewt, si-si-si.* . . . Drums loudly on bamboo; *TRAra-TRAra* . . . , *rra-rra-rra* . . . , which can sound like a large amphibian (see "Vocalization . . . "). Forest edges. Paraná to Rio Grande do Sul (where common), Uruguay, Argentina (Misiones). Includes *P. iheringi* (Rio Grande do Sul).

TAWNY PICULET, *Picumnus fulvescens,* Pica-pau-anão-de-Pernambuco   BR

10 cm. Mantle uniformly brown, underside light ferruginous, streaked white, similar to *P. nebulosus.* VOICE: a descending sequence of *driEE*s . . . " (G. Coelho pers. comm.). Open arboreal vegetation, caatinga that is not very dry; also humid forests where it meets *P. exilis.* Pernambuco, Alagoas.

RUSTY-NECKED PICULET, *Picumnus fuscus*

Underparts with vestiges of interrupted barring. Only in western Mato Grosso, Bolivia.

RUFOUS-BREASTED PICULET, *Picumnus rufiventris,* Pica-pau-anão-vermelho

10–11 cm. Relatively "large." Nape and underparts uniformly chestnut, mantle green. Upper Amazon from Rio Purus to Bolivia, Colombia. There is no similar species.

OCHRACEOUS PICULET, *Picumnus limae,* Pica-pau-anão-da-caatinga   BR

10 cm. Upperparts brown, underparts uniformly yellowish. VOICE: a high hum, *sirr-sirr-sirr,* resembling a hummingbird. Caatinga. Ceará to Alagoas.

CAMPO FLICKER, *Colaptes campestris,* Pica-pau-do-campo   PL 25.3

32 cm. Large, terrestrial, unmistakable in form and color. Sides of head and neck yellow like upper breast, brighter in male. Mantle and belly barred, lower back conspicuously white, prominent in flight. Male usually, not always, with red on malar region. Southern population has white, not black, throat (Field Flicker, (*C. c. campestroides*). Typical yellow rachis of flight feathers becomes more intense with molt to adult plumage. Underparts frequently soiled by ashes and glutinous substances from grasses. VOICE: quite varied, a loud *keyewk* . . . with timbre of Greater Yellowlegs, *Tringa*

melanoleuca; a tremulous *wewww* . . . , *gwik, ewuh.* In small flocks in savanna regions where it is among most conspicuous birds. Also above tree line in mountains of southeastern Brazil and in caatinga. Searches for food (ants, termites) mainly on ground among stones, even on road. Surveys landscape from tops of mounds, posts, isolated trees, cacti, rocks. Hops in an erect position on horizontal branches. Walks a little; occasionally perches for long periods on telephone wires, strange behavior for a woodpecker. During hottest hours seeks scarce shade of a fence post or such. Northeastern Brazil to Uruguay, Paraguay, Bolivia, Argentina; also savannas of lower Amazon (Monte Alegre, Pará), Suriname. Starting to invade Hylaea from south and to extend its domain in eastern Brazil, taking advantage of deforestation. Exploits low-quality overgrazed pastures with gullies or badlands where termite nests are built; also ruined and useless areas recently created over vast areas alongside Belém-Brasília and Transamazon highways. Also called *Chá-chá, Pica-pau-de-manga* (Minas Gerais). *C. c. campestroides,* formerly considered a separate species, ranges from Paraná southward.

GREEN-BARRED WOODPECKER, *Colaptes* (= *Chrysoptilus*) *melanochloros,* Pica-pau-verde-barrado   PL 25.8

26 cm. Relatively large, green with white on sides of head and red on nape (and on malar stripe in male). Upperparts barred, underparts with heart-shaped spots. Yellow rachis as in *C. campestris.* SOUNDS: voice is a full *kwiewk-kwik-kwik,* similar to *C. campestris;* a melancholy *klewa* . . . , *guh-a* . . . in a short sequence; *krrew* . . . ; *bewtra; pikwarrr.* Drums. Forest edge, cerradão, gallery forests. Typical of cerrado and caatinga, penetrates into open areas almost devoid of tall vegetation. Seeks top spikes of palm trees, from where it calls for extended periods. Perches on horizontal branches (see "Behavior"). Sometimes feeds while hanging under a branch. Descends to bushes and ground in search of ants, like *campestris.* Mouth of Amazon (Marajó) to northeast, from there to Rio Grande do Sul, Goiás, Mato Grosso (Rio Araguaia, Corumbá), Paraguay, Argentina, Uruguay. Two geographic races of somewhat different size occur in Brazil. Sometimes found in same areas as *Celeus flavescens* and *Melanerpes candidus.* Frequently alongside Narrow-billed Woodcreeper, *Lepidocolaptes angustirostris,* which has similar voice; in western Rio Grande do Sul it is a neighbor of *Drymornis bridgesii.* Also called *Pica-pau-carijó* (Rio de Janeiro).

SPOT-BREASTED WOODPECKER, *Colaptes* (= *Chrysoptilus*) *punctigula*

19.5 cm. Throat spotted, not streaked. VOICE: *key* . . . , resembling *C. campestris,* and like it frequently found on ground among sparse trees. Replaces *C. melanochloros* in northwestern Brazil. Central America to Bolivia, Brazil: upper Amazon to upper Rio Xingu (Mato Grosso) and Rio Tapajós (Pará); also Amapá, French Guiana.

YELLOW-THROATED WOODPECKER, *Piculus flavigula*, Pica-pau-bufador   PL 25.9

17.5 cm. Greenish, medium sized, widely distributed. Sides of head uniformly yellow, red on crown (male) or nape (female). Mantle uniformly green, belly with large spots. Southern form (*P. f. erythropsis*) has red throat, especially on male, unlike Amazonian form (see plate). VOICE: warning a surprisingly loud snort: *shaa, gheh*. Forests at medium height, frequently alongside *Veniliornis*. The Guianas to upper Rio Xingu (Mato Grosso), southern Pará (Serra do Cachimbo), northeastern and eastern Brazil to São Paulo. Also called *Pica-pauzinho-amarelo, Pica-pau-de-cabeça-amarela*. See *P. aurulentus*.

WHITE-BROWED WOODPECKER, *Piculus aurulentus*, Pica-pau-dourado

20 cm. Southern species that differs from *P. flavigula* by olive sides of head crossed by 2 horizontal yellow stripes. Throat yellow; top of head and malar stripe (only nape in female) red; remiges barred with chestnut. VOICE: a plaintive, descending sequence, *eeeww, eeeww, eeeww*. Forests. Mountainous regions of Espírito Santo, Minas Gerais, and Rio de Janeiro to Rio Grande do Sul, Argentina (Misiones), Paraguay. See *P. chrysochloros*.

GOLDEN-GREEN WOODPECKER, *Piculus chrysochloros*, Pica-pau-dourado-escuro

21 cm. Similar to *P. aurulentus* but with only 1 yellow stripe on side of head; iris white; remiges with chestnut base but, like *P. flavigula*, not barred. Forest, cerradão, cerrado. Panama to the Guianas, Bolivia, Paraguay, Argentina, southern Mato Grosso, Maranhão, northeastern and eastern Brazil to Minas Gerais, Rio de Janeiro, Espírito Santo.

WHITE-THROATED WOODPECKER, *Piculus, leucolaemus*

18 cm. Also with only 1 stripe on head; throat white. Forests alongside rivers. Upper Amazon; also Ilha do Bananal (Goiás).

GOLDEN-OLIVE WOODPECKER, *Piculus rubiginosus*

Sides of head white. In Brazil only in extreme north. Mexico to northern South America, including at 1500 m on massif of Pico da Neblina in Brazil.

BLOND-CRESTED WOODPECKER, *Celeus flavescens*, Pica-pau-de-cabeça-amarela   PL 25.6

27 cm. Considerable geographic variation in color: southern form, *C. f. flavescens* (see plate), yellow; northern *C. f. ochraceus*, from Pará to northeast, caramel with bars on upperparts reduced to spots. Underparts uniformly black,

unlike *C. elegans*. VOICE: strongly resonant, descending sequence, with syllables well pronounced and separated; territorial song *tsew tsew (tsew tsew)*; anger *ttttrrr*. Forest edge, gallery forest, orchards. Although arboreal, liking berries and fruits, descends to ground to eat ants and termites. Northern bank of lower Amazon to Rio Grande do Sul, Paraguay, Argentina (Misiones). Also called *João-velho, Bico-chã-chã* (Rio Grande do Sul), *Cabeça-de-velho*. See *C. flavus, C. torquatus, C. lugubris*.

PALE-CRESTED WOODPECKER, *Celeus lugubris*

27 cm. Wings barred, tail coverts and underparts chestnut brown. Replaces *C. flavescens* in southwestern Mato Grosso. To Bolivia, Paraguay, Argentina.

CHESTNUT WOODPECKER, *Celeus elegans*, Pica-pau-chocolate   PL 25.5

27 cm. Chocolate-colored Amazonian species with yellow rump, red (male) malar stripe. North of Amazon has yellowish crest (*C. e. elegans*), not chestnut like populations on south bank (*C. e. jumana*, see plate). SOUNDS: voice a melodious, descending sequence, *wewa ew-ew-ew-ew-ew-ew;* a hard *keeaa;* a smooth *gwarrr*. Bisyllabic drumming, *dop-dop*. Tall forest, gallery forest, seeks fruit trees, sometimes goes to ground. The Guianas, Venezuela, and Colombia to Bolivia, Mato Grosso (upper Rio Xingu), southern Pará (Rio Cururu, Serra do Cachimbo), Maranhão. See *C. grammicus*.

SCALE-BREASTED WOODPECKER, *Celeus grammicus*, Pica-pauzinho-chocolate

20 cm. Chestnut with black barring; rump and under surface of wings uniformly yellow. VOICE: a loud whistle, *doit-gua*. Forests, sometimes alongside *C. elegans*. The Guianas to upper Amazon, Bolivia, Pará (Rio Tocantins), northern Mato Grosso (upper Rio Xingu).

WAVED WOODPECKER, *Celeus undatus*

20 cm. Replaces *C. grammicus* in lower Amazon. Similar to it but with rump and tail barred. VOICE: a loud *wit-koa*, quite typical and almost identical to *C. grammicus*. Terra-firme forest. The Guianas to Rio Branco region and along Rio Negro and Amazon to Amapá (see fig. 193). Also eastern Pará from Belém to lower Xingu.

CREAM-COLORED WOODPECKER, *Celeus flavus*, Pica-pau-amarelo

25 cm. Widely distributed. Similar to *C. flavescens*, with high, soft crest and all plumage light yellow except wings and tail which are brownish black. Male has red malar stripe. VOICE: a sequence of 6 melancholic *glew*s, last note lower. Thin woodland, cacao plantations, etc. Sometimes descends to ground and becomes soiled with earth. Northern South America to Bolivia, Mato Grosso (Rios das Mortes and

Xingu), eastern Pará (Belém), Maranhão. Also Bahia to Espírito Santo.

RUFOUS-HEADED WOODPECKER, *Celeus spectabilis*

27 cm. Rare western species. Head rusty, back and underparts almost uniformly cinnamon, breast plate and tail black. Bolivia to Ecuador, locally in northeastern Brazil in Piauí (Uruçuí, Rio Parnaíba, August 1926) (Short 1973).

RINGED WOODPECKER, *Celeus torquatus*, Pica-pau-de-coleira

27 cm. Head carmel-colored, mantle chestnut bordered black, foreneck and breast black, belly whitish heavily spotted black. Tall forest. Northern South America to upper Rio Tapajós, upper Xingu, upper Rio das Mortes (Mato Grosso), Goiás (Rio Maranhão), Pará (Belém). *C. tinnunculus*, all densely barred with black and which I formerly accepted as a full species, is now considered a population of *torquatus*. It is endemic and endangered. Found on high trunks. VOICE: monotonous whistles, *peeee*, recalling song of Least Pygmy-Owl, *Glaucidium minutissimum*, which occurs in same region: Espírito Santo (Comp. Vale do Rio Doce forest, Linhares, Fazenda São Joaquim, formerly Klabin), Bahia (Monte Pascoal National Park, CVRD Reserve in Porto Seguro). Sympatric with *C. flavescens* and *C. flavus* (Gonzaga et al. 1988).

LINEATED WOODPECKER, *Dryocopus lineatus*, Pica-pau-de-banda-branca   PL 25.1

33 cm. One of largest and most frequently encountered species. White line links bill to sides of breast. Throat spotted, belly barred, female has black forehead. White scapular spot sometimes missing (Espírito Santo and Minas Gerais to Paraná, *D. "erythrops*," see "Morphology . . . "). SOUNDS: territorial song of both sexes a prolonged sequence of loud, sonorous *wets* . . . ; a sonorous *bet-wehrrr, GHI gogogo, BAY-be-be-kwa* (warning). Prolonged drumming *torrrrrr* (both sexes). Forest and cerrado, from where it may move into cultivated fields with trees. Sometimes in same area as *Campephilus melanoleucos*, without becoming as "savannalike" as it. Mexico to Bolivia, Paraguay, Argentina, throughout Brazil. Very similar to *C. melanoleucos*. See also *D. galeatus*.

HELMETED WOODPECKER, *Dryocopus galeatus*, Pica-pau-de-cara-amarela   EN R PL 44.6

29 cm. Rare southern form, similar to *D. lineatus*. Also has barred underparts, but face and throat light cream- or cinnamon-colored; auricular region vermiculated (and not uniformly black); upper back black. Lower back, as far as upper tail coverts, cream like *Campephilus robustus*. Tall forest. There are very few recent records. Rio Grande do Sul (Taquara 1883, Torres 1928), Santa Catarina (Trumbudo Alto

1946), Paraná (Porto Camargo 1954), São Paulo (Intervales, Capão Bonito, February 1987, E. Willis; Carlos Botelho State Park, November 1988, C. Yamashita), Paraguay (Itaipu, December 1986, N. Perez, Scherer Neto), Argentina (Misiones). Information on nesting in Iguaçu, Brazil/Argentina, and on vocalization (obtained by T. Parker) has recently become available (Short 1989 pers. comm.).

YELLOW-TUFTED WOODPECKER, *Melanerpes* (= *Tripsurus*) *cruentatus*, Benedito-de-testa-vermelha

20 cm. Amazonian replacement of *M. flavifrons*, which it resembles in color pattern. Head, neck, breast, and mantle black; crown red (male). Yellowish line extends from eye to nape but may be lacking (*M. "rubrifrons*," see "Morphology . . . "). Rump extensively white, belly red, flanks barred black and white. Immature occiput red, later becomes black. VOICE: *trrr-eh; treh-treh-treh-treh*. Gregarious. Forest, usually in treetops. The Guianas to Bolivia, Mato Grosso (upper Xingu), Pará (Belém).

YELLOW-FRONTED WOODPECKER, *Melanerpes* (= *Tripsurus*) *flavifrons*, Benedito-de-testa-amarela PL 25.2

19.5 cm. Noisy, multicolored; southern replacement for *M. cruentatus*. Forehead and throat bright yellow, rear crown and nape red (male). SOUNDS: voice a strident *kikiki, tsilidit*, uttered frequently in flight; pair, perched, give a repeated *chlit*. . . . Drums on tall trees, flies from treetop to treetop crying *benedito* (onomatopoeic). Comes to orchards, cane fields, palm groves. Gregarious (see "Behavior"). Bahia and Minas Gerais to Rio Grande do Sul, southwestern Mato Grosso, Goiás, Paraguay, Argentina (Misiones). Also called *Bereré* (Rio Grande do Sul). See *M. cruentatus* and *M. cactorum*.

WHITE WOODPECKER, *Melanerpes* (= *Leuconerpes*) *candidus*, Birro   Fig. 195

28.5 cm. Unmistakable black-and-white savanna species with abdomen and nape (male) or only abdomen (female) yellowish. Region around eye bare and orange-colored. VOICE: very distinctive, resembling a tern (*Sterna*): in flight a sharp *kirr-kirr-kirr*; perched, *ghirreh*. During breeding makes display flights. Savannas with sparse trees, cerrado, palm groves (e.g., buriti), orchards. Arboreal, lives in small flocks. Amazon estuary and Óbidos through the rest of Brazil to Bolivia, Argentina, Paraguay, Uruguay; also Suriname. Also called *Cri-cri, Pica-pau-branco*.

WHITE-FRONTED WOODPECKER, *Melanerpes* (= *Trichopicus*) *cactorum*, Pica-pau-de-testa-branca

18 cm. Southern species with upperparts black and white, crown red (male). Underparts yellowish gray, throat yellow. VOICE: a loud *weep-weep, wee-beep*. Gregarious. Trees in

Fig. 195. White Woodpecker, *Melanerpes candidus*.

palm groves. Paraguay, Argentina, Bolivia, Peru, Mato Grosso (Pantanal, perhaps only as a visitor, October 1958, A. Aguirre).

WHITE-SPOTTED WOODPECKER, *Veniliornis spilogaster*, Pica-pauzinho-verde-carijó

17.5 cm. Southern species, largest of a group of small, greenish woodpeckers. Crown dark brown (or reddish, male) with 2 white lines on side of head. Upperparts clearly barred with greenish yellow, underparts spotted (not barred as in *V. maculifrons*). VOICE: an unmistakable *ti-rra-rra, prio-rr-rr-rr-rr, reh-reh-reh-reh*. Forests. Rio de Janeiro (mountainous regions, e.g., Itatiaia) and Minas Gerais to Rio Grande do Sul, Uruguay, Paraguay, northern Argentina.

LITTLE WOODPECKER, *Veniliornis passerinus*, Pica-pauzinho-anão

15 cm. Smallest *Veniliornis*. Distinguishable by upper wing coverts speckled with yellow, nape (and sometimes crown) red (male). VOICE: *ki, ki, ki, ki*. Low levels in capoeira, gallery forests (Mato Grosso, Goiás, abundant) caatinga. Venezuela to Bolivia, Paraguay, central Brazil as far as western São Paulo and northeastern interior. Includes *V. agilis*. In upper Xingu, Mato Grosso, meets *V. affinis*.

YELLOW-EARED WOODPECKER, *Veniliornis maculifrons*, Pica-pauzinho-de-testa-pintada
BR PL 25.10

16 cm. Common in southeast Brazil. Crown brown, forehead streaked with white, nape red (male). Wide, yellowish collar, mantle with indistinct yellow spots. Immature has reddish crown. SOUNDS: voice a tremulous, sonorous *ew, ew, ew, ew . . .* , slightly rising and then descending; song quite different. Drums a *trrrrr*. Secondary forest, parks, both in lowlands and Serra do Mar (Rio de Janeiro), sometimes in same area as *Piculus flavigula*. Espírito Santo to Rio de

Janeiro (including ex-Guanabara), southern Minas Gerais. Also called *Pica-pau-de-bochecha-amarela*.

RED-STAINED WOODPECKER, *Veniliornis affinis*, Pica-pauzinho-avermelhado

16.5 cm. Amazonian. Mantle tinged red, wings with tiny reddish spots. Crown red (male). VOICE: *ghighighi*. Tall forests. Northern South America to Mato Grosso (Rios Guaporé and Xingu), Pará (Serra do Cachimbo), Maranhão. Also Bahia, northern Espírito Santo. Also called *Ipe-cui* (Kaiabi, Mato Grosso).

GOLDEN-COLLARED WOODPECKER, *Veniliornis cassini*

Upper wing coverts with eyelike spots, underparts densely barred. North of Amazon.

RED-RUMPED WOODPECKER, *Veniliornis kirkii*

Similar to *V. affinis* but rump and upper tail coverts red. On Venezuelan border.

CHECKERED WOODPECKER, *Picoides* (= *Dendrocopos*) *mixtus*, Pica-pau-chorão
PL 25.7

13.8 cm. Small, lacking any green, with pale brown mantle densely barred white, top of head sooty, male with red nape. Underparts whitish and streaked. VOICE: a high, horizontal sequence, like *weeping, we-we-we. . . .* Low, sparse woods with spiny vegetation. Uruguay, Argentina, Paraguay, and Bolivia to southern Mato Grosso, Goiás, Minas Gerais (Pirapora, Serra do Cipó), São Paulo, Rio Grande do Sul (espinilho parkland). Appears to migrate, beginning in May, from Porto Murtinho (Mato Grosso) region, returning in January (A. Schneider). Includes *P. cancellatus*, a larger and more northerly form (Minas Gerais, western São Paulo, southeastern Mato Grosso).

CRIMSON-CRESTED WOODPECKER, *Campephilus* (= *Phloeoceastes*) *melanoleucos*, Pica-pau-de-topete-vermelho

31 cm. Very similar to *Dryocopus lineatus*, having, like it, barred belly and white V on back. Distinguished by red sides of head, conspicuous white spot at base of bill, small black-and-white spot under ear. Black throat has no white streaking, foreneck and breast uniformly black. "Roof" of female crest black. Wide, white stripe from sides of neck (both sexes) reaches bill, which is usually whiter in this species than in *D. lineatus*. Some individuals have whitish spot on tips of primaries (Mato Grosso). Young male has red feathers on top of head. SOUNDS: voice a not-very-loud sequence, *kye-kye-kye . . .* ; a low *dewk-rororo*. Drumming very loud and 2-phrased, *DO-dododo, TR-trtrtr*; a monotonous *torrrrr*. Sparse woodland in savanna regions, gallery forests, palm groves. Panama to Bolivia, Paraguay, Argentina, south-

central Brazil to Paraná, Minas Gerais, Mato Grosso (Pantanal, Rio das Mortes), Goiás. Sometimes *D. lineatus* occurs in same area.

CREAM-BACKED WOODPECKER,
Campephilus (= Phloeoceastes) leucopogon,
Pica-pau-de-barriga-preta

32 cm. In Brazil only in extreme south and southwest. Large, crested, with head and back similar to *C. robustus,* differing in all-black underparts. Female has "roof" of crest black like *C. melanoleucos.* SOUNDS: voice a *pi-ow.* Drumming bisyllabic. Groves. Bolivia, Paraguay, Argentina, Uruguay, Brazil in Mato Grosso Pantanal, Rio Negro (nesting, September, B. Dubs, pers. comm.), Porto Murtinho (Schneider), possibly Rio Grande do Sul (see Belton 1984 p. 595).

RED-NECKED WOODPECKER,
Campephilus (= Phloeoceastes) rubricollis,
Pica-pau-de-barriga-vermelha

34 cm. Resembles *C. robustus* but underparts and wing speculum uniformly chestnut (sometimes reddish). Upperparts all black. SOUNDS: voice a loud *kyuh;* drumming *to-RO.* Forests, riverine woodland. Venezuela and the Guianas to Mato Grosso, southern Pará, Maranhão. Also called *Pica-pau-de-penacho, Uari* (Juruna, Mato Grosso). Includes *C. trachelopyrus.*

ROBUST WOODPECKER, *Campephilus* (= *Phloeoceastes*) *robustus,* Pica-pau-rei   PL 25.4

36 cm; average 200 g. Largest Brazilian woodpecker. Head and neck red, male with small black-and-white auricular spot, female with large white malar stripe bordered with black. Both sexes have extensive cream color on back. Inner vane of flight feathers barred with chestnut, prominent in flight. SOUNDS: voice *PSO-ko, po-po-po-po-rrat;* drumming a bisyllabic *do-PLOP.* Araucaria forests in southern Brazil, where not rare. In northern part of range (Espírito Santo) occurs both in mountains and hot lowlands (Rio Doce). Goiás, Minas Gerais, and Bahia to Rio Grande do Sul, Argentina (Misiones), Paraguay. Also called *Pica-pau-galo, Pica-pau-soldado, Pica-pau-de-cabeça-vermelha.* Sometimes alongside *Dryocopus lineatus.* See *C. leucopogon, C. melanoleucos,* and *Dryocopus galeatus.*

Picidae Bibliography
See also General Bibliography

Bitancourt, A., J. P. da Fonseca, and M. Autuori. 1935. *Man. de Citricultura,* 164–67. [Feeding]

Bock, W. J. 1963. *Am. Naturalist* 97:265–85. [Phylogeny]

Bock, W. J., and W. D. Miller. 1959. *Am. Mus. Nov.* 1931. [Anatomy]

Bock, W. J., and L. L. Short, Jr. 1971. *Ibis* 113:234–36. [Resinous secretion]

Burt, W. H. 1930. *Univ. California Publ. Zool.* 32:455–524. [Morphological adaptations]

Coimbra Filho, A. F. 1972. Aspectos inéditos do comportamento de saguís do gênero *Callithrix* (Primata). *Rev. Bras. Biol* 32(4):505–12.

Eichler, W. D. 1936. *Orn. Mber.* 44:173–75. [Ants as transmitters of Cestoda]

Fry, C. H. 1983. Birds in savanna ecosystems. In Bourlier, ed., *Tropical Savanna.* Amsterdam: Elsevier.

Gonzaga, L. P. 1980. *An. Acad. Bras. Ciênc.* 53(1):207–8. [Fungi and yeast in plumage]

Gonzaga, L. P., D. A. Scott, and N. J. Collar. 1988. Registros recentes do picapau *Celeus torquatus tinnunculus* nos estados do Espírito Santo e da Bahia. *XV Cong. Bras. Zool.:*476.

Goodge, W. R. 1972. *Auk* 89:65–85. [Anatomy, phylogeny]

Hofer, H. 1945. Untersuchungen über den Bau des Vogelschädels, besonders über den der Spechte und Steisshühner. *Zool. Jahrb. Anatomie* 69(1):1–158.

Müller, F. 1878. See Möller, A. 1915–20, in General Bibliography.

Posnanin, L. P. 1941. *Compte Ren. Acad. Sci. URSS* 31:173–76. [Adaptive morphology]

Selander, R. K. 1965. Sexual dimorphism in relation to foraging behavior in *Dendrocopos villosus. Wilson Bull.* 77(4): 416.

Selander, R. K. 1966. *Condor* 68:113–51. [Sexual dimorphism]

Short, L. L. 1969. *Wilson Bull.* 81:468–70. [*Colaptes,* behavior]

Short, L. L. 1970a. *Ostrich,* suppl. 8:35–40. [Distribution]

Short, L. L. 1970b. *Am. Mus. Nov.* 2413. [Behavior]

Short, L. L. 1971. The evolution of terrestrial woodpeckers. *Am. Mus. Nov.* 2467.

Short, L. L. 1972. *Bull. Am. Mus. Nat. Hist.* 149. [*Colaptes,* monograph]

Short, L. L. 1973. *Wilson. Bull.* 85:465–67. [*Celeus spectabilis* found in Brazil]

Short, L. L. 1980. *17th Cong. Int. Orn., Berlin* 1978:1268–72. [Speciation of South American woodpeckers]

Short, L. L. 1982. *Woodpeckers of the World.* Delaware Mus. Nat. Hist. Monogr. no. 4.

Sick, H. 1961. *J. Orn.* 102:401–3. [*Melanerpes cactorum, Campephilus leucopogon,* distribution]

Sielmann, H. 1959. *My Year with the Woodpeckers.* London.

Skutch, A. F. 1943. *Scient. Mon.* (N.Y.) 56:358–64. [Ecology]

Skutch, A. F. 1948. The life history of the Olivaceous Piculet (*Picumnus*) and related forms. *Ibis* 90:433–49.

Skutch, A. F. 1948. Life history of the Golden-naped Woodpecker *Tripsurus chrysauchen. Auk* 65:225–60.

Skutch, A. F. 1985. *Life of the Woodpecker.* Santa Monica Ibis Publ.

Steinbacher, J. 1955. *Senckenbergiana Biol.* 36:1–8. [Tongue morphology]

Winkler, H. 1979. Foraging ecology of *Picoides stricklandi. Wilson Bull.* 91(2):244–54.

ORDER PASSERIFORMES: PASSERINE BIRDS

The Passeriformes, or Passeres, include almost 5300 species throughout the world, or about 58.5% of the slightly more than 9000 bird species alive today. Passeriformes originated in the Southern Hemisphere, in Gondwanaland, the great southern continent whose western half separated to become South America and whose eastern half became Africa. Various indications lead me to believe that the oldest Passerines were terrestrial, resembling formicariids such as the *Grallaria* antpittas.

As Sibley and Ahlquist (1985) state, "the DNA-based phylogeny of the Passerines and the geological evidence of continental drift since the Cretaceous make it possible to reconstruct a partial biogeographic history of the Passeriformes. The Passeriformes originated from non-Passeriformes about 90 million years ago." They would have been related to the Piciformes and "Alcediniformes" (Alcedinidae, Todidae, Momotidae, and Meropidae).

Thus, appearance of the Passeriformes is not a more recent event, as is frequently speculated based on the fact that the Oscines became the most developed, most "modern" group. Evolution of the granivorous Passeres may have accompanied the evolution of monocotyledonous plants, among them the Gramineae.

The taxonomy of the order, which aims at better understanding the relationships and phylogeny of the group, is extremely difficult because the morphology of these birds is little differentiated compared with that of non-Passerine families and orders. Use has been made of such taxonomic characters as bill shape, tarsal scutellation, number of primaries, mandibular musculature, syringeal structure (various pairs of syringeal muscles, which non-Passerines usually lack), and skeletal details (skull: aegithognathous arrangement of the palatal bones). Spermatozoa of the Passeriformes are unique, showing tremendous specific variation which has not yet been sufficiently studied for taxonomic purposes (McFarlane 1963). The phylogenetic value of tarsal scutellation is only relative, as becomes evident when it cannot be said that the variations are adaptive in either Oscines or Suboscines. Interpretation of morphological differences is frequently questionable, especially because the change may be functional, an analogous development, a parallelism, rather than phyletic. Recently, biochemical data and ecological elements such as vocalization, behavior, and nesting have been used.

The Passeriformes can be divided into two groups, or suborders, organized primarily by syringeal structure, a long-recognized distinguishing factor that was studied by P. L. Ames (1971). Thus, recognition has been given to Suboscines, with about 1100 species in the world, and to Oscines, with about 4200 species. Feduccia (1974) discovered that the inner-ear anatomy also provides opportunities to determine phylogenetic relationships because of the distinctive shape of the columella, or stapes, a tiny bone only a few millimeters long (fig. 196). The stapes is simple in most birds, including the Oscines, resembling the stapes of reptiles, but it is complex in the Suboscines. It is very probable that such a small part of the internal apparatus is, to a certain extent, independent of secondary alterations, such as those caused by the environment during the geologic epochs.

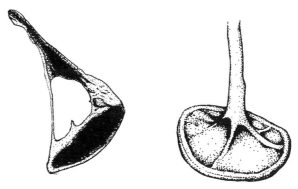

Fig. 196. Avian stapes. Columella of (left) a South American Suboscine, Rufous Hornero, *Furnarius rufus* (Furnariidae), and (right) an Asiatic Oscine, a Cuckoo-shrike, *Coracina* sp. (Campephagidae). The stapes are only a few millimeters long. After Feduccia 1980.

SUBORDER SUBOSCINES

The Suboscines, also called Clamatores or Tyranni, in Brazil include two superfamilies: Furnarioidea (Rhinocryptidae, Formicariidae, Furnariidae, and Dendrocolaptidae) and Tyrannoidea (Tyrannidae, Pipridae, Cotingidae, and Phytotomidae). They are supposedly the phylogenetically most primitive Passerines, but the problem is to know what is

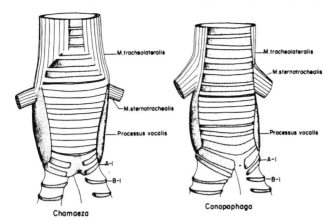

Fig. 197. Syringes of two Suboscines: Short-tailed Antthrush, *Chamaeza campanisona,* and Hooded Gnateater, *Conopophaga roberti,* both formicariids. After P. L. Ames 1971.

"primitive." This is also based on current zoogeography, since there are extremely few Pleistocene fossils. The Suboscines, also designated *Passeres mesomyodae,* have only two to four pairs of syringeal muscles (Oligomyodae) (fig. 197). The syrinx may, however, be very capable of producing sounds, and their calls are among the most impressive in South America (e.g., that of a forest species such as the Short-tailed Antthrush, *Chamaeza campanisona*), although they are stereotyped and have a relatively simple structure. Suboscines stand out more because of the volume of their voices and less because of modulation, which is the strong feature of the Oscines. Frequently both sexes sing. The statement that Suboscine social life is less dependent on vocalization than that of the Oscines cannot be applied generally, for in various species (e.g., tyrannids such as the *Elaenia*) acoustic communication is at least as intense as visual communication.

The Furnarioidea can be better classified by the syrinx, for it is quite complex, unlike that of the Tyrannoidea. The Furnarioidea are also called Tracheophonae, having a tracheal syrinx, and the Tyrannoidea are known as Haploophonae, having a tracheal-bronchial syrinx with intrinsic muscles.

The middle-ear ossicle, the columella or stapes (see above), shows that all Suboscines of both the New and Old worlds, although they have a wide variety of differences, are a close, monophyletic group. Biochemical data are confirming these morphological conclusions. The Suboscines are related to the "Alcediniformes" (see above). The complex stapes of the Suboscines distinguish Suboscine families that are natural entities.

The Rhinocryptidae and a few Formicariidae have a fournotched sternum (fig. 198) (Heimerdinger and Ames 1967). The *Scytalopus* (Rhinocryptidae) flying apparatus is much reduced.

All Suboscines have ten well-developed primaries, unlike

many Oscines (see Suborder Oscine). This is considered a primordial character: evolution has not tended to perfect flying activity, unlike what happened in the Oscines. Suboscines reach their greatest diversity in South America, with a Suboscine/Oscine relationship of two to one, or even three to one (Haffer 1985). In Brazil 582 Suboscine species compare with 325 Oscines, comprising 64.2% of the 907 Brazilian Passerines. The eight autochthonous Brazilian Suboscine families are only slightly more than half as many as the 15 families and subfamilies of Oscine immigrants. Suboscine diversity in Brazil is greatest in the Tyrannidae (200 species), Formicariidae (167), and Furnariidae and Dendrocolaptidae (99 and 37).

Almost all Suboscine species belong to the Neotropical region. Their numbers increase toward the south (Haffer 1985). Whereas in Mexico only 20% of local Passeriformes are Suboscines, in central South America about 60% are. This increase is impressive in the case of the Formicariidae: Mexico has 9 species, Honduras 19, Costa Rica 29, Colombia 136, and Brazil 167.

The Suboscines were late in immigrating to North America. The Tyrannidae were the most effective in this colonization, along with the hummingbirds. It was also a Tyrannidae (Large Elaenia, *Elaenia spectabilis ridleyana*) that colonized Fernando da Noronha Island.

Most Brazilian Suboscines are arboreal forest birds. The Neotropical forest has offered them a most favorable environment and has permitted an "evolutionary explosion." The greatest number of Suboscines are in the Amazonian forest. The current destruction of South American forests is felt more acutely by Suboscines than by Oscines. In southern and Andean South America there has been large-scale speciation of savanna and terrestrial Suboscines.

Most Suboscines (all the Furnarioidea) are insectivorous.

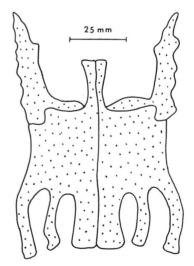

25 mm

Fig. 198. Sternum of Spotted Bamboowren, *Psilorhamphus guttatus,* showing the four incisions in the posterior edge, or metasternum. After Plotnick 1958.

Pipridae and Cotingidae are omnivorous or frugivorous. There are no granivorous Suboscines.

Among Old World Suboscines, the Eurylaemidae, broadbills, show a certain similarity to Neotropical Cotingidae: both are distinguished by broad bills, an adaptation for eating large fruits. The few non-American Suboscines are generally restricted to islands such as Madagascar and New Zealand and to India and Africa, giving the impression of being remnant populations. Only three Suboscines occur in the great Congolese forest. This situation has been interpreted as the result of a process of substitution of Suboscines by Oscines. There appear to be no indications of such having occurred in South America, at least partly because it was isolated by oceans until the end of the Tertiary (5 million years B.P.), thereby permitting its early fauna to be conserved and to evolve without disturbance, although certain Oscines must have reached this part of the world in very ancient times.

In Brazil I think it reasonable to give priority study to the Suboscines, the autochthonous birds of this continent. I count 95 endemic Suboscine species for Brazil.

SUPERFAMILY FURNARIOIDEA

This group comprises three entities: Rhinocryptidae, Formicariidae (including the "Conopophagidae"), and Furnariidae/Dendrocolaptidae, all endemic to the Neotropics with a total of about 520 species, 311 of which occur in Brazil. They form a natural grouping within the Suboscines, considering the character of syrinx, pterylosis, and osteology of the skull and sternum. The unique structure of the syrinx (exclusively tracheal: Tracheophonae) separates the Furnarioidea from all other Passerines. Apparently there is no non-American family related to members of this super-family; however, Feduccia and Olson (1982) found great similarities between our Rhinocryptidae and the Menurae, lyrebirds, of Australia. Considering the probable phylogeny of the group, the sequence should commence with the Rhinocryptidae, the most primitive, and end with the Dendrocolaptidae, the most specialized. The sequence that has been traditional since Wetmore (1960) began with the Dendrocolaptidae. The Furnariidae show so much morphological variation that Feduccia (1980) said they "may be the most diverse of all the passerine families."

FAMILY RHINOCRYPTIDAE: TAPACULOS (8)

Tapaculos comprise a relatively small group of Neotropical birds best represented in areas with moderate climate, such as Chile and the Andes. In the same Chilean forest one can find four species belonging to such various genera as *Pteroptochos*, *Scelorchilus*, *Eugralla*, and *Scytalopus*. Few species occur in Brazil. Most are restricted to mountainous regions of the southeast, but two, the Collared Crescentchest, *Melanopareia torquata*, and Brasilia Tapaculo, *Scytalopus novacapitalis*, occur in central Brazil, and one, the Rusty-belted Tapaculo, *Liosceles thoracicus*, in the upper Amazon.

Feduccia and Olson (1987) consider the osteology of the Rhinocryptidae and Menurae (lyrebirds of Australia) to be similar: both represent an ancestral type of Passerine. A Quaternary fossil has been found.

The inelegant name *tapaculo* is onomatopoeic, referring to the song of the White-throated Tapaculo, *Scelorchilus albicollis*, a Chilean species, and has been adopted as the English name of the family. The word means "cover your ass," and has also arisen from the way certain species raise their tail and exhibit the crissum.

Morphology

Related to the *Conopophaga* gnateaters and terrestrial antbirds such as the *Grallaria* (Formicariidae), tapaculos have, like them, the same four incisions in the posterior margin of the sternum (see fig. 198). The keel of *Scytalopus* is much reduced and the clavicle is unattached, indicating that the birds are close to renouncing the ability to fly. The nostrils are covered by a membrane (hence the technical name of the family; fig. 199). Tapaculos are similar to the *Chamaeza* antthrushes in syrinx structure and have a pair of syringeal muscles like *Grallaria* and *Conopophaga*.

Brazilian species such as the Spotted Bamboowren,

Fig. 199. Bill of Spotted Bamboowren, *Psilorhamphus guttatus,* showing covered nostrils. After Sick 1954.

Psilorhamphus guttatus, and the *Scytalopus* resemble the wrens, whereas *Melanopareia torquata* resembles the *Synallaxis* spinetails (Formicariidae). *Liosceles thoracicus* and the bristlefronts, *Merulaxis* spp., are like the *Chamaeza* antthrushes. The *Merulaxis* are notable for a rigid frontal tuft, a unique plumage feature found in certain Formicariidae (e.g., *Pyriglena*) and Furnariidae. As for size, the two *Merulaxis* are the largest tapaculos in eastern Brazil. The male Slaty Bristlefront, *M. ater,* reaches 37.2 g; the smallest rhinocryptid, the Mouse-colored Tapaculo, *Scytalopus speluncae,* weighs only 15 g.

The wings are rounded, ordinarily being used only to help maintain balance while hopping. Pectoral musculature is reduced (see keel above), but the legs are disproportionately long and strong with long toes. The "soft," wrenlike tail is graduated and in the process of atrophying (*Psilorhamphus guttatus* has only eight rectrices), thus losing its function as a rudder in flight. The *Scytalopus* are an exception to this, the Brazilian species being long tailed.

Plumage is somber, like that of forest antbirds, except for *Melanopareia torquata,* which inhabits open, sunny areas and is more similar to a savanna furnariid; it has hidden white on the back like certain antbirds. Sexes are the same, except in the *Merulaxis. Psilorhamphus guttatus* has a typical musky odor.

A notable feature of all *Scytalopus* is the large eyes, a consequence of their continuous residence in very shady places.

Vocalization

The songs of *Liosceles thoracicus* and the *Merulaxis* are melodious, resembling those of the *Chamaeza* antthrushes. The prolonged, squeaky vocalization of *Scytalopus speluncae* is somewhat like that of certain dendrocolaptids and furnariids such as the *Dendrocincla* and the Sharp-tailed Streamcreeper, *Lochmias nematura.* The White-breasted Tapaculo, *Scytalopus indigoticus,* has two entirely different song types. Voice recognition is essential for finding the extremely shy birds of this family. Females also sing, at times with the male (e.g., *Melanopareia torquata*), sometimes singing a different melody (*Scytalopus novacapitalis*). *M. torquata* customarily goes up to a high limb to sing; singing activity may be greatest in the hottest hours of the day (*M. torquata, S. novacapitalis*). Both these species sing all year.

Feeding and Behavior

Tapaculos eat small insects, spiders, centipedes, mollusks, etc. The *Pteroptochos* of Chile scratch the soil, standing on one leg while moving the other rapidly, even pulling out clumps of earth.

Most are terrestrial, hopping on the ground or low through the branches like terrestrial wrens such as *Microcerculus.* The *Scytalopus* may get caught in rat traps, as occurs with the *Grallaria.* The *Merulaxis* walk, run, and hop on the ground. In non-Brazilian species, such as those of the chaco and pampa, adaptation to terrestrial life is even more developed, with the birds being called *gallitos,* "small roosters." *Psilorhamphus guttatus* will climb as high as several meters into dense vegetation to catch caterpillars.

Tapaculos reveal the slightest nervousness by lifting the tail. *P. guttatus* and *Melanopareia torquata* move the tail a bit to the sides, holding it slightly open. The birds bathe in rainwater pools and sleep on perches (*Liosceles thoracicus*).

Breeding

A *Scytalopus indigoticus* nest in a heap of leaves on the ground alongside a tree trunk was built of roots and moss with some feathers on the inside. Two white eggs took 15 days to hatch (Ruschi pers. comm.). Tapaculo eggs are large, rounded, and lacking in sheen, resembling those of furnariids. *Melanopareia* eggs are lightly speckled on the large end. In Espírito Santo *S. indigoticus* apparently breeds twice a year, *Merulaxis ater* only once, around the end of the year.

Habitat, Distribution, and Evolution

Except for *Melanopareia torquata,* all Brazilian species are forest dwellers, living in shady areas of heavy vegetation and acting highly photophobic. *Scytalopus novacapitalis* lives in flooded thickets inside dense gallery forests among the open cerrados of central Brazil where no one would expect to find it. Such drastic ecological and geographic isolation, together with the fact that rhinocryptids are not very mobile, has favored speciation (fig. 200). The *Scytalopus* genus occupied the entire Andean massif, where it occurs even above 4000 m, and invaded southern Brazil. One relict (*S. novacapitalis*) remained on the central plateau at 1000 m. The fact of its immigration from the Atlantic forest, together with other species such as the Southern Antpipit, *Corythopis delalandi,* is supported by the existence of plants from eastern Brazil, such as tree ferns, in the same planalto forests (fig. 201).

It was a surprise to find *S. novacapitalis* later in Minas Gerais mountains at the same altitude as the Federal District. The fragmented distribution of certain *Scytalopus* demonstrates profound climatic and floristic changes, recently intensified by human intervention. A *Scytalopus* that now scarcely flies (see "Morphology") is incapable under present conditions of colonizing a neighboring mountain. Centuries ago the currently isolated mountain wilderness biomas were united.

Of the eight Brazilian species, three (*Scytalopus novacapitalis, Merulaxis ater,* and Stresemann's Bristlefront, *M. stresemanni*) are endemic to the country. Three others (*Scytalo-*

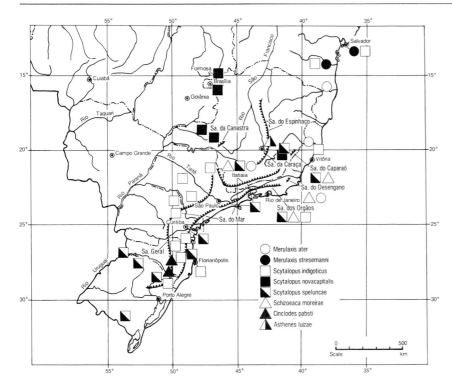

Fig. 200. Distribution of Patagonian/Andean elements (Rhinocryptidae and Furnariidae) in southeastern and central Brazil and Bahia: the very incomplete distributional information available on these species dictated the use of this type of symbol. Two additional species, *Asthenes baeri* and *A. hudsoni,* occur in the extreme west and south, respectively, of Rio Grande do Sul.

Fig. 201. Some types of plant dispersal in Brazil. After Rizzini 1963. The Atlantic forest as the center of dispersal: line 1, relations with northeastern forests; line 2, relations with central Brazil forests; lines 3 and 3A, relations with Tucuman-Bolivian forests and Acre; line 4, relations between the northeastern caatinga, Monte-Chaco, and Mato Grosso Pantanal. Line 2 matches the migration of the Brasilia Tapaculo, *Scytalopus novacapitalis,* which followed the flora of the Atlantic forest.

pus speluncae, S. indigoticus, and *Psilorhamphus guttatus*) are among the many southern "almost" endemics, being also found in bordering countries to the south.

Research and Taxonomy

Tapaculo research requires much care, for information is lacking on many aspects, both taxonomic and biological, which to a certain degree is explained by the fact that these birds lead such a retiring life that usually not even ornithologists find them. The best source of data on Rhinocryptidae biology is Johnson's book on Chile, volume 2, 1967 (see General Bibliography).

Melanopareia and *Psilorhamphus* were formerly included in the Formicariidae. The Rhinocryptidae were previously called Pteroptochidae. Strangely, the specimen that became the type of *Merulaxis stresemanni* was in the Berlin Museum for over 100 years, identified as a male *M. ater,* because of lack of a true male of the latter species (see Chapter 2.4).

Rusty-belted Tapaculo, *Liosceles thoracicus,* Corneteiro-da-mata

19 cm. Largest rhinocryptid, reaching size of a small thrush. Terrestrial bird of upper Amazon, upperparts dark brown, underparts and mandible white except for sulfur-and-chestnut breast. Flanks have blackish, scaly design. VOICE: song very loud and sonorous, with timbre of a *Crypturellus* tinamou, descending an octave or more. Lives in not-too-shady, dry woodland. Somewhat resembles a *Formicarius*

but with long tail. Peru, Ecuador, Colombia, upper Solimões of Brazil, south of Amazon from left bank of Tapajós (Jacareacanga) to Madeira (Amazonas).

COLLARED CRESCENTCHEST, *Melanopareia torquata,* Tapaculo-de-colarinho

14 cm. Typical of sunny cerrados of central Brazil. Similar to a *Synallaxis* (Furnariidae), distinguishable by black collar on upper breast. Superciliary white, sides of head black. VOICE: song a monotonous *dew-eh,* sounding at a distance like a monosyllabic *tewt* (reminiscent of Long-tailed Ground-Dove, *Uropelia campestris*) uttered spaced out in series and audible at long range; warning *rrreww.* Hops on ground or low above it in branches. Campo cerrado, savanna with ample termite nests, campos sujos. Cerrado ralo supports a larger population than campos sujos, the species not being photophobic (Federal District census 1985). Southern Pará, Piauí, Bahia, Goiás, Mato Grosso, and São Paulo to Bolivia. Originally classified as a Furnariidae, later placed in Formicariidae (based on appearance of eggs; see "Breeding"). It belongs to a more widely distributed superspecies. Collar recalls a *Herpsilochmus* antwren. Sometimes alongside Sooty-fronted Spinetail, *Synallaxis frontalis,* and Ochrecheeked Spinetail, *S. scutata.*

SPOTTED BAMBOOWREN, *Psilorhamphus guttatus,* Tapaculo-pintado   PL 29.5

12.5 cm; 11.3 g. Slender with long, narrow tail; long legs; thin, wrenlike bill. VOICE: song a liquid sequence of monotonous *wood-wood-wood*s . . . continuing 15–20 seconds, surprisingly low for a bird so small and slender; somewhat reminiscent of phrase of a Ferruginous Pygmy-Owl, *Glaucidium brasilianum,* heard at a distance. Edge of dense secondary forests, at average height of 2 m. Hops tirelessly through branches, forepart of body held low and tail cocked, wrenlike. Espírito Santo and Minas Gerais to Rio de Janeiro, São Paulo, Paraná, and Misiones, Argentina. In Espírito Santo and Rio de Janeiro restricted to mountains above 600 m. Extreme rarity of this species in collections and complete lack of data on its biology (no one knew voice, which identifies it immediately) before I began work in 1939 hampered recognition of true relationship of this bird, which had been attributed to such disparate families as Formicariidae, Troglodytidae, and Sylviidae.

SLATY BRISTLEFRONT, *Merulaxis ater,* Entufado   BR

17 cm; 37.2 g (male), 33 g (female). Restricted to southeast. Notable for elongated frontal feathers. Lead-black with brownish rump and abdomen; long, wide, tail; strong legs. Female brown with cinnamon underparts. VOICE: song a particularly melodious phrase on a rapidly descending musical scale of an octave, followed by a varied mixture of full notes with same timbre that are partly ventriloquial and tremulous; warning a sonorous *tsewk-tsewk, pit;* impressive notes given

by bird when frightened; there are longer sequences, *ik, ik, ik, ik;* differences of timbre probably relate to sex. Hops or runs on ground and through low branches. Thickets in tall virgin or secondary forests. Bahia to Paraná. In Espírito Santo and Rio de Janeiro found only in mountains, sometimes alongside *Psilorhamphus guttatus* and/or *Scytalopus indigoticus, S. speluncae,* and Large-tailed Antshrike, *Mackenziaena leachii.*

STRESEMANN'S BRISTLEFRONT, *Merulaxis stresemanni* BR   R

20.7 cm. Recorded only from Bahia. Similar to *M. ater* but larger with thicker bill, tarsi, toes, and claws. Known only from 2 specimens, a male collected between 1831–38 in Recôncavo region (Salvador) and a female collected in Ilhéus in 1945. Weights for this species are lacking. Should occur in densest forest of mountainous areas; must be highly endangered by almost total devastation of region's woodlands (see Chapter 3.2.4).

MOUSE-COLORED TAPACULO, *Scytalopus speluncae,* Tapaculo-preto   Fig. 202

10.5 cm; 15 g. Minuscule mountain bird of southeast Brazil. Male uniformly slate gray ("color of the black rat," *Rattus rattus*), female brownish with scaly-looking flanks; immature almost entirely covered with this scaly pattern. VOICE: *it, it-eet, gweea;* warning *birret;* song a dry, monotonous *tseh-tseh-tseh* . . . for 6–20 seconds but sometimes lasting 3 minutes or more; can be reminiscent of a *Dendro-*

Fig. 202. Mouse-colored Tapaculo, *Scytalopus speluncae,* in a typical stance, close to the ground.

cincla song. Hops on ground or through lowest branches. Edge and interior of thick, shady forests and bamboo groves; often the only bird in thickets of crisciuma-bengala (*Chusquea pinnifolia*) at top of Serra do Caparaó at 2000–2500 m. Minas Gerais and Espírito Santo to Rio Grande do Sul and Misiones, Argentina. Reaches highest populational density between 2000–2300 m on Serra do Caparaó. In northern part of range (e.g., Rio de Janeiro) does not occur below 1000 m. A close relative of numerous congeners in Andes and Patagonia. I have compared type specimen in Leningrad Museum, collected by E. Ménétriès (see Chapter 2.3) in São João del Rey, Minas Gerais, and described by him in 1835, with the type of *S. novacapitalis* to convince myself of the difference, which is very clear.

BRASILIA TAPACULO, *Scytalopus novacapitalis*, Tapaculo-de-Brasília   BR   R   PL 45.12

11 cm; 18.9 g. Upperparts dark gray, underparts light gray. Lores whitish; bill dark, mandible a bit lighter; legs light, yellowish brown, or pink (not dark brown as in smaller *S. speluncae*). VOICE: song resembles *speluncae* and thus is measured: *shet-shet-shet . . . , ewk-ewk-ewk . . . ,* or *tok-tok-tok . . . ,* with much less hurried rhythm than *speluncae*. This slightly rising sequence may continue uninterruptedly for 2 minutes or more. Sometimes a 2d individual (probably female) responds with higher sequence, *wit . . . ;* warning *cheh-teh-teh;* when aroused in defense of territory by playback, the long, monotonous sequence I describe becomes short and ends with a harsh *tsa, tsa, tsa . . .* that corresponds to warning. On ground or low above it in deeply shaded, flooded riverine forest with abundant ferns (*Blechnum brasiliense*) and palmito-juçara (*Euterpe edulis*). Discovered in May 1957 at Córrego Fundo in region of new capital, NOVACAP, then under construction; found again in 1981. White-striped Warbler, *Basileuterus leucophrys,* and *Lochmias nematura* occur in same area. In a census done by A. Negret and R. Cavalcanti (1985) using playback, 68 individuals were found in flooded gallery forests of IBGE Reserve and surrounding areas of Lago Paranoá watershed of Federal District. Has also appeared in Formosa, Goiás (J. Hidasi). Later I found it 500 km to southeast in Minas Gerais, in mountains between Rios São Francisco and Paranaíba watersheds: Serra da Canastra, 1200 m (1980 and subsequent years) and high on Serra Negra, Lagoa Chapadão de Ferro, 1000 m. (Sponsorship of G. Mattos 1981).

WHITE-BREASTED TAPACULO, *Scytalopus indigoticus,* Macuquinho

11 cm; 18 g. Similar to *S. novacapitalis* and *S. speluncae*. Upperparts bluish black, rump reddish, underparts very white, flanks cinnamon barred brown, mandible and legs whitish. VOICE: call *tec,* like a tree frog; song a sequence of muffled *ksh, ksh, kshs . . .* beginning hesitantly, then accelerating and ending tremolo, following song pattern of a *Thamnophilus* antshrike but much weaker. Another, totally different vocalization, with timbre of a *Crypturellus* tinamou (see *Liosceles*), consists of a loud, ascending, 2-second trill. Behavior similar to *novacapitalis*. Edge of extremely dense forests, sometimes alongside *Psilorhamphus guttatus,* locally on coast to about 1000 m (Rio de Janeiro), perhaps meeting *speluncae*. Bahia and Minas Gerais to Rio Grande do Sul and Misiones, Argentina. In certain parts of Serra do Mar, in São Paulo and Santa Catarina (at sea level) not uncommon.

Rhinocryptidae Bibliography
See also General Bibliography

Feduccia, A., and S. L. Olson. 1987. Morphological similarities between the Menurae and Rhinocryptidae, relict Passerine birds of the southern hemisphere. *Smithsonian Contr. Zool.* 366.

Negret, A., and R. Cavalcanti. 1985. Censo populacional de duas aves da região de Brasília: *Scytalopus novacapitalis* e *Melanopareia torquata. XII Cong. Bras. Zool., Campinas:* 271.

Olalla, A. M. 1938. *Rev. Mus. Paul.* 23:281–86. [Behavior]

Olson, S. L., and E. N. Kurochkin. 1987. Fossil evidence of a tapaculo in the quaternary of Cuba. *Proc. Biol. Soc. Wash.* 100(2):353–57.

Plotnick, R. 1958. *Physis* 21:130–36. [Anatomy]

Sick, H. 1954. *Bonn. Zool. Beitr.* 5:179–90. [*Psilorhamphus*, morphology, behavior]

Sick, H. 1958. *Bol. Mus. Nac. Rio de Janeiro, Zool.* 185. [*Scytalopus novacapitalis*]

Sick, H. 1960. *J. Orn.* 101:141–74. [*Merulaxis stresemanni*, taxonomy, biology]

Sick, H. 1964. Tapaculo. In A. L. Thomson, ed., *A New Dictionary of Birds.* New York: McGraw-Hill.

Sick, H. 1985. Observations on the Andean-Patagonian component of southeastern Brazil's avifauna. In *Neotrop. Ornithol.,* Ornith. Monogr., no. 36.

FAMILY FORMICARIIDAE: ANTBIRDS (167)

This exclusively Neotropical family vies with the Trochilidae for having the second largest number of species in South America (the Tyrannidae has the most). Fossils from the upper Pleistocene (20,000 years B.P.) have been found in Minas Gerais.

Antbirds occur from Mexico to northern Argentina in areas rich in brushy vegetation or forest. They are more diversified in warmer regions. Antbirds are related to tapaculos (Rhinocryptidae). The gnateaters, *Conopophaga,* were recently included in the Formicariidae.

Morphology and Signaling

Species vary considerably in size, with very small ones, such as the *Myrmotherula*, weighing 10 g or less and large ones, such as the *Grallaria* and the Giant Antshrike, *Batara cinerea,* weighing as much as 120 g or more. As a consequence their appearance varies appreciably. Some, such as the *Terenura*, are similar to flycatchers; others, such as *Batara* and the *Mackenziaena*, resemble cuckoos. Genera such as the *Taraba, Thamnophilus, Dysithamnus,* and *Myrmotherula* are spoken of as "typical" antbirds and form a morphological grouping based on a pair of syringeal muscles, distinct from the usually long-legged "terrestrial" antbirds, *Grallaria, Chamaeza,* and *Formicarius,* which have no intrinsic syringeal musculature. The *Conopophaga* also belong to the latter group, besides being anatomically close to the Rhinocryptidae. *Conopophaga* are unique in the group in having developed sound-producing wing feathers.

The so-called typical antbirds are recognizable by their soft plumage, especially on the back and flanks, and their subdued coloring, often black and gray in the male, brown in the female. An eye-catching contrast is created by a white pattern often found on the upper wing and tail coverts and frequently by a white area at the base of the dorsal feathers. This spot remains hidden except when purposely displayed in moments of excitement, such as before rivals and during agonistic behavior, when the feathers are raised to produce a "stoplight" signal. The importance of this mechanism is demonstrated by its wide diffusion throughout the family. The spot may be barely outlined or so extensive it rarely remains hidden, as in the Dot-winged Antwren, *Microrhopias quixensis*. At times it occurs only in certain geographic races of a species or in only one of the sexes. In the Rufous-throated Antbird, *Gymnopithys rufigula,* the bases of the "signal" feathers differ in color between the sexes, being white in the male, buff in the female. The presence of white under the wing is common, on under wing coverts or the underside of the flight feather vanes. This is displayed when the wings are raised, as in the Cinereous Antshrike, *Thamnomanes caesius,* and White-flanked Antwren, *Myrmotherula axillaris*. There are also white tufts on the flanks that are revealed by fascinating movements, as in *M. axillaris*. The half-concealed white on the crown of the Barred Antshrike, *Thamnophilus doliatus,* remotely resembles the vividly colored, concealed median stripe on the crown of many Tyrannidae. The *Conopophaga* have a different signal, a flashy postocular stripe exposed only when the bird is excited, rising as a brilliant tuft that ornaments the lateral contour of the head.

Another notable feature is the bare, brightly colored periophthalmic region of the *Gymnopithys, Rhegmatorhina,* and *Phlegopsis,* which in the deep Hylaean shadows appears almost phosphorescent on the Bare-eyed Antbird, *Rhegmatorhina gymnops*. When the bird is calm this area is restricted to a supraorbital zone, but it enlarges with excitement by retraction of the adjacent feathers and becomes an extensive, vivid periorbital patch. It is less colorful in immature birds. The same process can be observed in toucans, aracaris, and *Neomorphus* ground-cuckoos.

Certain semiterrestrial species, such as the Wing-banded Antbird, *Myrmornis torquata,* have a rather confusing plumage pattern, difficult to describe. The contrasts in the streaking on the flanks of *Chamaeza* imitate the play of light and shadow in the Hylaea and obscure the bird's body contours. Long crests occur in *Batara, Mackenziaena, Taraba, Sakesphorus, Pithys, Percnostola,* and *Rhegmatorhina;* some, such as *Thamnophilus,* appear crested when they elevate their crown feathers.

The wings are well developed though generally rounded, and in certain cases, such as *Myrmornis torquata* and the Banded Antbird, *Dichrozona cincta,* are quite large and strong. The tail is soft and varies in size from almost rudimentary, as in the *Grallaria,* to wide and longer than the body, as in *Batara cinerea* and the Spot-backed Antshrike, *Hypoedaleus guttatus*. Large, dark eyes, as in *D. cincta* and the *Grallaria,* are evidence of constant residence in heavily shaded areas. Red irises are common, as in the *Pyriglena,* but there are also light, whitish irises, as in certain *Myrmotherula*. The color may change with age, as for example, in *Dysithamnus* and *Thamnophilus*.

The bill is somewhat hooked and in the larger species strong. The maxilla has a "tooth" that lends itself well to catching and breaking up arthropods with hard exoskeletons. The Black Bushbird, *Neoctantes niger,* of Amazonia, has a chisel bill. Tarsi vary from black to white. Antbirds have their own characteristic odor.

Sexual differences are sometimes recognizable in nestlings, as in *Pyriglena*. In genera such as *Taraba* young males resemble females, later molting to definitive male plumage. Sexes are similar in the Star-throated Antwren, *Myrmotherula gularis,* and in the *Hypocnemis, Pithys, Formicarius, Chamaeza, Phlegopsis,* and *Grallaria*. Female coloring is particularly useful in identifying similar species, such as those of the *Formicivora* and *Cercomacra*. There are many similar species; see, for example, the Eastern Slaty Antshrike, *Thamnophilus punctatus*. It is important to note that female coloring has diversified more than that of males in various Amazonian species. In other words, while the aspect of males has scarcely altered over vast regions, their respective females have become quite diverse and now provide the basis for description of geographic races. This phenomenon (heterogynism, C. E. Hellmayr 1929; it is not "heterogeny") occurs, for example, in the *Thamnophilus, Dysithamnus, Thamnomanes, Myrmotherula, Formicivora, Cercomacra, Pyriglena, Myrmoborus,* and *Hylophylax*. In addition to geographic heterogynism there is specific heterogynism: diversification among females of species whose males are very similar, as in *Thamnophilus punctatus* and the Amazonian Antshrike, *T. amazonicus.* Also see heterogynism of Black-legged Dacnis, *Dacnis nigripes,* in Thraupinae, "Morphology."

Vocalization

Antbird songs are often ascending and/or descending sequences of harsh, ventroloquial whistles, as in *Thamnophilus,* or clear and limpid, as in *Thamnomanes* and *Myrmoborus. Thamnophilus* stanzas may resemble cuckoos such as the *Coccyzus;* the tremolos of *Hypoedaleus guttatus,* the *Myrmoborus,* and the Black-cheeked Gnateater, *Conopophaga melanops,* resemble, respectively, the Long-billed Gnatwren, *Ramphocaenus melanurus* (Sylviidae), the *Sclerurus* (Furnariidae), and the *Merulaxis* (Rhinocryptidae). The profusion of such trills in a Neotropical forest can be difficult to decipher. The components of a genus, *Thamnophilus* for instance, generally follow the same song pattern, so it is easily possible to distinguish the songs of congeneric species in nature or on recordings (noting timbre and rhythm when they can be compared), but a description in words is very difficult.

Allospecies usually have the same or very similar vocalization, as in *Pyriglena,* confirming taxonomic judgments based on morphology. Related genera, for example *Thamnophilus, Taraba,* and *Sakesphorus,* or *Gymnopithys, Rhegmatorhina, Phlegopsis,* and *Pithys,* have similar voices. In these cases vocalization is less differentiated than morphology.

The vocal repertoire of certain species is composed of six or more different types. In Central America 14 different vocalizations have been noted for the Bicolored Antbird, *Gymnopithys bicolor* (Willis 1967). The Ferruginous Antbird, *Drymophila ferruginea,* is unique for its call that can be heard at a distance as the bird wanders through the forest canopy outside the breeding season.

Among the most impressive vocalizations of Brazilian birds are the musical scales of the *Chamaeza* antthrushes, sung in the morning and late afternoon. These songs, together with those of the White-browed Antpitta, *Hylopezus ochroleucus*; Thrush-like Antpitta, *Myrmothera campanisona*; and Formicarius, may recall tinamous (see also Rusty-belted Tapaculo, *Liosceles thoracicus*). That of the Variegated Antpitta, *Grallaria varia,* low and lugubrious, given only at dawn and dusk, in timbre resembles a large owl. The loudest voice is that of *Batara cinerea* which can be heard at a distance of well over 1 km. The extraordinary prolongation of *Chamaeza* stanzas makes one wonder how the bird breathes while singing.

Females also sing, with a voice that may be higher and weaker, as in *Dysithamnus* and *Herpsilochmus,* softer and more melodious, as in the Dusky Antbird, *Cercomacra tyrannina,* or lower, as in the Stripe-backed Antbird, *Myrmorchilus strigilatus.* They generally respond to the male, and pairs sing duets, as in *Formicivora* and *Sakesphorus,* the

sexes occasionally singing different songs, as for example the Blackish Antbird, *Cercomacra nigrescens.* In the Scale-backed Antbird, *Hylophylax poecilinota,* some chase each other around their territory, singing and fluttering their wings. A few species, the "whistlers," *Pyriglena* and *Formicarius,* call loudly when they become agitated while following ant swarms (see "Feeding"), like thrushes when roosting at dusk.

From an evolutionary standpoint it is interesting that voice may be more stable than morphology, as in the *Myrmeciza,* suggesting that the respective species might be grouped as semispecies or geographic races.

Playback of the voice of certain very shy species, such as the *Grallaria,* can bring the bird out like magic to permit observation.

The male Rufous Gnateater, *Conopophaga lineata,* can produce a resonant rustling with its peculiarly shaped primaries ("sonorous remiges"), although its flight is normally silent. *Pithys* and *Gymnopithys* snap their bills.

Feeding

Antbirds seek insects and other arthropods such as spiders, daddy longlegs, millipedes, scorpions, etc., and enjoy caterpillars. *Pyriglena* catch geckos; *Mackenziaena* and *Batara,* having strong beaks, even kill mice, small snakes, nestling birds (they also like eggs), and frogs. These two genera and the *Myrmeciza* like snails. *Chamaeza* and *Grallaria* also eat seeds and are sometimes caught in traps baited with corn. The Short-tailed Antthrush, *Chamaeza campanisona,* is attracted by the succulent fruits of pokeweed (*Phytolacca decandra*).

Thamnomanes and others capture insects in flight. *Thamnophilus* and *Cercomacra* frighten up insects by beating their wings among the foliage, a tactic also employed by owls against sleeping birds. In searching for food, terrestrial species throw forest litter to the sides with rapid movements of the bill, without scratching the earth as the *Sclerurus* (Furnariidae) do. These bill movements resemble a similar technique of pigeons.

The name *antbird* is derived from the fact that certain, relatively few, species take advantage of army-ant swarms that serve as beaters to frighten up prey. These are primarily large, red ants (*Eciton burchelli*), or small, blackish "rain ants" (*Labidus praedator*). In both species the ant hordes, following an annual cycle of alternating nomadic and sedentary periods, march along the ground in broad formations or narrow columns, creating unique predatory fronts that advance through the dry, terra-firme forests, especially in Amazonia. These ants frighten all living things in their path, so the forest ahead appears to boil as the many animals, primarily crickets and cockroaches, flee the "front." The whole atmosphere is saturated with a crackling rustle produced by the ants and by fleeing animals, some of which, such as slow and languid caterpillars, are immediately overcome. Where daddy longlegs and bugs are abundant, the caustic odor these arthropods emit on fleeing can be smelled at a distance.

It is not well known that, unlike driver ants (*Dorylus*) of Africa, Neotropical army ants, *Eciton* and *Labidus,* cannot dismember vertebrates, for they lack cutting mandibles (Schneirla 1960, Willis 1985). Army ants live on insects and other arthropods, including other ants.

All this agitation attracts "army-ant birds" and, among these, antbirds. The "bridgehead" of the ant swarms, where the richest booty is guaranteed, is occupied by the strongest birds—adult males and the most aggressive species—which gorge themselves while screeching and driving away their rivals, even with bodily force. Competition is great, and an intra- and interspecific hierarchy is established as to who pecks and who gets pecked. Under favorable conditions a bird can capture one prey per minute, and on days when there are many swarms the most assiduous birds move from one front to another. Not only birds whose territories are invaded take advantage of the swarms, but also those attracted from the vicinity and even from more distant areas. The voices of certain species, when excited, carry more than 300 m and serve as a lure. There is a certain amount of interspecific vocal understanding, so not only antbirds but woodcreepers and tanagers attend the call to participate in the feast and react to alarms, but the antbirds, especially the *Pyriglena* with their very loud voices, are the noisiest. The most regular followers of army ants that obtain the greater part of their food thanks to these insects are called "professionals" (Willis 1967). They include, for example, in the Belém, Pará, region, the Black-spotted Bare-eye, *Phlegopsis nigromaculata;* White-backed Fire-eye, *Pyriglena leuconota;* and *Hylophylax poecilinota*. North of the Amazon *Gymnopithys leucaspis* stands out. Elsewhere in the country or continent other species may be more involved. Troglodytidae, Turdidae, Momotidae, Bucconidae, and others are also among ant-swarm followers. Large swarms may attract ten or more individuals of the same species plus other isolated birds. The situation varies greatly, with species participation depending very much on location. For instance, in the Belém region there might be seven species. The phenomenon is most common in Amazonia but may be absent in small patches of forest.

Prey frightened up by the ants are caught not far above ground on branches, leaves, or trunks by birds that fly, hop rapidly on the ground, etc., according to species. Antbirds hop, for instance, woodcreepers creep. Antbirds frequently use vertical perches low above ground. This would be impossible with driver ants, so dangerous they would attack and devour a bird that came so close; in Africa birds that follow driver ants, such as thrushes, perch higher on horizontal branches. Terrestrial species such as *Grallaria* and the *Neomorphus* ground-cuckoos run swiftly through the boiling ant swarm to snatch a morsel. Great confusion appears to reign,

but there is a well-established hierarchy: the strongest occupy the best sites. When an ant reaches a bird's foot, the bird shakes the foot violently or nips at it to free itself from the insect. Ants themselves are not hunted, but a bird may unintentionally catch one while chasing another insect. The technique used to catch such fleeing prey can be classified as follows: (1) catch the victim without leaving the perch: perch-glean; (2) fly to get prey that is on the substrate: sally-glean; or (3) capture the insect in flight: aerial-hawk (Fitzpatrick 1980a). Other types of ants are hunted, as I verified with a *Taraba major* (which infrequently associates with ant swarms) specimen that had 418 ants, including 109 pupae, belonging to three species in its stomach. *Dichrozona cincta* and *Conopophaga lineata* also eat ants sometimes.

The temporary association of certain antbirds such as the *Thamnomanes, Myrmotherula, Herpsilochmus,* and *Terenura* in flocks with other birds such as spinetails, woodcreepers, and tanagers also has a nutritional basis. Flying termite swarms, a major attraction for so many birds, also attract antbirds, although they do not like to fly in the open. Silva (1986) found eight White-fringed Antwrens, *Formicivora grisea,* participating in one termite flight in Amazonia, which also shows the high populational density of this species. Antbirds drink rainwater accumulated on leaves.

Behavior

The tail and crown are the best indicators of antbird nervousness. Various tail movements are characteristic for entire groups of species and can be important in systematic determinations. A slow lowering and raising of the tail, for example in *Pyriglena, Sclateria, Myrmoborus,* and *Myrmeciza,* accompanied by a spreading of the rectrices sometimes reveals white spots that otherwise are invisible or almost so, as in *Hypocnemoides* and the Scaled Antbird, *Drymophila squamata. Pithys* and *Gymnopithys* move the spread tail slowly forward and then throw it back to the original position as if pulled by a spring. The Brazilian Antthrush, *Chamaeza ruficauda,* does the opposite, lowering the tail rapidly and raising it slowly. *Mackenziaena, Myrmorchilus, Hylophylax, Rhegmatorhina,* and *Phlegopsis* also are noted for much tail movement, with the rectrices open. Wagging the tail is common with *Thamnophilus punctatus.* Species with very short tails, such as the *Formicarius* and *Grallaria,* walk almost constantly with the tail cocked like tapaculos and rails, their occasional neighbors on the shady Hylaean floor. See "Morphology . . . " re display of white areas normally covered by cryptic plumage.

Hylopezus ochroleucus makes strange to-and-fro body movements when alarmed, vaguely like the Sunbittern, *Eurypyga helias.* Some antbirds, such as *Cercomacra,* snap the beak when caught in a mist net.

Antbirds move predominantly by hopping or jumping,

whether on the ground or through the branches, having strong thigh muscles. Semiterrestrial species show great variation in tarsus and toe development. Legs may be long and thick, the toes long and strong, and the claws large and sharp, as in *Gymnopithys rufigula, Myrmornis torquata,* and the *Phlegopsis. G. rufigula* and others select and defend certain vertical shoots, common in the Amazonian forest, on which they perch to broaden their visual horizons and drive away intruders pausing nearby. These species rest and preen on horizontal perches, descending to the ground only to capture prey. Sometimes they hop or fly short distances but rarely walk. *Conopophaga* behave similarly with reference to horizontal branches.

In *Grallaria, Myrmothera, Myrmeciza,* and *Hylophylax* the tarsus is long and slender, an arrangement that seems to facilitate hopping; long toes are not suitable for moving on the ground. *Grallaria varia* could pass for a rabbit as, half hidden, it hops through vegetation in the twilight. In its constant use of certain routes it leaves trails resembling those of leaf-cutter ants. The *Chamaeza* run like gallinules, without making the slightest noise, as do *Grallaria.* Antbirds such as the *Formicarius, Dichrozona,* and *Myrmorchilus* also walk on tree branches. Surprisingly, terrestrial types such as *Grallaria* and *Hylopezus* flee by flying straight and swift as an arrow.

The custom of associating in mixed flocks must be advantageous for less-watchful species such as the *Myrmotherula,* which profit from the vigilance of others such as the *Habia* (Thraupinae) and *Thamnomanes* that are more alert and noisier, drawing attention in time of danger.

Antbirds such as *Grallaria varia* and *Conopophaga lineata* bathe in shallow, shady waters or in the cups of bromeliads, as does *Microrhopias quixensis.* The habit of anting has been observed in *Grallaria, Gymnopithys,* and *Rhegmatorhina;* a *Grallaria varia* used a caustic millipede for this purpose. It is common to rub the bill to clean it. Yawning occurs.

Breeding

Males customarily offer food to females, often before copulation. Many species appear to mate for a year, remaining constantly in the same territory. The reproductive cycle of antbirds that associate with army ants must be adapted to the annual cycle of these insects (see "Feeding"), since the period of the ants' greatest activity is the time of greatest food abundance for the birds and their young. In Trinidad *Thamnophilus doliatus* occupies nests for more than ten months each year; pairs, however, have a shorter breeding cycle. *Formicivora grisea* defends territory all year and probably nests in every month. It is not yet known whether one pair of this species produces two clutches per year, as has been suggested for the Black-headed Antbird, *Percnostola ruffifrons.*

Shapes of antbird nests are diverse, as follows:

1. An open basket made of fibers, stems, moss, etc., suspended in a horizontal fork: *Thamnophilus; Sakesphorus; Taraba; Thamnomanes; Myrmotherula axillaris;* Plain-throated Antwren, *M. hauxwelli,* Streaked Antwren, *M. surinamensis* (its nest is always constructed above water); and *Formicivora.* Among the materials used is "vegetable horsehair," a black fungus (*Marasmius*) very similar to horsehair (see Icterinae, "Breeding").

2. A deep bag made of dry fibers and leaves with a high, side entrance, suspended among dense branches: *Cercomacra.*

3. A large, closed ball about 10 cm in diameter placed low or on the ground with a high, side entrance: *Pyriglena;* or a small sphere: Brown-bellied Antwren, *Myrmotherula gutturalis.* The nest of the Slender Antbird, *Rhopornis ardesiaca,* conforms to this pattern also, being constructed among gravatás (Bromeliaceae) with a large lateral entrance prolonged into a short tunnel.

4. An open saucer made of dry materials such as leaves, stems, etc., set on a firm base in any sort of conical cavity in a tree trunk, in a bunch of leaves among plants on the ground, or in a wide, open, low hole in a tree: *Myrmeciza, Chamaeza, Formicarius, Grallaria, Gymnopithys,* and *Hylophylax.* When nesting in holes, as with *Hylopezus ochroleucus,* the entrance may be 2 m above ground but lead to the base of the trunk. *Conopophaga* gather a high pile of dry leaves on the ground in a patch of plants, *Eryngium* for instance, to support their saucers.

Antbirds normally lay two eggs, unequally shaped at the ends for smaller species and for *Formicarius,* or almost round, as with *Chamaeza.* They may be white, light pink, yellowish, or light brownish with chestnut, sepia, red, lilac, etc., spots generally concentrated on the more rounded end, sometimes recalling those of certain flycatchers. The two eggs of *Conopophaga melanops* are brownish cream with an ample ring of chocolate or violet specks on the large end. *Chamaeza* and *Formicarius* lay pure white eggs. The large eggs of *Grallaria varia* are greenish blue, resembling those of the Solitary Tinamou, *Tinamus solitarius.*

Parents take turns both in nest construction and in caring for the young; each sex has a brood patch. The female remains on the nest at night. Incubation lasts 14 days in the Black-crested Antshrike, *Sakesphorus canadensis,* 15 in the Plain Antvireo, *Dysithamnus mentalis,* 16 in *Myrmotherula axillaris,* and 17 to 18 in *Taraba major.* Young *D. mentalis* abandon the nest after 9 days, those of *Thamnophilus doliatus* in 12 to 13 days, and those of the Black-faced Antthrush, *Formicarius analis,* and *Conopophaga melanops* in 18 days. The parents clean the nest by swallowing the nestlings' excrement, as with *Sakesphorus,* and feign injury to draw the attention of a potential predator away from the nest. In doing so they make movements resembling those made when bathing. Fledglings sometimes draw attention by their incessant whistling, as in the Chestnut-backed Antshrike, *Thamnophilus palliatus,* and *Conopophaga lineata.* Tham-

nophilus and *Dysithamnus* are sometimes hosts to the Pavonine Cuckoo, *Dromococcyx pavoninus.*

Habitat, Abundance, Evolution, and Distribution

Antbirds are among the most abundant birds wherever there is suitable vegetation in South America's hot regions.

Congeneric species (e.g., various *Thamnophilus* and *Formicivora*) customarily exclude each other ecologically, but other very similar ones, such as *Dysithamnus mentalis* and the Spot-breasted Antvireo, *D. stictothorax,* may occur side by side, sometimes perching on the same branch without evidence of clashing, although it is not always easy to observe such interactions. In certain genera there has been pronounced diversification, the *Myrmotherula* being a good example. Some are semiterrestrial, some live 10 m or more high, others are found in intermediate strata. Most formicariids live at medium heights in shaded woodland, but the *Herpsilochmus* wander through the Hylaean canopy where the Rufous-backed Antvireo, *Dysithamnus xanthopterus;* Streak-capped Antwren, *Terenura maculata;* Gray Antbird, *Cercomacra cinerascens;* and *Drymophila ferruginea* are also found.

Adaptation of many *Thamnophilus* and *Myrmotherula* to diverse strata of the Amazonian Hylaea and to other ecological conditions permits the ornithologist to predict the presence or absence of respective members of these groups. Bamboo thickets in the forest may be attractive to certain species. Further research should be undertaken to determine morphological differences originating from the habitat of the birds in question.

The populational density of the Rusty-backed Antwren, *Formicivora rufa,* and *F. grisea,* for instance, in certain types of sunny capoeira and in the caatinga of central and eastern Brazil is impressively large. *F. grisea* is a good colonizer of altered environments in Amazonia, reaching high densities in landscapes opened by people and thereby constantly extending its geographic distribution. In Central Brazil *F. grisea* and *F. rufa* replace each other ecologically: *F. grisea* occurs in denser vegetation (cerradão, but does not enter the forest). *F. rufa* lives in open cerrado. The Black-bellied Antwren, *F. melanogaster,* occupies tangles at river edges. The *Pyriglena* are encountered with great frequency in deeply shaded forests, both in Amazonia and the southeast. In the caatinga of Rio das Contas, Bahia, we found during two visits of a few days (October 1977, December 1978) a total of 11 antbird species: Silvery-cheeked Antshrike, *Sakesphorus cristatus;* Rufous-winged Antshrike, *Thamnophilus torquatus;* Salvadori's Antwren, *Myrmotherula minor;* Pileated Antwren, *Herpsilochmus pileatus;* Narrow-billed Antwren, *Formicivora iheringi;* White-shouldered Fire-eye, *Pyriglena leucoptera; Taraba major; Thamnophilus punctatus; Rhopornis ardesiaca; Myrmochi-*

lus strigilatus; and a *Hylopezus* antpitta. This picture was further amplified by Teixeira (1987) in a new visit to the same place in October 1983: 18 antbird species were recorded in the various ecological niches.

In a census carried out over various years in an area near Belém, Pará (Rio Guamá, Novaes 1971), using mist nets, the antbird family provided the largest number of species (13) of which *Pyriglena leuconota* was the most abundant in capoeira and terra firme and *Myrmotherula hauxwelli* in várzea forests. In the study areas, which had already been altered by people, antbirds were outnumbered in density and frequency only by the Wedge-billed Woodcreeper, *Glyphorynchus spirurus.* The Rufous-capped Antthrush, *Formicarius colma,* is an example of a species with low populational density.

In a second area (Rio Acará) in the same region, in capoeira and partially altered forests, 12 Formicariidae species were found alongside 12 Fringillidae species and 17 Tyrannidae species. For the entire Belém, Pará, area of 736 sq km, 31 antbird species have been found; for the Municipality of Rio de Janeiro, formerly the state of Guanabara, with 1356 sq km, there are 22 species, but only 19 for the whole state of Rio Grande do Sul with 282,184 sq km. In Peruvian Amazonia, probably the world's richest area in bird life, 40 antbird species may occur in just one locality, and in one day it is possible to see 10 *Myrmotherula* species.

A real explosion occurred in the evolution of this group in Amazonia because of the region having the most ecologically diversified forest spectrum on the entire globe, and also because of the evolution of an immensely rich fauna providing sustenance for birds. Antbirds and flycatchers have best adapted themselves to this situation, which requires the most varied specializations for effective exploitation of the myriad creatures that live there and do their best to elude their predators. This process has resulted in Amazonia having a great number of insectivorous bird species with relatively low populations.

Speciation was even more stimulated by repeated fragmentation the region underwent during the Pleistocene and post-Pleistocene eras. Climatic changes in those times produced successive wet and dry periods, dividing the forest and segregating woodland fauna and flora into isolated refuges (see Cotingidae and Ramphastidae, "Distribution . . . "). Reflecting the fact that these environmental alterations are relatively recent (in geological time), differentiation in many cases only reached the level of geographic races, as for instance in *Thamnophilus, Myrmotherula,* and *Hypocnemis;* more than six races of *Thamnophilus doliatus* are known in Brazil.

Sometimes more differentiated allopatric forms, called allospecies, evolved. These make up superspecies, as in *Gymnopithys* and *Rhegmatorhina.* The effects of such differentiation normally are manifested more in morphology than in behavior, including vocalization (see "Vocalization"). In certain regions, such as the Venezuelan/Colombian boundary, *Gymnopithys rufigula* and *G. leucaspis* interbreed, forming a mixed population (*G. rufigula pallidigula*); analogous cases will perhaps be discovered in Brazil. Speciation is only complete when the congeneric species involved are sympatric in a certain area without interbreeding (e.g., in *Dysithamnus*). There are various cryptic species, as in the *Chamaeza* and *Formicarius*.

Distribution of certain species, for instance the *Chamaeza* and *Thamnophilus palliatus,* is disjunct and sometimes limited even in forests that are now continuous. Evidently many populations have died out. The wide, lower courses of some rivers frequently act as barriers to dispersal, which is not surprising considering that many antbirds are photophobic and do not even cross narrow rivers in spite of their good flying ability. Apparently the intricate Amazonian river system has changed over the centuries; previously narrow rivers have widened while others have diminished or disappeared, creating new ecological problems that are not always conquered by the fauna.

When weak-flying *Thamnophilus* or other antbirds are found on forested islands in the middle of large Amazon tributaries they may represent an earlier, easy, spontaneous invasion or a forced colonization caused by strong winds that carried these photophobic birds out of riverside vegetation to distant islands when they did not succumb to the waves. Living in the trees they are not forced out by the periodic floods, unlike the terrestrial Tinamidae.

Some widely distributed genera in Amazonia have an isolated representative in the forests of southeastern Brazil, for example, the Rio de Janeiro Antbird, *Cercomacra brasiliana.* This is evidence of earlier Amazonian incursions southward during the previously mentioned climatic changes, when Amazonian formations approached or met southeastern Brazilian forests. I consider the three *Pyriglena* to be geographic species that evolved as a result of such phytogeographic modifications and that can be accepted as allospecies.

Among the most notable antbirds of the southeast are the *Batara, Mackenziaena, Biatas,* and four *Myrmotherula,* which suggests a former center of evolution in this part of the country. The *Myrmotherula* constitute the most diversified group within the antbirds, with 25 species, some extremely similar, in Brazil.

Rhopornis ardesiaca of the dry interior forest of southeastern Bahia is a unique endemic; the Rufous-tailed Antbird, *Drymophila genei,* is another interesting case, being restricted to high mountains of the southeast and one of our few real mountain birds. *Batara* and *Chamaeza* "connect" southeastern Brazil to the Andes. *Chamaeza campanisona* reaches Guyana, passing from one mountain range to another, whereas the Noble Antthrush, *C. nobilis,* penetrates into the upper Amazon region. Equally peculiar is the distribution of *Myrmorchilus strigilatus* which inhabits

northeastern caatinga and reappears in corresponding formations in Mato Grosso and Paraguay, showing that the two areas were certainly united not so long ago.

Parasites and Diseases

Chamaeza campanisona may host large numbers of blood protozoans, *Trypanosoma dabbenei* having been identified in Misiones, Argentina. The majority of antbirds investigated by teams from the Evandro Chagas Institute in Belém, Pará, revealed a high rate of antibodies against the *Oropouche* virus, an arbovirus transmitted by blood-sucking insects that is widespread among the population of Amazonia (see also Troglodytidae, "Parasites . . . ").

Decline and Conservation

Problems are accumulating in eastern Brazil where environmental destruction is going to compromise the survival of *Rhopornis ardesiaca, Formicivora iheringi,* and the Fringe-backed Fire-eye, *Pyriglena atra.* As Willis (1979) showed, *Pyriglena leuconota* does not survive in forests of 21 to 250 ha, only in those of 300 ha or more. The situation of *P. atra* and *Rhopornis* must be the same due to the destruction of Atlantic forests and the "vine forests" in the caatinga caused by the human population explosion. The case of the Black-hooded Antwren, *Formicivora erythronotos,* was recently clarified: it survives without problems in an area that had been poorly investigated.

Synopsis of the Principal Brazilian Antbirds

Classification by size and ecology, the criteria adopted here, provides only an approximation to reality; nevertheless I hope it will help beginners find their way through this unquestionably confusing multitude. Identification of many species requires a complete listing of morphological characters, which is impractical here.

Antbird specialists recently decided to exclude four genera from the Formicariidae: *Psilorhamphus, Melanopareia, Ramphocaenus,* and *Microbates.* The first two have been included in the Rhinocryptidae, the latter two in the Sylviidae. The genus *Conopophaga* has been added, brought from the old, now dismembered Conopophagidae family.

1. Large; bushy crest; long, barred tail; low: *Batara* (see fig. 203), *Mackenziaena* (see fig. 204), both from southeastern Brazil, and *Frederickena,* from Amazonia; see also *Hypoedaleus.*
2. Large; long legs and short tail; low or on the ground: *Grallaria* (Pl 29.1), *Chamaeza, Formicarius* (Pl 29.2).
3. Medium size; low or on the ground:
   3.1. Periorbital region bare and brightly colored: *Gymnopithys, Rhegmatorhina,* and *Phlegopsis* (Pl 29.3), all in Amazonia; also *Myrmeciza melanops* and *M. fortis.*

3.2. Long legs; short tail: *Hylopezus, Myrmothera,* both resembling *Grallaria,* and *Myrmornis.*

4. Medium size; tail medium or long; legs not very long; at medium height above ground with incursions into higher and lower strata:

4.1. Prominent crest: *Sakesphorus.*

4.2. Crest slight or absent: *Thamnophilus* (Pl 28.1, fig. 205), *Dysithamnus* (Pl 28.2), and *Cymbilaimus* (this one barred all over, Amazonian).

4.3. Black or slate gray: *Pyriglena* (see fig. 207),*Thamnomanes,* and *Cercomacra* (males).

5. Small or medium size; tail and legs long; low or on the ground: *Myrmeciza* (Pl 28.7), *Myrmorchilus* (this one in the northeast and Mato Grosso).

6. Small or medium size; tail and legs long; low, descending to the ground: *Myrmoborus, Conopophaga* (Pl 29.4), *Hypocnemis, Hypocnemoides, Hylophylax* (Pl 28.8), and *Pithys;* all except *Conopophaga* restricted to Amazonia.

7. Small; tail long:

7.1. Low: *Formicivora* (Pl 28.5), *Drymophila* (Pl 28.3), and *Myrmeciza* (Pl 28.7).

7.2. At medium height and in the canopy: *Herpsilochmus* (Pl 28.6), *Terenura,* and *Microrhopias* (the latter in Amazonia).

8. Small; tail short or medium; both on the ground and in the canopy: *Myrmotherula* (Pl 28.4) and *Dysithamnus mentalis.*

FASCIATED ANTSHRIKE, *Cymbilaimus lineatus,* Papa-formigas-barrado

16.5 cm. Amazonian. Related to *Thamnophilus.* Male all black finely barred with white. Female yellowish brown barred with black, crown chestnut. VOICE: a leisurely sequence of full *eweeups,* crescendo, then decrescendo, resembling *Thamnophilus.* Phlegmatic. Middle levels and borders of dense secondary forest. The Guianas and Venezuela to Bolivia, northern Mato Grosso (upper Rio Xingu), eastern Pará (Rio Tocantins); more common north of Amazon. See *Thamnophilus doliatus.*

BAMBOO ANTSHRIKE, *Cymbilaimus sanctaemariae*

Rondônia, upper Purus, Acre, Peru, Bolivia. Restricted to bamboo thickets. In Rondônia alongside *C. lineatus* (Pierpont and Fitzpatrick 1983).

SPOT-BACKED ANTSHRIKE, *Hypoedaleus guttatus,* Chocão-carijó

20.5 cm. Rather long tailed, black above, sprinkled with white (male) or yellowish (female) with concealed white spot on back; tail barred, underparts yellowish white. VOICE: call *kayewrrr;* song a melodious, ascending tremolo that then descends and rapidly accelerates. Medium and upper forest levels. Bahia and Minas Gerais to Santa Catarina, Rio Grande do Sul, southern Goiás, Paraguay, and Misiones, Argentina. Also called *Papa-formigas-grande* (Minas Gerais).

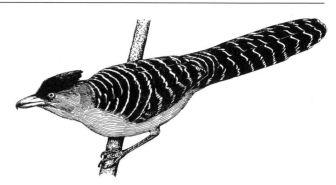

Fig. 203. Giant Antshrike, *Batara cinerea,* male.

GIANT ANTSHRIKE, *Batara cinerea,* Matracão
Fig. 203

34 cm; 134–56 g. Largest Formicariidae. With crest and long, wide tail resembles a terrestrial cuckoo, e.g., *Neomorphus,* or jay. Upperparts black barred with white, underparts uniformly gray (male); female brown with mantle and tail barred black. VOICE: very loud and hard but sonorous; call *klew-aarrr;* warning *tsewk-tsewk-tsewk;* song a prolonged sequence, *rrrrr-kyuh kyuh kyuh . . . jok.* Low in densest thickets and at edge of forest; descends to ground. Difficult to see but betrays itself by voice. Espírito Santo to Rio Grande do Sul, Argentina, Paraguay, eastern Bolivia; in Espírito Santo and Rio de Janeiro restricted to mountains. Also called *Galo-do-mato, Borralhara, Batará* (an Indian name used in Argentina for various antbirds similar to *Thamnophilus*).

LARGE-TAILED ANTSHRIKE, *Mackenziaena leachii,* Borralhara-assobiadora

26.5 cm. Notable for long tail, comprising ¹/₂ total length. Black speckled with white (male) or yellowish (female). VOICE: call a harsh whistle, *kree-kree;* song a prolonged sequence of clear, limpid whistles, first ascending, then descending, with timbre of a *Galbula* jacamar, *bee bee bee . . . .* Dense thickets. Espírito Santo and Minas Gerais to Rio Grande do Sul, Paraguay, and Misiones, Argentina. In Espírito Santo, Minas Gerais, and Rio de Janeiro in mountains, including *Chusquea* open country above tree line, e.g., heights of Serra de Caparaó of Minas Gerais and Espírito Santo. Also called *Papa-ovo, Brujarara, Chororó.*

TUFTED ANTSHRIKE, *Mackenziaena severa,* Borralhara   Fig. 204

23 cm. Prominently crested and long tailed; male uniformly slate with black head; female completely barred light yellow with uniformly rusty crest. VOICE: warning *greh;* call, *SEE-ew;* song an ascending sequence of 6 long, plaintive, raucous whistles, *eww-ew . . . .* Lurks in dense foliage of forests and capoeira. Espírito Santo and Minas Gerais to Rio Grande do Sul, Paraguay, and Misiones, Argentina; re-

Fig. 204. Tufted Antshrike, *Mackenziaena severa*, female.

stricted to mountains in Espírito Santo; reaches ex-Guanabara in Pedra Branca massif but descends to sea level near Mangaratiba and Parati, Rio de Janeiro. See *M. leachii*.

BLACK-THROATED ANTSHRIKE, *Frederickena viridis*
North of lower Amazon, where it can be considered a geographic replacement for *Mackenziaena severa*.

UNDULATED ANTSHRIKE, *Frederickena unduligera*
Upper Amazon, also as a replacement for *Mackenziaena severa*.

GREAT ANTSHRIKE, *Taraba major*, Choró-boi
20.5 cm. Almost like a large *Thamnophilus*. Male black above with hidden white dorsal patch, white bars on wings and tail, underparts white, iris red. Female uniformly rufous on upperparts with hidden white dorsal patch. Immature barred. VOICE: a loud, ventriloquial, ascending and accelerating sequence, *do, do, do* . . . , ending with 1–3 *kraaa*s, in pattern of a *Thamnophilus* song. Sunny, river-edge capoeira. The Guianas and Venezuela to Bolivia, Argentina, Paraguay, Uruguay; almost all of Brazil, south to Mato Grosso, Goiás, western São Paulo, Rio de Janeiro.

GLOSSY ANTSHRIKE, *Sakesphorus luctuosus*, Choca-d'água   BR
16. cm. Amazonian. Prominent crest; black with fine white line on wings, white at tips of axillaries and tail feathers. Female has chestnut crest. VOICE: an accelerating sequence of *kew-ok*s . . . , like *Thamnophilus*. Thickets. Northern bank of Amazon to Mato Grosso, Goiás, southeastern Pará. See *Pyriglena* and *Cercomacra brasiliana*.

SILVERY-CHEEKED ANTSHRIKE, *Sakesphorus cristatus*, Choca-do-nordeste   BR
12.7 cm. Bill slightly more pointed than in *S. luctuosus*. Back brown, crest black (male) or rufous (female); underparts whitish, throat and foreneck black (male); tail all spotted with white as if barred. VOICE: call a melodious and descending *oo;* other notes, e.g., a *bok* that resembles Creamy-bellied Thrush, *Turdus amaurochalinus; tewrr-tewrr-tewrr;* song relatively weak, similar to a *Thamnophilus;* a descending sequence ending in *ga-ga*. Caatinga; locally common, along with *Myrmorchilus strigilatus*. Piauí, Ceará, Bahia, Minas Gerais (Almenara).

BLACK-CRESTED ANTSHRIKE, *Sakesphorus canadensis*
Amazonia.

BAND-TAILED ANTSHRIKE, *Sakesphorus melanothorax*
Amazonia.

WHITE-BEARDED ANTSHRIKE, *Biatas nigropectus*, Papo-branco   R
18 cm. Southern species, brown, male with black cap and pectoral plaque, pure white throat. Female without any black, chestnut cap and white collar, similar to White-collared Foliage-gleaner, *Anabazenops fuscus,* which may be its near neighbor in bamboo thickets of Serra do Mar. VOICE: a series of whistles, *fe, FAYoo, FAYoo-FAYoo-FAYoo* . . . , that can be reminiscent of Green-barred Woodpecker, *Colaptes melanochloros* (G. Mattos). Rio de Janeiro in mountains, e.g., Teresópolis, Itatiaia; also Nova Friburgo (Bescke, from Burmeister 1856; Tinguá, Berla 1979 pers. comm.), Minas Gerais (Viçosa, Itabira, specifically in spiny wild bamboo thickets, G. Mattos), São Paulo, Santa Catarina. Also Misiones, Argentina, where not rare.

BARRED ANTSHRIKE, *Thamnophilus doliatus*, Choca-barrada
16 cm. Male abundantly barred white (yellowish in immature) and black; iris yellow. Female almost uniformly rusty brown with lighter underparts, sides of head streaked blackish brown. VOICE: call a melodious *dee-oh,* song (duet of pair) an accelerating sequence with 2d half descending, ending with conspicuous emphasis, *gagaga* . . . *GA*. Sunny, thin capoeira, várzea forest, caatinga, etc. Mexico to

Fig. 205. Chestnut-backed Antshrike, *Thamnophilus palliatus*, male.

Bolivia, northern Argentina, Brazil to São Paulo. Fourteen geographic races have been described for this species, 7 of them in Brazil. Also called *Chorró-cocá* (Minas Gerais), *Piolho-de-onça* (Mato Grosso), *Mbatará*. See *Cymbilaimus* and *T. palliatus*.

CHESTNUT-BACKED ANTSHRIKE, *Thamnophilus palliatus*, Choca-listrada   Fig. 205

16 cm. Unmistakable. Head and underparts densely barred with white (yellowish in female), mantle and tail chestnut. Male's cap black, female's chestnut. Immature has dark brown, wavy markings on mantle. VOICE: call (diagnostic) a melodious *a-EE, kew-EE;* song a hurried, descending sequence, *ga . . . GWA,* similar to *T. doliatus.* Young utter an ascending series of high peeps. Forests, including sparse but shady secondary woodlands. Frequents cities, e.g., Belém, Rio de Janeiro, in trees with dense canopy. Colombia through upper Amazon to Bolivia. In Brazil in 3 disjunct areas: extreme west (upper Madeira and Guaporé); Rio Tapajós, Pará, to Maranhão; the east from Paraíba to Rio de Janeiro. See also *T. doliatus, T. ruficapillus,* and *T. torquatus,* which are equally barred.

EASTERN SLATY ANTSHRIKE, *Thamnophilus punctatus*, Choca-bate-cabo   PL 28.1

14 cm. Varies geographically, with 5 races in Brazil. Very similar to *T. amazonicus:* basal portion of feathers of superciliary region gray in *punctatus;* in *amazonicus* black contrasting with white tips. VOICE: call quite variable, e.g., a *grrr;* song an ascending sequence of 6–10 well-pronounced *go*s, ending in muffled tremolo. Shakes tail. Forest edges, including secondary forests. Typical of hot lowlands of Rio de Janeiro and central Brazil. East of Andes south from Venezuela and Colombia to Peru, Bolivia, southern Mato Grosso, western São Paulo, Rio de Janeiro. Also called *Batará, Borralhara.* See *T. caerulescens* and *Herpsilochmus pileatus.*

VARIABLE ANTSHRIKE, *Thamnophilus caerulescens*, Choca-da-mata

15 cm. Very much like *T. punctatus* but darker (both sexes) and no white on inner secondaries, though it has concealed white spot on back. Female lacks rufous mark on crown and tail. VOICE: call a melodious *gwew-o, gow, ga-EE;* song an ascending, accelerated sequence ending in a deep *gaaaa.* Lowers tail slowly. Forest margins; tall, dense capoeira; bamboo thickets; etc. Replaces *punctatus* in mountains of Rio de Janeiro and Espírito Santo, being typical of Serra do Mar. The northeast to Rio Grande do Sul, Goiás, southern Mato Grosso, Uruguay, Paraguay, Argentina, Bolivia, Peru (slopes of Andes). Also called *Choró-da-mata* (Minas Gerais).

RUFOUS-WINGED ANTSHRIKE, *Thamnophilus torquatus*, Choca-de-asa-vermelha

13.5 cm. Very small with chestnut wings, black cap, underparts white barred with black, black tail spotted white (male); female has reddish cap, underparts uniformly yellowish, tail rufous without spots. VOICE: typical *Thamnophilus* song, phonetically similar to *T. ruficapillus* but distinguishable from it in field. Locally in cerrado, cerradão, marshy tangles. Southern Pará and northeast to central Brazil and Bolivia, São Paulo, Rio de Janeiro (Muri, April 1960 pers. obs.).

RUFOUS-CAPPED ANTSHRIKE, *Thamnophilus ruficapillus*, Choca-de-chapéu-vermelho

15.5 cm. Very like *T. torquatus* but larger with olive-brown wings almost same as back, no barring on underside (male); both sexes with rusty cap. VOICE: warning (very typical) a *baaaarri;* song a sequence with 1st half slightly ascending, 2d half descending and accelerating, ending in a *kwar* or *kweh.* Low levels from where it descends to ground and hops, in sparse bushes in open country and low, thin, secondary forest. Minas Gerais, Espírito Santo, and Rio de Janeiro (in mountains, especially on top of high ridges such as Serra do Caparaó and Serra dos Órgãos, e.g., in latter at Campo das Antas alongside Itatiaia Thistletail, *Schizoeaca moreirae,* a mountain bird) to Rio Grande do Sul, Uruguay, Paraguay, Argentina, Bolivia.

In Brazilian Amazonia there are seven other *Thamnophilus:*

WHITE-SHOULDERED ANTSHRIKE, *Thamnophilus aethiops*

Also reaches Pernambuco and Alagoas.

The others are:

BLACKISH-GRAY ANTSHRIKE, *Thamnophilus nigrocinereus*

CASTELNAU'S ANTSHRIKE, *Thamnophilus cryptoleucus*

PLAIN-WINGED ANTSHRIKE, *Thamnophilus schistaceus*

MOUSE-COLORED ANTSHRIKE, *Thamnophilus murinus*

AMAZONIAN ANTSHRIKE, *Thamnophilus amazonicus*
See *T. punctatus.*

STREAK-BACKED ANTSHRIKE, *Thamnophilus insignis*

Three other related Formicariidae are also found in Amazonia:

SPOT-WINGED ANTSHRIKE, *Pygiptila stellaris*

PEARLY ANTSHRIKE, *Megastictus margaritatus*
13 cm. Female resembles that of *Myrmotherula guttata* but is larger.

BLACK BUSHBIRD, *Neoctantes niger*
All black with concealed white area on black and upturned bill like a *Xenops* (Furnariidae).

RONDONIA BUSHBIRD, *Clytoctantes atrogularis*
BR   R
Recently described species with upturned mandible, found in terra-firme forest near Rio Jiparaná, eastern Rondônia (Lanyon et al 1990). See Translator's Comments, which precede Part One of this book.

SPOT-BREASTED ANTVIREO, *Dysithamnus stictothorax*, Choquinha-de-peito-pintado   PL 28.2
12 cm. Woodland species common in southeast, with speckled breast diagnostic in separating it from *D. mentalis.* VOICE: call a *tshewrr;* warning *tsharaaew;* song a slow, descending sequence, accelerating at end, like a *Thamnophilus.* Forests at mid and upper levels, frequently in association with other antbirds, particularly smaller congener. Bahia to Santa Catarina and Misiones, Argentina.

PLAIN ANTVIREO, *Dysithamnus mentalis,*
Choquinha-lisa
11 cm. Small, much like *D. stictothorax* but without breast spots. Female has reddish cap reminiscent of Rufous-crowned Greenlet, *Hylophilus poicilotis.* VOICE: a weak, descending sequence. Mexico to Bolivia, Brazil (western Pará to Rio Grande do Sul), Paraguay, and Misiones, Argentina.

RUFOUS-BACKED ANTVIREO, *Dysithamnus xanthopterus*   BR
13 cm. Relatively large, unmistakable with chestnut mantle. VOICE: descending sequence of loud whistles. High forest canopy, sometimes associated with *D. mentalis* and *D. stictothorax.* Rio de Janeiro (where restricted to mountains) to Paraná. See *Herpsilochmus rufimarginatus* and *Formicivora erythronotos.*

PLUMBEOUS ANTVIREO, *Dysithamnus plumbeus*
BR
14 cm. Another species from southeastern Brazil, size of a *Thamnophilus.* Male slate colored with a bit of white in upper wing coverts, concealed white at base of wings. Female olivaceous. VOICE: song has same pattern as *D. stictothorax* and *D. mentalis* but is fuller, not surprising since bird is larger; call a *grra;* warning a very low *wot, wot-di, di, di, di.* Lower level of high forests, from Bahia to Espírito Santo, where, in mountains, found in same forests with *stictothorax* and *mentalis,* though they usually frequent upper levels. Included by some authors in *Thamnomanes.*

CINEREOUS ANTSHRIKE, *Thamnomanes caesius,*
Ipecuá
14.5 cm. One of most noticeable antbirds because of loud voice. Long-tailed, like *Cercomacra,* with wide bill; male uniformly slaty, underside of wings white. Female olivaceous brown and rufous. VOICE: warning, alarm a strident *tse-tse-tse . . . , raaad-raaad-tsetsetse, buit, buit;* a hurried sequence of limpid notes, first ascending, then descending, ending with lower tone. Nervous, moves body and flicks wings and tail. One of most common birds in mixed flocks, revealing its presence by noisy calling. Forest interior at medium level. The Guianas and Venezuela to northern Mato Grosso, southern Pará, Maranhão; also eastern Brazil from Pernambuco to Minas Gerais and Rio de Janeiro, including ex-Guanabara. Also called *Uirapuru-do-bando.*

In Brazilian Amazonia there are three other related species:

DUSKY-THROATED ANTSHRIKE, *Thamnomanes ardesiacus*

SATURNINE ANTSHRIKE, *Thamnomanes saturninus*

BLUISH-SLATE ANTSHRIKE, *Thamnomanes schistogynus*

STREAKED ANTWREN, *Myrmotherula surinamensis,*
Choquinha-estriada
8.5 cm; 8.6 g. One of smallest Formicariidae, with short tail, upper- and underparts streaked black and white, back with concealed white. Female has chestnut streaking on crown. VOICE: *gwieh;* song an ascending sequence of weak whistles. Gallery forests, generally in canopy, although it nests in low foliage over water. Panama to Amazonia, in

Brazil as far as northern Mato Grosso (upper Xingu), eastern Pará.

STAR-THROATED ANTWREN, *Myrmotherula gularis*, Choquinha-da-garganta-pintada   BR

9.5 cm. Restricted to southeast. Distinct because of white-speckled throat in both sexes and for buff-spotted wings with concealed white at base. VOICE: call *drii-eh drii-eh;* warning *ch-ch-ch;* song a sharply descending sequence of 6 *shrew*s . . . , with lower volume than *Drymophila squamata,* sometimes found nearby. Stream edges in lowest branches of high, humid forests; descends to ground. Minas Gerais and Espírito Santo to Rio Grande do Sul; also ex-Guanabara.

BROWN-BELLIED ANTWREN, *Myrmotherula gutturalis*

10 cm. Male has spotted throat similar to *M. gularis;* female brown. The Guianas and Venezuela to north of lower Amazon (Óbidos, Pará).

WHITE-FLANKED ANTWREN, *Myrmotherula axillaris*, Choquinha-de-flancos-brancos   PL 28.4

9.5 cm. One of best-known small antbirds. Male distinguished by tuft of elongated white feathers on flanks and concealed white at base of wings. VOICE: call a high *juit, ch-chi, ghee-eh;* song a descending sequence of loud *ji-jew-jew-jew*s. . . . Forests, usually at medium heights of 4–5 m, but goes into canopy and descends to ground. Central America to Bolivia, Amazonian and southern Brazil to Rio de Janeiro. Occasionally found with *M. unicolor* in Rio de Janeiro or with *M. urosticta* and *M. minor* in Espírito Santo. Joins mixed flocks.

SALVADORI'S ANTWREN, *Myrmotherula minor*, Choquinha

8.4 cm. Dark gray with black throat, white-spotted wings. In southeast from Espírito Santo to São Paulo. Reported occurrence in Amazonia is unconfirmed. See *M. axillaris.*

Three other *Myrmotherula* are restricted to the forests of southeastern Brazil:

RIO DE JANEIRO ANTWREN, *Myrmotherula fluminensis*   BR

11.5 cm. Similar to *M. iheringi,* without white on flanks and tail, typical of *M. axillaris,* which occurs in same region. Known from only 1 male, collected in Santo Aleixo (Maié), Rio de Janeiro (Gonzaga 1988).

UNICOLORED ANTWREN, *Myrmotherula unicolor*, [Choquinha-cinzenta]   BR

9.5 cm. Like *M. axillaris* but without white on upper wing coverts; underparts gray, throat black. VOICE: relatively long, descending whistle. Espírito Santo to Rio Grande do Sul.

BAND-TAILED ANTWREN, *Myrmotherula urosticta*   BR

9.5 cm. Gray with black throat, extensive white tips on tail. Bahia to Minas Gerais, Espírito Santo.

The frequency of *Myrmotherula* individuals and species in Amazonia is puzzling. One flock of birds may contain 4 or more species. The greatest concentration of *Myrmotherula* species (11) has been recorded in Rondônia. There are 18 more *Myrmotherula* species in Amazonian Brazil, some of them abundant:

PLAIN-THROATED ANTWREN, *Myrmotherula hauxwelli*
See "Habitat . . . ."

RUFOUS-BELLIED ANTWREN, *Myrmotherula guttata*
North of Amazon (Manaus, etc.). Wings broadly spotted with cinnamon; large concealed dorsal spot; rufous belly.

WHITE-EYED ANTWREN, *Myrmotherula leucophthalma*
South of Amazon. Throat spotted black and light gray.

STIPPLE-THROATED ANTWREN, *Myrmotherula haematonota*
Upper Amazon. Also with throat spotted black and light gray but back chestnut.

ORNATE ANTWREN, *Myrmotherula ornata*
South of Amazon. Also has chestnut back.

RUFOUS-TAILED ANTWREN, *Myrmotherula erythrura*
Upper Amazon. Chestnut back and tail.

PYGMY ANTWREN, *Myrmotherula brachyura*

SHORT-BILLED ANTWREN, *Myrmotherula obscura*

SCLATER'S ANTWREN, *Myrmotherula sclateri*

YELLOW-THROATED ANTWREN, *Myrmotherula ambigua*

KLAGES' ANTWREN, *Myrmotherula klagesi*   BR

CHERRIE'S ANTWREN, *Myrmotherula cherriei*

LONG-WINGED ANTWREN, *Myrmotherula longipennis*

RIO SUNO ANTWREN, *Myrmotherula sunensis*

IHERING'S ANTWREN, *Myrmotherula iheringi*

PLAIN-WINGED ANTWREN, *Myrmotherula behni*

GRAY ANTWREN, *Myrmotherula menetriesii*

LEADEN ANTWREN, *Myrmotherula assimilis*

BANDED ANTBIRD, *Dichrozona cincta*, Tovaquinha

11 cm. Small, terrestrial, Amazonian. Reminiscent of *Microcerculus* wrens, to whose family it was formerly attributed. Long, slender neck; very short tail; quite large wings and long legs. Upperparts chestnut brown, concealed white on upper back, wings black with 2 distinct buffy bars, lower back with showy white band (buffy in female). Underparts white with black spots on breast. VOICE: a hurried series of whistles, *hewit*. Runs along ground in high, shady forests without too much undergrowth. Found in pairs. Venezuela to Bolivia, to Rio Negro and west of Rio Tapajós (upper Rio Cururu, Pará).

STRIPE-BACKED ANTBIRD, *Myrmorchilus strigilatus*, Piu-piu

14.5 cm. Typical of caatinga and other sunny but dense woodlands. Large and terrestrial, looks like a strange *Formicivora rufa*. Upperparts light rufous streaked with black; wings black and white; external tail feathers have white, visible when long tail is opened. Underparts white with black throat (male) or streaked breast (female). VOICE: a high, plaintive, 3- or 4-syllable stanza repeated at short intervals, e.g., *di-di-aDEE, tzree, tzree, ieh*, sometimes followed by descending sequence; *bch, bch, bch . . . ;* a prolonged whistle, *see-oo-eeoo*, recalling Lesser Nothura, *Nothura minor*, which occurs in same region. Runs on ground like Rufous Hornero, *Furnarius rufus*, which, with rufous color, it resembles, but differs by frequently cocking tail. Forests, low thickets in caatinga and cerrado. The northeast as far as Minas Gerais (Almenara), sometimes alongside *Hylopezus ochroleucus*, and "Espírito Santo" (Ruschi, without evidence). There is a 2d, widely disjunct population in southwestern Mato Grosso (Corumbá), Paraguay, Bolivia, Argentina. Also called *Tovaca, Tem-farinha-aí*.

RUFOUS-WINGED ANTWREN, *Herpsilochmus rufimarginatus*, Chororozinho-de-asa-vermelha
PL 28.6

10.5 cm. Slender, arboreal species, notable for chestnut in wings. VOICE: call *dew-dew-dew;* song a rapidly ascending sequence that falls and becomes tremolo at end, slightly reminiscent of *Dysithamnus*. Forest canopy. Panama to Bolivia, northern Mato Grosso, eastern Pará, Maranhão, Pernambuco, and southward as far as Paraná, Paraguay, and Misiones, Argentina. Common in Rio de Janeiro and easy to find by voice. See *Dysithamnus xanthopterus*.

Studies by Davis and O'Neill (1986) have made it clear that there are three *Herpsilochmus* that are extremely similar in appearance. Two of them occur in Brazil:

BLACK-CAPPED ANTWREN, *Herpsilochmus atricapillus*, Chororozinho-de-chapéu-preto

12.5 cm. Coloring similar to *Thamnophilus punctatus* (which is much more robust) but sides of tail all white, something like a *Polioptila* gnatcatcher. Thickets. The northeast across central Brazil to Bolivia, Paraguay, Argentina.

PILEATED ANTWREN, *Herpsilochmus pileatus*

Practically identical to *H. atricapillus* but found in caatinga, on both sides of central stretches of Rio São Francisco. Separation of the 2 species is possible, aside from morphology, by voice and habitat, although they are sympatric in Bahia.

TODD'S ANTWREN, *Herpsilochmus stictocephalus*

The Guianas to Venezuela. One specimen from Rio Paru de Oeste, Pará, taken June 1960.

Two endemic species from dry woodlands are:

PECTORAL ANTWREN, *Herpsilochmus pectoralis* BR

13 cm. Male has black spot on throat. VOICE: a full, descending sequence reminiscent of a *Thamnophilus*. Maranhão, Rio Grande do Norte, Bahia.

LARGE-BILLED ANTWREN, *Herpsilochmus longirostris* BR

14 cm. Similar to *H. atricapillus* but larger, sides of breast spotted. VOICE: similar to a *Thamnophilus*. When singing fans out long tail, displaying white tips of rectrices. Piauí, Goiás, Mato Grosso, northern São Paulo.

There are three more *Herpsilochmus* north of the Amazon:

SPOT-TAILED ANTWREN, *Herpsilochmus sticturus*

SPOT-BACKED ANTWREN, *Herpsilochmus dorsimaculatus*

RORAIMAN ANTWREN, *Herpsilochmus roraimae*

DOT-WINGED ANTWREN, *Microrhopias quixensis*, Papa-formigas-de-bando

11.5 cm. Long-tailed Amazonian species. Male velvety black with glittering white on wings, semiconcealed on back, and on sides of frequently opened tail as seen from below. Female has bright chestnut underparts. VOICE: *BEEeh*, reminiscent of *Myrmotherula axillaris*. Behavior reminiscent of arboreal *Myrmotherula* and wood-warblers. Gregarious. Mexico to Bolivia, northern Mato Grosso, eastern Pará (Rio Tocantins).

RUSTY-BACKED ANTWREN, *Formicivora rufa,*
Papa-formigas-vermelho   PL 28.5

13 cm. Similar to *Herpsilochmus* and *Drymophila* in general aspect. Tail relatively long, plumage quite loose on lower back and flanks. Accentuated sexual dimorphism, with females of genus sometimes more easily separated than their respective males. VOICE: call *tak-eet;* warning *it . . . , gheeeh, gheeA, rrrew,* a hard *trra-trra-trr;* song a smooth tremolo *rrrew, dewdewdew. . . .* Open bushes and cerradão. Locally abundant. Non-Amazonian plains regions, from northeastern and central Brazil to Rio de Janeiro, Minas Gerais, Paraguay, Bolivia. Also Suriname. See Willis and Oniki 1988 and other *Formicivora* and *Myrmorchilus.*

WHITE-FRINGED ANTWREN, *Formicivora grisea,*
Papa-formigas-pardo

11.5 cm. Similar to *F. rufa* but with upperparts brown, not reddish. Male has black extending to abdomen; flanks white, not rusty. Female different, with uniformly buffy, unstreaked underparts. VOICE: call a distinct, bisyllabic note, *dewpplewp;* pairs frequently sing together, a sequence of *drewp . . . , tsok . . . , tsok-SOK. . . .* On border of forest, capoeira, dense cerrado; sometimes near *rufa.* Panama to northeastern, central, and eastern (to Rio de Janeiro and Minas Gerais) Brazil. See *F. melanogaster.*

BLACK-BELLIED ANTWREN, *Formicivora melanogaster*

Central Brazil. Much like *F. grisea* but more slender, with more extensive white superciliary, etc. Female has almost uniformly white underparts. VOICE: similar to *F. rufa* but with less volume. Dense river-edge thickets, grottoes, forest edges, sometimes alongside *grisea.* The northeast to Goiás, western São Paulo, Mato Grosso, Bolivia. See *F. serrana.*

SERRA ANTWREN, *Formicivora serrana*   BR

12.5 cm. Like *F. melanogaster* (both sexes), sharing extensive white superciliary, but mantle somewhat rufous. VOICE: similar to *F. rufa;* warning *eet-eet-eet-eet-ewt;* a hard *ghiA-ghiA;* song a sequence of smooth *jewes. . . .* Low secondary forest, between 200–1000 m. Espírito Santo, Minas Gerais, Rio de Janeiro. Locally common in mountain regions. An isolated population, *F. s. littoralis* (Gonzaga and Pacheco 1990), occurs in Cabo Frio restinga; male has extensive black on head, lacks white superciliary.

NARROW-BILLED ANTWREN, *Formicivora iheringi*
EN

11 cm. Resembles *Myrmotherula axillaris* with long tail. Song reminiscent of neighbor, *Rhopornis ardesiaca,* but much weaker. In mountainous country, on tablelands and slopes, not below 600 m. Bahia (Bonfim, Boa Nova), Minas Gerais (Divisópolis, Almenara, Geraldo Mattos). See *Cercomacra brasiliana.* Has also been found in Peru.

BLACK-HOODED ANTWREN, *Formicivora erythronotos*
BR   R   PL 45.4

10.5 cm. Immediately recognizable as a *Formicivora* due to long tail and voice. Colorful, with chestnut back (recalling certain *Myrmotherula* and *Terenura*), black head and breast (whitish in female), white flanks. VOICE: a monotonous sequence of *tsak, tsak . . . ,* reminiscent of *F. grisea;* loud cry, *kiAK, kiAK;* song *chewk, chewk . . . ,* recalling *F. serrana.* Correctly described in 1852 by Hartlaub as a *Formicivora* (type specimen is in Hamburg) from "Brazil." In 1858 Sclater transferred it to *Myrmotherula.* Few specimens, all collected in 1800s, are in museums, and there had been no other findings. It was thus a great surprise when F. Carvalho and C. Carvalho of Rio de Janeiro Bird Observers Club found the species near Angra dos Réis, Rio de Janeiro, at sea level in September 1987, later confirmed by F. Pacheco (1988).

FERRUGINOUS ANTBIRD, *Drymophila ferruginea,*
Trovoada   BR

13.5 cm. Color and voice distinctive. Upperparts black and white, back with lots of concealed brilliant white, rump chestnut, underparts uniformly bright rufous. Female similar but paler. VOICE: call a clear *ti-tweIT,* given by male (female gives *ditWEE-ditWEE*) and audible at great distance, especially during local migrations. Also voices this call in its territory, responding immediately to playback. Forests, frequently in canopy with other birds. Very conspicuous because of clear notes. Bahia to Santa Catarina. Only in mountains in Espírito Santo and Rio de Janeiro, reaching ex-Guanabara on Pedra Branca massif. See *D. rubricollis.*

BERTONI'S ANTBIRD, *Drymophila rubricollis,*
Trovoada-de-Bertoni

Very similar to *D. ferruginea;* color lighter, female's forehead yellowish. Descending song. Rio de Janeiro to Rio Grande do Sul in bamboo thickets. In mountains of Rio de Janeiro (Itatiaia) and São Paulo lives alongside *ferruginea.* To Argentina and Paraguay, from where it was described in 1901 by Bertoni. Later included in *D. ferruginea.* Only now recognized as a valid species by E. O. Willis (1988).

RUFOUS-TAILED ANTBIRD, *Drymophila genei,*
Choquinha-da-serra   BR

13 cm. Strictly in mountains. Similar in color to *D. ochropyga* but has rufous tail, a bit like Streaked Xenops, *Xenops rutilans.* Male has concealed white on back. VOICE: reminiscent of *ochropyga;* warning *graa-eet, PSEEep-chehcheh;* song *eet-eet-eet-gleh-gleh, di-dlewit-dlewit.* Lowest level of high, humid forest, e.g., Serra de Bocaina, São Paulo, at 1500 m, where common; also páramo (Serra da Mantiqueira, Minas Gerais, at more than 1900 m; Serra do Caparaó, Minas Gerais/Espírito Santo; Itatiaia, Rio de Janeiro) where it is a neighbor of *Schizoeaca moreirae* and of Mouse-colored Tapaculo, *Scytalopus speluncae.*

OCHRE-RUMPED ANTBIRD, *Drymophila ochropyga*,
Choquinha-de-dorso-vermelho   BR   PL 28.3

13.5 cm. Common in lower levels of thickets in mountains
of Espírito Santo and Rio de Janeiro, where sometimes a
neighbor of *D. malura* and *Psilorhamphus guttatus*. VOICE:
alarm *ghiehh;* song *ghiehh-tshrrr, hee-tshrra-hee*. Reaches
ex-Guanabara in Pedra Branca massif. Also called *For-
migueiro*.

STRIATED ANTBIRD, *Drymophila devillei*

13 cm. Only in Amazonia (Rio Curuá, Pará, Rondônia)
and from Bolivia to Ecuador.

DUSKY-TAILED ANTBIRD, *Drymophila malura*,
Choquinha-carijó

14 cm. Tail longer than congeners'. Dark gray, head and
underparts streaked with black and white, tail without white.
Female brown. VOICE: warning *raait;* song a harsh sequence
somewhat reminiscent of Pallid Spinetail, *Cranioleuca pallida*. Thickets, sometimes alongside *D. ochropyga*. Near Rio
de Janeiro found only in mountains. Espírito Santo to Rio
Grande do Sul, Paraguay, and Misiones, Argentina.

SCALED ANTBIRD, *Drymophila squamata*,
Pintadinho   BR

12 cm. Black all scaled with white (male) or brown scaled
with pale buff (female). VOICE: call *bit-bit*, reminiscent
of White-throated Spadebill, *Platyrinchus mystaceus;*song
a descending sequence *DREEeh*, reminiscent of *Myrmotherula gularis,* a frequent neighbor. Low in deeply shad-
owed, high forests. Bahia to Santa Catarina. Locally common, e.g., on Corcovado in city of Rio de Janeiro. Also in
Alagoas.

STREAK-CAPPED ANTWREN, *Terenura maculata*,
Zídede

9.5 cm. Small with narrow tail; somewhat flycatcherlike.
Crown streaked black and white (male), back chestnut, underparts whitish, breast streaked with black. VOICE: a high
whistle, *TSEE-dede*. Medium to upper levels. Espírito Santo
and Minas Gerais to Santa Catarina, Paraguay, and Misiones,
Argentina. See *Formicivora erythronotos*.

ALAGOAS ANTWREN, *Terenura sicki*,
Zídede-do-Nordeste   BR   PL 45.9

10 cm. According to documentation of its discoverers,
D. Teixeira and L. Gonzaga, a typical *Terenura* in voice and
behavior. Streaked black-and-white pattern of male recalls
certain *Myrmotherula*, e.g., in Brazil, *M. surinamensis*
(with short tail, unlike *Terenura*). Female distinct in orange-
shaded underparts. Canopy, where its nest, under construction, was also found, 11 m above ground (November 1983).
See fig. 206 for a display of female. In pockets of escarpment

Fig. 206. Alagoas Antwren, *Terenura sicki,* female
ceremony in front of male. After Teixeira and Gonzaga
1987. Sketch by J. B. Nacinovic.

forest (300 m). Alagoas, Pernambuco. A northeastern replacement of *T. maculata*.

CHESTNUT-SHOULDERED ANTWREN, *Terenura
humeralis*
Amazonia.

ASH-WINGED ANTWREN, *Terenura spodioptila*
Amazonia.

GRAY ANTBIRD, *Cercomacra cinerascens*,
Chororó-pocuá

15 cm. Arboreal Amazonian species, more slender than a
Thamnophilus. Male uniformly dark gray with concealed
white on back, white-speckled upper wing coverts, extensive
white at tip of tail. Female olivaceous brown with white
design on wing. VOICE: warning *CAcacaca;* song a sequence
of *doc*s . . . " reminiscent of *Formicivora grisea;* about 6
loud, low, bisyllabic cries, *po-KWA*. Canopy of high terra-
firme and várzea forests. The Guianas to Bolivia, northern
Mato Grosso, Maranhão.

RIO DE JANEIRO ANTBIRD, *Cercomacra brasiliana*,
Chororó-cinzento   BR   PL 45.10

15.5 cm. Only *Cercomacra* in southeastern Brazil. Like
C. cinerascens but with even longer tail (7.5–8.3 cm), male
with white design on rectrices, concealed white spot on back.
Female olive brown with tail tip slightly yellowish. VOICE:
warning a loud, trisyllabic *ca-ca-ca*, reminiscent of a thrush.
Low, up to 3 m above ground, inside and at the edge of forest
in capoeira, caatinga tangles, bamboo thickets. Adapts well
to secondary vegetation. Minas Gerais (Muriaé, Divisópolis
at 950 m; Felisburgo at 600 m, E. Snethlage, G. T. Mattos),
Rio de Janeiro (Iguaçu, Estrela).

DUSKY ANTBIRD, *Cercomacra tyrannina*,
Chororó-escuro

15.2 cm. Gray, male usually without white on tail tip,
female underparts bright rufous. VOICE: duet a sequence of

clear whistles, *di-hileh, hileh, hileh, hileh,* female softer. Low in capoeira and terra-firme forests. Mexico to Amazonia as far as north bank of Amazon.

BELEM ANTBIRD, *Cercomacra laeta*   BR

Similar in plumage but smaller and with different voice than *C. tyrannina.* South and east from Belém and east bank of Tocantins. (R. O. Bierregaard and M. Cohn-Haft, pers. comm.). See Translator's Comments, which precede Part One of this book.

BLACKISH ANTBIRD, *Cercomacra nigrescens,* Chororó-preto

15.2 cm. Typical of flooded forests of Amazonia. Male plumbeous with upper wing coverts finely edged white. Female olivaceous brown with forehead, sides of head, and underparts bright rufous. Both sexes have large, concealed white spot on back. VOICE: a loud duet in which voice of each sex can be distinguished: male *jo-jew-JEW-ew-ew-ew,* female a monotonous, ascending sequence, *jew. . . .* Low levels, sometimes with *Myrmoborus leucophrys* and *Hypocnemoides* (Mato Grosso). The Guianas to Bolivia, northern Mato Grosso (upper Rio Xingu, Rio Araguaia), southeastern Pará.

There are five more *Cercomacra* in Brazil:

BANANAL ANTBIRD, *Cercomacra ferdinandi*   BR
Goiás, Ilha do Bananal.

BLACK ANTBIRD, *Cercomacra serva*
Southwestern Amazonia.

JET ANTBIRD, *Cercomacra nigricans*
Roraima.

RIO BRANCO ANTBIRD, *Cercomacra carbonaria*
BR
Roraima.

MATO GROSSO ANTBIRD, *Cercomacra melanaria*
Western Mato Grosso.

WHITE-BACKED FIRE-EYE, *Pyriglena leuconota,* Papa-taoca

17 cm. Distinctive forest antbird with extremely wide Amazonian distribution and 2 southern congeners. Male shiny black with red eyes and concealed interscapular white spot. Wing has no white. Female brown with lighter underparts and same concealed white. One form, *P. l. similis,* found between Tapajós and Xingu, has black head and tail. VOICE: song a descending sequence of identical, melodious notes, *dew, dew, dew . . . ,* frequently 6 times; scolds and other voices. Voice very similar (with certain exceptions) to *P. atra*

and *P. leucoptera,* which justifies grouping the 3 into a superspecies. Low in forests and dense secondary vegetation; also near human habitation, where its loud voice can be heard. One of most assiduous heralds of army ants (see "Feeding"), like its congeners. Bolivia to southwestern Mato Grosso and south of Amazon to eastern Pará, Maranhão. Also Pernambuco, Alagoas, Colombia, Ecuador. Also called *Mãe-da-taoca, Piadeira.*

FRINGE-BACKED FIRE-EYE, *Pyriglena atra,* Papa-taoca-da-Bahia   BR   EN

Male similar to *P. leuconota* but interscapular spot of white feathers with black elliptical mark always visible. Female interscapular like *P. leuconota.* VOICE: loud descending notes and some other vocalizations very similar to other *Pyriglena,* but alarm call different (Willis and Oniki 1982). Very local today north of Rio Paraguaçu, Bahia, at Boa Nova (Willis in 1974), and Santo Amaro (pers. obs. 1977 and Ridgely et al. 1987). It is a relict population in scattered secondary forest. "Espírito Santo" (Ruschi, without evidence). Severely menaced by destruction of woodlands in its area.

WHITE-SHOULDERED FIRE-EYE, *Pyriglena leucoptera,* Papa-taoca-do-Sul   Fig. 207

Male has 2 white wing bars, concealed dorsal white spot lacking in female. VOICE: see *P. leuconota.* Normally most penetrating voice in any thick forest from southern Bahia to Espírito Santo, Rio de Janeiro, Minas Gerais (Rio Doce) as far as Rio Grande do Sul, Uruguay, Argentina (Misiones), Paraguay. In Bahia may be sympatric with *Rhopornis ardesiaca* and *Formicivora iheringi.*

SLENDER ANTBIRD, *Rhopornis ardesiaca,* Gravatazeiro   BR   EN   PL 45.11

18 cm. Distinctive species found in bromeliad-rich caatinga. Long-tailed, male slate colored with black throat and black upper wing coverts lightly edged white. Lores and area under eyes bare and brilliant blue. Female has rufous

Fig. 207. White-shouldered Fire-eye, *Pyriglena leucoptera,* male.

crown and nape, gray back, light gray underparts with white throat and belly; wings and tail like male's. Red eyes. VOICE: a descending sequence of loud whistles, *EWoo, EWoo, EWoo . . .* with range of 500 m and audible in neighboring woods; voice reminiscent of *Pyriglena* and *Mackenziaena leachii.* Female responds to male with a shorter stanza. Warning, *ksht* (bird flips tail downward), like a *Conopophaga.* Hops on ground, perches to sing. Low, dense forests (*matas de cipó,* "vine forests") on top of low mountains in places abounding in large terrestrial and arboreal bromeliads (gravatás, *Aechmea* sp.) whose flowers are regularly visited by Ruby-topaz Hummingbird, *Chrysolampis mosquitus.* Known only from caatinga of southern Bahia, upper and middle reaches of Rio das Contas. I recorded it in Boa Nova region at 700 m (where it was observed by Wied, Kaempfer, and Willis) and Irajubá, as far as left bank of Rio das Contas: Ituaçu and Jequié. Although still well represented in patchy woodland of area, it is threatened by rapid destruction of these isolated stands resulting from demand for firewood by constantly increasing human population. Lives alongside *Formicivora iheringi* and *Herpsilochmus pileatus.* In same region but in various habitats I found 11 other antbird species. See Willis and Oniki 1981 and "Habitat . . . ."

WHITE-BROWED ANTBIRD, *Myrmoborus leucophrys,* Papa-formigas-de-sobrancelha

12.5 cm. Amazonian. Short tail and long legs, slightly like a *Conopophaga.* Male slate colored with black throat and sides of head; white forehead and superciliary; no white on wings or tail. Female is brown above with buffy forehead, superciliary, and wing markings; black cheeks; white underparts resembling male *Conopophaga melanops.* VOICE: warning *tsirr-tsirr;* song a sharply descending sequence of melodious whistles ending in a croak. Dense, lower levels of riverine, floodable forests, along with *Hylophylax poecilinota, Cercomacra nigrescens,* and *Hypocnemoides maculicauda.* In upper Xingu, Mato Grosso, sometimes with *Myrmoborus myotherinus.* The Guianas and Venezuela to Bolivia, northern Mato Grosso, Pará. See *Hypocnemoides maculicauda.*

In Brazilian Amazonia there are two more *Myrmoborus:*

ASH-BREASTED ANTBIRD, *Myrmoborus lugubris*
13.5 cm. Without white in wing.

BLACK-FACED ANTBIRD, *Myrmoborus myotherinus*
11.5 cm. Upper wing coverts edged with white.

WARBLING ANTBIRD, *Hypocnemis cantator,* Papa-formigas-cantador

10 cm. Amazonian. Short, narrow tail and long legs; black and olivaceous brown back; streaked crown; white underparts with black-speckled breast and rufous flanks. VOICE:

song varied, e.g., a prolonged stanza, initially ascending and melodious, then becoming harsh and descending, ending in some croaks. Low forests. The Guianas and Venezuela to Bolivia, Mato Grosso (upper Xingu), Goiás, Pará (Tocantins, Marajó).

YELLOW-BROWED ANTBIRD, *Hypocnemis hypoxantha* Amazonia.

BAND-TAILED ANTBIRD, *Hypocnemoides maculicauda,* Solta-asa

11 cm. Typical of shady, flooded forests of Amazonia. More slender than *Myrmoborus,* with plumbeous on throat; black on tail and wings, latter lightly bordered white; concealed white spot on back; large white spot on tail feathers, displayed when tail is raised and opened. VOICE: call *tir-rIT . . . ,* etc.; song an ascending, accelerating tremolo which promptly descends, becoming crescendo and turning harsh. Hops in mud or through branches leaning over water, tilting tail; sometimes alongside *Sclateria naevia.* Northeastern Peru to Bolivia, south of Amazon as far as Mato Grosso (upper Rio Xingu), Pará (Rio Tocantins), Maranhão.

BLACK-CHINNED ANTBIRD, *Hypocnemoides melanopogon*

Northern Amazonia. A geographic replacement for *H. maculicauda* from south of Amazon. See fig. 208.

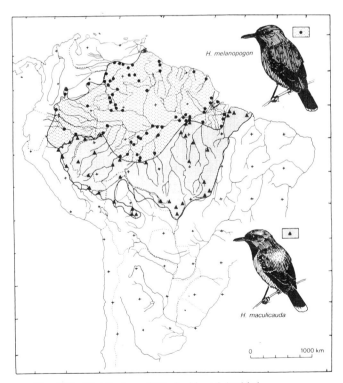

Fig. 208. Distribution of Black-chinned Antbird superspecies, *Hypocnemoides melanopogon.* After Haffer 1987a.

Five other Amazonian representatives of this family are:

BLACK-AND-WHITE ANTBIRD, *Myrmochanes hemileucus*

BLACK-HEADED ANTBIRD, *Percnostola rufifrons*
See Willis 1982.

SLATE-COLORED ANTBIRD, *Schistocichla schistacea*

SPOT-WINGED ANTBIRD, *Schistocichla leucostigma*

CAURA ANTBIRD, *Schistocichla caurensis*

SILVERED ANTBIRD, *Sclateria naevia,*
Papa-formigas-do-igarapé
14 cm. Flooded, shady forests of Amazonia. Bill long. Male gray with white throat and wingtips, white streaking on breast and belly. Female brown above with rufous flanks. VOICE: warning *bsh-bsh-bsh;* an ascending, then descending sequence of clear, hurried notes, higher than *Myrmoborus leucophrys,* sometimes found nearby. Lives at water's edge, hops on ground, bobs tail downward. Reminiscent of a *Sclerurus,* including bill. Upper Amazon and along right bank to Mato Grosso (upper Rio Xingu), eastern Pará (Belém), Maranhão. Also Venezuela, the Guianas.

WHITE-BIBBED (INCLUDES SQUAMATE) ANTBIRD, *Myrmeciza loricata,* Papa-formigas-de-grota
BR   PL 28.7
14.5 cm. Southern terrestrial species with whitish feet and concealed white dorsal spot but no white in long tail. VOICE: alarm a loud *bsh-bsh,* etc.; song a soft sequence, *tsisisisi . . . ,* followed by soft and melodious trill ending in another muffled, descending sequence. Beginning of stanza is like song of Sharp-tailed Streamcreeper, *Lochmias nematura,* but so much higher it could pass for a hummingbird song. Sometimes gives a simple, sonorous trill, first ascending, then descending; typical descending sequence heard in Espírito Santo, Rio de Janeiro, and Santa Catarina is *tsiBEE, tsiBEE, tsiBEE. . . .* Tall, humid forests with lots of undergrowth and fallen leaves, frequents shady grottoes. Bahia, Minas Gerais, and Espírito Santo to Rio Grande do Sul. In mountains in Espírito Santo. "Sooretama" (Ruschi, without evidence). Southern form, *M. squamosa,* has been included in *loricata.* This lumping needs to be better justified than it has been to date. See *M. ruficauda.*

SCALLOPED ANTBIRD, *Myrmeciza ruficauda*   BR
14 cm. Similar to *M. loricata* but without light superciliary; breast and belly black with whitish edges, creating scaly appearance. Female has white underparts with blackish, scaly design on breast. Hot, forested lowlands of Rio Doce, Espírito Santo, to Pernambuco and Paraíba.

The following ten *Myrmeciza* are found in Brazilian Amazonia; their voices, which are sometimes very similar to that of certain southern species, suggest that the latter are, in part, only geographic replacements of the northern ones:

WHITE-BELLIED ANTBIRD, *Myrmeciza longipes*

FERRUGINOUS-BACKED ANTBIRD, *Myrmeciza ferruginea*

GRAY-BELLIED ANTBIRD, *Myrmeciza pelzelni*

CHESTNUT-TAILED ANTBIRD, *Myrmeciza hemimelaena*

PLUMBEOUS ANTBIRD, *Myrmeciza hyperythra*

GOELDI'S ANTBIRD, *Myrmeciza goeldii*

WHITE-SHOULDERED ANTBIRD, *Myrmeciza melanoceps*

SOOTY ANTBIRD, *Myrmeciza fortis*

BLACK-THROATED ANTBIRD, *Myrmeciza atrothorax*

SPOT-BREASTED ANTBIRD, *Myrmeciza stictothorax*
BR

WHITE-PLUMED ANTBIRD, *Pithys albifrons,*
Papa-formigas-de-topete
12.5 cm Unique in long, white, frontal plume and prominent white throat tuft, a spectacular decoration lacking in immature. Upperparts slate colored, underparts and tail chestnut. SOUNDS: whistles a *psieww,* etc.; snaps bill. Lives hidden in lower levels of dense forests; locally common. Closely linked to army ants, where easy to see. The Guianas and Venezuela to Amazon (Amazonas, Pará, Amapá), Colombia, Peru. The *Gymnopithys, Rhegmatorhina, Phlegopsis,* and *Skutchia* are closely related to this genus.

RUFOUS-THROATED ANTBIRD, *Gymnopithys rufigula,*
Mãe-de-taoca-de-garganta-vermelha
13.5 cm. Amazonian. Characterized by bare, bluish white periorbital region (see "Morphology . . ."); red iris; olivaceous brown plumage (lighter on underparts); chestnut throat; white (male) or rufous (female) concealed spot on back; strong, whitish tarsi and toes. SOUNDS: warning a high *irrr;* song long or short sequences of melodious whistles of varying volume; various other vocalizations and some snapping. Low in forests, prefers to perch on vertical shoots, hops on ground. An assiduous follower of army ants. The Guianas and southern Venezuela to Amazon from Rio Negro (Amazonas) to Amapá.

BICOLORED ANTBIRD, *Gymnopithys leucaspis*

Replaces *G. rufigula* west of Rio Negro. Underparts white, sides of head, neck, and breast black. Female has concealed yellow on back.

WHITE-THROATED ANTBIRD, *Gymnopithys salvini*

Replaces *G. rufigula* south of Solimões. Male with white throat, superciliary, and tail bars. Female chestnut with tail barred black. See Willis 1968a.

BARE-EYED ANTBIRD, *Rhegmatorhina gymnops,*
Mãe-de-taoca-de-cara-branca   BR

13.5 cm. Related to *Gymnopithys;* also has bare, brilliant white, almost phosphorescent, periorbital region. Male crested with slender, black neck, dark brown mantle. Brown female has whitish mandible. VOICE: like *Gymnopithys.* High, terra-firme forest. Only between Rio Tapajós, south to Rio Teles Pires in Mato Grosso, and Rio Xingu in Pará. See Willis 1969.

In other regions of Amazonia *R. gymnops* is replaced by other forms that can be considered semi- or allospecies that make up a superspecies:

HARLEQUIN ANTBIRD, *Rhegmatorhina berlepschi*
BR

CHESTNUT-CRESTED ANTBIRD, *Rhegmatorhina cristata*

WHITE-BREASTED ANTBIRD, *Rhegmatorhina hoffmannsi*   BR

HAIRY-CRESTED ANTBIRD, *Rhegmatorhina melanosticta*

SPOT-BACKED ANTBIRD, *Hylophylax naevia,*
Guarda-floresta   PL 28.8

11 cm. Relatively short tail; long, whitish legs; slate-colored head; black (male) or white (female) throat; black back with white concealed spot and white speckling; cinnamon belly. VOICE: warning a loud *beea* and soft *bsh-bsh bsh-bsh;* song a sequence of high whistles, briefly ascending, then descending, *dee-eh dee-eh DEEeh dee-eh . . . .* Hops on ground to feed, mounts up onto shoots to observe surroundings. Sometimes alongside *Sclateria naevia* and *Myrmeciza atrothorax* (Mato Grosso). Riverine forests. Suriname and Venezuela to Bolivia, northern Mato Grosso (upper Xingu), Pará (Tocantins). Various geographic races differ primarily in color of females (heterogynism, see "Morphology . . . ").

SCALE-BACKED ANTBIRD, *Hylophylax poecilinota*

12 cm. Tail feathers crossed by a series of white spots, back scaled with black and white. Female has uniformly brown back and gray underparts (*H. p. nigrigula,* Rio Tapajós), spotted brown mantle and bright rufous on sides of head (*H. p. poecilinota,* left bank of lower Amazon), or even with other variations in upper Amazon. VOICE: warning *tshirr;* song a sharply ascending sequence of 10 very high *we* notes, last ones more prolonged, very reminiscent of Blue-throated Piping-Guan, *Pipile pipile* (Cracidae) heard at a distance. Terra-firme and adjacent riverine forests, alongside *Myrmoborus leucophrys* and *Thamnophilus amazonicus* (Mato Grosso). The Guianas and Venezuela to Mato Grosso (upper Rio Xingu and upper Rio Paraguay), Pará, Maranhão.

DOT-BACKED ANTBIRD, *Hylophylax punctulata*

Another Amazonian species.

BLACK-SPOTTED BARE-EYE, *Phlegopsis nigromaculata,* Mãe-de-taoca   PL 29.3

17 cm; 44 g. Heavy bodied, semiterrestrial, with large head and bill; slender neck; large wings; thick, black tarsi and toes; strong, sharp claws. A bit of white at base of wings. Bare periophthalmic region of immature black instead of red. VOICE: alarm a nasal *ee-eh, shiarrr;* a short, descending stanza with notes becoming successively longer and more nasal; various other vocalizations. Hops on ground and among lowest branches, tilts tail upward, perches on vertical shoots. It is one of species most attached to army ants, along with *Pithys, Gymnopithys, Rhegmatorhina,* and *Skutchia.* Colombia and Ecuador to Bolivia, Acre, Pará (upper Rio Cururu, Rio Tocantins, Belém), Maranhão. Locally common.

Two other related species in Amazonia are:

REDDISH-WINGED BARE-EYE, *Phlegopsis erythroptera*

PALE-FACED ANTBIRD, *Skutchia* (= *Phlegopsis*)
borbae   BR

SHORT-TAILED ANTTHRUSH, *Chamaeza campanisona,* Tovaca-campainha

20 cm; average 69 g. Large, gallinaceous-looking, terrestrial, quite long-legged with relatively short toes, medium-sized tail. Upperparts olivaceous brown, crown reddish, prominent white postocular stripe, blackish streak across lower tail. White or buffy tail tips may be worn off. Underparts buffy, streaked black; legs whitish. VOICE: warning *dwewt;* song, a remarkable musical scale comprising an interval of a fourth or fifth, is a long sequence of monotonous whistles that go up little by little with complete phrase lasting 25–40 seconds; another song type, generally accepted as a variation of former, is a shorter sequence ending in some croaking notes, *gwa, gwa, gwa* ("laugh"). Both can be heard in same area, as I noted in 1940 in Limoeiro-Jatiboca, Espírito Santo; short phrase was less frequent and stopped being used before the other in summer, suggesting it might be voice

of female. In some regions, e.g., Macaé de Cima, Rio de Janeiro, I noted only the sequence without the croaks. Song usually given from a low perch up to 5 m above ground (higher than *C. ruficauda*) (Ridgely pers. comm.) Walks zigzagging, with body lowered and hindparts raised and slightly oscillating. Excitement of any sort shown by bobbing tail. Flies low, rapidly, silently. The Guianas and Venezuela, following Andes as far as Bolivia; also Paraguay; Argentina, (Misiones), southeastern Brazil from Rio Grande do Sul to southern Bahia, Minas Gerais (Serra do Caparaó), Ceará (Serra do Baturité); in Espírito Santo and Rio de Janeiro usually restricted to mountains. May or may not occur at same altitude as *ruficauda*. Also called *Tobaca* (Rio de Janeiro). See *C. ruficauda, Grallaria,* and *Hylopezus.*

NOBLE ANTTHRUSH, *Chamaeza nobilis*

Upper Amazon from lower Tapajós (Santarém, Pará) Purus, Juruá, and Solimões (south side) to Peru, Ecuador, Colombia.

BRAZILIAN ANTTHRUSH, *Chamaeza ruficauda,* Tovaca-de-rabo-vermelho   Fig. 209

20 cm. Extremely similar to *C. campanisona* (a cryptic species) but with greenish crown and back, bright auburn tail coverts, tail feathers with only a suggestion of or entirely lacking white spots. Flank feathers extensively black in center with showy white edge. VOICE: completely unlike *campanisona*. Announcement or warning a short, ascending stanza, *rrrew;* song a sonorous, ascending, more prolonged trill, with same pattern as call but with notes more widely spaced. This is delivered while lifting body and ruffling throat. Distribution highly disjunct, from Venezuela to Colo-

Fig. 209. Brazilian Antthrush, *Chamaeza r. ruficauda,* singing.

mbia, also southern and southeastern Brazil from Rio Grande do Sul to São Paulo, Rio de Janeiro. Sometimes in same place as *campanisona* (e.g., Itatiaia and Serra dos Órgãos, Rio de Janeiro). Also called *Capoeira-cachorra* (Rio de Janeiro).

RUFOUS-CAPPED ANTTHRUSH, *Formicarius colma,* Galinha-do-mato   PL 29.2

17 cm; 43.7 g. Terrestrial, with very erect, rail-like stance. Long, brown legs and dark plumage blend well with shady forest habitat. Sexes similar, as with *Chamaeza* and *Grallaria.* VOICE: *pit;* a bisyllabic *psee-eh* (reminiscent of a domestic chick); a melodious, horizontal trill (observed in Espírito Santo) or a more varied phrase, a tremolo that briefly descends, then ascends, latter part (observed in Pará) recalling *Chamaeza ruficauda* in southeast. A short ascending tremolo, *rrrewEE.* Walks with tail cocked; an occasional patron of army ants. The Guianas and Venezuela to northern Mato Grosso, Pará, Maranhão; also eastern Brazil from Pernambuco and Bahia to Rio Grande do Sul. Also called *Pinto-do-mato, Winá* (Kaiabi, Mato Grosso). Includes *F. ruficeps.* May occur in same forest with *F. analis* (Maranhão).

BLACK-FACED ANTTHRUSH, *Formicarius analis*

17 cm. Very similar to *F. colma,* without brick-colored cap but with clear, white spot on lores and chestnut under-tail coverts which can be seen in field. VOICE: alarm a sonorous *prrri;* song a hurried, descending sequence of sonorous notes, the 1st with a strong accent, preceded by a diatonic note, *ew-EW, ew, ew, ew, ew;* at dusk produces more prolonged phrases. Throughout Amazonia, south as far as Bolivia, and to northern Mato Grosso, Pará (Belém), Maranhão, and north as far as the Guianas and Venezuela.

WING-BANDED ANTBIRD, *Myrmornis torquata,* Pinto-do-mato-carijó

14 cm. Peculiar-looking terrestrial species with long, slender neck, large head and bill, strong, wide wings, heavy body; legs light-colored and long but much less so than *Grallaria;* tail rudimentary. Plumage complicated, upperparts washed with chestnut, throat extensively black or rufescent (female), sides of head with white design, back black with concealed white in center, wings black, barred buffy, tail chestnut, underparts grayish. VOICE: call *EEew;* warning a loud rasp; song a sharply ascending sequence of strident whistles. Hops on ground, turns over leaves, perches low. In pairs in tall forests. Nicaragua to northern Mato Grosso (Rio Teles Pires), southern Pará (Belém, Rio Tocantins); also southern Bahia (Pinto 1938, p. 522). Also called *Winá* (Kaiabi, Mato Grosso).

VARIEGATED ANTPITTA, *Grallaria varia,* Tovacuçu   PL 29.1

19.5 cm; height when standing 20 cm; 125 g; one of largest formicariids. Terrestrial, with large head and eyes, relatively small body, rudimentary tail, long, strong, whitish legs.

VOICE: a basso-profundo stanza of approximately 10 *boo*s in an accelerating, crescendo sequence with timbre of a large owl, given only at dawn and dusk (originating the name *mãe-da-noite,* "mother of the night"). Hops on ground with very erect stance, tail cocked, sometimes walking and running. Wary, thus difficult to see. Flees with swift, low, short flights. Perches close to ground for long periods, sleeps perched. Tall, shady forests in a variety of climatic conditions; e.g., in Rio de Janeiro both in lowlands and highest parts of Serra do Mar. The Guianas and Venezuela to Rios Madeira and Xingu (southern Pará); also eastern Brazil (Pernambuco to Rio Grande do Sul), Paraguay, and Misiones, Argentina. Also called *Galo-do-mato, Tovaca, Tovacão, Bo-bo-bó* (Rio de Janeiro), *Pé-lavada* (Rio de Janeiro), *Boca-da-noite* (Rio de Janeiro).

SCALED ANTPITTA, *Grallaria guatimalensis*
Extreme north on Brazilian-Venezuelan border.

WHITE-BROWED ANTPITTA, *Hylopezus ochroleucus,* Pinta-do-mato

12.5 cm; 28 g. Medium size, extremely long-legged. Upperparts uniformly olivaceous, underparts yellowish white dotted with black. VOICE: a sequence of 8–12 soft whistles, with 2d part of phrase ascending and last syllables slowing (Rio de Janeiro); voice of northeastern form, *H. o. martinsi,* of Piauí, Ceará, and Bahia, distinctly different. Low in bamboo tangles, etc., both in Serra do Mar and caatinga; when wary lifts itself to full height on perch and makes slow lateral movements with body, swaying sideways to and fro. Flies rapidly, in absolute silence. Piauí and Ceará to Bahia, Minas Gerais, Rio de Janeiro (mountain regions), São Paulo, Rio Grande do Sul. Also Paraguay and Misiones, Argentina. Also called *Grallaria.* Includes *G. nattereri.* It is appropriate to separate the genera *Hylopezus* and *Grallaria* based on morphology and behavior.

There are two *Hylopezus* in Brazilian Amazonia:

SPOTTED ANTPITTA, *Hylopezus macularius*
Bill much larger than *H. ochroleucus.*

AMAZONIAN ANTPITTA, *Hylopezus berlepschi,* Torom-torom

THRUSH-LIKE ANTPITTA, *Myrmothera campanisona,* Tovaca-patinho

14 cm. Terrestrial Amazonian species related to *Hylopezus,* with very long legs and rudimentary tail. Upperparts uniformly reddish brown, underparts white with olivaceous streaking on breast. VOICE: warning a short, horizontal tremolo, *rrro;* song a horizontal or almost horizontal sequence of 5–10 low, monotonous whistles without crescendo, timbre like *Grallaria varia.* Perches to sing. Tall forests. The Guianas and Venezuela to Amazon (Amapá), on upper Amazon south to Rio Juruá and to right bank of Tapajós (Pará). Also called *Patinho* (Amapá).

TAPUI ANTPITTA, *Myrmothera simplex*
Along mountainous border with Venezuela.

SUBFAMILY CONOPOPHAGINAE: GNATEATERS

The *Conopophaga* were originally considered to be Formicariidae. Later they were separated into a separate family, the Conopophagidae, to which the genus *Corythopis*[1] was added. After further study the *Conopophaga* were reintegrated into the Formicariidae, eliminating the Conopophagidae family. An understanding of their life history and morphological discoveries show that the gnateaters constitute a peculiar group, justifying establishment of a subfamily, the Conopophaginae, near the Grallarinae in the Formicariidae. It should be noted that there are similarities in morphology and behavior between the *Conopophaga* and the tapaculos.

Morphology

With short neck and tail and long legs and toes, *Conopophaga* recall the *Myrmoborus.* There is a surprising similarity between the coloring of the male *Conopophaga melanops* and female *Myrmoborus leucophrys.* The postauricular tuft, the most distinctive characteristic of the group, is absent from the remainder of the most typical antbirds. This mechanism plays a significant role because its display is so noticeable in the shadows where gnateaters live.

Anatomical and morphological research supporting the current systematic definition of the gnateaters is based on study of the cranium, bill, sternum, syrinx, and pterylosis. Sibley et al. (1988) reinstated the Conopophagidae, placing it in a superfamily, Formicarioidea.

Sounds

Their calls and warnings have given rise to the common names *chupa-dente,* "tooth-sucker," and *cuspidor,* "spitter." The song of *C. melanops* is a limpid phrase reminiscent of those of *Myrmoborus* and *Ramphocaenus* (Silviidae).

The male *C. lineata* has specialized flight feathers (fig. 210) with which it makes a high buzz, another characteristic

[1]The genus *Corythopis* was added to *Conopophaga* in the Conopophagidae because of certain anatomical characters. However, the similarities between the two are minimal. With abandonment of the Conopophagidae, *Corythopis* was transferred to the Tyrannidae.

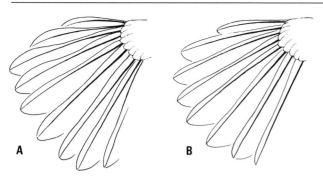

Fig. 210. Wing of Rufous Gnateater, *Conopophaga lineata:* (A) male, outer primaries modified as sound-producing remiges; (B) female, primaries unmodified. After Sick 1965.

not shared by the antbirds (Sick 1965). It turns on this "musical instrument" from one minute to the next at dusk, as if suddenly starting a machine. It then flies around its territory, sometimes at considerable height, and becomes one of the most conspicuous crepuscular birds, whereas during the day it passes almost unnoticed.

Behavior

Gnateaters stay perched on low, slender branches in shady forest, remaining quiet for long periods, tranquilly observing the surroundings, unlike most antbirds, which have restless dispositions. Sometimes they make a rapid wing movement (Chestnut-belted Gnateater, *C. aurita*); they fly to the ground to catch insects, then return to their perch. Sometimes on the ground they hop and do a bit of scratching, recalling tapaculos. They are curious and spontaneously approach observers. They take advantage of army ants. See also "Breeding" in antbirds.

BLACK-CHEEKED GNATEATER *Conopophaga melanops,* Cuspidor-de-máscara-preta
BR   PL 29.4

11 cm. Common in thickets of coastal lowlands and slopes of Serra do Mar. Male outstanding for contrast between chestnut cap and black sides of head. VOICE: call *schit, shist, kssrr;* warning *psEEeh;* song a prolonged sequence of short, limpid whistles with timbre of common canary but much higher, forming an unhurried, ascending phrase. Low in dense forests. Eastern Brazil from Paraíba to São Paulo, Santa Catarina; also ex-Guanabara. In mountainous regions of Espírito Santo and Rio de Janeiro sometimes alongside *C. lineata.*

RUFOUS GNATEATER, *Conopophaga lineata,*
Chupa-dente

11 cm. Typical of mountainous regions, especially of eastern Brazil. Sexes almost identical, male similar to female *C. melanops* but lacking black pattern on back. Maxilla

whitish (not black); prominent white postocular tufts. Lower throat often has white patch. Immature uniformly brown. SOUNDS: voices a *chic, chr,* not as loud as *melanops;* song a sequence of 5–10 cheeps in a phrase with a crescendo ending, *eeOO-eeOO-eeOO-we-we-we.* At dusk in breeding period, male, in addition to singing, produces a loud *brrro-brrro-brrro* with broadened tips of primaries, especially 2d and 3d outer primaries. It can even modulate and prolong this noise according to length of flight (e.g., *rrrro-ch, ch, ch*) and continues with this buzzing well into night. Outside breeding season flies silently. Edge of primary and secondary forests, in dense vegetation close to ground. Ceará to Rio Grande do Sul, Goiás, eastern Mato Grosso, Paraguay, and Misiones, Argentina. In Itatiaia (Rio de Janeiro) reaches *Chusquea* tangles in high open country at 2400 m where it lives alongside *Schizoeaca moreirae.* Locally sympatric with *C. melanops.* Also called *Limpa-dente.* Includes *C. cearae.*

BLACK-BELLIED GNATEATER, *Conopophaga melanogaster*

13 cm. Large, head and underparts black, mandible and postocular tuft white. South of Amazon from Rio Tocantins to lower Tapajós (Pará), Rio Madeira (Amazonias), Bolivia.

HOODED GNATEATER, *Conopophaga roberti*   BR

11.5 cm. Head, throat, and breast black; postocular tuft and belly white. Female lacks black. The Tocantins to Pará (Belém), Maranhão, Piauí, Ceará.

ASH-THROATED GNATEATER, *Conopophaga peruviana*
Also Amazonia.

CHESTNUT-BELTED GNATEATER, *Conopophaga aurita*
Also Amazonia. See "Behavior" under Conophophaginae.

Formicariidae Bibliography
See also General Bibliography

Ames, P. L., M. A. Heimerdinger, and S. L. Warter. 1968. *Postilla* 114. [*Conopophaga,* taxonomy]

Ataguile, B. S. 1988. Deslocamento e territorialidade de *Drymophila ferruginea* em mata mesofila semidecídua na região do Rio Claro, São Paulo. *XV Cong. Bras. Zool., Curitiba:*479.

Davis, T. J., and J. P. O'Neill. 1986. A new species of Antwren (*Herpsilochmus*) from Peru with comments on the systematics of other members of the genus. *Wilson Bull.* 98(3):337–52.

Fitzpatrick, J. W. 1980a. See Tyrannidae Bibliography.

Gonzaga, L. P., and J. F. Pacheco. 1990. Two new subspecies of *Formicivora serrana* (Hellmayr) from southeastern Brazil, and notes on the type locality of *Formicivora deluzae* Ménétriés. *Bull. B.O.C.* 110.

Hellmayr, C. E. 1929. On heterogynism in formicarian birds. *J. Orn.* 77, suppl. vol., comm. E. Hartert:41–70.

Lanyon, S. M., D. F. Stotz, and D. E. Willard. 1990. *Clytoctantes atrogularis,* a new species of antbird from western Brazil. *Wilson Bull.* 102:571–80.

Lowery, G. H., and J. P. O'Neill. 1969. *Auk* 86:1–12. [*Grallaria, Conopophaga,* systematics]

Naumberg, E.M.B. 1934. Rediscovery of *Rhopornis ardesiaca* (Wied), *Auk* 51:493–96.

Novaes, F. C. 1961. *An. Acad. Bras. Ciênc.* 33:11–117. [*Thamnophilus palliatus,* distribution]

Novaes, F. C. 1969. *Bol. Mus. Paraen. Zool.* 69. [Ecological analysis, Acará, Pará]

Novaes, F. C. 1971. *Bol. Mus. Paraen. Zool.* 71. [Ecological distribution and abundance, Guamá, Pará]

Novaes, F. C. 1982. *An. Soc. Sul-Riogr. Orn.* 3:5–8. [*Thamnophilus amazonicus,* behavior]

Oniki, Y. 1975. *An. Acad. Bras. Ciênc.* 47(3–4):477–515. [*Thamnophilus punctatus,* behavior, ecology]

Oniki, Y. 1979. Nesting of *Pyriglena leuconota* at Belém, Pará. *Rev. Bras. Biol.* 39(4):841–77.

Pacheco, F. 1988. Black-hooded Antwren *Formicivora (Myrmotherula) erythronotos* re-discovered in Brazil. *Bull B.O.C.* 108(4):179–82.

Pierpont, N., and J. W. Fitzpatrick. 1983. Specific status and behavior of *Cymbilaimus sanctaemariae,* from southwestern Amazonia. *Auk* 100(3):645–52.

Schneirla, T. C. 1960. The Army Ants. In *The Smithsonian Treasury of Science.* New York: Simon and Schuster.

Schulenberg, T. S. 1983. Foraging behavior, ecomorphology, and systematics of some antshrikes (*Thamnomanes*). *Wilson Bull.* 95(4):505–21.

Sick, H. 1964, 1981. Antpipit article. In A. L. Thomson, ed., *A New Dictionary of Birds.* New York: McGraw-Hill.

Sick, H. 1965. *An. Acad. Bras. Ciênc.* 37:131–40. [*Conopophaga,* sound-producing feathers]

Silva, J. M. C. 1988. Aspectos da ecologia e comportamento de *Formicivora g. grisea* (Boddaert, 1789) (Aves: Formicariidae) em ambientes amazônicos. Rev. Bras. Biol. 48:797–805.

Skutch, A. F. 1969. *Life Histories of Central American Birds,* vol.

3. Pacific Coast Avifauna 35:164–295. Berkeley, Calif.: Cooper Orn. Soc.

Teixeira, D. M. 1987. Notes sobre o gravateiro, *Rhopornis ardesiaca. Rev. Bras. Biol.* 47(3):409–14.

Teixeira, D. M., and L. P. Gonzaga. 1983. A new antwren from northeastern Brazil. *Bull. B.O.C.* 103(4):133–35.

Teixeira, D. M., and L. P. Gonzaga. 1987. Notas sobre *Terenura sicki* Teixeira e Gonzaga, 1983. *Bol. Mus. Par. E. Goeldi, Zool.* 3(2):241–51.

Willis, E. O. 1967. *Univ. Calif. Publs. Zool.* 79. [*Gymnopithys bicolor,* behavior]

Willis, E. O. 1968a. Studies of the behavior of Lunulated and Salvin's Antbirds. *Condor* 70:127–48.

Willis, E. O. 1968b. Taxonomy and behavior of Pale-faced Antbirds. *Auk* 85(2):253–64.

Willis, E. O. 1969. On the behavior of five species of *Rhegmatorhina,* ant-following antbirds of the Amazon. *Wilson Bull.* 81(4):363–95.

Willis, E. O. 1981. Diversity in adversity: The behavior of two subordinate antbirds. *Arq. Zool. S. Paulo* 30:159–234.

Willis, E. O. 1982. The behavior of *Percnostola rufifrons. Rev. Bras. Biol.* 42:233–47.

Willis, E. O. 1985. Survey of African ant-following birds. *Nat. Geo. Soc. Research Reports* 21(1980–83):515–18.

Willis, E. O. 1988. *Drymophila rubricollis* (Bertoni, 1901) is a valid species. *Rev. Bras. Biol.* 48(3):431–38.

Willis, E. O., and Y. Oniki. 1981. Notes on *Rhopornis ardesiaca. Wilson Bull.* 93(1):103–7.

Willis, E. O., and Y. Oniki. 1982. Behavior of *Pyriglena atra:* A test for taxonomy versus conservation. *Rev. Bras. Biol.* 42(1):213–23.

Willis, E. O., and Y. Oniki. 1988. Nesting of the Rusty-backed Antwren, *Formicivora rufa. Rev. Bras. Biol.* 48(3):635–37.

Zimmer, J. T. 1931. *Am. Mus. Nov.* 500 and subsequent publications. [Taxonomy]

FAMILY FURNARIIDAE: HORNEROS, SPINETAILS, FOLIAGE-GLEANERS, ETC. (99)

One of the largest exclusively Neotropical families, the Furnariidae extends from Mexico to Tierra del Fuego.[1] So far no fossils are known. See the Dendrocolaptidae for a discussion of joining it with that family; the Philydorinae would be the transition group.

There are many representatives of the family in savanna areas of southern South America and in the Andes, in temperate or cold climates. This Patagonian-Andean orientation makes Rio Grande do Sul by far the richest Brazilian state in Furnariidae (40 species). In Minas Gerais, a state twice as large but situated north of the Tropic of Capricorn, only 25 species have been recorded. Some of Brazil's best-known birds, the Rufous Hornero, *Furnarius rufus,* for instance, are in this family. Being related to dendrocolaptids, furnariids

share their rusty-colored plumage, concentrated primarily in the tail and sometimes in bars on the flight feathers, visible only when the wings are open.

Morphology

Size varies almost as much as in the Dendrocolaptidae. The largest Brazilian species, the Brown Cacholote, *Pseudoseisura lophotes,* reaches 90 g (male); the smallest, the Plain Xenops, *Xenops minutus,* weighs only 9.5 g. The Striolated Tit-Spinetail, *Leptasthenura striolata,* is only 10.5 g and Spix's Spinetail, *Synallaxis spixi,* only 14 g. *Furnarius rufus,* at 49 g, and the Long-tailed Cinclodes, *Cinclodes pabsti,* at 53 g, are good-sized species.

---

[1]The great monograph on Furnariidae by Charles Vaurie (1980), published post mortem (Vaurie died in 1975), is the work of a museum systematist. It includes data received from colleagues in the Neotropics or taken from the literature. I do not accept, for instance, the inclusion of *Cra-*

nioleuca in *Certhiaxis* or the elimination of various genera resulting from theoretical museum studies that obscure obvious differences among the live birds.

Tail structure is characteristic for many species and varies greatly within the family. No rigid tail generally used as a support on tree trunks, as found in the Dendrocolaptidae and Picidae, exists among the Furnariidae. There are slender species with extremely long tails, such as the *Leptasthenura* and the Chotoy Spinetail, *Synallaxis phryganophila,* whose central tail feathers comprise two-thirds of their total length. Such long and delicate feathers may wear so much during nesting that they frequently break. At another extreme are the *Sclerurus,* which have reinforced tail feathers although they do not use them for support (these species are terrestrial), for which reason the genus has been considered a precursor of the Dendrocolaptidae. A certain amount of tail reinforcement (a bare, needlelike tip) is also found in the Wren-like Rushbird, *Phleocryptes melanops,* and Sharp-tailed Streamcreeper, *Lochmias nematura.*

In *Synallaxis* (with more than 20 species) the number of rectrices varies from 8 to 12. The outermost are rudimentary. Ten rectrices are frequent (e.g., *S. spixi*); the Rufous-capped Spinetail, *S. ruficapilla,* has 8; the Red-shouldered Spinetail, *S. hellmayri,* 12. Variation occurs even within the same species. Bill variety reflects usage. Relatively thin but strong mandibles, such as those of the *Sclerurus,* resemble those of the Formicariidae (in which *Sclerurus* was formerly included), whereas others, such as those of the *Xenops* and *Megaxenops,* are real chisels with which the birds hammer like woodpeckers. Chisel-shaped bills also occur in the Formicariidae. The front toes are separate or only slightly joined, unlike the dendrocolaptids.

Vocalization

Voices are generally similar to those of dendrocolaptids. Pairs frequently give their song, loud cry, or coarse laugh together, as for example, with *Phacellodomus, Furnarius, Leptasthenura, Lochmias, Pseudoseisura, Schizoeaca, Synallaxis phryganophila,* and Yellow-chinned Spinetail, *Certhiaxis cinnamomea;* Rusty-backed Spinetail, *Cranioleuca vulpina;* Firewood-gatherer, *Anumbius annumbi;* and Point-tailed Palmcreeper, *Berlepschia rikeri.* The White-collared Foliage-gleaner, *Anabazenops fuscus,* has a peculiar technique of giving two different phrases at almost the same time, creating the impression of two, not one, individuals singing. Many species, such as the *Furnarius* and *Synallaxis,* are more active in the hottest and brightest hours of the day, unlike dendrocolaptids, which the Buff-browed Foliage-gleaner, *Syndactyla rufosuperciliata,* resembles in its custom of dawn and dusk vocal activity. The Rufous-breasted Leaftosser, *Sclerurus scansor,* is the same, its melodious song recalling certain antbirds such as the Black-cheeked Gnateater, *Conopophaga melanops,* or the *Merulaxis* (Rhinocryptidae). Voices of the sexes are usually slightly or distinctly different (see *Synallaxis spixi*).

Savanna species such as the *Geositta* sing in flight, over-

seeing in this way from a distance the demarcation of their territory. In the *Synallaxis* the song (a short, often bisyllabic whistle repeated ceaselessly in certain seasons) is an important aid in identifying these birds that rarely show themselves. The Pale-breasted Spinetail, *Synallaxis albescens,* adds a visual surprise to the sound effect by inflating its throat, thus revealing the black bases of the throat feathers which form a temporary black spot. Furnariid voices are dominant in certain habitats, as is the song of the Rufous Cacholote, *Pseudoseisura cristata,* in the caatinga.

Feeding

As with the Dendrocolaptidae, food consists of insects and their larvae, spiders, harvestmen, and other arthropods, mollusks, etc. There is not always a specialized technique for seeking food, the method recalling that of large wrens like *Campylorhynchus.* The Sharp-billed Xenops, *Heliobletus contaminatus,* and other arboreal furnariids tear away small epiphytes to uncover hidden animals, their technique resembling that of woodcreepers such as the *Lepidocolaptes.* In their searches for food *Syndactyla rufosuperciliata* and the *Xenops* and *Automolus* peck at soft wood and large, dry leaves like those of the tajá (*Caladium bicolor,* Araceae) of Amazonia or the cecropia that have fallen and become lodged in tree branches. The Pale-browed Treehunter, *Cichlocolaptes leucophrus,* exploits dry, rolled-up leaves of gravatás. In a survey made in Bolivia, 11 furnariid and formicariid species were identified as specializing in these dead leaves suspended among branches, which harbor a world of arthropods; Remsen and Parker (1984) calculated that such specialists obtain 75% of their food from those leaves. Some, like the Tail-banded Hornero, *Furnarius figulus,* and the *Sclerurus,* use their bills to turn over leaves and branches fallen on the forest floor. The Lark-like Brushrunner, *Coryphistera alaudina,* flips over cattle dung with its feet. *Lochmias nematura* is unique in its adaptation to life on stream edges, sometimes fishing in shallow water or pulling out larger items with its bill, even a leaf fallen in the water, and then stepping on it to examine it. Neither it nor the *Cinclodes* swim or submerge like the dippers, *Cinclus* (Cinclidae), of the Andes and Northern Hemisphere, the only Passerines that hunt underwater.

The *Furnarius* catch swarming termites as they appear on the surface of their nests. *Sclerurus scansor* sometimes devours the young of small Passerines. In Argentina a *Pseudoseisura lophotes* reportedly frightened away a brooding domestic hen and pecked at a hatching egg. *Furnarius rufus* occasionally eats seeds; the Common Thornbird, *Phacellodomus rufifrons,* is reputed to be a spreader of mistletoe. Vegetation remains found in the stomach contents of *Cinclodes,* for example, must originate with caterpillars they have eaten. All seven Itatiaia Thistletails, *Schizoeaca moreirae,* I collected on the Serra do Caparaó, Minas Gerais, in

March 1941 had drupes of capororoca (*Rapanea* sp., Myrsinaceae), and thus vegetable material, in their stomachs. This finding was fully confirmed by examination of the feces of seven individuals captured in mist nets in upper Itatiaia, Rio de Janeiro, all of which also contained these seeds (Pineschi 1990). Other *S. moreirae* were seen eating these little fruits. It is very interesting that a member of the Furnariidae, a typically insectivorous family, would systematically collect *Rapanea* fruits, which may perhaps be a supplement at times when insects are scarce, as in the winter. In Itatiaia 140 bird species were recorded eating fruits of seven *Rapanea* species (see also Ramphastidae, "Feeding"). Furnariids (*Lochmias nematura*) cough up pellets containing chitin. The *Xenops* drink rainwater accumulated in tree holes, as do dendrocolaptids and other birds.

Behavior

The White-browed Foliage-gleaner, *Anabacerthia amaurotis,* the *Automolus,* and others draw attention by suddenly opening the wide, light rufous tail against the light, and others, such as the *Cinclodes,* by bobbing it downward. The Common Miner, *Geositta cunicularia,* even rubs and soils the tips of its tail feathers against the ground. *Schizoeaca moreirae* reveals nervousness by lateral tail movements.

Flight ability varies. Whereas the *Synallaxis,* with round, soft wings, fly only as a last resort and then aim low for the closest thicket, the *Philydor* spend the greater part of the day wandering in the canopy and flying at the least provocation. *Berlepschia rikeri* flies in a straight line from one buriti palm to another. The longest and strongest wings are those of the Bar-winged Cinclodes, *Cinclodes fuscus,* which undertakes substantial migrations.

Capacity for moving around on the ground also varies substantially. Certain family members, such as the *Lochmias, Sclerurus,* and *Geositta,* live predominantly on the ground, with *Geositta* able to run like a sandpiper. Some have a surprising ability to change velocity (e.g., in *Furnarius*), like an automobile changing gears. *Furnarius figulus* also walks on large branches. The *Geositta* almost never perch above ground. The *Xenops* have a peculiar technique for scaling vertical trunks and, among other species, never descend to the ground.

They bathe in clear, shallow waters in the forest shade (*Sclerurus*) or in the dust of fields under a blazing sun (Campo Miner, *Geobates poecilopterus*). *Syndactyla rufosuperciliata* is active even at dawn and dusk, revealing its presence with its calls and loud song, a situation analogous to that found in the Plain-brown Woodcreeper, *Dendrocincla fuliginosa.*

Outside the breeding season forest species such as the *Philydor, Cichlocolaptes,* and *Xenops* that live in the highest levels of the forest join other birds (e.g., dendrocolaptids) to wander. In these mixed flocks there is a certain advantageous cooperation through reciprocal understanding of the alarm notes of the different species comprising them.

Population Census

The density of a *Pseudoseisura cristata* population was calculated by a census of the number of nests visible from a distance. In 90 km of road between Curuçá and Juazeiro, Bahia, 262 nests were counted and studied, including identification of the trees that served as substrate (Azevedo 1989).

Breeding

The shape of the nest, typical for each genus, is very important for making taxonomic determinations in the Furnariidae. This situation was well reviewed by Charles Vaurie (see below). It became evident that nest construction is one of the most conservative taxonomic characters of this family and thus very useful for making phylogenetic decisions. In the Furnariidae the evolution of nesting led to a series of models obtained independently from various species; the different nests do not, however, make up a linear sequence that begins with simple types and ends with the most perfected techniques. A tendency is always noticeable toward hiding the clutch and nestlings, using the most varied means. Taking Brazilian species as a base, I have arrived at the following classification:

1. Oven-shaped nest, made of mud, with two chambers, the inner one lined: *Furnarius rufus* and Pale-legged Hornero, *F. leucopus.* There is an interesting variety in the nesting instinct within the *Furnarius:* (A) well-known ovens, made only by *F. rufus* and *F. leucopus;* (B) construction of a simple, open nest instead of a protected one, by *F. figulus;* and (C) occupation of nests of other furnariids, including *F. rufus* and *F. leucopus,* and stick nests such as those of *Phacellodomus,* by *F. leucopus* (fig. 211).
2. A heap of dead, hard sticks with one or two chambers and an entrance (sometimes two) through a tunnel that may be long, twisting, and go up, down, or sideways. In the incubation chamber there is a mat of fluffy or flexible material under the eggs: the *Synallaxis; Certhiaxis; Phacellodomus; Anumbius; Coryphistera; Pseudoseisura;* Stripe-crowned Spinetail, *Cranioleuca pyrrhophia;* and Striated Softtail, *Thripophaga macroura* (fig. 211).
3. An ovoid nest, almost vertical, with the body made of very soft moss encapsuled within a covering of twigs, and an upper side entrance: *Schizoeaca moreirae* (fig. 212).
4. A spheroid nest of soft, fine material, such as Spanish moss, with a side entrance through a tunnel (sometimes widened into a second chamber) within the "ball": Pallid Spinetail, *Cranioleuca pallida* (fig. 212).
5. An oval nest, placed vertically and made of well interwoven, wide, soft material like piripiri leaves, with an upper side entrance. Constructed in reed beds: *Phleocryptes melanops* and Curve-billed Reedhaunter, *Limnornis curvirostris.* When dry, the walls of a *P. melanops* nest have the

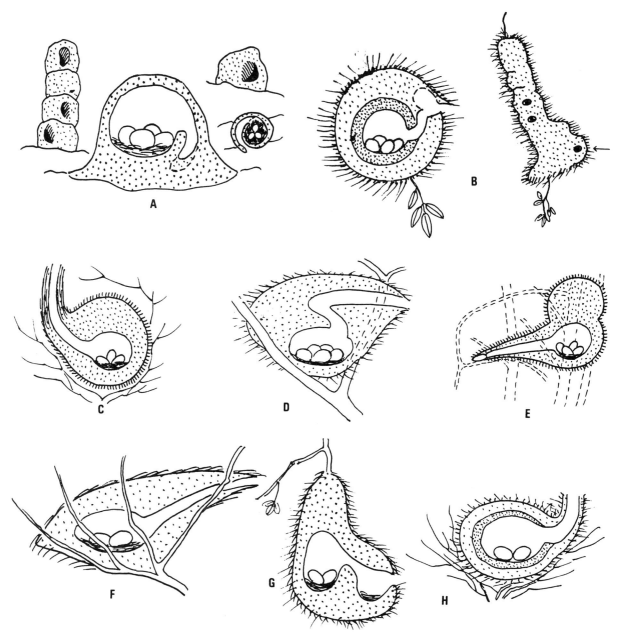

Fig. 211. Sketches of furnariid nest types, group I; nests have been reduced to the same size. (A) Rufous Hornero, *Furnarius rufus,* mud nest, longitudinal cross section (center); transverse cross section (right); four superimposed nests from Minas Gerais (left). (B) Common Thornbird, *Phacellodomus rufifrons,* hanging nest of sticks, built at the tip of a branch; the chamber is carpeted with soft material and there is a start of an antechamber; at right, more distant, a complex of half a dozen nests, but only the lowest nest is in use (Bahia). (C) Yellow-chinned Spinetail, *Certhiaxis cinnamomea,* a retort-shaped nest of sticks in a bush (Espírito Santo). (D) Firewood-gatherer, *Anumbius annumbi,* a stick nest placed firmly on branches (Rio de Janeiro). (E) Spix's Spinetail, *Synallaxis spixi,* stick nest, built in a coffee tree; above the chamber is a solid addition (Espírito Santo). (F) Rufous Cacholote, *Pseudoseisura cristata,* a large nest of sticks on branches. (G) Red-eyed Thornbird, *Phacellodomus erythrophthalmus,* boot-shaped hanging next of sticks, with a well-finished antechamber (Rio de Janeiro). (H) Freckle-breasted Thornbird, *Phacellodomus striaticollis,* retort-shaped stick nest with lined chamber (Santa Catarina). Original, H. Sick.

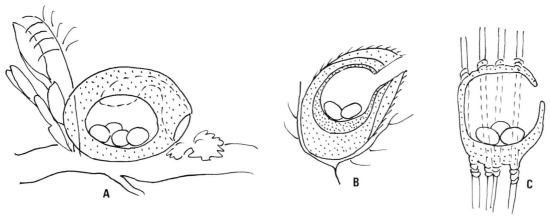

Fig. 212. Sketches of furnariid nest types, group II. (A) Pallid Spinetail, *Cranioleuca pallida*, nest of soft material, resting on a thick branch among epiphytes (Rio de Janeiro). (B) Itatiaia Thistletail, *Schizoeaca moreirae*, nest of moss in various layers, in a bush (Rio de Janeiro). (C) Wren-like Rushbird, *Phleocryptes melanops*, nest built of wet material, wound about cattail stems, hardened like papier-mâché (Rio de Janeiro). Original, H. Sick.

consistency of cardboard, a great advantage in view of the instability of its supports, for the nest is fastened to various reed stalks that wave in all directions and would tear apart a less solid edifice (see Many-colored Rush-Tyrant, *Tachuris rubrigastra* (Tyrannidae), whose nest is fastened to only one stem) (fig. 212).

6. A basket made of reeds and grass, well hidden in the most tangled base of the reeds; the leaning vegetation provides a good protective dome so the nest looks almost spherical: Bay-capped Wren-Spinetail, *Spartonoica maluroides*.

7. A nest in a tree hollow, either excavated by the same bird (in soft wood) or in woodpecker holes or other natural cavities: *Xenops*, *Syndactyla rufosuperciliata*, *Leptasthenura striolata*, and *Anabazenops*; probably also *Heliobletus*.

8. Subterranean nests, really excavated (fig. 213):

   8.1. A gallery having an enlarged end with a stem-lined cup forming a sometimes well-woven receptacle: *Geositta; Cinclodes;* Buff-fronted Foliage-gleaner, *Philydor rufus;* Black-capped Foliage-gleaner, *P. atricapillus;* White-eyed Foliage-gleaner, *Automolus leucophthalmus;* Henna-capped Foliage-gleaner, *A. rectirostris;* and *Sclerurus. Cinclodes* and *P. rufus* occasionally nest inside houses. I think it possible that certain *Philydor* use tree cavities and probably also nest among epiphytes (southeastern Brazil).

8.2. A closed nest, made of soft, long, wide leaves, with a side entrance, placed in a hole in the earth at the end of a horizontal gallery excavated by the bird; *Lochmias nematura*. Building a globe-shaped nest inside a cavity appears to me to be a waste of energy; such a habit suggests heredity from an ancestor that nested in the open.

9. A simple, open nest in a protected place, as already mentioned for *F. figulus*. See also *Spartonoica maluroides*.

Furnariids customarily sleep in their nests all year; they may use less elaborate nests as dormitories (*Phacellodomus*).

To make covered nests such as those of *Phacellodomus rufifrons*, *Phleocryptes melanops*, and *Schizoeaca moreirae*, the birds usually first build a deep bag open at the top and then build the top, picking up the sticks with the bill, not the toes (*Phacellodomus rufifrons*). The use of spiny twigs (e.g., the esporão de gallo, "cockspur," *Vismia brasiliensis*) guarantees the intertwined sticks greater firmness, further increased by their long length, which often exceeds that of the builder. Beyond this, the spines protect the nest against marauders. *Certhiaxis cinnamomea* immediately repairs small damages that occur. Certain irregularities in construction can be interpreted as false entrances that help camouflage the real en-

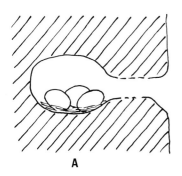

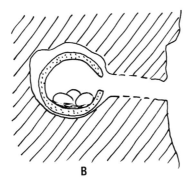

Fig. 213. Sketches of furnariid nest types, group III. Subterranean nests at the end of a gallery (shortened in sketches). (A) Long-tailed Cinclodes, *Cinclodes pabsti;* the eggs are placed on straw (Santa Catarina). (B) Sharp-tailed Streamcreeper, *Lochmias nematura*, a spherical nest of soft material with a side access, within a cavity in the earth. Original, H. Sick.

trance. Nests may have two entrances, a construction type that may save the owner's life, as I have observed in the *Anumbius* and *Certhiaxis*. Two entrances are also found in *Synallaxis phryganophila* nests. The complexity of the great heaps of branches of *Phacellodomus rufifrons* misleads as to what part the nest is really in. Yet not even the perfect oven of *Furnarius rufus* provides absolute protection, for it can crack and, beyond this, be invaded by the Guira Cuckoo, *Guira guira,* which eats eggs and nestlings, or by the Shiny Cowbird, *Molothrus bonariensis,* which lays its contraband eggs there.

The establishment of a pair of *Phacellodomus rufifrons, Anumbius annumbi,* or *Pseudoseisura* in a given territory results in an accumulation of numerous nests distributed over various parts of a tree. These have generally been constructed successively by the same pair and therefore do not represent colonies. Nevertheless, the resident pair tolerates the presence of other bird species occupying their abandoned nests. It can happen, however, that two furnariid species, both twig users, who set up housekeeping in the same tree may end up fighting when one steals sticks from the other. I have seen an *Anumbius annumbi* thus raid the nest of a *Synallaxis phryganophila.* Species that excavate in the earth periodically appear with the bill encrusted with soil (e.g., *Lochmias*). A *Phacellodomus rufifrons* or *Pseudoseisura cristata* nest may at times be attended by various individuals.

Eggs are pure white, sometimes greenish or bluish (*Synallaxis*), or even blue or greenish blue (*Phleocryptes melanops, Limnornis curvirostris*) or light green (*Synallaxis hellmayri*).

Mates take turns caring for the young. They attempt to deceive enemies to lure them away from the nest. A *Furnarius* may enter an unoccupied neighboring nest to draw away attention from the one it really uses. Incubation lasts 16 to 17 days in the case of *F. rufus,* 20 days for *F. figulus* (E. Studer). Although parents systematically remove nestling feces, the nest does not remain entirely clean for the evacuations are semiliquid. Nestlings defend themselves in the nest by hissing like snakes (*Furnarius, Certhiaxis*), sometimes while making an automatic aggressive movement with the bill, without aiming at anything. By 14 days of age *Furnarius* young start to sing a bit of subsong, interspersing it with the cries they use to call for food. Thus, large nestlings reveal from a distance the location of the nest (*Furnarius* and Streaked Xenops, *Xenops rutilans*). *Furnarius rufus* nestlings abandon the nest at about 23 days of age and do not return to sleep. They are frequently parasitized by botflies.

The practice of helpers at the nest occurs: one nest is attended by various individuals of the species helping to rear the nestlings. In the case of *Phacellodomus rufifrons* this can lead to the erroneous conclusion that there is a nesting colony.

The *Synallaxis* and *Certhiaxis cinnamomea* are the principal hosts of the Striped Cuckoo, *Tapera naevia,* although the following are also parasitized: *Phacellodomus rufifrons;* Red-eyed Thornbird, *P. erythrophthalmus;* Freckle-breasted Thornbird, *P. striaticollis;* and Greater Thornbird, *P. ruber. P. ruber, Anumbius annumbi,* and *Pseudoseisura cristata* are sometimes imposed upon by the parasitic icterine, *Molothrus bonariensis;* in Argentina *Furnarius rufus* is often its host.

Phacellodomus rufifrons nesting is sometimes associated with a wasp. *Guira guira* is reported to be a predator of oventype nests.

Habitat, Distribution, Abundance, and Migration

Habitats exploited by furnariids include almost the entire gamut of Neotropical landscapes. In Brazil three principal types of ecosystems where they live can be defined.

1. Forests and thickets: according to the species, *Sclerurus, Automolus, Philydor, Xenops,* and *Synallaxis* occur from the ground to the highest branches. There are interesting endemics, some with a very limited range, among various Atlantic forest species such as *Thripophaga macroura, Anabazenops, Cichlocolaptes,* and *Heliobletus. Megaxenops* and *Synallaxis hellmayri* are restricted to the caatinga, *Berlepschia* to certain palms. Bamboo groves can be attractive. The Araucaria Tit-Spinetail, *Leptasthenura setaria,* is the most typical bird of the araucaria forests. Its adaptation to a single plant, the araucaria, is almost unique among Brazilian birds. It can be compared with a related furnariid, *Schizoeaca moreirae* (see below) which, as an Andean bird, has occupied the tops of mountains covered with *Chusquea,* an Andean bamboo. This recalls the important ecological adaptation of another Brazilian furnariid, *Berlepschia rikeri,* which lives exclusively in palm groves in the most tropical areas, as well as the probable coevolution of the Scale-throated Hermit, *Phaethornis eurynome,* and the heliconia, *Heliconia velloziana. Automolus* has many species in the Amazonian forest. Various furnariids live in transitory areas between forest and open country, feeding on the ground but needing trees or bushes for nesting, as with *Phacellodomus, Anumbius, Coryphistera,* and *Pseudoseisura.*

2. Open country lacking high vegetation: *Geositta, Geobates,* and *Cinclodes.* This group becomes dominant in the south of the continent and in the Andes. Included here also is *Schizoeaca moreirae* of the high-altitude grasslands of southeastern Brazil. *S. moreirae* and *Cinclodes pabsti* have ancestors that belonged to an ancient Patagonian fauna living in mild or cold climates from where they colonized the Andes and southeastern Brazil in the Pleistocene or post-Pleistocene era when temperate climates had moved farther north as a result of progressive Antarctic glaciations. The very limited ability of these birds to colonize new areas indicates that the high-altitude areas where they are today isolated were once connected. The immense populations living at lower alti-

tudes that connected the high points were later eliminated by the climate which warmed and altered the habitat. The present remnants, which reached their respective areas thousands of years ago as pioneers, may be considered "glacial relics." The distribution of *C. pabsti* coincides with the area of coldest climate in present-day Brazil. It is significant, therefore, that *S. moreirae,* one of the few typically mountain birds of Brazil, is of Andean descent. The Sooty-fronted Spinetail, *Synallaxis frontalis,* and Gray-bellied Spinetail, *S. cinerascens,* live in open regions of central Brazil in contiguous formations that have different amounts of sunlight, as is also the case with *Furnarius leucopus* and *F. figulus.*

3. Marshes (reeds and cattails): *Limnornis, Phleocryptes, Certhiaxis,* and *Spartonoica.*

The multiplicity of Brazilian furnariids is all the more impressive when various species of the same genus occur in a single place; for instance, in just one Serra do Mar forest (southeastern Brazil) one can find three *Synallaxis* (*spixi, ruficapilla,* and *cinerascens*), one alongside the other occupying different ecological niches. In secondary forests of the lower Amazon (Rio Acará), the Olive-backed Foliage-gleaner, *Automolus infuscatus,* is one of the most common birds alongside the Wedge-billed Woodcreeper, *Glyphorynchus spirurus. Certhiaxis cinnamomea* and *Schizoeaca moreirae* are normally abundant in their respective habitats. Various groups such as *Synallaxis, Phacellodomus,* and *Furnarius* adapt well to human modifications of the environment; the immigration of *F. rufus* into Espírito Santo, for example, reflects the "catingaaization" of that area.

Migrations resulting from the southern winter are obvious in the case of *Cinclodes fuscus* but also occur with other forms, especially with the southernmost (Argentine) populations of *Phleocryptes melanops.*

Use of Furnariid Nests by Other Animals; Nest Fauna

The nests of some furnariids play an important role in the lives of a great variety of beings. Abandoned nests of *Phacellodomus rufifrons* and *Anumbius annumbi* are frequently occupied by the Bay-winged Cowbird, *Molothrus badius,* and Troupial, *Icterus icterus jamacaii,* and occasionally by the Gray Monjita, *Xolmis cinerea;* White-rumped Monjita, *X. velata;* Cattle Tyrant, *Machetornis rixosus;* Saffron Finch, *Sicalis flaveola;* and House Sparrow, *Passer domesticus.* Near Rezende, Rio de Janeiro, an *Anumbius annumbi* nest was taken over by *Passer domesticus* that set up a colony there. A spacious antechamber near the surface in the *Phacellodomus rufifrons* nest is attractive to Rufous-collared Sparrows, *Zonotrichia capensis,* and Ruddy Ground Doves, *Columbina talpacoti.* The nests are also used by lizards,

small snakes, toads, and even small forest rats, such as the rato-da-palmatória (*Thomasomys pyrrhorinus*) in the caatinga. I surprised a rato-de-espinho (*Proechimys* sp.) sleeping in a *Cranioleuca vulpina* nest during the day (Rio Xingu, Mato Grosso), whereas a recently constructed *Schizoeaca moreirae* nest harbored a mother and brood of a small *Oryzomys* rat (upper Itatiaia, Rio de Janeiro). It should be added that sometimes social wasps move into *Phacellodomus* nests.

The rich arthropod fauna (nest fauna) that use nests are a special case. In Minas Gerais and Pernambuco, *Phacellodomus rufifrons* and *Anumbius annumbi* nests may each harbor a score of different arthropods, primarily Hexapoda. Thus, small beetles, cimicid bugs, flesh flies, forest cockroaches, mites, spiders, pseudoscorpions, millipedes, etc., can be distinguished in a population of sometimes hundreds of "guests" per nest. The beetles, among others, are coprophagous and may even survive in empty nests. Some of these guests, however, especially the Triatominae, *Psammolestes coreodes* and *P. tertius*[2], depend on the presence of birds and are very similar to assassin bugs, vectors of Chagas disease; they can be experimentally infected with *Trypanosoma cruzi.* In almost all the *Phacellodomus rufifrons* nests examined by J. C. M. Carvalho in Goiás and Sergipe, *P. coreodes* was found, occasionally ten or more individuals per nest. The entire life cycle of these Hemiptera occurs in the nests of these birds, with everything from larvae to adults being found. When the *Phacellodomus* are breeding, the bugs gorge themselves on their blood. In a *Phacellodomus* nest in Uruguay, *Triatoma delpontei,* an assassin bug naturally infected by *Trypanosoma cruzi,* has been found, and *Triatoma platensis,* also a Chagas disease vector, has been found in *Pseudoseisura lophotes* nests. Ticks and fleas, also bloodsuckers, likewise require the presence of birds, especially unfeathered nestlings. The same is true for the cimicid bug, *Caminicimex furnarii,* that lives in *Furnarius rufus* ovens in Uruguay and Argentina but has not yet been found in Brazil (see also Hirundinidae, "Nest Fauna," and Ciconiidae, "Tenants of Arboreal Nests"). Possibly the nest fauna changes when a nest is occupied by another bird species, as when *Passer domesticus* installs itself in an *F. rufus* house.

The advantage for these tenants of periodically having new nests added to the old ones is obvious, for it guarantees the continuity of their residence, a situation they also enjoy with the Monk Parakeet, *Myiopsitta monachus.* This is not the case with fragile constructions such as the bags of the Red-rumped Cacique, *Cacicus haemorrhous.* Arthropods reach nests in part thanks to the twigs carried their by the builders. For some, such as arboreal spiders, these edifices are merely extensions of their natural habitat among the branches. The numerous stink bugs found in *Anumbius annumbi* structures in Uruguay must be primarily predators of other insects.

---

[2]A third species, *Psammolestes arthuri,* has been found in Venezuela in *Phacellodomus rufifrons* nests.

*Furnariid Nests as Obstacles
on Electric Systems*

In Rio Grande do Sul much damage to rural electrical systems has been caused by *Anumbius annumbi* nests (Tessmer 1989). Its frequent use of wire and other metallic objects increases the danger of short circuits and even fires. Preventive measures include removing and burning nests (so the birds won't immediately use the material again) and greasing posts; the nest owners are thus saved from electrocution. *Furnarius rufus* and *Myiopsitta monachus* nests can also become a problem.

SUBFAMILY FURNARIINAE

CAMPO MINER, *Geobates poecilopterus*, Andarilho   BR   PL 27.1

12 cm. Terrestrial, open-country bird of central Brazil with short tail and wings, resembling a European lark (*Alauda*, Alaudidae) or a pipit (*Anthus*). Wings and tail bright, light ferruginous, noticeable in flight, especially if bird sings while flying, when it soars and undulates like a large butterfly. VOICE: call *pit-pit;* song a monotonous, prolonged phrase of hurried whistles, *tslirpe.* . . . Nest is underground. Bird walks and runs like a sandpiper; with erect posture dips tail so tips of tail feathers almost touch ground (*abanacauda,* "fantail," Minas Gerais). Thinly vegetated open country, areas with sparse grasses among bushes and trees of cerrado. Restricted to Goiás, Mato Grosso, São Paulo, Minas Gerais. Could be included in *Geositta,* which has more than 10 species in pampas and Andes. Also called *Batebunda* (Goiás).

COMMON MINER, *Geositta cunicularia*, Curriqueiro

15 cm. Similar to *Geobates poecilopterus,* with breast clearly spotted dark brown, secondaries extensively pale rusty (in flight), tail brown, sides of tail feathers white at base. VOICE: call *truit;* song a tremulous phrase, *bewbew* . . . *trrri-bewbew* . . . , slightly undulating and somewhat reminiscent of song of Cliff Flycatcher, *Hirundinea ferruginea,* sung in flight with body erect and feathers ruffled. Excavates a long, horizontal gallery in earth (hence the name *miner*), lining incubation chamber with straw and leaves. Open fields without tall vegetation, plains, road edges, sloping fills, near dunes, overflies marshes, feeding in ponds in ocean tidal zone like a *Calidris* sandpiper. Perches on ground, avoiding posts. In behavior resembles Old World chats (*Saxicola*). Southern South America, including Tierra del Fuego and high areas of Andes (Bolivia and Peru) to Uruguay, Rio Grande do Sul.

LONG-TAILED CINCLODES, *Cinclodes pabsti*, Pedreiro   BR   Fig. 214

22 cm; 53 g. One of largest furnariids; may remind one of Chalk-browed Mockingbird, *Mimus saturninus,* or Fur *narius rufus,* each of which is sometimes found close to it. Posture erect, legs strong, tail long. Earth-colored with superciliary and underparts yellowish white. Wings have intricate design with wide, light yellowish bar on blackish brown background. Tips of outer tail feathers white. VOICE: warning a loud, descending, bisyllabic whistle, *tsio, ghee-eh;* song *tsiewrrrrrrr* . . . , crescendo and then diminuendo, reminiscent of *Anumbius annumbi,* sung either perched, sometimes with wings lifted, or in flight. Nests (November, Santa Catarina; September, November, Rio Grande do Sul) and overnights in galleries excavated in embankments, sometimes in dark attics of houses. Eggs placed on a lining of grass, feathers, and string. Open country and ranches near houses. Less dependent on presence of water than other *Cinclodes.* Walks and runs on ground, perches on posts, stone fences, rocks. Flies well but unlike *C. fuscus* does not migrate; large wings have rounder shape. Resident in uplands of northeastern Rio Grande do Sul and southeastern Santa Catarina above 800 m (see "Habitat . . . "). Described only in 1969, it is 1 of 2 Brazilian representatives of a genus widely distributed in Patagonia and Andes. See *C. fuscus,* which there is no indication it meets, since it lives constantly in Planalto. Also called *Terezinha* (Rio Grande do Sul), *Pedreirinho* (Santa Catarina).

Fig. 214. Long-tailed Cinclodes, *Cinclodes pabsti.*

BAR-WINGED CINCLODES, *Cinclodes fuscus*,
Pedreiro-dos-Andes   SV

18.5 cm. Occurs only as a migrant. Similar to *C. pabsti* but with shorter tail, white throat spotted brown, 2 yellow wing bars. Beaches of rivers, estuaries, lakes; also at oceanside where it seeks insects among trash left by tide, a biotope rarely exploited by a Passerine. Rio Grande do Sul (Rio Grande, Pelotas, Osório, Taquara, July–September), coming from Argentina where it is widely distributed. Also northern Andes (e.g., Colombia) up to 4000 m and breeds in Peru above 2000 m.

RUFOUS HORNERO, *Furnarius rufus*,
João-de-barro   PL 27.2

19 cm. One of best-known birds of southeastern Brazil. Yellowish streak can be seen at base of flight feathers in open wing. Sexes very similar but female can be identified by habit of occupying nest at night alone with eggs or nestlings. VOICE: call *krip;* song a strident *keekeekee* . . . in prolonged, rhythmic sequences, rising and falling in festive song; pair synchronizes in duet (male and female phrases slightly different in pitch and rhythm), showing great vivacity by singing on top of or alongside nest with head raised, bill wide open, while shaking half-drooping wings and trembling whole body.

Construction of Nest, Breeding: Builds an oven-shaped nest (see fig. 211A) (thus the name *Furnarius* [*forno,* "oven"] which provided name for Furnariidae family), 1 each year, though sometimes it remodels an old one. Uses wet mud and a little dung mixed with straw. In sandy regions more dung than earth is used. Quantity of straw used varies, it being actively gathered by builder and not a product of dung. Mortar may be used if available.[3] Birds select a good, open situation for installation, e.g., isolated trees, utility poles, etc. When a tall support is unavailable they build on ground, e.g., on earth thrown up from excavation of a canal (Espírito Santo). Pair works together, each placing material it brings and not passing it over to its partner. Irregularities in support, such as cracks, are filled. The technique of working the mud must be such that the material, after being baked by sun, has consistency of adobe. Wall is 3–4 cm thick, being thicker in nests in south. During last phase of construction half wall is erected that separates spacious incubation chamber from narrow vestibule that impedes entry of breezes and predators. Interior space thus acquires a conch shape.

Fifteen to 16 days after work has started the house may be practically ready, lacking only final touches. At end of 18 days nest is completed; 3 days after they finish working the mud, pair begins to prepare and line incubation chamber.

Work is more productive when there is a fine, continuous rain to supply abundant building material without washing away what has been built. When rain is scarce, construction may continue for a month. Wet mud stimulates constructing instinct of *F. rufus*, which will then build all year; a pair may work on several nests at same time. Durability of nest is not very great, and in a few months walls become weak and brittle, there also being much violent destruction resulting from winds, people, cattle. A pair may reach a point of not having an oven in good condition available in which to nest, although the inverse may occur, with 2 usable nests available.

Antechamber faces right or left according to which direction is most convenient for reaching nest on wing. Of 400 ovens examined by Hermann and Meise (1966) in Argentina in 1956–57, fewer than 60% had a right-hand entrance. Weather conditions (nest microclimate) also have their influence, for the birds normally place the opening on the side opposite the prevailing winds and rain, though on this there is no absolute rule. For instance, nests built one on top of the other or in the same tree have had entrances facing in different directions, having possibly been built by same pair in a certain period. Of 315 nests studied in Argentina that were exposed on all sides, 249 (79%) had entrance facing the direction opposite that of prevailing rains and cold winds (in this case south and southeast). Placement of nests on top of each other may involve 6 or even 11 units, all with entrances facing the same way (Minas Gerais). Average weight of a dry nest is 4.1 kg, whereas bird itself weighs only 49 g. Nests on lamp posts can interfere with functioning of lighting system. In a census by state electric company in Rio Grande do Sul in December 1987, there were 580 *F. rufus* nests on company structures, with 265 in risk of provoking short circuits. See also *Anumbius annumbi*, Tessmer 1989.

Three to 4 eggs are laid beginning in September. *F. rufus* is a host of *Molothrus bonariensis*. Abandoned nests are used by *Sicalis flaveola; Forpus* parrotlets; *Passer domesticus;* Brown-chested Martin, *Phaeoprogne tapera;* and occasionally by White-winged Swallow, *Tachycineta albiventer;* House Wren, *Troglodytes aedon;* Chopi Blackbird, *Gnorimopsar chopi;* and *Machetornis rixosus,* among others (see "Use of Furnariid Nests . . . "). These tenants (except *Forpus*) make their own lining. There are cases where the invaders, e.g., pairs of parrotlets, drive out the owners. *Guira guira;* Roadside Hawk, *Rupornis magnirostris;* and Black-chested Buzzard-Eagle, *Geranoaetus melanoleucus,* occasionally manage to raid one. Bees may seal a nest with black wax and build a tube for their own entrance.

Distribution: Found in savanna country, being abundant on southern ranches, parks, and even in cities, where it seeks human neighbors. Crosses patios and streets walking and running. Occurs from Argentina to Bolivia, Paraguay, northwestern Bahia, and southern Piauí. There are or have been

---

[3]The cocks-of-the-rock, *Rupicola,* also work with mud. I further recall certain seabirds, like the Lesser Noddy, *Anous tenuirostris,* that cement their nests with guano.

great gaps in its range. For example, it did not exist near the city of São Paulo in the early 1800s (1818–23) or in Campinas, where it appeared only around 1900. It colonized the Blumenau (Santa Catarina) region only from 1950 on, coming from the coast, but immigrated into the Santa Catarina mountains earlier. It did not exist formerly in the Paraíba Valley or in Rio de Janeiro. The cause of this unbridled recent expansion has been the ruthless deforestation of eastern Brazil, which has permitted the invasion of open-country species from the centralwest.

Folklore: Rivals sometimes assault each other, grappling until they fall to ground. This has given rise to anthropomorphic legends, one of most famous being that of punishment of the unfaithful wife whose husband walled her up alive in nest; sealed nests do occur, e.g., 2 in Vale do Jequitinonha, Minas Gerais, in 1970 and 1974. In one the skeletons of 2 nestlings were found (G. Mattos). Another legend is that the birds are "Catholic" and don't work on Sundays. Tradition has it that *F. rufus* taught the Caxinauá Indians the art of making clay pots. In Argentina the hornero is the national bird, and the scientific periodical of the La Plata Ornithological Association is called the *Hornero.* Also called *Barreiro* (Rio Grande do Sul), *Forneiro.* See the following 3 species.

PALE-LEGGED HORNERO, *Furnarius leucopus,* Casaca-de-couro-amarelo

17 cm. Slightly smaller than *F. rufus,* color closer to that of *F. figulus.* Upperparts light cinnamon, cap and postocular stripe sooty, superciliary white, legs whitish. VOICE: a sequence of *bzh, bzh, bzh*s . . . crescendo, relatively soft, unlike other *Furnarius.* Pair duets. Builds an oven nest similar to that of *rufus,* using ample quantity of dung and with other slight differences in comparison with *rufus* (G. T. Mattos, Minas Gerais); occupies abandoned nests of *F. rufus, Phacellodomus rufifrons* (Minas Gerais), and *Pseudoseisura cristata* (Bahia). Habitat similar to that of *rufus* but shadier (groves, riverine forest). The Guianas and Venezuela through savanna areas as far as Bolivia, Mato Grosso, Goiás, northeastern Brazil. Sometimes found in same regions as *F. rufus* and *F. figulus* (e.g., Minas Gerais, Bahia) but has different ecological requirements. Includes *F. torridus* of upper Amazon. Also called *João-de-barro.*

TAIL-BANDED HORNERO, *Furnarius figulus,* Casaca-de-couro-da-lama   BR

16 cm. Riveredge species similar to *F. leucopus* but smaller, with dark rusty cinnamon upperparts with rusty upper primary coverts (not black like *leucopus*). Tail feathers have black spot near end. Brown or gray legs relatively dark. VOICE: call a typical *chibit, chep;* song a loud sequence, *chewk, chik, chik, chik;* a loud cry, *KWEEeh, KWEEeh.* . . .

Does not build an oven; makes a simple, open nest of grass, etc., in a well protected place, e.g., beneath roof tiles, hidden amidst epiphytic bromeliads (Alagoas, A. Studer, pers. comm.), or among bases of large erect palm leaves, e.g., those of babaçu (*Orbignya*). There has been a great deal of confusion regarding nesting since various authors attributed ovens occupied by *figulus* to it without investigating their construction. A. Ruschi saw an *F. figulus* (recently immigrated into Espírito Santo) defend a nest it was occupying against a Blue-winged Parrotlet, *Forpus xanthopterygius.* The fact that in certain regions (as I noted on Pernambuco/Paraíba border) *F. figulus* is common but mud nests are not seen leads to conclusion that this species does not build ovens. Sunny edges of marshes, rivers, dug ponds, islands. Walks on mud, jumps from one stalk to another. The northeast to Mato Grosso, Goiás, Minas Gerais (Pirapora), Espírito Santo, Pará (both banks of lower Amazon). Reports concerning Espírito Santo, Minas Gerais, and apparently perhaps Rio de Janeiro are recent and may originate from a colonizing vanguard that could partially dissipate after some time (see "Habitat . . . ").

LESSER HORNERO, *Furnarius minor*

14.5 cm. Locally in Amazonia. Similar to *F. figulus* but clearly smaller, without black spots on tail feathers. Colombia, Peru, and south of Amazon, eastward to Rio Tapajós. Also Pará (Óbidos, Santarém).

SUBFAMILY SYNALLAXINAE

CURVE-BILLED REEDHAUNTER, *Limnornis curvirostris,* Junqueiro-bico-curvo

17 cm. Southern wetland species with long, curved, light bill. Brown with white superciliary and underparts. Tail relatively short. Rushes, cattails. Argentina and Uruguay to Rio Grande do Sul. See *L. rectirostris.*

STRAIGHT-BILLED REEDHAUNTER, *Limnornis rectirostris,* Junqueiro-de-bico-reto

16.3 cm. Southern species with long, slender, black, almost straight bill, unlike that of *L. curvirostris,* which it otherwise resembles. Tail long and reddish. VOICE: call *tzig;* song *tsrrrrrr-tsee-tsee* . . . , *psi, psi, psi . . psrrrr.* Builds an oval-shaped nest vertically disposed with a side entrance, using leaves of caraguatá (*Eryngium horridum*) or twigs. Wetland bird; frequents marshes with caraguatá. Uruguay to Rio Grande do Sul, northeastern Argentina. Previously placed in *Limnoctites*. Also called *Barreiro-do-brejo*.

WREN-LIKE RUSHBIRD, *Phleocryptes melanops*, Bate-bico

13.5 cm. Another southern, wetland furnariid. Upperparts brown clearly streaked with black. Wings have reddish bands visible in flight. VOICE: *tsla, tsek,* resembling a tree frog; a prolonged, monotonous sequence of *tatata . . . ,* like noise of wind in rushes or cattails. Nest, carefully bound to stems of aquatic reeds, is a well-finished, elongated ball with a small entrance high on side. Material (e.g., fresh, wet, well-woven piripiri, *Rhynchospora cephalotes,* leaves) is plastered with mud; after drying has strength of cardboard and loses green color it had when fresh (see fig. 212C). Rio de Janeiro to Rio Grande do Sul, Uruguay, Argentina, Chile, Paraguay, Bolivia. Also called *Tico-tico-do-biri, Cachimbo.* Found in Rio Grande do Sul alongside *Limnornis curvirostris* and *Tachuris rubrigastra.*

ARAUCARIA TIT-SPINETAIL, *Leptasthenura setaria*, Grimpeiro   Fig. 215

18.5 cm. Completely linked to occurrence of Paraná pine (*Araucaria angustifolia*). Tail extremely long and sharply graduated, 2 central feathers comprising ²/₃ of bird's total length. Top-knotted, brightly colored, top of head black with

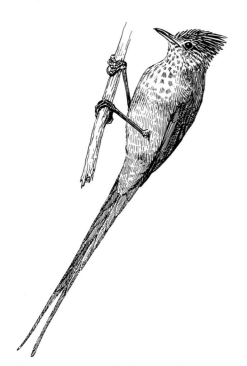

Fig. 215. Araucaria Tit-Spinetail, *Leptasthenura setaria.*

white streaks, back uniformly chestnut, throat white speckled black. VOICE: a high, descending phrase, accelerated at end, reminiscent of *Cranioleuca pallida,* sometimes its neighbor. Builds a pile of flexible material among araucaria, branches and fronds, frequenting tree crowns and exploring them from every possible position. Also hops along heavy branches. Occurs throughout range of *Araucaria angustifolia,* from Rio de Janeiro (Itatiaia) and São Paulo (Campos do Jordão, Serra da Bocaina) to Paraná (even in isolated araucarias in Curitiba estates), Santa Catarina, Rio Grande do Sul, and Misiones, Argentina. Also called *Grinfeirinho* (referring to *grinfar,* "chatter," of its voice).

Presence of this species among some planted araucaria (at 900 m at Peroba, Rio Grande de Cima, Nova Friburgo, Rio de Janeiro) draws attention to fact that araucaria forests once existed there. In Rio Grande do Sul there is a saying "Where there is no araucaria, there is no 'grimpeiro'" ("*grimpa* = araucaria frond). Formerly called *Dendrophylax.* See *L. striolata,* sometimes its neighbor in Rio Grande do Sul. The *Leptasthenura* genus is more widely distributed in south of continent and in Andes.

STRIOLATED TIT-SPINETAIL, *Leptasthenura striolata,* Grimpeirinho   BR

13.3 cm; 10.5 g. One of smallest furnariids. Less crested than *L. setaria,* with entire upperparts dirty brown with whitish stripes. VOICE: call distinctly weaker and with shorter phrases than *setaria; psi, psi-psi, ks-ks-ks-ks-ks.* Not closely linked to presence of *Araucaria,* or at least less so than *setaria. Podocarpus* woods or low, nonconiferous trees. Paraná to Rio Grande do Sul.

TUFTED TIT-SPINETAIL, *Leptasthenura platensis,* Rabudinho

17 cm. Crested, with uniformly gray back. VOICE: a short, descending phrase, *tsi . . . tsirrrrr,* with timbre of *L. striolata* and of Short-billed Canastero, *Asthenes baeri,* its neighbor in espinilho parkland of Rio Grande do Sul, where *L. platensis* is most common furnariid. Occupies holes such as those made by Checkered Woodpecker, *Picoides mixtus,* lining them with soft material. Replaces *L. striolata* in extreme southwestern Rio Grande do Sul, Uruguay, Argentina.

ITATIAIA THISTLETAIL, *Schizoeaca (= Oreophylax) moreirae,* Garricha-chorona   BR

18 cm. One of Brazil's few truly montane birds, an endemic of open country on tops of highest ranges of southeastern Brazil (see "Habitat . . ."). Tail very long (11 cm), fuller than *Leptasthenura.* Uniformly brown with yellow spot on chin. VOICE: a high *psee, trtrtr, berrrit;* song a decrescendo phrase, *dew-dee-dee-dee-DEEeeeeeeee.* Nest, placed in bushes, is a moss ovoid with a few twigs outside and a high side entrance without protecting tunnel (fig.

212B). Nest is very similar to that of Black-throated Thistletail, *S. harterti* (also only recently described), in similar habitat at 3480 m in Bolivian Andes (Vuilleumier 1969). I have concluded from nest and voice that bird is not a *Synallaxis* (as Miranda Ribeiro classified it in 1906; in 1925 Hellmayr made a very nice new genus, *Oreophylax*) but a member of Andean genus *Schizoeaca*. Thus, *S. moreirae* has no relatives in Brazil, being a relict of Pleistocene immigration to which *Cinclodes pabsti* and all the Rhinocryptidae belong (see fig. 200). Abundant in *Chusquea pinifolia* thickets between 1900 and 2800 m above tree line. Occurs in Serra do Caparaó (Minas Gerais, Espírito Santo); Serra dos Órgãos, Itatiaia; heights of Parque Desengano, 1800 m (Rio de Janeiro). It undoubtedly will be found on similar high peaks with *Chusquea* in southeast. Also called *Rabo-de-palha*.

SHORT-BILLED CANASTERO, *Asthenes (= Thripophaga) baeri*, Lenheiro

14.5 cm. In Brazil restricted to extreme south. Resembles *Schizoeaca moreirae* but with shorter tail. Bill short; plumage pale brown, lighter below; orange-chestnut chin looks black at a distance. Outer tail feathers light rufous, central ones black. VOICE: *tsewrrrr . . . , tsi . . . tsewrrr,* an often descending sequence reminiscent of *S. moreirae* and of *Leptasthenura platensis,* the latter its neighbor in espinilho parkland (Rio Grande do Sul). Like other *Asthenes* builds a globe-shaped nest of sticks solidly placed on branches or cacti. Open country with small trees, drops to ground where it hops with tail cocked. Argentina to Paraguay, Uruguay, Rio Grande do Sul. The *Asthenes* genus comprises more than 20 species occurring in Andes and southern part of continent to Chile and Tierra del Fuego.

HUDSON'S CANASTERO, *Asthenes hudsoni*

17 cm. Long-tailed like its congeners, streaked (like *Spartonoica maluroides* and *Phleocryptes melanops*), chin yellow. Marshes. Uruguay-Brazil border (Chuí, Rio Grande do Sul), Argentina.

CIPO CANASTERO, *Asthenes luizae,* Lenheiro-da-Serra-do-Cipó   BR

Similar to *A. baeri,* with prominent rufous at base of tail but no yellow on chin. First studied by B. C. Forrester in July 1988. Walks, runs, and hops over rocks, carrying tail vertically or even farther forward. VOICE: sings a descending phrase of sharp notes from a bare branch in low arboreal vegetation. Lives alongside other endemics: Gray-backed Tachuri, *Polystictus superciliaris;* Hyacinth Visorbearer, *Augastes scutatus;* and Pale-throated Serra-Finch, *Embernagra longicauda.* In stony campos of Serra do Cipó National Park, Minas Gerais, at 1400 m (Vielliard 1990).

BAY-CAPPED WREN-SPINETAIL, *Spartonoica maluroides,* Boininha

14 cm. Slender wetland species with rigid tail (7.7 cm), rusty cap, black-streaked bird. Reeds. On nest, see "Breeding."

CHOTOY SPINETAIL, *Synallaxis (= Schoeniophylax) phryganophila,* Bichoita   PL 27.4

20 cm. Very characteristic open-country species, more long-tailed than most *Synallaxis,* with bright sulfur yellow chin design reminiscent of *Certhiaxis cinnamomea.* Back streaked with black (typical of various savanna birds). VOICE: a ventriloquial, descending phrase, *go-go-go . . . , kwoaak . . . ,* surprisingly low for such a small bird, which might perhaps come from a Dark-billed Cuckoo, *Coccyzus melacoryphus,* or a *Thamnophilus* antbird; this vocalization is totally unlike a true *Synallaxis.* Nest spherical, built of twigs and elastic material with a side entrance through a horizontal or upward-sloping tunnel. Walls of incubation chamber "felted." Old nest accumulations may resemble structure of *Anumbius annumbi* or *Myiopsitta monachus.* Savannas with bushes and trees. Interior of Bahia, Minas Gerais, and São Paulo to southern Mato Grosso, Rio Grande do Sul; also Uruguay and Argentina to Bolivia. Also called *Titisiri* (Rio Grande do Sul), *Cabritinha-de-mama* (Mato Grosso).

SPIX'S SPINETAIL, *Synallaxis spixi,* João-tenenem   PL 27.3

16 cm. One of most common and best-known furnariids of eastern Brazil. Tail long, graduated, soft; wings short, round; bill slender. Cap and wings chestnut, tail olive brown like back. Underparts varied in color, usually with distinct black throat mark. Immature lacks red on head and wings. VOICE: *tre-te-wet, teteh-te (te), WET-te-te-te-te* (= onomatopoeic *Bentereré*); there is apparently sexual dimorphism in vocalization of pair, one calling *wat-TENneNENG,* the other *cheh, cheh, cheh, cheh.* Lives hidden in bushes and low capoeira mixed with sapé thatching grass at edge of forest. Sea level to high-altitude campos where it meets *Schizoeaca moreirae;* also near dwellings. Feeds in lowest levels of bushes, sometimes hopping on ground. Nest (fig. 211E) is a dense, long heap of sticks, mostly spiny, almost always with cast-off snake and lizard skins; access is from side through horizontal corridor that leads directly to center. Above incubation chamber there is a notable accumulation of heavy pieces of bark and branches that sometimes form a high, conical protuberance that apparently provides protection against rain. Incubation chamber has floor carpeted with green leaves, vegetable cotton, etc., that are felted in center. In city of Rio de Janeiro an assemblage of 3 nests was found that were built largely of wire, including barbed wire, that birds collected in a nearby factory; estimated weight of the whole was 15 kg. Espírito Santo and Minas Gerais to Rio Grande do Sul, Uru-

guay, Argentina, Paraguay. Also called *João-tiriri, Bentereré, Bentererê*. See *S. ruficapilla*.

RUFOUS-CAPPED SPINETAIL, *Synallaxis ruficapilla*, Pichororé

16 cm. Cap, wings, tail dark chestnut. Distinct yellowish stripe behind eye (lacking, together with chestnut on wings, in immature). VOICE: warning (diagnostic) a loud, low *tshrrr; terreTET*, harder and shorter than phrase of *S. spixi*. Nest similar to *spixi* but has top entrance like *S. albescens*. Interior thickets and forest edge, where it may encounter *S. spixi;* at times encounters *S. cinerascens* in forest interior. Eastern Brazil from Pernambuco to Rio Grande do Sul, Uruguay, Argentina (Misiones), Paraguay. In mountainous regions of Rio de Janeiro and Espírito Santo.

SOOTY-FRONTED SPINETAIL, *Synallaxis frontalis*, Petrim

16 cm. Common in interior. Chestnut cap, wings, and tail, like *S. ruficapilla,* but lacks light postocular stripe; forehead blackish. VOICE: song *dluh-dlooeet;* a low *joit,* a territorial *tsew-kli* (origin of Argentine name *Chicli*). Inside shady thickets of cerrado; low, dense capoeira; coffee plantations (northern Paraná). Sometimes alongside *S. scutata,* which has somewhat similar voice, and Collared Crescentchest, *Melanopareia torquata* (e.g., Goiás, Minas Gerais). The northeast and centralwest (including interior of São Paulo) to Rio Grande do Sul, Uruguay, Argentina, Paraguay. Also called *Dia-trinta* (Paraná), *Casaca-de-couro* (Ceará), *Garricha* (Minas Gerais).

PALE-BREASTED SPINETAIL, *Synallaxis albescens*, Ui-pí

16 cm. Common in central Brazil. Cap and wings chestnut, tail olive brown as in *S. spixi* but forehead grayish black. Underparts yellowish white. When singing displays black bases of throat feathers, which form a black spot invisible in silent bird but always present in stuffed specimens. VOICE: song *spi-di;* a bisyllabic *brrri-drrr, wi-deh*. Sunny cerrado, sometimes alongside *S. gujanensis* and near *S. frontalis,* and cattails, where it meets *Certhiaxis cinnamomea*. Open areas of Amazonian and northeastern, centralwestern, and southern Brazil; also Paraguay, Bolivia, Argentina. Also called *Garricha* (Minas Gerais), *Teutônio*.

GRAY-BELLIED SPINETAIL, *Synallaxis cinerascens*, João-teneném-da-mata

14 cm. Dark, southern, forest species, dark grayish brown with chestnut wings and tail. VOICE: call a high *see-eet;* song *sweet-peDEETZ*. Interior of dense, dark forests. Mountains in Rio de Janeiro, sometimes alongside *S. ruficapilla*. Rio de Janeiro to Rio Grande do Sul, Uruguay, Argentina, Paraguay.

PLAIN-CROWNED SPINETAIL, *Synallaxis gujanensis*, João-teneném-becuá

16 cm. Northern species with chestnut wings and tail like *S. cinerascens* but with underparts, but not cap, whitish yellow. VOICE: song a loud, low *be-KWA; tetetete*. Forest edges, edges of roads, and marshes, possibly meeting *S. albescens*. Venezuela to Bolivia, Paraguay, Mato Grosso, Goiás, Maranhão.

RUDDY SPINETAIL, *Synallaxis rutilans*, João-teneném-castanho

15 cm. Strangely colored, almost entirely dark chestnut with black throat and tail. VOICE: *tac, tac-owet,* reminiscent of *S. gujanensis; wetetet*. Forest, frequently in association with antbird flocks. Amazonia south to Bolivia, Mato Grosso, Maranhão.

Brazil has 11 more *Synallaxis:*

PINTO'S SPINETAIL, *Synallaxis infuscata*   BR
Pernambuco, Alagoas.

RIO BRANCO SPINETAIL, *Synallaxis* (= *Poecilurus*) *kollari*   BR
Roraima.

DUSKY SPINETAIL, *Synallaxis moesta*
Roraima.

CABANIS' SPINETAIL, *Synallaxis cabanisi*
May include *S. moesta*. Roraima.

The following five species occur in the north, northeast, and central-west of Brazil and in adjacent countries:

CINEREOUS-BREASTED SPINETAIL, *Synallaxis hypospodia*
Amazonia, central Brazil, the northeast.

SLATY SPINETAIL, *Synallaxis brachyura*
Goiás.

DARK-BREASTED SPINETAIL, *Synallaxis albigularis*
Western Amazonia.

WHITE-BELLIED SPINETAIL, *Synallaxis propinqua*
South of Amazon.

CHESTNUT-THROATED SPINETAIL, *Synallaxis cherriei*
Mato Grosso and Carajás, Pará.

RED-SHOULDERED SPINETAIL, *Synallaxis* (= *Gyalophylax*) *hellmayri*, João-chique-chique   BR
19 cm. Northeastern endemic, reminiscent of an *Asthenes,*

with strong bill and long, wide, graduated tail. Grayish brown with wide chestnut area on wing; lower throat has large black patch. VOICE: a repeated, bisyllabic *tetray* or *CHEE-krrr*. Terrestrial. Nest is a great conglomeration of chique-chique cactus spines. Caatinga. Piauí to Pernambuco, Bahia. Also called *S. griseiventris*. Also called *Sis-tré* (onomatopoeic, Bahia), *Maria-macambira*.

OCHRE-CHEEKED SPINETAIL, *Synallaxis* (= *Poecilurus*) *scutata*, Estrelinha-preta

14 cm. Back, wings, and tail reddish, underparts yellowish. Lower throat has black patch set off by white above. VOICE: a high, 2-part whistle, 2nd part initially lower than 1st, *duEET duEET*, a pattern similar to *S. frontalis*, sometimes its neighbor (Rio das Mortes, Mato Grosso). Lower level of dense, low forest. Maranhão and Piauí to Mato Grosso, Goiás, Bahia, Minas Gerais, São Paulo, northwestern Argentina, Bolivia.

YELLOW-CHINNED SPINETAIL, *Certhiaxis cinnamomea*, Curutié

14.5 cm. Generally most common wetland furnariid. Has look of a *Synallaxis spixi*, with long, quite rigid tail. Upperparts rusty brown, underparts whitish, chin with small sulfur yellow spot, inconspicuous at a distance. VOICE: a hard *krip;* song a hard, monotonous phrase that drops at end, resembling voice of Rufous-sided Crake, *Laterallus melanophaius*, but with lower volume. Pairs duet. Builds a pile of sticks above or very close to water, with access through a tube or vertical chimney made of perpendicularly placed branches (fig. 211C). Shape of nest may be compared to a retort. Chamber is a small cup lined with some leaves and a bit of vegetable wool. I found one of these structures near a large wasp nest in Piauí. Bird is one of principal hosts of *Tapera naevia*. Abundant where habitat is extensive. Colombia and the Guianas to Bolivia, Argentina, Paraguay, Uruguay, throughout Brazil. Also called *Marrequito-do-brejo*, *Corruíra-do-brejo*, *João-teneném-do-brejo*, *Corrucheba*, *Xexeuzinho-do-brejo* (Minas Gerais).

RED-AND-WHITE SPINETAIL, *Certhiaxis mustelina*
Amazonia.

SULPHUR-BEARDED SPINETAIL, *Cranioleuca sulphurifera*, Arredio-de-papo-manchado
Yellow, longitudinal streak on throat; breast spotted. Reeds. Rio Grande do Sul.

GRAY-HEADED SPINETAIL, *Cranioleuca semicinerea* BR
Reddish back. Ceará, Bahia, Goiás.

PALLID SPINETAIL, *Cranioleuca pallida*, Arredio-pálido   PL 27.5   BR

13.5 cm. Slightly resembles a *Synallaxis* but tail shorter and more rigid, but does not serve as a support as in dendrocolaptids. Cap red (brown in immature). VOICE: call *TSEEssik, TEEssi-sick;* song a more prolonged sequence of monosyllabic whistles, beginning slowly, then accelerating, *psi-psi-psi . . . psrrrrr*, sometimes repeated consecutively and mixed with more melodious whistles. Nest (fig. 212A), built in trees among epiphytic plants, is a ball of soft material, e.g., Spanish moss (*Tillandsia usneoides*), lichens, mosses. Side entrance leads to interior of sphere through a corridor that curves around to enter unlined chamber from above. Canopy at forest edge. In Espírito Santo and Rio de Janeiro in mountains where it prefers coniferous trees planted there. Customarily hangs head-down, like *Leptasthenura setaria*, which it meets in Serra da Bocaina (São Paulo) and with which it shares a similar voice. Southeastern Brazil from Espírito Santo and Minas Gerais to São Paulo.

OLIVE SPINETAIL, *Cranioleuca obsoleta*, Arredio-meridional

12.5 cm. Southern species without red on top of head. VOICE: similar to *C. pallida* (but lacking loud *TSEEssik*) and to *Leptasthenura setaria*, sometimes its neighbor in mixed araucaria forests, although *C. obsoleta* does not depend on this tree. Lower levels at forest border, sometimes alongside *Synallaxis spixi*. São Paulo to Rio Grande do Sul, Paraguay, Argentina.

STRIPE-CROWNED SPINETAIL, *Cranioleuca pyrrhophia*, Arredio

Replaces *C. obsoleta* in southern Rio Grande do Sul and parts of Uruguay, Argentina, Paraguay. They are closely related but occur together in southeastern Rio Grande do Sul (Belton 1984a).

TEPUI SPINETAIL, *Cranioleuca demissa*
Venezuelan border.

RUSTY-BACKED SPINETAIL, *Cranioleuca vulpina*, Arredio-do-rio

15 cm. Upperparts all ferruginous. VOICE: call a full *dlo-it;* song a sharply descending sequence of resonant whistles *gluh, gluh, gluh . . .*, or a drier *che, che, che . . .*, when duetting, the latter is probably that of female. Opens tail and wings while singing. Sometimes a 3d individual participates. Nest, built in branches drooping over a river or lake, is a ball of flexible material (roots, grass, vines, vegetable wool, feathers) that looks like a bunch of trash carried by a flood and caught in branches. Panama to Bolivia, Mato Grosso,

Goiás, São Paulo, Paraná. Also called *Hoch-tkai* (Trumai, Mato Grosso).

SCALED SPINETAIL, *Cranioleuca muelleri*   BR
Scaly underparts. Amazonia.

SPECKLED SPINETAIL, *Cranioleuca gutturata*
Spotted underparts. Amazonia.

STRIATED SOFTTAIL, *Thripophaga macroura,*
Rabo-amarelo   BR

16.7 cm. Looks like a *Philydor.* Light rusty yellow, long, wide tail. Body distinctly streaked above and below, chin extensively rusty yellow. VOICE: a loud *kit-kit-kit,* recalling *Syndactyla rufosuperciliata* (generally found at lower levels); song a descending scale of loud *che, che, che*s . . . sung in duet with female. Nest apparently a ball of sticks. Hops around among bromeliads on branches at middle levels of forest. Inspects trunks, climbs into canopy of humid, high forests. Sometimes in mixed flocks. Restricted to eastern Bahia and Espírito Santo, both in lowlands and mountains. Considerably larger than *Heliobletus contaminatus.*

PLAIN SOFTTAIL, *Thripophaga fusciceps*
Amazonia.

COMMON THORNBIRD, *Phacellodomus rufifrons,*
João-de-pau   PL 27.6

16 cm. Although responsible for most stick nests seen in interior (especially in Minas Gerais, São Paulo, Bahia), the bird is not easy to find if it is not tending nest. Stocky with long tail; red on forehead, although bright, not particularly conspicuous. VOICE: a hurried sequence, *tsitsitsi* . . . , rising or unmodulated, then descending and ending in tremolo. Tail oscillates in rhythm with song, which is sung by pair near nest. Male voice louder. Singing extends all year. Nest (figs. 211B and 216), a heap of sticks, is usually situated at end of branch on isolated tree. Most sticks are spiny and of same size. First nest made by a pair is a small but sturdy ball (perhaps 26 × 28 cm, without projections) of spiny sticks that offer stability and defense. Roof is more compact. Access is through a tunnel of variable length and direction that runs through sphere. Incubation chamber is lined with small, thick, spherical layer of feathers, vegetable wool, etc., so well compacted and so solid within rough frame of dry twigs that it doesn't come apart even if sticks are removed. Each year pair adds another nest, generally above former one, although lower nest sometimes is occupied. Material from an old nest in another tree may be used. Frequently there are 2 chambers per nest, with 2d, near surface and next to entrance, having a simple mat of broken leaves that provides a sleeping place.

When, as is usually the case, the support is a flexible limb,

Fig. 216. Nest of Common Thornbird, *Phacellodomus rufifrons.* After A. Studer 1983.

the tip sags with the progressive accumulation of weight. Some nest agglomerations are more than 1 m high and weigh several kilograms (this increasing greatly during rain) and may eventually break the limb. I have found nests made of 2 hanging cylindrical sections united at the base. It is not easy to inspect and understand the organization of these voluminous complexes; only 1 pair of birds lives even in these complicated nests full of appendages. Other individuals appearing in area of nest must be owners' offspring; now grown, they sleep there and sometimes work on edifice and even help feed younger siblings. Work continues on nest all year. Re occupation by other animals, nesting fauna, etc., see "Use of Furnariid Nests . . . ."

Nests may be confused with those of *Myiopsitta monachus* and in the case of nonhanging nests with those of *Anumbius annumbi,* when attached, for example, to crosspiece of a utility pole or placed on a heavy horizontal limb.

Although this thornbird nests in trees, it feeds on ground, weaving its way among fallen leaves and tangled grass, sometimes mounting into dense branches of a savanna bush. Northeastern and centralwestern Brazil to Bolivia, Paraguay, Argentina; also savanna regions from Venezuela to northern Peru. Also called *Carrega-madeira* (Bahia), *Teutônio, João-garrancho* (Minas Gerais), *Casaca-de-couro* (Pernambuco).

RED-EYED THORNBIRD, *Phacellodomus erythrophthalmus,* João-botina   BR

17.5 cm. Restricted to coastal strip. Eyes red; forehead, throat, and breast chestnut. VOICE; a 2-part song, first a horizontal introductory sequence followed by a descending series of loud cries, *chree, chree, chree-TSREEeh TSREEeh TSREEeh* . . . , sometimes a duet by pair. Nest (fig. 211G) is a large, boot-shaped mass of dead branches suspended from tip of a branch with entrance on lower projecting extremity. It has 2 rooms, both lined with grass and connected by a narrow opening. Edge of forest and marsh. Bahia to Rio Grande do Sul, in mountainous regions near Rio de Janeiro.

GREATER THORNBIRD, *Phacellodomus ruber*, Graveteiro

19 cm. Relatively large species of central Brazil. Cap, wings, and tail reddish; iris light yellow. VOICE: call *cheep;* song a loud, short, descending phrase composed of short or medium-short cries, e.g., *chip, chip, chip. . . ;* pairs duet frequently. Builds a heap of branches it installs solidly on a support, e.g., frond base of a buriti palm. Edge of lakes or rivers, feeds both in tops of palms and in vegetation only slightly above ground. Bahia, Minas Gerais, Mato Grosso, Goiás, Rio Grande do Sul, Argentina.

FRECKLE-BREASTED THORNBIRD, *Phacellodomus striaticollis*, Tio-tio

17 cm. Cap chestnut, breast streaked. VOICE: song: after 3 short, low notes gives a descending sequence of resonant cries, *psep, psep, psep-kleek, kleek, kleek. . . .* Makes a pile of branches, firmly placed on branches of a bush or tree; chamber, sometimes double (fig. 211H), is carpeted with vegetable felt and has an upper entrance. Low levels at edge of marshes or savannas with tall vegetation. Paraná to Rio Grande do Sul, Uruguay, Argentina, Bolivia.

CANEBRAKE GROUNDCREEPER, *Phacellodomus* (= *Clibanornis*) *dendrocolaptoides*, Cisqueiro

22 cm. Little-known southern resident with strong bill and feet; long, rigid tail; white throat ornamented on sides with black-tipped feathers; long, wide, whitish postocular stripe; reddish crown. Low in dense forest vegetation at edge of streams. Misiones, Argentina, to Rio Grande do Sul, Paraná.

LARK-LIKE BRUSHRUNNER, *Coryphistera alaudina*, Corredor-crestudo

16 cm. Terrestrial furnariid with bizarre frontal crest the color of light earth. Upper- and underparts streaked, tail ferruginous with black tip. VOICE: a tremulous, high *rrrrrew.* Nest, built in a tree, is a heap of sticks with a side entrance and a chamber well lined with soft vegetable material, horse hair, etc. Runs fast on ground with long steps. Lifts cattle dung with feet to find insects, at times throwing pieces of dry excrement violently aside as it turns them over. Flees to small, scattered trees of native savannas. Argentina to Bolivia, Paraguay, Uruguay, Rio Grande do Sul (Barra do Quaraí, Uruguaiana), where it is a neighbor of *Pseudoseisura lophotes* and *Furnarius rufus.*

FIREWOOD GATHERER, *Anumbius annumbi*, Cochicho

19.5 cm. Like *Phacellodomus rufifrons,* well known as a builder of stick nests in interior of Minas Gerais and São Paulo. Relatively large, brown above, yellowish below, with upperparts and white throat speckled black. Tail quite long and wide with white tip, noticeable when it fans tail like a *Mimus saturninus,* a larger bird that is sometimes its neighbor. VOICE: call a dry trill, *tsi-tsi-tsi-tsrrrrrr,* repeated consecutively while agitating wings like a *Furnarius.* Pairs duet.

Usually builds a globe-shaped accumulation of sticks in solid forks of tree branches in a pasture or on utility poles or houses (fig. 211D). High side access is a tunnel, sometimes 2, that often curves. Chamber lined with vegetable wool and grass; sometimes there are 2 interconnected chambers. Nest, well protected against rain, is rebuilt each year, as with *Phacellodomus rufifrons.* Frequently, serious problems with short circuits on lines of state electric company, CEEE, in Rio Grande do Sul are caused by *A. annumbi* nests (see also *Furnarius rufus,* Tessmer 1989). With sturdy feet runs on ground, impregnating plumage with earth. To sing it seeks a prominent spot, e.g., a post top. Goiás, Minas Gerais, and Rio de Janeiro to Rio Grande do Sul, Uruguay, Paraguay, Argentina. Also called *Tiri-tiri* (Rio Grande do Sul), *Añumbi* (Guarani).

ORANGE-FRONTED PLUSHCROWN, *Metopothrix aurantiacus*

10.7 cm. Small, unique; forepart of head olivaceous; forehead feathers erect; throat ferruginous orange. Flooded forest. Rios Purus and Solimões (upper Amazon) to Bolivia, Ecuador. May recall Orange-headed Tanager, *Thlypopsis sordida.*

SUBFAMILY PHILYDORINAE

RORAIMAN BARBTAIL, *Roraimia adusta*

15 cm. Streaked breast. Only from Brazil-Venezuela border (Roraima) to the Guianas.

POINT-TAILED PALMCREEPER, *Berlepschia rikeri* Limpa-folha-do-buriti

20 cm. Endemic of buriti (*Mauritia vinifera*) and miriti (*M. flexuosa*) palm groves and babassu (*Orbignya martiana*) in Maranhão. Head, neck, and underparts prominently streaked black and white; back and tail bright chestnut; tail feathers black. VOICE: a limpid trill, *tew, ew, ew . . . ,* ascending slightly then descending at end. Male and female respond to each other, with one, probably female, having higher timbre. Resembles voice of Campo Flicker, *Colaptes campestris.* Nests among wide bases of fronds in palm tops, where it is frequently invisible. Clutches green buriti leaflets,

Fig. 217. Nest of Rufous Cacholote, *Pseudoseisura cristata*. After A. Studer 1983.

sometimes hammering at them. Seeks food, head down, under bases of palm fronds. Flies rapidly from crown of one palm to another. The Guianas and Venezuela to lower Amazon (Rio Acará), Maranhão, Goiás (Rio Araguaia), Bahia (Rio Sapão).

RUFOUS CACHOLOTE, *Pseudoseisura cristata*, Casaca-de-couro   PL 27.7

21.5 cm. One of typical birds of caatinga and similar arid landscapes. Thrush sized with high crest and entirely light ferruginous except for black wing tips. Eyes yellow. VOICE: call *tshlip;* song of pair duetting is a sequence of harsh or nasal *ch-ch-ch . . . psee-psee-psee . . . ch . . . psee . . . ,* descending sharply, reminiscent of *Furnarius rufus.* Builds a great heap (sometimes 50 × 90 cm, figs. 211F and 217) of dead branches laced with vulture feathers, bones, etc., firmly placed on trees; often has a horizontally elongated shape and an entrance through a corridor that runs from base of nest to spherical chamber. This is cushioned with pieces of bark, reptile skins, etc. Latter are also used by various other furnariids and are valued as talismans by many people. Dung and mud are also carried into nest. In completely open places constantly whipped by wind, most of branches making up a nest may be oriented in same direction, showing from where wind blows strongest (Bahia). Bird walks on ground through low grass among sparse trees but perches higher to sing. In northeastern Brazil during recent years has extended range throughout Bahia because of primary forest destruction. Also in western Mato Grosso, Paraguay, Bolivia. Also called *Carrega-madeira-do-sertão, Carrega-madeira-grande* (Bahia). Nest sometimes used by *Icterus i. jamacaii* (Pernambuco).

BROWN CACHOLOTE, *Pseudoseisura lophotes*, Coperete

25 cm; 90 g (male). Largest furnariid, almost jay size. Color of dark earth with head and tail reddish. VOICE: call *krok;* song a harsh, prolonged, descending *zhayot-zhayot-zhayot . . . , ksh . . . kiOW. . . .* Pair vocalizes together. Nests on low trees, making a large ball of sticks with access through long external tunnel (see fig. 17, Chapter 1). Chamber padded with dung. Walks, runs, hops on ground. Turns over dry dung with brusque motions of head searching for prey. Argentina, Bolivia, and Paraguay to Rio Grande do Sul (espinilho parkland), Uruguay; alongside *Coryphistera alaudina* and *Furnarius rufus.* Also called *Casaca-de-couro-gaúcho.*

STRIPED WOODHAUNTER, *Hyloctistes subulatus*

17 cm. Streaked, like *Pseudoseisura lophotes.* Amazonia (in Brazil in upper Rio Negro, Rio Madeira). Related to the *Philydor.*

CHESTNUT-WINGED HOOKBILL, *Ancistrops strigilatus*

17 cm. Streaked, with heavy, hooked bill, reminiscent of certain Formicariidae. In Amazonia (Rio Tapajós to Acre, Ecuador). Related to the *Philydor.*

WHITE-COLLARED FOLIAGE-GLEANER, *Anabazenops fuscus*, Trepador-coleira   BR   Fig. 218

19 cm. One of most typical of large forest furnariids of southeastern Brazil. Striking with pure white collar and throat, former quite expandable through ruffling of feathers. VOICE: warning a strident *GHEEeh;* a hard, hurried rhythmic sequence, *wat-wat-wat . . . , dada-RAHP . . . ,* song an unmistakable, far-sounding phrase, at times given with a hard squeal that may be reminiscent of *Dendrocincla* or *Sittasomus* (see "Vocalization"). Nests in tree cavities. In Rio de Janeiro and Espírito Santo found in mountains, frequently among bamboos. Middle levels of forest, often head down. Inspects fallen palm and cecropia leaves caught in branches. Hammers like a woodpecker. Sometimes descends to ground. Espírito Santo and Minas Gerais to Santa Catarina. Also called *Papo-branco* (Minas Gerais).

BUFF-BROWED FOLIAGE-GLEANER, *Syndactyla rufosuperciliata*, Trepador-quiete   PL 27.8

17.5 cm. Usually most common forest species in southern Brazil but difficult to see. VOICE: call a loud and unmistakable *shet, SHETtete;* warning *kssr,* similar to *Conopophaga melanops;* song a hard sequence, *kit-kit-kit . . . ,* slow and rising at beginning, then hurried and falling (sung at first light and late at dusk). Nests in tree holes. Entrance to nest may be high (4 m perhaps). Low levels in densest thickets in forest and on edges; occasionally goes up for epiphytes. Hammers hard. Espírito Santo and Minas Gerais to Rio Grande do Sul, Uruguay, Paraguay, Argentina, Bolivia. See *Anabacerthia amaurotis.*

PERUVIAN RECURVEBILL, *Simoxenops ucayalae*

Eastern Peruvian species; 1 specimen found in Acre by Novaes (1978b).

WHITE-BROWED FOLIAGE-GLEANER, *Anabacerthia amaurotis*, Limpa-folha-miuda

15.7 cm. Quite similar to *Syndactyla rufosuperciliata* but with less sturdy bill and wide, pure white (not yellowish)

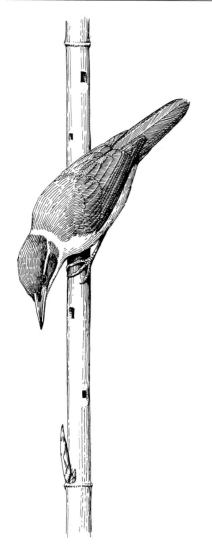

Fig. 218. White-collared Foliage-gleaner, *Anabazenops fuscus*, inspecting a perforated bamboo (Serra do Mar, Rio de Janeiro). On the rectangular cuts in the bamboo, see Picidae, "Feeding."

postocular stripe. Feathers on top of head have black and white bases. VOICE: call a high, insectlike *tsip tsip tsip*. . . . Low in thickets in forest. Descends to ground. Sometimes a few individuals move around together. Rio de Janeiro to Rio Grande do Sul and Misiones, Argentina. Formerly considered a *Philydor*, but voice proves it is not one.

BLACK-CAPPED FOLIAGE-GLEANER, *Philydor atricapillus*, Limpa-folha-coroada

17 cm. Distinctly colored southern species, bright cinnamon with black cap, black stripe through eye, rufous tail. VOICE: call *pt-wit;* warning *ch-ch-ch* . . . *shPEEeh*. Breeds in holes in embankments in forest interior. Southeastern Brazil, Paraguay, and Misiones, Argentina. Also called *Arapaçu*. Related to *P. novaesi*.

ALAGOAS FOLIAGE-GLEANER, *Philydor novaesi*   BR

In northeast, Alagoas (Teixeira and Gonzaga 1983). Related to *P. atricapillus*.

RUFOUS-RUMPED FOLIAGE-GLEANER, *Philydor erythrocercus*

Amazonia.

CINNAMON-RUMPED FOLIAGE-GLEANER, *Philydor pyrrhodes*

Amazonia (see *P. dimidiatus*).

PLANALTO FOLIAGE-GLEANER, *Philydor dimidiatus*, Limpa-folha-do-brejo

17 cm. Central Brazil. Bright greenish rust above; underparts, sides of head, and superciliary dark cinnamon rufous; tail reddish. Western Minas Gerais to Goiás, Mato Grosso, Paraná, Paraguay. Related to *P. pyrrhodes*.

OCHRE-BREASTED FOLIAGE-GLEANER, *Philydor lichtensteini*, Limpa-folha-ocrácea   PL 27.12

16.5 cm. Relatively common forest species in southeastern Brazil. Wanders through leafy and vine-entangled canopies in mixed flocks searching for insects and their larvae. Often hangs under branches. Espírito Santo and Minas Gerais to Rio Grande do Sul, Goiás, southern Mato Grosso, Paraguay, and Misiones, Argentina. Also called *Limpa-folha, Inturmado, Arapaçu*. See *P. rufus*.

BUFF-FRONTED FOLIAGE-GLEANER, *Philydor rufus*, Limpa-folha-testa-baia

19 cm. Twin of *P. lichtensteini;* a bit larger with yellowish forehead contrasting with grayish crown. VOICE: *shirrr*. Nests in embankments or crevices in houses in forest. Panama to Bolivia and Argentina; central and southern Brazil. Sympatric with *P. lichtensteini* over a large area. Also called *Arapaçu*. See also Brown Tanager, *Orchesticus abeillei*.

CHESTNUT-WINGED FOLIAGE-GLEANER, *Philydor erythropterus*

Amazonia.

RUFOUS-TAILED FOLIAGE-GLEANER, *Philydor ruficaudatus*

Amazonia.

WHITE-EYED FOLIAGE-GLEANER, *Automolus leucophthalmus*, Barranqueiro-olho-branco   PL 27.10

19 cm. Forest furnariid common in eastern Brazil. Similar to *Anabazenops fuscus* but without white collar and superciliary. Snowy eye conspicuous. VOICE: a typical *TEH-koee*, warning *kit-kwat, drewit-rewt-rewt-rewt*. Makes an underground nest; an almost horizontal gallery leads to chamber

lined with dry leaf stems. Northeastern and eastern Brazil south to Rio Grande do Sul, southern Goiás, eastern Mato Grosso, Paraguay, and Misiones, Argentina.

OLIVE-BACKED FOLIAGE-GLEANER, *Automolus infuscatus*
Amazonia.

RUDDY FOLIAGE-GLEANER, *Automolus rubiginosus*
Amazonia.

WHITE-THROATED FOLIAGE-GLEANER, *Automolus roraimae*
Brazilian-Venezuelan border. "*Philydor hylobius*" is synonymous with *Automolus roraimae* (Dickerman et al. 1986).

BUFF-THROATED FOLIAGE-GLEANER, *Automolus ochrolaemus*
Amazonia.

CHESTNUT-CROWNED FOLIAGE-GLEANER, *Automolus rufipileatus*
Amazonia.

BROWN-RUMPED FOLIAGE-GLEANER, *Automolus melanopezus*
Amazonia.

HENNA-CAPPED FOLIAGE-GLEANER, *Automolus rectirostris*, Fura-barreira   BR
21.5 cm; 48 g. Largest *Automolus*. Brown with head, rump, wings, and tail intensely rufous; iris sulfur yellow. VOICE: warning a loud *wat, ka, ka, ka . . . ; co-co-co-REK*, reminiscent of a setting hen. Excavates a horizontal gallery in a bare bank, ending in sizable chamber where it makes nest of dry leaves and grass. Lays 4 eggs (G. T. Mattos). Low or on ground in riverine vegetation. Bahia, Minas Gerais, western São Paulo, Paraná, southern Goiás, Mato Grosso.

PALE-BROWED TREEHUNTER, *Cichlocolaptes leucophrus*, Trepador-sobrancelha   BR   PL 27.11
20 cm. Large, arboreal species of southeastern Brazil. Characterized by intensely streaked underparts, reminiscent of dendrocolaptids such as *Lepidocolaptes*. VOICE: call a loud *krip, shrip*. Tall forests; seeks insects in dry, twisted, and hanging leaves of epiphytic bromeliads. Associates with mixed flocks. Bahia to Santa Catarina.

SHARP-BILLED XENOPS, *Heliobletus contaminatus*, Trepadorzinho
13 cm. Small, southern, forest species, streaked above and below. Seen from ground resembles *Xenops rutilans* but lacks uptilted bill. Canopies, often under large branches pull-

ing off lichens and moss in search of insects. Flies in mixed flocks. Espírito Santo to Rio Grande do Sul, Paraguay, and Misiones, Argentina. Also called *Arapaçu*. See also *Thripophaga macroura*.

RUFOUS-TAILED XENOPS, *Xenops (= Microxenops) milleri*
Has streaked pattern similar to *X. rutilans*. Amazonia.

SLENDER-BILLED XENOPS, *Xenops tenuirostris*
Has streaked pattern similar to *X. rutilans* and white "mustache." Amazonia.

PLAIN XENOPS, *Xenops minutus*, Bico-virado-miudinho   PL 27.13
11.5 cm; 9.5 g. Smallest furnariid, distinguished by uptilted bill (culmen straight), whitish "mustache" that stands above level of other plumage, and bright rusty markings on wings and tail. VOICE: a limpid whistle, *dlewit*, similar to Yellow-breasted Flycatcher, *Tolmomyias flaviventris*. Can excavate its own nest in soft wood; also nests in already existing holes, including abandoned *Picumnus* nests, where it also sleeps. Hops through branches, often on periphery, hanging under branches and vines, resembling *Picumnus* in its movements though it does not have such powerful feet. Moves vertically up tree trunks, hopping with feet together and switching direction of body axis with each jump. Does not use tail for support but can hammer forcefully. Likes company of other furnariids, antbirds, tanagers. Forests. Mexico to Bolivia, Paraguay, Argentina, throughout Brazil south to Santa Catarina. Also called *Arrebitado*. See *X. rutilans*.

STREAKED XENOPS, *Xenops rutilans*, Bico-virado-carijó
12.5 cm. Similar to *X. minutus* but with underparts entirely streaked with white. VOICE: song a phrase of a few syllables, *tsi-TSEE-tsi-tsi-tsi, chirp*. Nestlings cry incessantly, *tip-tip-tip. . . .* Behavior similar to *minutus*, with which it sometimes shares same forest (e.g., Rio de Janeiro). Costa Rica to Bolivia, Paraguay, Argentina; throughout Brazil. See *X. milleri*, *X. tenuirostris*, *Heliobletus contaminatus*, and *Megaxenops parnaguae*.

GREAT XENOPS, *Megaxenops parnaguae*, Bico-virado-da-caatinga   BR   PL 45.8
14.8 cm. Arboreal, typical of heart of northeast. Bill exceptionally strong and uptilted (awl-bill), culmen straight. Plumage light cinnamon, an adaptation to very sunny environment. Throat shiny white; tail quite large and soft. Large feet match strong bill. Low, dense woodlands of caatinga. Hops vivaciously through branches inspecting leaves and bark, of which it pulls off pieces. Does not creep

up trunks. Accompanies mixed flocks of Passerines: Pileated Antwren, *Herpsilochmus pileatus;* Rufous-crowned Greenlet, *Hylophilus poicilotis;* and Golden-crowned Warbler, *Basileuterus culicivorus* (Teixeira 1989). Ceará, Piauí, Pernambuco, northern Bahia. Also recorded in Brasília (Negret et al., 1984), Minas Gerais (Buritis and Triângulo Mineiro, Andrade 1990). It is a very different bird from the *Xenops.*

RUFOUS-BREASTED LEAFTOSSER, *Sclerurus scansor*, Vira-folhas PL 27.14

19.5 cm. Unusual terrestrial species. Forest bird; keeps hidden in darkest parts of woods where it is impossible to distinguish details of color. Shows syndactylism (connection between 3d and 4th toes) which may be an adaptation to standing on vertical perches. VOICE: reveals presence by loud *spix, spix-spix-spix,* which may recall *Lochmias nematura;* song a prolonged, trilled phrase of limpid whistles in a slightly undulating sequence resembling song of a canary, a *Myrmoborus* antbird, or a *Merulaxis* tapaculo. Uses existing holes in embankments for nesting, in which it excavates a gallery broadened at end where it prepares a mat of dry, well-intertwined leaf stems. When embankments are lacking it will install itself in earth caught among roots of a fallen tree. Phlegmatic (opposite of *Lochmias nematura*). Hops on ground, noisily throwing aside fallen leaves and bits of earth with rapid bill movements, leaving marks on ground as if chickens had been scratching there. Flees with fast, straight, low flight similar to that of various antbirds. Ceará to Rio Grande do Sul, western Goiás, southern Mato Grosso, Paraguay, and Misiones, Argentina. Also called *Pincha-cisco, Varradeira, Papa-formigas, Ciscador.*

TAWNY-THROATED LEAFTOSSER, *Sclerurus mexicanus*

This and following 3 species distinguishable by song. There are places, e.g., Rio São José, north of Rio Doce, Espírito Santo (1941–42), where it has been found in same forest with *S. scansor* and *S. caudacutus.* Amazonia to Espírito Santo.

SHORT-BILLED LEAFTOSSER, *Sclerurus rufigularis*

See comments under *S. mexicanus.* Amazonia to Mato Grosso.

BLACK-TAILED LEAFTOSSER, *Sclerurus caudacutus*

See comments under *S. mexicanus.* Amazonia to Espírito Santo.

GRAY-THROATED LEAFTOSSER, *Sclerurus albigularis*

Collected in Rondônia November 1986 (Stotz pers. comm.).

SHARP-TAILED STREAMCREEPER, *Lochmias nematura*, João-porca PL 27.9

14 cm. One of few Brazilian birds that lives constantly at edge of running water. Unmistakable, though in its shady

habitat diagnostic pattern of underparts can hardly be discerned; furthermore, it is almost always upperparts, which are dark, that are seen. May recall a small thrush with a short tail. Has a nervous temperament. VOICE: call and warning *tsi-sik, tsissi-SIK;* song—(pair together): a prolonged sequence of softer whistles, crescendo and then diminuendo, *si-sisi . . . ;* call resembles both *Cranioleuca pallida* and Grey Wagtail, *Motacilla cinerea,* of Europe, which occupies a similar biotope (edge of mountain streams). Nests in shady embankments, using bill to excavate horizontal gallery with terminal chamber in which it builds voluminous, spherical nest with side entrance, using roots and flexible stems on outside and long, well-woven bamboo leaves on inside (fig. 213B; also see "Breeding"). Large eyes testify to shady habitat. Densely vegetated stream edges where it hops on ground or from stone to stone, even entering water in search of insects and larvae. Sometimes picks up whole leaves fallen in water in search for prey (see "Feeding"). Inspects mud of pig pens and sewer outlets (hence the series of inelegant vernacular names it has accumulated), turns over leaves and clods of earth with bill. Central and southeastern Brazil from Espírito Santo and Minas Gerais to Rio Grande do Sul, Mato Grosso, Uruguay, Paraguay, Argentina, and up the Andes as far as Colombia, Venezuela, Panama. Also called *João-suiriri, Capitão-da-porcaria, Presidente-da-porcaria, Tridi, Tiriri.*

Furnariid Bibliography
See also General Bibliography

Achaval, F. 1972. *Bol. Soc. Zool. Uruguay* 21. [Nesting fauna]

Andrade, M. A. 1990. O bico-virado-da-caatinga, *Megaxenops parnaguae. O Charão* 16:14.

Azevedo, S. M., Jr. 1989. Notes on the biology of *Pseudoseisura cristata. XVI Cong. Bras. Zool., João Pessoa:*139.

Belton, W. 1984a. Taxonomy of certain species of birds from Rio Grande do Sul, Brazil. *Nat. Geo. Soc. Research Rep.* 17:183–88.

Carvalho, J.C.M. 1969. *Notas de viagem à região das caatingas.* Fortaleza. [Nesting fauna]

Dickerman, R. W., G. F. Barrowclough, P. F. Cannel, et al. 1986. *Philydor hylobius* Wetmore and Phelps is a synonym of *Automolus roraimae* Hellmayr. *Auk* 103:431–32.

Fraga, R. M. 1980. *Condor* 82:58–68. [*Furnarius rufus,* breeding]

Hermann, H., and W. Meise. 1966. *Abh. Naturw. Ver. Hamburg* 10. [*Furnarius,* behavior]

Narosky, S. 1973. *Ibis* 115:412–13. [*Spartonoica,* nesting]

Narosky, S., R. Fraga, and M. de la Peña. 1983. *Nidificación da las aves argentinas, Dendrocolaptidae, Furnariidae.* Ass. Orn. del Plata.

Novaes, F. A. 1961. *Rev. Bras. Biol.* 21:179–92. [*Automolus,* nesting]

Remsen, J. V., and T. A. Parker III. 1984. Arboreal dead-leaf-searching birds of the Neotropics. *Condor* 86:36–41.

Schirch, P. F. 1931. *Bol. Mus. Nac. Rio de Janeiro* 7:91–92. [*Synallaxis,* nesting]

Sick, H. 1969. *Beitr. Neotrop. Fauna* 6:63–79. [*Cinclodes pabsti*]

Sick, H. 1970. *Bonn. Zool. Beitr.* 21:251–68. [*Schizoeaca*, nesting]

Sick, H. 1970. O rabo-de-palha, *Oreophylax moreirae*, Furnarídeo andino no sudeste do Brasil. *IV Cong. Bras. Zool., Curitiba.*

Sick, H. 1973. *Rev. Bras. Biol.* 33:109–17. [*Cinclodes*, ecology]

Sick, H. 1979. *Bull. B.O.C.* 99(4):115–20. [*Berlepschia rikeri*, distribution]

Skutch, A. F. 1969. *Wilson Bull.* 81:1–2. [*Phacellodomus*, ecology]

Teixeira, D. M. 1989. Observações preliminares sobre *Megaxenops parnaguae*. *XVI Cong. Bras. Zool., João Pessoa:*134.

Teixeira, D. M., and L. P. Gonzaga. 1983. Um novo Furnariidae do

Nordeste do Brasil: *Philydor novaesi* sp. nov. *Bol. Mus. Para. E. Goeldi. Zool.* 124.

Vaurie, C. 1971. *Classification of the Ovenbirds (Furnariidae).* London: Witherby, Ltd.

Vaurie, C. 1980. *Taxonomy and geographical distribution of the Furnariidae. Bull. Am. Mus. Nat. Hist.* 166:1.

Vielliard, J. 1990. Uma nova espécie de *Asthenes* da Serra do Cipó, Minas Gerais, Brasil. *Ararajuba* 1:121–122.

Vuilleumier, F. 1969. Field notes on some birds from the Bolivian Andes. *Ibis* 111:599–608.

Zimmer, J. T. 1934. *Am. Mus. Nov.* 757 and subsequent publications. [Taxonomy]

FAMILY DENDROCOLAPTIDAE: WOODCREEPERS (37)

This family is restricted to the Neotropics, ranging from southern Mexico to northern Argentina, and is very well represented in Brazil. There is a 20,000-year-old upper Pleistocene fossil from Lagoa Santa, Minas Gerais. Although related to the furnariids, with which woodcreepers share various characters, there are differences in skeletal structure, syrinx, etc. At various times it has been proposed to unite the Dendrocolaptidae and Furnariidae into one family. Feduccia (1973) considers the Dendrocolaptidae to be the more specialized.

As essentially woodland birds, woodcreepers evolved primarily in the Hylaea, unlike the furnariids. Their extreme adaptation to arboreal life is like that of the woodpeckers, a cosmopolitan group, in a remarkably analogous evolution that is a notable feature of the Neotropics. The way this adaptation was achieved, however, was fundamentally different in woodpeckers and woodcreepers.

Morphology

Size varies considerably. In the smallest species, the Wedge-billed Woodcreeper, *Glyphorynchus spirurus*, the male averages only 14.4 g, whereas the male Long-billed Woodcreeper *Nasica longirostris*, reaches 99.5 g and the female Strong-billed Woodcreeper, *Xiphocolaptes promeropirhynchus*, reaches more than 120 g. Woodcreeper bills are generally long and curved, accounting for more than a quarter of the body length in *Nasica*. The extreme curvature of the bill of the *Campylorhamphus* results in a distinctive location of the eyes. The tongue is short and fixed. The feet are anisodactyl (fig. 219): three toes—the second, third, and fourth—point forward together, and one, the first, to the rear, as with most birds and all Passeriformes. The toes are not as strong as those of woodpeckers.

The tail is used for support, as with woodpeckers, as they mount tree trunks (in fact, they hop), but the rectrices are differently constructed: whereas the shafts of woodpeckers'

tail feathers are straight and thus meet the substrate at an oblique angle, the hardened points of woodcreepers' rectrices are curved inward like claws, touching the trunk almost at a right angle relative to the shafts, which lie parallel to the trunk (fig. 220). The wings and tail are intense rusty red, similar to many furnariids.

Sexes are identical, the male larger, particularly in *Deconychura*. Immatures have shorter bills, noticeable, for instance, in the *Lepidocolaptes* and *Campylorhamphus*. Broadly speaking, bill shape characterizes some genera, such as *Lepidocolaptes*, *Xiphocolaptes*, *Dendrocolaptes*, and *Campylorhamphus*, and bill color is also significant. Plumage color of most species appears quite similar, at least at first glance. The specific pattern of the underparts, used to identify museum specimens, is scarcely visible in the live bird clinging to a tree trunk. Color may vary considerably within species according to geographic region (see "Distribution . . ."); identification of the various species requires a fuller description of characters than is possible here.

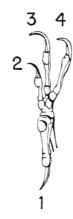

Fig. 219. Anisodactyl foot, left, of Narrow-billed Woodcreeper, *Lepidocolaptes angustirostris*, seen from below; compare the position of the toes with that of woodpeckers. After Böker 1935.

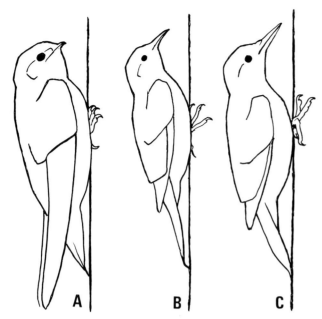

Fig. 220. Differential evolution of the structure of the tail as an instrument for body support in three orders of birds: (A) swift (Apodiformes, Chaeturinae); (B) woodcreeper (Passeriformes, Dendrocolaptidae); and (C) woodpecker (Piciformes, Picidae). Note the different form and position of the tail tip.

Recognition in the field is facilitated by the occurrence of various species side by side; for example, the White-throated Woodcreeper, *Xiphocolaptes albicollis,* and Planalto Woodcreeper, *Dendrocolaptes platyrostris,* may appear on the same tree at the same height within minutes of each other. Various species, such as *Lepidocolaptes, Dendrocincla, Campylorhamphus,* and *Sittasomus,* commonly live in the same area. *Glyphorynchus spirurus* is one of the most abundant birds of the Amazonian forest. Woodcreepers have a typical odor which is peculiar to themselves.

Vocalization

Song is closely associated with breeding in most woodcreepers; their voices are frequently among the most impressive to be heard, with monotonous but melodious, occasionally somewhat prolonged, phrases recalling those of certain furnariids, woodpeckers, or small rails. Unlike woodpeckers, woodcreepers sing more on rainy days and at dawn and dusk. They are heard at first light and are among the last diurnal birds to become silent, stopping only when nightjars and owls start to call. In the Brazilian southeast *Xiphocolaptes albicollis* is usually the last singer of the evening. In Amazonia this honor goes to the Straight-billed Woodcreeper, *Xiphorhynchus picus,* or Striped Woodcreeper, *X. obsoletus.*

Outside the breeding period they sometimes give forth just one burst during a whole afternoon to close out the day's business (e.g., *Xiphocolaptes albicollis*). Both sexes sing, the female voice being weaker and harsher, as in *X. albicollis.* Some, such as the Scimitar-billed Woodcreeper, *Drymornis bridgesii,* can diminish or amplify voice volume according to circumstances. The *Sittasomus, Dendrocincla,* and *Xiphorynchus* can prolong their stanzas for well over a minute. Young draw attention from within the nesting cavity by a loud phrase similar to the parents' song, as with the Narrow-billed Woodcreeper, *Lepidocolaptes angustirostris.* They continue its use even after abandoning the nest, as in *Xiphorhynchus picus,* it possibly serving as a location call.

Food, Behavior, and Habitat

Arboreal and insectivorous, woodcreepers use the bill, which is very different from that of woodpeckers, more like pincers than like a chisel. They explore cracks in the wood and bark of trees, pull or break off fragments of bark, and tear moss and lichens with sideways blows. Among the richest sources of food they exploit are epiphytic bromeliads, ripping off dead leaves and perforating live ones, scattering the heaps of humus accumulated in the plants and letting it fall noisily on the branches below. In the process they take whatever arthropods—from millipedes, spiders, and scorpions to flies—they find, as well as tree frogs, tadpoles, and lizards. *Xiphocolaptes albicollis* occasionally eats bird eggs it finds in tree holes. Scythebills, endowed with an extremely long, curved, but weak bill, manage with great dexterity to probe the centers of bromeliads and to reach the bottom of narrow holes, such as the rectangular cuts of unknown origin on bamboos in eastern Brazil (see Picidae, "Feeding"). When a *Campylorhamphus* catches an insect with the tip of its immense, curved bill, it drops the prey and catches it again with the mouth wide open, as do some toucans and hummingbirds. The bill of the Red-billed Scythebill, *C. trochilirostris,* appears weak and is elastic.

It is not unusual for woodcreepers to hammer forcefully; it is common in *Glyphorynchus spirurus* and has also been observed in *Xiphocolaptes* and even in *Campylorhamphus.* Each bill type is related to exploitation of a given niche. Apparently there is little competition with woodpeckers. Woodcreepers do not drum (see Picidae, "Vocalization . . . "). Happily, E. Willis has carefully analyzed the different techniques of various species, demonstrating that it is impossible to generalize.

The Black-banded Woodcreeper, *Dendrocolaptes picumnus,* opens nests of meliponine honey bees, whereas *D. platyrostris* occasionally catches bees and takes advantage of army ants as beaters, as do certain antbirds, by perching close to the ground and watching for insects frightened up by the ants to catch them with their bills. The Plain-brown Woodcreeper, *Dendrocincla fuliginosa,* and Barred Woodcreeper, *Dendrocolaptes certhia,* obtain more than half their food this way (E. O. Willis and Y. Oniki).

Adult dragonflies found in *Dendrocincla* stomachs are probably captured on cold days or in the early morning while perched. *Dendrocincla* beat their wings against tree trunks to frighten up arthropods. They sometimes eat seeds. Both they and the Olivaceous Woodcreeper, *Sittasomus griseicapillus*, catch small insects in flight, like flycatchers. Woodcreepers beat their larger prey violently against the substrate to kill them.

Frequently they mount tree trunks spirally, sometimes interspersing abrupt backward descents, keeping the head always upward, it being exceptional for a woodcreeper to descend head first, as I saw a Lineated Woodcreeper, *Lepidocolaptes albolineatus*, do while going down an oblique branch. This head-down method of creeping is very reminiscent of *Certhia* tree-creepers, Oscines, one of which, the Brown Creeper, *C. americana*, which ranges from Canada to Nicaragua, can sometimes be seen in the same trees with woodcreepers. Some, such as the *Lepidocolaptes*, frequently move along large horizontal limbs. From high on a tree trunk woodcreepers swoop down with open tail and wings to begin the ascent again, or from the crown they may rapidly fly to a more distant tree. They feed more on trunks than on branches. The larger species prefer thick trunks, the smaller ones more slender ones. Adaptation to a certain method of feeding may be distinctly different between male and female (different bill form or size). The result is a preference for different habitats and avoidance of competition. They fly silently, passing like shadows.

Nervousness is revealed by shaking their wings; when threatened they hide behind tree trunks with wings half open. They scratch themselves like woodpeckers, holding on to the substrate with only one foot. They use insects for anting. The formic acid, it appears, serves less for plumage and skin hygiene than as a stimulant.

Various family members, such as *Sittasomus griseicapillus*, *Glyphorynchus spirurus*, *Dendrocolaptes platyrostris*, and the *Xiphorhynchus*, *Lepidocolaptes*, and *Campylorhamphus*, associate after the breeding season in mixed flocks with birds such as furnariids, antbirds, and tanagers. Some are found in these flocks all year, especially in Amazonia. Certain ones, such as the *Lepidocolaptes*, are almost always found in pairs, whereas others, like the *Deconychura*, are more solitary. The radius of action of individuals appears to be limited. Woodcreepers do not leave the protective forest. They seek holes for sleeping and are even found in residential chimneys or on beams under roofs (*Xiphocolaptes albicollis*).

Few woodcreepers adapt themselves to life in open savannas, unlike the furnariids; however, *Lepidocolaptes angustirostris* has partially adjusted, whereas *Drymornis bridgesii* and the Great Rufous Woodcreeper, *Xiphocolaptes major*, have achieved accentuated adaptation. *D. bridgesii* manages to resemble a curlew, *Numenius* sp., as it runs through the sparse grass of the espinilho parkland of Rio Grande do Sul, but when seeking refuge it heads for trees.

Breeding

Woodcreepers nest in tree holes but are unable to excavate such holes themselves; they use well-rotted trees, trunks gutted by fire, and woodpecker holes (*Lepidocolaptes angustirostris* and the Scaled Woodcreeper, *L. squamatus*). They prefer very narrow entrances (*Lepidocolaptes*, *Sittasomus*), but nests in wide open trunks occur. *Drymornis bridgesii* apparently uses abandoned Rufous Hornero, *Furnarius rufus*, nests in the espinilho. *Xiphorhynchus picus* may nest in gaps between bromeliads or epiphytic orchids or in palm tops. Woodcreepers are shy on the nest, making observation difficult.

Normally they lay two pure white eggs with little gloss on a lining of bark bits or dry leaves. The pair may or may not take turns incubating and rearing the young, which are born blind and covered with down. Incubation of the Streak-headed Woodcreeper, *Lepidocolaptes souleyetii*, in Central America lasted 15 days, and the young abandoned the nest at 19 days. The nest is not kept clean for the full time, with the result that grown nestlings may dirty their tails (*Xiphorhynchus picus*). Nestlings are parasitized by larvae of the bird botfly (Diptera).

Distribution and Evolution

Geographic races have evolved in many species, sometimes in a long clinal sequence, as in *Sittasomus griseicapillus*, where more than ten subspecies have been described. In genera such as *Hylexetastes* the various geographic replacements may be quite different. The pattern of allopatric distribution—evident in many forest birds—is common in Amazonia, where effective separation may be enforced by large rivers. In genera such as *Dendrocolaptes* information is still lacking for a decision on whether certain forms are subspecies or allospecies. Among "good" species such as *Dendrocolaptes certhia* and *D. picumnus*, there is distributional overlapping, or sympatry. In cases of widely disjunct distribution, as in *Xiphocolaptes promeropirhynchus* and *X. albicollis*, we can use vocalization, very similar in the two, as evidence of relationship, showing that behavioral characters can be more conservative than morphological ones.

The *Dendrocincla* and *Xiphocolaptes* are evidence of a former linkage between the forests of eastern Brazil and Amazonia. The contrary is the case with *Lepidocolaptes angustirostris*, whose vast area of distribution, including cerrado, caatinga, and espinilho parkland, was broken up by development of Amazonia; it reappears in corresponding ecosystems to the north of Amazonia and has immigrated recently into deforested eastern Brazil.

Decline

Woodcreepers are among the Passeriformes that are abundant in Neotropical forests, especially in virgin stands; in impoverished secondary forests with a reduced number of plant species and few large, old trees, their numbers are greatly diminished. I believe this decline, beyond the scarcity of food, is due to lack of the natural or woodpecker-made cavities these birds need for nesting and sleeping. An exception is *Glyphorynchus spirurus*, a small understory species that achieves a high populational density in human-disturbed forests of lower Amazonia (Lovejoy 1974).

It would perhaps help to keep woodcreepers in impoverished forests of the type cited above if nest boxes, much used in the Northern Hemisphere, were set out. I have noted that *Lepidocolaptes angustirostris* and *L. squamatus* occasionally nest in holes in buildings.

PLAIN-BROWN WOODCREEPER, *Dendrocincla fuliginosa*, Arapaçu-liso   PL 26.7

21 cm. Only dendrocolaptid almost uniformly olive-brown, without black barring; rump and tail rufous like wings; head feathers generally raised. VOICE: warning a low, spitting *kta*, sometimes bisyllabic; song a hard, monotonous *klip klip klip* . . . , quite prolonged and slightly undulating, reminiscent of song of Mouse-colored Tapaculo, *Scytalopus speluncae;* dusk song (Mato Grosso) a more melodious, tremulous phrase, *prrrrrri-prrrrrrew*, initially ascending, then descending, resembling Russet-crowned Crake, *Laterallus viridis*. Forests; is still active in late evening when owls, e.g., Tropical Screech-Owl, *Otus choliba*, begin to call. Accompanies army-ant swarms, sometimes with *D. merula*. Amazonia from the Guianas to Maranhão, Mato Grosso, Rondônia, Bolivia.

PLAIN-WINGED WOODCREEPER, *Dendrocincla turdina*

21 cm. Replaces *D. fuliginosa* in southeastern Brazil. Similar in various aspects, including voice, but lacks rusty wings, rump, and tail; may be considered an allospecies or subspecies (if they interbreed). Southern Bahia to southern Goiás, Rio Grande do Sul, Paraguay, and Misiones, Argentina.

WHITE-CHINNED WOODCREEPER, *Dendrocincla merula*

19 cm. Smaller, chocolate colored, chin whitish. VOICE: warning *tsiriRIT;* song a tremulous phrase. Lower level of forest. Amazonia south to Serra do Cachimbo and Belém, Pará.

LONG-TAILED WOODCREEPER, *Deconychura longicauda*

See *D. stictolaema*.

SPOT-THROATED WOODCREEPER, *Deconychura stictolaema*

These 2 species are extremely similar to *Dendrocincla* but are less robust, with even longer tails and shorter bills. Head densely spotted (in *Dendrocincla* color is uniform). VOICES:

also resemble *Dendrocincla*. *Deconychura longicauda* larger and usually forages higher, but both sometimes found in same forest (e.g., Manaus). Humid Amazonian forests. Uncommon.

OLIVACEOUS WOODCREEPER, *Sittasomus griseicapillus*, Arapaçu-verde   PL 26.10

15.1 cm. One of most common woodcreepers, unmistakable in slender appearance and thin bill; back olive, rest of plumage variable. Seven geographic races in Brazil alone. Open wing always shows prominent light rusty streak. VOICE: song an unmistakable, prolonged sequence of clear whistles, *kwip* . . . , slightly ascending or descending; a strong *ttt* . . . , at times for minutes on end, resembling a *Dendrocincla*. All types of forest. Mexico to Bolivia, Paraguay, Argentina, throughout Brazil. Also called *Trepadeira, Cutia-de-pau-pequena* (Minas Gerais).

WEDGE-BILLED WOODCREEPER, *Glyphorynchus spirurus*, Arapaçu-de-bico-de-cunha   PL 26.5

14.2 cm. Our smallest woodcreeper, typical of Amazonian forests. With short, chisel-shaped bill somewhat resembles furnariid genus *Xenops;* has less prominent wing stripe than *Sittasomus griseicapillus*. Superciliary and throat rusty yellow, foreneck characteristically streaked. VOICE: a strident *psieh*, muffled *ksh, ksh, ksh*. Dense forest, climbs trees of all sizes, hammers forcefully. One of most abundant birds of várzea and terra-firme forests of lower Amazon. Mexico to Bolivia, Mato Grosso, southern Bahia, Espírito Santo (Rio Doce). Also called *Ra-pau-i* (Kamaiurá, Mato Grosso), a name also used for other woodcreepers).

SCIMITAR-BILLED WOODCREEPER, *Drymornis bridgesii*, Arapaçu-platino

29 cm. In Brazil only in extreme south, where it is unique in appearance and behavior. Bill extremely curved, resembling a *Campylorhamphus;* plumage brown; superciliary, throat, and streaking of underparts white. VOICE: song a hurried sequence, *deWEEdel-DLEEdel-DLEEdel* . . . , often descending; warning a loud *tsissik*. Espinilho parkland savanna in Rio Grande do Sul. Seeks food on ground, runs and hops through low, sun-bleached grass, its silhouette suggesting a curlew, *Numenius* sp. From time to time moves into sparse, low trees, perching on larger branches but also on trunks, supporting itself with tail. Found with *Lepidocolaptes angustirostris; Furnarius rufus;* Campo Flicker, *Colaptes campestris;* and Green-barred Flicker, *C. melanochloros*. Patagonia to Uruguay, Rio Grande do Sul (Barra do Quaraí), Paraguay. First recorded in Brazil in 1970.

LONG-BILLED WOODCREEPER, *Nasica longirostris*, Arapaçu-de-bico-comprido   PL 26.1

35 cm. Largest woodcreeper, unmistakable with enormous (7.2 cm), white, sabre-shaped bill. Narrow head, scarcely distinguishable from slender neck. VOICE: warning

ktaa; song a phrase of 3 prolonged whistles. Tall riverine forests, forested islands in large rivers. Amazonia south to upper Xingu (Mato Grosso), Maranhão.

STRONG-BILLED WOODCREEPER, *Xiphocolaptes promeropirhynchus,* Arapaçu-vermelho

30 cm. Amazonian version of *X. albicollis,* with even larger bill (5 cm); bright rufous plumage, more evident on wings and tail, less pronounced on barred design of belly. VOICE: very similar to *albicollis;* warning *gay-wat;* song a descending sequence of 4–8 loud whistles, *shaBEEeh . . . .* Tall forests. More than 20 geographic races extend from Mexico to upper Amazon, Bolivia, Mato Grosso (upper Xingu).

WHITE-THROATED WOODCREEPER, *Xiphocolaptes albicollis,* Arapaçu-de-garganta-branca
PL 26.2

29 cm. Largest woodcreeper in southeastern Brazil. Shiny black bill, somewhat long and curved, gives it a different aspect than *Dendrocolaptes platyrostris,* its frequent neighbor, from which it is also differentiated by pure white throat and lack of creamy streaking on back. VOICE: warning *ewehwet,* initial note prolonged, forceful, ending with a pop; song a sharply descending sequence, last notes softer, *sswidoBEEa doBEEa doBEEa . . . ,* sung almost exclusively at dusk, to which female responds with hoarse but weaker voice. Forests at all levels, frequently quite low. In Rio de Janeiro more common in mountains (Serra dos Órgãos, Itatiaia, etc.). Bahia and Minas Gerais to Rio Grande do Sul, Paraguay, and Misiones, Argentina. Also called *Agarradeira, Assobiadeira, Arapaçu, Pica-pau-cutiá.* May be considered allospecific with *X. promeropirhynchus.* See "Distribution . . . ."

MOUSTACHED WOODCREEPER, *Xiphocolaptes falcirostris*   BR

29 cm. Similar to *X. albicollis* but with lighter, chestnut-colored, and more slender bill, paler plumage, distinct yellow superciliary. No or almost no black barring on belly. Woodlands, riverine forest. Maranhão to Paraíba, Bahia. West of Rio São Francisco (Brejo S. Januário, Minas Gerais) *X. f. franciscanus* occurs. It is quite terrestrial, turning over leaves on ground and pecking strongly against earth itself. Its method of eating on ground resembles that of chickens (G. Mattos 1985 pers. comm.) It is restricted to a very limited area greatly menaced by woodcutting for charcoal.

GREAT RUFOUS WOODCREEPER, *Xiphocolaptes major,* Arapaçu-do-campo.

31 cm. Large, southern species with long (6 cm), sturdy bill, less curved than that of *Drymornis bridgesii;* almost uniformly dark rusty plumage contrasts with light grayish bill. VOICE: a bisyllabic *kwai-kwai* as it flies from tree to tree. Open country with sparse trees or palms. Descends to ground. Bolivia, Argentina, and Paraguay to southern Mato Grosso (Corumbá).

In Brazilian Amazonia there are three other large species similar to *X. major:*

CINNAMON-THROATED WOODCREEPER, *Dendrexetastes rufigula*

27 cm. Scaly pattern on throat (whitish streaks edged with black), bill without reddish tones. Belém and north of Amazon.

RED-BILLED WOODCREEPER, *Hylexetastes perrotii*

28 cm. Throat and line on side of head gray; bill heavy, red. Venezuela, etc.; east of Rio Negro, between Madeira and Tapajós; northern Mato Grosso.

BAR-BELLIED WOODCREEPER, *Hylexetastes stresemanni*

29 cm. Throat streaked with white, belly finely barred, bill red. Upper Amazon to Rios Negro and Purus.

PLANALTO WOODCREEPER, *Dendrocolaptes platyrostris,* Arapaçu-grande   PL 26.4

26 cm. Similar to *Xiphocolaptes albicollis* but smaller with barred belly and only slightly reddish tail; whitish throat, streaked crown and breast. Bill shorter, almost straight, black with chestnut tip. VOICE: song a sequence of simple, ascending, crescendo whistles that then descend and diminish in volume, *chree. . . .* Forests, cerrado (Mato Grosso), buriti groves (Bahia). Piauí to Rio Grande do Sul, Goiás, Mato Grosso (up to Rio Xingu), Paraguay, northern Argentina, including Misiones. Also called *Subideira, Cutia-de-pau* (Minas Gerais), *Ipekazin* (Kamaiurá, Mato Grosso), *Atú-ja-kalú* (Waurá, Mato Grosso), *Wos-wos* (Trumai, Mato Grosso).

BARRED WOODCREEPER, *Dendrocolaptes certhia*

26 cm. Scaly-looking crown, breast lightly barred, bill black or brownish. Various geographic races widely distributed in Amazonian forests. Mexico to the Guianas and south to upper Teles Pires and upper Xingu, Serra do Roncador (Mato Grosso), Rondônia (Stotz pers. comm.), Bolivia. Population east of Rio Madeira (Amazonas) is called *D. c. concolor;* there is a remnant population in northeast (Pernambuco, Alagoas). Meets *D. platyrostris* in upper Rio Xingu (Mato Grosso) and *Hylexetastes perrotii uniformis* on Rio Teles Pires (Mato Grosso). Partial to açai (*Euterpe oleracea*) palms, which abound with insects.

BLACK-BANDED WOODCREEPER, *Dendrocolaptes picumnus*

28 cm. Another sizable species, reminiscent of *D. platyrostris* in streaked pattern of crown, but larger. Brazilian Amazonia, Serra do Cachimbo (Pará), western Mato Grosso,

Bolivia, northeastern Argentina; regularly found alongside *D. certhia* in Roraima, Manaus area, and sometimes Amapá.

HOFFMANN'S WOODCREEPER, *Dendrocolaptes hoffmannsi* BR

29 cm. Crown scaly, rump and upper tail coverts red, belly vermiculated. Between Rios Xingu and Madeira (Pará, Mato Grosso, Amazonas), also Rondônia (Stotz pers. comm.).

STRAIGHT-BILLED WOODCREEPER, *Xiphorhynchus picus,* Arapaçu-de-bico-branco PL 26.8

20 cm. Easily recognized, common in Amazonia. Straight, white bill; wings, rump, and tail quite red; breast scaly. VOICE: warning *chik . . . ;* song a characteristic, resounding, strongly descending phrase, slowing toward end. Lowland forests near rivers and lakes, typical of forested islands of great rivers of Amazonia, várzeas of igapó, and buriti palm groves where it can be found with Point-tailed Palmcreeper, *Berlepschia rikeri.* Panama to Bolivia, Mato Grosso, eastern Pará, Maranhão, Piauí; also Bahia, Espírito Santo (Rio Doce). See *X. guttatus.*

BUFF-THROATED WOODCREEPER, *Xiphorhynchus guttatus,* Arapaçu-de-garganta-amarela PL 26.3

24 cm. Abundant in Amazonia. Slightly smaller than *Dendrocolaptes platyrostris,* with long, relatively slender, curved, light-colored bill. VOICE: a descending sequence, *chew-chew-chew-chew;* a loud, prolonged (up to 4 minutes) phrase, fast and tremulous at first, then slowing, *dew . . . chewwa. . . .* One of dominant voices at dawn and dusk, like that of *X. picus.* Forests, generally frequenting higher levels, often above 10 m; one of dominant birds along lower and upper Amazon. Guatemala to Mato Grosso, Goiás; also eastern Brazil from southern Bahia to Rio de Janeiro. Also called *Pica-pau-vermelho.*

There are seven other *Xiphorhynchus* in Brazilian Amazonia, all generally more difficult to identify:

ZIMMER'S WOODCREEPER, *Xiphorhynchus necopinus* BR

STRIPED WOODCREEPER, *Xiphorhynchus obsoletus*

OCELLATED WOODCREEPER, *Xiphorhynchus ocellatus*

SPIX'S WOODCREEPER, *Xiphorhynchus spixii*

ELEGANT WOODCREEPER, *Xiphorhynchus elegans*

CHESTNUT-RUMPED WOODCREEPER, *Xiphorhynchus pardalotus*

DUSKY-BILLED WOODCREEPER, *Xiphorhynchus eytoni* BR

Also in Ceará; may be considered a geographic race of *X. guttatus,* from which it differs by having white, not yellow, throat.

NARROW-BILLED WOODCREEPER, *Lepidocolaptes angustirostris,* Arapaçu-do-cerrado

20 cm. Characteristic woodcreeper of cerrado, caatinga, and similar open country with sparse trees; unmistakable with bright white superciliary and underparts. VOICE: call a melodious *jew-rewt;* song a sequence of melancholy, tremulous whistles, *drewEEew. . . .* Nestling reveals presence at a distance with melodious, descending stanza that slows toward end. Although typical of open country, continues to be arboreal; at times found with woodpeckers such as *Colaptes melanochloros,* which it resembles in voice timbre (habitat voice[1]), and *C. campestris.* Sympatric with *Drymornis bridgesii* in Rio Grande do Sul. Marajó to rest of non-Amazonian Brazil, Uruguay, Argentina, Paraguay, Bolivia. Also savannas of southern Suriname. Starting to invade Rio de Janeiro littoral. See *L. squamatus* and *L. fuscus.*

SCALED WOODCREEPER, *Lepidocolaptes squamatus,* Arapaçu-escamado

19 cm. Woodland species common in many areas of eastern Brazil; similar to *L. fuscus* but clearly larger, back with light pattern, underparts broadly streaked with sharply contrasting black, breast scaly looking. VOICE: call *BEEarrr;* song a phrase that descends in steps and ends very softly, *piCHAY. . . .* Forests from Piauí to Rio Grande do Sul, Paraguay, and Misiones, Argentina; in mountains of Rio de Janeiro (Serra dos Órgãos, Itatiaia, etc.); sometimes sympatric with *fuscus* (Minas Gerais). Also called *Cutia-de-pau-rajada* (Minas Gerais).

LESSER WOODCREEPER, *Lepidocolaptes fuscus,* Arapaçu-rajado PL 26.9

17 cm. Similar to *L. squamatus* but smaller, pattern on underparts indistinct. VOICE: call *speel;* song a clear laughing *kwip-KWIP-kwip-kwip-kwip-kwip-kwip,* faster and louder than *Sittasomus griseicapillus.* Forest, both in lowlands (e.g., ex-Guanabara and on Rio Doce, Espírito Santo) and mountains, often with *S. griseicapillus* and *Dendrocolaptes platyrostris.* Ceará to Rio Grande do Sul, Paraguay, and Misiones, Argentina. Also called *Cutia-de-pau-vermelha* (Minas Gerais), *Arapaçu-pequeno.*

STREAK-HEADED WOODCREEPER, *Lepidocolaptes souleyetii*

In Brazil only in Roraima.

---

[1]In certain habitats, such as open country and cattail and reedy marshes, voices of unrelated birds are similar, even on different continents. (See Emberizinae and Cardinalinae, "Vocalization").

LINEATED WOODCREEPER, *Lepidocolaptes albolineatus*

Brazilian Amazonia.

BLACK-BILLED SCYTHEBILL, *Campylorhamphus falcularius,* Arapaçu-de-bico-torto   PL 26.6

24 cm. Unmistakable with long neck and long (6 cm), slender, greatly decurved, laterally compressed, black bill. VOICE: song a sequence of 3 harsh but melodious, descending whistles followed by 1 ascending whistle: *tshrEEeh-tshrEEeh-tshrEEeh-tshri-EE,* sometimes in more prolonged phrases; warning a strident *spieh*. Forests and bamboo thickets at any altitude. Sinks oversized bill up to forehead into holes, cracks in trees, epiphytic plants; having caught a chrysalis or spider, etc., with tip of mandibles, bends neck backward and lets captive fall into its wide open gullet (See "Food . . . "). Espírito Santo to Rio Grande do Sul, Paraguay, and Misiones, Argentina.

RED-BILLED SCYTHEBILL, *Campylorhamphus trochilirostris*

Except for reddish bill, very similar, including voice, to *C. falcularius,* which it replaces in center of continent. Colombia and Venezuela to Mato Grosso, Paraguay, Argentina.

CURVE-BILLED SCYTHEBILL, *Campylorhamphus procurvoides*

Similar to *C. trochilirostris;* darker but also with red bill. Northern South America to south of Amazon (Tapajós).

Dendrocolaptidae Bibliography

See also General Bibliography

Belton, W. 1973. Some additional birds for the state of Rio Grande do Sul, Brazil. *Auk* 90:94–99.

Brooke, M. de L. 1983. Ecological segregation of woodcreepers (Dendrocolaptidae) in the state of Rio de Janeiro. *Ibis* 125:562–67.

Feduccia, A. 1973. Evolutionary trends in the Neotropical oven-birds and woodhewers. *Ornithol. Monogr.* 13. [Evolution]

Ihering, H. v. 1914. *Rev. Mus. Paul.* 9:469–75. [General]

Oniki, Y. 1970. *Condor* 72:233. [Behavior]

Sick, H. 1950. *Orn. Ber.* 3(1):23–26. [*Dendrocincla fuliginosa trumaii*]

Skutch, A. F. 1969. *Life Histories of Central American Birds,* vol. 3. Pacific Coast Avifauna 35:374–418. Berkeley, Calif.: Cooper Orn. Soc.

Willis, E. O. 1966. *Ecology* 47:667–72. [Behavior]

Willis, E. O. 1972. *Wilson Bull.* 84:377–420. [Behavior]

Willis, E. O. 1982. Three *Dendrocincla* woodcreepers as army ant followers. *Ciência e Cultura* 35(2):201–4.

Zimmer, J. T. 1934. *Am. Mus. Nov.* 728 and subsequent publications. [Taxonomy]

SUPERFAMILY TYRANNOIDEA

In this group of Suboscines are gathered the Tyrannidae, Pipridae, Cotingidae (where I include "Rupicolidae," *Rupicola,* and "Oxyruncidae," *Oxyruncus*), and Phytotomidae, having been defined by S. L. Warter (1965, from Traylor 1977) as Tyrannoidea through their osteology. They have a tracheobronchial syrinx (Haploophonae). The Tyrannoidea includes more than 500 species, nearly the same number as the Furnarioidea. There are 271 in Brazil. Over the millenia many Tyrannidae have emigrated to North America.

FAMILY TYRANNIDAE: TYRANT-FLYCATCHERS (200)

Tyrant-flycatchers are confined to the Western Hemisphere and constitute its largest family. A fossil from the middle Pleistocene (100,000 years B.P.) had been found in Florida.

New World tyrant-flycatchers rival Eastern Hemisphere flycatchers (the Oscine Muscicapidae), the two families having almost the same number of species. Tyrant-flycatchers are among the world's most diversified group of birds and in Brazil are the birds most seen and heard. They constitute about 18% of the Passerine species in South America. With 375 species ranging from Alaska to Tierra del Fuego, the greatest concentration is in the Neotropics. Evolution of the incredibly diverse Tyrannidae on this continent was greatly favored by a total absence of Oscines, Northern Hemisphere Passerines that immigrated here only after the two Americas came together in the late Pliocene. The Suboscine tyrannids adapted themselves to the highly varied ecological niches of this continent whose habitats correspond to the same or similar habitats occupied by Oscines in the Northern Hemisphere. Thus the most surprising analogies were created: Suboscines (non-Oscines) versus Oscines.

The Tyrannidae is the most important group in the Suboscines. Some of the most popular birds of Brazil, such as the Great Kiskadee, *Pitangus sulphuratus,* and Tropical Kingbird, *Tyrannus melancholicus,* are among its members. The family shows substantial similarity to cotingids and manakins.

Morphology and Identification

New World flycatchers compose the most heterogeneous family in the Suboscines. Although a "typical" tyrannid might be characterized as a small, olive green bird with a broadened, hooked bill surrounded by prominent bristles, there are more "atypical" species. Heterogeneity begins with size: *Pitangus sulphuratus*, at 60 g, is 12 times heavier than the Short-tailed Pygmy-Tyrant, *Myiornis ecaudatus*, at 4.9 g one of the smallest birds in the world. There are many small species. Some tyrannids, such as the Long-tailed Tyrant, *Colonia colonus;* Streamer-tailed Tyrant, *Gubernetes yetapa;* Strange-tailed Tyrant, *Alectrurus risora;* and Fork-tailed Flycatcher, *Tyrannus savana,* have very long tails with various shapes. One of the weirdest tail shapes known among birds has evolved in the *Alectrurus.* Although of only relative value, the tarsus type is an external morphological character often used to distinguish tyrannids. The tarsus is generally exaspidean: starting from the forward edge of the tarsus (the acrotarsus) the scales encircle the entire perimeter of the tarsus, leaving only a groove on the rear edge (the sole of the tarsus) too small for one or more lines of scales. *Attila, Casiornis, Rhytipterna,* and *Xenopsaris* are exceptions. The *Rhytipterna* tarsus is extraordinary, resembling that of toucans.

The widespread tendency in this family to have bright red or yellow concentrated on top of the head reaches its extreme in the Royal Flycatcher, *Onychorhynchus coronatus,* which has acquired a formidable crest that is folded and invisible when the bird is at rest. Such crests occur also in the *Lophotriccus.* There are various larger species with bright yellow bellies, such as the *Tyrannus, Tyrannopsis, Conopias, Megarynchus, Myiozetetes,* and *Pitangus.* Smaller species with yellow underparts are found among the *Platyrinchus, Tolmomyias, Todirostrum, Phylloscartes, Pseudocolopteryx, Tachuris,* and *Inezia.* Several species are distinguished by one or two light wing bars, differing in this way from female manakins.

The beautiful red of the Vermilion Flycatcher, *Pyrocephalus rubinus,* is due to the carotenoid cantaxanthin, a lipochrome found in the mushroom *Cantharellus cinnabarinus,* a substance only isolated in 1960 from the feathers of red birds, including the Scarlet Ibis, *Eudocimus ruber,* and Roseate Spoonbill, *Platalea ajaja.* The species with the greatest variety of colors is the Many-colored Rush-Tyrant, *Tachuris rubrigastra,* a wetland bird.

Some species are predominantly white (*Xolmis*) or black (*Knipolegus*). Various color phases or mutations occur in the *Attila,* independent of age, sex, or geographic region. A pattern of transverse barring such as that in *Onychorhynchus coronatus* is rare in Tyrannids. The inside mouth color (gray or orange) of the live bird sometimes facilitates identification of similar species (see *Mionectes*).

Sometimes immatures lack the yellow in the crown that characterizes adults. The immature Variegated Flycatcher, *Empidonomus varius,* resembles the adult Crowned Slaty Flycatcher, *Griseotyrannus aurantioatrocristatus,* but lacks yellow in the crown. The immature of the latter resembles the adult *Empidonomus varius. Tachuris rubrigastra,* the Crested Doradito, *Pseudocolopteryx sclateri,* and the Suiriri Flycatcher, *Suiriri suiriri,* also have different immature plumages.

After breeding the male of the southern population of *Pyrocephalus rubinus* molts to an eclipse plumage, it having arrived in Amazonia by this time (see also Thraupinae, "Morphology," *Cyanerpes*).

Sexes are generally similar, with a few exceptions such as the *Alectrurus, Pyrocephalus rubinus,* and Spectacled Tyrant, *Hymenops perspicillatus,* although sometimes there is sexual dimorphism in one or more species in a genus, as in the *Xolmis, Knipolegus,* and *Fluvicola.* In species with long tails, the male's tail is even longer than the female's, as in *Colonia colonus, Gubernetes yetapa, Tyrannus savana,* and the Shear-tailed Gray-Tyrant, *Muscipipra vetula.*

Among notable points of flycatcher morphology is modification of the flight feathers of various species. There are two categories:

1. The two or three outer primaries are sharply indented toward the tip as in various hawks, apparently improving flight, as with *Tyrannus savana* (fig. 221); the respective tips of the primaries may be soft (White Monjita, *Xolmis irupero*); the transformation normally is more distinct in males and absent in immatures.

2. One or more primaries are profoundly modified in various ways, most pronounced in the *Pachyramphus* (fig. 222). Certainly this relates to sound-producing feathers. The phenomenon is usually confined to males, as in the *Alectrurus, Pachyramphus, Pseudocolopteryx sclateri,* and White-headed Marsh-Tyrant, *Arundinicola leucocephala.* Both sexes of the Amazonian Black-Tyrant, *Knipolegus poecilocercus,* have these sharpened remiges.

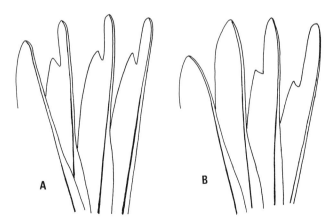

Fig. 221. Fork-tailed Flycatcher, *Tyrannus savana,* male, outer primaries of left wing: (A) *T. s. savana* (Chapada dos Veadeiros, Goiás); (B) *T. s. monachus* (Santarém, Pará).

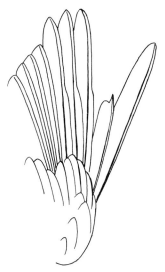

Fig. 222. Sound-producing remige in the left wing of the male Green-backed Becard, *Pachyramphus v. viridis.*

The greatest difficulties in identification are not caused by cases of wide divergence but by the similarity of many species, some of which are not even closely related. Figuring here is the legion of greenish birds, such as the elaenias (*Elaenia* and *Myiopagis*), the *Myiarchus* group, and the considerable number of small birds known in Brazil as *cagasebos,* such as the *Hemitriccus, Phylloscartes,* and *Empidonax.* Sometimes cryptic or twin species occur alongside one another, being sympatric, like the Ochre-bellied Flycatcher, *Mionectes oleagineus,* and McConnell's Flycatcher, *M. macconnelli* (these two are also syntopic and occasionally perch on the same branch); Crested Black-Tyrant, *Knipolegus lophotes,* and Velvety Black-Tyrant, *K. nigerrimus; Tyrannus melancholicus* and White-throated Kingbird, *T. albogularis;* Rusty-margined Flycatcher, *Myiozetetes cayanensis,* and Social Flycatcher, *M. similis;* Sulphur-rumped Flycatcher, *Myiobius barbatus,* and Black-tailed Flycatcher, *M. atricaudus;* and various *Elaenia* and *Myiarchus.* The male *Knipolegus poecilocercus* is extremely similar, by analogy, to the Black Manakin, *Xenopipo atronitens,* which is sometimes its neighbor, whereas the two females are completely different and immediately reveal their family relationships. In the *Myiopagis* (Tyrannidae) both sexes are similar to the *Neopelma,* which I consider to be manakins.

Identification of many tyrannids is possible only by thorough study of color and measurements. In the *Empidonax* group, for instance, the wing formula (relative length of the outer primaries) is decisive and serves even to distinguish geographic races of several species. Museums still have specimens awaiting correct identification. Outstanding among specialists dedicated to tyrannid taxonomy are J. T. Zimmer (deceased), W. E. Lanyon, W. J. Smith, J. W. Fitzpatrick, and M. A. Traylor, the latter with the Field Museum in Chicago, with Traylor responsible for writing up the Tyran-

nidae family for *Peter's Check-list of Birds of the World,* vol. 8 (1979), currently the last word on the matter. At the generic level Traylor used the work of S. L. Warter (1965), who analyzed the skulls of 160 species, including 84 genera, out of 850 tyrannids studied. After Warter the most profound anatomical studies were made by P. L. Ames (1971) and W. E. Lanyon (1978–86). The latter especially studied the *Myiarchus* and *Empidonax,* citing ecological data, with results that have been confirmed by biochemical analyses. It became evident, for example, that the genera *Pitangus, Megarynchus, Myiozetetes, Conopias, Myiodynastes, Legatus, Empidonomus, Tyrannopsis,* and *Tyrannus* are monophyletic. *Sirystes, Machetornis,* and *Muscipipra* were excluded from this complex. Relationships are so often unconvincing when only external morphology is observed, as for example, with *Myiarchus* and *Attila.*

Vocalization, behavior, and breeding (prenuptial displays and nesting) offer data that complement morphology. Vocalizations become the most efficient method for field identification of extremely similar species such as the *Elaenia* and *Myiarchus.*

Certain genera formerly considered cotingids have been included in the tyrannids: *Attila, Casiornis, Laniocera, Rhytipterna, Xenopsaris,* the *Pachyramphus* group (including *Platypsaris*), and *Tityra.* Their syringes and other characters, as well as their ecology, indicate closer relationship to the tyrannids than to the cotingids. For me, knowing these birds in life, it was a relief to remove them from the cotingids, especially considering that their nest types do not occur among cotingids. The *Corythopis,* very peculiar birds, have also been included, having formerly been placed in the Conopophagidae, a family abolished as not constituting a taxonomic unit. The Crested Becard, *Pachyramphus validus* (= *Platypsaris rufus*), has a hidden white patch on the back that it displays spontaneously, like various Formicariidae do, a character foreign to the Tyrannidae.

Sounds

Tyrannids produce strident, harsh cries, low chirpings, and melodious whistles. The Sirystes, *Sirystes sibilator,* and the *Attila* are among the most vigorous screamers in their respective regions, vocalizing untiringly during mating and then becoming as silent as if they had disappeared. Various species, such as the *Myiarchus, Elaenia,* and Southern Beardless-Tyrannulet, *Camptostoma obsoletum,* enjoy a wealth of vocalizations, demonstrating that communication among these birds is primarily acoustic and not visual. The difficulty of transmitting one's knowledge of voices often becomes insuperable when it is impossible to demonstrate with live birds, recordings, or sonagrams. Here I can give only the barest idea.

Mated pairs of the Boat-billed Flycatcher, *Megarynchus pitangua,* and Yellow-bellied Elaenia, *Elaenia flavogaster,* sing duets. Dawn songs of tyrannids are of major interest. Various species, such as the Gray and White-rumped Monjitas, *Xolmis cinerea* and *X. velata,* respectively; Pale-bellied Mourner, *Rhytipterna immunda;* Mouse-colored Tyrannulet, *Phaeomyias murina;* White-winged Becard, *Pachyramphus polychopterus; Tyrannus melancholicus;* and the *Myiarchus* and *Elaenia,* sing by preference or even exclusively at the first light of day and sometimes at dusk with a similar degree of light, during a period of 15 to 30 minutes. As for dusk singing, the Streaked Flycatcher, *Myiodynastes maculatus,* begins to sing on its night perch but sometimes moves as night falls. Identification of these twilight songs is usually a problem, for close approach is difficult in the thick tropical vegetation, birds such as the small *Myiopagis* perch in the upper canopy, and in the dark one cannot see the singer in the foliage. These songs usually comprise the same elements as those sung during daytime, but the combination of phrases and the intensity with which the bird sings (often one phrase following another with little or no pause) may obscure their identity. Lanyon (1978) has produced a key to identify nine South American *Myiarchus* species solely by their dawn songs. At the peak of the breeding period *Xolmis velata* and *Pyrocephalus rubinus* sing in the middle of the night on the perch. The *X. velata* song is extremely simple. It is worth noting that in this family, whose singing is not the best, crepuscular songs have frequently evolved which the birds use to proclaim territory and a disposition to breed. A theory exists that dawn songs are primordial and have phylogenetic significance. The dawn song phenomenon manifests itself in a common name for *Elaenia* species, *Maria-já-é-dia,* "Maria, it's daytime!"

Savanna and wetland species, such as *Tyrannus savana, Hymenops perspicillatus, Pyrocephalus rubinus,* the *Alectrurus,* and certain *Xolmis,* often sing in flight while displaying with special acrobatics designed to enhance the visual impression. There are certain resemblances to voices from other families, as for instance that of *Sirystes sibilator* to cotingids; the Rufous-sided Pygmy-Tyrant, *Euscarthmus rufomarginatus,* and Sooty Tyrannulet, *Serpophaga nigricans,* to furnariids; the Gray-hooded Flycatcher, *Mionectes rufiventris,* to formicariids; and *Rhytipterna immunda* to emberizids. The voice of *Pseudocolopteryx sclateri* is as high as the squeak of a mouse. Sometimes females also sing, their songs being higher and shorter, as in the Bran-colored Flycatcher, *Myiophobus fasciatus.*

Generally there is little geographic variation in tyrannid voices, as I have verified by comparing the voices of individuals living in regions as separated as southern Brazil, Venezuela, and Colombia; one can immediately identify species such as *Myiodynastes maculatus;* the Greenish Elaenia, *Myiopagis viridicata; Myiophobus fasciatus;* and *Elaenia flavogaster.* Sonagrams should reveal any local differences. Many tyrannids sing all year.

There is no shortage of instrumental music in the form of whirring produced by flight feathers. The *Pachyramphus* occasionally produce a short wing noise, *rrra,* when flying from one perch to another in the canopy. Detailed observations on such instrumental music are lacking. Snaps and rattles originate from the bill area, and in the case of *Pitangus sulphuratus* and *Suiriri suiriri* may be quite loud. It appears to me that snapping does not always come simply from the mandibles striking each other but from articulation of the mandibles with the skull, analogous to what I have observed in Old World muscicapids in flight cages where it was possible to see at close range that the snaps were produced when birds opened and closed the bill, not by striking the mandibles together. A *tak* or *tik* indicates nervousness in the Yellow-lored Tody-Flycatcher, *Todirostrum poliocephalum,* when chasing the female. In the *Corythopis* a snap replaces the warning call, whereas in the Serra do Mar Tyrannulet, *Phylloscartes difficilis,* snapping becomes the most frequent form of acoustic communication a restless bird produces while hopping and flying through vegetation in search of prey. The *Corythopis* also snap in flight. The snapping of the *Phylloscartes* is weak, similar to that produced in flight by the rainha-do-coqueiro, or reco-reco, butterfly (*Ageronia,* Nymphallidae), which occurs in the same regions. We must remember the important role of snapping to the White-bearded Manakin, *Manacus manacus,* of a related family, which produces this noise only in connection with prenuptial displays. I do not refer here to snaps that regularly occur when birds catch insects in flight, clicking their mandibles impressively, as in the case of the Cliff Flycatcher, *Hirundinea ferruginea,* that hunts close to my window. Instrumental music occurs in ritual courtship flights of the *Alectrurus* and of *Pseudocolopteryx sclateri.*

Feeding

Food consists primarily of arthropods caught with the tips of the mandibles, apparently without using the bristles around the bill. What could be the function of the very long bristles of *Onychorhynchus coronatus?* The elegance with which small beetles and swarming termites are caught is impressive. The Blue-billed Black-Tyrant, *Knipolegus cyanirostris,* sometimes turns a somersault while catching an insect, then returns to its lookout post. *Tyrannus melancholicus, Empidonomus varius,* and *Griseotyrannus aurantioatrocristatus* fearlessly hunt wasps and bees (both wild, stingless bees, Meliponidae, and domestic ones). It is said that *Suiriri suiriri* and *Pitangus sulphuratus* frequent apiaries only when there are drones, thus becoming friends of the beekeeper. The greater speed and corresponding buzz of worker bees are suggested as the reasons they are less often pursued by birds. It cannot be fear of the sting, for the insect is only swallowed after it is dead or the tip of the abdomen, with the stinger, has been pulled off. It is common to see *Tyrannus albogularis, T. savana,* and *T. melancholicus* hunting small, swarming ants. The *Myiarchus,* kiskadees, kingbirds, and similar species keep watch over leaf-cutter ant hills so they can eat the queens as they come out to establish new nests. *Suiriri suiriri* catches horseflies (Tabanidae), even off the bodies of people working in the open (Santa Catarina). *Megarynchus pitangua* catches large spiders (Nephila) and *Xolmis velata* small ones. The existence in the forest of large spider webs offering an abundant supply of insects leads small tyrannids such as the *Myiornis* to defend such places against other interested parties. The *Platyrinchus* and others occasionally take advantage of army ants as beaters. The Cattle Tyrant, *Machetornis rixosus,* perches on cattle, runs near their mouths while they graze, and like anis, *Crotophaga* spp., catches insects flushed up by these animals. The *Xolmis* are good at hovering, an art perfected by *X. irupero,* which greatly outperforms the American Kestrel, *Falco sparverius. Xolmis cinerea, Tyrannus melancholicus,* and others attend burning fields in the cerrado to catch insects carried by the strong air currents rising above the fire. The *Myiozetetes* and *Pitangus sulphuratus* are nest predators. The kiskadee may tear apart a Bananaquit, *Coereba flaveola,* nest to get at the contents without using the small side entrance. Sometimes it even carries the entire nest away to examine it elsewhere. It may even catch a hummingbird drinking from a bottle; it likes to fish in rivers, lakes, swimming pools, and hatchery tanks; it examines stones in the intertidal areas of the sea to find small crustaceans, and it catches tree frogs. It will perch on a capybara (*Hydrochoerus*), using it to scare up small animals from aquatic vegetation (Mato Grosso, Pantanal). It hunts nocturnal insects that perch during the day near streetlights. One *P. sulphuratus* investigated an air conditioner as a possible source of food, attracted by the machine's noise. To cite one more original source of food for this species, it even inspects offerings to voodoo saints left at night on the streets of Rio de Janeiro. *Megarynchus pitangua* also occasionally indulges fish-catching tendencies. Larger animals captured by tyrannids are beaten against the perch to kill them, or in the case of insects, to break their wings and destroy the stinger. The stomach of a Green-backed Becard, *Pachyramphus viridis,* may be replete with caterpillars.

Food is frequently varied and at times (e.g., with the *Mionectes* and *Elaenia*), predominantly vegetable, involving small fruits like the berries of Loranthaceae, fruits of the sororoca (*Ravenala*), camboatá, etc. I have seen *Myiozetetes cayanensis* regurgitate sticky mistletoe seeds and paste them on a nearby branch, the best place for the seed to germinate later. *Griseotyrannus aurantioatrocristatus* also takes a good number of seeds, among them species of *Maytenus* (Celastraceae). *Tyrannus savana* likes blackberries, and *Pitangus sulphuratus* uses fruits of the African dendê palm (*Elaeis guineensis,* Pernambuco). Tyrannids regurgitate pellets containing chitin, seeds, and pieces of fruit skin. The Piratic Flycatcher, *Legatus leucophaius,* is frugivorous.

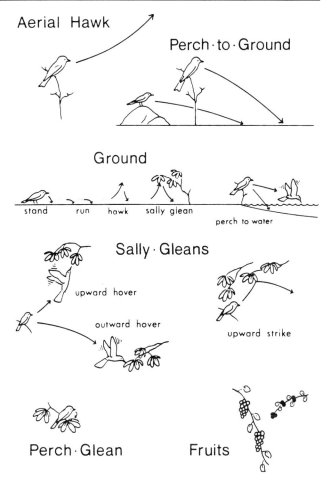

Fig. 223. Important prey-capture techniques used by tyrant flycatchers. Each capture is preceded by a stationary search period on the perch. After Fitzpatrick 1980a.

Various species use bananinhas-da-mata (*Heliconia*) fruits. Diet changes in the winter: insectivorous species become frugivorous. Analyzing 94 tyrannid species (25% of the family) Fitzpatrick (1980a, 1985) defined the principal foraging modes and developed a standardized nomenclature (fig. 223). The result is a unique catalogue recording the foraging behavior of these birds, with material sufficient even to confirm relationships of the taxa and their systematic position.

Behavior

Tyrannids generally perch erectly, like cotingids. Nervousness is frequently revealed by brusque wing movements. This behavior, at times accompanied by similar tail movements, as in *Onychorhynchus coronatus,* may be only sketchy but in some cases is highly developed. The Sepia-capped Flycatcher, *Leptopogon amaurocephalus,* for instance, fully stretches just one wing vertically and stays in this position for an instant, recalling the Red-headed Manakin, *Pipra rubrocapilla. Mionectes oleagineus* raises its wings alternately. The Ruddy-tailed Flycatcher, *Tereno-*

triccus erythrurus, rapidly lifts both wings at the same time. The *Attila* make brusque tail movements. The exceptional nervousness of the *Myiobius,* especially their way of spreading the tail, is reminiscent of the American Redstart, *Setophaga ruticilla.* The habits of the *Muscisaxicola* (constant tail movements while on the ground) much resemble those of the European wheatears, *Oenanthe* spp. (Muscicapidae), in a corresponding environment.

Onychorhynchus coronatus reacts in a unique fashion when it wants to intimidate enemies: it moves its head slowly from side to side with its fanlike crest open, like certain cockatoos with large crests which they also spread under similar circumstances. This frightening effect recalls the snake display, another strange ceremony of certain birds such as the young Striped Cuckoo, *Tapera naevia.* It is especially interesting that *O. coronatus* moves its head sideways, not toward the spectator (the presumed danger) like many tyrannids and other birds that move the head or crest in defense. Doubtless this display evolved to attract the opposite sex—an epigamic function—and only reappears in agonistic situations involving maximum agitation.

Tyrannids like to bathe in the rain or on wet foliage. Anting, the use of ants in bodily hygiene, has been observed with *Mionectes oleagineus* (see also Dendrocolaptidae and Emberizinae, "Behavior"). When two *Suiriri suiriri* chase a vulture feather falling from the sky it must be more play (perhaps mixed with a bit of fear of a large, black bird) than agonistic behavior. Certain forest tyrannids accompany mixed flocks of antbirds, tanagers, spinetails, etc. I have noted this with the *Myiobius, Mionectes,* and *Pachyramphus.*

In central Brazil (Mato Grosso) and the northeast (Piauí) I have recorded tyrannid movements arising from their custom of sleeping in groups or of looking for a sheltered place to spend the night. *Tyrannus savana* along Rio das Mortes, Mato Grosso, continues to frequent collective roosts even after it has established a nesting territory and laid eggs; one of a pair, the female, stays at the nest, a situation resembling that of certain parrots (*Amazona*). The flock gathering to sleep is composed partly of outside migrants traveling to more southerly regions, such as Argentina, where they breed (see "Migration"). In the Serra Roncador region of Mato Grosso in August–September, *Tyrannus melancholicus* regularly flies high between open cerrado, where it feeds during the day, and dense riverine forest 6 or more km away, where it sleeps; it is not gregarious like *T. savana.* I have noted a nervousness at dusk in certain species, *Myiozetetes cayanensis,* for instance.

Tyrannids are often quarrelsome. A *Tyrannus melancholicus* or *T. savana,* for instance, will attack any bird, even a vulture, overflying its territory, or a person approaching its nest, exercising its role of small tyrant. The alarms of *T. melancholicus* and of *Pitangus sulphuratus* immediately attract the attention of all birds in the area to the appearance of a hawk or, if not common in the area, a Guira Cuckoo, *Guira guira,* or even an escaped cage bird when it is a species unknown in the region. Several *P. sulphuratus* will immediately gather and assume a menacing attitude toward the stranger, a fact that illustrates a facet of the problem of liberating cage birds without careful previous consideration.

Even *Pitangus sulphuratus* is sometimes attacked by weaker tyrannids such as the Masked Water-Tyrant, *Fluvicola nengeta,* or *Tyrannus savana.* The predatory habits of *P. sulphuratus* are well known (see "Feeding"). It steals material from the nests of other birds, especially *Coereba flaveola.* One kiskadee tore up the entire nest of a Common Waxbill, *Estrilda astrild,* and another took a *Todirostrum* nest and used the material for its own structure. The colorful black-and-white plumage and erratic flight of *Xolmis cinerea* irritate *Tyrannus melancholicus* and *Pyrocephalus rubinus,* which pursue it exactly as if it were a bird of prey. Such competition does not stop *Pitangus sulphuratus* and *Myiozetetes cayanensis,* for instance, from coexisting peacefully in foraging, bathing, etc. A *P. sulphuratus* nested amidst a colony of House Sparrows, *Passer domesticus,* in a jar in the gardens of the National Museum in Rio de Janeiro.

The generalized use of mercury lamps for street lighting has caused various insectivorous birds to extend their foraging time into the night hours. It is logical that this custom would manifest itself first in synanthropic species, such as, among tyrannids, *Pitangus sulphuratus, Tyrannus melancholicus, T. savana,* and *Hirundinea ferruginea.* The first such observations were for hummingbirds. Other synanthropic tyrannids are *Myiophobus fasciatus* and *Todirostrum poliocephalum.*

Association with Icterines

On the association of *Legatus leucophaius* with icterines and some other builders of bag-shaped nests, see "Breeding" (see also *Conopias*). A unique association also exists between the Black-and-white Monjita, *Heteroxolmis dominicana,* and Saffron-cowled Blackbird, *Xanthopsar flavus.*

Breeding

Tyrannids provide one of the best examples of why more than 92% of all birds are monogamous and insectivorous (Lack 1968): it is advantageous for both parents to feed the young and defend a common territory.

During courtship tyrannids perform characteristic displays. The peak epigamic performance is display of the fan of *Onychorhynchus coronatus,* which I have described under "Behavior" because its agonistic function is much more easily observed. Open-country species make flights during which they sing, as with the White-winged Black-Tyrant, *Knipolegus aterrimus; K. lophotes; Hymenops perspicillatus* (fig. 224); and *Pyrocephalus rubinus. Tyrannus albogularis*

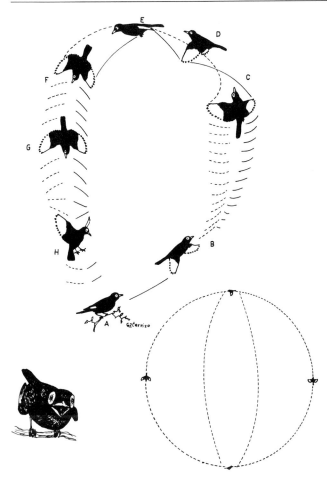

Fig. 224. Spectacled Tyrant, *Hymenops perspicillatus,* territorial flight. After Straneck and Carrizo 1983.

has a slow display flight with accelerated wing beats, resembling the famous song flight of the Eurasian Skylark, *Alauda arvensis,* of Europe. The male *Fluvicola pica* makes ascending flights and chases the female in zigzags.

Tyrant-flycatchers perform open-wing displays. *Fluvicola nengeta,* perched on a water-lily leaf or among water ferns, stretches and opens both wings laterally to display their black undersides frontward—an exhibitionist pose in the presence of the female. *Myiornis ecaudatus* has a similar display. The Yellow-olive Flycatcher, *Tolmomyias sulphurescens,* stands trembling with the wings stretched. The Campos Suiriri, *Suiriri suiriri affinis,* holds both wings vertically when it sings. The Common Tody-Flycatcher, *Todirostrum cinereum,* wiggles its short, narrow tail sideways when it chases the female. The numerous species with bright color more or less hidden in the center of the crown, such as *Pitangus sulphuratus,* display this ornament by ruffling these feathers, a unique spectacle with *Onychorhynchus coronatus.* Various tyrannids engage in behavior resembling the displays of lek birds such as the Pipridae and Cotingidae. For example, the Tropical Pewee, *Contopus cinereus,* jumps in solitary action. The Yellow Tyrannulet, *Capsiempis flaveola;* Planalto Tyran-

nulet, *Phyllomyias fasciatus;* the *Myiobius* and *Mionectes,* and others perform group displays and chases very similar to those of cotingids and manakins. Observing these may lead to more accurate conclusions on evolution of the complicated manakin behavior that has resulted in total emancipation of the females.

Mionectes males remain for long periods on certain branches—display grounds—where they sing intensely, agitate the wings, and ruffle the crown, typical irritation for lek birds. The females care for the young alone. It has even been suggested that a *Mionectes* female would drive the male away from the nest to prevent him from competing in foraging. This behavior leads to promiscuity (Willis et al. 1978).

The two *Alectrurus,* with their grotesque tails, make impressive display flights (the acoustic aspect is insignificant) and are suspected of being polygamous. Such extravagance occurs in male versus male competition, as in the birds of paradise of Australasia, but also in wetland birds of our hemisphere (Orians 1980).

Tyrannid nesting is a subject that would fill a voluminous book. The nesting pattern becomes important even in systematics: as in separating genera (e.g., Lesser Kiskadee, *Philohydor lictor*). Pairs usually build together. The male sometimes carries food to the female as a prelude to copulation, as I have seen in *Pyrocephalus rubinus.* The male generally does not participate in brooding. For exceptions see "Eggs . . . ."

There are five basic types of nest in this family:

1. Open saucer, basket, or cup-shaped nests with various finishes are made by *Knipolegus cyanirostris; Pyrocephalus rubinus; Contopus cinereus; Megarynchus pitangua;* White-throated Spadebill, *Platyrinchus mystaceus;* Tawny-crowned Pygmy-Tyrant, *Euscarthmus meloryphus;* Sharp-tailed Grass-Tyrant, *Culicivora caudacuta;* White-crested Tyrannulet, *Serpophaga subcristata;* White-naped Xenopsaris, *Xenopsaris albinucha; Suiriri suiriri;* the *Tyrannus* and *Empidonomus;* and some *Xolmis.* Among the best-constructed nests of this type are those of the *Elaenia* and of *Tachuris rubrigastra.* Whereas *Elaenia* nests, carefully covered with pasted lichens (a technique like that of hummingbirds), are firmly placed on a branch, the *T. rubrigastra* nest is a tiny cup with quite a long lower section attached to a reed swaying over the water. *Tachuris* employs wet materials (pieces of reed leaf) which, after drying, become as hard as cardboard, a great "invention" that reduces the danger of the structure coming apart on such an insecure base as a reed stalk in constant motion. A similar technique is used by the Wren-like Rushbird, *Phleocryptes melanops.*

Platyrinchus mystaceus, one of the smallest forest interior species, builds a deep basket with "vegetable horsehair" (*Marasmius* sp., a fungus, see Icterinae, "Breeding") and uses a good amount of spider web and dry bamboo leaves to make a homogeneous cap extending around the nest and to wrap firmly the branch holding the nest.

Fig. 225. Cliff Flycatcher, *Hirundinea ferruginea*, start of nest construction on a church console; the bird brings rock chips which it arranges in a circle of the same circumference as the future nest. Only afterwards does it begin to bring straw, etc. Limoeiro, Espírito Santo, November 1940. Original, H. Sick.

Among poorly built nests are those of *Empidonomus varius*, which comes apart with the slightest pressure, like doves' nests, and of *Tyrannus savana:* a badly built small cup placed near the tips of branches from where it is frequently torn by the wind. In one case the bird voided mistletoe seeds into the nest; by fortunate coincidence they glued the loose material together and soon sprouted.

Hirundinea ferruginea, which nests on rocks or on stone or cement buildings (in cities on building facades alongside an air conditioner or such), gathers pieces of decomposing rock (fig. 225) on which it makes a shallow cup of roots and straw held together with saliva.

One of the most common small forest species, Euler's Flycatcher, *Lathrotriccus euleri,* makes a deep saucer on a stump ¹/₂ m above ground in the forest. *Xolmis cinerea,* a savana species, sometimes places its saucer on top of the nest of a Firewood Gatherer, *Anumbius annumbi,* a good solution in open country where there are few trees on which to build.

2. Spherical nests with side entrances, firmly placed on branches, are built by *Pitangus sulphuratus,* the *Myiozetetes,* and *Camptostoma obsoletum.* The *Corythopis* make a small "oven" of moss on the ground.

There is some variation, both individual and regional, in the construction of these nests, as with *Pitangus sulphuratus* and *Myiozetetes similis,* which frequently rob material from one another. The former builds its soccer-ball-sized nest in the fork of a branch in open places such as trees with sparse foliage, using dry grass, vegetable wool, etc. The chamber, placed in the center, has a wide entrance (8 cm in diameter) protected by a slight overhang. Sometimes an outer layer of sticks is added to the usual ball of soft material (Mato Grosso). The roof is built last. I saw a *P. sulphuratus* install itself in the walls of the colossal nest of a Jabiru, *Jabiru mycteria,* which was in the only tree in a vast surrounding area in the Pantanal (Mato Grosso). It is interesting that *P. sulphuratus* is content to build only an open saucer if it is in a sheltered place, as among the bases of palm leaves.

The *Pachyramphus* becards build a large ball of moss and other soft materials high in a tree. The nest has a protected

side entrance and a small incubation chamber in the upper part. The *P. validus* nest is usually pendant and not firmly seated as with other *Pachyramphus;* all of them like to build in isolated trees (compare the Icterinae). The *Fluvicola* build on branches over water in marshes.

3. Enclosed, bag-shaped, hanging nests with a side entrance protected by a porch roof are built by the Helmeted Pygmy-Tyrant, *Lophotriccus galeatus; Terenotriccus erythrurus;* and the *Myiornis, Todirostrum,* and several *Hemitriccus. Tolmomyias sulphurescens* builds a long, narrow structure of black, shiny vegetable horsehair and similar material suspended from a branch. It is composed of three parts: the roof, the chamber in the form of a bag, and for an entrance a perpendicular chimney pointed downward (fig. 226). There is a certain amount of variation in the construction. The nest of the Olivaceous Flatbill, *Rhynchocyclus olivaceus,* is also a long bag, perhaps suspended over a trail in the woods and appearing as a larger edition of the *T. sulphurescens* structure. Frequently two or three are nearby, the latest nest and earlier ones.

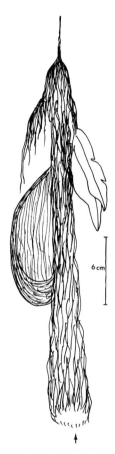

6 cm

Fig. 226. Sketch of Yellow-olive Flycatcher, *Tolmomyias sulphurescens,* nest. The entrance is underneath, through the hanging sleeve. The principal materials are thin vines and "vegetable horsehair." Upper Xingu, Mato Grosso, November 1947. Original, H. Sick.

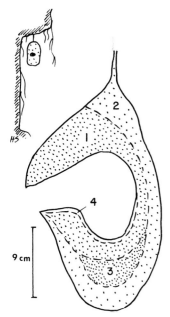

Fig. 227. Nest of Sepia-capped Flycatcher, *Leptopogon a. amaurocephalus.* Four kinds of material can be seen: (1) soft, fresh moss and some silky seeds; (2) dry moss and some seeds, making up the surface of the nest; (3) woolly seeds and fibers, worked like felt and forming a hard mass; and (4) a layer of soft fibers. Ilha Grande, Rio de Janeiro, May 1944. Original, H. Sick.

Such nests may look like those of icterines, but the material is more glued together than woven. In further contrast to the architecture of icterine hanging nests, the branch holding a tyrannid nest is built into the wall as far as the middle of the nest, giving it greater stability against swaying. When the nest is ready, the owner arrives and leaves so fast that its identification becomes a bit difficult; it never again clings to the outside of the nest.

I found that *Leptopogon amaurocephalus* works for more than a month on its oval, compact nest with a small side entrance (fig. 227). This is firmly lined with moss and vegetable wool in four easily observed layers—an "artistic" structure hanging on a root below the undercut of an embankment or other place protected from rain. The *Mionectes* and others build on branches over forest streams.

The large hanging nests of *Myiobius* and *Onychorhynchus coronatus* may appear at first glance to be heaps of dead leaves caught in large spider webs or between branches and vines, this to some degree being a protective camouflage against predators.

The nests of species such as the *Tyrannus, Myiozetetes, Pachyramphus, Rhynchocyclus,* and *Tolmomyias sulphurescens* are often found near wasp nests (e.g., of the genus *Chartergus*) or in trees full of ants, thereby better guaranteeing their safety. There is no doubt that birds assiduously seek these places, for nests of more than one species often appear in the vicinity. In Suriname, of 54 Yellow-breasted Flycatcher, *Tolmomyias flaviventris,* nests, 41 (76%) were near wasp nests (Haverschmidt 1974).

4. A few species, such as *Colonia colonus, Myiodynastes maculatus,* and the *Tityra, Myiarchus,* and *Ramphotrigon,* nest in holes or cavities. They build a true nest with ample material inside the hole. All occasionally install themselves in holes made by woodpeckers. Generally *Myiodynastes maculatus* and the *Myiarchus* occupy cavities with a wide entrance. *Myiodynastes maculatus* sometimes nests on a stump without protection above, but it also nests in holes in the walls of houses and under tile roofs. Curiously, *Colonia colonus,* one of the species with the longest tail, seeks a tight hole for breeding. The Rufous Casiornis, *Casiornis rufa,* which was transferred from the cotingids to the tyrannids, also nests in tree holes. The same is true for *Sirystes sibilator* and apparently for the Grayish Mourner, *Rhytipterna simplex.* The Gray-hooded Attila, *Attila rufus,* uses cavities in embankments, tree trunks, and tree ferns. The *Tityra* nest in abandoned woodpecker holes and in holes in the tops of dead palms, lining the cavity with dry material.

A tendency toward hole nesting is evident in *Serpophaga nigricans* and *Knipolegus lophotes,* which build under embankments and bridges in places that are well protected overhead and consequently dark. *Knipolegus nigerrimus* nests in burrows among rocks near streams. *Machetornis rixosus* also prefers protected places for nesting (e.g., among the bases of palm fronds or in any hole) and sometimes occupies nests of *Furnarius, Anumbius, Phacellodomus,* and woodpeckers, contenting itself with an abandoned one. *Xolmis irupero* has similar requirements: it uses, for instance, nests of the Chotoy Spinetail, *Synallaxis phryganophila,* or Firewood Gatherer, *Anumbius annumbi,* or simply the hollow trunks of palms. I have found *Xolmis velata* in the nest antechamber of a Common Thornbird, *Phacellodomus rufifrons,* and in a hole in a terrestrial termite nest made by a Field Flicker, *Colaptes campestris* (Minas Gerais).

5. Nest parasitism. *Legatus leucophaius* is a special case, occupying nests of various birds that build enclosed structures, preferably the hanging bag nests of the *Cacicus,* both those that gather in colonies and those nesting alone, such as the Golden-winged Cacique, *Cacicus chrysopterus.* It takes over the large globular nests of the *Myiozetetes* and *Pachyramphus* and the hanging nests of small tyrannids such as the *Tolmomyias.* It expels the owner, even if it is brooding, and throws out the eggs. Then it brings in some, sometimes many, dry leaves on which it lays its own eggs and broods them normally. Its impertinence sometimes forces a whole colony of Yellow-rumped Caciques, *Cacicus cela,* to abandon their nests (fig. 228). Nest parasitism might be called kleptoparasitism. It is always a single pair of *Legatus leucophaius* that installs itself in one of these colonies. The Three-striped Flycatcher, *Conopias trivirgata,* also associates with icterines. I have seen a *Pachyramphus polychopterus* occupy the nest of a *Myiozetetes similis.*

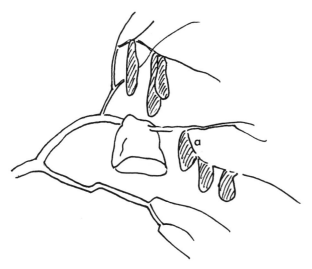

Fig. 228. A small Yellow-rumped Cacique, *Cacicus cela,* colony alongside a wasp nest. A Piratic Flycatcher, *Legatus leucophaius,* molested all these nests and finally occupied nest "a." The colony was abandoned by the caciques. Upper Xingo, Mato Grosso, 1947. Original, H. Sick.

Eggs, Incubation, and Parasitism

Oology can be of service in classifying the Tyrannidae (Schönwetter 1979). For example, it permits delimitation of the genera. The great similarity between the eggs of the *Myiodynastes* and of *Attila rufus* is interesting and an impressive corroboration of the correctness of including the *Attila* in the Tyrannidae. When *Attila* was still considered a cotingid, the color of its eggs was always a problem. Many species with closed nests, such as *Onychorhynchus coronatus* and *Legatus leucophaius,* have colored eggs, demonstrating their descent from ancestors with open nests. This also applies to *Pachyramphus* and *Tityra.* Incubation, carried out solely by the female, takes 14 days for *Myiozetetes cayanensis,* 14 to 15 days for *Pitangus sulphuratus,* 17 to 19 days for *Tolmomyias sulphurescens,* 19 to 21 days for *Mionectes oleagineus,* and 18 to 19 days for *Pachyramphus polychopterus.* The brood patch is usually restricted to females. However, Davis (1945b), working in the Teresópolis region, Rio de Janeiro, listed four tyrannids on which he found male brood patches: *Myiodynastes maculatus; Lathrotriccus euleri;* Gray-capped Tyrannulet, *Phyllomyias griseocapilla;* and Black-tailed Tityra, *Tityra cayana,* emphasizing that both the male and female *Tityra* were observed incubating.

Pachyramphus nestlings become noisy and "sing" like their parents in the nest. A *Pitangus sulphuratus* with young was observed also feeding the young of a neighboring *Myiozetetes similis. Fluvicola* have been seen protecting the nest by feigning. *Tolmomyias sulphurescens* nestlings fledge after 22 to 24 days, those of *Pitangus sulphuratus* after 25 to 26 days. The Masked Tityra, *Tityra semifasciata,* may rear three or even five young (Mato Grosso). *Myiozetetes* and

Pitangus nestlings are frequently infested with shade-loving fly larvae that later retreat to the bottom of the large nest to pupate.

A minuscule Ochre-faced Tody-Flycatcher, *Todirostrum plumbeiceps,* was seen rearing a young Pavonine Cuckoo, *Dromococcyx pavoninus,* the adult of which weighs eight times more than the tody-flycatcher. *Myiornis* and *Hemitriccus* also foster *Dromococcyx* young. *Xolmis cinerea, Arundinicola leucocephala, Serpophaga nigricans,* and other tyrannids are sometimes molested by the Shiny Cowbird, *Molothrus bonariensis.*

Habitat, Numbers, Distribution, and Evolution

Tyrannids occupy every type of Brazilian habitat. The majority are arboreal and live in forests, each species adapting to a certain environment it shares with other tyrannid species. Competition is reduced by differences in species size, food needs (requiring different bill shapes), hunting techniques, size of insect prey, feeding and nesting heights, territory size, and preferences as to vegetation density. The great variety of ecological niches in Neotropical forests is highly advantageous to insectivorous birds such as tyrannids and formicariids.

We are indebted to Traylor and Fitzpatrick (1982) for an exhaustive ecological analysis of the tyrannids, resulting in the illustration reproduced here (fig. 229) that demonstrates this complicated situation in the most understandable form,

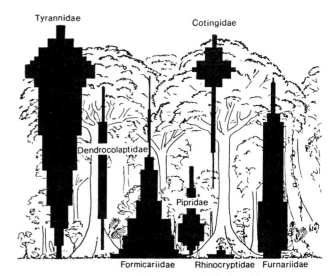

Fig. 229. Relative densities and ecological positions among the six principal non-Oscine families in the Neotropical rain forest. Overall relative diversity for each family at each forest layer is indexed by the horizontal width of the black bar. Note that Tyrannidae is the only family represented at all heights, including the aerial feeding zone above the canopy. Flycatchers are least diverse at the forest floor and increase steadily toward the canopy. After Traylor and Fitzpatrick 1982.

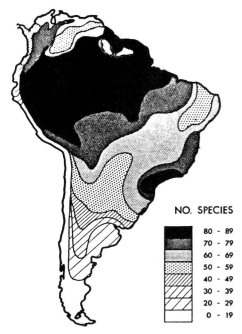

Fig. 230. Species density isoclines of breeding Tyrannidae in South America. After Fitzpatrick 1980b.

NO. SPECIES

80 - 89
70 - 79
60 - 69
50 - 59
40 - 49
30 - 39
20 - 29
0 - 19

with the tyrannids alongside the other principal non-Oscine families: Furnariidae, Dendrocolaptidae, Formicariidae, Rhinocryptidae, Cotingidae, and Pipridae.

The Tyrannidae are the only family represented at all forest levels, including an area above the treetops where they capture insects. Only one forest genus is terrestrial, *Corythopis,* but there are terrestrial savanna genera, such as *Muscisaxicola* and *Lessonia.*

Fitzpatrick's range map (fig. 230) shows how the largest concentration of Tyrannidae (89 species), in the center of Amazonia, has an equivalent (80 species) in the humid forests of southeastern Brazil where some Amazonian elements, such as the Cinereous Mourner, *Laniocera hypopyrrha,* recall ancient links with the Hylaea through a series of Atlantic coastal forests that are either residual or gone today.

When indexes of density and frequency, indicators of abundance, are calculated, *Mionectes oleagineus* is one of the most common birds after the Wedge-billed Woodcreeper, *Glyphorynchus spirurus,* and Plain-throated Antwren, *Myrmotherula hauxwelli,* in várzea forest of the lower Amazon (Novaes 1970). Certain tyrannid species, such as *Onychorhynchus coronatus,* have a low population density, as I have verified both in the south and in Amazonia.

Some, such as *Pitangus sulphuratus* and *Tyrannus melancholicus,* invade towns and cities by using urban trees and are among the most common birds in metropolitan centers such as Rio de Janeiro.

The cerrado, a special category of climax woodland whose avifauna is still insufficiently investigated, is rich in flycatchers (see Fry 1970). The slender *Culicivora caudacuta* is a campo cerrado endemic. It is noteworthy that another

long-tailed species, the Rufous-sided Pygmy-Tyrant, *Euscarthmus rufomarginatus* (like *C. caudacuta,* resembling a savanna furnariid), which inhabits even more open cerrado, reappears in savannas north of the Hylaea. This shows that the development of Amazonia is relatively recent and that it cut up the ancient, vast savanna region of the continental interior, dividing it into areas that are today disjunct.

In the arid diagonal, the large savanna area that separates the Hylaea from the Atlantic forest, Fluvicolinae such as *Xolmis irupero* and the Greater Wagtail-Tyrant, *Stigmatura budytoides,* each with subspecies, connect the Brazilian northeast with the Paraguayan chaco. Fitzpatrick (1980b) draws attention to "pairs" of species, such as the Graybacked Tachuri, *Polystictus superciliaris* (north) and Bearded Tachuri, *P. pectoralis* (south), that evolved in this area (fig. 231).

In Brazil there is less variation in savanna tyrannids than farther south in the continent or in the Andes, and I have observed the same with furnariids. Rarely have both savanna and forest species evolved in one genus, as in the *Knipolegus: K. lophotes* is one of the few tyrannids resident in high-altitude campos of the southeastern mountains; the Blue-billed Black-Tyrant, *K. cyanirostris,* lives in adjacent forests. The only Brazilian tyrannid adapted to life on rocks is *Hirundinea ferruginea.* It finds an ecological substitute in cities where it nests on the sides of buildings.

The *Fluvicola, Gubernetes,* and *Alectrurus* occur in riverine and marshy regions. A group of terrestrial species, *Muscisaxicola* and *Ochthornis,* resemble the pipits (*Anthus*), certain furnariids, and the *Oenanthe* of the Old World: they run on the ground, frequently fan their tails momentarily, and fly like swallows. They are widely distributed in the Andes and the south but penetrate only into southern and western Brazil. The Austral Negrito, *Lessonia rufa,* is a southern terrestrial marshland species. Some, such as the *Pseudocolopteryx* and *Tachuris rubrigastra,* live hidden in marshes.

Migration

Among Suboscines the tyrannids move about freely. Many species from southern Brazil and the mountainous regions of Rio de Janeiro and Espírito Santo migrate in the winter, a fact to which vernacular bird names such as *primavera* ["spring"] and "verão" ["summer"] refer; these species remain in their breeding areas only during the hotter months. Included in this group are *Xolmis, Colonia, Hymenops, Pyrocephalus, Machetornis, Sirystes, Tyrannus melancholicus, T. savana, Empidonomus, Megarynchus, Myiodynastes, Pitangus, Casiornis, Myiarchus,* and *Elaenia.* Migration is not always easy to understand, for two reasons: (1) all members of a population do not always migrate, and (2) individuals that breed only in the summer in southern regions invade tropical regions, where northern populations of the same species reside, during their March to September nonbreeding period.

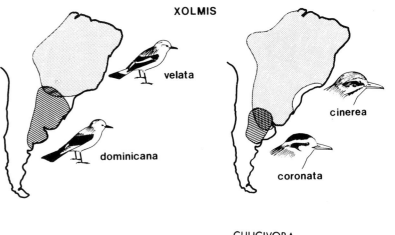

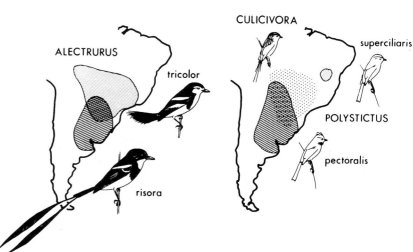

Fig. 231. Distribution of four pairs of species of savanna tyrannids. The overlapping of the ranges of three pairs is interpreted as secondary. The genera *Culicivora* (one species) and *Polystictus* (two species) are closely related. *Culicivora*, of more ancient origin, now separates the ranges of the two *Polystictus*. Isolated populations of *Xolmis cinerea* and *Polystictus pectoralis* exist farther north. Fitzpatrick 1980b; after Haffer 1987a.

Thus, there is a periodic, puzzling superimposition of various populations that can sometimes be deciphered by recognition of the various geographic races, such as those of *Tyrannus savana,* one of the most important migratory species.

Subtropical migratory populations of *Tyrannus melancholicus* and *Empidonomus varius* have more sharply pointed wings, interpreted as an adaptation for long-distance flights, unlike populations that live in the tropics, undertake little or no migration, and have more rounded wings. Such modification of the wing formula also occurs in the White-crested Elaenia, *Elaenia albiceps chilensis,* from Patagonia and Chile, which emigrates to Amazonia: it has a sharp-pointed wing, with the tenth (outermost) primary usually longer than the fifth. In Andean races that do not migrate, the tenth is shorter than the fifth. *E. a. chilensis* appears abundantly in the Municipality of Rio de Janeiro and in Itatiaia, Rio de Janeiro, in March and April, then disappears completely. One individual was even found on the high seas, 100 km off the coast of Rio Grande do Sul, in April. The Lesser Elaenia, *E. chiriquensis,* becomes the most abundant bird in the Mato Grosso cerrado in August–September while en route from the west. The Plain-crested Elaenia, *E. cristata,*

appears there at the same time, migrating in the same direction but in lesser numbers. As a result of these migrations the species involved have enormous distribution ranges that are only in part breeding areas, as in the case of some swallows. Southern populations (Argentina to São Paulo) of Swainson's Flycatcher, *Myiarchus s. swainsoni,* migrate as far as Suriname. *Tyrannus savana* and *Myiodynastes maculatus* resident in central Brazil migrate with a timing very similar to that of populations resident in extreme southern Brazil: they arrive in the local spring, nest, and disappear at the end of summer. It is interesting to note the impressive punctuality in arrival and departure dates of the migratory birds in our gardens (see *Tyrannus melancholicus*).

Some southern migrants reach only extreme southern or western Brazil during the southern winter: the Chocolate-vented Tyrant, *Neoxolmis rufiventris;* Black-crowned Monjita, *Xolmis coronata;* and *Lessonia rufa* are terrestrial savanna/riverine species typical of the Patagonian-Andean region. Everything leads me to believe that Hudson's Black-Tyrant, *Knipolegus hudsoni,* and *Elaenia albiceps,* also southern elements, are in Brazil only on migration, with the latter continuing north beyond the equator. These small tyrannids migrate at night. Because of the lack of banded individuals it is not clear whether visitors such as *Serpophaga subcristata* and the Rough-legged Tyrannulet, *Phyllomyias burmeisteri,* which I find annually in winter in Rio de Janeiro, have come from the south or have descended from the neighboring Serra do Mar, in the latter case performing a vertical migration such as that made by *Knipolegus nigerrimus* in Itatiaia, Rio de Janeiro.

Davis (1945a) noted that certain species such as *Lathrotriccus euleri; Attila rufus;* the Black-goggled Tanager, *Trichothraupis melanops;* and Uniform Finch, *Haplospiza unicolor,* are absent or present only in reduced numbers in winter in Teresópolis, Rio de Janeiro (900 m), but the supposition that they descend to the lowlands at this season still lacks proof.

A *Pitangus sulphuratus* banded in Argentina was recovered in Brazil. Migrants from the north also come to Brazil in small numbers during the northern winter: the Eastern Kingbird, *Tyrannus tyrannus;* Gray Kingbird, *T. dominicensis;* Olive-sided Flycatcher, *Contopus borealis;* Eastern Wood-Pewee, *C. virens;* and Willow Flycatcher, *Empidonax traillii,* all from North America, have been recorded in Amazonia and central Brazil in September, November, February, and March.

It is amusing to realize that hot-climate tyrannids that over the centuries conquered North America periodically return to the continent where they originated millions of years ago in search of warm weather.

The wide wanderings of tyrannids have led to colonization even of Fernando da Noronha: the Large Elaenia, *Elaenia spectabilis ridleyana,* is one of three landbirds living on that island 400 km away from the continent; see also Noronha Vireo, *Vireo gracilirostris* (Vireonidae), and Eared Dove, *Zenaida auriculata* (Columbidae). A *Tachuris rubrigastra* and a *Pyrocephalus rubinus* have been found on the high seas, 92 and 135 miles respectively, off the coast of Rio Grande do Sul.

On the subject of daily movements related to collective roosts and membership in mixed flocks, see "Behavior."

Perils and Parasites

In Espírito Santo I saw a Red-breasted Toucan, *Ramphastos dicolorus,* attack a *Pitangus sulphuratus* nest. It began by tearing out large pieces of material from the side opposite the entrance. Afterwards it hopped around the nest, and by tearing out material from the front it soon penetrated the chamber and took out a fully feathered chick. It carried the chick in its bill, with difficulty, to a distant perch and dismembered it.

I know of two carefully documented cases where *Leptodactylus* frogs captured good-sized birds (see also Turdidae, "Popularity . . ."). A *Leptodactylus ocellatus,* a relatively small species, caught a *Pitangus sulphuratus* by the legs when the bird flew close to the water surface in search of

minnows. The frog did not manage to pull the bird underwater, and the bird's cries attracted a human who saved it. The technique of a frog overcoming a large victim by drowning it recalls that of the anaconda (*Eunectes murinus*), which I observed in Central Brazil.

Nematode worms have been found living under the eyelids of *Tityra cayana.*

Synopsis of Brazilian Tyrannidae Subfamilies
(Classification of M. A. Traylor 1977, 1979)

Traylor tried to establish a phylogenetic sequence, moving from the most generalized or primitive forms to those more specialized or evolved. There follows a full list of genera recorded for Brazil, with some synonyms. In the following text I frequently give only the species' name and distribution, to help those wanting to find such birds in more specialized literature or in books on birds of neighboring countries, especially for Amazonia.

Subfamily Elaeniinae

Phyllomyias (includes *Oreotriccus, Xanthomyias,* and *Acrochordopus*), *Zimmerius* (includes *Tyranniscus*), *Ornithion, Camptostoma, Phaeomyias, Sublegatus, Suiriri, Tyrannulus, Myiopagis, Elaenia, Mecocerculus, Serpophaga, Inezia, Stigmatura, Tachuris, Culicivora, Polystictus* (includes *Habrura*), *Pseudocolopteryx, Euscarthmus, Mionectes* (includes *Pipromorpha*), *Leptopogon, Phylloscartes* (includes *Pogonotriccus* and *Leptotriccus*), *Capsiempis, Corythopis, Myiornis, Lophotriccus* (includes *Colopteryx*), *Poecilotriccus* (includes *Taeniotriccus*), *Hemitriccus* (includes *Idioptilon* and the subgenera *Snethlagea, Microcochlearius,* and *Ceratotriccus*), *Todirostrum, Cnipodectes, Ramphotrigon, Rhynchocyclus, Tolmomyias,* and *Platyrinchus.*

Subfamily Fluvicolinae

Onychorhynchus, Terenotriccus, Myiobius, Myiophobus, Contopus (includes *Nuttallornis*), *Empidonax, Lathrotriccus, Cnemotriccus, Pyrocephalus, Ochthornis, Xolmis, Neoxolmis, Heteroxolmis, Muscisaxicola, Lessonia, Knipolegus* (includes *Phaeotriccus* and *Entotriccus*), *Hymenops, Fluvicola, Arundinicola, Colonia, Alectrurus* (includes *Yetapa*), *Gubernetes, Satrapa, Hirundinea, Machetornis,* and *Muscipipra.*

Subfamily Tyranninae

Attila (includes *Pseudattila*), *Casiornis, Rhytipterna, Laniocera, Sirystes, Myiarchus, Pitangus, Philohydor, Megarynchus, Myiozetetes, Conopias, Myiodynastes, Legatus, Empidonomus, Griseotyrannus, Tyrannopsis, Tyrannus* (includes *Muscivora*), and *Xenopsaris.*

Subfamily Tityrinae

Pachyramphus (includes *Platypsaris*) and *Tityra*.
Based on syrinx morphology, nest type, and general morphology, Lanyon (1986) assembled five groups of tyrannids that are phylogenetically related. They are listed below, but I have included only genera occurring in Brazil. The relationships of the genus *Satrapa* remain to be determined, and *Machetornis* also appears to be an isolated case. This makes additional observation of these flycatchers all the more important.

1. *Arundinicola, Fluvicola,* and *Alectrurus*
2. *Empidonax, Lathrotriccus, Contopus, Cnemotriccus,* and *Ochthornis*
3. *Knipolegus, Lessonia, Hymenops,* and *Pyrocephalus*
4. *Muscisaxicola, Xolmis, Heteroxolmis, Neoxolmis, Gubernetes,* and *Muscipipra*
5. *Myiophobus* and *Hirundinea*

SUBFAMILY ELAENIINAE

PLANALTO TYRANNULET, *Phyllomyias fasciatus,* Piolhinho   PL 34.8

11.5 cm. Distinctly larger than *Camptostoma obsoletum,* yellower below (abdomen), a bit of white on lore and behind eye. VOICE: *eweet,* fuller and firmer than *C. obsoletum,* repeated 3 times when animated, then moving into song, a hurried and confused phrase, changing back and forth from crescendo to diminuendo, with clear whistles standing out, *dliewt . . . , ra-ewt.* Displays of 3, 4, or even more individuals nervously flying and hopping through leafy vegetation, like Pipridae, is useful diagnostic character (see "Breeding"). Forest edge, capoeira, canopy. Northeast, east, and south (Rio Grande do Sul), Argentina (Misiones), Paraguay, Goiás, southern Mato Grosso. In mountains in Rio de Janeiro.

ROUGH-LEGGED TYRANNULET, *Phyllomyias* (= *Acrochordopus*) *burmeisteri*

Mountain species, from Espírito Santo and Minas Gerais to Rio Grande do Sul and (depending on taxonomy) as far as Central America (see "Migration"). Parks, forest canopies, revealing its presence readily by a descending series of about 6 loud *EEeets.*

GREENISH TYRANNULET, *Phyllomyias* (= *Xanthomyias*) *virescens*

Piauí to Santa Catarina, Rio Grande do Sul, Paraguay. Includes *P. reiseri.*

GRAY-CAPPED TYRANNULET, *Phyllomyias* (= *Oreotriccus*) *griseocapilla*   BR

Minas Gerais to Espírito Santo, Santa Catarina.

SOOTY-HEADED TYRANNULET, *Phyllomyias griseiceps*

North of Amazon.

SLENDER-FOOTED TYRANNULET, *Zimmerius* (= *Tyranniscus*) *gracilipes*

Amazonia.

WHITE-LORED TYRANNULET, *Ornithion inerme*

Colombia to Amazonia, the northeast, Rio de Janeiro (Poço das Antas, D. A. Scott).

SOUTHERN BEARDLESS-TYRANNULET, *Camptostoma obsoletum,* Risadinha   PL 34.7

10 cm. Small, arboreal, common in many places and conspicuous because of cheerful voice. Bill small, head grayish, back greenish, 2 light rusty wing bars. VOICE: call a high whistle, frequently a bit indecisive, *ewit;* laugh a descending sequence of short, well-pronounced whistles, *glew-gli-gli-gli-gli-gli;* also a more elaborate song and other vocalizations. Forest edge, capoeira, gardens, canopy. Costa Rica to Bolivia, Argentina, throughout Brazil to Rio Grande do Sul; common also in east (e.g., ex-Guanabara) and south. Also called *Alegrinho, Assovia-cachorro.*

MOUSE-COLORED TYRANNULET, *Phaeomyias murina,* Bagageiro

Panama to Amazonia, the northeast, São Paulo.

SOUTHERN SCRUB-FLYCATCHER, *Sublegatus modestus*

Costa Rica to Amazonia, the northeast, Paraná.

AMAZONIAN SCRUB-FLYCATCHER, *Sublegatus obscurior*

Colombia and Suriname to Amapá, Pará (Tocantins). Probably a geographic race of *S. modestus.*

SUIRIRI FLYCATCHER, *Suiriri s. suiriri,* Suiriri-cinzento

15 cm. Unique arboreal species, gray above with black wings and tail. Tail tip and outer vane of outer rectrices light brown; upper wing coverts and tertiaries have wide whitish edges. Light gray below with white belly. Immature speckled white above. VOICE: surprisingly loud and harsh, *bay-eh, WEtetete;* dawn chirping is swallowlike. Cerrado, espinilho parkland. Argentina and Uruguay to Rio Grande do Sul, Mato Grosso, Minas Gerais (Pirapora).

Campos Suiriri, *S. s. affinis,* is a bit larger with yellow belly, rump and base of tail light yellow. VOICE: call a soft *BEE-jewt;* song *jew-BEE-di, di, di,* repeated while lifting both wings vertically. During breeding (November, Piauí) a pair, after moving from one tree to another, became very noisy, dueting vigorously every few minutes. When quietly perched occasionally flicks tail quickly downward, behavior that distinguishes it from certain other tyrannids that may be present. Cerrado, caatinga. Northern bank of lower Amazon (Monte Alegre) to Mato Grosso, Goiás, São Paulo, Paraná, Minas Gerais (Lagoa Santa), the northeast. Difference in voices of the 2 subspecies raises a question as to whether they may be 2 species, not just geographic races.

YELLOW-CROWNED TYRANNULET, *Tyrannulus elatus*
Northern South America to Amazonia, Maranhão.

GREENISH ELAENIA, *Myiopagis viridicata,*
Guaracava-de-olheiras

12.6 cm. Very similar to *M. gaimardii* but distinguished by white eye-ring; lacks light wing bars. VOICE: dawn song a squeaky whistle, *tsibit TSEE-tsigheh,* repeated insistently. Forest canopies, like a small *Elaenia.* Mexico to Bolivia, Paraguay, Argentina; locally in Brazil in centralwest, east, northeast, Minas Gerais, Santa Catarina, Rio Grande do Sul.

FOREST ELAENIA, *Myiopagis gaimardii*
Considerable white in center of crown, wing with notable yellowish pattern. VOICE: distinctive, a clear whistle, *seww-sewwit.* Riverine forest canopy. Amazonia to Mato Grosso, São Paulo, Panama.

YELLOW-CROWNED ELAENIA, *Myiopagis flavivertex,*
Guaracava-de-penacho-amarelo   PL 34.5

13 cm. Crested Amazonian forest species. Blackish crown with considerable sulfur yellow in center, conspicuous from a distance and resembling a *Neopelma* tyrant-manakin (Pipridae) when bird sings with crest raised. Two distinct wing bars; inner secondaries have light edges; breast streaked. VOICE: an unmusical, descending sequence, *bsh-bsh-bsh tsh-tsh-tsh,* sung in hot hours of day. Low in low woodland. Venezuela south to right bank of Amazon, Belém, Marajó (Pará).

GRAY ELAENIA, *Myiopagis caniceps,*
Guaracava-cinzenta

The Guianas to Argentina. Bananal Tyrannulet, *Serpophaga araguayae* Snethlage, is identical to *Myiopagis caniceps* (Silva 1990).

YELLOW-BELLIED ELAENIA, *Elaenia flavogaster,*
Guaracava-de-barriga-amarela   PL 34.6

15 cm. One of best-known resident species of a group whose identification requires a specialist's most skilled techniques. Crest has white that is usually hidden, throat whitish, 2 whitish wing bars. VOICE: bird immediately recognizable by voice, but voice is as difficult to describe as plumage; song a series of scratchy whistles, *chreeee-j, j chreeee-j, j,* the same in places as far apart as Rio de Janeiro and Amapá. Another very different song, used especially at dawn, sounds like a series of questions (the phrases rising) followed by the answer, *deLEE, deLEE, deLEE deli-de-DEE.* Edge of capoeira, cultivated fields with trees, gardens. Favored by disturbed habitat; as an insectivorous-frugivorous opportunist it has an important potential for dispersing secondary vegetation (Marcondes-Machado 1985). Mexico to Bolivia, Argentina, throughout Brazil. Also called *Maria-tola* (Minas Gerais), *Bobo* (Mato Grosso), *Cucurutado* (Espírito Santo), *Maria-acorda, Maria-já-é-dia, Guracava* (sic, São Paulo).

LARGE ELAENIA, *Elaenia spectabilis,*
Guaracava-grande

17.6 cm. Relatively large but only slightly crested, usually without white in crown but with 3 distinct whitish wing bars, light edges on inner secondaries, all-black bill. VOICE: a loud, isolated whistle, *WEEEEa.* Forest edge, capoeira, isolated trees. Frequently seen in canopy. Occasional in almost all of Brazil, e.g., Pernambuco, Rio de Janeiro, ex-Guanabara, São Paulo, Rio Grande do Sul; also Argentina, Bolivia, Peru.

E. s. ridleyana (BR) is a subspecies restricted to Fernando de Noronha whose subspecific status needs to be confirmed by study of its vocalization. It is one of 3 landbird species presently found on that island and is called *Cebito* there (see "Migration").

WHITE-CRESTED ELAENIA, *Elaenia albiceps*   SV
See "Migration."

SMALL-BILLED ELAENIA, *Elaenia parvirostris,*
Guaracava-de-bico-pequeno

14.5 cm. Southern species with smaller bill than *E. flavogaster,* no crest, but with small amount of white in crown and 2–3 light wing bars. VOICE: a low *kwewe, pit, tshilll, tsishili* (pair, near nest). There are 2 song types: a more common *priti-drew-it* and a bisyllabic *TSEE-ew* sung only at start of breeding. Nests in Bolivia, Argentina, Rio Grande do Sul (November); migrates to northern South America.

OLIVACEOUS ELAENIA, *Elaenia mesoleuca,* Tuque

15 cm. Locally abundant in southeast, lacking crest and white in crown but with whitish eye-ring, light mandible, and 2–3 whitish green wing bars. VOICE: song unmelodious and unmistakable but difficult to transcribe, *prrrt prr-PRREE-rrr.* Argentina and Paraguay to Rio de Janeiro (Nova Friburgo, Itatiaia, a typical mountain species), Goiás, Federal District, Mato Grosso, Bahia. Also called *Maria-tola* (Minas Gerais).

BROWNISH ELAENIA, *Elaenia pelzelni*
Amazonia, in riparian scrub and on islands.

PLAIN-CRESTED ELAENIA, *Elaenia cristata,*
Guaracava-de-topete-uniforme

14 cm. Small, crested, with blackish crown lacking white, back brownish with little green, 2 whitish wing bars. VOICE: *kweweh;* a squeaky *chrrr JElele JElele;* dawn song, from top of a tree, a 3-part *je-BEE dodo BEE.* See "Migration." Cerrado, sparse capoeira. Venezuela, Amazonia, and Amapá (where typical of campo cerrado) south to Mato Grosso, Goiás, São Paulo, northeast. Also called *Maria-é-dia.*

RUFOUS-CROWNED ELAENIA, *Elaenia ruficeps,*
Guaracava-de-topete-vermelho

13.5 cm. Crested Amazonian species, even smaller than *E. cristata,* distinguished from other elaenias by reddish in crown. Breast streaked with gray and pale yellow. VOICE: a loud, full *krrr-krrr.* Low, sparse woods. The Guianas to northern Amazonia, southern Pará (Cururu). Also called *Maria-tola.*

LESSER ELAENIA, *Elaenia chiriquensis*
See "Migration."

HIGHLAND ELAENIA, *Elaenia obscura,* Tucão

17.8 cm. Even larger than *E. spectabilis.* No white in crown. Dark brownish olivaceous green above, underparts uniformly green, mandible light brown. VOICE: *krrra . . . ,* resembling warning of House Wren, *Troglodytes aedon; pewrr; psiorr; gray-gray;* song *jewlew-jewrrit.* Also other vocalizations. Forest edge. Argentina and Paraguay to Rio de Janeiro (where nests), Minas Gerais, Mato Grosso, Bolivia, Peru. Also called *Maria-tola, Guaracava, Tonto* (Pernambuco).

SIERRAN ELAENIA, *Elaenia pallatangae*
Extreme north, near Venezuelan border.

WHITE-THROATED TYRANNULET, *Mecocerculus leucophrys roraimae*
Extreme north, from Pico da Neblina to the Andes.

RIVER TYRANNULET, *Serpophaga hypoleuca*
Amazonia.

SOOTY TYRANNULET, *Serpophaga nigricans,*
João-pobre

12 cm. Riverine, terrestrial, almost uniformly dark gray with lighter throat, black tail and wings. VOICE: a high *tsik;* song a series of these whistles ending in a buzz, the combination appearing to come from a furnariid. Tail constantly in motion, ceaselessly opening and closing. Moist edges of lakes, reservoirs, canals, or rivers, where it hops on ground.

Argentina to Rio de Janeiro, Minas Gerais, in mountains in north (Itatiaia, Bocaina). See River Warbler, *Phaeothlypis rivularis* (Parulinae).

WHITE-CRESTED TYRANNULET, *Serpophaga subcristata,* Alegrinho   PL 34.4

10 cm. Small, easily recognizable arboreal flycatcher of eastern Brazil with almost permanently erected crest. VOICE: a diagnostic *tsit-tsit tseRItitit* with timbre of Pallid Spinetail, *Cranioleuca pallida;* also a sequence of high *tsee-tsee-tsees. . . .* Capoeira, cultivated fields with trees. More common in mountainous regions. Also on coast in winter (Rio de Janeiro, ex-Guanabara, Espírito Santo). Piauí, Bahia, and Minas Gerais to Rio Grande do Sul, Argentina. Name *Serpophaga* is derived from Greek *serphos,* "mosquito" or "fly," and has nothing to do with serpents. Includes, disputedly, White-bellied Tyrannulet, *S. munda,* which has white instead of yellowish underparts and is found in Goiás, western Mato Grosso, Rio Grande do Sul, and adjacent countries.

PLAIN TYRANNULET, *Inezia inornata*
Paraguay, Bolivia, Argentina, Mato Grosso.

PALE-TIPPED TYRANNULET, *Inezia subflava,*
Amarelinho

9.5 cm. Amazonian. Similar to *Capsiempis flaveola* but smaller, underparts not so intensely yellow, and wing bars and tail tip white, not yellowish. VOICE: a sequence of strident whistles, *eet-HEE, i, i, i, i.* River edges. The Guianas and Colombia to northern Mato Grosso, the Tocantins (Pará).

LESSER WAGTAIL-TYRANT, *Stigmatura napensis,*
Papa-moscas-de-sertão   Fig. 232

13 cm. Arboreal, with long, thin legs. Brownish above, pale yellow below, long, graduated tail white at base and tip. VOICE: a trisyllabic *jew-didl-tshrrr.* Tail constantly in motion. Trees and bushes scattered across sunny savanna. Northeast (Pernambuco, Bahia), locally in upper Amazon (Rios Tapajós and Juruá and river islands) to Peru.

GREATER WAGTAIL-TYRANT, *Stigmatura budytoides*

Very similar to *S. napensis* but back greenish, black tail crossed by white strip and has white tip. Northeast (Pernambuco, Bahia), sometimes in same region as *napensis* (Bahia); also Bolivia, Paraguay, Argentina.

MANY-COLORED RUSH-TYRANT, *Tachuris rubrigastra,* Papa-piri   PL 34.14

10.5 cm. Multicolored, southern wetland tyrant. Green on back sometimes appears blue. Female similar but smaller. Immature different: greenish black above; head lacks yellow, black, or red; does have white postocular stripe and, like adult, white pattern on wings and tail. Low in high reeds and cattails, hiding like *Phleocryptes melanops* (Furnariidae),

Fig. 232. Lesser Wagtail-Tyrant, *Stigmatura napensis.*

often its neighbor and with which it shares unusual technique of wetting leaves of reeds to use as nest-construction material (see "Breeding"). Chile and Argentina to Rio Grande do Sul, São Paulo, Rio de Janeiro. Most northerly individuals found in Brazil are migrants. One individual was found on high seas, 92 mi from city of Rio Grande (Rio Grande do Sul, March 1960).

SHARP-TAILED GRASS-TYRANT, *Culicivora caudacuta*, Papa-moscas-do-campo   Fig. 233

10.2 cm. Savanna species of central Brazil with quite long, graduated tail having singularly narrow feathers. Upperparts light cinnamon streaked black, crown blackish streaked white, superciliary white or yellowish; underparts yellowish white. VOICE: low, sometimes buzzing, *jew, wit, jeh-pewrr,* somewhat like *Todirostrum plumbeiceps.* Wet or dry stands of tall grass, halfway up stalks where it catches insects. Flees by flying openly over grasslands, the same as emberizines such as *Sporophila.* Flies in small flocks. Argentina and Paraguay to Mato Grosso, Goiás, Federal District, Paraná, São Paulo. See *Polystictus pectoralis* and *P. superciliaris.*

BEARDED TACHURI, *Polystictus pectoralis,* Papa-moscas-canela

9.8 cm. Crested savanna species with cinnamon brown upperparts, cinnamon rump and wing bars, crown streaked white. Underparts yellowish white, throat slightly streaked, sides bright cinnamon. Uruguay to eastern Bolivia, central

Brazil: Goiás (Aragarças), Mato Grosso (Campo Grande, Cuiabá), São Paulo, Rio Grande do Sul; also in north (Venezuela). See *P. superciliaris* and *Culicivora caudacuta.*

GRAY-BACKED TACHURI, *Polystictus superciliaris,* Papa-moscas-de-costas-cinzentas   BR

10.2 cm. Upperparts uniformly gray with white around eye, on lores, and in hidden streaks on crown. Underparts bright cinnamon with white in center. VOICE: *kwirrLIP,* resembling squeak of *Euscarthmus meloryphus* but less loquacious. A mountain bird; high, rocky, open country, perching on branches of bushes and low trees. Minas Gerais in Serra do Espinhaço region—Mariana, 1000 m; Serra do Cipó, 1000 m (G. Mattos 1973); Serra da Piedade, 1750 m; Serra da Gandarela, Serra do Caraça—alongside Pale-throated Serra-Finch, *Embernagra longicauda,* and Hyacinth Visorbearer, *Augastes scutatus,* also endemics. Bahia (Morro do Chapéu, E. Kaempfer 1928), São Paulo (Serra da Bocaina, J. L. Lima 1961). See *Euscarthmus meloryphus, E. rufomarginatus,* and *P. pectoralis,* for which it probably could be considered a geographic replacement (see "Habitat . . .").

CRESTED DORADITO, *Pseudocolopteryx sclateri,* Tricolino   PL 34.3

9.8 cm. Wetland species with crest that, when seen from front, seems divided into 2 horns. Has 4–5 outer primaries modified for sound production whose function is still unknown. Immature brown, not yellow. VOICE: warning a coarse *shat;* song a high, squeaky *fit-fit, BEETsi-BEETsi.*

Fig. 233. Sharp-tailed Grass-Tyrant, *Culicivora caudacuta.*

Open várzea, seeking food by hopping through low vegetation and bases of marsh plants. Sings from tips of reeds. Bahia to Rio Grande do Sul, Argentina; also Venezuela, Trinidad, Guyana.

WARBLING DORADITO, *Pseudocolopteryx flaviventris*

11.5 cm. Dark brown above, crown rusty, yellow below. VOICE: call *plit*. Unlike *P. sclateri*, has no modified flight feathers. Bushes at marsh edges. Only in extreme south, from Chile, Argentina, Paraguay, and Uruguay to Rio Grande do Sul, São Paulo.

TAWNY-CROWNED PYGMY-TYRANT, *Euscarthmus meloryphus*, Barulhento   PL 34.2

11 cm. Small, brownish, with inconspicuous wing bars but red visible in crown. VOICE: loud and squeaky, difficult to describe, *przl-lidl, TREEde,* endlessly alternating with trills. Hard to see but tireless voice insistently attracts attention. Bushes in open country, pasture, sparse capoeira, caatinga. Venezuela to Bolivia, Uruguay, central and eastern Brazil, Maranhão to Rio Grande do Sul; city of Rio de Janeiro. In Mato Grosso sometimes near *E. rufomarginatus.* See also *Polystictus.* Also called *Arrelia* (Minas Gerais), *Traz-farinha-aí.*

RUFOUS-SIDED PYGMY-TYRANT, *Euscarthmus rufomarginatus*

In Brazil restricted to central area. Similar to *E. meloryphus* but tail long and narrow, tarsi long, underparts bright rusty on sides, yellow in middle. VOICE: call *blewt, blewt-blewt-blewt;* song *jic-jic-jic-tshrrrewdi,* resembling a furnariid. Low or hopping on ground. Open cerrado with little vegetation but many termite nests (Minas Gerais). Maranhão and Piauí to northern São Paulo; also savannas in southern Suriname.

OCHRE-BELLIED FLYCATCHER, *Mionectes oleagineus* (= *Pipromorpha oleaginea*), Supi, Abre-asas   PL 34.10

11.5 cm. Unique forest flycatcher, both in color (see *M. macconnelli*) and behavior (see "Breeding"). VOICE AND DISPLAYS: Each male periodically occupies a territory in which it flies nervously from one side to the other. While perching lifts wings alternately and sings song: a squeaky phrase, *PEEor, PEEor . . . ,* audible as far as territory of next male, with which it occasionally enters into contact by engaging in mutual chasing, recalling *Xenopipo atronitens.* Lower level of dark forests. In várzea forest of lower Amazon (Pará) it is one of most common birds (see "Habitat . . ."). Mexico and the Guianas to Bolivia, Mato Grosso, Pará, Maranhão; also along coastal strip where there is forest cover, from Alagoas to Espírito Santo (littoral, north of Rio Doce), Rio de Janeiro (Magé, Tinguá, L. P. Gonzaga);

in Tinguá (300 m) found alongside *M. rufiventris* (October).

MCCONNELL'S FLYCATCHER, *Mionectes* (= *Pipromorpha*) *macconnelli*

11.5 cm. Similar to *M. oleagineus* but lacking yellowish wing bar and with mouth interior lead colored (orange in *M. oleagineus*). Amazonia. The Guianas to Bolivia, Amazonas, Pará (Belém), often alongside *oleagineus,* even perching in same trees. Includes *M. roraimae.*

GRAY-HOODED FLYCATCHER, *Mionectes* (= *Pipromorpha*) *rufiventris*   BR

13 cm. Relatively large with rusty-washed, dark gray throat (not green). VOICE: song a low, descending, and accelerating sequence resembling that of a *Thamnophilus, bayo-bayo-bayo. . . .* Moves wings at brief intervals as if wanting to lift them. Restricted to south: Espírito Santo (mountainous regions), Minas Gerais, Rio de Janeiro (Petrópolis, Teresópolis, Itatiaia), ex-Guanabara to Rio Grande do Sul, Argentina (Misiones), Paraguay.

SEPIA-CAPPED FLYCATCHER, *Leptopogon amaurocephalus*, Cabeçudo   PL 34.9

13 cm. Forest flycatcher easily recognized by blackish spot on side of head, resembling Oustalet's Tyrannulet, *Phylloscartes oustaleti,* but with dark brownish crown (not green) and 2 yellowish wing bars but no light eye-ring. VOICE: *psewrrr,* a fuller *rrr-EEo, psorriulT,* conspicuous and resembling *Rhytipterna simplex;* a weak *wet,* similar to voice of a marmoset (*Callithrix* sp.); an ascending sequence of limpid, soft whistles ending with a coarse *ew ew ew ew ew ew . . . PSEEoo.* See fig. 227 for nest. Frequently lifts only 1 wing to a vertical position, an impressive sight. Medium heights in forest. Mexico across upper Amazon (apparently does not exist in lower Amazon) to Mato Grosso, Bolivia; northeast, east, and south to Rio Grande do Sul, Argentina (Misiones), Paraguay. Also called *Jawú-aíb* (Kaiabi, Mato Grosso), *Úri* (Rio de Janeiro).

CHAPMAN'S BRISTLE-TYRANT, *Phylloscartes chapmani*

Tepuis in Roraima and Venezuela.

SOUTHERN BRISTLE-TYRANT, *Phylloscartes* (= *Pogonotriccus*) *eximius*, Barbudinho

11.4 cm; 7.5 g. Characteristic southern woodland species with high, wide head, numerous bristles around bill, long tail, small feet. Green with plumbeous crown; large white spot above lore and another on side of head toward rear; large yellowish area below eye set off by half-moon-shaped black stripe behind it. Belly yellow. Inside forests, alongside *Leptopogon amaurocephalus* and *Mionectes rufiventris,* from

Minas Gerais and Espírito Santo to Rio de Janeiro, São Paulo, Santa Catarina, Rio Grande do Sul, Paraguay, Argentina (Misiones).

BAY-RINGED TYRANNULET, *Phylloscartes* (= *Leptotriccus*) *sylviolus*

Another southern species; northeastern Argentina, Paraguay, Santa Catarina, Minas Gerais, Espírito Santo.

MINAS GERAIS TYRANNULET, *Phylloscartes roquettei* BR

Minas Gerais.

MOTTLE-CHEEKED TYRANNULET, *Phylloscartes ventralis,* Borboletinha-do-mato

11.5 cm. Subtropical with relatively long tail, similar to *P. oustaleti* but lacking its characteristic pattern on sides of head, although there is some white on face; has 2 yellow wing bars. VOICE: call loud, resembling a furnariid or dendrocolaptid, *spit, tirrr, TSEE-ti, ti, ti, ti;* song *spit-spit-spit-tewtewtewtew-spit.* Tail is always carried a bit elevated, with frequent slight upward movements. Forest. Rio de Janeiro and Minas Gerais to Rio Grande do Sul and to Andes; in Rio de Janeiro in mountains (Bocaina, etc.). See *P. oustaleti* and *P. flaveola.*

ALAGOAS TYRANNULET, *Phylloscartes ceciliae*   BR

Alagoas.

SÃO PAULO TYRANNULET, *Phylloscartes paulistus*

Espírito Santo to Santa Catarina, Paraguay.

BLACK-FRONTED TYRANNULET, *Phylloscartes nigrifrons*

Tepuis in Roraima and Venezuela.

OUSTALET'S TYRANNULET, *Phylloscartes oustaleti,* Papa-mosca-de-olheiras   BR   PL 35.11

12.5 cm. Well characterized by golden yellow circle around eye and blackish spot at edge of auriculars. Lacks clear wing bars, unlike *P. nigrifrons.* VOICE: a hard, diagnostic *teck.* Customarily lifts long tail slightly. Forest, usually mountainous (e.g., Teresópolis, Rio de Janeiro). Rio Grande do Sul to Paraná; also Municipality of Rio de Janeiro (Corcovado). See *Leptopogon amaurocephalus* and Eye-ringed Tody-Tyrant, *Hemitriccus orbitatus.*

SERRA DO MAR TYRANNULET, *Phylloscartes difficilis,* Estalinho   BR

11 cm. Southeastern endemic, easily recognized by contrast between intense green upperparts and uniformly dark gray underparts. Clear white ring around whitish eye. VOICE: *prrit . . . ;* song a strident *tsi-ree.* More noticeable because

of a regularly produced popping *tak,* frequently bisyllabic, *tak-tak,* and sometimes a continuous clatter as it moves from one perch to another (see "Vocalization"). Some meters up at edge of forest; Minas Gerais, Rio de Janeiro, São Paulo (where restricted to mountains: Serra dos Órgãos, Bocaina, Itatiaia, Caparaó), Santa Catarina, Rio Grande do Sul.

YELLOW TYRANNULET, *Capsiempis flaveola,* Marianinha-amarela   PL 35.12

11 cm. Relatively long tail, long superciliary, intense yellow underparts and double wing bars. VOICE: an ascending *bewrr-bewrr* that, in spite of certain differences, resembles *Todirostrum plumbeiceps;* song *taytiREEti. . . .* Engages in group activities (see "Breeding"). Forest edge, coffee plantations, restinga. Nicaragua to Bolivia, Paraguay, throughout Brazil to Rio Grande do Sul. Also called *Sebinho.*

SOUTHERN ANTPIPIT, *Corythopis delalandi,* Estalador   PL 29.6

12 cm. Distinctive forest bird, resembling a pipit (*Anthus*) although it lives in darkest forests. May recall an antbird. VOICE: call *DLEEa;* song *di-driEET dewDREE ew ew ew,* interpreted locally (Bahia) as *eu sou terríbili* [I am terribly"]. Warning note is substituted by a popping sound (see "Vocalization"). Walks swiftly on ground (long, whitish legs), flies well (large wings), has relatively long tail. The northeast to Rio Grande do Sul, through Goiás and Mato Grosso to Bolivia, Paraguay, Argentina. The genus *Corythopis* was formerly considered part of Conopophagidae, a now-abandoned family grouping. *Corythopis* is certainly not related to *Conopophaga,* now included in Formicariidae. Placing *Corythopis* among tyrannids is based on characters of syrinx, skull, and pterylosis; there are bristles around bill. In my opinion the systematic position of *Corythopis* continues to be *incertae sedis.* Also called *Peixe-frito* (Maranhão). See *C. torquata.*

RINGED ANTPIPIT, *Corythopis torquata*

Replaces *C. delalandi* in Amazonia. Very similar, also having distinctive pattern on breast (faint brownish in immature), but under wing coverts blackish, not white. Voice and popping very similar to or same as *delalandi.* Northern Mato Grosso (upper Xingu, where it meets *delalandi*) and northern Maranhão to the Guianas, Venezuela.

EARED PYGMY-TYRANT, *Myiornis auricularis,* Miudinho

7 cm. One of smallest flycatchers, with short tail. Unmistakable head pattern: behind whitish auricular regions is a large, black, half-moon-shaped mark; crown brownish green, throat white streaked with black, belly yellow. VOICE: quite high, *tewk-tewk-tewk,* and an ascending *brrrew.* Forest edge. Southeastern Brazil (Bahia to Rio Grande do Sul),

Argentina (Misiones), Paraguay. Also called *Sebinho, Úri* (Municipality of Rio de Janeiro).

SHORT-TAILED PYGMY-TYRANT, *Myiornis ecaudatus,* Caçula   PL 34.13

6.5 cm; 4.9 g. Smallest Tyrannidae. Unlike *M. auricularis,* lacks black design on head, has gray crown. VOICE: *bit, TSEEbit,* a descending *tsewrrr;* warning *tsewrrit.* Stretches wings laterally, displaying their underside toward front. In flight produces a wing buzzing similar to that of a *Phaethornis* hummingbird. Riverine forest canopy. Amazonia to northern Mato Grosso (Xingu) and Pará (Belém), the Guianas, Colombia. Also called *Cigarra-bico-chato.*

LONG-CRESTED PYGMY-TYRANT, *Lophotriccus eulophotes*

Small. Amazonia.

DOUBLE-BANDED PYGMY-TYRANT, *Lophotriccus vitiosus*

Small. Amazonia.

HELMETED PYGMY-TYRANT, *Lophotriccus* (= *Colopteryx*) *galeatus,* Caga-sebinho-penacho PL 35.5

9.5 cm. Small, crested, forest flycatcher. Light yellow iris, underparts like those of Pearly-vented Tody-Tyrant, *Hemitriccus margaritaceiventer.* VOICE: a strident *eek, tic-tic-tirrr,* very loud considering small size of bird. Forest, at various levels. Amazonia south to southern Pará and Maranhão; the Guianas, Colombia.

TRICOLORED TODY-FLYCATCHER, *Poecilotriccus* (= *Todirostrum*) *tricolor*   BR

Rio Jamari, Rondônia. Probably identical to Black-and-white Tody-Tyrant, *P. capitalis,* of Peru, Ecuador, and Colombia (R. Ridgely pers. comm.).

BLACK-CHESTED TYRANT, *Poecilotriccus* (= *Taeniotriccus*) *andrei*

Somewhat larger than other tyrannids described here as "small." Amazonia.

SNETHLAGE'S TODY-TYRANT, *Hemitriccus* (*Snethlagea*) *minor*   BR

Small. Amazonia. I now classify this as an endemic because Blake's record (Meyer de Schauensee 1966) of this species in Suriname was based on a specimen of *H. josephinae* (Traylor pers. comm.).

BOAT-BILLED TODY-TYRANT, *Hemitriccus* (*Microcochlearius*) *josephinae*

Small. Amazonia in Amapá and near Manaus (Ridgely pers. comm.).

DRAB-BREASTED BAMBOO-TYRANT, *Hemitriccus diops,* Olho-falso   Fig. 234

11.5 cm. Dark, southeastern forest flycatcher, green above, slightly pinkish gray below, with whitish spot on lores and another larger one (less visible in life) on lower throat. Mandible light gray. VOICE: *bit, sewit, bit-biWIT,* like *Platyrinchus mystaceus.* Forest interior at midlevels. In north restricted to mountainous regions (Santa Teresa, Espírito Santo; Teresópolis and Itatiaia, Rio de Janeiro). Bahia and Minas Gerais to Rio Grande do Sul, southeastern Paraguay. Also called *Cigarrinha.*

BROWN-BREASTED BAMBOO-TYRANT, *Hemitriccus obsoletus,* Catraca   BR

Similar to *H. diops* but washed all over with brown, especially on underparts. VOICE: *tik, tik, tik, tik, tik.* Forest. Rio de Janeiro (Itatiaia, where it meets *H. diops*), São Paulo (Bocaina), Paraná, Santa Catarina, Rio Grande do Sul.

FLAMMULATED BAMBOO-TYRANT, *Hemitriccus flammulatus*

Western Mato Grosso.

WHITE-EYED TODY-TYRANT, *Hemitriccus* (= *Idioptilon*) *zosterops*

Amazonia to Pernambuco.

ZIMMER'S TODY-TYRANT, *Hemitriccus* (= *Idioptilon*) *aenigma*   BR

Amazonia, lower Rio Tapajós, Caxiricatuba.

EYE-RINGED TODY-TYRANT, *Hemitriccus* (= *Idioptilon*) *orbitatus,* Tiririzinho-do-mato   BR

11.5 cm. Forest species, dark green above with white eye-ring, throat and breast streaked, belly yellow. VOICE: *tirrit, tirririt.* Forest. Espírito Santo and Minas Gerais to São Paulo, Rio Grande do Sul; also ex-Guanabara. Also called *Oculista.*

JOHANNES' TODY-TYRANT, *Hemitriccus* (= *Idioptilon*) *iohannis*

Rios Solimões, Juruá, and Purus.

STRIPE-NECKED TODY-TYRANT, *Hemitriccus* (= *Idioptilon*) *striaticollis,* Sebinho-rajado-amarelo PL 35.9

10 cm. One of several extremely similar small flycatchers in Brazil. This one easily recognized by intense yellow belly; throat and breast streaked. VOICE: *bewt-bewit BEE-bibit.* Riverine vegetation and bamboo at both high and low levels. Amazonia, from Peru to Mato Grosso, Goiás, Maranhão, Bahia.

Fig. 234. Drab-breasted Bamboo-Tyrant, *Hemitriccus diops*.

HANGNEST TODY-TYRANT, *Hemitriccus* (= *Idioptilon*) *nidipendulus,* Tachuri-campainha BR

9.5 cm. Restricted to small area of southeast. Uniformly olivaceous green upperparts, uniformly olivaceous gray throat and breast, white belly, whitish eye. VOICE: call resembles a *Todirostrum, tic, prrew-prrew-prrew;* song (diagnostic) a clear, high phrase, *tiREE-TEElili TEElili TEElili.* Restinga woods, samambaia-das-taperas (*Pteridium aquilinum*) thickets in mountainous regions. Bahia to São Paulo.

PEARLY-VENTED TODY-TYRANT, *Hemitriccus* (= *Idioptilon*) *margaritaceiventer,* Sebinho-de-olho-de-ouro

10 cm. Typical of cerrado and caatinga. Grayish green above, white beneath, all streaked with gray. VOICE: *tewk-eek, tewk-eek, ik, ik, tic-tic-TIC-tic-tewk-tewk-tewk,* resembling *Xenopipo atronitens;* a low, croaking *sha.* Bushes in central savannas. Venezuela to Bolivia, Argentina, Paraguay, central and northeastern Brazil. Includes *H.* (= *Idioptilon*) *inornatus.*

BUFF-BREASTED TODY-TYRANT, *Hemitriccus* (= *Idioptilon*) *mirandae* BR

Northeast. See plate, Fitzpatrick and O'Neill 1979.

KAEMPFER'S TODY-TYRANT, *Hemitriccus* (= *Idioptilon*) *kaempferi* (= *Idioptilon mirandae kaempferi* Zimmer 1953) BR

Santa Catarina (Piraí, Joinville). See plate, Fitzpatrick and O'Neill 1979. [Rediscovered in 1991, less than 1 km from site where type and sole specimen was found in 1929. (*World Birdwatch* 13(4):3).]

FORK-TAILED PYGMY-TYRANT, *Hemitriccus* (= *Ceratotriccus*) *furcatus,* Papa-mosca-estrela BR R

9.2 cm. Rare and distinctive endemic of southeast with aspect of a *Todirostrum,* but male has forked tail with white tips, green back, brown head, dark gray breast, white belly, and white spot on throat. Rio de Janeiro (Nova Friburgo, Parati, in bamboo thickets), eastern São Paulo (Ubatuba). "Espírito Santo" (Ruschi 1954, without justification).

BUFF-CHEEKED TODY-FLYCATCHER, *Todirostrum senex* BR

Rio Madeira, Amazonas. Known only from type specimen.

RUDDY TODY-FLYCATCHER, *Todirostrum russatum* Extreme north.

YELLOW-LORED TODY-FLYCATCHER, *Todirostrum poliocephalum,* Teque-teque, Ferreirinho BR PL 34.11

8.8 cm. Common, very small arboreal flycatcher of southeast, easily recognized by yellow spot on lores. VOICE: utters a *spit-spit-spit* and other syllables; sometimes snaps (see "Vocalization"). Swift moving, almost never stays immobile. Treetops; also gardens of cities such as Rio de Janeiro, being temporarily satisfied with a few leafy street trees, e.g., some oitís (*Moquilea tomentosa*) in the Praça Pio X. Espírito Santo to Santa Catarina, sometimes alongside *T. cinereum.* Also called *Marrequinha, Patinho.*

COMMON TODY-FLYCATCHER, *Todirostrum cinereum,* Relógio, Ferreirinho

8.8 cm. Similar to *T. poliocephalum* but lacks lore spot; outer tail feathers have broad white tip. VOICE: *tsrrr-tsrrr-tsrrr, tsewk.* . . . During courtship wags tail sideways. Sparse woodland, restinga, gardens, canopy. Mexico to Bolivia, throughout Brazil south to southern Mato Grosso, Paraná. Also called *Tirri* (Bahia).

SPOTTED TODY-FLYCATCHER, *Todirostrum maculatum,* Ferreirinho-estriado

9 cm. Underparts, except belly, densely streaked with black. VOICE: a rhythmic sequence, *TSEE-tic TSEE-tic TSEE-tic.* . . . Forest edge, gardens and canopies, sometimes alongside *T. cinereum* (Pará). Amazonia to Maranhão, Venezuela.

OCHRE-FACED TODY-FLYCATCHER, *Todirostrum plumbeiceps,* Ferreirinho-de-cara-canela PL 34.12

9 cm. Lower level of dense secondary vegetation, also samambaia-das-taperas (*Pteridium aquilinum*) thickets. VOICE: a soft *brrew-brrew.* Hides in densest low tangles but reveals

its presence by distinctive voice. Southeast: Espírito Santo to Rio Grande do Sul, Argentina, Paraguay; also southern Andes; only in mountains in Rio de Janeiro and Espírito Santo. Also called *Tororó* (Rio Grande do Sul).

SMOKY-FRONTED TODY-FLYCATCHER, *Todirostrum fumifrons*
Suriname to Pará, Maranhão, Bahia.

RUSTY-FRONTED TODY-FLYCATCHER, *Todirostrum latirostre*
Amazonas to western São Paulo, Paraguay.

SLATE-HEADED TODY-FLYCATCHER, *Todirostrum sylvia*
Underparts slate colored; lores, throat, and belly white; 2 yellow wing bars. VOICE: *prrew*, similar to *T. plumbeiceps*. Low in edge of heavy, sometimes flooded forest (igapó). Amazonia south to Maranhão, Piauí.

PAINTED TODY-FLYCATCHER, *Todirostrum pictum*
North of Amazon.

YELLOW-BROWED TODY-FLYCATCHER, *Todirostrum chrysocrotaphum*
Upper Amazon.

BROWNISH TWISTWING, *Cnipodectes subbrunneus*
16 cm. Unique in twisted primaries. Tail long and reddish, bill wide, upperparts and breast dark olivaceous brown, wings edged yellowish brown, belly whitish. Upper Amazon, west of Rios Negro and Madeira as far as Central America. There is no information on function of its peculiar wing structure.

LARGE-HEADED FLATBILL, *Ramphotrigon megacephala*
Amazonia and from Minas Gerais to Espírito Santo, Rio de Janeiro, São Paulo, Paraguay.

RUFOUS-TAILED FLATBILL, *Ramphotrigon ruficauda*, Bico-chato-de-rabo-vermelho   PL 35.8
15 cm. Characterized by bright rusty tail. VOICE: a full, tremulous whistle, *eww-ewewew-eww.* Tall forest. The Guianas to Bolivia; in Amazonian Brazil to the Xingu, Mato Grosso.

OLIVACEOUS FLATBILL, *Rhynchocyclus olivaceus*, Bico-chato-grande
15.7 cm. Much heavier-bodied than *Tolmomyias*, with very wide bill with white mandible, dark olivaceous green plumage, yellowish belly. The Guianas to Bolivia, Amazonian, and eastern Brazil to Rio de Janeiro. See *Tolmomyias sulphurescens.*

YELLOW-OLIVE FLYCATCHER, *Tolmomyias sulphurescens*, Bico-chato-de-orelha-preta   PL 35.13
14.5 cm. Medium-sized, common forest flycatcher. VOICE: a typical squeaky whistle, *sheet, shi-eet* (frequently 3 times), often heard from southeastern population, *T. s. sulphurescens.* Canopy of tall forests, sometimes lower. Its presence is revealed by conspicuous, long, hanging nest (see "Breeding"). Mexico to Bolivia, Argentina, throughout Brazil to Rio Grande do Sul. Also called *Úri* (Rio de Janeiro).

YELLOW-MARGINED FLYCATCHER, *Tolmomyias assimilis*
Amazonia.

GRAY-CROWNED FLYCATCHER, *Tolmomyias poliocephalus*
Amazonia, Pernambuco, southern Bahia, Espírito Santo.

YELLOW-BREASTED FLYCATCHER, *Tolmomyias flaviventris*
12 cm. Eye-catching because of intense yellow underparts. VOICE: unusual, *tsew-it*, quite like Plain Xenops, *Xenops minutus.* Edge of sunny restinga and caatinga woodland, prominent because of black bag nests. Venezuela to Bolivia, Mato Grosso, Goiás, eastern Brazil to Rio de Janeiro.

CINNAMON-CRESTED SPADEBILL, *Platyrinchus saturatus*
Cinnamon orange crown. Amazonia.

WHITE-THROATED SPADEBILL, *Platyrinchus mystaceus*, Patinho   PL 35.6
9.8 cm. Small forest flycatcher with broad range. Head large, bill unusual. Has distinctive head pattern, with hidden yellow in crown more prominent in male. Strong legs, large wings. VOICE: a high whistle, *bit*, similar to that of *Hemitriccus diops; sip-sip-sip;* song *iew-ch, ch, ch, ch-wit.* Dark, low levels of tall forest (big eyes). Mexico to Bolivia, Argentina, eastern and southern Brazil including Rio Grande do Sul and centralwest. Also called *Bico-chato.*

GOLDEN-CROWNED SPADEBILL, *Platyrinchus coronatus*
Yellow and chestnut crown. Amazonia.

WHITE-CRESTED SPADEBILL, *Platyrinchus platyrhynchos* (= *P. senex*)
White crown. Amazonia.

RUSSET-WINGED SPADEBILL, *Platyrinchus leucoryphus*, Patinho-gigante
12.6 cm. Little-known southern species, similar to *P. mystaceus*, with same facial pattern but much larger. Tail rela-

tively long; center of crown white; dark spot on side of breast. VOICE: a loud call, *EEo,* similar to *Leptopogon amaurocephalus;* song a full trill with pattern similar to *P. mystaceus.* Medium levels of secondary forest, alongside *P. mystaceus* (Parque Desengano, 500 m, Rio de Janeiro).

Espírito Santo (forested mountain regions) to São Paulo, Paraná (Londrina), Rio Grande do Sul (Torres), eastern Paraguay. Also called *P. platyrhynchos,* which is correct name for another species formerly called *P. senex* (see *P. platyrhynchos).*

SUBFAMILY FLUVICOLINAE

ROYAL FLYCATCHER, *Onychorhynchus coronatus,* Maria-leque PL 35.10

15–17.5 cm; 13–14 g (male, Mato Grosso). Famous for crest, which when normally closed and invisible rises above crown plumage like a low, narrow sheaf and gives head a special, hammer-headed appearance. Light rusty tail, resembling that of a furnariid, conspicuous in forest shadows. Bill long and flattened with long bristles. Tarsus short. Individuals of southeastern Brazil population (*O. c. swainsoni;* BR, R; about 17.5 cm overall) have uniformly cinnamon underparts. Bird may emanate a strong odor. VOICE: a whistle that could come from a furnariid. When silent easily escapes detection.

Crest Display: Only exceptionally does one see the open fan (red in male, yellow in female), it usually being seen only partially, as when bird is preening. Its full opening produces one of the most notable epigamic effects among the world's birds. When captured, the bird, feeling its life threatened, regularly opens its fan until it reaches a half-moon shape (180°), then swings the head alternately 90° to the right and left (fig. 235). Strangest of all, it performs these movements slowly and silently, although it holds the bill wide open, showing the orange mouth. The bird keeps the plane of the fan directly in front of the focus of supposed danger, accompanying all the movements of its adversary (e.g., the eyes of the observer; also see "Behavior"). Brilliant blue spots in middle of fan disk are concentrated at certain points, thus augmenting their effect as supplementary eyes. Fanning the crest makes the bird appear bigger and more vigorous than it really is. It is a fascinating and even frightening spectacle for the spectator, comparable to the shock caused by the presence of a snake, as I myself have had the opportunity to experience. The large, resplendent disk of feathers and the slender neck stretched toward the danger can look like a strange flower on the tip of a slender stem waving in the breeze. I have noted that the first phase of fan opening, preceding its full spread, involves display of a narrow, blood red, vertical stripe arising from the bird's forehead.

More than 100 years ago Descourtilz (1944) lamented the fact that this bird had become rare, assuming the cause to be hunting for the crest, which was sold for an adornment. Surprisingly, Pinto (1944) said the species was "formerly abundant, especially in São Paulo." The Central American form *Onychorhynchus coronatus* (= *mexicanus*) may be even more common in secondary forests (Terborgh 1974). Lower forest levels in vicinity of shady streams, above which it builds its nest, a disorderly looking ball of dry leaves in branches. Locally from Mexico to Bolivia, Mato Grosso, Maranhão, also in eastern Brazil to Paraná, in mountains in southeast (Serra do Mar and Serra da Mantiqueira, Itatiaia, 1965). Also called *Lecre* (corruption of *leque,* "fan"), *Pavãozinho.*

RUDDY-TAILED FLYCATCHER, *Terenotriccus erythrurus,* Papa-moscas-uirapuru PL 34.15

9.7 cm. Small forest bird, notable for light rusty color and grayish crown (lacks bright color in center that characterizes Cinnamon Manakin, *Neopipo cinnamomea*). VOICE: a high phrase that may recall *Corythopis, see-ew-srrWIT;* also *bibist* that may recall Gray-bellied Spinetail, *Synallaxis cinerascens.* Frequently lifts both wings. Lives 4–7 m up in dense forest or coconut groves. Amazonia, northern Mato Grosso, and Maranhão to Mexico, Bolivia. Also called *Uirapuru* (Amazonas). Plate does not show surprising resemblance of plumage to *Neopipo cinnamomea* but does emphasize relatively heavy bill with long bristles.

SULPHUR-RUMPED FLYCATCHER, *Myiobius barbatus,* Assanhadinho PL 35.3

12.5 cm. Forest flycatcher, unmistakable in combination of bright yellow rump, long tail, and restless disposition.

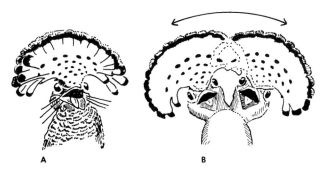

A   B

Fig. 235. Royal Flycatcher, *Onychorhynchus coronatus:* (A) head still, with fan open; (B) moving the head from side to side. After Dick and Mitchell 1979. The basic function of the fan is epigamic, but the display also appears in cases of death threats, when it becomes an antipredatory action.

VOICE: generally silent but sometimes utters a high *tsip.* Flies and hops unceasingly with drooping wings and tail fanned, displaying rump which stands out in dim light of lower forest levels. Usually travels in small flocks whose members, in demonstrating a degree of cooperative behavior, resemble manakins. Mexico to Amazonia and Mato Grosso, eastern Brazil to Santa Catarina.

BLACK-TAILED FLYCATCHER, *Myiobius atricaudus*

Very similar to *M. barbatus,* with even longer tail that is graduated, not rectangular, and equal in length or longer than wing. Breast brownish, not light yellow. Distribution similar to *barbatus;* sometimes they are even in secondary forest, e.g., mountains of Espírito Santo. Costa Rica to Paraná.

RORAIMAN FLYCATCHER, *Myiophobus roraimae*

Serra da Neblina, Roraima; Venezuela.

BRAN-COLORED FLYCATCHER, *Myiophobus fasciatus,* Filipe PL 35.4

12.2 cm. Common in open capoeira; only flycatcher in this habitat with dark streaking on underparts. Female has less yellow in crown. VOICE: call *chlep, jewleh;* daytime song a muffled squeak; dawn song a sequence of fuller whistles, *jili-juh jili-juh.* Sparse capoeira, gardens. Costa Rica to Argentina, all regions of Brazil, including ex-Guanabara. See female *Knipolegus cyanirostris,* a larger forest species with reddish tail.

OLIVE-SIDED FLYCATCHER, *Contopus* (= *Nuttallornis*) *borealis* NV

Lower Amazon; Carajás, Pará, February and October 1984 (P. Roth, L. Gonzaga); Itatiaia, Rio de Janeiro, November 1986 (T. A. Parker). Migrant from North America.

EASTERN WOOD-PEWEE, *Contopus virens* NV

Western Brazil, upper Juruá, Rondônia, as a migrant from North America. May reveal its identity by characteristic song, *piWEE.*

TROPICAL PEWEE, *Contopus cinereus,* Papa-moscas cinzento

13.5 cm. Small, long-tailed, woodland species, sooty with blackish crown, yellow mandible. VOICE: a weak whistle, *bit-bit-bit,* frequently with more syllables; song a more sonorous phrase, *WITjew.* . . . Frequently beats wings and shakes tail; male has a display in which it squats, opens and closes wings and tail, and turns around in a flying jump reminiscent of a *Pipra* manakin. Middle and upper forest levels. Southeastern and central Brazil to Bolivia and Argentina, northern Amazonia to Mexico.

BLACKISH PEWEE, *Contopus nigrescens*

Itapiranga, Tocantins, 14 June 1967, J. Hidasi (São Paulo Museum). Northern South America.

WHITE-THROATED PEWEE, *Contopus albogularis*

Northeast, Amapá, Suriname, Guyana.

SMOKE-COLORED PEWEE, *Contopus fumigatus*

Roraima.

WILLOW FLYCATCHER, *Empidonax traillii* NV

Found at Santarém, Pará, Mojui dos Campos, 24 February 1978 (F. C. Novaes pers. comm.). Specimen, deposited in Museu Goeldi, Belém, Pará, was identified by E. Eisenmann and A. R. Phillips as eastern race, *E. t. traillii.*

EULER'S FLYCATCHER, *Lathrotriccus* (= *Empidonax*) *euleri,* Enferrujado PL 35.1

12.7 cm. Woodland flycatcher, common in many places. Brown with 2 light wing bars, whitish mandible. Underparts lack striations, crown has no bright color. VOICE: call a muffled *BEACH-bich;* song *shpaye-shpaye-wileh.* Forest interior a few meters above ground level. Venezuela to Bolivia, Argentina, Paraguay, throughout Brazil. See *Myiophobus fasciatus* and *Cnemotriccus fuscatus.*

FUSCOUS FLYCATCHER, *Cnemotriccus fuscatus,* Guaracavuçu

15 cm. Almost a larger version of *Lathrotriccus euleri* but with lores and superciliary whitish, breast dark brown, bill black. VOICE: a muffled sequence, *aag-aag-aag* . . . , that sounds like a frog; *bsh-bsh-bsh.* Lives quietly in shady interior of low forest. The Guianas to Bolivia, Argentina, throughout Brazil. See *Knipolegus poecilocercus.*

VERMILION FLYCATCHER, *Pyrocephalus rubinus,* Verão, Príncipe PL 33.9

13 cm. Male is one of most beautiful tyrannids. Female and young male generally recognizable by traces of pink in under tail coverts, sometimes mixed with yellow. For analysis of red color, see "Morphology. . . ." VOICE: a weak *pst;* song a sequence of high *tee-LINGs* while overflying territory with fluttering, well-raised wings. Also sings perched, using same phrase, singly. At height of breeding season dawn and dusk song extends almost throughout night. Savanna and cerrado regions.

Migration: Emigrates in southern winter, invading areas of populations resident in more northerly regions, e.g., central Brazil, Amazonia. Southern race, *P. r. rubinus,* migrates to Ecuador and Colombia. At this time (May for a caged individual in Rio de Janeiro, August in Pará) it is in eclipse plumage with varying quantity of brown feathers. Adults of Argentine population, which emigrates to Amazonia, leave at peak of hot season (January) immediately after young of their 2d brood become independent. Young, which stay 3 months longer, reach adolescence during this time and emigrate only when cold begins (end of April, Hudson 1920). In certain regions, e.g., Paraná, known only as a migrant in winter. In August 1973, 7 individuals in poor physical condition that later died were found on Currais Island, Paraná (Pedro Scherer Neto). One individual came aboard a vessel 135 mi off coast opposite Torres, Rio Grande do Sul (September 1973). California and Mexico to Argentina, Bolivia; also Galapagos islands, throughout Brazil. Also called *São-joãozinho* (Mato Grosso Pantanal), *Canário-sanguinho* (Minas Gerais).

DRAB WATER-TYRANT, *Ochthornis* (= *Ochthoeca*) *littoralis*

13.5 cm. similar to Little Ground-Tyrant, *Muscisaxicola fluviatilis,* but with white around eye, black bill, sooty tail, white (not yellowish) abdomen. Sandy beaches of white-water rivers; nests on banks. Extreme north and west from the Guianas to Roraima, Óbidos, Tapajós, and more to west, Rondônia.

GRAY MONJITA, *Xolmis cinerea,* Maria-branca, Primavera   Fig. 236

22.5 cm. Thrush-sized savanna and cerrado species widely distributed south of Amazon. Gray and white, in flight reveals clear black-and-white wing pattern. VOICE: call high, with timbre of domestic chick, *PEEa;* song *PEEeh-PEEeh-ili, dew-dlee-ew,* a limpid whistle sung at dawn and during day. Flies skillfully, frequently with legs dangling and toes closed like a fist, resembling a bird of prey such as White-tailed Kite, *Elanus leucurus.* At times surrounded and pursued by other birds as if it were a hawk. Nuptial flight undulating. Savanna and cerrado regions. On migration appears in metropolitan areas, e.g., Rio de Janeiro, singing and perching on TV antennas of buildings in city center and at National Museum, Qunita da Boa Vista. Right bank of lower Amazon as far as Tapajós south to Rio Grande do Sul, Uru-

guay, Argentina, Paraguay, Bolivia; also Amapá, savanna regions of Suriname. Some birds migrate during local winter, announcing spring by their return. Recorded in Rio Grande do Sul all year (Belton 1985) and in state of Rio de Janeiro, numbers augmented in midyear by migrants from south (R. Pineschi). Also called *Mocinha-branca, Pombinha-das-almas, Para-bala-branco* (Minas Gerais).

BLACK-CROWNED MONJITA, *Xolmis coronata,* Noivinha-coroada   SV

22 cm. Large, gray above, white below, wings and tail black. Cap bordered with white. Female smaller but similarly colored. Open country. Only in extreme south (Rio Grande do Sul, Santa Catarina, Argentina, Paraguay, Bolivia).

WHITE-RUMPED MONJITA, *Xolmis velata,* Noivinha-branca

20 cm. Similar to *X. coronata* but with head whitish, rump, upper tail coverts, and base of tail white (the last very clear in flight). VOICE: silent during day; intense dawn song surprising, a monotonous song *jew* repeated at intervals of 1–5 seconds; infrequently this whistle is also heard at night, when it is easily confused with an insect voice. Hovers. Savanna, sometimes alongside *X. cinerea,* e.g., Rio de Janeiro, Minas Gerais. Migratory. Mouth of Amazon to São Paulo, Mato Grosso, Paraguay, Bolivia. Also called *Lavadeira, Pombinha-das-almas.*

WHITE MONJITA, *Xolmis irupero,* Noivinha Fig. 237

17 cm. In purity of white and elegance of flight one of our most beautiful birds. Lacks slightest camouflage except

Fig.236. Gray Monjita, *Xolmis cinerea.*

Fig. 237. White Monjita, *Xolmis irupero.*

when seen against a sky full of white clouds, which often occurs. VOICE: a weak *ghiks,* a whining *piew;* usually silent. Master of hovering, staying as if fixed in air for a considerable period. Then dives down, usually braking just above ground and flying away. May resemble a large butterfly. Visible from a distance as a white spot when it is watching from a branch tip or post. If chased hides among dense spiny branches. Savannas with sparse bushes and trees, marsh edges, sometimes alongside *X. cinerea.* Northeastern and southern Brazil, southern Mato Grosso, Santa Catarina, Rio Grande do Sul, farther south. Also called *Viuvinha-alegre* (Rio Grande do Sul).

BLACK-AND-WHITE MONJITA, *Heteroxolmis* (= *Xolmis*) *dominicana,* Noivinha-rabo-preto

20 cm. White with black wings and tail, tips of primaries white, a rare occurrence in birds. Female grayish above with wings and tail like male; immature has rusty back. Marsh edges and burned areas in open country where it hovers and descends to ground, sometimes alongside *X. cinerea.* Silent. Restricted to south with very local occurrence. Paraná to Rio Grande do Sul, Uruguay, Argentina (where migratory), Paraguay. Frequently found with *Xanthopsar flavus,* as I noted from 1966 forward in Rio Grande do Sul. Separation of this species from the genus *Xolmis* is well justified by its anatomy (Lanyon 1986). Apparently becoming rare, but there are recent records from Rio Grande do Sul. See *X. irupero.*

CHOCOLATE-VENTED TYRANT, *Neoxolmis rufiventris,* Gaúcho-chocolate   SV

22 cm; 77 g. Southern terrestrial migrant, resembling a large thrush. Draws attention by rapidly opening and closing long tail. Gray with black wings and tail, wing with noticeable white-and-chestnut speculum, belly ferruginous. One of largest and heaviest tyrannids. Frequents pastures, running on ground in small flocks. Breeds in Patagonia, occasional in winter in Rio Grande do Sul (May).

LITTLE GROUND-TYRANT, *Muscisaxicola fluviatilis* SV

13.5 cm. Brownish gray, inconspicuous, resembling a pipit, *Anthus,* noticeable when it opens and lifts white-sided black tail. Runs on beaches and rocks, appearing alongside migrant sandpipers. May enter Brazil only on migration. Appears in upper Purus and Madeira, Gi-Paraná. Genus is represented by many species in Andes. See *Ochthornis littoralis.*

AUSTRAL NEGRITO, *Lessonia rufa,* Colegial, Negrito   SV

12.5 cm. Terrestrial southern migrant, black except on back which is intense rufous (resembling backpack of a student, thus the name *colegial,* "schoolboy"). Female smaller,

Fig. 238. Crested Black-Tyrant, *Knipolegus lophotes.*

grayish brown with faded reddish back. Water's edge, runs like a sandpiper although legs are short. Tierra del Fuego to Rio Grande do Sul, where it appears in good numbers May–August; also Bolivia, Peru. Common in southern Chile and Argentina.

CRESTED BLACK-TYRANT, *Knipolegus lophotes,* Maria-preta-de-penacho   Fig. 238

20 cm. Open-country bird with permanently erect, high crest. Steely black with bases of flight feathers white, forming a large stripe in open wing. Unlike congeners, sexes similar, but female slightly smaller. VOICE: usually silent; night song of a perched bird is bisyllabic, composed of a modulated, ascending note and a modulated descending note with a short trill, *dewEE-kwirr* (Serra da Canastra, Minas Gerais, L. P. Gonzaga, October 1983.) Savanna regions from Minas Gerais to Rio Grande do Sul, Uruguay, Goiás, Mato Grosso; also highlands, e.g., of Itatiaia and Caparaó, where it meets *K. nigerrimus,* which attacks it when meeting occurs near nest. There is a surprising convergence between *K. lophotes* and male Phainopepla, *Phainopepla nitens* (Ptilogonatidae) of southwestern North America, resident in a very similar environment.

VELVETY BLACK-TYRANT, *Knipolegus nigerrimus,* Maria-preta-de-garganta-vermelha   BR

17.5 cm. Similar to *K. lophotes* but smaller and lacking crest. Has white streak hidden in wing, whitish bill. Female different, black with throat streaked chestnut. Makes the transition between forest and open country in mountains, usually above 1800 m, in Espírito Santo, Minas Gerais, Bahia (Raso da Catarina), Paraná, Rio Grande do Sul; also on highest points in city of Rio de Janeiro (Corcovado, Pico da Tijuca, Pico da Gávea). Migratory, coming partway down in winter from high campos of Itatiaia to about 1000 m.

WHITE-WINGED BLACK-TYRANT, *Knipolegus aterrimus,* Maria-preta-do-nordeste

16.2 cm. Male very similar to *K. nigerrimus* but smaller with white stripe in wing. Female similar to female *K. cyanirostris* but less streaked below. Male makes short, vertical display flight (white in wing) and utters a mechanical *toc-tec* at highest point (Straneck and Carrizo 1983). Caatinga, forest openings. Upper São Francisco (Bahia, Minas Gerais) to Bolivia, Argentina, Peru.

RUFOUS-TAILED TYRANT, *Knipolegus poecilurus* Amazonia.

RIVERSIDE TYRANT, *Knipolegus orenocensis* Amazonia.

BLUE-BILLED BLACK-TYRANT, *Knipolegus cyanirostris,* Maria-preta-de-bico-azulado PL 33.5

15 cm. Uniformly black forest species lacking white in flight feathers but with light gray bill. Female brown with 2 yellowish wing bars, underparts heavily streaked with blackish brown and dirty white. Upper and lower tail coverts and inner vanes of rectrices bright ferruginous. VOICE: a high *it* while perched. Male, with wings raised, glides silently down in front of female. Hunts insects (see "Feeding"). Migratory (Espírito Santo, Rio de Janeiro). Espírito Santo and Minas Gerais to Rio Grande do Sul, Mato Grosso, Argentina, Paraguay, Uruguay, in mountainous regions in northern part of range. Female similar to *Myiophobus fasciatus,* which is much smaller, less clearly streaked below, and lacks reddish in tail. See also female of *K. poecilocercus.*

AMAZONIAN BLACK-TYRANT, *Knipolegus* (= *Phaeotriccus*) *poecilocercus,* Pretinho-do-igapó

12.5 cm. Amazonian. All black, male extremely similar to *Xenopipo atronitens* but with dark bill. In both sexes 3 external primaries are pointed (instead of "normally" rounded); female different, resembles *Myiophobus fasciatus:* greenish chestnut above, 2 whitish wing bars, underparts light brownish, breast more darkly streaked, tail (including coverts) light ferruginous. VOICE: male a high *tsik,* like an insect, while opening wings slightly; female a louder *pit-pit.* In pairs in interior of dark, flooded forest at low levels. Amazonia south to Xingu (northern Mato Grosso), Tocantins (Pará). Sometimes not far from its counterpart, *X. atronitens.* See *Cnemotriccus fuscatus.*

HUDSON'S BLACK-TYRANT, *Knipolegus* (= *Phaeotriccus*) *hudsoni* SV

Nests in Argentina, migrates to Paraguay, Bolivia, Mato Grosso (Descalvados, Serra do Roncador, August–September).

CINEREOUS TYRANT, *Knipolegus* (= *Entotriccus*) *striaticeps* SV

Another southern species found in Argentina, Bolivia, southern Mato Grosso.

SPECTACLED TYRANT, *Hymenops perspicillatus,* Viuvinha-de-óculos Fig. 239

14 cm. Southern wetland species. Male unmistakable, black with bare, swollen area around eye in form of a

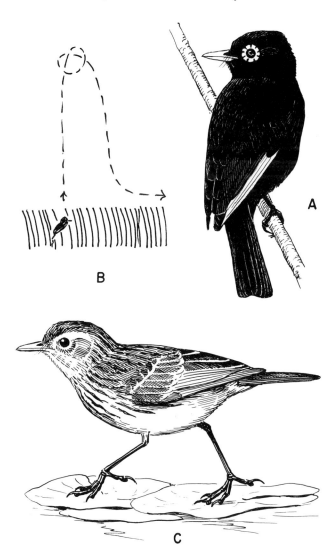

Fig. 239. Spectacled Tyrant, *Hymenops perspicillatus:* (A) the male perched; (B) in the background, in territorial flight over reedbeds (see also fig. 224); and (C) female walking on floating vegetation.

wrinkled, light yellow rosette; primaries almost entirely white, suddenly revealed in flight. Female and young male streaked brown with large ferruginous area on wing like furnariids, so different from adult male that they were long considered another species. SOUNDS AND DISPLAYS: during breeding performs a perpendicular flight displaying black-and-white wings most impressively. Rising, takes 28–30 wing beats per second and produces a loud humming like a hummingbird. Then throws itself on back and at peak, 4–6 m above ground, does a somersault. Afterward, while descending, utters a cry, *zheeeeee*. Flight always swift, with a whistling sound. Walks, runs, hops over mud, stops abruptly to stand well erect and make a rapid movement of wings and tail. Catches insects on ground and in flight. Chile and Patagonia to Mato Grosso, Santa Catarina, Rio Grande do Sul, sometimes migrating as far as Rio de Janeiro (August).

PIED WATER-TYRANT, *Fluvicola pica,*
Lavadeira-de-cara-branca

12.6 cm. Riverine species with white face and underparts, black upperparts from crown back except for some white spots on wings and narrow white band across rump (*F. p. albiventer*). Specimens from Roraima and farther north have white scapulars. Female similar but tail edged white. VOICE: call (pair) *tika* (*albiventer*). Performs prenuptial flights. Locally from the Guianas through Amazonia and the northeast (also Pirapora, Minas Gerais) to central Brazil, Paraná, Bolivia, Uruguay. Sometimes alongside *F. nengeta* in western Bahia, although there is a certain ecological separation in the sense that *F. pica* is even more dependent on open water. Also uses artificial lakes, like *F. nengeta*. See female *Arundinicola leucocephala*.

Fig. 240. Masked Water-Tyrant, *Fluvicola nengeta,* walking on floating *Salvinia* leaves.

Fig. 242. Long-tailed Tyrant, *Colonia colonus,* male.

Fig. 241. White-headed Marsh-Tyrant, *Arundinicola leucocephala,* male.

MASKED WATER-TYRANT, *Fluvicola nengeta,*
Lavadeira-mascarada   Fig. 240

15 cm. Similar to *F. pica* but larger with white head, black stripe behind eye, light gray back. Female similar. VOICE: call soft, typical, *tsewk;* song a soft, repeated, tremulous *dewdelewdel-dewdel.* Male raises himself to full height with tail fanned and displays black underside of wings by spreading them horizontally. Muddy shores. Runs on floating vegetation. Eastern Brazil and the northeast, typically at edge of any kind of waterhole or reservoir. South to Rio de Janeiro and ex-Guanabara since 1950s, when it began to appear at Rio Botanical Garden and later at Zoological Garden, Catete Palace gardens, and Sernambetiba, Marambaia, and other places. Occasionally near *F. pica* (Piauí, Bahia). There is a population in Peru and Ecuador. Also called *Maria-lencinho.*

WHITE-HEADED MARSH-TYRANT, *Arundinicola leucocephala,* Lavadeira-de-cabeça-branca   Fig. 241

12.4 cm. Widely distributed water-edge species. Male unmistakable. Female resembles *Fluvicola nengeta* but stockier and lacks black streak on sides of head and white on rump. Wings brownish, mandible yellowish. VOICE: *biriririt,* but usually silent. In nuptial flight rises rapidly at 45° angle to a good height, uttering repeatedly at short intervals a low phrase, *dew-de-lewde.* Marshes. Perches regularly on branches but does not move around on ground like *Fluvicola,* sometimes its neighbors. The Guianas and Colombia to

Bolivia, Paraguay, Argentina, throughout Brazil. Also called *Viuvinha, Freirinha.*

LONG-TAILED TYRANT, *Colonia colonus,*
Viuvinha   Fig. 242

13.3 cm, not counting lengthened central tail feathers which add 9 cm (sometimes more than 10 cm) to male, 2 cm to female. Tip of tail before molt is frequently worn or even broken. Unmistakable. Black with whitish cap and rump. Immature has short tail, no white at all. VOICE: *WEEeh,* a high penetrating whistle, timbre resembling call of Barefaced Curassow, *Crax fasciolata.* During courtship birds chase each other crying *prrri, bi-bibi. . . .* Hunts insects, spying them out from high leafless branches of tall trees. Migratory. The Guianas and Ecuador to Bolivia, Paraguay, central and eastern Brazil, Maranhão to Rio Grande do Sul. More often found in mountains in Espírito Santo and Rio de Janeiro. Also called *Viuva, Freirinha-da-serra* (Minas Gerais).

STRANGE-TAILED TYRANT, *Alectrurus*
(= *Yetapa*) *risora,* Bandeira-do-campo

15 cm, 33 cm including male's "flags." Color similar to *A. tricolor* but differs in having enormously elongated outer tail feathers that are elastic, twisted, and broadened at ends into long black flags. Female resembles female *Colonia colonus* but has elongated tail (body and tail = 20.5 cm).

Fig. 243. Cock-tailed Tyrant, *Alectrurus tricolor,* mated pair. In the background, a male flying, seen from behind, showing the vertical position of the tail, resembling a DC-10.

Little-known southern savanna species, becoming rare. Uruguay, Argentina, and Paraguay to Rio Grande do Sul (exceptionally), São Paulo, western Mato Grosso. Also called *Tesoura-do-campo*. See *Gubernetes yetapa*.

COCK-TAILED TYRANT, *Alectrurus tricolor*, Galito   Fig. 243

13.5 cm; with tail prolongations may reach 19 cm. Male's tail shape extraordinary: the 2 wide, stiff middle rectrices twist 90°, so their vanes are in a vertical position like ship's rudder and rise above head level like tail of a domestic rooster. Tail seems to be pulling bird backward, as if it weighs too much, an impression enhanced by black color. Lateral rectrices form an inclined plane on either side of "rudder" and serve as stabilizers in flight. In drawing the illustration to show the normal position of the rectrices I have used a specimen mounted by Prince Maximilian of Wied (see Chapter 2.4). Body pattern is a confusing black-and-white mixture with prominent white V on upperside and incomplete black breast band. Bill yellow. Female brown with darker, "normal" tail and wings, white throat.

SOUNDS AND DISPLAYS: During courtship, when male flies up obliquely some 4 m and then lets himself fall, tail proportions cause an even stranger impression, especially on descent: the spectator confuses wings with tail, not knowing which end is which. During this descent birds utters a weak *tic-tic-tic . . .* sequence, like an insect. On reproduction, see "Breeding." Marshes, humid savannas, cerrado. Locally from Minas Gerais to Paraná, Rio Grande do Sul, Federal District (where it migrated after lake was created). Mato Grosso, Bolivia, Paraguay (where migratory), and Misiones, Argentina. Broadening and vertical placement of central tail feathers remotely resemble that of Eastern Paradise-Whydah, *Vidua paradisaea*, of Africa (Ploceidae, Viduinae).

STREAMER-TAILED TYRANT, *Gubernetes yetapa*, Tesoura-do-brejo   Fig. 244

42 cm including long, graduated, forked tail. Upperparts gray; wings and tail black with large ferruginous speculum; white throat bordered by chestnut band. Female has shorter tail (total length 35 cm). VOICE: call a harsh *shrewip;* a fuller 2- to 3-syllable descending phrase, *jew-jew-jew.* Also has a dawn song. Rhythmically fans tail, lifting wings and displaying light reddish streak in front of female. Hunts flying low over marshes. Open marshes and buriti palm groves (Mato Grosso, Goiás). Bahia and Minas Gerais to São Paulo, Rio Grande do Sul, Paraguay, Argentina (Misiones), Bolivia. Also called *Tesoura*. See *Alectrurus risora*.

YELLOW-BROWED TYRANT, *Satrapa icterophrys*, Suiriri-pequeno

16.5 cm. Resembles *Myiozetetes* and *Philohydor lictor.* Short bill; intense olive green upperparts; sides of head,

Fig. 244. Streamer-tailed Tyrant, *Gubernetes yetapa*.

wings, and tail blackish; wide superciliary and entire underparts intense yellow; 2 whitish wing bars. Edge of secondary forest, restinga, lake edges. Eastern and central Brazil to Bolivia, Uruguay; also Venezuela. Smaller and yellower than *Tyrannus melancholicus*.

CLIFF FLYCATCHER, *Hirundinea ferruginea*, Gibão-de-couro   PL 35.7

17.5 cm. Unmistakable in appearance and ecology, being almost only Brazilian bird that lives in quarries and rocky escarpments without being entirely montane. VOICE:

TSREEdew, WEEewrr, birrr, from which one vernacular name is derived. Accustomed to life among rocks, easily adapts to cities, where it hunts insects by launching out from parapets of office buildings, churches, etc., to which it then returns. Also nests in these spots (see "Breeding"). Also appears far from stony environments, especially since it migrates and may then be found any place. The Guianas to Bolivia, Argentina, Uruguay, central and eastern Brazil, often in isolated places because of adaptation to rocky environment. Typical of karstic region of Minas Gerais, an ideal habitat for its nesting. Also called *Birro, Bem-te-vi-gamela* (Ceará). Includes *H. bellicosa.*

CATTLE TYRANT, *Machetornis rixosus,* Bem-te-vi-do-gado

18.5 cm. Resembles *Tyrannus melancholicus* but is smaller and paler with the upperparts greenish brownish, outer tail feathers with yellowish white tip prominent in flight. VOICE: reveals its identity by voice, more strident than *T. melancholicus* and differently phrased: song *tip-tip, tsi-tsip-tsiLIP-tsiLIP; tsirrrrr.* Cultivated fields, other open areas, city parks. Walks on ground (unlike *T. melancholicus*), accompanies cattle to catch insects they stir up while grazing; penetrates marshes perched on backs of cattle. Partially migratory in south. Venezuela to Bolivia, Argentina, Uruguay, eastern and central Brazil. Also called *Cavaleiro.*

SHEAR-TAILED GRAY-TYRANT, *Muscipipra vetula,* Tesoura-cinzenta

22 cm. Kingbird-sized, southern arboreal species, unlike any other. Uniformly dark gray with black wings and long, forked, black tail. VOICE: a muffled but far-reaching, attention-getting, bisyllabic whistle, *jew-bewt.* Hunts insects flying around canopy. Edge of secondary forest. Espírito Santo and Minas Gerais to Rio Grande do Sul, Argentina (Misiones), Paraguay. Mountains in Espírito Santo and Rio de Janeiro but reaches Municipality of Rio de Janeiro at Pedra Branca (August).

SUBFAMILY TYRANNINAE

GRAY-HOODED ATTILA, *Attila rufus,* Capitão-de-saíra   BR PL 30.9

20 cm. Forest bird of southeast, thrush sized, slender, with long, sturdy, slightly hooked bill. Immature's bill black. VOICE: quite varied, *the voice of tall forest,* resembling *Sirystes sibilator:* a bisyllabic *EE ew,* a melodious *ewee-i, i, i, i, i, i, i, i, i, i-ew;* a prolonged, ascending sequence of well-pronounced whistles, terminating with lower *ewEE-ewEE . . . ew-eh;* warning a hard shrieking *tseREtek, tsek.* When excited moves tail slowly forward and shakes it upward without opening it. Forest in lowland and mountains, from floor to canopy, frequently searching for food on ground. Hammers on rotten wood, catches butterflies in flight, eats ants, tree frogs, berries, etc. Sometimes in mixed flocks. Southeastern Bahia and Minas Gerais to Rio Grande do Sul. Also called *Tinguá-açu.* The *Attila* genus was transferred to the tyrannids from the cotingids for anatomical reasons (osteology, syrinx structure), as were *Laniocera, Rhytipterna,* and *Casiornis.*

BRIGHT-RUMPED ATTILA, *Attila spadiceus,* Capitão-de-saíra-amarelo

17 cm. Resembles a *Myiarchus* but has bright yellow rump with remaining colors quite variable, back green or brown, etc. There are 3 or 4 color phases, or morphs. VOICE: loud and full, resembling *A. rufus:* a rhythmic, ascending sequence of bisyllabic whistles, a loud *tirrit,* etc. Widely distributed in Amazonia; reaches coastal forests as far south as Alagoas, Espírito Santo (Rio Doce), Rio de Janeiro.

CINNAMON ATTILA, *Attila cinnamomeus* Amazonia to Maranhão.

CITRON-BELLIED ATTILA, *Attila citriniventris* Amazonia.

WHITE-EYED ATTILA, *Attila bolivianus* Amazonia.

RUFOUS-TAILED ATTILA, *Attila (= Pseudattila) phoenicurus,* Capitão-castanho

17.6 cm. Similar to *A. rufus* but only cap is gray. VOICE: a rhythmic, ascending sequence, *bee-bi BEE-bit* (November, December, Itatiaia), tirelessly repeated; a sonorous mewing, *ew-EE-eh* (February). Fans tail backward and forward. Forest canopies. Rio de Janeiro, São Paulo, Paraná, Santa Catarina, Rio Grande do Sul, and centralwest (southern Goiás, Mato Grosso) to Misiones, Argentina; in Itatiaia alongside *rufus.*

RUFOUS CASIORNIS, *Casiornis rufa,* Caneleiro PL 30.8

16.5 cm. Not uncommon locally in central Brazil. Resembles a female *Tachyphonus* or *Attila cinnamomeus* but bill light, crown rusty. VOICE: a trisyllabic descending sequence of high whistles, *pseep-pseep-pseep.* Middle levels of cerrado groves, clearings at edge of cerradão. Central Brazil: Goiás, Federal District, Mato Grosso (Rio das Mortes) to western Minas Gerais, São Paulo; Argentina, Paraguay, Bolivia; in north to Pará (Monte Alegre) and Maranhão, apparently a visiting migrant in north in winter. Also called *Bem-te-vi-castanho* (Minas Gerais). Formerly considered a cotingid (see *Attila rufus*). See *C. fusca*.

ASH-THROATED CASIORNIS, *Casiornis fusca,* Caneleiro-enxofre   BR

Very similar to *C. rufa* but with brown back contrasting with reddish cap and rump. Underparts whitish sulfur (not rusty yellow). Capoeira, tall forest, cerrado, caatinga, sometimes in canopy. South of lower Amazon from Rio Tapajós to northern Mato Grosso (upper Xingu), Goiás (Bananal), Minas Gerais (Rio São Francisco), the northeast (Maranhão, northern Bahia). Appears to be northern geographic replacement of *rufa*. I have not found the two in the same place in Mato Grosso.

GRAYISH MOURNER, *Rhytipterna simplex,* Wissiá

19.5 cm. Resembles a *Lipaugus* in almost uniformly gray color but differs in that sole of tarsus has very rough scales. Slightly crested with light brown iris. Female and immature have rusty spots on wings and tail feathers. VOICE: a full, crescendo phrase, *o, o, o, o, o, o-EEo;* a monosyllabic *psorr,* both resembling *Leptopogon amaurocephalus;* a steeply ascending short phrase with last 2 notes separated. Forest interior. Southern Amazonia to Bolivia, northern Mato Grosso, Maranhão; also coastal forests of Alagoas to Rio de Janeiro (Ilha Grande), ex-Guanabara. Previously considered a cotingid but transferred to tyrannids because of skull and syrinx morphology. Distinctive modification of rear face of tarsus (resembling that of a young toucan) may be an adaptation for perching in a cavity with a hard, wood bottom.

PALE-BELLIED MOURNER, *Rhytipterna immunda,* Wissiá-cantor

18 cm. Little known, rare in museum collections. Very similar in appearance to *Myiarchus ferox* but tarsus serrated like *R. simplex,* bill narrower than a *Myiarchus.* Belly pale yellow. VOICE: a sequence of loud, limpid, well-pronounced notes, *deww-deww-di-WEETye,* resembling a robust frigillid such as Common Rosefinch, *Carpodacus erythrinus,* of Northern hemisphere. Sings only at dawn or dusk, proclaiming territory, shifting its perch 50 m or more after each song. Eats large, hairy caterpillars, grasshoppers, other arthropods, spiders, berries. Edge of cerrado and cerradão, open gallery forest, sparse forest rich in terrestrial lichens (sandy soil) between savanna and deep forest, alongside *Myiarchus tyrannulus, Elaenia ruficeps, Hemitriccus aenigma, Neopelma pallescens, Xenopipo atronitens, Basileuterus flaveolus, Turdus ignobilis,* and *Tachyphonus phoenicius* (Cururu), companion fauna similar to that noted by Haverschmidt (1975) for *R. immunda* in Suriname. I found this species in 1949 and 1957 and made the first notes on its ecology, but it was identified only in 1972 by W. E. Lanyon. Savanna bordering Amazonian forest, including campinas of white sand.

Locally from the Guianas and Colombia to northern Mato Grosso (upper Xingu, Serra do Roncador), southwestern Pará (upper Rio Tapajós, headwaters of Cururu), Santarém (Pará), Manaus, Iaunari (Rio Negro, Amazonas).

CINEREOUS MOURNER, *Laniocera hypopyrrha,* Chorona-cinza   PL 31.6

20.7 cm. Forest bird, widely distributed in Amazonia, resembling a *Lipaugus* in plumage. Tarsal covering exaspidean, like that of manakins. VOICE: a high, prolonged, descending whistle, similar to *Oxyruncus cristatus* but fuller and sometimes repeated; a bisyllabic shriek; *weet-jeh,* repeated, resembling *Lipaugus* and *Casiornis.* Lives quietly at middle levels in forest interior. The Guianas to Bolivia, northern Mato Grosso (Rios Tapajós, Xingu), eastern Pará (Belém). Also southern Bahia, northern Espírito Santo. Also called *Sanhaçu-da-mata* (Pará). Previously included in Cotingidae (near *Laniisoma*), with which it has considerable biological similarity. I have known it for many years and have always considered it to be a cotingid.

SIRYSTES, *Sirystes sibilator,* Gritador   Fig. 245

17.8 cm. Relatively large forest species, notable for loud voice. Cap, sides of head, wings, and tail black; upper- and underparts gray; wing feathers with whitish edges; bill large. VOICE: a resonant whistle, *ewe-ewe-ewe, wee, wee, wee-WEEeh, tew, tew, ti, ti, ti, ti, ti, ti, ti, tew,* with timbre similar to *Attila rufus.* Tall forest canopy. Migratory (Rio Grande do Sul, Rio de Janeiro, Espírito Santo). Suriname to Bolivia,

Fig. 245. Sirystes, *Sirystes s. sibilator.*

Paraguay, Argentina (Misiones), throughout Brazil. Common in mountainous areas of Rio de Janeiro and Espírito Santo. May recall *Pachyramphus validus*.

SHORT-CRESTED FLYCATCHER, *Myiarchus ferox*, Maria-cavaleira

19.5 cm. One of 4 Brazilian *Myiarchus*, extremely similar to *M. swainsoni*. Usually has black bill; more easily identified by voice. VOICE: song a short, simple, horizontal trill, *TREE, i, i*, especially at dawn; call a descending, short *trrrew* or *prrew*, the most frequent vocalization during day; a long, hurried, sharply descending sequence resembling a corresponding phrase of *Camptostoma obsoletum: SPREE, i, i, i, i . . .*, without parallel among other *Myiarchus*. All *Myiarchus* have habit of ruffling crown feathers. Edge of woods and capoeira. Central, eastern, and Amazonian Brazil, including Rio de Janeiro and western Rio Grande do Sul; also Bolivia, Uruguay. See *Rhytipterna immunda*.

BROWN-CRESTED FLYCATCHER, *Myiarchus tyrannulus*, Maria-cavaleira-de-rabo-enferrujado   PL 33.6

19.5 cm. Inner vane of all except central tail feathers bordered with ferruginous, visible when tail is opened. Outer vane of primaries also edged, more or less clearly, with same color. VOICE: dawn song a hurried, rhythmic phrase, last note lower, *wit tewtewletewt;* calls short, ascending whistles, *wit*, and repeated *wit, wit . . .* , sometimes compounded, *wit-trelit*. Sparse forest, cerrado, caatinga. Locally migratory. Arizona and Mexico to upper Rio Branco, the Guianas, lower Amazon, and eastern Brazil to western Rio Grande do Sul, Goiás, Mato Grosso, Paraguay, Bolivia. Also called *Maria-tola* (Minas Gerais). Occasionally (Mato Grosso) in same areas as *M. swainsoni* and *M. ferox*.

SWAINSON'S FLYCATCHER, *Myiarchus swainsoni*, Irrê

19.5 cm. Even more similar to *M. ferox* but with mandible usually light brown, not black. VOICE: dawn song 2 sonorous whistles separated by a distinct interval, a slow sequence, 1st whistle deeper and descending, *ewo ewEEo;* dawn song (Marajó, Pará) an unmusical *spch-jrrreww*. Has many other vocalizations, as do other *Myiarchus*. Secondary forest. Migratory. Venezuela to Bolivia, Argentina, Paraguay, Uruguay, throughout Brazil, including Rio Grande do Sul.

DUSKY-CAPPED FLYCATCHER, *Myiarchus tuberculifer*, Maria-cavaleira-pequena

16 cm. Recognizable by smaller size and blackish crown. VOICE: similar to *M. swainsoni*, a bit higher (smaller bird) but also characterized by deep, descending whistle, *ewo*, and bisyllabic song, 2d syllable higher, shriller. Treetops of secondary forest. Arizona and Mexico to Bolivia, Argentina, Amazonia (Itacotiara, Amazonas, and Carajás, Pará), eastern Brazil to Rio de Janeiro.

GREAT KISKADEE, *Pitangus sulphuratus*, Bem-te-vi, Bem-te-vi-de-coroa   PL 35.2

22.5 cm; 54–60 g. Probably our best-known bird, much more robust than other similar species, with long, powerful bill. VOICE: call a trisyllabic *beng-te-vee*, or *bi-HEEeh* or *CHEEeh;* song a 4-syllable phrase, *beeeww-biew-prrrr-beeeww*, sung periodically at dawn, with sonorous rattle, *prrrr*, most notable. Young, after abandoning nest, cry *ieh* incessantly. Impressive in its vivacity, adapting to any environment and constantly discovering new food sources (see "Feeding"). Hovers well; regularly seen fishing at water's edge (see "Perils . . ."). Cultivated fields, cities, perches on buildings, its cries penetrating most remote recesses. Sometimes lives semidomesticated. Migrates from highest and coldest regions of south (e.g., northern Rio Grande do Sul); migration more evident in Argentina. An individual caught in Santa Catarina (January) had been banded in Santiago del Estero, Argentina, 1300 km to west. Texas, where it nests, to Argentina, throughout Brazil.

LESSER KISKADEE, *Philohydor* (= *Pitangus*) *lictor*, Bem-te-vizinho-do-brejo

18 cm. Small, water-edge species, resembling *Myiozetetes cayanensis* but with quite long, slender bill. Crest sulfur yellow, edges of outer flight feathers rusty. VOICE: an inconspicuous, high *sirr*, a bisyllabic *tsri-tsri*. Low along edges of lakes and marshes. Panama to Bolivia, Brazil: northwest (Amazonia), center, and east, south to Mato Grosso, Rio de Janeiro. This species was removed from the *Pitangus* for 2 reasons: syrinx structure is different, and it builds an open-saucer nest rather than a closed nest with a side entrance. Owing to erroneous data, ball-shaped *Myiozetetes* nests were thought to have been made by *Philohydor*. New name, "friend of the water." refers to its ecology.

BOAT-BILLED FLYCATCHER, *Megarynchus pitangua*, Nei-nei, Bem-te-vi-de-bico-chato

21.5 cm. Very similar to *Pitangus sulphuratus* but with extremely, but variably, wide, flat bill. Short tarsus. VOICE: call a characteristic *nay-nay;* territorial song a repeated *chewlewlew*, sung periodically, somewhat similar to *Myiodynastes maculatus*. Pairs' duets badly synchronized. Forest canopy. Mexico to Argentina, almost all of Brazil, including the east and south as far as Rio Grande do Sul. Migratory. Also called *Bem-te-vi-gameleiro* (Minas Gerais).

RUSTY-MARGINED FLYCATCHER, *Myiozetetes cayanensis*, Bem-te-vizinho-de-asa-ferrugínea PL 33.7

17.5 cm. One of several small, kiskadee-type flycatchers difficult to identify; recognizable by blackish sides of head, yellow or orange center stripe on crown, and particularly by clearly rusty edges of flight and tail feathers. VOICE: easy to identify; call a soft, prolonged whistle, *eww-ew, ew-EE-ew;* song a repeated *TSLEElidi.* Wing-rustle *prrrew-prrrew.* . . . Trees near water. Panama across Amazonia to Bolivia, Mato Grosso, Goiás, Minas Gerais, Pará, Maranhão; also Rio de Janeiro. Migratory (Rio de Janeiro). See *M. similis.*

SOCIAL FLYCATCHER, *Myiozetetes similis,*
Bem-te-vizinho-penacho-vermelho

17.5 cm. Much like *M. cayanensis* but usually lacking rusty edges on wings and tail feathers (except in young) and with red streak in cap that appears when bird is excited. VOICE: different; call a strident *PSEEeh, GLEEeh;* song *see-gli, gli, gli, gli, TSEElili-TSEElili.* Independent of water; inhabits edge of secondary forest, parks, gardens, street trees. Mexico to Bolivia, Argentina, and eastern, southern, and Amazonian Brazil to Santa Catarina, Rio Grande do Sul. Also common in Rio de Janeiro (state and municipality). Migratory (Rio de Janeiro). See *Philohydor lictor.*

GRAY-CAPPED FLYCATCHER, *Myiozetetes granadensis*
Only in extreme west.

DUSKY-CHESTED FLYCATCHER, *Myiozetetes luteiventris*
Upper Amazon.

THREE-STRIPED FLYCATCHER, *Conopias trivirgata,*
Bem-te-vi-pequeno   PL 34.1

15 cm. Resembles the *Myiozetetes* but has heavier bill, wide, white, auricular streak that extends to nape, and black cap without red or yellow in center. VOICE: a muffled *j, j, j,* best way to distinguish it from a *Myiozetetes.* Forests and canopy (unlike *Myiozetetes*), establishes itself in *Cacicus* colonies, is aggressive against *Myiodynastes maculatus.* Locally in southeast: Bahia, Espírito Santo, São Paulo, Santa Catarina (Florianópolis), Amazonia (Solimões, Tapajós); also Argentina, Paraguay.

YELLOW-THROATED FLYCATCHER, *Conopias parva*
Primarily north of Amazon.

STREAKED FLYCATCHER, *Myiodynastes maculatus,*
Bem-te-vi-rajado   Fig. 246

21.5 cm. Unmistakable in combination of large size, streaked pattern, and rusty-edged rump and tail feathers. VOICE: *chock, chock-i;* song at dusk a trisyllabic, resonant, descending phrase, *dlui-dluee-gwik,* repeated. Forest canopy. Common in many places; may be most numerous species in northeast, showing that low, young, secondary forests may also offer enough retreats for nesting. Mexico to Bolivia, Argentina. Includes *M. m. solitarius,* widely distributed in south, which migrates in winter to Amazonia (e.g., Manaus). Also called *Pintado, Bem-te-vi-do-mato, Bem-te-vi-preto.* See much smaller *Empidonomus varius.*

Fig. 246. Streaked Flycatcher, *Myiodynastes m. maculatus.*

PIRATIC FLYCATCHER, *Legatus leucophaius,*
Bem-te-vi-pirata

15 cm. Looks like *Empidonomus varius* but smaller with short bill. Superciliaries meet on nape, but voice and behavior are completely different. VOICE: a strident, far-reaching whistle, *DEE, dew, dew-WEEeh,* sung tirelessly. Its impertinent voice in distance usually indicates presence of an icterine colony where it is installed as a nest parasite (see "Breeding"). Tall forest and treetops. Widely distributed from Mexico to Argentina, throughout Brazil to Rio Grande do Sul. Also called *Bem-te-vi-pequeno.* See fig. 228.

VARIEGATED FLYCATCHER, *Empidonomus varius,*
Peitica   Fig. 247

19 cm. Dark brown above; center of crown yellow; long, white superciliaries meeting on nape; white mustache. Upper tail coverts and tail feathers rusty edged. Underparts dirty white, streaked brown. Immature has no streaking on underparts or yellow in crown. VOICE: a high whistle, *tsri, si, si, si* . . . . Treetops, parks, secondary forest edges. Throughout Brazil, not uncommon in east (Rio de Janeiro), to Venezuela, Argentina. Migratory. See immature *Griseotyrannus aurantioatrocristatus* and *Legatus leucophaius.*

CROWNED SLATY FLYCATCHER, *Griseotyrannus* (= *Empidonomus*) *aurantioatrocristatus,*
Peitica-de-chapéu-preto

18 cm. Common central Brazil. Almost uniformly dark gray with black cap having yellow in center. Immature resembles larger *Empidonomus varius,* with white supercili-

Fig. 247. Variegated Flycatcher, *Empidonomus v. varius.*

ary, rusty edges on flight feathers, upper wing coverts, and upper tail coverts, and brown crown with no yellow. VOICE: high whistles; song a 2-part phrase, *tsi-tsitsewbit tsitsewttsi-TSEbidit.* A loud wing rustle, *ewrrrr.* Cerrado, etc. Migratory. Venezuela to Pará, Maranhão, Piauí, Goiás, Mato Grosso, Minas Gerais, Rio Grande do Sul, Argentina.

SULPHURY FLYCATCHER, *Tyrannopsis sulphurea,* Suiriri-de-garganta-rajada

19.5 cm. Very similar to *Tyrannus melancholicus* and *T. albogularis* but with throat extensively streaked with gray and white. VOICE: different; call a loud, harsh *ksi;* song *ks, ks, ks, ks-ksi-gay.* Edge of forests and marshes in canopy. Amazonia, including Solimões, Amapá, Pará, to Maranhão, Goiás.

FORK-TAILED FLYCATCHER, *Tyrannus savana* (= *Muscivora tyrannus*), Tesoura   Fig. 248

40 cm, including long, forked, 29-cm tail. Gray above, white below, with head, wings, and tail black, center of crown sulfur yellow. VOICE: call *tzik;* song a hurried sequence, *tzik-tzik-tsitsitsi . . . ag, ag, ag, ag,* uttered perched or while letting itself fall in a spiral with tail open wide and wings positioned so they resemble a parachute. When chasing insects frequently perches on ground. Takes berries from camboatá [Sapindaceae and Meliaceae]. When resting in a tree customarily leans tail on a branch. Flocks for roosting (see "Behavior"). Savanna and cerrado areas.

Migration, Geographic Races, and Distribution: Outside breeding period assembles in flocks that migrate long distances, sometimes at great heights, resembling swallows. They gather in Amazonia by the hundreds or thousands (e.g., Manaus, August). In southern Minas Gerais largest concentrations occur October–November. In Rio Grande do Sul disappears in March, returns in September. Routes to and from wintering grounds apparently are not always the same. Existence of various geographic races characterized by shape of external primaries (see fig. 221) enables determination of origin of certain individuals forming part of the enormous mixed congregation in Hylaea in southern winter. Adult males of southern race (*T. s. savana,* Argentina to Mato Grosso) have 3 primaries indented at tip; northern races (e.g., *T. s. monachus,* Mexico to Solimões, in Amazonas, and *T. s. circumdatus,* lower Tapajós, Pará) have only 2 modified primaries. *T. s. savana* migrates to Ecuador, Colombia, the Guianas, Curaçao, Trinidad, Texas. Also called *Tesourinha.*

Fig. 248. Fork-tailed Flycatcher, *Tyrannus s. savana,* in territorial flight. Rio das Mortes, Mato Grosso.

TROPICAL KINGBIRD, *Tyrannus melancholicus*, Suiriri PL 33.8

21.5 cm. One of our best-known birds. VOICE: call *siriri;* clatters with bill; dawn song, also frequently sung during day, *srree-srree-srree-srree-it.* Wherever there are trees, common also in cities, where it is first to vocalize each day, even when still dark. Undertakes long flights to find suitable night roost (see "Behavior"). Migratory in south (Rio Grande do Sul, Rio de Janeiro in mountains, Espírito Santo), mostly disappearing in winter. Texas to Argentina, all of Brazil. Also called *Pára-bala* (Minas Gerais). See *T. albogularis.*

Over 8 consecutive years in Itapema, Santa Catarina, P. Raulino Reitz (1988, Alto Biguaçu, Lunardelli, Florianópolis) recorded departure and arrival on migration of a pair of *T. melancholicus* that showed impressive regularity. The schedule was as follows:

Departure	Arrival
1 April 1978	2 October 1978
1 April 1979	4 October 1979
8 April 1980	5 October 1980
3 April 1981	4 and 6 October 1981
3 April 1982	26 September 1982 (after a warm winter)
8 April 1983	7 October 1983 (after a cold winter)
11 and 20 April 1984	5 October 1984 (cold spring)
7 April 1985	5 October 1985

WHITE-THROATED KINGBIRD, *Tyrannus albogularis*, Suiriri-de-garganta-branca

20 cm. Very similar to *T. melancholicus* but with lighter gray crown, clearly greenish back, pure white instead of gray throat. VOICE: very different from *T. melancholicus;* call *tsip, tsip-tsip-tsip;* song *tsi, i, ii-tsi, i, i, i.* Produces a loud hum with wings in swift, horizontal flight (see "Breeding"). Trees around houses, near edge of secondary forest and rivers. Migratory. Suriname and Venezuela to northwestern and central Brazil, Mato Grosso, Goiás, Minas Gerais, São Paulo.

Sometimes alongside *T. melancholicus,* e.g., western Bahia, Amapá.

EASTERN KINGBIRD, *Tyrannus tyrannus* NV

19.5 cm. Sooty above, white below, with conspicuously white-tipped tail. VOICE: a low *tsr.* Generally silent in Brazil, appearing only as a migrant in nonbreeding season. Cultivated fields, cerrado: Mato Grosso, November; Amazonas, October; northwestern Bahia, Rio Preto, December, at river edge. Migrates as far as Paraguay, coming from North America where it is well known. Sometimes picks berries from same fruit trees as *T. melancholicus* (Bahia).

GRAY KINGBIRD, *Tyrannus dominicensis* NV

22 cm. Another migrant, very similar to *T. melancholicus* but with white, not yellow, underparts. Roraima, Maracá Ecological Station (Moscovits et al. 1985). Northern South America, southern U.S.

WHITE-NAPED XENOPSARIS, *Xenopsaris albinucha*, Tijerila

12.5 cm. Typical caatinga bird, slender with long tail, shiny black cap (female cap chestnut). White lores linked by white line above bill. Edges and undersides of wings white. Back gray, wings and tail brown. VOICE: a squeaky, slightly undulating screech. Perches on top of thin, sometimes spiny bushes. Builds nest in shape of a small, compact basket in treetops of open caatinga. Piauí, Ceará, Pernambuco, Alagoas, western Bahia, Roraima; also Venezuela, Bolivia, Paraguay, Argentina, in similar habitats. Its inclusion in Tyrannidae (and not Cotingidae, although tarsus structure is different) has been corroborated by nest type, only recently described. Recent research has suggested placing *Xenopsaris* in a separate "*Schiffornis* group," together with *Laniocera* and *Pachyramphus* (Tyrannidae) and *Laniisoma* and *Iodopleura* (Cotingidae) (see Prum and Lanyon 1989).

SUBFAMILY TITYRINAE

GREEN-BACKED BECARD, *Pachyramphus viridis*, Caneleirinho-verde PL 30.7

14 cm. One of many species of a genus typified by large head, broad bill, narrow tail, and 2d external primary modified for sound production (see fig. 222 and *P. castaneus*). Nape grayish, breast and eye-ring yellow. Female has green crown and back, chestnut upper wing coverts (may be green in immature female). VOICE: call *jew . . . ;* song a sequence of about 6 limpid, clearly enunciated *ew-LEE ew-LEE ew-LEE*s. . . . Forest edges, capoeira. Venezuela to Bolivia, Argentina, Paraguay, northern, southwestern, and eastern Brazil. In many places common. Sometimes alongside

P. castaneus and *P. polychopterus* (Rio de Janeiro). Also called *Bico-grosso.*

CHESTNUT-CROWNED BECARD, *Pachyramphus castaneus*, Caneleirinho

14.8 cm. Upperparts ferruginous, cap with scaly appearance, sides of head and nape gray, underparts yellowish. Female similar. VOICE: a high, ascending tremolo, *tewi, i, i, i, i, i, i,* or a descending sequence, *bi-bi-bi-bi (-bi),* and other very high notes with timbre of *Oxyruncus cristatus.* An explosive *tic,* heard when male perches near female in breeding season, may originate from sound-producing primaries (see

Fig. 249. White-winged Becard, *Pachyramphus polychopterus*, male.

P. viridis). Forest edges. Venezuela to Bolivia, Paraguay, Argentina (Misiones), and northern, eastern, and southern Brazil to Rio Grande do Sul. May recall Buff-fronted Foliage-gleaner, *Philydor rufus*. See also Brown Tanager, *Orchesticus abeillei* (Thraupinae).

WHITE-WINGED BECARD, *Pachyramphus polychopterus*, Caneleirinho-preto   Fig. 249

15.5 cm. Male plumage resembles Variable Antshrike, *Thamnophilus caerulescens,* but becard is more slender and has broader bill. Cap has strong, steely sheen. Female olive green with rusty-bordered tail and wing feathers, yellowish underparts. VOICE: a loud, full, attention-getting *juh-it jut-jut-jut . . .* with other variations. At dawn and dusk in breeding season incessantly intones a similar, more stereotyped phrase at 5-second intervals (Rio de Janeiro, northeastern Bahia). Forest borders, frequently the most common *Pachyramphus,* sometimes alongside *P. castaneus* (Rio de Janeiro). Like congeners, sometimes joins mixed flocks. Central America and the Guianas to Bolivia, Argentina, Uruguay, throughout Brazil. Also called *Araponguinha* (Minas Gerais).

BLACK-CAPPED BECARD, *Pachyramphus marginatus*

13.5 cm. Very similar to *P. polychopterus* but smaller. Male back spotted with black and gray, forehead and lores white, underparts whitish. Female has ferruginous cap. VOICE: higher and more melodious than *polychopterus, ewEE-ewEET,* repeated. Amazonia (the Guianas to Bolivia) and eastern Brazil, in canopy, sometimes alongside *polychopterus* (e.g., Lagoa de Juparanã, Espírito Santo).

GLOSSY-BACKED BECARD, *Pachyramphus surinamus*

13.8 cm. Amazonia, from Pará (Óbidos) to Suriname.

CINEREOUS BECARD, *Pachyramphus rufus*

12.9 cm. Smallest *Pachyramphus.* Gray back, black cap, whitish underparts. Female ferruginous, like *P. castaneus,* but lacks grayish collar. Maranhão (P. Roth) and eastern Pará to upper Amazon, the Guianas, Panama.

CRESTED BECARD, *Pachyramphus validus* (= *Platypsaris rufus*), Caneleiro-de-chapéu-negro

17.8 cm. Physique may give it appearance of giant *Pachyramphus,* with heavy bill and relatively short tail. Upperparts dark gray, cap black, back with hidden white patch that is suddenly displayed spontaneously, as in certain antbirds. Underparts brownish. Ferruginous female lighter on underparts, has dark gray cap. VOICE: a shrill whistle, *tsree,* resembling *Empidonomus varius* or a *Phaethornis* hummingbird; *si-i-it, tewit.* Forests. Periodically follows mixed flocks. Western Pará and the northeast to Rio Grande do Sul, Mato Grosso; also Argentina (Misiones), Paraguay, Bolivia, Peru. Inclusion of this species in *Pachyramphus* is unsatisfactory.

PINK-THROATED BECARD, *Pachyramphus* (= *Platypsaris*) *minor*

16.8 cm. Widely distributed in Amazonia. Male black with large, bright pink gular patch. Female similar to female *P. validus.* Amazonia to Maranhão and northwestern Mato Grosso, Venezuela to Bolivia.

BLACK-TAILED TITYRA, *Tityra cayana,* Anambé-branco-de-rabo-preto   Fig. 250

21 cm. Sturdy bill and relatively short tail give bird a somewhat robust aspect. Black-and-grayish-white male has bare red flesh around eye and on lores, red at base of bill. Typical form, from Amazonia, smaller. VOICE: a nasal, grunting *ed, rek.* Forest edges. The Guianas and Venezuela to Bolivia, Peru, locally throughout Brazil. Also called *Gui-kú* (Waura, Mato Grosso), *Araponguinha* (see next 2 species). At times all 3 *Tityra* are found in same region (e.g., Mato Grosso) although they occupy different habitats, which explains why they are not usually found side by side.

MASKED TITYRA, *Tityra semifasciata,* Anambé-branco-de-máscara-negra

20.5 cm. Similar to *T. cayana* but with black mask, white tail with wide, black subterminal band. Female similar to male but has brownish head. VOICE: a rhythmic, repeated cry, *ghe-RAK gherik;* a snorted *gaaaa;* a soft *eg-eg.* Male makes a sonorous hiss with wings that becomes louder as he brakes to perch. With a female present, male will run back and forth on a horizontal branch, stooped with drooping wings while

Fig. 250. Black-tailed Tityra, *Tityra cayana braziliensis:* (A) male, (B) female.

making a croaking sound. Female quite active and will pursue male. I have seen 4 birds "dancing" together near an occupied nest. Edges of groves and palm stands. Amazonia south to central Mato Grosso, also northern Maranhão. Extends as far as Mexico, with various geographic races, like *T. inquisitor.*

BLACK-CROWNED TITYRA, *Tityra inquisitor,* Anambé-de-bochecha-parda

17 cm. Like *T. cayana* but smaller with face feathered black. Bill also black, chin white. *T. i. albitorques,* with white sides on head, occurs on Rio Negro, *T. i. pelzelni,* with base and tip of tail white, in Mato Grosso. Sides of female's head chestnut, cap black, back brownish. Forest borders. Widely distributed from Mexico and Venezuela to Paraguay, Argentina (Misiones), locally throughout Brazil, including Rio de Janeiro and Rio Grande do Sul. Migratory.

Tyrannidae Bibliography
See also General Bibliography

Belton, W. 1974. Two new southern migrants for Brazil. *Auk* 91:820.

Bó, N. A. 1969. Acerca de la afinidad de las formas de *Serpophaga.* *Neotrop.* 15(47):54–58.

Borrero, J. I. 1972. *Mitt. Inst. Colombo-Alemán Invest. Cient.* 6:113–33. [(*Pyrocephalus rubinus,* biology, distribution]

Borrero, J. I. 1973. *Ardeola* 19:69–87. [*Fluvicola pica,* biology]

Carvalho, C. T. 1960. *Pap. Avuls. Zool. S. Paulo,* 14:121–32. [*Myiozetetes cayanensis,* behavior]

Cavalcanti, R. B. 1988. Morfometria de espécies de *Elaenia. XV Cong. Bras. Zool., Curitiba:*480.

Dick, J. A., and R. M. Mitchell. 1979. Um comportement anti-predateur du Gobemouche royal. *L'Oiseau* 5(49):155–57.

Fitzpatrick, J. W. 1976. Systematics and biogeography of the Tyrannid genus *Todirostrum* and related genera. *Bull. Mus. Comp. Zool.* Harvard 147(10):435–63.

Fitzpatrick, J. W. 1980a. Foraging behavior of Neotropical tyrant flycatchers. *Condor* 82:43–57.

Fitzpatrick, J. W. 1980b. Some aspects of speciation in South American flycatchers. *17th Cong. Int. Orn., Berlin:*1273–79.

Fitzpatrick, J. W. 1985. Form, foraging behavior, and adaptive radiation in the Tyrannidae. In *Neotrop. Ornith.,* Ornith. Monogr. no. 36.

Fitzpatrick, J. W., and J. P. O'Neill. 1979. A new tody-tyrant from northern Peru. *Auk* 96(3):443–47.

Haverschmidt, F. 1961. Nests of *Empidonomus varius, Pitangus lictor,* and *Myiozetetes cayanensis. Auk* 78:276–78.

Haverschmidt, F. 1974. *Wilson Bull.* 86:215–20. [*Tolmomyias flaviventris,* ecology]

Haverschmidt, F. 1975. *Bull. B.O.C.* 95:140–41. [*Rhytipterna immunda,* ecology]

Ihering, H. v. 1904. *Auk* 21:313–22. [Systematics, biology]

Johnston, D. W. 1971. *Auk* 88:796–804. [Ecology]

Lanyon, W. E. 1963. *Am. Mus. Nov.* 2126. [*Myiarchus,* vocalization]

Lanyon, W. E. 1978. *Bull. Am. Mus. Nat. Hist.* 161(4):427–628. [*Myiarchus* of South America, monograph]

Lanyon, W. E. 1984. A phylogeny of the kingbirds and their allies. *Am. Mus. Nov.* 2797.

Lanyon, W. E. 1985. A phylogeny of the Myiarchine flycatchers. In *Neotrop. Ornith.,* Ornith. Monogr. no. 36.

Lanyon, W. E. 1986. Phylogeny of the thirty genera in the *Empidonax* assemblage of tyrant flycatchers. *Am. Mus. Nov.* 2846.

Lanyon, W. E., and C. H. Fry. 1973. *Auk* 90:672–74. [*Rhytipterna immunda,* taxonomy, distribution]

Lanyon, W. E., and S. M. Lanyon. 1986. Genetic status of Euler's Flycatcher, a morphological and biochemical study. *Auk* 103:341–50.

Marcondes-Machado, L. O. 1985. *Elaenia flavogaster* como dispersor de plantas de áreas perturbadas. *XII Cong. Bras. Zool., Campinas:*586.

McKitrick, M. C. 1985. Monophyly of the Tyrannidae: Comparison of morphology and DNA. *System. Zool.* 34:34–45.

Meise, W. 1949. In *Ornithologie als Biologische Wissenschaft,* Heidelberg. [*Tyrannus* and *Empidonomus,* systematics]

Meise, W. 1954. Notes on the flat-bills of the genus *Platyrinchus. Auk* 71:285–92.

Moojen, J. 1936. *O Campo.* September 1936. [Feeding]

Morton, E. S. 1977. Intratropical migration in *Vireo flavoviridis* and *Legatus leucophaius. Auk* 94:97–106.

Moscovits, D., J. W. Fitzpatrick, and D. W. Willard. 1985. Lista preliminar das Aves da Estação Ecológica de Maracá, Território de Roraima, Brasil, e Areas adjacentes. *Pap. Avuls. Zool. S. Paulo.* 36(6):51–68.

Orians, G. H. 1980. *Some Adaptations of Marsh-nesting Black-birds.* Monogr. Pop. Biol. no. 14. Princeton, N.J.: Princeton University Press.

Parker, T. A. III. 1984. Notes on the behavior of *Ramphotrigon* flycatchers. *Auk* 101:186–88.

Sibley, C. G., S. M. Lanyon, and J. F. Ahlquist, 1984. The relationships of the Sharpbill, *Oxyruncus cristatus. Condor* 86: 48–52.

Sick, H. 1951. *Auk* 68:510. [*Tyrannus tyrannus*, first discovery in Brazil]

Silva, J. M. C. 1990. A reevaluation of *Serpophaga araguayae* Snethlage, 1928. *Goeldiana, Zoologia* 1.

Skutch, A. F. 1960. *Life Histories of Central American Birds,* vol. 2. Pacific Coast Avifauna 34:287–577. Berkeley, Calif.: Cooper Orn. Soc.

Smith, W. J. 1966. *Publ. Nuttall Orn. Club* 6. [*Tyrannus,* relationships]

Smith, W. J. 1971. *Condor* 73:259–86. [Serpophaginae, behavior]

Smith, W. J., and F. Vuilleumier. 1971. Evolutionary relationships of some South American ground tyrants. *Bull. Mus. Comp. Zool. Harvard* 141:179–268.

Straneck, R. J., and G. R. Carrizo. 1983. El despliegue de proclamación territorial de *Knipolegus aterrimus* y *Hymenops*

perspicillata. Com. Mus. Argent. Ciênc. Nat. Ecologia 1, no. 5.

Teixeira, D. M. 1987. A new tyrannulet (*Phylloscartes*) from northeastern Brazil. *Bull. B.O.C.* 107(1):37–41.

Teixeira, D. M. 1989. Observações sobre *Xenopsaris albinucha* no Nordeste do Brasil. *XVI Cong. Bras. Zool., João Pessoa:*131.

Teixeira, D. M., and J. Nacinovic. 1985. Notas sobre *Pseudocolopteryx sclateri. An. Soc. Sul-Riograndense Orn.* 6:3–7.

Traylor, M. A., Jr. 1977. *Bull Mus. Comp. Zool. Harvard* 148(4):129–84. [Tyrannidae, systematics]

Traylor, M. A., Jr., ed. 1979. *Peters' Check-list of Birds of the World,* vol. 8. Cambridge, Mass.: Harvard University Press.

Traylor, M. A., Jr., and J. W. Fitzpatrick. 1982. A survey of the tyrant flycatchers. *Living Bird* 19:7–50.

Warter, S. L. 1965. Thesis. "The cranial osteology of the New World Tyrannoidea and its taxonomic implications." Baton Rouge, La.: Louisiana State University.

Willis, E. O. 1962. Another nest of *Pitangus lictor. Auk* 79:111.

Willis, E. O., D. Wechsler, and Y. Oniki. 1978. On behavior and nesting of *Pipromorpha macconnelli:* Does female rejection lead to male promiscuity? *Auk* 95:1–8.

Zimmer, J. T. 1937. *Am. Mus. Nov.* 930 and numerous subsequent publications. [Systematics]

FAMILY PIPRIDAE: MANAKINS (34)

The manakins, a group of Neotropical forest birds related to the cotingas and tyrant flycatchers, are especially attractive because of their bright colors and prenuptial displays, some of which they perform in groups. Like the cotingids and many other Suboscines, they evolved together with the various types of tropical forest. The Blue Manakin, *Chiroxiphia caudata,* is one of the best-known birds in Brazil; its behavior aroused the interest of sixteenth-century colonists and has formed the basis of romantic legends.

Morphology

Manakins are small birds, no larger than a Rufous-collared Sparrow, *Zonotrichia capensis.* The Tiny Tyrant-Manakin, *Tyranneutes virescens,* weighing 6 to 7 g, is one of the smallest birds on the continent, excepting hummingbirds. Male manakins are generally splendidly multicolored with scarlet, gold, blue, or white, often concentrated on the head. There are even opalescent effects, as in the Opal-crowned Manakin, *Pipra iris;* this unusual feather feature is also found in birds of paradise of Australasia. Iris color is a prominent feature in some species. There are bizarre crests in the Scarlet-horned Manakin, *Pipra cornuta;* Helmeted Manakin, *Antilophia galeata;* and Blue-backed Manakin, *Chiroxiphia pareola.* The Wire-tailed Manakin, *Pipra filicauda; Chiroxiphia caudata;* and Pin-tailed Manakin, *Ilicura militaris,* have unusually long tails. The variety and extravagance of male plumage obscure the relationship between species (see *Pipra filicauda*).

Most females are green, their reputed similarity being less obvious when seen alive instead of as museum specimens, for in the live bird one can better appreciate the general aspect and bill and leg colors. The presence of males also helps in female identification, as does the fact that usually only species that are quite separable are found in the same place. The female may be larger than the male, as in *Pipra, Tyranneutes,* and *Manacus.*

Unlike many tyrannids, green-plumaged manakins do not have light wing bars. Both sexes of the Striped and Fiery-capped Manakins, *Machaeropterus regulus* and *M. pyrocephalus,* are striking in appearance. Both sexes of the *Tyranneutes* tyrant-manakins are green. The yellow crest (only *T. virescens* has this) indicates a relationship with tyrannids, increasing the importance of recognizing that their behavior is that of manakins. However, not even in behavior is there a clear-cut separation between these families. Syndactylism—adhesion of the third and fourth toes at the base—is a feature of manakin anatomy. This detail occurs in birds such as the *Rupicola* cock-of-the-rock (Cotingidae) and other unrelated ones, such as *Sclerurus* leaf-scrapers (Furnariidae), and is a useful adaptation for perching on vertical sticks. The tarsus is exaspidean. Syrinx structure is extremely varied. On the basis of behavior *Antilophia galeata* appears to be the piprid most closely related to the cotingids.

Females frequently show androgynous tendencies, having, for example, some red feathers on the head, as in the Red-headed Manakin, *Pipra rubrocapilla,* and also *Antilophia galeata, Chiroxiphia caudata, C. pareola, Machaeropterus pyrocephalus,* and *M. regulus,* or white in the iris, as in *Pipra rubrocapilla.* See also "Vocalization." Male *Chiroxiphia caudata* require some years (3½–4 in captivity, A. Assumpção) to complete their definitive plumage. Although the red cap appears first, it being the main display feature of this genus, it comes only little by little, with full development taking six months. In Belém, Pará, immature green *C. pareola* have been found with areas of reddish brown feathers on the breast and upper wing coverts and light pink legs. The molt of the White-bearded Manakin, *Manacus manacus,* begins on the throat, its principal display area, and adult plumage is attained during the second year, as in some other manakins, the genus *Pipra,* for instance.

Vocalization

Males proclaim or advertise their presence by a call tirelessly repeated at intervals—each minute or every few minutes by the White-crowned Manakin, *Pipra pipra;* each six seconds by *Tyranneutes virescens*—while perched alone in a normal stance on a favorite branch, in a limited area and in hearing distance and at least partially visible to some neighboring males. Manakins sometimes utter other whistles while dancing. Because of these sounds they easily attract attention. They almost entirely lack warning notes except in a few instances, for example *Pipra iris* and the *Chiroxiphia.* Whereas the advertising call that individuals use to signify readiness to dance clearly demonstrates phylogenetic relationships (e.g., *Pipra iris* and Snow-capped Manakin, *P. nattereri;* or Crimson-hooded Manakin, *P. aureola,* and Band-tailed Manakin, *P. fasciicauda),* other vocalizations may be unique, such as the alarm or bother call of *Pipra iris.*

Females are generally silent, having only a weak call. Sometimes they behave like males, as when a *Pipra rubrocapilla,* whose autopsy revealed an egg almost ready to be laid, advertised like a male. A female *Manacus manacus* with a brood patch cried *tsierr* like a male.

Instrumental Music

This term, originated by Darwin[1] (1871), refers to sounds produced by various birds independent of their vocal apparatus. Sound-producing flight feathers have developed in the *Chiroxiphia, Ilicura, Corapipo, Manacus,* and *Machaeropterus.* Sound-producing tail feathers appear in the Golden-headed Manakin, *Pipra erythrocephala; Tyranneutes virescens;* and the *Machaeropterus.* One of the most extreme modifications is in the *Machaeropterus,* whose secondaries are heavily reinforced and twisted. Mechanical sounds, designated instrumental music, are produced with these modified feathers, contrasting with vocal music uttered with the syrinx. The purpose of such feathers is normally the production of noise in flight, reaching its peak in the loud *prrrrAK* of *Ilicura militaris.* The male *Machaeropterus pyrocephalus* makes noise even while preening, for when it shakes itself a sharp rattling can be heard coming from the fluffed tail feathers, which serve as a resonance chamber. Understanding of the responsible mechanism is lacking in most cases, even as to whether the "music" under consideration is vocal or mechanical. Sometimes instrumental music is encountered without any recognizable special structure for creating it, as in the Pale-bellied Tyrant-Manakin, *Neopelma pallescens,* which produces a gonglike sound by simply beating its wings together, although they show no special modification. Certain populations (northern Mato Grosso) lack this feature, hopping about silently, permitting us to speak of an ethological race. *Pipra fasciicauda* makes a distinctive noise with the impact of its feet on the branch at the moment of perching.

Manacus manacus is the champion of instrumental music, making a violent, sharp, crackling sound resembling the rattle of crushed rock which it can intensify to a very loud clatter. The source of these noises is usually attributed to friction of the secondaries, which are thicker and more mobile than in other birds. I have observed, however, that green males and females with little or even no reinforcement of the flight feathers can also produce such noises, though they are weaker. Analogously, it has been reported that cracking noises produced in flight by a Peruvian hummingbird, the Marvelous Spatuletail, *Loddigesia mirabilis,* believed to have been made by the secondary flight feathers and tail racquets, are occasionally produced by perched individuals and even by birds lacking outer tail feathers, suggesting that the noise comes from the bill (Ruschi 1964). Perhaps my thoughts about snapping sounds produced by tyrannids, probably in the articulation between the mandible and skull, are applicable here. The loud, sonorous poppings made by *Manacus manacus* are similar to the noises produced by friction when the tendons and bones of certain mammals rub together, as in the foot joint of the reindeer (*Rangifer tarandus*), a Northern Hemisphere cervid (Sick 1959a). I can conceive of a similar occurrence in the case of *M. manacus* poppings: that the noise could originate from any joint; this might also be the case with the *prrrrAK* of *Ilicura militaris.* Modified flight feathers may be responsible only for the whisper of the wings in normal flight. Irritated male and female *Manacus* produce a muffled mechanical noise of uncertain origin that has been noted by A. Assumpção in his flight cages.

Food, Habitat, and Behavior

Manakins eat berries, such as those of the abundant Melastomataceae, which bear fruit all year. In Trinidad, off

[1]Darwin wrote (1871): "We have as yet spoken only of the voice, but the males of various birds practice, during their courtship, what may be called instrumental music" (see Sick 1969).

the coast of Venezuela, Snow (1962a) recorded 17 species of this plant family (among them 15 different *Miconia*) eaten by *Manacus manacus,* which also ate 15 Rubiaceae (various species of *Psychotria* in Brazil) and 4 Moraceae (including two *Ficus*). Manakins also like hard fruits, such as those of the magnolia (*Michelia champaca,* Rio de Janeiro). They turn them about in the bill before swallowing them whole (*Ilicura militaris*) or tear off small pieces (*Chiroxiphia*); a few minutes later they regurgitate the pits, like the Swallow Tanager, *Tersina viridis,* and cotingids do. They like bananeirinhas-do-mato (*Heliconia*) fruits. *Antilophia galeata* contributes appreciably to the dispersal of mistletoe (Loranthaceae), regurgitating the seeds which, with their sticky coating, are wiped onto a branch in the act of cleaning the bill and later germinate (Motta 1988). Manakins catch small insects and spiders on leaves. The Thrush-like Mourner, *Schiffornis turdinus,* is more insectivorous than the syntopic *Pipra pipra* (Belém, Pará).

Most manakins live at midlevels of the forest, but *Antilophia galeata, Ilicura militaris,* and *Machaeropterus pyrocephalus* keep to higher levels. *Chiroxiphia caudata* and *Manacus manacus* are frequently found at the edge of urban centers in southeastern Brazil, which has contributed to their popularity. Manakins are good fliers but do not normally leave the leafy forest. Some show real acrobatic ability during their prenuptial displays. Males, sometimes smaller and lighter than females, are more agile in their movements. Some, such as *C. caudata,* pick up ants to rub against the wings and base of the tail (anting).

Prenuptial Displays and Sexual Selection

Manakins, like cotingids, are considered to be polygamous, a situation apparently facilitated by the abundance of food (fruits): the female is able to rear the young alone. However, it has been possible to prove with color banding that many *Manacus* females are monogamous (Lill 1974).

In the hottest regions manakins conduct certain prenuptial rituals most of the year (except during molt). As with the Cotingidae, these have evolved in various ways within the group. I have also found clear rudiments of such demonstrations in the Tyrannidae.

This behavior, beginning with advertising (see "Vocalization"), attracts females and induces other males to participate in the displays. Male participants may still be entirely green but have well-developed testes, as with *Pipra rubrocapilla* and *Manacus manacus,* or have still-immature gonads and totally or partially green plumage, as with *Chiroxiphia caudata.* Dances may take place without females being present. However, the display postures are intensified and sometimes changed or amplified if a female appears; when the female leaves the court (= arena, lek), the male stops his activity but does not delay long before starting it again. The demonstrations progress with such speed that it is difficult to keep up with them and even harder to describe them; certain displays are relatively rare and easily escape observation. The scope of this book permits only a quick look at this subject.

In most species males have a rich behavioral repertoire involving intricate rituals. They require the presence of another male in their court, which consists of one or more nearby branches between which the birds move constantly back and forth. In the case of *Manacus manacus* the court extends down to the ground, which is actively cleaned (see also Guianan Cock-of-the-Rock, *Rupicola rupicola*), a practice of both manakins and cotingids that display among the branches. Such sites are used for years on end if there are no changes in the forest. Some dominant males take over certain courts and hold them for various years. When one disappears, the vacancy is filled by another male in a position to assume it. Color banding has shown how one *Manacus* male rose in the hierarchy from "visitor" to dominant individual. These birds may live a long time. A male *M. manacus* at least 14 years old occupied the same lek for more than 11 years (Snow and Lill 1974).

In the case of *Chiroxiphia caudata,* groups of males are linked to the principal courts and apparently do not mingle with other groups, dancing separately. The courts are so spaced that their respective attendants can hear but not see each other. *Pipra fasciicauda* and *Neopelma pallescens* occasionally use for a display perch a flexible branch that shakes and bounces when the bird alights, producing a visual effect that can be seen from a distance.

Displays comprise certain features that are repeated, mutatis mutandis, in the different species, such as crouching, leaning forward, rhythmic stomping, and sidestepping. A bird will also make sudden changes of position, including turning around immediately after perching, or even in the air before perching, to then look back in the direction from which it came. It will jerk, vibrate, open, stretch, beat, and lift the wings (sometimes only one), exposing their interior surfaces to its companion. *Pipra rubrocapilla* displays just its red and white "pants", standing sideways to its companion, stretching and displaying one leg while drawing in the other. Some males, such as those of *P. rubrocapilla* and *P. fasciicauda,* stay strictly apart at a safe distance from one another, as if envious, but constantly glance back alertly: competitive displays (see also *Ilicura* and *Corapipo*). This tension does not always exist, such as among *Chiroxiphia* individuals, which perch side by side. Two *Pipra aureola* or *Chiroxiphia pareola* males will cooperate perfectly, as will two or more *C. caudata* males, with such cooperation perhaps including a duet (*Chiroxiphia*). Re cooperative displays, see also the superspecies *P. aureola.* The display process takes place with machinelike precision. The displays of *Chiroxiphia pareola* and *C. caudata* are basically the same, proving that the two species are monophyletic.

Ilicura militaris makes a single jump-flight on a thick branch or board, producing a very loud noise; see the log and chin-down display of the Golden-winged Manakin, *Masius chrysopterus* (not Brazilian), and the *Corapipo*.

Chiroxiphia caudata has a ceremony with different roles: near the males, which are moving agitatedly in one ebullient mass, is an immobile, green individual that may be a female (even one ready to lay), immature, all-green male, or sub-adult male with a red cap. The substitution of a green male for a female, which I discovered by collecting a *C. caudata* specimen, is among the most surprising details observed in prenuptial displays, not only among manakins but also in the world of birds. This male must assume the attitude of a female, behavior inconsistent with the male sex (Sick 1942). This probably occurs when the females are busy with nesting duties, in which males do not participate. Often "only" adult or young males (with undeveloped testes) dance among themselves, but in such cases they are less organized.

The activity of males participating in group displays may be interpreted as cooperation to attract females, especially benefiting the dominant male (observation of color-banded individuals). Such prenesting cooperation is a characteristic of polygamous species (Foster 1985). In monogamous species, association with a certain pair is common (helpers at the nest).

Manacus manacus, the virtuoso of instrumental music, has a different kind of dance. I have noted half a dozen different mechanical sounds, the most impressive being the *click* previously mentioned. Its spectacular solitary exhibition, which is the crystallization of confused group displays performed away from the court, lacks any vocal manifestations, giving way entirely to the most arresting mechanical noises. Manakins also have other kinds of rites, such as those of the *Machaeropterus* and *Tyranneutes*. It is interesting that *Antilophia galeata*, a very dimorphic species, has not developed any lek activity; it engages in violent chases (see below).

Tyranneutes males do not maintain visual contact, distant mutual auditory stimulation being sufficient, as is the case with some cotingids.

Some species have evolved floating display flights, for instance *Chiroxiphia pareola* and *Tyranneutes virescens*. In various others, intense amorous chases with fast flights through the forest make up part of the prenuptial display, similar to the cotingids. These activities may be diagnostic, as in the Black Manakin, *Xenopipo atronitens*, for its tyrannid double, the monogamous Amazonian Black-Tyrant, *Knipolegus poecilocercus*, does not share the same behavior. Other manakins much given to chasing are *Antilophia galeata; Ilicura militaris;* the White-throated Manakin, *Corapipo gutturalis;* and the Flame-crested and Yellow-crested Manakins, *Heterocercus linteatus* and *H. flavivertex*. Such chases also occur in the *Myiobius, Pipromorpha,* and Planalto Tyrannulet, *Phyllomyias fasciatus*, all classified as Tyrannidae.

Displays are similar within groups of superspecies, such as *Pipra aureola, P. fasciicauda,* and *P. filicauda;* or *P. erythrocephala, P. rubrocapilla,* and the non-Brazilian Red-capped Manakin, *P. mentalis;* or the *Chiroxiphia*. Dominant, or alpha, males are calculated to spend 90% or more of their day in their courts (see below).

It appears obvious that in Pipridae and Cotingidae, selection by females, which seek out males or groups of males on their courts, has led to the evolution of males that are showier in form (luxuriantly elongated feathers) and color, and that make extravagant sounds and movements. It is quite surprising how the head of a male *Pipra rubrocapilla,* for instance, draws so much attention in the semidarkness of the forest and is the only part of the bird's body that can be seen at a distance. When a female visits a group of males displaying in their courts, she probably does not manage to "choose," but instead the dominant male assumes control over her. *Chiroxiphia* have a special mating display. It is impossible to know how many copulations occur away from the courts, with males not connected to the arenas.

Display postures precede the acquisition of bright colors, both ontogenetically and phylogenetically. For example, the young male *Pipra rubrocapilla* goes all out to exhibit his pants even before they are scarlet. Both the male of this species and of *P. erythrocephala* display the interior surface of the wing, although only the former has a showy underwing pattern.

The continuity of males on their courts over months is fundamental to the proper functioning of this polygamous system. In a banded population of *Manacus manacus* and *Pipra erythrocephala* studied by D. W. Snow (1962a, 1962b) in Trinidad, males stayed on their courts about 90% of the daylight hours; thus it is reasonable to speak of this group as the most "festive" of tropical birds, in the sense that they spend a minimum of time eating, bathing, etc. Certain males have more success attracting females than others, as can be shown with *Manacus manacus* when there are neighboring courts. I have observed single males of *Pipra rubrocapilla* and *Chiroxiphia caudata* receive simultaneous visits from two females, which fought each other. I have not seen copulations in the courts except when a stuffed female was used. There are simulated copulations between males. Display by green males is common in all species.

Among the few species with simple displays is Wied's Tyrant-Manakin, *Neopelma aurifrons,* whose display apparently is limited to a call that serves as a song; neighboring males remain in hearing range of each other's voices but do not assemble, remaining alone (as do the *Tyranneutes*) and assuming special poses when they see a female.

Interspecific Relations

There is no shortage of evidence of courtship between different species, even if accidental and not very intense. I have had the impression that the frenetic dances of *Manacus*

manacus might stimulate neighboring *Pipra rubrocapilla* and *Machaeropterus regulus,* causing them to intensify their respective displays in their own courts.

Some strange-appearing specimens in museum collections have been interpreted as intergeneric hybrids, for example between *Manacus* × *Pipra* and *Heterocercus* × *Pipra.* Currently *Chiroxiphia* × *Antilophia* crossing is occurring in the interior of São Paulo; apparently the constant capture of *Antilophia* males for the clandestine live-bird trade has deprived females of the species of opportunities for normal mating, the more so because numerical equilibrium appears to exist between the sexes in *Antilophia*—as it appears to with *Pipra erythrocephala* and *Manacus manacus*, unlike the case of *Chiroxiphia caudata*, where there are more males than females (Sick 1979, see also Emberizinae, "Hybridization").

I have observed that *Machaeropterus regulus* is driven away by the stronger *Pipra rubrocapilla* and *Manacus manacus* when they want to feed in the same fruit tree.

Nesting

Discrete in the modest, cryptic dress that guarantees their own and their offsprings' survival, females stay close to the nest. They alone take care of nesting, building a loose basket (shallow for *Pipra* and *Ilicura,* deeper for *Chiroxiphia* and *Antilophia*) fastened to a forked limb, often using black fungus mycelia (*Marasmius*) that may hang from the nest like a curtain (*Chiroxiphia caudata*), breaking up its outline and camouflaging it. Large amounts of spider webbing are used to hold together the material of the structure, which is often situated relatively high (4 m in *Ilicura militaris*), near water and even above it, sometimes quite close to other nests (e.g., *Chiroxiphia* and *Pipra filicauda*). I have learned some curious details on nest construction from A. Assumpção (1965 pers. comm.): a *C. caudata* female, before starting her nest, suspended herself between the branches of a forked limb, leaning on her tail and her forward-stretched feet, and made a back-and-forth rotating motion as if measuring the width of the gap to calculate the size of the nest to build.

Schiffornis turdinus prepares its nest in the cavity of a broken tree trunk, cushioning it with dry leaves, a procedure totally unlike that of typical manakins and more like that of a cotingid.

Manakins lay two eggs (sometimes only one) with a brownish background and dark brown markings. Incubation, carried out with dedication by the mother (who will lure away intruders from the nest), lasts 17.5 to 19 days in *Pipra coronata* and 18 to 19 in *Manacus manacus.* Nestlings receive berries and/or insects and spiders, partly regurgitated, partly pressed into balls, with saliva coming out of the mother's mouth during the act of feeding (*Pipra rubrocapilla*). The mother swallows feces and regurgitated seeds of the young, but grown nestlings defecate from the edge of the nest and soil the ground below. *Chiroxiphia caudata* nestlings have a

vocalization, audible at short distances, resembling the advertising of *Ilicura militaris.* At times the confines of the nest may be such that the nestlings have difficulty finding room, so sleep with the neck hanging vertically over the edge (*P. rubrocapilla*). They are badly tormented by mosquitoes, which even manage to get through the bottom of the nest to sting the nestlings' bellies, as I observed along the Xingu, Mato Grosso. The mother will drive away horseflies that perch on the edge of the nest (*P. rubrocapilla*). Young fledge at 13 to 14 days in *P. rubrocapilla*, at 13 to 15 days in *Manacus manacus.*

Distribution, Evolution, and Numbers

Manakins offer additional, better-studied examples of parapatric distribution, that is, of closely related species that inhabit adjacent but not overlapping areas. Thus, *Pipra coronata* appears to be the upper Amazon replacement of the White-fronted Manakin, *P. serena.* My Golden-crowned Manakin, *P. vilasboasi,* also belongs to this complex and may provide proof of the former existence of a refuge in Rondônia (see Chapter 4.1.3). *P. iris* replaces *P. nattereri,* and *P. erythrocephala* replaces *P. rubrocapilla* north of the Amazon and Solimões. *P. erythrocephala* in turn is replaced by *P. mentalis* in Ecuador and Central America. *P. fasciicauda* is the southern representative of *P. aureola* and *P. filicauda* (fig. 251). See also *Chiroxiphia* and Haffer 1970.

There are other instances of geographic replacement among Brazilian manakins forming superspecies: *Machaeropterus regulus* and *M. pyrocephalus; Heterocercus linteatus* and *H. flavivertex* (see fig. 63); *Tyranneutes virescens* and the Dwarf Tyrant-Manakin, *T. stolzmanni.* The situation of *Machaeropterus* is complicated: *regulus* occurs in two disjunct areas, Amazonia and eastern Brazil; *pyrocephalus* lives only in Amazonia.

Allospecies making superspecies in Amazonia are often separated by the great rivers, although they may cross them on certain occasions. Up to the present, specimens intermediate between the species in question have practically never been found. Manakin behavior (prenuptial displays and vocalization), which is very similar in these cases, generally proves to be more conservative than morphology (e.g., as between *Pipra aureola* and *P. fasciicauda*). Although very different, the various forms of *P. coronata* show areas of hybridization and therefore constitute geographic races of a single species.

When various manakin species occur in the same region they usually belong to different genera. This is the situation in the forests of ex-Guanabara, for instance, where four manakin species have been recorded: *Chiroxiphia caudata, Ilicura militaris, Manacus manacus,* and *Machaeropterus regulus.* In one area in the upper Xingu I found nine species in more or less diverse habitats: *Pipra rubrocapilla, P. nat-*

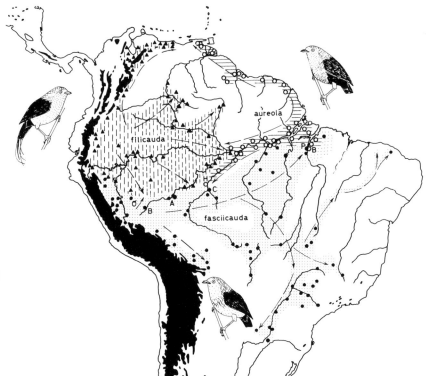

Fig. 251. Distribution of the Crimson-hooded Manakin and allies, *Pipra aureola,* super-species; males illustrated (slightly modified after Haffer 1970). Open circles and horizontal hatching: Band-tailed Manakin, *P. fasciicauda;* closed triangles and vertical dashes: Wire-tailed Manakin, *P. filicauda.* Symbols denote locality records.

tereri, P. fasciicauda, Chiroxiphia pareola, Manacus manacus, Machaeropterus pyrocephalus, Xenopipo atronitens, Heterocercus linteatus, and *Tyranneutes stolzmanni.*

Pipra erythrocephala and *P. rubrocapilla* may be among the most abundant birds in their respective regions, which is also the case in local situations for *Chiroxiphia caudata* and *Manacus manacus.* It appears to be a fact that frugivorous birds achieve larger populations than insectivorous ones. The distribution of *Chiroxiphia pareola* is an impressive example of how far Amazonian influence has extended, with only a relict population remaining today in the Brazilian southeast (fig. 252).

Names and Folklore

The term *tangará* is said to be derived from the Tupi *ata,* "to walk," and *cará,* "around." This would be the equivalent of the Spanish name *Saltarín.* Some confusion exists, for *tangará* is also used for the Red-capped Cardinal, *Paroaria gularis,* in Amazonia, and for some thraupines (formerly tanagrids) in Paraguay and Argentina, a designation also used in scientific nomenclature (genus *Tangara*). Further, the name *pipira* is used indiscriminately for manakins and thraupines in Bolivia, Brazil, and Peru.

In northern Brazil *uirapurus* (*Pipra* spp. with either red or white heads) enjoy great fame, being linked to a variety of legends, superstitions, and witchcraft. In Amazonia they are prized as amulets. Dried skins or whole birds, preserved in alcohol and stored in large, used, glass jars originally used for storing penny candy, are traded in the markets of Belém. However, it is widely claimed that a uirapuru obtained in the market is valueless as an infallible talisman, for it must be "conditioned" or "blessed" by certain women to attract a man's or woman's love, or for ordinary tasks such as producing financial success or bringing luck to a home, where it must be placed in a box buried under the entrance.

In Amazonia the name *uirapuru* is also used for certain wrens (Troglodytidae) and even for an antbird, *Thamnomanes.* The term *manaquim* (consecrated by the English word *manakin*), perhaps derived from an indigenous word of the upper Amazon, was used by M. J. Brisson (1760) to designate a genus (*Manacus*), and in 1830 the traveling naturalist, Prince Maximilian of Wied used *manakin* in the way it is now used by English-speaking peoples, as a general designation for the family.

Synopsis of Brazilian Manakins
(number of species in parentheses)

Identification of adult males generally offers no difficulty. The similar species of *Heterocercus, Neopelma, Tyranneutes,* and *Schiffornis* usually are geographically exclusive and may in part be considered allospecies. Green individuals (immature and female) require careful attention; they frequently appear together with adult males. I exclude the genus *Piprites* from the Pipridae (see Cotingidae), for it does not at all conform in behavior. I include *Schiffornis* and *Neopelma*, both *incertae sedis*.

1. Black and red or orange: *Pipra erythrocephala, P. rubrocapilla* (Pl 32), *P. cornuta, P. aureola, P. fasciicauda* (Pl 32), *P. filicauda*, and *Antilophia galeata* (Pl 32)
2. Black and white: *Pipra pipra* (fig. 254), *Corapipo gutturalis, Manacus manacus* (fig. 259)
3. Black or green, with more (back, body) or less (cap, rump) blue: *Pipra coronata* (Pl 32), *P. serena* (Pl 32), *Chiroxiphia pareola*, and *C. caudata* (Pl 32)
4. All black: *Xenopipo atronitens*
5. Green with cap:
   5.1. White: *Pipra nattereri*
   5.2. Opalescent: *Pipra iris* (Pl 32)
   5.3. Yellow: *Pipra vilasboasi* (Pl 45)
6. Green with or without yellow or red on crown: *Neopelma* (4, Pl 32), *Tyranneutes* (2, Pl 32), *Chloropipo uniformis*, and *Schiffornis* (3)
7. With green or pinkish brown back, crimson or reddish yellow cap: *Machaeropterus* (2, Pl 32)
8. Intensely rufous: *Neopipo cinnamomea* (Pl 33.3)
9. Polychrome, with long tail: *Ilicura militaris* (Pl 32)
10. Relatively large size, black cap, center of crown red: *Heterocercus linteatus* (2, Pl 32)

GOLDEN-HEADED MANAKIN, *Pipra erythrocephala*, Cabeça-de-couro

9 cm. Restricted to northern Amazonia, similar to *P. rubrocapilla* but smaller (quite noticeable in live birds) with shorter, stiff tail. Head yellow (not red), edged with scarlet on nape. Under wing coverts solid black, iris white. Prenuptial displays involve many special details and culminate in a display flight, almost identical to that of *rubrocapilla*, in front of female; emits a loud *buzz* when it perches after an exhibition flight. Forests. North of Amazon and Solimões from Amapá to Peru, Colombia, Venezuela, the Guianas. Also called *Uirapuru*.

RED-HEADED MANAKIN, *Pipra rubrocapilla*, Cabeça-encarnada ‎ ‎ PL 32.6

9.7 cm. Widely distributed south of Amazon, where it replaces *P. erythrocephala*. SOUNDS AND DISPLAYS: call a weak *pseep* (both sexes). Male advertises his court with vocalizations (*tslit, tsi-gheh*) and, assuming vertical posture and shaking tail, flies back and forth to a nearby branch; with growing excitement he crouches and leans backward and forward, stomping and shaking wings and tail, stretching

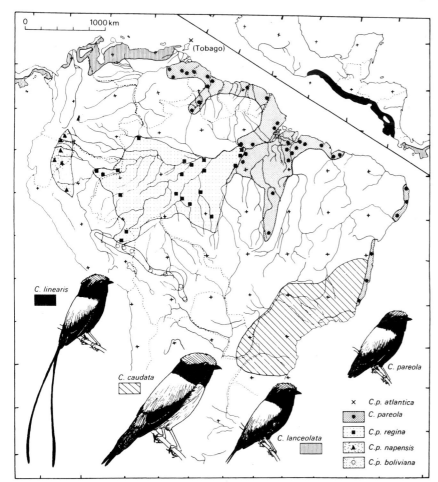

C. linearis

C. caudata

C. pareola

C. lanceolata

× C.p. atlantica
C. pareola
C.p. regina
C.p. napensis
C.p. boliviana

Fig. 252. Distribution of the four species of *Chiroxiphia*. After Haffer 1985.

Fig. 253. Red-headed Manakin, *Pipra rubrocapilla,* sketch of some phases of its dance. (a) The male tap-dances at the side of the immobile female. (b) The male displays the red spot of his "pants" to the female, stretching his leg and shaking his tail. (c) Two males display together, the one on the left leaning forward under the branch, the one on the right exposing the underside of its wings where a white spot is prominent. In all these phases the active male keeps carefully turned away from his partner (male or female) as if prepared to flee. (d) The male makes a zooming flight before the female, ending with copulation if she does not depart at the last moment. After Sick 1959a.

wings horizontally and immediately closing them, then lifting them when he whistles a *seeeeew-gheh* (fig. 253). When a female approaches, he accelerates stomping and displays red spot on pants, for which he presents himself obliquely to the recent arrival, although he frequently changes the direction he is facing by jumping. At peak of display he undertakes an impressive flight, moving off about 30 m in silence, then returning immediately with a *tsi-ewww, tsi-ewww, tsi-ewww* that changes to a *seeeeeeee* when he rises in a zooming S to a 2d display perch above female. He cries a sharp *weet* when he perches, ending demonstration with strident *gheh-gheh* (*-gheh*)s if female did not permit copulation. He may execute same type of flight in complete silence; in absence of a female male displays alone or with another male.

Terra-firme forest. South of Solimões and Amazon to Bolivia, Mato Grosso, Pará, Maranhão, through residual forests of northeast to north of Rio Doce (Espírito Santo) and Cantagalo (Rio de Janeiro). Also called *Uirapuru, Maria-lenço* (Espírito Santo). Often treated as a subspecies of *erythrocephala,* from which it clearly differs in morphology. All of my observations cited in other publications for *P. erythrocephala* refer to *P. e. rubrocapilla.* See *P. pipra* on distinctions between females.

SCARLET-HORNED MANAKIN, *Pipra cornuta*

12 cm. Similar to *P. rubrocapilla* and *P. erythrocephala* but much larger and crested, with 2 "horns" pointing to rear.

Red of head more extensive. Displays similar to *erythrocephala* and *rubrocapilla.* Extreme north, restricted to mountainous region between Brazil (upper Rio Branco) and Venezuelan and Guyanese borders where it should meet *erythrocephala.*

WHITE-CROWNED MANAKIN, *Pipra pipra,* Cabeça-branca   Fig. 254

9.2 cm. Unobtrusive, black, white-capped species, widely but locally distributed. Female similar to female *P. rubrocapilla* but recognizable by dark green color, grayish crown and throat, lack of yellow on thighs, blackish bill and legs,

Fig. 254. White-crowned Manakin, *Pipra pipra,* adult male.

and red iris like male. VOICE AND DISPLAYS: displays inconspicuous (Espírito Santo); advertises with a muffled *shrra* or a *tsirrr* similar to a locust chirp, sometimes finished off by a *tshrra-tewk* or *wieh* that may recall *rubrocapilla;* also a weak *eh* resembling *Machaeropterus regulus.* Solitary male may describe an S curve as it moves between 2 branches. Reportedly can make a silent, floating flight, almost like a butterfly, around female (Snow 1961; observed in Guyana). Tall forest. The Guianas to northeastern Peru, Rio Juruá, Mato Grosso, Maranhão; also eastern Brazil from southern Bahia to Rio de Janeiro. Also called *Uirapuru-catimbozeiro.*

BLUE-CROWNED MANAKIN, *Pipra coronata,*
Uirapuru-de-chapéu-azul   PL 32.3

8.5 cm. Amazonian species with at least 2 quite different plumages: black with blue cap (*P. c. carbonata, P. c. coronata*), from Costa Rica, Venezuela, and Rio Negro (both sides) to Rio Juruá; green with blue cap (*P. c. caelestipileata, P. c. exquisita,* and other races), from Rios Madeira and Purus to eastern Peru and Bolivia. South of middle and lower Solimões and on lower Purus intermediate populations occur (*P. c. chloromelaena, P. c. arimensis, P. c. hoffmannsi*). Female green with dark green upperparts, yellow belly, blackish bill, with variations in geographic races. Active male's vocalization is a trill and harsh call. Low levels in dense forest, where it makes short, whirring, to-and-fro flights in a limited area, 2 neighbors sometimes participating together. Dense forest. Appears to be geographic replacement for *P. serena.*

WHITE-FRONTED MANAKIN, *Pipra serena,*
Uirapuru-estrela   PL 32.7

8.7 cm. Only north of Amazon (Amapá, north of Manaus). Shiny white of forehead extends to light bill and is outlined behind by blue. Chestnut iris does not stand out against plumage. Rump, displayed by lifting black wings, same blue as *Morpho* butterflies in same region. Female bluish green above with white throat, yellow abdomen. VOICE AND DISPLAYS: aroused male ruffles yellow "necktie" and advertises with a harsh, ventriloquial *shrrewd-shrrewd (-shrrewd)* (fig. 255). Prenuptial display consists of silent movements back and forth between 2 branches, bird diving and rising vertically, with 1 or more neighbors participating without organizing a coordinated display as in *P. coronata.* Terra-firme forest in rugged terrain, sometimes alongside *P. pipra* and *P. rubrocapilla.* See *P. coronata.*

OPAL-CROWNED MANAKIN, *Pipra iris,*
Cabeça-de-prata   BR   PL 32.5

8.8 cm. Only south of lower Amazon. Notable for strongly opalescent cap. Light gray bill quite thick, as is that of female, which also has bright yellow belly. VOICE: advertises with a harsh, bisyllabic *jew-bewt* resembling *P. vilasboasi;*

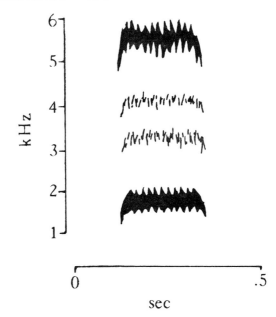

Fig. 255. Spectogram of call of White-fronted Manakin, *Pipra serena.* After Prum 1985.

alarm call a strident *ewEE.* Terra-firme forest, alongside *P. rubrocapilla* and *P. pipra.* Eastern Pará to lower Rio Tapajós (Santarém, Rio Jamanxim) and upper Xingu, Mato Grosso. See *P. vilasboasi* and *P. nattereri.*

GOLDEN-CROWNED MANAKIN, *Pipra vilasboasi*
BR   PL 45.3

7.7 cm. Green with yellow cap and belly (colors of Brazilian flag), whitish gray iris. VOICE: advertises with a *tak-ewt,* revealing its relationship to *P. iris* and *P. nattereri.* Terra-firme forest, alongside *P. rubrocapilla* and other noncongeneric manakins. Known only from upper Rio Cururu of southwestern Pará. Discovered only in 1957, and region has not been investigated since by an ornithologist.

In *P. vilasboasi* area I collected a *Pipra* female that was clearly larger than the adult male *vilasboasi.* Its upperparts were dark green tending toward blue, the edges of the outer vanes of all flight feathers were bluish, the throat and breast were dark green, and the belly was yellowish green. In the same area I collected a green male *Pipra,* with ossified skull and very small testes, that resembled this female, and a nest with eggs. At the time it did not occur to me that I might be dealing with 2 *Pipra* species. Later, on examining the specimens in the museum, and advised by Alexander Wetmore, doubts arose, so I described *P. obscura,* using a name that reflected my doubts. With the better understanding of the general situation that is possible today because of more complete knowledge of the distribution of related forms, I believe *P. obscura* to be the female and immature plumage of *vilasboasi* and that this belongs to the superspecies *P. iris,* being another geographic replacement of *P. nattereri.*

SNOW-CAPPED MANAKIN, *Pipra nattereri*,
Uirapuru-de-chapéu-branco   BR

8 cm. Similar to *P. iris* but more slender (evident in bill and feet), with shiny white cap and rump, black maxilla, whitish iris. Female has bluish green upperparts. Sexes may be quite different in size, e.g., male 8.5 cm, 6.8 g; female 9.2 cm, 9.6 g. Greater thickness of female bill is noticeable (Tapajós National Park, Pará). VOICE: advertises with a *takeet, bew-trr*. Terra-firme forest. Upper Xingu, Tapajós, and Madeira, reaching Amazon via latter two. Apparently *P. nattereri, P. iris,* and *P. vilasboasi* replace each other geographically. Also called *Tangará* (Kaiabi, Mato Grosso).

CRIMSON-HOODED MANAKIN, *Pipra aureola*,
Uirapuru-vermelho

10 cm. Very similar to *P. fasciicauda* in color and behavior. Breast scarlet, abdomen black, and tail lacks white band, but bases of flight feathers white as in *P. fasciicauda* and *P. filicauda*. SOUNDS AND DISPLAYS: advertises with *ee-eh, wee-eep;* 2 males jumping between 2 neighboring branches produce a sharp *click* (mechanical) when they perch; they emit another kind of instrumental music after a longer flight; after going to their court, 2 males exchange places several times with great precision. Seasonally flooded forest and várzea. Both sides of lower Amazon and lower Madeira, coast of Amapá to Venezuela. See *P. fasciicauda* and *P. filicauda*.

BAND-TAILED MANAKIN, *Pipra fasciicauda*,
Uirapuru-laranja   PL 32.4

10 cm. Southern replacement of *P. aureola* and *P. filicauda*. SOUNDS AND DISPLAYS: advertises with an *EEE-eh, ew-eet;* when very excited trills *i, i, i, i, i, i, i, i.* Two males (1 dominant) dance together with backs to each other, stomping, holding themselves crouched, trembling and opening wings and tail, thereby displaying white on inner vanes of flight feathers and bases of tail feathers. When one rises in zooming flight and perches on display perch, it makes a dull mechanical sound, *brrr-dlock*. Lone male has a different display (when a 2d male is on a neighboring limb), bowing on a flexible limb and making it sway. Also a slow display fight from one perch to another, which reveals magnificent contrast of white area in flight feathers (fig. 256). Riverine woodlands, adjacent forests. Southern tributaries of Amazon as far as Peru, Bolivia, upper Rio Paraguay, upper Rio Paraná, Goiás, Minas Gerais, Ceará. See *P. filicauda*.

WIRE-TAILED MANAKIN, *Pipra* (= *Teleonema*)
filicauda, Rabo-de-arame   PL 32.13

10.5 cm, with another 4.5 cm for bristlelike, elongated tips of tail feathers. Tail not only decorative but serves as a tactile organ—a brush with which mates touch each other on throat during dances fundamentally similar to those of

Fig. 256. Adult male Band-tailed Manakin, *Pipra fasciicauda*, displaying. After Robbins 1983.

P. aureola and *P. fasciicauda*, species also quite close to it in color and with which it comprises a superspecies (Schwartz and Snow 1979). Rios Negro and Purus west; Venezuela, Colombia, Peru; also right banks of lower Solimões and lower Purus, where range of *aureola* begins. Replaced by *fasciicauda* in upper Purus and Juruá.

HELMETED MANAKIN, *Antilophia galeata*,
Soldadinho   PL 32.14

13.9 cm. One of outstanding species of central Brazil, distinctive with large frontal tuft and long tail. Female dark green with only suggestion of a crest. VOICE AND DISPLAYS: quite loquacious; advertises with a loud, sonorous *glaa-ew;* a composite phrase, *kwewa-kwa kwa, kwa, kwa,* etc.; some males chase each other crying *trrra;* male points crest forward, covering bill. Bellicose disposition. Mounts into canopy from where it makes flights of 80–100 m to other tall trees (see "Prenuptial Displays . . ."). Gallery forest, groves, swampy forests, buriti palm groves. Its nest and hybridization with *Chiroxiphia* confirm that bird is truly a manakin, not a cotingid. Distribution peculiar: Maranhão, Piauí, and Bahia to Mato Grosso, Goiás, western Minas Gerais, Paraná, Paraguay. "Espírito Santo, Sooretama" (Ruschi, without basis). In northeastern São Paulo (e.g., Pirassununga, Campinas) found in same area as *Chiroxiphia caudata*, with which it occasionally hybridizes (see *C. caudata*). Loud voice and general aspect may suggest a cotingid, and it has a certain resemblance to Wing-barred Piprites, *Piprites chloris*. Also called *Testudo* (São Paulo), *Manaquim*.

BLUE-BACKED MANAKIN, *Chiroxiphia pareola,*
Tangará-falso

12 cm. Replaces *C. caudata* in northern Brazil. Tail not
elongated. Plumage black with sky blue back and crest extending backward in 2 "horns." Re immature plumage, see
"Morphology." VOICE AND DISPLAYS: advertises with a loud
weet-weet; as it becomes more animated moves to a gargled
kwa-ka-ka, then a sonorous *churr-churr,* after which it immediately proceeds to dance. Two males will associate in
complete harmony on display perch. One crouches, other
jumps vertically into air, hovers momentarily above its
watching companion, then returns to branch while other
takes flight to go through same display, combination giving
impression of a slowly rotating wheel. Homogeneity of performance is emphasized by a rhythmic, purring duet; finally a
strident *tic-tic* resounds during flight of 1 participant, ending
demonstration (pers. obs. 1947, Xingu, Mato Grosso). Prolonged purring may last for minutes: 2 participants perched
right next to one another do a highly synchronized duet.
Display said to differ in presence of a female: male flies
silently around female in a floating flight, perching at brief
intervals and finally copulating on display perch (Snow
1963, Trinidad). Terra-firme forest, riverine woodland. The
Guianas and Venezuela to Bolivia, northern Mato Grosso,
Maranhão, Alagoas, Pernambuco, the southeast: southern
Bahia, Espírito Santo, Rio de Janeiro. Also called *Cabeça-
encarnada, Tangará* (Pernambuco), *Uirapuru.* See
C. caudata.

BLUE MANAKIN, *Chiroxiphia caudata,*
Tangará, Dançador   PL 32.10

13 cm, plus 2 cm more for elongated central tail feathers.
Much-discussed bird in southeast because of dances. Female
dark green, recognizable by slight elongation of tail. SOUNDS
AND DISPLAYS: dominant male advertises with a loud *drew-
vet,* calling companions and females. A highly coordinated
ceremony then develops: 2–3 (sometimes 6) males form a
compact, moving queue on display perch, preferably an
oblique branch, all facing same direction (fig. 257). They
squat, quiver bodies, and stomp rhythmically, gliding upward toward a green individual (female or immature male,
see "Prenuptial Displays . . .") perched at their side, immobile in an erect posture with head raised, watching. When
queue gets close to quiet spectator, nearest male jumps into
air and hovers for a few moments in front of and slightly
above immobile individual while all other birds watch; he
then goes to far end of line, turns in direction from which he
came, and rejoins team of "tap dancers." Immediately 2d
male, which in meantime has "tap-danced" up to calm spectator, goes through same routine and moves to end of line
alongside 1st. This continues with each member of queue

until eventually 1st male repeats. This ritual is accompanied
by constant cries from dancers: a muffled *tiOO-oo, oo, oo
tiOO-oo, oo, oo . . .* that blends into a monotonous, waver-
ing, purring sound. At beginning, rhythm of both movements and voices is slow. Toward end, rhythm accelerates
and jumps become lower. Last individual, which takes wing
and then brings spectacle to a definite close, soars higher
and longer over spectator, beats wings more rapidly, skids
in air with back arched, turns back to female, and vibrates
tail, giving at the end a very high *tic-tic-tic.* Afterward he
perches above spectator, especially if it is a female, on a
higher branch or on trunk of the small tree where all this
takes place, flying there with a spurt resembling the final
jump of *Manacus manacus.* Penetrating *tic . . .* marks end
of ceremony. Other males immediately abandon court with
only female remaining. Apparently the male ending the display is dominant bird of group and runs the show. Ritual
normally lasts about 30 seconds but may go on as long as 2
minutes.

A few minutes later dance recommences. All attention is
drawn to dancer's fiery, fluffed-up cap, displayed with head
bent forward to show white bases of feathers. Ritual may
vary by beginning with last male, the one at end of queue,
which flies up to perch alongside female (Sick 1959a). When
there are many males, a line sometimes forms on either side
of her, with several males wanting to hover at same time and
all ending in confusion. When there is no female, 1 male may
jump over another. If only 2 males dance together, display
resembles "rotating wheel" performed by *C. pareola.* A male
may perform a floating flight around the still calmly perched
female. Before or after dance a male sometimes chases a
female, uttering a series of *trrrr*s. I have never seen copulation on the court. Another ritual that precedes copulation, the
mating display, has been well described by A. Assumpção[2]:
"A female leaves her accustomed tranquillity and moves
through the branches, crouching forward or backward on
them with the body arched upward and the head bent back
over the nape. Repeatedly, at every shift of position, she
makes a short, rapid move on the branch until a male enters
the area and starts to court her. He follows her and they
execute the same choreography while constantly accelerating
and moving toward each other. If more males approach, each
participates, with the one that finally proves his leadership
winning the mating." Assumpção adds that this ceremony-
for-two may also resemble display of *C. pareola.*

During more prolonged intervals between dances, members of a group sit quietly at some distance from one another,
from time to time producing different chirps. The species has
a warning whistle, *dwewt, dwewot.* There is obviously a
considerable excess of males.

Dense forests of southern Bahia and Minas Gerais to Rio

[2]Armando Assumpção, a São Paulo bird fancier, had a large flight cage
imitating the natural habitat with 20 male and 5 female *C. caudata* that bred

there. From 1956 to 1967 he kept me informed of his most interesting
observations.

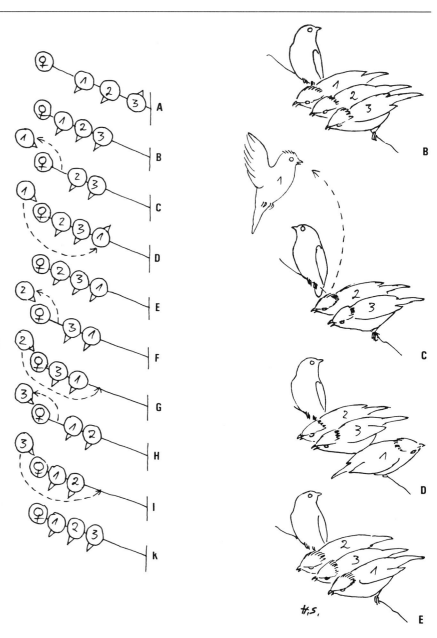

Fig. 257. Three Blue Manakin, *Chiroxiphia caudata*, males (1,2,3), dancing before an immobile female, which could be substituted by a young (green) male. Sketch, A–K: the three males, one after the other, take flight to hover in front of the female in a rhythmic process like a turning wheel. The triangles attached to the circles representing the males in the left column indicate their bills. The four sketches at the right give details of phases B, C, D, and E. (A) Two males (1 and 2) alongside the female, ready to dance. A third male, recently arrived, has not yet joined the line of dancers. (B) Formation of the line is complete, with the three males, all facing the same direction, tap-dancing and "purring." (C) The first male takes off to display before the female. (D) The first male returns to the branch while the second male, now at the head of the line, prepares for his display flight. (E) The three males tap-dancing and purring, as in B, but they have changed places. (F) The second male has taken off for his display flight. (G) The second male returns to the branch, while the third heads the line. (H) The third male has taken off for his display flight. (I) The third male returns to the branch, while the first heads the line, as in A and B. (K) The three males tap-dancing and purring with their positions the same as in B. Original, H. Sick.

Grande do Sul, Paraguay, and Misiones, Argentina. In northern part of range (Espírito Santo) restricted to or more widespread in mountains. Apparently does not meet *C. pareola*, which it replaces in southeast. Represented in northwest of continent by Lance-tailed Manakin, *C. lanceolata,* and in Central America by Long-tailed Manakin, *C. linearis.* There is a good description of *C. caudata* dance by Fernão Cardim, a contemporary of Anchieta (sixteenth century). Also called *Dançarino, Canto-de-macaco, Pavãozinho* (Minas Gerais), *Ticolão.* In northeastern São Paulo sometimes in same forests as *Antilophia galeata.* Occasional appearance of a *rei-dos-tangarás* ["king-of-the-manakins"] in that region refers to hybrids between the 2 species (Sick 1979, see also "Interspecific Relations").

PIN-TAILED MANAKIN, *Ilicura militaris,*
Tangarazinho   BR   PL 32.11
12.8 cm, including slightly upturned elongation of tail, which contrasts with straight tail of *Chiroxiphia caudata.* An important endemic of southeast. Female green with tail a bit elongated. SOUNDS AND DISPLAYS: advertises with a descending phrase as high as a hummingbird's, *bee-bi-bi-bibibibi.* Male displays alone in tops of large trees, using a thick branch divested of its epiphytic vegetation for a court, or in captivity, a board, perhaps 80 × 5 cm; he flies lengthwise along court (fig. 258). At takeoff point he crouches with wings drooping slightly and tail half-raised, resting breast on branch with throat almost touching substrate and revealing, in this position, a small white spot on either side of lower

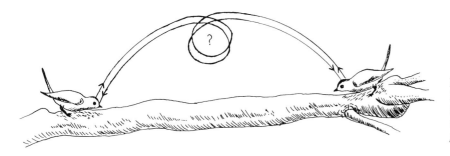

Fig. 258. Solitary ceremony of Pin-tailed Manakin, *Ilicura militaris*. It makes a jump-flight to the end of its runway on an unobstructed heavy limb while producing a loud *prrrrák* halfway along. Original, H. Sick.

back. He stays in this vigilant position for a few seconds, as if concentrating. Suddenly he takes flight at full speed, rising about 30 cm above perch and producing a loud *prrrrAK*, a noise similar to that of a stick being run along an iron grating. I suspect he does a somersault (Sick 1967). Perching at end of runway, he turns around to face direction from which he came and immediately crouches again on branch, ready to return over same course (see *Corapipo* and "Prenuptial Displays . . ."). Appearance of other *I. militaris* is a stimulus for this performance. Rattle must be produced by reinforced, specially implanted external primaries, and these are likely source of intense whistle made by adult male whenever it flies. It can, however, fly silently when it wishes. Common for males to chase each other. Forests of Serra do Mar and Serra da Mantiqueira: Espírito Santo, Minas Gerais to Santa Catarina, also ex-Guanabara. Also called *Estalador* (Minas Gerais).

WHITE-THROATED MANAKIN, *Corapipo gutturalis*

8.6 cm. Black with white throat. DISPLAYS: male, crouching on fallen tree trunk, lifts bill vertically to display bright, white throat; in flight another white area appears on flight feathers. Makes rapid to-and-fro flights, then lowers head and flutters wings. Males do not cooperate (Davis 1949, Prum 1986). North of Amazon in Serra do Navio (Amapá), the Guianas, Venezuela.

WHITE-BEARDED MANAKIN, *Manacus manacus,* Rendeira Fig. 259

11 cm. Unmistakable. One is alerted to bird's presence by crackling noise that can be heard before seeing it. Black and white, distinguished by large beard, long legs with strong musculature, bright orange tarsi. Female green, recognizable by yellow shins, same general aspect.

SOUNDS AND DISPLAYS: Voice quite varied. Loudest cry is a penetrating *tsierr*. Most interesting mechanical noise is the crackling already mentioned. Birds ready to dance gather in small groups among branches and yield themselves to a confused game of shrieking, croaking, wing whirring, popping, etc. Suddenly 1 male separates from group and occupies his private court nearby, close to ground: a roughly triangular space about 80 cm on a side (fig. 260). He starts to jump from 1 vertical sprig to another, touching 2–4 fixed points, the last

being near the 1st. Rhythm of this solitary dancer's moves is greatly accentuated by crackling that resounds at each jump like clicks of a metronome. This is all the more crisp and exciting because now there is no wing whirring; bird only hops, does not fly. At next-to-last jump he goes to ground and from there rises vertically in a more violent spurt, half between jumping and flying, to reach a higher perch and make a loud *buzz* resembling wing rustle of certain hummingbirds. There it ends. After a short interval he repeats show in same or reverse direction (clockwise or counterclockwise). Air currents caused by bird's movements sweep arena clean, and he carries away twigs and dry leaves, so it is visible at a distance. When so disposed, neighboring males also move into their courts, resulting in an explosion of activity, each stimulating the others.

Forest and capoeira, abundant in terra firme in Amazonia (see "Distribution . . ."). The Guianas and Venezuela to Bolivia, almost all of Brazil south to southeastern Mato Grosso, São Paulo, Santa Catarina, Paraguay, and Misiones, Argentina. Also called *Atangará-tinga*. Name *Rendeira* ["lacemaker"] comes from similarity of clicking produced during dance to sound of bobbin heard in lace-making. Various geographic races have evolved, 6 of them in Brazil: e.g., *M. m. gutturosus,* with slate gray belly (instead of

Fig. 259. White-bearded Manakin, *Manacus m. manacus,* adult male.

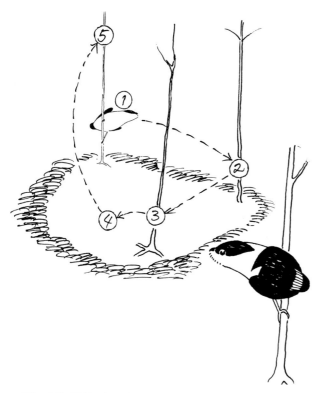

Fig. 260. White-bearded Manakin, *Manacus m. manacus,* court with five stations, the fourth on the ground, which has been swept by the dancer's abrupt wing movements. In the foreground is a neighboring male, owner of another court, watching with interest the solitary dance of his neighbor. Original, H. Sick.

white) in southeastern Brazil from Bahia to southeastern Mato Grosso.

FIERY-CAPPED MANAKIN, *Machaeropterus pyrocephalus,* Uirapuru-cigarra

7.6 cm. Similar to *M. regulus* but even smaller, crown yellow with scarlet center (*M. regulus* cap is all red), back greenish brown (not green). SOUNDS AND DISPLAYS: advertises with a far-ringing metallic *ting* that sounds like a cicada song. Male displays while perched on vertical branch, head down, uttering a whispered *ts, s, s, s, s, s, s* . . . similar to a grasshopper (Locustidae) or cicada buzz, a noise similar to that produced by *regulus*. Also shifts position on branch and draws attention by flaunting a series of black spots on wings that stand out like eyes in a light gray, convex framework. Flight produces a loud rattling sound, recalling noise a large beetle of region makes with wing covers when flying. Tall forest canopy. Amazonia south to Rio das Mortes, Mato Grosso, Rio das Almas, Goiás, Amapá. See *M. regulus.*

STRIPED MANAKIN, *Machaeropterus regulus,* Tangará-rajado   PL 32.2

8.6 cm. Small, may pass unnoticed if one does not know voice. Sexes similar, female having green cap corresponding

Fig. 261. Striped Manakin, *Machaeropterus r. regulus,* male displaying before another male. After Sick 1959a.

to rest of upperparts. SOUNDS AND DISPLAYS: advertises with a nasal *gheh*. When analyzed at close range, evident that this sound comprises 2 tones given at same time: 1 high (the already mentioned *gheh*), 1 low that sounds like *Oa* and could be voice of a tiny owl. Displaying male clutches a slender vertical branch and remains suspended sideways with head down, producing a buzzing similar to *M. pyrocephalus* that lasts 5–20 seconds. He stretches wings, spreads and shakes tail, and makes extremely rapid changes of position that create impression he is turning a somersault around perch (fig. 261); also spreads crest and projects it forward. Two, sometimes more, males are on hand. Tangled tropical forest. Bahia to Rio de Janeiro and extreme western Brazil (Rio Javari), from there to Peru, Venezuela. Also called *Atangará.*

BLACK MANAKIN, *Xenopipo atronitens,* Pretinho

12.2 cm. Uniformly black with black-tipped, light gray bill. Female resembles various other female manakins, being dark green with black bases to feathers. VOICE AND DISPLAYS: a weak *bit-bit,* a loud *tsit-krr-krr-krr;* a few males will chase each other crying a penetrating *ikeh.* . . . Terra-firme forest. At transition with floodable forests sometimes meets Amazonian Black-Tyrant, *Knipolegus poecilocercus,* male of which is similar but has different behavior, female of which is different. The Guianas and Venezuela to upper Amazon as far as upper Xingu, northern Mato Grosso. Also called *Uraí-um* (Kaiabi, Mato Grosso).

OLIVE MANAKIN, *Chloropipo uniformis*

13.8 cm. Green, resembling the *Schiffornis* but with gray throat, no brown in wing. Only on Brazil/Venezuela border, Cerro Uei-tepui.

CINNAMON TYRANT-MANAKIN, *Neopipo cinnamomea,* Enferrujadinho   PL 33.3

9.9 cm. Small Amazonian species resembling Ruddy-tailed Flycatcher, *Terenotriccus erythrurus,* but with more slender bill, no bristles. Center of crown yellow in male, red in female. I found it in Cururu in canopy of low, dry forest. The Guianas and Venezuela to Peru, Madeira, Tapajós,

Fig. 262. Flame-crested Manakin, *Heterocercus linteatus,*
adult male, displaying its resplendent white whiskers.
After Sick 1959a.

Cururu (Pará), Amapá. Its phylogenetic relationships have
not yet been clarified.

FLAME-CRESTED MANAKIN, *Heterocercus linteatus,*
Coroa-de-fogo   PL 32.12

13.8 cm; 24 g. Large and distinctive piprid. Tail long,
graduated. Female lacks red crest; head olive, underparts
brownish. VOICE AND DISPLAYS: advertises with a sharp *pit-
eeew.* When displaying spreads shiny white throat feathers to
side, like a broad beard (fig. 262). A few males will chase
each other calling *psieh.* Dark riverine forests subject to
flooding. South of Amazon from Xingu, Mato Grosso, to
Peru (fig. 263). Also called *Tangará* (Kamaiurá, Mato
Grosso). See *Neopelma aurifrons.*

YELLOW-CRESTED MANAKIN, *Heterocercus flavivertex*
Crest yellow instead of red, but behavior similar to
H. linteatus. Replaces it north of Amazon.

WIED'S TYRANT-MANAKIN, *Neopelma aurifrons,*
Fruxu   BR   PL 32.9

13.3 cm. Resembles the *Myiopagis* and *Elaenia* (Tyrannidae) in aspect and color but lacks their light wing bars. Iris
yellowish brown, unlike these tyrants, which have dark
chestnut iris. Female similar, with less yellow on crown, a
decoration not always well developed even in males. VOICE
AND DISPLAYS: male, sitting low and alone, utters a squeaky
phrase of 3–4 syllables, *chewp-chewp-chip, chak-chak-
tsirrew-chak.* Thick forest, restricted to mountains (Teresópolis, etc.) in Rio de Janeiro. Bahia and Minas Gerais to
São Paulo. See *Heterocercus linteatus* and Greenish
Mourner, *Schiffornis virescens.*

PALE-BELLIED TYRANT-MANAKIN,
Neopelma pallescens   BR

14 cm. Aspect similar to *N. aurifrons* except for much
larger bill. Iris yellowish, throat streaked. Prenuptial display

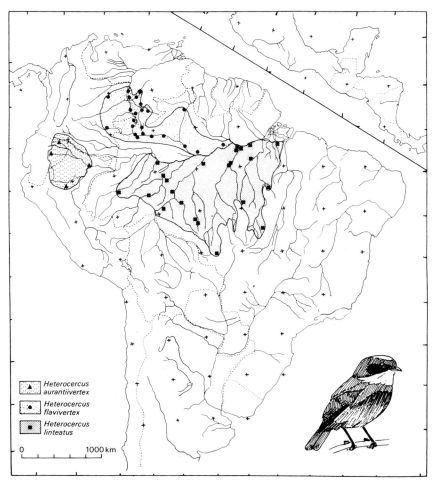

Heterocercus
aurantiivertex

Heterocercus
flavivertex

Heterocercus
linteatus

0   1000 km

Fig. 263. Distribution of the Flame-crested
Manakin superspecies, *Heterocercus
linteatus.* After Haffer 1985.

more elaborate. SOUNDS AND DISPLAYS: even when alone male jumps vertically, displaying the always extensively sulfur yellow crown and beating wings, *dop-dop* (sounding like hammering of a small woodpecker), then returns to perch where he raucously calls *heh-gheh-gheh*, voice resembling Squirrel Cuckoo, *Piaya cayana*. At times jumps without beating wings (Teles Pires, Mato Grosso). May shake foliage when jumping near end of a branch (Kuluene, Mato Grosso). Warning call a loud cry, *wet-wet-wet*, like a tree frog. Forest, cerradão. Minas Gerais and São Paulo to Rio Tapajós, north bank of lower Amazon, Maranhão, Alagoas.

SAFFRON-CRESTED TYRANT-MANAKIN, *Neopelma chrysocephalum*

Quite similar to *N. pallescens* with similar prenuptial display (jumps and hovers over perch; a 3- to 5-syllable phrase). Upper Amazon from Rio Negro to the Guianas, Colombia.

SULPHUR-BELLIED TYRANT-MANAKIN, *Neopelma sulphureiventer*

Also similar to *N. pallescens*. Upper Amazon in Brazilian/Bolivian border region.

TINY TYRANT-MANAKIN, *Tyranneutes virescens*, Uirapuruzinho-do-norte

7 cm; 7 g. Smallest piprid. Similar to *T. stolzmanni* but with more yellow in crown and short, stiff tail that probably produces sharp mechanical trill occasionally heard in display flights. VOICE AND DISPLAYS: lone bird assiduously advertises with a 3- to 4-syllable descending phrase, *WIje-bew, tsew-dewdewdew*, volume of which leads one to expect a larger bird. Sometimes makes a hovering flight, like a butterfly, with body and head lifted, crest raised, legs dangling, moving from one branch to another. When perching between such flights holds itself well erect and makes slow lateral movements with neck, looking fixedly forward (fig. 264). Tall forest. Amapá to Rio Negro, Venezuela, the Guianas.

DWARF TYRANT-MANAKIN, *Tyranneutes stolzmanni*, Uirapuruzinho   PL 32.8

8 cm. Similar to *T. virescens*, sometimes with a bit of yellow in crown. Sexes similar but female larger. VOICE: a weak, bisyllabic *dew-plewp*. Like *virescens*, vocalizes only when perched on branch of a leafy tree. At times utters a series of *jewit*s . . . and is answered by neighbor advertising in distance but within sound of its voice. Venezuela and Rio Negro to Peru, Bolivia, Mato Grosso (upper Xingu), eastern Pará, Maranhão. It is geographic replacement of *virescens*.

GREENISH MOURNER, *Schiffornis virescens*, Flautim   PL 33.4

15.6 cm. Bird of southeast, dark olivaceous green with brown wings and tail. VOICE AND BEHAVIOR: a somewhat confused and not very loud phrase, usually with typical accent at start, *tsew-TSWEET-tsew-tsew, tsiEW-che-delewt,*

Fig. 264. Tiny Tyrant-Manakin, *Tyranneutes virescens*, adult male, making lateral head movements. After Snow 1961.

tiu-tiu-brootui, sung by male perched alone low in dense capoeira. Likes vertical perches. Bahia and Minas Gerais to Rio de Janeiro (Itatiaia), ex-Guanabara, Rio Grande do Sul, Goiás (Anápolis), Paraguay, and Misiones, Argentina. In Espírito Santo only in mountains. Voice recalls *S. turdinus* (its replacement to north) and *Antilophia galeata*. Behavior, nesting, and feeding (see *S. turdinus*) do not conform to manakin pattern. I lean toward grouping genus with the Cotingidae. See *Neopelma aurifrons* and *S. turdinus*. It has been suggested that *Schiffornis* be taken out of the Pipridae and grouped with 5 other genera that are difficult to place: *Laniisoma* and *Iodopleura* (Cotingidae) and *Laniocera, Xenopsaris,* and *Pachyramphus* (Tyrannidae) (Prum and Lanyon 1989).

THRUSH-LIKE MOURNER, *Schiffornis turdinus*

17.7 cm (Espírito Santo), smaller in Amazonia proper (16.5 cm). Amazonian replacement for *S. virescens*, which it resembles. Locally (e.g., Espírito Santo) uniformly olivaceous brown. VOICE: song a prominent, clear, 3-part phrase, *dew-dewit-dewee*, that when imitated immediately attracts bird; warning *terAY-tete*. Eats large, hairy caterpillars, fruits with large pips. Solitary, like *virescens*. Male takes no interest in nest (see "Nesting"). Throughout Amazonia and eastern Brazil, in Amazonian-type forest to hot lowlands north of Rio Doce, Espírito Santo, and to Central America and Mexico.

CINNAMON MOURNER, *Schiffornis* (= *Massornis*) *major*

15.6 cm. Usually included as a 3d *Schiffornis*. Entirely ferruginous, sometimes with gray cap; resembles Rufous-tailed Attila, *Attila phoenicurus*. Upper Amazon.

Pipridae Bibliography
See also General Bibliography

Antas, P.T.Z., and S.L.R. Leeuwenberg. 1987. Dados sobre a biologia reprodutiva de *Antilophia galeata* no P. Nac. de Brasília. *III ENAV*:37.

Assumpção, A. 1985. O tangará dançarino. *SOBoletim* 1(5):13–16.

Assumpção, A. 1985. Observações sobre a reprodução do tangará dançarino em cativeiro. *SOBoletim* 1(6):13–16.

Brisson, M. J. 1760. *Ornithologie* 4:442.

Crandall, L. S. 1945. A brilliant flash—that's the manakins' display. *Animal Kingdom* 48(3):67–69.

Davis, T. A. W. 1949. Display of the White-throated Manakin, *Corapipo gutturalis. Ibis* 91:146–47.

Foster, M. S. 1976. Nesting biology of the Long-tailed Manakin. *Wilson Bull.* 88(3):400–420.

Foster, M. S. 1981. Cooperative behavior and social organization of *Chiroxiphia caudata. Behav. Ecol. Sociobiol.* 9:167–77.

Foster, M. S. 1985. Pre-nesting cooperation in birds: another form of helping behavior. In *Neotrop. Ornith.*, Ornith. Monogr. no. 36.

Foster, M. S. 1987. Delayed maturation, neoteny, and social system differences in two manakins of the genus *Chiroxiphia. Evolution* 41:547–58.

Gilliard, E. T. 1959. Notes on the courtship behavior of the Blue-backed Manakin (*Chiroxiphia pareola*). *Am. Mus. Nov.* 1942.

Hellmayr, C. E. 1906. A revision of the species of the genus *Pipra. Ibis:*1–46.

Hellmayr, C. E. 1915. Ein bisher verkannter Pipride aus Brasilien (*Pipra aureola* und ihre Rassen: *P.a. scarlatina* n. subsp.). *Verh. Ornith. Ges. Bay.* 12:12.

Lill, A. 1974. Sexual behavior of lek-forming White-bearded Manakins (*Manacus m. trinitatis*). *Z. Tierpsych.* 36:1–36.

Lill, A. 1976. Social organization and space utilization in the lek-forming White-bearded Manakin (*Manacus m. trinitatis*). *Z. Tierpsych.* 36:513–30.

Lill, A. 1976. Lek behavior in the Golden-headed Manakin (*Pipra erythrocephala*), Trinidad. *Z. Tierpsych.*, suppl. 18.

Motta, J. C., Jr. 1988. Observações sobre a dispersão de sementes de *Psittacanthus robustus* (Loranthaceae) por aves. *VII Cong. Soc. Bot. S. Paulo.*

Parkes, K. C. 1961. *Condor* 63:345–50. [Hybrids]

Prum, R. O. 1985. Observations of the White-fronted Manakin, *Pipra serena*, in Suriname. *Auk* 102:384–87.

Prum, R. O. 1986. The display of the White-throated Manakin, *Corapipo gutturalis*, in Suriname. *Ibis* 128:91–102.

Prum, R. O., and A. E. Johnson. 1987. Display behavior, foraging ecology, and systematics of the Golden-winged Manakin, *Masius chrysopterus. Wilson Bull.* 99(4):521–39.

Robbins, M. B. 1983. The display repertoire of the Band-tailed Manakin, *Pipra fasciicauda. Wilson Bull.* 95:321–42.

Robbins, M. B. 1985. Social organization of *Pipra fasciicauda. Condor* 87(4):449–56.

Ruschi, A. 1964. Os movimentos controlados das retrizes em *Loddigesia mirabilis* e o estalido produzido pelo macho. *Bol. Mus. Biol.*, Ser. Biol. 44.

Schwartz, P., and D. W. Snow. 1979. *The Living Bird* 17:51–78. [*Pipra filicauda*, behavior]

Sick, H. 1942. *Orn. Mber.* 50:18. [*Chiroxiphia caudata*]

Sick, H. 1959. *J. Orn.* 100:111–12. [*Pipra vilasboasi*, description]

Sick, H. 1959a. *J. Orn.* 100:269–302. [Displays]

Sick, H. 1959b. *Bol. Mus. Nac. Rio de Janeiro, Zool.* 213. [Displays]

Sick, H. 1959c. *Rev. Bras. Biol.* 19:13–16. [*Pipra vilasboasi*]

Sick, H. 1959d. *J. Orn.* 100:404–12. [*Pipra vilasboasi*, general, color plate]

Sick, H. 1960. *Proc. 12th Int. Orn. Cong., Helsinki:* 672–80. [Displays]

Sick, H. 1967. *The Living Bird* 6:5–22. [Displays]

Sick, H. 1979. *Bull. B.O.C.* 99(4):115–20. [Hybrids between *Chiroxiphia caudata* and *Antilophia galeata*]

Snow, D. W. 1961. *Ibis* 103:110–13. [*Pipra pipra, Tyranneutes virescens*, displays]

Snow, D. W. 1962a. *Zoologica* (N.Y.) 47:65–104. [*Manacus manacus*]

Snow, D. W. 1962b. *Zoologica* (N.Y.) 47:183–98. [*Pipra erythrocephala*, monograph]

Snow, D. W. 1963. *Zoologica* (N.Y.) 48:167–76. [*Chiroxiphia pareola*, displays]

Snow, D. W. 1975. *Bull. B.O.C.* 95:20–27. [Classification]

Snow, D. W. 1979. Pipridae. In J. L. Peters, *Check-list of Birds of the World*, vol. 8. Cambridge, Mass.: Museum of Comparative Zoology.

Snow, D. W., and A. Lill. 1974. *Condor* 76:262–67. [Longevity]

Wagner, H. 1945. Observaciones sobre el comportamiento de *Chiroxiphia linearis* durante su propagación. *An. Inst. Biol. Univ. Nac. Auton. Mex.* 16(2):539–46.

Willis, E. O. and Y. Oniki. 1988. Bright crowns of female and young male Swallow-tailed Manakins, *Chiroxiphia caudata. Rev. Bras. Biol.* 48(3):439–41.

FAMILY COTINGIDAE: COTINGAS (36)

Typically Neotropical, this is one of the most famous South American families because of the exuberant forms and colors of its members, which to some extent rival the beauty of the birds of paradise of Australasia. They also have distinctive behavior. They occur from Mexico to southern Brazil, northern Argentina, and Bolivia, reaching their greatest diversity in Amazonia. Fossils are so far unknown. Cotingidae are related to Tyrannidae and Pipridae. The Cotingidae are said to show certain affinities with the peculiar Eurylaimidae, Suboscines of the Old World, which may be the most primitive Passeriformes now in existence.

Morphology and Definition of the Family

Cotingids vary widely in appearance. Generally of average size, some large species such as the Red-ruffed Fruitcrow, *Pyroderus scutatus*, and the *Cephalopterus* umbrellabirds are even bigger than jays (Corvidae). The

Cephalopterus are about the same size as the Red-throated Caracara, *Daptrius americanus*, an occasional neighbor. Although some Cotingidae are among the largest Passerines in the world, there are some very small species, such as the *Iodopleura* purpletufts and Kinglet Calyptura, *Calyptura cristata*.

Cotingids have large heads and sturdy bills, and their mouths and wings are large and wide. Sometimes bristlelike feathers appear around the bill, as in the *Lipaugus* pihas and *Querula* and *Pyroderus* fruitcrows. Their legs are short, but their feet are large enough to perch comfortably on branches. Large species such as the *Cephalopterus;* Capuchinbird, *Perissocephalus tricolor;* and *Rupicola* cocks-of-the-rock have sharp, powerful claws.

Interestingly, powder down is a well-developed aspect of the plumage structure of the Bare-necked Fruitcrow, *Gymnoderus foetidus*. This powdery plumage (see Mealy Parrot, *Amazona farinosa*) is a distinctive character rare in Passeriformes, but it also occurs to a limited extent in the *Iodopleura* and is abundant in the Black-faced Cotinga, *Conioptilon mcilhennyi*, of Peru.

Based on a large number of cotingid skins, Snow (1976) verified the coincidence of molt and breeding (which usually occur separately) with the period of greatest food abundance, near the end of the dry season.

The Crimson Fruitcrow, *Haematoderus militaris*, and Black-necked Red-Cotinga, *Phoenicircus nigricollis*, are almost entirely red. The *Rupicola* are bright orange. It is surprising to find extensive white occurring in forest species: the White Bellbird, *Procnias alba*, is one of the world's few entirely white nonmaritime birds. The *Xipholena* cotingas have white wings, creating a marked contrast against the green forest. Together with the Scarlet and Red-and-Green Macaws, *Ara macao* and *A. chloroptera*, they are among the birds that most attract attention as they fly low over the Hylaea. When seen against a sky with bright white clouds, so common in the tropics, the bellbird becomes almost invisible, like a white bird in the snow.

It is common for cotingids to have a brightly colored throat, as in the *Cotinga*, *Querula*, and *Pyroderus;* the feathers are sometimes stiffened, increasing reflectiveness. The throat feathers of the Purple-throated Fruitcrow, *Querula purpurata*, have a peculiar structure. Species with somber dress, such as the *Lipaugus*, are not lacking.

Analysis of the feather colors of cotingas presents certain problems, reflected in the name *kotingin* for the violet of the *Cotinga*, reported to consist of blue (due to light reflected from a spongy structure, not to pigmentation) and of a red carotenoid pigment. Rodoxanthin, a pigment known from vegetable matter, has been extracted from *Phoenicircus* feathers. The bright orange of the Andean Cock-of-the-rock, *Rupicola peruviana*, is derived from zeaxanthin, a pigment found in corn (*Zea mays*), which fades rapidly both in prepared specimens and captive individuals, although in the latter case it can be restored by supplementing the bird's diet with cantaxanthin. The *Cephalopterus* are noted for their bizarre shapes, with a long "necktie" and a large crest like a small umbrella ("umbrellabird"). Two *Procnias* species have stringy protuberances on the head that look like strange worms. The beautiful lilac tuft of *Iodopleura* males, hidden beneath the bird's wings, is displayed by excited individuals in a way reminiscent of the *Tachyphonus* (Thraupinae) that show the white underside of their wings.

Another high point in cotingid evolution is the replacement of feathers by areas of bare, sometimes brightly colored, skin, a privilege of adult males of *Procnias* and even more notably of *Gymnoderus* and *Perissocephalus*. Sexes may differ, and the female is generally smaller, as in *Querula*, *Pyroderus*, *Cephalopterus*, and *Procnias*. Whereas female Purple-breasted and Banded Cotingas, *Cotinga cotinga* and *C. maculata*, are much smaller, the female Plum-throated Cotinga, *C. maynana*, has longer wings than the male. We need to discover the functional reasons for these and other morphological peculiarities. This difference in the *Cotinga* is thought to involve one more sophisticated means of producing instrumental music. See "Sounds."

After losing their natal plumage but while still in the nest, young Swallow-tailed Cotingas, *Phibalura flavirostris*, and *Gymnoderus foetidus* acquire another plumage different from that of the adult. *Phibalura* becomes all speckled with black and white; *Gymnoderus* turns grayish white like a *Sterna* tern nestling. The male Bare-throated Bellbird, *Procnias nudicollis*, acquires adult plumage in its third year; during earlier molts it acquires white feathers marbled with gray, intermediate in appearance between the juvenal and adult pattern; the throat becomes half bare during the first year.

The Cotingidae were reexamined based on syrinx structure (Ames 1971) and taxonomic characters in general (Snow 1973b). Transfer of five genera (*Attila, Pseudattila, Casiornis, Laniocera,* and *Rhytipterna*) to the Tyrannidae was recommended, and recently the same was done for *Pachyramphus, Platypsaris,* and *Tityra* (Peters 1979). D. W. Snow's excellent monograph of the Cotingidae (1982) provides detailed information. Later research such as that of Prum and Lanyon (1989) has resulted in minor modifications. My own observations confirm that the problem is complex. On scrutinizing live birds one notes a combination of tyrannid and cotingid characters in various species that to me suggest the existence of intermediate genera. Obviously a linear sequence is not adequate for satisfactory definition of these intricate relationships.

I include *Oxyruncus* (up to now in a monotypic family) and *Piprites* (generally listed with the Pipridae) in the Cotingidae. Ames (1971) considers the syrinx of *Oxyruncus* similar to that of *Pachyramphus* and *Piprites*. The syrinx of *Iodopleura* is also said to be close to those of the Tyrannidae. An evaluation of *Schiffornis* is equally difficult. It is usually aligned with the *Pipridae*, where I leave it, although in my opinion it is closer to the Cotingidae. A more precise conclusion on the systematic position of these birds awaits study of other taxonomic characters. I also include the *Rupicola* in the Cotingidae. I exclude the White-naped Xenopsaris, *Xenopsaris albinucha* (see Tyrannidae).

Sounds

Male cotingids have many cries (corresponding to the song of most species) that are given tirelessly during the breeding period. Otherwise they are generally silent, although some species, such as the Black-and-Gold Cotinga, *Tijuca atra,* can be heard all year. Several, such as the *Tijuca* and the Sharpbill, *Oxyruncus cristatus,* have extremely high, clear whistles, a type of vocalization also found in birds classified by their syringeal structure as tyrannids (e.g., *Laniocera*). The song of a group of *Querula purpurata* is melodious and rhythmic, remotely resembling that of *Monasa* (Bucconidae) heard at a distance. Male *Pyroderus scutatus* sing a kind of duet; their "pounding" can be heard for more than 2 km. These sounds reach their peak in the din of *Procnias nudicollis,* which has one of the loudest bird voices in the world. The Screaming Piha, *Lipaugus vociferans,* is the most persistent shrieker of the Hylaea, acoustically dominating the forests where it lives. Its whistle blasts have earned it the title "the voice of Amazonia," which it amply confirms in the Amazonian-type forests north of the Rio Doce in Espírito Santo.

Pyroderus, Cephalopterus, and *Perissocephalus* have deep voices like the mooing of a cow. They increase volume by an expandable extension of the foreparts of the trachea and pharynx, similar to certain anatids. *Procnias nudicollis* has a very muscular syrinx, but to make such a racket it also depends on interclavicular air sacs that are probably inflated before the cry. Its spectacular "hammering" is followed by a high, strident sound believed to originate in a part of the vocal apparatus (the other bronchus) different from that responsible for the preceding noise. Vocal changes at puberty can be detected in this species: the hammering only reaches perfection after the second or third year. The female *P. nudicollis* has been considered mute, but I think it probable that the warning call I have noted for males and immatures of unknown sex may also originate with females. *Phibalura* nestlings make a notably melodious trill.

In some species, such as the *Cotinga* and *Xipholena,* vocalization is almost entirely replaced by noises produced by the wings, easily heard when they fly or fight (instrumental music, see Pipridae). The sound-producing feathers responsible for these effects may be the narrow, saber-shaped outer primaries. I have noticed that wing noise in the *Cotinga, Xipholena,* and *Procnias* is controlled by the individual bird, which can increase, decrease, or even eliminate it according to circumstances. The *Rupicola,* which make a loud hiss in flight, also have a sound-producing remige at the tip of the wing. In the service of better instrumental music, the wing of the male *Phoenicircus* has become appreciably shortened, producing a change in wing-beat frequency and, consequently, in the sound produced. It also has a single, highly modified remige hidden among the normal primaries whose function is poorly understood. Generally even ornithologists do not know of the existence of this feather. *Xipholena* makes a noisy display flight, moving from one distant branch to another. The *Rupicola* make popping noises, attributed to snapping of the mandibles.

Feeding

Cotingids are primarily frugivorous, exploiting the copious and relatively easy food source supplied by Neotropical fruits (Snow 1981). They often take not only little ones, such as those of the palmito, açaí (*Euterpe*), and exotic *Livistonia,* but also and especially large fruits with voluminous seeds that they pick from Lauraceae and Burseraceae trees in the primary forest and which completely fill their wide gapes and are swallowed whole. The extremely large mouth of *Procnias nudicollis,* combined with the short bill and broad head that create a vague, froglike impression, are special adaptations for swallowing large mouthfuls.

Cotingids also eat berries, such as of Loranthaceae and Melostomataceae, which are more often the food of opportunists with "normal" bills, such as thraupines. *Iodopleura* are the birds most devoted to mistletoe berries. I have seen *Tijuca* and *Procnias* satiate themselves with berries of the capororoca (*Rapanea ferruginea,* Myrsinaceae; Bocaina, São Paulo, April). Cecropia fruits and pitangas are prized; *Pyroderus scutatus* and *Procnias nudicollis* can be attracted by small red paper imitations of these fruits. I have seen *Phibalura, Carpornis, Cotinga,* and *Xipholena* go down to lower levels of the forest to gorge themselves in bushes, especially on the purple berries of caruru (*Phytolacca*). As hunters well know, *Pyroderus scutatus* eats the same fruits as toucans.

Favorite fruit trees are often visited on a morning and late-afternoon schedule with an interval of some hours between. Fruits are taken in full flight, like trogons do, and are eaten while perched on a bunch or hopping through the branches. They toss food into their mouths like toucans. Larger seeds are regurgitated, whereas smaller ones pass through the digestive tract; their pellets sometimes contain several husks (*Oxyruncus*).

The Elegant Mourner, *Laniisoma elegans; Lipaugus vociferans; Haematoderus militaris; Querula purpurata; Cephalopterus* umbrellabirds; and others complement their fruit diet by eating insect adults and larvae, especially when fruits become scarce, as during the rainy season. The Wing-barred Piprites, *Piprites chloris,* catches caterpillars as well as butterflies. The White-browed Purpletuft, *Iodopleura isabellae,* sometimes chases insects in flight, recalling the

Swallow-wing, *Chelidoptera tenebrosa* (Bucconidae). *Gymnoderus foetidus* catches swarming termites flying above the forest.

Cotingids are among the most efficient disseminators of plants whose fruits they eat. The advantage for the plants is that the seeds or stones of the fruits the birds swallow are not harmed, being promptly regurgitated, or even better, having passed through the intestines, sprout faster (Snow 1971b).

The abundant food offered by Neotropical forests to fruit-eating birds such as the Pipridae and Cotingidae saves these birds both time and effort. Females are able to rear their young by themselves, and males devote themselves to displaying on their courts. The result is polygamy. On this point it is interesting to remember that most monogamous birds are insectivorous (Lack 1968).

Behavior

Cotingidae perch erectly but generally move slowly and have phlegmatic dispositions, keeping absolutely quiet when perched. They can fly well, as already mentioned for *Gymnoderus foetidus*. *Querula purpurata* has developed a special aptitude for flying among branches. *Rupicola* have a heavy, pigeonlike flight. Cotingids such as *Tijuca, Procnias,* and *Oxyruncus* have a characteristic way of letting themselves drop vertically through the leafy canopy, thus unexpectedly disappearing like a hawk diving on prey (see fig. 268). Most live in the highest forest levels where it is difficult to observe them. Ecologically speaking they are relatively homogeneous.

I have observed aggression between cotingids feeding in the same fruit tree: a *Procnias nudicollis* expelled a female White-winged Cotinga, *Xipholena atropurpurea*. The *Piprites, Querula purpurata,* and *Oxyruncus cristatus* regularly join mixed flocks.

Prenuptial Displays

The male *Procnias nudicollis* selects certain branches from which he calls while alone, but he also receives visits from neighbors, including females, there. Such spots are traditional, being used for years on end and probably by generation after generation of bellbirds if the tree lasts long enough (see also Pipridae, "Prenuptial Displays . . ."). Males of other species, especially *Querula purpurata, Pyroderus scutatus, Perissocephalus tricolor,* the Guianan Red-Cotinga, *Phoenicircus carnifex,* and *P. nigricollis,* gather to display and sing together in courts like manakins and birds of paradise (the latter are polygamous Oscines of Australasia).

In certain trees *Perissocephalus tricolor* prepares real courts. Each male, one alongside the other, actively takes over and strips an appropriate branch from which he intones his *moos*. In Brazil there are certain regional names for such meeting places: *cemas* for *Pyroderus scutatus* (Espírito

Santo) and *paradas de galos* ["cock parades"] for *Rupicola rupicola* (Roraima).

There is usually a certain amount of coordination of calling, with one group vocalizing alternately with its neighbors, not all calling at the same time, as I verified with the *Lipaugus* and *Perissocephalus*. This may also occur to some extent with bellbirds when several individuals are in hearing distance. Two northern species, *Procnias alba* and the Bearded Bellbird, *P. averano,* put on interesting exhibitions. Surprising visual effects supplement the acoustic displays of most cotingids and in the case of *Rupicola* reach a high point when the bird stands immobile and silent on the ground, as if frozen, in a purely visual display, very different from those of other cotingids and manakins—and all the more impressive when a breeze catches the feathery filigree covering the rear of the statuesque bird. Although *Rupicola* display alone, they require the presence of the other males of their group, either as spectators or acting on neighboring stages. To such mutual stimulation is added the advantage of a fortuitously formed network of sentinels. Cotingids stay on their courts almost all day for months; if not displaying they rest or preen there or feed in the vicinity. Females seek out the males at their display sites.

Gymnoderus foetidus displays in full flight, executing its stunts high over the Amazonian forest. Some males perform together. The male *Haematoderus militaris* displays alone in a spiral flight, silently like *G. foetidus*. The *Xipholena*, with wide, brilliant, white wings, create a great effect flying through the highest treetops. The White-tailed Cotinga, *X. lamellipennis,* is even more spectacular with its long white tail. *Phibalura flavirostris* and the *Carpornis* berryeaters live in pairs.

Nesting

The *Cotinga* and *Xipholena, Querula purpurata, Perissocephalus tricolor, Lipaugus vociferans, Procnias averano,* and Amazonian Umbrellabird, *Cephalopterus ornatus,* all make a small platform of sticks in a fork, frequently so thin the eggs can be seen through the cracks (fig. 265). This usually doesn't make any difference, for the nests, situated high in trees and sometimes atop compact tangles of vegetation, pass totally unnoticed. I measured an *L. vociferans* nest built of corkscrew vine in the fork of a dead branch 7 m above ground in Cururu, Pará, at 7 × 7 cm (relatively large for a cotingid). The nest of a *Cotinga maculata* was found in an empty arboreal termite nest (Espírito Santo, A. Ruschi pers. comm.). Gonzaga, Scott, and Collar saw a female *C. maculata* nesting on a pile of twigs in the crotch of a treetop in October 1986 at Porto Seguro, Bahia.

Phibalura flavirostris and *Gymnoderus foetidus* build a shallow cup of loose, flexible materials, lichens, and tender stems covered with white mycelia on a thick limb densely covered with lichens, moss, and small orchids. (I found a

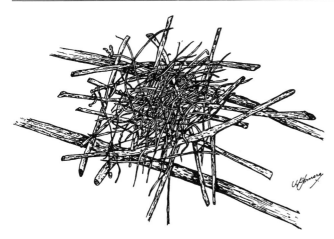

Fig. 265. Nest of Screaming Piha, *Lipaugus vociferans*. After Oniki 1986.

G. foetidus nest in the upper Xingu, Mato Grosso, in September 1947.) Near Belém, Pará, in November 1977 I saw an *Iodopleura isabellae* build in a treetop 19 m above ground, the nest being placed on a clean, thin, horizontal branch without any protection whatever. It was a tiny cylindrical structure resembling a hummingbird nest, made mostly of "vegetable horsehair" (*Marasmius* fungus) and algae (Cyanophyceae and Chlorophyceae), all bound firmly by spider webs (see fig. 266).

I saw *Oxyruncus cristatus* work on the base of a nest in the same way as *Iodopleura*, applying spider webs and probably saliva to a thick limb 10 m up in the top of a broken tree in the middle of the forest at Itatiaia, Rio de Janeiro, on 30 September 1974. An *O. cristatus* nest found in Tinguá, Rio de Janeiro, in October 1980 by D. A. Scott and M. Brooke was a cup made of leaf stems (it had no vegetable horsehair) well worked on the outer surface with heavy spider webs combining moss and algae to produce a homogeneous surface. Although an *Oxyruncus* nest in the hand does not appear so small (unlike that of *Iodopleura*), the *Oxyruncus* individual I saw incubating appeared to overlap the edges of the nest entirely, as if its body would not fit in.

Gymnoderus and *Iodopleura* nests are so small it is hard to imagine how the incubating bird manages to stay on. The *Rupicola* build a solid pan of clay mixed with vegetable fibers and covered with lichens inside caverns in cliffs or ravines, frequently over a small stream. Cementing of this mass appears to be done with the bird's own saliva; the weight of the nest may reach 900 g. Some females place their nests close to each other. *Rupicola* nesting practices are different from those of the typical cotingid group but conform basically to the *Iodopleura* and *Oxyruncus* type.

R. Krone (from Ihering 1914) reported that the nest of *Procnias nudicollis* is a shallow cup similar to a pigeon nest with a diameter of 16 cm. This has been confirmed twice by informants of mine who compared the nest, placed openly on branches, with that of the White-tipped Dove, *Leptotila ver-*

reauxi. The nest may be well hidden among the leaf bases of a large bromeliad situated high in a tree, as I observed from a distance in the Serra da Bocaina (São Paulo 1977). I recorded a similar nesting for *Xipholena atropurpurea* in Espírito Santo. Various people have informed me that *P. nudicollis* gathers very little construction material. Reports from Rio de Janeiro, São Paulo, and Santa Catarina of use of a "hollow tree" still need to be investigated.

I have been informed by inhabitants of the Serra da Bocaina (São Paulo) that *Tijuca atra* has a "thrush-type" nest made with Spanish moss (*Tillandsia usneoides*). This requires further research for it could even indicate occupation of a structure built by another bird. A woodsman in Amapá reported finding two young *Haematoderus militaris* in an arboreal termite nest.

From the viewpoint of the type of nest constructed, exclusion of the genus *Pachyramphus* (which makes a large, enclosed nest) from the Cotingidae was appropriate and strengthens its inclusion in the Tyrannidae.

Querula purpurata has a tendency to install its nest in isolated trees, which should improve its chances against monkey predation. I saw four *Phibalura flavirostris* vehemently attack a Red-breasted Toucan, *Ramphastos dicolorus*. Toucans must be a great threat to the totally open (though well-camouflaged) nest of *Phibalura*. I found a *Gymnoderus* nest in the upper Xingu region of Mato Grosso in a group of souari nut trees inhabited by legions of biting ants. *Phibalura* and *Rupicola* mend old nests and reuse them. In monogamous species such as *Phibalura* the male helps with construction.

Various species, such as the *Lipaugus*, *Cephalopterus*, *Perissocephalus tricolor*, *Querula purpurata*, *Procnias averano*, and Buff-throated Purpletuft, *Iodopleura pipra*, lay a single egg. With *I. pipra* it is obvious that not more than one egg would fit into its miniscule nest. Egg color in the different species is so variable that a generalized description is impossible; background color may be yellowish, brownish, greenish blue (*Phibalura*), or dark green (*Lipaugus vociferans*), with chestnut blotches and dense spotting on the rounded end. The *Procnias nudicollis* egg is oval and reddish brown with a crown of dark brown spots around the rounder end.

The female alone incubates in the *Cotinga* and *Querula*. *Iodopleura* and *Phibalura* mates take turns on the nest. Sometimes the male *Phibalura* brings food for his mate. I have noticed that *Querula purpurata* is apt to attack any bird that comes close to its nest, and I have even seen it advance on a human. *Lipaugus vociferans* also assumes threatening attitudes near its nest in the canopy.

Incubation takes 25 days for *Q. purpurata*, 26 to 27 days for *Perissocephalus tricolor*, and 27 to 28 days for the *Rupicola*.

Chicks hatch blind and featherless. Those of *Gymnoderus foetidus* are black but develop a nestling plumage that perfectly imitates the nest color and white bark of the tree where

Fig. 266. Buff-throated Purpletuft, *Iodopleura pipra,*
brooding in erect position. After Willis and Oniki 1988.

it is situated. The *Iodopleura* do the same. The size of the
brood varies: *Procnias averano* in Trinidad has only one
nestling, whereas *P. nudicollis* has two; *Phibalura flavirostris* has two or three.

In the *Cotinga* and *Procnias* the mother alone cares for the
young. With the *Phibalura* and *Iodopleura* the parents take
turns feeding them. In *Querula* various adults help feed the
young of one nest. *Phibalura* brings a large ball of food that it
administers by sinking its bill deep into the immense mouth
of the young. The reverse can also occur. Female *Procnias*
give the brood regurgitated fruits and clean the nest of feces
and regurgitated pits. *Querula* feeds its young solely on insects. *Phibalura* nestlings beg for food with soft whistles;
those of *Gymnoderus* give a weak croak. We are indebted to
Willis and Oniki (1988) for interesting behavioral details of
adult and young *Iodopleura pipra* on the nest. The birds
incubate in a vertical position (fig. 266), simulating a broken
branch like the *Nyctibius* potoos (Nyctibiidae) or even more
like the *Batrachostomus* (Podargidae, of Sumatra, Indonesia) which build a completely open, miniscule nest of
feathers and moss on a smooth branch.

Procnias averano nestlings abandon the nest after 33 days.
The sex of *Rupicola* chicks can be ascertained as soon as they
hatch by the color of the bill and feet: yellow in males, black
in females.

I have verified that at least *Phibalura flavirostris* and
Cephalopterus ornatus breed more than once a year. This is
announced by the restart of singing by *C. ornatus* males and
by reuse of the nest by *P. flavirostris.*

Distribution and Evolution

The family contains clear examples of allospecies, species
descended from a common ancestor that have differentiated
because of isolation in forest pockets or refuges formed during arid Pleistocene or Quaternary epochs. Such allospecies
make up a superspecies, a category that includes a certain
number of particularly closely related species in a genus and

thereby provides a more realistic picture of relationships.
There are analogous situations in the Cracidae, Psittacidae,
Formicariidae, and Pipridae, among others. Among cotingids the *Cotinga, Xipholena,* and *Phoenicircus* genera
provide good models of allospecies that are geographically
mutually exclusive and even quite distant from each other,
such as *Xipholena atropurpurea* and *X. lamellipennis* (fig.
267). When they do enter into contact, as in the case of the
two *Phoenicircus* in Amazonia, they usually keep apart and
do not invade each other's territory, showing that the forms
have achieved reproductive isolation and cannot be treated
merely as subspecies or geographic races.

Widely disjunct distribution occurs with *Laniisoma elegans* and *Iodopleura pipra,* indicating disappearance of
many intermediate populations. It appears that *Laniisoma*
and *Phibalura* evolution was centered in the mountains of
southeastern Brazil, from where they expanded as far as the
Andes. Endemics in this part of the country include *Tijuca
atra* and the Gray-winged Cotinga, *T. condita;* Hooded and
Black-headed Berryeaters, *Carpornis cucullatus* and *C. melanocephalus;* Cinnamon-vented Piha, *Lipaugus lanioides;*
Black-capped Piprites, *Piprites pileatus;* and *Calyptura
cristata.* Colonization of the Atlantic forest by Amazonian
species such as the *Lipaugus, Xipholena,* and *Cotinga* was
more frequent; subsequent separation occurred because of
Amazonia later receding, which has been aggravated more
recently by destructive human activity.

The diverse ecological requirements of two similar
cotingids are not always as clear-cut as they are in the case of
Lipaugus lanioides and *L. vociferans,* which live in different
climatic regions, the former in mountains, the latter in lowlands, and even then there is a lowland record of *lanioides.*

Frequently it can be seen that vocalization has evolved
more slowly than morphology (e.g., in Dendrocolaptidae
and Pipridae), but the contrary is the case with the two Brazilian *Lipaugus* and the *Carpornis. Procnias* evolution is also
of great interest with regard to both morphology and behavior
(Snow 1973a).

Migration

Migration occurs outside the breeding season and is usually discernible by the disappearance (sometimes partial) or
appearance of various species. Observation of this phenomenon is difficult, for the birds do not vocalize at this season or
form flocks. Instead they lurk in the canopy where they are
easily overlooked unless they reveal their presence by the
whir of their flight or by letting fruits fall as they eat.

Migration is generally in the form of altitudinal movements, induced by the abundance of wild fruits at other levels. Thus, *Tijuca atra* descends from 1000 m to 500 m in Bocaina, Rio de Janeiro. *Phibalura flavirostris* and *Iodopleura
pipra* emigrate, the latter to breed in the lowlands in winter.
There are also movements in Amazonia during which birds

Fig. 267. Distribution of the Pompadour Cotinga and allies, *Xipholena punicea,* superspecies; males illustrated (slightly modified after Haffer 1970). Open circles and shading: *X. punicea.* Closed circles and stippling: White-tailed Cotinga, *X. lamellipennis.* Open triangles and vertical hatching: White-winged Cotinga, *X. atropurpurea.* Symbols denote locality records.

such as *Haematoderus militaris* and the *Phoenicircus* red-cotingas become very fat.

Parasites

Nematode worms have been found living under the eyelids of *Lipaugus vociferans.*

Usefulness

Brilliant cotingid feathers are used in indigenous feather costumes. In the upper Amazon the Plum-throated Cotinga, *Cotinga maynana,* is one of the most sought, whereas whole, stretched skins of the Spangled Cotinga, *C. cayana,* are used by the Kaiabi of the Rio Tapajós, Mato Grosso, as pendants. Various other tribes use *Cephalopterus* wattles for adornment. The emperor of Brazil used a mantle made of *Rupicola* feathers (see also Ramphastidae, "Enemies . . ."). Various species, especially the *Phibalura, Cotinga, Xipholena, Pyroderus,* and *Tijuca,* are considered game birds by local people.

Decline and Conservation

Because of habitat destruction and unrestricted hunting, various species have become rare, the most affected being species in eastern and northeastern Brazil: *Procnias averano, Cotinga maynana,* and *Xipholena atropurpurea. Pyroderus scutatus* is also disappearing. Their protection is made more difficult by the fact that small refuges are not effective; the birds must be in sizable numbers, and they migrate periodically.

Synopsis of Brazilian Genera
(number of species in parentheses)

Cotingids are morphologically diverse, with various monotypic genera, sometimes without any other similar species. Where there is more than one species in a genus, they may be allospecies (e.g., see *Xipholena* and *Phoenicircus*). I provisionally include *Oxyruncus* and *Piprites,* genera of *incertae sedis,* and also *Rupicola,* for all of which it would be appropriate to establish a subfamily. The genera *Attila, Pseudattila, Pachyramphus, Platypsaris, Tityra, Casiornis, Laniocera, Rhytipterna,* and *Xenopsaris* have been transferred to the Tyrannidae, as already mentioned.

1. *Laniisoma* (1), *Phibalura* (1, Pl 30), *Calyptura* (1), *Carpornis* (2, Pl 30), *Tijuca* (2, fig. 268), and *Oxyruncus* (1, Pl 33)
2. *Cotinga* (4, Pl 30), *Xipholena* (3, Pl 30), and *Porphyrolaema* (1)
3. *Iodopleura* (2, fig. 269)
4. *Lipaugus* (2)
5. *Piprites chloris* (Pl 33)
6. *Piprites pileatus* (Pl 32)
7. *Haematoderus* (1, Pl 31), *Querula* (1, Pl 31), *Pyroderus* (1, Pl 31), and *Phoenicircus* (2, Pl 30)
8. *Cephalopterus* (1, fig. 271), *Perissocephalus* (1, Pl 31), and *Gymnoderus* (1, fig. 273)
9. *Procnias* (3, figs. 274–77)
10. *Rupicola* (1, Pl 31)

ELEGANT MOURNER, *Laniisoma elegans*, Chibante

17.7 cm. Stocky; uniformly green upperparts (male with black cap); sulfur yellow underparts, belly with black scaly markings. Mandible and legs whitish. VOICE: a high, short whistle or sequence of clearly enunciated, crescendo notes, *pseee pseee pseee*, with timbre of a *Callithrix* monkey. Hops freely through high canopy. Eastern Brazil from Bahia to São Paulo; also in Andes from Venezuela to Peru, Bolivia. Vaguely resembles *Phibalura* and *Oxyruncus*, sometimes inhabiting same areas as latter. Also called *Assobiador.*

SWALLOW-TAILED COTINGA, *Phibalura flavirostris*, Tesourinha-do-mato   PL 30.3

21.5 cm. Unique because of long, forked tail, always held well spread. Bill short, thick, yellow. Sexes similar, though female differs in various details, e.g., shorter tail, less pronounced color, green upper wing coverts, etc. Young have shorter tail, black bill, black upperparts speckled with creamy white, creamy underparts spotted black. VOICE: a high guttural whistle, *ghewt ghewt;* a tremolo. Perches on dead limbs, preferring highest branches of canopy. Forest edge, gardens. Rather tame. Breeds in mountains (Itatiaia and Bocaina, Rio de Janeiro; Campos de Jordão, São Paulo) September–February, with a 2d clutch in same nest (H. Gouvêa, Itatiaia), then emigrates, appearing also in ex-Guanabara and Rio de Janeiro. Espírito Santo to Rio Grande do Sul, southern Goiás, Argentina (Misiones), Bolivia. See *Laniisoma* and *Oxyruncus.*

BLACK-AND-GOLD COTINGA, *Tijuca atra*, Saudade, Assobiador   BR   Fig. 268

26.7 cm. Outstanding endemic of mountainous regions of southeastern Brazil. Superficially resembles Yellow-legged Thrush, *Platycichla flavipes*, but is much larger with long tail. Male black with yellow bill and speculum; bill may be orange. Female green with yellowish abdomen. VOICE: male perches in a high treetop, usually well in open, and utters a pure, high, prolonged whistle with frequency of 3100–3150 Hz (Snow and Goodwin 1974) for about 3 seconds. A slight crescendo can be noted that might be taken for an upscale trend, *eweeeeeeee*. Whistle has an "imprecise" quality, with volume increasing and decreasing and sometimes a short interruption before end of each sector. In Serra dos Órgãos on 13 June 1959 I observed a subadult male (or was it *T. condita?* See that species.) produce a much shorter whistle. It sings with drooping wings, displaying yellow speculum that sometimes appears longitudinally "cut" by a black streak, created by inner vane of a secondary showing through.

Several males will station themselves within hearing of each other, at distances of perhaps 80 m on a rugged slope. Sometimes 2 will sing from neighboring trees or even from same tree. Perfect similarity of their voices makes it difficult to distinguish them individually. During periods of max-

Fig. 268. Black-and-gold Cotinga, *Tijuca atra,* male singing. In the background is an individual letting itself fall from canopy to a lower level (Serra dos Órgãos, Rio de Janeiro).

imum activity whistles of such congregations unite into an almost uninterrupted drone, a common occurrence because interval between any individual's performances may amount to only a few seconds. Voice remotely resembles *Oxyruncus cristatus*, whose whistle is downscale. Said to nest in November. High montane forest in Serra do Mar (Serra dos Órgãos, Serra da Bocaina) and Serra da Mantiqueira (Itatiaia), above 1000 m, alongside *Procnias nudicollis, Carpornis cucullatus,* and *Oxyruncus cristatus,* with only *C. cucullatus* being a cold-climate species. Migrates vertically, descending to 500 m in coldest months (Parati, Rio de Janeiro), probably in search of certain fruits. Espírito Santo (Serra do Caparaó, "Sooretama" ?, Ruschi), Minas Gerais to northern São Paulo. Despite generic name *Tijuca*, ex-Guanabara never had suitable conditions for this species. *Tijuca* = muddy or dirty water in Guaraní.

GRAY-WINGED COTINGA, *Tijuca condita*   BR

24 cm. Female olive green with yellowish belly and rump, grayish (not yellowish green) remiges. Apparently there is little or no sexual dimorphism, but male has not yet been collected. High-altitude (1370–1980 m) patches of low *Myrcia* sp. (Myrtaceae) of Serra do Mar, where found by D. Scott and M. Brooke in 1980. VOICE: similar to *T. atra* but whistle shorter, a bisyllabic *suee-ssueeee*. Tinguá and Serra dos Órgãos, Rio de Janeiro. First described in 1980 by D. Snow

based on a female specimen now in São Paulo Museum collected by Pedro Brito in 1942 on Fazenda Guinle at Teresópolis, Rio de Janeiro. Could be confused with juvenal or subadult male *atra* but is smaller.

HOODED BERRYEATER, *Carpornis cucullatus,* Corocochó   BR   PL 30.2

23 cm. Restricted to eastern Brazil. Well known because of distinctive voice. Female has streaked belly, head and lower throat greenish. VOICE: warning a low *GRAAoo,* in flight *krrra;* "conversation" between a pair *bibibi.* For song male gives a loud, 2-parted whistle with 2d part accented, *kewewt wewEEDyoo,* interpreted onomatopoeically as *corocochó, corocoteu, cavalo-frouxou* (Rio de Janeiro), or *Prost-Otto* (Espírito Santo). Calls insistently July–August, just like *Procnias nudicollis* (Espírito Santo). Tall, humid forest, palm groves, sometimes alongside *P. nudicollis.* Espírito Santo to Rio Grande do Sul. Restricted in northern part of range (Espírito Santo, Rio de Janeiro) to mountains, usually above 400 m (unlike *C. melanocephalus*).

BLACK-HEADED BERRYEATER, *Carpornis melanocephalus,* Sabiá-pimenta   BR

21 cm. Only on our southeastern littoral. Similar to female *C. cucullatus* but with back uniformly green (no chestnut). Male has black bill and head. VOICE: a sonorous, bisyllabic *jewwew* or a *kewow* with timbre of *Lipaugus vociferans.* Tall forest. Southern Bahia and Espírito Santo (lower Rio Doce, where it lives alongside *L. vociferans*) to Rio de Janeiro, São Paulo.

PURPLE-THROATED COTINGA, *Porphyrolaema porphyrolaema*

18 cm. Recorded only from upper Amazon. Resembles a *Cotinga.* Upperparts black patterned with white. Underparts white, throat purple. Female underparts have black streaks. Peru and Colombia to Rios Negro, Solimões, and lower Purus.

SPANGLED COTINGA, *Cotinga cayana,* Anambé-azul   PL 30.5

20 cm. Beautiful, widely distributed across Amazonia. Its voice is usually replaced by an intense whistle produced by sound-producing remiges. Canopy of riverine forests. The Guianas, Venezuela, and Colombia to Bolivia, northern Mato Grosso (upper Rio Xingu, Rio Teles Pires), eastern Pará (Belém). Also called *Bacaca, Catingá, Quiruá.* See *C. maynana.*

PLUM-THROATED COTINGA, *Cotinga maynana*

Known only from upper Amazon. Somewhat larger and even more spectacular than *C. cayana.* Has smaller throat patch; blue body feathers have lilac subterminal band followed by intermediate white area and black bases (feathers of *cayana* are bicolored, blue with ample black base). Female has light cinnamon underparts. Colombia and Bolivia to Rios Purus, Madeira, Roosevelt, and Negro.

PURPLE-BREASTED COTINGA, *Cotinga cotinga,* Anambé-de-peito-roxo

18 cm. Small *Cotinga* of northwestern Brazil. Color similar to *C. maculata* but anterior underparts uniformly purple, abdomen blue. Female blackish brown, speckled above with small whitish dots and below with scaly whitish pattern. SOUNDS: a croaking *ooaa, ooaa,* indicating fear. A loud clinking produced by wings in flight. The Guianas and Venezuela to Rio Uaupés, Rio Tapajós, and eastern Pará; found at Capitão Poço in 1977 alongside *Haematoderus militaris.*

BANDED COTINGA, *Cotinga maculata* Crejoá BR   EN   PL 30.4

20 cm. Replaces *C. cotinga* in southeastern Brazil. Relatively large, characterized by blue pectoral band. Female and immature similar to those of *cotinga* and of *Xipholena atropurpurea,* which occurs in same region, but are larger and have more contrasting scaly pattern. SOUNDS: low cries with little volume. A loud noise produced by wings, including those of brown individuals. Tall virgin forest. Southern Bahia to Rio de Janeiro, Minas Gerais. Rare, menaced with extinction by habitat destruction and hunting. Also called *Pássaro-azul.*

POMPADOUR COTINGA, *Xipholena punicea,* Anambé-pompadora

19 cm. Northern Amazonia. Silky purple with stiffened feathers that hang over the large white wings. Tips of primaries black, iris yellow. Female grayish sooty with lighter abdomen. Upper wing coverts and inner secondaries have whitish bars. VOICE AND DISPLAYS: gives gargling shrieks. Two or 3 males will chase each other, flying from one high canopy to another with swift, straight flight. Over longer distances alternates several wing beats with a brief folding of wings. North of lower Amazon (Amapá) to the Guianas, Venezuela, Manaus (where not uncommon), and upper Amazon, reaching eastern bank of Rio Madeira and also lower Tapajós. Closely related to *X. lamellipennis* and *X. atropurpurea* (allospecies, see fig. 267).

WHITE-TAILED COTINGA, *Xipholena lamellipennis,* Anambé-de-rabo-branco   BR

19 cm. Replaces *X. punicea* south of lower Amazon. Black with purple sheen, seemingly transparent white tail and wings. Makes short, upward flights out of a treetop rising above surrounding forest, returning to point of origin or elsewhere while offering a spectacular display of white wings and tail. Maranhão and Pará to left bank of lower Rio Tapajós

and Serra do Cachimbo (Pará), where range of *punicea* begins.

WHITE-WINGED COTINGA, *Xipholena atropurpurea*, Anambé-de-asa-branca   BR   EN   PL 30.6

19 cm. Close relative of *X. lamellipennis* and *X. punicea,* which it replaces on coastal strip of eastcentral Brazil. Blackish purple with white wings. Female and immature similar to those of other 2 *Xipholena,* female having yellow iris. SOUNDS: meowing. Makes a loud hiss with wings, but on short flights can move silently. Same habitat as *Cotinga maculata,* occasionally its neighbor. Paraíba to Rio de Janeiro, in much diminished numbers because of deforestation. In danger of extinction. Also called *Bacacu, Crijuá.*

BUFF-THROATED PURPLETUFT, *Iodopleura pipra,* Anambezinho   Fig. 269

9.3 cm. One of smallest cotingids, a singular species with long wings, short tail, and soft, short plumage. Gray with brownish pink under tail coverts and throat. Underparts barred with white and gray, remotely resembling a *Picumnus* piculet (Picidae). Male has tuft of long, silky, violet feathers at edge of breast, hidden under wing, that is absent in female. VOICE: call a sharp, bisyllabic, descending whistle, *see-see,* resembling Purple-throated Euphonia, *Euphonia chlorotica,* but even thinner; song a sequence of limpid notes with short, repeated motifs. Phlegmatic; sits absolutely quiet on thin, dead branches in canopies of tall trees in primary forest or capoeira; likes mistletoe (Loranthaceae) berries, catches small insects. When excited displays lilac tufts by erecting them and holding wing out a bit. I found the species migrating in small flocks in summer (November) at 900 m in mountains of Espírito Santo. An adult male was collected that had inactive testicles and was molting. There was no indication of breeding, and the nest of species, and even of genus, was still unknown at that time (1940). This observation has been nicely complemented by records of Willis and Oniki (1988), who found the species breeding at sea level in midwinter on

Fig. 269. Buff-throated Purpletuft, *Iodopleura pipra.*

São Paulo littoral. Minas Gerais to São Paulo, the northeast (Alagoas, Pernambuco, Paraíba); replaced in Amazonia by *I. isabellae.* It has been proposed to place *Iodopleura* and *Laniisoma* in the *Schiffornis* group together with *Laniocera* and *Pachyramphus* (Tyrannidae).

DUSKY PURPLETUFT, *Iodopleura fusca*

Observed in December 1984 by D. F. Stotz north of Manaus, Amazonas, in area of Minimum Critical Size of Ecosystems Project.

WHITE-BROWED PURPLETUFT, *Iodopleura isabellae*

10.7 cm. Amazonia. Stocky, blackish brown, with 3 facial spots, white rump, underparts with central band of whitish, whitish under tail coverts. Flanks streaked, and there is a pectoral tuft as in *I. pipra.* VOICE: a thin *wewwt WEEli-WEElili.* Forest edges, cerrado; perches on bare branches in bushes and high treetops, from where it launches out on short forays to catch insects, like *Chelidoptera tenebrosa.* Venezuela and Colombia to Bolivia, northern Mato Grosso, eastern Pará. A northern replacement of *I. pipra.*

KINGLET CALYPTURA, *Calyptura cristata,* Tietê-de-coroa   BR   EN   PL 45.2

7.6 cm. Smallest cotingid, with unusual proportions: short, thick bill, very short tail, crest. In color resembles certain tyrannids, having green upperparts and 2 wing bars. Forehead, rump, and underparts yellow, top of head scarlet (yellowish in female) bordered black. VOICE: call short, harsh, loud (Descourtilz 1944). Reported to live in pairs and to be constantly in movement, keeping to medium levels at forest edge in search of berries and insects. A few specimens are known from Nova Friburgo and from areas surrounding city of Rio de Janeiro. "Espírito Santo," Ruschi, without basis. Descourtilz was the only person to provide information on this bird, which no one has found since.

SCREAMING PIHA, *Lipaugus vociferans,* Cricrió, Tropeiro

24 cm. Noisiest of all Amazonian birds. Size of a large thrush, with long tail, sturdy, black bill, and uniformly grayish plumage. VOICE: call a low *goo-o;* a loud sequence of 4–5 phrases with increasing volume: in 1st 2 bird appears to grunt or inhale (recalling short cries of *Querula*); last 2 more violent, given with head thrown up, *kurrrO-kurreh WEET-WEETew.* Certain individuals, a few trees away from each other, will sing in same limited area, coordinating voices, sometimes chasing each other in rapid flight through forest. Middle levels of tall forests. All over Amazonia, from the Guianas to Bolivia, Mato Grosso, Maranhão; also remnant forests of centraleast, from northeast to Espírito Santo (north of Rio Doce, in formations very similar to those of Amazonia). Also called *Namorador* (Pará), *Poaieiro* (Mato Grosso), *Seringueiro* (Amazonas), *Wissiá* (Kaiabi, Mato

Grosso), *Ha-wi-já* (Kamaiurá, Mato Grosso), *Gritador* (Pernambuco). See *L. lanioides.*

CINNAMON-VENTED PIHA, *Lipaugus lanioides,* Tropeiro-da-serra   BR

26.8 cm. Larger, northern replacement of *L. vociferans,* which it resembles in plumage. The 2 species usually are not sympatric. VOICE: entirely unlike *vociferans,* consisting of a series of 2–4 strident phrases, *SWEEssa-SWEEssa-SWEEssak,* last sometimes more bland, like an echo with timbre of a thrush. Calling, which peaks July–August (Espírito Santo), accepted by local people as a forecast of rain. Mountainous regions from Espírito Santo to Minas Gerais, Santa Catarina. Found in Sooretama Reserve (Linhares, Espírito Santo) December–January but in a different forest type from that inhabited by *vociferans* (Scott and Brooke 1985). Also called *Gardena* (Espírito Santo).

ROSE-COLLARED PIHA, *Lipaugus streptophorus*

Cerro Uei-Tepui (Cerro del Sol) on Brazilian/Venezuelan border, Roraima, at 1500 m. Three specimens were collected (Phelps and Phelps 1962).

CRIMSON FRUITCROW, *Haematoderus militaris,* Anambé-militar   EN   PL 31.4

34 cm. One of most beautiful cotingids. Male red with blackish wings and tail. Female crimson red only on head and underparts, back dark brown. Immature preponderantly sooty. VOICE: a bisyllabic *wow-wow* resembling a barking dog. Mooing resembles *Cephalopterus ornatus.* Solitary. Displays in spiral flight above forest, flying with rapid, horizontal wing beats, then returning to perch (Bierregaard et al. 1987). Tall terra-firme forest canopy (35 m high with emergents to 45 m, Manaus). Frequents fruiting trees where it meets *Phoenicircus, Xipholena, Cotinga cotinga, C. cayana,* toucans, and parrots. North of Amazon occurs with *Perissocephalus tricolor.* The Guianas to lower Amazon (Óbidos), south of Serra de Tumucumaque (Pará), Amapá (Rio Araguari), lower Rio Tocantins (Cametá), Rios Acará, Acaraí, and Ourém to Gurupi (Pará), where it appears in adornments of the Kaapor (which may have been traded from neighbors, B. Ribeiro 1957 pers. comm.). Formerly occurred even in city of Belém, though only occasionally. Never common, now endangered by road construction, etc., which brings environmental destruction and unlimited hunting (eastern Pará), as on Belém-Brasília Highway, km 75 (1959); Capitão Poço, 1977; Amazonas (Manaus). Also called *Anambé-raio-do-sol* (Amapá).

PURPLE-THROATED FRUITCROW, *Querula purpurata,* Anambé-una   PL 31.3

27 cm. Common Amazonian species. Voice can be heard at considerable distance. Wings and tail quite long. Female, at 25.5 cm, smaller than male, lacks red gular shield. VOICE

AND DISPLAYS: in company with other individuals gives a soft, triphrased, strongly accentuated *keweh-keweh oh-ew,* with last syllable drawn out. This basic sequence is preceded by shorter, lighter cries, *ow-A, owA-owA,* also made by other individuals present. When calling shakes wings and especially tail while raising elongated, stiffened, resplendent throat feathers toward sides into 2 large tufts (if seen from below), 1 on either side of neck. Lives in pairs or small flocks of 3–4 individuals that periodically sing for long stretches; voice resembles *Monasa* (Bucconidae). Tall forest below canopy, frequently near *Lipaugus.* The Guianas and Venezuela to Bolivia, Mato Grosso (Rio Xingu), northern Goiás, eastern Pará. Also called *Anambé-preto, Mãe-de-tucano.*

RED-RUFFED FRUITCROW, *Pyroderus scutatus,* Pavão-do-mato   EN   PL 31.2

46 cm. Largest Brazilian cotingid outside Amazon. Female only 39 cm, throat pale red. Immature wings and belly mixed with chestnut; red on throat appears gradually, becoming complete probably only in 3d year.

VOICE AND DISPLAYS: in company with other individuals sings a series of hollow, ventriloquial, deep, low, mooing sounds, *shoo,* given at short intervals in a sequence of about 6. Timbre similar to curassow (Cracidae) vocalization; may also be compared to sound produced by blowing into an empty bottle or pounding a pestle in a mortar. When it wants to *moo,* bird stoops and, shaking head, fills gular sac (it is not a crop), which it then shakes from side to side. Bird finally rises and, throwing head back, displays fully inflated red balloon and, with bill closed, releases *moo,* which is bisyllabic when heard up close (fig. 270). This display is reminiscent of inflated gular sac display of Magnificent Frigatebird, *Fregata magnificens.* I have heard 2 individuals collaborating on 1 phrase, 1 singing 2 syllables with 2d adding a lower one, thus making it trisyllabic. The flock (at times up to

Fig. 270. Red-ruffed Fruitcrow, *Pyroderus scutatus,* mooing. Original, H. Sick.

Fig. 271. Amazonian Umbrellabird, *Cephalopterus o. ornatus,* adult male. At left, a female perched on a leaf of the inajá palm (*Pindarea concinna*). After Sick 1954.

10 individuals) meets in morning under canopy to display by ruffling resplendent throat feathers, whose structure produces a somewhat frizzled appearance that is augmented by shaking action. During intervals between vocalizations they fly back and forth in a certain forest sector. These meetings, known locally in Espírito Santo as *cemas,* resemble displays and chases of Pipridae. I have also noted another type of vocalization, an individual warning call, equally low, as if muffled, *ek, ok-OK-ok,* that bird gives with neck horizontally extended and tail brought a bit forward. Other vocalizations resemble those of large Corvidae.

Tall forests, including araucaria. Bahia to Rio Grande do Sul, southeastern Goiás, Paraguay, and Misiones, Argentina. Also upper Amazon (eastern Peru, etc.) to the Guianas. Range much reduced in southeastern Brazil (Sooretama, 1939, 1961); in Rio de Janeiro still occurs in Itatiaia and Ilha Grande, and in Paraná in Iguaçu National Park. Also called *Pavoa* (Espírito Santo), *Jacu-toro* (Misiones), *Pavó.*

AMAZONIAN UMBRELLABIRD, *Cephalopterus ornatus,* Anambé-preto   Fig. 271

48 cm. Largest cotingid and only one to boast characteristic hat-shaped topknot that is similar to hairstyle of upper-Amazonian native peoples. Has long "necktie" or wattle (15 cm in adult male). Uniformly black plumage with steel blue sheen; only iris and shafts of front feathers of topknot are white. Female decidedly smaller (43 cm), almost without topknot, necktie, or sheen.

VOICE AND DISPLAYS: both sexes give a growling *rrro* resembling Greater Ani, *Crotophaga major;* territorial cry of male is a low, deep, melodious, ventriloquial bellow or roar, *moo,* with timbre of a large pigeon or bull heard at a distance. The Indians, having no knowledge of cattle, compared it to sound of their large flutes. Act of roaring takes place in 3 phases: while still silent, bird leans forward and down so topknot falls forward and opens to sides, covering bill and

eyes like bangs, while at same time feathers of dangling "necktie" are erected; it then lifts itself slowly, making regurgitation and quivering motions and producing a low squeak; finally gives a sudden forward thrust of the neck accompanied by a loud roar. The first 2 phases must be to fill trachea and pharyngeal sac with air (fig. 272), to amplify resonance, recalling similar situation in *Pyroderus scutatus.* To sing it

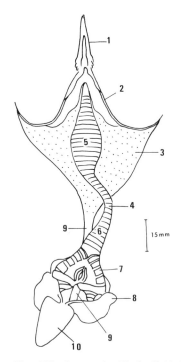

Fig. 272. Amazonian Umbrellabird, *Cephalopterus o. ornatus,* adult male, upper Xingu, Mato Grosso, internal anatomy (3–7 comprise the sound apparatus): (1) tongue, (2) hyoid, (3) pharyngeal cavity, (4) trachea, (5) broadened upper portion of trachea, (6) broadened lower portion of trachea, (7) syrinx, (8) lungs, (9) esophagus, (10) heart. After Sick 1954.

perches in canopy of tall trees rising above surrounding forest. I have not seen an adult male vocalize in presence of any individuals other than a single female.

Edge of moderately low forests with plenty of palms (Xingu, Mato Grosso). Undulating flight jaylike. Sometimes performs aerial displays above forest, as if playing, and in this is like *Gymnoderus foetidus,* being very agile. Crosses wide rivers flying at an altitude of 30–40 m. Upper Amazon and Rio Xingu (Mato Grosso) to Rio Negro (Amazonas) west to upper Rio Paraguay and the Guianas to Colombia. Has close relative, Long-wattled Umbrellabird, *Cephalopterus penduliger,* with even longer "necktie," in Colombia and Ecuador. Also called *Pássaro-trovão, Macaná* (Trumai, Mato Grosso), *Ua-ri-ri* (Juruna, Mato Grosso), *Toro-pishu* (Peru).

CAPUCHINBIRD, *Perissocephalus tricolor,*
Maú, Pássaro-boi   PL 31.5

35.5 cm. Characterized by bare face and forehead, which give plumage on back of top of head a hoodlike aspect. Plumage brown like a monastic habit (hence the name Capuchinbird). Sexes similar. VOICE AND DISPLAYS: call *ehh, ehhg;* gathers in groups on a court to give a loud, harsh, nasal cry, *shrow-ehh-ohh-ahh,* that resembles bellow of a steer or deer, one of weirdest sounds in Amazonia. In preparation for this bird leans forward, "filling itself" with air and croaking *shrow;* then lifting itself vertically and erect, it lets go a prolonged meow, *ehh;* finally it leans back and utters full-force roar, *ohh-ahh.* During last phase ruffles feathers of upperparts and compresses bright orange under tail coverts, which thus project from sides of tail and become visible from behind. Individuals performing this display remain with their backs to one another. As sites for these performances they use open canopies from which males remove branches that might impede their movements during meeting. When away from such courts they also roar, but with little emphasis. Lives in small flocks in fairly low forests, sometimes alongside *Phoenicircus* and *Lipaugus.* The Guianas and Venezuela to Amapá, Rios Uaupés and Branco; Manaus, alongside *Haematoderus militaris.* Also called *Pássaro-maú, Mãe-de-balata.*

BARE-NECKED FRUITCROW, *Gymnoderus foetidus,*
Anambé-pombo   Fig. 273

36 cm. Similar in general aspect to a pigeon. Head appears small because of sparse, short, plushlike plumage. Eyelid thickened, and there is a lobe on each side of throat. Sides of neck bare and bright blue. Sides and underparts (except in center, see below) have dense black plumage. Wings and tail long; predominantly whitish gray wing has rounded end. Plumage full of powder, like American Swallow-tailed Kite, *Elanoides forficatus.* Center of underside bare and blue, breast blackish (these areas are normally covered by feathers on sides of body). Female smaller, neck more feathered, wings slate colored without light areas. Young grayish white

Fig. 273. Bare-necked Fruitcrow, *Gymnoderus foetidus,* adult male. At left above, in display flight over the forest.

with vermiculations; underparts entirely white with black streaks (see "Nesting"). VOICE AND DISPLAYS: a sonorous growl. During breeding season a few males, perhaps 4, can be seen amusing themselves with acrobatic group flights high over forest and adjacent rivers; they fly to and fro, closing and opening ranks and resembling in their way of flying *Chelidoptera tenebrosa.* Forest in substantial groups. Amazonia: the Guianas and Venezuela to Bolivia, upper Rio Paraguay, upper Rio Xingu (Mato Grosso), eastern Pará. In upper Xingu sometimes alongside *Cephalopterus ornatus.*

WHITE BELLBIRD, *Procnias alba,*
Gainambé, Araponga-da-Amazônia   Fig. 274

All white, including tips of remiges and feathered throat. White-feathered, stringlike protuberance on forehead hangs loosely alongside bill (never stands erect, contrary to what was formerly believed). Female and young similar to those of *P. nudicollis* but have green heads, dark backs without gray. Young has only scarcely perceptible start of a wattle on forehead. VOICE AND DISPLAYS: male displays by crouching forward and silently agitating head violently back and forth, thereby shaking wattle which becomes elongated. He then opens mouth wide and utters 1st "anvil strike"; after this he

Fig. 274. White Bellbird, *Procnias alba,* adult male, the frontal protuberance hanging loosely alongside the bill.

moves head to left, pulling wattle that was hanging to right of bill so it is in a horizontal position and, without closing bill, gives another cry (observations by B. K. Snow in the Guianas, 1973). Voice similar to *P. nudicollis* and *P. averano* but distinguished by more resonant timbre, principal anvil strike being prolonged as in an echo; bisyllabic strikes occur in connection with above-described display, *ting-ting, ting-ting*, 2d syllable being higher. Locally from the Guianas and Venezuela to lower Rio Negro (Manaus); a relict population was discovered in 1983 in Serra dos Carajás, the area where Rio Doce Valley Company is working, between Xingu and Tocantins, Pará. Range overlaps that of *P. averano*. There is another species in Central America, Three-wattled Bellbird, *P. tricarunculata*, with 3 pendant wattles.

BARE-THROATED BELLBIRD, *Procnias nudicollis*,
Araponga, Ferreiro   Figs. 275, 276

27 cm. One of most famous and most typical birds of southeastern Brazil, frequently kept as a cage bird. White, at a distance resembling a carrier pigeon, with greenish bare throat and face as if covered with verdigris. Smaller female has green upperparts except for gray head; underparts streaked greenish yellow and gray; throat gray and streaked. Immature male similar to female but with black head and throat; its green feathers are replaced successively by green-

Fig. 276. Bare-throated Bellbird, *Procnias nudicollis*, female.

Fig. 275. Bare-throated Bellbird, *Procnias nudicollis*, adult male, "anvil striking."

ish gray and white ones, the latter partly vermiculated with gray; becomes entirely white at 3 years of age.

VOICE AND DISPLAYS: song is composed of 2 elements. (1) An "anvil strike" resembling a blow on a blacksmith's anvil—violent *peng* uttered by bird with its mouth wide open—one of loudest vocalizations produced by birds on this continent and most notable music of back country, a fact mentioned 400 years ago by Fernão Cardim (see Chapter 2.1), who said the voice could be heard for half a league (3 km). Guimarães Rosa has expressed it poetically: "Tense silence—like the pause of an araponga." This cry may be repeated at intervals of 5 seconds but always sounds like an isolated anvil strike. (2) Less loud cries that sound like a file passing over metal (*reigns, reigns, reigns*), repeated at 1-second intervals; these *reigns* merit careful attention because of high, strident sound with which they end, a feature only outlined in the main anvil strike (see "Sounds"). Periodically these cries, weaker and ventriloquial, are given in a more hurried series of, say, 25 seconds.

There is no fixed sequence to various types of cry, in the sense of a gradual buildup. Bird may begin with loudest strike, although to give it he reserves a longer preliminary period as if to prepare for an all-out effort. Unique timbre of voice appearing to come from all sides, makes finding the bellbird in the forest difficult, but it is easy if one is at the same level as bird. Immature males have a croaking voice and seem to caw, requiring 2–3 years to achieve adult perfection. Warning cry a low *kwo-ak*. In certain months (July–August, mountains of Espírito Santo), adult male establishes his court in a group of trees in forest, frequenting certain branches where he sings perseveringly during most of day (see "Prenuptial Displays"). Breeding occurs at end of year (Bocaina, Rio de Janeiro, Rio Grande do Sul).

Primary forest but also invades capoeira if there are fruit

trees. In both mountains and lowlands. Migratory. Pernambuco (Berla 1946 pers. comm.) and Minas Gerais to Rio Grande do Sul, southern Mato Grosso (Rio Amambaí), Argentina (Misiones), southeastern Paraguay. Much sought after by commercial cage-bird trade and for this reason becoming scarce near large cities. See *P. averano* and *P. alba*.

BEARDED BELLBIRD, *Procnias averano*,
Araponga-do-nordeste, Guiraponga   EN   Fig. 277

27 cm. Similar to *P. alba* and *P. nudicollis* but with black wings, chocolate-colored head, and spectacular, shiny black, stringy "beard" on throat in form of pendants so delicate they oscillate at least movement. Female is green, like that of *nudicollis*, but top of head not as gray. Immature male green with brown head, black throat; subadult male has sooty black primaries, black-and-white marbled tertiaries.

VOICE AND DISPLAYS: voice similar to *P. nudicollis* but lacks strident sound that follows cries of that species. I have noted a principal anvil strike (that may be repeated at intervals of 3–8 seconds), and I counted 91 continuous lesser strokes at intervals of 1 second (Piauí, Maranhão). Also even weaker and more hurried cries and various series of hurried *reigns* or *tring* (18 in a row). Call low, deep, crowlike *krrro*. When a singing male receives visit of another male or female at his court, he reacts with rapid jumps between 2 branches, displaying beard at its best and perching with tail fanned, a display resembling those of Pipridae (Snow 1970, Trinidad). The Guianas, Venezuela, and Colombia to Roraima (Rio Branco), Trinidad; also northeastern Brazil (where it replaces *nudicollis*), Maranhão (where not uncommon), southwestern

(a)

(b)

Fig. 277. Bearded Bellbird, *Procnias averano carnobarba*, Trinidad: (a) male bowing before the female before copulation; (b) male in erect position. After Snow 1970.

Piauí (1975), northwestern Bahia (1974), Alagoas (1979). Rare in captivity. In southernmost states of northeast it is in danger of extinction. Also called *Ferreiro* (Bahia, Piauí, Alagoas), *Guiraponga* (Pernambuco, Marcgrave 1648).

GUIANAN RED-COTINGA, *Phoenicircus carnifex*,
Saurá   PL 30.1

21 cm. Predominantly crimson red with brown secondaries. Female has greenish mantle and foreneck, grayish throat and breast. VOICE: a loud, harsh *KWA-ka-ka* and low, ventriloquial cries. Various males gather and fly about in a small area in forest, uttering their strange cry and "whispering" with wings (a hidden primary has become modified as a sound-producing feather; see "Sounds"). North of lower Amazon (Amapá) to Rio Negro, lower Rios Tapajós, Xingu, and Tocantins to Belém (eastern Pará). Also called *Anambé-raio-de-sol-pequeno* (Amapá).

BLACK-NECKED RED-COTINGA, *Phoenicircus nigricollis*

22 cm. Sides of head, throat, and mantle black. Replaces *P. carnifex* in upper Amazon. Range extends to Rio Negro and, south of range of *carnifex*, to Tocantins (Marabá).

BLACK-CAPPED PIPRITES, *Piprites pileatus*,
Caneleirinho-de-chapéu-preto   PL 32.1

12.6 cm. Distinctive and unmistakable with black cap contrasting with short, thick, yellow bill and intense ferruginous and chestnut color of most of plumage. Small white wing speculum. Tarsi and toes orange. Female has green back, chestnut rump. VOICE: high notes, *eeoo, eeoo-bibibibi-eeoo*, and more varied murmuring between mates (noted with W. Belton, São Francisco de Paula, Rio Grande do Sul, 840 m, September 1972). Locally in various types of high-altitude forest (Itatiaia, 1500 m), high capoeira, and mixed forests of araucaria and podocarpus, as in Campos de Jordão and Serra da Bocaina (1600 m). Has been seen pecking at fruits of *Geonoma* sp. palms, a type that attracts many fruit-eating birds, as well as *Rapanea ferruginea* (Myrsinaceae) and *Leandra sulfurea* (Melastomataceae, R. B. Pineschi, Itatiaia). Rio de Janeiro to São Paulo, Paraná, Santa Catarina, Rio Grande do Sul, and Misiones, Argentina. Species was discovered and named by Natterer (later Temminck used the name given by Natterer on the label) near Curitiba, Paraná, where he collected 10 specimens in October 1820. A species of *incertae sedis*, as is *P. chloris*.

WING-BARRED PIPRITES, *Piprites chloris*,
Papinho-amarelo   PL 33.2

12.8 cm. Widely distributed but uncommon. Thick, dark bill. Predominantly green and gray, resembling certain tyrannids. Forehead brownish. Tips of internal secondaries and of upper greater wing coverts have distinct design, suggesting they may be displayed. Female similar. VOICE: surprisingly loud and full, a rhythmic, liquid series of monosyllabic notes interrupted by an accentuated, higher sequence, *wut, wut, wut, wut, wew-dew-dew, wut, wut*. Mate responds with same phrase but higher. This frequently heard call (or song) would suggest a larger bird and resembles a *Pachyramphus* in timbre. Canopy of tall forests both in Amazonia and araucaria forests of south. At times joins mixed flocks. The Guianas and Venezuela to Bolivia, Paraguay, Argentina (Misiones), throughout Brazil. There are various geographic races. Commonly included in Pipridae, as is *P. pileatus*. The relationship of the 2 *Piprites* is questionable.

SHARPBILL, *Oxyruncus cristatus*, Araponga-do-horto   PL 33.1

18 cm; 41.5 g (male). Unique, up to now in a monotypic family (Oxyruncidae). Has affinities with tyrannids. Bill extraordinarily sharp in spite of wide base, perhaps indicating a feeding adaptation. In general aspect resembles a *Laniisoma* or *Phibalura*. Sexes similar but adult male more deeply colored and has serrations on outer edge of outer primary. Immature lacks red in crown. VOICE: an extremely sharp but firm whistle, prolonged (1–3 seconds) and descending, *ieww, ee-ee*, extending over a wide interval (from a fourth to an octave). Timbre similar to voice of Chestnut-crowned Becard, *Pachyramphus castaneus* (Tyrannidae), and to song (this one ascends) of *Tijuca atra*, both of which are occasional neighbors in mountains of southeastern Brazil. Apparently voice of *O. cristatus* was unknown before I began my work in Espírito Santo in 1939. Has other vocalizations, e.g., a weak *tet*, a high, tremulous *tsirrr*.

Solitary, perching quietly in treetops with erect posture resembling (when seen from below) female Swallow Tanager, *Tersina viridis*. Feeds on large and small fruits, e.g., merendiba (*Terminalia*), and hunts caterpillars at end of leafy branches, where it hangs upside down. When male fights, vertically held silky red of his crown can be seen shining at a distance. It took a long time before anything was known about reproduction of species (see "Nesting"). After beginning of year associates with migrant flocks (Espírito Santo, Rio de Janeiro). Mountains, where it appears to be spreading, and lowlands, e.g., ex-Guanabara. Range quite discontinuous: Costa Rica to Paraguay, Pará, Goiás (Rio Tocantins); Guyana, southern Venezuela, eastern Peru; Espírito Santo and Minas Gerais to Santa Catarina. It is difficult to explain extremely wide distribution of this species (Chapman 1939), subdivided into more than 6 subspecies—with underparts yellowish (southeastern Brazil and Central America) or white (along Tocantins and north of Amazon). Its inclusion in Cotingidae is my own proposal, confirmed by DNA hybridization (Sibley et al. 1984).

GUIANAN COCK-OF-THE-ROCK, *Rupicola rupicola*, Galo-da-serra   PL 31.1

28 cm. One of most spectacular birds of continent, comparing with birds of paradise of Australasia. Headpiece of male (cock) is a broad crest, erected in a semicircle like a Roman helmet and capable of being moved by bird back and forth like a fan so it can cover bill and delude observer as to true position of bird's head, the more so because a feathered ring around eye may also be closed, hiding it. Large white speculum formed by white bases of primaries is prominent when bird holds wings open while perched. Beautiful orange feathers of male appear in 2d year, with adult plumage complete in 3d year. Female (hen) so dark she looks black at a distance.

SOUNDS AND DISPLAYS: Caws like a crow or meows, *gayoo;* male makes cracking sounds like White-bearded Manakin, *Manacus manacus*. In flight makes a whispering sound (see below). Each male has his own court, a special place among stones on forest floor that is clean from so much wing beating; bird immediately displays splendid plumage by ruffling it and remaining statuesquely immobile. He does not make the slightest movement, but the lightest breeze will stir the filigree of elongated secondaries that meet highly developed upper tail coverts to form a single, large, almost horizontally opened fan. According to angle of light, plumage color shifts from orange to gold to red, becoming brownish or dull in shade. Although various males live together, there is no mutual cooperation on court according to statements of various observers; individual courts are grouped along a perimeter of some meters (cocks' walk) and used simultaneously. Before and after displaying birds perch on nearby branches where immature (brown) individuals also appear and may outnumber adult males.

Frugivorous, as is usual with cotingids. Seeks tree fruits and those produced by palmito (*Euterpe* sp.) The Olallas (1956), who had a great deal of experience with fauna of the upper Orinoco and upper Amazon (see Chapter 2.5), describe in detail how cock-of-the-rock hunts insects and catches geckos and frogs. Male, on alighting and taking off, makes a strident whistle with external primaries (sound-producing feathers), recalling the *Cotinga* and *Xipholena*. When perched remains erect and immobile like other typical cotingids. Nests in eroded or rocky rough terrain in humid, shady, primary forest, female building a saucer-shaped nest of mud and sticks on projections of wall. Lays 2 spotted eggs that she broods herself.

Escarpments covered with forests and broken by shady streams. Border forests between Brazil, the Guianas, Venezuela, Colombia. Up to now still common there. Until recently was only accessible through cooperation of Indians. Gradual advance of colonization may endanger it, especially because it is highly prized by cage-bird collectors, although most birds die when caged. Andean Cock-of-the-Rock, *R. peruviana*, a close relative in Andes from Colombia to Bolivia, has even more intense reddish orange color, black wings and tail, gray tertiaries; iris light blue, unlike our *rupicola*, which has orange eyes and feet.

Systematic position of the *Rupicola* has been much discussed, and the genus has been placed in a separate family, the Rupicolidae, or even considered to be an enormous manakin (Pipridae). To me it is evident that the *Rupicola* are more closely linked to the Cotingidae, including by the type nest they build (see *Iodopleura* and *Oxyruncus*).

Cotingidae Bibliography

See also General Bibliography

Bierregaard, R. O., Jr., D. F. Stotz, L. H. Harper, et al. 1987. Observations on the occurrence and behavior of the Crimson Fruitcrow, *Haematoderus militaris,* in central Amazonia. *Bull. B.O.C.* 107(3):134–37.

Brooke, M. de L., D. A. Scott, and D. M. Teixeira. 1983. Some observations made at the first recorded nest of the Sharpbill, *Oxyruncus cristatus. Ibis* 125:259–61.

Camargo, H.F.A., and E. A. Camargo. 1964. Ocorrência de *Iodopleura pipra* no Estado de São Paulo e algumas notas sobre *Iodopleura isabellae. Pap. Avuls. Zool. S. Paulo* 14(4):45–55.

Carvalho, J.C.M., and G. R. Kloss. 1950. *Rev. Bras. Biol.* 10:65–72. [*Rupicola,* behavior]

Chapman, F. M. 1939. The riddle of *Oxyruncus. Am. Mus. Nov.* 1047:1–4.

Gilliard, E. T. 1962. On the breeding behavior of the Cock-of-the-Rock, *Rupicola rupicola. Bull. Am. Mus. Nat. Hist.* 124:31–68.

Goeldi, E. A. 1894. *Ibis* 36:484–94. [*Phibalura,* nesting]

Lowery, G. H., Jr., and J. P. O'Neill. 1966. A new genus and species of Cotinga from eastern Peru. *Auk* 83:1–9.

Olalla, A. M. 1943. *Pap. Avuls. Zool. S. Paulo,* 3:229–36. [Behavior]

Olalla, A. M. 1956. *Bibl. Zool.* 2:26–40 [*Rupicola,* behavior]

Oren, D. C., and F. C. Novaes. 1985. A new subspecies of White Bellbird, *Procnias alba,* from southeastern Amazonia. *Bull. B.O.C.* 105:23–25.

Phelps, W. H., and W. H. Phelps, Jr. 1962. Nueve aves nuevas para la avifauna brasileira del Cerro Uei-Tepui. *Bol. Soc. Venez. Ciênc. Nat.* 23, no. 101.

Roth, P. 1985. Observações preliminares na araponga-de-asa-preta, *Procnias averano. XII Cong. Bras. Zool.:*560.

Roth, P., D. C. Oren, and F. C. Novaes. 1985. The White Bellbird, *Procnias alba,* in the Serra dos Carajás, southeastern Pará, Brazil. *Condor* 86:343–44.

Schuchmann, K. L. 1984. Zur Ernährung des Cayenne Felsenhahns, *Rupicola rupicola. J. Orn.* 125(2):239–41.

Sibley, C. G., S. M. Lanyon, and J. E. Ahlquist. 1984. The relationships of the Sharpbill, *Oxyruncus cristatus. Condor* 86:48–52.

Sick, H. 1951. *Wilson Bull.* 63(4):338–39. [*Cephalopterus ornatus,* egg]

Sick, H. 1954. *J. Orn.* 95(3/4):233–44. [*Cephalopterus ornatus,* ecology]

Sick, H. 1955. *Rev. Bras. Biol.* 15:361–76. [*Cephalopterus,* morphology, behavior]

Sick, H. 1970. *J. Orn.* 111:107–8. [*Xipholena,* eggs]

Sick, H. 1971. *Bonn. Zool. Beitr.* 22:255–60. [*Oxyruncus,* behavior]

Sick, H. 1979. *J. Orn.* 120(1):73–77. [*Iodopleura, Xipholena,* nesting]

Skutch, A. F. 1969. *Life Histories of Central American Birds,* vol. 3. Pacific Coast Avifauna 35:10–96. Berkeley, Calif.: Cooper Orn. Soc. [Behavior]

Snow, B. K. 1961. *Auk* 78:150–61. [*Procnias alba, Lipaugus, Perissocephalus,* behavior]

Snow, B. K. 1970. *Ibis* 112:299–329. [*Procnias averano,* behavior]

Snow, B. K. 1972. *Ibis* 114:139–62. [*Perissocephalus,* behavior]

Snow, D. W. 1971a. *J. Orn.* 112:323–33. [*Rupicola,* biology]

Snow, D. W. 1971b. *Ibis* 113:194–202. [Feeding]

Snow, D. W. 1971c. *The Living Bird* 10:5–17. [*Querula,* behavior]

Snow, D. W. 1973a. *Bull. Brit. Mus. Nat. Hist, Zool.* 25:367–91. [*Procnias,* ecology, evolution]

Snow, D. W. 1973b. *Breviora* 409:1–27. [Classification]

Snow, D. W. 1976. The relationship between climate and annual cycles in the Cotingidae. *Ibis* 118(3):366–401.

Snow, D. W. 1980. *Bull. B.O.C.* 100(4):213–15. [*Tijuca condita,* description]

Snow, D. W. 1982. *The Cotingas.* Ithaca, N.Y.: Cornell University Press.

Snow, D. W., and D. Goodwin. 1974. *Auk* 91:360–69. [*Tijuca atra,* behavior]

Teixeira, D. M., G. Luigi, and A.C.C. Almeida. 1990. A redescoberta de *Iodopleura pipra leucopygia* no Nordeste do Brasil. *Resumos XVII Cong. Bras. Zool., Londrina:* 179.

Traylor, M. A., Jr. 1979. *Peter's Check-list of Birds of the World,* vol. 8. Cambridge, Mass.: Harvard University Press.

Vieira, C. C. 1935. *Rev. Mus. Paul.* 19:327–97. [Brazilian species]

Willis, E. O., and Y. Oniki. 1988. Winter nesting of *Iodopleura pipra* (Lesson, 1831) in southeastern Brazil. *Rev. Bras. Biol.* 48(2):161–67.

Wünschmann, A. 1966. Die Balz von *Pyroderus scutatus. Gef. Welt* 90(3):46–48.

FAMILY PHYTOTOMIDAE: PLANTCUTTERS (1)

The plantcutter family, with only three species, is restricted to the southern part of South America. These birds resemble emberizines but belong to the Suboscine group. Morphologically they have substantial affinity with the Cotingidae, through skeleton, podotheca, syrinx, arteries, and pterylosis, but they differ in reproduction. The nest (they do not breed in Brazil) is a large basket made of heavy branches and lined with soft material—a type cotingas do not make. Biochemical research suggests inclusion of *Phytotoma* in the *Ampelion* genus, with this transferred from the Cotingidae to the Phytotomidae (Lanyon and Lanyon 1989). There is accentuated sexual dimorphism in coloration. The serrated bill is unique, and their peculiar way of cutting leaves makes them pests in orchards and gardens. They are migratory, partially abandoning their breeding areas in Chile and Argentina in winter when they move to adjacent areas northward.

WHITE-TIPPED PLANTCUTTER, *Phytotoma rutila*
Corta-ramos-de-rabo-branco   SV   Fig. 278

18 cm; 32 g. Male colorful, with rusty red forehead and underparts, similar to Eurasian Bullfinch, *Pyrrhula pyrrhula;* back grayish, spotted with black; iris red. Female modestly colored: spotted with black without any red, with small crest remotely resembling that of a young Rufous-collared Sparrow, *Zonotrichia capensis,* though much larger; wings and tail similar to adult male. VOICE: call a coarse *jep.* Sluggish, perches calmly on bushes and trees. Cuts buds and leaves, even hard ones, using a rapid sideways movement of head to tear off pieces to eat. Also eats berries and seeds. Patagonia to Bolivia, Paraguay; migrates to Uruguay and Rio Grande do Sul (espinilho parkland, May, Belton 1978).

Fig. 278. White-tipped Plantcutter, *Phytotoma rutila.* The serrated bill is a unique feature. Original, M. Grabert.

Phytotomidae Bibliography

Belton, W. 1978. Supplementary list of new birds for Rio Grande do Sul, Brazil. *Auk* 95(2):413–15.
Daskam, T., and J. Rottmann. 1984. *Aves de Chile.* Calderón.
Küchler, W. 1936. *J. Orn.* 84:352–62. [Anatomy]
Lanyon, S. M., and W. E. Lanyon. 1989. The systematic position of the plantcutters (Phytotomidae). *Auk* 106:422–32.

SUBORDER OSCINES

With almost 4200 species, the Oscines include a little less than half the world's approximately 9000 extant bird species. They have reached their highest development in the tropical regions of the Old World and Australia.

The taxonomic problem with Oscines is a reflection of the same problems encountered in the Suboscines. Beyond the lack of conclusive evidence, the need to present a linear system is perturbing because the relationships are tridimensional. Also, I feel that the 1983 AOU *Check-list of North American Birds* presents a problem by downgrading to subfamilies various former families that are important in the Neotropics, such as the Sylviidae and Turdidae, causing them to lose their prominence. These now form part of the Muscicapidae superfamily, being grouped with about 400 species of the Northern Hemisphere and Old World that are little known in a Neotropical county such as Brazil. The Muscicapidae broadly correspond to the Tyrannidae.

Similar problems arise with establishment of the Emberizidae superfamily, which includes as subfamilies, along with the Cardinalinae and Emberizinae, the former families Parulidae, Thraupidae, Coerebidae, and Icteridae. The Fringillidae family is represented by the Carduelinae.

The nectariniids of the Old World (Africa, etc.) also belong to the Oscines. Their evolution is clearly analogous to that of the nectivorous, Neotropical Coerebinae and the Trochilidae (the latter non-Passerines). The existence of ecologically similar niches in various parts of the globe stimulated the convergence of nonrelated families.

The Oscines are considered the most evolved group in the Class Aves. Although "primitive" and "progressive" charac-

ters are found in almost all the families, it is possible to establish a sequence in the Oscines that demonstrates a certain evolutionary tendency (Amadon 1957, Delacour and Vaurie 1957). The Suboscines are not ancestors of the Oscines.

The Oscine syrinx is complex (fig. 279), having at least six and generally seven (and up to nine) pairs of syringeal muscles (Polymyodae). The structure of the Oscine syrinx is less varied than that of the Suboscines, or Clamatores, which suggests that the Oscine group is monophyletic (Ames 1971). Although song in the Oscines is frequently a male privilege, syrinx structure is the same in both sexes, but the musculature of the male vocal apparatus is more powerful. In certain families (e.g., Troglodytidae) females also sing; sometimes females even sing better than males, as in certain icterines.

The complexity of the syrinx does not mean that vocalization by Oscines, often called "singing birds," is always superior to that of Suboscines. Suboscine voices are in many cases as impressive as those of Oscines, and the vocalization of certain Suboscines may even "outdo" that of Oscines. The lyrebirds, *Menura,* of Australia, considered the most primitive Oscines judging by their anatomy, have a simple syrinx but a notable song; they are considered unparalleled in their imitation of other birds. It is therefore the central nervous system and genetic factors that govern the efficiency of the vocal apparatus. The Brazilian bird that best imitates other birds is Lawrence's Thrush, *Turdus lawrencii,* of Amazonia.

The middle-ear ossicle (columella, or stapes) is less complex than in the Suboscines and little used in the study of Oscine taxonomy.

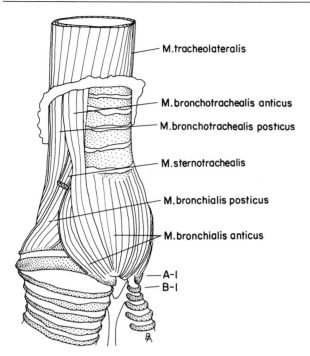

M.tracheolateralis

M.bronchotrachealis anticus

M.bronchotrachealis posticus

M.sternotrachealis

M.bronchialis posticus

M.bronchialis anticus

A-I
B-I

A

Fig. 279. Syrinx of a member of the Oscines, the Diademed Tanager, *Stephanophorus diadematus*. It has six syringeal muscles. A and B are cartilaginous materials. Original, P. L. Ames.

There is a great deal of variation in development of the primaries. The tenth, or outer, primary, a tiny, rigid feather shorter than the greater primary coverts, is rudimentary in varying degree. Among the most cited members of the so-called *Passeres novempennatae* is the American nine-primaried assemblage: the present Emberizidae (see above), all very important in this hemisphere, probably of tropical North American origin (Mayr 1946) and considered the most progressive Passerine group. The tenth primary is also lacking in the Hirundinidae and Motacillidae, both having relatively long, pointed wings. Some families, such as the Vireonidae, are transitional so far as the outer wing feather is concerned. The number of primaries is one of the key characters in Passerine classification, but it does not always indicate close relationship. Apparently there is a tendency toward reducing the number of flight feathers in various groups, reflecting a general evolutionary trend.

Aerodynamic analysis shows clearly that this relates to perfection of flight: a tendency to develop the most appropriate wing for long-distance flights. It is an adaptation of birds living in open habitats that have become migratory—conditions entirely foreign to the Suboscines.

In Brazil the Oscines, with 325 species, make up only 35.8% of the Passeriformes. However, they represent 15 families or subfamilies, almost double the number of Suboscine families living in the same region. There are three large groups of Oscines on this continent: the Thraupinae with 96 species in Brazil, Emberizinae and Cardinalinae with

81 species in Brazil, and Icterinae with 35 species in Brazil. Two other Oscine families were introduced: the Passeridae (House Sparrow, *Passer domesticus*) and Estrildidae (Common Waxbill, *Estrilda astrild*). The Oscines are of the greatest importance in the Old World, where they predominate among the Passeriformes.

Most Oscines in South America are relatively recent immigrants, having originated in two groups: (1) apparently North American families such as the Troglodytidae (remote descendants of pre-Muscicapidae of the Old World), Mimidae, Vireonidae, Icterinae, Parulinae, and Thraupinae; and (2) families based in the Old World that invaded North America more recently across the Bering Straits and that from there came to South America: Hirundinidae, Corvidae, Turdinae, Silviinae, and Motacillidae. The colonizing abilities of the immigrants varied. One Oscine species, the Noronha Vireo, *Vireo gracilirostris,* has managed to establish itself on Fernando de Noronha in mid-Atlantic where it lives alongside a Suboscine representative, the Large Elaenia, *Elaenia spectabilis ridleyana* (Tyrannidae). Oscines have reached the extreme tip of South America: two Troglodytidae, the Grass Wren, *Cistothorus platensis,* and House Wren, *Troglodytes aedon,* breed in Tierra del Fuego as well as in the United States, where they are well known as local birds.

Some nine-primaried Oscines must have reached South America during the Tertiary, before the two continents were definitively united, and established their principal center of evolution here. This also appears to be the case for the Icterinae. Icterines and emberizines have been called "Pan Americans," for their evolution has been almost equal in the two American subcontinents. Over the centuries there must have been constant interchange of winged fauna between the two areas.

Oscine immigration to South America began well before formation of the Orinoco and Amazon basins, as is proven by many populations of nonforest species that today inhabit regions north and south of the Hylaea and are separated by it in a notably discontinuous distribution (e.g., see Emberizinae, "Distribution . . .").

Early Oscine immigration must frequently have followed the Andes. Other, more recent immigrants penetrated northern Brazil and found the Amazon to be an obstacle. This happened with the Crested Bobwhite, *Colinus cristatus,* and Eastern Meadowlark, *Sturnella magna,* a descendent of North American meadowlarks.

There are North American Oscine Tertiary fossils of emberizines, corvids, turdines, and parulines from 10 to 25 million years old. Brazil has fossil documentation only from the Pleistocene (20,000 years B.P.), comprising vireonids, icterines, and thraupines. Brazil has 32 endemic Oscine species.

Oscines must compete on this continent with Suboscines that were here first. Although there are various typically forest Oscines, such as the Troglodytidae, Oscines frequently live in open areas and many are not adapted to life in the forest, the principal Suboscine habitat. This ecological difference is one of the reasons there should not be much competition between Oscines and Suboscines. In marshlands and open country, Oscines such as icterines and emberizines are Brazil's most abundant birds. The decrease in forest habitats on this continent, either by natural climatic causes or human intervention, favors the spread of many Oscines. For this reason the erroneous impression often arises that avifauna is richer on cultivated land than under natural conditions. Impoverishment of our flora through human action only stimulates the spread of certain ordinary synanthropic species, be they Oscines or Suboscines.

Oscines are among the few birds that the Portuguese, on arriving in America, recognized as relatives of birds of their homeland, which explains the use of names of European species such as *andorinha* (swallow), *gralha* (jay), *melro* (oriole), *rouxinol* (nightingale), and *canário* (canary). This has given rise to confusion, for the Brazilian species in question appeared like those of Europe but weren't always the same. The solution has been to adopt indigenous names, available in abundance, for local fauna (see Chapter 4.2.3).

FAMILY HIRUNDINIDAE: SWALLOWS (15)

Swallows are well known, widely distributed throughout the world, and frequently synanthropic. There are upper Tertiary (Pliocene, 4 million years B.P.) fossils from North America. The family comes first among the Oscines because the structure of the vocal apparatus is considered relatively primitive. Swallows are, however, highly evolved in various other aspects.

Morphology, Special Adaptations, and Vocalization

This is one of the most distinctive Oscine families. The resemblance of swallows in flight to swifts (Apodiformes, Apodidae, *Chaetura*, etc., see Pl 19) is superficial. Swallows' wings are shorter, wider, and less rigid than those of swifts, resulting in more agile and less sweeping flight. Swallows are considered the most graceful fliers among all birds. The most noticeable difference between swallows and swifts is that swallows perch at will on wires, TV antennas, and branches, whereas swifts are completely incapable of perching, being able only to clutch rough walls or lie on their bellies. Thus, swifts are only seen flying. Swallows are the birds most frequently found perched on electric and telephone wires, making them easy to observe. At dusk small swallow species can be confused with bats. The White-winged Swallow, *Tachycineta albiventer,* when perched on rocks in a river or flying just above the water's surface may appear to be a sandpiper. In flight the Brown-chested Martin, *Phaeoprogne tapera,* resembles a small, imaginary hawk. One should not use the term *andorinhão* ["superswallow"] when discussing this family, but instead *andorinha grande* ["big swallow"], because *andorinhão* is the word for swifts of all sizes.

The neck of a swallow is short and the bill very short and flat, perfectly adapted for capturing small insects in flight, like the Apodidae, with which swallows also share the peculiarity of two focal centers on the retina: a centered binocular one (to focus on longer distances) and another that is pe-ripheral and monocular. The legs are short, the toes strong, suitable for grasping a perch. Walking ability is weak. Sexes are similar. The voice is chittering or chirping and similar in related species. Sometimes individuals sing on the nest at night (Blue-and-white Swallow, *Notiochelidon cyanoleuca*). In Rio Grande do Sul *Phaeoprogne tapera* and the White-rumped Swallow, *Tachycineta leucorrhoa,* have a notable dawn song, uttered in flight like the famous daytime song of the Eurasian Skylark, *Alauda arvensis.* It has been proven that *T. leucorrhoa* can make different sounds with each of the two bronchi (see Bare-throated Bellbird, *Procnias nudicollis,* Cotingidae).

Feeding

In general swallows are strictly insectivorous and together with swifts are the principal consumers of aerial plankton. Swallows are the first to take advantage of flying swarms of termites, ants, mayflies, flies, etc. They also take bees and even wasps. It is not unusual to find Hymenoptera with large stingers in the crop of a swallow. With bees, probably mostly drones and stingless bees are involved, for swallows engulf insects without killing them (see Tyrannidae, "Feeding"). They catch insects one by one, like swifts and nightjars do.

The stomach of one *Phaeoprogne tapera fusca* specimen collected on the upper Rio São Francisco, Minas Gerais, late on a September afternoon, from a large migrating flock, contained 402 insects belonging to more than 20 families. Among them were 295 winged termites and 10 drones. It has been calculated that in Europe a pair of Barn Swallows, *Hirundo rustica* (a species whose North American population migrates to Brazil) and its young (two sets per year of three or four each) consume about 291,000 insects. When swallows fly close to a water surface it is not always easy to see whether they are catching insects, drinking, or taking a quick bath.

Swallows have been seen together with dragonflies exploiting a flying swarm of termites. It is not true that swallows are great consumers of mosquitoes. Newspapers say they eat 700 to 2000 per day. Insects, yes. Swallows do not hunt in twilight, nor do they enter enclosed habitats, the domain of mosquitoes.

Behavior

Like swifts, swallows suffer in strong winds and heavy rains; bad weather is a serious menace for them. Also like swifts, they try to fly against the wind, being the smallest of all birds capable of making long soaring flights to catch insects. Swallows are not fast. Their normal velocity when feeding is 20 to 30 km/hr. During flights before roosting it is 80 km/hr.

The alarm given by swallows at the appearance of a hawk is as impressive as are the cries of the Tropical Kingbird, *Tyrannus melancholicus,* or Great Kiskadee, *Pitangus sulphuratus. Notiochelidon cyanoleuca* will call and fly like a swarm of flies around a hawk circling close to their roost. They appear able to distinguish whether the hawk is just "out for a walk," resting, or hunting. If the last, they flee and hide. I saw an *N. cyanoleuca* chase a vulture feather falling from the sky, an action that could be interpreted as play. In the same category, mutatis mutandis, is a Southern Rough-winged Swallow, *Stelgidopteryx ruficollis,* chasing a *Pitangus sulphuratus* high in the sky. See Aplomado Falcon, *Falco femoralis.* Swallows also like to bathe in rain.

Swallows sleep under roofs or in holes. The pair sleeps together on the nest, something uncommon in birds. Migrating flocks of *Hirundo rustica, Stelgidopteryx ruficollis, Phaeoprogne tapera,* and others roost in cattails, cane fields, patches of tall grass, and on bushes on riverine islands in Amazonia. On migration the *Progne* also roost in trees in public plazas of certain cities. Everyone knows of the immense lines of swallows perched on electric wires. When one hears of "swallows" roosting or nesting in chimneys, alone or in colonies, they are almost certainly not swallows but swifts (*Chaetura*). When "swallow waterfalls" and "swallow grottoes" are mentioned, it is certainly *Cypseloides* and *Streptoprocne* swifts that are being referred to. At dusk swallows become restless, like thrushes, etc, increasing their cheeping and chattering until they occupy their roost.

Breeding

Swallows nest in holes of various kinds, making a padding of grass, leaves, and feathers. The Gray-breasted Martin, *Progne chalybea,* makes a tray of mud or dung to which it adds saliva which gives it extraordinary strength. It then arranges a soft padding. It may spend 20 days fixing its nest. *P. chalybea, Notiochelidon cyanoleuca,* and sometimes *Tachycineta leucorrhoa* have been found nesting in human-made cavities such as rafters under tile roofs, wall linings, and drain holes in walls. The White-banded Swallow, *At-*

ticora fasciata; White-thighed Swallow, *Neochelidon tibialis;* Tawny-headed Swallow, *Alopochelidon fucata;* and *Stelgidopteryx ruficollis* all like burrows in embankments; the last-named can excavate tunnels and occasionally installs itself in road embankments or holes of the Swallow-wing, *Chelidoptera tenebrosa* (Espírito Santo). *Tachycineta albiventer* nests in holes in rocks in the middle of rivers and in banks or hollow branches leaning over the water. *Atticora fasciata* and *Tachycineta leucorrhoa* also nest in hollow limbs. I found *Progne chalybea* nesting in an arboreal termite nest in the upper Xingu, Mato Grosso. At the beginning of the eighteenth century *P. chalybea* started abandoning rocks in favor of houses, a process now about complete. The same can be said of its North American congener, the Purple Martin, *P. subis.* They are unable, however, to keep up with verticalization of the modern city. Exceptionally one finds *P. chalybea* still nesting in rocks (e.g., Chapada das Mangabeiras, Bahia 1976).

Phaeoprogne tapera regularly occupies houses of the Rufous Hornero, *Furnarius rufus,* in which it prepares a soft saucer using dung. I have seen this swallow nest in a wall drain (Rio de Janeiro) and in a hollow, arboreal termite nest excavated by a parakeet (upper Xingu, Mato Grosso).

Progne chalybea is well known for having several pairs nesting together, and *Stelgidopteryx ruficollis* tends toward this. Except for *P. chalybea,* we do not find large swallow colonies in Brazil, in contrast to the situation in the Northern Hemisphere.

The usually pure white eggs are incubated by the female. Young *Notiochelidon cyanoleuca* hatch after 15 days. The parents take turns feeding them. Chicks leave the nest at about 26 days but return to it. At this age various swallow species are brown above instead of shiny black. *N. cyanoleuca* lays two or three times a year (Rio de Janeiro). It is not always the same pair that uses a nest for the second time, as has been proven by banding.

Sometimes swallows and the House Sparrow, *Passer domesticus,* compete for a nesting place. In the Xingu, Mato Grosso, I saw *Phaeoprogne tapera* chase away a pair of Chestnut-eared Aracaris, *Pteroglossus castanotis,* that had approached its nest.

Migration

Swallows are a symbol of bird migration. After breeding, all swallow species living in southern Brazil, but not all individual swallows, undertake more or less extensive migrations northward where food is more abundant. Some cross the equator, *Progne chalybea domestica,* for instance, reaching the Rio Uaupés (Amazonas) and southern Venezuela (July, April). Southern populations penetrate farther north. *Phaeoprogne tapera fusca,* for instance, from southern and central Brazil, regularly appears in quantity in Central America, like the Ashy-tailed Swift, *Chaetura andrei merid-*

ionalis. One of the longest journeys undertaken by birds on this continent is the migration of *Notiochelidon cyanoleuca patagonica,* which has been collected in Costa Rica, more than 4000 km away in a straight line from its breeding area.

To separate migrant individuals from residents caught in the same place, plumage condition can be useful up to a point. *Progne chalybea* migrants, for example, are in molt while the residents, which are breeding, are not. Exceptions may occur, however, for it is not unusual near the equator for molt to occur during the breeding period (Eisenmann 1959). See more on this subject below.

During migration swallows often assemble in hundreds, and at times in thousands, especially before roosting. They form clouds, immense sinuous veils. Although they fly in tightly packed formation, it is noteworthy that there are no midair collisions. The same applies to northern sandpipers, which, together with swallows, are among the birds that form the largest flocks known in Brazil. Swallows far outdo the Fork-tailed Flycatcher, *Tyrannus savana,* whose flocks are on the move at the same time. These Amazonian accumulations of swallows could lead someone traveling in the region between February and August who sees only rivers, open fields, and adjacent forest openings to believe these are the dominant birds of Amazonia, whereas actually the great majority are only visiting from distant southern regions. When swallows from the south begin the return to their homeland, then the Bank Swallow, *Riparia riparia;* Cliff Swallow, *Hirundo pyrrhonota; H. rustica;* and *Progne subis* begin to arrive from the north, sometimes in mixed flocks, to stay in Brazil until March or April. Some individuals banded in the U.S. have been captured in Brazil, revealing their birthplace (see *H. pyrrhonota*). Through 1987, 12 swallows banded in North America had been recorded in Brazil: 7 *Progne subis,* 1 *Riparia riparia,* 1 *Hirundo rustica,* and 3 *H. pyrrhonota.*

In recent years the press has reported on the large swallow flocks that periodically roost in dense trees in the plazas of cities of the interior, especially São Paulo. Television has shown their arrival at these group dormitories. They are not well received because they soil automobiles. Attempts have been made to frighten them away with exploding rockets, jets of water, and even torches. One effort tried to route them to a neighboring forest, which was illuminated while the central plazas were kept dark. Interestingly, swallows, being typical synanthropic birds, have become accustomed over hundreds of years to roosting during migration under strong illumination, such as modern mercury lights, which may help ward off predators such as opossums, owls, and bats. The illumination of that forest was not sufficiently dazzling to attract the swallows, so the city authorities reacted by cutting down the plaza trees.

Concentrations of swallows in the state of São Paulo are said to have increased considerably. At the beginning of the 1970s about 8000 swallows were in the São José do Rio Preto area, with *Progne chalybea* dominant. In 1975 *P. subis* of North America was in the majority, and this species gradually increased. In recent years it has been calculated that 70% are *P. subis,* 20% *Phaeoprogne tapera,* and 10% *Progne chalybea.* In February 1990 *Phaeoprogne tapera* was the dominant species in concentrations surveyed in São Paulo (E. S. Morton pers. comm.). It is easy to identify swallow species when the birds perch on wires.

At a petroleum refinery on the banks of the Rio Negro, Amazonas, in November–December 1984, a concentration of about 100,000 martins was discovered: 60% were *Progne subis,* the remainder *P. chalybea* and *Phaeoprogne tapera* (Sanotti 1985). These martins perch on tubing, ladders, platforms, piping, and wires between 1.5 m and 40 m high. Within this intensely lighted area are large jets of steam, tremendous heat, loud noise, and an odor insupportable to humans, but for the birds it is a safe and adequate roost. Martins come to this refinery all year. Much about it remains to be explained. When individuals can be examined, as during banding that took place in the Mato Grosso Pantanal at the same time, it is interesting to pay attention to molt, which can provide information on the annual cycle of these birds. In the case at hand, 89% of the 46 *Progne subis* specimens examined showed total molt (meaning nonbreeding status for the birds that arrived from their northern homeland), whereas 85% of the 40 *Phaeoprogne tapera* caught had fresh plumage without any molt and were ready to nest.

Installations of the Companhia Vale do Rio Doce's Carajás iron project south of Marabá, Pará, built since 1981, have been discovered as a suitable shelter by *Progne chalybea, Phaeoprogne tapera,* and *Notiochelidon cyanoleuca* flocks from the south that winter in Amazonia from May to October. The birds perch on slender beams that support the aluminum roofs of the highest (30–50 m) open buildings but do not use lower buildings or houses. In late May 1990 their droppings, which created problems by soiling machinery, were mixed with many loose feathers, indicating that these migrants had undergone a complete molt.

Marking by microdots of paint sensitive to ultraviolet light, a technique developed by the U.S. Fish and Wildlife Service, was successfully applied in 1985 by Luis Dino Vizotto of Rio Preto, São Paulo. Thousands of birds were marked in the flocking areas by spraying pigments only visible to the human eye under ultraviolet light. Pigment distribution was as follows: Rio Preto received violet; Barretos fiery orange; Ribeirão Preto golden yellow; Araraquara green; Rio Claro blue. Thus the birds returned to their breeding grounds in Carnival fancy dress. The color lasts only until the next molt, perhaps half a year. Of the 200,000 martins microtagged, 29 were found in the U.S. and 1 in Canada. In 60 years of banding only an occasional martin has been recovered. In North America they returned to their wooden or aluminum houses, prepared by local residents, where the painted ones were recorded. Some molted microtagged feathers were also found and examined in the banding laboratory in Laurel, Maryland. Most of the 30 recovered came from the Rio Claro and Ribeirão Preto roosts.

It is probable that the now-ended, famous swallow concentration in the old market in Campinas, São Paulo, also involved primarily the North American *Progne subis* in migration and not our local *P. chalybea* (see *P. chalybea*).

A different type of migration is involved in a collective roost, or "club," of the common *Notiochelidon cyanoleuca* I found in the center of Rio de Janeiro in a small group of palm trees (*Phoenix* sp.) in the middle of a heavily used traffic circle. This roost was used all year by just the one species but with considerable variation in the number of birds using it. The birds were not from the neighborhood, where there are many places for them to breed, but from distant areas. They appeared high over the palms at dusk and flew in circles awaiting deeper twilight, then finally dove vertically in an impressive funnel formation into the palms. Only occasionally did one or another swallow arrive from the immediate neighborhood in a low, horizontal flight to join the flock that came from beyond. Attendance varied greatly: from many hundreds and even thousands in April 1986 and January–February 1987 to just 100 in November 1986.

Between September and April of this same period I recorded two to three reproductive cycles of this swallow in the surrounding city. Attendance at the swallow club continued independent of the breeding of the species in the same area. Compare clubs of *Chaetura* and *Streptoprocne* swifts. Because it was not possible to examine individuals to learn their age and molt state, it is impossible to draw satisfactory conclusions regarding the nature of this concentration, in contrast to a *Chaetura andrei* club in Minas Gerais (see Apodidae, "Swift Grottoes . . .").

Parasites

Swallows are sometimes hosts to louse flies. I have found *Ornithomyia* (= *Pseudornithomyia*) *ambigua* on *Notiochelidon cyanoleuca* (Rio de Janeiro). See also "Nest Fauna."

Nest Fauna

Occurrence of some nest insects, such as lice, fleas, pupiparous flies, and bugs (e.g., Emisinae), in nesting material gathered by swallows does not involve danger for humans. Nevertheless, as a preventative sanitary measure one can remove excess accumulations during the months the birds are gone. This, however, sometimes involves the risk of their not returning.

In some places, Minas Gerais, for instance, *Ornithocoris pallidus* (Haematosiphoninae, Cimicidae), a close relative of the Brazilian chicken-bug (*Ornithocoris toledoi*[1]), lives in the straw nest of *Notiochelidon cyanoleuca*. These bloodsucking bed-bug relatives are exclusively bird parasites and do not attack people.

Usefulness, Popularity, Dangers, and Decline

Swallows are popular with people, their return in spring brings joy ("One swallow maketh not summer"), and their usefulness is evident to everyone, although it is clear that insecticides are much more efficient against insects than swallows. They are symbols of peace and happiness.

The popularity of swallows in old Rio de Janeiro was reflected in the designation of the horse carts used for moving, called *andorinhas*, "swallows" (a name still used by moving companies), which may have been an allusion to the migratory habits of these birds.

However, there have been cases where even force was applied to scare them away, as happened recently in Belém, Pará, and in Ceará (1969) in a demonstration of gross stupidity. Swallows are linked with Padre Anchieta [a sixteenth-century Brazilian Jesuit missionary]. It is said that a swallow's nest brings luck and that when one shoots a swallow the gun is damaged (northeast).

Among the dangers threatening swallows around their nests are spider webs (*Nephila* sp.), in which they sometimes get caught, especially young birds going in or out under the webs, as has been observed with *Notiochelidon cyanoleuca*. Apparently such occurrences are accidental, producing no advantage for the spider (see also Trochilidae, "Parasites . . ."). The Barn Owl, *Tyto alba*, occasionally becomes an enemy of *Progne chalybea* when the owl is installed in the same attic as the swallow, as observed in Santarém, Pará. I recorded a case of army ants entering a *Stelgidopteryx ruficollis* nest in an embankment and killing the young (Rio de Janeiro).

In 1869 the well-known naturalist R. F. Hensel documented a surprising incident from Blumenau, Santa Catarina, where a bat (probably a *Phyllostomus*) caught a *Notiochelidon cyanoleuca* on the nest in a house under good light. In this case the light did not save the bird (see above).

Regrettably, the existence of swallows is threatened by the use of pesticides. Swallows ingest poisoned insects and perch on branches to which contact poisons are adhering. Polluted rivers are abandoned by riverine swallows. Everyone in Brazil complains about the decline in the number of swallows (see also Apodidae, "Enemies . . ."). Prolonged

---

[1]The Brazilian chicken-bug, *Ornithocoris toledoi,* has until now been found only in chicken houses (a habitat created by people after the discovery of America) and not in American wild bird nests, where it might be pre-

sumed to exist. It has now become rare because of the use of residual insecticides with hexachlorides (Usinger 1966).

rains are another serious danger for swallows in any part of the world—unlike swifts, which have the ability to become torpid when occasion demands.

Recent reports have appeared both in Brazil and the United States that American martins, the popular *Progne subis,* have died by the thousands as a result of unrestricted use of organochloride pesticides in Brazil. The American, James Hill (1986), who studied martins in Brazil in 1986, concluded that these reports of widespread mortality from pesticides were unverified and greatly exaggerated (Hill pers. comm.). Hill felt that prolonged rains were what affected the birds adversely. Martins were found dead in their flock roosts. Two autopsies showed extensive worms. Hill founded the Purple Martin Conservation Association at Edinboro University of Pennsylvania, with a quarterly review for its 3500 members (December 1989). It organizes wildlife trips to Brazil from December to March to visit various *P. subis* roosts.

In Rio Grande do Sul about 50 unidentified migrant swallows were electrocuted by a high-tension line in São Leopoldo in January 1989. The flock suddenly took flight, causing a short circuit and blowing fuses in the power house (H. Tessmer pers. comm.).

Identification Key

More than with many other birds, perception of swallow plumage color is subjective, for it changes with the light. For example, the color of a *Notiochelidon cyanoleuca* appears to have, instead of blue, a greenish sheen when it flies over a green tile swimming pool. The green or blue sheen may be the diagnostic character for the species, as in *Tachycineta albiventer* and *T. leucorrhoa,* but it may also change with molt (e.g., *T. albiventer*). Some species commonly fly together, at times mixed with swifts (*Chaetura* spp.), providing an opportunity for instructive observation.

1. Large: brown: *Phaeoprogne tapera* (Pl 36.3); royal blue and white: *Progne chalybea* (Pl 36.2) and *P. modesta,* the latter as a migrant in the upper Amazon; or all blue: *P. subis*
2. Medium or small, blackish and white:
   2.1. White rump: *Tachycineta albiventer* (Pl 36.4) and *T. leucorrhoa* (Pl 36.5)
   2.2. Upper side uniformly black: *Notiochelidon cyanoleuca* (Pl 36.1), *Atticora fasciata* (Pl 36.8), and *A. melanoleuca,* the last two with a band on the underside
3. Medium or small, brown: *Neochelidon tibialis* (Pl 36.5), *Alopochelidon fucata* (Pl 36.7), *Stelgidopteryx ruficollis* (Pl 36.6), and *Riparia riparia* (Pl 36.10)
4. Distinctive species: *Hirundo rustica* (Pl 36.9) and *H. pyrrhonota*

WHITE-WINGED SWALLOW, *Tachycineta albiventer,* Andorinha-do-rio   PL 36.4

13.5 cm. Typical river-edge swallow with bluish green sheen that is clear green in fresh plumage. Rump, wide

edges of inner flight feathers and corresponding upper wing coverts, and base of inner vanes of outer tail feathers white. Wing white gradually erodes with use. Immature brown with white band. VOICE: call a soft *schrreet, chewrr;* song *drewit-drewIT-drewit-drewit.* Perches preferentially on rocks, stakes, or snags in middle of rivers. Common in Amazonia, where frequently alongside *Atticora fasciata.* The Guianas and Venezuela to Bolivia, Argentina, throughout Brazil. Also called *Andorinha-ribeirinha.* See *T. leucorrhoa.*

WHITE-RUMPED SWALLOW, *Tachycineta leucorrhoa,* Andorinha-de-sobre-branco   PL 19.5

13.5 cm. Southern species very similar to *T. albiventer* but lacking wide white wing bars and hidden white on tail feathers. Has white mark over lores. Upperparts clear shiny blue, sometimes slightly greenish. Southern race, *T. l. leucopyga,* a bit smaller with steel blue upperparts, no white on face; Tertiaries have clear white spots. VOICE: high, ringing. On dawn song, see "Morphology. . . ." Flies low over grassy areas and roads, appears at edges of rivers and in flood plains; only rarely found with the *albiventer.* Argentina, Chile, and Bolivia to Mato Grosso, Minas Gerais, Espírito Santo. *T. l. leucopyga* appears as a migrant (Rio Grande do Sul, August; Rio de Janeiro, July–September), sometimes alongside type race.

BROWN-CHESTED MARTIN, *Phaeoprogne tapera,* Andorinha-do-campo   PL 36.3

17.5 cm. Large, sooty with white throat, belly, and under tail coverts that are prominent in flight. Never has blue feathers, unlike immature *Progne.* VOICE: call a rough, metallic *chree,* a bisyllabic *tch-tch;* song a more melodious *jew-il-jew, chri-chri-chrruit.* In Rio Grande do Sul in January sings a continuous half-hour dawn song until daylight while fluttering alone about 40 m up over an area of 20 sq m. Open country, cultivated areas. In Rio de Janeiro immigration of *Furnarius rufus,* on whose structures it is extensively dependent for nesting, has facilitated its propagation. Uses various hollow places for breeding (see "Breeding"). Argentina, Uruguay, Paraguay, and Bolivia to northern part of continent, where southern population (*P. t. fusca,* of southern and central Brazil) is found in migration (see "Migration") together with resident northern race (*P. t. tapera,* with slightly different coloration) which breeds in Amazonia. In south only in hottest months, nesting there. Migratory assemblages are seen in February (Rio de Janeiro). Also called *Uiriri* (Amazonas). Its inclusion in *Progne* is under study.

GRAY-BREASTED MARTIN, *Progne chalybea,* Andorinha-doméstica-grande   PL 36.2

19.5 cm; 43 g. Fork-tailed *Andorinha-grande-de-casa* ("large house swallow") is largest native Brazilian swallow. Royal blue and white with highly variable markings on underparts. Immature sooty on upperparts, similar to *Phae-oprogne tapera*. VOICE: a resonant *jeep-jeep-jewp*, etc. Ranches, rural towns, cities, preferentially in churches (*andorinha-católica*, "catholic swallow"). Does not take so easily to larger cities, unlike *Notiochelidon cyanoleuca*. See also "Breeding." Swarms of swallows in the old market ("the house of the swallows") in Campinas, São Paulo, were an extraordinary spectacle described by Rui Barbosa [famous Brazilian statesman and author, 1849–1923] and studied by R. von Ihering, who in one afternoon counted 30,000 in an open, tile-covered shed where they stayed all night, making a noise like that of a machine churning broken glass, as if none of them slept. At dawn all left together.

It is clear today that the thousands of Campinas martins were probably not *P. chalybea* but *P. subis* in migration, coming from North America and meeting the local *P. chalybea*, its close relative, which bred there. Calculations can be made based on the period (summer or winter) in which old observations were recorded. The market was demolished, but there is still a mosaic portraying a swallow on the sidewalk around it.

Mexico to Argentina. In Brazil divided into 2 geographic races: southern *P. c. domestica* which starts nesting August–September (Rio de Janeiro, Mato Grosso) and leaves southern and central Brazil (Goiás, Rio Araguaia) in autumn, emigrating to northern South America where Amazonian population, smaller-sized *P. c. chalybea*, lives. Large migrant flocks appear in February in Espírito Santo, July in Amazonas, October in Mato Grosso (see "Migration"). Recorded on Ilha Trindade. Also called *Taperá*. *P. chalybea* may be considered a southern replacement of *P. subis*, with which, together with *P. modesta*, it forms a superspecies.

PURPLE MARTIN, *Progne subis*   NV

20 cm; 55 g. A bit larger than *P. chalybea* and most popular swallow in U.S. Adult male uniformly dark blue, female less lustrous and with white on underparts, similar to *P. chalybea*. Forehead and sketchy collar whitish (these are lacking in *P. chalybea*). VOICE: because of close relationship, vocalizations of *P. subis*, *P. chalybea*, and *P. modesta* are very similar. *P. subis* in U.S. is a popular synanthropic species that emigrates in September, going to Bolivia and southern Brazil: São Paulo, Rio de Janeiro (November, March, April, May), Espírito Santo (October, February), Amazonas (November, March still in large numbers), Pará (January, February). Seven individuals banded in U.S. have been caught in Brazil. It is this species that gathers in great flocks in interior of São Paulo, including in Campinas, at end and beginning of year (see *P. chalybea* and "Migration").

SOUTHERN MARTIN, *Progne modesta elegans*   SV

Only in extreme west as a migrant from south. Uaupés, Rio Negro, Amazonas. See *P. subis* and *P. chalybea*.

BLUE-AND-WHITE SWALLOW, *Notiochelidon cyanoleuca*, Andorinha-pequena-de-casa   PL 36.1

12 cm; 12 g. Small, synanthropic, common in eastern Brazil. No white on rump. Immature has brown upperparts and yellowish breast, resembling *Riparia riparia*. VOICE: call *tseeeeh, chee-chee-cheeeeh;* warning, as when a hawk appears, *chreeee-chreeee . . . .* Song a modest, tremulous trill. Lives in towns and cities; a dominant species in Rio de Janeiro. Occurs in quarries, road cuts, embankments, along walls. In south, including Rio de Janeiro, present in large numbers only in warmest months, periodically augmented by migrants. Also common at crests of high mountains, e.g., Itatiaia. Costa Rica to the Guianas, Bolivia, Argentina, eastern and southern Brazil. In central Brazil and Amazonia appears only in reduced numbers on migration (Goiás, June; Mato Grosso, July–August; Pará, September). Most southerly non-Brazilian population, *N. c. patagonica*, migrates annually as far as Panama, where there is a resident population.

WHITE-BANDED SWALLOW, *Atticora fasciata*, Peitoril   PL 36.8

14.7 cm. Riverine species of Amazonia with long, forked tail. VOICE: song (when repeated) *tirIT, tewrewt*. In various regions it is dominant river-edge swallow. Perches on rocks in midstream and on branches hanging over water, often alongside *Tachycineta albiventer*. The Guianas and Venezuela to Bolivia, northern Mato Grosso (Xingu), eastern Pará.

BLACK-COLLARED SWALLOW, *Atticora melanoleuca*, Andorinha-de-coleira

14.7 cm. Behavior same as *A. fasciata*. Underparts white with black breast band. Immature brown instead of black. Amazonia, central Brazil, locally in Goiás, Bahia, Pernambuco, and Foz do Iguaçu, Paraná (July 1976, P. Roth). See *Riparia riparia*.

WHITE-THIGHED SWALLOW, *Neochelidon tibialis*, Calcinha-branca   PL 36.5

12.3 cm. Small forest swallow, easily overlooked except when in flocks on migration. Uniformly sooty except pants, which are not easily seen in life. In flight looks much like a *Chaetura* swift, differing in forked tail and by perching on wires and small, bare branches like other swallows. Roosts in embankments. Lives at forest edge. São Paulo (Alto da Serra), Rio de Janeiro (Parati, Nova Friburgo, March–May in flocks; Itatiaia, August and November), Espírito Santo (Chaves), Bahia (Salvador), across central Brazil (Goiás; Mato Grosso; Pará, Tapajós, April) to Panama.

TAWNY-HEADED SWALLOW, *Alopochelidon fucata*, Andorinha-morena   PL 36.7

12.5 cm. Small savanna species with relatively short tail, recognizable by intense rufous on sides of head, nuchal band,

and breast. Blackish cap prominent. VOICE: *zi-zi-zi . . . zulit.* Fairly common locally and periodically, even becoming numerous in central Brazil. Can be confused with *Stelgidopteryx ruficollis.* Argentina through southern and central Brazil (Minas Gerais, Goiás, Federal District, Mato Grosso) to northern South America, probably on migration.

SOUTHERN ROUGH-WINGED SWALLOW,
Stelgidopteryx ruficollis, Andorinha-serrador
PL 36.6

14 cm; 13.5 g. Medium sized, definitely larger but slimmer than *Alopochelidon fucata,* with almost rectangular tail. Reddish cinnamon throat contrasts with sooty breast, sides of head, and entire upperparts. Belly and under tail coverts pale yellow. At postjuvenal molt male acquires distinctive outer primary with roughened outer edge (*serrador,* "sawyer") of as yet unknown function. VOICE: a soft *jlid-jlid, schree-schree.* Cultivated fields near rivers, etc. Central America to Argentina, throughout Brazil. Migratory in southern Brazil. In North America replaced by Northern Rough-winged Swallow, *S. serripennis,* formerly included in *ruficollis.*

BANK SWALLOW, *Riparia riparia,*
Andorinha-do-barranco   NV   PL 36.10

12.5 cm. Small savanna species from North America. Diagnostic mark is white underparts crossed by wide brown breast band. VOICE: *zrrr-zrrr-zrrr,* shorter and lower than *Stelgidopteryx ruficollis.* Migrates as far as Argentina; may appear anywhere in Brazil but most likely in low-lying areas, e.g., Amazonas (October), Pará (September, March, April), Bahia (December, March), Mato Grosso (Pantanal, October and November), Rio Grande do Sul (December). Also Old World. See *Stelgidopteryx ruficollis, Atticora melanoleuca, Alopochelidon fucata,* and immature *Notiochelidon cyanoleuca.*

BARN SWALLOW, *Hirundo rustica,*
Andorinha-de-bando   NV   PL 36.9

15.5 cm. Migrant from Northern Hemisphere, unique with long, deeply forked tail crossed by white streak (invisible from above in closed tail). Immature, with much shorter tail, pale rusty underparts, and whitish forehead and belly. Is not very similar to adult; more easily recognized by voice. VOICE: a soft *wit, ewit-ewit,* diagnostic; melodious song twittered and hurried. Savannas, flood plains, ranches, and in breeding range highly synanthropic, but does not enter into cities such as Rio de Janeiro. Occurs periodically throughout Brazil, sometimes in hundreds and thousands September–March. In October (Amapá) and November (Rio de Janeiro)

immatures usually predominate; in March (Rio de Janeiro) adults do. In migration reaches as far as Tierra del Fuego. *H. r. erythrogaster* of North America is a geographic replacement of *H. r. rustica* of Old World, with same voice, etc. European populations migrate to southern Africa. Recorded on Ilha Trindade.

CLIFF SWALLOW, *Hirundo* (= *Petrochelidon*)
pyrrhonota, Andorinha-de-dorso-acanelado   NV

14.3 cm. Migrant from north, stocky with relatively short tail and complicated color pattern: whitish forehead, shiny blue cap, chestnut upper throat and nuchal band, rusty rump. Open country. Arriving from north in flocks, goes as far as Argentina. Recorded in various parts of Brazil, e.g., Amazonas (November), Rio de Janeiro (January), ex-Guanabara (November), São Paulo (January, February, March), Santa Catarina (January), Rio Grande do Sul (March). Near Viamão, Rio Grande do Sul, on a windy, misty January day, a flock of many hundreds, probably thousands, was seen perched on tips of a bamboo grove (W. Voss). An individual taken near São Paulo on 13 January 1961 was banded as a nestling on 19 June 1955 in New York State. Another taken on 20 January 1951 near Florianópolis, Santa Catarina, was banded as a nestling on 22 June 1950, also in New York.

Hirundinidae Bibliography

Eisenmann, E. 1959. *Auk* 76:529–32. [Migration]
Gómez, G.M.R. 1988. "Eto-ecologia evolutiva e adaptiva da comunicação sonora em andorinhas neotropicais." Thesis. Univ. Estad. Campinas.
Hill, J. R., III. 1986. Manaus refinery—is "the most unlikely spot on earth." *Nat. Soc. News* 21:(6)2–3, June (also March, April, and May).
Oliveira, R. G. 1987. O antigo mercado ou casa das andorinhas em Campinas, São Paulo. *Sulornis* 8:12–17.
Oren, D. C. 1980. Enormous concentration of Martins, *Progne* spp., in Iquitos, Peru. *Condor* 82:344–45.
Ricklefs, R. E. 1972. *Auk* 89:826–36. [*Stelgidopteryx ruficollis,* variation]
Sanotti, J. M. 1985. Grande concentração de andorinhas do gênero *Progne* em Manaus. *XII Cong. Bras. Zool., Campinas:*561.
Sick, H. 1979. *Bull. B.O.C.* 99(4):115–20. [*Atticora melanoleuca,* distribution]
Stiles, F. G. 1981. The taxonomy of Rough-winged Swallows (*Stelgidopteryx*) in southern Central America. *Auk* 98:282–93.
Valle, M. P., C. Yamashita, and P.T.Z. Antas. 1985. Contribuição ao conhecimento de andorinhas no município de Poconé, Mato Grosso. *XII Cong. Bras. Zool., Campinas:*562.
Vizotto, L. D. 1985. Andorinhas. *O Estado de São Paulo* 28/8/85.
Zimmer, J. T. 1955. *Am. Mus. Nov.,* 1723. [*Progne,* taxonomy]

FAMILY CORVIDAE: JAYS (8)

This nearly cosmopolitan family of large Passerines is better developed in the moderate climates of the Northern Hemisphere. There are tertiary fossils (Miocene, 18 million years B.P.) from North America. Molecular taxonomy, or DNA hybridization, has revealed that the Corvidae evolved in Australia, like the marsupials. They colonized Africa, Eurasia, and North America (Sibley and Ahlquist 1986). These birds began to emigrate early from Asia to North America, with the invasion continuing even in recent times. Today some species occupy both the Old World and North America. South America was invaded last.

On this continent the *gralhas,* a collective term used for the corvid group known as *jays* in English, are the only representatives of the family. Here they formed a new evolutionary center, diversifying much more than in the Old World. South America lacks the Common Raven, *Corvus corax,* the world's largest Passerine (about 61 cm total length and weighing 1.3 kg) and a species well-known in the Northern Hemisphere because of its cleverness. It reaches Nicaragua in Central America. The name *corvo,* "crow," used in São Paulo for the vulture, has a pejorative or deprecatory meaning in Brazil.

Morphology and Identification

Brazil has no other birds with a similar aspect, with the possible exception of certain cuckoos (*Piaya*), antbirds (*Batara*), or cotingas (*Cephalopterus*). Jays have broad wings, a long tail, frequently elongated feathers on the crown, and often vividly colored markings on the sides of the head. The principal color is dark violet blue, with white on the belly. The blue is produced by the microscopic structure of the melanin-colored feathers. The same reflective phenomenon causes the blue of the sky. The yellow of the Plush-crested Jay, *Cyanocorax chrysops,* may be lost in captivity. Sexes are identical.

In many American corvids the bill of the immature is a different color than that of the adult, interpreted by Hardy (1976) as a protection against aggression by adults (see Azure Jay, *Cyanocorax caeruleus*).

Vocalization

The voices of certain species, especially *Cyanocorax chrysops* and the White-naped Jay, *C. cyanopogon,* are quite varied. Fourteen basic cries have been recorded for *C. caeruleus* in captivity. There are cries of alarm, contact, flight, courtship, and more. Often there is a different tonality in consecutive stanzas from the same individual, creating the impression of a conversation between two birds. In a young

C. caeruleus, evidence was found of two harmonically related sounds being emitted by the two bronchi.

Sometimes sounds are produced that may not originate with the syrinx (instrumental music). There is an unending richness of motifs, induced by the capacity to imitate other sounds, such as voices of other birds and even human words (*C. chrysops*). These, often performed as subsong and frequently sung during rest, appear to serve for amusement and have nothing to do with proclaiming territory. I found a *C. cyanopogon* that was singing nothing but cries of the Roadside Hawk, *Rupornis magnirostris,* even holding to the characteristic rhythm of that species. When the jay noted my presence it shortened the intervals and finally changed to its own cries, *kuh, kuh.* I found another *C. cyanopogon* in the middle of an imitation of a Yellow-headed Caracara, *Milvago chimachima;* the jay was part of a flock I had seen previously amusing itself with various calls. When the hawk arrived and called, the jay copied it exactly, although it had not previously been using the caracara voice. Social and alarm vocalizations of jays are loud, simple cries or whistles.

Feeding, Behavior, and Intelligence

Being omnivorous, jays eat animals as well as seeds and berries. *Cyanocorax cyanopogon,* for example, will gorge itself with termites swarming out of a nest in a tree. The Purplish Jay, *C. cyanomelas,* will nibble at dry meat exposed to the sun at the forest edge. Jays eat small dead animals and steal bait from snares set for small mammals. Occasionally they depredate bird nests; the Curl-crested Jay, *C. cristatellus,* even breaks chicken eggs to extract the contents. Jays hunt at any level. The rural population in southern Brazil generally believes that *C. caeruleus* plants araucarias; in the northeast there is a corresponding belief that *C. cyanopogon* plants corn. These ideas have a basis in fact, for as with *C. caeruleus,* jays have the habit of hiding and storing seeds they then forget, which permits germination and growth of plants whose seeds are hidden in moss on the ground or in rotted tree ferns. Corvids living in cold regions make heavy use in winter of seeds they store in summer, even taking them out from under the snow. They probably find the seed stores either by memorizing the locales or by chance through constant search.

Young araucarias rooted high in other trees must truly be planted by jays. The fact that the jay does not stay in the tree where it found the nut, but flies to the next or a more distant tree to eat it, also serves to spread these seeds. To reach a cone located at the tip of a branch among the fronds, *C. caeruleus* may hover in the air or hop along the branch. It never picks up a nut from the ground; that is to say, it never recovers a dropped seed, so it is a good disseminating agent.

C. caeruleus does aid in araucaria dissemination by tearing apart cones on the branch. It eats, or carries away to eat later, only the odd nut; the majority fall, disappearing on the ground where they germinate if not found by other lovers of these flavorful delicacies, such as rats and pacas (see also Cracidae, "Feeding," re Dusky-legged Guan, *Penelope obscura,* "planting" erva mate). The jay ordinarily cuts the "head" of the nut, which is a great benefit to the seed since it is in this part that insects like to deposit their eggs and the larvae then invade the seed. *C. cyanopogon* likes the succulent fruits of the mandacuru (*Cereus jamacaru*), a tree cactus of the northeast, and *C. cristatellus* likes the pequi (*Caryocar* sp.), a typical cerrado plant. Small, hard seeds pass unharmed through the digestive tract of jays without losing their capacity to germinate.

Jays use their toes to hold food, and they share a technique with icterines: that of inserting the sharp bill in a crack which is then forced open by opening the mandibles ("gaping").

Flocks of *C. cyanopogon* (5, 10, or 12 individuals, usually probably representing families consisting of parents with offspring of more than one clutch), in search of food and guided by cleverness and curiosity, discover whatever is new in their area, be it food or danger. Thus they confront a snake (*acusacobras,* "snake-confronter," northeast) as readily as an owl, hawk, or concealed human. They approach immediately if someone makes a squeaking noise. The discovery is "discussed" with such clamor by the flock that this hubbub is an ideal warning for local fauna or for a human when a poisonous snake is involved.

In remote areas jays are tame and easy to observe. They adopt a multiplicity of postures. The most common demonstration is to lean forward and down while stretching the neck alternately to left and right and rhythmically lifting the tail. They fly well and sometimes move about high above the trees with a slightly undulating flight (*C. cristatellus*). The rhythm of the wing beats is sometimes altered. Descent to a perch is normally by gliding. Their agility in moving through trees, half jumping and half flying, reminds one of the Squirrel Cuckoo, *Piaya cayana,* or of a monkey (*Callithrix* sp.).

The vivacity of jays arises out of the fact that corvids possess, after psittacids, the second-highest intracerebral index of the Class Aves (18.95 for Common Raven, *Corvus corax;* 28.07 for Blue-and-yellow Macaw, *Ara ararauna,* Portmann 1947).

The following event could be folklore if it weren't true (J. C. Guix pers. comm.): in São Paulo at a feeder with fruit, the resident Rufous-bellied Thrush, *Turdus rufiventris,* had mounted guard and was driving away other birds. One morning a *Cyanocorax chrysops* was sneaking toward it; when about 8 to 10 m away, it called like a Roadside Hawk, *Rupornis magnirostris,* a common species in the area feared by other birds. The thrush fled, and the jay immediately perched on the feeder and began to eat the fruit.

The superior mental capacity of corvids has led many ornithologists, especially in Europe, to award them, not the fringillids, the highest rank in the sequence of Passerine families, a ranking constructed in an effort to express progressive phylogenetic evolution. This process has been criticized as being an anthropomorphic interpretation and because high mental capacity also exists in the psittacids, although in an analogous development.

Our jays (*Cyanocorax*), like many other birds—Dendrocolaptidae, Tyrannidae, and Fringillidae, for instance—use ants for plumage hygiene (as commonly believed), rubbing the live insects on the wings to take advantage of the effects of the formic acid.

Breeding

Mates usually preen each other, one bending down in front of the other to pull at the throat feathers (*C. cyanopogon*). The almost constant movement of the crown feathers is the best indicator of the emotional state of these birds. They are very pugnacious. In the Mato Grosso Pantanal, two male *C. cyanomelas* were found on the ground, exhausted after a bitter struggle, apparently over a nearby female (Aguirre 1958).

Little is known about the nesting of South American jays. The nest, located in a tree, may have a structure even sparser than that of a pigeon and is difficult to find (*C. cyanopogon,* "Whoever finds the nest of the White-naped Jay gets rich," northeastern proverb). *C. cristatellus* nests in cerrado trees (A. Negret pers. comm.). Sometimes a jay will occupy the abandoned stick nest of another bird. They lay three or four eggs. *C. caeruleus* eggs are light greenish blue with numerous light brown spots that are larger on the rounder end.

Incubation in non-Brazilian jay species takes 16 to 18 days, and the young, fed by the parents, develop slowly, leaving the nest after 23 or 24 days in the case of a Central American species, the White-tipped Brown-Jay, *C. mexicanus*. It is practically a rule that various individuals cooperate in attending a nest and its nestlings, such groups probably consisting of the parents with young of a previous clutch. In Japan in a completely banded population of a Eurasian species, the Azure-winged Magpie, *Cyanopica cyana,* it was noted that one individual helper appeared at four nests. Helpers help bring nesting material and build the nest, feed brooding females and nestlings, and clean the nest (carry away fecal sacs). Helpers do not participate in laying or brooding.

Habitat, Distribution, and Evolution

Jays are arboreal, living in gallery forests and groves. *Cyanocorax caeruleus* and *C. chrysops* also go into high forests. *C. cyanopogon* moves from forest to cerrado and is one of the most typical caatinga birds. Apparently *C. chrysops* and *C. cyanopogon* are geographically mutually exclusive. Although they are closely related both morphologically and ecologically, I know of no cases of hybridization between them. It seems they show allopatric distribution and do not invade each other's ranges, so can be considered allospecies forming a superspecies.

C. cristatellus inhabits open cerrado. In transition areas between open country and more densely forested places, *C. cristatellus* and *C. cyanopogon* may perch on the same branch, one after the other, without acknowledging each other's presence (northwestern Bahia). In certain regions *C. chrysops* lives regularly in the same forests as *C. caeruleus* (Rio Grande do Sul) or *C. cyanomelas* (Mato Grosso do Sul), reciprocally ignoring each other. *C. chrysops* rarely encounters *C. cristatellus*, although they are often sympatric (Mato Grosso, Pará), because they occupy different ecological niches. The various species are common in their typical habitats.

Parasites

Notable among parasites of our jays is the nematoid *Oxyspirura matogrossensis* which lives under the nictitating membrane of *C. cyanomelas*. E. Béraut of Rio de Janeiro extracted a still-unidentified leech of the same color as the eyelid from the eyelid of a *C. caeruleus* (see also Tinamidae, "Parasites"). A louse fly, *Ornithoica confluenta,* has been found on *C. chrysops*. I have noted that *C. cristatellus* nestlings in the cerrado are always severely parasitized by larvae of a small *Philornis* fly.

Reaction of Other Birds to Jays

Corvids are often feared by the local avifauna as a possible source of danger. I have observed that the Chivi Vireo, *Vireo chivi,* responds to the presence of *C. chrysops* as if it were a raptor.

Alleged Harmfulness, Use, Longevity, and Popularity

Jays are often accused of damaging corn, cane, vegetables, orchards, and pineapple and potato plantings. The harm, however, is not so great as to justify their elimination. Jays are sought as pets, especially *C. cyanopogon* of the northeast. They grow quite old in captivity: a *C. chrysops* in New York lived more than 37 years.

C. cyanopogon is one of the most popular birds of the northeast, and its cries may be symbolic of the region, taking on the role of "the voice of the caatinga."

AZURE JAY, *Cyanocorax caeruleus,* Gralha-azul
PL 37.1

39 cm. Robust, shiny blue southern species with forepart of body (head, foreneck, breast) black. Short, bristly feathers on forehead; eye dark. Nestling shows yellow mark at base of mandible (see "Morphology . . ."). VOICE: call and warning a loud, repeated, cawing, *kayo; gray, gray, gray; kuh-kuh-kuh.* Forests; likes Paraná pine groves (*Araucaria angustifolia*) but is not dependent on this vegetation, which it often leaves, at least at certain seasons (Rio Grande do Sul). Popular belief that this is a bird typically and exclusively of araucaria forests is myth. In some regions, e.g., Santa Catarina Island and along coast of Paraná, lives regularly in Atlantic rain forest where Paraná pine does not exist and never has. Even occurs on forested islands in Paranaguá Bay. Flies at some height from one forest to another, stops even in eucalyptus groves. Regarding its fame as a planter of araucaria, see "Feeding. . . ." It has been declared official bird of Paraná, just as araucaria has been named its official tree. São Paulo to Rio Grande do Sul, northern Argentina, Paraguay, sometimes alongside *C. chrysops*. See *C. cyanomelas.*

PURPLISH JAY, *Cyanocorax cyanomelas,* Gralha-do-pantanal

35 cm. Only in extreme southwest. Similar to *C. caeruleus* but differs in color: has soft, violet color that also invades black or sooty forepart of body. From a distance in forest shade appears all black (see Hyacinth Macaw, *Anodorhynchus hyacinthinus,* alternative Brazilian name = *arara-preta*). VOICE: a monotonous *gray,* a whistled *tshEEew.* Cerradão and gallery forests far from civilization. Southern Mato Grosso (Cuiabá, Coxim, Pantanal, edge of Rio Paraguay) to Bolivia, Paraguay, Argentina. It has been proposed to group *C. cyanomelas* and *C. caeruleus* as allospecies forming a superspecies, or even to consider them geographic races of the same species (Short 1975), but this needs to be supported by more data (existence or otherwise of intermediate individuals, voice comparisons). Sometimes alongside *C. chrysops*. Also called *Aka-á* (Guarani, Mato Grosso).

In Amazonia there are two other violet-colored species whose color extends to the belly but that have extensive bluish white on the back of the head. They are:

VIOLACEOUS JAY, *Cyanocorax violaceus*
The Purus to Roraima and farther north.

AZURE-NAPED JAY, *Cyanocorax heilprini*
Upper Rio Negro, Venezuela, Colombia. Has bluish white "mustache," white-tipped tail.

CAYENNE JAY, *Cyanocorax cayanus*
Similar to *C. chrysops* but with back of head, face pattern, belly, and tail-tip white. North of Amazon in Amapá (Oiapoque), northern Pará (Rio Paru), Manaus (Amazonas), Roraima, the Guianas, Venezuela.

Fig. 280. Curl-crested Jay, *Cyanocorax cristatellus*.

CURL-CRESTED JAY, *Cyanocorax cristatellus*,
Gralha-do-campo BR Fig. 280

33 cm. Typical open-country species of central Brazil with long wings, relatively short tail. Unmistakable with elongated frontal crest, separate from top of head. Mantle dark violet blue, belly and end two-thirds of tail white. Immature recognizable even at 6 months by short crest. VOICE: a loud *gray, graa, gray-gray-gray,* sometimes repeated 8–10 times. Cerrado, even in sparse, sunny stretches interrupted by open country. Piauí, Maranhão, and southern Pará (Cachimbo) to Mato Grosso, Goiás, Minas Gerais, São Paulo. Formerly called *Uroleuca.* Locally sympatric with *C. cyanopogon* or *C. chrysops,* although ecologically distinct. Also called *Gralha-do-peito-branco, Pega* (Piauí).

PLUSH-CRESTED JAY, *Cyanocorax chrysops*,
Gralha-picaça

34 cm. Slender-appearing woodland species of southern and central Brazil, closely related to *C. cyanopogon.* Black feathers on top of head form high, velvet cushion, rising from hind head like a ball. Spot behind eye, shiny whitish blue nape, blue pattern under eye, and "mustache" all attract attention. Iris sulfur yellow. Belly and end of tail yellowish white (pure white in Amazonian populations, *C. c. diesingii* and *C. c. inesperatus,* Madeira, Amazonas, as far as Serra do Cachimbo, Pará).

VOICE: a metallic *kuh-kuhkuh (-kuh)* with frequent changes of pitch (difference of a third); a resonant *iyok-iyok-iyok, wow, caang-caang,* ventriloquial notes, tremulos, sounds of tapping on wood, gargles, croaks. Song babbling, full of perfect imitations of other birds and mammals, e.g., *Rupornis magnirostris;* Boat-billed Heron, *Cochlearius cochlearius; Penelope* guans; *Cebus* monkeys. Imitations are realistic, for they are given one by one, in isolation. I heard a wild individual imitate chatter of a tame parrot in our camp at edge of woods, including various Portuguese words. Most were not recognizable but some, such as *loro,* "parrot," and *Raimundo,* name of one of our crew, were. Imitation of human voice was in this case processed through a parrot. Same jay also imitated the *piewrrr* used by local residents to call their chickens. Jay vocalizations can be very soft and delicate, reminiscent of an emberizine song.

Forest. Argentina, Paraguay, and Bolivia to Mato Grosso (southern Mato Grosso, upper Xingu and Tapajós), Amazonas (lower Madeira), Pará (Cachimbo), and Rio Grande do Sul to São Paulo. Sometimes alongside *C. caeruleus* (Santa Catarina, Rio Grande do Sul) or *C. cyanomelas* (Mato Grosso); in forest surrounded by cerrado, it is within hearing distance of voice of *C. cristatellus* (Mato Grosso, Pará). I do not know of any meeting with *C. cyanopogon,* probably its geographic replacement. Also called *Buka-ne-héne* (Trumai, northern Mato Grosso), *Aka-á, Uraca, Gráia* (southern Mato Grosso).

WHITE-NAPED JAY, *Cyanocorax cyanopogon*,
Cancã BR PL 37.2

31 cm. Abundant in northeast, very similar to *C. chrysops* but with sooty instead of dark blue mantle, black wings and tail instead of blue, belly and end of tail always pure white. VOICE: call ("voice of the caatinga," see "Alleged Harmfulness . . .") *kuhkuh-kuhkuh-kuhkuh;* warning *gheeeh, ghep-ghep; gray, gray, gray; krrro,* similar to noise of reco-reco [a Brazilian percussion instrument made of notched bamboo]. Song extremely varied; depends greatly on imitations of local fauna, copying perfectly, for instance, cries of Burrowing Owl, *Speotyto cunicularia,* and resonant phrases of Red-throated Caracara, *Daptrius americanus* (Rio das Mortes, Mato Grosso). See "Vocalization" on imitation of a *Milvago chimachima* that suddenly appeared. Song reminiscent of varied chatter, chirping, and huffing of European Starling, *Sturnus vulgaris.* Same individual often vocalizes with varying volume and pitch, like *C. chrysops.* Among voices of caatinga birds, *C. cyanopogon* is dominant. Dense cerrado, cerradão, rather open places in gallery forest, caatinga. All of northeastern and eastcentral Brazil to southeastern Pará (Gorotire), Goiás, eastern Mato Grosso (Rio das Mortes), Minas Gerais, Bahia. Invading Espírito Santo, taking advantage of deforestation. Locally in northwestern Bahia in same area as *C. cristatellus,* from which it is easily distinguished by voice. *C. cyanopogon* usually cries *kuh, kuh, kuh; C. cristatellus gray, gray, gray.* Also called *Quem-quem, Pion-pion* (Bahia).

Corvidae Bibliography
See also General Bibliography

Aguirre, A. 1958. *A caça e a pesca no Pantanal de Mato Grosso.* Rio de Janeiro: Min. Agricultura.
Anjos, L. de. 1988. "Eto-Ecologia e Análise do sistema de com-

unicação sonora e visual da gralha azul, *Cyanocorax cae-ruleus.*" Thesis. Univ. Estat. Campinas.

Hardy, J. W. 1969. A taxonomic revision of the New World Jays. *Condor* 71:360–75.

Hardy, J. W. 1976. Comparative breeding behavior and ecology of *Cyanocorax melanocyanea* and *C. sanblasiana*. *Wilson Bull.* 88: 96–120.

Hardy, J. W. 1984. *Voices of New World Jays, Crows and Their Allies*. Gainesville, Fla.: Ara Records.

Komeda, S., S. Yamagishi, and M. Fujioka. 1987. Cooperative breeding in *Cyanopica cyana* living in a region of heavy snow-fall. *Condor* 89:835–41.

Rodrigues, H. O. 1963. *Rev. Bras. Biol.* 23:239–42. [Nematoda]

Woolfenden, G. E., and J. W. Fitzpatrick. 1984. *The Florida Scrub Jay: Demography of a Cooperative-breeding Bird*. Princeton, N.J.: Princeton University Press.

Zusi, R. L. 1987. A feeding adaptation of the jaw articulation in New World Jays (Corvidae). *Auk* 104:665–80.

FAMILY TROGLODYTIDAE: WRENS (18)

This group, although remotely descended from Old World birds (predecessors of the Muscicapidae), is restricted to the Americas except for a single, non-Brazilian species, the Winter Wren, *Troglodytes troglodytes,* which has invaded Eurasia, conquering from the Far East to Europe and thereby posing a zoogeographic mystery. There are Pleistocene fossils (100,000 years B.P.) from Florida. The greatest diversification of the family has occurred in tropical America. The House Wren, *Troglodytes aedon,* with a range from Canada to Tierra del Fuego, is one of the most popular birds in all Brazil.

Morphology and Identification

With somber colors, species of the same genus, such as *Thryothorus,* are generally very similar, being best distinguished by the color pattern of the head, especially the face. Similarity with various Suboscines and other Oscines is purely analogous.

The *Microcerculus,* with extremely short tails, strong feet, and semiterrestrial habits, are much like tapaculos of the *Scytalopus* genus, which, to a certain extent, they replace in Amazonia. It is difficult to give an exact idea of the size of these species, for the legs (tarsus and toes) do not enter into calculation of the total length measurement (tip of bill to tip of tail), and in the *Microcerculus* they are much longer than the tail, which in museum specimens is hidden between the wing tips. The *Campylorhynchus,* with an elongated shape and large tail, may resemble thrushes. Sexes are similar.

The Black-capped Donacobius, *Donacobius atricapillus,* previously classified with the Mimidae, has been transferred to the Troglodytidae, near *Campylorhynchus*—a solution that is also unconvincing because of its tail movements, open-cup type nest, etc.

In Brazil the name *uirapuru* refers to species both of wrens and manakins, creating considerable confusion.

Vocalization

The high-quality, versatile vocalizations of this family are of special interest but difficult to paraphrase. The wealth of motifs is impressive. I have observed an individual Moustached Wren, *Thryothorus genibarbis,* sing four times within 20 minutes, each time rendering a basically different song. No two individuals have the same voice. In *Thryothorus* and *Henicorhina* each individual of a pair sings a different song in duet. Each sex enjoys roughly the same vocal riches. Members of a *Thryothorus* pair, when established on a territory, synchronize their songs perfectly and develop modalities of phrasing different from those of neighboring pairs. Nobody would suspect it is two individuals singing, and the researcher can only determine this when situated between them, something quite difficult because they normally perch close to each other. Pair members differ slightly in phraseology and accentuation, the female perhaps intoning a discrete counterpoint to the song of the male. Sometimes there is a surprisingly sudden acceleration of the tempo. The rhythm may also change from one stanza to the next. To achieve such complicated synchronization each pair member must learn the individual phrasing of its companion. This means that only the true mate is capable of giving the correct "answer"—a factor that must be a decisive help in maintaining the pair bond. One must conclude that a third individual, whose song is not well adjusted to the situation, would be unable to interfere successfully with the duet of the mated pair.

Field identification of certain *Thryothorus* species by their song may be difficult or impossible. Two related species living sympatrically customarily evolve contrasting songs. This was found among Mexican *Thryothorus* in a comparison of ten species (Brown and Lemon 1980).

Dueting also occurs in the *Campylorhynchus* and *Donacobius atricapillus,* accompanied by rhythmic tail movements. Dueting is provoked by the dueting of neighboring pairs. The calls and songs of *Donacobius* are among the most powerful voices of the wetlands environment.

Duet-singing wrens are apparently long-time residents of the same area and are probably mated for life. Seemingly it is not always the male who initiates the duet. Phrasing of the duet is not entirely individual, for certain elements are used by various individuals of the species, or at least of the population of a certain region, thereby forming a dialect. The dialogue does not always function mechanically either, for sometimes one of the singers begins after or stops before the other. Large-scale dueting occurs only in the breeding season. Duets reflect an aggressive attitude toward rivals and constitute a strong territorial manifestation.

In assessing female song we must remember that female birds are heterogametic, that is, they possess hormones of both sexes. It can be conjectured that song originally existed in both sexes but that in some cases the female preserved and even perfected the ability to sing while in other cases it was lost.

Although female song in response to the male occurs in various Brazilian birds, such as in some Suboscine Furnariidae and Formicariidae, it would be difficult to find other dueting so perfect as that of *Thryothorus*. In other birds (including *Troglodytes aedon*) it is more common for the female to respond after the male has finished. Some non-Passerines, such as Capitonidae, also duet.

The phenomenon of dueting has been diligently researched in recent years in Africa, especially with voices of *Laniarius* shrikes (Thorpe 1972).

One distinctive vocalization of *Thryothorus* is a solitary territorial call, probably sung only by the male. The most simple phrase, loud and not repeated, may recall the sonorous call of an *Icterus* oriole (see Long-billed Wren, *Thryothorus longirostris*). Each territory holder has its own phraseology, different from its neighbor's. Other less characteristic phrases, quite varied and sometimes repeated in long series, are sung by solitary *T. longirostris* individuals, apparently of either sex. These change during the day, and according to popular belief, vary depending on whether the weather is good or bad. Other *Thryothorus* vocalizations can be classified as songs or calls, such as a short, melodious phrase that may be the prelude to the solitary territorial song of *T. longirostris*.

The ability to sing is evident shortly after the young bird abandons the nest (*Thryothorus, Troglodytes*). The song of the immature is different from that of the adult, being very soft and sounding like a conversation, without any well-defined character. Although the tendency to repeat motifs (*Thryothorus*) is noticeable, there are no duets.

The Musician Wren, *Cyphorhinus aradus,* enjoys the greatest fame as a singer. *Microcerculus* song is also unique, being outstanding for its musical qualities as well as for its extraordinary length. I have noted regional differences in the song of the Southern Nightingale Wren, *M. marginatus.* The *Campylorhynchus* voice is typically ventriloquial in character and can be recognized immediately in all species of the genus.

Brazilian wrens sing all year except during molt. Their singing is intensified during the breeding season, which may be prolonged. The Thrush-like Wren, *Campylorhynchus turdinus,* sings at dawn; its voice periodically becomes one of the most notable in certain regions, as in the forests north of the Rio Doce in Espírito Santo. I have sometimes had the impression that the vigorous singing of *Thryothorus* stimulates singing activity in other nearby, nontroglodyte birds. All species have low warning cries (*tac, ta, ta, ta, krrra,* etc.) that immediately reveal them as Troglodytidae.

Troglodytes aedon can emit a snap that may be increased to a real rattle, apparently produced in the articulation of the mandibles and not by snaps of the bill. It is a sign of excitement (instrumental music).

Feeding

Wrens are omnivorous. Arthropods and their larvae predominate in their menu. *Cyphorhinus aradus* also takes spiders, harvestmen, and even millipedes, not being bothered by the defensive glands or caustic secretions of these animals. Sometimes pieces of the miniscule bones of geckos, seeds, and remains of small fruits appear in the stomach contents of *Troglodytes aedon* and other species. Just one pair of *T. aedon* catches scores of insects each day. They beat larger insects against branches to kill them, or tear off the wings. I have seen this same technique used by a *T. aedon* holding a chicken feather in its bill. I have seen *Microcerculus* and *Cyphorhinus* take advantage of army ants, which in their marches cause thousands of insects and other small animals to leave their hiding places and become easy prey for birds. *T. aedon* has been seen to start foraging under intense artificial light.

Behavior

Wrens are all restless, even the larger ones such as the *Campylorhynchus.* They sometimes hop along the ground through the undergrowth. Species recognition and control over the mate must be largely visual but would function only over short distances in the heavy thickets that are the regular habitat of these birds. *Thryothorus* frequently reveal their presence by the noise they make stirring and turning dry leaves at low levels or on the ground, resembling furnariids such as *Automolus* and *Sclerurus.* Those species best adapted to terrestrial life walk and run on the ground like diminutive rails or certain antbirds. *Microcerculus,* when walking on the ground with long steps, constantly tilt the body in the peculiar fashion of the Spotted Sandpiper, *Actitis macularia.* Wren flights are short, although their wings are long. A *Microcerculus* comes flying fast when lured by an imitation of its voice. *Cyphorhinus aradus* frequently appears as a member of mixed flocks (see also "Folklore . . ."). *Donacobius* makes peculiar lateral tail movements.

Wrens sleep in their nests, sometimes the pair together (e.g., *Thryothorus, Campylorhynchus*), or even the whole family, but an individual may make a small nest in which to sleep alone. They like to bathe by immersion, especially when already partially wet from rain (*Troglodytes aedon*).

Campylorhynchus takes dust baths on the ground, sometimes several birds together.

Breeding

Pairs are affectionate, engaging in mutual preening (e.g., *Campylorhynchus turdinus*). When members of a pair duet they stay close together, opening wings and tail, trembling and displaying the bars on flight and tail feathers (*Thryothorus genibarbis*).

Wrens build a covered nest with a side entrance. *Thryothorus* construct a long extension above the entrance that hides it completely so the opening points downward. The chamber is a deep basket. Construction material is straw, roots, etc. The nest is placed 1–2 m high in branches. The Buff-breasted Wren, *T. leucotis,* builds its nest (fig. 281) over water. In a small area monitored in Minas Gerais, eight *T. genibarbis* nests were built on cansação, or ortigão (Loasaceae), a stinging, nettlelike plant, an eminently antipredatory adaptation (A. Studer). *C. turdinus* makes a great ball of soft material, including rags and tow, high in trees; sometimes (Mato Grosso) it uses the stick nests of *Phacellodomus* thornbirds (Furnariidae) as a base on which to build its own nest, stuffing everything generously with feathers and other flexible material. The Grass Wren, *Cistothorus platensis,* hides its ball-shaped nest in the grass. More experienced male Marsh Wrens, *C. palustris,* of North America build the best nests. This is advantageous for their females and young (Verner and Engselsen 1970).

Wrens are generally much inclined toward nest building. In addition to the nest for breeding, *Thryothorus longirostris* makes a sleeping nest for one individual that has a shallower basket and lacks the extension that points the entrance downward. The *Campylorhynchus* and *Cyphorhinus* are said to try

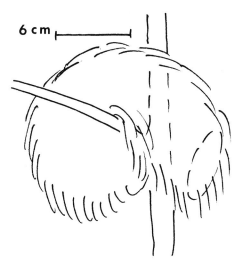

6 cm

Fig. 281. Sketch of nest of the Buff-breasted Wren, *Thryothorus leucotis.* The entrance is at the right. Mato Grosso Pantanal. Original, H. Sick.

to build their nests on trees (except *Cecropia* spp.) harboring large colonies of biting ants, for these provide excellent protection against enemies. The ants do not attack the birds living in their midst. *Donacobius* makes a deep basket swathed with spider webbing, fixed to tall grass or other low plants in or at the edge of a marsh. The eggs are light ferruginous, the color denser at the rounder end. Its chicks have red mouths and three black spots on the tongue, one on the tip and two farther back. The mouth of *Donacobius* adults becomes entirely black. *Troglodytes aedon* will nest in and line any kind of cavity, be it a hollow tree, hole in a house, or abandoned Rufous Hornero, *Furnarius rufus* (Furnariidae), nest. *T. aedon* nests have been found in an open drawer and in the pocket of an old pair of pants forgotten in a shed. One pair settled into the body of a pickup truck and was not disturbed even when it was occasionally used, the female incubating and both parents later feeding the chicks (Rio de Janeiro). Rats sometimes take over nests, such as those of *Thryothorus.*

Troglodytes aedon eggs are light red, densely speckled with darker spots mixed with flecks of pale gray. This species is among the birds that continue to lay for a considerable time after losing their original clutch. The normal clutch is 3 to 4 eggs (Rio de Janeiro). A female whose eggs were constantly removed produced 30 eggs in 43 days (experiment carried out in the United States).

Eggs are incubated only by the mother and hatch after 15 days. The parents take turns feeding the nestlings, which leave the nest after 17 or 18 days in *T. aedon,* a period also valid for *Donacobius atricapillus.* The nest is clean, the fecal sacs being removed or sometimes swallowed by the parents. Apparently the parents also catch parasites infesting the nest cavity. The female *T. aedon* sometimes begins to lay again when she is still caring for the grown young of the previous clutch. These later help feed the younger siblings. In Rio de Janeiro *T. aedon* has been known to lay in June and July (winter); in São Paulo and Rio Grande do Sul the reproductive period is restricted to the summer months. The presence of one or more individuals associated with the breeding pair is regularly observed with *Campylorhynchus* and *Donacobius. T. aedon* is frequently polygamous in the northern part of its range.

After the young leave the nest the family still maintains contact for some time. I have seen this with *Cyphorhinus aradus,* for instance, while it associated with mixed flocks of other birds, such as antbirds, moving through lower levels of the Amazonian forest.

Perils

Among the dangers *T. aedon* face near their nests are spider webs (*Nephila* sp.) on houses, where the birds infrequently become entangled. I once found a *T. aedon* on the ground with all its toes firmly entwined with webbing. Sometimes the House Sparrow, *Passer domesticus*, expels *T. aedon* from its nesting place in a house. Eggs of the Shiny Cowbird, *Molothrus bonariensis*, are occasionally found in *T. aedon* nests. In Ecuador *Thryothorus* species are also parasitized by this cowbird.

Habitat, Distribution, and Evolution

The majority of wrens are forest birds living at lower levels, with the exception of *Campylorhynchus turdinus*, which inhabits the canopy. *Cistothorus* uses grasslands or marshes. *T. aedon*, adaptable to any habitat, has become perfectly synanthropic; locally it is a wetland bird (Minas Gerais).

Certain *Thryothorus* live sympatrically and sometimes syntopically, although slight ecological differences may exist, as in the preference for a higher or lower level; they feed in a very similar manner (the different bill sizes must indicate trophic differences), breed at the same period, and make similar nests.

Various species (e.g., *Campylorhynchus*, *Cistothorus*) have widely discontinuous ranges. Possibly some populations have become extinct because of ecological changes. *Cistothorus platensis*, a very small species whose flight capacity seems limited, has managed to colonize an immense area, from Canada to Tierra del Fuego and the Falkland Islands. Populations of this species on the South American continent are very sparse. In Amazonia rivers frequently impose barriers that appear to be insuperable for small birds. The range of *T. aedon*, which includes *musculus*, in the three Americas is unsurpassed by any other Passerine of the hemisphere.

Parasites and Diseases

Wrens are among the Amazonian birds having the highest levels of antibodies against arboviruses (see Formicariidae, "Parasites . . .").

Troglodytes aedon nestlings are sometimes severely parasitized by bird botflies (*Philornis angustifrons*, Rio de Janeiro). I found ten larvae on one nestling. Larvae that are squeezed out and fall in reach of nestlings are eaten by them.

T. aedon is occasionally host to louse flies (Hippoboscidae). One that has been identified is *Ornithoica confluenta*, a species also found on other birds (Corvidae, Ramphastidae).

Folklore and Popularity

The name *uirapuru* is used for various Amazonian birds but most commonly for certain Pipridae that are considered talismans or mascots. In the upper Amazon this same significance is given to *Cyphorhinus aradus* when it is killed and mummified according to magic ritual. The *Microcerculus* are considered hunting charms, called *uirapuru-veado*, "deer-uirapuru." The bird must be caught on a Thursday or Friday with a waxing moon, according to the curious belief of local countrypeople (Tapajós, Pará).

In legend, *C. aradus*, with its beautiful song, attracts other birds which form a flock around it. In reality this species follows an already existing flock searching for food and has no role different from the other birds there, which have no interest in its song. This became the subject of a musical work by the Brazilian composer Villa-Lobos: "O pássaro encantado, o uirapuru," "The enchanted bird, the Musician Wren."

Outside Amazonia even more mystery and sensationalism is created around the uirapuru, exploiting the ignorance of uninformed people about a bird that is not unusual. To enhance interest in the uirapuru, absurdities have been invented such as "the uirapuru sings only one week per year, during five minutes each morning."

THRUSH-LIKE WREN, *Campylorhynchus turdinus*, Catatau, Garrinchão   PL 38.7

20.5 cm; 39 g. Large, thrush-sized, with long tail and bill. Lives in canopy. Population of southern Mato Grosso and Bolivia (*C. t. unicolor*) uniformly cream color on underside, contrasting with *C. t. turdinus* (and other subspecies, see Pl 38.7) of northeastern Brazil with brown speckled underparts. VOICE: far-reaching, a rhythmic, sonorous, ventriloquial song like sound of blowing in water; e.g., *kyoh-KYO-kyok*, *cho-cho-CHOL*, *ko-kiOKe-KOke*, with 1–2 diatonic notes (Espírito Santo, *C. t. turdinus*); a slightly ascending sequence of 4 syllables, *yok-glok-glok-glok* (Mato Grosso, *C. t. unicolor*). Pairs duet, with phrasing of female different from male. Lofty, vine-covered trees of primary forest (Espírito Santo) or isolated trees in open country and in palms (Pantanal, Mato Grosso). Panama to Bolivia, Mato Grosso, Rio Grande do Sul, northwestern Brazil to south of Amazon (Amazonas, Pará) as far as the Tocantins; Roraima, northern Pará; Maranhão to Goiás, Bahia, northern Espírito Santo. Also called *Nicolau* (Mato Grosso), *Rouxinol* (Maranhão), *Catiço* (Minas Gerais).

BICOLORED WREN, *Campylorhynchus griseus*

Closely related to *C. turdinus*, with cap and stripe through eye blackish, upperparts uniformly brown, underside pure white, outer tail feathers with large white spots. VOICE: sonorous and ventriloquial, with much the same character as *turdinus*. Canopy of densely foliaged trees; also around houses and occasionally enters under roof tiles. In extreme north to Colombia, Venezuela, Guyana.

BLACK-CAPPED DONACOBIUS, *Donacobius atricapillus*, Japacanim, Batuquira   PL 37.3

23 cm; 43 g. Unique marsh bird, thrush sized with short, rounded wings, lengthy, graduated tail. Black and yellow;

wings and tail show impressive white markings when opened. Has an area of yellow, thickened, bare skin at side of neck, wrinkled when bird is at rest but inflated when singing. Immature has whitish postocular streak, brown instead of yellow iris, lacks yellow spot on neck. VOICE: loud cries, given with bill wide open so black interior of mouth is exposed, while perched on tips of reeds. Warning *shrra-schrra, kreh-kreh;* resonant sequences, sometimes prolonged, with motifs repeated various times, e.g., *BEEek-booIK BEEeh-booIK,* etc., *tseh-tseh-tseh . . . , tew-tew-tew . . . , gooEE-gooEE-gooEE,* etc., song sometimes sung together with female (whose voice is a bit different) perched nearby (duet). Does not imitate other birds. In a pair display they open tails and fan them laterally. On other occasions they shake tail vigorously to sides. Reed beds, where it is frequently dominant bird species. Seeks food (arthropods) in interior of marsh and on water surface, thus remaining hidden most of time. Panama to Bolivia, Argentina, throughout Brazil south to Mato Grosso, Paraná. May recall Dark-billed Cuckoo, *Coccyzus melacoryphus* (which lacks white on wing, among other differences). Also called *Saci-do-brejo, Sabiá-do-brejo* (Minas Gerais), *Assobia-cachorro* (Rio de Janeiro), *Gaturamo-do-brejo* (Espírito Santo), *Casaca-de-couro* (Amazonas), *Pássaro-angu.*

Donacobius classification is a problem. Grouping it with the Troglodytidae is more satisfactory than other linkages. The species most closely related to it are the *Campylorhynchus.* By analogy it resembles a *Coccyzus* cuckoo.

TOOTH-BILLED WREN, *Odontorchilus cinereus,* Cambaxirra-cinzenta   BR

11.8 cm. Male similar to *Troglodytes aedon* but uniformly dark gray above, cap brownish, tail light gray with wide black bars. Upper Madeira to lower Tapajós (Santarém) and Xingu (Iriri). See Gray Wren, *Thryothorus griseus.*

GRASS (= SEDGE) WREN, *Cistothorus platensis,* Corruíra-do-campo   PL 38.5

10.2 cm; 7 g. Small, open-country wren with back streaked black and white, wings and tail clearly barred, white superciliary. VOICE: quiet, inconspicuous song with prolonged, staccato, fast, even-tempoed phrase composed of short motifs separated by brief intervals, each motif consisting of a sound repeated 3–4 times, frequently interspersed with a croaked motif and another chirped one, sometimes the 2 motifs combined, *t, t, t, t-klieh, klieh, klieh tak, tak, tak-glew, glew, glew, glew trrr.* Character of song recalls other marshbirds; phenomenon of "habitat voice" again (see Emberizinae, "Vocalization"). Lives hidden in tall grass and open marshes, revealing its presence by song. Locally from Canada to Argentina and Chile, with few records for Brazil: Goiás, Federal District, Minas Gerais, São Paulo, Paraná, Santa Catarina, Rio Grande do Sul (see "Habitat . . ."). It is one of the outstanding colonizers among wrens.

MOUSTACHED WREN, *Thryothorus genibarbis,* Garrinchão-pai-avô

17 cm. Largest *Thryothorus,* with color very similar to *T. leucotis* but usually distinguishable by wide black malar stripe and pure white superciliary. VOICE: sharp, loud, with tone similar to *leucotis* but different cadence, e.g., *tirrAYo-okLUK, dwewo-WEEo, schrr-bo-WEEo, pai-avoh, didew-didi-dewdo,* etc. Each of these phrases is repeated (see "Vocalization"); warning *wew-tew-tew.* Forest edge and interior. South of Amazon and Solimões southward to Bolivia, Mato Grosso, and Goiás, northeast and east (Minas Gerais, Rio de Janeiro); also Venezuela, Peru. Also called *Piô-vovô* (Minas Gerais), *Pai-avô* (Maranhão).

CORAYA WREN, *Thryothorus coraya,* Garrinchão-coraia

Widely distributed in Amazonia. Similar to *T. genibaris* but with lower cheeks intensely and solidly black. VOICE: call a loud and typical *chaAYo.* The Guianas and Venezuela to southern edge of Amazon as far as lower Tapajós and Tocantins and Amapá.

BUFF-BREASTED WREN, *Thryothorus leucotis,* Garrinchão-de-barriga-vermelha   PL 38.2

14.5 cm. Widely distributed in interior. Very similar to *T. genibarbis;* wings and tail finely barred with black, similar to congeners; belly reddish. VOICE: song a series of well-pronounced and sonorous motifs, with male and female of mated pair singing antiphonally; one of pair sings, e.g., *juh-dulT, juh-dulT-juh-dulT,* etc; other sings *TREEbie-luh, TREEbie-luh, TREEbie-luh,* etc.; same individual or pair will periodically change motifs, e.g., *caDAY-mayoo-boy, cadaDAY-mayoo-boy,* etc., *tebeNEEru, tebeNEEru,* etc. *DAYu-divahn, DAYu-divahn,* etc., *bebiZHOO, bebiZHOO,* etc., *beniro-KWEEra, beniro-KWEEra,* etc.; call and warning *dro-KAHT, chrraaaa-chrraaaa, ta, ta, ta.* Lives low above ground in densest thickets, like other *Thryothorus.* Riverine brush and gallery forests. Panama to Amazonia, central Brazil, Mato Grosso, Goiás, São Paulo, Minas Gerais, Piauí, Maranhão, the Guianas, Venezuela. Locally in same region and even in same area as other *Thryothorus,* especially *genibarbis* (Mato Grosso). Also called *Marido-é-dia.*

FAWN-BREASTED WREN, *Thryothorus guarayanus*

Closely related to *T. leucotis.* Only from western Mato Grosso to Bolivia.

LONG-BILLED WREN, *Thryothorus longirostris,* Garrinchão-de-bico-grande   BR

Dominant species along coast, very similar to *T. leucotis* but with extremely long bill (25 mm instead of 18 mm). VOICE: a sonorous *jip-JEEP joh, joh, joh, joh;* territorial song of a lone individual (see "Vocalization") *newt-je-HEW.* Male and female sing slightly different phrases, one singing *de-lewIT-de-deweh*, other *dewLIT-deweh-dewLIT-deweh*, superimposing them in a duet; phrases not as loud as territorial song are repeated by both sexes without synchronization; call *jo-WIT, dwo-doIT;* warning *cha-cha-cha, charrr.* Forest edge, dense secondary forest, caatinga (where voice may be confused with whistle of Troupial, *Icterus i. jamacaii*). Also frequents mangroves. Piauí to Santa Catarina, also ex-Guanabara, on hills covered with dense capoeira. May be geographic replacement of *leucotis*. Also called *Curruiruçu, Rouxinol* (Bahia), *Framato* (Ilha Grande, Rio de Janeiro), *Cambaxirra-grande*.

GRAY WREN, *Thryothorus griseus*   BR

12.5 cm. Gray, similar to *Odontorchilus cinereus* but with very short tail. Only south of upper Amazon, from the Javari to upper Purus.

HOUSE WREN, *Troglodytes aedon,* Corruíra, Cambaxirra   PL 38.6

12.2 cm. One of our most familiar and common birds. Brown wings and tail with thin, black barring, back uniformly brown (unlike *Cistothorus platensis*), underparts light brownish with pinkish cast. VOICE: male song short, fast, continuous stanza of high, resonant notes; female responds with sequence of harsh, monotonous tones; warning *kret-kret,* etc. When excited male sometimes produces cracking noises (*tak*) and in presence of female even mixes in rattles at intervals with songs. Anywhere, typically ubiquitous, around houses, in gardens, even enters into rooms, where it sings. Also in center of cities, e.g., Rio de Janeiro. In most diverse natural habitats, e.g., forest edges, cerrado, caatinga, marshes, open country in high mountains of southeast, etc. Occupies islands along coast, e.g., Ilha Alfavaca (Rio de Janeiro), Ilhas Moleques do Sul (Santa Catarina). North and South America from Canada to Argentina, Chile, all of Brazil. Lumping Neotropical form *T. musculus* with *T. aedon* of North America (which breeds as far south as southern Mexico) is justified by character of voices, which are same or form a cline. Although normally people have nothing against the companionship of this tireless singer, which also helps so efficiently in eliminating household insects, there is a local belief in Rio de Janeiro that it brings bad luck. There is a cinnamon-colored mutant (Minas Gerais). Also called *Cur-ruíra, Garricha, Curipuruí* (Pará, Amazonas), *Rouxinol* (Maranhão), *Barattenvogel* (Santa Catarina).

TEPUI WREN, *Troglodytes rufulus*
Only in extreme north, Roraima to Venezuela.

WHITE-BREASTED WOOD-WREN, *Henicorhina leucosticta,* Uirapuru-de-peito-branco   PL 38.1

11 cm. Semiterrestrial forest species with large feet, found north of lower Amazon. Characterized by black-and-white design on head and by pure white of underparts, which stands out in deep shade of its habitat. VOICE: song reminiscent of *Thryothorus* but lower in volume, with some high cheeping, e.g., *BEEeh-BEEeh-BEEeh tsililili, tsewkeLEE-klo, klo, klo;* warning *ta-ta-ta, trrr, kat.* Heavy thickets inside high forest. Hops through lowest branches with tail carried vertically, perches on vertical shoots, descends to ground frequently to catch insects. Behavior may recall Collared Gnatwren, *Microbates collaris,* sometimes its neighbor, or *Thryothorus coraya.* Amapá and Roraima to Mexico.

SOUTHERN NIGHTINGALE WREN, *Microcerculus marginatus,* Uirapuru-veado   PL 38.4

10.7 cm. Forest wren of Amazonia with long, relatively slender bill, disproportionately large feet, extremely short tail. Upperparts uniformly chestnut, throat and breast shiny white mixed with brown edges, giving a scaly appearance. VOICE: song a sequence of limpid whistles, both short and prolonged, with very special, sharp timbre. There is one relatively short song, another surprisingly extended one that may be prolonged for some minutes. Latter begins with some animated, consecutive notes, e.g., *dew-DEE-dew-dew-dew,* but immediately turns more pensive, with intervals between notes becoming successively longer, to 2, 4, and 5 seconds; each new note is a repetition of previous one (sometimes there are 3–4 repetitions) or is higher or lower, with up or down leaps of, for example, a third or fourth interspersed; interval of entire stanza covers a sixth or an octave; there are perfect, descending scales; finally intervals are prolonged to 8–9 seconds until stanza finally dies out. Separation of parts of this song is unique among bird voices of Brazil so far as I can judge. Phrasing and timbre may resemble Rufous-brown Solitaire, *Myadestes leucogenys.* Warning *tsack.* Interior of tall forests, walks and runs on ground with long steps as if it were a diminutive rail, with body slightly tilting. Sometimes clings to side of heavy tree trunks. Widely distributed in Amazonia, except for left bank of lower Amazon east of Rio Negro. South to Bolivia, northern Mato Grosso (Teles Pires), Pará (Cururu, Cachimbo, Belém), and to Venezuela, Mexico. Found in same terra-firme forests as *Cyphorhinus aradus* (Tapajós). Sought on Tapajós, Pará, as a talisman for deer hunts. Responds to imitation of its voice.

FLUTIST WREN, *Microcerculus ustulatus*
Only in extreme north, Roraima to Venezuela.

WING-BANDED WREN, *Microcerculus bambla,* Uirapuru-de-asa-branca

10.6 cm. Very similar in aspect and behavior to *M. marginatus* but with different coloring: wings black, crossed by wide and prominent white streak; foreneck and breast gray; belly densely vermiculated. North of Amazon: Amapá (replacing *marginatus*), northern Pará (Óbidos), north of Solimões, Manacapuru, Amazonas, Ecuador, Venezuela, the Guianas.

MUSICIAN WREN, *Cyphorhinus aradus,*
Uirapuru-verdadeiro, Músico   PL 38.3

12.6 cm. Amazonian species famous for song. Has robust, high bill, large feet. Color varies according to region: populations of upper Amazon (as far as Rios Negro and Tapajós, see plate, *C. a. rufogularis*) have uniformly reddish brown head, bare blue circle around eye; populations on both sides of lower Amazon (*C. a. aradus, C. a. griseolateralis,* etc.) distinguished by white pattern on sides of head, lack red on belly, etc., but have rusty throat and breast, unlike *Microcerculus.* VOICE: song notable, comprising a series of relatively short, fast, much-varied phrases. These have a ventriloquial base from which arise beautiful, clear, clarinet- or flutelike tones, partly in scales, partly in admirably high leaps of a sixth or even an octave, all the notes connected, unlike the *Microcerculus* song. May recall tuning of instruments before a concert. Periodically an individual will not go beyond a ventriloquial trill. Call, warning a low *k-k-k, krrra.* Lower level of tall forests, likes to perch on side of shoots, like various antbirds. Shakes tail. Lives in pairs and small flocks. Seen frequently in same terra-firme forests as *Microcerculus.* Honduras to Bolivia, Amazonas, Pará (south as far as Cur-

uru, Cachimbo), Amapá, the Guianas. Includes *C. modulator.* Also called *Corneta.* See "Folklore . . . ."

Troglodytidae Bibliography
See also General Bibliography

Brown, R. N., and R. E. Lemon. 1980. The effect of sympatric relatives on the evolution of song. *XVII Cong. Int. Orn., Berlin:*742–47.
Grant, P. R. 1966. The coexistence of two wren species of the genus *Thryothorus. Wilson Bull.* 78:266–78.
Haverschmidt, F. 1952. *Condor* 54:292–95. [*Troglodytes,* nesting]
Kiltie, R. A., and J. W. Fitzpatrick. 1984. Reproduction and social organization of *Donacobius atricapillus* in southeast Peru. *Auk* 101:804–11.
Olalla, A. M. 1959. *Geográfica* 9:46–48. [*Cyphorhinus,* behavior]
Skutch, A. F. 1960. *Life Histories of Central American Birds,* vol. 2. Pacific Coast Avifauna 34:116–210. Berkeley, Calif.: Cooper Orn. Soc.
Skutch, A. F. 1968. *Condor* 70:66–82. [*Donacobius,* behavior]
Slud, P. 1958. *Condor* 60:243–51. [*Microcerculus,* behavior]
Thorpe, W. H. 1963. *Nature* 197:774–76. [Dueting]
Thorpe, W. H. 1972. Duetting and antiphonal song in birds. *Behaviour,* suppl. 18.
Verner, J., and G. H. Engelsen. 1970. Territories, multiple nest building, and polygyny in the Long-billed Marsh Wren. *Auk* 87:557–67.

FAMILY MUSCICAPIDAE
SUBFAMILY SYLVIINAE: GNATCATCHERS AND GNATWRENS (6)

These are small, very active, insectivorous, arboreal birds represented in Brazil by the genera *Microbates, Ramphocaenus,* and *Polioptila.* The *Polioptila* are typical representatives of the Sylviinae, a large and very diverse Oscine subfamily of the Old World with more than 300 species. I include this group and the Turdinae in the Muscicapidae, following the 1983 AOU *Check-list of North American Birds.*

The relationship of the genera *Microbates* and *Ramphocaenus* (with which *Psilorhamphus,* presently included in the Rhinocryptidae, was erroneously grouped) has been a subject of continuous controversy. Originally they were considered Troglodytidae (Oscines), then Formicariidae (Sub-

oscines), and finally were brought back to the Oscines where, because they have aftershafts and because of their syrinx structure, they are placed in the Sylviinae.

There has been an effort to explain the great difference between *Ramphocaenus* and *Microbates* on the one hand and *Polioptila* on the other as due to a second invasion of America by Silviinae, which would imply that the two groups had even more remote ancestors; finally, it has been proposed to establish a separate family, in the Oscines and related to the Sylviinae, to cover *Ramphocaenus* and *Microbates.* There are no known sylviine fossils in the New World.

MICROBATES AND *RAMPHOCAENUS* TRIBE

Distribution and Morphology

Exclusively Neotropical, these birds are distinguished by the very long bill and long, slender legs with strong musculature. The toes are relatively short; the birds are not terrestrial.

Birds in both genera have abundant silky plumage on the flanks. All things considered, the similarity of the two genera appears to me to be very superficial; for instance, both their bills and feet are different. Sexes are identical. In external aspect they resemble wrens.

Vocalization

The calls and warning notes of both genera are similar to those of wrens. The song of the Long-billed Gnatwren, *Ramphocaenus melanurus,* is a limpid tremolo, like the song of some antbirds. I sometimes hear a sharper response, which apparently does not come from any neighboring bird but from the respective mate, giving rise to the belief that both sexes sing.

Behavior

R. melanurus fans its tail and raises it vertically until the tips of the rectrices touch its back. It also makes lateral tail movements.

I have seen *Microbates* only at very short distances above ground level, whereas *Ramphocaenus* frequently mounts to the tops of trees. Both periodically join mixed flocks. They take advantage of army ants as beaters to frighten prey out of hiding.

Breeding

Birds of both genera live in pairs. The nest of the Collared Gnatwren, *Microbates collaris,* placed on a spiny palmetto leaf ½ m above ground level, is a high, coarse pile of dry leaves with a small, open cup in which it lays two white eggs that are spotted on the rounded end. The nest of *Ramphocaenus melanurus,* built among shoots a few inches above the forest floor, is a 20-cm-high loose pile of dry leaves with a cup so deep and narrow that the bird, when sitting on it, is forced to hold its head vertically upward, letting the long bill be seen from a distance like a small vertical stick. It lays two yellowish white eggs, speckled with red, which are incubated by both parents. In the case of *R. m. rufiventris* of Costa Rica, the incubation period is 17 days, the same long time as an antbird of identical size. The young hatch naked (like *Polioptila*) and abandon the nest after 12 days. *R. melanurus* has two breeding periods, June and October, in Mato Grosso.

COLLARED GNATWREN, *Microbates collaris,*
Bico-assovelado-de-coleira   Fig. 282

11 cm. Northern Amazonian species with peculiar physique, including long (18 mm) bill, medium-length tail, extraordinarily long tarsi, short toes. Upperparts brown; superciliaries and underparts white, particularly visible in forest shade. Has postocular streak, malar stripe, and black upper breast band, the last remotely resembling that of *Corythopis* (Tyrannidae). VOICE: call *tak, tsrrr* (weak); a loud whistle,

Fig. 282. Collared Gnatwren, *Microbates collaris.*

iew, repeated every 3–4 seconds; song a loud, hurried trill. Lives hidden in interior of tall forests. Like small Amazonian wrens, hops about in low, dense, deeply shaded foliage, from where it descends to ground to pursue insects. Holds narrow tail in horizontal position, only tending to lift it when it picks up something from ground. North of Amazon (Amapá) and Solimões (Amazonas) to Colombia, Venezuela, the Guianas. Appears alongside *Henicorhina* (Trogolodytidae). A second, non-Brazilian species reaches Central America.

LONG-BILLED GNATWREN, *Ramphocaenus melanurus,*
Bico-assovelado   PL 38.8

15 cm; 8.5–9 g. Widely distributed, characterized by exceptionally long (21 mm), thin bill. Compared with *Microbates,* bill is more slender and differently shaped, tail larger and graduated, tarsi less sturdy. Underparts have no dark marking of any kind except occasional black bases on throat feathers. VOICE: call *tseck-tseck,* warning *krra.* Song consists of a trill with or without modulations, ascending or descending, with timbre of a canary with some preliminary notes, *ttt-ew, ew, ew, ew, ew. . . .* Primary or secondary forests and on their edges. In places with average-height forest climbs vine-covered trees from 8 m or more to crown, but also comes down to low levels, where it builds nest. Constantly in action, attracts attention by small size, but even then only easy to discover through song, which it sings all year. Timbre sometimes resembles certain antbirds, e.g., Spot-backed Antshrike, *Hypoedaleus guttatus.* If excited cocks tail, frantically fanning it up and down, recalling Spotted Bamboowren, *Psilorhamphus guttatus* (Rhinocryptidae); also makes lateral tail movements. Mexico to Amazonia, from there south to Mato Grosso (Guaporé, Gi-Paraná, upper Xingu), eastern Pará, northeastern and eastern Brazil, including Municipality of Rio de Janeiro, as far as Santa Catarina. Relatively common in various regions. Also called *Garricha-do-mato-virgem* (Mato Grosso), *Ma-träbino* (Kamaiurá, Mato Grosso).

POLIOPTILA TRIBE

Distribution and Morphology

This genus is widely distributed in the Americas but is more common in the tropical sectors. In Brazil there is no way to confuse it with any other group because of its characteristically slender shape, its short, thin bill, and especially its long, narrow tail. The body is gray and white, frequently with some black shading on the head, which is more extensive in the male. There are several quite similar species.

Vocalization

The song, sung when the birds are standing erect as if swallowing water, is extremely high, the timbre comparable to the whistle of a sandpiper. The various populations of the Masked Gnatcatcher, *Polioptila dumicola,* have different dialects. I have heard a dawn song from this species in Rio Grande do Sul.

Behavior

The tail is kept constantly in motion, whether vertically or laterally. When excited the birds fan the tail, displaying contrasting black and white. Live openly in treetops, exposed to the wind and strong sun. Like arid regions.

Breeding

The birds are aggressive during breeding, attacking any animal entering their territory. The small nest, firmly attached to a tree branch, is a durable little saucer, covered on the outside with lichens fastened with spider webbing, like those of the *Elaenia* (Tyrannidae) and hummingbirds. The resulting camouflage is perfect. When constructing a nest for a second clutch, sometimes material is taken from the first nest. The eggs are white with small, chestnut spots and are incubated by the pair for 13 days (Tropical Gnatcatcher, *P. plumbea*); the young, fed by both parents, as in *Ramphocaenus,* leave the nest at 14 to 15 days of age (Black-tailed Gnatcatcher, *P. melanura,* of the southwestern United States).

Evolution

Usually only one species of the genus occurs in each locale, but there is some overlapping in Amazonia. In certain species distinctive geographic races occur, forming intermediate populations in the zones of contact, as for example, with *P. dumicola* in southern Mato Grosso; such intergradation spreads as a consequence of the destruction of forests that previously separated the populations of these light-loving birds.

TROPICAL GNATCATCHER, *Polioptila plumbea,* Balança-rabo-de-chapéu-preto

11 cm. Slender, arboreal bird with long tail always in motion. Upperparts gray with top of head as far as nape black; wing and tail feathers black. Inner remiges have wide, white, longitudinal border; outer remiges have areas of white. Underparts grayish white. Female lacks black cap. VOICE: draws attention by frequently producing a strident call, *PSEEeh; tsewk,* descending *eet, eet, eet, eet* with timbre of Spotted Sandpiper, *Actitis macularia.* Song a high whistle, somewhat varied and with rapid tempo, beginning with a series of monotonous *glis* . . . Bird untiringly hops and flits among trees and bushes, always fanning tail up and down and to sides. Arid regions with abundant acacia and cactus, e.g., caatinga. Mexico to Peru, the Guianas, Brazil, in sparse open country of Brazilian Amazonia (Rio Branco, lower Tapajós, lower Xingu, Pará), Tocantins, eastern Pará (Belém, Marajó, etc.); northeastern Brazil south to Bahia, Minas Gerais. Also called *Miador* (Minas Gerais).

CREAM-BELLIED GNATCATCHER, *Polioptila lactea,* Balança-rabo-leitoso

10.9 cm; 7 g. Especially distinguished by intensely yellowish underparts; lores, superciliary, and around eye white. Male has black similar to *P. plumbea.* Paraguay, Argentina (Misiones), eastern Brazil from Rio de Janeiro to Rio Grande

Fig. 283. Masked Gnatcatcher, *Polioptila d. dumicola,* male.

do Sul (São Borja). See Black-capped Warbling-Finch, *Poospiza melanoleuca* (Fringillidae).

GUIANAN GNATCATCHER, *Polioptila guianensis*

Amazonia between Belém and Rio Tapajós and from upper Rio Negro to Venezuela, the Guianas.

MASKED GNATCATCHER, *Polioptila dumicola*, Balança-rabo-de-máscara   Fig. 283

11.5 cm; 6 g. Very similar in appearance to other species described above, with gray upperparts, male with black mask (or only black postocular stripe). Female lores and superciliaries white. Underparts white (*P. d. berlepschi,* central Brazil except southeastern Mato Grosso) or as dark as upperparts (*P. d. dumicola,* southwestern Mato Grosso, Rio Grande do Sul). VOICE: call *grehh, tseRET-greh* (warning). Song limpid, with timbre of a *Hylophilus* greenlet (Vireonidae); an individual may use a variety of motifs in a half hour of song. In Mato Grosso I noted the following sequences: (1) a strongly descending sequence, *DLEEew . . . ;* (2) an unmodulated sequence, *dip, dip, dip-DEEew, DEEew, DEEew;* (3) *dewdew-WEEa dewdew WEEa . . .* From another individual, in Rio Grande do Sul, I noted: (1) *wit, wit, wit . . . ;* (2) *bewEET, bewEET, bewEET . . . ;* (3) *WEEje, WEEje, WEEje.* Also has a more varied and flowing song, with much more rapid tempo, reminiscent of a *Sporophila* seedeater (Emberizinae) or a *Euphonia* (Thraupinae), that may be sung over a long period. I encountered a similar song with *P. plumbea.* Cerrado and open regions with scattered trees. Southeastern Pará, Goiás, and Minas Gerais to São Paulo, Rio Grande do Sul, Mato Grosso (including upper Xingu); also Bolivia, Paraguay, Argentina, Uruguay. Also called *Sebinho* (Rio Grande do Sul).

Sylviinae Bibliography

Oniki, Y., and E. O. Willis. 1979. A nest of the Collared Gnatwren, *Microbates collaris. Condor* 81:101–02.

Rand, A. L., and M. A. Traylor, Jr. 1953. *Auk* 70:334–37. [*Ramphocaenus, Microbates,* taxonomy]

Sick, H. 1954. *Bonn. Zool. Beitr.* 5:179–90. [*Ramphocaenus,* taxonomy]

Skutch, A. F. 1960. *Life Histories of Central American Birds,* vol. 2. Pacific Coast Avifauna 34:43–65. Berkeley, Calif.: Cooper Orn. Soc.

Skutch, A. F. 1968. *Condor* 70:66–82. [*Ramphocaenus,* behavior]

SUBFAMILY TURDINAE: THRUSHES AND SOLITAIRES (18)

This large, cosmopolitan subfamily of more than 300 species is of eastern origin but has long been established in the Americas where it reaches the extreme south in Tierra del Fuego and the Falkland Islands. I follow the 1983 AOU *Check-list of North American Birds* and include the "Turdidae" and "Sylviidae" in the Muscicapidae family (see Passeriformes, Suborder Oscines). In the Neotropics Turdinae are more common in mountainous regions such as the Andes. There are fossils from the Tertiary (Miocene, 20 million years B.P.) from California.

Morphology and Identification

The distinctive character of this subfamily is well known to all, with the only departures from the *Turdus* pattern being the unique *Myadestes* (= *Cichlopsis*) genus and *Catharus* (= *Hylocichla*). The latter are small North American species that reach Brazil as migrants.

Size runs between 17 and 25 cm. The Rufous-bellied Thrush, *Turdus rufiventris,* the largest Brazilian species, weighs approximately 75 g. All have modest plumage except the Yellow-legged Thrush, *Platycichla flavipes,* and Black-hooded Thrush, *Turdus olivater.* It takes some experience to distinguish between common species such as the Pale-breasted Thrush, *T. leucomelas,* and Creamy-bellied Thrush, *T. amaurochalinus.* Throat color is prominent; a white spot on the lower throat becomes more visible when the bird sings or stretches its neck. Bill color is important, for in certain species, such as *T. amaurochalinus,* it is bright yellow during breeding, at least in the male. The same can be said in some cases about the feet and eyelids, especially in *Platycichla.* During molt, which occurs at the beginning of the year in the south, the bare parts lose their bright color. In *T. amaurochalinus* the bill becomes entirely black, in *P. flavipes* only vestiges of yellow finally remain. By August the bill again becomes yellow.

Sexes are mostly similar, differing only in *Platycichla, Turdus olivater,* and the Eastern Slaty-Thrush, *T. subalaris.* The initial plumage of immatures of most species is similar and spotted, a typical pattern for thrushes (Fig. 284). This plumage protects the immature against attack by adults who see it as a noncompetitor. *Platycichla* nestlings already show sexual dimorphism. Albino individuals occur, being occasional but universal phenomena in cities. Albinos are usually solitary outsiders that are eliminated by predators (natural selection). They are not so rare among *T. rufiventris* females or in *P. flavipes* and are usually noted around human habitations where elimination of these individuals so visible to raptors is less likely. I have seen a completely white *T. rufiventris,* although it had dark eyes (not red) and yellow eyelids (Rio de Janeiro). An albino pair, reported from São Paulo in 1987, *is* unusual. I have also recorded cinnamon-colored

Fig. 284. Creamy-bellied Thrush, *Turdus amaurochalinus,* immature

mutants of *P. flavipes* (male and female, Petrópolis, Rio de Janeiro) and of *T. rufiventris* and the White-necked Thrush, *T. albicollis* (females). The Rufous-brown Solitaire, *Myadestes leucogenys,* is a distinctive species whose inclusion in this family has been disputed.

Vocalization

Various species, such as *Turdus rufiventris* and *T. leucomelas,* have many different vocalizations, including various calls—a fact rarely or never mentioned in the literature, which almost always refers only to songs. Certain calls are more useful for field identification than the songs, the more so because they serve all year and not only during the singing seasons, which are short. There are, for example, cries that immediately identify *T. amaurochalinus, T. albicollis,* and *T. leucomelas. T. amaurochalinus* has a whistle it makes only when it takes flight or is flying. Certain calls, for instance a *psib,* are similar in various species. It is difficult to ascertain the meaning of certain thrush vocalizations, such as those of *T. rufiventris* and *T. leucomelas.*

A prolonged, extremely high whistle is used as an alarm when a raptor is discovered hunting (see *Platycichla flavipes*). Because of its high timbre, its source is hard to locate, so the sentinel producing this whistle cannot be found by the predator. This vocalization is also understood by other birds. On vocalizing in twilight, see "Behavior."

Thrush songs are praised everywhere on earth, each country pointing with pride to the species that is the best singer in its area, claiming it to be superior to all others. João Guimarães Rosa, whom I have cited several times, emphasized the natural beauty of thrush song: "a thrush sings without sugar." Thrush songs have a certain similarity all over the world. There is scarcely a woodland where these characteristic voices are not heard. Judging song quality is subjective, but it also depends on the singer, its age, and the region. There are regional modifications (see *T. rufiventris*). *Platycichla flavipes* is the species most sought by bird fanciers in southern Brazil. It has a well-varied song and is capable of

imitating other birds. Lawrence's Thrush, *T. lawrencii,* is unique in our area in its capacity for imitation. The Cocoa Thrush, *T. fumigatus,* is also an excellent singer. *T. rufiventris* can sing very well but is disappointing in certain regions; in Rio de Janeiro, for example, there is a marked impoverishment of its song, perhaps related to life in a large city, a phenomenon for which there are parallels in Europe (Stadtamseln). The songs of *T. rufiventris, T. leucomelas, T. amaurochalinus, T. fumigatus,* and *T. albicollis* sound similar to each other to the novice. *Platycichla flavipes* and *T. amaurochalinus* are among the species that sing openly on treetops. Others, like *T. albicollis,* sing hidden in the forest. *T. subalaris* usually sings in groups in dense woods. Immatures, and especially adults at the beginning of the breeding season, such as *T. rufiventris* and *T. amaurochalinus,* sing distinctively: pianissimo, prolonged, and full of motifs. When the appropriate season has passed they stop singing entirely. Even more notable is the fact that *T. rufiventris* and *T. fumigatus* have evolved, in addition to their song (intimately related to breeding), a second territorial vocalization: a loud, descending sequence used almost as a substitute for song outside the breeding season. In captivity *T. rufiventris* may sing all year, even at night under artificial light. The female generally does not sing, but there is some confusion about this in the northeast, where the word *sabiá,* "thrush," is feminine. The name *sabiá* comes from Tupi, being a contraction of *haá-piy-har,* "he who prays a lot" (Baptista Caetano), an allusion to the abundant song of thrushes.

Feeding

Thrushes are omnivorous. They like the fruits of various palms such as sweet palmito and açaí (*Euterpe*) and of introduced species such as the oil palm (*Elaeis guineensis*), *Livistonia,* and *Archontophoenix.* Six thrush species have been recorded in Espírito Santo on the enormous bunches of *Livistonia australis* fruit: *Platycichla flavipes, Turdus rufiventris, T. leucomelas, T. amaurochalinus, T. fumigatus,* and *T. albicollis.* They regurgitate the pits after about an hour, thus contributing to the spontaneous dissemination of these plants. They seek out the fruits of yellow magnolia (see Swallow Tanager, *Tersina viridis,* Thraupinae), *Cecropia,* falsa-erva-de-rato (*Hamelia patens,* Rubiaceae), pimenta-malagueta (*Capsicum*), blackberries, Myrtaceae, etc. They feast on ripe oranges and papayas. They take arthropods, etc., scared up by army ants. They are among the few birds recorded foraging under electric light (*T. leucomelas,* Santarém, Pará; see Trochilidae, "Behavior" and "Pollination"). They drink rainwater from tree holes.

Behavior

Behavior of most thrushes, such as the way they hop and run on the ground, turn over leaves, and peck into the earth with the bill, is similar in any part of the world. Tail movements are characteristic for various species; *Turdus amaurochalinus* is the most active in shaking its tail vertically. All fly well. They are wary and like to remain under cover. They are belligerent, as can be observed when a fruit tree in the territory of one pair becomes an attraction for various birds, including other thrushes.

I have seen a *Platycichla* rub garlic under its wing, a process that must be a substitute for anting; a *T. fumigatus* used red pepper; both were captive birds.

No matter what time of year, thrushes become a bit restless in the late afternoon, flying around the area where they intend to sleep, voicing calls and warnings. The phenomenon is most impressive with species such as *T. rufiventris* and *T. leucomelas* whose calls are very vigorous. This nervousness of thrushes, observed also on other continents, must be linked to the "fear" of not obtaining a good, safe roost for the night. Such twilight agitation is more widespread in the Class Aves than is generally realized, but it goes unnoticed when not combined with vocalization. It occurs even among non-Passerines such as guans and trumpeters. Sometimes thrushes also show a certain nervousness at dawn, when light conditions are similar to those at dusk.

Breeding

The nest is a deep dish with thick walls made of roots, other plant parts, and moss, reinforced with varying amounts of mud. *Turdus leucomelas* uses a lot of mud; some species use almost none. There are also individual differences in this regard within the same species. Clay is not used in the cup or on its edge. *Platycichla* apparently do not use mud. Thrush nests are solidly located in the foliage, on thick limbs, stumps, or slanting trunks covered with epiphytes, among gravatás, and sometimes on banks (*T. leucomelas* = sabiá-barranco = "bank thrush"; *T. fumigatus*). *T. leucomelas* often builds on a banana or palm stump. The female alone constructs the nest. Thrushes originally nested in low situations but learned to build high in trees where they escape human depredation (observations from Mexico).

A bird may sometimes become confused in constructing its nest, as when it builds in the spaces between numerous identical beams of a roof: it mistakes the spaces and makes nests in several of them at the same time. I once found five completed nests and four more in different phases of construction in the spaces between adjacent beams (*T. rufiventris*, Macieiras, Itatiaia, Rio de Janeiro). The same thing may occur if a bird builds in the spaces between the steps of a ladder lying horizontally, as I observed with a Rufous Hornero, *Furnarius rufus*, in Rio Grande do Sul.

Eggs are bluish green, speckled with sepia (*T. rufiventris*). They are incubated by the female for 12 days (*T. leucomelas*). Both parents care for the young, which leave the nest after approximately 17 days. There are at least two clutches per

season. Surveys are lacking on the ecology of the different species under the diverse climatic conditions of Brazil's various regions.

Habitat

Most Brazilian thrushes are forest birds, unlike mockingbirds (Mimidae). There are almost always at least two syntopic species in the same area, such as *Turdus albicollis*, *T. rufiventris*, and *T. fumigatus* (forest, Rio de Janeiro, Espírito Santo); *T. albicollis*, *T. rufiventris*, and *T. subalaris* (forest, Santa Catarina, Rio Grande do Sul); and *T. amaurochalinus* and the Black-billed Thrush, *T. ignobilis* (cerrado, southern Pará). *T. leucomelas* and *T. amaurochalinus* are found at the forest edge. The coexistence and reduced competition of such similar and relatively large species must be due to ecological reasons that are not easily recognized. In the south *T. rufiventris* and *T. amaurochalinus* adapt well to life in cultivated fields and even cities.

Distribution

Ranges of some subtropical thrushes (*Myadestes, Platycichla, Turdus subalaris*) are widely discontinuous. Ancient climatic conditions that were different from those of today apparently made direct contact possible between southeastern Brazil and the Andean region.

Migration

After breeding, southern populations from regions extending as far north as Espírito Santo migrate on a large scale toward warmer northern regions. Notable in this are *Turdus amaurochalinus* and *Platycichla flavipes,* which appear in waves in Rio de Janeiro (both the municipality and state) in autumn (end of April and beginning of May) and disappear northward. *T. amaurochalinus* reaches the Amazon. Because of lack of banded individuals we do not yet know the origin of the migrant thrushes that cross our coastal area, but I suspect they come from the far south and not, or at least in lesser numbers, from adjacent high altitudes whose populations are also migratory and probably also head north. They pass through rapidly on their return in July (Rio de Janeiro). The dates and quantities of birds vary according to the weather. In hot years the migration is scarcely perceived, at least in more northerly regions such as Rio de Janeiro. At times I have recorded the arrival of *T. amaurochalinus* at the Quinta da Boa Vista [site of the National Museum in Rio de Janeiro] on the same day, as for instance 20 April 1970 and 1977, during its northward migration.

The repeated use of the same routes and "vacation" spots by migratory thrushes was demonstrated by a Swainson's Thrush, *Catharus ustulatus,* a species coming from Alaska and Canada, that was banded in Jujuy, northern Argentina, in

January 1964 and recaptured in the same place in January 1968. These small thrushes migrate at night, revealing their presence only by their calls. Sometimes they fly into light-houses, lighted TV towers, etc., (see also Parulinae, "Northern Migrants"). *C. ustulatus* covers distances of 300 km in one night.

Parasites

Turdus amaurochalinus reportedly is sometimes attacked by the chigger *Tunga penetrans.*

Popularity and Enemies

Everyone likes thrushes. Gonçalves Dias [a famous Brazilian writer] immortalized the Brazilian thrush: "My land has palms, where the thrush sings," which is perhaps the best-known literary quotation in the country. It is almost certain, however, that the poet was not even referring to a *Turdus* thrush but to a *Mimus* mockingbird, a bird that often perches on palms in his homeland on the Maranhão coast.

A group of cage-bird fanciers in São Paulo suggested *Turdus rufiventris* for the national bird. Thrushes are distributed throughout the world, particularly in the Northern Hemisphere, and are highly esteemed because of their beautiful song. Since such a symbol should have a strong national identity, it is evident that it would be more appropriate to have a Brazilian endemic, such as the Golden Parakeet, *Guaruba guarouba* [known in Brazil as *ararajuba* or *guaruba*]; it is among the most beautiful birds in the world and has the same colors as the Brazilian flag (see the species account in Psittacidae). Two Northern hemisphere countries (Sweden and Malta) have thrushes as national birds. The name *sabiá* appears as a name for people, a publisher, pharmaceutical products, a play, music, etc. Thrushes may survive many years in captivity. A *Platycichla flavipes* lived 18 years in perfect health, singing until the end. The pursuit of thrushes as game birds, practiced by descendants of Italians, is a scandal.

Among the natural enemies of thrushes (or of any small animal that moves on the ground) are frogs of the genus *Leptodactylus* when, during rains, they come out of the water. I know of one of the largest (20 cm not counting the legs) in Paraná that caught an adult *T. rufiventris* by the head; the bird would have been lost had a man not interfered. See also Tyrannidae, "Perils . . ."

RUFOUS-BROWN SOLITAIRE, *Myadestes*
(= *Cichlopsis*) *leucogenys*, Sabiá-castanho
EN PL 37.4

21 cm; 61 g. Woodland species of southeast, of very local occurrence. Long-tailed with slender body, small feet; resembles a female *Platycichla*. Throat and foreneck uniformly ochraceous brown, maxilla black, mandible yellow. Sexes similar. VOICE: a penetrating whistle, *tsrreeee* (weak),

Fig. 285. Occurrence of the Rufous-brown Solitaire, *Myadestes leucogenys*, a highly disjunct distribution in mountainous regions. (A) The Brazilian population, *M. l. leucogenys*. Adapted from Mayr and Phelps 1967.

sueeeet (loud), similar to alarm of various other thrushes; song a penetrating, unmelodious chirping, relatively homogeneous and continuous but composed of short, poorly separated phrases with a metallic timbre, reminiscent of *Turdus subalaris*. Lives concealed in primary forests of mountainous (750–850 m) regions in Espírito Santo and southeastern Bahia as a remnant or relict population, *M. l. leucogenys* (BR) (fig. 285). Species occurs in Andes (Peru, Ecuador, Venezuela) and Guyana. Genus is more diversified in mountainous regions of northwestern South America and in Central America, Mexico, and Antilles, where it is known for its flutelike song that may recall Veery, *Catharus fuscescens*. See also *Platycichla flavipes*. Anatomy of syrinx separates *Myadestes* from other thrushes.

VEERY, *Catharus fuscescens*,
Sabiá-norte-americano NV Fig. 286

17 cm. Quite small migrant to Amazonia from North America. Upperparts rusty chestnut, throat and belly white, breast yellowish with brownish spots that extend to sides of throat. VOICE: a loud *KWEEeh*, characteristic of species. Occasionally the song of these travelers is heard in Brazil. Lower and middle levels of forest. Amazonas (Rio Negro, October; Javari, October), Rondônia (Porto Velho, November), Mato Grosso (upper Xingu, December; Cuiabá, December; Chapada, February). Three races have been recorded in Brazil as migrants from Canada and U.S.: *C. f. fuscescens*, *C. f. fuliginosa*, and *C. f. salicicola*. See *C. ustulatus* and *C. minimus*.

SWAINSON'S THRUSH, *Catharus ustulatus* NV

Northern migrant, less common than *C. fuscescens*, more common that *C. minimus*. Similar to *fuscescens* but with upperparts olive instead of reddish and with yellowish eye-

Fig. 286. Veery, *Catharus fuscescens.*

ring. VOICE: call *ooit; it* given in flight at night on migration. By end of November, or in March at latest, before returning to breeding area in distant north, begins to sing: limpid, flutelike phrases, each motif with an ascending swirl. Forest. Recorded in Amazonas (Rio Tucanos, November; Rio Negro, February, March); goes as far as Argentina.

GRAY-CHEEKED THRUSH, *Catharus minimus minimus* NV

Third northern migrant; occasional in Brazilian northwest.

YELLOW-LEGGED THRUSH, *Platycichla flavipes,* Sabiaúna Fig. 287

20.5 cm; 64 g (male), 72 g (female). Southeastern species. Black-and-gray male unmistakable (gray often appears black at a distance). Bill, eyelids, and feet yellow. In nonbreeding season bill becomes spotted with black (see "Morphology . . ."); female dark olive brown with underparts a little lighter, throat whitish streaked with brown, belly whitish, eyelids and feet yellowish (unlike *Turdus amaurochalinus* and *T. leucomelas*). Male recognizable even as a juvenile (black wing and tail feathers); acquires yellow bill only gradually, however.

VOICE: *tsreep, tshreh-tshreh-tshreh, tsrip-tsip-tsip;* a loud, highly varied song with abundant and diverse motifs of varying lengths, well separated from each other by irregular intervals; limpid whistles, moving from high to low, with changes in amplitude and speed; repetition is usual but may be limited; certain individuals, especially captives, imitate other birds, e.g., Buffy-fronted Seedeater, *Sporophila frontalis;* Tropical Kingbird, *Tyrannus melancholicus;* Australian Budgerigar, *Melopsittacus undulatus;* Blue-and-white Swallow, *Notiochelidon cyanoleuca* (warning); Roadside Hawk,

Rupornis magnirostris. Two wild individuals, in Espírito Santo and Rio de Janeiro respectively, mimicked American Swallow-tailed Kite, *Elanoides forficatus,* and a *Pionus* parrot. Likes to sing from highest trees. Song peaks in October (Espírito Santo). Has strange alarm whistle, *seeeet,* similar to that of several other birds, which serves as alarm for various species.

Forest, in mountainous regions in Rio de Janeiro and Espírito Santo, where it is generally most common species, but not lacking on coast where it also nests (ex-Guanabara) and increases considerably in numbers on migration. Abandons southern mountain regions in winter, as far north as Espírito Santo (see "Migration"). Eastern Brazil from Paraíba to Rio Grande do Sul, Paraguay, and Misiones, Argentina. Also on boundary with Venezuela and in more northerly mountains (Venezuela, Colombia). Also called *Sabiá-da-mata.* There is little reason to separate out this genus. The *Platycichla* bill is more robust than that of *Turdus.*

PALE-EYED THRUSH, *Platycichla leucops*

Only in Roraima and mountainous regions outside Brazil.

EASTERN SLATY-THRUSH, *Turdus subalaris,* Sabiá-ferreiro

21 cm. Small, southern, woodland species with yellow bill (at least mandible); upperparts olive gray, head blackish; throat white, densely covered with nearly black streaks with white spot below; breast dark grayish, belly white. Female brown, similar to that of *T. amaurochalinus.*

VOICE: call (reminiscent of *amaurochalinus*) *tsuk.* Song unmistakable in unique, metallic timbre (thus its name "Blacksmith Thrush"). Motifs short, frequently only 2–3 or a

Fig. 287. Yellow-legged Thrush, *Platycichla f. flavipes,* male, singing.

few more, separated by characteristic interval. Phrases normally begin with a penetrating whistle, *tsree*, also followed by an interval, e.g., *tsree tsing, tsing chewluh chewluh chuh, tsree ting, ting, ting sing, sing, sing kile, kile, kile, kile, kle, kli, kli, sree*, etc.; Repetitions (3–5) are notable. Certain individuals with greater variety of motifs are also recognizable by their metallic timbre (recalling certain *Myadestes*) and by trials of *teling, teling*. Sings hidden in forest, often in flocks, revealing its presence immediately on its return in spring in October (Rio Grande do Sul, Santa Catarina) or September (Rio de Janeiro, Minas Gerais, Itatiaia).

Araucaria groves, dense riverine forests, woodlands on mountain slopes, etc., alongside *Platycichla flavipes, T. albicollis*, and *T. rufiventris*. Argentina, Paraguay, and Bolivia locally as far as Rio de Janeiro (Itatiaia), Minas Gerais; in winter in Goiás, Mato Grosso (upper Xingu); also Peru, Ecuador. Because of distinctive song and appearance in flocks on migration, it is very conspicuous, as in Brasília in September and early October, where it sings before returning south. A good number have been banded in Brasília. Closely related to Andean Slaty-Thrush, *T. nigriceps*, of Andes (Ecuador to Argentina). Also called *Sabiá-campainha, Ferreirinho, Sabiá-pita*. See *Platycichla flavipes*.

BLACK-HOODED THRUSH, *Turdus olivater*

21.8 cm. Head to breast black, also tail. Upperparts olive brownish, belly pale brownish, bill yellow; female lacks black. Roraima (Pico da Neblina, Maracá) to Guyana, Colombia.

RUFOUS-BELLIED THRUSH, *Turdus rufiventris*, Sabiá-laranjeira   PL 37.6

25 cm; 68 g (male), 78 g (female). Best-known thrush in southeast. Unmistakable with intense orange-rufous belly, less colorful in worn plumage. Eyelid sometimes yellow. VOICE: multiple calls: *djok;* warning *tsri;* a resonant *juh-JOEit, drew-wip;* a descending sequence of approximately 9 *drewuh*s . . . , a conspicuous, territorial vocalization that replaces song in nonbreeding season and increases at beginning of breeding. Song loud and continuous with distinctive and varied motifs that can be very attractive because of full tone. Locally (e.g., ex-Guanabara) song may be simple and monotonous, e.g., *dewee-dewo dewee-dewo, fewri-tewri*, carried on endlessly (*oitenta-e-oito, teófilo-vai-teófilo-vem*), constituting a degraded form of song, a sort of dialect, a "carioca"[1] of thrushes (see "Vocalization"). Forests, parks, estates, even in center of cities such as Rio de Janeiro when gardens are available. Eastern and central Brazil from Maranhão to Rio Grande do Sul, Minas Gerais, Goiás, Mato Grosso, Bolivia, Paraguay, Argentina, Uruguay. Partially emigrates in winter (Espírito Santo). Also called *Sabiá-de-barriga-vermelha, Sabiá-coca* (Bahia). See *T. fumigatus*.

PALE-BREASTED THRUSH, *Turdus leucomelas*, Capoeirão, Sabiá-barranco   PL 37.8

22 cm. Widely distributed semiwoodland species, recognizable (compared with smaller *T. amaurochalinus*) by rusty wings contrasting with grayish olive head. Under wing coverts intensely rusty; whitish throat has pale brownish striations; under tail coverts white with clear brownish centers; bill always dark (blackish). VOICE: multiple vocalizations: call *shreh, shreh, shreh* (characteristic of species), reminiscent of *Platycichla;* warning *cha, cha; pseep, shuh-DEE-dididi; shrewee* . . . (at dawn and dusk); mellow, continuous song softer than *T. rufiventris* and made up of relatively simple motifs repeated once or twice, e.g., *chrewIT, chrewIT glewo CHEWluh, CHEWluh TIrewd TIrewd*, etc. Forest edges, parks, gallery forests, palm groves, coffee plantations (*Sabiá-do-café*, "Coffee Thrush," Paraná), etc. The Guianas and Venezuela to Bolivia, Argentina, Paraguay; southern and central Brazil to mouth of Tapajós and north of lower Amazon (Amapá, Marajó, etc.); also Espírito Santo, Bahia, Minas Gerais. In Rio de Janeiro more common in mountains. Also called *Capoeirão, Sabiá-branco, Caraxué* (Pará). See *T. amaurochalinus*.

CREAMY-BELLIED THRUSH, *Turdus amaurochalinus*, Sabiapoca   PL 37.7

21.9 cm. Southern species, common in semiopen landscapes. Head and upperparts, including wings, uniformly olive brown. Area in front of eye black. White throat has dense brown streaking but there is white or yellowish spot on lower throat. Under wing coverts pale yellow, under tail coverts pure white. During breeding male's bill is pure, waxy yellow; at other times uniformly blackish like female and immature (see fig. 284). VOICE: call *bok, bak* (very low, like a cork coming out of a bottle; when perched); *pseep* (in flight or before flying, especially on migration when predisposed to fly); warning a sharp *pshewo* like a kitten; song can be a bit dry and monotonous ("sad"), composed of short, simple motifs, each followed by a characteristic interval that produces a halting effect in great regularity of entire sequence, which can be extensive. A popular transcription that imitates rhythm well is *Eu plantei, não nasceu, apodreceu, frio, frio* [yo PlantAY, nAAo nasSAYoo, apodraySAYoo, FREEo, FREEo], "I planted, it didn't sprout, it rotted, cold, cold." Shakes tail vertically when perched or when it stops to stand erect while walking on ground. Forest edges, parks, estates; also cities, cerrado. The northeast, east, and south to Argentina, Bolivia, central Brazil (Mato Grosso, upper Xingu, singing locally August and September), Goiás, Acre (September); lower Amazon (Belém, probably only on migration). Frequent appearance of migrating individuals (nonsingers) may obscure picture of resident populations; species is not Amazonian. Also called *Sabiá-branco, Sabiá-pardo,*

---

[1] A carioca is a native of Rio de Janeiro, where Portuguese is spoken in a distinctive way.

Sabiá-bico-amarelo. Name *Sabiapoca* is most suitable; *poca* from Tupi: *poc,* "pop," an allusion to call.

BLACK-BILLED THRUSH, *Turdus ignobilis,* Carachué-bico-preto

21.5 cm. Only in Amazonia. Very similar to *T. amaurochalinus* but dark olive gray instead of brownish, breast grayish, throat streaking indistinct, abdomen white, bill always uniformly black. VOICE: call *bok, sree;* song said to resemble American Robin, *T. migratorius.* Cerrado and dry, low woods. Venezuela to upper Amazon, Bolivia, right side of Tapajós (Teles Pires, Mato Grosso; Cururu, Pará); syntopic in last region with *amaurochalinus.*

LAWRENCE'S THRUSH, *Turdus lawrencii,* Carachué-de-bico-amarelo

21.6 cm. Only in upper Amazon. Deep olive brown, almost as dark as *T. fumigatus* and almost without rusty tones except on under wing coverts. Belly and under tail coverts white. Bill yellow with black tip during breeding, otherwise dark chestnut. Edge of eyelid yellowish. VOICE: song notable for variety of very broad motifs, regularly separated by long intervals. Capacity for mimicking is greatly enhanced by complete separation of motifs. Examples of birds imitated are Squirrel Cuckoo, *Piaya cayana;* Pavonine Cuckoo, *Dromococcyx pavoninus;* Wing-barred Piprites, *Piprites chloris;* also *Galbula, Thamnomanes, Campylorhynchus, Microcerculus,* and *Pitylus* (recordings of José Carlos Magalhães, Rio Peixoto Azevedo, Mato Grosso). A single individual imitated 35 different species, and it is said that one bird imitated more than 60. Probably world's best bird imitator. Treetops. Relatively common in upper Amazon, southward as far as southern Pará (Cururu), northern Mato Grosso (Gi-Paraná, etc.), and Acre, north as far as Venezuela.

Fig. 288. White-necked Thrush, *Turdus a. albicollis.*

COCOA THRUSH, *Turdus fumigatus,* Sabiá-da-mata
PL 37.5

24 cm. Large woodland species, entirely intense rufous with white chin, streaked throat, relatively light belly, white and brownish under tail coverts. VOICE: call *bak* (less resonant than *T. amaurochalinus*); warning *chat-shat-shat;* a descending scale of about 6 melodious *deww-eh*s . . . , territorial, see "Vocalization"; song a vigorous, continuous warble, reputed to be best Brazilian thrush song; sometimes phrases end with a high *sree,* resembling alarm note. See "Vocalization." Forest, cultivated areas with plenty of trees. Colombia, Venezuela, and the Guianas to eastern Amazonia, Maranhão, eastern Pará, Mato Grosso. Also Atlantic forest of northeastern Brazil south to Rio de Janeiro. Also called *Carachué-da-capoeira* (Amazonia), *Sabiá-verdadeiro, Chapéu-de-couro, Pardão* (São Paulo). Sometimes alongside *T. albicollis.* See *T. rufiventris.*

PALE-VENTED THRUSH, *Turdus obsoletus*

Very similar to *T. fumigatus.* Only in upper Amazon, from Solimões to Madeira and from Bolivia to Central America.

HAUXWELL'S THRUSH, *Turdus hauxwelli*

Only in upper Amazon. Very similar to *T. fumigatus* but with white crissum and white in center of belly. Replaces *fumigatus* west of Rio Madeira and in Ecuador, Colombia, Peru, Bolivia.

BARE-EYED THRUSH, *Turdus nudigenis,* Carachué

22 cm. Amazonian. Similar to *T. amaurochalinus* but immediately recognizable by wide, bare, bright yellow eyering; bill yellowish. VOICE: call *shuh-ey, uhEEuh,* with timbre reminiscent of *amaurochalinus* (like mewing of a kitten); *tak-tak-tak;* low-volume song is a sequence of short phrases comprising 3–4 distinctly pronounced and connected motifs, with little repetition and each phrase separated by a characteristic interval. Forest edges, semiopen areas. The Guianas and Venezuela to Amazon and locally farther south: Santarém, Belém, Pará; Maranhão (Snethlage, P. Roth).

WHITE-NECKED THRUSH, *Turdus albicollis,* Sabiá-coleira, Carachué-coleira   Fig. 288

22 cm. Widely distributed in deep forest. Characterized by throat, so densely streaked with black that it appears all black when seen from side. Lower throat has pure white patch, immediately visible in deep shade of forest. Flanks and under wing coverts intensely rufous (*T. a. albicollis,* southeastern Brazil) or gray (*T. a. phaeopygus,* Amazonia); abdomen pure white, eyelids and mandible yellow. VOICE: call *jup, jew-up;* warning *tsri;* song smooth, prolonged, and uninterrupted phrases (intervals between motifs are so short they are scarcely noticeable) with simple, relatively quiet motifs and less variation that those of *T. leucomelas* and less intensity than those of *T. rufiventris* and *T. fumigatus.* Middle levels of forest, both in lowlands and mountains, and according to region, alongside

T. fumigatus, T. rufiventris, or *T. subalaris.* Throughout Brazil: extreme north (Amapá, Roraima) to extreme south (Rio Grande do Sul); also north and south beyond Brazil. Inclusion of smaller *T. phaeopygus* as a geographic race in this species is justified by similarity of their voices.

Turdinae Bibliography

Ames, P. L. 1975. The application of syringeal morphology to the classification of the Old World Insect Eaters (Muscicapidae). *Bonn. Zool. Beitr.* 26:107–34.

Antas, P. T. Z., and M. P. Valle. 1987. Dados preliminares sobre *Turdus nigriceps* no Distrito Federal. *II ENAV, Rio de Janeiro*:213–220.

Carvalho, C. T. 1957. *Bol. Mus. Paraen. Zool.* 4. [*Turdus leucomelas,* nesting]

Hardy, J. W., and T. A. Parker III. 1985. *Voices of New World Thrushes.* Gainesville, Fla.: ARA Records.

Olrog, C. C. 1971. *Neotropica* 17:97–100. [Banding]

Ripley, S. D. 1952. *The Thrushes.* Post. Yale Peabody Mus. 3.

Ruschi, A. 1950. *Bol. Mus. Biol. Prof. Melo Leitão,* Bot. 1. [Feeding]

Snow, D. W. 1985. Systematics of the *Turdus fumigatus/hauxwelli* group of thrushes. *Bull. B.O.C.* 105:30–37.

Snow, D. W., and B. K. Snow. 1963. *Wilson Bull.* 75:27–41. [Annual cycle]

Wagner, H. O. 1941. *Orn. Mitt.* 49:142–43. [Ecology]

Family Mimidae: Mockingbirds (3)

Like the Troglodytidae, mockingbirds are restricted to the Americas but are remote descendants of Old World birds. Molecular taxonomy indicates affinity with the Sturnidae, a group widely distributed in the Old World. The Mimidae have achieved greatest diversity in the arid regions of southwestern North America. There are Pleistocene fossils (100,000 years B.P.) from Florida. The *Donacobius* genus has been transferred to the Troglodytidae.

Morphology

At first glance the *Mimus* resemble thrushes, to which they are distantly related, but they are differentiated by many features. They are more slender, appearing to have a longer neck and more curved bill. The tail is graduated and quite long. The legs are long and sturdy, something that catches one's attention even with small nestlings (Chalk-browed Mockingbird, *M. saturninus*). Sexes are similar. The small gray spots on the breast of the immature Tropical Mockingbird, *M. gilvus,* resemble the respective plumage of the true thrushes (Turdinae).

Vocalization

Mimus vocalization is notable for the masterful way some, such as *M. gilvus,* imitate the songs and calls of other species, but there is great individual and specific variation in this peculiar capacity: often this vocalization is no more than mediocre, as with *M. saturninus,* but the voice of the White-banded Mockingbird, *M. triurus,* is justifiably spoken of as a perfection matched with difficulty by any other Oscine.

Feeding

Mockingbirds are omnivorous and eat insects and spiders as well as small fruits and seeds. Seeds of 20 plants, mostly invasive types, were found in the feces of *M. saturninus* in one year (São Paulo). Seeds of ten of these species germinated. Large seeds are regurgitated, as are pellets. The *Mimus* prefer to find their food on the ground. Occasionally they prey on eggs in other birds' nests.

Behavior

Mimus move in long hops or run on the ground, becoming soiled with earth (Paraná). They fly well. They show unusual agility by being able to perch with one foot on each of two different branches. Mockingbirds are notable for the way they stretch their necks vertically to scrutinize their surroundings while hiding with only the head exposed.

The tail reveals every emotion and is held sharply cocked in *M. saturninus. M. gilvus* is much less expressive in this gesture, but both species spread their tail feathers when perching, showing the white tips.

Breeding

The nest of *M. saturninus* is a shallow bowl, coarsely constructed in the crown of a tree in open country and often built on top of an old nest, including that of another species, such as the Rufous Cacholote, *Pseudoseisura cristata,* in Bahia, or the Firewood-gatherer, *Anumbius annumbi,* in Rio Grande do Sul; the center of the nest is lined with soft material. Eggs are greenish with rust-colored spots. *M. saturninus* chicks hatch after 12 days and leave the nest 15 days later. The inside of the nestlings' mouths is orange-yellow. Individual *M. saturninus* nestlings may vary considerably in size. *M. gilvus* and *M. saturninus* pairs attending a nest sometimes have two or three associates, possibly young from a previous clutch. Nestlings are sometimes infested with botfly larva.

M. saturninus is occasionally host to the Shiny Cowbird, *Molothrus bonariensis.*

Habitat, Distribution, and Migration

The *Mimus* are open-country birds, living in semiarid regions and generally in open landscapes, including sometimes marshy areas. To some degree they may constitute evidence of the botanical evolutionary process of Amazonia. For instance, *M. s. saturninus* is restricted to the savannas of Monte Alegre and Santarém, areas that are today isolated in the middle of the Hylaea as remnants of an extensive savanna zone that existed in times of drier climate and was inhabited by a widely distributed, light-loving fauna. Being good fliers, however, the *Mimus* can easily colonize distant areas. *M. saturninus* populations in Rio de Janeiro or more southerly regions are migratory. The same is true of *M. triurus* in Mato Grosso and Argentina. *M. saturninus* and *M. gilvus* ordinarily are interspecifically territorial.

TROPICAL MOCKINGBIRD, *Mimus gilvus,* Sabiá-da-praia

26 cm. Typical of Atlantic coastal strip, very similar to *M. saturninus* but with slighter build. They are same length, however, because of longer, more graduated tail of *M. gilvus.* Upperparts light gray instead of brown; forehead, superciliary, and underparts pure white; flanks streaked with black. In old plumage back becomes brownish and white tips of tail feathers are frazzled. Iris red, gray in immature. VOICE: call, characteristic of species, a resonant *PREEew;* female call a *shick;* warning, irritation a snorting *ga, kweh-kweh;* song short or more prolonged, soft, melodious stanzas, quite varied and absolutely limpid, e.g., *DREEdro-DREEdro dridew-DREEdew-drideww, drew-DEEdewdew-DEE drew-DEEdewdew-DEE.* Repetitions and intervals between motifs typically give song a staccato character. Certain individuals are clever in imitating other birds to perfection and even learn music (e.g., national anthem). In eastern Brazil restricted to sandy and saline coastal regions with sparse vegetation (restinga) with abundant cactus on which it perches, supporting itself on clusters of spines. In such regions it is most prominent bird, replacing *M. saturninus.* Mexico to the Guianas and to Brazilian coast as far as Rio de Janeiro. Also plains of upper Rio Branco. *M. gilvus* must be the "sabiá" to which Gonçalves Dias (1823–64, see Turdinae, "Popularity . . ."): referred in his song on exile.

CHALK-BROWED MOCKINGBIRD, *Mimus saturninus,* Sabiá-do-campo, Arrebita-rabo Fig. 289

26 cm; 73 g. Widely distributed in interior. Upperparts dark brown, superciliary white with long, contrasting, blackish postocular streak (lacking in *M. gilvus*); wings and tail brownish black, upper tail coverts with white bars, tail with more extensive white tip than *gilvus.* Underparts white, often

Fig. 289. Chalk-browed Mockingbird, *Mimus saturninus frater,* singing.

yellowish or reddish from soil, breast grayish, flanks streaked. Iris sometimes yellow. VOICE: call, characteristic for species, a sharp, penetrating *tshrip, tshik;* warning, irritation a snorting *sha-sha-sha, krrrra.* Song can be very good, e.g., in Rio Grande do Sul, but commonly attracts so little attention that species is generally known for "not" singing or for singing "poorly." I heard a wild individual imitate Roadside Hawk, *Rupornis magnirostris,* and American Kestrel, *Falco sparverius.* Any open situation with groups of trees or bushes, ranches, caatinga; also mountains of southeast (Serra do Mar and Mantiqueira), buriti groves (Mato Grosso, Goiás). Locally reaches Atlantic coast, e.g., Bahia (Recôncavo), replacing *M. gilvus.* Prairie regions of lower Amazon and across central Brazil, the northeast, east, and south to Uruguay, Paraguay, Argentina, Bolivia. Also called *Galo-do-campo, Sabiá-cara-de-gato, Sabiá-do-sertão, Tejo* (Paraná), *Calandra* (Rio Grande do Sul).

WHITE-BANDED MOCKINGBIRD, *Mimus triurus,* Calandra-de-três-rabos SV

22 cm. Southern species, much smaller than *M. saturninus* and *M. gilvus,* with upperside brownish, becoming reddish brown on rump. Wide white band on wing extends to some of secondaries. Tail "tripartite": black in middle with sides entirely white. Iris orange-yellow. VOICE: call resembles *saturninus;* song has prolonged, melodious, and resonant phrases mixed with good imitations of many birds, including, appar-

ently, songs learned in winter migrations to more northern areas, e.g., Brazil. Xerophytic woodland, water-edge vegetation. Chile and Argentina to Bolivia, southern Mato Grosso, Rio Grande do Sul, Uruguay. Because of small size, amount of white (though it lacks white on rump), and restless temperament, may recall White-rumped Monjita, *Xolmis velata* (Tyrannidae).

FAMILY MOTACILLIDAE: PIPITS (5)

This is a cosmopolitan savanna group represented in South America only by the *Anthus* genus. It reaches Tierra del Fuego and even South Georgia (where the South Georgia Pipit, *Anthus antarcticus,* one of the landbirds that gets closest to the South Pole, nests). It also reaches Andean plateaus. There are no known fossils of this group from the New World. Pipits on the savannas of South America remind the ornithologist who knows other continents of the open country and savannas of those distant regions, inhabited by other *Anthus* species very similar to ours.

Morphology and Identification

Pipits are the size of a Rufous-collared Sparrow, *Zonotrichia capensis,* but are more slender. The bill is thin and straight, the wings and legs long, the tail medium. The toes are long and sharp, with the claw of the hallux modified into a sort of spur whose length and degree of curve are typical for each species. The plumage is modest, brownish, and extremely similar for all members of the genus. The color varies according to the condition of the feathers, for which reason individuals of one species with different degrees of plumage wear may differ more among themselves than from another species, even though it may also have equally worn plumage. Their constant activity in and under sharp grass rubs away the plumage on the upperparts of the body and particularly affects the tip of the tail, especially the central rectrices, which may be so worn they lose 1 cm of their normal length. The tertiaries are also severely affected. These are greatly developed in this family, extending, when not worn, even beyond the tips of the primaries (with the wings closed) to form a shield that protects the wing tips from abrasion in grasslands, which if it occurred, could interfere with flight. The same adaptation is found in other savanna birds, such as certain emberizids.

The color of the earth may influence coloration. Outer tail feathers have a white or light brownish design conspicuous when the tail is open. There is no sexual dimorphism.

Vocalization

The song is a simple, squeaky phrase sung with a high voice while flying. The singer sometimes stays flying for an

Mimidae Bibliography

Oliveira, M.M.A. 1987. *Mimus saturninus* como dispersor de sementes no Estado de São Paulo. *XIV Cong. Bras. Zool., Juiz de Fora*:699.

Sales, O. 1987. Alguns dados sobre a biologia de *Mimus saturninus frater. Atualidades Orn.* 17:5.

hour or more, so high (perhaps 70–80 m) that an observer has difficulty linking its movements with its voice because of the time lag of the sound reaching earth. The birds define and announce their territories by these song flights. Having finished singing, they come sailing down with the wings elevated obliquely and the legs dangling. When not very excited they sing on the ground. Song recognition is indispensable for field identification of species.

Feeding

Pipits eat small insects, especially beetles, termites, ants, etc., that they catch on the ground. Sometimes they ingest seeds, perhaps more in the winter when animal food is scarce.

Behavior

They walk and run low to the ground, in such a way that the spur helps locomotion, dragging along and leaving a visible trail if the earth is sufficiently soft. They also appear to use the spur as an offensive weapon when fighting among themselves. They perch little and avoid flight, although perfect at it. When pursued they squat on the ground, hiding behind a clod or bunch of grass.

Pipits are similar to certain terrestrial furnariids (*Geobates, Geositta*) that have almost the same build and color and that sometimes live in the same locales. They differ from these birds in lacking their characteristic habit of bobbing the body and in having smaller bills. They may also resemble certain emberizines, their neighbors, such as the *Sicalis* and *Ammodramus,* and in southwestern Amazonia, terrestrial tyrannids of the *Muscisaxicola* genus. They take dust baths and occasionally use ants for plumage hygiene.

Breeding

Pipits nest on the ground, building a rough, deep nest under a grass clump. They lay white eggs densely speckled with brown, gray, etc.; the design varies greatly even within a species. The female incubates alone, but the male helps rear the young. They lay more than one clutch per breeding season. At times they are parasitized by the Shiny Cowbird, *Molothrus bonariensis.* They feign injury to lure a potential predator away from the nest.

Habitat and Migration

Frequently their occurrence is very local: groups of pairs can be found concentrated in appropriate habitats. They generally prefer low-lying meadows. Two species may live so close as to be within hearing of each other, although each inhabits a given area according to its own requirements. I observed this in Rio Grande do Sul, where the Yellowish Pipit, *A. lutescens,* occupied a humid low sector and Hellmayr's Pipit, *A. hellmayri,* occupied the drier environment of an adjacent hill. *A. lutescens* has no problem colonizing reclaimed land. Pipits are more common in the southern regions of South America and occupy the tops of high mountains in southeastern Brazil.

They migrate after the breeding season. Several species can then be found alongside one another in the same place, without their ecological preferences then being evident. At this time their numbers increase considerably in southern regions. Individuals coming from the south form flocks, parts of which must come from afar. They do not sing during migration (*A. lutescens*).

SHORT-BILLED PIPIT, *Anthus furcatus,* Caminheiro-de-unha-curta   Fig. 290

14.5 cm; 20 g. Southern species with short, broad-based bill and hallux with relatively short, sharply curved claw. Color pattern of upperparts has little contrast but may create a very pale, scaly effect if plumage is worn. Sides of body only slightly streaked, unlike Correndera Pipit, *A. correndera;* outer tail feathers pure white or light brown. VOICE: call *tslit, chip;* song consists of simple, 2-part phrase with latter part higher, composed of a diatonic note scarcely perceptible at a distance: *tsree-tse, tse, tse si, si, si, tree-chi, chi, chi, chi, chi.* Bird sings while flying, remaining at considerable altitudes for 10–30 minutes. Every 5 seconds it sings a phrase accompanied by a slight loss of altitude because, at this moment, it is soaring with wings open and immobile. Termi-

nates this display with a flying dive toward ground, where it alights without a sound. Dry fields. Argentina to Peru, Bolivia, Paraguay, Uruguay, Brazil in Rio Grande do Sul. Sometimes shares same fields with *A. hellmayri* and is within sound of *A. lutescens* and *A. correndera.*

HELLMAYR'S PIPIT, *Anthus hellmayri,* Caminheiro-de-barriga-acanelada

14.8 cm. Southern species with relatively broad distribution. Hallux claw greatly curved and longer than in *A. furcatus.* Breast and sides of body sharply streaked. In fresh plumage, underparts, particularly breast, and edges of all wing feathers tinged cinnamon. Outer tail feathers brownish white, not white. VOICE: call *tslip, schep;* song *tsillT, tsillT, tsillT . . . , spile, spile, spile . . . ,* sung while gaining altitude on a very steep trajectory; generally does not reach great heights and returns promptly to ground. If it sings while perched, it produces greater variation, emphasizing a motif such as *tsidel-tsi tsi aarrr.* Dry fields alongside Greater Rhea, *Rhea americana,* and Spotted Nothura, *Nothura maculosa* (Rio Grande do Sul), rocky areas, high open country in mountains of Brazilian southeast, e.g., Serra dos Órgãos and Itatiaia (2350 m); also at any altitude in south (Santa Catarina, Rio Grande do Sul). Argentina and Chile to Bolivia, Paraguay, Uruguay, Brazil north to Espírito Santo, Minas Gerais, Rio de Janeiro. See *A. nattereri.*

YELLOWISH PIPIT, *Anthus lutescens,* Caminheiro-zumbidor   Fig. 291

13 cm; 13–18 g. Widely distributed, smaller-sized pipit. Easily recognized by light sulfur yellow of underparts. Bill small; hallux has long, curved claw; tail relatively short. VOICE: call *wist, wist, wist, wist, sluit;* song much different than other *Anthus,* consisting of a single, sharply descending sizzle similar to noise made by fireworks when set off: *tsitsi-tsieh.* Flies to sing, vocalization coinciding with a loss of altitude when bird lets itself fall. This can be observed both in long, high flights (when loss is small, 2–3 m, and bird quickly regains it, repeating sequence several times) and shorter flights, when bird makes only 1 dive toward ground and alights. Also sings while perched but with slightly modified version of aforementioned motif. Fields, edges of lakes,

Fig. 290. Short-billed Pipit, *Anthus furcatus.*

Fig. 291. Yellowish Pipit, *Anthus l. lutescens.*

rivers, and marshes. Promptly moves into fills resulting from road construction; e.g., it was 1st bird to inhabit fill slopes (still almost lacking vegetation and difficult to walk on) made for construction of Rio-Niterói bridge in 1974. Hot, open country from Panama to Chile, Argentina, all of Brazil, but does not go into mountains of southeast. Also called *Codorninha-do-campo* (São Paulo), *Foguetinho, Peruinho-do-campo, Peruzinho, Martelinha* (Minas Gerais). Also called *A. chihi,* an indigenous name, perhaps of onomatopoeic origin.

CORRENDERA PIPIT, *Anthus correndera,* Caminheiro-de-espora

14.5 cm. Long-billed, southern species, hallux with very long but only slightly curved claw. What draws attention is characteristic blackish color pattern on both upper- and underparts, including densely spotted breast and sides. Back has large, contrasting yellowish streaks. Outer tail feathers have pure white, noticeable when bird starts to fly. VOICE: call *tsip, tsilip;* song a short phrase ending with a loud *gheh* or *tsieh,* characteristic of species, e.g., *tsiTSIdelew-tseeeh,* repeated without interruption while bird mounts vertically to a considerable height where it stays for some minutes still singing; then it suddenly sails down, sometimes almost vertically, voicing a shortened phrase, *tseLIT-gheh,* in a slower

rhythm than the other, until it alights on ground. May perform a series of these flights, making them consecutively without alighting. Wetlands, dunes with low vegetation. Peruvian Andes to Chile, Bolivia, Argentina, Uruguay, southern Brazil from Rio Grande do Sul to São Paulo coast. Not infrequently within hearing of voice of *A. lutescens* (Rio Grande do Sul).

OCHRE-BREASTED PIPIT, *Anthus nattereri,* Caminheiro-grande

15 cm. Larger, little known. Bill, tarsus, toes, and hallux claw all quite long, claw reaching same 15 mm length as hallux. Tail feathers pointed, not rounded as in *A. hellmayri.* Stony fields, sometimes alongside *hellmayri* (Minas Gerais, Poços de Caldas, April) or *A. furcatus* (Rio Grande do Sul, Conceição do Arroio, August). Minas Gerais to São Paulo, Paraná, Rio Grande do Sul, northern Argentina.

Motacillidae Bibliography

Hudson, W. H. 1920. *Birds of La Plata* 1:20–23. [Behavior]
Sick, H. 1969. *Beitr. Neotrop. Fauna* 6:63–79. [Plumage wear]
Straneck, R. L. 1987. Aportes sobre el comportamento y distribución de *Anthus lutescens* y *A. chacoensis. Rev. Mus. Arg. Ciên. Nat. Bernardino Rivadavia* 14(6):95–102.

FAMILY VIREONIDAE: VIREOS, SHRIKE-VIREOS, PEPPERSHRIKES, AND GREENLETS (16)

This is a New World Oscine family, especially well represented in northern South America and Central America. *Vireo* fossils from the middle Pleistocene (100,000 years B.P.) have been found in Florida and *Cyclarhis* fossils from the upper Pleistocene (20,000 years B.P.) in Minas Gerais.

Morphology and Identification

Four genera representing four diverse types are united in this family. They are little-known arboreal birds with dull green upperparts, the bill hooked at the tip, and relatively strong feet. Birds of two of the four genera, *Cyclarhis* and *Smaragdolanius,* are larger and relatively colorful, each having been assigned formerly to separate families, Cyclarhidae and Vireolaniidae, respectively. In the field *Cyclarhis* might be confused with a thraupine, whereas *Smaragdolanius,* a Central American and Amazonian species, may resemble a small Great Kiskadee, *Pitangus sulphuratus.* The third type is that of the *Vireo* genus, extremely well known in North America where the Red-eyed Vireo, *V. olivaceus,* is among the most abundant species. This group is characterized by lack of the outermost primary (the tenth, counting from in-

side), this perhaps being linked to the migration problem (see "Migration").

The last genus, *Hylophilus,* contains small species the size of the Bananaquit, *Coereba flaveola,* that are exclusively tropical and similar to Parulinae such as *Basileuterus* or the North American warblers. In the field they may be confused (as may the *Vireo*) with small tyrannids, but they differ in having a posture that is usually different, more inclined forward (see also Thraupinae, *Dacnis* and *Conirostrum*). The iris is frequently brightly colored. Although sexes are similar, the male may be larger.

Vocalization

Voices consist of resonant and melodious whistles, though they are simple and monotonous in Brazilian species except the Rufous-browed Pepper-Shrike, *Cyclarhis gujanensis,* which has standardized but more varied phrases. The voice of *C. gujanensis* is one of the most prominent Passerine voices in the Neotropics, so much the more so because it sings a lot all year, sometimes even while on the nest. I have noticed a certain geographic variation to its phrasing, although there is a basic resemblance between areas as separate as Mexico and southern Brazil. The vireos are famous for their tireless singing. *Vireo o. olivaceus* of North America repeats its whistle 40 times per minute. The frequency of its Brazilian relative, the Chivi Vireo, *V. chivi,* whose voice is very much the same, is only half, or a bit more, of that. The *Hylophilus* species in Brazilian Amazonia have developed a much faster rate, giving as many as three cheeps per second. They sing, with short intervals, for hours and hours, particularly at the hottest time of the day, with the head lifted while moving it constantly from side to side. The Lemon-chested Greenlet, *Hylophilus thoracicus,* sometimes sings, in addition to its monotonous phrase, a varied, smooth trill. I have noted the reply of the female to the song of the male Rufous-crowned Greenlet, *H. poicilotis:* it is not like the male phrase, but a series of harsh cries, like the warning note of the species and comparable to the reply of the female House Wren, *Troglodytes aedon,* to the song of her mate. The perseverance with which vireonids sing creates the impression that they are more numerous than they really are. It remains to be verified if the intensive singing of *H. thoracicus* that I registered in Rio de Janeiro (ex-Guanabara) in certain autumns and winters really corresponds to the breeding season.

Feeding

Vireonids eat insects and larvae. The *Cyclarhis* and *Smaragdolanius* hold large caterpillars (including hairy ones, often caught by *Cyclarhis*) with their toes against their perch to pick them to pieces. They catch them on leaves and branches while hopping through the foliage, often jumping sideways. They cling to the dense foliage hanging upside down. They also eat small fruits in quantities that may exceed even the insect numbers (e.g., *Hylophilus poicilotis*).

Behavior

Vireo chivi acts as a forest scout, sounding the alarm when, for instance, a jay is patrolling the forest in search of bird nests. Amazonian *Hylophilus,* such as the Tawny-crowned Greenlet, *H. ochraceiceps,* join mixed flocks.

Breeding

The nest, fitted into a forked branch to which it is firmly attached, is a deep, open cup made of fiber, leaves, Spanish moss, vegetable hair (*Marasmius*) etc., coated on the outside with moss secured by spider webbing. The nest is situated at midheights, sometimes near the top of a tree. Eggs are white or reddish white with a few black and reddish white spots and speckles, or in *Vireo olivaceus,* almost none. The pair generally takes turns incubating. This lasts 12 or 13 days in *V. o. olivaceus* and 16 days in the Lesser Greenlet, *Hylophilus decurtatus,* of Central America. They sit more closely than many other birds. The male customarily participates in feeding the young, which abandon the nest at 10 to 11 days in *V. olivaceus.* The Shiny Cowbird, *Molothrus bonariensis,* lays its eggs in the nests of *V. olivaceus* and *Hylophilus poicilotis.*

Distribution and Evolution

Each species has its own ecological requirements. In southeastern Brazil *Hylophilus thoracicus* and *H. poicilotis* replace each other over a wide range. In Panama there are three resident *Vireo* species; periodically three other *Vireo* appear there as migrants. One of the factors governing the existence of vireonids is vegetation density. It is common for one representative of each genus to occur in the same habitat. The widely disjunct distribution of *H. thoracicus* documents the extinction of the species over a vast area that has been phytogeographically altered over the centuries. The Noronha Vireo, *Vireo gracilirostris,* and an *Elaenia* (Tyrannidae), both endemics, are the only Passerines on the island of Fernando do Noronha off the coast of Rio Grande do Norte.

Migration

Various *Vireo* species are migratory. Both northern and southern migratory species are found in Amazonia, where there is already a resident equatorial population. Thus *V. olivaceus* from North America appears as a migrant in northwestern Brazil (Amazonas, October; Mato Grosso), living there for some time alongside the local *V. chivi* and migrant ones from Argentina that at this season begin returning to their southern homeland. Even *Vireo* resident in Central America migrate to South America. Perhaps elimination of the outer primary (the tenth, counting from inside) of *V. olivaceus* (and also of *V. chivi*) is related to their migratory activities, during which they take advantage of their more pointed wings. However, there are also nonmigratory *Vireo* with long wings.

Rufous-browed Peppershrike, *Cyclarhis gujanensis,* Pitiguari   Pl 40.8

16 cm; 28 g. Unmistakable forest bird with large head and high, blunt, laterally compressed bill, slightly resembling a parrot bill. Wings short, plumage fluffy. Forehead and superciliaries rusty brown or chestnut, contrasting with gray sides of head. Breast intense yellowish green; iris yellow, orange, or red. *C. g. gujanensis,* with slate gray crown and long reddish superciliary, occurs in Amazonia.

voice: call (warning, male and female) *kreh, krraa; kep, kewp.* Song may be 1 of 3 distinct melodies with clear tone and plenty of intensity, timbre reminiscent of a large emberizid and impressive enough to inspire a number of common names for bird (see below): (1) a strongly descending sequence, *chewY-chewY (-chewY);* (2) a phrase rising at end,

Fig. 292. Slaty-capped Shrike-Vireo, *Smaragdolanius leucotis simplex*.

dewa-dewa-hiew, usually repeated more quietly a 2d time; (3) a horizontal phrase repeated 3–4 times at short intervals that appears to be true song of male. It varies to a degree according to region, e.g., *JIli-duh JIli-duh JIli-duh* (Rio de Janeiro), *plit-hewa-wooIT* (Mato Grosso), *tsewlew-DIlew-dewlo* (Amapá). Bird sings for an hour or more, varying intervals, then stays quiet for some time; becomes extremely active when a rival threatens its territory, and the 2 then have a singing duel. Sometimes moves to another melody. Easy to attract either sex by imitating these whistles, even outside breeding season. In any region it is one of most prominent voices.

Bird remains hidden in dense foliage at midheight or above, where it easily escapes observation, especially because it avoids flying. Forest edge, capoeira, groves in caatinga, parks and estates with plenty of trees. Near Rio de Janeiro more common in mountains. Mexico to Bolivia, Argentina, throughout Brazil. Includes *C. ochrocephala* of southeast. Also called *Gente-de-fora-vem*, *Tem cachaça-aí* (Espírito Santo), "We don't believe it," "Do you wash every week?" (Central America). Name *Pitiguari* also is used as a family name, being best known through a song of northeast. See *Hylophilus thoracicus*, which has similar color on breast and iris.

SLATY-CAPPED SHRIKE-VIREO, *Smaragdolanius leucotis*, Assobiador-do-castanhal   Fig. 292

14.5 cm; 25 g. Characteristic Amazonian species whose relationships have not yet been clarified. In aspect remotely similar to *Cyclarhis gujanensis* but less stocky and with bright color reminiscent of *Pitangus sulphuratus*. Head slate gray with wide superciliary, spot over eye, and entire underparts golden yellow; mantle and tail green. North of Amazon has white area on sides of head (*S. l. leucotis*) lacking in southern form (*S. l. simplex*); iris red. VOICE: a single, sharp, descending, monosyllabic whistle, *iewuh*, repeated at well-spaced intervals over an extended period. Perches openly in leafy canopy of high trees in primary forest, where difficult to

see. Flies straight from one canopy to another and will heed mimicking of a hunter without descending. At edge of forest meets *Cyclarhis gujanensis*, which lives at lower levels. The Guianas, Venezuela, Colombia, and Peru to Bolivia, Brazil from north of Amazon south to Rondônia, lower Tapajós, lower Tocantins (Marabá, Pará). There are 2 other, non-Brazilian, species that reach Mexico.

CHIVI VIREO, *Vireo chivi*, Juruviara   PL 40.6

14 cm; 15 g. Widely distributed forest bird with relatively long bill, gray cap, and white superciliary outlined with black; wings lack bars. Underparts pure white, except under tail coverts yellow and sides of body sometimes washed with yellowish green. Iris dark brown or grayish brown, not red like *V. olivaceus*. VOICE: call (warning) *gweh, greh;* song a monotonous bisyllabic whistle, *klewp-kleep, chewle-chew*, 20–24 times a minute, sung tirelessly in breeding season (also see "Vocalization"). Lives at middle levels of any kind of forest, also canopy. Greater part of South America, south to Argentina and throughout Brazil. Also called *Trinta-e-um* (ex-Guanabara).

RED-EYED VIREO, *Vireo olivaceus*, Juruviara-norte-americano   NV

Extremely similar to *V. chivi* but with red eye. Seasonal migrant from North America to northwestern Brazil (Amazonia, Mato Grosso) during northern winter.

I have adopted the concept of an *olivaceus* superspecies, uniting *V. olivaceus* of North America and *V. chivi* of South America. The surest means of distinguishing them (beyond iris color, which must be further studied, considering the existence of immatures), is by wing formula (fig. 293): in *olivaceus*, outer primary (9th counting from inside) is longer than 5th; in *chivi*, it is same length or shorter (see also "Mi-

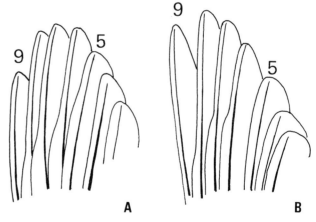

Fig. 293. Relative length of outer primaries (wing formula) of: (A) a Chivi Vireo, *Vireo chivi*, from Recife, Pernambuco, and (B) a Red-eyed Vireo, *V. olivaceus*, from Tapuruquara, Amazonas, that certainly originated in North America.

gration"). Short (1975) verified from abundant material in American museums that variation in *chivi* is so great it overlaps with *olivaceus*. Consequently *chivi* and *olivaceus* may be considered geographic races of 1 species. I prefer to keep the 2 separate so as not to obscure the definite differences. The voices of *olivaceus* and *chivi* are extremely similar. There are, however, other cases in which *Vireo* species that certainly are separate have very similar voices.

NORONHA VIREO, *Vireo gracilirostris*   BR

Only on Fernando de Noronha Island. Slender-billed, long-tailed (longer in male than female), abundant in island's low woodlands where it feeds from canopy to ground level by pursuing insects (Oren 1984). A close relative of Yucatan Vireo, *V. magister*, of Caribbean but not of *V. chivi* of continent. Also called *Sebito*. Incidentally, maritime birds resident on Fernando de Noronha also show affinity to those of Caribbean region.

BLACK-WHISKERED VIREO, *Vireo altiloquus*

Like *V. chivi* but with clearly stronger bill, distinct black malar stripe. VOICE: similar to *V. chivi*, tri- or bisyllabic, poorly rendered as *Julian Chivi*. Flooded forests, mangroves. In Brazil only in Amazonia, from Amazonas and Pará (January, July, December) south to lower Madeira and lower Tapajós and north to Antilles (principal center of species) and Florida, from where there is a partial migration to northern South America near end of year.

RUFOUS-CROWNED GREENLET, *Hylophilus poicilotis*, Verdinho-coroado   PL 40.7

12.4 cm; 11.8 g. Forest bird with short, sharp-pointed bill, relatively long tail. Unmistakable with rusty cap (both sexes) and black design on light gray sides of head. VOICE: call (warning) *chaa, chaa, chaa, chaa*. Male song a phrase of limpid, monotonous whistles, frequently in groups of 6: *jili, jili, jili . . . , tseLIT, tseLIT, tseLIT . . .* , reminiscent of song of Coal Tit, *Parus ater*, of Europe. Sometimes a standard 3 whistles, *chivil, chivil, chivil*, like *V. chivi*. Female responds with series of *kray, kray, kray*s. . . . Densely foliaged forests, generally in treetops, preferably in mountains in Rio de Janeiro and Espírito Santo and in caatinga of northeast (Bahia). Eastern Brazil from Piauí to Santa Catarina, Rio Grande do Sul, southeastern Mato Grosso, Bolivia, Paraguay, and Misiones, Argentina. Has a superficial resemblance to female Plain Antvireo, *Dysithamnus mentalis* (Formicariidae). Also called *Chenenéu* (Minas Gerais).

GRAY-EYED GREENLET, *Hylophilus amaurocephalus* BR

New studies (Willis 1990) have proven that this bird, recognized until now as a northern (São Paulo to northeast) subspecies of *H. poicilotis*, must be considered a separate species. The 2 may be sympatric in São Paulo.

LEMON-CHESTED GREENLET, *Hylophilus thoracicus*, Vite-vite

12.5 cm. Similar to *H. poicilotis* but with head olivaceous gray, forehead intensely greenish, breast bright lemon yellow like *Cyclarhis gujanensis*, abdomen white, iris yellowish white. VOICE: call (warning) *kray*. Song a flowing sequence of whistles, *dewEE, dewEE, dewEE . . .* , at times mixed with low *spet, spet*, at times sounding like *deBIDje, deBIDje, deBIDje . . .* or *tsewlit, tsewlit, tsewlit . . .* in slightly fuller tone than *poicilotis*. Low, sparse, sunny woodland, restinga, open capoeira in hot lowlands, forest edges, city districts with trees, e.g., Laranjeiras and Santa Tereza in Rio de Janeiro. Ecologically separated from *poicilotis*. The Guianas and Venezuela to upper Amazon (Amazonas, Acre), Bolivia, southeastern Brazil: Espírito Santo, Minas Gerais, Rio de Janeiro. See Green-backed Becard, *Pachyramphus viridis*.

GRAY-CHESTED GREENLET, *Hylophilus semicinereus*, Verdinho-da-várzea

11.3 cm. Like *H. thoracicus* but with gray breast, sides gray mixed with olivaceous yellow. VOICE: call (warning) *graay;* song a prolonged, 10-second or more, sequence of monotonous, resonant whistles, *ewEE, ewEE, ewEE . . .* , with crescendo noticeable at each start. In hottest hours of day scarcely stops. I registered 18 calls in 5 seconds from one individual that was not collected but I believe was of this species. Bird continued for 20 seconds without slightest alteration in rhythm but twice inserted a slightly weaker note. Thus it sang 72 consecutive notes. After a 2-second interval, as if to catch its breath, it continued with same song (see also "Vocalization"). Upper level of dense but low riverine or flooded forests, where song may be dominant voice (e.g., Mato Grosso, September). The Guianas and Venezuela to Brazilian Amazonia, south to upper Juruá, upper Xingu, eastern Pará, Maranhão. Also called *Ba-kama-kama* (Juruna, Mato Grosso). See Black-faced Dacnis, *Dacnis lineata*.

ASHY-HEADED GREENLET, *Hylophilus pectoralis*

Similar to *H. semicinereus* but with white throat and belly; intense greenish yellow breast. VOICE: very similar to *H. thoracicus*. Widely distributed in Amazonia to northeast (Alagoas), Goiás, Mato Grosso (upper Xingu), Bolivia.

TEPUI GREENLET, *Hylophilus sclateri*
Only in Roraima.

BUFF-CHEEKED GREENLET, *Hylophilus muscicapinus*
Amazonia.

BROWN-HEADED GREENLET, *Hylophilus brunneiceps*
Amazonia.

DUSKY-CAPPED GREENLET, *Hylophilus hypoxanthus*
Only in upper Amazon.

TAWNY-CROWNED GREENLET, *Hylophilus ochraceiceps*
Only in upper Amazon.

Vireonidae Bibliography
See also General Bibliography

Eisenmann, E. 1962. *Condor* 64:505–8. [*Vireo*, taxonomy]
Hamilton, T. H. 1958. *Wilson Bull.* 70:307–46. [*Vireo*, variation]
Hamilton, T. H. 1962. *Condor* 64:40–68. [*Vireo*, taxonomy]

Johnson, N. K., R. M. Zink, and J. A. Marten. 1988. Genetic evidence for relationships in the avian family Vireonidae. *Condor* 90:428–45.
Oren, D. C. 1984. As relações taxonômicas dos Vireonidae. *XI Cong. Bras. Zool., Belém*:331–32.
Sibley, C. G., and J. E. Ahlquist. 1982. The relationships of the Vireos indicated by DNA-DNA Hybridization. *Wilson Bull.* 94:114–28.
Skutch, A. F. 1960. *Life Histories of Central American Birds*, vol. 2. Pacific Coast Avifauna 34:11–42. Berkeley, Calif.: Cooper Orn. Soc.
Skutch, A. F. 1967. *Publ. Nuttall Orn. Club* 7:123–29. [*Cyclarhis*, behavior]
Willis, E. O. 1990. *Hylophilus poicilotis* and *H. amaurocephalus*, espécies simpátricas. *XVII Cong. Bras. Zool., Londrina*: 167.

FAMILY EMBERIZIDAE
SUBFAMILY PARULINAE: WOOD-WARBLERS (19)

Members of this large American subfamily of Oscines are regularly found from Alaska and Canada to Argentina. The group is most diversified in North America. It has relatively recently (AOU 1983) been included in the Emberizidae family, along with the Icterinae, Coerebinae, Thraupinae, Cardinalinae, and Emberizinae. There are Miocene (25 million years B.P.) fossils from Florida.

In the Neotropics the greatest number of species occur in the Antilles and mountainous regions of Central and South America. They belong to the nine-primaried Oscines and are related to the Thraupinae, Coerebinae, and Emberizinae. In life they resemble vireonids, such as *Hylophilus*, and small tyrannids. Brazil has 11 resident species. Eight additional nonbreeding tropical species appear, fleeing the North American winter, but according to Morton (pers. comm.) they should not be considered visitors.

Morphology

Wood-warblers are forest birds that are little known in Brazil. Their dominant colors are green and yellow, and there is frequently some distinctive design on the head. In Brazil there is only one brightly colored resident species, the Rose-breasted Chat, *Granatellus pelzelni*, an unusual Amazonian bird reminiscent of a strange saíra tanager. Bills are slender but strong, as in other insectivorous birds, and sometimes broad and surrounded with whiskers. Wings are sizable and the tail in many cases relatively long. Sexes are similar in Brazilian species, excepting the Masked Yellowthroat, *Geothlypis aequinoctialis*, and *Granatellus pelzelni*, but different in migrant species from the north—the North American warblers—whose males have extremely varied coloring and whose females and immatures appear modest and indistinct. Whereas Brazilian species keep their attractive dress—similar in males, females, and immatures—all year, northern species acquire a dull plumage (similar to the regular dress of their females) in the nonbreeding season, which coincides with a long migration to the tropics. They molt to this modest plumage before leaving for the south and change it for their nuptial plumage before returning to their homeland in the extreme north, the only region where they breed.

Vocalization

The voice is generally attractive. Brazilian species sing all year, preferring the warmer hours of the day. Melodies are rhythmic. *Geothlypis aequinoctialis* and *Basileuterus* songs are loud and melodious, although standardized. The song of the White-rimmed Warbler, *B. leucoblepharus*, is one of the most notable voices in the forested region of the Serra do Mar. The same can be said for that of the White-striped Warbler, *B. leucophrys*, in gallery forests of the planalto, a completely different habitat. *G. aequinoctialis* has, in addition to its sweet song, a crackling phrase corresponding to a fighting song. The female River Warbler, *Phaeothlypis rivularis*, sings nicely, at times in response to the male. The female *B. leucophrys* gives a squeaky counterpoint, closely accompanying the melody of her mate.

As has been shown in North America, wood-warblers that inhabit treetops generally have voices with higher frequencies or pitch than those residing at middle levels or on the ground. The lower frequencies can be heard at a greater distance and are more appropriate for penetrating the dense vegetation of the lower forest levels (see also forest tinamous) or for competing with the noise of streams with rapids. The Blackpoll Warbler, *Dendroica striata*, which lives in the canopy, has one of the highest voices known, with an average frequency of 8900 Hz; semiterrestrial species, such as the *Seiurus* waterthrushes, which live at the edge of streams, as does our *Phaeothlypis rivularis,* have an average frequency of 4000 Hz.

Feeding

The Tropical Parula, *Parula pitiayumi,* is insectivorous, finding small arthropods and caterpillars in the corollas of flowers and sometimes catching flying insects. It eats *Cecropia* corpuscles (white ovoid grains the size of a pinhead, well hidden in the felt at the base of the leaves). These corpuscles, discovered by Fritz Müller in Santa Catarina, are rich in proteins and therefore much sought after by the symbiotic ants of cecropia (see also Thraupinae, "Feeding"). *P. pitiayumi* also feeds on the sweet excretion of plant lice while hovering (see Trochilidae and Thraupinae, "Feeding"). Some, such as the Flavescent Warbler, *Basileuterus flaveolus; B. leucoblepharus;* and *Phaeothlypis rivularis,* prefer to seek their sustenance on the ground or very low in the foliage. Note that migrant wood-warblers from the north become frugivorous in subtropical and tropical zones.

Behavior

Wood-warblers are quite restless and given to much tail movement. Three principal types of movement can be observed that are performed habitually and not just as display poses during courtship: (1) tilting the tail up and down continuously, opening it and moving it to the sides (*Phaeothlypis rivularis*); (2) raising the tail upward, without any regular rhythm (Golden-crowned Warbler, *Basileuterus culicivorus*), while opening it wide (*B. leucoblepharus, B. flaveolus, Granatellus pelzelni*); (3) opening the tail and holding it open (American Redstart, *Setophaga ruticilla;* Slate-throated Redstart, *Myioborus miniatus*); this demonstration recalls the behavior of the Sulphur-rumped Flycatcher, *Myiobius barbatus.* Tail movements are frequently accompanied by wing movements, more commonly, for example, in *P. rivularis* in a rapid stretching of the wings. *Granatellus pelzelni* opens and even raises its wings.

Wood-warblers move by hopping, not walking, as is the way of arboreal, nonterrestrial birds. They make noise among dry leaves like wrens or furnariids when looking for food on the ground. They bathe in streams (*B. flaveolus*).

Species such as *B. culicivorus* and *G. pelzelni* periodically accompany mixed flocks of small birds. This can also be said of *Dendroica striata,* a migrant from North America. Wood-warblers are curious and come at once when another bird warns, for instance, of the presence during the day of an owl.

Brazilian Residents: Breeding

The *Basileuterus* build a nest on the ground, among dry leaves and living plants, covered on top to a degree that varies with the species, sometimes with a very projecting overhang (*B. flaveolus*). They prefer to find niches in embankments (*B. culicivorus, Phaeothlypis rivularis*). *Parula pitiayumi* constructs a small open basket in dense epiphytic vegetation high in trees or weaves its nest in hanging, swinging pieces of Spanish moss (*Tillandsia usneoides*) (Rio de Janeiro). *Geothlypis aequinoctialis* makes a deep, open, well-finished cup in clumps of grass, especially in marshy terrain. The nest of the Red-breasted Chat, *Granatellus venustus,* of Mexico is an open cup with thin walls placed in the fork of a tree.

Whereas *Granatellus* eggs are pure white, those of *Parula pitiayumi* have purplish speckles on a white field; *Basileuterus culicivorus* eggs have a crown of bluish and red spots, and those of *Geothlypis aequinoctialis* have a reddish background with violet and red spots. *Phaeothlypis rivularis* incubation in Costa Rica is performed only by the female and takes 16 to 19 days. The young are fed by the parents. The inside of the nestlings' mouths is orange or red.

Parent birds are very diligent in their efforts to mislead possible intruders who come near the nest. *Basileuterus flaveolus* appears to sweep the ground with its widely opened tail, opens and shakes its wings, and ruffles up the feathers of its rump; it also pretends to preen or to work on a nest, and it picks at imaginary insects; meanwhile it moves from the ground to lower branches and back to the ground, calling and attracting attention. I have seen similar behavior with *Geothlypis aequinoctialis.*

Young *Phaeothlypis rivularis fulvicauda* abandon the nest at 12 to 15 days. *G. aequinoctialis* and *Basileuterus leucophrys* are sometimes victims of the Shiny Cowbird, *Molothrus bonariensis.*

Distribution, Evolution, and Habitat

The development of Amazonia left widely separated populations of *Basileuterus culicivorus* in various geographic races and in localities that today are north and south of the Hylaea as far away as Mexico. The *hypoleucus* population [referred to as White-bellied Warbler, *B. hypoleucus,* in Meyer de Schauensee 1970] underwent long geographic separation because of ancient geoclimatic events that produced a great change in its coloration, whereas its voice remained the same as that of *B. c. auricapillus* (see this phenomenon also in Dendrocolaptidae, ("Distribution . . .") and Formicariidae "Vocalization"). This confirms that the two are cospecific and that *B. hypoleucus* should be called *B. c. hypoleucus,* for the two forms interbreed where they now meet. Consideration has been given to treating *B. leucophrys* and *B. leucoblepharus* as conspecific, but their voices do not support this.

B. culicivorus and *B. leucoblepharus* live in the forests of the Serra do Mar and their extensions, such as the forest of the Rio Iguaçu in Paraná. *B. c. hypoleucus* and *B. leucophrys* may be syntopic in the planalto (humid gallery forests). *B. c. culicivorus* is a neighbor of *B. flaveolus* in Ceará. *B. flaveolus* is one of the typical birds of the caatinga in the northeast; it inhabits the dry, low woodland presently interspersed with the Hylaea in Pará as well as the high, humid riverine forest of Mato Grosso. Its distribution has become discontinuous because of the relatively recent interposition of Amazonia, although the bird is managing to occupy certain Hylaea areas through subsequent invasion. *Phaeothlypis rivularis,* forced away from the river edge during floods, enters adjacent forests moistened by rains and thereby reaches other river systems. Thus it is easy to imagine how its notable dispersion occurred. Nevertheless, there has not been sufficient segregation for various geographic races to evolve. *P. rivularis* is one of the few Brazilian Passerines adapted to a forest river habitat (see Sharp-tailed Streamcreeper, *Lochmias nematura,* a furnariid, and Sooty Tyrannulet, *Serpophaga nigricans*). All Brazilian *Basileuterus* can be abundant in their respective regions.

TROPICAL PARULA, *Parula pitiayumi,*
Mariquita   PL 40.9

9.8 cm; 7.5 g. Smallest Brazilian wood-warbler, widely distributed. Unmistakable with bluish upperparts, 2 white wing bars, yellow underparts, breast tending toward caramel. Outer tail feathers have white spot. VOICE: call a high, shrill *tsik, tsit-tsik;* very high song is a fast-tempo sequence that rises in crescendo, then goes undulatingly down or ends in ascending tremolo. Tree canopies where it would be easily overlooked were it not for untiring song, sung even in hottest hours. Texas, Mexico, and Central America through greater part of South America, except Amazonia, to Bolivia, Argentina, Paraguay, Uruguay, eastern and central Brazil: Roraima, Maranhão to Rio Grande do Sul, Mato Grosso. Also called *Figuinha-baiana* (Minas Gerais), *Vira-folhas* (ex-Guanabara), *Pitiayumi* (Paraguay, Argentina). It is a geographic replacement of Parula Warbler, *P. americana,* of North America, including Canada.

MASKED YELLOWTHROAT, *Geothlypis aequinoctialis,*
Pia-cobra   PL 40.10

13.5 cm; 11 g. Widely distributed, common wetland species. Tail long and wide. Male has black mask and gray cap, lacking in female and immature. VOICE: call a harsh *CHAlap* (reminiscent of House Sparrow, *Passer domesticus*); has 2 entirely different "songs": (1) a smooth, sweet, descending sequence reminiscent of our Ultramarine Grosbeak, *Passerina brissonii,* and Willow Warbler, *Phylloscopus trochilus,* of Europe; (2) a descending, croaking sequence, *chip-chap-chap,* at times repeated, used to confront a rival. Marshy areas with bushes, buriti palm groves, riverine tangles, flooded gallery forest. Panama across major part of South America to Bolivia, Paraguay, Argentina, Uruguay, all of Brazil. Also called *Canário-sapé, Canário-do-brejo,*

Vira-folhas, Caga-sebo, Curió-do-brejo (Minas Gerais). See immature female *Basileuterus flaveolus* and female Yellow-backed Tanager, *Hemithraupis flavicollis,* both forest species but not syntopic; also see Connecticut Warbler, *Oporornis agilis.*

ROSE-BREASTED CHAT, *Granatellus pelzelni,*
Polícia-do-mato   PL 40.12

11.8 cm. Unique Amazonian species, only one with its coloration, female also unmistakable with cinnamon face, etc., and red crissum. Immature male lacks black on head and throat. VOICE: call a smooth *jew-jew* (reminiscent of a tyrannid) and a loud, descending, trisyllabic chirp, *dreww-dreww-dreww;* song a descending sequence of 7 mellow notes. Medium levels in dense riverine forests. Bobs and opens tail, simultaneously raising wings. Suriname and Venezuela to Bolivia, Mato Grosso (upper Xingu), eastern Pará (Belém), Maranhão.

The following two species are found in Brazil only in northern Amazonas and Roraima, near the Venezuelan frontier, their distribution being broader outside Brazil, where they live in mountainous regions of the continent. They resemble *Basileuterus culicivorus,* even to the song, and have yellow underparts. Both attract attention by their nervous opening of the white-edged tail (like *Setophaga ruticilla*). They are:

SLATE-THROATED REDSTART, *Myioborus miniatus*
Black throat.

BROWN-CAPPED REDSTART, *Myioborus brunniceps*
White eye-ring and superciliary, brownish back.

FLAVESCENT WARBLER, *Basileuterus flaveolus,*
Canário-do-mato

14.1 cm; 12 g. Semiterrestrial species of hot, interior regions, with upperparts olive green; lores, short superciliary, and underparts yellow. Bill black with base of mandible a bit lighter. Tarsi yellow. VOICE: call (warning) a high *tik;* melodious song quite rhythmic, jumping from high to low in repeated motifs, e.g., *deDI, deDI, deDI-tseh, tseh, tseh, tseh, DIdel, DIdel-tslew, tslew-tsiew, tsiew,* one of most noticeable songs in its area. Riverine woods, dry woodland edges, dense cerrado, caatinga, etc. See also "Distribution. . . ." Found among lowest branches or rustling on ground. Venezuela to Bolivia, Paraguay, eastern and central Brazil: northeast, Bahia, Minas Gerais, São Paulo, Santa Catarina, Goiás, Mato Grosso. Sometimes alongside *B. culicivorus.* Meets *B. leucoblepharus* in interior of Santa Catarina. Also called *Canário-do-chão* (Pernambuco), *Canário-de-chapada* (Minas Gerais). See *Geothlypis aequinoctialis,* whose female is more slender than female *B. flaveolus.*

TWO-BANDED WARBLER, *Basileuterus bivittatus*

Only in extreme north, from Roraima to Venezuela and northwestern Argentina.

GOLDEN-CROWNED WARBLER, *Basileuterus culicivorus auricapillus*, Pula-pula

12.2 cm; 10.5 g. Widely distributed. Olive green upperparts, whitish superciliary outlined above and below by blackish line, reddish gray central stripe on cap. Underparts yellow. VOICE: call *ks, tsi;* song an ascending sequence of high whistles at 3 levels, *ji, ji-ji, ji-ji, ji* or *tsew, tsew-tshi, tshi-tsi.* Forest interior at middle heights, tirelessly hopping through foliage. Mexico and Central America through greater part of South America to Bolivia, Paraguay, Argentina, Uruguay; northern Brazil (Roraima), eastern Brazil (Maranhão to Rio Grande do Sul), central Brazil (Mato Grosso, southern Pará [Cachimbo], Goiás).

Replaced in central Brazil, southern and western Minas Gerais, southern Goiás, Federal District, Mato Grosso, part of interior of São Paulo, and northern Paraguay by *B. c. hypoleucus* (Pl 40.11), which has grayish white underparts with only crissum and thighs yellowish. In vocalization and ecology identical to *B. c. auricapillus,* with which it interbreeds.

WHITE-STRIPED WARBLER, *Basileuterus leucophrys*, Pula-pula-de-sobrancelha   BR

15.3 cm. Largest *Basileuterus,* similar to *B. leucoblepharus* but with brownish back and blackish cap and ocular stripe contrasting with wide, white superciliary and white underparts; under tail coverts brownish. VOICE: sonorous and with high timbre (suggesting song of an imaginary icterine or wren), very different from *leucoblepharus;* there are surprising shifts between very clear high and low notes, e.g., *tsidelidel-dee tsidelidel-deww;* other individuals (nearby males in Federal District) sing a beautiful ascending trill, e.g., *di, di, di-rrewit di, di, di;* female accompanies song of male with a very high squeak while hopping and flying around him. Flooded gallery forests where it is one of most typical birds, attracting attention by voice. A dawn singer. Northwestern São Paulo, Mato Grosso, Goiás, Federal District, in last-mentioned area sometimes alongside *B. c. hypoleucus;* also western Bahia (Rio das Pedras), Minas Gerais (Patrocínio). On its relationship to *B. leucoblepharus,* see "Distribution. . . ."

WHITE-RIMMED WARBLER, *Basileuterus leucoblepharus*, Pula-pula-assoviador

14.4 cm. Typical inhabitant of high, forest-covered mountains of southeast and adjacent areas with humid climate. Relatively large with long, broad tail; upperparts dark green, center of cap gray, eye-ring and narrow superciliary white; underparts white with grayish sides; under tail coverts yel-lowish. VOICE: call a sharp *pist, tsi;* a notably loud and melodious song starting with a hurried warble, then passing to a clear, descending scale. Interior of heavily shaded forest; semiterrestrial, staying at low levels or hopping along ground. Rio de Janeiro (mountains) to Rio Grande do Sul, at Foz do Iguaçu in Paraná; also Argentina (Misiones), Paraguay, Uruguay. Frequently alongside *B. culicivorus,* which lives at higher levels. To some extent resembles *Seiurus* of North America (see "Vocalization"). Also called *João-conquinho* (Rio de Janeiro).

RIVER WARBLER, *Phaeothlypis* (= *Basileuterus*) *rivularis*, Pula-pula-ribeirinho

14.2 cm; 14.5 g. Exclusively riverine forest species. Upperparts greenish, underparts white and cinnamon; superciliary and sides of head cinnamon. VOICE: call (warning) a soft *tsig, tsig, tsig, tsig;* song a resonant, crescendo sequence of 8 monotonous, sonorous whistles preceded by 3 lower diatonic notes. Edge of streams running though forest, hops on roots and stones under branches overhanging water, almost constantly bobbing tail vertically and horizontally and slightly opening and agitating wings. Locally from Honduras to Bolivia, Paraguay, and Misiones, Argentina; Amazonia (Amazonas, Pará, northern Maranhão), southeastern Brazil from Bahia to Rio Grande do Sul, Paraná as far as Foz do Iguaçu. Includes *P. fulvicauda* of upper Amazon. Also called *Lavadeira-do-mato.* See also introductory headings and riverine Sooty Tyrannulet, *Serpophaga nigricans,* which has somewhat similar behavior.

Northern Migrant Species

At least eight North American migrant species, known as warblers in the United States and Canada and as reinitas or candelitas in Venezuela, Colombia, etc., congregate in Brazil north of the Amazon. Of the 57 warbler species in North America, 17 come to South America during the northern winter, some continuing as far as northern Argentina.

Males arrive on this continent in dull nonbreeding or immature plumage, similar to that of the female for each respective species. They resemble small Tyrannidae, Vireonidae, and Coerebinae. Discovery of additional migrant warbler species is to be expected, even in southeastern Brazil. Their identification is not easy; I recommend consulting U.S. field guides, which treat them exhaustively.

They migrate only at night, making extraordinary efforts. In the U.S. it has been calculated that a warbler in nocturnal migration loses 1% of its total weight per hour of flight, an expenditure a bird can afford only after accumulating a large fat reserve. At night they are attracted and disoriented by light sources such as large illuminated windows into which they fly and die. Thousands die annually at illuminated TV towers in the U.S. They rest and eat during the day.

The best known of these, with respect to its migration, is

Dendroica striata, many of which are reported regularly to cross extensive stretches of the North Atlantic, starting in New England (Massachusetts) in September and, when the weather is favorable, flying directly to the Antilles or coast of Venezuela. This involves nonstop flights that cover thousands of kilometers over various days and nights. Murray (1989) thinks information obtained primarily from radar should be reviewed and consideration to given to statistics on migrant weight that reveal the readiness of the birds to undertake long flights. The normal weight of a blackpoll is 12 g. Fat migrant individuals reach more than 19 g and even up to 23 g (compare Charadriidae, "Visiting Species . . .").

It is of particular interest to note the ecological conditions under which these birds live on this continent, these being generally very different from those of their homeland. They choose a certain area for their "winter vacation." I found a *Dendroica striata* that remained for three months (February–April) in a group of leafy trees in the middle of Rio de Janeiro, living there peacefully with various Brazilian birds resident in the same habitat (Sick 1971). Although having adapted to a particular northern biotope (exclusively coniferous forest in high latitudes with a late spring), *D. striata* is able to adapt to certain tropical environments where it stays for a longer time on its lengthy migrations. Perhaps it finds here, in the delicate foliage of the tamarinds (*Tamarindus indicus*) to which it gives preference in the Municipality of Rio de Janeiro, an adequate substitute for conifers. In Amazonia migrant wood-warblers accompanying flocks of local birds appear especially on forest edges and in semiopen areas, which makes observing them easier.

These visiting Passerines generally don't sing, their only aural signals being calls. Only at the end of their stay on this continent do they begin to sing. Being one of the most northern species, *D. striata* seeks extreme southern regions (it sometimes continues traveling to Argentina and rarely Chile), a regular occurrence already discussed in the case of the Peregrine Falcon, *Falco peregrinus tundrius*.

YELLOW WARBLER, *Dendroica petechia*   NV

12 cm. Typical paruline. With predominantly yellow coloring remotely resembles Orange-fronted Yellow-Finch, *Sicalis columbiana*. Forehead and tail spots yellow. Underparts streaked with chestnut, but this is lacking in immatures, which are frequent among migrants here. VOICE: call *tsip* (similar to various *Tangara* (Thraupinae). Bushes, forest edges, mangroves (*canário-de-mangue*, "mangrove canary," a name used in Antilles). Recorded in Amapá (November), Marajó (Pará), Purus (Amazonas, February), and Roraima in good numbers at edge of flooded fields (R. Cavalcanti). There is resident population in Venezuela. Includes *D. aestiva*.

CERULEAN WARBLER, *Dendroica cerulea*   NV

Observed by D. Scott on 24 October and 13 November 1980 in forests of Tinguá, Rio de Janeiro.

BLACKBURNIAN WARBLER, *Dendroica fusca*   NV

12 cm. In nonbreeding season and when immature, has yellow superciliary that extends behind cheek. Throat also yellow, becoming orange in male nuptial dress. Two white wing bars. Recorded in Roraima (March) and Nova Lombardia, Santa Tereza (Espírito Santo, December, T. Parker).

BLACKPOLL WARBLER, *Dendroica striata*   NV

13 cm. When it arrives in September–October, it is greenish white or yellowish below with vestiges of blackish streaking on sides and 2 white wing bars. At beginning of year male molts into nuptial plumage: cheeks and underparts white, contrasting with black cap and black streaking, yellow legs. VOICE: call *tsep;* warning *tsep tsep tsep;* begins to sing from April on with very high, crescendo squeak, *tsi, tsi, tsi* . . . (see "Vocalization"). Tree canopies where it associates with mixed flocks (Amazonia). Roraima, Amazonas (Manaus, October), Pará (Belém), ex-Guanabara (January–May, see "Northern Migrant Species"), São Paulo (March), migrates as far as Argentina. Principal wintering areas in South America are Orinoco and upper Amazon regions. Many winter in Mexico. In October arrives in flocks in Central America, together with many other North American migrants.

NORTHERN WATERTHRUSH, *Seiurus noveboracensis*   NV

On Rio Alto Paru de Leste in Pará (November).

CONNECTICUT WARBLER, *Oporornis* (= *Geothlypis*) *agilis*,   NV

13.5 cm. Upperparts and from throat to breast uniformly olive green. No wing bars but clear, white eye-ring. Belly yellowish. VOICE: a strident *pic*. Low levels in dense vegetation. Observed on Solimões (Amazonas, April), Madeira (November), Rio São Lourenço (Mato Grosso; December, January).

CANADA WARBLER, *Wilsonia canadensis*   NV

12.5 cm. Upperparts grayish, no white in wing, lores and eye-ring yellow. Underparts yellow with breast more or less streaked. Low levels in dense vegetation. Recorded in Roraima (April).

AMERICAN REDSTART, *Setophaga ruticilla*   NV

12 cm. Unmistakable with large orange (male) or yellow (female, immature) spots in wings and tail, displayed frequently by opening wing and tail feathers as it hops restlessly through foliage, recalling a small *Myiobius* tyrannid (see "Behavior"). Recorded in Roraima (April).

Parulinae Bibliography

Brand, A. R. 1938. *Auk* 55:263–68. [Vocalization]

Cherry, J. D., D. H. Doherty, and K. D. Powers. 1985. An offshore nocturnal observation of migrating Blackpoll Warblers. *Condor* 87:548–49.

Ficken, M. S., and R. W. Ficken. 1962. *The Living Bird* 1:103–22. [Behavior]

Keast, A. 1980. Spatial relationships of migratory parulid warblers and their ecological counterparts in the neotropics. In: Keast and Morton, eds)., *Migrant Birds in the Neotropics: Ecology, Behavior, Distribution, and Conservation.* Washington, D.C.: Smithsonian Institution Press.

Murray, B. G., Jr. 1965. On the autumn migration of the Blackpoll Warbler. *Wilson Bull.* 77:122–33.

Murray, B. G., Jr. 1989. A critical review of the transoceanic migration of the Blackpoll Warbler. *Auk* 106(1):8–17.

Nisbet, I.C.T. 1963. Weight loss during migration 2. Review and other estimates. *Bird Banding* 34(3):139–59.

Nisbet, I.C.T., W. H. Drury, and J. Baird. 1963. Weight loss during migration 1. Deposition and consumption of fat by the Blackpoll Warbler, *Dendroica striata. Bird Banding* 34(3):109–38.

Parkes, K. C. 1964. Warbler chapter. In A. L. Thompson, ed., *A New Dictionary of Birds.* New York: McGraw-Hill.

Pough, R. H. 1949. *Audubon Bird Guide, Small Land Birds.* Garden City, N.Y.: Doubleday. [And other North American field guides showing migrants that come periodically to Brazil, all with illustrations]

Sick, H. 1971. *Wilson Bull.* 83:198–200. [*Dendroica striata* in Rio de Janeiro]

Skutch, A. F. 1954. *Life Histories of Central American Birds,* vol. 1. Pacific Coast Avifauna 31:339–86. Berkeley, Calif.: Cooper Orn. Soc.

Skutch, A. F. 1967. Life Histories of Central American Highland Birds. *Publ. Nuttall Orn. Club* 7:137–64.

Stiles, F. G., and R. G. Campos. 1983. Identification and occurrence of Blackpoll Warblers in southern Middle America. *Condor* 85:254–55.

FAMILY EMBERIZIDAE
SUBFAMILY COEREBINAE: BANANAQUIT (1)

With abandonment of the Coerebidae family, the Bananaquit, *Coereba flaveola,* remains as the only member of the Coerebinae.

BANANAQUIT, *Coereba flaveola,*
Cambacica, Mariquita   PL 40.2

10.8 cm; 10 g. One of our most abundant species, very common in gardens. Awl-billed, with wide, white superciliary, gray throat, lemon-yellow belly. Popularly described as a miniature Great Kiskadee, *Pitangus sulphuratus.* Immature has almost no streak above eye, gray underparts. Difference in size sometimes noted among birds approaching hummingbird feeders (e.g., in Rio de Janeiro) may be attributed to sexual dimorphism, male being larger. VOICE: call a high-pitched *tsri.* Song a hurried, undulating, loud sibilance, *tsi, tsi-tsiA, tsiA, tsiA-tsi, tsi.* Locally song may be more melodious, reminiscent of a wood-warbler. It is one of most tireless and assiduous singers, being heard at any hour of day and any time of year. Female *Coereba* also sings but only a little and for shorter periods. Recent fledglings get attention of their parents with a continuous twittering, *psi* (location call).

Coereba, one of the most anthophilous/nectarivorous species, is unique in various morphological and biological characteristics compared with some of the species, now in the Thraupinae, with which it shared the now dismantled Coerebidae family, e.g., Green Honeycreeper, *Chlorophanes, Cyanerpes,* and *Diglossa,* formerly associated with the Coerebidae, a family name now abandoned. The true reaching the nectar (see Thraupinae, "Feeding"). More than two-thirds of the food of *Coereba* is nectar. With its curved, awl-sharp bill it perforates the calyx of flowers whose nec-taries it cannot reach directly. In this way the flower is cheated of fertilization, as with, for instance, cultivated malvaceas having large red flowers (see Pl 40.2). As the flower wilts, the holes made this way become larger, permitting hummingbirds and insects to reach the nectary easily. *Coereba* is able to exploit flowers of widely varying types, including those with very small corollas united in panicles.

In Rio de Janeiro I have sometimes seen *Coereba* try to hover, apparently unsuccessfully, in front of a sugar-water bottle in hope of sipping the coveted liquid. To achieve its goal it usually clutches the feeding tube. Even in heavily populated places it takes over feeders placed out for hummingbirds. In Rio de Janeiro (Laranjeiras) it has begun to exploit planted verandas on buildings of whatever height, from where it also sings. A nest has been found on a veranda in the Leblon area of Rio de Janeiro. It uses a wide variety of flowers, beginning with hibiscus and going on to those of bromeliads, etc., and to banana inflorescences (which would justify the name *bananaquit,* for it has little interest in bananas).

Because of frequent contact with sticky liquid nectar, *Coereba* bathes often. It occasionally bathes in rainwater accumulated in bromeliads, where at the same time it feeds on small animal life found there, e.g., mosquito larvae (Serra do Mar, Rio de Janeiro). It also drinks from leaf imbrications and cleans the bill by wiping the sides on a branch, as do many birds. *Coereba* and *Chlorophanes spiza* occasionally use ants to enjoy the stimulus of the formic acid (anting).

Coereba has a peculiar technique it quite commonly uses for various purposes: "gaping" (see also Icterinae, "Feeding") is also used by the *Dacnis* and Red-legged Honeycreeper, *Cyanerpes cyaneus*. A captive *Coereba* speared ant pupae and then opened its mandibles, permitting examination of the inside of the casing which it explored with its tongue. Gaping must also be useful in separating petals to reach a nectary.

Bananaquits are always on the move, similar to woodwarblers searching for food, often hanging with head or back down while clutching firmly with their sharp claws. They are very quarrelsome and even fall grappling to the ground where they continue the struggle. To frighten a rival, *Coereba* stands, stretches its body, and vibrates its wings, a gesture even more impressive in northern races that have a large white speculum.

The spherical nest, built at various heights and poorly concealed, may be of 2 types: (1) relatively high and well finished with thick walls and a small, high entrance leading downward, covered by a long porch that reaches from the base of the nest and completely hides the entrance; it is constructed by the pair and serves for rearing the young; or (2) a smaller, loosely constructed nest, wider than it is high, with a low, wide entry; it serves only as a resting place and overnight roost. Many nests of the latter type are found; they are built in 2–4 hours by 1 individual at any season of the year and are commonly uninhabited. Two individuals of a pair are never found in the same nest. Nests dedicated to rearing the young require 6–8 days work. Some examined in Tobago were composed of 404–650 individual pieces.

Incubation is performed exclusively by the female and takes 12–13 days. The inside of the nestlings' mouths is red, as is that of the Blue Dacnis, *Dacnis cayana*. The male helps feed the young. Whereas tanagers of the *Cyanerpes, Chlorophanes,* and *Dacnis* genera bring food for the young in the mouth or bill, *Coereba* regurgitates the rations of its young, in which insects play an important part. *Coereba* nest hygiene is performed with care: the mother swallows the nestlings' fecal sacs or carries them far away. The young fledge at 17–19 days.

Coereba lives in all kinds of secondary forests where there are flowers, from Mexico and the Guianas to Bolivia, Paraguay, and Misiones, Argentina, and throughout Brazil south to Rio Grande do Sul. Numerous geographic races have evolved in its vast range; a melanistic variant, almost all black (polymorphism), is found on islands off the coast of Venezuela. Also called *Caga-sebo, Sebito, Chiquita* (ex-Guanabara), *Papa-banana* (Rio Grande do Sul), *Saí, Temtem-coroado* (Pará).

Coerebinae Bibliography

Beecher, W. J. 1951. Convergence in the Coerebidae. *Wilson Bull.* 63:274–87.

Carvalho, C. T. 1958. *Bol. Mus. Paraen., Zool.* 10. [*Coereba,* behavior]

Gross, A. O. 1958. *Wilson Bull.* 70:257–79. [*Coereba,* behavior]

Winkel, W. 1968. Zirkeln bei Zuckervögeln (Coerebidae) *Z. Tierpsychol.* 25:533–36.

SUBFAMILY THRAUPINAE: TANAGERS (96)

[Translator's note: Dr. Sick groups certain tanager genera under headings for which there are no English-language equivalents and whose components may vary with circumstances. In these cases I have adhered to his Brazilian terminology. Thus, "tiés" (tee-AIS), refers primarily to *Tachyphonus, Habia,* and *Ramphocelus;* "sanhaços" (san-YA-sues) refers primarily to *Thraupis* and *Stephanophorus;* "saíras" (sa-EER-as) refers to *Tangara* and *Chlorophonia;* and "saís" (sa-EES) refers to *Dacnis, Cyanerpes,* and *Chlorophanes.*]

The Thraupinae, formerly considered a separate family, is one of the great groups of American birds. Its broadest speciation has occurred in warm climates. There is a Pleistocene (20,000 years B.P.) fossil from the Dominican Republic. Tanagers are nine-primaried Oscines. The group has become quite complex with inclusion of the genera *Dacnis, Chlorophanes, Cyanerpes,* and *Diglossa,* formerly associated with the Coerebidae, a family name now abandoned. The true affinity of the former Coerebidae with the Thraupinae is demonstrated by hybrids produced in captivity, such as Red-legged Honeycreeper, *Cyanerpes cyaneus,* × Masked Tanager, *Tangara nigrocincta.* Sometimes tiés, such as the Brazilian Tanager, *Ramphocelus bresilius,* and Ruby-crowned Tanager, *Tachyphonus coronatus,* and saíras, such as the Seven-colored Tanager, *Tangara fastuosa,* and Blue-necked Tanager, *T. cyanicollis,* hybridize in captivity. Some species, such as the Black-faced Tanager, *Schistochlamys melanopis,* and Diademed Tanager, *Stephanophorus diadematus,* are quite close to the Emberizinae. The Opal-crowned Tanager, *Tangara callophrys,* is similar to the *Cyanerpes,* and the Dotted Tanager, *Tangara varia,* is like the *Dacnis.*

Morphology

The tanagers, also called thraupines and tanagrids, contribute decidedly to the reputation for beauty held by Neotropical avifauna. The most colorful are in the largest genus, *Tangara,* with more than 40 species, (Brazil having "only" 20). Among them are representatives having the greatest number of colors known in one species. The *Cyanerpes* compete with the *Tangara* in beauty. The brilliant color effect is often reinforced by a metallic or opalescent sheen and by a difference in head feather structure, as in the Paradise Tanager, *Tangara chilensis.*

The intense red of *Ramphocelus bresilius* is caused by astaxanthin, a lipochrome relatively common in other animals, including invertebrates, but rare in birds; it also occurs in the Roseate Spoonbill, *Platalea ajaja.* In the Black-backed Tanager, *Tangara peruviana,* there is color polymorphism. Individuals in the wild sometimes exhibit a cinnamon mutation, for example in the *Euphonia* females.

Some, such as the Gray-headed Tanager, *Eucometis penicillata;* Black-goggled Tanager, *Trichothraupis melanops;* and *Stephanophorus diadematus,* are crested. The bills of the *Ramphocelus* appear to be phosphorescent white, whereas the Red-billed Pied Tanager, *Lamprospiza melanoleuca,* has a carmine bill. Adult iris color may be bright: yellow in the *Nemosia* and Magpie Tanager, *Cissopis leveriana,* and red in the Brown Tanager, *Orchesticus abeillei.*

Among the most notable morphological features is the practical elimination of the muscular gizzard in the *Euphonia,* a unique alimentary adaptation (see also "Feeding.")

In various cases, such as the Blue-naped Chlorophonia, *Chlorophonia cyanea,* the *Tangara,* and the *Thraupis,* sexes are similar; in the *Euphonia* and tiés the females are modestly colored and different from the males. Occasionally one or another species of a genus normally lacking sexual dimorphism breaks the rule, as in the Burnished-buff Tanager, *Tangara cayana,* and Blue-and-yellow Tanager, *Thraupis bonariensis,* in which sexual dimorphism is accentuated.

Female *Hemithraupis* and White-shouldered Tanagers, *Tachyphonus luctuosus,* look like vireos or wood-warblers, and wood-warblers are considered to be related to tanagers. The Rufous-browed Peppershrike, *Cyclarhis gujanensis,* a vireo, can be mistaken in the field for a tanager. There are also similarities of appearance with icterines and cotingids, as in the case of the Scarlet-throated Tanager, *Sericossypha loricata.* The fact of superficial similarities having arisen among clearly unrelated groups creates confusion. *Trichothraupis melanops* has bristles around the bill like flycatchers and a yellow crown like some of them. On the nape there are hairlike feathers (found on various tanagers.) *Orchesticus abeillei,* another distinctive type, has various color analogies with furnariids; its bill resembles that of a *Saltator,* a genus previously included in the Thraupinae and later transferred to the Cardinalinae. The White-rumped Tanager, *Cypsnagra hirundinacea,* is another distinctive species: its voice identifies it as a tanager. See also the Swallow Tanager, *Tersina viridis.*

Juvenal males and females of sexually dimorphic tanagers, such as the tiés, usually still have the modest plumage of the female when they fledge. Later, during the postjuvenal molt, *Tachyphonus* and *Lanio* males (see Pl 42.7) become a totally mixed black and brown, reminiscent of the corresponding dress of the Screaming Cowbird, *Molothrus*

rufoaxillaris (Icterinae). Various *Tangara* whose adults sport multicolored dress leave the nest in almost uniformly green plumage. The Red-crowned Ant-Tanager, *Habia rubica,* and Yellow-backed Tanager, *Hemithraupis flavicollis,* require a second molt to complete their definitive dress. The immature *Schistochlamys melanopis* is green, completely unlike its parents which are gray and black and not sexually dimorphic. Immature White-banded Tanagers, *Neothraupis fasciata,* and *Thraupis bonariensis* also diverge radically from the adults.

After the breeding season the male *Cyanerpes cyaneus* shifts to a green dress similar to that of the female and immature male (postnuptial molt). Thus it acquires nonbreeding plumage, also called eclipse plumage, analogous to that of northern waterfowl and corresponding to the winter plumage of Northern Hemisphere birds such as the wood-warblers. It is interesting that this phenomenon does not occur in the other *Cyanerpes.* This type of molt was unknown in Neotropical Passerines until discovered in 1953 in Costa Rica by the great naturalist Alexander F. Skutch, who observed certain individuals at a feeder. Shortly afterward I found that the fact was recognized in bird-fancying circles in the former state of Guanabara, where I had a chance to study it. The postnuptial molt occurs at the end of summer. It is short-lived, the period varying each year according to the weather. Winter plumage is often incomplete, blue and black patches remaining on the back. Simultaneously leg color becomes light red. The molt is complete, for flight and tail feathers are also renewed. The new remiges are identical in color to those replaced: the distinctive black and yellow of the adult male. The green flight feathers of the immature male are successively replaced by definitive ones during the first winter.

I have verified that the local springtime replacement of the blue-and-black dress is not due to a prenuptial molt but comes simply through daily abrasion of the tricolored feathers, which are black at the base, blue in the middle, and green on the outer edge. When the green tip is worn, the feather appears blue. Color change of this type without molt occurs in various birds; see, for instance, Red-breasted Blackbird, *Sturnella militaris* (Icterinae).

I know of few analogous cases in Brazil of eclipse plumage: for example, *Sporophila* (Emberizinae), *Sturnella militaris,* and *Heliomaster* (Trochilidae). A Green Honeycreeper, *Chlorophanes spiza,* gynandromorph has been found (see also Emberizinae, "Morphology").

The bill is sharp, slender, long, and curved in the *Cyanerpes* and *Chlorophanes;* nevertheless, its shape varies considerably from one genus to another. The hypothesis has been advanced that the notable difference in bill shape of the various *Cyanerpes* is not merely a nectar-eating specialization but also an adaptation to different ways of catching insects. The *Diglossa* have a hooked bill (see "Feeding"). The bill of immature but already independent *Cyanerpes cyaneus* is clearly shorter than that of adults. The color of the legs (red, yellow, or black) and of the iris (red, yellow, or dark chestnut) is sometimes diagnostic. In the Black-legged Dacnis, *Dacnis nigripes,* the female is easier to identify than the male (heterogynism, see Formicariidae, "Morphology").

Vocalization

The voice of various tanagers, such as most *Tangara,* is squeaky and unattractive. Thus, some of the most beautiful birds are among those least gifted in voice, although they are quite communicative. Tanager voices are sometimes as high as the noises produced by insects and may bring to mind the squeal of a bat or the chitter of a hummingbird. *Euphonia* calls are loud and sometimes more characteristic than their songs, serving as diagnostic indicators; when imitated, individuals of the respective species are immediately attracted. *Chlorophonia cyanea* and other tanagers give a certain note only when flying. The calls of *Cypsnagra hirundinacea* and *Sericossypha loricata* are like those of icterines such as the Chopi Blackbird, *Gnorimopsar chopi. Tangara peruviana* and *T. cayana* sometimes voice a sharp whistle, recalling the alarm note of certain thrushes.

The songs of the *Thraupis, Habia rubica,* and *Eucometis penicillata* are resonant and generally a bit squeaky. The *Thraupis;* Orange-headed Tanager, *Thlypopsis sordida;* and others sing all year. *Thraupis bonariensis, Neothraupis fasciata, Habia rubica,* and the Green-headed Tanager, *Tangara seledon,* have developed a special dawn song; at the first light of day *Thraupis bonariensis* engages in angry intraspecific chases interspersed with songs hastily sung from constantly changing perches. *Sericossypha loricata* has a spectacular dawn "song," a loud, single cry similar to that of certain cotingas, which it sings with unique perseverance. The Fawn-breasted Tanager, *Pipraeidea melanonota,* can produce two essentially different song types: in addition to its common, simple song, it sometimes gives a varied one reminiscent of the subsong of thrushes, with elements of mimicry. The Violaceous Euphonia, *Euphonia violacea,* is a well-known master at mimicking other birds; although these imitations are notably faithful, they do not delude, being generally sung rapidly one after the other. Occasionally, however, one of these euphonias will "amuse itself" for a considerable time singing, for example, only the whistle of a Tropical Kingbird, *Tyrannus melancholicus,* at varying intervals. However, it reveals its true identity by the lower volume of its voice. In captivity this species also learns to mimic clicks of the tongue. The Thick-billed Euphonia, *Euphonia laniirostris,* and Chestnut-bellied Euphonia, *E. pectoralis,* can also imitate, but I think the virtuosity of *violacea* is unequalled. Imitations are usually of alarm or contact calls, not of songs.

Females commonly sing also, but their song is less developed. *Cypsnagra hirundinacea* pairs sing in perfectly synchronized duets, the male and female perched near each other, each singing entirely different phrases. They only sing together and in each other's presence; a second pair might sing in a neighboring tree in the presence of two other silent individuals. *Neothraupis fasciata* pairs also sing in duet but with simple, similar phrases.

The *Ramphocelus* and Olive-green Tanager, *Orthogonys chloricterus,* get together for collective noisemaking, mutually stimulating one another and even attracting other birds; the situation sometimes reaches the point of becoming confusing and alarming; their racket also may result from a snake appearing. Some *Tangara,* the Brassy-breasted Tanager, *T. desmaresti,* for example, are also attracted to these noisy assemblages.

The *Cyanerpes, Chlorophanes,* and *Dacnis,* with their high, squeaky voices, are inconspicuous in spite of having plenty of vocal variety. Thus, some of the most beautiful Oscines are among the least gifted vocally.

Feeding

Tanagers feed primarily on vegetable matter: small, frequently hard fruits of trees, bushes, and their epiphytes as well as small fruits from vines and pieces of larger fruits and their juices, leaves, buds, and nectar. Requirements vary from species to species. Tanagers are among the birds that contribute most to the dispersal of plant seeds. However, certain species, such as the Sayaca and Palm Tanagers, *Thraupis sayaca* and *T. palmarum,* do this poorly because they chew on the berries and let the seeds fall on the mother plant.

The *Euphonia* and *Chlorophonia* are fond of the fruits of mistletoe (Loranthaceae), whose succulent berries they swallow whole. The food passes without obstacle from the esophagus to the small intestine, for the gizzard has degenerated (fig. 294). Only a wide, short tube with elastic walls remains. This peculiarity was studied by Lund (1829) and is reflected in the public impression that euphonias "don't have intestines." In fact, after a few minutes (mistletoe berries are purgative), the seeds and torn skins of the berries appear in the feces; this limits their dissemination. The seeds come out unharmed, protected against digestion by a viscous external coating that, after defecation, fixes the seed to the bark of a branch where it germinates. Passage through the intestine of the bird appears to be even necessary for germination of the seeds of certain Loranthaceae. *Euphonia violacea* also likes the fruits of flagelliform cactus (*Rhipsalis*), which it sometimes takes while fluttering in front of the plants.

The *Ramphocelus* and others like fruits of cecropia (*Cecropia* spp.). They perch on the pendulous spikes, head down, and rip off pieces of pulp with their bills, working from the tip to the base of the spike.

Euphonias also use the cecropia's Müller corpuscles, protein deposits that are the principal food of *Azteca* ants living in cecropia trunks. Alexander Skutch (1945), working in

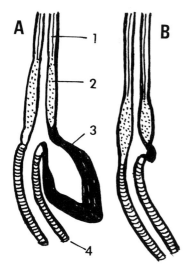

Fig. 294. (A) Well-developed stomach of a species of *Dicaeum* (Nectariniidae), of the Indo-Australian region, that lives on a mixed diet of insects and fruits. (B) Much reduced muscular stomach of a frugivorous Brazilian euphonia, *Euphonia* sp. In A, note (1) esophagus, (2) glandular stomach (proventriculus), (3) muscular stomach (ventriculus, eliminated in the euphonia), (4) duodenum. After Desselberger 1931.

Costa Rica, titled one of his publications *The Most Hospitable Tree,* referring to the cecropia, the most characteristic tree of tropical America, and explaining the immense value of these plants for fauna and especially for birds. Apparently germination of cecropia seeds is accelerated by their passage through bird intestines.

The wide diversity in bill size and tongue shape of certain euphonias suggests essential differences in their food. The Green-chinned Euphonia, *E. chalybea,* has a bill similar to a parakeet and a fleshy tongue with a cartilagenous double tip. It feeds on cactus fruits. Saíras like the fruits of *Schinus* species (Anacardiaceae) and of *Syzygium jambolanum,* a Mirtaceae from India. Sanhaços seek magnolia (*Michelia champaca*) fruits, as do *Tersina viridis* and thrushes. The various Melastomataceae are of the greatest importance for fruit-eating birds such as tanagers. Fruit-loaded specimens attract enormous congregations not only of tanagers but of numerous other species and individuals. It has been shown that a fruit diet permits a greater concentration of individuals of a species in one area (Snow 1971). Flowers and fruits are very visible, for plants have to attract the animals necessary for their own propagation. Tanagers are among the creatures whose orientation is primarily visual. The superabundance of food provided by a single bush or tree reduces competition between its visitors. Sometimes there are differences in "visiting hours." These extraordinary food sources are located outside the breeding territory of most of their customers.

Certain Melastomataceae, such as species of *Miconia,* offer an additional advantage because of their long fruiting period: fruits of a single pixirica (*Leandra* sp.) plant, for example, ripen over a period of several weeks, guaranteeing good nourishment for a *Tachyphonus coronatus* that might be living nearby, enabling it to avoid long flights to find adequate food. Choice of a fruit source is regulated by specific preferences and physical conditions; birds with small bills, for example, generally eat small fruits, whereas those with large bills eat both large and small fruits.

Once in Mato Grosso on an almiscar (*Protium* sp., Burseracea) bush, I saw 13 Passerine species, among them 8 tanagers, mostly in pairs, and 1 thrush with young. This shows that such gatherings are not limited to the nonbreeding season, when there is more freedom to wander.

The fruits of falsa-erva-de-rato (*Hamelia patens,* Rubiaceae), a bush of capoeiras and gallery forests of the central-west region, are avidly sought by various tanagers: *Euphonia violacea, Tangara seledon, T. cayana, Thraupis sayaca, Cissopis leveriana,* and *Tersina viridis* (Gomes et al. 1975). Bananeirinhas-do-mato (*Heliconia* sp.) fruits are extremely popular.

Palm fruits are also an important source of food, like those of the Cuban Royal Palm (*Roystonea regia*) and of *Livistonia australis;* on ripe bunches of *L. australis* in Espírito Santo, 28 birds species have been found, among them 7 tanagers, including all 4 *Thraupis* in the region. The fruits are eaten whole. Both these palms are exotic, as is the magnolia. Species such as *Cissopis leveriana* and the Cinnamon Tanager, *Schistochlamys ruficapillus,* periodically gorge themselves on fruits of pokeweed (*Phytolacca decandra*), an herbaceous plant of newly cultivated land. Thus, sometimes the stratigraphic designation "in the treetops" is inexact. Pits and stones, such as those of magnolia fruits, are regurgitated by saíras, as well as by *Tersina viridis* and manakins, and rarely appear in feces. A diet of vegetable matter requires a large quantity of food and consequently produces intense defecation, as is frequently noted with caged specimens.

I have seen *Tachyphonus coronatus* exploit bromeliads of *Neoregelia.* It looks for small fruits hidden in the base of the rosette, each fruit having stiff, upward-projecting sepals which the bird pulls at until it finds a ripe one that comes off; it then squeezes it and swallows as much as it can of the juice and seeds, leaving the fiber. It eats *Nidularia* fruits in a similar manner. This is an interesting specialization, reminiscent of the hummingbirds that know how to find the flowers of these plants. *Tangara seledon* is among those that use the inflorescences of bromeliads. *Tachyphonus coronatus;* the Turquoise Tanager, *Tangara mexicana;* and others like cecropia fruits. They also tear off chunks of ripe orange and sometimes completely smear themselves with juice.

Thraupis sayaca regularly eats leaves and buds of trees and shrubs, among them canudo-de-pito (*Cassia* sp.) in Espírito Santo and Rio de Janeiro. *T. bonariensis* devours large pieces of papaya and chuchu [*Sechium edile*]. *Tachyphonus coronatus* eats goiaba-do-campo leaves; in addition to insects and fruits, *Pipraeidea melanonota* eats buds and flowers.

Nectar is taken by *Euphonia laniirostris; Thraupis sayaca;* the White-lined Tanager, *Tachyphonus rufus;* and Silver-beaked Tanager, *Ramphocelus carbo. R. carbo* seeks the large red inflorescences of the Amazonian vine *Norantea,* perforating the base of the calyx to reach the nectar deposit. In Minas Gerais and Rio Grande do Sul I have seen *Thraupis sayaca* and *T. bonariensis* eat eucalyptus flowers. Euphonias, such as *E. violacea,* take nectar from the *Psittacanthus* mistletoe. In Rio de Janeiro I have seen *E. pectoralis* cling to feeders put out for hummingbirds to sip the sweetened water. In southeastern Brazil the sweet excretion of plant lice is a food coveted by *Tangara peruviana, Stephanophorus diadematus,* and *Tachyphonus coronatus.* I saw a female *T. coronatus* hover to drink this liquid and scare away other birds visiting the host mimosa, as do some Trochilidae and Parulinae.

In Trinidad, B. K. and D. W. Snow (1971) showed that the Blue Dacnis, *Dacnis cayana,* was highly insectivorous (49% of its diet), with fruit (44%) being the other important ingredient in its diet. Nectar only amounted to 7%. In Rio de Janeiro L. Gonzaga proved that *D. nigripes* is more nectivorous than *D. cayana.* In Trinidad the food of *Cyanerpes cyaneus* consisted of 44% insects, 44% fruit, and 12% nectar. *Chlorophanes spiza* was highly frugivorous (63%). In Brazil it seeks, for example, the fruits of *Protium, Clusia, Michelia* (see *Tersina viridis*), *Hamelia patens, Cecropia* (imbaúba), *Miconia* (quaresmeira) and other Melastomataceae, and succulent berries of *Rhipsalis.* The raceme of *Lasiacis* grass, falsely appearing to resemble a bunch of small fruits, reportedly attracts *Chlorophanes spiza* and other frugivorous birds such as the *Manacus* (Pipridae) and *Myiarchus* (Tyrannidae) but is ignored by seed-eating species such as the Blue-black Grassquit, *Volatinia jacarina,* or small doves. Seeds passing through the digestive tube germinate normally (Davidse and Morton 1973).

I have observed *Cyanerpes cyaneus* feeding on oranges and persimmons. The *Dacnis* sometimes tear pieces off larger fruits. I have found seeds in the stomach that were the residue of small fruits eaten whole. The Bananaquit, *Coereba flaveola* (Coerebinae), "knows" the value of cecropia corpuscles (see Parulinae, "Feeding," Tropical Parula, *Parula pitiayumi*). It also sucks juice from jaqueira [*Artocarpus integra*] fruits.

Nectar is of particular interest as a food of the *Cyanerpes, Dacnis,* and *Coereba,* as it is of the Trochilidae and the Old World (Africa, etc.) Nectariniidae (sunbirds). This food is difficult to trace through stomach examinations. I have seen nectar run from the bill of a collected *Coereba flaveola* specimen. The same has happened with hummingbirds. *C. flaveola, Cyanerpes cyaneus,* and *Dacnis cayana* seek *Psittacanthus* flowers, for example, and encounter various hummingbirds there. The liquid is absorbed by a brush on the tip of the tongue and drawn into the mouth by two capillary tubes that make up the tongue. *Cyanerpes cyaneus* has a long and "heavy" semitubular tongue whose function must be similar to the tongue of hummingbirds. To obtain nectar these birds clutch the flower firmly like Nectariniidae do. They usually cannot hover near flowers as hummingbirds do and lack bills or tongues long enough to reach nectaries in deep, tubular calyxes.

Some attempt to hover, especially *C. cyaneus,* a species with long, pointed wings that often catches insects in the foliage this way and also learns to drink from hummingbird feeders. The Greater Flower-piercer, *Diglossa major,* has developed a more specialized technique: encircling a calyx with its hook-shaped maxilla, it perforates the corolla with its very sharp, upturned mandible and introduces its tongue to sip nectar. It thus becomes a nectar "thief" by avoiding pollinization (see Trochilidae, "Feeding . . ."). Carrying out observations in a well-planted flight cage, Winkel (1967) showed that a *C. cyaneus,* although it was stealing nectar, had been covered with the pollen of a Gesneriaceae.

It is common for various tanagers to be found in flowering trees also frequented by hummingbirds, sometimes for different reasons: either to sip nectar or to hunt insects attracted by the flowers. They must also take pollen, since I sometimes find it on the forehead of a *Dacnis.* They catch small insects and their larvae and miniscule spiders on branches, leaves, buds, and flowers, either while resting or in flight. They even catch swarming termites; I have seen *Cyanerpes cyaneus* do this.

Arthropods constitute an important complementary food for tanagers such as *Tangara cayana.* They catch insects, caterpillars, etc., on or under leaves and on branches, often hanging upside down like they do when taking certain fruits. *Thraupis sayaca, Orchesticus abeillei, Trichothraupis melanops,* and others also catch flying insects, swarming termites or butterflies, for example. The Summer Tanager, *Piranga rubra,* catches bees. The Fulvous Shrike-Tanager, *Lanio fulvus,* is also a specialist in catching flying insects, having a tooth on the maxillar tomia (see fig. 299), remotely reminiscent of the *Lanius* shrikes (Laniidae) of North America, Africa, etc., and of the falcons; this is a very effective means of holding insect prey having a thick chitinous covering. *Thraupis palmarum* sometimes catches insects flying near its perch.

Trichothraupis melanops and *Eucometis penicillata* accompany army ants and obtain the greater part of their food that way. They hunt in the understory, frequently descending to the ground to catch prey but immediately reentering the vegetation. I have seen *Habia rubica* do the same in Espírito Santo. *Cypsnagra hirundinacea,* an open-country species, is more insectivorous than frugivorous. Like other birds, tanagers (tested in *Ramphocelus carbo*) learn to avoid taking aposematically marked noxious insects such as heliconid butterflies. However, in São Paulo *Pipraeidea melanonota* has been recorded preying extensively on Ithomiinae, lepidoptera universally accepted as protected by their disagreeable taste; the birds treated the insects as if they were fruits with a bitter rind, eating only the "pulp" of the abdomen (Brown and Vasconcellos Neto 1976).

Euphonia violacea avidly seeks out small terrestrial snails, as I observed in a flight cage: it extracts the body of the mollusk from the shell, which it then lets fall. The White-vented Euphonia, *E. minuta,* is largely insectivorous. Individual birds may also discover new food sources: I saw a *Ramphocelus bresilius* diligently exploit a colony of *Thoropa* tadpoles on a wet rock in Rio de Janeiro; it carries insects, spiders, geckos, and frogs to its young. The occasional presence of feather fragments in the stomach of a *Ramphocelus,* for instance, must come from swallowing this material while preening. I have seen the Gilt-edged Tanager, *Tangara cyanoventris,* drink rainwater accumulated in tree holes.

Behavior

Tanagers seek light, like the more colorful hummingbirds. They are good flyers. Some, such as the *Euphonia* and *Tachyphonus,* can hover to pick a small fruit or catch a sitting insect. *Cissopis leveriana,* which makes short flights, produces a hissing noise that can be heard at a distance. I know of only a few Brazilian species that make characteristic tail movements: *Euphonia minuta* and the Golden-sided Euphonia, *E. cayennensis,* move their short tails to the sides, whereas *C. leveriana* teeters its long tail vertically.

Tanagers use ants for anting, as I have observed with *Tangara cyanoventris, T. desmaresti, T. cyanicollis,* and the Golden-chevroned Tanager, *Thraupis ornata.* They clean their bills by wiping them on a branch, like so many other birds, and enjoy bathing. I have seen *Dacnis cayana* and *Cyanerpes cyaneus* gaping. In this way *Dacnis* opens gaps in the foliage while searching for insects; it even gapes in its own plumage, perhaps to facilitate removal of parasites.

The drinking of nectarivorous and frugivorous species such as the *Dacnis* and *Coereba* (and, for that matter, of hummingbirds also, with their specially adapted tongue) is really sucking. In Rio de Janeiro I have seen a *Thraupis palmarum* drink from a hummingbird feeder where a perch had been placed for *Coereba flaveola.*

Several times a day flocks of saíras, *Orthogonys chloricterus,* and other tanagers pass through those sections of the forest having trees with edible fruits, such as ingazeiros [*Inga* spp.]. Insectivorous species such as the Flame-crested Tanager, *Tachyphonus cristatus,* and *Lanio fulvus* also join these flocks. *Orchesticus abeillei* merits special attention because of its unique behavior. In winter great mixed flocks assemble in which tanagers may predominate, both in number of species and individuals. A flock I recorded at Itatiaia, Rio de Janeiro, in July 1952 had 21 species, 7 of which were tanagers: *Tangara desmaresti, T. cayana, Thraupis sayaca, Tachyphonus coronatus, Trichothraupis melanops, Orchesticus abeillei,* and *Cissopis leveriana.* In Amazonia

Lamprospiza melanoleuca can be heard announcing the presence of a flock of birds while still far off, a role filled in the south by the *Caryothraustes* grosbeaks. Congregations of this kind must be useful in detecting the presence of enemies, such discovery being easier when several individuals are on watch. Frequently nesting pairs, such as of *Sericossypha loricata* and the *Ramphocelus,* are accompanied by other individuals of their species acting as helpers at the nest.

In agonistic situations, *Cyanerpes cyaneus* displays the bright yellow underside of its flight feathers. The *Cyanerpes, Chlorophanes,* and their allies are very bellicose.

For sleeping *Euphonia violacea* selects the densest clumps of mistletoe, which provide perfect protection against storms; several individuals will assemble in one plant.

Reproduction

During the breeding period tanagers display the brightly colored parts of their plumage. *Tachyphonus* males rhythmically open and close their wings before a female or a rival, showing the resplendent white of the under wing coverts and epaulets. *Encontro-de-prata,* "silver epaulet," is a name used for *T. rufus. Thraupis* also display their epaulets, the white, blue, or yellow being characteristic of each species. The scarlet on the crown of *Tachyphonus coronatus,* invisible when the bird is at rest, is spread over the whole top of the head on these occasions. Progressive development in the color of these bright parts of the plumage can be noted across several species: they provide signals fundamental to specific social behavior. The white spots on the tail feathers of some euphonias are an important decoration, being constantly displayed by *Euphonia minuta* when it shakes its half-open tail. One population of *E. laniirostris* (*melanura* of the upper Amazon) lacks white on the tail.

Sericossypha loricata has developed a surprise display of the white bases of the back feathers, reminiscent of certain antbirds. The wing bar of *Trichothraupis melanops* is uniquely arranged and produces an exceptional effect. Male *Ramphocelus* lift their heads vertically, providing maximum display for the relucent base of the mandible. *R. carbo* is sometimes called *bico-de-prata,* "silver-beak."

The nest is usually an open, well-constructed basket, as with *Thraupis sayaca,* located among branches at various heights. The saíras, *Tangara desmaresti,* for instance, make a deep, well-lined saucer at the tip of a branch such as araucaria. *Ramphocelus carbo* builds in dense vegetation (sometimes it even uses palms) and likes to use fresh, green material on the outside. The *Tachyphonus* make their little baskets in undergrowth inside the forest. *Habia rubica* and the Hepatic Tanager, *Piranga flava,* build a loose, sometimes almost transparent saucer high in the trees. The nest of the Hooded Tanager, *Nemosia pileata,* is transparent but strong, well fastened with spider web in a high place among trees of the cerrado. The Red-shouldered Tanager, *Tachyphonus phoe-*

nicius, and *Schistochlamys melanopis,* semisavanna species, build in grass on or somewhat above the ground. On exceptional occasions *Ramphocelus carbo* does this too.

Thraupis palmarum; the Blue-gray Tanager, *T. episcopus;* and *Sericossypha loricata* hide their nests in the base of palm foliage or in tree holes. *Sericossypha* also uses woodpecker holes or occupies stick-heap nests of the Rufous Cacholote, *Pseudoseisura cristata* (Bahia). *Thraupis palmarum* and *T. ornata* sometimes build among large epiphitic bromeliads (Rio de Janeiro). *T. episcopus* occasionally sets up housekeeping under roofs (Amapá). *S. loricata* carries long sticks. *Tangara peruviana* from time to time uses the remains of a bulky Monk Parakeet, *Myiopsitta monachus,* structure in setting up its own nest. *Chlorophonia cyanea* and the *Euphonia* require a maximum of protection and darkness; their spherical nests, with side entrance, are placed in protected places such as amidst a palm crown, among epiphitic bromeliads, or in an interlaced tangle of Spanish moss (*Tillandsia usneoides*). Male and female *Euphonia* and *Thraupis* work together in nest construction; in the *Ramphocelus* only the female labors.

Euphonias sometimes occupy nests of other species. In Brazilian Amazonia *Euphonia violacea* eggs were found in an abandoned nest of the Rusty-margined Flycatcher, *Myiozetetes cayanensis,* and *E. cayennensis* eggs in an occupied nest of the Ochre-bellied Flycatcher, *Mionectes oleaginea,* which also held eggs of its legitimate owner; possibly the euphonia had expelled the *Mionectes.* A pair of *E. laniirostris* built inside the abandoned nest of a Great Kiskadee, *Pitangus sulphuratus.* In Central America *Thraupis episcopus* is reported sometimes to take over recently built nests of other birds, such as the Boat-billed Flycatcher, *Megarynchus pitangua,* and saíras, including also saíra eggs. *Cyanerpes cyaneus* nest is a shallow saucer well fixed with spider webbing to a rather high tree fork. *Chlorophanes spiza* and *Dacnis* nests are similar.

The customary two or three eggs, or with *Euphonia violacea* up to five (Pará), vary greatly in color according to species. *Ramphocelus bresilius* lays shiny greenish blue eggs sprinkled with black. *Thraupis sayaca* and other sanhaços have such heavily mottled eggs that the yellowish white background can scarcely be seen. *Chlorophonia cyanea* and the *Euphonia* lay eggs with pale red and white backgrounds, respectively, with rusty speckles. *Cyanerpes* eggs have a white or slightly pink background with brown spots, usually concentrated on the large end. Those of *Diglossa* have a blue background. The statement that *Cyanerpes cyaneus* lays "blackish" eggs (sepia colored) in a hanging nest of the Red-rumped Cacique, *Cacicus haemorrhous,* type is evidently erroneous. The female alone incubates; 12 to 14 days have been recorded for *Thraupis episcopus* and "at least" 17 days for *E. minuta* in Costa Rica.

The inside of the mouth of young birds is red. They are fed by the parents, who deliver meals in their bills in the case of *Ramphocelus, Thraupis,* and *Tangara,* or regurgitate it in mushy form in *Chlorophonia* and *Euphonia.* Not infrequently more than two individuals care for the brood; they may be young of the same pair by an earlier nesting, as I verified in the case of a *Tangara cyanoventris,* or adults—another pair, or unpaired individuals, as has been shown with *T. mexicana.* Various individuals attending one nest appears to be a frequent occurrence with *Sericossypha loricata.*

Ramphocelus carbo may indulge in polygamy, judging from its building of neighboring nests in Pará. *R. bresilius* nests are sometimes attended by more than two adults. In Central America *Habia rubica* and *Thraupis episcopus* are said occasionally to practice bigamy. I observed *H. rubica* using the trick of feigning injury to lead intruders away from the nest, regularly practiced only by birds that build on the ground, and it has also been seen with *Eucometis penicillata,* although both had nests some meters high. *Sericossypha loricata* attacks hawks that come near the nest, and *Cissopis leveriana* becomes aggressive if a person catches another of that species and it screeches. It is reported that nestlings fledge after 18 days in *Thraupis* species and after approximately 22 days in *Euphonia violacea.*

Up to the present, 13 Brazilian tanagers are known to be parasitized by the Shiny Cowbird, *Molothrus bonariensis.* *Ramphocelus bresilius* is so severely parasitized by this icterine in certain areas that it scarcely manages to raise its own young. I have seen as small a species as *Thlypopsis sordida* feeding an *M. bonariensis.*

Habitat and Abundance

Tanagers are numerous on this continent. They are most abundant in the Andean foothills, far from Brazil, where more than ten *Tangara* may occur together. I have already mentioned the diversity of species and the great number of individuals that gather at certain fruit trees. *Ramphocelus carbo,* one of the most abundant birds in Amazonia, lives on the forest edge, in the canopy, and in riverine vegetation. Thus it adapts easily to secondary vegetation on abandoned cultivations, where forest is in its first stages of growth. Usually it is the most abundant species there. In capoeira of the lower Amazon (Rio Guamá), in a special study area, *R. carbo;* the White-bearded Manakin, *Manacus manacus;* and Red-headed Manakin, *Pipra rubrocapilla,* were the predominant species. The feeding behavior of the two manakins is similar to that of the tanagers; all prefer vegetable substances and are therefore predominantly primary consumers in the food chain. In a similar area in the same region (Caratateuá Island), *R. carbo* was also the most numerous species, followed by *M. manacus.* In a third area (Rio Acará) the most abundant species was *Manacus,* second place was occupied by the Pectoral Sparrow, *Arremon taciturnus,* and "only" third place by *R. carbo* (Novaes 1969, 1970).

Notwithstanding the abundance of individuals and the respectable number of species tanagers supply to certain tropical ecosystems, they do not match, in number of species, families such as the Formicariidae and Tyrannidae, birds that are basically insectivorous and therefore secondary consumers adapted to a multiplicity of ecological niches in forests.

The sanhaços are among the most common city birds, readily adjusting to people. *Thraupis sayaca* penetrates even into big cities such as Rio de Janeiro; it nests, for example, in oiti trees [*Moquilea tomentosa*] planted on narrow streets such as Avenida Rio Branco, and *T. palmarum* populates the royal palms among skyscrapers in any section of the city. *Piranga flava* is expanding its distribution, taking advantage of the deforestation of eastern Brazil.

Distribution and Evolution

Tanager distribution presents interesting problems. There are an appreciable number of endemics in eastern Brazil such as *Orchesticus abeillei, Orthogonys chloricterus,* and various *Tangara,* some of them, such as *T. fastuosa,* of very limited distribution. On the coastal strip within the range of *Thraupis sayaca,* the cryptic and syntopic Azure-shouldered Tanager, *T. cyanoptera,* occurs, whereas *Dacnis nigripes* is found within the broad range of *D. cayana;* the two live syntopically, as do certain *Cyanerpes.* In Espírito Santo, for instance, four *Thraupis* live in the same area. *Sericossypha loricata* is a unique endemic of the northeast. Some southern species, such as *Trichothraupis melanops,* reach the slopes of the Andes. *Chlorophonia cyanea* and *Pipraeidea melanonota* occupy, in addition to the Brazilian southeast, vast stretches of the Andes and reach as far as the northern part of the continent (disjunct distribution).

The originally unitary range of savanna species such as *Tangara cyanicollis* was cut by the intrusive development of Amazonia, resulting in various distinct populations. The situation of the Orange-bellied Euphonia, *Euphonia xanthogaster,* a forest species, is comparable.

The Amazonian counterparts of *Tangara mexicana* and *Cissopis leveriana* are considerably smaller than their southern representatives from milder climates (see Emberizinae, "Distribution . . . ," *Oryzoborus*); great differences in color may also occur; see the geographic races, for example, of *Tangara cayana.*

Ramphocelus carbo is an example of a semispecies, being the Amazonian counterpart of *R. bresilius;* they meet and interbreed in the upper Rio Doce (Minas Gerais). Each has evolved into geographic races in other regions. The same status of geographic speciation can perhaps also be attributed to the Guira Tanager, *Hemithraupis guira,* and Rufous-headed Tanager, *H. ruficapilla,* for which some hybrids are known.

Euphonia cayennensis and the Rufous-bellied Euphonia, *E. rufiventris,* which can be considered Amazonian counterparts of *E. pectoralis,* are examples of allospecies, that is, species with allopatric distribution that are totally separated geographically (fig. 295); neither geographic races nor areas of hybridization are known for them. *Lanio fulvus* replaces the White-winged Shrike-Tanager, *L. versicolor; Thraupis episcopus* is apparently a northern counterpart of *T. sayaca.* *Tachyphonus rufus* and *T. coronatus* also appear to form a superspecies. In these cases ethological characters, such as voice and behavior, are of great interest as a means of testing the degree of relationship.

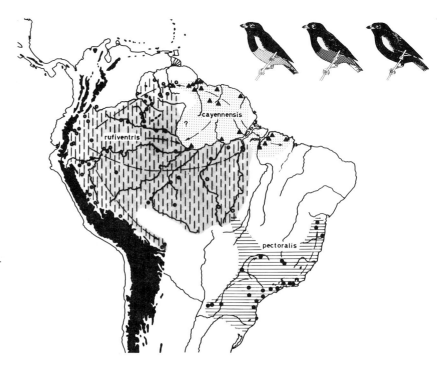

Fig. 295. Distribution of the Golden-sided Euphonia and allies, *Euphonia cayennensis* superspecies; males illustrated (slightly modified after Haffer 1970). Closed triangles and stippling: *E. cayennensis.* Open circles and vertical dashes: Rufous-bellied Euphonia, *E. rufiventris.* Closed circles and horizontal hatching: Chestnut-bellied Euphonia, *E. pectoralis.* Symbols denote locality records.

Migration

In winter certain species appear in regions where, in other months, they either do not occur or are scarcer. Examples of this are found in the former state of Guanabara, for example, with *Thraupis ornata* and *Piranga flava* representing the first case and *Tachyphonus coronatus* the second, its numbers increasing in August and September with the ripening of oranges. In the winter of 1940 in the mountainous region of Espírito Santo I noted an appreciable reduction of certain species such as *Tangara desmaresti* and *Orchesticus abeillei;* the Purple-throated Euphonia, *Euphonia chlorotica,* had already disappeared completely. Determination of these facts is not easy, for generally not all of a population moves, as with swallows and other migratory birds. In central Brazil the two *Schistochlamys* disappear periodically. Cone-billed Tanager, *Conothraupis mesoleuca,* migrations related to the rainy season occur in Amazonia. Tanagers, especially *Cyanerpes* and *Dacnis,* associate with mixed flocks. *Piranga rubra* is a Northern Hemisphere migrant that penetrates into upper Amazonia.

Intergeneric Hybridization

A male *Cyanerpes cyaneus* and a female *Tangara nigrocincta* twice reared two young in the Zoological Garden of San Diego, California. There is no record of whether the descendants were fertile (Delacour 1972).

Alleged Harmfulness, Usefulness, and Scarcity

Because of their abundance, sanhaços and tíes are not popular in orchards. These birds have already paid tribute to the Indians, who valued their feathers for use in making adornments, using the Masked Crimson Tanager, *Ramphocelus nigrogularis,* for instance, in the upper Amazon. Because of their magnificent plumage, the *Cyanerpes* have always been much pursued; formerly by Indians, later by hunters of ornamental birds who used their skins in the fashion trade and, in our times, for the illegal commerce in cage birds.

The very restricted range of endemics such as *Tangara fastuosa,* a bird still common in the northeast, increases the risk of extinction, given the progressive alteration of the environment and their unrestricted capture for the cage-bird trade. Thus, in this subfamily also, we must see to the protection of certain species.

Although it was assumed to have become extinct some time ago, I have included the Cherry-throated Tanager, *Nemosia rourei,* herein, having seen it myself in Espírito Santo.

Terminology

The tanagers were called tanagridae, based on the Indian name *tangará* formerly used (e.g., in Pernambuco) for *Tangara fastuosa,* as can be seen in Marcgrave's work (1648), the first scientific treatise on our plants and animals. The name *tangará* continues to be used for *Habia rubica* in Amazonia (Pará). There has been some confusion, for Linnaeus, by transposing the letters, created the generic name *Tanagra* for the euphonias, a name revoked (1966) by the International Commission on Nomenclature and replaced by *Euphonia. Tangará* is also used for Thraupinae in Paraguay and adjacent regions of Bolivia and Argentina. In Brazil at present, *tangará* is more used for members of the Pipridae family, especially *Chiroxiphia.* In Amazonia it also refers to a cardinal, Red-capped Cardinal, *Paroaria gularis* (see Emberizinae).

Synopsis of Brazilian Thraupines

1. Gaturamos: *Chlorophonia* and *Euphonia,* 14 small species with short bills in which most of the males have a yellow belly; females are green (Pls 41.2, 41.4)
2. Saíras, saís, saíra-diamante, and allies: *Tangara, Dacnis, Chlorophanes,* and *Cyanerpes,* 29 frequently multicolored species; sexes generally similar (Pls 41.5, 41.9)
3. Sanhaços and sanhaço-frade: *Thraupis* and *Stephanophorus,* 7 large species, bluish-gray or greenish, the *Thraupis* with relucent upper wing coverts, 1 species (*T. bonariensis*) with orange belly (Pls 41.10, 41.11)
4. Tié-sangue, tié-fogo, and allies: 12 species with aspect similar to that of the sanhaços but with color predominantly red (*Ramphocelus* males, *Piranga* males, and *Habia* males) or green and yellow (*Piranga* females, *Cyanicterus, Orthogonys, Eucometis,* and *Mitrospingus* (Pls 42.1, 42.3)
5. Tié-preto and allies: *Tachyphonus* (8 species) and *Lanio* (2 species) with aspect similar to the two previous groups but including some smaller species. *Tachyphonus* males are black, with the epaulet (see also *Cypsnagra,* item 6) and underside of wings white, and there are sometimes bright marks on the crown, throat, or rump. The *Lanio* have rusty yellow backs and bellies; (Pls 42.5, 42.7)
6. Various medium-sized species, some with a black mask: *Pipraeidea* (Pl 42.4); *Neothraupis* and *Trichothraupis* (crested, yellow crown, fig. 301); *Cypsnagra* and *Schistochlamys* (Pl 42.6); black and white: *Lamprospiza* (with red bill) and *Conothraupis;* rufous-brown with heavy bill: *Orchesticus* (fig. 296)
7. Various species the size of a saíra or more slender, with thin bills, relatively long tails, and black, brown, or yellow throats: *Hemithraupis guira* and *ruficapilla* (Pl 42.2); *Hemithraupis flavicollis* and *Thlypopsis sordida;* or red throat: *Nemosia rourei;* plumage lead gray with chestnut head: *Pyrrhocoma ruficeps;* gray, black, and white: *Nemosia pileata* (fig. 298)
8. Two large species, all black or with a scarlet throat: *Sericossypha* (= *Compsothraupis*); or black and white with a long tail: *Cissopis* (fig. 297)
9. *Diglossa,* only in Roraima and Venezuela
10. *Conirostrum,* a genus of *incertae sedis,* similar in aspect to the Parulinae, in which it was for a time included, now brings up the rear of the Thraupinae.

Fig. 296. Brown Tanager, *Orchesticus abeillei,* about to catch a hymenopteron.

BROWN TANAGER, *Orchesticus abeillei,*
Sanhaço-pardo   BR   Fig. 296

17.5 cm; 31.5 g. Arboreal, southern species. Reminiscent of *Schistochlamys melanopis* but unique in emberizine-like bill and spinetail-like coloring (*Philydor,* see below); this combination may also remind one of Chestnut-crowned Becard, *Pachyramphus castaneus.* Brown; forehead and superciliaries pale rufous like entire underparts; crown, lores, and postocular stripe grayish brown; iris red; tail and wings reddish rufous; upper wing coverts and bend of wing olivaceous. Has hairlike feathers on nape. VOICE: high and shrill, sometimes similar to a *Thraupis.* Canopy of high or low forests; catches insects by sudden sallies; also eats fruits. Bahia to Paraná; only in mountains of Espírito Santo and Rio de Janeiro, from where a portion of population apparently migrates in winter. Associates in mixed flocks with birds such as saíras, tíes, and saltators. Sometimes joins certain furnariids, among them occasionally Buff-fronted Foliage-gleaner, *Philydor rufus.* Resemblance between these two gives rise to the thought that *Orchesticus,* an endemic of Brazilian southeast, may have adapted to imitate the *Philydor,* a widely distributed genus with various similar species. However, I know of no other contact between the two beyond the superficial association existing in migrating flocks (social mimicry).

CINNAMON TANAGER, *Schistochlamys ruficapillus,*
Bico-de-veludo   BR   PL 42.6

17.8 cm; 38.2 g. Emberizine-like, with small, black mask contrasting sharply with typical cinnamon forebody. Belly normally white. VOICE: call a low *kwat, che-it;* song similar to an emberizine, a smooth, sweet-sounding trill with frequent trisyllabic stanzas, e.g., *ji, jew, joo-ji-JOOi* or *wewlDje-wewlDje, wewlDje,* sometimes repeated. Brushy open country and low, open woods; perches on top of small trees and bush clumps to observe and sing. Widely distributed in partially open country, e.g., cerrado and caatinga, abundant above tree line in high montane meadows with cold climate (e.g., Serra do Caparaó, Minas Gerais). The northeast, east, and south of Brazil to Santa Catarina, Goiás, eastern Mato Grosso (Rio das Mortes), southern Pará (Cururu, Cachimbo). Sometimes alongside *S. melanopis* in cen-

tral Brazil. Also called *Sanhaço-do-campo, Sanhaço-pardo, Saí-veludo, Zorro* (Rio de Janeiro).

BLACK-FACED TANAGER, *Schistochlamys melanopis,*
Sanhaço-de-coleira

18 cm. Species with wide extra-Amazonian distribution. Adult gray except for head, throat, and foreneck which are black in both sexes. Immature olive green, lighter below. VOICE: call a loud *tsic;* song a trilled stanza rising and descending several times. Low riverine forests, marshes (e.g., buriti groves), cerrado, restinga, brushy open country. South of lower Amazon from Santarém to Belém, central, northeastern, and eastern Brazil to São Paulo, and northern South America. Sometimes host to *Molothrus bonariensis.* See *S. ruficapillus.*

WHITE-BANDED TANAGER, *Neothraupis fasciata,*
Cigarra-do-campo

15.5 cm. Arboreal and savanna species of interior. Upperparts grayish; black mask; upper wing coverts black with white stripe. Throat and belly equally white; breast grayish. Eyes and feet dark. Female similar to male but browner. Immature has brown upperparts, yellowish gray underparts, lacks both mask and black-and-white wing pattern. VOICE: call a strident *wit, bit;* song a short, squeaky phrase. Has extensive dawn song. Pairs duet. Cerrado, groves; associates with mixed flocks. Maranhão and Piauí to Goiás, Minas Gerais, São Paulo, Mato Grosso, eastern Bolivia. There is a curious similarity between this tanager and Northern Shrike, *Lanius excubitor,* of Northern Hemisphere (see also *Nemosia pileata,* which is more slender).

WHITE-RUMPED TANAGER, *Cypsnagra hirundinacea,*
Bandoleta

15.5 cm; 28.5 g (male). Central Brazilian species with black upperparts, 2 white wing bars, white rump. Underparts whitish except for rufous throat. Sexes alike. Immature lacks rufous spots on throat. VOICE: call a low *kwet, chat;* a rattly *tshrararara* generally precedes song, which in male consists of a loud, rhythmic stanza of a few syllables, e.g., *wadje-WEET-ja-ja,* flowingly repeated about 6 times while accompanied by female with a simple, time-marking counterpoint, *cha, cha, cha . . . ;* sometimes a more melodious *chewluh, chewluh, chewluh. . . .* (see "Vocalization"). Song seems to confirm that *Cypsnagra* is really a Thraupinae, not an Emberizinae. Brushy open country; feeds on ground and among foliage, being predominantly insectivorous (see "Feeding"). Perches on branches of bushes and low trees to sing. Northeastern Brazil to Minas Gerais, São Paulo, Goiás, Mato Grosso, Bolivia, Paraguay.

CONE-BILLED TANAGER, *Conothraupis mesoleuca*
BR

14.5 Known only from central Brazil (Mato Grosso). Black with greenish sheen, center of breast and belly white like speculum and underside of wings. Bill and feet black. Originally called *Rhynchothraupis.* Related to Black-and-white Tanager, *C. speculigera,* of eastern Peru (black with purple sheen, grayish rump and flanks, white crissum) and which probably also occurs in Brazilian Amazonia (upper Purus) in partially open, secondary vegetation. The two perhaps are nothing more than geographic replacements of each other (Storer 1960). See *Lamprospiza melanoleuca.*

RED-BILLED PIED TANAGER, *Lamprospiza melanoleuca,* Pipira-de-bico-vermelho

15.5 cm. Amazonian. Upperparts, throat, and center of breast black with blue sheen. Rest of underparts white except for 2 black stripes running from breast to flanks. Very strong bill is scarlet, black in immature. Female has grayish back, yellowish underparts. VOICE: call *hewtsi-hew, wist-wist,* audible at a distance; song a sharp-sounding, stereotyped stanza, *SEE-sisili.* Lives in small flocks in tops of trees. The Guianas to lower Amazon, from east of Tapajós to Belém (Pará), northwestern Mato Grosso (Rio Roosevelt), Peru. See *Conothraupis.*

MAGPIE TANAGER, *Cissopis leveriana,* Tietinga
Fig. 297

29 cm; 27.8 g (male), 67.5 g (female). Large, unusual, with very long tail, unmistakable both in general aspect and in black-and-white coloring. White forms a V on upperparts. Iris yellow. VOICE: call a strident *spix-spix;* song a stereotyped cadence of screechy notes, frequently 3-phrased, e.g., *tsibi-SWEE-tsiew,* rapidly repeated. Moves through branches with long hops, making violent motions with tail; makes short flights with loud whistling of wings. Medium heights on edge of dense forests and riverine woodlands in small flocks, sometimes with Black-throated Grosbeak, *Pitylus fuliginosus* (Espírito Santo). The Guianas and Venezuela to Bolivia; Amazonian Brazil from south of Solimões to Tapajós (Tapirapoã, Mato Grosso), southern Pará (Gorotire), Maranhão; Pernambuco to Minas Gerais, Goiás, São Paulo, Rio Grande do Sul, Argentina (Misiones), Paraguay; in Espírito Santo and Rio de Janeiro in mountainous regions. Amazonian form is considerably smaller, has white back. Also

Fig. 297. Magpie Tanager, *Cissopis leveriana major.*

called *Pipira* (Mato Grosso), *Probexim, Sanhaço-tinga* (São Paulo), *Pintassilgo-do-mato-virgem, Sabiá-tinga.* Considered by backcountry people to be a jay (Corvidae), *Pega* (Pernambuco) remotely resembles Black-billed Magpie, *Pica pica,* of Northern Hemisphere.

SCARLET-THROATED TANAGER, *Sericossypha loricata,* Carretão   BR

23 cm; 72.5 g (male). Interesting endemic of northeastern Brazil. One of largest tanagers, with appearance of a curve-billed, heavy-billed sanhaço with relatively short tail. All black with bluish sheen except for scarlet patch in middle of throat and upper breast. Bases of back and flank feathers white, visible only when bird is preening. Female all black, lacking even above-mentioned white. Young males lack scarlet patch but can breed in this plumage; some are soot-colored. All-black individuals are more numerous than those with scarlet throat and are similar to icterines such as *Cacicus haemorrhous, Gnorimopsar chopi,* and *Molothrus bonariensis.* Color pattern may also suggest a cotinga.

VOICE: call *kwatt,* quite similar to cry of *Cacicus haemorrhous* but harsher; song repeated, loud, harsh, but resonant cry, *kyeh* or *kyuh.* This monotonous clamor, which could be a cotinga vocalization, is infrequently given during lighter hours of day but is produced insistently at dawn, commencing with first light. At that time interval between calls customarily lasts a second, sometimes less, with bird continuing to vocalize for perhaps 7 minutes. It then stops for a few seconds or up to a minute but renews its cries uninterruptedly for another 4 minutes or more. I have found that these periods of intense early morning vocalization may continue 18–45 minutes, with very short intervals. Such extraordinary perseverence in singing is reminiscent of certain vireos. Trees at river edges, frequently in small groups, even during nesting. Maranhão to Alagoas, Bahia, Minas Gerais (e.g., Rio Jequitinhonha and Rio São Francisco, Pirapora), Goiás. Also called *Boiadeiro, Espanta-vaqueiro, Guaxe* (Pernambuco, Minas Gerais), *Azulão* (Ceará), *Tejo* (Bahia). See *Sturnella* and Giant Cowbird, *Scaphidura oryzivora.* Public confuses it with these icterines and, also erroneously, attributes to it parasitism of *Molothrus bonariensis.*

CHESTNUT-HEADED TANAGER, *Pyrrhocoma ruficeps,* Cabecinha-castanha

14 cm. Restricted to southeastern littoral. Head and throat chestnut; forehead and region around eyes black; rest of plumage slate gray. Female olive green with cinnamon crown. VOICE: a high, squeaky *tsip* and a stanza that may end in 2 lower, fuller syllables, *seep-seep-seep-tsiew-tsiewwi,* reminiscent of song of *Arremon taciturnus,* sometimes its neighbor. Low in densest tangles and bamboo thickets. Espírito Santo to Rio Grande do Sul; Misiones, Argentina; Paraguay. Also called *Pioró* (São Paulo).

ORANGE-HEADED TANAGER, *Thlypopsis sordida*, Canário-sapé

13.5 cm. Slender, arboreal, well known to backcountry people. Immediately recognized by yellow face and throat, reminiscent of Saffron Finch, *Sicalis flaveola;* top of head rusty, mantle olivaceous, underparts brownish white. Female similar to female *Hemithraupis*, being green above with face and underparts yellow, belly brownish. VOICE: call *tsree, tsip, tsip, tsip, tsi-tsiewi;* has various song types: a well-pronounced one recalling *S. flaveola, tsap-tsip, tsip, tsip-tsop-tswit;* a very high trill, *tsi . . . tsrrrri,* that could come from a hummingbird; and a high, rapid warble, reminiscent of *Tangara cayana.* Treetops, including cities. Venezuela to Bolivia, Argentina, Paraguay; in Brazil to Paraná. Reminds one of a wood-warbler. Sometimes host to *Molothrus bonariensis.*

GUIRA TANAGER, *Hemithraupis guira*, Saíra-de-papo-preto

13 cm; 10 g (female). Similar to *H. ruficapilla* but distinguished by black mask and throat bordered with sulfur yellow. Female and immature olive green with region around eye and underparts yellowish, mandible yellow. VOICE: in flight *tsip-tsip; jewt;* song a sequence of high notes that rise slightly, *tsi, tsi, tsi-tseh, tseh, tseh.* General aspect and habitat very similar to *ruficapilla.* The Guianas and Venezuela to Bolivia, Paraguay, Argentina. Locally throughout Brazil but generally not encountered in same places as *ruficapilla,* for which it is a geographic replacement. They interbreed in areas where they enter into contact (Bahia, São Paulo). Also called *Pintassilgo-do-papo-preto.*

RUFOUS-HEADED TANAGER, *Hemithraupis ruficapilla*, Saíra-da-mata   BR   PL 42.2

12.8 cm; 13 g. Slender forest species, restricted to littoral of southeastern Brazil. Dark rufous head unmistakable. Breast and rump ochraceous, sides of neck bright yellow, mandible whitish. Female and immature greenish, lighter on underparts, reminiscent of a *Hylophilus* (Vireonidae) or *Basileuterus* (Parulinae). VOICE: identical to *H. guira,* apparently its geographic replacement. Treetops, forests, parks, etc. Southern Bahia and Minas Gerais to Santa Catarina. Also called *Figuinha-amarela* (Minas Gerais), *Pintassilgo-da-mata.*

YELLOW-BACKED TANAGER, *Hemithraupis flavicollis*, Saíra-galega

14 cm. Forest species notable for yellow throat, with lower back, rump, and under tail coverts also yellow. Rest of upperparts black, wing with large white speculum. Underparts white, breast speckled black. Female and immature similar to those of 2 previous species but smaller. VOICE: *tsri;* song *si, si, si . . . ,* like an insect. Canopy. Panama to Bolivia; Brazilian Amazonia south to northern Mato Grosso and

Fig. 298. Hooded Tanager, *Nemosia pileata*, male.

southern Pará and to north of lower Amazon (Amapá); Pernambuco to Rio de Janeiro (Cabo Frio), ex-Guanabara (immature individuals predominating, e.g., in March). Sometimes associates with *H. ruficapilla.* Also called *Pintassilgo-da-mata* (Minas Gerais, Rio de Janeiro).

HOODED TANAGER, *Nemosia pileata*, Saíra-de-chapéu-preto   Fig. 298

13 cm; 14 g (female). Arboreal species of well-lighted places, drawing attention with pure white lores and underparts that contrast with black of crown. Mantle gray; iris and legs yellow (brown in immature). Female lacks black pattern; has yellowish underparts, white mandible. VOICE: high like a *Dacnis;* song, *si-si-SLEE,* repeated several times. Sparse arboreal vegetation, e.g., caatinga, cerrado, etc. The Guianas and Venezuela across savanna areas of Amazonia to northeastern and eastern Brazil as far as São Paulo and Rio Grande do Sul, central Brazil, Bolivia, Paraguay, Argentina. See *Neothraupis fasciata* (much larger) and Black-capped Warbling-Finch, *Poospiza melanoleuca.*

CHERRY-THROATED TANAGER, *Nemosia rourei*, Saíra-apunhalada   BR   EN   PL 45.5

14 cm. Upperparts gray; sides of head, wings, and tail back; crown whitish. Underparts white; throat and lower neck blood red, forming a pointed shield. Described in 1870 but known in recent times only from a single specimen from left margin of Rio Paraíba do Sul (Muriaé, Minas Gerais), in collection of Berlin Museum. Collector, J. de Roure, stated he did not see another individual of this species in more than 30 years of intense study of the birds of the area (see Chapter 2.4). However, I saw a flock of 8 in treetops in mountainous region of Espírito Santo (Limoeiro-Jaboticaba, 900–1000 m) on 8 August 1941.

OLIVE-BACKED TANAGER, *Mitrospingus oleagineus*

Only in extreme north, in mountains of Roraima, Venezuela, the Guianas.

OLIVE-GREEN TANAGER, *Orthogonys chloricterus*, Catirumbava   BR

19 cm. Restricted to Serra do Mar and Serra da Mantiquera. Lacks distinctive marking but bill relatively slender and black. Upperparts olive green, underparts greenish yellow. Legs yellowish brown. VOICE: call a strident and prolonged *tsee* (louder than call of Yellow-legged Thrush, *Platycichla flavipes*, frequently its neighbor), *pix;* song a squeaky stanza, *TSEE-si, si, si, TSEE-si, si, si.* Sometimes several join in a collective clamor. In flocks in forest canopy. Espírito Santo to Santa Catarina. Also called *Sanhaço-de-bando, Imbaraí, Selvagem* (Rio de Janeiro). See female *Piranga flava* (lighter) and *Eucometis penicillata.*

GRAY-HEADED TANAGER, *Eucometis penicillata*, Pipira-da-taoca

18 cm. Widely distributed in Amazonia. Crested, with olive green upperparts and gray head, normally with semiconcealed white in center of crown. Throat white, belly bright yellow. Immature all green, including head. VOICE: call *chip;* alarm a loud *tseh;* song a sequence of high whistles with 2d part of stanza descending, *tsee, tsee, tsee, tsi, tsi, tsi, tsi, tsi, tsi,* perhaps reminiscent of an *Arremon* sparrow; sometimes more varied and prolonged. Interior of thick forests, frequently near water alongside narrow channels among açaí palm groves and *Montrichardia* sp. (Araceae). One of most assiduous frequenters of army-ant swarms. Mexico to Bolivia, Paraguay, all of Brazilian Amazonia to Mato Grosso (Xingu, Rio das Mortes), Goiás, western São Paulo, eastern Pará, Maranhão.

The genus *Lanio,* which occurs from Mexico to Amazonia, is a small group similar in plumage to *Tachyphonus,* with an extensive white area on the wing and a relatively long tail. Members are characterized by having a tooth on the maxilla.

FULVOUS SHRIKE-TANAGER, *Lanio fulvus*, Pipira-parda   Fig. 299

18 cm. Ochraceous yellow, darker on breast and rump; head, wings, and tail black; concealed white epaulet. Female lacks black, giving it appearance of a small *Tachyphonus.* See "Morphology" regarding subadult. Treetops, open secondary vegetation, palm groves. North of Amazon from Solimões to Amapá, replacing *L. versicolor.*

Fig. 299. Fulvous Shrike-Tanager, *Lanio fulvus,* showing the maxillar tooth. Rio Paru, Pará. Original, H. Sick.

Fig. 300. Flame-crested Tanager, *Tachyphonus cristatus,* male.

WHITE-WINGED SHRIKE-TANAGER, *Lanio versicolor,* Pipira-de-asa-branca   PL 42.7

16 cm. Similar to *L. fulvus,* its geographic replacement, but shows only a hint of maxillar tooth. Center of crown and throat greenish, extensive white on upper wing coverts. Riverine forests. Peru and Bolivia to southern Amazonia, south to northwestern Mato Grosso (Jamari), Pará (Cururu, Tocantins).

FLAME-CRESTED TANAGER, *Tachyphonus cristatus,* Tié-galo   Fig. 300

15.5 cm; 19 g (male). Widely distributed, common, much smaller than *T. coronatus* and with nuchal crest. All black with yellowish brown throat and rump, extensive scarlet on crown that is always visible (unlike *coronatus*). Partially hidden epaulet and under wing coverts white. Female and immature brown with lighter throat, blackish forehead. VOICE: an insignificant, low *chat; tseh, tseh, tseh, tsititit.* Forest canopy, frequently associated with *T. luctuosus* (Amazonia) and various *Tangara,* sometimes also with *T. rufus.* The Guianas and Venezuela to Amazonia, central Brazil (Mato Grosso, etc.), the northeast and east, south to São Paulo. Also called *Gurricha* (Pará).

NATTERER'S TANAGER, *Tachyphonus nattereri*   BR

In extreme west. Similar to *T. cristatus* but even smaller, throat black instead of yellow. Recorded in Cáceres (Mato Grosso) and Rio Guaporé (Rondônia). Can be considered a geographic race of *cristatus.*

FULVOUS-CRESTED TANAGER, *Tachyphonus surinamus,* Tem-tem-de-topete-ferrugíneo

15.5 cm. Like *T. cristatus.* Underside all black except for yellow spot on side of breast; flanks chestnut; crown and rump reddish yellow. Female and immature differ from those of *T. rufus,* with gray head, yellow area around eyes, green mantle, brownish or whitish underparts. VOICE: a weak *si-si.* Low and medium levels of tall forest, often in mixed flocks. The Guianas and Venezuela to Rios Juruá and Tocantins, Belém. Also called *Pipira.*

RED-SHOULDERED TANAGER, *Tachyphonus phoenicius,* Tem-tem-de-dragona-vermelha

15.5 cm. Uniformly silky black; some of inside feathers of white lesser upper wing coverts red, creating a flashy mark that is concealed when bird is at rest. Female has blackish brown upperparts and sides of head, a concealed ferruginous epaulet, and grayish underparts, darker on breast. Open vegetation and plantations, sometimes alongside Rufous-collared Sparrow, *Zonotrichia capensis.* The Guianas and Venezuela to the Guaporé and Tapajós (Teles Pires, Mato Grosso, in the Cururu and Serra do Cachimbo, Pará), Araguaia (southeastern Pará). Also called *Curió* (Pará).

YELLOW-CRESTED TANAGER, *Tachyphonus rufiventer,* Tem-tem-de-crista-amarela

15.5 cm. Black with yellow crown and rump, semiconcealed white epaulet. Center of underparts rusty yellow. On Juruá, Javari (Amazonas), and in adjoining countries.

WHITE-SHOULDERED TANAGER, *Tachyphonus luctuosus,* Tem-tem-de-dragona-branca

12.5 cm. Smallest *Tachyphonus.* Black with conspicuous white epaulet. Female has gray head, olive green back, whitish throat. Breast and belly yellowish, reminiscent of a vireo. VOICE: soft, call resembling a canary's. Middle heights on forest edge, sometimes alongside *T. cristatus* and *T. rufus.* The Guianas and Venezuela to Bolivia and Brazil, Mato Grosso (Rio das Mortes), Goiás, eastern Pará (Belém).

RUBY-CROWNED TANAGER, *Tachyphonus coronatus,* Tié-preto   PL 42.5

17.7 cm; 29 g (male). Typical of southeastern Brazil, where it replaces *T. rufus,* which it resembles except for being less stocky. Center of crown has scarlet patch that stays entirely hidden except when elevated. Female similar to female *rufus* but with more sombre coloring; head and breast grayish, foreneck and breast lightly streaked. Subadult males of all *Tachyphonus* and *Lanio* retain for some time a mixture of brown and black plumage that reminds one of *Molothrus rufoaxillaris.* VOICE: a loud *ghep* similar to *Ramphocelus bresilius;* a monotonous, staccato, leisurely repeated phrase of 3–4 syllables, like *chep-chep-cho, tsewLEE-tsuk, tsewLEE-tsuk.* Forest edges, capoeria, parks, etc. Near Rio de Janeiro abundant in Serra do Mar; in ex-Guanabara area more frequent in winter. Espírito Santo to Rio Grande do Sul, southern Mato Grosso, Paraguay, Argentina. Found with *T. rufus* in western São Paulo. Sometimes host to *Molothrus bonariensis.* Also called *Gurundi* (São Paulo), *Azulão.*

WHITE-LINED TANAGER, *Tachyphonus rufus,* Pipira-preta

18 cm. Common in interior and very similar to *T. coronatus,* its geographic replacement. Uniformly silky black except for concealed white epaulets, under wing coverts, and axillaries. Female and immature uniformly rufous brown but lighter on underparts. VOICE: in flight *wist-wist;* principal call *jep, ieh, ieh, ieh . . . ,* reminiscent of peeps of a baby chick; song of male in presence of female is given sotto voce and is similar to a *Thraupis.* Medium and low levels; also descends to ground. In any arboreal vegetation. Outside Amazonia on edge of tangles, occasionally associated with other tanagers, e.g., *T. cristatus,* woodcreepers, etc. Costa Rica to Venezuela, the Guianas, Peru, Paraguay, Argentina. In Brazil south of Amazon (between Tapajós and Belém), northeastern and central Brazil to Minas Gerais, São Paulo, Mato Grosso. Also called *Encontro-de-prata.*

BLACK-GOGGLED TANAGER, *Trichothraupis melanops,* Tié-de-topete   Fig. 301

17.5 cm; 23 g (male). Southern, crested species. Male always displays extensive sulfur yellow of crown which contrasts with black mask. Back dark olive gray, wings and tail black. Flight feathers have unique pattern of white markings, visible only on open wing, which forms a contrasting band interrupted in middle, serving as 2 alarm signals on each side, for a total of 4 conspicuous stripes. Underparts yellowish brown. Female has no black on face, little yellow on crown; immature lacks least vestige of yellow crest. VOICE: call *tshik,* characteristic for species; song a rapid trill reminiscent of a *Thraupis.* Forest bird, lives low in dense woods, descends to ground. Gregarious, one of principal frequenters of army-ant swarms. Bahia and Minas Gerais to Rio Grande do Sul, southern Mato Grosso, Argentina (Misiones), Para-

Fig. 301. Black-goggled Tanager, *Trichothraupis melanops,* male.

guay, Bolivia, Peru. Abundant in mountains of Espírito Santo and Rio de Janeiro, reaches ex-Guanabara on Pedra Branca massif. See *Pipraeidea melanonota,* which lacks white in wing.

RED-CROWNED ANT-TANAGER, *Habia rubica,* Tié-do-mato-grosso

19.5 cm; 40 g. Relatively large and common, widely distributed. Slight crest. Uniformly dull red (appearing sooty chestnut in forest shadows) except shiny scarlet crown. Female and immature all brown, adult female with yellow in center of crown. VOICE: call and warning a copious *tsak,* a noisy *cha-cha;* song—whistles reminiscent of *Thraupis;* soft, melodious phrases; a different, monotonous dawn song. Understory inside dark forests; frequently descends to ground. Accompanies army ants (Espírito Santo), both with family members and in association with spinetails, etc. Mexico to northern South America, from there to Argentina, Paraguay, Bolivia. In Brazil south of Amazon, from Juruá and western Mato Grosso, and from southern Bahia to Rio Grande do Sul. Also called *Tangará* (Pará), *Tié-da-mata.* See *Tachyphonus rufus* and *T. coronatus,* which have smaller bills.

HEPATIC TANAGER, *Piranga flava,* Sanhaço-de-fogo   PL 42.3

17.5 cm; 38 g (male). Widely distributed, notable for bright coloring and accentuated sexual dimorphism. Male almost all carmine, becoming brownish on upperparts; female bright yellow below; immature male has mixed green and orange plumage in 1st year. VOICE: call a loud *chip, chap, cherIT;* song a melodious but little-varied stanza, *jip-jewlo jewlo jip.* Perches conspicuously on tops of tall trees (unlike *Ramphocelus*), moves with headlong flight at canopy height. Thin, deciduous forest, cerrado, eucalyptus groves. Expanding range on our coastal strip, taking advantage of forest devastation. Southwestern U.S. and Mexico to northern South America, from there to Bolivia, Argentina, Uruguay, except in forested Amazonia. Sometimes host to *Molothrus bonariensis.* Southern replacement of *P. rubra.* Also called *Canário-do-mato, Queima-campo.* See *P. rubra, P. olivacea, Habia rubica,* and females *Orthogonys chloricterus* and *Eucometis penicillata,* which live more secluded.

SUMMER TANAGER, *Piranga rubra*   NV

16.5 cm. Migrant from North America, similar to *P. flava* but both sexes with yellowish bill, not black and gray of *flava.* Immature male plumage a mixture of red and green. Recorded in Amazonas (Rio Negro, December; Rio Madeira).

SCARLET TANAGER, *Piranga olivacea*   NV

Seen at Manaus, Amazonas, in December 1984 (Bierregard and Stotz).

WHITE-WINGED TANAGER, *Piranga leucoptera*

Only 14 cm. Mountains of northern border. Red, masked, with black wings and tail, 2 white wing bars. Female greenish yellow but recognizable by wing bars. Along Andes and its slopes from Mexico to Venezuela, Bolivia; Roraima in Brazil.

MASKED CRIMSON TANAGER, *Ramphocelus nigrogularis,* Pipira-de-máscara

18.5 cm. Only in upper Amazon. Similar to *R. bresilius* but distinguished by black mask and back. VOICE: unlike other *Ramphocelus.* Low, thick forests. Western Pará, Amazonas, adjacent countries. Sympatric with *R. carbo* in certain areas. Considered to be the species that most resembles the supposed ancestral form of this genus.

SILVER-BEAKED TANAGER, *Ramphocelus carbo,* Pipira-vermelha

18 cm. Replaces *R. bresilius* in central Brazil and Amazonia as an allopatric form or semispecies. General color velvety black, changing toward purple, particularly on throat and breast. Base of male mandible swollen and white with phosphorescent appearance. Female similar to female *bresilius* but generally darker, underparts tending more definitely toward red. VOICE: call, warning *ghep, tshik, spit;* song a repeated sequence of soft whistles, *pse-bit, pse-bit, pse-bititit,* sung especially at dawn and reminiscent of corresponding twitter of *Tachyphonus coronatus;* about 6 or more individuals may get together and vehemently cry *chik.* Riverine vegetation and low capoeira; along lower Amazon is customarily most abundant species, this impression being created in part because it lives in small groups (see "Vocalization") The Guianas and Venezuela to Bolivia, Paraguay, Amazonian Brazil, extending east to Piauí and south through central Brazil to western Paraná, southern Mato Grosso. Host to *Molothrus bonariensis.* Also called *Bico-de-prata, Pipira-de-prata, Pipira-de-papo-vermelho, Pepita, Chaubaêta* (Mato Grosso).

BRAZILIAN TANAGER, *Ramphocelus bresilius,* Tié-sangue   BR PL 42.1

19 cm; 31 g (male). One of world's most spectacular birds, endemic to eastern Brazil. Superb, vivid red-and-black plumage of male acquired only in 2d year. Female brownish. An important feature of genus, occurring exclusively in males, is shiny white callosity at base of mandible. Immature male similar to female but bill all black, not brown. VOICE: call, warning a hard *jep, jip, ist, sst-sst;* song a melodious 3-part trill, sounding like *jewle-jewle-jewle,* leisurely repeated; a few individuals together may indulge in harsh, rapid chattering. Low capoeira, restinga, plantings, etc. Paraíba to Santa Catarina; in upper Rio Doce region interbreeds with *R. carbo* (see "Distribution . . ."). Frequently is

host to *Molothrus bonariensis*. Also called *Sangue-de-boi, Tié-fogo, Tapiranga* (Bahia). See female *Tachyphonus coronatus*, which is less stocky, has similar call, and frequently occurs in same places.

BLUE-GRAY TANAGER, *Thraupis episcopus*, Sanhaço-da-amazônia

16.5 cm. Very similar to next 2 species but with white or bluish white epaulets. VOICE: a high, strident twitter, like *T. palmarum*. Low capoeira, plantations, open vegetation, palm groves. Abundant in Amazonia. The Guianas and Venezuela to south of Amazon as far as Rio Juruá, Belém (Pará), Maranhão. A geographic replacement for *T. sayaca*. Also called *Saí-açu*.

SAYACA TANAGER, *Thraupis sayaca*, Sanhaço-cinzento

17.5 cm; 42 g (male). One of most abundant birds of eastern Brazil. Slightly bluish gray with somewhat lighter underparts. Epaulets and edges of flight and tail feathers dull greenish blue (unlike *T. cyanoptera*, as noted below). VOICE: call *jewluh, cheweet, CHEEeh;* song a descending cadence of well-pronounced notes, some soft and melodious, frequently ending with a long, ascending note. When a male is preparing to attack another, his song becomes harsh and monotonous like that of *T. palmarum*. Trees anywhere, in rural open country, cultivated areas, or cities (center of Rio de Janeiro, Belo Horizonte, etc.). Eastern and central Brazil from Maranhão to Rio Grande do Sul, Goiás, Mato Grosso; Bolivia, Paraguay, Argentina, Uruguay, Venezuela, Colombia. Sometimes host to *Molothrus bonariensis*. Locally alongside *T. cyanoptera* or *T. ornata;* frequently with *T. palmarum*. Southern replacement for *T. episcopus* but voice significantly different. Also called *Saí-açu, Sanhaço*.

AZURE-SHOULDERED TANAGER, *Thraupis cyanoptera*, Sanhaço-de-encontro-azul PL 41.10

18 cm; 43 g (male). Extremely similar to *T. sayaca*, differing in bright blue epaulets and in more contrasting, brilliant blue edges of flight feathers. VOICE: a rapid and somewhat harsh twitter, reminiscent of *T. palmarum;* lower and more melodious phrases reminiscent of *Schistochlamys ruficapillus*. Capoeira, forest edge. In Espírito Santo and Rio de Janeiro more common in mountains, where it lives locally more or less alongside *T. sayaca*, *T. ornata*, and *T. palmarum* (see "Feeding"). Stockier than *sayaca*, which it drives away when they meet (Petrópolis, Rio de Janeiro). Espírito Santo to Rio Grande do Sul, Paraguay.

GOLDEN-CHEVRONED TANAGER, *Thraupis ornata*, Sanhaço-de-encontro-amarelo BR

18 cm. Easily identifiable southern species; very dark grayish blue with yellow median wing coverts. Immature a bit darker than *T. sayaca*. VOICE: call *tswit;* song loud and rapid, similar to *T. palmarum* but with a shorter phrase; at

times sings penetrating phrases, e.g., *tshlit, chit, chit . . . , kleh, kleh, kleh, kleh*. Edge of forests and capoeria; in mountainous region of Rio de Janeiro it is most common species, sometimes found alongside *T. sayaca* and *T. cyanoptera*. In winter appears in reduced numbers in ex-Guanabara, and I have noted a decrease in population in mountains of Espírito Santo in same season. Bahia to Santa Catarina. Sometimes host to *Molothrus bonariensis*. Also called *Sanhaço-de-encontros*.

PALM TANAGER, *Thraupis palmarum*, Sanhaço-do-coqueiro PL 41.11

18 cm. Widely distributed, generally closely associated with palm trees. Unmistakable, being all greenish with back changing toward sepia gray. VOICE: call a metallic *tsiep;* song squeaky, impetuous, with little variation, distinctly louder than *T. sayaca* and much less melodious. Tops of isolated trees, preferably palms. Likes to perch on tip of top spike of a palm to sing. Costa Rica and northern South America to Bolivia, Paraguay, throughout Brazil. Sometimes host to Shiny Cowbird, *Molothrus bonariensis*. Also called *Saí-açú-pardo* (Pará).

BLUE-AND-YELLOW TANAGER, *Thraupis bonariensis*, Sanhaço-papa-laranjas

18 cm. Brightly colored southern species. Head and wings blue; back black; rump and breast orange; belly lighter yellow. Female much different, brownish green with lighter underparts and no special markings, difficult to identify in absence of male. Immature male has bluish crown with yellowish rump and underparts. VOICE: song a simple, unaccelerated sequence, *tsli-tsi, tsli-tsi, tsli-tsi;* at dawn sings a more complex but still stereotyped *tsip, tsip, tsip-tsiewli*, tirelessly repeated in rapid rhythm. Moves frequently from perch to perch, engages in intraspecific chasing. Gallery forests and groves. Paraná (nesting, P. Scherer Neto) to Paraguay, Argentina, Chile, Colombia, following Andes. Also called *Papa-queijo* (Santa Catarina), *Papa-ameixa* (Santa Catarina).

BLUE-BACKED TANAGER, *Cyanicterus cyanicterus*, Pipira-azul

18.5 cm. Only in northern Amazonia. Dark blue with yellow belly, yellow iris, large bill. Female has greenish blue upperparts. Tops of fruiting trees, together with other tanagers. Flies rapidly from one treetop to another (Silva and Willis 1986). The Guianas to Rio Negro (Manaus), Amapá (Serra do Navio, Grantsau 1985), Borba (Rio Madeira). There are few records.

DIADEMED TANAGER, *Stephanophorus diadematus*, Sanhaço-frade

19 cm; 41.5 g (male). Large, southern species with heavy, cardinaline-type bill and a crest. Dark purplish blue, face black, top of head whitish with carmine in center. Female

paler, immature sooty, somewhat reminiscent of immature *Molothrus bonariensis.* VOICE: call *kwatt, pitz;* song melodious and varied, soft or loud, reminiscent of *Passerina brissonii* (Emberizinae). In pairs in dense, low forests, e.g., on tops of mountains such as Caparaó and Itatiaia (above line of high forests), where it is one of most typical birds. Espírito Santo and Minas Gerais to Rio Grande do Sul (in Rio de Janeiro restricted to mountainous regions), Uruguay, Argentina, Paraguay. Also called *Cabeça-de-velha, Frade* (Rio Grande do Sul), *Azulão-da-serra* (São Paulo).

FAWN-BREASTED TANAGER, *Pipraeidea melanonota,* Viúva PL 42.4

15 cm. Unmistakable with brilliant light blue on top of head, black mask, and rusty yellow underparts. Female and immature similar but paler, with mask barely outlined or absent. VOICE: call *tsi,* reminiscent of a saíra; song a rapid, monotonous series of 6–8 very high, sharp notes, *si, si, si . . . ,* somewhat reminiscent of Uniform Finch, *Haplospiza unicolor;* a varied trill recalling spring song of a thrush. In pairs in canopy, also frequents restinga vegetation. Bahia and Minas Gerais to Rio de Janeiro, Rio Grande do Sul, Uruguay, Argentina, Paraguay, and following slopes of Andes, to northwestern Amazonas and Venezuela. Also called *Gaturamo* (Rio de Janeiro).

Key for Identification of Male Euphonias:
Euphonia *(13 species) and* Chlorophonia cyanea

1. Underparts yellow or yellowish:
   1.1. Underparts pure yellow, including throat: *E. violacea, E. laniirostris*
   1.2. Underparts yellow with greenish wavy marks, throat white: *E. chrysopasta*
   1.3. Head and foreneck green: *Chlorophonia cyanea* (Pl 41.2)
   1.4. Sides of head and throat black, cap blue: *E. musica*
   1.5. Head, throat, and foreneck black or bluish gray, respectively: *E. rufiventris* and *E. plumbea*
   1.6. Head and throat black, forehead or forehead and top of head yellow: *E. xanthogaster, E. minuta, E. finschi, E. chlorotica* (Pl 41.3), and *E. chalybea*
2. Underparts without yellow except an area on side of breast:
   2.1. Throat to breast black, belly chestnut: *E. pectoralis* (Pl 41.4)
   2.2. Underparts all black: *E. cayennensis*

PLUMBEOUS EUPHONIA, *Euphonia plumbea,* Gaturamo-anão

9 cm; 8.8 g. Tiny, with upperparts, throat, and foreneck dark bluish gray, rest of underparts orange-yellow. Female back green. VOICE: 2–3 ascending whistles; sings well. Canopy of high terra-firme forest, but sometimes in low fruit trees outside woods. The Guianas and Venezuela to Manaus (Amazonas), Amapá.

PURPLE-THROATED EUPHONIA, *Euphonia chlorotica,* Fi-fi verdadeiro, Vivi PL 41.3

9.5 cm; 8 g (male). Together with *E. violacea,* best-known *Euphonia.* Small and also with black throat, it is reminiscent of *E. xanthogaster,* but bill more slender, yellow cap lighter and less extensive. There are white spots on 2 outer tail feathers on each side. Female olivaceous green with yellowish forehead. Belly frequently whitish. VOICE: call a penetrating *dee-dee, wee,* (used by both sexes and diagnostic for species); a soft *telewt-telewt;* song a weak, rapid trill that might recall a siskin, *Carduelis* sp. Thin, low woods, cerrado, caatinga, palm groves, mountain forests (southeastern Brazil). Most of northern South America, south to Uruguay, Argentina, Paraguay, Bolivia, throughout Brazil. Individuals of northern populations are smaller (total 9 cm). In south sometimes alongside *E. musica* and *E. violacea.* Also called *Vem-vem, Gaturamo-miudinho.*

FINSCH'S EUPHONIA, *Euphonia finschi*
On Venezuelan-Brazilian border (Roraima). Lacks white in tail feathers.

VIOLACEOUS EUPHONIA, *Euphonia violacea,* Gaturamo-verdadeiro

12 cm; 15 g (male). Best-known and most appreciated singer in genus. Relatively large, black above with strong bluish sheen, forecrown, throat, and underparts dark yellow. Two outer tail feathers on each side have large white spot, inner vane of secondaries has white that is normally hidden. Female dark olivaceous green with forehead and underparts lighter.

VOICE: call *kweh, shewit, slit, ghep, ghep, ghep, sprrr;* song a persistent, rapid warble that at times includes many imitations of other birds of area: in Rio de Janeiro usually includes Tropical Kingbird, *Tyrannus melancholicus;* Yellow-lored Tody-Flycatcher, *Todirostrum poliocephalum;* Rufous-bellied Thrush, *Turdus rufiventris; Passer domesticus;* Roadside Hawk, *Rupornis magnirostris;* Great Kiskadee, *Pitangus sulphuratus;* Three-striped Flycatcher, *Conopias trivirgata;* Southern Beardless-Tyrannulet, *Camptostoma obsoletum;* Southern Rough-winged Swallow, *Stelgidopteryx ruficollis;* Golden-crowned Warbler, *Basileuterus culicivorus; Thraupis sayaca;* and Common Waxbill, *Estrilda astrild.* In Rio de Janeiro Botanical Garden I also heard it imitate Plain Parakeet, *Brotogeris tirica;* White-shouldered Fire-eye, *Pyriglena leucoptera;* and Blue Manakin, *Chiroxiphia caudata;* and in forests of Corcovado, Plain-brown Woodcreeper, *Dendrocincla fuliginosa;* White-necked Thrush, *Turdus albicollis;* and *Ramphocelus bresilius.* In Santa Teresa section of Rio de Janeiro I heard an imitation of the impressive night song of Rufous-collared Sparrow, *Zonotrichia capensis.* In upper Xingu of Mato Grosso typical species of that region are mimicked, e.g., Rufous-tailed Jacamar, *Galbula ruficauda;* Swallow Wing,

Chelidoptera tenebrosa; aracaris; toucans; and Fiery-capped Manakin, *Machaeropterus pyrocephalus.* Generally the euphonia does not separate the imitations, singing them in uninterrupted sequence; only when it starts to sing does it separate them and may thus fool listeners.

Forest borders, orchard fruit trees, dense trees in parks, etc., more common in Amazonia. The Guianas and Venezuela to Rio Grande do Sul, Argentina (Misiones), Paraguay. Might be considered an eastern geographical replacement for *E. laniirostris.* Also called *Guiratã* (female of species, Rio de Janeiro), *Guipara* (female, Santa Catarina), *Guiratã-de-coqueiro* (Pernambuco), *Tem-tem-de-estrela, Gaturamo-itê.* See *E. chlorotica,* female.

THICK-BILLED EUPHONIA, *Euphonia laniirostris,* Gaturamo-de-bico-grosso

12.5 cm. Very thick-billed. Stockier than *E. violacea* but with much the same coloring, including lack of black throat. Yellow on top of head extends behind eyes; population of upper Amazon (Juruá, Madeira, *E. l. melanura*) has no white on tail feathers. VOICE: a harsh *shrew,* various other whistles; also a *dee-dee,* reminiscent of certain congeners; song a varied warble; sometimes mimics. Deciduous forests. Costa Rica to Venezuela, upper Amazon, central Brazil (Rio das Mortes, Mato Grosso), Bolivia.

GREEN-CHINNED EUPHONIA, *Euphonia chalybea,* Cais-cais

12.5 cm. One of largest *Euphonia,* restricted in Brazil to south. Has surprisingly heavy, deep bill (see "Feeding"). Upperparts and upper throat blue with distinctive greenish sheen; forehead and rest of underparts dusky yellow. Female similar to female *E. pectoralis* but with under tail coverts green like flanks. VOICE: reminiscent of *E. violacea,* song being given very rapidly, like a siskin, *Carduelis* sp., being a bit monotonous and generally without mimicking. Syllables such as *cais-cais* are prominent. Canopy. Rio de Janeiro (in mountainous regions, Teresópolis) to Rio Grande do Sul; Misiones, Argentina; Paraguay. In Rio de Janeiro sometimes alongside *E. musica* and *E. chlorotica.*

GOLDEN-RUMPED EUPHONIA, *Euphonia musica aureata,* Gaturamo-rei

11 cm. Only euphonia with light blue cap; mask, throat, and mantle black with bluish reflections, rump and underparts yellow tending toward caramel; female green but with blue cap and ochraceous forehead; immature with green cap but recognizable by small bill that is typical of species. VOICE: call full and a bit harsh, a slow *uurt-uurt-uurt* (characteristic of species); a rapidly trilled song, mixed with louder notes, *ew, tehtehteh,* etc. Edge of high or low forest. Mexico to Bolivia, Argentina, Paraguay; in Brazil north of lower Amazon, from Bahia and Minas Gerais to Rio Grande do Sul, southern Mato Grosso. Formerly called *Tanagra,* like

the other species presently included in *Euphonia* (see "Terminology"). Sometimes alongside *Chlorophonia cyanea* or *E. laniirostris.* Also called *Bonito-canário, Bonito-fogo* (São Paulo). See *E. rufiventris* and *E. xanthogaster.*

WHITE-LORED EUPHONIA, *Euphonia chrysopasta,* Gaturamo-verde

11 cm; 12 g. Upperparts relucent dark green, occiput and nape dark gray, lores and chin white; rest of underparts greenish yellow with breast barred. Female like male but center of underparts gray. Forest edges, descends to fruiting bushes. Northern South America to Bolivia, Amapá, and on Rios Madeira and Roosevelt (Mato Grosso). Sometimes alongside *E. minuta* and *E. violacea.*

WHITE-VENTED EUPHONIA, *Euphonia minuta,* Gaturamo-de-barriga-branca

8.5 cm. Amazonian. Very similar to *E. chlorotica* but even smaller. Only forehead is yellow; belly and thighs white. Three outer tail feathers (only 2 in *chlorotica*) on each side have white spot. Female green with olivaceous yellow breast, grayish white throat and belly. VOICE: call a high, repeated whistle; song a very ordinary trill. Moves tail sideways in a characteristic way, male displaying white in outer tail feathers with this gesture. Edge of forest, among planted trees. Mexico to Bolivia, Brazil in northern Mato Grosso (Xingu), eastern Pará (Belém).

ORANGE-BELLIED EUPHONIA, *Euphonia xanthogaster,* Fi-fi-grande

10.5 cm. Throat black, like *E. chlorotica,* but bill heavier. Top of head all yellow, belly orange-yellow; white spot on outermost tail feather, easily seen from below. Female olivaceous green with yellowish brow, grayish brown nape and underparts. VOICE: call a nasal *buur-buur(-buur),* a bit less sonorous and more rapid than *E. musica;* harsh *esht, esht, esht, gaya, sui, bitz,* high like *Coereba flaveola;* song trilled. Forests, river edges. Panama to upper Amazon (including Rio Tapajós), Bolivia; Bahia and Minas Gerais to São Paulo. In southeastern Brazil sometimes alongside *E. chlorotica.* See also *E. musica* and *E. pectoralis,* female. Also called *Gaturamo-de-barriga-laranja.*

RUFOUS-BELLIED EUPHONIA, *Euphonia rufiventris,* Gaturamo-do-norte

11 cm. Only in Amazonia, where apparently replaces *E. pectoralis* and *E. cayennensis* (see fig. 295). Upperparts, including top of head, forehead, throat, and front of neck, bluish black; belly rusty yellow; sides of breast golden yellow, similar to *pectoralis* and *cayennensis.* Female like female *pectoralis* but with crissum yellowish brown. VOICE: pair alongside nest, *bi-bit-bit;* song soft and melodious. Tall forests. Venezuela to upper Amazon, Tapajós and Xingu

(Mato Grosso), Bolivia. Seen from below similar to *E. musica.*

CHESTNUT-BELLIED EUPHONIA, *Euphonia pectoralis,* Ferro-velho   PL 41.4

11.5 cm; 16.5 g (male). Well known in southeast, where it replaces *E. rufiventris* and *E. cayennensis.* Like them, has striking, bright yellow tufts on sides of breast but differs in chestnut belly. Female similar to female *rufiventris* and *cayennensis* but has gray only in center of underparts. Under tail coverts chestnut. VOICE: call a loud, metallic *shri, shri, shri* (*serrador,* "sawyer") reminiscent of *cayennensis; chewlew;* song a somewhat harsh warble, sometimes with imitations that are repeated. Canopy of tall forest. Paraguay; Misiones, Argentina; central and eastern Brazil from Bahia and Minas Gerais to Rio Grande do Sul, southern Goiás, Mato Grosso (Rio das Mortes, upper Xingu). In upper Xingu overlaps with *rufiventris.* Also called *Tieté, Gaita, Serrador, Alcaide, Gaturamo-rei* (Minas Gerais). See also *E. chalybea* and *E. chrysopasta* females.

Apparently *E. vittata,* also known as *Tanagra catasticta,* of which there is only 1 specimen (from Rio de Janeiro?), is a hybrid of *E. pectoralis* × *E. xanthogastra.*

GOLDEN-SIDED EUPHONIA, *Euphonia cayennensis,* Gaturamo-preto

11.3 cm. Replaces *E. rufiventris* north of lower Amazon and east of Pará, and *E. pectoralis* in Amazonia (see fig. 295). All steel blue except sides of breast, which are orange-yellow like *rufiventris* and *cayennensis;* underside of wings resplendent white. Female similar to female *pectoralis* but with under tail coverts gray like belly. VOICE: a low *che, che, che* similar to *pectoralis;* a soft *si-si,* much less strident than *E. chlorotica.* Moves tail sideways like *E. minuta.* Canopy. The Guianas and Venezuela to lower Rio Negro (Manaus, Amazonas), Amapá, Pará (Belém), northern Maranhão. Relatively rare in Brazilian Amazonia.

BLUE-NAPED CHLOROPHONIA, *Chlorophonia cyanea,* Bonito-do-campo   PL 41.2

10.8 cm; 13.8 g (female). Small with short tail, well known to commercial bird-catchers in southeast. Easily recognized by bright blue eye-ring and collar of same color on hind neck. Belly yellow (male) or greenish (female). VOICE: a conspicuous, melodious, descending *ewuh;* soft notes *hewtew, tew, tew, jet,* etc.; *wewit* while flying; song a low chatter. Forest edge in hilly regions and lowlands, generally in canopy in families and in association with saíras. Bahia and Minas Gerais to Rio Grande do Sul, Argentina (Misiones), Paraguay, along Andes from Bolivia to Venezuela and Guyana. In ex-Guanabara sometimes alongside *E. musica.* Also called *Bandeirinha* ("Little Flag"; it has colors of Brazilian flag), *Canário-assobio* (Santa Catarina), *Gaturamo-filó.*

TURQUOISE TANAGER, *Tangara mexicana,* Cambada-de-chaves, Coleiro-de-bando

13–14.2 cm; 26 g (southern race). Gregarious and widely distributed. Upperparts black except for blue bands crossing top of head and rump. Sides of head, throat down to breast, and upper wing coverts blue. Southern race, called *Cambada-de-chaves* (*T. m. brasiliensis*), distinctly larger than Amazonian forms (*T. m. mexicana,* among other races), called *Coleiro-de-bando,* which in addition to being noticeably smaller, have brighter blue parts and yellow abdomen, not white like *T. m. brasiliensis.* VOICE: a high and strident, attention-catching, repeated *tsri, tsik,* reminiscent of a bat squeak. Always in groups of 5–10 in forest canopy, capoeira, farms with trees. The Guianas and Venezuela to Amazonia, Bolivia, northern Mato Grosso (upper Xingu), eastern Pará; Bahia to Rio de Janeiro. In spite of name, has never been found in Mexico.

PARADISE TANAGER, *Tangara chilensis,* Sete-cores-da-amazônia

13.5 cm. Notable for light green hood of hardened, spatulate feathers. Mantle black; lower back and rump red or orange; throat dark blue; abdomen black; rest of underparts turquoise blue. VOICE: extremely high whistle, *tsilip, chip chip . . . ;* song prolonged sequences reminiscent of a marmoset (*Callithrix jacchus*), demonstrating that the most varicolored birds may have unmusical voices. Medium heights in forests, especially in várzeas; abundant in Amapá and Acre. The Guianas and Venezuela to upper Amazon, Rio Negro, Rio Juruá, Rio Guaporé; also northwestern Mato Grosso. In spite of name, has never been found in Chile.

SEVEN-COLORED TANAGER, *Tangara fastuosa,* Pintor-verdadeiro   BR EN

13.5 cm. Notable northeastern endemic, similar to *T. seledon* but with orange not only on lower back and rump but also on edges of inner secondaries and upper tail coverts, a combination that, seen from side, looks like a brilliant yellow triangle on base of tail; head and neck turquoise blue, lacking relucent green collar of *seledon;* tail feathers black with blue lateral borders. VOICE: in a dispute between males: *it-it-it-it.* Restricted to northeastern littoral from Pernambuco to Alagoas; was mentioned in Marcgrave (1648) as *tangará* (see "Terminology"). Highly prized by commercial bird-catchers, it was still common in 1974 in clandestine bird traffic. Its systematic persecution now appears to be a problem, for there has been a sharp decline in species in recent years. Situation is even more acute because of its restricted range.

GREEN-HEADED TANAGER, *Tangara seledon,* Sete-cores   PL 41.9

13.5 cm; 18 g. One of most abundant *Tangara* in southeast. Easily recognized by relucent yellowish green sides of neck, bright orange rump. Female paler; immature lacks bright rump color. VOICE: an insignificant *tsri,* a strident *tsEEe, cheIT, tsewk.* Loud, trisyllabic, descending dawn song. In flocks in treetops both in hot lowlands (where more abundant) and mountainous regions. Individuals with modest plumage are frequently seen. Bahia and Minas Gerais to Rio Grande do Sul, Paraguay. Associates with *T. cyanocephala, Tachyphonus, Dacnis cayana,* etc. Also called *Saíra-de-bando.*

RED-NECKED TANAGER, *Tangara cyanocephala,* Saíra-militar, Saíra-lenço   PL 41.7

13.5 cm. Unmistakable with scarlet on sides of head and hind neck (*lenço* = "scarf"). Female paler, has green streaking on back. Immature lacks red scarf. VOICE: a high *pst,* a sharp *tsit-tsit-tsit;* song a rapid twitter. Forest edges, frequently in association with *T. seledon* and in mountains with *T. cyanoventris.* Ceará to Rio Grande do Sul, Argentina (Misiones), Paraguay. Also called *Soldadinho, Saí-de-bando, Saíra-fogo.*

BRASSY-BREASTED TANAGER, *Tangara desmaresti,* Saíra-lagarta   BR

13.5 cm. Mountain dweller, like *T. cyanoventris.* Black forehead; celestial blue area around eyes; yellow foreneck and breast; distinctive black spot on upper throat. Rest of body green with black streaking on back. VOICE: a sharp *TSEEeh, tsi, tsi, tsi, tsirrr, tseep,* these notes sometimes repeated as a song by several individuals together. Capoeira, forests. Espírito Santo to Paraná; also Minas Gerais (Serra do Caraça, alongside *T. cyanocephala*). Also called *Saíra-da-serra.*

GILT-EDGED TANAGER, *Tangara cyanoventris,* Douradinha   BR

13.5 cm; 20 g. Head yellow; forehead and throat black; breast blue; back streaked with black and yellow; edges of flight and tail feathers green. Most abundant in mountainous regions (e.g., those of Rio de Janeiro), where it occurs alongside *T. desmaresti,* which it resembles. Bahia and Minas Gerais to São Paulo. Also called *Serra.*

GREEN-AND-GOLD TANAGER, *Tangara schrankii,* Saíra-ouro

13.5 cm. Upper Amazon. Green with black mask and black spots on mantle; cap, rump, and center of underparts golden yellow. Female's cap and rump spotted with black and green. Medium heights in várzea forest, alongside *T. chilensis.* Abundant, e.g., in Acre. Colombia to the Solimões, Purus, Bolivia.

SPOTTED TANAGER, *Tangara punctata,* Negaça PL 41.6

12 cm. Relatively small Amazonian species. Plumage has contrasting, scaly appearance, uncommon in tanagers; black

lores. Canopy. The Guianas and Venezuela to northern side of lower Amazon and Belém area. Also Ecuador, Bolivia. See *T. guttata* and *T. xanthogastra.*

SPECKLED TANAGER, *Tangara guttata*

Similar to *T. punctata.* Green with black spots, with golden yellow forehead and eye-ring. Costa Rica to Venezuela; also Roraima.

YELLOW-BELLIED TANAGER, *Tangara xanthogastra*

Also like *T. punctata.* Green with black spots but has blue-bordered mantle, yellow in center of abdomen. Rio Negro to Acre; Bolivia.

DOTTED TANAGER, *Tangara varia,* Saíra-carijó

11 cm; 10 g. Very small Amazonian species. Relucent green with black speckling on underparts. Lores black, wings and tail blue, similar to female *Dacnis cayana* (which is larger and has sharper-pointed bill). The Guianas and Venezuela to Rios Negro and Tapajós (Cururu, Pará).

BAY-HEADED TANAGER, *Tangara gyrola,* Saíra-de-cabeça-castanha

13.5 cm. Amazonian. Unmistakable with chestnut head. Rest of plumage varies greatly according to region. Form found in Brazil has bright blue underparts and rump. VOICE: singularly plaintive whistles. Forest edge, frequently low. Costa Rica and the Guianas to Bolivia, Guaporé, southern and northeastern Pará (Serra do Cachimbo and Belém, respectively). Also called *Saí.*

BURNISHED-BUFF TANAGER, *Tangara cayana,* Saíra-amarelo   PL 41.8

14.2 cm. Easily recognized despite existence of quite diverse races. Silvery yellow color predominates. In eastern and central Brazilian populations black mask extends to throat and along center line of entire underside. Female less colorful, has no black. VOICE: reminiscent of a *Thraupis;* song a monotonous, prolonged, rapid, whispering twitter, sounding as if it were made by several individuals at once; locally (Piauí) conspicuous for a sharp *pseeeeee* that recalls alarm note of certain thrushes. Capoeira, cerrado, gardens, etc. Common in mountains around Rio de Janeiro. The Guianas and Venezuela to Amazonia, central and northeastern Brazil, Paraná, Paraguay. Also called *Saí-amarelo, Saíra-de-asas-verdes, Cara-suja, Sanhaçuíra* (Rio de Janeiro, São Paulo), *Guiriatã* (Pernambuco).

BLACK-BACKED (= CHESTNUT-BACKED) TANAGER, *Tangara peruviana,* Saíra-sapucaia

14.2 cm. Unusual southern species, with crown and sides of head chestnut with coppery sheen. This color may extend to lower neck and back; upper wing coverts and rump silvery yellow; underparts relucent bluish green. Female grayish green, recognizable by chestnut on top of head and crissum. Polymorphic: males of northern populations (e.g., Rio de Janeiro) normally have black backs. Species was called *T. peruviana* because of an error in origin, for it has never been found in Peru, but the name is now fixed for the species because of the rules of nomenclature. VOICE: reminiscent of *Thraupis sayaca;* in Santa Catarina I noted a whistle, *seeeeee,* recalling *T. cayana.* Dense xerophytic vegetation (restinga in ex-Guanabara; June, August, September), edges of araucaria groves (Santa Catarina, November), groves in open country (Rio Grande do Sul, November, nesting). Migratory. Rio de Janeiro to Rio Grande do Sul, Uruguay, Argentina, Paraguay. Also called *Cara-suja, Saíguaçu* (Rio de Janeiro). Also called *T. preciosa* and formerly *T. castanonota.*

BLUE-NECKED TANAGER, *Tangara cyanicollis,* Saíra-de-cabeça-azul

12 cm; 14 g. Handsome Amazonian species, distinguished by turquoise blue head and neck contrasting with black on back and underparts. Upper wing coverts copper green, rump greenish blue. VOICE: *tsiBIT-tsiBIT,* reminiscent of a siskin, *Carduelis* sp. Palm groves. Mato Grosso (Chapada dos Parécis, Rio das Mortes, Rio Xingu) to Goiás (Chapada dos Veadeiros), southern Pará (Serra do Cachimbo); also Venezuela, Bolivia.

MASKED TANAGER, *Tangara nigrocincta*

Another Amazonian species, similar to *T. cyanicollis.* Sides of body blue, center of abdomen white. Mexico and the Guianas to upper Amazon, Rio Madeira, southern Pará (Serra do Cachimbo, Carajás).

BLACK-HEADED TANAGER, *Tangara cyanoptera whitelyi*

12 cm. Only on Venezuelan border, in Roraima. Head, wings, and tail black, rest of plumage relucent pale greenish yellow.

OPAL-RUMPED TANAGER, *Tangara velia,* Saíra-diamante   PL 41.5

13.8 cm; 19.5 g. Slender-billed, multicolored, like so many other saíras. When seen from below, chestnut belly stands out. Breast light bluish gray (eastern Brazil subspecies, *T. v. cyanomelaena*) or purplish blue (northern Brazil, *T. v. velia*). Canopy. The Guianas and Venezuela to upper and lower Amazon (Rio Tapajós to Belém, Pará, etc.), northeastern and eastern Brazil to Rio de Janeiro, northwestern Argentina to Colombia. Also called *Pintor-estrela.*

OPAL-CROWNED TANAGER, *Tangara callophrys*

Only in upper Amazon. Similar to northern forms of *T. velia,* which it seems to replace. Top of head and long superciliary opalescent, abdomen black. South of Solimões, from the Purus to Javari, and adjacent countries.

WHITE-BELLIED DACNIS, *Dacnis albiventris,* Saí-de-barriga-branca

11.5 cm. Rather dark, shiny, purplish blue with black feather bases, mask, and tail; white belly. Female green above, greenish yellow below. Canopy of tall forest in flocks with other birds, among them *Cyanerpes caeruleus* and Rufous-tailed Xenops, *Xenops milleri.* Upper Amazon south to east of Tapajós (Cururu, Pará).

BLACK-FACED DACNIS, *Dacnis lineata,* Saí-de-máscara-preta

Amazonia. Similar to *D. cayana* but mask continuous with black of back. Underparts light blue (without black on throat); belly and underside of wings white. Eye golden yellow; legs blackish. Female greenish brown above, uniformly brownish gray below, yellow eye. VOICE: *tsree.* Forest edge and in trees in plantations, sometimes with *D. cayana, D. flaviventer, Cyanerpes cyaneus,* and *Tangara chilensis.* The Guianas and Venezuela to Bolivia, northern Mato Grosso (upper Xingu), Pará (Belém). Shiny white belly and black mask are reminiscent of *Tersina viridis.*

YELLOW-BELLIED DACNIS, *Dacnis flaviventer,* Saí-amarelo

11.3 cm. Distinctive Amazonian species, black with yellow V on upperparts (including rump); underparts yellow; throat black; cap greenish; eye red. Female similar to female *D. lineata* but with underparts slightly streaked, eye red. Riverine forests, sometimes in association with *lineata.* Upper Amazon to Rio Negro, northern Mato Grosso (Xingu), Bolivia. See *Hemithraupis flavicollis,* which is stockier.

BLACK-LEGGED DACNIS, *Dacnis nigripes,* Saí-de-pernas-pretas   BR

12 cm; 14 g. Little known, found only in southeast. Smaller and with much shorter tail than *D. cayana.* Male very similar to male *cayana* but has less black on throat, smaller and very thin bill, plumbeous tarsi (not pink, and relatively slender appearing). Female easily recognized by sooty back, cinnamon brown underparts (not green), plumbeous legs. In fruiting and flowering trees, where it sips nectar and catches insects. Appears in flocks in winter at sea level (Magé, Rio de Janeiro, July, L. P. Gonzaga), Minas Gerais (Lagoa Santa), Espírito Santo (mountain region), Rio de Janeiro (Novo Friburgo, Petrópolis, Tinguá), São Paulo, Santa Catarina (Blumenau). Its restricted range is entirely within that of *cayana.* Also called *Saíra.*

BLUE DACNIS, *Dacnis cayana,* Saí-azul, Saíra   PL 40.4

13 cm; 16 g. Common, widely distributed. Short, pointed bill. Male blue and black with light red legs. Female green with bluish head and upper wing coverts, gray throat, orange legs. VOICE: a sharp *tsit,* a soft *tsri;* song a weak warble.

Forest edge at various heights and in canopy of high forest. Depends relatively little on flowers (see "Feeding"). Normally appears in small mixed flocks with *Cyanerpes* and *Tangara*. Central America and greater part of South America south to Bolivia, Paraguay, Argentina, throughout Brazil, including northeast and south, to Rio Grande do Sul. Also called *Saí-bicudo, Bico-fino* (Minas Gerais). See *D. lineata* and *D. nigripes*.

GREEN HONEYCREEPER, *Chlorophanes spiza*, Saí-verde, Tem-tem   PL 40.3

13.5 cm; 18.5 g. Largest species of honeycreeper group except for *Diglossa*. Bill relatively broad with light yellow mandible. Unmistakable with large black mask. Eye red. Female green like a parakeet but recognizable by bill. VOICE: a strident *SPEEeh* but generally silent. Forest canopies and among fruiting and flowering trees (see "Feeding"). Mexico and Central America to northern South America and Amazonia, south as far as Bolivia, Mato Grosso (Xingu), southern Pará (Cururu), Maranhão, locally in eastern Brazil: Pernambuco to Minas Gerais, Rio de Janeiro, Santa Catarina. Generally scarce. See *Cyanerpes cyaneus* and male *Tersina viridis*.

SHORT-BILLED HONEYCREEPER, *Cyanerpes nitidus*, Saí-de-bico-curto

10 cm. Bill quite curved but relatively short. Plumage brilliant blue, with throat and breast black; back blue (opposite of *C. cyaneus*); no yellow on flight feathers. Legs orange. Female similar to female *cyaneus* but with throat, belly, and legs yellowish. Venezuela to upper Amazon, northwestern and northern Mato Grosso (upper Xingu), Goiás.

PURPLE HONEYCREEPER, *Cyanerpes caeruleus*, Saí-de-perna-amarela

9.3 cm. Very like *C. nitidus* but with yellow legs, longer bill (17 mm), black only on throat. Female has rusty lores. The Guianas and Venezuela to Bolivia, Brazilian Amazonia as far as the Guaporé, Tapajós (Pará), Belém, northern Maranhão.

RED-LEGGED HONEYCREEPER, *Cyanerpes cyaneus*, Saí-azul-de-pernas-vermelhas, Saíra-beija-flor   PL 40.1

11.7 cm; 14 g. Best-known *Cyanerpes*, being widely distributed and one of continent's most colorful birds. Cap brilliant bluish green; inner vein of flight feathers yellow, a surprising adornment when wings are opened. After breeding molts to green plumage (see "Morphology"). Legs red. Female and immature greenish, including flight feathers, with pale red legs. Young male requires several months to acquire definitive plumage. VOICE: a weak *st, st, tsee*. In small flocks, both in canopy of large trees and in low woods,

Fig. 302. Greater Flower-piercer, *Diglossa major*, showing distinctive bill shape. Original, H. Sick.

e.g., restinga (Espírito Santo, Rio de Janeiro). Mexico to northern South America and to Bolivia, northern, central (Mato Grosso, Goiás), and eastern Brazil: Maranhão to Rio de Janeiro (Cabo Frio), occasionally in Municipality of Rio de Janeiro. Common in various parts of Amazonia. Also called *Saí-verdadeiro, Sapitica* (Bahia). See *Chlorophanes spiza*.

GREATER FLOWER-PIERCER, *Diglossa major*, Diglossa-grande-do-roraima   Fig. 302

18 cm. Recorded only in Venezuelan border region. Especially straight bill, ending in a hook; long tail; bluish black plumage; chestnut under tail coverts. VOICE: high-pitched and squeaky, slightly reminiscent of *Coereba flaveola*. In spite of being nectarivorous (see "Feeding"), hunts insects on leaves of mountain bushes. Has restless temperament. Observed in Roraima. This genus is rich in Andean species.

SCALED FLOWER-PIERCER, *Diglossa duidae*

Slightly smaller than *D. major*, with gray underparts. Pico da Neblina region.

CHESTNUT-VENTED CONEBILL, *Conirostrum speciosum*, Figuinha-de-rabo-castanho   PL 40.5

10.5 cm; 8.4 g. Very slender with conical bill. Belly and speculum white; under wing coverts chestnut in male only. Female may recall a *Hylophilus* (Vireonidae). VOICE: call a high-pitched *eest, eest* in flight, characteristic of species; *tsi-tsi-see*, repeated while perched; song is rapid, high-pitched whistles. Canopy of dense trees, forest, capoeira, gardens. Frequently a group of individuals will associate with *Dacnis cayana*. Likes mistletoe berries, eats primarily insects and caterpillars. Comes to sugar-water bottles, where it supports itself clinging to outlet. Likes to wander in small, single-species flocks, probably composed of family groups. Before parents and young separate, their movements could involve real migration. The Guianas and Venezuela to Bolivia, Paraguay, Argentina, throughout Brazil as far as Rio Grande do Sul. Also called *Vira-folhas* (ex-Guanabara). Compare female with *C. bicolor*.

BICOLORED CONEBILL, *Conirostrum bicolor*, Figuinha-do-mangue

Replaces *C. speciosum* in mangroves, where easily overlooked. Both sexes similar in appearance to female *speciosum* but entire upperparts bluish gray, face and underside light brownish, legs orange-yellow. Immature somewhat different: greenish above, light yellow below, reminiscent of Yellow Warbler, *Dendroica petechia.* VOICE: call a high-pitched *tsri,* like squeak of a mouse; song a rhythmic twitter, *TSEEdi, TSEEdi-didelide, TSEEdi, LEEdiLEE-zrrr.* Has specialized in occupying immense mangroves and low, flooded forests of Atlantic coast from Venezuela to São Paulo, ascending Amazon and its tributaries, following this type of vegetation to Óbidos and Borba (Rio Madeira), an ecosystem to which few birds are confined. Also called *Sanhaço-do-mangue, Avezinha-do-mangue* (Rio de Janeiro).

PEARLY-BREASTED CONEBILL, *Conirostrum margaritae*

Very similar to *C. bicolor* but paler. Only in Amazonia, in Parintins, Borba, Peru.

There is one species whose relationships are still under discussion. Based on morphology, tanagers appear to be its nearest relatives, and the 1983 AOU Check-list includes it as a member of this subfamily, in the Tribe Tersini. There is a Pleistocene (20,000 years B.P.) fossil from Minas Gerais:

SWALLOW TANAGER, *Tersina viridis,* Saí-andorinha   PL 41.1

14 cm; 30 g. Typically bright colored, appearing blue when seen against light or from below and brilliant green when seen with light; shiny white collar. Female and immature green but show some wavy design on sides and are also immediately recognizable by general aspect. Definitive plumage of adult male (black instead of gray mask, entire plumage shiny) acquired only after 3–4 years. Adult iris in both sexes reddish. VOICE: strident whistle, *tsit, tseh-IT,* attracts attention at long distances; song a weak twitter, reminiscent of sanhaços; only male sings.

Morphology, Behavior, and Feeding: Tersina viridis is unique in several ways. It differs in appearance from sanhaço and saíra tanagers. The head is flat. The bill is quite broad at the base and has a slight hook at the tip. Skull structure, especially the palate, is distinctive. The esophagus is expandable, with internal folds permitting formation of a generous gular sac, highly useful when tearing off flesh of fruits. The wide bill also helps capture insects in flight and in accumulating food adults carry to young. Large wings imply good flying ability. The tarsus is short. There is accentuated sexual dimorphism.

It does not associate with other birds, which it encounters only in fruit feeding areas or when perched in certain trees also used by others as "hangouts." It is not aggressive, unlike sanhaços, for example. Rather even-tempered and arboreal, it perches in an upright position similar to a Bare-throated Bellbird, *Procnias nudicollis,* often for long periods, in which it also differs from sanhaços, etc., which never stay still. This also explains one of its common names, *saíra-araponga.* It prefers bare branches such as those of cecropia. Aspect and behavior are in fact similar to those of cotingas such as Swallow-tailed Cotinga, *Phibalura flavirostris,* something already recognized by early investigators such as Pelzeln (1871), influenced by reports of Johann Natterer who, at beginning of 1800s, had ample opportunity to study the bird in its natural habitat. When *Tersina* pursues insects such as swarming termites and ants and shows its slightly forked tail, it may remind one of a swallow. This is the origin of its most-used common name, *saí-andorinha,* "swallow tanager." In flight, when seeking prey, also resembles Cliff Flycatcher, *Hirundinea ferruginea.* Sometimes catches various insects, one after the other, without swallowing them, such small animals, as well as small fruits, being easily retained in the esophagus. Depending on weather of the day or season, it may be more insectivorous (in summer rains) or more frugivorous (winter). It hops easily along branches to reach a fruit. Unlike *Tangara,* it does not hang upside down. Its method of turning fruits in its spacious, wide-open mouth to scrape off the fleshy pericarp, finally letting the pip fall, is unique. Strange as it may seem, this technique is reminiscent of a snake preparing an overlarge mouthful for swallowing. It also swallows whole fruits and regurgitates larger seeds after approximately 20 minutes, as do manakins, cotingas, thrushes, etc., thereby actively contributing to dispersal of these plants. In southern Brazil certain fruits, e.g., those of magnolia (*Michelia champaca,* Magnoliaceae), are among the most sought because of their thick and nutritive aril, rich in carotenoids. *Tersina* rapidly swallows about 6 of these small fruits one after the other and later expels the pips. Germination tests on *Michelia* seeds have shown that seeds that passed through digestive tracts of birds had a high rate of germination (Motta 1988).

It carries relatively large fruits in its open bill to some distant place to tear off and devour the flesh. Although not very eager for berries, it likes mistletoe fruits, which are also much sought after by euphonias and saíras. It also makes good use of cecropia fruits, the small nuts of *Livistonia* palms, etc. It also eats flower buds, e.g., those of the flamboyant, which it "chews" like a snake in the same way as larger fruits.

Breeding: In southeastern Brazil *T. viridis* nests in mountainous regions, in Tinguá and Novo Friburgo, Rio de Janeiro, in September and October, and Uberlândia, Minas Gerais, in July. In central Brazil (upper Xingu, Mato Grosso) I found it with active reproductive organs in July, August, and October. At the beginning of breeding season I saw some males gather in neighboring branches and silently raise and lower themselves alternately, jumping from one branch to another, sometimes chasing each other. It forms faithful pairs, nesting in holes in cliffs and river banks and in stone buildings in the forest, e.g., walls of ruins; also under bridges and in a grain storage building in Minas Gerais. It can dig its own galleries in earth, explaining the name *saíra-bura-*

queira, "burrowing-saíra." It uses tree holes (Minas Gerais) and holes in other substrates previously used by spinetails, swallows, jacamars, and puffbirds. In the hole it constructs a voluminous saucer. Male always accompanies female but does not work, remaining as a nearby sentinel.

Three or 4 pure white eggs are laid. They are incubated by the female alone for approximately 15 days. Nestlings are fed primarily by the female. When gathering food for young, parents fill the esophagus so full with fruits and insects that the throat protrudes noticeably. Small nestlings also accumulate food in the mouth to swallow later. The interior of the empty mouth is red. Excrement of nestlings is swallowed or carried away by the female. Young abandon nest at 24 days. Males reportedly reach maturity in their 1st year without having acquired full nuptial plumage.

Migration: In ex-Guanabara appears as a migrant (February–August) in varying numbers and not every year. Remains only a few days, like thrushes, reappearing only half a year later. Peak of magnolia fruiting is the big time for *Tersina*. Concentrations of migrant *Tersina* in places where there is an abundance of fruiting magnolias (e.g., Viçosa and Juiz de Fora, Minas Gerais) are among the largest assemblages of fruit-eating birds in Brazil. This has been so only in post-Columbian times, for the magnolia, used for ornamental planting in streets, parks, and gardens, was brought from Asia. Birds arrive in Viçosa in March and disappear in May and early June (Erickson and Mumford 1976). Not discouraged even by intense traffic, *Tersina* invades metropolitan centers such as Belo Horizonte, where there is an abundance of magnolias fruiting June–August.

Treetops at forest edges and in gallery forests. Central America (Panama) and northern South America south to Bolivia, Paraguay, and northeastern Argentina; eastern, south-central, and westcentral Brazil; also southern and eastern Pará (Cachimbo in August, October; Gorotire in July, August, September; Belém) and Maranhão (January); also Santa Catarina, Rio Grande do Sul. Also called *Saíra-araponga*, *Saíra-buraqueira* (Minas Gerais), *Saí-arara*. See Sharpbill, *Oxyruncus cristatus* (with similar horizontal pattern on underparts) and *Chlorophanes spiza*.

Thraupinae Bibliography
See also General Bibliography

Berlioz, J. 1946. *L'Oiseau,* n.s., 16:1–6. [*Conothraupis mesoleuca*]

Borrero, H.J.J. 1972. Explotación de las flores de Guayacan (*Tabebuia chrysantha*) por várias espécies de aves e insectos. *Biotrópica* 4(1):28–31.

Brower, L. P., J.V.Z. Brower, and C. T. Collins. 1963. *Zoologica* (N.Y.) 48:65–83. [Feeding]

Brown, K. S., Jr., and J. Vasconcellos Neto. 1976. *28. Reun. Soc. Bras. Progr. Ciênc.:902. [Pipraeidea,* feeding]

Carvalho, C. T. 1957. *Bol. Mus. Paraen., Zool.* 5. [*Ramphocelus,* behavior]

Carvalho, C. T. 1958. *Bol. Mus. Paraen., Zool.* 20. [*Cyanerpes,* nesting]

Davidse, G., and F. Morton. 1973. *Biotrópica* 5:162–67. [Feeding]

Delacour, J. 1972. *Avicult. Mag.* 78:187–88. [Hybrid between *Cyanerpes cyaneus* and *Tangara nigrocincta*]

Desselberger, H. 1931. *J. Orn.* 79:353–70. [Digestion]

Gomes, V., Ney Carnevalli, and M. B. Ferreira. 1975. *Cerrado* 6(24):9–11. [Feeding]

Gonzaga, L. P. 1983. *Iheringia,* Zool. (63):45–58. [*Dacnis nigripes,* general]

Grantsau, R. 1985. *SOBoletim* 2(7):2. [*Cyanicterus* in Amapá]

Haverschmidt, F. 1956. *Wilson Bull.* 68:322–23. [*Tachyphonus,* behavior]

Ingels, J. 1983. Habitat preference of *Thraupis episcopus* and *T. palmarum* in Surinam. *Le Gerfaut* 73:85–97.

Isler, M. L., and P. R. Isler. 1987. *The Tanagers: Natural History, Distribution, and Identification.* Washington, D.C.: Smithsonian Institution Press.

Leck, C. F. 1971. *The Living Bird* 10:89–106. [Behavior]

Lund, P. W. 1829. *De Genere Euphones.* Kopenhagen.

Moermond, T. C. 1983. Suction-drinking in tanagers, etc. *Ibis* 125:545–49.

Motta, J. C., Jr., 1988. *VII Cong. Soc. Bot. S. Paulo.* [Use of seeds of *Michelia champaca* as bird food]

Norgaard-Olesen, E. 1970. *Tangarer.* Skibby.

Novaes, F. C. 1959. *Bol. Mus. Paraen., Zool.* 22. [*Ramphocelus,* variation]

Parkes, K. P. 1963. *Proc. Biol. Soc. Washington* 76:81–84. [*Hemithraupis,* variation]

Ruschi, A. 1950. *Bol. Mus. Biol. Prof. Melo Leitão,* Bot. 1. [Ecology]

Schäfer, E. 1953. *Auk* 70:403–60. [Monograph]

Sibley, C. G. 1973. *Bull. B.O.C.* 93:75. [Taxonomy]

Sick, H. 1957. *Wilson Bull.* 69(2):187–88. [*Tangara,* anting]

Sick, H. 1960. *Condor* 62:66–67. [*Dacnis albiventris,* 1st record for Brazil)

Sick, H. 1979. *Bull. B.O.C.* 99(4):115–20. [*Nemosia rourei,* live observation]

Silva, W. R. 1988. Ornitocoria en *Cereus* na Serra do Japí, São Paulo. *Rev. Bras. Biol.* 48(2):381–89.

Skutch, A. F. 1954. *Life Histories of Central American Birds,* vol. 1. Pacific Coast Avifauna 31:123–261. Berkeley, Calif.: Cooper Orn. Soc.

Skutch, A. F. 1954. *Life Histories of Central American Birds,* vol.1. Pacific Coast Avifauna 31:387–438. Berkeley, Calif.: Cooper Orn. Soc.

Skutch, A. F. 1962. *Condor* 64:92–116. [*Cyanerpes,* behavior]

Skutch, A. F. 1972. Studies of Tropical American Birds. *Publ. Nuttall Orn. Club* 10:182–208.

Snow, B. K., and D. W. Snow. 1971. *Auk* 88:291–322. [*Euphonia, Thraupis, Ramphocelus, Tachyphonus, Cyanerpes, Chlorophanes, Dacnis,* behavior]

Steinbacher, G. 1935. *Orn. Mber.* 43:41–45. [*Euphonia,* stomach]

Storer, R. W. 1960. *Auk* 77:350–51. [*Conothraupis,* taxonomy]

Storer, R. W. 1969. *The Living Bird* 8:127–36. [Family definition]

Teixeira, D. M. and F.J.M. Pinto. 1988. *XV Cong. Bras. Zool.:* 482. [*Tangara fastuosa,* breeding]

Wetmore, A. 1914. *Auk* 31:458–61. [*Euphonia,* stomach]

Willis, E. O. 1960. *Auk* 77:150–70. [*Habia,* behavior]

Willis, E. O. 1966. *Auk* 83:479–80. [Frugivorous birds]

Willis, E. O. 1976. *Ciência e Cultura* 28(12):1492–93. [Similarity of *Orchesticus abeillei* and *Philydor rufus*]

Winkel, W. 1967. Blumenvögel, Vogelblumen. *Kosmos* 63:265–69.

Winkel, W. 1969. *Z. Tierpsychol.* 26:573–608. [Behavior]

Winkel, W. 1972. *Zool. Gart.,* N.F., 42:143–58. [*Chlorophanes spiza,* ethology, breeding]

Subfamilies Emberizinae and Cardinalinae: Finches, Grosbeaks, and Sparrows (81)

With acceptance of the great Emberizidae family, the name "Fringillidae" for seed-eating birds with heavy, conical bills, long used for this group (Pinto 1944; Meyer de Schauensee 1966, 1970; Hilty and Brown 1986) took on a different meaning. The Emberizidae are of New World origin and are Pan-American, ranging from Greenland to Tierra del Fuego. Fossils from the Pleistocene (100,000 years B.P.) and the Pliocene (10 million years B.P.) have been found in Florida. The Emberizinae are the only American Passerines that have colonized the Old World, and this only to a limited extent.

One must remember that zoogeography, while revealing the history of continental colonization by these birds, at the same time shows something regarding their relationships. The recent discovery that hybridization is possible between the Common Canary, *Serinus canaria* (Carduelinae, Fringillidae), and Chestnut-capped Blackbird, *Agelaius ruficapillus* (Icterinae, Emberizidae), shows a close relationship between the two families.

The Emberizidae, as defined in Peter's *Check-list of Birds of the World,* volume 13 (1970), includes seven subfamilies previously considered to be families: Emberizinae, Cardinalinae, Thraupinae, Tersininae, Coerebinae, Parulinae, and Icterinae. The first two subfamilies, together with the present Fringillidae, correspond to the former grouping of "Fringillidae."

I have prepared a single family text to cover the Emberizinae and Cardinalinae. The assignment of various species to the Emberizinae or Cardinalinae is still a subject in dispute among various experts. An example is the case of the *Paroaria* genus, which some attribute to the Cardinalinae and others to the Emberizinae. *Tiaris* has been shifted from the Cardinalinae to the Emberizinae.

Morphology

The largest members of the group, such as the *Saltator, Pitylus,* and *Embernagra,* are thrush sized. The Green-winged Saltator, *Saltator similis,* weighs 38 to 46 g, whereas others, such as the Marsh Seedeater, *Sporophila palustris,* scarcely reach 10 g. The long tail results in relatively high total length, although the body may be small (e.g., Wedge-tailed Grass-Finch, *Emberizoides herbicola,* and Long-tailed

Reed-Finch, *Donacospiza albifrons*). The wing has nine well-developed remiges, with traces of a tenth.

The bill is one of the most distinctive features (fig. 303). Its form may vary considerably, even within a single genus, such as *Saltator, Paroaria,* and *Sporophila.* There is even considerable variation within a species when heavy billed birds such as the Buffy-fronted Seedeater, *Sporophila frontalis,* and the *Oryzoborus* are concerned. The situation found in Temminck's Seedeater, *Sporophila falcirostris,* and the Slate-colored Seedeater, *S. schistacea,* is extraordinary, for the maxilla is much more slender than the mandible, almost an inversion of the "norm." The bill is frequently brightly colored (e.g., *Paroaria, Arremon, Embernagra, Porphyrospiza,* and *Pitylus*) and changes with age. There are also regional and individual variations, as occur with the Plumbeous Seedeater, *Sporophila plumbea;* Double-collared Seedeater, *S. caerulescens;* and Great-billed Seed-Finch, *Oryzoborus maximiliani.* If the adult male has a yellow bill (e.g., *S. caerulescens*), this paler color in the immature serves for sexual differentiation. (For more on the bill, see "Feeding"). Leg color may also be distinctive (e.g., *Paroaria*). The bright yellow claws of the adult male *Sporophila schistacea* are a curiosity, giving the impression the bird has had a pedicure.

Sexes are different, with the male well colored and the female modest and sober in the *Passerina, Sporophila, Oryzoborus,* and *Amaurospiza. Sporophila* females are notably similar, their identification being easier with live individuals than with museum specimens. There is no sexual dimorphism in the *Saltator,* except for the Thick-billed Saltator, *S. maxillosus.*

Male *Sporophila frontalis* and *S. falcirostris* are slow to develop their typical, showy, definitive plumage, remain-

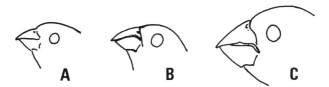

Fig. 303. Bill shape in three closely related species:
(A) Plumbeous Seedeater, *Sporophila plumbea;*
(B) Temminck's Seedeater, *S. falcirostris;* and (C) Great-billed Seed-Finch, *Oryzoborus maximiliani.*

ing "immature" for several years or, apparently in certain cases, for their entire lives. Interestingly, a race of the Capped Seedeater, *S. bouvreuil crypta,* can be called "hen-plumaged," for the males of this group never acquire the colored plumage of their sex like other geographic races of this species.

Females of the *Porphyrospiza, Volatinia, Haplospiza,* and Saffron Finch, *Sicalis flaveola,* are streaked below. The *S. flaveola* female may occasionally have the splendid plumage of the male. Sexes are similar in *Pitylus, Caryothraustes, Paroaria, Gubernatrix, Arremon, Ammodramus, Zonotrichia, Emberizoides, Poospiza,* and *Embernagra.*

In the lingo of commercial cage-bird hunters, young males that are similar to females are designated *pardos,* "browns," in the *Passerina, Sporophila, Oryzoborus,* and *Sicalis* (in the *Sicalis* they are not even brown). When they begin to acquire adult plumage (*virando,* "turning") and show a mixture of colors corresponding to the subadult stage, they are called *pintão,* "big chick," or *maracajá,* "ocelot." The *Sporophila* that begin to show the collar, such as *S. caerulescens,* are called *golão,* "big collar"; once the molt is over they are *virados,* "turned."

Immature *Saltator, Ammodramus, Zonotrichia, Emberizoides,* and *Embernagra* usually have streaked or spotted underparts. Immature Red-rumped Warbling-Finches, *Poospiza lateralis,* and the *Paroaria* show other differences. These juvenal plumages protect immatures from aggression by adults with established territories. However, individuals that are not entirely "turned," big chicks that is, breed, as in the *Sporophila* and *Sicalis.*

It is said that young *Oryzoborus maximiliani* must molt three times to acquire definitive adult plumage. These molts occur (1) at 3 months of age, with the individual continuing to be entirely brown; (2) at 7 or 8 months, with mixed plumage; and (3) at more or less 12 months, when it obtains the black adult plumage. After this it molts normally, once a year, beginning each February (Ignácio L. Campos). Some Lesser Seed-Finches, *O. angolensis,* acquire their definitive plumage at the second molt.

In certain *Sporophila* and in the Blue-black Grassquit, *Volatinia jacarina,* a nonbreeding winter, or eclipse, plumage occurs in which adult males appear similar to females and juvenals (see also Thraupinae, "Morphology," *Cyanerpes*). This pattern is frequently incomplete, however. This phenomenon is found only in the most southerly regions of Brazil, as is evident in *S. bouvreuil,* a widely distributed species in which only the southern population, *S. b. pileata,* assumes nonbreeding plumage; the northern population, *S. b. bouvreuil,* molts at the same time to plumage identical to its previous one. Note that the southern form simultaneously undergoes a change in bill color. For southern species such as the Dark-throated Seedeater, *S. ruficollis,* and Black-bellied

Seedeater, *S. melanogaster,* eclipse plumage appears to be the rule.

Eclipse plumage is acquired through a complete postnuptial molt, with not only the body feathers but the remiges and rectrices changing (as is generally the case with Passerine, molt, which occurs in Brazil beginning in February). Restoration of breeding plumage (which occurs in August–September in Rio de Janeiro) is a partial molt involving only the body feathers. Thus, *Volatinia jacarina,* for example, reacquires its all-black plumage by this process and not by abrasion of the brown tips of the black feathers, as happens with the Red-breasted Blackbird, *Sturnella militaris* (Icterinae).

Various "natural color mutants" are known, referring to color not acquired in captivity. Cinnamon mutants have been found in *Zonotrichia* (relatively frequently); the White-throated Seedeater, *Sporophila albogularis; S. plumbea* (females); *S. caerulescens* (males); *Coryphospingus* (males and females); and the Ultramarine Grosbeak, *Passerina brissonii* (females). Lutescent individuals have been found in *Sicalis flaveola* males. I have even seen a melanistic *Oryzoborus angolensis* from Goiás that was similar to the western (Ecuador to Mexico) race of the species, *O. a. funereus,* except that it lacked the white speculum of *funereus.* All-black Red-crested Cardinal, *Paroaria coronata,* individuals have been found in the market of Cuiabá, Mato Grosso. Flecha (1987) cites six *O. angolensis* mutants he has recorded and others of *Sicalis* and *Sporophila* (1985).

Wild albino individuals have been found among the Lined Seedeater, *Sporophila lineola;* Rusty-collared Seedeater, *S. collaris; S. schistacea* (males); and Rufous-collared Sparrow, *Zonotrichia capensis.* Variations of this sort appear more frequently among captive specimens (see *Sicalis flaveola*).

Hermaphrodites and gynandromorphs occur among the Emberizinae and Cardinalinae that can be carefully studied in cage birds. They show the division of the sexual characteristics more or less exactly on the median line of the body: one side, generally the right, is masculine and the other feminine, reflecting the fact that in birds only the left ovary is developed. I have seen two *Sporophila caerulescens* individuals of this type. One case of *Sicalis flaveola* has been cited (Oliveira 1984a). Inverted gynandromorphs, with the left side masculine and the right feminine, are even rarer, but I have seen a captive *Oryzoborus maximiliani* of this type.

Vocalization

Because of their exceptional singing abilities, the Emberizinae and Cardinalinae are the most discussed and best-known birds of Brazil. The song types of the various species are extremely varied. Here I can only draw attention to certain distinctive aspects that help in specific identification.

Whereas seed-finches, cardinals, saltators, and *Passerina brissonii* produce loud songs that are first-rate by our musical standards, *Sporophila frontalis* produces only a raucous chatter. It is believed that notable singing ability might indicate low population density; in fact *S. frontalis* periodically becomes extremely numerous (see "Feeding").

Soothing songs characterize most of the *Sporophila*, varying from a simple tune of *S. caerulescens* to the complex, flowing, and variable phrases of *S. plumbea, S. collaris,* and others. When a male *Oryzoborus angolensis* confronts another male of its species he shifts from the normal territorial song to a different "fighting song" to demonstrate his aggressive qualities.

Some seedeaters, such as *Sporophila collaris, S. albogularis,* and *S. bouvreuil,* may be good imitators of the voices of other birds of their own natural habitat, although they mix everything together, singing one song after another consecutively without separating them. Small Emberizinae such as the Yellow-browed Sparrow, *Ammodramus aurifrons,* are among the Passerines with the highest voices, rivaling certain wood-warblers in this respect. Some songs are arranged like a question and answer to form a complete harmony (Buff-throated Saltator, *Saltator maximus,* and *Emberizoides herbicola*).

Birds of these two subfamilies usually sing from the tip of a branch or the top of a grass stem (e.g., *Saltator, Passerina brissonii, Sporophila, Oryzoborus, Embernagra*), sometimes closing their eyes as they sing (*Sporophila*). Some open-country species sing in flight: *Volatinia jacarina* makes a short vertical flight, returning to its takeoff point; the Grassland and Stripe-tailed Yellow-Finches, *Sicalis luteola* and *S. citrina,* sing during a long, high flight from which they descend at a distance, like the *Anthus* (Motacillidae); and the Black-throated Saltator, *Saltator atricollis,* often sings during a horizontal flight between two separate treetops in midsavanna.

Saltator similis, a forest species, also occasionally sings while flying from one tree to another. An exceptional case is that of the Uniform Finch, *Haplospiza unicolor,* which vocalizes in dense forest while flying from one branch to another, probably a heritage of savanna ancestors. It is normal for certain marsh species to sing while flying, for instance *Sporophila bouvreuil, Donacospiza albifrons,* and the Lesser Grass-Finch, *Emberizoides ypiranganus.* With these, especially the last-named, it should be noted that their songs resemble those of other marsh birds, even those of other families and other continents, such as, for example, the Old World warblers (*Acrocephalus* spp., Muscicapidae). This "habitat voice" phenomenon is also noticeable in other biotopes.

Few emberizines or cardinalines sing at dawn in the wild, but I have noted this behavior with the Golden-billed Saltator, *Saltator aurantiirostris; Passerina brissonii; Sporophila frontalis;* Coal-crested Finch, *Charitospiza eucosma;* and Red and Gray Pileated-Finches, *Coryphospingus cucullatus* and *C. pileatus.* Surprisingly, the Pale-bellied Mourner, *Rhytipterna immunda,* a tyrannid, has a dawn song which, to judge by the timbre, could be that of an emberizine. Dawn songs are generally more common among less gifted singers such as the tyrannids.

Group songs occurs among male *Volatinia* and *Sicalis. Saltator atricollis* is unrivaled in making a group din that recalls thraupines such as *Ramphocelus.*

Zonotrichia capensis has a night song much different from its daytime vocalization and unrelated to the dawn songs of other birds. Extremely frightened individuals also use it during the day. I know of no parallel situation with any other bird in the world.

In the nonbreeding season *Z. capensis, Passerina brissonii,* and the *Paroaria* sing an incomplete song as whisper song, corresponding to autumnal vocalizations of Northern Hemisphere birds. Mixed flocks of savanna and marsh species, such as various *Sporophila,* produce a quieter song distinguishable from the loud, simple territorial song.

In various cases, such as with *Passerina* and *Oryzoborus,* both sexes sing well. Sometimes the female *Oryzoborus maximiliani* sings better than the male. An incubating female may sing in reply to the male vocalizing nearby (*Arremon*). The *Paroaria* duet. In the *Saltator* there are differences between the songs of each sex, and a pair may synchronize, as do Grayish Saltators, *Saltator coerulescens.* There is plenty of individual and geographic variation (dialects) in song among the *Saltator, Passerina, Oryzoborus, Sporophila, Zonotrichia,* and in *Emberizoides herbicola,* a fact well known to commercial cage-bird fanciers, who even apply their own onomatopoeic nomenclature or refer to the origins of the bird (see *Sporophila caerulescens, Oryzoborus maximiliani, O. angolensis*). Individuals react better to a voice (or playback) that corresponds to their own dialect. Sometimes an individual may not recognize the dialect of another population as the voice of its own species, according to tests of the Black-throated Grosbeak, *Pitylus fuliginosus,* in various places in São Paulo, using playback (J. C. Magalhães pers. comm.) Song is not entirely hereditary. Cage birds, especially those so reared from youth, learn songs of other species that may be available when they do not have a "teacher" of their own species. Thus a *Sporophila caerulescens* may sing, with great perfection, only like the *S. lineola* with which it was reared. Apparently there is no Brazilian emberizine or cardinaline that can learn to imitate human melodies like the Eurasian Bullfinch, *Pyrrhula pyrrhula,* of Europe. The young *Oryzoborus maximiliani* reportedly develops its song by beginning to twitter at 20 days. At five months it begins to sing a little, and from seven months on the song becomes loud and complete, turning pure and crystalline like the notes of a flute after one year (information from various breeders). The young male *Zonotrichia capensis* adopts the song of the adult at five to six months, when it reaches breeding age. In very old males, as with an *O. maximiliani* that was captive for 18 years, the song becomes higher. In their natural habitat these groups sing well only during the breeding period, afterwards either stopping or singing listlessly and without taking an interest in other individuals of their own species. During migration and foraging, when *Sporophila* and *Volatinia* gather in flocks, there is collective singing. In captivity they sing all year except during molt. The enthusiasm of cage-bird fanciers for the singing of *Oryzoborus maximiliani* and *O. angolensis* is so great that they organize competitions (see *O. angolensis*) as used to be done in Europe with the common Chaffinch, *Fringilla coelebs*. A cage bird treated with affection will concentrate all its activity on singing.

Feeding

Most emberizids are predominantly granivorous, a specialization considered to be a recent evolutionary development. At the same time there is reduced sensitivity to bitterness (by human taste standards), an adaptation advantageous in permitting consumption of seeds that are frequently extremely bitter (Rensch 1925, Berkhoudt 1985). It is evident that Emberizinae and Cardinalinae are more often predators (destroyers) of seeds and not dispersers, unlike Thraupinae.

The functional morphology of the bill reveals existence of two basic techniques employed in seed eating: crushing or splitting. The crushing process (fig. 304) practiced by Emberizinae such as *Sporophila*, *Coryphospingus*, *Paroaria*, and many others is like the action of a vise, being carried out by a simple vertical movement of the mandible toward the palatine, which is fixed and acts as a grater. Grass seeds, frequently the principal food, are picked while still green and squeezed out of their hulls, which fall away (Ziswiler 1965). On the splitting process, see Fringillidae, "Feeding."

The great variety of conical bills found in this group demonstrates multiple adaptations to the most varied trophic con-

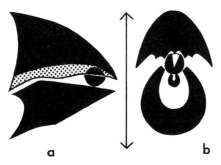

Fig. 304. Bill movements in the process of opening a round seed, in an Emberizinae seedeater, *Sporophila* sp.: (a) side view, tomia stippled; (b) front view, the arrow indicating the direction of movement of the mandible. After Ziswiler 1965.

ditions, such as hardness and size of the seeds or consistency of the shoots and fruits that are eaten. One must not forget that occasionally and temporarily these birds become insectivorous. Some seed eaters are synanthropic, being attracted by the planting or semispontaneous dispersion of grasses, such as, for instance, introduced *Panicum* species (see also "Habitat . . .").

Among the favorite seeds of *Oryzoborus angolensis* are those of the tiritica (*Cyperus rotundus*) and navalha-de-macaco (*Hypolytrum schraderianum*). For other types of seeds consumed, see *Sporophila melanogaster*.

An extraordinary phenomenon in the mountainous regions of southeastern Brazil is the appearance of thousands of *Sporophila frontalis* during the fruiting of bamboo (*Merostachys* sp.), which provides them abundant food ("bamboo rice"), sometimes accumulating in layers several centimeters deep. Because this happens only at long intervals (periods of 8–16 years have been recorded, with an average of 12 and even 20, 30, and 34 years), a single individual would not have more than one chance in the same place during its lifetime to profit from such an unusual food source. They must come mostly from a distance, perhaps sometimes many kilometers. The concentration reaches such levels that the chatter uttered by the host of males participating in the festival creates a unique roar that echoes strangely in the mountain forests. I have seen *Haplospiza unicolor* and the Sooty Grassquit, *Tiaris fuliginosa*, also participate in these gatherings (Itatiaia, Rio de Janeiro 1952). Other species, such as *Sporophila falcirostris*, *S. schistacea*, the Blackish-blue Seedeater, *Amaurospiza moesta*, and Purple-winged Ground-Dove, *Claravis godefrida*, have also been reported.

Two categories of bird participate in these gatherings: (1) resident species, considerably increased in numbers by the participation of outsiders, and (2) species that have come from elsewhere and that disappear completely when the bamboo rice is gone.

Usually bamboo flowering occurs around the end of the year (Pereira 1941), as I saw in November 1981 in Rio de Janeiro, with the seeds appearing in the early months of the following year. However, in 1952 the fruiting occurred in July. It has been conjectured that this cycle corresponds with sun-spot cycles. Apparently bamboo flowering occurs in very dry years and may be a defensive strategy of the plant before dying, leaving an abundance of seeds. A similar thing happens with bamboos of Africa (Zambia), where the fruiting attracts Estrildidae species whose distribution is erratic both in space and time (Jackson 1972). A frightening upsurge of rodents occurs at the same time, the "rice rats" (various species, among them *Oryzomys* and the house rat, *Rattus rattus*), which later invade planted crops and finally succumb in mass mortality. The "bamboo rats" (*Kannabateomys amblyonyx*) do not participate, for they are not granivorous (see Picidae, "Feeding").

Various species, such as *Saltator coerulescens* and the

Yellow-billed Cardinal, *Paroaria capitata,* eat cecropia fruits and those of the bananeirinhas-do-mato (*Heliconia* sp.). *Poospiza lateralis* likes the aril of pinherinho fruits (*Podocarpus* sp.). Saltators are among the numerous consumers of fruits of the *Livistonia* palm (see Thraupinae "Feeding"). The *Caryothraustes* and *Saltator* eat shoots. *S. similis* eats canema (*Solanum* sp.) leaves. Two forest species, the Pectoral Sparrow, *Arremon taciturnus,* and *Passerina cyanoides* of Amazonia, are essentially frugivorous. I have seen *S. similis* and *Zonotrichia capensis* sip the sweet fluid excreted by aphids (see Trochilidae, "Feeding . . .").

A mixed diet is common. I have seen *Sporophila caerulescens* take insects caught in spider webs, going from one web to another and even making short hovering flights. I have also seen *S. schistacea* chase small insects on the wing. In feeding the young, arthropods have a large place, even for species such as *Oryzoborus angolensis* which is highly granivorous. *Zonotrichia capensis* nourishes its young exclusively with food of this type.

Behavior

Seeds are taken directly from the stalk or on the ground. To eat more comfortably the *Sporophila* bend a grass stem to the ground after seizing it in full flight. They take the seeds by pushing the panicle under the toes to hold it while they take out the edible part. Many arboreal Neotropical species descend to the ground to feed, moving around by hopping. Some, such as *Zonotrichia capensis* and the Black-striped Sparrow, *Arremonops conirostris,* have a unique means of removing a covering layer of leaves or loose earth that may be on top of food such as seeds or arthropods: while scrutinizing the ground in front of them they hop vertically twice (*Zonotrichia* as many as four times) without altering the position of their legs, scratching the ground with both feet together and tossing behind them the overlying material. With *Z. capensis* the tendency to do this is so strong that even when it is eating something on a cement surface or in a yard, it hops the same way. This behavior, linked to relatively large feet and to a distinctive scale covering at the base of the outer two toes, is typical of various Emberizinae that move on the ground by hopping. The *Atlapetes* brush-finches, with the same foot structure (one instead of two basal scales), toss detritus to the side with a rapid bill movement, like thrushes. *Z. capensis* sometimes pulls vigorously at fallen leaves with its bill.

The most terrestrial, such as those in the genera *Paroaria, Ammodramus, Gubernatrix, Porphyrospiza, Sicalis, Emberizoides,* and *Embernagra,* walk on the ground and even run a bit. *Ammodramus* show a tendency to squat and not to fly if being chased. *Sicalis citrina* may be mistaken in the field for a pipit, *Anthus* sp. These species also have a rapid walk or hop. *Emberizoides herbicola* shows remarkable ability in moving through reeds and tall grasses, sometimes supporting itself on two separate stems or branches like marsh species such as rails and herons (a technique linked to long toes).

It is amazing to see the *Paroaria* flocks that gather at the edge of riverbed wells in the caatinga of the northeast or at natural waterholes and river edges in the Mato Grosso Pantanal to drink and bathe. In extremely dry regions, such as the cerrado, dew is a source of water for bathing for *Coryphospingus*. *Sicalis luteola* takes sand baths. *Sporophila* and *Sicalis* enjoy rubbing the sides of their heads above their eyes, which are kept closed. I have seen anting occur with *Zonotrichia capensis* and *Saltator similis*. The ant used by *Z. capensis* was *Camponotus blandus* (Galileu Coelho, Pernambuco 1975). A few Cardinalinae, such as the *Saltator, Caryothraustes,* and *Pitylus,* follow noisy, mixed flocks in the forest. *Sporophila* sleep in patches of high grass, reeds, and cane fields, the stems on which they roost bending down as they crowd together on them.

In captivity *Volatinia* and *Sporophila* learn to pull up a water receptacle tied under a perch. This trick has been used since the Middle Ages in Europe with the European Goldfinch, *Carduelis carduelis*. The motions required to gather in the string holding the receptacle are the same as the bird makes to pull a spike of grass through its foot.

Breeding

During the breeding season emberizines and cardinalines stay strictly in pairs and are extremely attached to their territory, which the male defends energetically against the approach of other males of his species. This makes them easy victims of bird catchers who use traps with a decoy. A *Zonotrichia capensis* will vigorously attack its own reflection in the hubcap of an automobile parked in its territory. This passionate reaction can also be observed when the cages of two male *Oryzoborus angolensis* are placed close to each other. Each becomes aroused and utters a shrill, penetrating song (called *serra,* "saw") to frighten and repel its adversary. In this same kind of agonistic behavior, the *Sporophila* stretch themselves vertically to show their full height and characteristic pattern of foreneck and belly, demonstrating the selective effect of this coloration. Contrariwise, when the *Sicalis* and *Zonotrichia* are going to fight, they lower themselves, open their wings, and lean forward with the bill half open.

In fights and in front of females, black or dark blue species such as *Oryzoborus, Amaurospiza, Volatinia,* and *Pitylus* open their wings to expose the white underside, ruffling the feathers like a *Tachyphonus* (Thraupinae). In doing this an *O. maximiliani* is almost hidden behind his raised wing, which is turned toward the female. In addition he vibrates his wings and moves his long tail upward and to the sides, stopping this movement with the tail in whatever position. Lateral tail movements are also typical in *Volatinia jacarina,*

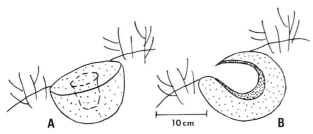

Fig. 305. Nest of the Pectoral Sparrow, *Arremon t. taciturnus*. Sketch of two phases of construction: (A) funnel, built of dry leaves, placed upright; between them an open cavity 6 × 6 cm, forerunner of the incubation chamber; (B) the finished nest nine days later, fitting perfectly into the natural layer of fallen leaves that cover the forest floor. The axis of the cavity (incubation chamber) turned about 30° and was carpeted with vines and roots, forming a solid construction in the natural carpet of fallen leaves. Limoeiro, Espírito Santo, December 1940. Original, H. Sick.

Emberizoides herbicola, and certain *Sporophila.* The *Paroaria* and *Saltator* use other types of tail movement.

Analysis of the nature of these movements is used in phylogenetic research. Three principal aspects are of importance: the amount of vertical movement, if the tail is open and how much, and lateral movements.

The male *Saltator similis* brings food for the female. The male *Sicalis luteola* regurgitates food for his mate.

The nest is an open cup, sparsely woven in some species (e.g., *Sporophila*) and thick in others (e.g., *Zonotrichia*), frequently built low or even on the ground under the grass, as with *Sicalis luteola.* Sometimes pairs of this finch locate their nests close to one another.

Tiaris fuliginosa builds a spherical nest with a side entrance among the foliage. It is said sometimes to construct a false "second entrance" that is obstructed but more visible than the first one, apparently an adaptation against predators (see Common Waxbill, *Estrilda astrild*).

Arremon taciturnus builds a large, spherical nest on the forest floor (fig. 305). *Sicalis flaveola* makes a small, neat basket in cavities, often in those of other birds, especially the Rufous Hornero, *Furnarius rufus.* Apparently *S. citrina* occupies holes in embankments, filling them with nesting material (Minas Gerais). Those species that nest on the ground, such as the *Ammodramus* and *Arremon,* customarily try to attract the attention of possible predators in an attempt to lure them away from the vicinity of the nest.

There is much variation in egg color. *Zonotrichia capensis* eggs, for instance, have a greenish background with a crown of reddish speckles on the more rounded end. I have recorded noticeable differences in form, color, and pattern in the same clutch both in this and other species. *Saltator similis* eggs are shiny with a blue-green background and a narrow crown of black streaks and dots. Although laid in enclosed nests, *Arremon* and *Sicalis* eggs are also spotted. The reverse is the case with the Grassland Sparrow, *Ammodramus humeralis,*

and *Coryphospingus cucullatus,* which although they build open nests, have uniformly bluish eggs. In *Volatinia jacarina* the incubation period and time the nestlings remain in the nest is very short, 10 and 9 days respectively (Stahl 1984). The incubation period is 12 to 13 days for *Zonotrichia capensis* (Rio de Janeiro) and 14 days for *Oryzoborus maximiliani* (Minas Gerais). It is said that more males than females are hatched of this latter species. Parents alternate in caring for the nestlings. Most, such as *Z. capensis,* bring a few arthropods crushed into a ball in the bill, or when the nestlings are larger, larger whole insects held between the mandibles. Some species, such as the *Sporophila,* do not carry nestling food in the bill but swallow and partially digest it in the crop for subsequent regurgitation and administration as a mush. It has been reported that all nestlings in these subfamilies have red mouths. Young *Z. capensis* abandon the nest 9 to 12 days after hatching, those of *Oryzoborus maximiliani* beginning on day 15. They are still fed by the parents for some days, both species becoming independent only at 20 to 30 days of age. Young *Z. capensis* establish their own territories between 5 and 11 months. A young female *O. maximiliani* can already breed at 9 to 10 months and the male a bit later.

O. maximiliani lays two to three consecutive clutches per year (Minas Gerais). The female reportedly starts a new clutch 30 or 40 days after the previous hatching, depending on the availability of rains to guarantee abundant food. In equatorial regions *Volatinia jacarina* appears to breed at any season. Each individual, however, has its own cycle, limited to three clutches per year. Eight successive clutches have been recorded in captivity.

Unlike most Passerines, birds of these subfamilies are not always careful of nest hygiene, especially after the young reach a certain age. I found a recently abandoned *Haplospiza unicolor* nest with the edges covered by nestling feces; the same has been observed with *Z. capensis.*

Various emberizines and cardinalines are victimized by the Shiny Cowbird, *Molothrus bonariensis.* Eggs of this parasite have been found in the nests of 12 species of these subfamilies (see *M. bonariensis*). However, *Z. capensis* is the only one that regularly rears *M. bonariensis,* with the result that it suffers heavy losses of its own chicks. This pressure is so great that in certain areas *Z. capensis* is practically eliminated by the icterine and not by the House Sparrow, *Passer domesticus,* as popularly believed.

Habitat and Numbers

Most emberizines and cardinalines live in open or semi-open landscapes, cultivated fields, secondary forest, forest or river edges, cerrado, caatinga, or marshes. Certain species, such as *Ammodramus, Emberizoides,* and *Coryphaspiza,* living in sharp-edged grasses suffer heavy abrasion to their plumage, especially on the tail and mantle, as do other terrestrial Passerines such as the Icterinae. To ameliorate the problem these birds usually carry the tail horizontally, thus reducing wear from vegetation rubbing the dorsal side as they walk on the ground. Regular contact with the earth may produce, as in *Ammodramus,* impregnation of the plumage with the color of the local soil, especially where this is red.

Various granivorous species become synanthropic. Since 1963 the numbers of *Sporophila caerulescens* and Yellow-bellied Seedeaters, *S. nigricollis,* have increased in the vicinity of Brasília as a result of the introduction of grasses producing abundant seeds, such as capim-colonião or murumbu (*Panicum maximum*), not previously found there. There has been a reduction, however, in species such as *Charitospiza eucosma* and *Sporophila plumbea* that depend more on seeds of native cerrado plants that are eliminated by human activity. I have observed that, because of this same problem in relation to riverine meadows and marshes of the region, *S. bouvreuil* and *Oryzoborus maximiliani* have become rarer or have even totally disappeared, although in these cases one must also remember that they are species much sought in the cage-bird trade. As a consequence of the introduction of forage grasses in the Corumbá (Mato Grosso) region *O. angolensis* immigrated there about 1962 and *O. maximiliani* more recently. See also "Feeding" (bamboo periodicity) and "Use . . . ."

Few emberizines or cardinalines have invaded forest biotopes; doubtless the most notable instance is that of the *Arremon* genus, semiterrestrial birds whose aspect is in no way that of a forest bird, suggesting that their adaptation to this environment is a relatively recent event. *Sporophila falcirostris* and its northern replacement, *S. schistacea,* also conquered the forest, nesting in its medium and upper levels (unlike *Arremon*). From there they fly high to riverine meadows and marshes. *S. schistacea* even overflies cities.

In capoeira of the lower Amazon (e.g., the Rio Guamá), *Saltator maximus* and *Arremon taciturnus* become abundant, being greatly outnumbered, however, by the Silver-beaked Tanager, *Ramphocelus carbo,* and Red-headed and White-bearded Manakins, *Pipra rubrocapilla* and *Manacus manacus.*

Distribution and Evolution

The ranges of Brazilian emberizines and cardinalines show the most varied patterns, evidence of large and repeated climatic changes. Since they are largely nonforest birds, the development of Amazonia created a great barrier, fragmenting the distribution of certain species so they now exist in widely disjunct areas to the north and south of Amazonia. This happened, for example, with *Sporophila plumbea* and *S. bouvreuil* and with the Hooded and Yellow-faced Siskins, *Carduelis magellanica* and *C. varrellii* (the latter two now Carduelinae), each under specific conditions. In each case, however, there is very little difference in external characteristics between northern and southern populations. This leads to the conclusion that these separations were relatively recent.

The situation of the *Coryphospingus* genus is more complex. A gray population, *C. pileatus,* and a red one, *C. cucullatus,* have evolved. Both are found in certain areas south of the Amazon where they interbreed, behaving like geographic races (see also Thraupinae, "Distribution . . . ," *Ramphocelus*), but I have never managed to find them in the same locale. Both reappear in northern Amazonia in disjunct populations.

Marked geographic speciation also has occurred in the *Paroaria,* there being two principal groups whose respective members, allospecies making up a superspecies, are geographically separated. In the first group are the Red-cowled Cardinal, *Paroaria dominicana,* of northeastern Brazil and *P. coronata,* its southern replacement. In the second group are the Red-capped cardinal, *P. gularis,* of Amazonia; Crimson-fronted Cardinal, *P. baeri,* of central Brazil; and *P. capitata,* a southern species. The ranges of *P. coronata* and *P. capitata,* each representing one of the groupings, overlap in the region of the Mato Grosso Pantanal.

Other open-country elements, such as the Blue Finch, *Porphyrospiza caerulescens,* and *Charitospiza eucosma,* are restricted to the cerrado and caatinga regions of central and northeastern Brazil. We find the Black-masked Finch, *Coryphaspiza melanotis,* a campo limpo species of central Brazil, in the Amazonian estuary, suggesting that the campos of Marajó Island are of ancient origin, not recent and anthropogenic. These areas having been flooded various times, settlement by the present open-country fauna was enabled 4000 to 5000 years ago. Because this terrestrial bird is difficult to find, it is probable that other populations may be encountered in previously contiguous but now separated campo regions.

Arremon, a forest genus, also demonstrates the phenomenon of geographic replacement. *A. taciturnus,* widely distributed in Amazonia and eastern Brazil, is replaced in the south by the Saffron-billed Sparrow, *A. flavirostris.* Both are found in central Brazil.

Southern Andean elements, such as the *Poospiza* that penetrated southern Brazil, have advanced north into the mountainous regions of Minas Gerais and Espírito Santo. There *Donacospiza albifrons,* related to the *Poospiza,* occupies high-altitude open country. *Saltator maximus* is an example of forest endemism in southeastern Brazil. It replaces *S. aurantiirostris,* which in turn reaches the Andes.

Very distinctively colored geographic races have evolved in *Sporophila collaris.* The same process, but with distinctions of size, can be observed in the subspecies of *Oryzoborus angolensis.* The two forms of seed-finch, however, constitute two species.

I have already called attention to *Sporophila bouvreuil,* in which a local, hen-feathered race exists. There are parallels in the avifauna of the oceanic islands of the Caribbean and in the Old World. Various endemisms exist among Brazilian emberizines, the most notable being the Pale-throated Serra-Finch, *Embernagra longicauda,* whose distribution is very similar to that of the *Augastes* hummingbirds. The *Sporophila* genus is a good ecological analogue of the large *Lonchura* genus (Lonchurinae, Estrildidae) of the Paleotropic regions (Fry 1983).

Migration

After breeding, many species migrate to a varying extent, a subject on which very little is known. Usually it is only noted that a species (e.g., *Sporophila lineola*) appears to nest in a given region and then disappears, destination unknown. We should band individuals of certain populations and conduct systematic observations throughout the year. It appears certain that in Brazil the motivator of migration is food, not climate. For example, *Sporophila caerulescens, S. melanogaster,* and the Tawny-bellied Seedeater, *S. hypoxantha,* leave the high plateau of Santa Catarina before the onset of cold weather (which becomes intense in that region) in search of seed-bearing grasses and sedges. Large migrant flocks of *S. hypoxantha* appear in November–December in the Mato Grosso Pantanal. The extent of these migrations is well exemplified by the fact that in the second half of September I have found many hundreds of migrant *Sporophila* in seed-loaded grasses (canevão, *Echinochloa crus-pavonis*) on an island in the upper Rio São Francisco, Minas Gerais. I noted 11 *Sporophila* species from a diverse range of geographic areas. There were southern species such as *S. hypoxantha, S. melanogaster, S. ruficollis,* and the Marsh Seedeater, *S. palustris,* alongside *S. b. bouvreuil* (the northern race of the species), *S. c. collaris* (from eastcentral Brazil), *S. caerulescens,* and *S. nigricollis.* Also present were the Chestnut Seedeater, *S. cinnamomea; S. albogularis;* and Chestnut-bellied Seedeater, *S. castaneiventris,* the last from Amazonia.

Another interesting case is that of *Sicalis luteola* in southern Brazil, where it arrives in flocks of thousands, becoming from May to July one of the most abundant birds of Rio Grande do Sul. Such bands (which associate with *S. flaveola* and *Volatinia jacarina*) probably come from adjacent countries to the south. *S. citrina* is also migratory.

I have recorded vertical migration of species such as *S. nigricollis* and *S. caerulescens* in mountainous regions of Espírito Santo. In Itatiaia, Rio de Janeiro, high-country species such as *Saltator maxillosus* and the Diademed Tanager, *Stephanophorus diadematus,* move to low altitudes (E. Gouvêa; see also Trochilidae, "Return to Territory . . . ," and Tyrannidae, "Migration"). Concentrations of *Sporophila frontalis* in bamboo groves, which also is in effect a migration, are discussed under "Feeding."

Only one species, the Dickcissel, *Spiza americana,* reaches Brazil as a northern migrant, coming from North America and reaching extreme northern Brazil. This species usually migrates at night, being detected by its voice, as is the Bobolink, *Dolichonyx oryzivorus* (Icterinae), another northern migrant.

Parasites

These birds are among the few Passerines occasionally known to be parasitized by hippoboscid louse flies. *Pitylus fuliginosus* is a host to *Olfersia fusca.*

Hybridization

A variety of hybridizations occur naturally in wild birds, especially in the genera *Oryzoborus* and *Sporophila.* Admittedly this has always been on a limited scale and not always recognized for what it was. Such is the case with the so-called *Oryzoborus specularis,* a hybrid from São Paulo that was described as a species in 1870.

Recently human intercession has been a principal factor in bringing about the current phenomenon, which occurs through (1) alteration or destruction of the original landscape, making possible contact between birds that previously lived apart; or through (2) reduction in the number of individuals, especially males, as a result of their being caught by people, leaving females without males of their own species with which to mate. I learned of one case in which a male *Sporophila caerulescens* was mated with three nesting females of his own species at the same time, thereby relieving them of the need to seek mates of other species (Petrópolis, Rio de Janeiro, Hugo Souza Lopes pers. comm.).

Hybrids acquired through commercial channels usually have no sure indication of origin, although we know they come from a variety of states such as Minas Gerais, São Paulo, Santa Catarina, and southern Mato Grosso. Behavior (movements of wings and tail, etc.) and vocalization contributed to identification. The song may be mixed or pure, in the latter case from either parental species, and sometimes cannot be used as an indication of ancestry. Furthermore, captive individuals easily learn the voices of other species, which increases the confusion even more.

Among wild Emberizinae of hybrid parentage that I recorded between 1959 (Sick 1963) and 1976 are the following belonging to the two genera mentioned above:

1. *Oryzoborus angolensis* × *Oryzoborus maximiliani*[1]
2. *Oryzoborus angolensis* × *Sporophila caerulescens*
3. *Oryzoborus angolensis* × *Sporophila leucoptera*
4. *Oryzoborus angolensis* × *Sporophila lineola*
5. *Oryzoborus angolensis* × *Sporophila collaris*
6. *Oryzoborus angolensis* × *Sporophila nigricollis*
7. *Sporophila caerulescens* × *Sporophila nigricollis*
8. *Sporophila caerulescens* × *Sporophila lineola*
9. *Sporophila b. bouvreuil* × *Sporophila lineola*
10. *Sporophila b. bouvreuil* × *Sporophila plumbea*
11. *Sporophila bouvreuil pileata* × *Sporophila lineola*
12. *Sporophila bouvreuil pileata* × *Sporophila plumbea*

---

[1]When a hybrid is referred to, the rule is to name the father first. Because the parentage of the hybrids cited here is unknown, I have named first the species whose characteristics are more pronounced in the hybrid.

In various of the above cases I have seen more than one hybrid individual of the same type. I also knew of a cross of *Sporophila frontalis* × *Sporophila falcirostris* produced in captivity. Such crosses demonstrate a relationship between the species in question that is closer than a museum scientist might expect but is not surprising to one who knows the live birds and knows that a quarrelsome *O. maximiliani* can be attracted by an *O. angolensis*. A hybrid of these two is called a *bicurió* [*bicudo* + *curió*].

Hybridization apparently also occurs in the wild between other genera, such as *Passerina* (= *Cyanocompsa*) × *Oryzoborus* and *Passerina* (= *Cyanoloxia*) × *Sporophila*. I advise against hasty conclusions as to the parentage of abnormal individuals on which genealogical information is lacking. Hybrids may show characteristics of distant genetic origin that were not manifest in their parents.[2]

The intense interest of cage-bird fanciers in any hybridization, and especially in emberizine hybrids, resulted in the early 1900s in systematic campaigns to liberate seedeaters such as *Sporophila nigricollis* in the interior of São Paulo to encourage hybridization (Sick 1963). To me this is a regrettable adulteration of wild fauna, whereas well-controlled crossbreeding in captivity provides valuable scientific information. Occasional crossbreeding in the wild does not present a problem for the "purity" of local fauna for two reasons: because the hybrids are sterile or, if not, because the difficulty of being accepted by individuals of pure parentage constitutes a serious obstacle to their propagation. In captivity *Paroaria dominicana* and *P. coronata* produce fertile hybrids. This is to be expected, for each is a geographic replacement of the other (see "Distribution . . .").

It remains to be said that, in captivity, crosses have been made between birds of more distant relationship, especially domestic canaries with various Brazilian species, such as *Sicalis flaveola* × a female canary; *Volatinia jacarina* × a female canary; and *Coryphospingus pileatus* × a female canary. The offspring were fertile. A single female *Paroaria coronata* has hybridized with both an *Agelaius ruficapillus* and a *Molothrus bonariensis* (Oliveira 1984b) (see also Icterinae, "Interfamilial . . . Crossing").

Use, Decline, Captive Breeding, Repopulations, and Longevity

The Emberezidae is the family most pursued by the clandestine wild-bird trade. *Oryzoborus maximiliani, O. angolensis,* and *Passerina brissonii* especially have become rare around larger population centers. *Sporophila plumbea* is also becoming scarce, and even *Sicalis flaveola* is disappearing. The time has finally passed when the skins of colorful species were exported to Europe for decorative purposes. Fashion has always shown similar destructive tendencies with fauna.

It should be added that low-flying species such as *Volatinia jacarina* and the *Sporophila* are frequently killed on highways. Holding fights between *Sicalis flaveola* is a disgraceful sport, as absurd as cockfights.

There is not yet much breeding of Emberizinae and Cardinalinae in captivity, for until recently it was easier to obtain wild specimens in the market. *S. flaveola* and *V. jacarina* are reputedly the easiest to breed. The former can be reared in semicaptivity with the door of the cage open. Rearing of *Oryzoborus maximiliani* and *O. angolensis* is interesting, with the latter considered to be the "king" of song birds (see competitions under the *O. angolensis* species account). One male *O. maximiliani*, active over a period of 18 years, had "47 children and scores of grandchildren and great-grandchildren" (G. Viana, in Nogueira Neto 1973).

Recently increased breeding of *Oryzoborus* species has become important as a substitute for captured specimens, which day by day become more difficult to obtain, less because of legislation prohibiting their sale than because of natural scarcity arising out of their unrestrained persecution. Individuals born and reared in captivity adapt better to such a life and survive well in small cages. Between 1976 and 1985, Ennio Flecha (1987), with an annual average of 10 pairs of *O. angolensis*, obtained 188 eggs and 58 hatched young. It is said, however, that individuals born under artificial conditions leave much to be desired in those qualities required for show birds (Coimbra Filho 1986). Efforts are being made to give abandoned clutches and hatchlings of both *O. maximiliani* and *O. angolensis* to domestic canaries, which care for them conscientiously.

The next step should be not to consider only the profit these birds can bring but also to rear them for repopulating areas from which they have been exterminated. Good results along these lines have been achieved in Minas Gerais, using females of *O. maximiliani* born in captivity. Individuals were freed during the latter part of August and first half of September, a time when they remained in appropriate habitat until males still living in the region appeared. Results were deemed favorable. Obviously care was taken, through careful surveillance, to protect the area from hunters (Hugo E. F. Werneck).

There have been partially successful attempts to transplant *Sicalis flaveola*. *Paroaria dominicana* has been introduced on Ilhas das Enxadas, Rio de Janeiro, and *P. coronata* onto the Hawaiian Islands. *Oryzoborus maximiliani* and *O. angolensis* have lived in the area of Itatiaia National Park. Presently they are beginning to leave, for the forest is protected and becoming dense, making open places with grasses, the habitat of those species, scarce (E. Gouvêa 1980 pers. comm.). It is comforting to note that both *O. angolensis* and *O. maximiliani* are expanding their ranges in certain locales as a result of the planting of introduced grasses (Mato Grosso 1972).

---

[2]See the Fringillidae appendix on hybridization between *Carduelis* and the domestic canary.

When well treated, birds of these groups can be quite long-lived in captivity. A *Sporophila caerulescens* may live in good health for 18 years, an *O. angolensis* 22 years, and an *O. maximiliani* 26 years. It is reported than an *O. maximiliani* lived to 41 years in captivity in Rio de Janeiro but with serious health problems at the end because of its advanced age.

Alleged and Real Harmfulness

The attraction of these birds as pets contrasts with accusations that some are harmful to crops. I have already spoken of the real hoards of *Sicalis* in southern Brazil, which are associated with another multitude of "blackbirds" (icterines and some *Volatinia jacarina*) accused of desolating rice fields. It is said that *Passerina brissonii* damages cornfields and that *Zonotrichia capensis*, with its habit of scratching the ground, digs up seeds, thus damaging gardens. *Z. capensis*, however, well repays any damage it may do by destroying great numbers of noxious insects, such as chrysomelid leaf beetles.

Synopsis of Brazilian Male Emberizinae and Cardinalinae

1. Saltators and allies: *Saltator*, relatively large, long tail, five species with light throat (Pl 42.8), one with black throat: *Saltator atricollis*. See also *Embernagra* (item 10).
2. Grosbeaks such as *Caryothraustes*, *Gubernatrix cristata* and allies, large like the preceding group, with yellow underparts: *Caryothraustes canadensis* (Pl 42.9), *Periporphyrus* female, *Gubernatrix* (Pl 42.11), and *Pheucticus*; with red underparts: *Periporphyrus* male

3. Cardinals: *Paroaria* (Pl 42.10), medium size, head more or less extensively red, five species
4. Blue grosbeaks: *Passerina*, three species (Pl 43.1), *Porphyrospiza* (with yellow bill), and *Amaurospiza moesta*, medium size or smaller, dark blue
5. Seed-finches: *Oryzoborus crassirostris*, *O. maximiliani*, and *O. angolensis* (the last with chestnut belly, Pl 43.2), medium size
6. Grassquits: *Volatinia jacarina* (fig. 308) and *Tiaris fuliginosa*, and *Haplospiza unicolor*, small size, black or soot-colored, the latter two lacking white under the wings
7. Seedeaters: *Sporophila*, 22 species with varied coloring, belly white, chestnut, or yellow, sometimes a collar, the bill black or yellow (Pl 43.3, figs. 309–11); one larger, greenish species: *Sporophila frontalis*
8. Yellow-finches: *Sicalis* (Pl 43.9), four yellowish species
9. Sparrows and finches: *Zonotrichia capensis* (Pl 43.4); *Arremon* (Pl 43.5), two species; *Ammodramus* (Pl 43.10), two small, open-country species; *Coryphaspiza melanotis*, an open-country species with a gaudy black-and-white design on the head; two species: *C. pileatus*, gray with a red streak on the crown, and *C. cucullatus* (Pl 43.8); warbling-finches: *Poospiza* (Pl 43.6), three species with bright rusty and two black-and-white species (fig. 307); see also *Diuca diuca* (extreme south) and *Arremonops conirostris* (extreme north).
10. Grass-finches: *Emberizoides* (Pl 43.11), two species; Pampa-finches: *Embernagra*, two species; and *Donacospiza albifrons* (fig. 306): long-tailed open-country species, mid-size or smaller, greenish or brownish
11. Eight species that do not fit into the above groups: *Charitospiza eucosma* (Pl 43.7); *Pitylus* (fig. 312), two species; *Caryothraustes humeralis*, from extreme western Brazil; and four species from the extreme north: *Spiza americana*, *Dolospingus fringilloides*, *Catamenia homochroa*, and Tepui Brush-Finch, *Atlapetes personatus*.

SUBFAMILY EMBERIZINAE (64)

RUFOUS-COLLARED SPARROW, *Zonotrichia capensis*, Tico-tico   PL 43.4

15 cm. One of best-known and best-loved birds of southeastern Brazil. Small crest, streaked head, and rusty collar characteristic of species, though less pronounced in female. Juvenals lack streaks on head, black spot on side of neck, and rusty collar but are speckled black on breast. VOICE: call *tic* (*tico-tico*); warning, near nest a high *tist;* song a melody of 4–5 clear, well-enunciated whistles with beginning of phrase accentuated, e.g., *dew-BEE chew-chew* (ex-Guanabara); phrasing and timbre of song vary with population and region, with diatonic notes and an additional whistle occurring in some places. Has other vocalizations, e.g., a quiet trill, and cries when it fights. Outside breeding season sometimes has an incomplete subsong; is singing by 6 months of age (see "Vocalization"). Tico-tico's mellow, insinuating tune has

won it admiration of public, which interprets phrase variously, e.g., *Maria acorda! É dia! É dia!* "Maria, wake up! It's day! It's day!" or *Nosso ranchinho assim 'tava bom,* "Our little cabin, how good it was!"

Night and Fright Songs: At dusk it sings a different, loud song, characterized by prolongation and accentuation of last notes, *hew, jew, jew tsieww-tsieww-tsieww.* This night song, heard from overnight roost (sometimes situated high, e.g., in a palm crown where bird almost never goes during day) is usually sung only once by an individual as night falls or shortly (approximately 1 hr) after dark; rarely it is given during night, even more extraordinarily at dawn. Sometimes an individual repeats it after an interval of 7–10 minutes. Only certain individuals sing night song. On rare occasions it is heard in full daylight, sung as subsong at intervals during regular loud, normal, daytime singing. This appears to be a kind of voice "training," as is known in many songbirds. There are individual differences in night song, but I have not noticed any geographic variation, unlike day song. I have noted night song since 1940 in the following regions: Espírito Santo, Rio de Janeiro, ex-Guanabara, Minas Gerais, São Paulo, Santa Catarina, Rio Grande do Sul, Goiás, southern Pará (Cachimbo, Cururu); also Chile, Peru. On exceptional occasions daytime song is sung at night.

Night song creates such a different impression from daytime song that someone unaware of it may take it for singing of another species. Interestingly, night song is produced during day, being given only once but with full force, when an individual is extremely frightened, as when a Roadside Hawk, *Rupornis magnirostris,* or Peregrine Falcon, *Falco peregrinus,* appears on the prowl. It is scarcely credible that the night song, sung regularly at nightfall, would be caused by fright. The night song, which has been familiar to me for 50 years, escaped the attention of researchers such as F. Nottebohm (1969), who studied 523 individuals and carefully studied the song of *Z. capensis* in Argentina. The only reference that perhaps applies to it is found in the work of the naturalist and poet W. H. Hudson (1920), who said "tico-tico" also sings at night and that in the dark silence its song sounds "strangely sweet and expressive." I have not managed to make a recording of this, so did not publish anything about it prior to the Brazilian edition of this book (Sick 1985). Finally, in 1988 the night song of *Z. capensis* was discovered by Lougheed and Handford (1989), who were unaware of my studies.

Habitat and Behavior: Inhabits open areas, cultivated fields, ranches, gardens, even patios and enclosed planted areas. Abundant in regions with temperate climate, e.g., mountains of southeast (Serra de Mantiqueira, etc.) up to highest peaks, exposed to strong winds and cold. Habitat is constantly increasing as a result of deforestation and drainage. Bird easily becomes synanthropic, penetrating into cities and nesting where there are enough gardens, as it did for years alongside Palácio da Cultura in center of Rio de Janeiro. Among interesting aspects of its behavior is its technique of scratching up food from ground by means of small hops (see "Behavior").

Scarcity and Competition: In Brazil it is principal host of Shiny Cowbird, *Molothrus bonariensis.* In areas most affected by this parasite, *Z. capensis* losses are so great its extinction would be imminent were it not for other areas where it breeds freely. Although too little is yet known on the subject, it may be that the 2 species have some difference in their breeding seasons, giving tico an advantage: in Rio de Janeiro I have found tico nests with eggs and nestlings in June (end of autumn), and in certain years I have noted intensive song in July and August (local winter).

Of 83 *Z. capensis* nests I monitored on Ilha Grande, Rio de Janeiro, in 1944, 51 (61%) were parasitized by *Molothrus bonariensis.* They contained a total of 152 *Z. capensis* eggs and 94 *M. bonariensis* eggs. Sixty-two (41%) of the *Z. capensis* eggs hatched. Of the *Z. capensis* nestlings, 37 (59%) fledged. The success of *Z. capensis* was reduced to 21 (25%) of the 83 nests. Of the 37 juvenals that fledged, 22 (59%) came from nests that were not parasitized. There were 3 cases in which sparrow and cowbird nestlings were successfully reared together, proving that generalized statements about the cowbird always winning lead to error. It may be that the sparrows' success came from cowbird nestlings being severely parasitized by bird botflies, even more so than those of the sparrow (see *M. bonariensis*).

It is generally thought, based on purely theoretical knowledge of the subject, that *Z. capensis* is being driven out by invading *Passer domesticus* (see that species also). This is found, for instance, in *Zoogeografia do Brasil* by C. Mello Leitão (1937): "The Rufous-collared Sparrow, formerly so common and giving a cheery air to Rio de Janeiro, from where it has been expelled by the invading House Sparrow." This erroneous interpretation is given by others who can't distinguish between the two, or who have not considered that the 2 species have radically different ecological requirements: *Z. capensis* lives in isolated pairs, each male furiously attacking its conspecific neighbor if it invades his approximately 30-m-diameter territory. It is not primarily a city bird but more adapted to country, capoeira, and rural properties. It builds its nest in midst of quite low vegetation, on embankments covered with false ivy (*Ficus pumila*), even on the ground under the grass.

Passer domesticus, in contrast, although it also lives in pairs, likes to associated in colonies for nesting, establishes itself in high places on buildings, and appears in flocks in search of food. Because of this *Z. capensis* will always be much less numerous than *P. domesticus* in cities. It is popularly affirmed that before introduction of *P. domesticus,* flocks of *Z. capensis* existed, but it is evident they were not tico-ticos, for *Z. capensis* flocks form only during winter migrations in extreme south. Hélio F. A. Camargo said it well: "The idea of the House Sparrow, the 'fortunate one,' expelling the Rufous-collared Sparrow comes from the House Sparrow being more abundant, thereby creating the impression that the former has been replaced by the latter."

The fact is that *Z. capensis* is little affected by the activity of *P. domesticus. Z. capensis* drives *P. domesticus* away from the feed tray. Neither is *P. domesticus* a competitor of the other in the breeding season, for the nesting requirements of the two are entirely different. *Z. capensis* is hurt by the lack of gardens in the cities, which it needs for food and nesting. Thus, with urban growth its natural habitat is disappearing and the bird moves to the suburbs where human population is less dense. It is, therefore, expelled by people, a victim of urbanization and of *M. bonariensis,* not of *P. domesticus.*

Distribution: Mexico and Central America throughout larger part of South America to Tierra del Fuego, with many gaps that usually correspond to regions of tropical climate not to its liking. Thus colonizes mountainous regions where it is usually abundant, as in Alto da Itatiaia, Rio de Janeiro. Many geographic races have developed. It is one of most abundant birds of Chile; in Andes reaches 5000 m (Andean Sparrow). Found in all regions of Brazil except forested areas of Amazonia, occurring there in certain savanna and mountainous regions with milder climate, e.g., Serra dos Carajás, 700 m (Pará). Exists in Amapá but appears to be missing in Belém region and on Ilha de Marajó, Pará. In south (Rio Grande do Sul, Paraná) migratory, appearing there in flocks that must come from adjacent countries to south. Considered a replacement for *Junco,* a genus widely distributed in North America (Mayr and Short 1970).

GRASSLAND SPARROW, *Ammodramus (= Myospiza) humeralis,* Tico-tico-do-campo-verdadeiro PL 43.10

22 cm. Small, terrestrial, savanna species, common outside Amazonia. Upperparts gray streaked black with rust-colored tints, prominent yellow spot before eye. Shoulder (hidden) also yellow. Young have breast spotted blackish. Modifications in plumage color occur (e.g., may appear reddish) from being soiled by earth. VOICE: a high, insectlike *tsip,* sometimes repeated; call *sooEET;* song high and ringing, *dee-diew DEE-ee, ee, ee.* Dry savannas with low grasses and sedges, cultivated lands. Runs and hops on ground, crouching like a mouse; easily overlooked. Perches to sing. In 2 quite disjunct areas, one north of Amazonia (the Guianas and Venezuela to Colombia and extreme northern Brazil in Roraima, Monte Alegre, Marajó, Pará), the other to south: some isolated savanna areas in Hylaea, e.g., Santarém and Humaitá (upper Madeira), and all of Brazil south of Hylaea; also Bolivia, Paraguay, Argentina, Uruguay. Also called *Tico-rato, Corre-corre, Canário-do-campo, Tico-tico-do-pasto* and *Tringolim* (Minas Gerais), *Salta-caminho.* See *Volatinia jacarina* immature (browner); *Haplospiza unicolor* female (greener, in forests); *Zonotrichia capensis* (larger); *Sicalis;* and *A. aurifrons.*

YELLOW-BROWED SPARROW, *Ammodramus (= Myospiza) aurifrons,* Cigarrinha-do-campo

Only in Amazonia. Distinguished from *A. humeralis* by wide yellow superciliary, more yellow around eye and on malar region. Differs from *Sicalis luteola* by having slimmer bill, white underparts (not yellow). VOICE: song a very high, monotonous, bisyllabic buzz, *tsewrrr-tsewrrr* (completely unlike *humeralis*). Runs and hops in savannas with low vegetation, moving tail slightly up and down, reminiscent of pipits, *Anthus.* In cities such as Santarém and Manaus sometimes perches on buildings in center of town to sing. Venezuela to Bolivia and along southern shore of Amazon from Acre and lower Tapajós and lower Tocantins to Belém, Pará. Appears to be a geographic replacement, particularly Ama-

zonian, for *humeralis.* However, I draw attention to the fact that the songs of the 2 species are basically different and so, apparently, are some other facets of their ecologies.

UNIFORM FINCH, *Haplospiza unicolor,* Cigarra-bambu

13 cm. Restricted to southeast. Plumage resembles *Tiaris fuliginosa* but conical bill extremely sharp. Plumage uniformly bluish gray, including underside of wings. Bill black, legs light rosy brown. Female dark olive above, whitish below with flanks and breast greenish, throat streaked with black. Mandible yellowish. VOICE: call a high *tsri, tsip;* a bisyllabic, monotonous phrase of fast, ringing cheeps, reminiscent of *Volatinia jacarina* or buzz of a cicada, *tsi, tsi-tshrEEE, ts, s, s, s, tslEEE, ts, ts, ts, ts-s, s, s, s, s,* 2d part of phrase faint like an echo. Sings frequently while flying between 2 branches some meters above ground in shady forest below canopy. On these occasions always moves with a horizontal or slightly descending trajectory, beating wings aimlessly with remiges spread obliquely downward and legs dangling. Rather open but shady bamboo groves occurring in great numbers when bamboo rice is available and then disappearing; see "Feeding"). Espírito Santo and Minas Gerais to Rio Grande do Sul, Argentina, Paraguay. Also called *Cigarra-coqueiro, Pichochó-bambu.*

LONG-TAILED REED-FINCH, *Donacospiza albifrons,* Tico-tico-do-banhado Fig. 306

14 cm. Savanna species with long, wide tail that is graduated, flexible, and occupies ¹/₂ of bird's total length. Sharp bill reminiscent of *Poospiza.* Lore and superciliary white, sometimes has white around eye. Sides of head and upperparts gray, back streaked black, edges of wing feathers brownish. Underparts light yellowish brown, throat whitish.

Fig. 306. Long-tailed Reed-Finch, *Donacospiza albifrons.*

Female and immature browner, more streaked; tail lacks white, as in adult. VOICE: a low *chet*, reminiscent of *Stephanophorus diadematus* (sometimes its neighbor in Santa Catarina) and *Schistochlamys ruficapillus;* squeaky song, *tseep, tseep, tseep . . .*, is repeated rapidly with very long sequences. Sometimes sings while flying, rising in a straight but oblique line to 2 m, then descending and moving some 15 m away. Cattail beds and marshy places in open country, seeking its sustenance (insects) in bases of plants. Argentina, Uruguay, and Paraguay to Rio Grande do Sul, Paraná, São Paulo, Rio de Janeiro (valleys of Piraí and Paraíba, upper Itatiaia), Minas Gerais (Serra do Caparaó, high-altitude savanna). Related to *Poospiza.*

COMMON DIUCA-FINCH, *Diuca diuca*, Diuca SV

17.5 cm. Southern species, size of a cardinal. Male upperparts light gray, as are breast and foreparts of body. Rest of underparts white, as are tips of outer tail feathers, frequently displayed by brief spreading of tail. Sides of crissum chestnut, bill black. Female brown. VOICE: *tslit, tslip*, reminiscent of a *Thraupis* tanager. Song melodious, resonant. Bushy savanna. Chile, where it is one of most abundant birds, and Argentina to Uruguay, Rio Grande do Sul (June).

BAY-CHESTED WARBLING-FINCH, *Poospiza thoracica*, Peito-pinhão BR

13.7 cm. Southern species of local occurrence, with long tail like congeners. Similar to *P. lateralis* but smaller, with more slender bill. Upperparts, sides of head, and rump dark gray tending toward greenish. Speculum, spot over eye, throat, and center of belly pure white. Breast and sides of body chestnut. Female paler. High-mountain forests of southeast from Caparaó (Minas Gerais), Itatiaia, and Bocaina (Rio de Janeiro) to São Paulo, Paraná, Santa Catarina, northeastern Rio Grande do Sul. Much less common than *lateralis,* from which it is immediately distinguishable by red pectoral band, lack of white superciliary, and white marks on tail. Also called *Vira-folhas.*

BLACK-AND-RUFOUS WARBLING-FINCH, *Poospiza nigrorufa*, Quem-te-vestiu

13.8 cm. Typical southern species, more slender than *P. lateralis,* which it somewhat resembles. Upperparts uniformly dark grayish brown. Superciliary, malar stripe, and chin white, resulting in curious X-shaped design when viewed from front. Sides of head black. Underparts vivid dark rusty except for white abdomen. Outer tail feathers tipped white. VOICE: a strongly accentuated *bis-BIS-tsiew, tsri-tsWEE-tsieh* (*Quem-te-vestiu,* Who-dressed-you; Glad-to-meet-you). In pairs low in dense bushes and riverine forest. Argentina to Bolivia, Paraguay, Uruguay, southern Brazil: Rio Grande do Sul, Santa Catarina (São Joaquim, Blumenau). Also called *Bigorrinho* (Rio Grande do Sul).

RED-RUMPED WARBLING-FINCH, *Poospiza lateralis,* Quete PL 43.6

15.5 cm. Abundant in high mountains of southeast and extreme south. Easy to confuse with *P. thoracica,* from which it can be distinguished by lack of chestnut breast band, large rusty area on rump, and if seen from below, large white spots on outer tail feathers. Female paler. Young have greenish upperparts, sulfur yellow superciliaries, forehead, and throat. VOICE: high like a saíra tanager; call *pix, tsip,* a quiet *jeh-it,* which may be repeated; *tsee* in flight; warning a deep *jep;* song sharp, metallic ringing, *tsaa-tse-lidle . . . ,* rapidly repeated; trilled phrases reminiscent of song of Whitevented Violetear, *Colibri serrirostris* (Trochilidae): *tsip, tsip, tsip-tsip, tsip, tsip, tsip, tsap, tsip, tsip, tsap,* constantly repeated. Any high-altitude forest, frequently in *Podocarpus* forests. Espírito Santo and Minas Gerais (Caparaó) to Rio de Janeiro (Itatiaia, Bocaina, Serra dos Órgãos), São Paulo, Paraná, to Rio Grande do Sul, where it reaches sea level; also Uruguay, Paraguay, Argentina. Sometimes alongside *P. thoracica* (Rio de Janeiro) and *P. nigrorufa* (Rio Grande do Sul). Also called *Quem-te-vestiu-da-serra, Monterita* (Argentina).

CINEREOUS WARBLING-FINCH, *Poospiza cinerea,* Capacetinho-do-oco-do-pau BR

13.3 cm. Similar to *P. lateralis* but larger, with only lores and auricular region blackish. Cap gray tending toward greenish of remaining upperparts. Underparts white, though breast slightly yellowish. Bill black, iris red. Immatures have sides of head brown. Cerrado. Restricted to Mato Grosso, Goiás, Minas Gerais, northern São Paulo. Probably a geographic replacement of *lateralis.* Also called *Andorinha-do-oco-do-pau.*

BLACK-CAPPED WARBLING-FINCH, *Poospiza melanoleuca*, Capacetinho Fig. 307

12.5 cm. Only in extreme south. Head black, rest of upperparts gray, tail black, outer tail feathers with large white

Fig. 307. Black-capped Warbling-Finch, *Poospiza melanoleuca.*

spots; underparts white, bill blackish, iris red. Female has only a vestige of black on crown. VOICE: a loud trill, repeating same simple phrase. Bushes in open country, dense grass, and along river edges, sometimes in small flocks. Argentina and Paraguay to Bolivia, southern Mato Grosso, Rio Grande do Sul, Uruguay. See *Polioptila* gnatcatchers (Sylviinae), which are much more slender, and *Sicalis citrina*.

STRIPED-TAILED YELLOW-FINCH, *Sicalis citrina*, Canarinho-rasteiro

12.3 cm. Slender canary-like species, distinguishable by white spot on 2 outer tail feathers of each side, visible from underside of closed tail. Small bill. Female less yellow, back brownish. VOICE: a strident whistle, *iew; tsi tsi;* song a heterogeneous mixture, beginning with a ventriloquial *tsle, tsle, tsle . . .* , then turning into a rapid, rising warble reminiscent of House Wren, *Troglodytes aedon*, and culminating with a descending series of resonant *iew*s. Sings in flight, ascending obliquely, then descending while voicing a melodious trill, finally perching on a post in a pasture or on a tree trunk. Open cerrado, campo limpo; is even more terrestrial than *S. flaveola*, with potential for being mistaken for an *Anthus* pipit. In Andes from Argentina to Colombia, mountains of Venezuela, Colombia, Brazil: Mato Grosso, southern Pará (Serra do Cachimbo, August), Goiás, Piauí, Minas Gerais, southern São Paulo, Paraná. Migratory, disappearing periodically (July, Minas Gerais).

ORANGE-FRONTED YELLOW-FINCH, *Sicalis columbiana*, Canário-do-amazonas

11.5 cm. Similar to *S. citrina* but clearly smaller. Male has same bright yellow of *S. flaveola* but lacks dark streaking on upperparts. Female has olive brown upperparts, almost without dark spots. Tail and wing feathers bordered with olive, underparts whitish with breast and flanks brownish. VOICE: *tsi-tsooEE, chiLEE,* similar to *flaveola*. Savannas, campinas, cerrado. Venezuela to Peru and Brazil as far as southern Pará, Maranhão, Minas Gerais, São Paulo, Goiás, Mato Grosso.

SAFFRON FINCH, *Sicalis flaveola*, Canário-da-terra-verdadeiro   PL 43.9

13.5 cm. Very well known in Brazil outside Amazonia. Males of northeastern populations (*S. f. brasiliensis*, Maranhão to São Paulo, see plate) resemble a domestic canary in their relatively large size, bright yellow color, and orange tinge on forecrown. Males of southern populations (*S. f. pelzelni*, Santa Catarina, Rio Grande do Sul, Mato Grosso, Argentina, Uruguay) similar to *S. citrina* males, being smaller and more olivaceous than typical form and with more blackish streaking on back and flanks. Females and young of both forms olive brown above with dense brown streaking, whitish below with brownish streaking. Breast and crissum

of female *brasiliensis* yellowish. Sometimes females appear similar to males. Frequently they become colored (e.g., purple) by local earth impregnating plumage if they are soiled with dust or wet dirt. VOICE: *tsit*, a resonant *tsewk*, a soft *sooit;* a flowing, continuous twittering interrupted by staccato cadences, as if choking, e.g., *tsip, tsip, TSIlip-tsewp, tsip-tsewlap,* etc. ("explosive song"; see also Orange-headed Tanager, *Thlypopsis sordida*); a confused, rapid warble. Female also sings.

Habitat, Behavior, Nesting, and Alleged Harmfulness: Lives in dry, overgrown savannas, cultivated fields, caatinga. Runs on ground in search of seeds and commonly appears with Shiny Cowbird, *Molothrus bonariensis,* but is more shy and cautious than it. Perches to sing. Unlike other *Sicalis*, nests in holes, commonly occupying *Furnarius* houses and sometimes competing for them with Cattle Tyrant, *Machetornis rixosus* (Tyrannidae) and *Passer domesticus.* Also uses stick piles of Firewood-gatherer, *Anumbius annumbi,* and of *Phacellodomus, Pseudoseisura,* and *Synallaxis* for its own nest. It is so adaptable in this respect that it will even take advantage of a hanging cow skull or arch of a tile on a house (thus the name *canarinho-da-telha,* "little canary of the tile"). Also accepts small boxes or perforated bamboo for nesting and even moves in among dense epiphitic plants. In available space always builds a comfortable little basket. Periodically moves about in flocks, in which immatures predominate, and may then cause damage to rice crops.

Captivity: Breeds without difficulty, even in captivity. Under these circumstances a series of plumage variations appear, known to breeders as canela, isabel, lutina, arlequim, and nevada. Hybridization with domestic canary is not easy to obtain, for it belongs to another subfamily (see "Hybridization") and has different behavior, building its nest on branches, not in cavities. Such hybrids are infertile.

Some people take advantage of very jealous and aggressive nature of certain males to use them as "fighting canaries," as in equally detestable "sport" of cockfighting. The 2 competitors are placed in a special large cage while spectators wager money on which will win. Such fights may go on for more than 1/2 an hour and end when one of combatants flees or falls wounded (with some serious injuries).

Distribution: In Brazil from Maranhão south to Rio Grande do Sul and west to Mato Grosso (Cuiabá, Pantanal). Also on islands off coast of Rio de Janeiro and São Paulo. Maintains itself well after introduction in protected places, e.g., islands in Guanabara Bay, Brocoió and Ilha das Enxadas. Reappears north of Amazonia from the Guianas to Colombia. Introduced in 1963 on Ilha Trindade where at last report it was only breeding landbird of native Brazilian origin. In 1975 it was still uncommon and did not extend beyond the area frequented by humans, the same as domestic pigeon (*Columba livia*) (see also Helmeted Guineafowl, *Numida meleagris*). Also called *Canário-da-horta, Canário-*

da-telha (Santa Catarina), *Canário-do-campo, Chapinha* (Minas Gerais), *Canário-do-chão* (Bahia), *Coroia* (female of fighting breed).

GRASSLAND YELLOW-FINCH, *Sicalis luteola*, Tipio

12.5 cm. Male differs from male *S. flaveola* in lack of yellow on crown but has distinctive yellow pattern on lores and around eyes. Throat and belly also bright yellow, contrasting with grayish malar stripe and breast. Mantle intensely streaked with blackish. Female similar but with less yellow. VOICE: call a characteristic whistle, *bi-ditz, tsi-tsss, tiPEEo;* song unlike *flaveola*, a high, melodious voice, singing flowing and well-varied phrases, moving from high to low notes, sometimes with trills reminiscent of domestic canary though much weaker. Also crescendos, resonant cadenzas, and series of calls all in rapid succession. Sings by preference in flight, gliding calmly to ground with wings obliquely extended upward and tail open. Sometimes also dangles legs like an *Anthus* pipit. Also sings with crown feathers erected while flying around female, which remains perched on ground. Terrestrial, running on ground like an *Ammodramus*. Always in flocks, even during breeding, and nests in groups. In migration gathers by hundreds in bamboo thickets to sleep, associating then with other species, e.g., *Agelaius ruficapillus* (Rio Grande do Sul). Open savanna, both dry and humid; in dry areas sometimes alongside *S. flaveola*. Mexico and Central America to Chile, Argentina, almost all of South America. Locally common in eastern and southern Brazil. In Amazonia only in certain savanna areas, e.g., Marajó Island. Reaches 3000 m in Andes. Also called *Canário-do-lote, Patativa* (Bahia), *Cigarrinha* (Minas Gerais), *Canário-do-rio-grande* (Rio de Janeiro), *Tico-tipió, Canário-da-horta*.

WEDGE-TAILED GRASS-FINCH, *Emberizoides herbicola*, Canário-do-campo   PL 43.11

20 cm. Common, widely distributed savanna species whose long, graduated tail occupies more than ½ its total length. Upperparts have contrasting black streaks; shoulder (usually hidden) yellow; bill strong, slightly curved, yellow with black along top of maxilla; legs yellow or pinkish. Young immatures have superciliary and underparts sulfur yellow instead of brownish white, sides of breast streaked, mandible whitish. VOICE: a high *spit*, a penetrating *tsik;* song a loud, resonant whistle trending upward like a question, *jewLEE*. After an interval it "responds" with downward phrase, *jewleh*, the 2 phrases forming a harmonic unit to human ears. Also a phrase with more syllables, e.g., *wewt-wewt hee-TSEEew*, which varies with locale. Among dry or humid tall grasses, walking or running on ground. Perches to sing and to scrutinize surroundings, moves tail sideways and up and down, flies with tail half-cocked. Costa Rica across northern South America to Bolivia, Argentina, Paraguay,

open parts of Brazil: Marajó (Pará) to northeast, east, and south to Rio Grande do Sul, Mato Grosso (upper Xingu, Chapada). Also called *Cabo-mole, Tibirro* (Espírito Santo). See *E. ypiranganus*.

LESSER GRASS-FINCH, *Emberizoides ypiranganus*, Canário-do-brejo

18 cm. Southern wetland species, similar to *E. herbicola* but distinctly smaller, with tail relatively shorter. Streaking on upperparts wider and blacker, sides of head gray instead of brownish, central tail feathers more graduated. Maxilla black, tomia and mandible yellow, legs light brownish. VOICE: entirely unlike *herbicola*: call and warning a low *tse, tse, tse, ch, ch, ch;* song made up of harsh, monotonous cadences, e.g., *wet, wet, wet . . . JAda, JAda, JAda . . . ,* reminiscent of other wetland birds such as *Cistothorus* (Troglodytidae) or *Acrocephalus* (Sylviinae, of Old World), a "habitat voice"; sometimes more melodious and resonant phrases, *widje, widje, widje . . . , tsleh, tsleh, tsleh . . . ;* sometimes sings in flight: rises 3–4 m, then continues horizontally with tail wide open, finally comes down silently. Marshes with *Sphagnum*, scattered about in savanna regions, sometimes in small, nearly dry, humid spots with clumps of carqueja (*Baccharis*). Feeds and shelters near base of vegetation but sometimes flies high and far. Described in 1907 by H. von Ihering of São Paulo; I rediscovered it again in Brazil (Santa Catarina, Paraná) in 1969, when for first time I entered range of species, not knowing that in meantime W. Partridge had collected bird in Argentina; in 1971 I also found it in Rio Grande do Sul. Occurs in Paraguay. Occurs with Masked Yellowthroat, *Geothlypis aequinoctialis;* Saffron-cowled Blackbird, *Xanthopsar flavus; Sporophila hypoxantha* (Santa Catarina, Rio Grande do Sul); Cock-tailed Tyrant, *Alectrurus tricolor;* and Black-and-white Monjita, *Heteroxolmis dominicana* (Paraná).

GREAT PAMPA-FINCH, *Embernagra platensis*, Sabiá-do-banhado

21.5 cm. Large, southern, savanna species with long, wide, rounded tail. Plumage full and soft, bill bright orange with top of maxilla black. Upperparts grayish olive green, sides of head blackish, wings intense green, shoulder yellow, underparts gray, sides and crissum brownish, belly whitish. Immature has sulfur yellow throat and foreneck, breast with black marks, reminiscent of corresponding plumage of *E. herbicola*, its occasional neighbor. VOICE: warning a loud *tsit, spit, spit, spit;* a short phrase of clear, resonant whistles alternating with squeaky cadences, e.g., *tsew-BEEeh, TSEEdelew-TSEEdelew-pryst, tsi, tsi, tsi, tsi-spiliEW, sewee-tsee-tsili*. Marshes with some tall vegetation; overgrown, humid fields; high open country of Mantiqueira (Itatiaia, Rio de Janeiro, 1800 m, and Caparaó, Minas Gerais). Walks on ground with long steps; perches on tips of bushes, sometimes clutching 2 branches of a fork; perches on rocks; moves tail sideways and vertically; flies heavily with legs dangling. Argentina, Uruguay, and Paraguay to Rio Grande do Sul, Santa Catarina, Paraná, São Paulo, Rio de Janeiro, Minas Gerais, Bolivia. Also called *Perdizinha-do-campo.* See *E. longicauda.*

PALE-THROATED SERRA-FINCH, *Embernagra longicauda,* Rabo-mole-da-serra   BR

21.5 cm. Endemic of chapadas of interior Minas Gerais and Bahia. Very similar to *E. platensis* but has narrow white or yellowish eye-ring (interrupted on front and back sides) and line of same color above blackish lores. All-green back (not slightly streaked like *platensis*), yellowish white throat (not dark gray). VOICE: call a loud *BEEtsi, ooLEE;* song *PAY-tiziEEoo.* Described in 1844 from "South America," it was rediscovered in 1926 by E. Snethlage near Marian, Minas Gerais, and in 1928 by E. Kaempfer in Morro do Chapéu, Bahia. Dry plains with dwarf palms and *Vellozia* species in Serra do Espinhaço, Minas Gerais, at altitudes above 900 m. In Serras da Moeda, Caraça, do Cipó, Gandarella, de Piedade (G. Mattos pers. comm.). Reappears in chapadas of central Bahia (Morro do Chapéu). In Serra do Espinhaço in high altitudes replaces *platensis,* a more southerly species, evidently involving competitive exclusion without twin species. I found *longicauda* on Serra do Cipó (1300 m) alongside *Augastes scutatus* (Trochilidae) and Gray-backed Tachuri, *Polystictus superciliaris* (Tyrannidae), other endemics of region. In area of Morro do Chapéu occurs with Hooded Visorbearer, *Augastes lumachellus.* See "Distribution. . . ."

BLUE-BLACK GRASSQUIT, *Volatinia jacarina.*
Tiziu   Fig. 308

11.4 cm. One of most common and best-known emberizines in Brazil. Black-billed male in nuptial plumage uniformly glossy bluish black with white axillaries and under wing coverts. In some regions of Amazonia (e.g., upper Rio Negro) these parts also black. After breeding season plumage changes to black feathers bordered whitish, more conspicuous on underparts. Before next breeding season there is another molt, changing bicolored feathers for all-black nuptial plumage (see "Morphology"). Female and immature brown on upperparts, whitish below. Immature male usually has some black on head. Subadult male (known as *pintão*) similar to adult male in nonbreeding plumage but differs in wide brown borders on feathers, more visible on upperparts; it may be sexually mature in this phase, which can last about 2 years. VOICE: call a strident *tsic;* warning a series of *ti-ti-ti . . . ;* song a short, squeaky, stereotyped *ti-ZEEoo,* emitted during a short, vertical jump which is very characteristic and is accompanied by a series of wing beats that not only display bright white of axillaries and under wing coverts but also produce a certain noise with remiges. Bird alights in same spot from which it took off and immediately jumps

Fig. 308. Blue-black Grassquit, *Volatinia jacarina,* male. At left, the jump-flight during song.

again, executing perhaps 12–14 jumps per minute. Open areas, tall grass, rice fields, even abundant around buildings. In Belém (Pará) area breeds all year (see "Breeding"). In more southerly regions (e.g., São Paulo) disappears in winter. Mexico to most of South America, including all of Brazil. Closely related to famous Darwin's Finches, Geospizinae of Galapagos Islands. Also called *Saltator,* "Jumper"; *Veludinho,* "Little Velvet"; *Papa-arroz,* "Rice-eater"; *Bate-estaca,* "Pile-driver" (ex-Guanabara); *Serrador,* "Sawyer"; *Serra-serra,* "Saw-saw"; *Alfaiate,* "Tailor" (last 4 obviously compare jumping movements to a pile driver, sawing of a carpenter, or arm movement of a tailor measuring cloth). See also *Haplospiza, Tiaris, Ammodramus.*

BUFFY-FRONTED SEEDEATER, *Sporophila frontalis,* Pichochó

13.4 cm. Largest *Sporophila.* Has thick bill that varies in size but is characterized by maxilla being more narrow than mandible, similar to *S. falcirostris* and *S. schistacea.* Male olive brown with narrow postocular stripe, throat and center of underparts white or whitish, center of abdomen yellow, 2 yellow wing bars. Color varies greatly, apparently because of age, with pure white sometimes on forehead, crown, and/or sides of neck (adult male with this is called *estrela,* "star"); may also have clear malar streak of same color; or upper back and top of head may be dark gray. Female similar to male but greener and without white postocular stripe. Females and males without white are called *taquara,* "bamboo." VOICE: strident *pitz;* song a violent sort of whip-snapping, *cho-cho-cho-chewt,* interpreted by people as *pichochó;* also a confused, liquid warble. In captivity becomes a most tireless songster. Apparently female also sings. Thick forest interiors, bamboo thickets (see "Migration"). In years when bamboo produces seed appears in great numbers and spreads into regions where it does not normally appear, e.g., on restinga of Marambaia (Rio de Janeiro), associated with *Haplospiza*. Has also occurred in cultivated areas (rice fields in Rio Grande do Sul, from beginning of year until end of harvest in April). Paraguay, Argentina (Misiones), Brazil from Espírito Santo to Rio Grande do Sul. Also called *Chanchão, Catatau* (Minas Gerais), *Estalador, Pichochó-estrela*.

TEMMINCK'S SEEDEATER, *Sporophila falcirostris*, Cigarra-verdadeira   BR

10.5 cm. Southern species notable for strange shape of bill, which has narrow, angular maxilla bent over mandible that is twice as thick. Male's bill corn-colored. Male completely slate-colored with under tail coverts brownish white, center of abdomen and speculum white. Sometimes has additional white, e.g., around eye, on superciliary, throat, sides of neck, or bar on upper wing coverts. Female and young brown with center of abdomen somewhat whitish or yellowish but immediately recognizable by bill shape. Captive males commonly keep their youthful brown plumage for several years, and this is probably also the case in nature, for few males are found in characteristic "adult" plumage. VOICE: a strident *tslit, eet;* call a bisyllabic *i, eet;* warning *tseeaa;* song melodious and varied but dominated by a sharp, penetrating, monotonous sound reminiscent of buzz of a cicada, *tsi, si, si, si . . . , tsirrrrr*, sometimes with a slow, sharp *s, s, s, s, s-s, s, s, s, s*. Lives in areas where forest has been felled and where sedge, navalha-de-macaco (*Hypolytrum* sp.), of whose seed this species is extremely fond, grows. Forest edges at medium height and even higher, where it nests and from where it travels on long, high flights to reach meadows, marshes, rice fields; also hot lowlands (e.g., Lagoa de Juparanã, Espírito Santo, in July, associated with *S. bouvreuil* and *S. collaris*) and mountainous regions (Teresópolis, Tinguá, Nova Friburgo in Rio de Janeiro, and Alto da Serra, São Paulo, where it is found with *S. frontalis*). Endemic to southern Brazil from Minas Gerais and Espírito Santo to São Paulo, Paraná. Apparently migrates, for it disappears periodically. Has already totally disappeared from certain localities (e.g., lowlands of Santos and Iguapé in São Paulo). Also called *Patativa-chiador, Chiadora* (Minas Gerais).

SLATE-COLORED SEEDEATER, *Sporophila schistacea*, Cigarrinha-do-norte

Replaces *S. falcirostris* in Amazonia and is very similar to it both morphologically and ecologically. Adult males stand out because of distinct and unique light yellow color of claws and deep yellow color of bill. VOICE: very similar to *falcirostris:* call a strident, bisyllabic *tsi, tsi;* a cicadalike buzz, phrase sometimes comprising diverse crescendo cadenzas, e.g., *tsit-ts, s, s, s, s, s, s-s, s, s, s-s, s, s, s*. Edge of tall forests; nests on tips of branches, preferably not too low (e.g., 8 m above ground); from there flies high to a river edge to feed, flying high enough to reach islands in middle of Amazon and to overfly Belém (Pará). Mexico to Bolivia and lower Amazon (Amapá, eastern Pará). Also called *Cigarra-bico-de-lacre*.

GRAY SEEDEATER, *Sporophila intermedia*

Similar to *S. schistacea* but much lighter, gray, with black claws (not yellow). Roraima (Rio Branco), Rio Mucajaí (Boa Vista), Maracá. Also the Guianas, Venezuela, Colombia (Silva 1988).

PLUMBEOUS SEEDEATER, *Sporophila plumbea*, Patativa-verdadeira

10.5 cm. One of most sought-after singers. Male bluish gray, lighter on underparts, with chin, short malar stripe (very typical for this specie), abdomen, and speculum white. Frequently has a white spot right below eye. Female and young brown, lighter on underparts. Bill color varies between black, gray, and yellow, with last found in Goiás and Minas Gerais alongside dark varieties. Yellow variety may already be distinguishable in juvenal (as I found in Minas Gerais) or may appear only in 2d year or later (as I saw in individuals in Rio Grande do Sul). VOICE: call a loud *jep;* song one of finest and most melodious of Brazilian emberizines and cardinalines. There are frequent motifs of 2–3 well-pronounced, repeated syllables, e.g., *jui-jui-jewluh-jewluh, dijewlp-dijewlp*. Has a rapid warble resembling *Carduelis magellanica* (Fringillidae); sometimes imitates other birds, e.g., Great Kiskadee, *Pitangus sulphuratus* (*bem-te-vi*), and tody-flycatchers, *Todirostrum*. Edge of low forest intermingled with open country, cerrado, riverine vegetation, buriti groves. Does not adapt to exotic grasses, as I observed in Federal District (see "Habitat . . ."). Argentina to Paraguay, Bolivia, and Brazil in Rio Grande do Sul, Santa Catarina, Paraná, São Paulo, Minas Gerais, Mato Grosso, Goiás, Federal District (where formerly occurred in flocks in December). Also most northerly parts of South America, Marajó (Pará), Roraima, adjacent countries. In southern part of range (e.g., Santa Catarina) disappears in winter, apparently because of lack of food. Also called *Patativa-da-serra* (Minas Gerais, given only to individuals with yellow bills), *Patativa-do-cerrado, Patativa-da-Amazônia*. See *S. leucoptera*.

VARIABLE SEEDEATER, *Sporophila americana*, Cola, Coleiro-do-norte

11 cm. Amazonian, with thick, black bill, related to *S. collaris*. Male has black upperparts except for gray rump, 2 white wing bars, white speculum. Underparts and sides of neck also white; narrow, black band across throat forms a sometimes-incomplete collar. Female and young brown, lighter on underparts, similar to those of *collaris* but differen-

Fig. 309. Rusty-collared Seedeater, *Sporophila collaris,* male.

Fig. 310. Lined Seedeater, *Sporophila lineola,* male.

tiated by bill shape and color. VOICE: call *jep;* song is reminiscent of *S. caerulescens* but more prolonged; sometimes imitates other birds. Overgrown open country, edge of cultivated fields, etc. Mexico into northern South America to Rio Juruá, lower Tapajós (Pará), Belém (Pará). Also called *Pintada* (Amapá), *Patativa* (Pará), *Coleiro-do-brejo-do-Amazonas.*

RUSTY-COLLARED SEEDEATER, *Sporophila collaris,* Coleiro-do-brejo   Fig. 309

11.5 cm. Colorful southern species with blunt, black bill. Male plumage has complicated black-and-white or black-and-yellowish-cinnamon pattern. Top and sides of head black with 2 small white spots before and below eye. Upper back, wings, and tail black; lower back gray; wide, black breast band. Speculum and throat white. Rest of plumage (nuchal collar, rump, and rest of underparts) may be almost pure white (*S. c. collaris*) or with a definite cinnamon in individuals originating in interior São Paulo and Mato Grosso, called *coleiros-do-brejo-do-oeste* (*S. c. ochrascens* and *S. c. melanocephala*). Female and young very similar to those of *S. americana* and *S. leucoptera* but larger and with thicker bill than those of *S. caerulescens.* VOICE: call *ghep,* fuller than *caerulescens;* song a rapid warble, ascending and descending a few times, mixed with twitters, often well-larded with imitations of other birds, e.g., anis, *Crotophaga;* elaenias, *Elaenia;* tody-flycatchers, *Todirostrum.* Repeats motifs. Marshes with tall vegetation. Espírito Santo to Rio Grande do Sul, Goiás, Mato Grosso, Paraguay, Uruguay, Argentina. Also called *Pássaro-frade* (Minas Gerais), *Coleira-do-sertão* (Espírito Santo). See *S. albogularis.*

LINED SEEDEATER, *Sporophila lineola,* Bigodinho   Fig. 310

11 cm. Male distinguished by white malar stripe and center steak on crown (latter sometimes smaller on *S. lineola* of northern Amazonia); female differs from others of genus in slimmer body lines, longer tail, and small bill with light yellow mandible. VOICE: a rapid, metallic warble that transforms into typical, quite resonant major cadence, *chuh,*

chuh, chuh, or even *ch, ch, ch, ch-HOOch,* with structure similar to shriller song of *S. falcirostris.* Song varies according to region. Uncultivated savannas, plantations, edge of capoeira. Migratory in Espírito Santo and Paraná, appearing in December to nest, disappearing in March and April. In eastern Maranhão appears only from May on; in Piauí has been observed nesting in May. The Guianas and Venezuela to Bolivia, Paraguay, Argentina, and Brazil to São Paulo, Mato Grosso, Goiás. In Venezuela migrants from northeastern Brazil reveal their presence by their different song (Schwartz, Vielliard pers. comm.). Also called *Estrelhinha, Cigarrinha* (Minas Gerais).

YELLOW-BELLIED SEEDEATER, *Sporophila nigricollis,* Baiano

11 cm. Male characterized by all-black head, throat, neck, breast, and tail. Back and wings olivaceous. No speculum. Underparts pale yellow or white (see below). Bill light gray. Female very similar to female *S. caerulescens* but can sometimes be differentiated by whiter throat. VOICE: a weak *plit,* a metallic *tsi* (shorter than *caerulescens*); song a short, rapid, unimpressive phrase, reminiscent of *caerulescens.* Cultivated fields, tall-grass areas; widely distributed, common in many places, having benefitted from introduction of forage grasses (see "Habitat . . ."). Costa Rica to Bolivia, Argentina, and throughout Brazil. Also called *Papa-arroz, Coleiro-baiano, Papa-capim-de-peito-preto.* Individuals with white underparts, called *Papa-arroz-de-barriga-branca,* "white-bellied rice-eater," belong to subspecies *S. n. ardesiaca,* which has sometimes been considered a separate species. It can be distinguished by gray mantle and primarily by white belly; bill may be yellowish, greenish, or whitish. This form is endemic to southeastern Brazil (southeastern Minas Gerais, Espírito Santo, Rio de Janeiro) and has a voice identical to that of yellow-bellied individuals. It nests in mountainous region of Espírito Santo from August on,

disappearing at beginning of year, but appearing periodically in other regions, e.g., Brasília (August–September), where it is called *coleiro-paulista* (P. Antas pers. comm.). Where their ranges overlap, it may occupy same locales and even hybridize with *caerulescens*.

HOODED SEEDEATER, *Sporophila melanops*   BR

11 cm. Known only in Goiás (Porto do Rio Araguaia). Similar to *S. nigricollis* but with larger, yellowish bill. Only head and throat black and shiny, contrasting with yellowish brown back. Very slight white line under eye; speculum white. Underparts brownish white, sides of breast speckled with chestnut. Along lake edges in company with other *Sporophila*.

DOUBLE-COLLARED SEEDEATER, *Sporophila caerulescens,* Coleirinho, Papa-capim   Fig. 311

11 cm. Most abundant and best-known *Sporophila* in southeastern Brazil. Male has dark gray upperparts, sometimes with tinge of green. Face, upper throat, and streak across upper breast black. Malar stripe, spot on lower throat, and belly white or yellowish. May or may not have speculum. Bill color variable: gray, yellow, greenish, or blackish, which gives rise to various popular names (*coleira-bico-laranja,* "Orange-billed Collar"; *coleira-bico-de-chumbo,* "Lead-billed Collar"; etc.). Female similar to those of *S. plumbea, S. nigricollis, S. albogularis*. VOICE: call *tsri, tslit, zheh;* song a rapid, somewhat weak warble, with phrase, after reaching its culminating point, followed by a brief, descending scale, e.g., *jewle, jewle, jewle, jewle-JEE-jewlo, jewlo-tshrrr*. Sometimes sings in flight. Different populations have different dialects even in neighboring valleys. Cage-bird fanciers have their own terminology for classifying these songs, e.g., "twi-twi" (referring to beginning of song), "sawing song" (when they fight). Female also can

Fig. 311. Double-collared Seedeater, *Sporophila caerulescens,* male.

sing. Cultivated fields, grassy patches. Centralwest and south (Bahia to Rio Grande do Sul), Uruguay to Bolivia, Peru, and on right bank of Amazon to east of Tapajós. Apparently does not occur in northeast, a region dominated by *albogularis*. Follows spread of forage grasses that produce abundant seed and has thus invaded areas where it did not formerly occur, e.g., Federal District. Disappears periodically, e.g., from mountainous regions of Espírito Santo and Rio Grande do Sul. Also called *Coleirinha-dupla, Coleira-da-mata, Paulista, Papa-capim-de-peito-amarelo;* last 3 refer to individuals with yellowish underparts.

WHITE-THROATED SEEDEATER, *Sporophila albogularis,* Golinho, Brejal   BR

10.5 cm. Typical of northeast. Male similar to male *S. caerulescens* but has less slender, conspicuously orange bill. Pectoral collar black, throat all white. Sides of neck also white, so this color can be seen even from behind. Rump and speculum also white. VOICE: a high, persistent, well-varied warble, possibly reminiscent of song of *Carduelis magellanica*. Mimics. Humid spots of caatinga, where usually abundant, and along with *S. bouvreuil,* 1 of only 2 *Sporophila* present. Northeastern Brazil in Piauí, Ceará, Pernambuco, Bahia, rarely as far south as northern Espírito Santo (Itaúnas, December) and Minas Gerais. Also called *Coleira-garganta-branca*. See *S. collaris,* which is much stockier.

WHITE-BELLIED SEEDEATER, *Sporophila leucoptera,* Chorão

12.5 cm. Relatively large, long-tailed, with heavy, yellow bill. Male, with uniformly gray upperparts, reminiscent of slender *S. plumbea*. Speculum and underparts white, latter sometimes washed with gray. Female and young brown, recalling *S. collaris* because of large bill and curved culmen. VOICE: warning, similar to *Passer domesticus,* a low *jayip, kwek;* characteristic part of song a plangent, ascending whistle, *ew-EE, ew-EE, ew-EE . . . ,* repeated unhurriedly. Low woodland intermingled among savanna and marshland. Argentina, Paraguay, Bolivia, Brazil: mouth of Amazon and northeast to Rio de Janeiro, Minas Gerais, Goiás, Mato Grosso (as far as upper Rio Xingu). Also called *Patativa-chorona, Boiadeiro* (Minas Gerais), *Bico-vermelho* (Espírito Santo). See female *Oryzoborus angolensis,* which has black bill.

BLACK-AND-TAWNY SEEDEATER, *Sporophila nigrorufa,* Caboclinho-do-sertão

10 cm. Male of this small, little-known species resembles male *S. b. bouvreuil* except that upperparts are all black, excepting ocraceous rufous rump, which is like underparts and sides of head. Also has heavier, brown-and-black bill. Open areas and savannas in central Brazil (western Mato Grosso) and eastern Bolivia. Also called *Caboclinho-campo-grande*.

CAPPED SEEDEATER, *Sporophila bouvreuil,*
Caboclinho   PL 43.3

10 cm. Generally best-known of a group of 9 small species called *caboclinhos.* There are notable color variations according to subspecies, with the following occurring in Brazil:

1. *S. b. bouvreuil (Caboclinho-verdadeiro, Fradinho).* Male reddish cinnamon with cap, wings, and tail black; large, white speculum. Northern and eastern Brazil from mouth of Amazon to Goiás and northeastern São Paulo.

2. *S. b. pileata (Caboclinho-paulista, Caboclinho-coroa-do).* Male has light grayish brown upperparts with cap black; underparts whitish, sometimes pinkish or yellowish. In Brazil restricted to São Paulo, Minas Gerais, southern Mato Grosso (see plate). Also Argentina and Paraguay.

3. *S. b. crypta (Bico-de-ferro).* Male all brown, lacking black cap of *S. b. pileata.* Never develops typical male plumage of species, remaining like female, with only certain individuals having vestiges of black on crown (which might erroneously suggest a subadult individual) or of tile red on underparts. Endemic to Rio de Janeiro (Lagoa Feia, Sick 1967b). Also called *Ferrinha.*

Female and young of all 3 subspecies brown, young males usually recognizable by larger speculum and blackish bill. After breeding season males of southern populations (*S. b. pileata* in São Paulo, *S. b. bouvreuil* in southern Minas Gerais) molt to a postnuptial or eclipse plumage, becoming similar to females. At this time not only plumage but also bill color changes, from black to yellowish (see "Morphology"). VOICE: call a strident *tslit, tsi* or a bisyllabic whistle, *ewt-eet;* song extremely varied, long, and hurried, at times resembling *Carduelis magellanica.* May also intermingle imitations among its well-pronounced, fluid, continuous phrases, composed of beautiful, resonant whistles such as *eet-ewt-ewlo-EET.* Penetrating, single whistles, e.g., *tsew-tsee, ewwist,* and rough cadences, *tserre-tserre, tarre-tarre,* resembling certain wetland birds (*Emberizoides ypiranganus* and Grass Wren, *Cistothorus platensis,* "habitat voice") are other typical components of song. Marshes, savannas with bushes, locally more abundant when grasses are in seed (see "Migration"). Amazon estuary (Amapá, Pará, Marajó Island to northeast, east, and central Brazil (to São Paulo, Goiás, and Mato Grosso south); also Argentina, Paraguay, Rio Grande do Sul (Passo Fundo), savannas north of Amazonia (Suriname). Also called *Caboclinho-lindo* (Amapá, Minas Gerais), *Coleirinho-do-brejo.*

RUDDY-BREASTED SEEDEATER, *Sporophila minuta,*
Caboclinho-lindo

10 cm. Black-billed Amazonian species. Male has olive brown upperparts except for chestnut rump. Speculum white, underparts rusty. VOICE: *tsi, tchew, tsep;* song melodious with cadences of clear, leisurely, well-pronounced whistles. Open country, cultivated fields, roadsides. In northern Amazonia common in many places. The Guianas and Venezuela to lower Amazon, Tapajós, and Tocantins; also Belém

(Pará), Amapá. Also called *Patativa* (Pará), *Curió* (Pará), *Caboclinho-do-norte.*

TAWNY-BELLIED SEEDEATER, *Sporophila hypoxantha,*
Caboclinho-de-barriga-vermelha

10 cm. Southern species, similar to *S. minuta* but with more slender, black bill. Male has light bluish gray upperparts with rump, underparts, and sides of head rusty cinnamon. Female brownish. VOICE: *tsi, tslit.* Squeaky song relatively monotonous. Savanna marshes. Migratory, e.g., appearing on São Joaquim (Santa Catarina) highlands near end of year (November, December) to nest, then disappearing immediately, as also happens with *S. melanogaster* in same area. Bolivia, Argentina, Paraguay, and Uruguay to Brazil: Rio Grande do Sul, Santa Catarina, Paraná, São Paulo, southern Mato Grosso, Goiás (migrant individuals). Also called *Caboclinho-roxinho* (Santa Catarina). See *S. ruficollis.*

DARK-THROATED SEEDEATER, *Sporophila ruficollis,*
Caboclinho-paraguai

10 cm. Adult male has bluish gray upperparts, subadult grayish brown. Upper tail coverts and underparts dark rusty, throat and upper breast black, large speculum white. Bill black or yellowish. See "Morphology" regarding non-breeding plumage. VOICE: a quiet *tsiew, jep, tsilew;* song, which resembles *S. minuta,* sung with wings half open, displaying undersides. Savannas. Argentina, Uruguay, Paraguay, and Bolivia to Brazil: Mato Grosso, Goiás, São Paulo, Minas Gerais (Pirapora, September). Individuals found for sale in markets are usually from Argentina or Paraguay. This species has been considered by some as a mutation of *S. hypoxantha,* which would then be polymorphic (Short 1969). Also called *Paraguai-ito.*

MARSH SEEDEATER, *Sporophila palustris,*
Caboclinho-de-papo-branco

9.6 cm. Small, rare, southern species, related to *S. ruficollis* and *S. hypoxantha.* Male has gray upperparts except for chestnut rump. Sides of head, throat, and breast pure, resplendent white. Belly chestnut, speculum white, bill yellowish brown. Subadult male has brown mantle, dirty white lower throat. VOICE: *tsieh, tsi-ee,* rising or falling, resembling *S. bouvreuil;* call *tslit.* Among tall grasses of types with abundant seeds, in marshes. Uruguay, Argentina, and Paraguay to Rio Grande do Sul, southern Mato Grosso (Campo Grande), Minas Gerais (upper Rio São Francisco, September); most northerly records must relate to migratory individuals fleeing effects of winter.

CHESTNUT-BELLIED SEEDEATER, *Sporophila castaneiventris,* Caboclinho-de-faixa

10 cm. Common in Amazonia. Male has bluish gray upperparts. Wings and tail black, edged gray; speculum white; bill black. Underparts have chestnut streak running down

center from throat to under tail coverts, giving bird a distinctive appearance. VOICE: *tsiep.* Grassy areas alongside rivers and lakes. The Guianas and Venezuela to Bolivia, Brazil: Acre, lower Tapajós (Pará) and São Francisco (Pirapora, Minas Gerais, September). Also called *Peito-roxo, Cabuculino* (Pará), *Caboclinho-amazonas.*

RUFOUS-RUMPED SEEDEATER, *Sporophila hypochroma*

10 cm. Gray, with sides of head, rump, and underparts chestnut, speculum white. Central Brazil, in Emas National Park, Goiás, October 1984 in a large mixed flock (*S. hypoxantha, S. palustris,* etc.) in a marshy area. (A Negret pers. comm.). Bolivia, Argentina.

CHESTNUT SEEDEATER, *Sporophila cinnamomea,* Caboclinho-de-chapéu-cinzento

10 cm. Male dark chestnut with gray cap; wings and tail black bordered with gray; larger white speculum; light yellow bill. Tall grasses. Northeastern Argentina, Paraguay, Brazil: Rio Grande do Sul (São Borja), Mato Grosso (Campo Grande, Aquidauana), Goiás, Minas Gerais (Rio São Francisco, September, see "Migration"). Also called *Caboclinho-goiano.*

BLACK-BELLIED SEEDEATER, *Sporophila melanogaster,* Caboclinho-de-barriga-preta   BR

10 cm. Typical of mountain and savanna regions of southern Brazil. Male light gray with throat, breast, belly, and under tail coverts back. Wings and tail also black. Speculum white, bill yellow or black. After breeding season adult males become brown, resembling females. VOICE: similar to *S. bouvreuil.* Nests in isolated marshes in high-altitude open country. Migratory, appearing in Santa Catarina (at 1000 m) to nest in October–November, disappearing at beginning of year (February–March). I observed it in Rio Grande do Sul while it was eating seeds of *Paspalum naumanni* (Gramineae), *Rhynchospora corymbosa* (Cyperaceae), and *Sisyrinchium macrocephalum* (Iridaceae). Southern Brazil from northeastern Rio Grande do Sul (at 980 m) to Santa Catarina, São Paulo, Minas Gerais (Campanha, Poços de Caldas, and September in Pirapora), Federal District (February, May). In Santa Catarina coexists with *S. hypoxantha* and *S. plumbea.* Also called *Caboclinho-bico-de-ferro.*

LARGE-BILLED SEED-FINCH, *Oryzoborus crassirostris,* Bicudinho

13.5 cm. Amazonian. Differs from *O. maximiliani* in smaller size, noticeable in brown individuals that are not much larger than *O. angolensis.* Another important difference is bill, which is smaller and smoother, lacking grooved bony structure on surface and any vestige of a maxillar tooth seen in *maximiliani.* VOICE: weaker than *maximiliani.* Marshy areas with bushes and trees. Relatively common on left bank of lower Amazon (e.g., Mazagão, Macapá) and in interior of Amapá (Porto Platon, during rice harvest) and

islands (Mexiana). Also on Rio Negro and farther north: the Guianas, Venezuela, Colombia, northeastern Peru. No geographic races have evolved, and there is no indication of hybridization in nature with *maximiliani,* which it meets in Amapá, proving that *crassirostris* and *maximiliani* are distinct species. Also called *Bicudo-do-norte.*

GREAT-BILLED SEED-FINCH, *Oryzoborus maximiliani,* Bicudo, Bicudo-verdadeiro

15 cm. Characterized by very thick bill which has irregular, fluted, bony structure on surface, giving it a streaked appearance. Also has a maxillar tooth. Male uniformly shiny black with greenish blue reflections, but speculum, under wing coverts, and axillaries white. Female and young dark brown, recognizable by body size and bill shape, identical to that of adult male. VOICE: a loud *jep, kwek, chok, chewk;* song rapid and flutelike, with jumps to both high and low tones and sometimes with metallic timbre. This varies considerably with origin of singer, and in classification of fanciers there are types known as "flauta," "cocotil," "araguari" (a city of Minas Gerais), etc. Female also sings, sometimes even more and better than male. Currently one of best-known and most sought-after of our songbirds, which because of changes in fashion, was not the case 50 years ago. Re singing contests, see *O. angolensis;* on song development, behavior, breeding, and molt, see subfamily introduction. Moist areas with bushes, edge of groves, marshes, etc. Central America to Bolivia, Colombia, Brazil: on northern bank of Amazon (Macapá and Mazagão in Amapá), Rondônia, Mato Grosso, Goiás, Federal District, Minas Gerais, São Paulo, Rio de Janeiro, Espírito Santo. Locally in Bahia (Poções, Boa Nova), Alagoas, southeastern Pará. Six geographic races have evolved, but only *O. m. maximiliani* is in Brazil; the others, e.g., *O. m. gigantirostris* of Bolivia, occur in north and west of continent. Wild hybrids, *O. maximiliani* × *O. angolensis,* known as bicuriós, are abnormal in appearance, spirited but lacking character, and infertile (see "Hybridization").

LESSER SEED-FINCH, *Oryzoborus angolensis,* Curió, Avinhado   PL 43.2

13 cm. Presently most highly prized songbird in Brazil. Male unmistakable, being all black except for chestnut belly, white shoulders and undersides of wings. May or may not have white speculum of widely varying size. Bill of male, female, and young varies greatly in size but is black with straight culmen. Female and young brown, without speculum, but recognizable by general appearance. VOICE: call *jewp, jep;* song a melodious, fluent phrase, distinguished by its so-called whistle or running song, a descending musical scale of loud, sonorous whistles making up a song unique among Brazilian birds. A male fighting with another gives a different vocalization, a hurried, rather unmelodious warble, commonly called *serra.* Sometimes female curió can also sing.

Variation in the Song; Contests: In this species diverse dialects have evolved in nature. Variations in song are classified by bird fanciers, usually with onomatopoeic designations (e.g., *viví-tetéo, vovô-víu, fili-fute* in Rio de Janeiro) or linked to origin of bird (*paracambi*, a city in state of Rio de Janeiro; *praia-grande* in centralsouth). A professional trainer of this species, N. P. Martins of Rio de Janeiro, has produced a cassette with a good paracambi song and had sold 50,000 through 1986. Fanciers let the tape run day and night near a young bird (singing starts at 6 months) for it to learn song. Most valued birds are those that do not "split" their song (i.e., do not interrupt melodious and fluent sequence with twitters) and those that repeat "whistle." There may be sequences of 6, 10, 13, or more repetitions in only 1 song. In fanciers' terminology, bird *está matando*, "is killing," if it sings more than any other, and is *grego*, "greek," if it does not do well. There are many enthusiasts who dedicate themselves to this pastime, many curió clubs, and a National Federation of Breeders of Bicudos and Curiós (FENABIO), with a publication, *O Bicurió*, founded in 1969.

Competitions are organized with as many as 200 curiós, where rating is based on number of points awarded, winner being bird that sings the most songs in a predetermined space of time, e.g., 5 or 30 minutes. A curió from Alagoas sang 223 songs in 30 minutes in 1972. The grand champion, "Patinho" (from Jundiaí and participant in 23 contests in 23 consecutive years, with 12 first places), achieved the notable score of 295 "singings" in ½ an hour. Three hundred to 350 songs in 25 minutes and 35–40 in 10 minutes have been claimed. Local bird, "Filipe," sang 80 songs in 5 minutes, winning National Curió Tournament in 1980. Nothing like this happens under natural conditions.

O. maximiliani also participates in contests. One in Jundiaí, São Paulo, in 1968 attracted 70 curiós and 62 bicudos. In above-mentioned 1972 contest, a bicudo achieved 292 singings in 10 minutes.

The value of a champion curió may be as high as the cost of a new car. The death of one is announced in newspapers like the passing of an important public personage. Clearly the sensational spectacle of competitions between selected cage birds becomes a sport and a business, far from the pure study of birds and their conservation. In fact, these competitions are illegal, for some participants are wild specimens captured without authorization. It is worth noting that certain types that were in great demand, e.g., the curió-tanoeiro of Jacarepaguá, Rio de Janeiro, have disappeared (Coimbra Filho 1986).

Habitat, Distribution, and Taxonomy: Lives at edge of woods and marshes, and in searching for tiririca (*Cyperus rotundus*) seeds enters forests. Mexico to Bolivia, Paraguay, Argentina. Throughout Brazil. Northern subspecies *O. a. torridus* (*curió-do-norte*) still common and differs from other in less robust bill, shorter tail. All-black individuals, with white only under wings and on speculum, can be found.

I saw 1 from Goiás. Also called *Bicudo, Peito-roxo* (Pará). Specific name, *angolensis*, is explained by an error regarding origin of first-known specimen of species (designated as coming from Angola) classified by Linnaeus in 1766. See also "Hybridization."

BLACKISH-BLUE SEEDEATER, *Amaurospiza moesta*, Negrinho-do-mato

13 cm. Strong, short, dark gray bill. Male entirely dull bluish schist color, appearing black at a distance. Only under wing coverts are white, visible just on certain occasions, e.g., when bird takes off in flight. Female rusty brown, lighter on underparts, resembles female *Oryzoborus angolensis*. VOICE: call *psit, pix;* song a sweet, soft warble with timbre of *Passerina brissonii* song: *dzew, dzew-tseweelo-dzew, dzew,* repeated regularly at short intervals. Two to 3 m above ground in interior of dense secondary forest or tall forest intermingled with araucarias (Rio Grande do Sul). Paraguay, Argentina (Misiones), Brazil: Maranhão, Rio de Janeiro (Itatiaia, Serra dos Órgãos), São Paulo, Paraná, Rio Grande do Sul. Very local in eastern Brazil. In Rio Grande do Sul sometimes alongside *P. brissonii*. See *Tiaris fuliginosa* and *Haplospiza unicolor*.

WHITE-NAPED SEEDEATER, *Dolospingus fringilloides*

12 cm. Thick, conical bill. Male black except for white on nape, shoulder, speculum, rump, and belly. Female cinnamon brown with throat and center of abdomen whitish. Secondary vegetation, plantations. Venezuela, extreme northern Brazil along upper Rio Negro.

PARAMO SEEDEATER, *Catamenia homochroa*, Patativa-da-amazônia

13.5 cm. Male blackish slate, set off by chestnut under tail coverts and yellow bill. Female olive brown with streaked upperparts, chestnut crissum. Bushy areas in mountains. Colombian Andes, Venezuela, Venezuelan-Brazilian frontier (Roraima).

SOOTY GRASSQUIT, *Tiaris fuliginosa*, Cigarra-do-coqueiro

12.3 cm. Male entirely dark sooty but sometimes tends toward coal black or olivaceous. Female has dark gray-brown upperparts almost totally lacking in greenish tonalities, light upperparts with whitish abdomen. Both sexes have dark brown legs. Bill thick, black in male, black with yellow mandible in female. VOICE: a high, strident phrase, *TSEEriri-ree*. Grassy areas at forest edge, marshes, gardens, etc. Frequents fruiting bamboos (see "Feeding"). Venezuela, Colombia, southeastern and southwestern Brazil, locally from Pernambuco to São Paulo, Minas Gerais, Mato Grosso. Also called *Trigolino* (Minas Gerais), *Cigarra-preta, Cigarra.*

May be confused with *Haplospiza unicolor* but is smaller, has heavier bill, dark legs, and lacks bluish cast of *unicolor*. Female not streaked underneath. Unlike *Volatinia jacarina* and *Amaurospiza moesta*, lacks white under wings. See also *Sporophila frontalis* and *S. falcirostris*.

PECTORAL SPARROW, *Arremon taciturnus*, Tico-tico-do-mato-de-bico-preto   PL 43.5

15.3 cm. Singular forest species, reminiscent of *Zonotrichia capensis* without a crest. Male head and breast sharply contrasting black and white, back green, chin black (not visible in plate). Bill all black, bend of wing and epaulet golden yellow in *A. t. taciturnus* of northern, central, and eastern Brazil; yellow in wing less pronounced and bill yellowish in southern subspecies. *A. t. semitorquatus*, of mountainous regions of Espírito Santo, Rio de Janeiro, São Paulo, Rio Grande do Sul. Female similar to male, differing in slightly brownish underparts, broken black collar. VOICE: call a high, mouselike *bis-bist;* a squeaky phrase of approximately 4 syllables, initially rising, then descending, *see-see-see-see*, resembling Chestnut-headed Tanager, *Pyrrhocoma ruficeps*, sometimes its neighbor. Constructs a voluminous, spherical nest on ground (see "Breeding"). Low levels, often hopping on ground at edges of thick forest, which it never leaves, conspicuous even in deepest shade because of bright color pattern. The Guianas and Venezuela to Bolivia; right bank of Amazon from Madeira, upper Tapajós and Xingu, and Rio das Mortes (Mato Grosso) to Goiás, eastern Pará, Maranhão, and Piauí to Pernambuco, Bahia; eastern Brazil from eastern Minas Gerais, Espírito Santo, and Rio de Janeiro (mountainous areas) to Rio Grande do Sul. Also called *Pai-pedro, Coroado, Salta-caminho* (Ceará), *Jesus-meudeus* (Bahia), *Tico-tico-coleiro* (Minas Gerais). See *A. flavirostris*.

SAFFRON-BILLED SPARROW, *Arremon flavirostris*, Tico-tico-de-bico-amarelo

Extremely similar to *A. taciturnus* but always with reddish yellow bill; also has white chin. Back may be green *A. f. flavirostris* of Bahia, western Minas Gerais, northern and central São Paulo, southern Goiás, Mato Grosso, western Pará, Paraguay, Argentina) or gray (*A. f. devillii* of western São Paulo, southern Mato Grosso, Bolivia). Reported as sometimes occurring in central Brazil (Bahia, Mato Grosso, northeastern São Paulo) alongside *A. taciturnus*, with which it appears to form a superspecies.

BLACK-STRIPED SPARROW, *Arremonops conirostris*

15.6 cm. Resembles an *Arremon* in appearance but with less color contrast. Head gray with 2 black stripes on either side, chin grayish green, underparts white with breast gray. Bill blackish with base of mandible yellowish. VOICE: totally unlike *Arremon:* a short, melodious phrase of well-pronounced notes, *tsieww-tsie, tsie, tsie, tsie, tsie-tsieww*, resembling an *Icterus* oriole. Honduras to Colombia and Andean foothills but only in extreme north of Brazil, in Roraima, where common.

TEPUI BRUSH-FINCH, *Atlapetes personatus*

16.5 cm. Stocky with aspect of a thraupine; dark gray above, yellowish below, sides of throat rusty. Low or on ground, lurking in thick vegetation. Only in Roraima in mountainous region of Venezuelan-Brazilian frontier; also Mexico to Argentina.

COAL-CRESTED FINCH, *Charitospiza eucosma*, Mineirinho   PL 43.7

11.3 cm. Notable for nuchal crest in both sexes. Bill very pointed. Male has unusual coloring: black, white, and rusty yellow (see plate). Female brown with black wings, white speculum (also present in male), yellowish underparts. VOICE: call a high, insectlike *tsi-tsi;* a dawn song comprising a modest 3-part phrase, *tsli-tsli-tslewi*, sung while perched prominently on end of a branch. Low in bushes or trees in cerrado or caatinga. Hops on ground to feed. Forms small flocks. Argentina (Misiones), Brazil: southeastern Pará and interior Maranhão to Piauí, Bahia, Minas Gerais, northern São Paulo, Goiás, Mato Grosso. In Goiás disappears at beginning of rainy season. Also called *Vigilante* (Minas Gerais), *Bavezinho* (São Paulo).

BLACK-MASKED FINCH, *Coryphaspiza melanotis*, Tico-tico-do-campo

13 cm. Unique savanna species. Cap and sides of head black; superciliary long, shiny, white (reminiscent of *Arremon*); underparts all white. Also white spots on tips of tail feathers. Mantle greenish with chestnut brown streaking, bend of wing yellow. Maxilla black, mandible yellow. Although referred to as "females," individuals with brown heads (without black), speckled breasts, and dull mandibles are probably immatures. VOICE: a strident *tsri*, a soft *spit*, resembling *Poospiza;* song a squeaky, bisyllabic *TSEErr-i*. Savannas with low vegetation, runs on ground, perches up on stems of grasses and herbs to sing. Goiás, Mato Grosso, Minas Gerais (Pocos de Caldas), São Paulo, Marajó (Pará, see "Distribution . . ."); also Bolivia, Paraguay, Argentina. Occurs with *Emberizoides herbicola* and *Ammodramus*.

YELLOW CARDINAL, *Gubernatrix cristata*, Cardeal-amarelo   PL 42.11

19.2 cm. Southern savanna species, unmistakable with long, black crest it raises vertically. Plumage green and bright yellow. Female has white superciliary and malar stripe, gray breast. VOICE: call *tsip;* a clearly pronounced 4- or 5-part cry with last note accented, *kewi-kewooee-tsi-WIT*, with an indistinctly pronounced following part as if bird had already outreached itself; a loud, squeaky whistle while vibrating wings. Overgrown savanna; walks on ground while feeding. Argentina and Uruguay to southern Rio Grande do Sul.

GRAY PILEATED-FINCH, *Coryphospingus pileatus*, Galinho-da-serra

13.3 cm. Closely related to *C. cucullatus*, which it replaces in eastcentral Brazil. Male has gray upperparts with black base to crest, center of which is scarlet, as in *cucullatus*. Underparts washed with gray. Female grayish brown on upperparts, whitish below with breast and sides streaked with gray. When bird is calm red does not show, with only a narrow longitudinal black streak in center of crown and no sign of a crest. As restlessness increases, a surprising red streak appears in midst of black which often is scarcely noticed. When excitement peaks, maximum effect is visible with all of crown feathers erected vertically, displaying a brilliant, large red area set off on each side by narrow black streaks that resemble 2 horns when seen from front. VOICE: call a soft *tsig*, similar to *cucullatus*; song a hurried sequence of approximately 6 low-volume *jiWIT-DWITs*; a more resonant cadence of repeated *ss-ss-szrs*, slightly resembling song of *Volatinia jacarina*. Low, dry, sparse woodlands, restinga, caatinga. Range is as disjunct as that of *cucullatus*: northern Venezuela, Colombia, and Brazil in northeast, east (to ex-Guanabara and Minas Gerais: Belo Horizonte, Sete Lagoas, Pirapora, Vale do Jequitinhonha, Januária), and center (Goiás, Federal District, Mato Grosso—upper Xingu, upper Juruena). May be conspecific with *cucullatus*. Also called *Cravina*, *Tico-tico-rei-cinza*, *Tico-tico-do-sertão* (Minas Gerais), *Abre-fecha* (Minas Gerais).

RED PILEATED-FINCH, *Coryphospingus cucullatus*, Tico-tico-rei   PL 43.8

13.3 cm. Widely distributed, replacing *C. pileatus* in southern, central, and western Brazil. Male unmistakable in generally dark brownish red color and crest distinguished by scarlet base. Female has dark brown upperparts; reddish rump and underparts; white around eyes and on chin. VOICE: call *tsik*; song a rapidly repeated 3-part phrase, e.g., *jewlew-jewlew jewlewt*, sometimes sung in flight at dusk; dawn song *tswit-TSWIT-tsit*, also rapidly repeated. Sparse, low secondary woodland and cerrado, close to ground or on it, moving around noisily with long hops in dry leaves. Abundant in certain areas. Present range includes 2 completely disjunct areas: 1st is in the Guianas and eastern Pará (Belém); 2d is from Mato Grosso (Cuiabá, Xavantina, Rio das Mortes) and Goiás to western Minas Gerais (Ituiutaba, Uberlândia, Uberaba, Araxá), São Paulo, Paraná, Santa Catarina, Rio Grande do Sul, Uruguay, Paraguay, Argentina, Bolivia, Peru. In Mato Grosso, Goiás, and western Minas Gerais approaches *pileatus* and overlaps with it in certain areas,

where they hybridize. I have a hybrid from Brasília and have seen various others in captivity, all of unknown origin except 1 from Minas Gerais. Because these hybrids are fertile (Machado 1980), *pileatus* may be considered a subspecies of *cucullatus*, which is the older species. I prefer to maintain them as species or semispecies. Also called *Vinte-um-pintado*, *Galo-do-mato*, *Cravina*, *Foguinho*.

RED-CRESTED CARDINAL, *Paroaria coronata*, Cardeal

18 cm. Southern species, quite similar to *P. dominicana* but unmistakable with large red crest (bright in male, pale in female) which is constantly held erect. Upperparts uniformly light gray, bill whitish. Immature brownish with rusty crest. VOICE: a harsh *chirip*, resembling *Passer domesticus;* a soft *wit;* the song varied, a cadence of short, full, separate whistles with timbre of a thrush, *tsilewp-jewp* repeated or *dew-dewe-duh-dew-diuh;* a fluent warble, phrases such as these sung together by pair; sometimes sings subsong; in captivity imitates other birds, e.g., thrushes. Savannas mixed with higher vegetation, along river edges. Sings from tops of trees or isolated bushes. Argentina to Bolivia, Paraguay, Uruguay, and Brazil in Rio Grande do Sul and southwestern Mato Grosso (Pantanal) where it meets *P. capitata*, with which it appears to compete, for number of pairs is reduced in that region in contrast with abundant *capitata*. Introduced into Hawaii and Caracas, Venezuela. Is a geographic replacement of *dominicana* of northeastern Brazil, with which it hybridizes in captivity, producing fertile offspring. Also called *Galo-de-campina* (Mato Grosso).

RED-COWLED CARDINAL, *Paroaria dominicana*, Galo-de-campina   BR   PL 42.10

17.2 cm. One of most typical birds of interior of northeastern Brazil. Red head plumage short and erect, with velvet appearance, especially on nape of male. Unlike *P. gularis*, lacks black "necktie." Upperparts gray except for upper back, which has feathers that are black at ends and white at base, giving area a black-and-white scaly appearance. Lower back and upper wing coverts spotted with black. Maxilla blackish, mandible light gray. Female crown appears smoother. Immature has blackish brown upperparts, white belly, rusty throat. VOICE: a hoarse cry, *qwaik, jeh-jet;* both sexes sing sonorously and monotonously, a series of 12 consecutive, loud, monosyllabic whistles, partly twittered and partly as subsong; also a flowing warble, resembling an Old World starling (Sturnidae). Low, sparse, sunny woodlands (caatinga), where sometimes is most abundant bird. Walks and hops on ground to feed. Northeastern Brazil from southern Maranhão to interior Pernambuco. Has expanded its range, occupying new areas (southern Bahia 1975; Minas Gerais, Pirapora 1973). Pairs escaping from cages may breed freely, as in Rio de Janeiro (Niterói, Santa Cruz, Ilha das Enxadas). It is one of species bearing heaviest burden of illegal wild-bird trade. Also called *Cabeca-vermelha, Cardeal-do-nordeste.*

RED-CAPPED CARDINAL, *Paroaria gularis,* Galo-de-campina-da-amazônia

Amazonian, a bit more slender than *P. dominicana.* Upperparts all black, throat red with black "necktie"; bill slender and black with base of mandible pinkish white; legs black. Immature head and rest of upperparts brown, throat cinnamon, maxilla and legs black, base of mandible white. VOICE: call *chap, chelep;* song a 2-phased *tooWiT-TSEEeh,* repeated unhurriedly; a varied, melodious, rapid warble. Sometime mimics. River edges, várzea forest. The Guianas, Venezuela, and Amazonia south to Bolivia, Acre, northwestern Mato Grosso (Guaporé), Pará (lower Tapajós—Jacareacanga, lower Araguaia, Tocantins), northwestern Goiás. Also called *Cardeal, Tangará* (Amazonia).

CRIMSON-FRONTED CARDINAL, *Paroaria baeri*　BR

Replaces *P. gularis* in heart of central Brazil. Black upperparts, "necktie," black also extending to head, where only cap and "mustaches" are very dark shade or red but feathers are bright with white shafts. Bill black, base of mandible lighter, legs dark gray. VOICE: a distinct *tshrik,* resembling a *Ramphocelus* tanager; song a vigorous, descending phrase of harsh whistles, *chewk-chik-chewk-chewk.* Riverside forests, low above water or in small flocks in canopy. Western Goiás (Rio Araguaia, Ilha do Bananal), Mato Grosso (Rio Cristalino, upper Xingu). Similar to *P. gularis* and *P. capitata;* all 3 may be considered allospecies composing a superspecies.

YELLOW-BILLED CARDINAL, *Paroaria capitata,* Cavalaria

Very similar to *P. gularis,* its geographic replacement, but with entire bill and legs light yellow, orange, pink, or whitish. Marshes, river edges, savanna. Bolivia to western Mato Grosso (Pantanal), Argentina, Paraguay. Common in Pantanal, where it occurs in dense flocks (from which it derives common name *cavalaria,* "cavalry"). Also called *Cardeal, Galo-de-campina-do-oeste.* See *P. coronata.*

A combined Emberizinae and Cardinalinae bibliography follows the Cardinalinae species accounts.

SUBFAMILY CARDINALINAE (17)

The introductory text on the Cardinalinae is combined with that of the preceding subfamily, the Emberizinae.

YELLOW-GREEN GROSBEAK, *Caryothraustes canadensis,* Furriel　PL 42.9

17 cm. Very characteristic species, yellow with black mask. Bright color and voice might suggest a thraupine. VOICE: song a short, loud, unmelodious whistle, squeaky at beginning, *chree GLEEeh-GLEEeh.* In small flocks, frequently associated with other birds, e.g., saíra tanagers, when they visit fruit trees. Edge of forest, orchards. Panama to Amazonia and eastern Brazil from Minas Gerais to Espírito Santo, Rio de Janeiro (ex-Guanabara, Serra do Mendanha). Also called *Canário-do-mato* (Espírito Santo). See *Periporphyrus* female.

YELLOW-SHOULDERED GROSBEAK, *Caryothraustes humeralis*

Upper Amazon (Rio Purus), Pará (Carajás).

RED-AND-BLACK GROSBEAK, *Periporphyrus erythromelas,* Bicudo-encarnado

20 cm. Only in Amazonia. Bill even larger than that of *Caryothraustes canadensis.* Plumage magnificent. Male has black head and throat, rest of body pink, a bit lighter on underparts. Female has black head like male but upperparts olivaceous, underparts orange. High terra-firme forests at middle levels. The Guianas and Venezuela to lower Amazon (Belém, Pará). See *Piranga* tanagers and Masked Crimson Tanager, *Ramphocelus nigrogularis.*

BLACK-THROATED GROSBEAK, *Pitylus fuliginosus,* Pimentão　Fig. 312

22.5 cm. Large, long-tailed, with enormous red bill. Plumage very dark bluish gray with blackish wings and tail.

Fig. 312. Black-throated Grosbeak, *Pitylus fuliginosus.*

Upper throat black in male, gray in female. Under wing coverts white. VOICE: call, warning a strident *psieh, ksee, gaoot, ksAAY;* song short, sonorous, often 2-phrased, *drewit-WOTju.* There are regional differences in song (see "Vocalization"). Dense forest, sometimes alongside Magpie Tanager, *Cissopis leveriana.* Bahia and Minas Gerais to Rio Grande do Sul, Argentina (Misiones), Paraguay. Also called *Bico-pimenta, Guaranisinga* (São Paulo).

SLATE-COLORED GROSBEAK, *Pitylus grossus*

19 cm. Replaces *P. fuliginosus* in Amazonia. Very similar to it but with center of throat white. VOICE: a song similar to *fuliginosus,* a bi- or tripart sequence, *dewlit-dewdewlit-deway.* Nicaragua to Bolivia, Juruá, (Acre, Amazonas), lower Tapajós, eastern Pará, northern Maranhão. Also called *Bico-de-pimenta-da-Amazônia.*

BUFF-THROATED SALTATOR, *Saltator maximus,* Tempera-viola

19.5 cm. Very similar to *S. similis* but with entire upperparts green, including both faces of tail. Upper throat white, lower throat and under tail coverts rusty, malar stripe and bill black. VOICE: call a soft *tsic, tsip,* a metallic *ting-ting-ting;* a short, soft, ascending sequence with questioning inflexion, *jewluh-JIT,* which is immediately "answered" by same individual with a descending sequence, *jew-luh-loh,* the 2 parts together resulting in a single, well-finished phrase that may recall Rufous-browed Peppershrike, *Cyclarhis gujanensis;* also more prolonged cadences. Edge of forests and plantings. Forages in medium-level foliage. Mexico to Paraguay, central and eastern Brazil. Locally syntopic with *S. similis* (e.g., lowlands behind Rio de Janeiro). Does not enter into mountainous areas. Also called *Sabiá-pimenta, Trinca-ferro, Sabiá-gongá* (Pará, Pernambuco), *Estevam* (Bahia). See *S. maxillosus,* which also has yellow throat; Olive-green Tanager, *Orthogonys chloricterus; Embernagra platensis,* a savanna species.

GREEN-WINGED SALTATOR, *Saltator similis,* Trinca-ferro-verdadeiro   PL 42.8

20 cm. Best-known *Saltator* south of Amazonia. Strong bill (thus the name *trinca-ferro,* "bite-iron," used for all *Saltator*), ample tail. Very similar to *S. maximus* and *S. coerulescens,* with upperside green except for tail, which is schist-colored below and above. Throat white (sometimes yellow in center), malar stripe bordered white, cheeks schistaceous. Juvenal breast and abdomen streaked black. VOICE: a loud *tsip,* a low *ghi-ghew-ghew;* song not as soft as *maximus* and very clear—a phrase of 5 limpid whistles with 2d and penultimate higher, latter with strong emphasis: *dew-dee dew-DEE-dew* (ex-Guanabara), interpreted as *bom-dia-seu-chico* (Petrópolis); phrasing changes according to region. Juvenal cheeps *iew.* Forest edge, both in lowlands (sometimes alongside *maximus*) and mountains. Central and south-

eastern Brazil from Bahia to Rio Grande do Sul; also Bolivia, Paraguay, Argentina, Uruguay. Also called *Esteves* (Bahia), *Tico-tico-guloso, Bico-de-ferro, Pixarro.*

GRAYISH SALTATOR, *Saltator coerulescens,* Sabiá-gongá

20 cm. Widely distributed, very similar to *S. maximus* and *S. similis* but differing from them in dark coloring, almost without green tints, of upperparts. Tail blackish, throat with vestige of yellow, abdomen rusty. Juvenal has greenish back and breast, gray spots on bill. VOICE: a phrase with 4–5 or a few more loud whistles, reminiscent of *Paroaria dominicana, joop, joop joop-dewuh;* at times duets with female, which sings simple phrases, rough sequences of *chap, chap, chap.* River edges, marshes, overgrown savannas. At any level in trees. Descends into grassy patches. Mexico to Bolivia, Argentina, Uruguay, Brazil (Amazonia, Bahia, Maranhão, Piauí, Mato Grosso). Also called *Trinca-ferro-da-Amazônia.*

THICK-BILLED SALTATOR, *Saltator maxillosus,* Bico-grosso

19.5 cm. Conspicuous because of high, thick bill, yellow at base. Male upperparts dark gray, almost without green. White superciliary starts at base of bill. Underparts ferruginous. Female has green back; immature has green upperparts, black bill. VOICE: a phrase with 4 loud notes, the 3rd higher. Sings from August on (Serra da Bocaina). Forest edges, gardens, locally in high mountains of southeastern Brazil where it is dominant *Saltator.* Sometimes alongside *S. coerulescens.* Espírito Santo (Serra do Caparaó) to Rio de Janeiro (Serra do Itatiaia, among others), from there to northeastern Rio Grande do Sul, eastern Argentina. Also called *Botió.* See *S. aurantiirostris.*

GOLDEN-BILLED SALTATOR, *Saltator aurantiirostris,* Patetão

20 cm. Quite similar to *S. maxillosus* but has "normal" bill, not exceptionally thick, with orange design on mandible. Wide, yellowish postocular stripe. Throat yellow with black collar across lower throat. VOICE: a short, resonant phrase with timbre of *Paroaria dominicana, tsew-tswee-eh, tsip, tsip-CHEEeh,* sung both at dawn and during day. Dense riverine forests, etc. Argentina to Bolivia, Peru, Paraguay, and Brazil in southern Mato Grosso, Rio Grande do Sul. Apparently hybridizes naturally with *maxillosus* in Corrientes, Argentina.

BLACK-THROATED SALTATOR, *Saltator atricollis,* Bico-de-pimenta

20 cm. Unmistakable savanna species with black mask and foreneck, reddish orange bill. Upperparts brownish gray, underparts light yellowish gray. Juvenal upperparts, head, and foreneck brown, bill blackish, underparts striated.

VOICE: call (diagnostic for species) resembles a *Forpus* parrotlet, a high *pist, biditz;* song a short, stereotyped phrase, *tsibele-BEETsehwi,* sung alone while in horizontal flight from one tree to another or in a small flock of 2–3 companions perched near each other with no show of aggression. Various individuals may make a collective clamor during early morning hours, calling *buit.* Behavior of *atricollis* differs from other *Saltator,* more resembling that of a thraupine such as *Ramphocelus.* Cerrado, similar open country; moves about on ground and on roads, cocks and lowers tail. Paraguay, Bolivia, and Brazil from Mato Grosso and Goiás to interior of eastern regions (e.g., Serra dos Órgãos, Rio de Janeiro) and the northeast. Also called *Batuqueiro.*

GLAUCOUS-BLUE GROSBEAK, *Passerina (= Cyanoloxia) glaucocaerulea,* Azulinho

14.5 cm. Southern species, almost a miniature *P. brissonii* but less stocky, with longer legs and relatively small bill, black on maxilla, whitish on mandible. Male bluish with gray or greenish tones. Lacks conspicuous bright blue areas on head and wings of *brissonii.* Female differs from female *brissonii* more in size than color. VOICE: warning *psit, jet;* song rapid and flowing, without appreciable modulation; smooth timbre may recall paruline *Geothlypis aequinoctialis* (which sometimes inhabits same areas). Edge of low forest, bushes in humid, riverine lowlands, marshes, river islands (e.g., upper Rio Paraná), sometimes alongside *Sporophila collaris.* Argentina and Uruguay to western São Paulo, southern Mato Grosso, Paraguay. See *Amaurospiza moesta.*

BLUE-BLACK GROSBEAK, *Passerina (= Cyanocompsa) cyanoides,* Azulão-da-amazônia

16 cm. In Brazil we have impression that this is Amazonian replacement for *P. brissonii,* which it greatly resembles, differing in a bit longer and less swollen bill. Female well distinguished from female *brissonii,* by being darker brown, especially on underparts. VOICE: warning a loud *spit;* song entirely unlike *brissonii* a sequence of 4–6 clear, monotonous notes followed by a lower one, less emphatic: *tsew, tsew, tsew, tsew, tsew-tsewlew.* Middle levels in forest interior, capoeirão, riverine vegetation, igapó forest. Mexico to northern South America, from there as far as Bolivia, northern Mato Grosso (upper Xingu), eastern Pará (where relatively common in secondary growths), northern Maranhão.

ULTRAMARINE GROSBEAK, *Passerina brissonii (= Cyanocompsa cyanea),* Azulão, Azulão-verdadeiro   PL 43.1

15.5 cm. Well known in southeastern Brazil through songbird traffic. Bulky, black bill. Male entirely dark blue except for brilliant blue forehead, superciliary, loral spots, and part of upper wing coverts. Female and immature all brown, a bit lighter on underparts. VOICE: call, warning *jet, kweh;* song full and melodious, quite intense, flowing, and extensive,

alternating higher cadences with some lower ones. Sings a different song at dusk and dawn. In tangles and at edge of marshes. Goes to top of bushes and trees of medium height to sing. If excited ruffles head feathers. Northeastern Brazil to Rio Grande do Sul; also central Brazil (Goiás, Mato Grosso to Rio das Mortes and Cuiabá), Bolivia, Paraguay, Argentina, northern Venezuela, Colombia. In Mato Grosso approaches range of *P. cyanoides.* By a decision of the International Commission on Zoological Nomenclature, species is now designated *Passerina brissonii* to avoid confusion with Indigo Bunting, *P. cyanea,* a North American species that migrates to South America. Also called *Azulão-bicudo, Gurundi-azul, Tiatã, Azulão-do-nordeste, Azulão-do-sul.* See *P. glaucocaerulea* and *Amaurospiza moesta.* See also "Hybridization."

BLUE FINCH, *Porphyrospiza caerulescens,* Campainha-azul

13 cm. Slender savanna species with thin, conical, orange bill, reddish legs. Male uniformly dark blue, female has reddish brown upperparts, brownish white underparts streaked brown. VOICE: very high and metallic, song a tinkling, reminiscent of *Ammodramus humeralis.* Open savanna and cerrado. Runs on ground among stones and low grasses, flies well, perches on high branches to sing. Bolivia and Brazil: Maranhão and southeastern Pará to Piauí, Bahia, western Minas Gerais, Goiás, Federal District, Mato Grosso. Also called *Azulinho-de-bico-de-ouro.*

BLACK-BACKED GROSBEAK, *Pheucticus aureoventris,* Rei-do-bosque   SV

20 cm. Upperparts, head, throat, and upper breast black; belly yellow; wings and tail with white design. Immature brown instead of black, has spots on underparts. VOICE: a soft *gooIP;* song resembles a *Paroaria* cardinal. Forests, in canopy. Venezuela to Bolivia, Argentina, Paraguay. Only in extreme southwestern Brazil (western Mato Grosso, Cáceres, Miranda, August). Appears occasionally in illegal bird trade, for it is a good singer.

DICKCISSEL, *Spiza americana*   NV

12.5 cm. Northern immigrant which, when it arrives in Brazil, is in nonbreeding plumage, resembling a female *Passer domesticus* but differing from it by chestnut epaulet, yellowish breast. Open country. Winters irregularly in northern South America, including Brazil, in Roraima (March). English name, Dickcissel, is onomatopoeic. See "Migration" and Bobolink, *Dolichonyx oryzivorus* (Icterinae).

Emberizinae and Cardinalinae Bibliography
See also General Bibliography

Andrade, F.F.M. 1976. *O Criador de Bicudos e Curiós.* São Paulo: Nobel.

Bock, W. J. 1964. *Wilson Bull.* 76:50–61. [Bill]

Carvalho, C. T. 1957. *Bol. Mus. Paraen., Zool.* 2. [*Volatinia jacarina,* behavior]

Clark, G. A., Jr. 1972. *Auk* 89:551–58. [Foot]

Coelho, A. Galileu M. 1975. *Not. Biol. Recife, PE* 4:25–27 [Anting]

Coimbra Filho, A. F. 1986. O aspecto negativo da participação de pássaros de procedência selvagem em competições de canto. *Bol. FBCN* 21:191–200.

Coimbra Filho, A. F., and D. M. Teixeira. 1982. Sobre um caso de ginandromorfismo bilateral em *Oryzoborus crassirostris. Rev. Bras. Biol.* 42:377–79.

Flecha, E. A. 1985. *SOBoletim* 1(5):1–7. [*Sicalis,* mutations, etc.]

Flecha, E. A. 1987. Criação e mutação de curió. *Atual. Orn.* 17:8.

Harrison, C.J.O. 1967. *Wilson Bull.* 79:22–27. [Scratching]

Henniger, J. 1962. *Farbenkanarien, Lehrbuch f. Farbenkanarienzüchter. Maximiliansau*:83–90. [Domestic canary × various "fringillids"]

Jackson, H. D. 1972. *Rhodesia Science News* 6:342–48. [Periodicity of bamboo and Estrildidae]

Kaiser, K. A. 1972. Manuscript. [Ethology]

Kumerloeve, H. 1954. *Ciência e Cultura* 6:7. [Gynandromorphism]

Lordello, L.G.E. 1951. Pequena contribuição à história natural de alguns Fringillidae do Brasil. *An. E.S.A. Luis de Queiroz* 8:650–62.

Lordello, L.G.E. 1957. Duas aves híbridas da fauna brasileira. *Rev. Bras. Biol.* 17(1):139–42.

Lougheed, S. C., and P. Handford. 1989. Night songs in the Rufous-collared Sparrow. *Condor* 91:462–65.

Machado, L.O.M. 1974, *Reun. Soc. Bras. Progresso da Ciência 26, Recife.* [*Tiaris fuliginosa,* nesting]

Machado, L.O.M. 1980. "Alguns aspectos do comportamento e da biologia de *Sicalis flaveola.*" Thesis. Universidade de São Paulo.

Machado, L.O.M. 1982. Notas sobre a reprodução de *Sporophila albogularis* em cativeiro. *Iheringia, Zool.* 61:81–89.

Machado, L.O.M. 1982. Poligamia em *Sicalis flaveola. Rev. Bras. Biol.* 1(1):95–99.

Meyer de Schauensee, R. 1952. A review of the genus *Sporophila. Proc. Acad. Nat. Sci., Philadelphia.* 104:153–96.

Meyer de Schauensee, R. 1970a. *Notulae Nat.* 428. [*Oryzoborus crassirostris,* distribution]

Miller, A. H., and V. D. Miller. 1968. *Caldasia* 10:83–154. [*Zonotrichia,* behavior]

Nottebohm, F. 1969. *Condor* 71:299–315. [*Zonotrichia capensis,* dialects]

O'Brien, C. E. 1968. *Auk* 85:323. [*Embernagra longicauda,* distribution]

Oliveira, R. G. 1984a. *An. Soc. Sul-Riogr. Orn.* 5:7–9. [*Sicalis flaveola,* gynandromorphism in]

Oliveira, R. G. 1984b. Hibridismo em "Cardeal-do-Sul," *Paroaria coronata. An. Soc. Sul-Riogr. Orn.* 5:11–14.

Oliveira, R. G. 1987. A reprodução do bicudo em ambiente doméstico. *Sulornis* 8:6–11.

Pereira, C. 1941. *Arqu. Inst. Biol. S. Paulo* 12:175–95. [Explosive proliferation of rats]

Schwartz, P. 1975. Solved and unsolved problems in the *Sporophila lineola/bouvronides* complex. *Ann. Carnegie Mus.* 45:277–85.

Short, L. L. 1969. *Wilson Bull.* 81:216–19. [*Sporophila,* relationships]

Sick, H. 1950. *Rev. Bras. Biol.* 10(4):465–68. [*Paroaria baeri xinguensis*]

Sick, H. 1962. *Bol. Mus. Nac. Rio de Janeiro, Zool.* 235. [*Sporophila ardesiaca*]

Sick, H. 1963. *Proc. 13th Cong. Int. Orn., Ithaca*:161–70. [Hybridizations]

Sick, H. 1967a. *J. Orn.* 108:218–20. [*Coryphaspiza melanotis marajoara*]

Sick, H. 1967b. *An. Acad. Bras. Ciênc.* 39:307–14. [*Sporophila bouvreuil crypta*]

Sick, H. 1979. *Bull. B.O.C.* 99(4):115–20. [*Emberizoides ypiranganus,* rediscovery in Brazil]

Silva, J. M. 1988. Novo registro de *Sporophila intermedia* para território brasileiro. *XV Cong. Bras. Zool., Curitiba*:482.

Skutch, A. F. 1954. *Life Histories of Central American Birds,* vol 1. Pacific Coast Avifauna 31:19–121. Berkeley, Calif.: Cooper Orn. Soc.

Stahl, J. 1984. *Gef. Welt* 108(4):105. [*Volatinia jacarina,* breeding]

Vaurie, C. 1964. Chapters Bunting and Finch in A. L. Thomson, ed., *A New Dictionary of Birds.* New York: McGraw-Hill.

Weber, T. 1985. *Condor* 87:543–46. [*Volatinia jacarina,* behavior]

Ziswiler, V. 1965. *J. Orn.* 106:1–48. [Use of bill]

Subfamily Icterinae: American Orioles and Blackbirds (35)

This Oscine subfamily is an exclusively New World group. Of North American origin, it soon spread to South America where it has achieved its greatest diversification. Today it is distributed from the Arctic to Tierra del Fuego. There are Pleistocene fossils from Florida and Minas Gerais. It is related to the Emberizinae, also of American origin. My observation that a Chestnut-capped Blackbird, *Agelaius ruficapillus,* has crossed with females of the domestic canary demonstrates clearly that affinity exists with the Carduelinae of the Old World. I have also learned of a cross between a male Shiny Cowbird, *Molothrus bonariensis,* and a female Red-crested Cardinal, *Paroaria coronata* (in captivity, Rio Grande do Sul). The pair produced two young, one of which developed normally. Icterines are nine-primaried Oscines (see also Oscines) that resemble the starlings (Sturnidae)[1] of the Old World because of what appears to have been analogous evolution.

Icterines have nothing in common with the weavers (Plo-

[1]The Common Starling, *Sturnus vulgaris* (Sturnidae), was introduced into the United States and the Antilles, where it has become a pest. It reached Venezuela clandestinely but disappeared (Sick 1968a). It seems to be starting to conquer the Buenos Aires, Argentina, area but has not yet been recorded in Brazil.

ceinae) of Africa, contrary to the opinion of some laypeople who are influenced by the woven nests of various icterines such as oropendolas. It can be said, however, that ecologically speaking, *Agelaius* corresponds to the ploceid *Euplectes*, whereas *Sturnella* (including *Pezites*) corresponds to *Macronyx*, an African motacillid (Fry 1983).

Morphology

The group is heterogeneous in size and color. All icterines have a smooth, conical bill, in many cases extremely sharp-pointed, like the tips of pincers or a compass. In the *Psarocolius* and *Cacicus* the upper base of the bill is swollen and projects over the forehead. In the *Psarocolius* oropendolas, which have often been grouped under the genus name *Gymnostinops*, there is a bare, light red area below the eye (see Olive Oropendola, *Psarocolius bifasciatus*). It is advantageous that none of the icterines have long plumage in front of the eyes so their view is not obstructed while indulging in their peculiar habit of scrutinizing the area between the tips of the open mandibles during the act of gaping (see "Feeding"). In icterines an adaptation of the skull evolved from the gaping technique, in the sense that the eye is at the level of the bill commissure and not above it. The bills of the *Molothrus* are similar to those of emberizines, but their behavior is typical of icterines. There are no bristles around the bill in this subfamily. The legs and toes are strong.

Black and yellow colors predominate. The yellow is frequently localized on the upper wing coverts, on the epaulet; it may be confined to the smaller coverts, next to the humerus, in which case it is visible only when the bird stretches its wings (Yellow-winged Blackbird, *Agelaius thilius*). It may be more extensive (Epaulet Oriole, *Icterus cayanensis*) or may reach the median coverts (Golden-winged Cacique, *Cacicus chrysopterus*), both cases in which it is quite visible even when the bird is at rest. Yellow in the tail, when present, as in the oropendolas and Yellow-rumped Cacique, *C. cela*, becomes very visible when the tail feathers are spread or in flight. Some, such as the *Icterus*, are among the most colorful birds on the continent. In captivity the bright yellow fades, but it may be reactivated at the next molt with doses of canthaxanthin. Splendid scarlets occur in the Red-breasted Blackbird, *Sturnella militaris*, and others.

In *Sturnella* (including *Leistes* and *Pezites*) there is a barred pattern on the tail and internal secondaries. *S. militaris* achieves its beautiful nuptial dress of red and black through wear on the feathers of its basic plumage. Abrasion thus becomes a desirable process for beautification. The contrary—unwanted abrasion of the plumage—comes in the case of this same terrestrial bird's wing feathers, which are greatly exposed to constant wear from the cutting effect of grass. This situation brought about the evolution of lengthened internal secondaries (tertiaries) that cover the wingtip, for abrasion affects the upper feathers first, excessive wear interfering with flight capacity. In such species molt of the tertiaries twice a year becomes necessary. The tip of the tail, which lacks any protection, continuously breaks (see also Motacillidae, "Morphology," *Anthus*). The Bobolink, *Dolichonyx oryzivorus*, a bird that makes extremely long migratory flights, molts its entire plumage twice a year (including wing and tail feathers). One of these molts, the prenuptial, occurs during its stay in South America.

The subadult male *Agelaius ruficapillus* is black with varying degrees of brown on the feather edges, apparently corresponding to the subadult Blue-black Grassquit, *Volatinia jacarina* (Emberizinae).

The oropendola have nuchal crests. The Chopi Blackbird, *Gnorimopsar chopi*, and Forbes' Blackbird, *Curaeus forbesi*, have shiny, stiff feathers on their crowns. In general, icterine plumage is thick and smooth. The birds give off a characteristic smell, similar to that of cockroaches, which is penetrating in the large species. Water in which they bathe becomes covered with a bad smelling scum. It is interesting that 400 years ago Fernão Cardim (see Chapter 2.1) noted that the oropendola has "a very strong smell when it becomes irritated." The smell, more noticeable in colonial species, is from the feathers, not the skin.

All icterines have this smell, which is typical for the subfamily. Even a small icterine colony can develop a strong odor that attracts insects. Bare nestlings have little odor, at least to our weak sense of smell, but enough to be a strong attraction to parasitic flies. I observed a *Molothrus bonariensis* chick in a Rufous-collared Sparrow, *Zonotrichia capensis*, nest. It was full of *Philornis* larvae, whereas the *Z. capensis* chicks had not been attacked by the flies. Cardim's comment may have been an example of anthropomorphism: equating the smell of the birds to the sweat of people.

Iris color is notable in various cases, for instance, yellowish white in the Troupial, *Icterus icterus; Cacicus chrysopterus;* and *Quiscalus;* light blue in *Cacicus cela, Psarocolius decumanus,* and *P. viridis;* and red in *P. bifasciatus* and *Scaphidura*. Iris color changes with age, and there are also sexual differences.

Some very similar species live alongside one another, such as *Molothrus bonariensis* and the Screaming Cowbird, *M. rufoaxillaris;* the two *Pseudoleistes;* and *Gnorimopsar chopi* and *Curaeus forbesi*. Identification of the numerous black species requires careful attention, for knowledge of the voices does not always facilitate the matter.

Sexes are different in color, as in the *Agelaius* and *Sturnella militaris*, which are marsh or savanna species, or similar, as in the Brazilian *Icterus* (there is accentuated sexual dimorphism in North American *Icterus*). Only the females of the various geographic races of the Unicolored Blackbird, *Agelaius cyanopus*, are recognizable (heterogynism, see Formicariidae, "Morphology"). Near the lower base of its mandible the male *Psarocolius bifasciatus* has a bare fleshy cushion that turns violet when filled with blood.

There are great size differences between the sexes in species in which the male and female are similar in color, such as the polygamous *Psarocolius, Cacicus,* and Giant Cowbird, *Scaphidura oryzivora,* the first-named living in colonies in the forest, the last a parasite. The male may weigh twice what the female does. I have learned that this size difference is interpreted by the Indians of Central Brazil and Amazonia as a mark of caste: the small females are the workers, the big ones the captains, or caciques (*cacique* = "chief" in Taino, the language of the Arawak tribe of Hispaniola, which has various representative groups in northern Brazil). I think it probable that the scientific name *Cacicus,* given in 1799 by Lacèpéde, is derived from the word *cacique,* brought with these birds by the first traveling naturalists. The name has been used in various languages, for example by Prince Maximilian of Wied in 1831, *die Cassicken* (covering *Cacicus* and *Psarocolius*), and in English, *caciques* (just for *Cacicus*).

Female and immature *Agelaius, Sturnella militaris,* and others are a modest, streaked brown that is difficult to describe in a few words. Cinnamon-colored mutants occur in nature in *Gnorimopsar chopi, Molothrus bonariensis,* and *Icterus icterus jamacaii,* for example; albinos have also been found in nature, in *G. chopi* in Minas Gerais, and individuals with isolated white feathers in *Scaphidura* on the Xingu in Mato Grosso and in *Psarocolius* (see Pl 39.2). There are almost no icterines that are similar to birds of other groups. *Dolichonyx oryzivorus* might pass for an emberizine. *Molothrus bonariensis* resembles a *Tachyphonus* tanager or a young Scarlet-throated Tanager, *Sericossypha loricata.* *Sturnella militaris,* with a scarlet throat, resembles *Sericossypha* in adult male plumage. It is noteworthy that the Eastern Meadowlark, *Sturnella magna,* distinctively icterine, is very much like an African Yellow-throated Longclaw, *Macronyx croceus,* of the Motacillidae: an example of convergent evolution having occurred in similar terrain—campos and savannas respectively.

Vocalization

Most of the voices are whistles. *Icterus icterus* and *Gnorimopsar chopi* are among those birds with the most melodious voices of Brazil, motivating the Portuguese colonists to call *I. icterus* "*rouxinol*", "nightingale," the name of the best singer of Europe (*Luscinia*). It is, however, entirely different in aspect and voice. It is impossible to convey a convincing impression of these songs through graphic descriptions, so one can only call attention to certain characteristic elements that may permit recognition of the species. Caged and wild *Cacicus cela,* for instance, sometimes imitate to perfection the voices of other birds and mammals, separating each imitation without mixing them. Sometimes they include voices of nightbirds and even group related species, imitating, for instance, first a toucan and then an aracari. Males of a *C. cela* colony have the same song type,

different from that of other colonies (Feekes 1977). Females of various species also sing but do not always achieve the mastery of the males; the female *Icterus cayanensis,* however, sometimes sings even better than the male.

Icterines assume the most grotesque positions when singing, making bows, sometimes hanging under the perch, or shaking the wings violently to produce an intense noise (instrumental music). A vertical stretch of the neck is frequent, in which the bird may touch its throat with its bill. Such displays are very characteristic of the subfamily and are duplicated, with certain modifications, in various species, suggesting a closer relationship of some groups, the "black" blackbirds, for instance, to which should be added the Oriole Blackbird, *Gymnomystax mexicanus,* a largely yellow species. In general these displays tend to make the individual appear larger than it really is.

In captivity *Icterus icterus* learns any sound and can also reproduce music, such as the national anthem. It switches, sometimes brusquely, the pitch and tonality of its voice and also the rhythm of the song, to the point of giving the impression that two birds are singing at once. Some, such as *Cacicus chrysopterus,* can also sing whisper song. Sometimes a voice will have a unique tone, nasal to our ears, resulting from certain simultaneous harmonics. The Bay-winged Cowbird, *Molothrus badius,* has a notable dawn song.

Marsh and open-country species such as the *Agelaius* and *Sturnella* often sing in flight; their voices ordinarily dominate in várzeas and swamps. They also sing at roosts, and when gathered in hundreds in a clump of bamboo *Agelaius ruficapillus* or the Red-rumped Cacique, *Cacicus haemorrhous,* make a stupifying clamor with their singing and screeching. The calls and warning notes of many species are very similar. The type of alarm given in a colony is different from that used outside the area. Other birds living near oropendola colonies also react to their alarm calls. Certain notes are uttered only by young after leaving the nest, to facilitate their being found by adults feeding them (location call, see *Molothrus bonariensis*).

Feeding

Food is mixed, varying even among individuals of the same species and depending on the season of the year. The method of locating hidden food is extraordinary: using a technique called "gaping," icterines introduce the closed, sharp-pointed bill into a fruit, or into elastic or fluffy material such as buds, rolled leaves, flowers, honeycombs, rotten wood, or under bark, and then open the mandibles, forcing open the material being inspected and making a hole that permits them to look inside and eventually withdraw the food or suck the juice. This activity involves a distinctive position for the eyes. Tame troupials force open the closed fingers or lips of their owners this way, showing with what great force they can apply this technique—a great natural invention that is also used in nest construction. They have a special muscular adaptation: enlargement and special insertion of the mandibular depressor (Beecher 1950, Zusi 1959). The purpose of this extremely sharp-pointed bill is thus not only to serve as a pincer. The Scarlet-headed Blackbird, *Amblyramphus holosericeus,* hammers like a woodpecker on soft vegetable materials then gapes and withdraws the food it finds. The European Starling, *Sturnus vulgaris,* and Sturnidae in general, as well as Corvidae, Coeribinae, and some non-Brazilian Passerines, use the same technique.

Among the fruits most sought by *Gnorimopsar chopi* and *Icterus icterus jamacaii* are the mature nuts of the buriti palm (*Mauritia*). The same *Icterus* adores the nectar contained in the flower of mandacaru (*Cereus jamacaru*), a tree cactus typical of the northeast, and it eats the flowers of the yellow ipê [*Tabebuia* sp.]. It also likes the large red mandacaru fruits, which it opens with its sharp bill, facilitating subsequent exploitation by other birds such as doves and the Red-cowled Cardinal, *Paroaria dominicana.* The Solitary Cacique, *Cacicus solitarius,* seeks flowers of the algodão-do-brejo (*Hibiscus tiliaceus*). I have found *Cacicus haemorrhous* in flowering mistletoe (*Psittacanthus*) bunches. I believe icterines, like thraupines, contribute greatly to pollenization. *Sturnella militaris* eats shoots of herbaceous plants as well as seeds and insects.

Scaphidura oryzivora turns over small stones, hunts ticks by perching on pigs, cows, and horses, rummages in garbage, and accompanies cattle to catch fleeing insects, the way anis and cowbirds do. Cowbirds perch on sheep to broaden their hunting horizon and on occasion pick insects from the thick wool of these animals. *Agelaius ruficapillus,* walking through a muddy pasture, will turn over any clod of earth, sticking its bill underneath, lifting and throwing it to the side to discover food. *Molothrus bonariensis, Gymnomystax mexicanus,* and *Gnorimopsar chopi* like to stir up cattle excrement (*Vira-bosta,* "turd-turner"), perhaps in search of undigested grains rather than fly larvae. *Agelaius thilius* and *A. cyanopus* inspect floating leaves with the typical technique of gaping. *Gnorimopsar chopi* and the *Molothrus* eat insects killed on roads. *Cacicus haemorrhous* sometimes catches insects in flight, like flycatchers do. Oropendolas, *Cacicus cela,* and Carib Grackles, *Quiscalus lugubris,* sometimes raid bird nests; they catch termites on termite nests or in the air and enjoy cecropia (*Cecropia* spp.) fruits. *Q. lugubris* doesn't even spurn centipedes. *Psarocolius bifasciatus* and *Sturnella militaris* sometimes use the toes to hold a prey item, including even a flower, before eating it.

Behavior

Icterines fly well, producing a noticeable, loud whisper with the remiges, as in *Icterus icterus* and *Scaphidura oryzivora.* After each few wing strokes they fold the wings against the body momentarily. *Amblyramphus holosericeus* flies with some difficulty. On the ground icterines walk with erect posture. The *Molothrus,* especially *M. badius,* run and hop on the ground with the tail half-cocked. The *Agelaius* run on top of floating plants and creep through reeds with each foot clinging to a separate stem, like rails and herons.

On the important and unique technique of gaping, employed during the search for food, see "Morphology" and "Feeding."

Surprisingly, the behavior of *Gymnomystax mexicanus,* which being predominantly yellow appears to be related to the *Icterus* group, more closely approximates that of certain "black" blackbirds.

The gregarious tendency of some icterines is more evident in the wetland types, which sometimes gather in hundreds or even thousands in one place during certain periods. *Agelaius ruficapillus* is the most numerous bird in some localities (e.g., Rio Grande do Sul). In certain regions *Molothrus bonariensis* flocks are just as large. The different species usually remain in separate flocks, but sometimes one flock will associate with another, as for example, 80 *M. bonariensis,* 20 Brown-and-yellow Marshbirds, *Pseudoleistes virescens,* and 6 Saffron-cowled Blackbirds, *Xanthopsar flavus,* seen together in Rio Grande do Sul.

The flocks of "black" blackbirds that attack rice fields demonstrate what is called "social mimicry" (Moynihan 1960), the association of bird species sharing similar color and plumage patterns (note our saying "birds of a feather flock together"). These birds, living in the same habitat, are usually related and have adapted to a similar diet. *Volatinia jacarina,* an emberizine, associates with black icterines.

In Amazonia oropendola flocks provide an impressive late-afternoon spectacle, sounding a certain call at short intervals as they fly over the forest on the way to their colonial roosting sites, perhaps on river islands. These flights recall the corresponding activity of parrots and macaws. In Espírito Santo during the breeding season I observed an intense movement of *Cacicus haemorrhous,* which in late afternoon flew very low toward certain cattail marshes and returned at dawn to the forest. Various icterine species may be found at roosting sites in reedbeds.

Breeding

Scaphidura oryzivora and Crested Oropendola, *Psarocolius decumanus,* pairs preen each other. There are outstanding prenuptial displays. I have seen interspecific courting, a presumed male *Molothrus rufoaxillaris* greeting an apparent female *M. bonariensis,* which, however, did not respond to his gallantry.

Icterine breeding is especially interesting, for it offers great variety: the full scale of normal conditions, from monogamous to polygamous species, even within the same genus: whereas *M. rufoaxillaris* is monogamous, *M. bona-*

riensis lives promiscuously. There is also unqualified parasitism. Three phases can be distinguished: (1) species that build and rear young in their own nests; (2) species that do not construct nests but use nests of other species, where they then rear young normally; and (3) parasitic species that have lost not only the ability to build a nest but also the instinct to care for their young.

1. Species that build a nest where they rear young. There are four types of nesting:

1.1. This group makes an open nest, deep and well lined (*Pseudoleistes* add mud), placed in a fork that may be low or some meters above ground, sometimes among palm fronds (*Agelaius ruficapillus, Gymnomystax mexicanus*); the nest may be arranged in the grass (*Xanthopsar flavus*), sometimes over water (*Agelaius thilius*). The *Agelaius* tend to form colonies: the Tricolored Blackbird, *A. tricolor,* of California gathers in groups of thousands of pairs. *Sturnella militaris* builds a shallow cup on the ground that is open above but well protected by the overhanging dry grass in which it is situated. Some *Sturnella* are said to make a covered or semicovered nest with side entrance. These semiterrestrial birds resort to feigning to lead possible enemies away from the nest.

1.2. The nest of *Amblyramphus holosericeus* is ellipsoid in shape with a small side entrance and is made of woven straw fixed to the reeds 1 m above the water.

1.3. These weave a bag suspended from a branch or end of a palm frond. The various species can be distinguished by the length and breadth of the bag, the form and placement of the entrances, the material used, and the finish. The nest of *Icterus cayanensis,* for example, is relatively short and loose, made of broad, dry stems that are conspicuous because they are yellow. The nest of *Cacicus chrysopterus,* likewise solitary, is long and densely woven of black "vegetable horsehair" (hyphas of the *Marasmius* fungus[2]) or Spanish moss (*Tillandsia usneoides*) (fig. 313). A slit in the narrow upper portion serves as an entrance—in contrast to the bag nests of certain Tyrannidae, such as *Tolmomyias,* in which access is below and whose walls are pasted instead of woven. It is interesting to compare these nests with those of African weavers, relatives of the House Sparrow, *Passer domesticus.*

Oropendola nests are also made of Spanish moss if it is available and reach 2 m in length. At the bottom of the bag is a cushion of dry leaves, etc. Two or three weeks are required to finish construction (*Psarocolius decumanus*). When two nests happen to touch each other along the surface, the respective owners lace them together.

While studying *Cacicus haemorrhous* I found three nests firmly united for their full length: one nest was normal, but the other two had entrances from underneath and presumably were serving just as dormitories. Icterines with hanging nests close up the entrances better when rain starts to enter. They usually make a new nest for each clutch, frequently alongside the old one (whose bottom sometimes falls out). This is more

[2]*Marasmius,* horsehair fungus, is also used by many birds in Africa (Collias and Collias 1964).

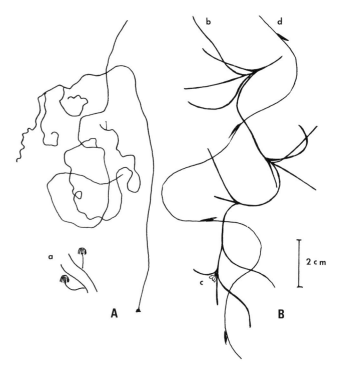

Fig. 313. Building material of Passerine nests: (A) "Vegetable horsehair" (*Marasmius* sp.) taken from the nest of a Golden-winged Cacique, *Cacicus chrysopterus,* Minas Gerais: (a) cap with spores of the fungus, enlarged; (B) Spanish Moss (*Tillandsia usneoides*), Teresópolis, Rio de Janeiro: (b) live stem, with (c) a flower; (d) dead stem, with the green part rubbed off, giving it a thinner appearance. Original, H. Sick.

easily observed in solitary species such as *Cacicus chrysopterus:* a neighboring nest is sometimes an unoccupied old one. Used nests may also be mended.

Strong winds may blow down hanging nests containing eggs or nestlings. I have known of cases where the parents continued feeding nestlings in a nest that had fallen to the ground. Nests are also destroyed by heavy rains, an important limiting factor as to the timing of the breeding season. *Psarocolius decumanus* lays two or three clutches per year (Rio de Janeiro). It is said that in Peruvian Amazonia, the Band-tailed Oropendola, *Psarocolius (= Ocyalus) latirostris,* binds its nests to the leaves of the tree with the result that all the nests fall periodically, together with the leaves (Koepcke 1972).

The *Cacicus* (excluding the two former *Archiplanus*) and *Psarocolius* form colonies. Each is normally confined to a single tree, such as a buriti palm (Mato Grosso, *P. bifasciatus*). Colony size varies greatly. I recorded one with 59 *C. haemorrhous* nests, not counting the old ones (Espírito Santo). There are much larger colonies of *C. cela* and of *Psarocolius.* Mixed colonies occur, with some *C. haemorrhous* associating with a flock of *P. decumanus,* or *C. cela* with *P. bifasciatus yuracares,* each species occupying a certain part of the tree, but with the *Cacicus* more concentrated. In the midst of these colonies it is customary to find a large wasp nest, a hive of bees, or various ant nests (see fig. 228, Tyrannidea); the bees (*Trigona,* Meliponidae) have no sting but often bite. This symbiosis, apparently self-evident and so easy to explain, in final analysis has a totally unexpected basis: saving icterine nestlings from a double parasitism that constitutes the greatest danger to their lives. Because of the strong odor of these birds (see "Morphology"), *Philornis* flies are attracted in incalculable numbers. As many as 30 flies may be seen flying around a nest. Further, the *Philornis* are parasitized by mites that then move onto the birds—a hyperparasitism that aggravates the problems of the nestlings, which often die (Smith 1978 and many other publications).

It has been discovered that the presence of Hymenoptera reduces the penetration of *Philornis* in an icterine colony to a minimum. The *Trigona,* installed in arboreal termite nests, circulate all day around the tree's canopy, preventing the passage of other insects, many of which are potential Hymenoptera predators. Among these insects are the *Philornis,* which have no interest in the Hymenoptera but are prevented from attacking the icterine nests. Active pursuit of *Philornis* by Hymenoptera has not been observed. When a Hymenoptera nest is removed from the colony, the icterine abandon the area.

It cannot be just coincidence that birds associating with Hymenoptera build closed nests. Nestlings are just as subject to attack by insects as are adults. Doubtless being covered with feathers is a good protection, but icterine feathers are no better protection against stings than feathers of other birds, such as toucans. When toucans want to raid icterine nests, they are driven away by the Hymenoptera, which also attack the icterines when they are building their nests but fail to expel them.

Although it is the birds that seek Hymenoptera as neighbors, the latter may also enjoy advantages from the relationship: protection of their honey and larvae from predatory birds (e.g., Black Caracara, *Daptrius ater,* and Gray-headed Kite, *Leptodon cayanensis*) that are attacked by the Hymenoptera but also, to a certain degree, by the associated birds, especially the quarrelsome Piratic Flycatcher, *Legatus leucophaius,* a sure resident of so many *Cacicus* colonies (see "Enemies . . ."). In Central America, where Smith (see above) worked, *Myiozetetes* flycatchers also associated with icterines.

Neither must it be purely by chance that *Cacicus* and *Psarocolius* frequently select trees with smooth, tall trunks. Another *Cacicus* defense consists of establishing themselves over water. Sometimes nests are placed so low they are almost reached by floods (*C. haemorrhous,* Espírito Santo).

Among forest species living in colonies (oropendolas, *C. cela, C. haemorrhous*), the female alone normally takes charge of nest construction (see fig. 316) and care of the young. With these icterines polygamy (polygyny) governs, especially in those cases where there is accentuated sexual dimorphism: the males are much larger but fewer than females (this is obvious in the oropendolas). The number of males in colonies is not constant, being greater during the founding period. Determination of the numerical relationship of the sexes in colonies is hampered by the presence of smaller, younger males not recognizable as such, for they share the plumage color of the females and are not obviously larger.

Color banding has begun to reveal some of the complicated details of hierarchy in colonies. Males become dominant adults at three to four years (they live five to six years). The larger, dominant females hold the safest nesting places in the colony; smaller, lower-ranking females must nest on the periphery.

Small colonies, such as ones with three *C. haemorrhous* nests, may be attended by three pairs, the males helping a little in building the nests and participating in feeding the nestlings. The principal function of large oropendola males in their colonies is that of sentinel; they aggressively attack invaders, sometimes with help from the females.

A group of oropendola nests swinging in a high tree is one of the most attractive sights offered by Neotropical forests. I have found them described in early reports on Brazil, among them that of Fernão Cardim in the sixteenth century.

1.4. Gnorimopsar chopi usually breeds in holes but manages to adapt to various conditions. It even uses eroded sandstone cliffs, such as those existing in Vila Velha, Paraná. In some cases it pads the chamber amply, at other times it uses little or none. It appears to be on the way to losing the instinct to build its own nest, approaching the situation of the species dealt with in the following section.

2. Species that occupy nests of others for breeding. Some icterines use other birds' nests to rear their young (nest parasitism or kleptoparasitism, the latter being more used for stealing food; see, for example, the Magnificent Frigatebird, *Fregata magnificens*). Among these are *Icterus icterus* and *Molothrus badius.* Both prefer the large stick nests of furnariids such as the Common Thornbird, *Phacellodomus rufifrons.* I have never seen *I. icterus* touch a piece of nesting material; it merely inspects the nests of others and finally lays in the one it likes best. *M. badius* is reportedly capable of building a nest of its own. *I. icterus* sometimes behaves aggressively against birds whose nest it occupies, expelling them and even pulling out the nestlings and throwing them to the ground when it lays its own eggs in the nest; it does incubate *Molothrus bonariensis* eggs. G. Mattos has seen an *Icterus i. jamacaii* feed a young *Cacicus solitarius* in two regions of Minas Gerais. Surprisingly, Anita Studer saw a pair of *I. icterus* in Alagoas carrying grass to build their nest in a hole in a palm tree.

3. Parasitic species. It is well known that *Molothrus bonariensis* lays its eggs in nests of the Rufous-collared Sparrow, *Zonotrichia capensis.* Up to the present 58 bird species have been recorded as victims of *M. bonariensis* in Brazil. This parasitic action is very different from that of the common cuckoo, *Cuculus canorus,* of Europe, whose parasitism evolved independently. One of the basic differences is that the recently hatched *M. bonariensis* does not have the unpleasant instinct that causes *C. canorus* to empty the nest by throwing out everything in it, be it eggs or nestlings. Compared with the perfected parasitism evolved in *C. canorus*, *Molothrus* adaptations are few. The young *M. bonariensis* is often reared along with its stepsiblings, but it is more common for the latter to die for lack of space and because they are less vigorous in requesting food. The parasites, developing more rapidly than the host young, move ahead from the start. *M. bonariensis* is polygamous and is distinguished by an excess of males.

Brazil has another parasitic species in the genus: *Molothrus rufoaxillaris*. Its parasitism is selective. In the south, in the center of its range, it lays in the nests of *M. badius* (see item 2). I have confirmed that in Paraná *M. rufoaxillaris* parasitizes *Gnorimopsar chopi*. One more parasite, *Scaphidura oryzivora*, is also selective, specializing in laying in the bag nests of *Cacicus cela* and the *Psarocolius*.

Eggs and Young

Eggs are elongated and have a thick shell both in nonparasitic and parasitic species. The shell of an *M. bonariensis* egg is 30% thicker than might be expected from the size of the egg (Spaw and Rohwer 1987). *Psarocolius decumanus* eggs in Rio de Janeiro had partially faded violet-red marbling on an off-white background. There are bluish gray eggs with a small black design (*Gnorimopsar chopi*, usually a clutch of four). *Amblyramphus holosericeus* lays light blue eggs speckled with black. The recently discovered egg of *Curaeus forbesi* is similar. In *Gnorimopsar chopi* incubation lasts 14 days and is performed by the female alone. The time the young remain in the nest varies; whereas *M. bonariensis*, a parasite, requires only 11 or 12 days, 18 days have been reported for *G. chopi* and 30 or more for large species such as *Psarocolius bifasciatus*. *M. bonariensis* nestlings lack the instinct of self-preservation: if a person disturbs a *Zonotrichia capensis* nest, for instance, the young sparrows jump from the nest, but the cowbird chick remains. *G. chopi* and *C. forbesi* nests are sometimes attended by various individuals, helpers at the nest.

Distribution and Evolution

The northwest corner of the continent has the greatest concentration of icterines, with 23 species. Another center is in the open-country and marshy regions of Rio Grande do Sul and Uruguay, where there are 17 or 18 species. In Rio de Janeiro (ex-Guanabara) I have recorded 7 species.

The distribution of icterines throughout vast regions of this continent and the separation of populations as a result of climatic and phytogeographic changes have resulted in the evolution of very distinct geographic races, as in *Gnorimopsar chopi*, *Icterus cayanensis*, *I. icterus*, and *Sturnella militaris*. Some populations, much altered during their prolonged isolation, later came into contact again and intermingled over extensive areas. This happened, for example, with two forms of *I. cayanensis* in the center of the continent and with *Psarocolius bifasciatus* south of the Amazon. The latter case was a phenomenon corresponding, to some extent, to what occurred with two toucans to the north and south of the Amazon (fig. 314).

Geographic races of *Agelaius cyanopus* have evolved that

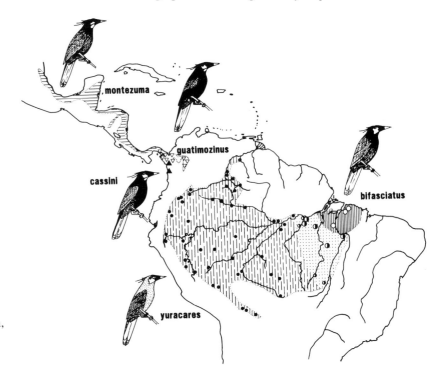

Fig. 314. Distribution of the Olive Oropendola and allies, *Psarocolius bifasciatus* superspecies (modified after Haffer 1974b). Open circles and vertical hatching: *P. b. bifasciatus*. Closed circles and vertical dashes: *P. b. yuracares*. Half-solid circles and stippling: *P. b. "neivae"* (hybrid zone between *P. b. bifasciatus* and *yuracares*). Open triangles: Black Oropendola, *P. guatimozinus*. Closed triangles: Baudo Oropendola, *P. cassini*. Horizontal hatching: Montezuma Oropendola, *P. montezuma* (individual records are not plotted). Symbols denote locality records.

are distinguishable only in the females and immatures, whereas the corresponding adult males are uniformly black in each region ("heterogynism," see Formicariidae, "Morphology").

Sturnella magna provides evidence of a recent invasion from North America. Populations living today in northern South America, including northern Brazil, are extremely similar to the eastern North American form, an interesting zoogeographic phenomenon. Among migrants, those originating in the eastern part of North America predominate, rather than those from the western part, as one might expect.

Species such as *S. magna* and *S. militaris* benefit from deforestation, constantly broadening their area of dispersal. On the invasion of eastern Brazil by the former, see Chapter 4.2.

Agelaius blackbirds are considered the most primitive icterines, whereas the *Psarocolius* oropendolas pass as the most evolved. *Molothrus badius,* a brown bird, appears to be an ancestral type as compared with its black congeners, *M. bonariensis* and *M. rufoaxillaris.* It is most interesting that the young *M. rufoaxillaris* has a plumage pattern very similar to that of the *M. badius* adults that rear it.

Migration

Species resident in the south, such as *Sturnella militaris* and *Molothrus bonariensis,* seek other climes during the winter. The tendency of icterines to move about becomes evident when, for instance, a flock of *Agelaius ruficapillus* appears on an oceanic island such as the Moleques do Sul, Santa Catarina (Lenir A. Rosário). *Dolichonyx oryzivorus,* a migrant from North America during the northern winter, crosses the Caribbean and comes from the Venezuelan coast directly to central Brazil and Argentina, apparently one of the most extensive migrations know for Passerines on this continent. After half a year's absence it returns to its breeding grounds in Canada and the United States. On movements at roosting time, see "Behavior."

Parasites and Nest Fauna

Nestlings are frequently infested by botflies. In a single *Zonotrichia capensis* nest in which one *M. bonariensis* and two sparrows were reared, I found 52 larvae of the dipteran *Philornis obscura* pupated in the bottom of the nest (Rio de Janeiro). In the Municipality of Rio de Janeiro, *M. bonariensis* nestlings in *Z. capensis* nests are sometimes so severely parasitized by these bloodsucking larvae that they die. In this way the sparrow nests are freed of the introduced cowbirds, permitting the sparrow nestlings to develop normally, for they are little or never parasitized by the botfly. In one *Z. capensis* nest in the Municipality of Rio de Janeiro I found an already grown cowbird parasitized by 14 *Philornis angustifrons* larvae. Its stepsibling had no larvae at all. I suppose the smell of *M. bonariensis* attracts the flies. Young

Scaphidura oryzivora pick off botfly eggs and larvae from their stepsiblings, thus even saving their lives (Smith 1978).

I have also found many botfly larva on *Cacicus cela, C. haemorrhous,* and *Psarocolius bifasciatus* nestlings. The last-named customarily have lice on the skin of the head. At night they are bothered by mosquitos. I have frequently found nematodes, perhaps transmitted by mosquitos, under the eyelids of *P. bifasciatus.* The parasite *Oxyspirura cassici* has been discovered in the eye of *Cacicus haemorrhous,* whereas *O. cephaloptera* lives in the eye of *Icterus i. croconotus.*

There is no special, abundant nest fauna in the hanging bag nests of icterines, for this type of nest is much less durable than, say, the compact homes of the furnariids. I have found casual residents in *Cacicus haemorrhous* nests, such as assassin bugs (*Emesa* sp.), ants, and tree frogs, all animals for which the bird nest is a simple extension of their natural habitat on tree branches.

Enemies and Relations with Other Birds

Among enemies that raid bag nests of *Cacicus cela,* etc., are snakes, monkeys, aracaris, and the Roadside Hawk, *Rupornis magnirostris.* I was amazed to see in Piauí how two nonpoisonous snakes, the caninana (*Spilotes pullatus*) and jararacuçu-do-brejo (*Dryadophis bifossatus*), managed to take *Gnorimopsar chopi* nestlings from nesting holes high above the ground in buriti palms.

It has been reported that a whole colony of oropendolas will sometimes attack aggressors with screeches, wing beats, and pecks. I have observed little defense in the case of attacks by toucans. When male oropendolas give the alarm, the females abandon their nests and dive into the lower level of the forest. I did see a *Cacicus haemorrhous* pursue a vulture that was flying by. *C. haemorrhous* will tolerate a Saffron Finch, *Sicalis flaveola,* occupying an old nest on the edge of the colony.

Neal Smith has called attention to the fact that bees and wasps are the best defense for a colony. He has seen these insects attack a *Daptrius* caracara, for instance. They also attack the icterines, but these are not much bothered by them.

Scaphidura oryzivora, a notorious parasite, creates serious problems when it comes to lay in a nest. This makes it all the stranger that *Scaphidura* nestlings pick off *Philornis* eggs and larvae from their stepsiblings. Fraga (1984) saw a *Molothrus badius* pull out botfly larvae from its parasitic stepsibling, *M. rufoaxillaris.* Birds pulling larvae off themselves is perhaps more widespread. A. Studer found vestiges of holes left by botfly larvae in the skin of young Crested Becards, *Pachyramphus validus,* taken from their large enclosed nests, that could only have come from mature larvae that left the birds and fell to the bottom of the nest to pupate— or from larvae extracted by the birds themselves, or perhaps more probably, by the parents.

The case of the Piratic Flycatcher, *Legatus leucophaius,* a regular tenant in *Cacicus cela* and oropendola colonies, is different. It is not a parasite in the same sense as *Scaphidura* but takes over a nest for its own breeding purposes (nest parasitism). Not content with an old nest, it demands a new one in which an icterine is laying or incubating. Its impertinence is so great that it may even expel an entire small colony (see fig. 228, Tyrannidae).

The indifference of most *M. bonariensis* victims to this dangerous parasite is surprising: they do not recognize any immediate peril from it. Yet the cowbird is aggressive and will attack a Yellow-headed Caracara, *Milvago chimachima*, that comes near, just like other Passerines. I mentioned under "Breeding" the aggressiveness of *Icterus icterus*. I once saw a female *Scaphidura oryzivora* inspect three nests in a *Psarocolius bifasciatus* colony without any oropendola reacting.

The frequent association of *Xanthopsar flavus* with the Black-and-white Monjita, *Heteroxolmis dominicana*, a tyrannid, still awaits a reasonable interpretation. While I noted it cursorily in Rio Grande do Sul in 1966, W. Belton made systematic observations over a period of years (Belton 1985). We have not discovered any interaction between the two species, such as, for example, feeding together. It has been confirmed that it is *Xanthopsar* that follows *Heteroxolmis*, and that *Heteroxolmis* does not follow the icterine.

Interfamilial and Intergeneric Crossing

A male *Agelaius ruficapillus* living in captivity with two female domestic canaries produced a total of seven descendants in eight months. Canaries belong to the Carduelinae (Fringillidae). Five of the offspring died while small, age 2 to 27 days. A sixth, which looked like a badly shaped canary, died at a bit less then eight months. Only one of the young, which looked like a female *A. ruficapillus*, grew well. Later it was proven really to be a female when mated with a male canary (Flávia Silveira Lobo). One young was hatched from their first clutch, thus proving the fertility of the hybrid female. I have known of other crosses between *A. ruficapillus* or *Molothrus bonariensis* and emberizines in captivity, such as with *Paroaria coronata*, *P. dominicana*, and *Sicalis flaveola* (see Oliveira 1984). In Mexico there has been hybridization between two *Icterus* species in the wild (Olson 1983). Such hybridization is not surprising when one considers the close relationship of these birds as indicated by electrophoretic and hemoglobin analyses (Sibley 1970).

Harmfulness, Use, Longevity, and Popularity

Rice, sorghum, and cereal crops in general are attacked, primarily by *Molothrus bonariensis* but also by some *Agelaius*, especially *A. ruficapillus*, *Gnorimopsar chopi*, and *Dolichonyx oryzivorus*; *G. chopi* also attacks recently planted corn, pulling up the shoots. In the interior of the country they often speak of "blackbirds," referring to various black species that are crop pests, such as *Molothrus*, *Agelaius*, and *Gnorimopsar*. These flocks are reminiscent of the hated flocks of starlings in Europe and the U.S. that are frightened away (not eliminated!) by broadcasting their alarm calls through an automatic electronic device, the modern successor of noisy urchin guards who stayed all day in the rice fields. We need more observations and stomach-content analyses to better understand the diet of these birds. It is possible that the great quantity of insects, including pest insects, consumed by species such as the *Agelaius* compensates for the damage they do to crops. The *Agelaius* and other birds make good use after the harvest of rice scattered and lost on the ground. Oropendolas sometimes damage cacao and bananas. In Rio Grande do Sul, breeding of *A. ruficapillus*, which Belton (1985) considers perhaps the most numerous bird in that state, is well synchronized with ripening of the rice crop; the young are fed with insects (Fallavena 1988).

I have already mentioned the damage *Molothrus bonariensis* does in exterminating *Zonotrichia capensis*, a situation frequently misinterpreted by blaming *Passer domesticus* for this disappearance.

Icterines pay their dues, for they are hunted for their meat (oropendolas) or for the illegal cage-bird trade, as a result of which *Gnorimopsar chopi* and *Icterus cayanensis* have become rare around cities such as Rio de Janeiro. Along the Rio de Janeiro/Bahia highway they are finishing off *Icterus icterus*. Hundreds and thousands are captured in the area of Mata Verde and Divisópolis and taken, already in poor condition, to centers such as Cândido Sales, Itaobim, and Vitória da Conquista. Most die in their cages of undernourishment.

Indians greatly value the golden tail feathers of oropendolas for making headdresses. Various tribes, such as the Kaiabi of Mato Grosso and Indians from the Rio Branco, use whole icterine skins (e.g., *Cacicus cela*) as pendant ornaments.

C. cela, *G. chopi*, and others become perfectly tame and will sing while perched on the finger of their owner. They seem to adopt a certain person as a substitute for an individual of their own species and do not try to flee. *C. cela* may live 23 years in captivity.

There is a legend relating to the association of wasps with icterine nests. The *Cacicus cela* had enemies that broke their eggs and killed their nestlings while they were out looking for food. They asked the wasps to be godmothers to their children, so the wasps built their house close to the bird nests in order to be able to look after the chicks.

In slang the term *ninho de guaxe*, "Red-rumped Cacique nest," is used to describe a messy confusion, reference presumably being made to the superficial appearance of these birds' nests, which to the eye of a naturalist are admirable structures.

Synopsis of Brazilian Icterines

(number of species in parentheses)

Not included in this list are *Molothrus badius, Agelaius ruficapillus, Sturnella magna, Dolichonyx oryzivorus,* or the females or immatures of some species such as the *Agelaius.*

1. Large, jay size, sides of tail yellow: *Psarocolius* (5, including *Gymnostinops*, Pls 39.1, 39.2, and *Psarocolius* [= *Ocyalus*] *latirostris*).
2. All black: *Molothrus bonariensis* (Pl 39.3), *M. rufoaxillaris* (see also item 3), *Scaphidura oryzivora* (fig. 321), *Cacicus solitarius* (whitish bill), *Quiscalus lugubris, Curaeus forbesi, Lampropsar tanagrinus, Gnorimopsar chopi* (fig. 319), *Agelaius cyanopus* (Pl 39.5), and *Amblyramphus holosericeus* (in the immature the color is more blackish brown; see item 3 re the adult)
3. Black and red: *Cacicus haemorrhous, Amblyramphus holosericeus, Sturnella* (= *Leistes*) *militaris* (Pl 39.6), *Sturnella* (= *Pezites*) *defilippi*; and *Molothrus rufoaxillaris* (see also item 2)
4. Black with yellow marks: *Cacicus cela* (Pl 39.4) *C. chrysopterus, Macroagelaius imthurni, Agelaius thilius, Icterus cayanensis* (the "epaulet" may be brown instead of yellow), and *I. chrysocephalus.*
5. Black with extensive areas of yellow: *Agelaius icterocephalus, Icterus icterus* (Pl 39.8), *I. nigrogularis, Gymnomystax mexicanus* (Pl 39.7), *Xanthopsar flavus,* and *Pseudoleistes* (2).

BAND-TAILED OROPENDOLA, *Psarocolius* (= *Ocyalus*) *latirostris*

31–34 cm. Base of maxilla swollen. Plumage black with chestnut on top of head, sides of neck, and back; sides of tail at base yellow. Only in upper Amazon. Forests. Ecuador and Peru to the Juruá, Amazonas. See "Breeding."

CRESTED OROPENDOLA, *Psarocolius decumanus,* Japu, Rei-congo   PL 39.2

34–45 cm; 155–360 g. Best known of large icterines. Conspicuous with long, yellow tail that characterizes all *Psarocolius*. Male distinctly larger. VOICE: call in flight a soft *gooEH;* song *go, go, go-tsEEo-go, go, go,* with middle part a strident, ventriloquial sound. When phrase is ended bird leans forward and violently shakes wings, producing a loud rustling. Lives in flocks; makes large, bag-shaped nests, a few to many together in very tall trees, like other oropendolas. Panama to northern South America, Bolivia, Argentina, throughout Brazil except Rio Grande do Sul. Scarce or absent where tall forest is lacking. Also called *Japu-gamela* (Bahia), *Japu-preto, Fura-banana* (Minas Gerais).

GREEN OROPENDOLA, *Psarocolius viridis,* Japu-verde

Size of *P. decumanus,* color similar to *P. bifasciatus yuracares* (which is larger) but with green instead of chestnut back, whitish bill with red tip, and lacking bare area behind

Fig. 315. Russet-backed Oropendola, *Psarocolius angustifrons,* male prenuptial display. After E. Schäfer 1957.

mandible. VOICE: warning *kwat;* call a low *kwoah;* song similar to *decumanus,* combined with a vigorous display, sometimes including a somersault around branch on which it is standing. The Guianas and Venezuela to southern Amazonas, from Juruá to middle Tapajós (Pará), Belém. Also called *João-congo.*

RUSSET-BACKED OROPENDOLA, *Psarocolius angustifrons,* Japu-pardo   Fig. 315

Large, like *P. viridis.* Chestnut brown except for green head; outer tail feathers have brown outer vane; bill black. Sometimes nests in *P. decumanus* colonies; upper part of nest wider than that of *decumanus.* Only in upper Amazon. Region of the Solimões and Juruá to Bolivia, Venezuela.

OLIVE OROPENDOLA, *Psarocolius bifasciatus,* Japuaçu, João-congo   PL 39.1

37–50 cm. Largest icterine, widely distributed in upper Amazon (*P. b. yuracares*), replaced in eastern Pará by *P. b. bifasciatus,* which is smaller (45 cm). Head, neck, and breast black; mantle, belly, and thighs chestnut. Bill black, with tip and bare area behind mandible red. Noticeable size difference in sexes, female being smaller. VOICE: warning a loud *tac;* call a full *drrOT;* in flight a soft *dwot,* which is also typically used when flocks are on their way to roost (see "Vocalization"); song, a loud, resonant *psooEE-OH, o, o, o, o, o, o, o,* ending with a deep bow forward and a noisy shaking of wings and tail. Lives in large flocks, sometimes with *P. decumanus.* Venezuela to Bolivia, western part of Brazilian Amazonia, northern Mato Grosso, western Pará (*P. b. yuracares*), left bank of lower Tocantins to northern Maranhão (*P. b. bifasciatus*). There is a broad zone of hybridization between *P. b. yuracares* and *P. b. bifasciatus,* from left bank of lower Tapajós and all of Xingu region to Araguaia; *P. b. "neivae"* is one of products of this (see fig. 314). Also called *Japu-de-bico-encarnado* (*P. b. yuracares*).

YELLOW-RUMPED CACIQUE, *Cacicus cela,* Xexéu, Japim   Fig. 316   PL 39.4

22–29 cm; 60–98 g. Very well known except in south. Robust, male much larger. Immature sooty instead of black. VOICE: call a noisy *cherp;* an individual's ventriloquial song is so varied it not infrequently gives impression of a chorus of various birds; wild birds commonly produce perfect imitations of birds and mammals, e.g., toucans, aracaris, parrots, parakeets, hawks (*Micrastur, Milvago*), kingfishers, Passerines such as *Todirostrum* flycatchers and *Thryothorus* wrens; among mammals copied, I have noted an imitation of an otter (upper Xingu, Mato Grosso 1947). While singing bird squats with wings drooping and rump feathers ruffled to show bright yellow, altering its appearance so much it is hard to tell which is front and which is back of bird. On dialects, see "Vocalization." Nests in large or small colonies, frequently in low cerrado trees at edge of gallery forest, often on branches covered with ant and wasp nests (see Fig. 228, Tyrannidae). Nest, made of palm leaflets, is a relatively short, wide bag. Nests are usually quite close together. In Amazonia it is one of birds whose flocks draw the most attention, especially in várzeas and river edges. Panama and northern South America to Bolivia, southern Mato Grosso, Goiás, southern Bahia. Also called *Japuíra, João-con-guinho.*

RED-RUMPED CACIQUE, *Cacicus haemorrhous,* Guaxe, Japira

23–26 cm. Steely black with rump and upper tail coverts red; bill light greenish yellow; immature sooty with rump slightly reddish. VOICE: call a harsh *guashe* mixed with whistles; a strident *chelp* and a breathy *ft-ft-ft* in flight; song a noisy *kwat, kwat-prrrEEo EEo-tik-EEo kwat, kwat . . . ;* I have not noted any mimicry. Display less elaborate than *C. cela.* Placement of colonies varies: low over water, high in trees in middle of forest, or in palms at woodland edge. Nesting material consists of a variety of vegetable products. Prefers hot lowlands with forests (e.g., Espírito Santo, Rio

Fig. 316. Yellow-rumped Cacique, *Cacicus cela,* constructing its nest.

de Janeiro). Northern South America across Amazonia locally to Juruá, lower Tapajós, Belém (Pará); eastern and southcentral Brazil; Pernambuco, Espírito Santo, Rio de Janeiro, São Paulo, Santa Catarina, Rio Grande do Sul, Goiás, southern Mato Grosso; also Paraguay, Argentina. Also called *Japi-im-do-mato, Japi-im-de-costas-vermelhas.*

GOLDEN-WINGED CACIQUE, *Cacicus* (= *Archiplanus*) *chrysopterus,* Soldado, Tecelão

20.5 cm. Slender southern species with long tail. Upper middle wing coverts and rump sulfur yellow (very visible); bill light bluish gray; iris white or light brown. VOICE: warning a nasal *kweh-ehh;* song melodious and very beautiful, timbre recalling *Icterus icterus: dew, dewliuh-dee, dee* repeated in leisurely fashion. Mimics, e.g., Plush-crested Jay, *Cyanocorax chrysops.* When singing sometimes hangs beneath branch like certain oropendolas. When singing on top of a branch bows rhythmically. Constructs a bag nest with black "vegetable horsehair" (*Marasmius,* see "Breeding"), woven with machinelike precision. Length of nest is 58 cm

(Minas Gerais). Unlike *Cacicus haemorrhous*, lives alone in pairs in forest interior. Argentina to Bolivia, Paraguay, Uruguay, and southeastern Brazil as far as Rio de Janeiro (where restricted to mountainous regions, e.g., Itatiaia, etc.), southern Mato Grosso (riverine forests). Formerly known as *Archiplanus albirostris*, a genus name also applied to *C. solitarius*, with which it appears to have more in common than with other icterines. Also called *Pega* (Mato Grosso), *Melro*, *Nhapim*. See *Icterus cayanensis*.

SOLITARY CACIQUE, *Cacicus* (= *Archiplanus*) *solitarius*, Iraúna-de-bico-branco

23–27 cm. Less robust than *C. haemorrhous*, with suggestion of a crest, large tail, all-black coloring, prominent greenish white bill, unremarkable brown iris. VOICE: call a loud *kweh-ah;* song variable, e.g., *ewit, ewit, ewit . . .* followed by a warble so different it seems to be coming from another individual; imitates well, e.g., neighboring kingfishers, (which are also mimicked by *C. cela* in same area, Pernambuco). Nest is a long, 80-cm bag, with widest point, 13 cm, at low end. It is well constructed of flexible yellow material, grass, and stems and hung perhaps from an *Avicennia* tree. Does not live in colonies. Normally scarce, occupies flooded forest, revealing its presence by voice. Venezuela to Bolivia and to south of Amazon (lower Tapajós, Pará), Marajó, northeast, Goiás, Mato Grosso, Paraguay, Uruguay, Argentina. Closely related to *Icterus cayannensis*. Also called *Bauá* (Pernambuco); *Bom-é* (Ceará). See *Gnorimopsar chopi*.

EPAULET ORIOLE, *Icterus cayanensis*, Inhapim, Encontro

21 cm; 43 g. Slender body, long tail, bill slender and curved; black, with epaulet varying in color according to region:

1. Epaulet sulfur yellow: Amazonia. *Primavera, Rouxinol-de-encontro-amarelo. I. c. cayanensis.* See also item 4.
2. Epaulet chestnut: southern Mato Grosso, western Paraná, Rio Grande do Sul. *Encontro. I. c. pyrrhopterus.*
3. Epaulet orange-yellow, lacking yellow on underwing. Southern Goiás, western Minas Gerais, western São Paulo, southeastern Mato Grosso. *Pega, Soldado. I. c. valenciobuenoi.* This is a mixed population, originating from crossing between *I. c. pyrrhopterus* and *I. c. tibialis*, and as such is not entitled to its own name; for this reason the name *I. c. valenciobuenoi* is synonymous with *I. c. pyrrhopterus*, an older name. The designation of such a hybrid would be *I. c. pyrrhopterus* ≳ *I. c. tibialis.*
4. Epaulet sulfur yellow with same color on under wing coverts and thighs: eastern Brazil, Maranhão to Rio de Janeiro. *Inhapim, Xexéu-de-banana, Pega, Soldado, Encontro. I. c. tibialis.*

VOICE: call (resembling Chalk-browed Mockingbird, *Mimus saturninus*) *chic*, a harsh *kwou;* song resonant and melodious, or staccato or flowing, with motifs such as *dlew-eet-trrreh*, sometimes with imitations of other birds, e.g., *Milvago* caracaras. Brusque tail movements draw attention. Solitary, makes a wide, bag-shaped nest. Lives at forest edge, in palm groves, etc. Northern South America to Bolivia, Paraguay, Argentina, Uruguay, throughout Brazil. See *I. chrysocephalus*.

MORICHE ORIOLE, *Icterus chrysocephalus*, Rouxinol-do-Rio-Negro

Similar to *Icterus cayanensis tibialis* but with more golden yellow areas: cap (prolonged on sides), rump, and band over crissum. VOICE: call *pit, chat;* song mellow, softer than *I. icterus,* and full of mimcry. May sing vehemently while hanging under its perch, spreading wings and tail. Builds bag nest in miriti palms (*Mauritia flexuosa*), binding it to leaflets of dead, drooping palm fronds. Gallery forests, palm groves. The Guianas and Venezuela to upper Rios Negro and Branco. Hybridizes locally in Solimões region with *I. cayanensis*, which it replaces in northern portion of upper Amazon. Can be considered a geographic race of *I. cayanensis*.

YELLOW ORIOLE, *Icterus nigrogularis*, João-pinto-amarelo

20.5 cm. More slender than *I. chrysocephalus*. Yellow with small mask; throat, wings, and tail black, wing feathers with white edges; dark iris. VOICE: melodious song. Builds a hanging bag nest. Marshes, along river edges. Only north of Amazon, from the Guianas and Venezuela to Rondônia.

TROUPIAL, *Icterus icterus*, Corrupião, Sofrê
PL 39.8

23 cm. One of most beautiful and most vocally gifted birds of South America, represented in Brazil by 2 geographic forms that are usually considered different species: (1) *Sofrê, Concriz, Corrupião, I. i. jamacaii*, with black head and back. Maranhão to Bahia, Minas Gerais; see plate. (2) *João-pinto, Rouxinol, I. i. croconotus*, with upper head and back orange. Northern part of continent and Amazonia to Rios Paraguay and Piquiri, Mato Grosso. VOICE: call, warning *crik;* song clear and sonorous, with plaintive sweetness, or a melancholy intonation, frequently with repeated bisyllabic motifs, e.g., *chew-chuh, chew-chuh, chew-chuh,* a resonant *tuhtuhtuh . . . , eeOHH, eeOHH, eeOHH . . . , kong-krEE.* Voice of *I. i. jamacaii* may sound very similar to Long-billed Wren, *Thryothorus longirostris,* its neighbor in caatinga. Also gives harsh, ventriloquial cries and imitations. Individuals living in semidomestication or in cages even learn to imitate musical passages (see "Vocalization"). Assumes grotesque positions when it sings, with head down or stretching neck exaggeratedly upward and "freezing" with tail raised. When flying produces a loud rustling sound, like *toLo-toLO-toLO. . . .*

Occupies enclosed nests made of dead sticks by furnariids:

Phacellodomus rufifrons and Rufous Cacholote, *Pseudoseisura cristata;* sometimes uses a *Cacicus cela* nest or one made by a Great Kiskadee, *Pitangus sulphuratus,* or even by a Rufous Hornero, *Furnarius rufus* (Bahia). At times builds its own nest (see "Breeding"). This bird is the most typical ornament of caatinga and of dry, uninhabited areas. Likes to perch on tall cacti. Guyana and Venezuela to Bolivia, Paraguay, Brazil. Introduced onto island of Itamaracá, Pernambuco, around 1928. Much sought after as a pet, being attractive because of its tameness and vivacity, and does not even flee when released from cage. Can learn various tricks. Quite similar to Northern Oriole, *Icterus galbula,* of U.S., although latter has pronounced sexual dimorphism. *I. icterus* is national bird of Venezuela.

SAFFRON-COWLED BLACKBIRD, *Xanthopsar flavus,* Pássaro-preto-de-veste amarela   EN

21 cm; 43 g. Increasingly scarce southern species, with head and entire underparts, epaulets, rump, and underside of wings bright yellow, breast tending toward caramel. Rest of plumage black. Female brownish above, streaked with black, but with superciliary, epaulets, rump, and underparts yellow. VOICE: call a bisyllabic *chewp-chap;* warning *dwat-dwat;* song a squeaky, not very resonant, short, simple phrase, *tsi-di-di-tsi.* Nest is a deep cup placed in grass. Lives in pairs in marshes in open country, perching in bushes and on tall umbelliferas (*Eryngium*). Argentina to Paraguay, Uruguay, southern Brazil: Rio Grande do Sul, Santa Catarina. Small flocks frequently associate with *Heteroxolmis dominicana* (Tyrannidae); it is almost the rule that the 2 species, so different from one another, appear together. In this association *X. flavus* is the active one, seeking out *Heteroxolmis* (see "Enemies . . .").

ORIOLE BLACKBIRD, *Gymnomystax mexicanus,* Iratauá-grande   PL 39.7

27–31 cm. Large Amazonian, with plumage reminiscent of *Icterus* but with "blackbird" (*Molothrus, Gnorimopsar, Quiscalus,* etc.) behavior. Mask and bare sides of throat black (gray in immature, which has black cap). VOICE: call a cry resembling a jay; a metallic *tic, TEElili, chewlewlew;* song resonant, somewhat monotonous, *jup-juh, juh, juh-jup, jup,* while ruffling body plumage. Nest is a basket in a fork, or may be installed in crown of a palm. Walks on ground; stirs up cattle dung like *Molothrus.* Humid open country, muddy beaches, flooded and riverine forests. Common in Amazon delta region, e.g., on Marajó. The Guianas to Amazonia and south to lower Tapajós and Tocantins.

YELLOW-WINGED BLACKBIRD, *Agelaius thilius,* Sargento

17 cm. Only in south. When perched appears all black but has sulfur yellow under wing coverts and epaulets; female and immatures streaked and edged with brownish but are also recognizable by epaulet when they open wings. VOICE: call *jak;* melodious song is of low intensity and a bit squeaky, *siuee-tsuee. . . .* Nests in grass. Lives in marshes, reed beds, treeless open areas; runs on floating plants. Chile and Argentina to Bolivian altiplano, Rio Grande do Sul, Santa Catarina.

YELLOW-HOODED BLACKBIRD, *Agelaius icterocephalus,* Iratauá-pequeno

17 cm. Black except for yellow head and throat. Female blackish olive, spotted, recognizable by yellow cap, superciliary, and throat. VOICE: call (in flight) *tchak;* song a sequences of limpid, resonant notes terminating with a prolonged *tsi-tsree.* Builds an open basket in a fork. Lives in marshes and várzeas, where locally common. The Guianas to Amazon, Amapá, Belém, lower Tapajós, Juruá, Rio Negro, Colombia, Peru.

UNICOLORED BLACKBIRD, *Agelaius cyanopus,* Carretão   PL 39.5

19.5 cm. All black with silky sheen. Female and immature have blackish brown upperparts streaked with olive and chestnut, wing feathers with rusty edges. Underside dirty yellow, slightly streaked with black. In Amapá and Maranhão head and breast black (*A. c. xenicus*). Bill extremely sharp, a diagnostic character different from *A. ruficapillus.* VOICE: call, reminiscent of *ruficapillus* and of *Passer domesticus, jep.* Sings with tail spread and plumage ruffled, even in flight. Certain phrases may recall Black-capped Donacobius, *Donacobius atricapillus* (Troglodytidae), sometimes its neighbor: *EEeh, EEeh, EEeh, EEeh, EEeh, EEeh, EEeh, EEeh,* perched with bill pointing upward. When frightening a rival moves forward obliquely and in silence (behavior unlike *A. ruficapillus*). Marshes. Occurs locally, generally infrequently, and may be syntopic with *I. icterocephalus.* North of lower Amazon, Maranhão, Minas Gerais (Teófilo Otoni). Rio de Janeiro (state and municipality), Rio Paraná system: São Paulo, Goiás, Mato Grosso; also Rio Grande do Sul, Paraguay, Bolivia, Argentina. Geographic races are recognizable only in females (heterogynism). See *Gnorimopsar chopi.*

CHESTNUT-CAPPED BLACKBIRD, *Agelaius ruficapillus,* Garibaldi

17.5 cm. Widely distributed, common wetland species. Shiny blue-black with rusty chestnut cap, throat, and breast. Olive-brown female lighter on underparts, has black and light brownish streaking on belly and upperparts, throat yellowish (unlike young *Molothrus bonariensis*). Bill "normal" and short, a diagnostic character differentiating it from *A. cyanopus.* Subadult male black, spotted with brown (see "Morphology"). VOICE: call *pewt, tsiew, chat;* song somewhat monotonous but melodious and pure, with canarylike timbre: *tsee-tsieh-dew, dew, dew, dew, dew, dee, dee, dee*

dee-di, di, di, di, di (dó-ré-mi), sometimes with some harsh *gahhs* and other rough elements; frequently sings in flight as it sails down with wings and tail well opened, forepart of body upright, and plumage ruffled; when perched produces a short phrase, *si, si, si-grahh*, while erect, ruffling feathers and vibrating wings.

Nest basket-shaped, well lined with wool, etc. in fork of a bush in a marsh or in a tree or palm. Male and female are both able to build, wetting straw before placing it in nest. A male living in a flight cage with 2 female canaries with which it hybridized (see "Interfamilial Crossing . . .") built a nest alongside nest of female with which it was mated at time. Very gregarious; forms flocks of hundreds in broad, marshy regions, outnumbering other species and dominating landscape with its mellow voice. French Guiana, mouth of Amazon, Maranhão, and the northeast to southern Goiás, Santa Catarina, Rio Grande do Sul, southwestern Mato Grosso, and adjacent regions, including Rio de Janeiro and São Paulo. Seminomadic; can become a pest. Also called *Casaca-de-couro* (Bahia) *Doremi* (Minas Gerais).

RED-BREASTED BLACKBIRD, *Sturnella* (= *Leistes*) *militaris*, Polícia-inglesa   PL 39.6

17–19 cm. Widely distributed wetland species. Broad wings identify it without any color being visible. Tail short. In breeding season male's coloring is very vivid; red of lesser upper wing coverts visible in flight when seen from behind. Almost all-black upperparts produced by abrasion of brownish edges of feathers; there is a similar process on underparts. White postocular stripe on males found only on non-Amazonian population, *S. m. superciliaris*; female brown, breast with vestige of red, and Amazonian females also with cream-colored wide superciliary. Immature similar to female but lacks red, underparts with some black streaking; may recall immature *Molothrus bonariensis*. Re abrasion as a danger to maintenance of wing feathers, see "Morphology."

VOICE: call (most common) *ee;* alarm (announcement of presence of a hawk) *pist; chit-chit, cha, kwak;* song squeaky *tsi-li-li-EE*, often given in flight and while making a soaring descent with wings and tail well opened. I have impression that call of *S. m. militaris* on Marajó Island is different from voice of southern *S. m. superciliaris* in Rio de Janeiro, where most-used call is a harsh *pshee*. Nest is an open basket on ground, hidden under grass. Constantly extending its range by taking advantage of tremendous deforestation and invading cultivated fields, airports, landfills, sometimes even dry areas. It was unknown in Rio de Janeiro even in 1950s, but I recorded it on Cabo Frio in 1960 and at Lagoa Feia in 1961. It immigrated into Rio Itabapuana region in 1961 and in 1962 to Itaguaí, at doors of ex-Guanabara. In 1964 it was common in Jacarepaguá, and in 1969 it appeared at Santos Dumont Airport and on Flamengo beach. At same time it immigrated into western São Paulo (Caraguatatuba, around

1960, São Sebastião in 1964; Hélio F. A. Camargo). It has been reported that at the beginning of the twentieth century it occupied deforested fields at mouth of Xingu, Pará. In most of these cases it became abundant in a short time, but occasionally it subsequently became scarce or disappeared. It is spreading in other countries, e.g., Colombia, also.

Várzea and humid fields with low vegetation. In most parts of continent, from Argentina to Panama and throughout Brazil. Also called *Papa-arroz* (Amapá), *Puxa-verão, Baieta* (Marajó), *Pipira-do-campo* (Pará), *Cheque* (Ceará), *Flamengo* (Rio de Janeiro).

A recent revision of the genera *Leistes, Pezites,* and *Sturnella* resulted in the decision to unite all of them under the generic name *Sturnella,* which does not conform to my own views on the subject. Morphology (juvenile plumage) and behavior (flocking, singing in flight) are more similar to that of *Agelaius.* It has been proposed to treat *S. m. superciliaris* as a separate species.

PAMPAS MEADOWLARK, *Sturnella* (= *Pezites*) *defilippi*, Peito-vermelho-grande   SV

22.5 cm. Seen only in extreme south. Similar to subadult *S. militaris* but much stockier with long, pincerlike bill and long whitish superciliary that becomes red between eye and bill. Epaulet and underside red except for gray and black sides and abdomen. Underside of wing black, like *militaris*. VOICE: call *cheep, ta, ta, ta;* sings in flight in same way as *militaris*. Thickets in dry grassy fields, cultivated areas. Argentina to Uruguay, southern Brazil: Rio Grande do Sul, sporadically to Paraná.

EASTERN MEADOWLARK, *Sturnella magna,* Pedro-celouro   Fig. 317

20.5 cm. Northern terrestrial species descended from North American meadowlarks, with even longer bill than *S. militaris* and large feet. Upperparts streaked with black,

Fig. 317. Eastern Meadowlark, *Sturnella magna praticola*.

chestnut, and whitish, recalling a tinamou (*Nothura* sp.), and with white postocular stripe and another on top of head. Underside yellow, breast crossed by a black collar. Tail edges white. VOICE: call *chit, chit;* song a short, melodious, undulating phrase, e.g., *jew-jiledieh-deh, tsew-TSI-deleh-dewduh.* Nests on ground. Runs on ground, hiding behind clumps of grass. When wary, lifts bill obliquely. Open fields. Resident in northern South America: *S. m. praticola* to Amazon (Uaupés), Roraima, Amapá, Marajó, lower Tocantins (Cametá, Pará); Central America and eastern North America as far as Canada: *S. m. magna;* see also "Distribution. . . ."

YELLOW-RUMPED MARSHBIRD, *Pseudoleistes guirahuro,* Chopim-do-brejo

24 cm. Blackish brown species of central and southern Brazil, with back becoming olivaceous and epaulet, rump, belly, and underside of wings yellow. VOICE: call (in flight) *tac-tac;* song a loud, somewhat harsh, monotonously repeated whistle, *grooeep-gruit-gruit,* with ruffled rump displayed. It is common for some individuals to sing together, perched a hand's breadth apart from each other. They also sing in flight when flock moves from one place to another. Nest is an open basket; inside on bottom is a sizable quantity of mud which makes it surprisingly heavy. Várzeas. Argentina, Uruguay, and Paraguay to southern Mato Grosso, Goiás, Federal District, Minas Gerais, Santa Catarina, Rio de Janeiro. In Minas Gerais esteemed locally as a cage bird because of its melodious song. Also called *Melro-amarelo, Melro-d'angola, Melro-mineiro, Pássaro-preto-soldado* (all from Minas Gerais). See *P. virescens.*

BROWN-AND-YELLOW MARSHBIRD, *Pseudoleistes virescens,* Dragão

24 cm; 74 g. Similar to *P. guirahuro* but more svelte. Lacks yellow on rump. Sides of body brown, bill longer. VOICE: call (warning) *TA, ta, ta, psEEew; Tszaka-TSEEah,* repeated by full flock in flight; song a short warble, beginning with *TSIah.* Marshes, open country. Argentina and Uruguay to Santa Catarina. Usually does not associate with *guirahuro.*

SCARLET-HEADED BLACKBIRD, *Amblyramphus holosericeus,* Cardeal-do-banhado

23 cm. Unique wetland species with extremely sharp, chisel-shaped bill, wide wings, heavy flight, long tail. Black, with head, breast, and thighs scarlet. Young uniformly sooty but recognizable by bill shape. VOICE: call *jak, jat-jat,* a very loud note, *ooeeeet;* song a limpid whistle with downward leaps of an octave or more, e.g., *HEElili-HOlolo.* Builds a closed nest with a side entrance. Re its peculiar technique for using its sharp bill, see "Feeding." Deep-water marshes, reedbeds, and cattails, edges of canals and rivers with dense marsh vegetation. Argentina to Bolivia, Paraguay, Uruguay, Brazil: Rio Grande do Sul, Santa Catarina, southern Mato Grosso (Pantanal), Gurupi (northern Goiás). Also called *João-pinto-do-brejo.* See *Sturnella militaris.*

Fig. 318. Nest of Forbes' Blackbird, *Curaeus forbesi,* hanging among branches. The support underneath is unnecessary. After Studer and Viellard 1988.

FORBES' BLACKBIRD, *Curaeus forbesi,* Anumará BR

23 cm. Frequently confused with *Gnorimopsar chopi* but has smooth, ungrooved mandible; culmen broadened; bare skin behind mandible all wrinkled. Plumage sooty black without blue sheen. Narrow feathers of top of head have shinier rachises; these also occur on breast and back. Wing shorter and rounder, covering only rump, as can be seen in perched bird. Frequently opens bill, conspicuously displaying red mouth (black in *G. chopi*). Always in small flocks, including during breeding. Until 1960s was a mystery bird. It has been studied in wild in Alagoas since 1981 by A. Studer and J. Vielliard, with Studer having prepared a well-illustrated monograph. VOICE: completely unlike *Gnorimopsar:* in flight utters a trisyllabic *pi-li-lit;* song a strange, loud, snorting *chaaaaaa.* Nests at edge of forest or marsh, perhaps in canopy of a mango tree, where it builds a well-finished basket (fig. 318). Lays 3–4 light blue eggs with slight black design. In Alagoas 64% to 100% of nests were parasitized by *Molothrus bonariensis* (Studer and Vielliard 1988), sharply reducing reproductive success. Two isolated areas of occurrence are known: northeast (Pernambuco, Alagoas) and Minas Gerais (Raul Soares, Rio Doce Park, Barra do Piracicaba). Also called *Agelaius forbesi.* The other species in genus, Austral Blackbird, *C. curaeus,* occurs in southern Chile, southern Argentina. It has a pleasant song and is sought by cage-bird fanciers; it reportedly can learn words, like a parrot.

CHOPI BLACKBIRD, *Gnorimopsar chopi,* Melro, Graúna   Fig. 319

21.5–25.5 cm. All black with silky sheen, head feathers narrow and pointed, bill black with deep grooves at base. Specimens from northeast (*graúna, graúna-verdadeira, melro, G. c. sulcirostris*) considerably larger and shinier than those from southern or central Brazil (*pássaro-preto, melro, vira-bosta, vira-campo, graúna, G. c. chopi,* 66–85 g).

Fig. 319. Chopi Blackbird, *Gnorimopsar chopi sulcirostris.*

VOICE: call a low *cot;* a sharp whistle, *EEeh, EEew-jewp, twep-eee;* song composed of highly varied, resonant, mellow whistles, some prolonged and repeated, mixed with short, harsh tones, e.g., *ee, ee, ee-jewlit, jewlit, tsiewrrr, choPEE-choPEE;* usually begins with well-spaced monosyllabic notes, moving to bisyllabic whistles, and only later goes into song with full vigor; there are transliterations of the song, e.g., *Planta Joaquim, planta Joaquim, eu arranco, eu arranco,* "You plant, Joaquim, You plant, Joaquim, I'll pull it out, I'll pull it out." One of loudest and most melodious bird songs of Brazil, even more impressive when sung by various individuals, as often happens in rural areas of interior. Sings in an erect position while vibrating wings. Female also sings but usually lacks *tsiewrrr.*

Nests in hollow trees, palm trunks, woodpecker nests, frequently well up but also in low places such as fence posts; also among bases of palm fronds, in dense tops of araucaria pines, in heaps of branches gathered by Jabiru, *Jabiru mycteria,* for its nest (Mato Grosso), or in abandoned hornero (*Furnarius* sp.) nest (Minas Gerais). Also occupies holes in embankments (Minas Gerais) and terrestrial termite nests with holes in them. Sometimes breeds in open nest situated in fork of a branch far out from trunk of a tall, dense tree, e.g., guapuruvu [*Schizolobium parahybum*], probably taking advantage of an old nest of some other bird (Paraná). Lives in cultivated fields, pastures, plantings with isolated trees, snags, forest remnants, buriti and other palm groves, araucaria areas. Non-Amazonian Brazil; northeast, east, south, and central west to Bolivia, Paraguay, Argentina, Uruguay. Much sought by local country people as a songbird and becoming scarce in most populated areas. Also called *Pássaro-preto, Chupão* (Mato Grosso), *Arranca-milho, Chopim;* word *chopi* is onomatopoeic indigenous name still used in Argentina; *gra-una* comes from indigenous *guira-una,* "bird-black." See *Curaeus forbesi, Scaphidura oryzivora,* and Scarlet-throated Tanager, *Sericossypha loricata.*

VELVET-FRONTED GRACKLE, *Lampropsar tanagrinus*

23 cm. Similar to *Curaeus forbesi* but with shorter bill, velvetlike plumage on forepart of head, chestnut-colored iris, small feet. Longer tailed than *Molothrus.* In flocks at river edges. Only in extreme west. Guaporé and Madeira to Javari and Rio Negro to Venezuela.

TEPUI MOUNTAIN-GRACKLE, *Macroagelaius imthurni*

27 cm. Black with white bases on rump feathers and yellow axillaries. Only in extreme north. Roraima to Venezuela, the Guianas.

CARIB GRACKLE, *Quiscalus lugubris,* Iraúna-do-norte

23 cm. Only north of Amazon. Size of *Gnorimopsar chopi* with longer, graduated, trough-shaped tail; long, slightly curved bill; large feet. All black with blue sheen. Iris yellow or white. VOICE: a penetrating *ksayk, ksayk . . . , squit. . . .* Builds a deep nest, using some mud. In flocks around houses and villages, sometimes with *Molothrus bonariensis.* Antilles to Amapá.

BAY-WINGED COWBIRD, *Molothrus badius,* Asa-de-telha

17 cm. Brown, sides of head and bill blackish, wings bay-colored with black tips, tail blackish brown. Sexes identical. VOICE: call a squeaky *chayt, chap;* song a series of melodious whistles (*Tordo-músico,* "Musician Thrush," Argentina) that may recall song of *Gnorimopsar chopi,* occasionally emphasizing a strident *tseee-EE;* frequently several males sing together, with females sometimes participating. *Tseee-EE* or *ee-ew* whistle has special role as a dawn song (Rio Grande do Sul, January).

Not a parasite; breeds normally, installing itself in large interwoven stick nests of furnariids such as Firewood Gatherer, *Anumbius annumbi* (Rio Grande do Sul); Common Thornbird, *Phacellodomus rufifrons;* Chotoy Spinetail, *Synallaxis phryganophila* (Mato Grosso); and Rufous Chacholote, *Pseudoseisura cristata* (Bahia), padding nest with grass, etc.; or builds its own nest, an open, loose cup in a fork. Male also builds. Has been reported that sometimes 2 or even more *M. badius* females lay in same nest. Regularly parasitized by *M. rufoaxillaris.* Small *M. badius* chick differs in dark subterminal spot on bill, lacking on *M. rufoaxillaris* and *M. bonariensis* (Fraga 1979, Buenos Aires area). *M. rufoaxillaris* chick grows larger than that of *badius.*

Usually in flocks of 4–6. Open landscapes with isolated trees and clumps, carnauba groves, caatinga. The northeast to interior Minas Gerais, southern Mato Grosso, Rio Grande do Sul, and adjacent countries, sometimes even to Chile. May recall *Passer domesticus,* a furnariid, or female *Tachyphonus* tanager. Very similar to young *rufoaxillaris.*

SCREAMING COWBIRD, *Molothrus rufoaxillaris,* Chopim-azeviche

18–21 cm; 47–63 g. Southern, very similar to *M. bonariensis* but a bit larger with longer tail, shorter bill, almost no sheen on plumage. Some of under wing coverts and axillaries chestnut on male, but this is very difficult to see in field. Sexes otherwise similar, except female smaller. Young and immature very different, with brown plumage believed to be of ancestral heritage and indistinguishable from that of *M. badius* when birds leave nest (at approximately 12 days).

Shortly, however, they start to molt into black on head and body, making it easy, in this plumage, to identify them for what they are. VOICE: a harsh cry, *kshrr, tsheh, tshree,* very different from *bonariensis,* immediately identifies species. When perched in front of female, male sings *tsiLIT-cheh* while spreading wings and tail horizontally and stretching head forward as if making a bow, a display much different than that of *bonariensis.* Male displays his reddish axillaries.

Lives in pairs (appears to be monogamous) or small flocks. A parasite, like *bonariensis;* apparently preys only on *badius* (Argentina). Eggs extremely variable: reddish, bluish, greenish, grayish, yellowish, or white, without showing any tendency to mimic host's eggs (Argentina, Fraga 1983). Incubation time 12–13 days in a *badius* nest. In Paraná (Rolândia), where *rufoaxillaris* immigrated a few years ago and where I have not seen *badius,* the *Chopim-marrão,* "Chestnut Cowbird," 1 of the names used for *rufoaxillaris,* parasitizes *Gnorimopsar chopi,* which rears the parasite along with its own young, the same as *badius.* In 1973 in Rolândia I observed the rearing of 3 *rufoaxillaris* and 1 *G. chopi* together; in a 2d case 1 *rufoaxillaris* and 3 *bonariensis;* and in a 3d case 1 *rufoaxillaris,* 3 *bonariensis,* and 1 *G. chopi.* There are cases where *chopi* rears only *rufoaxillaris.*

Open country with sparse trees; also ranches. Argentina, Uruguay, Paraguay, and Bolivia to southern Mato Grosso, Rio Grande do Sul, Paraná, and rarely farther north: Rio de Janeiro (28 August 1959, 2 immatures). A record from Pernambuco refers to *M. bonariensis.* May look like *G. chopi;* brown immature resembles female Ruby-crowned Tanager, *Tachyphonus coronatus.* Also called *Namura* (Paraná), *Chorão* (Paraná), *Chupim.*

SHINY COWBIRD, *Molothrus bonariensis,*
Chopim, Gaudério, Maria-preta   PL 39.3

16.5–21.5 cm; 42–52 g. Well known throughout Brazil. Male shiny violet-blue with relucent greenish wings. Smaller female sooty chestnut with black back, varying greatly in size (as does male) and color, with some all black but less shiny than adult male. Immature black above, without sheen (male), or spotted brownish (female), underparts in both more or less streaked with whitish and black. Sex recognizable even in juvenile plumage: male blackish, female sooty chestnut. VOICE: warning call a high, strident *spitititi . . . ;* a very low *jok;* snorts when it fights; sings perched in front of female, *prro-prro-prro-TSLEEyew,* while stretching vertically, touching bill to throat and ruffling all its feathers; song a hurried tinkling, often prolonged, given in flight or when it files around perched female.

Parasitism and Hosts: Apparently there are more males than females, and polygamy is the rule. Breeding period is lengthy, calculated at 6 months. The species has become entirely dependent on other species to care for its eggs and young. There is documentation for Brazil on 58 species representing 12 Passerine families or subfamilies in whose nests *M. bonariensis* eggs have been found or that have been observed feeding its young. Only species in 2d category (feeding adoptees) can be designated hosts. There follows a list of all known species affected by *M. bonariensis* in Brazil[3]:

Furnariidae (5): *Furnarius rufus, Cranioleuca obsoleta, Phacellodomus ruber, Anumbius annumbi, Pseudoseisura cristata*

Tyrannidae (10): *Xolmis cinerea, Fluvicola nengeta, Arundinicola leucocephala, Satrapa icterophrys, Tyrannus savana, T. melancholicus, Empidonomus varius, Pitangus sulphuratus, Serpophaga nigricans, Tityra cayana*

Troglodytidae (1): *Troglodytes aedon*

Turdidae (1): *Turdus rufiventris*

Mimidae (1): *Mimus saturninus*

Motacillidae (1): *Anthus lutescens*

Vireonidae (2): *Vireo chiri, Hylophilus poicilotis*

Parulinae (2): *Geothlypis aequinoctialis, Basileuterus leucophrys*

Thraupinae (13); *Thraupis sayaca, T. ornata, T. palmarum, T. bonariensis, Ramphocelus bresilius, R. carbo, Piranga flava, Tachyphonus coronatus, Neothraupis fasciata, Cypsnagra hirundinacea, Hemithraupis guira, Thlypopsis sordida, Schistochlamys melanopis*

Emberizinae (10): *Paroaria gularis, Sporophila caerulescens, Oryzoborus angolensis, Sicalis flaveola, Coryphospingus cucullatus, C. pileatus, Ammodramus humeralis, Zonotrichia capensis, Emberizoides herbicola, Poospiza lateralis*

Cardinalinae (2): *Pitylus fuliginosus, Saltator similis*

Icterinae (9): *Cacicus chrysopterus, Curaeus forbesi, Gnorimopsar chopi, Agelaius ruficapillus, A. cyanopus, Icterus cayanensis, I. icterus jamacaii* breeding in a nest of *Phacellodomus rufifrons, Pseudoleistes guirahuro, Sturnella militaris*

Passeridae (1): *Passer domesticus*

In the entire range of *M. bonariensis,* 201 species (even a small dove) (Friedmann et al. 1985) have been recorded having its eggs in their nests. Many of these do not rear the parasite because they abandon its eggs. Cowbird eggs have been found even in *Sporophila* nests (which were then abandoned). This total of more than 200 species includes many Brazilian birds that have not yet been recorded as cowbird victims here. With more observations the list of parasitized Brazilian birds should rise substantially. However, I have the impression that in Brazil the concentration of this parasite on certain species, especially *Zonotrichia capensis,* limits the number of hosts.

In southeastern region of Brazil and in Argentina and Uruguay, this cowbird primarily seeks out *Z. capensis* as host. Most people are only aware of *Z. capensis* as a foster parent for rearing *M. bonariensis.* In 95 nests of this emberizine on Ilha Grande, Rio de Janeiro, I found 57 (60%) had

---

[3]Documentation on many of these cases is found in the publications of H. Friedmann, most recently in Friedman and Kiff 1985, and of H. Sick 1958; almost all recent data is taken from the author's diary.

been invaded by this cowbird. Estimates for other parts of Brazil, e.g., Viçosa, Minas Gerais, raise percentage to 75%, a figure that should be valid for other southern states, e.g., Paraná. The percentage can go even higher, as I verified in Rio de Janeiro (municipality and state), where it is very difficult to find a *Z. capensis* nest that does not have 1 or more cowbird eggs. Under these conditions it is obvious that reduction and even elimination of this sparrow is the work of the cowbird, not of *Passer domesticus*. There are, however, places where the number of cowbird offspring reared by *Z. capensis* is controlled by excessive botfly larvae (see "Parasites . . ."). Increase of *M. bonariensis* may be so great that in an area poor in birds, e.g., Quinta da Boa Vista in Rio de Janeiro, there may not be enough nests for the icterine to lay its eggs in.

Other species are affected only exceptionally. In southeastern Brazil *M. bonariensis* is not commonly reared by sanhaço tanagers. In Jacarepaguá area of Rio de Janeiro, it lays so often in nest of Brazilian Tanager, *Ramphocelus bresilius,* that this bird scarcely manages to save its own offspring. In Pirapora region of Minas Gerais it is reared with some frequency by *Icterus icterus jamacaii* in abandoned Common Thornbird, *Phacellodomus rufifrons,* nests; the principal host there also, however, is *Z. capensis*.

It has been reported that in Amazonia *M. bonariensis* lays regularly in nest of the White-headed Marsh-Tyrant, *Arundinicola leucocephala,* a marsh bird. In northern Argentina the Rufous Hornero, *Furnarius rufus,* is most prejudiced species; in Brazil I have only 1 record, from Rio Grande do Sul, of parasitism of *M. bonariensis* on this hornero. In Buenos Aires region, Fraga (1985) found 78.1% of Chalk-browed Mockingbird, *Mimus saturninus,* nests parasitized by this cowbird.

One of latest additions to my list of hosts is *Passer domesticus* (Rio de Janeiro, São Paulo). It was even hoped that *M. bonariensis* might keep the *P. domesticus* population under control in Ribeirão Preto and Rio Claro, São Paulo (W. E. Kerr pers. comm.); I suppose in this case the situation could be influenced by the nesting place of the sparrows, possibly of easier access to the cowbirds, and by preadaptation of cowbirds already raised in *P. domesticus* nests (see *P. domesticus*).

During my surveys of *M. bonariensis* on Ilha Grande, Rio de Janeiro, in 1943–44, I was often surprised that it did not parasitize more species. A Creamy-bellied Thrush, *Turdus amaurochalinus,* for example, had a nest for 2 successive years in same place, where cowbirds could not have failed to see it, but it was not molested.

Begging of *M. bonariensis* chick is addressed to any bird that approaches. It also induces neighbors to participate in feeding it. Normally chicks beg only from their parents, as do the young of *M. badius,* which is not a parasite.

Eggs and Development of Chicks: M. bonariensis eggs are extremely variable. There are 2 basic shapes, oval and round, sometimes almost spherical. Shell may be dull or lustrous. Color in many cases, e.g., Rio de Janeiro, is generally a light red or green tone covered with spots and speckles. Eggs that are uniformly greenish white have also appeared in Bahia and Rio Grande do Sul. In each region certain types dominate. Although there are *M. bonariensis* eggs that greatly resemble those of *Z. capensis, Mimus saturninus,* or even a furnariid (pure white), all kinds are found everywhere. Hosts usually accept all these different eggs, in complete contrast with the highly selective acceptance by Old World hosts only of cuckoo eggs that match their own. This notable adaptation evolved through the selective attitude of the layer: she lays only in nests of the species that reared her. *Scaphidura oryzivora* also lays mimetic eggs. In Argentina *Mimus saturninus* throws out almost all white cowbird eggs (Fraga 1985).

Although eggs of various females of the same area may be quite similar to each other, the Rey quotient (multiplying the length of the egg by its width, in millimeters, and dividing that product by the weight of the empty shell, in milligrams) reveals significant differences among individuals and demonstrates the near homogeneity of the eggs of an individual female, thereby permitting classification of eggs according to the layer (J. Ottow, in Sick 1958)[4]. We thus reach the conclusion that a female *M. bonariensis* does not lay more than one egg in each nest, but that up to 7 of them visited 1 *Z. capensis* nest, 4 during the course of the same early morning. Females do not exclude one another from an area. The range of a female is 21–48 ha (Fraga 1983). A nest may be overloaded with eggs; I have counted 6 in a *Z. capensis* nest (Rio de Janeiro, Minas Gerais); with 2 cowbird eggs and 2–3 of the sparrow, the nest is full. Up to 14 eggs, laid possibly by 14 different females, have been recorded in the spacious nest of a *Mimus saturninus*. The record is 37 *M. bonariensis* eggs in a *Furnarius rufus* nest (Argentina). Laying capacity of an *M. bonariensis* female is said to be 4–5 eggs or more, there being an interval of 2–3 days between layings. Number of layings must vary according to region. A female *M. ater* of North America lays 40 eggs a year in 6 weeks, the highest productivity known among Passerines. She lives only 2 productive years, so lays a total of 80 eggs in her lifetime (Scott et al. 1980).

Overloaded nests are abandoned by their owners. Since a female *M. bonariensis* customarily pecks open eggs she finds (this is also done by males, who participate in search for nests and apparently may sometimes suck out a bit of contents), each visit of a parasite increases the danger for the entire contents of the nest, including the *Molothrus* eggs. Perhaps the more curved surface of the *bonariensis* egg, and its thicker shell (see "Eggs . . ."), offer some protection against the danger of being pecked open. Sometimes females

---

[4]Detailed studies on the House Wren, *Troglodytes aedon,* have shown that the eggs of each female have very similar dimensions; the variation is less than that occurring among various females (Kendeigh 1975). The shape

of the eggs laid by the same female may be different, as with the Cracidae (*Crax* spp.).

Fig. 320. Rufous-collared Sparrow, *Zonotrichia capensis*, feeding a young Shiny Cowbird, *Molothrus bonariensis*.

throw eggs out of the nest. Although uncommonly, they also lay in old, abandoned nests. As a result there is a tremendous loss of parasite eggs. Of a total of 94 *M. bonariensis* eggs laid in 83 *Z. capensis* nests, 41 (44%) hatched, showing a slight advantage over the sparrow, of whose eggs only 41% hatched (Sick 1958). In Buenos Aires, Fraga (1985) noted that 102 cowbird eggs resulted in only 6 chicks that fledged.

Incubation of an *M. bonariensis* egg in a *Z. capensis* nest takes 11–12 days, 1 day less than the host's eggs, an advantageous adaptation of the parasite. Prompt laying of parasite eggs in the host nest, i.e. on the same day or even before the sparrow lays its 1st egg, is of maximum importance. I have verified that the sparrows normally do not continue to incubate for more than 3 days after 1st egg has hatched. Cowbirds sometimes hatch simultaneously with sparrows. I have not noticed the slightest indication of cowbird nestlings trying to get rid of nest contents, although a cowbird nestling may unintentionally sit on top of a smaller stepsibling; cowbirds beg more insistently than sparrow chicks; their food consists of insects. It is only after leaving the nest that cowbirds become granivorous. The inside of the mouth of these cowbirds is red, like that of the sparrows.

It is not unusual for a cowbird and 1–2 sparrows to grow up together; sometimes there are 2 cowbirds, exceptionally 3, or 2 cowbirds and 2 sparrows. A Masked Water-Tyrant, *Fluvicola nengeta*, nest was found holding a tiny (3 g) *Fluvicola* nestling and a 25-g cowbird nestling. Both managed to fledge (A. Studer pers. comm.). I have verified that *Gnorimopsar chopi* may rear 4 *M. bonariensis* at a time (Paraná). In my own records, of 51 parasitized *Zonotrichia capensis* nests, 25 (49%) were successful, producing 24 cowbirds and 15 sparrows that fledged. Of the cowbirds that hatched, 59% fledged, so the parasites were 26% successful, the sparrows not quite 24%. After leaving the nest, young cowbirds still accompany their stepparents for 2 weeks, drawing their attention through a high *klip* (location call) that has nothing to do with their coarse begging during or before feeding (fig. 320). Sometimes a young cowbird will continue

to follow its stepmother when she has started another clutch. Possibly the very loud begging of the insatiable cowbird chick is an important factor in the elimination of *M. bonariensis* young by hawks such as *Milvago chimango, Accipiter,* and *Circus.*

Habitat, Distribution, Harmfulness, and Popularity: Inhabits semiopen landscapes, cultivated fields, pastures. Associates with cattle, on which it perches to broaden its horizons. Flocks may become a problem for agriculture (see "Harmfulness . . ."); periodically invades cities, alighting on lawns and roosting at night in trees in parks and along streets with *Passer domesticus.* Panama and Antilles throughout greater part of South America to Argentina, Chile, and all over Brazil. Also called *Vira-bosta, Iraúna* (Amazonia), *Azulão, Papa-arroz, Parasita, Anu* (Rio Grande do Sul), *Maria-preta, Engana-tico, Grumará* (Espírito Santo). Nickname *chopim* is popularly used for lazy and worthless husbands who live off the work of their wives. See *M. rufoaxillaris* and *M. badius.*

GIANT COWBIRD, *Scaphidura oryzivora,*
Iraúna-grande   Fig. 321

30–35 cm; 130–76 g. Largest black icterine, uniformly shiny black with long tail and neck thickened by prolongation of feathers, causing head to look small; bill heavy and black. Immature female larger-bodied than *Gnorimopsar chopi,* male larger than Smooth-billed Ani, *Crotophaga ani.* Iris chestnut, green, or whitish. VOICE: generally silent; calls—a cry *che-che-che;* a meowing; a low *dak;* song a strident but melodious phrase, *jewli, chi, chi, chi, chi,* while puffing up neck and lowering bill. Display in front of female recalls that of *Molothrus bonariensis:* stretching neck upward and holding bill against throat, at same time fluffing out ample neck plumage. Lives alone or in small flocks, walking erectly in pastures near cattle, horses, or pigs (from which it removes ticks); perches on half-submerged capybaras (Pantanal, Mato Grosso), walks on river beaches or on rocks in rivers.

Fig. 321. Giant Cowbird, *Scaphidura oryzivora*, male display before female. Xavantina, Mato Grosso, 1947.

Turns over stones, perches in tall, isolated trees. Flight unusual and noisy (see "Behavior").

Parasitic. Lays in bag-shaped nests of other icterines (*Cacicus cela*, *C. haemorrhous*, *Psarocolius decumanus*). Egg green with black spots and considerably larger than those of *Cacicus*. There are also eggs with a light blue background, still others with white (Suriname). In Central America eggs have been found that are highly adapted to background color of host eggs. It has been reported that incubation period for *S. oryzivora* eggs may be 5–7 days shorter than for hosts' eggs. Open country, feeding at edge of woodlands where birds it parasitizes nest. Mexico to Bolivia, Argentina, throughout Brazil except Rio Grande do Sul; scarce outside Amazonia. Also called *Melrão* (Rio de Janeiro), *Rexenxão*, *Graúna*, *Chico-preto*, *Vira-bosta-grande*, *Lau-na-ná* (Juruna, Mato Grosso). See also *Cacicus solitarius*.

BOBOLINK, *Dolichonyx oryzivorus*, Triste-pia
NV   Fig. 322

16 cm. Recorded only as a migrant from North America. In nonbreeding plumage in which it arrives in Brazil at end of year resembles a sparrow or female *Sturnella militaris*, though with rigid tail, long rear claw, and white superciliary emphasized by blackish postocular line and another on side of crown. Underparts yellowish. January–March, before returning to breed in extreme north (Canada and northern U.S.), undergoes a full molt. Male then acquires nuptial dress: front of head and entire underparts all black (feathers frequently barred yellow), upperside with large white V. VOICE: a monosyllabic, tinkling, or metallic *pink*, voiced in flight and also at night on migration, revealing its presence. I have not heard it sing in Brazil. Marshes, rice and sorghum plantations, fields, often associated with *Molothrus* and

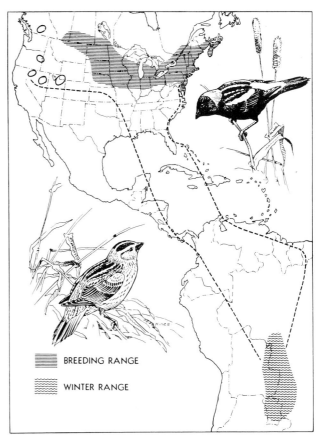

Fig. 322. Migration of Bobolink, *Dolichonyx oryzivorus*. It migrates from its breeding area in North America to the center of South America. At right, male in nuptial plumage; at left, nonbreeding plumage. After Lincoln 1950.

Agelaius. Observed in Amazonas (Rios Negro and Juruá, October), Mato Grosso (November, March), Rio Grande do Sul (December); occasional in eastern Brazil in summer in small flocks. Also captured in Marambaia and Cabo Frio in Rio de Janeiro, where on sale as a cage bird. Goes as far as Argentina, Paraguay, Bolivia. *Charlatan* (Argentina). One of most popular birds of North America, the "rice bird." In nonbreeding plumage easily overlooked. American banders are marking *D. oryzivorous* with 6 different colors on tail. When a bird is found, it should be reported to the Bird Banding Laboratory, Laurel, MD 20708. This species makes one of the most extensive annual migrations for landbirds known in Americas, covering well over 20,000 km on its yearly round trip.

Icterine Bibliography
See also General Bibliography

Ankney, C. D., and S. L. Johnson. 1985. Variation in weight and composition of Brown-headed Cowbird eggs. *Condor* 87:296–99.

Beecher, W. J. 1950. *Wilson Bull.* 62:51–86. [Evolution]

Beecher, W. J. 1955. Adaptations for food-getting in the American blackbirds. *Auk* 68:411–40.

Cavalcanti, R. B., M.N.F. Silva, M. N. Lemos, et al. 1984. Parasitismo interespecífico, existem adaptações para evita-lo? *XI Cong. Bras. Zool.*:313.

Collias, N. E., and E. C. Collias. 1964. Evolution of nest-building in the Weaverbirds (Ploceidae). *Univ. Calif. Publ. Zool.* 73.

Davis, D. E. 1942. *Condor* 44:10–12. [*Molothrus*, laying]

Fallavena, M.A.B. 1988. Alguns dados sobre a reprodução do garibaldi, *Agelaius ruficapillus*, en lavouras de arroz no Rio Grande do Sul. *Rev. Bras. Zool.* 4(4):307–17.

Feekes, F. 1977. *Ardea* 65:197–202. [*Cacicus cela*, colony-specific song]

Ferolla, M. I. 1981. *Soc. Bras. Progr. Ciênc. 33a Reun., Resumos*:764. [*Molothrus bonariensis*, hosts]

Fraga, R. M. 1979. *Wilson Bull.* 91(1):151–54. [*Molothrus bonariensis* and *M. badius*, young]

Fraga, R. M. 1983. *J. Orn.*:187–93. [*Molothrus rufoaxillaris* and *M. badius*, variation in eggs]

Fraga, R. M. 1983. *Hornero* 12:245–55. [*Molothrus bonariensis* parasitizing *Zonotrichia capensis*]

Fraga, R. M. 1984. *Biotrópica* 16:223–26. [*Molothrus* parasitism]

Fraga, R. M. 1985. Host-parasite interactions between Chalk-browed Mockingbirds and Shiny Cowbirds. In *Neotrop. Ornith., Ornith.* Monogr. no. 36.

Fraga, R. M. 1988. Nest sites and breeding success of *Molothrus badius. J. Orn.* 129(2):175–83.

Friedmann, H. 1929. *The Cowbirds.* Springfield. [*Molothrus*, monograph]

Friedmann, H. 1971. *Auk* 88:239–55. [*Molothrus*, hosts]

Friedmann, H., and L. F. Kiff. 1985. The parasitic cowbirds and their hosts. *Proc. West. Found. Vert. Zool.* 2:225–304.

Haverschmidt, F. 1967. *Bull. B.O.C.* 87:136–37. [*Scaphidura*, eggs]

Howell, T. R. 1964. *Condor* 66:511. [*Psarocolius*, displays]

Hoy, G., and J. Ottow. 1964. *Auk* 81:186–203. [*Molothrus*, parasitism]

Kendeigh, S. C. 1975. *Auk* 92:163–64. [Eggs, individual characteristics]

Koepcke, M. 1972. *J. Orn.* 113:138–60. [Nesting]

Lent, H. 1939. *Bol. Biol.* 4:260. [Nest fauna]

Lorenz, K. 1949. Über die Beziehungen zwischen Kopfform und Zirkelbewegung bei Sturniden und Icteriden. In *Orn. als Biol. Wissenchaft, Memor. E. Stresemann.* Heidelberg: Carl Winter.

Lowther, P. E. 1975. *Wilson Bull.* 87:481–95. [Geographic and ecological variation]

Mason, P. 1986. Brood parasitism in a host generalist, the Shiny Cowbird. *Auk* 103:52–60.

Mason, P. 1987. Pair formation in Cowbirds. *Condor* 89:349–56.

Moojen, J. 1938. *O Campo* 9. [*Molothrus*, parasitism]

Müller, P. 1968. *Orn. Mitt.* 20:107–8. [*Leistes*, distribution]

Oliveira, R. G. 1984. Hibridismo em "Cardeal-do-sul" *Paroaria coronata. An. Soc. Sul-Riogr. Orn.* 5:11–14.

Olson, S. L. 1983. A hybrid between *Icterus chrysater* and *I. mesomelas. Auk* 100:733–35.

Orians, G. H. 1985. *Blackbirds of the Americas.* Seattle: University of Washington Press.

Parkes, K. C. 1966. *Proc. Biol. Soc. Washington* 79:1–12 [*Agelaius*, taxonomy]

Peña, M. R. de la. 1979. *Cyta* 10:11–16. [Photos of nests of 41 species of birds parasitized by *Molothrus bonariensis*]

Pinto, O.M.O. 1967. *Hornero* 10:447–49. [*Icterus*, breeding]

Pinto, O.M.O. 1975. *Pap. Avulsos Zool. S. Paulo* 29:35–36. [*Icterus*, nest parasitism]

Robinson, S. K. 1986. Social security for birds. *Nat. Hist.*:38–47.

Rodrigues, H. O., and J. T. Teixeira de Freitas. 1964. *Atas Soc. Biol. Rio de J.* 8:33–35. [Nematoda]

Schäfer, E. 1957. *Bonn. Zool. Beitr.* Supl. [*Psarocolius*, behavior]

Scott, D. M., and C. D. Ankney. 1980. Fecundity of the Brown-headed Cowbird in Southern Ontario. *Auk* 97:677–83.

Short, L. L. 1968. *Am. Mus. Nov.* 2349. [*Leistes*, etc., taxonomy]

Short, L. L., and K. C. Parkes. 1979. The status of *Agelaius forbesi. Auk* 96:179–83.

Sick, H. 1957. *J. Orn.* 98:421–31. [*Psarocolius, Icterus*, nesting material]

Sick, H. 1958. *Rev. Bras. Biol.* 18:417–31. [*Molothrus bonariensis*, parasitism]

Sick, H. 1979. *Bull. B.O.C.* 99(4):115–20. [Hybrids between *Agelaius ruficapillus* and *Serinus canaria*]

Sick, H., and J. Ottow. 1958. *Bonn. Zool. Beitr.* 9(1):40–62. [*Molothrus bonariensis*, parasitism, eggs]

Skutch, A. F. 1954. *Life Histories of Central American Birds,* vol. 1. Pacific Coast Avifauna 31:263-337. Berkeley, Calif.: Cooper Orn. Soc.

Skutch, A. F. 1967. *Hornero* 10:379–88. [*Gymnomystax*, behavior]

Smith, N. G. 1968. *Nature* 219:690–94. [Advantages of parasitism]

Smith, N. G. 1978. Some evolutionary, ecological and behavioral correlates of communal nesting by birds with wasps or bees. *Acta 17 Cong. Internat. Orn., Berlin*:1199–1205.

Spaw, C. D., and S. Rohwer. 1987. A comparative study of eggshell thickness in cowbirds and other passerines. *Condor* 89:307–18.

Studer, A. 1982. "La redécuverte de l'Ictéridé *Curaeus forbesi* ao Brésil." Ex. D.E.S. Univ. Nancy.

Studer, A., and J. Vielliard. 1988. Premières données étho-écologiques sur l'Ictéridé brésilien *Curaeus forbesi. Rev. Suisse Zool.* 95(4):1063–77.

Zusi, R. C. 1959. The function of the depressor mandibulae muscle in certain passerine birds. *Auk* 76:537–39.

FAMILY FRINGILLIDEA, SUBFAMILY CARDUELINAE: SISKINS (2)

The Fringillidae are a typically Old World family of the Palearctic, from where they colonized the New World, Africa, etc. The designation *fringillid* has been applied to any granivorous songbird of the Oscine suborder, including various families and subfamilies of different ancestry (see Emberizidae). In systematics the name Fringillidae was used until

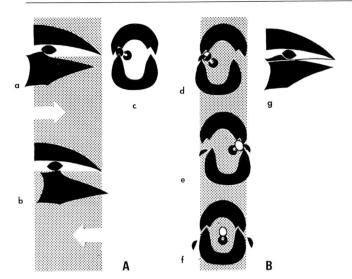

Fig. 323. Bill movements while working a seed in members of the Carduelinae (Hooded Siskin, *Carduelis magellanica*). (A) Method of cutting: (a) and (b) side views; (c) front view. (B) Method of hulling: (d), (e), and (f) front views; (g) side view. The stippled plate shows the position of the immobile maxilla, and the white arrows indicate the direction of movement of the mandible; the maxillar tomia has been left white to show the position of the seed in the bill. After Ziswiler 1965.

recently to bring together the present group and what are now the Emberizinae and Cardinalinae of the Emberizidae family.

The Fringillidae as presently accepted are represented in South America only by the siskins[1] of the Carduelinae subfamily. The Carduelinae is a large group (more than 120 species) widely distributed in North America and the Old World, their place of origin. Outstanding among them is the canary (see Fringillidae Appendix). There has been hybridization with *Icterinae*.

On our continent a total of 13 Carduelinae species, all in the *Carduelis* (= *Spinus*) genus, live primarily in the Andes region, some at considerable altitudes. In the Andes, which they easily colonized from Central America, the Carduelinae found a climate similar to that of their place of origin. They have reached Tierra del Fuego and have also invaded some subtropical and tropical regions.

The *Carduelis* genus is quite homogeneous, not only in morphology (there is variation in bill shape, indicating different food habits) but in vocalization, which has a typical pattern recognizable wherever in the world siskins occur, be it Brazil, the Andes, or Europe. Only two species are found in Brazil.

The existence of the Yellow-faced Siskin, *Carduelis yarrellii*, in both northeastern Brazil and northeastern Venezuela appears to confirm that there was a continuous extension of a caatinga (or similar formation) ecosystem from the Brazilian northeast to Venezuela in arid Pleistocene times. This area

was divided by intrusion of the mouths of the Orinoco and Amazon.

Feeding

The Carduelinae are the most specialized granivorous group in the Passerines, which appear originally to have been eaters of berries and arthropods. In feeding on grass seeds, *Carduelis* use a technique similar to that of the *Sporophila* (see Emberizinae/Cardinalinae, "Behavior"), holding a spike of grass on the ground under the foot. To split open dicotyledonous seeds with a hard covering, Carduelinae use a more complicated movement (fig. 323) than the Emberizinae; the knife-sharp mandible moves back and forth, cutting the seed, which the bird secures by holding it against the palatine (a variable structure) with the tongue. The *Carduelis* have a long, narrow tongue to match their slender and relatively long bill. *Carduelis* feed their young only on seeds. They do not carry nestling food in the bill but swallow and partially digest it in the crop for subsequent regurgitation and administration as a mush.

Behavior

It is especially characteristic of the Carduelinae (the *Carduelis* in our case) when frightening an opponent to lower themselves, open their wings, and lean forward with the bill half open.

YELLOW-FACED SISKIN, *Carduelis* (= *Spinus*) *yarrellii*, Coroinha, Pintasilgo-do-nordeste

A northeastern bird, one of our smallest granivorous birds. Differs from *C. magellanica* by having only cap black, sides of head and entire underparts yellow, as are rump and upper tail coverts. Female lacks black cap. VOICE: a rapid, ringing warble. Happily the time has passed when *S. yarrellii* skins were exported to Europe for decorative purposes, but it is endangered by its range being so limited. Ceará, Pernambuco, Alagoas, and northern Bahia where, in 1970s, it was not rare; also northeastern Venezuela. On its disjunct distribution, see Emberizinae/Cardinalinae, "Distribution. . . ." Superficially resembles American Goldfinch, *C. tristis*, which does not reach this continent. Also called *Pintassilvio* (Pernambuco), *Pintassilgo-baiano*.

HOODED SISKIN, *Carduelis* (= *Spinus*) *magellanica*, Pintassilgo   Fig. 324

11 cm. Widely distributed in South America and well known in southern Brazil as a cage bird. Head and upper neck black, back green. Underside, 2 wing bars, and rump yellow. Female's head and underparts olive, but she is more easily recognized by yellow wing bars, which are same as male's. VOICE: call *jay-ehh, tsewahee;* in flight *jet-jet;* a high, much varied, extremely rapid warble, with long phrases intermin-

[1]The other subfamily, Fringillinae, is a small Palearctic group to which the Common Chaffinch (*Fringilla coelebs*), one of the popular birds of Europe, belongs. It does not occur on this continent.

Fig. 324. Hooded Siskin, *Carduelis magellanica*, male.

gling imitations of other birds, e.g., Social Flycatcher, *Myiozetetes similis;* Rufous-bellied Thrush, *Turdus rufiventris;* Tropical Parula, *Parula pitiayumi;* Yellow-bellied Elaenia, *Elaenia flavogaster;* warning call of Rufous-collared Sparrow, *Zonotrichia capensis,* etc. Group song occurs among males when birds migrate or gather in evening to roost. Has very restless temperament; shakes wings and tail; flight extremely undulating. Open, secondary forest, tree plantations, estates, araucaria groves (mountainous regions of southeast, *pintassilgo-dos-campos-de-altitude* = "high-country siskin"), cerrado, etc. Nests in tops of tallest araucarias, also coffee plantations. Appears in all types of habitat on winter migrations, then disappears entirely. In north and northwest of continent, often in isolated populations, e.g., in upper Rio Branco (Roraima). South of Amazonia, locally in southeastern and centralwestern Brazil to Argentina (Rio Negro Province). Also called *Pintassilva, Pintassilgo-mineiro.*

Fringillidae Appendix

Male *C. magellanica* and *C. yarrellii* are crossed with small canary females. The hybrid obtained, called *Pintagol,* is highly prized for its excellent singing virtues.

The canary, a bird found worldwide that was domesticated more than 300 years ago, is a descendant of the Island canary, *Serinus canaria,* from the Canary archipelago. Thanks to breeding and hybridizing techniques, it has been possible to produce innumerable color, plumage, and song varieties of this bird. The ease of crossing the canary with American siskins, *Carduelis,* is explained by the fact that both belong to genera of the Old World Carduelinae subfamily, unlike the Brazilian "ground canary," *canário-da-terra* (Saffron Finch, *Sicalis flaveola*), which belongs to the Emberizinae, an American subfamily.

The Red Siskin, *Carduelis cucullata, pintassilgo-da-Virginia* or *pintassilgo-da-Venezuela,* a beautiful red and black species, is crossed with the canary to produce colored canaries, also called *Pintagol,* which are fertile. *C. cucullata* comes from Venezuela and Colombia and is endangered. The name Virginia is explained by the fact that trade in these birds has been in the hands of Americans. In the Northern Hemisphere *C. cucullata* is readily bred in captivity; it crosses with *C. magellanica.* The offspring are fertile.

Fringillidae Bibliography

Mayr, E., R. J. Andrew, and R. A. Hinde. 1956. Die systematische Stellung der Gattung *Fringilla. J. Orn.* 97:258–73.
Ziswiler, V. 1965. *J. Orn.* 106:1–48. [Use of bill]

FAMILY PASSERIDAE: OLD WORLD SPARROWS (1)

This large Oscine family of the Old World (Africa, Eurasia, Malaysia, etc.) is related to the weavers, Ploceidae. It has also been treated as a subfamily of the Ploceidae: the Passerinae. It includes several genera with a substantial number of species. The House Sparrow, *Passer domesticus,* was introduced from Europe (see below).

Morphology and Behavior

The bill is strong and conical, appropriate for crushing seeds. Insects are also eaten, with *P. domesticus* being omnivorous. The voice is harsh and noisy, and the song is poorly developed, unlike the Emberizidae. They also differ in prenuptial displays, in the lack of rivalry among males, in not establishing a territory around the nest (they only defend the nest itself), and in building a covered nest, a rarity among emberizids.

They move in vegetation and on the ground by hopping and have short tarsi and toes. They are gregarious and usually nest in colonies. See also the Ploceidae Appendix: Subfamily Ploceinae.

HOUSE SPARROW, *Passer domesticus,* Pardal
Fig. 325

14.8 cm; 30 g. Adult male distinguished by black "necktie" and bill and uniformly gray crown, never crested and with no black streaks, unlike Rufous-collared Sparrow, *Zonotrichia capensis.* Bill becomes yellowish in nonbreeding season. Female, known in Brazil as *pardoca,* and immature more similar to *Z. capensis* but heavier-bodied, with

Fig. 325. House Sparrow, *Passer d. domesticus* (A) Male and (B) female.

B   **A**

heavier bills, and without crest; Plumage brownish, postocular stripe light, underside uniformly dirty white, bill white. Individuals sometimes have white feathers, and there are cinnamon and yellow morphs.

Vocalization: The voice is coarse and noisy, more noticeable when birds gather in evening at a collective roost. It is interesting how on these occasions the chirping of a large flock becomes organized into a regular, almost unisonal rhythm, like the Greater Ani, *Crotophaga major.* Flocks also make a noisy clamor during day (see *Breeding*). Although modest, a quiet, prolonged, staccato song is interlaced with a soft note, *rrrew-rrrew.* I have observed this song from black-billed adult males and from male juvenals (ex-Guanabara).

Breeding: The male courts female by hopping around her with wings drooping and tail cocked while cheeping loudly. This noise attracts other males and leads to general confusion until female flees. Pairs are said to mate for life.

In Brazil *P. domesticus* nests on walls and other building parts that provide cavities and recesses, usually quite high. Modern verticalization of cities has created housing problems for it and has diminished its numbers in metropolitan centers. It has been able, however, to find new opportunities to hide its nest in hollowed walls, inside mercury streetlamps, and even in frames of traffic signal lights. It also uses dovecotes. The nest of Rufous Hornero, *Furnarius rufus,* must be very much like a hole in a stone building for *P. domesticus* (Rio Grande do Sul, Santa Catarina, Minas Gerais). Sometimes it establishes itself in holes of dead trees, in base of the crown of a palm, e.g., of macaúba (*Acrocomia sclerocarpa*), or on upper part of trunk of oil palm (*Elaeis guineensis*). Occasionally it occupies stick houses of Firewood Gatherer, *Anumbius annumbi.* 1 of which can accommodate several pairs of sparrows (Rio de Janeiro, Rio Grande do Sul), and it also uses Common Thornbird, *Phacellodomus rufifrons,* nests (Minas Gerais). Very rarely poorly built, spherical-shaped nests are placed on tree branches (as I saw in Nova Friburgo, Rio de Janeiro). These are rather large with a side entrance and as poorly woven as nests that are inside holes, scarcely having the outline of a roof. Such nests may resemble a Thrush-like Wren, *Campylorhynchus turdinus,*

nest. *P. domesticus,* especially male, is very prone to gather a lot of building material which it heaps into a loose, disorderly pile, differing in this respect from Ploceidae weavers (see appendix). It arranges an abundant lining of grass, cotton, and rags, sometimes so much that this material falls out through entrance and stops up gutters, etc. Interior of nest chamber is carpeted with feathers and sometimes, at Carnaval time, with confetti (ex-Guanabara). The warm nest protects the sparrow in cold regions to which it has also emigrated (it has even crossed Arctic Circle). The nest is used more than once.

Eggs (4 in ex-Guanabara) are densely spotted, with color varying considerably in the same clutch. They are incubated 12 days by pair. Chicks hatch naked (unlike emberizids, which are feathered) and are fed by parents, which at the beginning furnish food stuck together in small balls. Later food is almost exclusively small arthropods and their larvae, carried by parents in their bills. A. Ruschi saw a female *P. domesticus* pick botfly larvae off her nestlings, eating some and giving others to nestlings to eat. When young fledge, at 10 days or more, they move to a more vegetarian diet. Parents clean nest. Young often return to nest for some time to sleep. Various clutches are laid in 1 breeding season. Adults bathe both in water and dust.

There is little information on *P. domesticus* being parasitized by Shiny Cowbird, *Molothrus bonariensis,* reflecting the fact that its nests are generally inaccessible to cowbirds. There are records for Rio de Janeiro (1929, 1969, and 1981, Sick 1971), Rio Claro, and Ribeirão Preto, São Paulo (W. E. Kerr since 1962). The situation in Rio Claro seemed to be reaching the point where the sparrow would be controlled by the cowbird (see *M. bonariensis*). In Ribeirão Preto *P. domesticus* nested on rafters on the open veranda of the Colégio Vita e Pax (W. Engels 1973–74 pers. comm.). The sparrow nests, visible from a distance, were regularly visited by cowbirds. Closing the veranda ended this situation, which could repeat itself anywhere. Two small *M. bonariensis* nestlings taken from the nest of a Chopi Blackbird, *Gnorimopsar chopi,* and placed in a *P. domesticus* nest were reared normally by the sparrows.

Habitat and Distribution: P. domesticus is a typically synanthropic bird that adapts to city life better than any other bird. Its dispersal center was in the Middle East. Today it inhabits a large portion of Palearctic and Asia. It was introduced in North America and Cuba in 1850, in Argentina in 1872. It now exists from Tierra del Fuego and Chile to Bolivia and the coast of Peru, Ecuador, and Colombia. In Brazil it has almost reached equator. Helping its spread in South America is the fact that, in contrast to Africa (where it was also introduced), there are no congeners with similar ecological requirements. It found an open niche here. It has also been introduced into Australia.

Spread in Brazil: P. domesticus is said to have been introduced into Rio de Janeiro in 1906 by Antonio B. Ribeiro, who brought 200 individuals from Leça da Palmeira, Portugal, to be liberated in Campo de Santana with the approval of the mayor, Pereira Passos. They claimed to be collaborating with Oswaldo Cruz in his campaign to clean up the city, for the sparrows were considered to be enemies of mosquitoes and other insects that were vectors of diseases then raging in Rio de Janeiro (Sick 1971)[1].

Part of the subsequent spread of this sparrow throughout Brazil has been due to a great deal of purposeful introduction, both with the idea of freeing them in a new place and of selling a bird unknown to interior people.

Occupation of Brazil by *P. domesticus* was thus more of an artificial than natural process. Road construction was decisive, especially after the founding of Brasília (1957)[2] and the resulting increase in traffic. Before this modern development, dissemination of the sparrow particularly followed the few existing railroad lines and the rivers that were important interior communication routes. In Pirapora in 1973 I saw the bird traveling as a stowaway on large vessels along the Minas Gerais part of the Rio São Francisco. Possibly this is how it reached Petrolina and Cabrobó (Pernambuco 1971) on the northern bank of that river. It also exists in Alagoas and Rio Grande do Norte. Ships also carried it from one coastal port to another. This is about the only way it could have reached Belém (Pará) more than 60 years ago. More recently it was taken from Santos (São Paulo) to Recife (Pernambuco). However, it does not lack initiative of its own to conquer new terrain. It appears on ranches distant from urban centers, as I noted along Rio das Mortes and in Pantanal (Mato Grosso). There have also been other introductions from Europe, e.g., from France, always with typical race, *P. d. domesticus*. One of the Brazilian areas most densely populated by the sparrow is Rio Grande do Sul, where occupation occurred between 1910 and 1923. In Belo Horizonte (Minas Gerais) it was already common in 1912, having been taken to the recently

founded city even before 1910. It reached Uberaba in 1930 and Poços de Caldas in 1934. In Mato Grosso it penetrated from Paraguay; by 1925 it had already approached close to the headwaters of the Araguaia. In Cuiabá, the geographic center of continent, it appeared only in 1952 and the same year in Rio das Mortes (Araés, Mato Grosso); in 1954 it was in Aragarças (Goiás). Twenty years later it had occupied all the microregions of Goiás, with Goiânia being the most densely populated area; out of 157 questionnaires sent to municipal offices, 156 came back with positive replies confirming the presence of *P. domesticus,* only 1 giving negative response (J. Wellington Lemos 1976). The bird has also reached the upper Xingu (Mato Grosso, Fontoura nucleus 1972, W. Bokermann), which has for some time been linked by road with the Rio Araguaia region.

Various private individuals introduced it into Brasília (Federal District) in 1959, and following the Belém-Brasília road, it arrived in Marabá (Tocantins, Pará, where it nested in 1964), Estreito, and Itinga (Maranhão-Pará line, 450 km south of Belém in 1973). It was also recorded in Itupiranga (Pará), north of Marabá (N. Smith, 1974 pers. comm.).

An effort to establish *P. domesticus* in Belém around 1928 failed. Perhaps individuals born along the Belém-Brasília highway adapt to support equatorial conditions better than birds brought from the south and released in the Amazonian climate. In December 1977 I found the sparrow in Capitão Poço, (Pará) and even in Salinópolis (Pará) on the coast, north of Belém, 70 km south of the equator. Finally, in November 1978 the bird was recorded in Belém (Smith 1980), reaching the area semispontaneously, apparently from the east (Zona Bragantina), not from the south. In 1985 it was well established in Belém (Novaes pers. comm.) In 1982 it was found in the Colégio do Carmo, Balbina, Rio Urubu, near Manaus, Amazonas.

Although taken to Vitória (Espírito Santo) in 1928, it delayed in its spread north of the Rio Doce (Córrego Bley 1959). It was found in Bahia (Potiraguá) only in 1969, and in Jequié and Itabuna in 1971. In 1974 I found it in Barreiras and Formosa do Rio Preto in northwestern Bahia, it having been introduced there some years previously. Today it is found in almost all parts of the Recôncavo Baiano. Only recently have I received information on its introduction into the city of Salvador (Bahia) (1981, J. Davidson).

There is little documentation on introduction onto Brazil's oceanic islands. It had not appeared on Fernando de Noronha as of January 1990. It was also absent from Ilha Trindade at that time, but apparently there was a record for it there in 1984. Surprisingly, in March 1971 it was found on the Atol das Rocas, islands lacking drinking water, 250 km from the

---

[1]It is also said that it was Garcia Redondo who sent to Europe for the House Sparrows, which were considered "very useful, being insectivores *par excellence*" and freed them in Rio de Janeiro in September 1907. As late as 1964 in an important newspaper of the northeast it was recommended that "House Sparrows be imported to beautify the parks and gardens and liqui-

date the thrips that infest the plazas." Another paper there, under "Ecology," described the House Sparrow as a "bad character."

[2]The citation of a year in this chapter refers to the date in which I or my collaborators recorded *P. domesticus* in the place referred to; in many cases it arrived there before.

continent and 150 km west of Fernando de Noronha, a pair being seen near the ruins of the lighthouse keeper's house with their plumage in very poor condition. They managed to survive, opportunists that they are, eating small succulents (beldroegas-da-praia, Portulacaceae?) and sand fleas (miniscule crustaceans). They bred, and 10 years later 16 individuals were counted, apparently in reasonable health (P. T. Z. Antas 1985 pers. comm.). They must have arrived there as stowaways from Natal, Rio Grande do Norte, where they have become acclimatized. They were still there in reduced numbers in February 1990 (Jaqueline Goerck pers. comm.).

Excessive humidity is a limiting factor for *P. domesticus,* as we know from Africa. In Brazil it has been noted that storms cause sparrow deaths (ex-Guanabara, Rio de Janeiro, São Paulo), as does hail, a rare occurrence in this country.

Nest Fauna, Disease, and Sanitation Problems: P. domesticus nests may harbor the assassin bug *Triatoma sordida,* a carrier of Chagas disease. Its nymphs were found affixed to *P. domesticus* feathers in São Paulo (Forattini et al. 1971). In Uruguay it has been discovered that the louse *Caminicimex furnarii,* which occurs in *Furnarius rufus* nests, also establishes itself in *P. domesticus* nests.

P. domesticus is one of the few Brazilian Passerines in which the presence of *Toxoplasma gondii,* the microbe causing toxoplasmosis, has been confirmed (Giovannoni 1954); see also Rock Dove, *Columba livea.* The sparrows could be disseminators of the avian pox virus and of Newcastle disease; many mites and ticks live in their nests.

In Rio de Janeiro 18 bird botfly larvae (*Philornis* sp.) were found on 1 juvenal sparrow and were apparently the cause of its death after leaving the nest, although it was fed to the end by its parents. All the larvae weighed 1.5 g, more than 10% of the bird's 14.5 g. The larvae, which were found in the bird's wings, legs, back, and malar regions, abandoned their victim immediately after its death.

Noxiousness: Everyone agrees *P. domesticus* harms gardens and orchards, damaging seedlings, corn, rice, and small trees that are sprouting. Overseas it followed the spread of wheat cultivation, and in America it accompanies rice and corn as well as animal husbandry, e.g., swine raising. It is extraordinary how it discovers new sources of food, thanks to the careful attention it gives to testing immediately if there is some advantage to a new dish. It learns, for instance, to drink from hummingbird feeders, clutching the nipples of bottles. It is among the regular customers for oil palm fruits. It has found seeds of forest plants stored in open boxes inside a closed compartment and accessible only under the edge of the roof (Rio de Janeiro, J. Lanna). It turns over clods of earth with rapid lateral movements of the bill to pick out food hidden by wind or rain (*Zonotrichia capensis* uses its legs). *P. domesticus* were said to have eaten a sack of rice in a warehouse (were they perhaps helped by rats?), to cite 1 more bit of mischief (Minas Gerais). It also is accustomed to looking for food remains in cans and trash piles.

In compensation it destroys considerable numbers of insects during its breeding season, including noxious ones such as plant lice, thrips, caterpillars, and spiders. Sometimes it catches swarming termites and ants and small moths, staying on the wing for extended periods. Occasionally it takes advantage of army ants to catch arthropods fleeing from them (ex-Guanabara).

Based on the questionnaire distributed in Goiás, Lemos (1976, see above) concluded that *P. domesticus* (1) damages agriculture and horticulture; (2) prefers rice, followed by corn, vegetables, other grains, and fruits; and (3) contributes to city sanitation by eating leftovers and garbage from houses.

The food of *P. domesticus* was investigated in the U.S., based on the stomach contents of 8004 individuals. Of the total consumption, 19.64% was useful (especially harmful insects), 24.78% was neutral, and 55.58% was harmful to human economy. The food of nestlings was 59.38% useful (Kalmbach 1940).

Menace to Other Birds: Another accusation is that *P. domesticus* chases away native birds. This is true in the case of species that have a similar mode of nesting (installation in building cavities), e.g., Saffron Finch, *Sicalis flaveola* (see that species); swallows; and House Wren, *Troglodytes aedon.* A sparrow was seen chasing a *Furnarius rufus,* pecking it on the head in flight. It did not manage to expel the hornero from its nest, but this was accomplished by a pair of Blue-winged Parrotlets, *Forpus xanthopterygius.* In Goiás I saw *P. domesticus* drive away birds living in palm trees (1959). The female is more aggressive than the male. There is no competition of this sort between *P. domesticus* and *Zonotrichia capensis,* for the latter has different nesting requirements (see *Z. capensis*). *Z. capensis* is by temperament more aggressive than *P. domesticus* and customarily drives away such intruders unless they arrive in a flock. I have even seen a young *Z. capensis,* still being fed by its parents, drive a dove and a *P. domesticus* away from a feeder. The accusation that *P. domesticus* drives away other birds from food sources is correct when, for example, a flock descends to the ground where *Sicalis flaveola* are feeding.

The simple presence of *P. domesticus,* with its din and petulance, threatens and bothers other birds and may end by driving them away once and for all as the number of sparrows increases. The number of *P. domesticus* in a certain locale is best indicated by the disturbance they make in the enclosed canopies of trees before sleeping. Sometimes *Molothrus bonariensis* joins them. *P. domesticus* has great biological potential and numerically is probably the 2d or 3d most common bird in the world. The most numerous is the domestic chicken, followed by the Starling, *Sturnus vulgaris,* another invader species (see Icterinae, introduction, footnote 1). *P. domesticus* has been able to multiply its range in the world for 100 years, using people as its quartermaster.

Rivalry and Longevity: Among the many natural enemies of *P. domesticus* in Brazil are rats, possums (*Didelphis* sp.), and possibly vampire bats (*Desmodus rotundus*) that inhabit the same attics of houses and churches. The Barn Owl, *Tyto alba,* catches *P. domesticus* in its collective roosts in trees. Nests are sometimes raided by the Guira Cuckoo, *Guira guira,* and Chimango Caracara, *Milvago chimango,* in Rio Grande do Sul and Chile. It is rare for *Molothrus bonariensis* to discover a *P. domesticus* nest in which to lay its egg, which helps reduce the population of this intruder (see *Breeding* above). The Roadside Hawk, *Rupornis magnirostris,* hunts *P. domesticus* in gardens. Mortality during the 1st year of life is very high, calculated at from 45% to 70% in Europe. *P. domesticus* 5, 7, and 13 years old have been recorded in their natural habitat in Europe, and up to 23 years old in captivity.

Methods of combating *P. domesticus* run into various difficulties, beginning with the intelligence of the bird: it is always alert and wary, never becoming tame. It immediately knows when it is being pursued and disappears. This attitude has brought it incomparable success in the world of birds: it resists all persecution and constantly occupies new areas.

The most efficient means of combating it, by means of poisoned wheat, would involve killing *Zonotrichia capensis,* finches, and other granivorous birds and would be a threat to children and domestic animals. Sound is used in the Northern Hemisphere: cries of fright and warning, recorded on magnetic tape when a cat was shown to a flock of caged sparrows, are played through loudspeakers. But this only drives the birds to some other place. A more elegant solution would be the use of a sterilizing agent added to wheat given to the birds as food, a method used against pigeons in the U.S. Affected individuals lay and incubate normally, but the eggs do not hatch. This method, however, has drawbacks similar to those for poisoned wheat: high cost and the possibility of eliminating other granivorous birds. There remain, however, simple methods that are less drastic: destroy nests, eggs, and nestlings and capture or drive away adults, all however, without involving children. I think it premature to promote a "Week for Combating the House Sparrow," as was proposed in 1972, in view of the fact that people frequently confuse it with other birds such as *Z. capensis.*

P. domesticus has been placed on the list of Brazilian animal pests by the Ministry of Agriculture (Decree No. 1 of 5-1-1957), occupying 1st place, followed by vampire bats, rats, and poisonous snakes. This attitude was commented on in 1965 by the late Vivaldo Coaracy: "Isn't there a lot of prejudice, perhaps even a bit of xenophobia in this, because the House Sparrow is an imported bird?"

P. domesticus has become immune to extermination. Therefore, let us at least take pleasure in the attractive appearance of this bird and not forget that we ourselves introduced it from overseas.

Ploceidae Appendix: Subfamily Ploceinae

Weavers, members of the Ploceinae subfamily, are bred in cages in Brazil, the Eastern Paradise-Whydah, *Vidua para-disaea,* being an example (see Tyrannidae, under *Alectrurus*). They do not occur in the wild here. They have reached a state of perfection in nest construction that is unlikely to be rivaled by other birds. In appearance, weaver nests remotely resemble the bag nests of Brazilian icterines such as the Red-rumped Cacique, *Cacicus haemorrhous.* Nesting of the Ploceinae is therefore very different from that of the Passeridae to which *P. domesticus* belongs. See also Estrildidae.

Passeridae Bibliography

Carvalho, J.C.M. 1939. *O Campo* 10:34–35. [Harmfulness]

Collias, N. E., and E. C. Collias. 1973. *Proc. 13th Cong. Int. Orn., Ithaca:* 518–30. [Nesting]

Deckert, G. 1969. Zur Ethologie und Ökologie des Hausspatzen, *Passer domesticus. Betr. z. Vogelkunde* 15(1):1–84.

Dott, H.E.M. 1986. The spread of the House Sparrow in Bolivia. *Ibis* 128:132–37.

Forattini et al. 1971. *Rev. Saúde Publ. S. Paulo* 5:193–205. [Nest fauna]

Giovannoni, M. 1954. *An. II Cong. Panam. Med. Vet.* 2:269. [*Toxoplasma gondii* in *Passer domesticus*]

Gliesch, R. 1924. *Egatea* 9. [Distribution]

Kalmbach, E. R. 1940. *Economic Status of the House Sparrow in the United States.* U.S. Dept. Agric., Techn. Bull. 711.

Lemos, José Wellington. 1976. *28 Reun. Soc. Bras. para o Progresso da Ciência.* [*Passer domesticus,* distribution in Goiás]

Löhrl, H., and R. Börhinger. 1957. *J. Orn.* 98:229–40. [Populations]

Long, J. L. 1981. *Introduced Birds of the World.* Sidney: Reed.

Matthew, K. L., and R. M. Naik. 1981. Interrelation between moulting and breeding in a tropical population of the House Sparrow, *Passer domesticus. Ibis* 128:260–65.

Müller, P. 1967. *J. Orn.* 108:497–99. [Distribution]

Nicolai, J. 1970. Viduinae. In Grzimek, *Tierleben.* Zurich.

Philippi B., R. A., 1954. *Rev. Chil. Hist. Nat.* 54:127–28. [Harmfulness]

Pinto, O.M.O. 1933. *Bol. Biol. S. Paulo,* n.s. 1:15–20. [Harmfulness]

Sick, H. 1957. *Die Vogelwelt* 78(1):1–18. [*Passer domesticus* in Brazil]

Sick, H. 1959. *Bol. Mus. Nac. Rio de Janeiro Zool.* 207. [Invasion of Latin America]

Sick, H. 1971. *Arq. Mus. Nac. Rio de Janeiro* 54:113–21. [Distribution, behavior]

Sick, H. 1979. *Bull. B.O.C.* 99(4):115–20. [*Passer domesticus* north of Belém, Pará]

Smith, N. J. H. 1973. *Condor* 75:242–43. [Distribution]

Smith, N. J. H. 1980. *Condor* 82:109–11. [Distribution in Amazonia]

Summers-Smith, D. 1963. *The House Sparrow.* London.

Vierke, J. 1970. *J. Orn.* 111:94–103. [Conditions in Africa]

Wolters, H. E. 1970. Ploceidae. In Grzimek, *Tierleben.* Zurich.

FAMILY ESTRILDIDAE: COMMON WAXBILL (1)

Estrildidae are Old World (Africa, Australia, etc.) Oscines that total 125 species, of which one, the Common Waxbill, *Estrilda astrild,* has been introduced into Brazil. They are related to the Ploceinae, a subfamily of the Ploceidae. Relationship with the House Sparrow, *Passer domesticus,* is distant (see *P. domesticus*).

Morphology

Estrildids are usually slight of build. The most prominent morphological feature is the shiny white protuberances on the base of the maxilla and on the mandible of the young (fig. 326). These reflect light and appear phosphorescent in the dark interior of the nest (which is enclosed, with a small side entrance), orienting the parents toward the heads of their nestlings when they want to feed them. The interior of the nestlings' mouths, primarily the palatine, has spots and lines that are bluish black, red, etc., according to the species. The protuberances disappear after the young leave the nest, but the design in the mouth remains. The plumage and bills of adults are vividly colored.

COMMON WAXBILL, *Estrilda astrild,*
Bico-de-lacre   PL 38.9

10.7 cm; 7.5 g. Gregarious savanna bird, similar in body shape to *Sporophila* seedeaters (Emberizinae). Tail relatively long and wide, bill and mask carmine, bill with lacquered appearance. Sexes similar, but crissum and under tail coverts black in male, dark brown in female. Immature has black bill, almost no wavy marks in plumage. VOICE: call *tseh, tseh, tseh;* song a short, stereotyped phrase, sometimes repeated, *gli, gli, deh-HEEa.*

Behavior: Likes tall, seedy grass, e.g., colonião or mur-

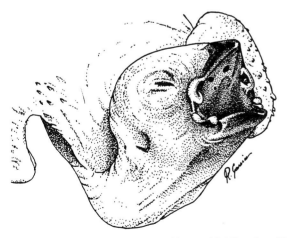

Fig. 326. Common Waxbill, *Estrilda astrild.* Nine-day-old nestling, showing the shiny protuberances in the mouth. Sketch by Raul Garcia, after a photograph by J. Nicolai.

umbu, *Panicum maximum* varieties, introduced from Africa along with waxbill itself, which comes from southern part of that continent. Adult lives exclusively on seeds of this grass. It drinks by sucking, like pigeons do.

Associates in flocks of about 6 or more, paying no attention to Emberizinae such as *Sporophila* seedeaters when they meet in grassy areas in search of seeds. There is therefore no conflict with native birds. In spite of having originated in an extremely hot climate, does not appear to migrate in winter from places such as cities of São Paulo and Porto Alegre, Rio Grande do Sul, but it must feed differently. Some movement does occur, for it disappears at end of fruiting period of local grasses, after having reared its young. Flocks periodically increase and diminish. In Brasília it is said to disappear in dry season.

Breeding: Male sings before female, bowing and wagging his tail sideways and sometimes holding a panicle of cut grass in his bill, a display that can be interpreted as a nest-construction ritual. Song of Estrildidae is an integral part of their prenuptial displays, not being used to announce or defend a territory. Males do not attack one another. Pair builds its nest together in dense bushes, including bougainvillea and hedges. Nest is spherical or oval with thick, resistant, but not woven walls composed of grass stems (of same species as grasses on which bird feeds) and some chicken feathers or cotton. The nest is accessible through a narrow, round tube protected by an awning leaning obliquely downward that makes it difficult to find the entrance.

Sometimes a small, loose, second-story nest is built with thin walls and a wide, easily visible side entrance, with level roof of nest below for a base (fig. 327). It is easy to believe that this addition is a false nest that would attract attention of any observer, and therefore of a dangerous predator, distracting it from true entrance to incubation chamber. It is said the male Black-rumped Waxbill, *Estrilda troglodytes,* which constructs a supplementary nest of this type in Africa, sometimes uses it for sleeping at night. Our *E. astrild* male usually sleeps in lower nest together with female. See Emberizinae, "Breeding," Sooty Grassquit, *Tiaris fuliginosa. E. astrild* sometimes makes an upper entrance to nest, right at the top, but such nests are abandoned shortly afterward. Some nests may be partly joined to one another. Some small, badly finished, egg-shaped nests appear to serve only as dormitories. Three miniscule, uniformly white eggs are incubated by pair for 11 days. Nestlings do not beg by raising themselves vertically but do so with the neck resting on surface and only the mouth turned upward, displaying its characteristic design (see "Morphology"). They are fed small balls that are regurgitated by parents and transferred in a prolonged process. In the 1st week these balls contain insects and later a mixture with green seeds. Normally nests are perfectly clean, which

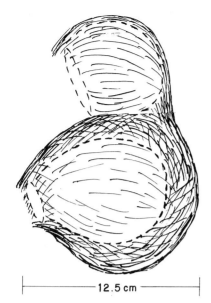

Fig. 327. Nest of the Common Waxbill, *Estrilda astrild*. A small upper nest was built above the principal nest and probably served as a place for the male to sleep. Rio de Janeiro, January 1982. Original, H. Sick.

is not always the case in the *Estrilda* genus. Young remain in the nest a long time, 17–19 days.

Spread in Brazil: According to indeterminate sources, the species was brought to Brazil in slave ships during reign of Dom Pedro I. It is certain that around 1870 José Torre Rossmann freed *E. astrild* in various places in interior São Paulo. Probably some seaman brought the species directly from Africa to Santos, where Rossmann's father was an important ship chandler (A. R. Carvalhaes pers. comm.). Meanwhile the waxbill was carried to other states, for it spreads even less spontaneously than *Passer domesticus* because of its more limited flying ability. It is found only in the vicinity of some cities.

Around 1918 it was living freely in Lins de Vasconcelos, and in 1924 it was not unusual in Santa Teresa (ex-Guanabara). Today it is also found on islands in Guanabara Bay. It occurs in various places in Rio de Janeiro and in Niterói and Petrópolis. It appeared wild in Vitória, Espírito Santo, after 1940 but in Salvador, Bahia, only after 1953. I saw it in Recife, Pernambuco, in 1967 and in the same year in Manaus, Amazonas, where it was taken by plane. In the northeast (Pernambuco) the name *Bico-de-lacre* ("Lacquer-bill") is used for a local wild rat, *Wideomys pyrrorhinos*. In Brasília, Federal District, the bird has occurred since 1964 when half a cageful of 100 birds escaped. In 1968 it was introduced in Campo Grande, Mato Grosso, and it is also found in Minas Gerais: in Nova Lima since 1950 and various other places, e.g., Belo Horizonte since 1967. It was recorded in Londrina, Paraná, in 1973 and liberated in Florianópolis, Santa Catarina, between 1928 and 1930 by Adolfo Konder. From there it conquered the adjacent continental coast. It appeared in Blumenau between 1940 and 1945. It occurs in Porto Alegre, Rio Grande do Sul, having been introduced before 1965 when it was brought from Santa Catarina. It was first seen in Belém, Pará, in 1977 (F. C. Novaes pers. comm.). Also called *Beijo-de-moça* (Minas Gerais). Introduced on Ilha Trindade.

Value; Other Captive Species: It continues to be sold, and there may have been new introductions from overseas. The species has various geographic races in Africa that interbreed in captivity. *Estrilda troglodytes* (= *cinerea*), quite similar to *E. astrild* but with white under tail coverts and white-margined outer tail feathers, is also sold in Brazil, though less frequently than *E. astrild*. So far it does not appear to exist in the wild here.

Other estrildids are sold in markets and bred in captivity in Brazil that do not occur here in the wild. They are frequently splendidly colored, e.g., Gouldian Finch, *Chloebia gouldiae*, with pointed tail, from Australia. Java Sparrow, *Padda oryzivora*, a large species with white cheeks and a large red bill, has been domesticated for centuries, as have the canary and budgerigar.

Estrildidae Bibliography

Immelmann, K. 1968. *J. Orn.* 109:284–99. [Song]

Sick, H. 1966. *An. Acad. Bras. Ciênc.* 38:169–71. [Identification, occurrence]

Wolters, A. E. 1970. Estrildidae. In Grzimek, *Tierleben.* Zurich.

General Bibliography

Ab'Saber, A. N. 1973. A organização natural das paisagens inter e subtropicais brasileiras. *Geomorf.* 41, São Paulo: IGEOB-USP.

Ab'Saber, A. N. 1977a. Espaços ocupados pela expansão dos climas secos na América do Sul por ocasião dos períodos glaciais quaternários. *Paleoclimas* 3. São Paulo: IGEOB-USP.

Ab'Saber, A. N. 1977b. Potencialidades paisagisticas brasileiras. Geomorf. 55. São Paulo: IGEOB-USP.

Ab'Saber, A. N. 1981. *Domínios morfoclimáticos atuais e quaternários na região dos Cerrados.* Craton and Intracraton 14.

Ackermann, F. L. 1964. *Geologia e fisiografia da região Bragantina (Estado do Pará).* ONPA.

Alvarenga, H. 1982. Uma gigantesca ave fóssil do Cenozoico brasileiro: *Physornis brasiliensis* sp.n. *An. Acad. bras. Ciênc.* 54(4):697–712.

Alvarenga, H. 1983. Uma ave ratita do Paleoceno brasileiro: Bacia Calcárea de Itaboraí, Estado do Rio de Janeiro, Brasil. *Bol. Mus. Nac. Rio de Janeiro, Geol.* 41:1–11.

Alvarenga, H. 1985a. Um Novo Psilopteridae (Aves-Gruiformes) dos Sedimentos Terciários de Itaboraí, Rio de Janeiro, Brasil. *VIII Cong. Bras. Paleont., 1983. MME-DNPM,* ser. Geologia no. 27.

Alvarenga, H. 1985b. Notas Sobre os Cathartidae (Aves) e Descrição de um Novo Gênero do Cenozoico Brasileiro. *An. Acad. bras. Ciênc.* 57(3):349–357.

Alvarenga, H. 1988. Ave Fóssil (Gruiformes: Rallidae) dos folhelhos da Bacia de Taubaté. *An. Acad. bras. Ciênc.* 60(3):321–328.

Amadon, D. 1957. Remarks on the classification of the perching birds, order Passeriformes. *Calcutta Zool. Soc. Proc., Mookerjee Mem.:* 259–268.

Amadon, D. 1966a. The superspecies concept. *Syst. Zool.* 15:245–249.

Amadon, D. 1966b. Avian plumage and molts. *Condor* 68:263–278.

Amadon, D. 1968. Further remarks on the superspecies concept. *Syst. Zool.* 17:345–346.

Amadon, D. 1973. Birds of the Congo and the Amazon Forest. In B. J. Meggers et al., *Tropical Forest Ecosystems in Africa and South America,* 267–277. Washington, D.C.: Smithsonian Institution.

American Ornithologists' Union. 1983. *Check-list of North American Birds.* 6th ed.

Ames, P. L. 1971. The morphology of the syrinx in passerine birds. *Bull. Peabody Mus. Nat. Hist.* 37.

Anchieta, Padre José de. 1900. *Cartas Inéditas.* S. Paulo: Ed. Inst. Hist. e Geográf.

Andersen, D. E., O. J. Rongstad, and W. R. Mytton. 1989. Response of nesting Red-tailed Hawks to helicopter overflights. *Condor* 91:296–299.

Andrade, G. A. 1982. *Nomes populares das aves do Brasil.* SOM-IBDF. Belo Horizonte.

Antas, P.T.Z. 1979. Reserva Biológica do Atol das Rocas. *Brasil Florestal* 9, 38:15–17.

Antas, P.T.Z. 1986. Migração de aves no Brasil. *An. II ENAV, Rio de Janeiro,* 153–184.

Antas, P.T.Z. 1990. Novos registros de aves para o Brasil. *Res. VI ENAV, Pelotas:* 51–52.

Ataliba, R. 1990. *XVII Congr. Bras. Zool.*

Azara, F. de. 1802–5. *Apuntiamentos para la historia de los Paxaros del Paraguay y Rio de la Plata.* 3 vols. Madrid.

Bang, G. B., and S. Cobb. 1968. The size of the olfactory bulb in 108 species of birds. *Auk* 85:55–61.

Bates, H. W. 1863. *A Naturalist on the River Amazons.* London: J. Murray.

Belton, W. 1984. Birds of Rio Grande do Sul, Brazil, Part 1: Rheidae through Furnariidae. *Bull. Amer. Mus. Nat. Hist.* 178(4):369–631.

Belton, W. 1985. Birds of Rio Grande do Sul, Brazil, Part 2: Formicariidae through Corvidae. *Bull. Amer. Mus. Nat. Hist.* 180(1):1–241.

Berkhoudt, H. 1985. Structure and function of avian taste receptors. In *Form and Function of Birds III:*463–468. London: Academic Press.

Berlepsch, H. von, and H. von Ihering. 1885. Die Vögel der Umgegend von Taquara do Mundo Novo, Rio Grande do Sul. *Zeitschr. Ges. Orn.* 1885:97–184.

Bock, W. J. 1963. Evolution and phylogeny in morphologically uniform groups. *A. Nat.* 97:265–285.

Böker, H. 1935–37. *Einführung in die vergleichende biologische Anatomie der Wirbeltiere.* 2 vols. Jena: G. Fischer.

Brown, K. S., Jr. 1987a. Areas where humid tropical forest probably persisted. In T. C. Whitmore and G. T. Prance, eds., *Biogeography and Quaternary History in Tropical America,* 45. Oxford Monogr. Biogeogr. 3. Oxford: Clarendon Press.

Brown, K. S., Jr. 1987b. Conclusions, synthesis, and alternative hypotheses. In T. C. Whitmore and G. T. Prance, eds., *Biogeography and Quaternary History in Tropical America,* 175–196. Oxford Monogr. Biogeogr. 3. Oxford: Clarendon Press.

Brown, K. S., Jr., and A. N. Ab'Saber. 1979. Ice-age forest refuges and evolution in the Neotropics. *Paleoclimas* 5. São Paulo: IGEOB-USP.

Brown, K. S., Jr., P. M. Sheppard, and J.R.G. Turner. 1974. Quaternary forest refugia in Tropical America: Evidence from race formation in *Heliconius* butterflies. *Proc. R. Soc. London* (B) 187.

Burmeister, H. 1853. *Viagem ao Brasil, através das provincias de Rio de Janeiro e Minas Gerais.* Bibl. Histor. Bras. XIX.

Burmeister, H. 1854–56. *Systematische Übersicht der Tiere Brasiliens, welche während einer Reise durch die Provinzen von Rio de Janeiro und Minas Gerais gesammelt und beobachtet wurden.* 2 vols. Berlin: G. Reimer.

Cabrera, A., and J. Yepes. 1940. *Mamíferos sudamericanos.* Buenos Aires.

Camargo and Posey. 1984. *XI Congr. Bras. Zool., Belém:* 477.

Caparella, A. P. 1988. Genetic variation in Neotropical birds: Implications for the speciation process. *Acta XIX Congr. Intern. Ornith.* (Ottawa 1986) 2:1658–1673.

Cardim, F. 1939. *Tratados da terra e gente do Brasil.* São Paulo: Brasiliana.

Carvalho, C. E. Souza. 1985. Massacre na feira. *ISTO-E* 31/7.

Carvalho, J.C.M. 1953. Contribuição da Ornis Brasileira na Confecção das Murças Imperiais. *Publ. Avuls. Museu Nacional* 10.

Castelnau, F. de. 1855. *Expedition dans les Parties Centrales de l'Amerique du Sud, de Rio de Janeiro à Lima, et de Lima à Pará, exécutéé en 1843 à 1847.* Oiseaux par M. O. des Murs. Paris.

Chandler, A. C. 1916. A study of the structure of feathers, with reference to their taxonomic significance. *Univ. Calif. Publ. Zool.* 13(11):243–246.

Chapman, F. M. 1917. The distribution of bird-life in Colombia: A contribution to a biological survey of South America. *Bull. Amer. Mus. Nat. Hist.* 36:1–729.

Choris, L. 1822. Voyage pittoresque autour du monde, avec de portraits de sauvages. In P. Berger (1979), Relatos de viajantes estrangeiros nos séculos XVIII e XIX em Santa Catarina. Florianopolis. *Assembl. Leg., Ass. Cult.:*257–261.

Clements, J. F. 1991. *Birds of the World: A Check List.* 4th ed. New York.

Cody, M. L. 1969. Convergent characters in sympatric species: A possible relation to interspecific competition and aggression. *Condor* 71:222–239.

Coelho, A.G.M. 1981. Observações sobre a avifauna do Arquipélago dos Abrolhos, Bahia. *Univ. Fed. Pernambuco, Publ. Avuls.* 1:1–7.

Colinvaux, P. 1987. Amazon diversity in light of the paleoecological record. *Quat. Sci. Reviews* 6:93–114.

Connor, E. F. 1986. The role of Pleistocene forest refugia in the evolution and biogeography of tropical biotas. *Trends in Ecology and Evolution* 1:165–168.

Cory, C. B., C. E. Hellmayr, and B. Conover. 1918–49. Catalogue of birds of the Americas. *Field Mus. Nat. Hist.* 13. 14 vols.

Cracraft, J. 1985. Historical biogeography and patterns of differentiation within the South American avifauna: Areas of endemism. *Ornith. Monogr.* 36:49–84.

Cracraft, J., and R. O. Prum. 1988. Patterns and processes of diversification: Speciation and historical congruence in some Neotropical birds. *Evolution* 42:603–620.

Darwin, C. 1868. *Variation of Animals and Plants under Domestication.* Vol. 2. London: John Murray.

Darwin, C. 1871. *The Descent of Man and Selection in Relation to Sex.* New York: Appleton.

Davis, D. E. 1945a. The annual cycle of plants, mosquitoes, birds and mammals in two Brazilian forests. *Ecol. Monogr.* 15:243–295.

Davis, D. E. 1945b. The occurrence of the incubation-patch in some Brazilian birds. *Wilson Bull.* 57(3):188–190.

Delacour, J., and C. Vaurie. 1957. A classification of Oscines. *Contrib. in Science, Los Angeles County Mus.* 16.

Descourtilz, J. T. 1944. *Ornitologia Brasileira, História Natural das Aves do Brasil.* Rio de Janeiro: Kosmos.

Dickerman, R. W., and W. H . Phelps, Jr. 1982. An annotated list of birds of Cerro Urutany on the border of Estado Bolivar, Venezuela and Territory Roraima, Brazil. *Am. Mus. Nov.* 2732.

Eisenmann, E., and H. Poor. 1946. Suggested principles of vernacular nomenclature. *Wilson Bull.* 58:210–215.

Ellenberg, H. 1981. Was ist ein Bioindikator? *Ökologie Vögel* 3(Sonderh.):83–99.

Emsley, M. G. 1965. Speciation in *Heliconius* (Lep., Nymphalidae): Morphology and geographic distribution. *Zoologica* (N.Y.) 50:191–254.

Engler, A. 1879–82. *Versuch einer Entwicklungsgeschichte der Pflanzenwelt.* Leipzig: Engelmann.

Erickson, H. T., and R. E. Mumford. 1976. *Notes on Birds of the Viçosa, Brazil, Region.* Dept. Forestry, Purdue University, West Lafayette, Indiana.

Euler, C. 1900. Descrição de ninhos e ovos das aves do Brasil. *Rev. Mus. Paul.* 4:9–148.

Fearnside, P. 1985. Processos predatórios na floresta úmida da Amazonia Brasileira. *Estudos Avançados* 3, no. 5. São Paulo.

Feduccia, A. 1974. Morphology of the bony stapes in New and Old World Suboscines: New evidence for common ancestry. *Auk* 91:427–429.

Feduccia, A. 1977. A model for the evolution of perching birds. *Syst. Zool.* 26, 1:19–31.

Feduccia, A. 1980. *The Age of Birds.* Cambridge, Mass.: Harvard University Press.

Feduccia, A., and S. L. Olson. 1982. Morphological similarities between the Menurae and the Rhinocryptidae, relict Passerine birds of the Southern Hemisphere. *Smithsonian Contr. Zool.* 336.

Feio, J. L. A. 1960. Contribuição à conceituação da Biogeografia. *Mus. Nacional, Rio de Janeiro, Publ. Avuls.* 36.

Ferreira, A. R. 1971. *Viagem Filosófica pelas capitanias do Grão Pará, Rio Negro, Mato Grosso e Cuiabá 1783–1792.* Iconografia, 2 vols. Rio de Janeiro: Cons. Fed. de Cultura.

Ferreira, D. F. 1899. *Arte da caça de altaneira* (Re-edition of the original published in 1616). Lisbon: Bibl. Cláss. Portug.

Fittkau, J. J. 1975. Productivity, biomass and population dynamics in Amazonian water bodies. In Golly and Medina, eds., *Tropical Ecol. Systems.* Berlin and New York.

Florence, H. 1876. Zoophonia. *Rev. Trim. Inst. Geogr. e Etnogr. do Brasil* 39:321–336.

Forbes, W. A. 1881. Eleven weeks in North-eastern Brazil. *Ibis* 4(5):315–362.

Fry, C. H. 1970. Ecological distribution of birds in North-Eastern Mato Grosso, Brazil. *An. Acad. bras. Ciênc.* 42, 2:275–318.

Fry, C. H. 1983. Birds in savanna ecosystems. In F. Bourlière, ed., *Tropical Savannas.* Amsterdam.

Fürbringer, M. 1888. *Untersuchungen zur Morphologie und Systematik der Vögel, zugleich ein Beitrag zur Anatomie der Stütz- und Bewegungsorgane.* 2 vols. Amsterdam.

Garcia, R. 1913. *Nomes de aves em língua Tupi.* Rio de Janeiro: Min. Agricult.

Gentry, A. H. 1988. Tree species richness of upper Amazonian forests. *Proc. Nat. Acad. Sci.* 85:156–159.

Gesner, C. 1555. *Historia animalium.* Zurich.

Gmelin, J. F. 1788. See Schaeffer, E. (1970).

Goeldi, E. 1893. *Os mamíferos do Brasil.* Rio de Janeiro: Ed. Alves.

Goeldi, E. 1894. *As aves do Brasil.* Rio de Janeiro: Ed. Alves.

Goeldi, E. 1897. Ornithological results of a naturalist's visit to the coastal region of South Guyana. *Ibis:* 149–165.

Goeldi, E. 1900–1906. *Album de aves Amazônicas.* Reedited 1981. Rio de Janeiro: Ed. Univ. Brasília/CNPq.

Gonzaga, L.A.P. 1988. A new antwren (*Myrmotherula*) from southeastern Brazil. *Bull. B.O.C.* 108(3):132–135.

Gould, J. 1854. *Monograph of the Ramphastidae.* London.

Gould, J. 1849–. *Monograph of the Trochilidae.* London.

Grassé, P. P. 1950. *Traité de Zoologie* 15: Oiseaux. Paris.

Haffer, J. 1967. Speciation in Colombian forest birds west of the Andes. *Am. Mus. Nov.* 2294.

Haffer, J. 1969. Speciation in Amazonian forest birds. *Science* 165:131–137.

Haffer, J. 1970. Art-Entstehung bei einigen Waldvögeln Amazoniens. *J. Orn.* 111, 3/4:285–331.

Haffer, J. 1974a. Pleistozäne Differenzierung der amazonischen Vogelwelt. *Bonn. Zool. Beitr.* 25:87–117.

Haffer, J. 1974b. Avian speciation in tropical South America. *Publ. Nuttall Ornith. Club* 14:1–390.

Haffer, J. 1975. Avifauna of northwestern Colombia, South America. *Bonn. Zool. Monogr.* 7.

Haffer, J. 1978. Distribution of Amazon forest birds. *Bonner Zool. Beitr.* 29:38–78.

Haffer, J. 1981. Aspects of Neotropical bird speciation during the Cenozoic. In G. Nelson et al., eds., *Vicariance Biogeography,* 371–405. New York: Columbia University Press.

Haffer, J. 1982. General aspects of the refuge theory. In G. T. Prance, ed., *Biological Diversification in the Tropics,* 6–24. New York: Columbia University Press.

Haffer, J. 1985. Avian zoogeography of the neotropical lowlands. *Ornith. Monogr.* 36:113–146.

Haffer, J. 1987a. Biogeography of neotropical birds. In T. C. Whitmore and G. T. Prance, eds., *Biogeography and Quaternary History in Tropical America,* 105–150. Oxford Monogr. Biogeogr. 3. Oxford: Clarendon Press.

Haffer, J. 1987b. Quaternary history of tropical America. In T. C. Whitmore and G. T. Prance, eds. *Biogeography and Quaternary History in Tropical America,* 1–18. Oxford Monogr. Biogeogr. 3. Oxford: Clarendon Press.

Hahn, E. 1989. Schwermetalle in Federn vom Habicht (*Accipter gentilis*) aus einem unterschiedlich belasteten Gebiet. *J. Orn.* 130:303–309.

Hahn, E., K. Hahn, and M. Stoeppler. In press. Zeeman SS-GFASS, an ideal method for the evaluation of lead and cadmium profiles in bird feathers. *Fres. Ztschr. f. anal. Chemie.*

Hartman, F. A. 1961. Locomotor mechanisms of birds. *Smithsonian Misc. Coll.* 143, 1.

Haverschmidt, F. 1968. *Birds of Suriname.* Edinburgh and London: Oliver and Boyd.

Heimerdinger, M. A., and P. L. Ames. 1967. Variation in sternal notches of Suboscines. *Postilla* 105.

Hellmayr, C. E. 1906. Revision der Spix'schen Typen brasilianischer Vögel. *Abh.d.II.Kl.d. Bayr Akademie d. Wiss.* 22, 3:563–726.

Hellmayr, C. E. 1910. The birds of the Rio Madeira. *Novit. Zool.* 17:257–428.

Hellmayr, C. E. 1912. Zoologische Ergebnisse einer Reise in das Mündungsgebiet des Amazonas, ed. L. Müller. II: Vögel. *Abhandl. Bayer. Akad. Wiss., Math.-phys. Klasse* 26:1–142.

Hellmayr, C. E. 1925. Review of the birds collected by Alcide d'Orbigny in South America (continuation). *Nov. Zool.* 32(1).

Hellmayr, C. E. 1929. A contribution to the ornithology of Northeastern Brazil (material Heinrich Snethlage). *Field Mus. Nat. Hist. Zool.,* ser. 12.

Hellmayr, C. E. See Cory.

Hershkovitz, P. 1977. *Living New World Monkeys (Platyrrhini).* Vol. 1. Chicago: University of Chicago Press.

Hickey, J. J., and D. M. Anderson. 1968. Chlorinated hydrocarbons and eggshell changes in raptorial and fish-eating Birds. *Science.*

Hilty, S. L., and W. L. Brown. 1986. *A Guide to the Birds of Colombia.* Princeton, N.J.: Princeton University Press.

Holdgate, M. W. 1987. Changing habitats of the world. *Oryx* 21:149–159.

Hudson, W. H. 1920. *Birds of La Plata.* Vols. 1 and 2. London.

Hueck, K. 1966. *Die Wälder Südamerikas.* Stuttgart: Fischer. (Translation, University of Brasilia.)

Hueck, K., and Siebert, P. 1972. *Vegetationskarte von Südamerika.* Stuttgart: Fischer.

Ihering, H. von. 1898. As Aves do Estado de São Paulo. *Rev. Mus. Paul.* 3:113–476.

Ihering, H. von, and R. von Ihering. 1907. *As aves do Brasil. Catálogo da Fauna Brasileira.* Vol. I. São Paulo: Museo Paulista.

Ihering, R. von. 1914. *O livrinho das aves.* São Paulo.

Ihering, R. von. 1967. *Da vida dos nossos animais.* 5th ed. São Leopoldo: Rotermund & Cia.

Ihering, R. von. 1968. *Dicionário dos animais do Brasil.* Editora Univ. de Brasília.

Johnson, A. W. 1965–67. *The Birds of Chile and adjacent regions of Argentina, Bolivia, and Peru.* 2 vols. Buenos Aires: Platt. [This is an English-language version of J. D. Goodall, A. W. Johnson, and R. A. Philippi B. (1946, 1951), *Las aves de Chile,* 2 vols.]

Kartchev, N. N. 1962. *J. Orn.* 103:297–298.

Koepcke, M. 1972. Über die Resistensformen der Vogelnester in einem begrenzten Gebiet des tropischen Regenwaldes in Peru. *J. Orn.* 113(2):138–160.

Krieg, H. 1948. *Zwischen Anden und Atlantik, Reise eines Biologen in Südamerika.* Munich.

Kuhlmann, M., and S. Jimbo. 1957. A flora na alimentação das aves brasileiras I. *Pap. Avuls. Zool. S. Paulo* 13(7):85–97.

Lack, D. 1968. *Ecological Adaptations for Breeding in Birds.* London: Methuen.

Léry, J. de. 1961. *Viagem à Terra do Brasil.* Rio de Janeiro. (Reprint of 1578 edition.)

Lincoln, F. C. 1950. Migrations of Birds. *U.S. Fish and Wildlife Service,* circ. 16.

Lisboa, Frei Cristóvão de. 1625–31. *História dos animals e árvores do Maranhão.*

Livingstone, D. A. 1980. History of the tropical rain forest. *Paleobiology* 6:343–344.

Lovejoy, T. E. 1974. Bird diversity and abundance in Amazon forest communities. *Living Bird* 13:127–191.

Lovejoy, T. E., and D. C. Oren. 1981. Minimum critical size of ecosystems. In R. L. Burgess and D. M. Sharp, eds., *Forest Island Dynamics in Man-dominated Landscapes.* New York: Springer.

Lumley, H., and M. Lumley. 1987. *L'Anthropologie* (Paris) 91(4):917–942.

Lynch, J. D. 1988. Refugia. In A. A. Myers and P. S. Giller, eds., *Analytical Biogeography,* 311–342. London: Chapman and Hall.

MacArthur, R. H., and E. O. Wilson. 1967. *The Theory of Island Biogeography.* Princeton, N.J.: Princeton University Press.

McFarlane, R. W. 1963. The taxonomic significance of avian sperm. *Proc. XIII Intern. Orn. Congr., Ithaca.* 1962:91–102.

Marcgrave, G. 1648. *Historia naturalis Brasiliae.* Amsterdam.

Martins Neto, R., and A. Kellner. 1988. Primeiro Registro de Pena na formação Santana (Cretáceo Inferior), Bacia do Araripe, Nordeste do Brasil. *An. Acad. Bras. Ciênc.* 60(1):61–68.

Martius, C.F.P. von. 1863. *Nomina animalium in lingua Tupí.*

Martius, C.F.P. von. 1967. *Flora Brasiliensis.* Vols. 1–15. New York: J. Cramer.

Maximiliano, Prince of Wied Neuwied. 1940. Viagem ao Brasil. *Brasiliana,* ser. 5a,1 (annotated by Olivério Pinto). São Paulo.

Maximiliano, Prince of Wied Neuwied. 1830–33. *Beitr. Naturg. Bras.* Vols. 3–4 (morphology and behavior of birds).

Mayr, E. 1942. *Systematics and the Origin of Species.* New York: Columbia University Press.

Mayr, E. 1946. History of the North American bird fauna. *Wilson Bull.* 58:3–41.

Mayr, E., and D. Amadon. 1951. A classification of recent birds. *Am. Mus. Nov.* 1496. New York.

Mayr, E., E. G. Linsley, and R. L. Unsinger. 1953. *Methods and Principles of Systematic Zoology.* New York: McGraw-Hill.

Mayr, E., and W. Phelps, Jr. 1967. The origin of the bird fauna of the south Venezuelan highlands. *Bull. Am. Mus. Nat. Hist.* 136, 5.

Mayr, E., and L. L. Short. 1970. Species taxa of North American birds. *Publ. Nuttall Ornith. Club* 9 (Cambridge, Mass.).

Mazza, S. T., E. Deautier, and A. Stellet. 1927. Investigación de Hemoparásitos en algunas aves de Misiones. *Hornero* 4:49–52.

Mello Leitão, C. 1937. Zoogeografia do Brasil. *Brasiliana,* ser. 5, vol. 77.

Meyer de Schauensee, R. 1966. *The Species of Birds of South America and Their Distribution.* Narberth, Pa.: Livingston.

Meyer de Schauensee, R. 1970. *A Guide to the Birds of South America.* Narberth, Pa.: Livingston.

Meyer de Schauensee, R., and W. H. Phelps, Jr. 1978. *A Guide to the Birds of Venezuela.* Princeton, N.J.: Princeton University Press.

Miller, R. R. 1986. *For Science and National Glory: The Spanish Expedition to America 1862–66.* Norman: University of Oklahoma Press.

Miranda Ribeiro, A. 1937. *Rev. Mus. Paul.* 23:36–90 (seriema monograph).

Miranda Ribeiro, A. 1938. *Rev. Mus. Paul.* 23:667–788 (tinamou monograph).

Mitchell, M. H. 1957. *Observations on Birds of Southeastern Brazil.* Toronto.

Möller, A. 1915/1920. *Fritz Müller, Werke, Briefe und Leben.* 3 vols. Coletânia.

Moraes, R. 1938. *Os Igaraúnas.* Rio de Janeiro: Civilização Brasileira.

Moynihan, M. 1960. Some adaptations which help to promote gregariousness. *Prox. XII. Cong. Internat. Ornith. Helsinki* (1958), 533–541.

Moynihan, M. 1969. Social mimicry: Character convergence versus character displacement. *Evol.* 22:315–331.

Müller, F. 1863. *Pro-Darwin.* Leipzig: Engelmann.

Müller, P. 1973. The dispersal centres of terrestrial vertebrates in the neotropical realm. *Biogeographica* 2 (The Hague).

Murphy, R. C. 1936. *Oceanic Birds of South America.* Vols. 1–2. New York.

Narosky, T., and D. Yzurieta. 1987. *Guía para la Identificación de las Aves de Argentina y Uruguay.* Buenos Aires: Vazquez Mazzini Eds.

Naumburg, E.M.G. 1930. The birds of Mato Grosso, Brazil. *Bull. Am. Mus. Nat. Hist.* 60:1–432.

Navas, J. R., T. Narosky, N. A. Bó, et al. 1991. *Lista Patrón de los Nombres Comunes de las Aves Argentinas.* Buenos Aires: Asoc. Orn. del Plata.

Negret, A. 1984. Sazonalidade da avifauna da Reserva Ecol. IBGE, Brasília. *Resumos XI Congr. Bras. Zool., Belém,* 352.

Negret, A., J. Taylor, R. C. Soares, R. C. Cavalcanti, and C. Johnson. 1984. *Aves da região geopolítica do Distrito Federal.* SEMA, Minist. Interior.

Neiva, A., and B. Penna. 1916. Viagem científica pelo norte da Bahia, sudoeste de Pernambuco, sul de Piauí e norte a sul de Goiás. *Memor. Inst. Oswaldo Cruz* 8(3):75–224.

Nice, M. M. 1964. *Studies in the Life History of the Song Sparrow.* 2 vols. New York: Dover.

Nogueira Neto, P. 1973. *A criação de animais indígenas vertebrados.* São Paulo.

Nomura, H. 1959. Zoofonia. *Almanaque Agrícola Chácaras e Quintais* 100(1):259–265.

Novaes, F. C. 1969. Análise ecológica de uma avifauna da região do rio Acará, Pará. *Bol. Mus. Para. E. Goeldi* Zool. 69.

Novaes, F. C. 1970. Distribuição ecológica e abundância das aves em um trecho da mata do baixo rio Guamá, Pará. *Bol. Mus. Para. E. Goeldi* (Zool.) 71.

Novaes, F. C. 1978a. Ornitologia do Território de Amapá II. *Mus. Para. E. Goeldi* (Publ. Avuls.) 29.

Novaes, F. C. 1978b. Sobre algumas aves pouco conhecidas da Amazonia Brasileira. *Bol. Mus. Para. E. Goeldi* (Zool.) 90.

Olrog, C. C. 1963. Lista y distribución de las aves argentinas. *Opera Lilloana* 9, Fund. Miguel Lillo, Tucumán.

Olrog, C. C. 1984. *Las aves argentinas "Una nueva guía de campo."* Admin. de Parques Nacionales. Buenos Aires.

Olson, S. L. 1973. Evolution of the rails of the South Atlantic Islands (Aves: Rallidae). *Smithsonian Contr. Zool.* 152.

Olson, S. L. 1977. A synopsis of the fossil Rallidae. In S. D. Ripley, *Rails of the World,* 509–525. Boston: Godine.

Olson, S. L. 1981. Natural history of vertebrates on Brazilian islands of the mid South Atlantic. *Nat. Geogr. Soc. Research Rep.* 13:481–492.

Olson, S. L. 1982. A critique of Cracraft's classification of birds. *Auk* 99:733–739.

Olson, S. L., and A. Feduccia. 1980. *Presbyornis* and the origin of the Anseriformes. *Smithsonian Contri. Zool.* 323.

Oniki, Y. 1986. "Nidificação de aves em duas localidades amazônicas: sucesso e adaptação." Thesis. Inst. Biol., Univ. Campinas.

d'Orbigny, A. D. *Voyage dans l'Amerique Meridionale 1835–38.*

Oren, D. C. 1984. Resultados de uma nova expedição zoológica a Fernando de Noronha. *Bol. Mus. Para. E. Goeldi* (Zool.) 1(1):19–44.

Padua, M.T.I., and A. F. Coimbra Filho. 1979. *Os Parques Nacionais do Brasil.* ICBF/INCAFO.

Pearson, D. L. 1971. Vertical stratification of birds in a tropical dry forest. *Condor* 73:40–55.

Pearson, D. L. 1977. A pantropical comparison of bird community structure on six lowland forest sites. *Condor* 79:232–244.

Pelzeln, A. von. 1867–71. *Zur Ornithologie Brasiliens. Resultate von Johann Natterers Reisen 1817 bis 1835.* Vienna: Pichlers.

Pernetty, A. J. 1979. Histoire d'un voyage aux isles Malouines, fait en 1763 et 1764. In P. Berger, ed., *Relatos de viajantes estrangeiros nos séculos XVIII e XIX,* 83–115. Florianópolis.

Peters, J. L. 1931–86. *Check-list of the Birds of the World.* Cambridge, Mass.: Harvard University Press.

Peterson, R. T. 1980. *A Field Guide to the Birds.* Boston: Houghton Mifflin. (Various other North American field guides cover North American birds that migrate to South America.)

Phelps, W. H., and W. H. Phelps, Jr. 1962. Cuarentinueve aves nuevas para la avifauna Brasileña del Cerro Uei-Tepui. *Bol. Soc. Venez. Cienc. Nat.* 23:101.

Pineschi, R. B. 1990. Aves como agentes dispersores de sete espécies de *Rampanea* (Myrsinaceae) no maciço do Itatiaia, Rio de Janeiro e Minas Gerais. *Ararajuba* 1:71–75.

Pinto, O.M.O. 1938. Catálogo das aves do Brasil. Part 1. *Rev. Mus. Paulista,* vol. 22.

Pinto, O.M.O. 1944. *Catálogo das aves do Brasil.* Part 2. São Paulo: Sec. Agric. Ind. e Comercio.

Pinto, O.M.O. 1950. Peter W. Lund e sua contribuição a ornitologia brasileira. *Pap. Avuls., Dept. Zool. São Paulo* 9, 18:269–283.

Pinto, O.M.O. 1953. Sobre a coleção Carlos Estevão de peles, ninhos e ovos de aves de Belém, Pará. *Papéis avuls. Zool. S. Paulo* 11, 13:113–224.

Pinto, O.M.O. 1954. Aves do Itatiaia. Lista remissiva e novas achegas à avifauna da região. *Minist. Agricult.,* Bol. 3.

Pinto, O.M.O. 1964. *Ornitologia Brasiliense.* Vol. 1, Depto. Zool. Secret. Agric. S. Paulo.

Pinto, O.M.O. 1978. *Novo catálogo das aves do Brasil.* Vol. 1. São Paulo: Empresa Gráfica da Rev. dos Tribunais.

Prance, G. T., ed. 1982. *Biological Diversification in the Tropics.* New York: Columbia University Press.

Prance, G. T. 1985. The changing forests. In G. T. Prance and T. E. Lovejoy, eds., *Amazonia,* 146–165. Oxford: Pergamon Press.

Prum, R. O. 1988. Historical relationships among avian forest areas of endemism in the Neotropics. *Acta XIX Congr. Intern. Ornith. Ottawa 1986,* vol. 2: 2562–2572.

Prum, R. O., and W. E. Lanyon. 1989. Monophyly and phylogeny of the *Schiffornis* group (Tyrannoidae). *Condor* 91:444–461.

Rappole, J. H., E. S. Morton, T. G. Lovejoy III, J. L. Ruos, and B. Swift. 1983. *Nearctic Avian Migrants in the Neotropics.* U.S. Fish and Wildlife Serv./World Wildlife Fund.

Räsänen, M. E., J. S. Salo, and R. J. Kalliola. 1987. Fluvial perturbance in the western Amazon basin: Regulation by long-term sub-Andean tectonics. *Science* 238:1398–1401.

Reguerio, A. M. 1983. *Por la Ciencia y la Gloria Nacional. La Expedición científica española a América (1862–1866).* Barcelona: Ed. del Serbal.

Reinhardt, J. T. 1881. Sobre os presumiveis restos de uma ave gigantesca das cavernas do Brasil, congenere de *Cariama. Com. Cinet. Soc. Hist. Nat. Copenhagen,* 141–153, in Portuguese by G. Hanssen. (Translated in *Ibis,* 1982).

Reiser, O. 1924. Bericht über die ornithologische Ausbeute der zool. Expedition der Akad. Wiss. nach Nordostbrasilien 1903. *Denkschrift Wien* 765:107–252.

Remsen, Jr., J. V., J. O'Neill, and T. A. Parker III. 1983. Contribution of river-created habitats to bird species richness in Amazonia. *Biotropica* 15:223–231.

Rensch, B. 1925. [Taste sensitivity.] *J. Orn.* 73:1–8.

Rensch, B., and R. Neunzig. 1925. Experimentelle Untersuchungen über den Geschmackssinn der Vögel, II. *J. Orn.* 73:633–646.

Ridgely, R. S., and G. Tudor. 1989. *The Birds of South America.* Vol. 1, *The Oscine Passerines.* Austin: University of Texas Press.

Rizzini, C. T. 1963. Nota prévia sobre a divisão fitogeográfica (florístico-sociológica) do Brasil. *Rev. Bras. Geograf.* 25, 1:1–64.

Rizzini, C. T. 1976–79. *Tratado de Fitogeografia do Brasil.* 2 vols. USP.

Rodrigues, J. Barbosa. 1903. *Sertum Palmarum Brasiliensium.* Brussels. (Facsimile: Expressão e Cultura, Rio de Janeiro, 1989.)

Ruschi, A. 1950. Fitogeografia do Estado do Espírito Santo. *Sér. Bot.* 1.

Ruschi, A. 1979. *Aves do Brasil.* São Paulo: Ed. Rios.

Ruschi, A. 1981. *Aves do Brasil.* vol. 2. São Paulo: Ed. Rios.

Ruschi, A. 1982. *Beija-flores do Espirito Santo.* Serves as *Aves do Brasil,* vol. 3. São Paulo: Ed. Rios.

Ruschi, A. 1982. *Aves do Brasil.* Vol. 4, *Beija-flores.* Rio de Janeiro: Ed. Expressão e Cultura. (Appeared in 1986.)

Ruschi, A. 1982. *Aves do Brasil.* Vol. 5, *Beija-flores.* Rio de Janeiro: Ed. Expressão e Cultura.

Saint-Hilaire. A. de. 1936. Viagem a Província de Santa Catarina (1820). *Brasiliana* 58.

Salo, J. V. 1987. Pleistocene forest refuges in the Amazon: Evaluation of the biostratigraphical, lithostratigraphical and geomorphological data. *Ann. Zool. Fennici* 24:203–211.

Sampaio, A. J. 1938. Phytogeographia do Brasil. *Brasiliana, ser.* 5, 35. Bibl. Ped. Bras. S. Paulo.

Santos, E. 1938. *Da Ema ao beija-flor.* Rio de Janeiro. (Republished.)

Santos, E. 1940. *Pássaros do Brasil.* Rio de Janeiro (Republished.)

Schaeffer, E. 1970. *Pássaros do Brasil, pintado por Albert Echhout no castelo de Hofloessnitz na Saxônia,* with commentary by H. Sick. Rio de Janeiro: Agir.

Schauensee. See Meyer de Schauensee.

Scherer Neto, P. 1980. *Aves do Paraná*. Zôo-botânica Mário Nardelli.

Schneider, A. 1938. Die Vögelbilder zur Historia Naturalis Brasiliae des George Marcgrave. *J. Orn.* 86, 1:74–106.

Schneider, A., and H. Sick. 1962. Sobre a distribuição de algumas aves do Sudeste do Brasil segundo coleções do Museu Nacional. *Bol. Mus. Nac. Rio de J. Zool.* 239.

Schönwetter, M. 1967. *Handbuch der Oologie*. Vol. 1. Berlin: Akad. Verlag.

Schönwetter, M. 1979. *Handbuch der Oologie*. Vol. 2. Berlin: Akad. Verlag.

Schubert, C. 1988. Climatic changes during the last glacial maximum in northern South America and the Caribbean: A review. *Interciencia* 13:128–137.

Scott, D. A., and M. L. Brooke. 1985. The endangered avifauna of southeastern Brazil: A report of the BOU/WWF expeditions of 1980/81 and 1981/82. *ICBP Technical Publ.* 4.

Selander, R. K. 1971. Systematics and speciation in birds. In D. S. Farner and J. R. King, eds., *Avian Biology* 1, 57–147. New York: Academic Press.

Short, L. L. 1969. Taxonomic aspects of avian hybridization. *Auk* 86:84–105.

Short, L. L. 1971. The affinities of African with Neotropical woodpeckers. *Ostrich* (suppl.) 8:35–40.

Short, L. L. 1975. A zoogeographic analysis of the South American Chaco Avifauna. *Bull. Am. Mus. Nat. Hist.* 154(3):165–352.

Shufeldt, R. W. 1916. A fossil feather from Taubaté. *Auk* 33:206–207.

Sibley, C. G. 1970. A comparative study of egg white proteins of Passerine birds. *Bull. Peabody Mus. Nat Hist.* 32.

Sibley, C. G., and J. E. Ahlquist. 1982. The relationships of some groups of non-Passerines based on data from DNA-DNA hybridization. Unpublished paper distributed at 13th Intern. Ornith. Congr., Moscow.

Sibley, C. G., and J. E. Ahlquist. 1985. The phylogeny and classification of the Passerine birds based on comparisons of the genetic material. *Proc. 18th Intern. Ornith. Congr. Moscow,* 82–121.

Sibley, C. G., and J. E. Ahlquist. 1986. Reconstructing bird phylogeny by comparing DNAs. *Scient. American* 254(2):82–92.

Sibley, C. G., J. E. Ahlquist, and B. L. Monroe, Jr. 1988. A classification of the living birds of the world based on DNA-DNA hybridization studies. *Auk* 105(3):409–423.

Sick, H. 1937. Morphologisch-funktionelle Untersuchungen über die Feinstruktur der Vogelfeder. *J. Orn.* 85, 2:206–372.

Sick, H. 1950b. [Twilight movements.] *Vogelwarte* 15:156–160.

Sick, H. 1958. Resultados de uma excursão ornitológica do Museu Nacional a Brasília, novo Distrito Federal. *Bol. Mus. Nac. Rio de J. Zool.* 185.

Sick, H. 1960. *Publ. avuls. Mus. Nac. Rio de J.,* 34 (*Falco peregrinus,* behavior).

Sick, H. 1965. A fauna do cerrado. *Arq. Zool. S. Paulo* 12:71–93.

Sick, H. 1966. As aves do cerrado como fauna arborícola. *An. Acad. bras. Ciências* 38, 2:355–363.

Sick, H. 1967a. Hochwasserbedingte Vogelwanderungen in den neuweltlichen Tropen. *Vogelwarte* 24, 1:1–6.

Sick, H. 1967b. Rios e enchentes na Amazônia como obstáculo para a avifauna. In H. Lent, ed., *Atas do simpósio sôbre a biota*

Amazônica 5 (Zoologia), 495–520. Rio de Janeiro: Conselho Nacional de Pesquisas.

Sick, H. 1968a. Vogelwanderungen im kontinentalen Südamerika. *Vogelwarte* 24, 3/4:217–242.

Sick, H. 1968b. Über in Südamerika eingeführte Vogelarten. *Bonn Zool. Beitr.* 19:298–306.

Sick, H. 1969. Aves brasileiras ameaçadas de extinção e noções gerais de conservação de aves do Brasil. *An. Acad. bras. Ciências* 41 (suppl.):205–229.

Sick, H. 1981. Zur frühen bildlichen Darstellung neotropischer Papageien. *J. Orn.* 122, 1:73–77.

Sick, H. 1983. Die Bedeutung von Johann Baptist von Spix für die Erforschung der Vogelwelt Brasiliens. *Spixiana* (suppl.) 9:29–31.

Sick, H. 1985. Observations on the Andean-Patagonian component of southeastern Brazil's avifauna. In *Neotropical Ornith., Ornith. Monogr.* 36:233–237.

Sick, H. 1985. *Ornitologia Brasileira, Uma Introdução*. Brasilia: Editora Universidade de Brasília.

Sick, H., L. A. do Rosário, and T. R. de Azevedo. 1981. Aves do Estado de Santa Catarina. *Sellówia,* ser. Zoologia, no. 1.

Silva, J.M.C. 1988. Atividade noturna de forageamento sob iluminação artificial de algumas aves amazônicas. *Bol. Mus. Para. E. Goeldi* (Zool.) 4(1):17–20.

Silva, J.M.C. 1989. "Análise biogeográfica da avifauna de florestas do interflúvio Araguaia-São Francisco." Thesis. Inst. Ciências Biol., Univ. Brasília.

Silva, J.M.C., and E. O. Willis. 1986. Notas sobre a distribuição de quatro espécies de aves da Amazônia Brasileira. *Bol. Mus. Para. E. Goeldi* (Zool.) 2:151–158.

Silva, J.M.C., and Y. Oniki. 1988. Lista preliminar da avifuana da estação ecológica Serra das Araras, Mato Grosso. *Bol. Mus. Para. E. Goeldi* (Zool.) 4(2).

Silva Santos, R. 1950. Vestígio de Ave Fóssil nos Folhelhos Betuminosos de Tremembé, São Paulo. *An. Acad. Bras. Ciências* 22:7–8.

Simpson, G. G., and J. Haffer. 1978. Speciation patterns in the Amazonian forest biota. *Ann. Rev. Ecol. Syst.* 9:497–518.

Sioli, H. 1962. Solos, tipos de vegetação e águas na Amazônia. *Bol. Mus. Para. E. Goeldi* (n.s., Avuls.) 1.

Skutch, A. F. 1945. The most hospitable tree. *The Scientific Monthly* 60:5–17.

Skutch, A. F. 1969. Life histories of Central American birds, III. *Pacific Coast Avifauna* 35:419–561 (Cooper Orn. Soc.).

Slud, P. 1976. Geographic and climatic relationships of avifaunas with special reference to comparative distribution in the neotropics. *Smithsonian Contr. Zool.* 212.

Snethlage, E. 1913. Über die Verbreitung der Vogelarten in Unteramazonian. *J. Orn.* 61:469–539.

Snethlage, E. 1914. Catálogo das aves amazônicas. *Bol. Mus. Para. E. Goeldi* 8:1–530.

Snethlage, H. 1928. Meine Reise durch Nordostbrasilien. Biologische Beobachtungen. *J. Orn.* 76:503–581.

Snow, D. W. 1971. Evolutionary aspects of fruit-eating by birds. *Ibis* 113:194–202.

Snow, D. W. 1981. Tropical frugivorous birds and their food-plants: A world survey. *Biotropica* 13(1):1–14.

Souza, G. S. de. 1938. *Tratado descritivo do Brasil em 1587*. São Paulo.

Spix, J. B. von. 1824–25. *Avium species novae Brasilian.* 2 vols. Munich: Hübschmann.

Spix, J. B. von, and C.F.P. von Martius. 1823–31. 3 vols. *Reise in Brasilien in den Jahren 1817–1820.* (Re-edition 1966.) Stuttgart: F. A. Brockhaus.

Spix, J. B. von, and C.F.P. von Martius. 1938. *Viagem pelo Brasil 1817–1820.* Rio de Janeiro: Imprensa Nacional.

Steinbacher, J. 1962. Beitrag zur Kenntnis der Vögel von Paraguay. *Abh. Senckenberg Naturf. Ges.* 502:1–106.

Stiles, F. G. 1985. On the role of birds in the dynamics of neotropical forests. *ICBP Technical Publ.* 4:49–59.

Storer, R. W. 1982. Fused thoracic vertebrae in birds: Their occurrence and possible significance. *J. Yamashina Inst. Ornith. 14:* 86–95.

Stotz, D. F. 1990. "Foraging ecology and morphology in the avian genus *Myrmotherula.*" Ph.D. diss. University of Chicago.

Stresemann, E. 1927–34. Sauropsida: Aves. In W. Kükenthal, *Handbuch der Zoologie,* vol. 7. Berlin and Leipzig: W. de Gruyter & Co.

Stresemann, E. 1948. Der Naturforscher Frederick Sellow (d. 1831) und sein Beitrag zur Kenntnis Brasiliens. *Zool. Jahrb. Syst. Ökol. Geogr.* 77(6):401–425.

Stresemann, E. 1950. Die brasilianischen Vogelsammlungen des Grafen von Hoffmannsegg aus den Jahren 1800–1812. *Bonn. Zool. Beitr.* 1:43–51, 126–143.

Stresemann, E. 1954. Ausgestorbene und austerbende Vogelarten, vertreten im Zoologischen Museum zu Berlin. *Mitt. Zool. Mus. Berlin* 30(1):38–53.

Stresemann, E., and V. Stresemann. 1966. Die Mauser der Vögel. *J. Orn.* 107 (Sonderheft).

Taunay, A. de E. 1918. O primeiro naturalista de São Paulo. *Rev. Mus. Paulista* 10:830–864. Extract of an unfinished treatise on Brazilian ornithology in the archives of the State of São Paulo, by Diogo Toledo Lara e Ordonhes.

Taunay, A. de E. 1934. *Zoologia Fantástica do Brasil.* São Paulo: Melhoramentos.

Teixeira, D. M., J. B. Nacinovic, and M. S. Tavares, 1986. Notes on some birds of northeastern Brazil. *Bull B.O.C.* 106(2):70–74.

Teixeira, D. M., J. B. Nacinovic, and G. Luigi. 1989. Notes on some birds of northeastern Brazil (4). *Bull. B.O.C.* 109(3):152–157.

Terborgh, J. 1974. Preservation of natural diversity: The problem of extinction-prone species. *Bio. Science* 24:715–722.

Terborgh, J. 1985. Habitat selection in Amazonian birds. In M. L. Cody, ed., *Habitat Selection in Birds.* 311–338. New York: Academic Press.

Terborgh, J., and J. S. Weske. 1969. Colonization of secondary habitats by Peruvian birds. *Ecology* 50:765–782.

Tessmer, H. 1989. Interferências de aves em redes aéreas. *Moderna Electricidade* 17(180):36–42.

Thevet, A. 1878. *Les singularités de la France Antarctique.* New ed. Paris: Maisonneuve.

Tomback, D. F. 1975. An emetic technique to investigate food preferences. *Auk* 92:581–83.

Trancoso, N.S.S., E. P. Coelho, P. B. Bernardo, M. L. Soneghet, V. S. Alves, L. M. Gomes, and C. S. Munita. 1985. Dados preliminares sobre a concentração de metais pesados na Baia da Guanabara. *Relat. Anual Fund. Univers. José Bonifácio. UFRJ.*

Udvardy, M. D. F. 1969. *Dynamic Zoogeography.* New York: Van Nostrand-Reinhold.

Ulrich, W. 1972. Hermann Burmeister, 1807 to 1892. *Ann. Rev. Entom.* 17:1–20.

Usinger, R. L. 1966. Monograph of the Cimicidae. *Thomas Say Found.* 7.

Van Tyne, J., and A. J. Berger. 1959. *Fundamentals of Ornithology.* New York: John Wiley and Sons.

Vanzolini, P. E., and E. E. Williams. 1970. South American anoles, the geographic differentiation and evolution of the *Anolis chrysolepis* species group (Sauria, Iguanaidae). *Arqu. Zool. S. Paulo* 19:1–124.

Velloso, Fr. J. M. da C. 1800. *Aviário Brasílico, ou galleria ornithologica das aves indígenas do Brasil.* Off. da Casa Litt. do Arco do Cego.

Vermeer, K., et al. 1974. Pesticide effects on fish and birds in ricefields of Suriname. *Environ. Pollut.* 7:217–236.

Villela, G. G. 1968. Carotenóide de penas de algumas aves amazônicas. *An. Acad. Bras. Ciências* 40(3):391–399.

Villela, G. G. 1976. *Pigmentos animais zoocromos.* Rio de Janeiro: Acad. Bras. Ciências.

Voss, W. A., and M. Sander. 1981. Aves observadas numa monocultura de acacia-negra, *Acacia mollissima,* nos arredores de S. Leopoldo, Rio Grande do Sul. *Brasil Florestal* 11(46):7–15.

Vuilleumier, F. 1978. Remarques sur l'echantillonage d'une riche avifauna de l'ouest de l'Ecuador. *L'Oiseau et R.F.O.* 48:21–360.

Wagener, Z. 1964. *Zoobiblion, Livro de animais do Brasil.* Brasiliensia Documenta 4. Ed. by E. Cerqueira Falcão and E. Schaeffer.

Wallace, A. R. 1853. *Narrative of Travels on the Amazon and Rio Negro.* London: Reeup and Co.

Wallace, A. R. 1876. *The Geographical Distribution of Animals.* New York: Harper.

Watson, G. E. 1975. *Birds of the Antarctic and Sub-Antarctic.* Washington, D.C.: American Geophysical Union.

Wetmore, A. 1960. A classification for the birds of the World. *Smithsonian Misc. Coll.* 139.

Wied. See Maximiliano.

Willis, E. O. 1976. Effects of a cold wave on an Amazonian avifauna. *Acta Amazon.* 6(3):379–394.

Willis, E. O. 1977. Lista preliminar das aves da parte noroeste e áreas vizinhas da Reserva Ducke, Amazonia. *Rev. Bras. Biol.* 37(3):585–601.

Willis, E. O. 1979. The composition of avian communities in remanescent woodlots in southern Brazil. *Pap. Avul. Zool.* 33(1):1–25.

Willis, E. O., and Y. Oniki. 1988. Aves observadas em Balbina, Amazonas e os prováveis efeitos da barragem. *Ciência e Cultura* 40(3):280–284.

Willis, E. O., and Y. Oniki. 1988. Na trilha das formigas carnívoras. *Ciência Hoje* 8(47):27–32.

Willis, E. O., and Y. Oniki. 1991. *Nomes Gerais para as Aves Brasileiras.* "Gráfica da Região" - Américo Brasiliense, São Paulo.

Winge, O. 1888. Fugle fra Knoglehuler i Brasilien. *E Lundi* 1(2):1–54.

Species Index: Scientific Names

For Brazilian birds, English name and location of species account and of plate, where applicable, follow genus listing. Numbers of all pages where name appears follow species listing. **Bold** type indicates species account.

maculatus, Rallus 209–10, **211,** 213
maculicauda, Hypocnemoides **417**
maculicaudus, Caprimulgus 304, 309, **310**
maculifrons, Veniliornis 9, 66, **393**
maculipennis, Larus 185, 236–37, **238,** 240
maculirostris, Selenidera 33, 373–74, 377, 378, **380**
maculosa, Columba 244–45, **247**
maculosa, Nothura 52–53, 74, 80, 93–101, **105,** 181, 201, 203, 245, 252, 283, 291, 552
maculosus, Nyctibius 302
magdalenae, Hoazinoides 204
magellani, Pelecanoides 75, **119**
magellanica, Carduelis 11, 13, 374, 593, 603, 605–6, **635,** 636
magellanicus, Spheniscus 75, **120,** 121
magister, Vireo 556
magna, Sturnella 12, 17, 60, 72, 202, 282, 521, 616, 621, 623, **627,** 628
magnifica, Lophornis 66, 322, 326, 329, 332, 334, **345**
magnificens, Argentavis 148
magnificens, Fregata 16, 71, 128, **129,** 130, 171, 513, 619
magnirostris, Rupornis 167–70, 172, **174,** 186, 211, 280, 292, 431, 529–30, 532, 546, 550, 579, 597, 621, 640
maguari, Ciconia 132, 144–45, **146,** 150, 153, 165
major, Crotophaga 78, 141, 176, 189, 205, 278–82, **283,** 514, 637
major, Dendrocopos 384
major, Diglossa 567, **584**
major, Podiceps 15, 110, **111,** 121
major, Schiffornis **502**
major, Taraba 404–6, **409**
major, Tinamus 96, 99–100, **102**
major, Xiphocolaptes 445, **447**
malachitacea, Triclaria 10, 66, 68, 252–55, 259, 262, **276**
Malacoptila 366–67
  fusca White-chested Puffbird **369**
  panamensis 367
  rufa Rufous-necked Puffbird **369**
  semicincta Semicollared Puffbird **369**
  striata Crescent-chested Puffbird **369,** Pl. 23.3
malaris, Phaethornis 325, 333, **341**
malura, Drymophila 69, **415**
maluroides, Spartonoica 427, **434**
Malvaviscus 338
Malvaviscus arboreus 325
Manacus 487, 567
  manacus White-bearded Manakin **499**
manacus, Manacus 452, 488–93, 497, **499,** 500, 518, 569, 593
mangle, Aramides 15, 36, 66, 210, **211**
mangle, Rhizophora 15
manilata, Orthopsittaca 12, 252, 254, 262, 264, **267**
mansoni, Oxyspirura 194
maracana, Propyrrhura 12, 253–54, 261–62, 264, 266, **267**
marail, Penelope 195–96, **197**
maranhaoensis, Phaethornis 342
Marasmius 405, 455–56, 491, 507, 554, 618, 624
margarettae, Phaethornis 341
margaritaceiventer, Hemitriccus 468, **469**
margaritae, Conirostrum **585**
margaritatus, Megastictus **411**
marginatus, Microcerculus 534, **538**
marginatus, Pachyramphus **485**
marinus, Bufo 173, 294
marinus, Larus 238
Marisa planosgyra 156, 206
martiana, Orbignya 438
martii, Baryphthengus **361**
martinica, Porphyrula 70, 72, 186, 210–11, **214,** 219, 318
Masius chrysopterus 490
Massornis 502
matogrossensis, Oxyspirura 531
Mauritia 6, 177, 184, 255, 617
Mauritia flexuosa 320, 438, 625
Mauritia vinifera 11, 317, 320, 438

maxillosus, Salminus 158
maxillosus, Saltator 69, 587, 594, **612**
maxima, Sterna 73, 239, **240**
maximiliani, Anodorhynchus 34
maximiliani, Oryzoborus 32, 587–96, **607,** 608
maximiliani, Pionus 32, 255–56, 258, 261, **273,** 387
maximum, Panicum 593, 641
maximus, Saltator 589, 593, **612**
maynana, Cotinga 504, 509, **511**
mays, Zea 504
Maytenus 453
Mazama simplicicornis 177
mcilhennyi, Conioptilon 504
Mecocerculus 461
  leucophrys White-throated Tyrannulet **464**
medius, Picoides 388
megacephala, Ramphotrigon **470**
Megarynchus 450–51, 459, 461
  pitangua Boat-billed Flycatcher **481**
Megastictus
  margaritatus Pearly Antshrike **411**
Megaxenops 424, 428
  parnaguae Great Xenops **441,** Pl. 45.8
melacoryphus, Coccyzus 280–81, **282,** 434, 537
melambrotos, Cathartes 150, **151**
melanaria, Cercomacra **416**
melancholicus, Tyrannus 24, 28, 170, 182, 281, 320, 449, 451–54, 459–60, 478–79, 483, **484,** 523, 546, 565, 579, 630
melancoryphus, Cygnus 14, 154, 156, 158, **160**
Melanerpes 383, 386, 388–89, 392
  cactorum White-fronted Woodpecker **392**
  candidus White Woodpecker **392**
  cruentatus Yellow-tufted Woodpecker **392**
  flavifrons Yellow-fronted Woodpecker **392,** Pl. 25.2
  formicivorus 325
  rubrifrons 383, 392
melanocephala, Pionites 259, 261, 264, **272**
melanocephalus, Carpornis 9, 10, 67, 508, **511**
melanoceps, Myrmeciza **418**
melanochloros, Colaptes 382–86, **390,** 409, 446, 448
melanogaster, Conopophaga **422**
melanogaster, Formicivora 406, **414**
melanogaster, Piaya 282, **283**
melanogaster, Sporophila 15, 67–68, 588, 590, 594, 606, **607**
melanogenia, Galbula 364
melanoleuca, Atticora 526, **527**
melanoleuca, Lamprospiza 564, 568, **573**
melanoleuca, Poospiza 542, 574, **599**
melanoleuca, Tringa 73, 225, 227, **228,** 230, 390
melanoleucos, Campephilus 383–87, 389, 392, **393,** 394
melanoleucus, Geranoaetus 169–70, **173,** 176, 185, 431
melanoleucus, Spizastur **177,** 178
melanonota, Pipraeidea 565–67, 570, 577, **579**
melanonota, Touit 9, 32, 66, **272,** 274
Melanopareia 398–99, 407
  torquata Collared Crescentchest **400**
melanopezus, Automolus **441**
melanophaius, Laterallus 111, 210–11, **212,** 213, 436
melanophris, Diomedea 75, 112, **113,** 114–15, 118
melanopis, Schistochlamys 563–64, 569, **572,** 630
melanopogon, Hypocnemoides **417**
melanops, Conopophaga 9, 66, 403, 405, 417, 421, **422,** 424, 439
melanops, Leucopternis 175
melanops, Phleocryptes 424–25, 427–29, **433,** 434–55, 464
melanops, Porphyriops 209, **213**
melanops, Sporophila 67, **605**
melanops, Trichothraupis 461, 564, 567–68, 570, **576**
melanosticta, Rhegmatorhina **419**
melanothorax, Sakesphorus 49, **409**
melanotis, Coryphaspiza 69, 593, 596, **609**
melanotos, Calidris 73, 223, 227, **229**

Species Index: English Names

PLATES

Index to Plates

PLATE 1
Tinamidae

1. Solitary Tinamou, *Tinamus s. solitarius* (p. 102)
2. White-throated Tinamou, *Tinamus guttatus* (p. 102)
3. Brown Tinamou, *Crypturellus o. obsoletus* (p. 102)
4. Undulated Tinamou, *Crypturellus u. undulatus* (p. 103)

5. Yellow-legged Tinamou, *Crypturellus noctivagus zabele*, female (p. 103)
6. Brazilian Tinamou, *Crypturellus strigulosus*, male (p. 104)
7. Dwarf Tinamou, *Taoniscus nanus* (p. 105)
8. Spotted Nothura, *Nothura m. maculosa* (p. 105)

9. Small-billed Tinamou, *Crypturellus parvirostris* (p. 104)
10. Red-winged Tinamou, *Rhynchotus r. rufescens* (p. 104)

PLATE 2
Diomedeidae (4), Sulidae (5), Phalacrocoracidae (2), Anhingidae (1), and Fregatidae (3)

1. Anhinga, *Anhinga a. anhinga*, female (p. 127)
2. Neotropic Cormorant, *Phalacrocorax brasilianus*, immature (p. 126)
3. Magnificent Frigatebird, *Fregata magnificens*, adult male; 3a. immature (p. 129)
4. Black-browed Albatross, *Diomedea melanophris*, adult (p. 113)
5. Brown Booby, *Sula leucogaster;* 5a. diving into the sea (p. 124)

PLATE 3
Ardeidae (1,2,4,8), Cochleariidae (3), Threskiornithidae (5–7), and Aramidae (9)

1. Rufescent Tiger-Heron, *Tigrisoma lineatum marmoratum,* adult; 1a. immature (p. 136)
2. Chestnut-bellied Heron, *Agamia agami* (p. 136)
3. Boat-billed Heron, *Cochlearius c. cochlearius* (p. 139)
4. Whistling Heron, *Syrigma sibilatrix* (p. 136)
5. Buff-necked Ibis, *Theristicus c. caudatus* (p. 141)
6. Scarlet Ibis, *Eudocimus ruber,* male in nonbreeding plumage (p. 141)
7. Roseate Spoonbill, *Platalea ajaja* male in breeding plumage (p. 143)
8. Green-backed Heron, *Butorides s. striatus* (p. 136)
9. Limpkin, *Aramus g. guarauna* (p. 206)

PLATE 4
Ardeidae (2,3), Ciconiidae (1), Threskiornithidae (4)

1. Wood Stork, *Mycteria americana* (p. 146)
2. Snowy Egret, *Egretta thula* (p. 134)
3. Least Bittern, *Ixobrychus exilis*, male (p. 137)
4. Green Ibis, *Mesembrinibis cayennensis* (p. 141)

PLATE 5
Anhimidae (5), Anatidae (1–4)

1. Black-bellied Whistling-Duck,
   *Dendrocygna autumnalis
   discolor* (p. 160)
2. Orinoco Goose, *Neochen jubata*
   (p. 160)

3. Brazilian Duck, *Amazonetta
   brasiliensis*, male flying; 3a. female
   standing (p. 162)

4. Brazilian Merganser, *Mergus
   octosetaceus*, male standing;
   4a. female flying (p. 163)
5. Southern Screamer, *Chauna
   torquata* (p. 166)

PLATE 6
Cathartidae (1–3), Pandionidae (6), Falconidae (4,5)

1. Black Vulture, *Coragyps atratus* (p. 151)
2. Turkey Vulture, *Cathartes aura ruficollis* (p. 151)
3. King Vulture, *Sarcoramphus papa* (p. 150)
4. Crested Caracara, *Polyborus p. plancus* (p. 185)
5. Yellow-headed Caracara, *Milvago chimachima*, immature (p. 184)
6. Osprey, *Pandion haliaetus* (p. 179)

PLATE 7
Accipitridae (1–5,7), Falconidae (6,8)

1. American Swallow-tailed Kite,
   Elanoides forficatus yetapa
   (p. 171)
2. Roadside Hawk, *Rupornis
   magnirostris* (p. 174)
3. White-necked Hawk, *Leucopternis
   lacernulata* (p. 174)

4. Plumbeous Kite, *Ictinia plumbea,*
   immature (p. 172)
5. Long-winged Harrier, *Circus buffoni,*
   adult female (p. 178)
6. Peregrine Falcon, *Falco peregrinus*
   subsp. (p. 185)

7. Snail Kite, *Rostrhamus sociabilis*
   (p. 172)
8. Yellow-headed Caracara, *Milvago
   chimachima,* adult (p. 184)

PLATE 8
Accipitridae (1,2,4), Falconidae (3,5–9)

1. Roadside Hawk, *Rupornis magnirostris magniplumis* (p. 174)
2. Double-toothed Kite, *Harpagus b. bidentatus* (p. 172)
3. Laughing Falcon, *Herpetotheres c. cachinnans*, immature (p. 183)

4. Pearl Kite, *Gampsonyx s. swainsonii* (p. 171)
5. Barred Forest-Falcon, *Micrastur r. ruficollis* (p. 183)
6. Collared Forest-Falcon, *Micrastur s. semitorquatus*, immature (p. 183)

7. Aplomado Falcon, *Falco f. femoralis*, subadult (p. 188)
8. American Kestrel, *Falco sparverius cearae*, male; 8a. female (p. 188)
9. Bat Falcon, *Falco r. rufigularis* (p. 187)

PLATE 9
Accipitridae

1. Ornate Hawk-Eagle, *Spizaetus o. ornatus*, subadult (p. 177)
2. Black Hawk-Eagle, *Spizaetus tyrannus*, immature (p. 178)
3. Hook-billed Kite, *Chondrohierax uncinatus* (p. 171)

4. Savanna Hawk, *Buteogallus meridionalis* (p. 176)
5. Crane Hawk, *Geranospiza caerulescens gracilis* (p. 178)

6. White-tailed Hawk, *Buteo albicaudatus* (p. 173)
7. Harpy Eagle, *Harpia harpyja* (p. 177)

P.B.

PLATE 10
Cracidae (1–7), Phasianidae (8), Opisthocomidae (9)

1. Amazonian Razor-billed Curassow, *Mitu tuberosa* (p. 199)
2. Nocturnal Curassow, *Nothocrax urumutum* (p. 200)
3. Bare-faced Curassow,*Crax f. fasciolata*, male; 3a. female (p. 198)

4. Dusky-legged Guan, *Penelope obscura* (p. 196)
5. Rusty-margined Guan, *Penelope superciliaris jacupemba* (p. 196)
6. Speckled Chachalaca, *Ortalis g. guttata* (p. 196)

7. Black-fronted Piping-Guan, *Pipile jacutinga* (p. 197)
8. Spot-winged Wood-Quail, *Odontophorus c. capueira* (p. 202)
9. Hoatzin, *Opisthocomus hoazin* (p. 204)

PLATE 11
Psophidae (1), Rallidae (2–6), Eurypygidae (7)

1. Dark-winged Trumpeter, *Psophia v. viridis* (p. 208)

2. Ash-throated Crake, *Porzana a. albicollis* (p. 212)

3. Gray-necked Wood-Rail, *Aramides c. cajanea* (p. 212)

4. Rufous-sided Crake, *Laterallus m. melanophaius* (p. 212)

5. Purple Gallinule, *Porphyrula martinica*, adult; 5a. immature, swimming (p. 214)

6. Common Moorhen, *Gallinula chloropus galeata* (p. 213)

7. Sunbittern, *Eurypyga h. helias* (p. 216)

PLATE 12

Haematopodidae (4), Scolopacidae (2,5,6), Recurvirostridae (1); Phalaropidae (3)

1. Black-winged Stilt, *Himantopus himantopus melanurus* (p. 232)
2. Lesser Yellowlegs, *Tringa flavipes*, nonbreeding plumage (p. 228)
3. Wilson's Phalarope, *Steganopus tricolor*, nonbreeding plumage (p. 232)
4. American Oystercatcher, *Haematopus palliatus* (p. 221)
5. Spotted Sandpiper, *Actitis macularia*, nonbreeding plumage (p. 228)
6. Sanderling, *Calidris alba*, nonbreeding plumage (p. 229)

PLATE 13
Charadriidae (1–5), Scolopacidae (6,7)

1. Lesser Golden-Plover, *Pluvialis
   dominica*, nonbreeding plumage
   (p. 225)
2. Southern Lapwing, *Vanellus
   chilensis* (p. 225)
3. Pied Lapwing, *Hoploxypterus
   cayanus* (p. 225)

4. Collared Plover, *Charadrius
   collaris* (p. 226)
5. Semipalmated Plover, *Charadrius
   semipalmatus*, immature (p. 225)

6. Whimbrel, *Numenius phaeopus
   hudsonicus* (p. 230)
7. Semipalmated Sandpiper, *Calidris
   pusilla*, nonbreeding plumage
   (p. 229)

PLATE 14
Stercorariidae (1), Laridae (2–6), Caprimulgidae (7)

1. Parasitic Jaeger, *Stercorarius parasiticus,* immature (p. 235)
2. Large-billed Tern, *Phaetusa simplex* (p. 239)
3. Kelp Gull, *Larus dominicanus* (p. 238)

4. Royal Tern, *Sterna maxima,* nonbreeding plumage (p. 240)
5. South American Tern, *Sterna hirundinacea,* breeding plumage; 5a. immature (p. 239)

6. Yellow-billed Tern, *Sterna superciliaris,* breeding plumage (p. 240)
7. Sand-colored Nighthawk, *Chordeiles rupestris* (p. 308)

PLATE 15
Columbidae (1–5), Cuculidae (6–10)

1. White-tipped Dove, *Leptotila verreauxi decipiens* (p. 250)
2. Ruddy Ground-Dove, *Columbina t. talpacoti,* male; 2a. female, irritated (p. 249)
3. Eared Dove, *Zenaida auriculata chrysauchenia* (p. 247)
4. Long-tailed Ground-Dove, *Uropelia campestris* (p. 249)

5. Scaled Pigeon, *Columba speciosa,* male (p. 247)
6. Squirrel Cuckoo, *Piaya cayana macroura* (p. 282)
7. Striped Cuckoo, *Tapera n. naevia* (p. 284)

8. Dark-billed Cuckoo, *Coccyzus melacoryphus* (p. 282)
9. Pavonine Cuckoo, *Dromococcyx pavoninus* (p. 285)
10. Rufous-vented Ground-Cuckoo, *Neomorphus g. geoffroyi* (p. 285)

PLATE 16
Psittacidae

1. Indigo Macaw,*Anodorhynchus leari* (p. 265)
2. Little Blue Macaw, *Cyanopsitta spixii* (p. 266)
3. Hyacinth Macaw, *Anodorhynchus hyacinthinus* (p. 264)
4. Red-bellied Macaw, *Orthopsittaca manilata* (p. 267)

5. Red-shouldered Macaw, *Diopsittaca nobilis cumanensis* (p. 267)
6. Blue-and-yellow Macaw, *Ara ararauna* (p. 266)
7. Red-and-green Macaw, *Ara chloroptera* (p. 266)
8. Golden Parakeet, *Guaruba guarouba* (p. 267)

9. White-bellied Parrot, *Pionites l. leucogaster* (p. 272)
10. Golden-tailed Parrotlet, *Touit surda* (p. 272)
11. Golden-winged Parakeet, *Brotogeris chrysopterus* (p. 271)

P.B.

PLATE 17
Psittacidae

1. Turquoise-fronted Parrot, *Amazona a. aestiva* (p. 275)
2. Vinaceous-breasted Parrot, *Amazona vinacea* (p. 275)
3. Orange-winged Parrot, *Amazona a. amazonica* (p. 275)
4. Red-browed Parrot, *Amazona rhodocorytha* (p. 274)
5. Red-fan Parrot, *Deroptyus a. accipitrinus* (p. 276)

6. Vulturine Parrot, *Pionopsitta vulturina* (p. 273)
7. Scaly-headed Parrot, *Pionus maximiliani siy* (p. 273)
8. Sun Parakeet, *Aratinga solstitialis jandaya* (p. 268)
9. Peach-fronted Parakeet, *Aratinga a. aurea* (p. 268)

10. Reddish-bellied Parakeet, *Pyrrhura frontalis chiripepe* (p. 269)
11. Maroon-faced Parakeet, *Pyrrhura l. leucotis* (p. 269)
12. Blue-winged Parrotlet, *Forpus x. xanthopterygius*, male (p. 271)
13. Yellow-chevroned Parakeet, *Brotogeris chiriri* (p. 271)

P.B.

PLATE 18
Strigidae (1–5), Nyctibiidae (6), Caprimulgidae (7,8)

1. Rusty-barred Owl, *Strix hylophila*
   (p. 297)
2. Tropical Screech-Owl, *Otus c.*
   choliba (p. 294)
3. Tawny-browed Owl, *Pulsatrix*
   koeniswaldiana, see text (p. 296)

4. Striped Owl, *Rhinoptynx clamator*
   (p. 297)
5. Ferruginous Pygmy-Owl, *Glaucidium*
   brasilianum, 5a ferruginous
   phase (p. 296)
6. Common Potoo, *Nyctibius griseus*
   (p. 302)

7. Pauraque, *Nyctidromus a. albicollis*
   (p. 308)
8. Long-trained Nightjar, *Macropsalis*
   creagra (p. 311)

PLATE 19
Caprimulgidae (1,2), Apodidae (3,4), Hirundinidae (5)

1. Scissor-tailed Nightjar, *Hydropsalis brasiliana torquata*, adult male; 1a. female (p. 310)
2. Lesser Nighthawk, *Chordeiles a. acutipennis*, male (p. 308)

3. Ashy-tailed Swift, *Chaetura andrei* (p. 319)
4. White-collared Swift, *Streptoprocne z. zonaris* (p. 318)

5. White-rumped Swallow, *Tachycineta l. leucorrhoa* (p. 526)

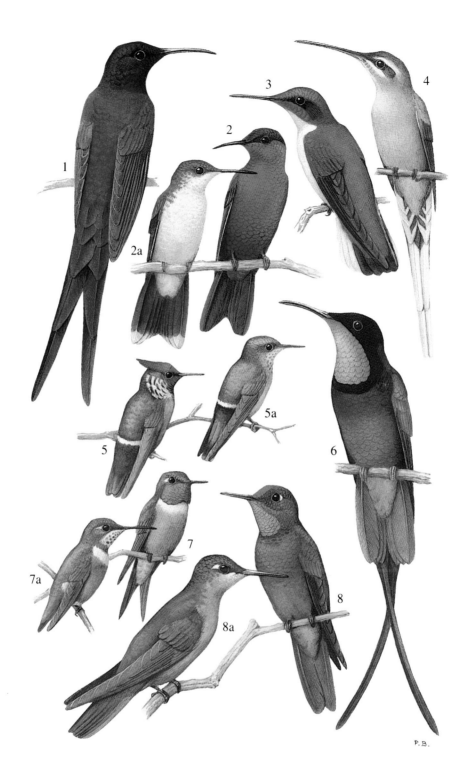

PLATE 20
Trochilidae

1. Swallow-tailed Hummingbird,
   Eupetomena macroura, male
   (p. 343)
2. Violet-capped Woodnymph,
   Thalurania glaucopis, male;
   2a. female (p. 347)
3. Black-eared Fairy, *Heliothryx aurita*,
   male (p. 349)

4. Planalto Hermit, *Phaethornis
   pretrei* (p. 342)
5. Frilled Coquette, *Lophornis
   magnifica*, male; 5a. female
   (p. 345)
6. Crimson Topaz, *Topaza pella*,
   male (p. 348)

7. Amethyst Woodstar, *Calliphlox
   amethystina*, male; 7a. female
   (p. 350)
8. Brazilian Ruby, *Clytolaema
   rubricauda*, male; 8a. female
   (p. 348)

PLATE 21
Trochilidae

1. Ruby-topaz Hummingbird,
   Chrysolampis mosquitus, male
   (p. 345)
2. Glittering-bellied Emerald,
   Chlorostilbon aureoventris, male;
   2a. female (p. 346)
3. Black-breasted Plovercrest,
   Stephanoxis l. lalandi, male;
   3a. female (p. 345)

4. White-throated Hummingbird,
   Leucochloris albicollis (p. 347)
5. White-vented Violetear, *Colibri
   serrirostris* (p. 344)
6. Black-throated Mango, *Anthracothorax nigricollis*, male;
   6a. female (p. 344)

7. White-chinned Sapphire, *Hylocharis
   cyanus viridiventris*, male;
   7a. female (p. 347)
8. Glittering-throated Emerald, *Amazilia
   fimbriata* (p. 348)
9. Sombre Hummingbird, *Aphantochroa
   cirrhochloris* (p. 348)
10. Stripe-breasted Starthroat, *Helio-
    master squamosus*, male
    (p. 350)

PLATE 22
Trogonidae (1–3), Alcedinidae (4,5), Momotidae (6)

1. White-tailed Trogon, *Trogon v. viridis*, male; 1a. female (p. 355)
2. Pavonine Quetzal, *Pharomachrus pavoninus*, male (p. 355)

3. Collared Trogon, *Trogon c. collaris*, male; 3a. female (p. 355)
4. Ringed Kingfisher, *Ceryle t. torquata*, female (p. 358)

5. American Pygmy Kingfisher, *Chloroceryle a. aenea*, male (p. 359)
6. Rufous-capped Motmot, *Baryphthengus r. ruficapillus* (p. 361)

PLATE 23
Galbulidae (1,2), Bucconidae (3–6), Capitonidae (7)

1. Great Jacamar, *Jacamerops a. aurea,*
   male (p. 365)
2. Rufous-tailed Jacamar, *Galbula*
   ruficauda rufoviridis, male (p. 365)
3. Crescent-chested Puffbird,
   Malacoptila striata (p. 369)

4. White-eared Puffbird, *Nystalus*
   chacuru (p. 369)
5. Spotted Puffbird, *Bucco tamatia*
   (p. 368)

6. Rusty-breasted Nunlet, *Nonnula*
   rubecula (p. 369)
7. Black-spotted Barbet, *Capito n.*
   niger, male; 7a. female (p. 372)

PLATE 24
Ramphastidae

1. Red-billed Toucan, *Ramphastos tucanus cuvieri* (p. 381)
2. Red-breasted Toucan, *Ramphastos dicolorus* (p. 381)
3. Channel-billed Toucan, *Ramphastos vitellinus ariel* (p. 380)

4. Toco Toucan, *Ramphastos toco albogularis* (p. 381)
5. Chestnut-eared Aracari, *Pteroglossus castanotis* (p. 379)
6. Curl-crested Aracari, *Pteroglossus beauharnaesii* (p. 380)

7. Saffron Toucanet, *Baillonius bailloni* (p. 380)
8. Spot-billed Toucanet, *Selenidera maculirostris,* male; 8a. female (p. 380)

PLATE 25
Picidae

1. Lineated Woodpecker, *Dryocopus lineatus* (p. 392)
2. Yellow-fronted Woodpecker, *Melanerpes flavifrons*, female; 2a. male (p. 392)
3. Campo Flicker, *Colaptes c. campestris*, male (p. 390)
4. Robust Woodpecker, *Campephilus r. robustus*, male (p. 394)

5. Chestnut Woodpecker, *Celeus elegans jumana*, male (p. 391)
6. Blond-crested Woodpecker, *Celeus f. flavescens*, male (p. 391)
7. Checkered Woodpecker, *Picoides mixtus*, male (p. 393)
8. Green-barred Woodpecker, *Colaptes melanochloros*, male; 8a. female (p. 390)

9. Yellow-throated Woodpecker, *Piculus f. flavigula*, male; 9a. female (p. 391)
10. Yellow-eared Woodpecker, *Veniliornis maculifrons*, male; 10a. female (p. 393)
11. White-barred Piculet, *Picumnus cirratus*, male; 11a. female (p. 389)

PLATE 26
Dendrocolaptidae

1. Long-billed Woodcreeper, *Nasica l. longirostris* (p. 446)
2. White-throated Woodcreeper, *Xiphocolaptes a. albicollis* (p. 447)
3. Buff-throated Woodcreeper, *Xiphorhynchus guttatus guttatoides* (p. 448)

4. Planalto Woodcreeper, *Dendrocolaptes p. platyrostris* (p. 447)
5. Wedge-billed Woodcreeper, *Glyphorhynchus spirurus* (p. 446)
6. Black-billed Scythebill, *Campylorhamphus falcularius* (p. 449)

7. Plain-brown Woodcreeper, *Dendrocincla f. fuliginosa* (p. 446)
8. Straight-billed Woodcreeper, *Xiphorhynchus p. picus* (p. 448)
9. Lesser Woodcreeper, *Lepidocolaptes fuscus tenuirostris* (p. 448)
10. Olivaceous Woodcreeper, *Sittasomus griseicapillus* (p. 446)

PLATE 27
Furnariidae

1. Campo Miner, *Geobates poecilopterus* (p. 430)

2. Rufous Hornero, *Furnarius rufus badius* (p. 431)

3. Spix's Spinetail, *Synallaxis s. spixi* (p. 434)

4. Chotoy Spinetail, *Synallaxis phryganophila* (p. 434)

5. Pallid Spinetail, *Cranioleuca pallida* (p. 436)

6. Common Thornbird, *Phacellodomus r. rufifrons* (p. 437)

7. Rufous Cacholote, *Pseudoseisura c. cristata* (p. 439)

8. Buff-browed Foliage-gleaner, *Syndactyla rufosuperciliata* (p. 439)

9. Sharp-tailed Streamcreeper, *Lochmias n. nematura* (p. 442)

10. White-eyed Foliage-gleaner, *Automolus l. leucophthalmus* (p. 440)

11. Pale-browed Treehunter, *Cichlocolaptes leucophrus* (p. 441)

12. Ochre-breasted Foliage-gleaner, *Philydor lichtensteini* (p. 440)

13. Plain Xenops, *Xenops minutus* (p. 441)

14. Rufous-breasted Leaftosser, *Sclerurus s. scansor* (p. 442)

PLATE 28
Formicariidae

1. Eastern Slaty Antshrike, *Thamnophilus punctatus sticturus*, male
   (p. 410)
2. Spot-breasted Antvireo, *Dysithamnus
   stictothorax*, male; 2a. female
   (p. 411)

3. Ochre-rumped Antbird, *Drymophila
   ochropyga*, male; 3a. female
   (p. 415)
4. White-flanked Antwren, *Myrmotherula axillaris melaena*, male;
   4a. female (p. 412)
5. Rusty-backed Antwren, *Formicivora
   r. rufa*, male; 5a. female (p. 414)

6. Rufous-winged Antwren, *Herpsilochmus r. rufimarginatus*, male;
   6a. female (p. 413)
7. White-bibbed Antbird, *Myrmeciza l.
   loricata*, male; 7a. female (p. 418)
8. Spot-backed Antbird, *Hylophylax
   naevia ochracea*, male (p. 419)

PLATE 29
Formicariidae (1–4), Rhinocryptidae (5), Tyrannidae (6)

1. Variegated Antpitta, *Grallaria varia imperator* (p. 420)
2. Rufous-capped Antthrush, *Formicarius colma ruficeps* (p. 420)
3. Black-spotted Bare-eye, *Phlegopsis nigromaculata paraensis* (p. 419)
4. Black-cheeked Gnateater, *Conopophaga melanops*, male;
   4a. female (p. 422)
5. Spotted Bamboowren, *Psilorhamphus guttatus* (p. 400)
6. Southern Antpipit, *Corythopis delalandi* (p. 467)

PLATE 30
Cottingidae (1–6), Tyrannidae (7–9)

1. Guianan Red-Cotinga, *Phoenicircus carnifex*, male (p. 517)
2. Hooded Berryeater, *Carpornis cucullatus* (p. 511)
3. Swallow-tailed Cotinga, *Phibalura flavirostris*, male (p. 510)

4. Banded Cotinga, *Cotinga maculata*, male (p. 511)
5. Spangled Cotinga, *Cotinga cayana*, male; 5a. female (p. 511)
6. White-winged Cotinga, *Xipholena atropurpurea* (p. 512)

7. Green-backed Becard, *Pachyramphus v. viridis* (p. 484)
8. Rufous Casiornis, *Casiornis rufa* (p. 479)
9. Gray-hooded Attila, *Attila rufus* (p. 479)

PLATE 31
Cotingidae (1–5), Tyrannidae (6)

1. Guianan Cock-of-the-Rock, *Rupicola*
   rupicola, male; 1a. female (p. 518)
2. Red-ruffed Fruitcrow, *Pyroderus s.*
   scutatus, male (p. 513)

3. Purple-throated Fruitcrow, *Querula*
   purpurata, male (p. 513)
4. Crimson Fruitcrow, *Haematoderus*
   militaris, male (p. 513)

5. Capuchinbird, *Perissocephalus*
   tricolor, male (p. 515)
6. Cinereous Mourner, *Laniocera*
   hypopyrrha (p. 480)

P.B.

PLATE 32
Cotingidae (1), Pipridae (2–14)

1. Black-capped Piprites, *Piprites pileatus*, male (p. 517)
2. Striped Manakin, *Machaeropterus r. regulus*, male (p. 500)
3. Blue-crowned Manakin, *Pipra coronata arimensis;* 3a. *P. c. carbonata;* adult males (p. 495)
4. Band-tailed Manakin, *Pipra f. fasciicauda*, adult male; 4a. female (p. 496)

5. Opal-crowned Manakin, *Pipra iris*, male (p. 495)
6. Red-headed Manakin, *Pipra rubrocapilla*, adult male; 6a. female (p. 493)
7. White-fronted Manakin, *Pipra s. serena*, male (p. 495)
8. Dwarf Tyrant-Manakin, *Tyranneutes stolzmanni*, adult male (p. 502)
9. Wied's Tyrant-Manakin, *Neopelma aurifrons*, adult male (p. 501)

10. Blue Manakin, *Chiroxiphia caudata*, male (p. 497)
11. Pin-tailed Manakin, *Ilicura militaris*, male (p. 498)
12. Flame-crested Manakin, *Heterocercus linteatus*, male (p. 501)
13. Wire-tailed Manakin, *Pipra filicauda*, male (p. 496)
14. Helmeted Manakin, *Antilophia galeata*, male (p. 496)

PLATE 33
Cotingidae (1,2), Pipridae (3,4), Tyrannidae (5–9)

1. Sharpbill, *Oxyruncus cristatus*
   (p. 518)
2. Wing-barred Piprites, *Piprites
   chloris* (p. 517)
3. Cinnamon Tyrant-Manakin, *Neopipo
   cinnamomea* (p. 500)

4. Greenish Mourner, *Schiffornis
   virescens* (p. 502)
5. Blue-billed Black-Tyrant, *Knipolegus
   cyanirostris*, female (p. 475)
6. Brown-crested Flycatcher, *Myiarchus
   tyrannulus bahiae* (p. 481)

7. Rusty-margined Flycatcher,
   Myiozetetes cayanensis (p. 481)
8. Tropical Kingbird, *Tyrannus
   melancholicus* (p. 484)
9. Vermilion Flycatcher, *Pyrocephalus r.
   rubinus*, male; 9a. female (p. 472)

PLATE 34
Tyrannidae

1. Three-striped Flycatcher, *Conopias trivirgata* (p. 482)
2. Tawny-crowned Pygmy-Tyrant, *Euscarthmus meloryphus* (p. 466)
3. Crested Doradito, *Pseudocolopteryx sclateri* (p. 465)
4. White-crested Tyrannulet, *Serpophaga subcristata* (p. 464)
5. Yellow-crowned Elaenia, *Myiopagis flavivertex* (p. 463)

6. Yellow-bellied Elaenia, *Elaenia flavogaster* (p. 463)
7. Southern Beardless-Tyrannulet, *Camptostoma obsoletum* (p. 462)
8. Planalto Tyrannulet, *Phyllomyias fasciatus brevirostris* (p. 462)
9. Sepia-capped Flycatcher, *Leptopogon amaurocephalus* (p. 466)
10. Ochre-bellied Flycatcher, *Mionectes oleagineus wallacei* (p. 466)

11. Yellow-lored Tody-Flycatcher, *Todirostrum poliocephalum* (p. 469)
12. Ochre-faced Tody-Flycatcher, *Todirostrum plumbeiceps* (p. 469)
13. Short-tailed Pygmy-Tyrant, *Myiornis ecaudatus* (p. 468)
14. Many-colored Rush-Tyrant, *Tachuris rubrigastra* (p. 464)
15. Ruddy-tailed Flycatcher, *Terenotriccus erythrurus* (p. 471)

PLATE 35
Tyrannidae

1. Euler's Flycatcher, *Lathrotriccus euleri* (p. 472)
2. Great Kiskadee, *Pitangus sulphuratus* (p. 481)
3. Sulphur-rumped Flycatcher, *Myiobius barbatus mastacalis* (p. 471)
4. Bran-colored Flycatcher, *Myiophobus fasciatus*, male (p. 472)

5. Helmeted Pygmy-Tyrant, *Lophotriccus galeatus* (p. 468)
6. White-throated Spadebill, *Platyrinchus mystaceus* (p. 470)
7. Cliff Flycatcher, *Hirundinea ferruginea* (p. 478)
8. Rufous-tailed Flatbill, *Ramphotrigon ruficauda* (p. 470)
9. Stripe-necked Tody-Tyrant, *Hemitriccus striaticollis* (p. 468)

10. Royal Flycatcher, *Onychorhynchus c. coronatus*, male (p. 471)
11. Oustalet's Tyrannulet, *Phylloscartes oustaleti* (p. 467)
12. Yellow Tyrannulet, *Capsiempis flaveola* (p. 467)
13. Yellow-olive Flycatcher, *Tolmomyias sulphurescens* (p. 470)

PLATE 36
Hirundinidae

1. Blue-and-white Swallow, *Notiochelidon c. cyanoleuca* (p. 527)
2. Gray-breasted Martin, *Progne chalybea domestica* (p. 526)
3. Brown-chested Martin, *Phaeoprogne tapera* (p. 526)
4. White-winged Swallow, *Tachycineta albiventer* (p. 526)

5. White-thighed Swallow, *Neochelidon t. tibialis* (p. 527)
6. Southern Rough-winged Swallow, *Stelgidopteryx r. ruficollis* (p. 528)
7. Tawny-headed Swallow, *Alopochelidon fucata* (p. 527)

8. White-banded Swallow, *Atticora fasciata* (p. 527)
9. Barn Swallow, *Hirundo rustica erythrogaster* (p. 528)
10. Bank Swallow, *Riparia riparia* (p. 528)

PLATE 37
Corvidae (1,2), Troglodytidae (3), Turdinae (4–8)

1. Azure Jay, *Cyanocorax caeruleus* (p. 531)
2. White-naped Jay, *Cyanocorax cyanopogon* (p. 532)
3. Black-capped Donacobius, *Donacobius a. atricapillus* (p. 536)

4. Rufous-brown Solitaire, *Myadestes leucogenys* (p. 545)
5. Cocoa Thrush, *Turdus f. fumigatus* (p. 548)
6. Rufous-bellied Thrush, *Turdus r. rufiventris* (p. 547)

7. Creamy-bellied Thrush, *Turdus amaurochalinus* (p. 547)
8. Pale-breasted Thrush, *Turdus l. leucomelas* (p. 547)

PLATE 38
Troglodytidae (1–7), Sylviinae (8), Estrildidae (9)

1. White-breasted Wood-Wren,
   Henicorhina leucosticta (p. 538)
2. Buff-breasted Wren, *Thryothorus
   leucotis albipectus* (p. 537)
3. Musician Wren, *Cyphorhinus aradus
   rufogularis* (p. 539)

4. Southern Nightingale Wren, *Microcerculus m. marginatus* (p. 538)
5. Grass (=Sedge) Wren, *Cistothorus p.
   platensis* (p. 537)
6. House Wren, *Troglodytes aedon
   musculus* (p. 538)

7. Thrush-like Wren, *Campylorhynchus
   turdinus* subsp. (p. 536)
8. Long-billed Gnatwren, *Ramphocaenus melanurus austerus* (p. 540)
9. Common Waxbill, *Estrilda astrild*,
   male, perched on a panicle of
   Panicum maximum (p. 641)

PLATE 39
Icterinae

1. Olive Oropendola, *Psarocolius bifasciatus yuracares* (p. 623)
2. Crested Oropendola, *Psarocolius decumanus maculosus* (p. 623)
3. Shiny Cowbird, *Molothrus b. bonariensis*, adult male; 3a. female (p. 630)

4. Yellow-rumped Cacique, *Cacicus c. cela* (p. 624)
5. Unicolored Blackbird, *Agelaius c. cyanopus*, subadult male; 5a. female (p. 626)

6. Red-breasted Blackbird, *Sturnella militaris superciliaris*, male; 6a. female (p. 627)
7. Oriole Blackbird, *Gymnomystax mexicanus* (p. 626)
8. Troupial, *Icterus icterus jamacaii* (p. 625)

P.B.

PLATE 40
Vireonidae (6–8), Parulinae (9–12), Coeribinae (2), Thraupinae (1,3–5)

1. Red-legged Honeycreeper, *Cyanerpes c. cyaneus*, male; 1a. female (p. 584)
2. Bananaquit, *Coereba flaveola chloropyga*, trying to perforate a flower of *Malvaviscus arboreus*, var. *penduliflorus*, to take nectar (p. 562)
3. Green Honeycreeper, *Chlorophanes s. spiza*, male (p. 584)
4. Blue Dacnis, *Dacnis c. cayana*, male; 4a. female (p. 583)

5. Chestnut-vented Conebill, *Conirostrum s. speciosum*, male; 5a. female (p. 584)
6. Chivi Vireo, *Vireo c. chivi* (p. 555)
7. Rufous-crowned Greenlet, *Hylophilus p. poicilotis* (p. 556)
8. Rufous-browed Peppershrike, *Cyclarhis gujanensis ochrocephala* (p. 554)

9. Tropical Parula, *Parula pitiayumi elegans* (p. 559)
10. Masked Yellowthroat, *Geothlypis aequinoctialis velata*, male (p. 559)
11. Golden-crowned Warbler, *Basileuterus culicivorus hypoleucus* (p. 560)
12. Rose-breasted Chat, *Granatellus p. pelzelni*, male; 12a. female (p. 559)

PLATE 41
Thraupinae

1. Swallow Tanager, *Tersina v. viridis*, male; 1a. female (p. 585)
2. Blue-naped Chlorophonia, *Chlorophonia c. cyanea*, male (p. 581)
3. Purple-throated Euphonia, *Euphonia chlorotica serrirostris*, male; 3a. female (p. 579)

4. Chestnut-bellied Euphonia, *Euphonia pectoralis*, male; 4a. female (p. 581)
5. Opal-rumped Tanager, *Tangara velia cyanomelaena*, male (p. 583)
6. Spotted Tanager, *Tangara p. punctata* (p. 582)
7. Red-necked Tanager, *Tangara c. cyanocephala*, male (p. 582)

8. Burnished-buff Tanager, *Tangara c. cayana*, male (p. 582)
9. Green-headed Tanager, *Tangara seledon*, male (p. 581)
10. Azure-shouldered Tanager, *Thraupis cyanoptera* (p. 578)
11. Palm Tanager, *Thraupis p. palmarum* (p. 578)

PLATE 42
Thraupinae (1–7), Emberizinae (10,11), Cardinalinae (8,9)

1. Brazilian Tanager, *Ramphocelus bresilius dorsalis*, male; 1a. female (p. 577)
2. Rufous-headed Tanager, *Hemithraupis r. ruficapilla*, male; 2a. female (p. 574)
3. Hepatic Tanager, *Piranga flava saira*, male; 3a. female (p. 577)
4. Fawn-breasted Tanager, *Pipraeidea m. melanonota*, male (p. 579)

5. Ruby-crowned Tanager, *Tachyphonus coronatus*, female (p. 576)
6. Cinnamon Tanager, *Schistochlamys r. ruficapillus* (p. 572)
7. White-winged Shrike-Tanager, *Lanio v. versicolor*, subadult male; 7a. female (p. 575)
8. Green-winged Saltator, *Saltator s. similis* (p. 612)

9. Yellow-green Grosbeak, *Caryothraustes c. canadensis* (p. 611)
10. Red-cowled Cardinal, *Paroaria dominicana* (p. 610)
11. Yellow Cardinal, *Gubernatrix cristata* (p. 609)

PLATE 43
Emberizinae (2–11), Cardinalinae (1)

1. Ultramarine Grosbeak, *Passerina brissonii*, male; 1a. female (p. 613)
2. Lesser Seed-Finch, *Oryzoborus a. angolensis*, male; 2a. female (p. 607)
3. Capped Seedeater, *Sporophila bouvreuil pileata*, male; 3a. female (p. 606)
4. Rufous-collared Sparrow, *Zonotrichia capensis subtorquata* (p. 596)

5. Pectoral Sparrow, *Arremon t. taciturnus* (p. 609)
6. Red-rumped Warbling-Finch, *Poospiza l. lateralis* (p. 599)
7. Coal-crested Finch, *Charitospiza eucosma* (p. 609)
8. Red Pileated-Finch, *Coryphospingus cucullatus rubescens*, male (p. 610)

9. Saffron Finch, *Sicalis flaveola brasiliensis*, male; 9a. female (p. 600)
10. Grassland Sparrow, *Ammodramus h. humeralis* (p. 598)
11. Wedge-tailed Grass-Finch, *Emberizoides h. herbicola* (p. 601)

PLATE 44

Rallidae (9), Columbidae (10), Psittacidae (4,5,7,8), Nyctibiidae (1), Galbulidae (2), Capitonidae (3), Picidae (6)

1. White-winged Potoo, *Nyctibius leucopterus*, adult (p. 302)
2. Three-toed Jacamar, *Jacamaralcyon tridactyla*, adult (p. 364)
3. Black-girdled Barbet, *Capito dayi*, adult male; 3a. adult female (p. 372)

4. Red-tailed (=Blue-cheeked) Parrot, *Amazona brasiliensis*, adult (p. 274)
5. Blue-bellied Parrot, *Triclaria malachitacea*, adult male (p. 276)
6. Helmeted Woodpecker, *Dryocopus galeatus*, adult male; 6a. adult female (p. 392)

7. Golden Parakeet, *Guaruba guarouba*, adult (p. 267)
8. Pearly Parakeet, *Pyrrhura perlata perlata*, adult (p. 269)
9. Little Wood-Rail, *Aramides mangle*, adult (p. 211)
10. Blue-eyed Ground-Dove, *Columbina cyanopis*, adult male (p. 248)

PLATE 45

Trochilidae (1,6,7), Rhinocryptidae (12), Formicariidae (4,9–11), Furnariidae (8), Pipridae (3), Cotingidae (2), Thraupinae (5)

1. Hyacinth Visorbearer, *Augastes scutatus,* adult male (p. 349)
2. Kinglet Calyptura, *Calyptura cristata,* adult male; 2a. adult female (p. 512)
3. Golden-crowned Manakin, *Pipra vilasboasi,* adult male; 3a. adult female (p. 495)
4. Black-hooded Antwren, *Formicivora erythronotos,* adult male; 4a. adult female (p. 414)

5. Cherry-throated Tanager, *Nemosia rourei,* adult (p. 574)
6. Broad-tipped Hermit, *Phaethornis gounellei,* adult (p. 342)
7. Hook-billed Hermit, *Glaucis dohrnii,* adult male (p. 340)
8. Great Xenops, *Megaxenops parnaguae,* adult (p. 441)
9. Alagoas Antwren, *Terenura sicki,* adult male; 9a. adult female (p. 415)

10. Rio de Janeiro Antbird, *Cercomacra brasiliana,* adult male (p. 415)
11. Slender Antbird, *Rhopornis ardesiaca,* adult male (p. 416)
12. Brasilia Tapaculo, *Scytalopus novacapitalis* (p. 401)

PLATE 46   Indian Feather Work

Kaapor (Urubu) Indian woman's collar from the Rio Gurupi region of Maranhão. The portion that goes around the neck is made of feathers from the upper breast of the Channel-billed Toucan, *Ramphastos vitellinus.* The "medallion," in the form of an insect, is made from the tail feathers of the Guianan Red-Cotinga, *Phoenicircus carnifex,* which are outlined by feathers, including some remiges and small throat feathers, of the Spangled Cotinga, *Cotinga cayana.* All three birds are found in Amazonia. Color photograph courtesy of Banco Safra.

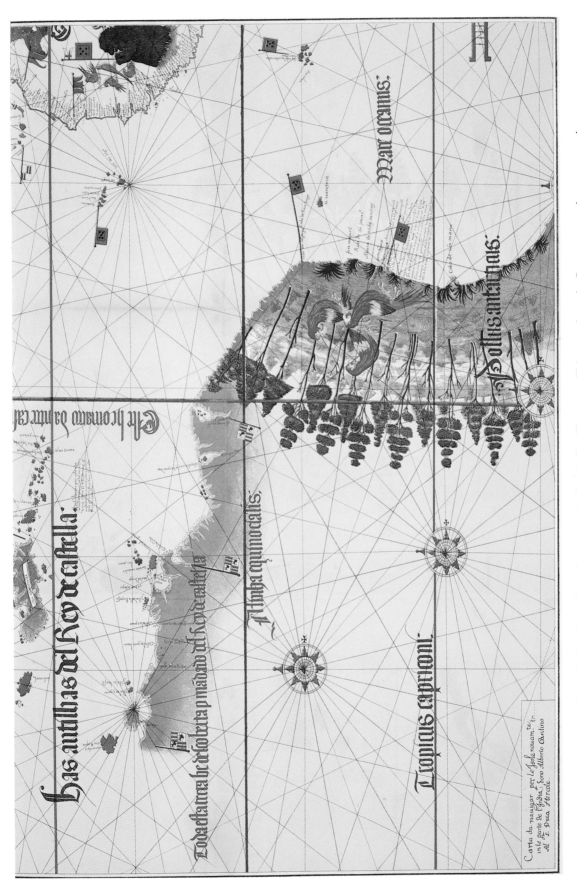

Cantino's 1502 Map of the World. Reproduction of a portion of the map, showing the Brazilian coast. This map, drawn by Portuguese explorers, was stolen in Lisbon by an Italian, Alberto Cantino, under orders from the Duke of Ferrara, Hercules d'Este. The original map is today in the Estense Library in Modena, Italy. The copy comes from the famous *História da Colonização Portuguesa do Brasil*, *"History of Portuguese Colonization of Brazil"*, vol. 1, 1921, Porto, Portugal: Litografia Nacional.